Epistle to the Hebrews

Other books in the BYU New Testament Commentary series:

The Gospel according to Mark by Julie M. Smith

The Testimony of Luke by S. Kent Brown

Paul's First Epistle to the Corinthians
by Richard D. Draper and Michael D. Rhodes

The Revelation of John the Apostle
by Richard D. Draper and Michael D. Rhodes

Epistle to the Hebrews

BRIGHAM YOUNG UNIVERSITY
NEW TESTAMENT COMMENTARY

Richard D. Draper
and
Michael D. Rhodes

BYU Studies
Provo, Utah

JOHN A. WIDTSOE FOUNDATION Significant support from the John A. Widtsoe Foundation in Los Angeles, California, as the Publication Sponsor for this Commentary Series is gratefully acknowledged. http://www.widtsoefoundation.org/

This Commentary Series is made possible by a generous gift from John S. and Unita W. Welch.
This volume received a generous grant from Belva and David Stone.

Published by BYU Studies. To contact any member of the board of editors or BYU Studies, write to 1063 JFSB, Brigham Young University, Provo, Utah, 84602, or visit http://byustudies.byu.edu or http://www.byunewtestamentcommentary.com.

Cover images (left to right): Left: Abel and Melchisedec sacrificing at the altar, mosiac, Ravenna, Italy, Basilica of Sant'Apollinare in Classe, circa AD 600–700, photo by John W. Welch. *Center:* a menorah carved into a stone lintel, from the Eshtemoa synagogue, circa AD 200–300. Rockefeller Archaeological Museum, Israel, photo by John W. Welch. *Right:* Carl H. Kraeling, *The Synagogue, The Excavations at Dura-Europos, Final Report 8, Part 1,* ed. A. R. Bellinger et al. (New Haven, Conn.: Yale University Press, 1956), plate 59, © Yale University Press, reprinted by permission of Yale University Press.

First time in print. Substantive corrections, additions, questions, or comments may be sent to byu_studies@byu.edu.

Library of Congress Cataloging-in-Publication Data

Names: Draper, Richard D., author. | Rhodes, Michael D., 1946- author.
Title: Epistle to the Hebrews / Richard D. Draper, Michael D. Rhodes.
Other titles: Bible. Hebrews. English. Authorized. 1611. | New Testament commentary (Brigham Young University)
Description: Provo, Utah : BYU Studies, [2020] | Series: Brigham Young University New Testament commentary series | Includes bibliographical references and index. | Summary: "A verse-by-verse commentary on the New Testament Epistle to the Hebrews. Provides a modern English version of the text. Cites scriptures of The Church of Jesus Christ of Latter-day Saints (Mormons). Focuses on Jesus Christ and his role as High Priest and Savior, highlighting the saving nature of faith in him"-- Provided by publisher.
Identifiers: LCCN 2020035469 | ISBN 9781942161721 (hardcover) | ISBN 9781942161738 (ebook)
Subjects: LCSH: Bible. Hebrews--Commentaries.
Classification: LCC BS2775.53 .D73 2020 | DDC 227/.87077--dc23
LC record available at https://lccn.loc.gov/2020035469

Printed in the United States of America
10 9 8 7 6 5 4 3 2 1

About the Brigham Young University New Testament Commentary Series

Welcome to the BYU New Testament Commentary, a project by a group of Latter-day Saint specialists offering to readers a careful, new look at the biblical records that witness the life and ministry of Jesus Christ and the first generation of his church. The commentary series seeks to make the New Testament more accessible to Latter-day Saint general readers and scholars by employing much of current biblical scholarship while reflecting important LDS insights. At the same time, this effort may also be helpful to interested readers of other faiths who want to learn how a group of Latter-day Saint scholars understands the Bible. A fundamental article of faith for Latter-day Saints (Mormons) affirms the Bible "to be the word of God" while adding, understandably, that it needs to be "translated correctly" in order for it to be accurately comprehendible to modern language speakers.

These objectives have helped shape the purposes and parameters of this commentary series. Serious LDS readers of the Bible search the scriptures, looking for depth and breadth in passages whose meanings and mandates may ultimately be plain but not shallow. Such readers and interpreters are served by treatments that unite faith and research, reason and revelation, in prayerfully confronting profound and difficult issues that arise in the texts and affect one's path of progression. The New Testament has served as an influential guide to western civilization for centuries. As such, its records have long been studied by lay people and scholars alike, resulting in a rich reservoir of information that illuminates the New Testament era culturally, historically, and linguistically. Selectively, the BYUNTC builds upon this vast body of knowledge, resting on the Greek texts of the New Testament and connecting helpful elements of linguistic, literary, historical, and cultural research and traditional scholarship together with LDS scriptures and doctrinal perspectives. The combination of all these features distinguishes the BYUNTC from other commentaries, which are readily available elsewhere and which readers may also want to consult for more encyclopedic or specialized discussions.

The tone of the BYUNTC aims to be informative rather than hortatory, and suggestive rather than definitive in its interpretation. The opinions expressed in this series are the views of its contributors and should not necessarily be attributed to The Church of Jesus Christ of Latter-day Saints; Brigham Young University, where many of those involved here are headquartered; or anyone else, though these works have benefitted from input and guidance from a number of colleagues, advisors, editors, and peer reviewers.

Each volume in this series sets in two parallel columns the King James Version (KJV) and a new working translation of the New Testament. Calling this a new "rendition" clarifies that it does not seek to replace the authorized KJV adopted by the LDS Church as its official English text. Rather, it aims to enhance readers' understanding conceptually and spiritually by rendering the Greek texts into modern English with LDS sensitivities in mind. Comparing and explaining the New Rendition in light of the KJV then serves as one important purpose for each volume's notes, comments, analyses, and summaries. This effort responds in modest ways to the desire President J. Reuben Clark Jr. expressed in his diary in 1956 that someday "qualified scholars [would provide] . . . a translation of the New Testament that will give us an accurate translation that shall be pregnant with the great principles of the Restored Gospel."

Depending on their personal skills and interests, the authors of these volumes approach their scholarly sources and LDS materials differently but always with careful exposition and engaging perspectives. In several ways, they employ various interpretive tools, including semantic considerations of Greek vocabulary; cultural, historical, critical, literary, and structural analyses; and intertextual comparisons with other biblical passages, the Book of Mormon, and other scriptural works including the Joseph Smith Translation of the Bible. Observations are also proffered about the doctrinal and spiritual reception of New Testament teachings and practices in the broad LDS religious tradition.

The format also varies moderately from volume to volume regarding introductory materials and the style of commentary. Throughout, Greek and Hebrew terms appear in transliterated form in conformity with standards adopted by the Society of Biblical Literature. In some cases, a volume reproduces the Greek New Testament text based on the Greek text published by the Society of Biblical Literature (2010) or draws upon the twenty-eighth edition of the Nestle-Aland text in *Novum Testamentum Graece* (2012).

Contents

Abbreviations

For ancient works, the footnotes follow the style of Patrick H. Alexander and others, *The SBL Handbook of Style for Ancient Near Eastern Biblical and Early Christian Studies* (Peabody Mass.: Hendrickson Publishers, 1999).

BDAG	Walter Bauer. *A Greek-English Lexicon of the New Testament and Other Early Christian Literature.* Ed. F. W. Danker. 3d English ed. Chicago: University of Chicago Press, 2000.
BDB	Frances Brown, Samuel R. Driver, and Charles A. Briggs. *A Hebrew and English Lexicon of the Old Testament.* 1952. Rpt., Oxford: Clarendon Press, 1987.
CR	Conference Report of The Church of Jesus Christ of Latter-day Saints. Salt Lake City: The Church of Jesus Christ of Latter-day Saints, 1897–1970.
D&C	Doctrine and Covenants. Salt Lake City: Church of Jesus Christ of Latter-day Saints, 1981.
HAL	L. Koehler, W. Baumgartner, and J. J. Stamm. *The Hebrew and Aramaic Lexicon of the Old Testament.* Trans. and ed. M. E. J. Richardson. 5 vols. Leiden: E. J. Brill, 1994–2000.
JST	Joseph Smith Translation of the Bible.
KJV	King James Version of the Bible.
LSJ	Henry G. Liddell and others, eds. *Greek English Lexicon.* Oxford: Clarendon Press, 1968.
LXX	Septuagint, Greek Old Testament.
MT	Masoretic Text of the Hebrew Bible.
NR	New Rendition.
NRSV	New Revised Standard Version of the Bible.
NID	Moisés Silva. *New International Dictionary of New Testament Theology and Exegesis.* Grand Rapids, Mich.: Zondervan, 2014.

NIV New International Version of the Bible.

NJB New Jerusalem Bible.

NR The New Rendition of the Greek text contained in this volume.

PG Migne, Jacques-Paul, ed. *Patrologia Graeca.* 161 vols. Paris: Imprimerie Catholique,1857–1866).

PL Migne, Jacques-Paul, ed. *Patrologia Latina.* 217 vols. Paris: Imprimerie Catholique, 1841–55.

REB Revised English Bible.

RSV Revised Standard Version of the Bible.

SBLGNT Michael Holmes, ed. *The Greek New Testament: SBL Edition.* Atlanta: Society of Biblical Literature; Bellingham, Wash.: Logos Bible Software, 2010.

SCI Stephen W. Liddle and Richard C. Galbraith. "LDS Scripture Citation Index." https://scriptures.byu.edu.

TDOT G. Johannes Botterweck and Helmer Ringgren, eds. *Theological Dictionary of the Old Testament.* Trans. John T. Willis. 15 vols. Grand Rapids, Mich.: Wm. B. Eerdmans, 1976–2004.

TDNT Gerhard Kittel and Gerhard Freidrich, eds. *Theological Dictionary of the New Testament.* Trans. Geoffery W. Bromiley. 10 vols. Grand Rapids, Mich.: Wm. B. Eerdmans, 1964–76.

TWOT Harris, R. Laird, Gleason L. Archer Jr., and Bruce K. Waltke, eds. *Theological Wordbook of the Old Testament.* 2 vols. Chicago: Moody Press, 1980.

Preface

The nascent Christian community did not develop in a vacuum. It matured in a specific historical and multicultural sphere, one interestingly not particularly favorable for its growth and advancement. The Christian movement developed around neither philosophical nor theological constructs but through events that took place between BC 6 and AD 100 that affected the first through the third generations of converts. During that period, they came to understand who they worshiped, including both how and why. In the process, they discovered who they were as a people, of what their belief system consisted, and how they were to apply those beliefs in the world they lived in.

The ground of their faith was Jesus Christ, and the structure of that faith was his teachings. However, the doctrines that grew out of his teachings developed line by line, here a little and there a little, as inspiration and revelation came and understanding increased. The Savior gave the responsibility for the doctrinal development and its practical application to the Apostles and prophets. In so doing, he kept the responsibility within the bounds of those who had his personal authority to declare his word and perform his ordinances.

These authorized followers were met with many challenges and worked diligently to overcome them. One of the ways they did so was through the power of the epistle. Written texts could do what the individual could not, namely reach across distances and bring instruction to disparate congregations. Admittedly, personal visits were imperative, but written communications conveyed teachings and instructions in a way that could be shared broadly and lay the ground work that made the visits all the more productive. Further, at least initially, on these letters rested the institutional memory the Christian community.

One of the major responsibilities of these leaders, then, was to teach the doctrine of the kingdom. Paramount among the teachings was detailing the importance of the life, ministry, work, and identity of the Savior. Among those who took up this remarkable if somewhat overwhelming task was the author of the Epistle to the Hebrews. He wrote to a certain body of Christians facing specific problems. Every word, phrase, and sentence that he wrote had both a historical and a social context. He wrote to his fellow Saints in a language that they could understand and did so with singular beauty and power.

This intent is the starting point of our work. We have tried diligently and to the highest degree possible to capture the thrust and trajectory of his ideas so the modern reader can understand the writings of this deeply spiritual and profoundly insightful leader in their context.

We spend little time addressing the relevance of the author's writings to the modern reader. That is not say we believe any relevance is absent. It is there! The author's writings contain insights, instructions, and admonitions that are grounded in revelation and testimony that transcends time and culture and therefore can meaningfully address similar conditions and situations met by the modern Saint. Our focus, however, as noted above, is on understanding the text as the author and his readers understood it. We fully believe, however, that one of the most important purposes of scripture is for the application of those who read it. But we also feel that when a text is understood in its context, it can then be better applied to conditions today. Otherwise, it is possible to give a passage a greater significance or make it have a different application than the original text warranted or the author intended.

The Book of Mormon does encourage its readers to "liken all scriptures" unto themselves that these timeless teachings might be for their "profit and learning" (1 Ne. 19:23), but it also warns that it is possible for people to "wrest [the scriptures] to [their] own destruction" (Alma 13:9). Likewise, as the Doctrine and Covenants points out, many err because "they do wrest the scriptures and do not understand them" (D&C 10:63). Placing a scripture in its context mitigates this problem. It is our hope that by placing the scriptures in their theological, historical, social, and cultural settings, modern readers can readily see their relevance and desire to apply the principles and doctrines in their lives. Believing that to be the case, we leave it up to the readers to make the proper application. When that happens, the underlying intent and primary motivation behind our writing of this commentary will be realized.

Our primary audience is the educated Latter-day Saint reader who wishes to distill more from the text than one can usually get from popular and less extensive works. Even so, we have not directed our efforts to the advanced student or those seeking a graduate level of study, although many of the sources we cite are directed to this audience, and readers who wish to gain that level of understanding can refer to these. We have often placed more technical details in the footnotes as well as references not only to the authorities we use but also to discussions and arguments that go beyond the reach of this study but which some may be interested in exploring.

Having noted that, we must say that the Translation Notes and Comments are of necessity more technical than the Analysis and Summary sections. This is because we wish both the Latter-day Saint and non–Latter-day Saint reader to understand both how and why we rendered a Greek or Hebrew word, phrase, or passage into English the way we have. Even here, however, we were careful not to overly use specialized technical terms unless these were necessary in interpreting and understanding the meaning of a word or phrase.

Some passages are dense with theological implications, nuances, and ramifications. Many of the terms have both denotative and connotative properties that both deserve and demand exploration and development. Though rendering the Greek into English demands that a specific word be used, the value of a commentary is that it allows the full range of a word's or phrase's meanings to be addressed and explored, thus permitting the reader to get a feel for a breadth of implications and nuances a word or phrase may carry.

All in all, our work is designed neither to be all inclusive nor definitive but tentative and suggestive. We expect and hope that others will come along who will improve our work. In the meantime, we hope what we have laid a firm foundation and put up a solid scaffolding that they can use to continue to build an ever better understanding of God's word as revealed through his New Testament Apostles and prophets.

Due to the size and complexity of this work, we have called upon many to assist us, and to them we give our heartfelt thanks. Our praises go out to a bevy of Brigham Young University research assistants and source checkers who not only helped the project move along but supplied much needed material and assistance. We are especially appreciative of the efforts of our graduate assistant Nathaniel Pribil who did both background research and also wrote a number of essays used as the basis of some of the sections of this work. Our thanks also go out to Julianne Nelson who read the full text for clarity, cohesion, and comprehension. To Professors Brent Schmidt and Avram Shannon we are particularly indebted for their insights and helpful suggestions on both our rendering of the Greek passages and insights into both Greco-Roman and Second Temple Jewish cultures in which the Epistle was written. Further, we wish to thank the participants in the BYU New Testament Seminar held in June and July 2016 for their very helpful suggestions and comments: Jacob Renneker, Christopher Morey, Ben Spackman, and Avram Shannon.

Finally, we give thanks to our wives, whose enthusiasm and support for our work has been most gratifying and encouraging.

Throughout this study, we have sought to faithfully interpret the Greek into English, to be in harmony with the doctrines of The Church of Jesus Christ of Latter-day Saints, to follow teachings found in the standard works of the Restoration, and to accurately represent to all readers the powerful testimony of the Epistle to the Hebrews. Even so, the assertions, conclusions, and the overall work represent our own thinking and not that of the Church, the publisher, the University, or any of those associated with this work.

Richard D. Draper
Michael D. Rhodes

Introduction

The Beauty and Challenges of This Early Christian Text

The Epistle to the Hebrews is "the most elegant and sophisticated, and perhaps the most enigmatic, text of first-century Christianity" while it is also "a masterpiece of early Christian rhetorical homiletics."[1] Among the preserved epistles in the New Testament, Hebrews is truly unique. No other work attains its grammatical correctness, style, organization, and force of argument. Even the author's choice of words for precision, clearness, and effectiveness are unmatched by any other contributor to this sacred volume of scripture. Unsurpassed is the author's testimony of the work, place, greatness, and majesty of Jesus Christ. Unrivaled is the author's witness of the truthfulness of the gospel and its necessity in the salvation process. With the exception of the book of Revelation, there is no clearer warning as to the consequences of turning from the truth. The work is exceptional, compelling, and forceful. The notable Latter-day Saint scholar Hugh Nibley called it "the great Christian tract on the Atonement" that "begins with an exhilarating prospect: 'God . . . hath in these last days spoken unto us by his Son, whom he hath appointed heir of all things, by whom also he made the worlds'" (1:1–2).[2]

Yet with all its many virtues, much of Hebrews remains a mystery. As one authority noted in 1991:

1. Harold W. Attridge, *The Epistle to the Hebrews: A Commentary on the Epistle to the Hebrews* (Philadelphia: Fortress Press, 1989), 1.

2. Hugh Nibley, *Approaching Zion,* ed. Don E. Norton, vol. 9 of The Collected Works of Hugh Nibley (Provo, Utah: Foundation of Ancient Research and Mormon Studies; Salt Lake City: Deseret Book, 1989), 555.

> Hebrews is a delight for the person who enjoys puzzles. Its form is unusual, its setting in life is uncertain, and its argument is unfamiliar. It invites engagement in the task of defining the undefined. Undefined are the identity of the writer, his conceptual background, the character and location of the community he addresses, the circumstances and date of his composition, its setting in life, the nature of the crisis to which the document is a response, the literary genre, and the purpose and plan of the work. Although these undefined issues continue to be addressed and debated vigorously, no real consensus has been reached.[3]

Fortunately, so far as the spiritual value and message of the work is concerned, it is unnecessary to resolve any of these issues. Admittedly, it would be both helpful and likely enlightening if we knew more about its background. But even so, the work is articulate enough that it can stand solidly alone. In short, the puzzles that surround it do not diminish the beauty of its central picture. It conveys in clear focus the importance of and the reward for faith in the Savior. Standing in central place is the Atonement of Jesus Christ and its effects for all.

Why This Commentary?

A question that should be asked and answered is this: why another commentary on the Epistle to the Hebrews? The question is valid since there is a plethora of commentaries reaching from medieval to modern times, many of which illuminate the text of this work beautifully. Further, the target audiences of these commentaries range from the novice to the highly trained, from the layman to the professional. There is hardly an educational level that one or another does not reach. Even so, there is something lacking in all of them—they are not written from the perspective of the Restoration. That fact is a major justification for this work. Not until the inception of the Brigham Young University New Testament Commentary Series has any Latter-day Saint set out to write a commentary exclusively on the Epistle to the Hebrews. That is not to say that the Epistle has been neglected in Latter-day Saint works dealing with the New Testament as a whole. All these have commented on it, but not one has presented an in-depth discussion of the book alone. This work fills that void.

3. William L. Lane, *Hebrews 1–8*, vol 47a of Word Biblical Commentary, ed. David A. Hubbard and Glenn W. Barker (Dallas: Word Book Publisher, 1991), xlvii.

Further, this work presents a rendering of the Greek text into modern English. In doing so, it makes plain many passages that are vague, oblique, or inaccurate in the King James Version (hereafter KJV). Because it is a commentary, it is able to explore the range of meanings that a word, phrase, or verse can have, thus giving the reader a greater understanding of the depth, breadth, and ramifications of a passage. This understanding is heightened by bringing to bear insights from Restoration scriptures, the Joseph Smith Translation of the Bible, and modern apostles and prophets. Indeed, these make up the foundation on which the work rests. But in addition to these, some of the best scholarly works both within and without the Latter-day Saint community have been consulted and their insights brought to bear in discussing the beautiful and enlightening text of this wonderful work. All the above give reason for why we have written this commentary on the Epistle to the Hebrews.

Relevance of the Book Today

The Epistle to the Hebrews is both a doctrinal and hortative text. Though the main issues that drove the author to write this beautiful and compelling treatise are not faced by modern Saints, the doctrine the author develops is still cogent in today's ever-more secular world. Many passages in this marvelous letter are of particular significance for members of The Church of Jesus Christ of Latter-day Saints.[4] Among the topics the author addresses are the Godhead (1:1–3; 12:9; 13:8), the obedient suffering of Jesus and its result (2:14–18; 4:15–16; 5:8–9), the eternal nature of the priesthood of Jesus Christ (chaps. 7–8), that a person must be called by God in order to hold the priesthood (5:1–4), and the nature of true faith, which motivates people to righteous action (chap. 11). These themes are essential pillars of the gospel of Jesus Christ and support the doctrines of the Restoration.[5]

Further, many of the author's exhortations remain relevant today, such as his warning not to slip into apostasy (2:1–4; 3:7–12; 5:11–14; 12:25); the need to move from the foothills of the doctrines of the Gospel in order to

---

4. From this point on, the Church will be referred to either as "the Church of Jesus Christ" or "the Church" and its members as "Latter-day Saints."

5. Richard D. Draper, "Hebrews, Epistle to the," in *Encyclopedia of Mormonism,* ed. Daniel H. Ludlow (New York: Macmillan, 1992), 2:581.

progress (5:11–14); the importance of going on "unto perfection" (6:1); and the necessity of enduring to the end (12:4–11).

But more important and significant than any of these are the author's unique insights into and testimony of the Savior Jesus Christ. In the author's writings, we find a marvelous description of the Lord, his work, and his station (1:1–4); his Sonship and oneness with the Father (1:5–9); his exaltation and locus sitting on the right hand of God (1:3, 13; 8:1); the eternal nature of the priesthood over which he presides (7:20–21); his position as the great High Priest (4:14–16; 8:1–2); his role as the surety of the new covenant (7:22); and most importantly, his exclusive role as the one who opened the way to salvation that allowed others to follow (2:10; 12:2–3).

In addition, the author witnesses the Savior's humanity, showing he became one with the Father's other children (2:10–14) and, like them, suffered the vicissitudes of life (2:5–18) and learned the cost of obedience by the things which he suffered (5:7–10).

In sum, the witness of Hebrews is that those who are determined in their faith and endure to the end will find themselves sustained and assisted along the way. The means will come through the enabling power emanating from the throne of grace (4:16) occupied by the Father and Son. Through their combined power, the faithful community of the righteous will find place in the eternal city (11:10; 12:22).

Background

Authorship

The question of who actually wrote the Epistle to the Hebrews has been debated from at least the early second century AD and continues unresolved up to the present time.[6] Since the text itself does not say who the author was, and the external evidence is meager and ambiguous, this question cannot be answered with certainty. The title found in KJV that assigns the Epistle to

6. This section was adapted from Michael D. Rhodes, "Some Thoughts on the Authorship of the Epistle to the Hebrews," paper presented at New Mormon Ideas about Mark and Hebrews, Fourth Annual BYU New Testament Commentary Conference, Provo, Utah, July 29, 2016; and also an unpublished paper by Nathaniel Pribil, "On the Author of Hebrews," in possession of the authors.

Paul is not found in any early Greek or Latin manuscript. The shorter, rather vague title πρὸς Ἑβραίους (*pros Hebraious*), "to [the] Hebrews," which is found in all extant Greek manuscripts, is almost certainly an editorial label added later rather than part of the original composition.[7]

Most Latter-day Saints believe the author was Paul. This view is often based on Joseph Smith's references that unite the Apostle with the Epistle.[8] Noteworthy, however, is the absence of any statement by the Prophet that he had spiritual confirmation or any other evidence as to the authorship of this work. It is most likely that, due to the general belief in his day that the Epistle was written by Paul, the Prophet never questioned the idea or sought divine validation or further instruction in this regard.

Therefore, among Latter-day Saint scholars, ample disagreement and debate concerning the author continue due to the lack of an "official" Church position on the subject. Many General Authorities and Apostles have used the phrase "the author of Hebrews" instead of "Paul" when referencing Hebrews.[9] There are differences between Latter-day Saint scholars concerning who wrote Hebrews ranging from those who continue to support Pauline authorship to those who support other candidates such as Apollos.[10] The Church has not issued a definitive statement declaring an official position on who wrote Hebrews. For these reasons, this commentary leaves this issue unresolved and speaks open-endedly of the author of this work. As discussed below, several other possible authors have been suggested, including the apostles Peter or Jude, Paul's first missionary companion Barnabas, Paul's convert Luke the Evangelist, and Clement,

---

7. F. F. Bruce, *The Epistle to the Hebrews,* rev. ed., The New International Commentary on the New Testament (Grand Rapids, Mich.: William B. Eerdmans, 1990), 4–5.

8. "The Elders of the Church in Kirtland, to Their Brethren Abroad," *Evening and the Morning Star* 2 (March 1834): 143, online as "Letter to the Church, circa March 1834," The Joseph Smith Papers, https://www.josephsmithpapers.org/paper-summary/letter-to-the-church-circa-march-1834/2. For the logic on this, see Bruce R. McConkie, *Doctrinal New Testament Commentary* (Salt Lake City: Bookcraft, 1973), 3:133.

9. Terrence L. Szink, "Authorship of the Epistle to the Hebrews," in *How the New Testament Came to Be: The 35th Annual Brigham Young University Sidney B. Sperry Symposium,* ed. Kent P. Jackson and Frank F. Judd Jr. (Salt Lake City: Deseret Book, 2006), 243–59.

10. Examples of those in favor of Pauline authorship are Richard Lloyd Anderson, *Understanding Paul* (Salt Lake City: Deseret Book, 1983), 197; and Szink, "Authorship," 243–59; and examples of those not in favor are Richard Neitzel Holzapfel and Thomas A. Wayment, *Making Sense of the New Testament: Timely Insights and Timeless Messages* (Salt Lake City: Deseret Book, 2010), 446–47; Richard Neitzel Holzapfel, Eric D. Huntsman, and Thomas A. Wayment, *Jesus Christ and the World of the New Testament* (Salt Lake City: Deseret Book, 2006), 254–56.

the first bishop of Rome. In any event, the Epistle communicates with highly authoritative confidence, and its acceptance within the canon of scripture dates to very early Christian centuries. In the important fourth-century codices Sinaiticus, Vaticanus, and Alexandrinus, the Epistle to the Hebrews is positioned right after 2 Thessalonians.

Because many readers are unfamiliar with the latest scholarship regarding the authorship of this letter, it seemed appropriate to look at this issue in some detail at the outset of this study. Because the answer to this question remains elusive, our analysis of the language and arguments of this epistle does not firmly presuppose any particular resolution.

Evidence for authorship (or the lack thereof) falls into two categories: internal evidence, that is, evidence within the text of Hebrews itself, and external evidence, sources other than the text. Let us assess the available information under these two categories in turn.

Internal Evidence

Although the author of Hebrews does not identify himself in the Epistle, it is clear that the original readers of the work knew who he was because he asked for their prayers that he might be able to visit them (13:18–19) and expressed the hope that Timothy would come with him (13:23). However, the author not identifying himself strongly argues against Paul being the author. In every other epistle attributed to this Apostle, he consistently identified himself with his name, Παῦλος (*Paulos*), which was invariably the very first word in each epistle.

This problem of authorship was recognized by early church fathers. Pantaenus (died c. AD 200), who was head of the catechetical school at Alexandria,[11] claimed that Paul did not include his name διὰ μετριότητα (*dia metriotēta*), "out of modesty."[12] Clement of Alexandria (c. AD 150–215), Pantaenus's successor as head of that school, suggested that "in writing to Hebrews who had conceived a prejudice against him, he [Paul] very wisely did not repel them at the beginning by putting his name."[13]

However, neither of these arguments is very convincing. Paul's Epistle to the Romans was addressed to an audience that included Jewish converts. In that letter he refers to "Abraham, our ancestor according to the flesh" (Rom. 4:1, our translation). Later in the letter he states, "For I speak to those who know the law [of Moses]" (Rom. 7:1, our translation). Why

11. Eusebius, *Hist. eccl.* 5.10.4.
12. Eusebius, *Hist. eccl.* 6.14.4.
13. Eusebius, *Hist. eccl.* 6.14.2–3.

would Paul choose here not to identify himself out of modesty or a desire not to offend, when he did not hesitate to do so in his Epistle to the Romans? Moreover, why would the recipients of the letter accept the authority of an anonymous letter rather than a letter from one having apostolic authority?

Eusebius summarized Clement of Alexandria's position on Hebrews, saying, "It is Paul's, but that it was written for Hebrews in the Hebrew tongue, and that Luke, having carefully translated it, published it for the Greeks."[14] A major problem with this proposal is that not only are all of the Old Testament passages in Hebrews from the Septuagint, the Hebrew Bible translated into Greek (hereafter noted by LXX), but "the author argues on the basis of a LXX deviation from the Hebrew text" in at least two passages.[15]

Another weighty argument against Paul's authorship of Hebrews is found in 2:3: "How will we escape if we disregard so great a salvation? This salvation was first spoken by the Lord, and was confirmed to *us* by those who heard him" (NR; emphasis added). The author here states that he learned of the gospel through others who had personally "heard" Jesus. But in Galatians 1:11–12, Paul boldly asserts to the contrary, "Now I want you to know, brothers and sisters, that the gospel that was preached by me does not have a human source. For I did not receive it from nor was I taught it by any man, but I received it through revelation from Jesus Christ" (our translation).

Several passages found at the end of the Epistle have been used in an attempt to support Pauline authorship. For example, in 13:25, the statement "grace be with you all" is in various forms found at the conclusion of all Paul's epistles but is not found in any other New Testament epistle. But this is hardly conclusive evidence for Paul being the author.

Also, 13:23 states, "Know that our brother Timothy has been released. If he comes soon, he will be with me when I see you" (NR). The assumption is this is the same Timothy who is Paul's companion with him in prison in Rome. But Timothy was known to many early Church members who could have called him "brother." Further, Timothy was a common name at the time and, therefore, may not refer to Paul's companion. Thus, the inclusion of this information about his being freed does not necessarily require the author to be Paul.

In 13:24, the author says, "Those from Italy send their greetings" (NR). This would make sense if Paul were writing while in prison in Rome, but

---

14. Eusebius, *Hist. eccl.* 6.14.2.

15. Bruce, *Epistle to the Hebrews,* 15 n. 61. The two passages are 9:15–20 and 10:5 (a quote from Ps. 40:6).

"they of Italy" could refer to people from Italy that were with the author in some other location.

The passages in 10:34, "You had compassion on those who were in prison" (NR), and 13:3, "remember those who are in prison" (NR), could also be taken to refer to Paul's imprisonment but are so general that it is most unlikely that they refer specifically to Paul.

Furthermore, there are noteworthy differences between the vocabulary used in Hebrews and that used by Paul in his epistles. These include terms associated with knowledge and revelation; expressions of emotion; words relating to life and death; references to power, conflict, and judgment; ethical terms; references to the people of God; and finally liturgical expressions.[16] Especially noteworthy is the rarity of the noun ἀγάπη, "love" (used only twice in Hebrews, in 6:10 and 10:24, and 65 times in the Pauline epistles) and the verb ἀγαπάω, "to love" (found only once in Hebrews, in 12:6, but 32 times in Paul's other writings). The author of Hebrews also uses technical philosophical terms such as αἰσθητήριον, "judgment"; θέλησις, "determination"; μετριοπαθεῖν, "to treat with moderation"; τελειόω, "to be whole, complete"; τέλος, "end, termination"; τιμωρία, "vindication"; and ὑπόδειγμα, "to instruct, admonish," that are not used by Paul.[17] In his epistles, Paul frequently uses the term Χριστὸς Ἰησοῦς ("Christ Jesus") whereas that phrase is not found in Hebrews at all.[18] At the same time, several points of doctrine in Hebrews are consonant with Paul's known teachings, such as the idea that Jesus died "one for many" (Rom. 5:12–15), which compares with "Christ was once offered to bear the sins of many" (9:28).

Another point in favor of non-Pauline authorship is the author's lack of a distinction between Jews and Gentiles throughout his Epistle. One of Paul's major concerns in his longer works is this difference and how God responds to each group.[19] But to the Jewish-Christian audience to whom Hebrews is directed, this division would not necessarily have been a relevant concern.

---

16. For a more detailed comparison, see Paul Ellingworth, *The Epistle to the Hebrews: A Commentary on the Greek Text,* The New International Greek Testament Commentary (Grand Rapids, Mich.: Wm. B. Eerdmans, 1993), 8–11.

17. James Moffatt, *A Critical and Exegetical Commentary on the Epistle to the Hebrews* (Edinburgh: T&T Clark, 1924), lxi. For a study of this issue see Craig R. Koester, *Hebrews,* vol. 36 of Anchor Yale Bible series (New Haven, Conn.: Yale University Press, 2001), 42–44, with nn. 81–85.

18. For example, see Rom. 3:24; 8:1–2, 39; 16:3; Eph. 1:1; 2:7, 10, 13.

19. Gareth Lee Cockerill, *The Epistle to the Hebrews,* New International Commentary on the New Testament (Grand Rapids, Mich.: Wm. B. Eerdmans, 2012), 20.

Further, Hebrews is written in some of the best Greek found in the New Testament. One scholar describes the overall structure of Hebrews as having "generally harmonious development, smooth rhetorical structure, and skillful use of Greek, contrasting with Paul's vigorous but sometimes obscure oratory and frequent anacolutha."[20] For additional information on the distinctive, if not unique, style used by the author of Hebrews, see the section entitled "The Nature of the Greek in Hebrews" below.

External Evidence

The pivotal issue in accepting or rejecting Paul as the author of Hebrews was canonicity. In general, the Eastern Church, with its center in Alexandria, accepted Paul as the author of Hebrews earlier than the Western Church, centered in Rome. The first known citations from Hebrews, however, actually occur in Clement of Rome's First Epistle to the Corinthians, which was probably written around AD 95, but he does not refer to Hebrews by name nor does he attribute to Paul any of his six uses of language from Hebrews.[21]

As noted above, Pantaenus, who was head of the catechetical school at Alexandria,[22] maintained that Paul was the author,[23] and his successor as head of that school, Clement of Alexandria, suggested that Hebrews had been translated by Luke from a Hebrew original authored by Paul.[24]

Clement of Alexandria's successor, Origen (c. AD 185–254), questioned Paul's authorship of the Epistle based on "style" and "the character of its diction," which he said was "much better Greek" than Paul's "rudeness in speech."[25] Origen went on to say, "If I were to state my own opinion, I should say that the thoughts are the apostle's, but that the style and composition belong to one who called to mind the apostle's teachings and, as it were, made short notes of what his master [that is, Paul] said" (our translation).[26]

The Muratorian Fragment (c. AD 170–90), which contains a list of books considered canonical by the Western church at that time, does not mention

20. Ellingworth, *Epistle to the Hebrews,* 12. "Anacolutha" are inconsistencies within a sentence often caused when the speaker or writer loses the point he or she is making.

21. *1 Clem.* 17:1 (compare Heb. 11:37, 39); 17:5 (compare Heb. 3:5); 21:9 (compare Heb. 4:12); 27:2 (compare Heb. 6:18); 31:3 (compare Heb. 11:20); *1 Clem.* 36:2–5 (compare Heb. 1:1–3).

22. Eusebius, *Hist. eccl.* 5.10.4.

23. Eusebius, *Hist. eccl.* 6.14.4.

24. Eusebius, *Hist. eccl.* 6.14.12.

25. Eusebius, *Hist. eccl.* 6.25.11.

26. Eusebius, *Hist. eccl.* 6.25.11–13.

Hebrews,[27] but then again, the letter was probably addressed to people in the East.

Chester Beatty Papyrus 𝔓[46], probably from Egypt and dated to around AD 200, places Hebrews immediately after Romans, probably indicating its collector considered Paul to be the author.[28]

Eusebius (c. AD 265–340), when discussing the canonicity of the books of the New Testament, notes that while he considers the fourteen letters of Paul (including Hebrews) to be obvious and plain, he does not think it right to ignore that some people dispute the Epistle to the Hebrews, saying that it was rejected by the Church of Rome as not being authored by Paul.[29] Eusebius specifically remarked that in his day some among the Romans did not consider the author to be Paul.[30]

To summarize, external evidence points to early doubts concerning Pauline authorship of Hebrews and that the deciding factor in ultimately attributing it to Paul was canonicity. Even though there was no compelling evidence for Pauline authorship, Hebrews obviously contained important gospel truths, and so to be formally accepted into the canon, it had to have apostolic authority behind it, and so even bishops dubious of its origin but liking its doctrine fell in line.[31]

The question naturally arises, if not Paul, then who? At least thirteen people have been suggested, over the years, as the actual author of Hebrews.[32] Five of them—Clement of Rome, Luke, Barnabas, Peter, and Jude—have surviving writings that have been attributed to them with which Hebrews may be compared. Stephen has also been suggested based on the speech attributed to him in Acts 7. The remaining six people—Philip the deacon, Aristion, Priscilla (and Aquila), Mary the mother of Jesus, Epaphras, and Apollos—have no ancient writing attributed to them. Of these, the females can easily be rejected since in 11:32 the author refers to himself using a masculine participle. In a detailed analysis of each of the

---

27. F. F. Bruce, *The Canon of Scripture* (Downers Grove, Ill.: InterVarsity, 1988), 165.

28. For a description of this manuscript, see Bruce M. Metzger and Bart D. Ehrman, *The Text of the New Testament: Its Transmission, Corruption, and Restoration,* 4th ed. (New York: Oxford University Press, 2005), 54–55.

29. Eusebius, *Hist. eccl.* 6.25.11–13.

30. Eusebius, *Hist. eccl.* 6.20.3.

31. For a scholarly review from a Latter-day Saint standpoint opposite ours, see Richard Lloyd Anderson, *Guide to Acts and the Apostles' Letters* (Provo, Utah: FARMS reprint, 1999), 89–90.

32. For a detailed analysis of these suggested candidates, see Ellingworth, *Epistle to the Hebrews,* 13–21.

candidates, a noted scholar concludes that "[Apollos] is perhaps the least unlikely of the conjectures which have been put forward."[33]

So what can we say in conclusion? Some eighteen hundred years ago Origen declared, "But who the author of the epistle was, God knows the truth."[34] As one scholar rightly stated, "Even today we have not got far beyond Origen's confession of ignorance."[35]

Concerning authorship, "the critical issue is not necessarily who said or wrote it, but whether the speaker or writer was inspired by the Holy Ghost and spoke or wrote the truth. . . . President J. Reuben Clark explained: 'I am not really concerned, and no man of faith should be, about the exact authorship of the books of the Bible.'"[36] What is certain is that the text of Hebrews exudes the spiritual force that enlightened the author's understanding and drove him to produce it.

There is an additional good thing that would come out of the work being non-Pauline. It would then stand as yet another witness of the understanding of Christ possessed by many of the Church's earliest leaders and spokesmen. Because its doctrine and witness align so closely with many of those found in the Pauline epistles, it would then show Paul did not stand alone in those views and would add support that the orthodox doctrine of Christ was consistently understood among the early leaders of the followers of Jesus Christ.

The Audience

Tied to the question of who wrote Hebrews is that of its audience.[37] The question becomes more relevant given the Jerusalem council's instructions that Paul (with others) was to bear the gentile ministry and Peter (with others) that to the Jews (Acts 15:1–29; Gal. 2:7–9). Would Paul be writing "to the Hebrews"? Two important factors play on the issues associated with the audience of the Epistle. The first is the constant use and argument from various passages in the Old Testament almost exclusively making use of the Greek Septuagint. The author's use of quotations either cited or alluded to assume that the references have meaning and even some authority to the

33. Ellingworth, *Epistle to the Hebrews*, 21.

34. Eusebius, *Hist. eccl.* 6.25.14.

35. Bruce, *Epistle to the Hebrews*, 20.

36. Quoted in Szink, "Authorship," 254.

37. The material in this section was adapted from papers written by Avram Shannon and Nathaniel Pribil.

Epistle's audience. This has suggested to some that the audience was largely Greek-speaking Jews,[38] and hence the title "To the Hebrews."[39] The knowledge of the Greek version of the Old Testament might play against the idea that the audience was primarily gentile converts. Not only is knowledge of the Old Testament required, but acknowledgement of its authoritative status is also necessary for the arguments in Hebrews to be taken seriously. However, one must take into account the possibility that there were "God-fearers" and proselytes (the two terms referring to gentile converts to Judaism) who composed part of the audience. God-fearers were Gentiles who shared the religious idealism and moral lives of the Jews and their reverence for the Hebrew Bible. However, for all their faithfulness, they refused to endure the rite of circumcision. Proselytes, on the other hand, were Gentiles who accepted Judaism fully, including circumcision.[40] Though of non-Jewish heritage, some of these converts seem to have become acquainted with at least the Pentateuch and accepted its teachings. The book of Acts shows that some of them accepted Christianity (Acts 10:2; 13:43) and could easily have made up part of the author's audience. And of course, Paul's Epistles to the Corinthians, Galatians, and especially the Romans also abound with copious quotations from the Septuagint. Even so, these facts do not diminish from the great depth of knowledge of the LXX that was necessary for the readers of Hebrews to understand and accept its arguments.

The second factor is the question of the Greek-ness of the audience of Hebrews. As noted above, the Greek of the Epistle is both elegant and complex and includes rhetorical devices from the broader Greco-Roman world.[41] The use of these devices suggests the author's readers could make connections from both the broader Greco-Roman and Jewish worlds and therefore had to have been fairly educated according to the standards of

38. On the problem associated with the category of "Jewish-Christian," see Daniel Boyarin, "Rethinking Jewish Christianity: An Argument for Dismantling a Dubious Category," *Jewish Quarterly Review* 99, no. 1 (Winter 2009): 7–36. In his work, Boyarin addresses the difficulty in categorizing ancient religion at all.

39. Alan C. Mitchell, *Hebrews* (Collegeville, Minn.: Liturgical Press, 2007), 12.

40. "Bible Dictionary," in the Holy Bible published by The Church of Jesus Christ of Latter-day Saints (1976), s.v. "Proselytes."

41. Brent Nongbri, "A Touch of Condemnation in a Word of Exhortation: Apocalyptic Language and Graeco-Roman Rhetoric in Hebrews 6:4–12," *Novum Testamentum* 45, no. 3 (2003): 265–79, suggests that these verses were derived from Jewish apocalyptic literature but were built on Aristotelian notions of rhetoric and fear, making Hebrews part and parcel with a tradition which combined Jewish and Greek cultural idioms.

their day,[42] a characteristic for which Jews were noted.[43] Even so, they appear to be living outside the Holy Land and were, therefore, comfortable with the greater language and culture.[44]

If members of the audience were primarily of ordinary gentile background, it is unlikely that they would have a strong interest in or an understanding of how Jesus had fulfilled and perfected the salvific powers of the Mosaic law and its associated temple cult.[45] The very fact that the primary argument in chapters 8 and 9 is that the Savior's sacrifice was superior to that offered in the Jewish system suggests that the temple sacrificial system was something of a moving concern for the audience of Hebrews. In short, the Epistle was written to an audience which still retained a great deal of respect for the old covenant and the old law.[46] In many ways, the situation in the Epistle parallels similar situations in the Book of Mormon where the gospel of Jesus Christ and his salvation were of greatest importance in spite of the place of the law of Moses.[47]

Because of the lack of geographic detail, opinions vary as to the location of the Epistle's readers. These opinions range from Jerusalem through its neighboring communities to Rome.[48] The author's note in 13:24 that "they of Italy salute you" unfortunately does not illuminate the broader context for the Epistle. This is because the Greek in this phrase can be taken two ways; it could refer either to those living in Italy or to those who had come from there.

---

42. Mitchell, *Hebrews,* 13.

43. Though literacy was very low in biblical times, among the Jews education was prized and many took advantage of it. For a study, see Catherine Hezser, *Jewish Literacy in Roman Palestine* (Tübingen: Mohr Siebeck, 2001).

44. The term "diaspora" refers to Jews living outside of Palestine. During New Testament times, there were many more Jews living outside of the Holy Land than within it. Notables among these were Paul and Barnabas.

45. There is an interesting argument that Jesus as priest is part and parcel with an argument of Jesus as brother, a notion that has strong resonances within Latter-day Saint thought. This image of Jesus as brother draws on Greco-Roman notions of brotherly love, which again nicely illustrates the hybrid nature of the Epistle to the Hebrews. See Patrick Gray, "Brotherly Love and the High Priest Christology of Hebrews," *Journal of Biblical Literature* 122, no. 2 (Summer 2003): 335–51.

46. On this point, see Matthew Thiessen, "Hebrews and the End of the Exodus," *Novum Testamentum* 49, no. 4 (October 2007): 353–69.

47. This tension is nicely encapsulated in the interaction between Abinadi and the priests of Noah in Mosiah 12:28–31. See also 3 Ne. 15:1–10; 4 Ne. 1:11.

48. Attridge, *Epistle to the Hebrews,* 9–13; Mitchell, *Hebrews,* 13.

One thing does seem clear: given the Epistle's specific subject matter, it seems likely that it was addressed to a definite group within the broader church membership of the targeted area,[49] and these had been followers of Jesus for some time.[50] Indeed, the author insists on a standard of knowledge that one would expect of members who were fairly experienced in Christian religious tradition (5:11–14) rather than newly minted converts. This suggests that the audience were mostly made up of second-generation Christians.

From the above we can conclude that, as with the issue of authorship, the audience of the Epistle remains an open question. Even so, it seems clear that the target audience consisted of Christians who had long been associated with both Christianity and Judaism and who were also well acquainted with Greek and Hellenistic ways of thinking. In many ways, it appears that the audience of the Epistle is as transitional as the Epistle itself—situated at the crossroads between the old and the new covenants, its audience clearly appreciated the Mosaic law and were apparently open to instruction that highlighted the old law in connection with Jesus' new one.

In sum, the Epistle was addressed initially to Jewish converts who were members within a local congregation that was comprised mainly of Christians who had been converted for many years but who were facing new threats and adversities. The result was lagging faith and even the thought that the cost of discipleship was too high. The temptation to abandon the church was getting ever more attractive. The Epistle was a sensitive, caring, well-executed response to their situation. Its objective was to strengthen their resolve to stand firm in face of the new crises.[51]

Dating

Like authorship and audience, getting a firm date on the writing of the Epistle is not possible. There are, however, a few pieces of information that can give a range of dates in which it was composed. First, we should note that some argue for a late date for Hebrews, even putting it into the post-apostolic or "early Catholic" period in the second century AD, because of the sophistication of its Christology. Those who hold this view insist that such an understanding of the nature, mission, and accomplishments of the

49. Peter T. O'Brien, *The Letter to the Hebrews* (Grand Rapids, Mich.: Eerdmans, 2010), 15; Cockerill, *Epistle to the Hebrews*, 16.

50. Cockerill, *Epistle to the Hebrews*, 16.

51. See Lane, *Hebrews 1–8*, xlvii.

Lord would have taken time to develop.[52] The Restoration, however, presents a window into how fast doctrine can solidify. In just fourteen years (AD 1830–44) Joseph Smith laid down the doctrinal foundation on which the theological framework of the modern Church has been erected with surprisingly little modification from that time to the present. Indeed, most modifications focus on implementation and not further doctrinal expansion. The same is likely true of earliest Christianity. One scholar noted that "an exalted significance of Jesus appears astonishingly early in Christian circles. Well within the first couple of decades of the Christian movement" (between AD 30 and 50).[53] As a result, the sophistication of the text's Christology is not a good indicator of the time of its composition.

An upper limit of the work's creation can be set due to an epistle sent to Corinth from Rome by its bishop, Clement. In it, to bolster the points he wishes to make, the bishop clearly cites passages from Hebrews.[54] His epistle dates to about AD 96 and therefore Hebrews had to have been written before that time. Clement's assumption that his readers were not only acquainted with the content of Hebrews but also considered it authoritative suggests the work had been in circulation for some time before he wrote and was viewed as authentic.

The author's mention of Timothy being freed from prison (13:23) may provide another clue. Though the name was popular at the time, it is likely that he is the same person that was converted by Paul around AD 52 and, according to tradition, died about AD 97. Since Timothy's ministry can be traced more or less until the death of the Apostle Paul, presumably in AD 67, and since Timothy was not known to have been incarcerated during that time, the Epistle was likely written after that date.

Some argue that the Epistle was written before AD 70, when the Romans destroyed Jerusalem with its temple. Because the author focuses on cultic rites which, they insist, he would not have done had the temple been destroyed, they argue for an earlier date.[55] The problem is that Hebrews

52. See Harold W. Attridge, "Hebrews, Epistle to the," in *Anchor Bible Dictionary,* ed. David Noel Freedman (New York: Doubleday, 1992), 3:97.

53. Larry W. Hurtado, *Lord Jesus Christ: Devotion to Jesus in Earliest Christianity* (Grand Rapids, Mich.: Eerdmans, 2003), 2.

54. Attridge, *Epistle to the Hebrews,* 6–7.

55. See A. M. Fairhurst, "Hellenistic Influence in the Epistle to the Hebrews," *Tyndale Bulletin* 7–8 (1961): 17–27; and Peter Walker, "Jerusalem in Hebrews 13:9–14 and the Dating of the Epistle," *Tyndale Bulletin* 45, no. 1 (1994): 39–71, who argue that Hebrews was written before the fall of Jerusalem because they see it as a warning of the physical

concentrates not on the practices of Second Temple Judaism but on the rituals of the Mosaic tabernacle, and therefore whether or not Herod's temple stood is irrelevant to the author's points.

That the author wrote a few decades after the death of the Lord and at a time the Church had been established quite widely within the Roman Empire is suggested by three comments the author makes: first, that he received the gospel message second hand (2:3); second, that his readers had been members for a considerable time (5:12); and third, that they had gone through a period of persecution (10:32–34). The latter does not provide a solid clue since the Christians were persecuted in Palestine from AD 33 onward and within in the Roman Empire from the time of Nero (AD 54–68).[56] Thus the plausible dates for the Epistle's creation range from AD 67 to 96.

Purpose in Writing[57]

Two factors seem to have both driven the author to write his Epistle and to have directed its content. First, as noted above, many Jewish converts to Christianity saw their new faith as a subset of Judaism, a sort of reformed Judaism built on the teachings of Jesus. They, therefore, missed the point that the Lord had introduced both a new covenant and gospel and, more importantly, that he was the Savior. Due to their lack of vision and the persecutions they faced, some were tempted to return fully to their old religion. The entire force of Hebrews is to convince them that such a move would not only be foolish but spiritually damaging. The author's challenge was not only to keep them from leaving the Church but also to have them actively engage in its work. As one scholar noted, the work is a specialized "reconversion" text focusing on "deconversion" from false "Jewish interpretations of Christ."[58]

Second, the audience seems to be second generation believers, and among these there were those who were discouraged because of the delayed Second Coming or Parousia. They had not yet realized the promises the eschaton was supposed to bring. God and Christ had not yet triumphed in the world, bringing with them the kingdom of God and the

---

judgments that would shortly come upon Judea and especially Jerusalem and all who remained therein.

56. The emperor Claudius expelled the Jews from Rome near AD 49, but the persecution does not seem to have followed them elsewhere.

57. This section, with a little adaptation, has been taken from Draper, "Hebrews," in Ludlow, *Encyclopedia of Mormonism*, 2:581–83.

58. Richard Lloyd Anderson, "Paul's Witness to the Early History of Jesus' Ministry," in *The Apostle Paul: His Life and His Testimony: The 23rd Annual Sidney B. Sperry Symposium* (Salt Lake City: Deseret Book, 1994), 1–33.

reward for the faithful. The author acknowledged this concern, admitting that the community did not yet see all things in subjugation to the Lord (2:8). Many were asking if the promised coming would be in their day. If not, they wondered if the price of commitment was too great. Even in their own communities they were unsettled and seem to suffer the insecurity of refugees (6:18). The author's concern was whether they would "drift away" (NR 2:1), "fall away" (NR 3:12; 6:6), or "be . . . carried about" (13:9). By whichever means, the author was concerned they would leave the kingdom.

Some have suggested a third motive for the author, specifically that he was presenting an anti-Jewish polemic designed to denigrate Jewish practices and malign the religion. These commentators' position is not without a basis and, indeed, dominated the scholarly view of Hebrews for centuries.[59] Looking at Hebrews as a whole, however, suggests that anti-Jewish feelings were not a driving force behind the author's work. The Epistle actually says nothing about the Jews directly and even suggests that many who had accepted the new covenant were Jews. Certainly, nowhere in the text, even in the most polemical of passages that concentrate on the inefficacy of the old covenant, is there any promotion of hatred of the Jews. Indeed, the Epistle never makes a distinction between Jews and Gentiles.[60] Likewise, the Epistle's comparisons are primarily with the scriptures in the Hebrew Bible rather than with Second Temple Jewish practices. Further, at this point, thinking members of the Christian community were as yet still trying to figure out just what the Church was and how it related to Judaism. Thus, they had not yet developed a consistent and stiffened position against the Jews. Among these was the author of Hebrews. All this suggests that pushing the idea that anti-Jewish sentiments motivated the author to write the Epistle seems overblown and unconvincing.[61]

---

59. The best articulation of this position by an early Christian is that of John Chrysostom, *Hom. Heb.* 13; Jacques-Paul Migne, ed., *Patrologia Graeca,* 161 vols. (Paris: Imprimerie Catholique, 1857–66), 63:103–5 (hereafter cited as *PG*); *Adv. Jud.* 7; *PG,* 48:915–28. For a study, see John Chrysostom, *Discourses against Judaizing Christians,* trans. Paul W. Harkins, vol. 68 of Fathers of the Church, ed. Hermigild Dressler and others (Washington, D.C.: Catholic University of America Press, 1979). Examples of modern authors who have followed his views are Rosemary R. Ruether, *Faith and Fratricide: The Theological Roots of Anti-Semitism* (New York: Seabury Press, 1974), 107–11; Stephen G. Wilson, *Related Strangers: Jews and Christians, 70–170 C.E.* (Minneapolis: Fortress Press, 1995), 110–27.

60. Cockerill, *Epistle to the Hebrews,* 20. On page 23, he also states "Hebrews *never* compares Christianity with Judaism" (emphasis in original).

61. For a study, see Jody A. Barnard, "Anti-Jewish Interpretations of Hebrews: Some Neglected Factors," *Melilah: Manchester Journal of Jewish Studies* 11 (2014): 25–48; Pamela Eisenbaum, "Hebrews, Supersessionism and Jewish-Christian Relations," presentation

In sum, it is clear that the author wrote primarily to correct his readers' various misunderstandings and propensities. To do so, the author brought to bear all of his considerable resources to teach them about their saving Messiah and what he had done for them.

The Epistle's Worldview and Conceptual Background

Dependence on Christian Tradition

Scholars have pointed out similarities between Hebrews and other books of the New Testament. Since dating Hebrews is still a fairly tenuous task, not to mention dating the other books in the New Testament, it is hard to know which books definitively influenced Hebrews.[62] However, these similarities, at the very least, suggest that parallel doctrines and ideas influenced this corpus. It is clear that Hebrews was not written in a vacuum but was influenced by both Christian thought and writings. Some scholars see Mark as having a large influence on Hebrews since both place similar emphasis on Christ's suffering.[63] Luke and Acts have also been cited as influencing Hebrews due to the synopsis found in 2:3 that resembles the narrative in these works.[64] First Peter and the Gospel of John have also been cited as having influence on Hebrews. For instance, 1 Peter and Hebrews both use Christ and his atonement to provide support and encouragement to a persecuted people.[65]

Paul's writings also share a number of similarities with Hebrews.[66] One example is the imagery that compares milk with solid food found in 5:11–14 and 1 Corinthians 3:1–3. However, whereas Paul emphasized how his audience was not yet ready for spiritual "solid food" (our translation), the author of Hebrews urges his readers to move beyond spiritual "milk" and partake of

---

at the SBL Annual Meeting, Philadelphia, 2005, accessed April 23, 2017, https://www.hebrews.unibas.ch/documents/2005Eisenbaum.pdf.

62. Much of this section comes from an unpublished paper by Nathaniel Pribil, in possession of the authors.

63. Mitchell, *Hebrews,* 10–11.

64. Luke Timothy Johnson, *Hebrews: A Commentary* (Louisville, Ky.: Westminster John Knox Press, 2006), 28.

65. Attridge, *Epistle to the Hebrews,* 31.

66. O'Brien, *Letter to the Hebrews,* 19; Attridge, *Epistle to the Hebrews,* 30.

the gospel's "solid food" (NR). This evidences that the author assumes that his audience is familiar with the same Christian tradition he is and wants them to build on that tradition.[67] One scholar wrote in reference to Hebrews and Paul, "Both share a large number of common Christian traditions, and both certainly derive from the same wing of the early church."[68]

Looking beyond similarities to specific writings, Hebrews contains teachings and themes that are present throughout many New Testament books. The basic doctrine Hebrews advocates is the same doctrine promoted elsewhere in the Gospels and other Epistles. As one scholar points out, "Hebrews advocates the classic triad of Christian virtues: love, hope, and above all, faith. Similarly, Hebrews calls for the practices that we recognize as standard in the early Christian movement: prayer; hospitality, care for prisoners, chaste sexual life, sharing possessions, avoiding love of money. Hebrews encourages attendance at assemblies and respect for leaders of the community."[69] Furthermore, the picture Hebrews gives of a helpful, caring Christ is the picture of Christ that the Gospels as a whole give of him.[70] Additionally, Hebrews interprets scripture, particularly LXX Psalm 109 (Ps. 110 in the Old Testament), like other books in the New Testament do.[71] While there are definitely various doctrines and teachings presented in Hebrews that are not taught or emphasized in the same manner elsewhere in the Bible, there are plenty of parallels between Hebrews and other books of the New Testament to suggest they are at least drawing from a common Christian tradition.

The Degree of the Influence of Apocalyptic Thought and Expectations of the Parousia

As noted above, many within the early Church believed that the kingdom of God would be established in their day. They expected the Parousia or Christ's Second Coming to bring this state into being. This was because of a misreading of the Savior's teachings. "There can be no doubt," stated President Brigham Young, "but they [the early Christians] were mistaken with regard to the time of the winding up scene, thinking it was much nearer than it really was."[72] There is little wonder that such thinking predominated Christian

67. Johnson, *Hebrews,* 29.
68. Attridge, *Epistle to the Hebrews,* 30.
69. Johnson, *Hebrews,* 29.
70. Bruce, *Epistle to the Hebrews,* 30.
71. Mitchell, *Hebrews,* 9.
72. Brigham Young, in *Journal of Discourses,* 26 vols. (Liverpool: F. D. Richards, 1854–86), 12:65.

thought. From the Church's inception, its teachings carried an apocalyptic urgency. John the Baptist's testimony to his followers concerning the coming One whose sandal laces he was not worthy to unloose also testified that "the kingdom of God was at hand," and that demanded immediate repentance and flight from "the wrath to come." Indeed, he taught, the ax was laid to the root of the trees and all that did not bring forth good fruit would be hewn down (Matt. 3:2, 7, 10, our translation). It is not surprising then that the earliest Christians were caught up in this fervor and looked forward to the time when God's kingdom would be established and Christ would reign.[73] It was based on this expectation that, after the Lord's resurrection, his disciples asked him, "Lord, wilt thou at this time restore again the kingdom to Israel?" The Lord's response was vague, stating simply that the Parousia was not their concern. They should rather concentrate on proclaiming the gospel "to the uttermost part of the earth" (Acts 1:6–8). And though the Apostles and others obediently set themselves to this task, they continued for a time to believe they would see the Second Coming (see, for example, 1 Thes. 4:14–17). Many converts were energized by this idea.

The Hebrew Bible itself fueled the desire for the coming kingdom when God would rule on the earth and when "the lamb would lie down with the lion" and all would be at peace (Isa. 11:6–9, our translation). Apocalyptic writers took up the theme.[74] These emphasized the evil nature and injustice

---

73. A stream within early Mormonism carried this same fervor. It was generated by such statements in the Doctrine and Covenants that the Lord would "come quickly to judgment, to convince all of their ungodly deeds which they have committed against me" (D&C 99:5). At that time, he would receive the Saints unto himself (D&C 88:126) and promised that his reward would be with him "to recompense every man according as his work shall be" (D&C 112:34). Mitigating against the idea that these statements meant the Lord's return would be immediate was Joseph Smith's teaching that the Lord would not come before 1890, if then (D&C 130:14–17). For a study, see Richard D. Draper, "Babylon in Zion: The LDS Concept of Zion as a Cause for Mormon-Gentile Conflict, 1846–1857" (master's thesis, Arizona State University, 1974), 22–30.

74. Though the writings of Second Temple Judaism have few references to an end-time messianic leader (an exception being 4Q521, known as the "Messianic Apocalypse") and the close of the present age, the idea was not unknown, and some Jewish converts could have been sensitized to the idea as Christianity developed. For a study, see S. Talmon, "The Concepts of *Māšîaḥ* and Messianism in Early Judaism," in *The Messiah: Developments in Earliest Judaism and Christianity,* ed. James H. Charlesworth (Minneapolis: Fortress Press, 1992), 79–115. According to Eric F. Mason, "Cosmology, Messianism, and Melchizedek: Apocalyptic Jewish Traditions and Hebrews," in *Reading the Epistle to the Hebrews: A Resource for Readers,* ed. Eric F. Mason and Kevin B. McCruden (Atlanta: Society of Biblical Literature, 2011), 76, the text from Qumran and other sources "are

of the present age that was dominated by Satan. This period would come to a cataclysmic end with the Second Coming, which would inaugurate the era of peace and divine rule.[75] The author of Hebrews confirmed the idea of the coming age and the glory that would attend it. God's intervention would occur in two stages through his Son. God would first send him to fulfill the requirements of the old covenant and open the way for the new through his Atonement. The Father would then send the Son again to usher his faithful followers into the eternal kingdom (1:13; 2:5–9; 9:26–28).[76] Thus the Second Coming would marshal in the overthrow of the current world order and both the resurrection and the final judgment.[77]

Between the two comings, the "old age" and "new age" will overlap. During that period, the righteous must live in an alien world as strangers and foreigners (11:1–21) subject to ostracism and persecution by the faithless (11:22–27, 35–38). Even so, though the old era was one in which evil dominated, it was also one of anticipation. Indeed, God, speaking through Moses and other prophets (1:1–2; 10:3–6), established his covenant, and though it may not have been the means of salvation, it pointed toward salvation. Christ then came and fulfilled the old law and what its covenant anticipated (7:11–19; 10:5–10) by instituting the new covenant (8:7–13). By this means, the new age asserted itself (10:15–18) through which the power of the Spirit would flow, cleansing the conscience and transforming the souls of the believers (4:15–16; 10:22). Thus, through his ministry, the Lord's first coming brought the present age of "drawing near" to God, a time of preparation for what was to follow.[78] The "new age" would then be followed by the final one in which Christ would return, judge the world, and bring all the faithful with him into the glory of the eternal city.[79]

A problem faced by the readers of Hebrews was that the promised age of glory had not yet come. Instead, they were bound in an age of persecution

---

useful for understanding the Epistle to the Hebrews" but provide only one of the conceptual influences that formed the background to the work.

75. See *2 Bar.* 44:8–15; 83:4–9; *1 En.* 17:15; *4 Ezra* 7:50, 112–13, 119; and *T. Levi* 10:2. For a study, see Scott D. Mackie, *Eschatology and Exhortation in the Epistle to the Hebrews* (Tübingen: Mohr Siebeck: 2007), 30–37.

76. The author's scheme does not allow for a millennial period. The Second Coming transitions the earth from its telestial standing to a celestial one without the intermediate terrestrial period found in Latter-day Saint theology.

77. Cockerill, *Epistle to the Hebrews,* 25–26.

78. Alma 42:10–13 emphasizes the nature of mortality as a "preparatory state" during which people must repent and come under the merciful power of the Atonement.

79. Cockerill, *Epistle to the Hebrews,* 27–28.

and ostracism with no hope of relief in sight. The author's task was then to give them an anchor on which to hold that they might endure to the end in faith (4:14–16; 10:19–25), as well as a warning of the consequences should they fail (2:1–4; 3:12–14; 6:4–6). He did this by building up the importance of the present age as a preparatory period for what was to come. Now was the time when the Saints, through the eternal Spirit, could have their conscience purged through the blood of Christ (9:14), resulting in no consciousness of sins (10:2). It was also a time that, with God's help, they could "go unto perfection" (6:1), the idea being they could continue to spiritually mature into an ever-growing state of holiness. It also meant, however, enduring the Father's discipline (12:5–10). Readers, however, could rest in God's promises that "I will never desert or abandon you." Thus, the faithful could declare, "The Lord is my helper; I will not be afraid. What can anyone do to me" (NR 13:5–6).

The Degree of Influence of Middle Platonism and Greek Culture

Platonic ideas dominated thought in the Greco-Roman world. So ingrained had they become among the various cultures in this large and diverse empire that many were not conscious of the degree of its influence. From the fourth century BC when Plato laid down the philosophy's foundation, his ideas evolved and ramified. By the first century AD, middle Platonism had been well established, and its undergirding ideas had become very popular among the well educated of all cultures.[80] Therefore, it is not surprising to find that the author of Hebrews, whose writing reveals his unusually high level of education, would echo middle-Platonic ideas like his near contemporaries Philo and Josephus.[81] The degree to which these ideas influence him, however, is debated.[82] What is obvious is that echoes and reverberations are found in the work.

---

80. For a detailed study see John M. Dillon, *The Middle Platonists, 80 B.C. to A.D. 220* (Ithaca, N.Y.: Cornell University Press, 1977).

81. There is a recognizable similarity between the Platonic language found in Hebrews and the writings of Philo of Alexandria. See James W. Thompson, "What Has Middle Platonism to Do with Hebrews?" in Mason and McCruden, *Reading the Epistle to the Hebrews,* 31–52.

82. For example, see L. D. Hurst, *The Epistle to the Hebrews: Its Background of Thought* (Cambridge: Cambridge University Press, 1990); and Mackie, *Eschatology and Exhortation,* who insist the influence was minimal. See also Brian E. Daley, *The Hope of the Early Church: A Handbook of Patristic Eschatology* (Cambridge: Cambridge University Press, 1991; rpt. Grand Rapids, Mich.: Baker Academic); and James W. Thompson, "*Ephapax*:

A close look at the author's ideas, however, reveals a rather large gulf between his theological views and that of the foundational principles of the Platonic system. For example, in Platonism, the ultimate reality was the sphere of ideas or "Forms," which were nonmaterial, eternal, and unchanging, of which things in this world were but poor and transitory copies. That the author of Hebrews described the work of the Levitical priests as "examples and shadows" (8:6) could suggest he agreed with certain middle-Platonic ideas. However, for him, heaven was a real place where Christ had already ascended and his people would also. There they would occupy a concrete, material city already built and sustained by God (11:10). Thus, the idea of the nature of the ultimate reality between Platonism and Hebrews was contradictory and incompatible.

The vast difference between Christian and philosophical views was not lost on people at the time. The great antagonist to Christianity, Celsus, insisted that there were irreconcilable differences between Christianity and Platonism, most notably the Christian ideas of creation and resurrection. He was not alone. Even some educated Christians recognized the tension between their ideas and that of the philosophers but nonetheless "employed Platonic language and categories in varying degrees to explain Christian beliefs" to those they were trying to attract or to whom they were defending their beliefs.[83] The church fathers eventually mixed the two belief systems together and adulterated Christianity during the later centuries that Latter-day Saints call the Great Apostasy.

In sum, "the author of Hebrews demonstrates neither a profound knowledge of Platonism nor a belief in all of the major tenets of its point of view."[84] However, like the works of other Christian theologians who would come after him, his would also carry nuances and echoes of Platonic assumptions but reworked for his own pastoral purposes. Responding to his readers' need for an anchor to hold them in place during their period of trial, the author provided stability for their hope and ground for their faithful endurance by reassuring them of the reality of the self-sacrificing, immortal, and transcendent Christ (1:10–12; 7:3, 23–24), who alone would not only sustain them but also bring them through an insecure existence

The One and the Many in Hebrews," in *New Testament Studies* 53, no. 4 (October 2007): 566–81, who see a very strong influence not only in Hebrews but in Christianity, running well into the Apostolic Fathers.

83. Thompson, "Middle Platonism," 31.

84. Thompson, "Middle Platonism," 51; for another study, see Koester, *Hebrews*, 98–99.

(6:19–20) to "the heavenly Jerusalem" and "church of the firstborn" (12:22–24) that was sure and eternal.

How the Author Develops His Message

Genre

Because Hebrews is unique, its genre has come into question. It is located among the Epistles of the New Testament, but does it belong there? The English term "epistle" is related to the verb ἐπιστέλλω (*epistellō*), "to send to," and especially referred to the sending of a message.[85] Thus, an *epistolē* was "anything sent by a messenger, message, order, commission, whether verbal or in writing" but in general commonly referred to a letter.[86] Although the "Epistles" in the New Testament were similar in form to the epistles of antiquity, they nevertheless constitute a special genre of a didactic or teaching communication.[87] Hebrews, therefore, falls generally into the category of an epistle. Its developed presentation, however, is unique when compared to the other Epistles in the New Testament. In genre and form, the work begins like a treatise, moves into a sermon, and ends like an epistle.[88] Taking the work as a whole, many identify it as a homily,[89] that is, a discourse on a religious theme. Various attributes within the text support this conclusion. Its homiletic style is evident through the way the author structures his arguments using scripture and examples and then makes them the ground for his appeals to his audience. The author was very effective in his use of homiletics, and the method served him well.

---

85. Henry G. Liddell and others, eds., *Greek English Lexicon* (Oxford: Clarendon Press, 1968), 660 (hereafter cited as LSJ).

86. LSJ, 660.

87. Rengstorf, *TDNT,* 7:593–94; J. Schneider, "Brief," in *Reallexikon für Antike und Christentum: Sachwörterbuch zur Auseinandersetzung des Christentums mit der Antiken Welt,* vol. 2, *Bauer–Christus,* ed. Theodor Klauser (Stuttgart: Hiersemann Verlag, 1954), 2:574–76.

88. H. E. Dana, *Jewish Christianity: An Expository Survey of Acts I to XII, James, I and II Peter, Jude, and Hebrews* (New Orleans: Bible Institute Memorial Press, 1937), 201.

89. Albert Vanhoye, *The Letter to the Hebrews: A New Commentary,* trans. Leo Arnold (New York: Paulist Press, 2015), 1–2; Ben Witherington III, *Letters and Homilies for Jewish Christians: A Socio-rhetorical Commentary on Hebrews, James, and Jude* (Downers Grove, Ill.: IVP Academic, 2007), 20–21.

Content and Problems the Epistle Addresses

The main point at the center of the Epistle is that Jesus Christ is the eternal "high priest, who sits on the right hand of the throne of the Majesty in the heavens; a minister of the sanctuary, and of the true tabernacle" of God (NR 8:1–2). This theme is developed throughout the Epistle, showing how eternal salvation comes through the greatness, sufficiency, and supremacy of Jesus Christ. The letter was written to devoted converts from Judaism to the early Christian church, who already understood the first principles of the gospel and had received its basic ordinances (6:1–4). Step by step, it systematically strives to persuade them to "hold firmly to our confession of hope" (10:23, our translation), to keep the covenant, and to realize the incomparable and irrevocable promises given to them by God through the sacrifice of Jesus Christ. With its explication of the Atonement in terms of priesthood, oaths, covenants, and temple imagery, this entire Epistle resonates and harmonizes with Latter-day Saint concepts and practices.

Chapter 1 begins by boldly declaring that Jesus is the sole mediator between God and all human beings; he is superior to and supersedes both prophets and angels. As a separate and distinct personage in the Godhead, he is the God of creation and the perfect revelation of godhood for all time. He is the express image of his Father, both spiritually and physically; he alone purged the sins of humankind and sits on the right hand of God the Father (1:1–3). The Father brought the Savior (who was his "first begotten" in the premortal existence) "into the world" (1:6; compare D&C 93:21; 1 Ne. 11:18). As the firstborn, Jesus is the heir of all things (1:2), and those who are faithful become joint-heirs with him.

Chapter 2 holds a strong warning to heed the word of God given through Jesus Christ (2:1–4). The next world is in subjugation to Christ alone (2:5–10). God made him a little lower than "the gods" (taking the Hebrew reading of Ps. 8:4–6). Because God is the Father of all, even Christ is subject to him. Thus, the Savior is second only to the Father, yet he is the spirit brother of humankind (2:17). Like his brothers and sisters in mortality, he suffered temptation, but unlike them, he never gave in to sin (2:18; 4:15–16). Through this suffering, he learned obedience and gained compassion for all God's children.

The admonition of chapter 3 counsels people to contemplate the greatness of the Lord and to commit themselves to him. The total obedience shown by the Savior to his Father marks the way to do so. The time for commitment is "today." The gospel is not always available to humankind, and so it is necessary to respond covenantally "this day," lest individuals be left like the rebellious Israelites to die in the deserts of their own lives (NR 3:7–17; compare Josh. 24:14–25; Jacob 6:5–7; D&C 64:23–25).

Chapter 4, drawing in part upon Israelite temple symbolism, admonishes the Saints to enter into the rest of the Lord (4:1, 11). This comes by believing, softening the heart, laboring, standing openly before God, relying on the compassion of Jesus the High Priest, and coming boldly to the mercy seat of God to find grace in time of need (4:7, 11, 13, 15, 16).

Chapter 5 explains how Jesus obtained his authority to act as Israel's great High Priest. He did not presume to take this honor upon himself. As with Aaron, God chose Christ and bestowed authority upon him, but in Christ's case, he would be "a priest for ever after the order of Melchisedec" (5:6; see also Ps. 110:4).

Chapter 6 calls upon all members of the church to "lay hold upon the hope" of perfection and eternal life, which has been extended to them by an immutable oath and covenant (6:1, 13–20). Diligence in serving Christ will bring a full assurance of extraordinary promises, as God covenanted with Abraham and promised him eternal increase (6:13–14; compare D&C 132:30). This hope, made possible in Christ, is an anchor for the soul, since God cannot lie. However, those who have once tasted the good word of God and have partaken of the Holy Ghost and then fall away and "crucify to themselves the Son of God afresh," the sin is so grievous that they cannot be renewed again unto repentance (6:6–10).

The author goes on to focus on God's promises to Abraham that are extended to all who come unto Christ, a covenant so important that God himself swore an oath to secure it. Based on that oath, Christians have "an anchor of the soul," firm and secure (6:19), for the Lord has entered heaven and works in the Christians' behalf. Indeed, he is a priest after the order of Melchizedek (who was the priest who blessed Abraham).

Chapter 7 focuses on the superiority of Christ's Melchizedek Priesthood over the Levitical Priesthood and the law of Moses. Melchizedek was a type of Christ. His priesthood was more enduring than the Levitical Priesthood, which was limited to bloodlines and was not given with an oath and whose priesthood did not continue after their death and also needed daily renewal (7:3, 21, 23, 27). The Melchizedek order of priesthood, however, was directed by Jesus Christ, who, unlike the high priest under the law of Moses on the annual Day of Atonement (Lev. 16:29–34), did not need to "offer sacrifice for his own sins, for he knew no sins" (JST Heb. 7:26). His priesthood was ἀπαράβατος (*aparabatos*), meaning "permanent, unchangeable, and incomparable" (7:24). No other priesthood will succeed it. It is "as eternal as God himself" and will administer "endless lives" to all who receive it.[90]

In chapters 8–10 the author focuses on the Savior's Atonement. As the great High Priest, Jesus offered himself as the eternal atoning sacrifice and became the mediator of this new and better covenant (8:6), putting the law of God into the hearts of his people (8:10; 10:16). The old law, with its performances and sacrifices, Jesus fulfilled. Through the new covenant, God promised to remember the sins of the repentant no more (10:17), and each Saint was challenged to enter into "a new and living way" through the blood of Christ (10:15–20). Those who were willing to do so in patience and faith would be justified and receive the promise (10:35–38).

Chapter 11 then concentrates on faith and its outward effects in the lives of Israel's spiritual heroes. Faith is the actual underlying substance, substantiation, or assurance (ὑπόστασις, *hypostasis*) and the evidence or evincing (ἔλεγχος, *elenchos*) of things not seen that are true (11:1; see Alma 32:21). True faith necessarily manifests itself in works of righteousness.

Chapter 12 thus exhorts the faithful to endure the chastening and correction of God, who is the Father of their spirits. By inheriting the blessings of eternity as sons and daughters of the living God, his Saints are able to come to the new Mount Zion, the heavenly Jerusalem, being made perfect, an assembly of "firstborns" (πρωτότοκοι, *prōtotokoi*), having inherited all with *the* Firstborn.

Chapter 13 concludes by noting, "Marriage is honourable in all," and by counseling all to "let brotherly love continue," to "be without covetousness," and to be loyal to Jesus alone, "bearing his reproach. For here [on earth] have we no continuing city, but we seek one to come" (13:1, 4–5, 13–14). Those who enter into this holy order and keep its covenants prepare themselves for eternal life, and fulfillment of the invocation that "the God of peace, that brought again from the dead our Lord Jesus, that great shepherd of the sheep, through the blood of the everlasting covenant, make you perfect in every good work to do his will" (13:20–21).

---

90. "Instruction on Priesthood, 5 October 1840," 1, in *Documents, Volume 7: September 1839–January 1841,* ed. Matthew C. Godfrey and others, The Joseph Smith Papers (Salt Lake City: Church Historian's Press, 2012), 435, https://www.josephsmithpapers.org/paper-summary/instruction-on-priesthood-5-october-1840/1; "History, 1838–1856, Volume E-1 [1 July 1843–30 April 1844]," 1708, Joseph Smith Papers, https://www.josephsmithpapers.org/paper-summary/history-1838-1856-volume-e-1-1-july-1843-30-april-1844/80.

Structure of the Work

By seeing how the author constructed his work, his message becomes all the more clear.[91] The view we have taken in this commentary looks at the broad literary organization, that is, at the work's form and content as a whole as supported by its individual pieces. In short, we have used content to determine the structure.[92]

As a whole, the work divides into five parts preceded by a carefully crafted introduction (1:1–4) and followed by a concluding heartfelt wish (13:20–21). In order to help his readers follow the development of his arguments, the author methodically states the purpose of each part: the first after the introduction (1:5) and the others at the conclusion of the preceding section (2:17; 5:9–10; 10:36–39; 12:13).

Part 1 (1:5–2:18) confirms the traditional view of Christ and very skillfully lays the groundwork for seeing him as the great High Priest because of his place as both the brother of humankind and the Son of God. As such he is the perfect mediator between the mortal and the Divine. In sum, he is the ideal High Priest. In this section, we see the author introducing a comparative/superlative rhetorical device he will use throughout the Epistle to emphasize the unmatched greatness of the Son along with his work and power compared to others.

Part 2 (3:1–5:10) contains the author's initial analysis of the Savior as High Priest, stressing the continuity between the Levitical Priesthood of the old covenant and that of Christ in the new. He shows that the Savior was "trustworthy . . . like Moses" (NR 3:2), and that he, like Aaron, was appointed to his priestly position by God (5:4–5).

Part 3 (5:11–10:39) contains the author's continued analysis of Christ as High Priest, but in this section the author stresses the difference and superiority of Jesus over the Levitical high priest. The author shows that the Lord is not a high priest after the Aaronic order but after the higher order of Melchizedek (7:1–28) and that the personal sacrifice Christ made was far different and vastly more profitable than the offerings of mere animals (8:1–9:28) because it was perfectly efficacious where the others were not (10:1–18). Based on this fact, the author concludes (10:19–25) with an

---

91. How one understands the structure of any scriptural piece influences how she or he interprets it. For a study on how viewing differing structures of Hebrews influences its interpretation, see Steve Stanley, "The Structure of Hebrews from Three Perspectives," *Tyndale Bulletin* 45, no. 2 (1994): 245–71.

92. In this we follow Bruce, *Epistle to the Hebrews,* xix–xxii; Ellingworth, *Epistle to the Hebrews,* 50–62; and particularly Vanhoye, *Letter to the Hebrews,* 15–20.

exhortation that defines and emphasizes the consequences of the Savior's act in the face of the situation in which the Saints found themselves and urges them to come to a unity with their Lord, the merciful High Priest, through faith (10:22), hope (10:23), and love (10:24–25).

Through the material he has presented in parts 2 and 3, the author has prepared his readers for the points he makes in the last two parts of his homily.

Part 4 (11:1–12:3) reviews the faith of the spiritual as well as physical ancestors of the Christians. The author shows both the blessings and the cost of obedience and highlights the faithful endurance of these heroes. He then admonishes his readers to follow their example by pushing forward in faith and loyalty to God.

Part 5 (12:14–13:18) addresses the two dimensions of charity. The author admonishes his readers, through love, to seek peace with their fellowmen (12:14) and then to seek sanctification with God (12:15–29). He then amplifies his first admonition, defining a Christian attitude toward one's neighbors and then urging his readers to so act in behalf of others (13:1–6) and then toward the greater Christian community (13:7–19).

The Developmental Process

In developing his arguments, the author of Hebrews appealed to various scriptures that he interpreted for his readers. His readers were able to follow and be persuaded by his arguments because he did not interpret in a cultural vacuum. He applied certain traditions, assumptions, and strategies to elucidate and communicate the message he wanted to bring forth that his readers were aware of and comfortable with.

In a format similar to the *pesharim* (a Hebrew word meaning "interpretation") found among the roughly contemporaneous Dead Sea Scrolls, the author quotes a passage and then provides an explanation of the scripture with a specific focus on how the authoritative text contributes to an understanding of the importance of the Savior and his work. To get his point across, the author often cites only a portion of a text, albeit with care. He then breaks down the passage explaining words and phrases. But in selectively quoting only a portion of a scripture and then analyzing it out of context, the author actually recontextualizes the passage and repurposes it in a way that fits his thesis.[93] Though this technique would be frowned upon today, it was part and parcel of the exegesis in the author's day.

---

93. David M. Moffitt, "The Interpretation of Scripture in the Epistle to the Hebrews," in Mason and McCruden, *Reading the Epistle to the Hebrews,* 96.

Among other strategies that he used in order to develop his arguments were those that were later canonized in the Midrash (a Hebrew word meaning "exposition"). This term refers to an exegetical methodology that pushes more deeply into a text than a literal understanding would allow in an attempt to get at the spiritual heart of the scripture.[94] It does so in ways and following a logic that can sometimes be different from traditional post-Enlightenment modes of thinking.[95] Therefore, midrashic readings of scripture sometimes fly in the face of more literal readings of the scriptures. Such is the case in a number of the author's developments. The Translation Notes and Comments sections of the various chapter analyses found below will point these out.

Two techniques the author used in bolstering his theses are of particular importance. Both of these eventually became standard rabbinical ways of stressing a point but were operating in the first century AD. The first is making a case by *qal waḥomer,* which is basically an *a fortiori* argument that pushes an idea by stressing that if a minor point "x" is important, then how much more so is the major point "y" (for examples, see 2:2–3; 8:6). Using this technique, a writer or orator makes a statement about a "lighter" matter which then infers even greater weight to the "heavier" matter he mentions next.

The second is making a case using the rabbinical interpretive tool that later became known as *gezērāh šāwāh,* which is "an argument by analogy that is based on the presence of an identical term or phrase in two different scriptural texts such that the two texts can be read together."[96] This is based on the rabbinical idea that "all of Scripture is meaningful and indeed has a single author, so that an occurrence of a word in one passage can be used to illuminate the use of a word in another passage. The two passages, indeed, can stand as mutually interpretive" (for an example, see the juxtaposition of Ps. 2:7 with 2 Sam. 7:14 in Heb. 1:5).[97] Again, using scriptures

94. Richard N. Soulen, *Handbook of Biblical Criticism,* 2d ed. (Atlanta: John Knox Press, 1981), 122, s.v. *midrash.* Attributing methods used by later rabbis to the first century opens the problem of anachronism, but in the cases reviewed here the practice can be found in texts dating to the Second Temple period.

95. Howard Eilberg-Schwartz, "Myth, Inference, and the Relativism of Reason: An Argument from the History of Judaism," in *Myth and Philosophy,* ed. Frank E. Reynolds and David Tracy (Albany: State University of New York Press, 1990), 247–85; Naomi Janowitz and Andrew J. Lazarus, "Rabbinic Methods of Inference and the Rationality Debate," *Journal of Religion* 72, no. 4 (October 1992): 491–511.

96. Johnson, *Hebrews,* 175.

97. Johnson, *Hebrews,* 175. For studies, see David H. Wenkel, "Gezerah Shawah as Analogy in the Epistle to the Hebrews," *Biblical Theology Bulletin: Journal of Bible Culture* 37,

in this manner violates traditional post-Enlightenment procedures but it fit easily into the mindset of Second Temple Judaism and thereby into earliest Christianity.

The author normally introduces these quotes as if falling from the lips of God himself, often using the verb λέγω (*lego*), "to say," to stress this point. Of the thirty-seven times he quotes scripture, he has God speaking twenty-three times, with Christ and the Holy Spirit each speaking four times. The only anomaly to his introductory formula is found at 2:6, where he states that somewhere someone testified, saying such and such. But even here, though the speaker is human, the ambiguity supports the author's insistence that God stands behind all revelation. Also, in 9:20, referring to Moses reciting a command from God, and in 12:21, describing Moses as being terrified of Jehovah's revelations, the author is still emphasizing the aspect of divine revelation. For the author, it is the force of the Father either speaking directly or prompting others to either speak or understand that is the authoritative ground of scripture and makes it not only relevant to but essential in understanding the mind and will of God.

The author fully believes that God has spoken in times past through the prophets (1:1), and these passages, from the author's point of view, have preserved those very words. Thus, they carry heavy weight and must be taken seriously. He can, therefore, use them to strengthen his exhortations inducing his readers to stay true to their Lord.

The author skillfully makes his appeals by presenting the new covenant as the fulfillment of the promises of the old. His use of the various biblical texts reveals just how important the Old Testament was for him. Indeed, it is impossible to fully understand "the significance of the spiritual realities of the New Covenant—[the transformation of the soul, the way to perfection, entrance into the heavenly realm, and the grace generated through the Atonement and exaltation of the Savior that made all these possible]—apart from their concrete prefigurements in Scripture."[98] Thus, the idea of "fulfillment" that stood behind and was revealed through the Old Testament scriptures validated the old covenant and gave it meaning, authority, and significance for those now living under the new covenant.

---

no. 2 (May 2007): 62–68; Saul Lieberman, *Hellenism in Jewish Palestine: Studies in the Literary Transmission, Beliefs and Manners of Palestine in the I Century B.C.E.–IV Century C.E.*, 2d ed. (New York: Jewish Theological Seminary of America, 1962), 58–63; Wilhelm Bacher and Jacob Zallel Lauterbach, "Talmud Hermeneutics," in *Jewish Encyclopedia,* accessed March 11, 2016, http://www.jewishencyclopedia.com/articles/14215-talmud-hermeneutics.

98. Steven K. Stanley, "A New Covenant Hermeneutic: The Use of Scripture in Hebrews 8–10," *Tyndale Bulletin* 46, no. 1 (1995): 204–6.

The Use of the Old Testament

As stated above, a notable feature of the Epistle to the Hebrews is the frequent use and exegetical exploration of passages from the Old Testament. These were not Hebrew but Greek texts found in translations of the books of the Old Testament known as the Septuagint (from the Latin word for "seventy"). Tradition ascribes the creation of this work to Jewish sages living in Egypt during the third century BC.[99] This work was the Bible for Jews living outside of the Holy Land because most of them knew neither Hebrew nor Aramaic but rather Greek.

In reaching to the scriptures as proof texts for his points, the author uses Psalms far more than he uses any other work. There he found a wealth of material in support for his Christological reading of the Old Testament. In total, he quoted from Psalms 19 times and made illusions to it in 15 more instances. He used the Pentateuch the next most often, requoting 9 verses (3 from Genesis, 2 from Exodus, 4 from Deuteronomy) and alluding to another 15 (9 from Genesis, 1 from Exodus, 2 from Leviticus, 2 from Numbers, and 2 from Deuteronomy). Most of these he used to illustrate God's work in redemptive history. The author did not overlook the prophets. He quoted Isaiah 3 times with 4 allusions, Jeremiah 2 times with 3 allusions, and once from Habakkuk, Haggai, Proverbs, and 2 Samuel, with 1 allusion to Joshua and likely also 1 from Proverbs and Job, although the latter two are rather oblique.

Each time the author begins an argument, he sets its foundation on one of these scriptures: by first appealing to these ancient and holy texts apart from Christ, he establishes common ground with his Jewish readers. On that ground, he is able to show both the futurity of the old covenant (what God designed it to do) and also its futility as the means of salvation. By appealing to the Old Testament alone, the author skillfully and forcefully excludes any counterarguments that insisted that the old covenant with its Levitical Priesthood had ever been adequate as a means of gaining purity

---

99. Though some disagree. The work had been around long enough to be widespread among Jews not living in the Holy Land during New Testament times. For these Greek-speaking people, the LXX was their contact with the law since most of the people knew neither Hebrew nor Aramaic. For a study, see Timothy Michael Law, *When God Spoke Greek* (New York: Oxford University Press, 2013). Concerning the LXX, we stress that a single, codified work did not exist. The various books were passed around in scrolls that had been copied and recopied. This copying resulted in variants and thus the single volume found today only approximates the original. Even so, it is a very good approximation. See Moffitt, "Interpretation," 78–79.

and thus clearing the way to approach God. Having done so, he is able to clearly demonstrate the logic of how God's revelation of the work of the Son, the great High Priest, "fulfills what the old order both intimated and lacked."[100] Unlike a *pesher* interpretation of textual mysteries that relied on esoteric revelation in order to gain an understanding of a text,[101] the author presents no revisionist history of God's Old Testament word, but rather of its God-intended fulfillment. In doing so, he demonstrates the full relevance of the old covenant for those who have yielded to the power of God's word as revealed through his Son.[102]

In sum, all this demonstrates that "far more than any other [New Testament] book, Hebrews, from beginning to end, *preaches* the [Old Testament]. The author's explanations of the text serve ultimately to communicate a forceful message aimed at convincing the hearers/readers to respond by persevering in following Christ and standing with his church. His Christology vies for a christocentric life. His hortatory material has but one aim: to present a resolute call to endurance and holy living. This is the task he takes up in taking up the [Old Testament] and he carries it out with rhetorical power and artistry."[103]

The Use and Function of Typology

The author of Hebrews is especially adept at using biblical typology as a means of bolstering a point he wishes to make. This interpretive method views an element "found in the Old Testament [as prefiguring] one found in the New Testament. The initial one is called the *type* and the fulfillment is designated the *antitype*."[104] On the surface, it seems just like another

100. Cockerill, *Epistle to the Hebrews,* 58.

101. The noun *pesher* comes from the Hebrew פֵּשֶׁר (*pēšer*), meaning "interpretation," but carries the nuance of "solution" and denotes a mystical interpretive commentary on an Old Testament text. Many models of this method are found among the Dead Sea Scrolls. For studies, see Maurya P. Horgan, *Pesharim: Qumran Interpretations of Biblical Books,* vol. 8 of Catholic Biblical Quarterly Monograph Series (Washington, D.C.: Catholic Biblical Association of America, 1979); James H. Charlesworth, *The Pesharim and Qumran History: Chaos or Consensus?* (Grand Rapids, Mich.: Eerdmans, 2002).

102. Cockerill, *Epistle to the Hebrews,* 58.

103. George H. Guthrie, "Hebrews," in *Commentary on the New Testament's Use of the Old Testament,* ed. D. A. Carson and G. K. Beale (Grand Rapids, Mich.: Baker Academic, 2007), 923.

104. "Biblical Typology," Theopedia, accessed August 27, 2014, https://www.theopedia.com/biblical-typology, italics in original. This source is an online conservative Christian encyclopedia.

form of symbolism where one thing represents something else. Typology differs, however, in at least three important ways.

First, a type is a "definite historical person or event . . . [that] exists with its own independent meaning and justification."[105] Therefore, a type differs from a symbol, which does not necessarily exist on its own merits in a particular place or time. For instance, the raising of the brazen serpent on the stick is a type of Christ being lifted up on the cross (see Num. 21:9 and John 3:14–15). It is not just any serpent on a stick; it is the specific event carried out by Moses that prefigures the actual event of Christ being raised on the cross. The raising of the serpent was the type; the actual crucifixion of the Lord was the antitype. Thus, a type "relates the past to the present in terms of a historical correspondence and escalation in which the divinely ordered pre-figurement finds a complement in the subsequent and greater event."[106]

Second, in the case of symbols, the author of the text deliberately uses one thing to stand for something else. It is unlikely that every single author in the Old Testament was cognizant of the future fulfillment of various types in Christ and so deliberately directed his narrative to that end. Nonetheless, as far as the author of Hebrews is concerned, a divine hand was at work both ordering history and inspiring its prophets, thus leaving a trail of spiritual insight. Thus, "the [Hebrew Bible's] authors and participants did not necessarily recognize any typological force in the original, but in the divine plan the early event did anticipate the later reality."[107]

Third, the type can highlight the similarities between it and the antitype or provide contrast between the two. This is known as "synthetic" and "antithetic" typology.[108] For instance, Adam can be viewed as both a synthetic and antithetic type. Adam is like Christ since he brought physical life to us all as Christ brought spiritual life. But Adam also stands as an antithetic type as Paul so eloquently states, "as in Adam all die, even so in Christ shall all be made alive" (1 Cor. 15:22).

While biblical typology has existed since the inception of Christianity, there have been some who have criticized its use.[109] Even so, it is one of the

105. Ursula Brumm, *American Thought and Religious Typology,* trans. John Hoaglund (New Brunswick, N.J.: Rutgers University Press, 1970), 23.

106. E. Earle Ellis, *The Old Testament in Early Christianity* (Tübingen: J. C. B. Mohr, 1991), 106.

107. "Biblical Typology," Theopedia.

108. Ellis, *Old Testament,* 108.

109. Some contend that "typology is forced exegesis rather than an interpretation rising naturally out of the Scriptures." Bernard Ramm, *Protestant Biblical Interpretation:*

earliest Christian ways of interpreting the Old Testament. In fact, "typology is the method of interpreting Scripture that is predominant in the NT and characteristic of it."[110] Christ implicitly defends the validity of typology when he tells his hearers to search the scriptures for "they are they which testify of me" (John 5:39). Additionally, he expounded the scriptures unto the disciples on the Road to Emmaus and showed how they testified of him (Luke 24:27).

The Book of Mormon also witnesses that the Hebrew Bible was full of Christological types. It notes that the things given of God "from the beginning" typified the Lord (2 Ne. 11:4). Further, through types, Jehovah showed his people many things "concerning his coming" (Mosiah 3:15). Indeed, the law of Moses itself was a type and shadow of that coming (Mosiah 13:30–31; 16:14).

The Epistle to the Hebrews is replete with use of types. For example, the author speaks about how the law of Moses was "a shadow of good things to come" (10:1) and how the tabernacle in the desert "was a figure for the time then present" (9:9) as well as a "type and shadow of what is in heaven" (NR 8:5). He notes that the Levitical high priest served as a model of Christ (8:1–2) as did Melchizedek (7:16–17). The author's purpose in using these types was to illustrate how Christ supersedes the elements of the law of Moses. The author's use of biblical typology helped him make the Old Testament relevant and important for his Christian readers. While it may be difficult to know if he was reading too much into a text, it is certain that, under inspiration, the author understood the nature and mission of the Lord and discerned the message within the old covenant that bore witness of the new.

Use of Chiasmus

Chiasmus is a literary device that uses mirroring or inverted parallelism to emphasize a point. A simple example is A B C B′ A′ where the symbols A and B can refer to words, sentences, ideas, or themes that are repeated in B′ and A′. Often an author uses this scheme to emphasize the middle element C. The scheme can involve a single verse, multiple verses, or even an

---

A Textbook of Hermeneutics, 3d ed. (Grand Rapids, Mich.: Baker Books, 1970), 215. Often those who make this case do not believe that prophecy exists and therefore discount any conclusions based on it.

110. Leonhard Goppelt, *Typos: The Typological Interpretation of the Old Testament in the New,* trans. Donald H. Madvig (Grand Rapids, Mich.: William B. Eerdmans, 1982), 198.

entire chapter.[111] In Latter-day Saint scripture, chiasmus has been famously identified in Alma 36 and other places in the Book of Mormon.[112]

Analysis of the use of chiasmus in Hebrews is a fairly recent development.[113] While the idea is not universally accepted, the possibility has caused many scholars to look at how the author of Hebrews may have used chiasms to emphasize various points.[114] Some are attracted to this device because it potentially provides a way to structure Hebrews, which has been notoriously hard to fit into a traditional structural framework or genre.

While Hebrews has many possible instances of chiasmus, scholars are still divided as to how many are intentional, that is, deliberate creations by the author, and how many are mere reflects of his thought processes.[115] Further complicating this challenge is that many proposed chiasms are based on connections between words that are synonyms or have similar meanings rather than instances of the repetition of same words or thoughts.[116] Also, for those not using a Greek text, chiasms can be harder to recognize in English since the differences in grammar and syntax between the languages can disguise a chiastic structure. Combining the work of various scholars, over seventy-five possible chiasms have been suggested.[117] We must stress, however, that among the proposed chiasms there is no universal agreement.

Scholars have identified different levels of chiasms in Hebrews. Some are contained in a single verse. An example of one proposal is 11:3:[118] "By faith we understand that the worlds were organized by the word of God, so that what is visible was made by what is invisible." The chiastic features can be illustrated as follows:

---

111. See John W. Welch, "Introduction," in *Chiasmus in Antiquity: Structures, Analyses, Exegesis* (Provo, Utah: Research Press, 1999), 9–16.

112. John W. Welch, "Chiasmus in the Book of Mormon," in *Book of Mormon Authorship: New Light on Ancient Origins,* ed. Noel B. Reynolds (Provo, Utah: Religious Studies Center, Brigham Young University, 1982), 33–52.

113. The scholar Albert Vanhoye helped bring this practice into prominence in the 1960s. See his work *La structure littéraire de l'Épître aux Hébreux* (Rome: Editrice Pontificio Istituto Biblico, 1963).

114. David M. Heath, "Chiastic Structures in Hebrews: With a Focus on 1:7–14 and 12:26–29," *Neotestamentica* 46, no. 1 (2012): 62.

115. Heath, "Chiastic Structures," 62.

116. Heath, "Chiastic Structures," 68.

117. Beyond the seventy-five mentioned in Heath, "Chiastic Structures," 65, see the chiasmus index on https://chiasmusresources.org/new-testament#21, which now lists over one hundred fifty.

118. Ellingworth, *Epistle to the Hebrews,* 568.

A organized
  B worlds
    C word of God
    C′ what is invisible
  B′ visible
A′ made

The justification for the chiasmus is that both halves of the verse have the same meaning. Though none of the terms are identical, they do express similar ideas.

Other chiasms stretch across multiple verses. An example proposed by William Lane in 1991 covering multiple verses is 7:1–10.[119] This chiastic structure can be outlined thus:

A Melchizedek met Abraham (v. 1)
  B Melchizedek blessed Abraham (v. 1)
    C Abraham paid tithes to Melchizedek (v. 2)
      D The greatness of Melchizedek extolled (vv. 3–4)
    C′ Abraham, paid tithes to Melchizedek (v. 4)
  B′ Melchizedek blessed Abraham (v. 6)
A′ Melchizedek met Abraham (v. 10)

In this example, the various elements of the chiasmus are not symmetrical in length. Even so, the themes are easily recognized in both the Greek and English texts. Further, this example illustrates how the style can be used to emphasize a point (in this case the greatness of Melchizedek).

An even more extended proposal of chiasmus, influentially launched by Albert Vanhoye in 1989, runs from 8:1 to 9:28, with the central focus at verse 9:11,[120] which reads, "But when Christ came, a high priest of good things that have come, he passed through the greater and more perfect tent that was not made by human hands, that is not of this creation." This structure marks the Savior as the great High Priest and focuses on the work he did. The structure makes this idea the focal point of not only this section but of the central chiasmus within the entire book of Hebrews. That being the case, 9:11 is the most important verse in the whole book and what

119. Lane, *Hebrews 1–8,* 159–60.

120. Albert Vanhoye, *Structure and Message of the Epistle to the Hebrews,* vol. 12 of Subsidia Biblica (Rome: Editrice Pontificio Istituto Biblico, 1989), 35–36.

everything in the book revolves around.[121] This idea can be seen in the following example, which views a major portion of the Epistle as a carefully structured chiasm.[122]

A Avoid the Company of the Faithless Generation (3:7–19)
  B Pursue the Blessing Lost to the Faithless Generation (4:1–11)
    C You are Accountable before the Word of God (4:12–13)
      D Embrace This Great High Priest (4:14–16)
        E Christ, the All-Sufficient High Priest (5:1–10:18)
      D′ Avail Yourself of This Great High Priest (10:19–25)
    C′ You are More Accountable Because of This High Priest (10:26–31)
  B′ Pursue the Blessing Promised the Faithful (10:32–33)
A′ Join the Company of the Faithful of Old (11:1–40)

Vanhoye's work was praised by Gabriella Gelardini in 2009 as having had a "most fruitful impact" on Hebrews scholarship. Building on that central work, she offered a "macrostructure consisting of a five-partite two-dimensional and concentric step-by-step arrangement" of the full letter to the Hebrews.[123]

At the same time, and most exhaustively, John Paul Heil, in 2010, published his structural and audience response analysis, dividing the entire Epistle into thirty-three sequential chiastic units, seeing their composition at "three macrochiastic levels."[124] Skillfully illustrating these various patterns "intricately at work in the elegant structure of the letter to the Hebrews," Heil provides a remarkable aid to modern readers. He concludes, "The ancient audience, of course, did not see [these patterns], but rather heard and experienced them as an essential vehicle orchestrating the author's rhetorical presentation . . . through its arresting artistry."[125]

121. Vanhoye, *Structure and Message,* 36.

122. The example follows Cockerill, *Epistle to the Hebrews,* 463. For a compatible early suggestion that the entire Epistle was centrally organized around 8:1–2, pronouncing "the main point of this letter is that we have just such a high priest," see John W. Welch, "Chiasmus in the New Testament," in Welch, *Chiasmus in Antiquity,* 220–21.

123. Gabriella Gelardini, "From 'Linguistic Turn' and Hebrews Scholarship to *Anadiplosis Iterata*: The Enigma of a Structure," *Harvard Theological Review* 102, no. 1 (2009): 59, 61–73.

124. John Paul Heil, *Hebrews: Chiastic Structures and Audience Response,* vol. 46 of Catholic Biblical Quarterly Monograph Series (Washington, D.C.: Catholic Biblical Association of America, 2010), 4.

125. Heil, *Hebrews,* 428.

As noted above, and while there has been considerable progress, no universal agreement has been reached among scholars as to which passages are deliberate constructs by the author or even which sections are really chiastic at all. Some among the more conservative have even felt that the continual looking for chiasms "says more about the determination of the modern scholar than about the structure of Hebrews."[126] Even so, the weight of the cumulative evidence certainly suggests that there are instances where the author deliberately used this rhetorical technique to buttress his arguments and emphasize his points. We note several of these in this commentary.

Having stated all that, we must emphasize that, although not every proposed chiasmus can be definitively determined as something deliberately designed by the author, looking closely at the more probable chiasms can help modern readers better understand not only the structural format of individual sections of Hebrews but also better appreciate the overall skill of the author in making a case for his position.

The Epistle's View of Christ

The Importance of Christology

In technical terms, this section deals with what students of the Bible call Christology, that is, the study and understanding of the Savior and his work.[127]

---

126. Barry C. Joslin, "Can Hebrews Be Structured? An Assessment of Eight Approaches," *Currents in Biblical Research* 6, no. 1 (October 2007): 111. Heath, "Chiastic Structures," 78, concludes that while the strength of the individual macrostructures within the text of Hebrews is not very compelling in and of themselves, the consistent nature of smaller units of chiastic structures is observable, and when the centers of these macrostructures are compared, then the positing of a chiastic book-level arrangement looks probable.

127. Christology is divided into two aspects. "High Christology" refers to approaches that begin with the divinity and preexistence of Christ as the *Logos* (the Word), as expressed in the prologue to the Gospel of John (John 1:1–14). These approaches interpret the works of Christ in terms of his divinity. The term "low Christology," on the other hand, refers to approaches that begin with the human aspects and the ministry of Jesus (including his teachings, miracles, and parables) and move toward his divinity. Those emphasizing this aspect explore the incarnation and its mystery, referring to how the physical form and nature of Jesus can be understood in light of his divinity. For a study, see Raymond E. Brown, "Christology," in *The New Jerome Biblical Commentary,* ed.

The term is not frequently used by Latter-day Saints, but it is very common in the world of New Testament studies. Christology is very important because our understanding of who and what Christ is sets our theological foundation and determines the degree of our willingness to follow him. Those who view him as just a man, and many do, see his teachings as, at most, ethical, beautiful, and even compelling statements that should be considered and even implemented for both their good and that of society.[128] On the other hand, those who view him as a God, and many do, understand his teachings, though still beautiful and compelling, as divine mandates carrying eternal ramifications and are not only good for themselves and society but absolutely necessary for their spiritual growth and eventual reunion with the Father and Son. There are high stakes and eternal consequences to one's Christological views. Can our natures really approach theirs? Is it really possible to become as they are? If the answer to these questions is "yes," then divinity becomes a possibility and Christ marks the way.[129]

The Christology of the Church of Jesus Christ can be summed up as follows:

> Jesus Christ descended from his high pre-existent station as a God when he came to earth to die for mankind's sins. . . . He was Jehovah come to earth in a physical body as the Only Begotten of the Father in the flesh. . . . While on earth he was still God, but he received from his Father "grace for grace," as do God's other children (D&C 93:12 . . .). The Book of Mormon and Doctrine and Covenants speak forcefully of the divine sonship of Christ and also of his humanity (Mosiah 15:2-3; Alma 6:8; 11:38; 13:16; 34:2; 3 Ne. 11:7, 28:10; D&C 93, . . .).
>
> Like Jesus Christ, all mortals live in a state of humiliation, but through the mediation of the Christ they may progress to a state of exaltation. . . . There is no ultimate disparity between the divine and human natures; Joseph Smith asserted that mankind is of the same species as God, having been made in God's image (theomorphism) and being eternal, with unlimited capacity (*TPJS*, pp. 345–46). One early LDS leader [President

Raymond E. Brown, Joseph A. Fitzmyer, and Roland E. Murphy (Englewood Cliffs, N.J.: Pearson Publishing, 1990), 1354–59.

128. A good example of this approach is Albert Schweitzer, *The Quest of the Historical Jesus* (Mineola, N.Y.: Dover Publications, 2005), which was originally published in English in 1910 by A. & C. Black. For more modern analyses, see Craig S. Keener, *The Historical Jesus of the Gospels* (Grand Rapids, Mich.: Eerdmans, 2012); or Richard Bauckham, *Jesus and the Eyewitnesses: The Gospels as Eyewitness Testimony* (Grand Rapids, Mich.: William B. Eerdmans, 2017).

129. A point made by Julie Smith to Richard Draper, May 21, 2017.

> Lorenzo Snow] proclaimed, "As man now is, God once was. As God now is, man may be. . . ." Latter-day Saints speak of man as a god in embryo and of Jesus Christ as mankind's elder brother.[130]

A close examination of the above statement demonstrates that "Latter-day Saint doctrine can be understood to have appreciation for Christ and applications for man that go beyond traditional Christology. It is the LDS teaching that all the Father's children possess the potential to strive toward the same godhood that the Godhead already has; because in their humanity there is a divinity that is progressing and growing according to the faith, intelligence, and love that abound in their souls. Like the attribute of perfection, divinity is not a static absolute but a dynamic progression."[131]

Before getting into the Christology of Hebrews, one more item seems noteworthy. The Church, like Hebrews itself, is unconcerned with what some feel is a major theological puzzle that the Epistle raises, namely, how can Christ be the express image of God, the creator of worlds, yet still learn obedience through suffering? How can God learn? How can he suffer?[132] These questions anchor on a distortion created by viewing Jesus, the Godhead, and godhood through the lens of Platonic philosophy, something neither Latter-day Saint theology nor Hebrews allows.

Having noted that, it is also true that many Latter-day Saints do not fully appreciate who and what the mortal Jesus really was or what he had to give up to "take upon him[self] flesh and blood, and go forth upon the face of the earth" (Mosiah 7:27; compare 13:34). The Book of Mormon witness, however, is clear: "God himself shall come down among the children of men, and shall redeem his people" (Mosiah 15:1). Indeed, he is "the Lord Omnipotent who reigneth, who was, and is from all eternity to all eternity" (Mosiah 3:5). And more, he is "the very Eternal Father of heaven and of earth, and all things which in them are; he is the beginning and the end, the first and the last" (Alma 11:39). It was this "God, the Father of all things" who took upon himself "the image of man" (Mosiah 7:27).[133] Thus, it was

130. Gary P. Gillum, "Christology," in Ludlow, *Encyclopedia of Mormonism,* 1:272–73; See also S. Kent Brown, "Man and Son of Man: Issues in Theology and Christology," in *Pearl of Great Price: Revelations from God,* ed. Charles D. Tate and H. Donl Peterson (Provo, Utah: Religious Studies Center, Brigham Young University, 1989), 57–72.

131. Gillum, "Christology," 273.

132. For a discussion, see Rowan A. Greer, "The Jesus of Hebrews and the Christ of Chalcedon," in Mason and McCruden, *Reading the Epistle to the Hebrews,* 233–34.

133. The Book of Mormon is consistently careful never to identify the Lord fully with humankind. For instance, it never says that Jesus became a man, but rather states that

no small question when the Holy Spirit asked Nephi, "Knowest thou the condescension of God?" (1 Ne. 11:16). To "condescend" means to waive the privileges of rank and dignity and descend to the station of an inferior. Though Jesus did not give up his godhood, he certainly suppressed it so he could fully experience the impotence, weaknesses, frailties, failures, and demands of life as did his mortal brothers and sisters. Thus, though he was a God, he was still fully mortal and identified completely with humankind. To drive this point home, the Spirit showed Nephi what condescension cost this God. Though this eternal and powerful being went forth healing, giving, teaching, and loving, "the everlasting God was judged of the world . . . [and] was lifted up upon the cross and slain for the sins of the world" (1 Ne. 11:32–33). The irony is incredible. Even so, as the author of Hebrews understood, Jesus learned the cost of obedience through what God called upon him to suffer. And in the process, he also gained compassion such that he ministers as the faithful and merciful High Priest into eternity.

Christology as Presented in Hebrews

Though the Epistle to the Hebrews does not share the uniqueness of the Latter-day Saint view, it certainly contributes to that view's broader understanding of who and what Christ was and is. Before developing that theme, however, one item needs to be kept in mind—the author of Hebrews has but one objective as he develops his brilliant Christological insights: to encourage his readers not just to maintain but to progress in their commitment and devotion to the Lord and their place in both his earthly and heavenly kingdoms. To stress the point, the author does not present his doctrinal

---

he took upon himself "the form of man" (Mosiah 13:34). It makes the point that Christ would "take upon him the image of man, and it should be the image after which man was created in the beginning; or in other words, . . . that man was created after the image of God, and that God should come down among the children of men, and take upon him flesh and blood, and go forth upon the face of the earth" (Mosiah 7:27). More fully developing the idea that some kind of separation exists between the Lord and humankind, the book focuses on his self-sacrifice and states clearly that it will not be a "sacrifice of man," indeed it "shall not be a human sacrifice; but it must be an infinite and eternal sacrifice" (Alma 34:10). Stressing the point, it states that the "great and last sacrifice will be the Son of God, yea, infinite and eternal" (Alma 34:14). From the Book of Mormon perspective, though Jesus was fully mortal, he was not actually "human." In this case the adjective refers to one whose paternal descent is from Adam. The Savior's was not. He was the direct Son of God. As the Book of Mormon puts it, he was "the Son, because of the flesh" (Mosiah 15:3). Even so, he shared the "image" and the "form" of his brethren and with them all the challenges and delights that form offered.

development for its own sake. Rather he continually links his Christological understanding with his readers' behavior. He shows them that because of what Christ is, they should behave in a certain way, but also because of what he is, they will receive serious consequences if they abandon his way.[134]

In a single well-crafted sentence running four verses long, the author introduces the station, power, position, and glory of Christ (1:1–4). He is God's spokesman and heir, the creator and sustainer of worlds, and the revelation of the Father's image and glory. After providing a way for human sin to be purged, he was exalted and sits on the right hand of the Father. The author concludes that because of what the Son has done, he became greater than the angels. The author then cites seven Old Testament scriptures to bolster this point (1:5–14). His purpose is not to denigrate the position of angels but rather to build on their exalted position to illustrate just how truly superior the Son is. Indeed, the Father put all things under the Son's power and gave him full honor and glory (2:5–8).

Once he had illustrated the exalted position of the Son, the author then turns to the Savior's station in mortality and its importance. This divine being voluntarily became lower than the angels and participated fully in human nature including suffering and especially death (2:9, 14, 17). By that means he gained compassion for all those who suffer. Indeed, he became "a merciful and faithful High Priest" serving his Father through making the Atonement for his brothers and sisters (2:17–18).

Having introduced the Savior as High Priest, the author develops and defines the Savior's place in the priesthood. He shows that Jesus' priesthood surpasses that of the Levitical order (4:14–7:28). This was due in large part because of the Lord's divine sonship that made him superior to both angels and Levitical priests (5:5–10; 7:28). To emphasize this point, the author again draws on scripture (Gen. 14:17–20; Ps. 110:4) to compare the Savior with the great priest Melchizedek (5:6–10; 6:20; 7:1–17). The author insists that his order of the priesthood stood higher than that of Aaron. By this means the author is able to establish the uniqueness and superiority of the Lord's position in the priesthood. He stands as "a priest for ever after the order of Melchizedek" (5:6; 6:20).

Once he had set the stage, the author presents the Lord's unique standing and redemptive work through a series of interconnected declarations. The author notes specifically that the Savior is the "great high priest" (4:14–5:10;

134. Note how he introduces the behaviors he wants them to adopt in 2:1; 3:1, 8; 4:1; 6:1; 10:19; 12:1.

7:1–28) who supersedes his Levitical counterpart, for he alone is able to "completely and eternally save those who come to God through him, since he always lives to make intercession for them" (NR 7:25). Because of his office, he becomes "the guarantee of a better covenant" (NR 7:22), indeed, a "new covenant" that will fulfill "better promises" as well as prophetic hope (8:1–13). This he does as he ministers in the heavenly sanctuary, the earthly tabernacle in all its glory being only its shadow (9:1–14). The author stresses that all priests give sacrifices, but Jesus' is superior because he offered himself (9:23–28). Certainly, the sufficiency of this self-offering superseded the law of the sacrifice. Indeed, those offerings acted only as the type of "good things to come" (10:1–18).

In the final chapter, the author makes three important declarations about the Lord. The first is that the Savior does not change but is the same continually (13:8) with the implication that he can be ever relied upon. Second, the author refers to the Lord's resurrection noting that, through the "blood of the everlasting covenant," he proved himself to be the great Shepherd of the sheep, whom God restored to life (13:20). Here the implication is that Jesus can continue to shepherd his people and lead them into the eternal city. Finally and poignantly, the author declared that through Jesus, the Father enables the Saints to be "complete in every good thing to do his will, working in them that which is pleasing before him" (NR 13:21). This last witness is very powerful. It declares the absolute necessity of the Savior's work. Through it, the Father enables the faithful to do all that is necessary to please him. By extension, he enables them to do all that is necessary to obtain eternal life.

From all this we can clearly see that the gospel stands at the heart of Hebrews as it does in the other New Testament writings. Its message is that Jesus, coming to earth, took upon himself the form of a man but never left his godhood behind. He ministered, blessed, taught, loved, suffered, and wrought the Atonement, after which he was exalted to sit on the right hand of the Father. These events, and particularly the accomplishing of the Atonement, "cannot be bypassed, demythologized, or reduced in translation to abstract terms, even the language of Christ's obedience and God's forgiveness, though such language is an essential dimension of the central message of Hebrews. The significance of the cross is essentially Christ's once-for-all self-offering in obedience to the will of God; yet that significance can clearly not stand apart from the event of the crucifixion itself."[135] The author's own

135. Ellingworth, *Epistle to the Hebrews*, 70.

summary of the role Christ played in our salvation cannot be bettered in simplicity, accuracy, or potency. It is this: "because Jesus Christ did what God wanted him to do, we are all purified from sin by the offering that he made of his own body once and for all" (10:10, Good News Bible).

Canonicity

Given its beautiful and powerful witness of Jesus and the role he plays in the salvation process, modern readers may be surprised to find that those who espoused the authenticity of the Epistle to the Hebrews struggled to gain its inclusion within the New Testament canon.[136] While this work was read widely and regarded highly by many first-century Christians, concerns about its authorship and teachings kept it from receiving full acceptance for about three centuries.

The earliest preserved citation of the Epistle, as noted above, is in a letter written by the Roman Bishop Clement to the Saints in Corinth in the late first century AD. Though the bishop does not give direct credit for his quotations and allusions, both the language and the ideas of Hebrews are clearly reflected there, and he does use the material as coming from an authoritative source. This fact indicates that the Epistle was already being read and used by some Christians in Rome and accepted as authoritative by some outside.[137] Another Christian document from Rome, the *Shepherd of Hermas* (dating roughly AD 120–140), indirectly refers to Hebrews. In it, the central figure, Hermas, mentions that "some teachers" claim there can be no postbaptism repentance. Many scholars believe this is a reference to 6:4–6; 10:26–31; and 12:17, which do seem to preclude repentance for serious sins after baptism.[138] Hermas, however, counters this strict view of repentance with a more lenient stance.[139] While some Christian writers

---

136. Much of the following is taken from an unpublished paper by Andrew Mickelson, in possession of the authors.

137. Passages that reflect literary acquaintance with Hebrews are *1 Clem.* 9:3–4 (compare Heb. 11:5–7); 12:1–3 (compare Heb. 11:31); 17:1 (compare Heb. 11:37); 19:2 (compare Heb. 12:1); 21:9 (compare Heb. 4:12); 27:2 (compare Heb. 6:18); 36:1–6 (compare Heb. 1:3–13; 2:17–18; 4:15–16); 43:1 (compare Heb. 3:2–5). See also Lane, *Hebrews 1–8,* cli.

138. Koester, *Hebrews,* 23; Erik M. Heen and Philip D. W. Krey, eds., *Hebrews,* vol. 10 of Ancient Christian Commentary on Scripture, ed. Thomas C. Oden (Downers Grove, Ill.: InterVarsity Press, 2005), xvii; Lane, *Hebrews 1–8,* clii.

139. A heavenly messenger told Hermas that what he heard (concerning no postbaptism repentance) was correct, but because of human weakness, the Lord allowed one repentance after baptism, although those who persistently sinned would perish. *Herm. Mand.* 4.3.1–7. Later, this rigorism was modified when Hermas learned that people could

agreed with the strict approach of Hebrews,[140] Christians in the western parts of the Roman Empire sided with Hermas's leniency. The controversy resulted in the western church being suspect of the Epistle for decades.

But an even greater challenge to Hebrews' acceptance was the question of authorship. Writers such as Irenaeus, Gaius of Rome, and Hippolytus (all third-century clerics) denied that Paul wrote Hebrews, and in a period where the authority of a text was inextricably linked to its author, the question of Hebrews's dubious provenance caused many to devalue it.[141] While a few Christian theologians in the West occasionally drew on Hebrews for support in theological debates,[142] the majority broadly held it as suspect and therefore disregarded it. This helps explain why Hebrews was not included in the Muratorian Canon, a list of works composed near the end of the second century in Rome considered as authoritative by a broad range of western Christian leaders.

In contrast, Christians in the eastern part of the empire were less concerned with the issues of doctrine that limited the appeal of Hebrews in the West. Eastern authors did not read Hebrews as prohibiting postbaptismal repentance.[143] Also, the question of authorship troubled eastern Christian authorities less. The earliest manuscript collection that includes Hebrews places the Epistle squarely in the Pauline writings, directly after Romans.[144] That is not to say the eastern authorities did not recognize the

---

repent of sins committed prior to this revelation, but those who sinned in the future would not obtain salvation. *Herm. Vis.* 2.2.4–5. A final statement seems to modify the rigor even further by saying that people may repent until the end of the age, for only after that time will repentance become impossible. *Herm. Sim.* 9.26.5–6.

140. Tertullian cites 6:4–8 as a rationale for barring lapsed Christians from repenting. See Tertullian, *Pud.* 20.3–5.

141. Lane, *Hebrews 1–8,* cliii, explains that "some church leaders in the West undoubtedly questioned the authority of Hebrews. Confusion over the distinction between authorship and authority was widespread. Divergent points of view over the authorship of Hebrews may have prevented the Church from listening to its witness."

142. Tertullian, who believed Barnabas wrote Hebrews, cited the book as a defense against what Tertullian considered an overly liberal approach to repentance. He based his position on the *Shepherd of Hermas*. See Tertullian, *Pud.* 20.3. It was also cited by the Novatians after the Decian persecution to argue that lapsed Christians should not be allowed to repent. See Koester, *Hebrews,* 23.

143. According to Koester, *Hebrews,* 20, "Clement and Origen did not find these warnings [6:4–6; 10:26–31; 12:17] especially troublesome, but understood them to give Christians incentive to persevere on their spiritual journey, not to cause them to despair (Clement, *Stromata* 2.13; 4.20)."

144. This is 𝔓[46], an Egyptian papyrus codex dating to the beginning of the third century.

difficulties inherent in attributing Hebrews to Paul, yet they found ways to justify the problem and thus preserve the apostolic authority of the text.[145] Origen, for example, as noted above, after recognizing the differences in style, opined that "the thoughts are the apostle's [that is, Paul's], but that the style and composition belong to one who called to mind the apostle's teachings and, as it were, made short notes of what his master said. If any church, therefore, holds this epistle as Paul's let it be commended for this also. For not without reason have the men of old time handed it down as Paul's."[146] Thus, Origen kept the apostolic quality of the Epistle while explaining the difference in style.

Given these distinct attitudes towards Hebrews in the East and West, it is unsurprising that early canon lists from the East (such as Athanasius's Festal Letter 39, written in AD 367) include Hebrews, while early canon lists from the West (such as the list in Codex Claromontanus, collected in the fourth century) omit Hebrews.[147]

Attitudes towards Hebrews in the West began to soften starting with Hilary of Poitiers in the fourth century, who under eastern influence began to regard Hebrews as Pauline and authoritative.[148] This stance was adopted by other church leaders as well, most notably Jerome and Augustine. Both church fathers acknowledged the controversies regarding the authorship of Hebrews yet still asserted its authority as scripture. Jerome argued, "It makes no difference whose it is, since it is from a churchman, and is celebrated in the daily readings of the Churches." He also noted that "ancient writers" cited Hebrews "as canonical and churchly."[149] Augustine, though also aware of controversy surrounding authorship, cited it as scripture and listed it among the letters of Paul.[150]

145. Besides Origen, a number of Eastern authors voiced their defense of Pauline authorship of Hebrews. Pantaenus claimed that Hebrews's anonymity was a mark of Pauline humility. Clement believed that anonymity was a strategy Paul used in Hebrews to ally Jewish suspicion of him, and Clement attributed the unique style to the fact that it was written in Hebrew by Paul and translated into Greek by Luke. See Koester, *Hebrews,* 21.

146. As cited in Eusebius, *Hist. eccl.* 6.25.13.

147. Athanasius's Festal Letter 39 dates to AD 367 (see Bruce, *Canon,* 208–9) while the list in Codex Claromontanus dates to the mid-fourth century (see Ellingworth, *Epistle to the Hebrews,* 35).

148. See Hilary, "On the Trinity," 4.11, which dates to AD 367. See Lane, *Hebrews 1–8,* cliv.

149. From Jerome's "Epistle 129," written in AD 414. See Ellingworth, *Epistle to the Hebrews,* 36.

150. Pertinent references include Christian Doctrine 2.8; City of God 16.22. Lane, *Hebrews 1–8,* cliv.

This shift in attitude towards Hebrews prepared a way for it to be formally accepted into the New Testament canon. The Synod of Hippo, held in AD 393, declared Hebrews as canonical, though somewhat unique among Paul's writings. The council recognized, according to its justification, the "thirteen Epistles of Paul, and the Epistle to the Hebrews, by the same."[151] The later Synod of Carthage (in AD 397) simply recognized fourteen Epistles of Paul, but placed Hebrews at the end of the Pauline corpus, "memorializing the West's earlier ambivalence regarding the letter's status."[152] From that point on, it has unquestionably remained part of the New Testament canon.

Manuscript Tradition and Nature of the Greek Text

Important Manuscript Variants

The earliest complete copy of the Epistle to the Hebrews is found in the famous papyrus 𝔓[46], which contains most of the Epistles of Paul, generally ordered according to length with Hebrews placed after Romans and before 1 Corinthians.[153] Since the provenance of the papyrus is unknown, its dating is based on paleography, with the most probable date being somewhere between AD 150 and 250.[154] It belongs to the Alexandrian Text-type, which predominates in the earliest surviving documents, including the Sinaiticus, Alexandrinus, and Vaticanus manuscripts.

Hebrews has few variant readings of the text.[155] In a detailed study of this subject, one scholar states, "All surviving copies of Hebrews go back to one archetype, the edition which was admitted to the Pauline corpus, is suggested by their having a number of errors in common, including a few primitive corruptions which were take over into the corpus."[156] The majority of these "corruptions" comprise minor spelling differences, the addition

151. Ellingworth, *Epistle to the Hebrews*, 36.

152. Heen and Krey, *Hebrews*, xviii.

153. F. F. Bruce, "Textual Problems in the Epistle to the Hebrews," in *Scribes and Scripture: New Testament Essays in Honor of J. Harold Greenlee*, ed. David Alan Black (Winona Lake, Ind.: Eisenbrauns, 1992), 27.

154. Bruce W. Griffin, "The Paleographical Dating of P-46," paper delivered to the Society of Biblical Literature, New Testament Textual Criticism Section, New Orleans, November 1996, http://www.biblical-data.org/P-46%20Oct%201997.pdf.

155. Bruce M. Metzger, *A Textual Commentary on the Greek New Testament*, 2d ed., 9th printing (Stuttgart, Ger.: Deutsche Bibelgesellschaft/German Bible Society, 2012), 591–607, lists only forty-nine for the entire work.

156. Bruce, "Textual Problems," 27.

or deletion of a word or words, or the replacing of one word with another.[157] It is important to note, however, that the few variants are of little importance and none are doctrinally significant. As a result, the principles as taught in this marvelous and insightful Epistle seem to have remained pure and virtually as it was written in the oldest extant copy.

The Nature of the Greek in Hebrews

The Epistle to the Hebrews, like the rest of the New Testament, was written in Koine Greek, an evolved and simplified form of classical Attic Greek. By the first century AD, it had become the *lingua franca* of the whole eastern part of the Roman Empire. "The language tended toward shorter, simpler sentences. Some of the syntactic subtleties [of classical Greek] were lost or at least declined." Although Koine did not have the precision and refinement of classical Greek, Koine was more explicit, thus allowing for a plainness and distinctness that left little room for difficulty in understanding.[158]

Hebrews, as noted above, is written in some of the best Koine Greek found in the New Testament. The prose of Hebrews stands apart from the rest of the New Testament writings in its skilled use of rhythmic oratorical cadences that were taught by the famous Athenian rhetorician Isocrates (436–338 BC),[159] suggesting the author's high state of education and his familiarity with the larger culture in which he lived.

An outstanding feature of the style of the author is the number of long, carefully constructed sentences, some as long as seven verses.[160] Even so, he is also able to use short sentences effectively.[161] The author loves a play on words or assonance, for example, καρδία πονηρὰ ἀπιστίας ἐν τῷ ἀποστῆναι (3:12, *kardia ponēra apisitas en tō apostēnai,* "an evil, unbelieving heart so that you rebel"), ἔμαθεν ἀφ' ὧν ἔπαθεν (5:8, *emathen aph' hōn epathen,* "he learned through the things that he suffered"), and καλοῦ τε καὶ κακοῦ (5:14, *kalou te kai kakou,* "good as well as evil").[162]

---

157. For a list of ancient documents containing Hebrews, see Lane, *Hebrews 1–8,* clvi–clvii.

158. Daniel B. Wallace, *Greek Grammar beyond the Basics: An Exegetical Syntax of the New Testament* (Grand Rapids, Mich.: Zondervan, 1996), 19.

159. Moffatt, *Critical and Exegetical Commentary,* lvi.

160. For example, 1:1–4; 2:2–4, 14, 15; 3:12–15; 4:12, 13; 5:1–3, 7–10; 6:4–6, 16–20; 7:1–3; 8:4–6; 9:2–5; 9:6–10, 24–26; 10:11–13, 19–25; 11:24–26; 12:1–2, 18–24.

161. For example, 2:18, 3:16–18, 4:8, 10:18. These examples are discussed by Moffatt, *Critical and Exegetical Commentary,* lix–lx.

162. Other examples include 3:13; 5:14; 9:28; 12:5; 13:14.

The author is especially fond of alliteration; one of the best examples is found in the very first verse of the Epistle: **π**ολυμερῶς καὶ **π**ολυτρόπως **π**άλαι ὁ θεὸς λαλήσας τοῖς **π**ατράσιν ἐν τοῖς **π**ροφήταις (1:1, ***polymerōs*** *kai* ***polytropōs palai*** *ho theos lalēsas tois* ***patrasin*** *en tois* ***prophētais***), **π**ᾶσα **π**αράβασις καὶ **π**αρακοή (2:2, ***pasa parabasis*** *kai* ***parakoē***).[163] He is also partial to sonorous compound words such as μισθαποδοσία (*misthapodosia*) and εὐπερίστατος (*euperistatos*), and adjectives in alpha-privative,[164] which Aristotle noted was a mark of elevated style.[165]

Another characteristic of the author's style is that he often inserts several words between a definite article, adjective, or pronoun and its associated noun. For example, 1:4 states, διαφορώτερον παρ' αὐτοὺς κεκληρονόμηκεν ὄνομα (*diaphorōteron par' autous keklēronomēken onoma*), literally "a better than them he has inherited name."[166]

In summary, the author of Hebrews was well trained in the rhetorical and stylistic techniques of educated Greco-Roman literature and used it skillfully and effectively in putting across his message.

Citation and Translation Philosophy

Citation Philosophy

The bibliography for the Epistle to the Hebrews is vast. For examples, see such exhaustive works as Paul Ellingworth, *The Epistle to the Hebrews* (Grand Rapids, Mich.: Wm. B. Eerdmans, 1993), xxiv–xcviii, or Garth Lee Cockerill, *The Epistle to the Hebrews* (Grand Rapids, Mich.: Wm. B. Eerdmans, 2012), xxiv–xlix. The purpose of this commentary, however, is not to note all who have commented or expounded on a specific word, phrase, verse, or issue in this inspired and wonderful Epistle. Therefore, rather than footnoting an entire field of referents, we cite from one to three that we deem the most useful and correct with an understanding that if readers

163. Other examples include 2:8; 3:1; 4:3, 12; 7:3, 18, 25; 9:15, 24, 26, 27; 10:3, 4, 33; 11:15; 12:11; and 13:19. See Moffatt, *Critical and Exegetical Commentary,* lx.

164. The alpha-privative prefix, α- (*a*-), performs the same function as the prefixes "un-" and "in-" in English—it negates the sense of the word, for example, "unhappy" = "not happy."

165. Aristotle, *Rhet.* 3.6.7; see also Moffatt, *Critical and Exegetical Commentary,* lx.

166. Other examples include 4:8; 10:11; 10:12; 10:27; and 12:3. See Moffatt, *Critical and Exegetical Commentary,* lxi.

are interested in following the breadth of a given argument, they can do so by looking up the full texts of the works we do cite and follow the arguments of those authorities.

Understanding words and phrases are critical in seeing the possible breadth of the author's ideas. Some words, however, have greater theological implications and nuances than do others. When we consider a lexical definition as sufficient, we cite only it. However, when a word is of particular theological importance, we list multiple sources so that the interested reader can appreciate the full semantic range of a word or phrase with its various nuances.

Our purpose is to present a Latter-day Saint perspective on this beautiful Epistle and to elucidate, from a Restoration perspective, so far as possible, the Epistle's most cogent insights and arguments for the educated reader but not for the specialist. We have used recent authorities both inside and outside of the Church as well as Church General Authorities. We have worked hard to fully address the issues or difficulties in translating and understanding the Greek text but have not dwelt on issues that are of little concern for Latter-day Saints. Even so, it is our intent to let the reader, through the Translation Notes and Comments section and the extensive use of footnotes, see where we are coming from and why.

In referencing ancient authorities, we have used the system in Patrick H. Alexander and others, eds., *The SBL Handbook of Style for Ancient Near Eastern, Biblical, and Early Christian Studies* (Peabody, Mass.: Hendrickson Publishers, 1999).

Translation Philosophy

Our translation philosophy concentrates on words, phrases, and grammatical insights that help the reader to understand the doctrine and make the text plain. In that same light, this work looks at only those few textual variants that may influence how a text is understood. It delves only lightly into the many opinions and scholarly issues that surround many of the passages in the work, but does not shy away from differing opinions when they are important to understanding a text and where there is no help from Restoration materials.

Though we are working with a language that could express thoughts and ideas with plainness and clarity, because of the great differences in syntax, style, and grammar between ancient Greek and modern English, it is no easy task to produce a clear and understandable translation. An overly literal translation can easily lead to confusion and misunderstanding. While the King James Version of the Bible was a remarkable achievement for its time, there has been significant progress in our understanding of ancient Greek in the intervening four hundred years. Moreover, English itself has evolved and changed significantly in those four hundred years—numerous words have become obsolete, or their meanings have changed substantially. For these reasons, we felt that a modern English translation was an important and necessary part of this commentary.

Also, the King James Version used the Textus Receptus, a late sixteenth-century version of the Greek New Testament that was less accurate than the much earlier manuscripts that are now available. Modern critical editions of the New Testament used today, such as the Nestle-Aland Greek New Testament and the Society for Biblical Literature Greek New Testament, carefully evaluate all available manuscripts (with the readings of the earliest being favored) to produce the best possible text. Unless there is a compelling reason to accept an alternate reading from a later source, we have followed the same philosophy.

Each section of this commentary, therefore, begins with the Greek text from the Society for Biblical Literature's Greek New Testament. This is followed by two parallel columns with the King James Version on the left and the Brigham Young University New Testament New Rendition on the right. We selected the noun "rendition" to describe our version because, although the term can be used as a synonym for "translation," when describing a person's performance of a dramatic role or the playing of a piece of music, rendition carries the sense of an "interpretation" of that role or music. Thus, our Rendition is our interpretation of the Greek text in which we present, as faithfully and clearly as possible, the best sense of the Epistle's meaning in modern English.

In creating this Rendition, we have constantly felt the need to balance the esoteric details of a text with the importance of communicating the breadth of its meaning as clearly as possible to English readers. Fortunately, because this is a commentary and not a stand-alone translation, the Translation Notes and Comments section allows us to further elucidate and expand the range of meanings of a word or phrase and, thereby, render it to a greater extent.

We were ever aware that individual words have both denotative and connotative properties that are best understood within their semantic fields. Further, meaning often does not reside in individual words alone but in collections of words found in clauses, phrases, sentences, and ultimately in whole discourses. Our task was to first determine the meaning of any given cluster of words in the biblical text and then convey that meaning as accurately as possible into *natural,* contemporary English. Sometimes grammatical and syntactical forms that make good sense in Greek or Hebrew seem stilted, odd, and even weird when translated word for word into English and, as noted above, cause misunderstanding. Our purpose has been to render the Greek in such a way that an earnest reader could readily understand its meaning. And so, because of the marked difference between English and Greek grammar and syntax, we have especially tried to avoid an overly "literal" translation, which we feel could often obscure the author's intent. We have, therefore, followed Bruce Metzger's dictum to be "as literal as possible, as free as necessary" in order to communicate to the modern reader the meaning of the text.[167]

We worked aware of a caution given by Elder Dallin H. Oaks: "One trouble with commentaries is that their authors sometimes focus on only one meaning, to the exclusion of others. As a result, commentaries, if not used with great care, may illuminate the author's chosen and correct meaning but close our eyes and restrict our horizons to other possible meanings. Sometimes those other, less obvious meanings can be the ones most valuable and useful to us as we seek to understand our own dispensation and to obtain answers to our own questions. This is why the teaching of the Holy Ghost is a better guide to scriptural interpretation than even the best commentary."[168] In light of his statement, where it can, this commentary points out the best solutions to translation issues and explains why that is the case. When ambiguity remains, for example, if a passage can be understood in two different ways, we have tried to preserve that ambiguity in English rather than force our own interpretation on it.

Still, individual words do count and, therefore, we have labored carefully to determine both how each word contributes to the clause, phrase, or sentence in which it is found and how each informs the whole. We are also aware of another matter that influences how words are understood. Very often the definitions of Greek words come from their use in philosophical

167. The dictum is found in the New Revised Standard Version of the Bible introduction, "To the Reader" (hereafter cited as NRSV). For discussion on the challenges of translation, see Douglas J. Moo, *We Still Don't Get It: Evangelicals and Bible Translation Fifty Years after James Barr* (Grand Rapids, Mich.: Zondervan, 2014); D. Stephen Long, "Sources as Canons: The Question of Canonical Coherence," *Modern Theology* 28, no. 2 (April 2012): 229–51.

168. Dallin H. Oaks, "Scripture Reading and Revelation," *Ensign* 25, no. 1 (January 1995): 9.

texts. As one scholar noted, "There is one particular vice in the theological picture (or rather caricature) of the Greeks. They are always represented as philosophical thinkers. . . . Such a description of the Greeks ignores the fact that many other Greeks at all the relevant times thought differently, and that a multitude of them did not think in this systematic way at all."[169] With this in mind, we have tried to determine the meaning of words in their biblical contexts especially when they have Hebrew connections.

Our intent has been to convey, to the best of our ability, the meaning of the whole. Even so, we can put only one word in a rendered passage even though others may have validity. Helping to overcome this limitation is the Translation Notes and Comments section. It allows us to identify other words that may have force and to explain why we chose the one we did but also allows the reader to see other possibilities. Therefore, our Rendition should not be seen as prescriptive but as descriptive. It is in no way intended to be the ultimate Latter-day Saint translation but, rather, a rendering and interpretation of the Greek to assist the modern reader in understanding the power and beauty of the witness of our Lord as contained in the Epistle to the Hebrews.

Where textual variants in the ancient manuscripts have significant impact on the meaning of a passage, we have tried to select the one that is the most likely to have been the original, but when the variants do not affect the understanding of the text, we have generally ignored them.

Further, there are times when the words in our Rendition will be exactly the same as those in other translations. This is because that is the best, and in some cases, the only way a Greek text can be rendered into English.

In sum, the translation is Restoration based and, therefore, looks for the insights and understandings that modern scripture and the official pronouncements of Church authorities provide. It also takes into consideration those insights provided by the Joseph Smith Translation of the Bible. It is also conscious of and takes into consideration the work of Latter-day Saint scholars as well as some of the best of those outside the Church.

---

169. J. B. Skemp, *The Greeks and the Gospel* (London: Carey Kingsgate Press, 1964), 3–4.

Latter-day Saints and the Epistle to the Hebrews

Latter-day Saint General Authorities' Use of Hebrews

The contribution that the Epistle to the Hebrews has made to Latter-day Saint theology and doctrine can easily be seen as we look at its use among the Church's General Authorities.[170] Indeed, only Matthew, Luke, John, Acts, 1 Corinthians, and Revelation have been cited more.[171]

Since specific verses from chapters 11 and 12 eclipse those from all the others, this analysis first focuses on material found in them. After that, it examines verses from other chapters from the most to the least quoted. We do not examine verses that authorities have cited less than ten times or where they have not offered explanatory insights. One overarching occurrence becomes obvious as we examined how Latter-day Saint leaders use the scriptures found in Hebrews: they rarely supply exegetical comments. Most often they use the scriptures as they stand, feeling they are sufficiently clear to bolster the point the Authority is making. There are, of course, a number of exceptions and this study brings these out.

Chapter 11

The General Authorities have referred to verses in chapter 11 far more than any other chapter. Some General Authorities have however commented on the meaning of the whole chapter. For example, President Hugh B. Brown said, "The writer of the Epistle to the Hebrews saw the intimate relationship between the quality of faith and the quality of life and called upon his readers to judge the Christian life by its consequences in character."[172] President George Q. Cannon also commented on the whole chapter,

---

170. Much of the material in this section has been taken from an unpublished paper written by Nathaniel Pribil and Christian Brockman, in possession of the authors.

171. The statistics are drawn from Stephen W. Liddle and Richard C. Galbraith, "LDS Scripture Citation Index," accessed May 28, 2017, https://scriptures.byu.edu/ (hereafter cited as SCI). That source shows that chapter 11 has 389 total citations, and these make up nearly 20 percent of all references to verses in this chapter. Though SCI cites talks that reach as far back as the Joseph Smith era, it does not include all conference talks given by General Authorities since that time. It does serve, however, to give a very good representative sample of scriptures these men and women have cited. A passage, however, could receive undue weight because it was a favorite of one General Authority who quoted it many times. We have taken this into account as we have analyzed the material.

172. Hugh B. Brown, in Conference Report of The Church of Jesus Christ of Latter-day Saints, October 1969, 105 (hereafter cited as CR).

saying, "a more comprehensive chapter than this, in its description of the effects of faith when properly exercised by the children of men, I think is not contained within the lids of the Bible. . . . The [author], in this chapter, pointed out the power which their fathers exercised through faith, and to the mighty works that had been wrought thereby, and he endeavored to stir up within them a desire to exercise the same faith."[173]

Some General Authorities, viewing the chapter as providing examples of what great faith can do, have used it to emphasize the idea that such faith has not died. For instance, President Gordon B. Hinckley, after referring to faith, stated, "It was by faith that [Joseph Smith] kept himself worthy of the remarkable manifestations which followed in bringing to the earth the keys, the authority, the power to reestablish the Church of Jesus Christ in these latter days. It was by faith that this marvelous record of ancient peoples . . . was brought forth. . . . It was by faith that a small band of early converts . . . left home and family to spread the word." President Hinckley concluded, "All of the great accomplishments of which I have spoken were once only 'the substance of things hoped for, the evidence of things not seen.' But with vision, with labor, and with confidence in the power of God working through them, they brought their faith to reality."[174] Thus, President Hinckley and other leaders have viewed the chapter as setting forth the standard of faith the Saints should follow as well as stating the rewards that come therefrom that the ancient Saints enjoyed and the modern Saints can.

11:40

Turning now to individual verses within the chapter, the most popular is v. 40.[175] It focuses on the promise of God to the Old Testament faithful that he had "something better" coming than the old covenant could give. That "something better" was that they would "reach perfection" through the assistance of the Christian Saints. Authorities have used this verse as part of the scriptural foundation for the Church's doctrine concerning work for the dead, most particularly the phrase "they without us should not be made perfect." The idea is closely paraphrased in D&C 128:15, where the words "should not" are strengthened by the phrase "cannot." Further, this modern scripture also adds that the living cannot be made perfect without doing the necessary work for the dead. Joseph Smith expanded on this idea in a

---

173. George Q. Cannon, in *Journal of Discourses,* 15:366–67.

174. Gordon B. Hinckley, "God Grant Us Faith," *Ensign* 13, no. 11 (November 1983): 52; Wilford Woodruff, in *Journal of Discourses,* 19:357–63, did much the same thing.

175. The SCI references this verse about 79 times.

discourse he gave on April 7, 1844, stating, "The greatest responsibility in this world that God has laid upon us, is to seek after our dead. The Apostle says, 'they without us cannot be made perfect'; for it is necessary that the sealing power should be in our hands to seal our children and our dead for the fulness of the dispensation of times."[176] At another time, the Prophet linked 11:40 with Malachi 4:6: "I would refer you to the Scriptures, where the subject is manifest that is, without us they could not be made perfect, nor we without them; the fathers without the children, nor the children without the fathers. I wish you to understand this subject, for it is important, and if you will receive it, this is the Spirit of Elijah, that we redeem our dead, and connect ourselves with our fathers which are in heaven and seal up our dead to come forth in the first resurrection."[177]

Throughout the *Journal of Discourses,* many General Authorities also cite 11:40 to emphasize the importance of temple work. For instance, President Wilford Woodruff stated, "The eyes of all the hosts of heaven are over us; the eyes of God Himself, and the eyes of all the Prophets and Apostles who have ever lived in the flesh are watching this people. They know that they are not neither can they be made perfect without you; and they fully understand that we cannot be made perfect without them."[178]

Because of the support that this verse gives to the doctrine of temple work, many other Latter-day Saint leaders have referenced it, although emphasizing that it is the Saints who cannot be made perfect without doing work in behalf of the dead. One example comes from Elder David A. Bednar, who stated, "We have the covenant responsibility to search out our ancestors and provide for them the saving ordinances of the gospel. 'They without us should not be made perfect.' And 'neither can we without our dead be made perfect.'"[179] His words illustrate how the General Authorities use the idea of "covenant responsibility" to promote temple work. Elder Russell M. Nelson took the idea a bit further by referencing the Greek that stands behind the verse. "The Greek term from which *perfect* was translated was a form of *teleios,*" and he concluded, on the basis of the Greek, "the perfection that the Savior envisions for us is much more than errorless performance. It is the eternal expectation as expressed by the Lord in his great intercessory prayer to his father—that we might be

176. "History, 1838–1856, Volume E-1," 1975.

177. "History, 1838–1856, Volume E-1," 1920.

178. Wilford Woodruff, in *Journal of Discourses,* 22:148.

179. David A. Bednar, "The Hearts of the Children Shall Turn," *Ensign* 41, no. 11 (November 2011): 25.

made perfect and be able to dwell with them in the eternities ahead." He went on to explain that the work we do does not necessarily change the spiritual nature of those who have died, but it does enable to them to have access to the ordinances that allow them to reach their full potential.[180]

Elder Mark E. Petersen, also citing this verse, explained why the dead cannot be made perfect without us: "The requirement of the Lord is that each couple must be married for eternity and each child must be bound to his or her own parents by the power of the holy priesthood. This process must be carried back into the past as far as we can obtain genealogical information to justify it. This is in addition to the baptisms we may perform for our dead. If we fail to do this work, we place our own salvation in question."[181] In this same light, Elder Ezra Taft Benson noted that "the work we are performing here has direct relationship to the work over there. Someday you will know that there are ordinances performed over there, too, in order to make the vicarious work which you do effective. It will all be done under the authority and power of the priesthood of God."[182] Clearly, as it stands, 11:40 has an important place in Mormon theology.[183]

11:1

The next most cited verse is 11:1, which provides a description of faith as "the substance of things hoped for, the evidence of things not seen."[184] This succinct description is quite popular among Latter-day Saint Authorities. However, most simply quote the verse without elucidating what the verse

180. Russell M. Nelson, "Perfection Pending," *Ensign* 25, no. 11 (November 1995): 87.

181. Mark E. Petersen, "The Message of Elijah," *Ensign* 6, no. 5 (May 1976): 15.

182. Remarks at the dedication of the São Paulo Brazil Temple, February 26, 1979, as quoted in *The Teachings of Ezra Taft Benson* (Salt Lake City: Bookcraft, 1988), 252–53.

183. The JST makes a major change to this verse, stating that "God having provided some better things for them through their sufferings, for without suffering they could not be made perfect." Since much of the chapter deals with the suffering and trials of the faithful in former ages, the change makes the verse fit that text very well. The change, however, does take the focus away from temple work. This is likely why the change has been ignored by the General Authorities. While the SCI lists eight references to the verse in the *Journal of Discourses*, there is no definite link that the General Authorities were actually thinking of JST 11:40. For instance, the SCI lists a citation from President John Taylor, who states, "Man might be made perfect through suffering." *Journal of Discourses*, 21:3. However, the SCI also lists 2:10 as a citation, which seems to be the more likely source of President Taylor's thought. In recent times, only Elder Dennis E. Simmons, "But If Not . . . ," *Ensign* 34, no. 5 (May 2004): 73, refers directly to the JST change of this verse.

184. The SCI lists thirty-two references to just 11:1. There are fourteen other references that include 11:1 with other verses, but not all of those citations discuss 11:1 as a distinct entity.

is saying. There are a few exceptions. One is its use by President Dieter F. Uchtdorf. Twice he explained the verse. The first was in a discourse he gave in 2008, where he used the verse in a fairly unique way to show how faith and hope are interconnected.[185] He stated, "Hope comes of faith, for without faith, there is no hope. In like manner faith comes of hope, for faith is 'the substance of things hoped for.'" While this is not an in-depth theological discussion of the nature of hope or faith, it is noteworthy that President Uchtdorf uses the text as more than a definition of faith—he ties faith and hope together. The second time he expanded on the verse was in an address given in 2016.[186] He began his discussion by quoting from the New International Version of the text rather than the KJV. It states, "Faith is being sure of what we hope for and certain of what we do not see." President Uchtdorf then proceeded to discuss how the Saints can be certain of what they do not see by using the eye of faith.

Elder Howard W. Hunter twice rephrased 11:1 to help explain its meaning. He stated that "faith is the assurance of the existence of a truth even though it is not evident or cannot be proved by positive evidence"[187] and that it "makes us confident of what we hope for and convinced of what we do not see."[188] This rephrasing, though no in-depth discussion of the scripture, does help to provide a more modern definition of faith for Latter-day Saints.

This verse has a modest JST variant that changes the word "substance" to "assurance." A few General Authorities, in general conferences, have noted the change but have not expanded on it. One notable exception is President J. Reuben Clark who, after quoting it, stated, "I have never been able quite to understand that."[189] This is a very interesting and frank acknowledgment from a General Authority that a popular scripture can still be confusing and not immediately understandable. President Clark then discussed how the *Lectures on Faith* helped him make sense of the verse.

11:6

Looking at the number of total references cited by the "LDS Scripture Citation Index," 11:6 has almost as many as 11:1.[190] This stems from two phrases

---

185. Dieter F. Uchtdorf, "The Infinite Power of Hope," *Ensign* 38, no. 11 (November 2008): 23.

186. Dieter F. Uchtdorf, "Fourth Floor, Last Door," *Ensign* 46, no. 11 (November 2016): 15.

187. Howard W. Hunter, "Faith—the First Step," *Ensign* 5, no. 5 (May 1975): 38.

188. Howard W. Hunter, "To Know God," *Ensign* 4, no. 11 (November 1974): 97.

189. J. Reuben Clark, in CR, April 1960, 21.

190. The SCI references 11:6 thirty times and 11:1 thirty-two times.

in the verse that have proved very popular among Church leaders, namely, "without faith it is impossible to please [God]" and "he is a rewarder of them that diligently seek him." These phrases are often used to highlight the importance of faith and the promise given to those who exercise it. The citations to the verse before 1962 frequently either quote just the first part of the verse or the whole thing. For example, Elder Francis M. Lyman stated, "In the first place, God requires us to have faith in Him, because it is not possible to please Him without faith. If we do not have faith in Him, we will not listen to Him, we will not accept His word, we will not be led and counseled by Him, hence it is necessary that this principle should be and abide with the Latter-day Saints."[191]

Since then, with but one exception,[192] General Authorities quote only the second half of the verse. An example comes from President Thomas S. Monson's 2007 General Conference address. He said, "As we offer unto the Lord our family and our personal prayers, let us do so with faith and trust in Him. Let us remember the injunction of the Apostle Paul to the Hebrews: 'For he that cometh to God must believe that he is, and that he is a rewarder of them that diligently seek him.'"[193] Note President Monson did not quote the whole verse but used the clause that directly spoke to his theme.

Other Verses

While nearly every verse of the chapter has been cited at one time or another usually as proof texts, it is rare for a General Authority to give any further elucidation or exegesis on the scripture. However, there have been some exceptions. For example, some leaders have used 11:3, which states God created the worlds through faith, to show that faith is not just belief but actual power. For instance, President Charles W. Penrose stated, "By the power of his faith the worlds were formed. Faith is a force. It is as much a force as magnetism or electricity."[194] President Spencer W. Kimball took the verse another way. He quoted the phrase "the worlds were framed by the word of God," but instead of saying this was done by faith, he noted the creation came by "hidden treasures of knowledge."[195] Here President Kimball equated faith with a kind of knowledge that is unavailable to mortals but essential in the creation process.

---

191. Francis M. Lyman, in *Journal of Discourses,* 22:248.

192. Patricia P. Pinegar, "Increase in Faith," *Ensign* 24, no. 5 (May 1994): 95, states, "'Without faith it is impossible to please him'; and to please him we must 'believe that he is.'"

193. Thomas S. Monson, "A Royal Priesthood," *Ensign* 37, no. 11 (November 2007): 61.

194. Charles W. Penrose, in *Journal of Discourses,* 21:230.

195. Spencer W. Kimball, in CR, October 1968, 129.

Joseph Smith used 11:4 in a fairly unique way. It states that Abel offered up an acceptable sacrifice to God through faith and God commended him for his righteousness. The Prophet interpreted this to mean that Abel knew of the plan of redemption: "It is said, that Abel himself obtained witness that he was righteous. Then certainly God spoke to him: indeed, it is said that God talked with him; and if he did, would he not, seeing he was righteous, deliver to him the whole plan of the gospel? And is not the gospel the news of redem[p]tion?"[196]

Chapter 12

After chapter 11, the General Authorities cite verses from chapter 12 the most.[197]

12:9

One verse, 12:9, has been quoted more than any other verse in chapter 12. It speaks of the Father of spirits disciplining those whom he accepts as sons and daughters. The one phrase in this verse that Authorities have quoted and commented on most is that God is the father of our spirits.[198] They use it as a proof text for the premortal existence of humankind. An excellent example of how General Authorities have used it is a statement by President Monson: "The Lord has declared that 'the spirit and the body are the soul of man' [D&C 88:15]. It is the spirit which is the offspring of God. The writer of Hebrews refers to Him as 'the Father of spirits.' . . . The spirits of all men are literally His 'begotten sons and daughters' [D&C 76:24]."[199] President Brigham Young cited this verse frequently to make an important point: "There is no spirit among the human family that was begotten in hell; none that were begotten by angels, or by any inferior being. They were not produced by any being less than our Father in heaven. He is the Father of our spirits; and if we could know, understand, and do His will, every soul would be prepared to return back into His presence. And when they get [to heaven], they would see that they had formerly lived there for ages, that they had previously been acquainted with every nook and corner, with the palaces, walks, and gardens; and they would embrace their Father, and He would embrace them and say, 'My [child], I have you again;' and the child would say, 'O my Father, my Father, I am here again.'"[200]

196. "The Elders of the Church in Kirtland, to Their Brethren Abroad," 143.

197. The SCI references this chapter a total of 322 times.

198. The SCI references this verse seventy-two times.

199. Thomas S. Monson, *An Invitation to Exaltation* (Salt Lake City: Deseret Book, 1997), 2–3.

200. Brigham Young, in *Journal of Discourses*, 4:268.

12:24

The second most-often cited verse is 24.[201] This verse speaks of Jesus as the mediator of the new covenant through the shedding of his blood. President John Taylor frequently referred to Jesus as the "the mediator of the new covenant."[202] For example, he referred to the appearance of God and Christ to Joseph Smith: "When they appeared to him, the Father, pointing to the Son, said, 'This is My Beloved Son, Hear Him!' [As if the Father were saying], 'I have not come to teach and instruct you; but I refer you to my Only Begotten, who is the Mediator of the New Covenant, the Lamb slain from before the foundation of the world; I refer you to Him as your Redeemer, your High Priest and Teacher. Hear Him.'"[203] Only once did President Taylor actually expand on the title: "'There is none other name under heaven given among men, whereby we must be saved,' and unto him every knee shall bow and every tongue shall confess, and hence he is called the Mediator of the New Covenant, and hence we are told to ask for blessings in the name of Jesus Christ and to approach the Father in his name. We are told that to know God and Jesus Christ whom he has sent is eternal life."[204]

Other Chapters Cited by General Authorities

Having looked at verses in the two most popular chapters, we now turn our attention to other chapters and verses that have appealed to the Church leadership.

5:8–9

General Authorities have cited 5:8–9 to teach about the role of trials and suffering in life.[205] These verses note that Jesus learned obedience through suffering and by that means became perfect and thereby the author of eternal life for the faithful. Concerning this idea President Howard W. Hunter stated, "He was perfect and sinless, not because he had to be, but rather because he clearly and determinedly wanted to be."[206] His words suggest

201. The SCI references this verse thirty-three times.

202. He cites or refers to this verse twenty-six times in his talks.

203. John Taylor, in *Journal of Discourses,* 26:106.

204. John Taylor, in *Journal of Discourses,* 10:117.

205. The SCI references these verses seventy-three times. The break shows 5:8 with twenty-four references; 5:8–9 with twenty-six, and 5:9 with twenty-three.

206. Howard W. Hunter, "The Temptations of Christ," *Ensign* 6, no. 11 (November 1976): 19.

that perfection was not something thrust upon the Savior without any agency on his part but something he willingly chose for himself.

Concerning the Lord's gaining perfection through suffering, Elder Marvin J. Ashton said, "Jesus, too, developed unique balance mentally, physically, spiritually, and socially as he labored and served under all types of trying circumstances." After quoting 5:8–9, Elder Ashton noted, "Difficulties can be a valuable tool in our pursuit for perfection. Adversity need have no necessary connection with failure."[207] Following this same theme, Elder Eldred G. Smith stated that "if it [the suffering] was necessary for Jesus, the Son of God, to learn obedience, then how much more is it necessary for us?"[208] President Monson taught about the consequences of both obedience and disobedience. Admonishing the Saints he implored, "Let us remember that the end result of disobedience is captivity and death, while the reward for obedience is liberty and eternal life."[209]

The Church's leaders also extrapolate from these verses that people must also suffer to one degree or another in order to reach perfection. For example, Elder Russell M. Nelson concluded that "so we must endure trials—as did He."[210] President Young put it this way: "It is recorded that Jesus was made perfect through suffering. If he was made perfect through suffering, why should we imagine for one moment that we can be prepared to enter into the kingdom of rest with him and the Father, without passing through similar ordeals?"[211] The point that the General Authorities make is that though no person will endure the same sufferings or the same trials that Christ did, some amount of suffering is necessary for all humankind in order to grow and obtain perfection.

13:8

Many leaders, and especially President Cannon, were fond of 13:8, which states, "Jesus Christ the same yesterday, and to day, and for ever."[212] On the basis of this scripture, President Cannon witnessed, as did others, that Jesus "lives. . . . He is the same today [as he] was 1,800 years ago, [and he is the same as] He was in the days of the Prophets and Patriarchs, [he is]

207. Marvin J. Ashton, "Adversity and You," *Ensign* 10, no. 11 (November 1980): 60.

208. Eldred G. Smith, in CR, October 1970, 16.

209. Thomas S. Monson, "The Paths Jesus Walked," *Ensign* 4, no. 5 (May 1974): 49.

210. Russell M. Nelson, "Doors of Death," *Ensign* 22, no. 5 (May 1992): 73.

211. Brigham Young, in *Journal of Discourses,* 8:66.

212. The SCI references this verse seventy-two times with President Cannon citing twenty-one of them.

the same kind, [benevolent], merciful, all-powerful Being."[213] Thus have Church leaders used this scripture to stress the immutability of the Lord and, on that basis, the trust the Saints can put in him. Typical of this witness is that of Elder Alma Sonne, who stated, "The Latter-day Saints believe in the divine mission of the Savior. The very first principle of the restored gospel is faith in the Lord Jesus Christ. It is the foundation of true worship. Without him there could be no gospel of salvation. He is its author. His gospel [as with him] is the same yesterday, today, and forever. It originated in the heavens and was restored to the earth in these modern times through Joseph Smith, the Prophet."[214]

1:3

Because 1:3 identifies five characteristics of the Lord, it is not surprising General Authorities have frequently appealed to it.[215] It describes the Savior as sharing in God's glory, having the Father's express image, upholding all creation by the word of his power, purging the sins of humankind, and finally, taking his place on the right hand of God. It is the reference to the Savior being in the "express image of his [God's] person" that accounts for the largest number of Authorities citing it. They mainly use it to support the Church's doctrine of the corporeality of God. They take the scripture at face value and use it to show Christ's physical appearance is similar to God's. As Elder Oaks stated, "The Bible contains an apostolic witness that Jesus was 'the express image' of His Father's person, which merely elaborates Jesus's own teaching that 'he that hath seen me hath seen the Father.'"[216] Supporting this idea, Elder Delbert L. Stapley said, "Like produces like, and any earthly son we know—and the earthly is typical of the heavenly—is in the image of his father."[217] Thus, Jesus as the Son would carry the image of his Father. A statement by President Cannon illustrates how literally Latter-day Saint leaders take this view. He stated that Jesus "was the Son of that Being, and was the express image of His person, like Him, having a head, having the senses that men have, having all the bodily features that we have, and His Father was precisely like Him, or He, in other words, was precisely

213. George Q. Cannon, in *Journal of Discourses,* 25:240.

214. Alma Sonne, in CR, April 1969, 31–32.

215. The SCI references this verse sixty-seven times.

216. Dallin H. Oaks, "The Godhead and the Plan of Salvation," *Ensign* 47, no. 5 (May 2017): 102.

217. Delbert L. Stapley, "Easter Thoughts," *Ensign* 6, no. 5 (May 1976): 76.

like His Father."[218] Thus, when 1:3 says "express image," this is not used in a mystical or allegorical sense, but a literal and descriptive one.

Elder Henry W. Naisbitt added another dimension to this idea. He stated that "this likeness was in [Christ] by virtue of the fact that he lived in possession of the inspiration of revelation; his course was marked out by that spirit. It animated every faculty, controlled every action, and prompted every motive, and because that spirit was poured upon him 'without measure,' he became the glory of his Father and exhibited in himself the 'express image of his person.'"[219] Expanding on this idea, President Brown stated that when Jesus "entered the presence of God, the Father, he was transformed into the express image of his person. He became not only the revelation of the Father but also the revelation of redeemed man."[220] Thus Christ became the express image after he had performed the Atonement and became perfect through his death and resurrection.

5:4

Another popular verse is 5:4. It refers to the necessity of a person being called of God "as was Aaron" in order to properly have priesthood authority. Given the Church's stress on this idea (see A of F 5), it is not surprising that many General Authorities have appealed to this verse as a proof text.[221] Though the biblical context specifically refers to the honor of becoming a high priest and does not say how Aaron's call came, General Authorities have adopted it to support the Church's practice. For example, Elder Nelson has said, "As in former days, [the priesthood] is again conferred by ordination, by the laying on of hands by those in authority."[222] Thus, the verse is used to justify Church practice of ordaining to all priesthood offices. As President Woodruff noted, "Men cannot legally and authoritatively go forth to preach the Gospel until they are sent."[223] In his view and that of other General Authorities, a strong, even propelling feeling that one must serve a mission does not constitute authority to do so. Missionaries must first be called by those in authority and then sent out to preach. Further, while 5:4 does not necessarily specify that every single position in the Church

---

218. George Q. Cannon, in *Journal of Discourses,* 25:155.

219. Henry W. Naisbitt, in *Journal of Discourses,* 21:107.

220. Hugh B. Brown, in CR, April 1967, 51.

221. The SCI references the verse sixty-one times.

222. Russell M. Nelson, "Combatting Spiritual Drift—Our Global Pandemic," *Ensign* 23, no. 11 (November 1993): 106.

223. Wilford Woodruff, in *Journal of Discourses,* 23:78.

should follow this model, the pattern has been extended to every calling from prophet and apostle to Relief Society president to Primary instructor—all must follow the Aaronic pattern.

Additionally, this verse has been cited to support the calling and authority of prophets and apostles in the Church. For instance, President Hinckley, in reference specifically to the General Authorities, said, "I believe that no better men are to be found in any cause anywhere on earth. They have not taken this honor unto themselves, but they have been called of God, as was Aaron."[224] In a similar vein, Elder David B. Haight said, "The Lord's spokesmen are not self-appointed, but called of God."[225] In both these quotations, 5:4 is invoked to show the leaders of the Church are there because God called them to the position, not through any ambition or glory-seeking on their part. The tacit point is that because prophets and apostles have been chosen by God, they deserve the support and loyalty of Church membership. Elder William J. Critchlow said, "No man taketh any office in the kingdom until he is called. Since priesthood is authority to act—even to call—for God, every call by those in authority to call is tantamount to a call from [Christ.]"[226] Thus, any person holding the position is bona fide as being placed there by divine will.

General Authorities have also used 5:4 to emphasize the need for continuing revelation. This requires some extrapolation, as seen in a statement by Elder Orson Pratt. After quoting 5:4, he stated, "If that be true there must be more revelation in order that there may be a calling."[227] His point is that those who deny modern revelation must also deny that people are, in this generation, called of God. Thus, Elder Pratt concludes, "For hundreds and hundreds of years, no man had authority to baptize, from the very fact that they all denied new revelation, and hence none of them could have been called as Aaron was."[228] Blunting any who might claim that the Old Testament requirements are no longer necessary, an article in the *Times and Seasons* said, "We have sufficient grounds to go on and prove from the bible that the [gospel] has always been the same; the ordinances to fulfil its requirements, the same; and the officers to officiate, the same."[229]

---

224. Gordon B. Hinckley, "My Testimony," *Ensign* 23, no. 11 (November 1993): 53.

225. David B. Haight, "The Keys of the Kingdom," *Ensign* 10, no. 11 (November 1980): 75.

226. William J. Critchlow, in CR, April 1963, 31.

227. Orson Pratt, in *Journal of Discourses,* 23:162.

228. Orson Pratt, in *Journal of Discourses,* 16:293.

229. Joseph Smith Jr., "Baptism," *Times and Seasons* 3, no. 21 (September 1, 1842): 904, https://www.josephsmithpapers.org/paper-summary/times-and-seasons-1-september-1842/10.

The inference is that both the Old Testament practice and the declaration in 5:4 are still binding until God through modern revelation determines to change them.

2:18 and 4:15

The verses studied from this point on have less than half the number of citations as those studied above. Nonetheless, Church leaders have often cited them in support of important doctrinal positions.

Because of the similarity of their content, Church leaders sometimes cite 2:18 and 4:15 together. When they do not, it is the latter that is cited.[230] Both verses deal with the suffering that the Savior endured, with 4:15 noting that even though Jesus was High Priest, he could be touched with human feeling and infirmities because he too, as a mortal, was fully tried, although he never yielded to sin. Elder D. Todd Christofferson touched on this idea, stating, "Jesus was also a being of flesh and spirit, but He yielded not to temptation. We can turn to Him as we seek unity and peace within, because He understands. He understands the struggle, and He also understands how to win the struggle." Based on 4:15, he continued noting that the suffering that Christ went through allows him to comfort the Saints as they go through their trials and provides an example for us to follow as we encounter temptations.[231] President Cannon explained the dynamic. He stated that Jesus "was tempted in all things like unto us, but he differed from us in being able to overcome temptation, in being sinless through the power that he had through his Sonship. But he set us the example. He knows through that which he had to contend against the weakness of human nature. He stands as mediator at the right hand of the Father, pleading for his brethren and sisters who, like himself, are subject to the trials, temptations and afflictions that exist in this mortal life."[232] Thus, through the use of this scripture, Church leaders have stressed that the Lord does understand, in a very personal way, the suffering mortality can impose, and because of that he can be reached by and support people during their troubles.

---

230. There are thirty-six SCI references to 4:15 while it references 2:18 only six times with four of these in connection with 4:15. It is noteworthy that General Authorities used the two in conjunction only after 1968.

231. D. Todd Christofferson, "That They May Be One in Us," *Ensign* 32, no. 11 (November 2002): 71.

232. George Q. Cannon, in *Journal of Discourses,* 22:239.

2:10

Connected to the idea in the scripture above is one in 2:10,[233] which states it was necessary for the Savior, though he is the sustainer of all things and the captain of salvation, to go through suffering in order to both bring God's children into glory and to become perfect. It is the phrase "the captain of our salvation" that has caught the attention of quite a number of General Authorities. For example, President Ezra Taft Benson said, "[Christ] is the captain of our salvation and the only means through whom we can return to our Father in Heaven to gain that fulness of joy."[234] However, it is the doctrinal implications of this verse that hold the greater importance, particularly Jesus being made perfect through suffering. President Lorenzo Snow succinctly said, "You and I cannot be made perfect except through suffering: Jesus could not."[235] Quite a number of Church leaders have supported this idea. Elder Amasa M. Lyman noted, "We are told . . . that [Jesus] was made perfect through sufferings; and therefore we must conclude that if he was made perfect, he must at some time (no matter when that time might have been), have lacked that perfection which he appears to have gained by the sufferings he experienced."[236] The Apostle went on to say that the opportunity to grow in perfection was not limited to the Savior alone. "The same privilege that is extended to [Christ] of attaining salvation is also extended to us."[237] President Taylor connected the idea of perfection through suffering with the people referred to in Revelation 7:13–14. He noted, "Certain people, described in the visions of John, . . . were clothed in white raiment, singing a song that no man knew or could sing excepting those that were acquainted with the principles that they were. And who were they? They were those that had come up through much tribulation. . . . And are we not told that we must be made perfect through suffering?"[238] Salvation apparently does not come easy, entailing suffering in order to reach perfection.

233. The SCI references this verse thirty-two times.
234. Ezra Taft Benson, "I Testify," *Ensign* 18, no. 11 (November 1988): 86.
235. Lorenzo Snow, in *Journal of Discourses,* 26:367.
236. Amasa M. Lyman, in *Journal of Discourses,* 7:297.
237. Amasa M. Lyman, in *Journal of Discourses,* 7:298.
238. John Taylor, in *Journal of Discourses,* 23:336.

6:1

This verse, as translated in the KJV, states that it is necessary to leave the foundational principles of the gospel in order to go on to perfection.[239] Interestingly, the verse has been cited as an example of the incorrectness of some biblical passages.[240] The Prophet Joseph Smith clearly articulated this idea. He was quite emphatic, stating that "if a man leaves the principles of the doctrine of Christ, how can he be saved in the principles? This is a contradiction—I don't believe it: I will render it, as it should be, 'therefore *not* leaving the principles.'"[241]

Others who have cited the verse have focused on the last half, particularly the phrase "let us go on unto perfection." A good example is the statement from President Brown, who, after quoting 6:1, stated, "The work of perfecting the Saints . . . must continue. . . . Salvation is a continuing, on-going process. It is eternally improving, achieving, becoming—yes, and overcoming."[242] His feelings echo that of other Church leaders. They emphasize continual improvement. Salvation is not a one-time event, but a process of enduring to the end in righteousness and then finding perfection.

7:3

This verse sits among others (7:1–21) that expand on the only two biblical references to the high priest Melchizedek (Gen. 14:18; Ps. 110:4).[243] As it is interpreted in the KJV, it appears to say that this priest, who was ordained after the order of the Son of God, was without father, mother, or any other ancestry. It also states that all those ordained after this order of the priesthood are made like the Son of God and remain priests forever. There is a JST change to this verse that makes it clear that the reference to a lack of parentage refers to the priesthood, not to the priest. General Authorities

239. There are additionally seven references to the JST version of this verse, which states, "not leaving the first principles of the gospel," and twenty-two other references which include verse 1.

240. Though the SCI references this verse thirty-three times, only once has it been noted by a General Authority since 1982—Elder Quentin L. Cook, but even then it was referenced only in a footnote in his conference address "Our Father's Plan—Big Enough for All His Children," *Ensign* 39, no. 5 (May 2009): 36 n. 27.

241. "History, 1838–1856, Volume E-1," 1755.

242. Hugh B. Brown, in CR, April 1962, 107.

243. The SCI notes that the KJV version of the verse has been cited twenty-seven times while the JST version has been cited thirty.

are quite aware of this change, for most quote the JST. For example, President Penrose said that the "priesthood had no beginning, and will never have an end. As we are told in Scripture it is 'Without father or mother, without beginning of days or end of years.'"[244] President Cannon, after reading the verse, explained, "The whole Christian world have gone astray over this expression of Paul, not being able to understand it, thinking that that which I read in your hearing referred to Melchizedek himself, when in reality it was the Priesthood he bore."[245] Thus, President Cannon interestingly placed the problem not on a mistranslation of the text but on the vagueness of its original author, suggesting that the modern Apostle recognized that at least this biblical writer could make mistakes.

6:4–6

These verses contain a single warning. That warning focuses on the impossibility of saving through repentance certain persons who fall away from Christ, "crucifying to themselves the son of God afresh" and "putting him to an open shame," once they have been enlightened by the Holy Ghost.[246] After quoting these verses, the Prophet Joseph Smith taught, "So there is a possibility of falling away, you could not be renewed again, and the power of Elijah cannot seal against this sin, for this is a reserve made in the seals and powers of the Priesthood."[247] Noteworthy is that this kind of sin is a breach of a priesthood contract that cannot be repaired. President Woodruff explained, "Any man who receives this Priesthood and tastes of the word of God, and of the powers of the world to come—any man that turns away from these things, apostatizes, and turns away from the Church of God, shall not, in accordance with the revelations of the Lord to Joseph Smith, 'have forgiveness of sins in this world nor in the world to come.'"[248] On that basis, President Clark warned, "Ours is the responsibility to see to it that no act or thought or teaching of ours shall in any way question . . . that [Jesus] was the Son of God, nor in any way question the atoning sacrifice which he made for us. If we do, we shall become guilty of that great offense where we shall crucify to ourselves the Son of God afresh."[249]

---

244. Charles W. Penrose, in *Journal of Discourses,* 26:27.
245. George Q. Cannon, in *Journal of Discourses,* 26:245.
246. The SCI references these verses eighteen times.
247. "History, 1838–1856, Volume E-1," 1921.
248. Wilford Woodruff, in *Journal of Discourses,* 23:331; his reference is to D&C 76:30–37.
249. J. Reuben Clark, in CR, April 1953, 65.

9:16–17

These verses focus on the need for a testator to die in order to put a testament (that is, a will) into force.[250] In this connection, President Woodruff said,

> God has called a class of men and women who, with the exception of a few, have been permitted to live out their days and die a natural death. It is true that Joseph Smith, who laid the foundation of this work, and others, have had to seal their testimony with their blood; and if I were to tell what I think about it, I would say it was ordained of God that our Prophet and head should be sacrificed in the manner that he was, as much as it was ordained of God that Jesus Christ should be sacrificed in the way that he was . . . in order that his testimony might remain in force upon all the world from the hour of his death.[251]

In his view, the "testament" was the restored gospel, now bona fide by the death of the Prophet.

Conclusion

The scriptures cited here evidence the many ways that the Epistle to the Hebrews has informed and inspired General Authorities and contributed to Latter-day Saint theology. Important doctrines such as the priesthood and the nature of God derive support from Hebrews. While there may be other scriptures, particularly in nonbiblical sources such as the Book of Mormon, which teach similar doctrines, Hebrews has provided a biblical foundation for General Authorities for nearly two hundred years.

Latter-day Saint Scholars' Work on Hebrews

Though verses from the Epistle to the Hebrews have both been cited and examined in many Church publications, no single work has focused exclusively on it. The Epistle, therefore, has received, at best, coverage that is limited and generally targeted to a popular audience.

The following present general overviews: Edward J. Brandt and J. Lewis Taylor, "New Testament Backgrounds: Thessalonians to Hebrews," *Ensign* 6, no. 4 (April 1976): 56–59; Richard D. Draper, "Hebrews, the Epistle to the," in *Encyclopedia of Mormonism,* ed. Daniel H. Ludlow (New York: Macmillan, 1992), 2:581–83; and Clarence F. Schramm, "Hebrews," in *CES*

250. The SCI references these verses twenty-seven times with President Woodruff accounting for thirteen of them.

251. Wilford Woodruff, in *Journal of Discourses,* 22:232.

New Testament Symposium (Salt Lake City: The Church of Jesus Christ of Latter-day Saints, 2000), 54–58.

More extensive treatments can be found in Richard Lloyd Anderson, *Understanding Paul* (Salt Lake City: Deseret Book, 1983), 195–229; Bruce R. McConkie, *Doctrinal New Testament Commentary,* 3 vols. (Salt Lake City: Bookcraft, 1970), 3:133–242; Richard Neitzel Holzapfel and Thomas A. Wayment, *Making Sense of the New Testament: Timely Insights and Timeless Messages* (Salt Lake City: Deseret Book, 2010), 446–59; D. Kelly Ogden and Andrew C. Skinner, *Verse by Verse: Acts through Revelation* (Salt Lake City: Deseret Book, 1998), 244–63; and Thomas Valletta, Robert Barrett, and Bruce L. Andreason, eds., *The New Testament for Latter-day Saint Families* (Salt Lake City: Bookcraft, 1998), 413–31.

The work by Gary P. Gillum, ed., *General Authority Commentary on the New Testament,* 2 vols. (Provo, Utah: Harold B. Lee Library, 2001–5), 2:536–63, differs from the others in that it presents a collection of statements on specific verses by Latter-day Saint General Authorities.

Chapter 1

The Majesty, Power, Station, and Work of the Son of God

INTRODUCTION

The first major section of Hebrews (1:1–2:4), its prologue, loosely follows a rhetorical format known as an *exordium* or exhortation, which would have been very familiar to the author's readers. Its design was twofold: first, to make the audience receptive to the speaker's message and, second, to motivate them to follow his admonition through the persuasive force of his arguments.[1] The opening lines were often used as an introduction to the subject or theme the person would next address.[2]

In Hebrews, this exhortation has three components. The first deals with God's speaking to his people through the prophets in the past but now speaking to them through his Son. This divine being, the author shows, is superior to all other agents of revelation including angels, prophets, and all previous prophetic agents (1:1–4). Next, he cites various biblical passages to support the description of the Son he has given (1:5–14). Finally, having backed up his position through scriptural authority, he appeals to his readers to take the action he prescribes (2:1–4).

---

1. Koester, *Hebrews,* 174; Lane, *Hebrews 1–8,* 1–2. The content and structure of these verses, though close, are not an exact match for an *exordium* as defined classically. Though Augustine referred to them as such, he was using the term in a nontechnical sense. See Jacques-Paul Migne, ed., *Patrologia Latina,* 217 vols. (Paris: Imprimerie Catholique, 1841–55), 44:137.

Theodoret used the term *prooemium,* that is, "a preface," to describe the whole of the first chapter. See *PG,* 82:675A; LSJ, supplement, 261. Because of the lack of a complete match, a number of modern authors prefer the word "prologue" to describe the opening verses. For example, see Johnson, *Hebrews,* 64; and Ellingworth, *Epistle to the Hebrews,* 89–90.

2. Quintilian, *Inst.* 4.1.30.

The emphasis of these verses is twofold. First, that God has spoken and continues to speak. His revelations are ongoing and progressive. His means of speaking, however, have changed. In the past, he spoke through various prophets—especially Moses—through whom God revealed and maintained the old covenant made at Sinai. He now speaks through his Son, through whom God has now established a new covenant. The movement from old to new is not, however, "from the less true to the more true, from the less worthy to the more worthy, or from the less mature to the more mature."[3] It is, rather, a movement from less complete to more complete, from partial to full. The progression has been, as the work shows (especially chapter 11), "from promise to fulfillment."[4]

The introduction's second emphasis is on the majesty, power, station, and work of the Son. Verses 2–4 present an exquisite Christology, that is, a theological study of the nature and work of the Savior. The author shows Christ to be the agent through whom God worked to bring about creation and redemption and who sustains all creation by his power. The Son is the one who reveals the Father through his brightness and image and now sits enthroned at the right hand of the Father (1:2–3). Finally, Jesus is greater than even the angels (1:4).[5]

These verses contain a very strong Greek poetic structure that emphasizes cadence, but unfortunately this cannot be captured in English.

God Has Spoken by His Son (1:1–4)

Greek Text

1 Πολυμερῶς καὶ πολυτρόπως πάλαι ὁ θεὸς λαλήσας τοῖς πατράσιν ἐν τοῖς προφήταις 2 ἐπ' ἐσχάτου τῶν ἡμερῶν τούτων ἐλάλησεν ἡμῖν ἐν υἱῷ, ὃν ἔθηκεν κληρονόμον πάντων, δι' οὗ καὶ ἐποίησεν τοὺς αἰῶνας· 3 ὃς ὢν ἀπαύγασμα τῆς δόξης καὶ χαρακτὴρ τῆς ὑποστάσεως αὐτοῦ, φέρων τε τὰ πάντα τῷ ῥήματι τῆς δυνάμεως, δι'

3. Bruce, *Epistle to the Hebrews,* 45.

4. Bruce, *Epistle to the Hebrews,* 45.

5. The author's skill in developing ideas later in the work that he initially introduced in the prologue is easily recognized. For example, the Savior's sonship (1:5) is developed in 2:1–3:6; his superiority over the angels (1:4, 14) in 2:6–9; his priesthood (only inferred in 1:3, but necessary for him to purge sin) in 2:17, 5:6, and all of chapter 7. See Ellingworth, *Epistle to the Hebrews,* 90.

αὐτοῦ καθαρισμὸν τῶν ἁμαρτιῶν ποιησάμενος ἐκάθισεν ἐν δεξιᾷ τῆς μεγαλωσύνης ἐν ὑψηλοῖς, 4 τοσούτῳ κρείττων γενόμενος τῶν ἀγγέλων ὅσῳ διαφορώτερον παρ' αὐτοὺς κεκληρονόμηκεν ὄνομα. [SBLGNT]

King James Version

1 GOD, who at sundry times and in divers manners spake in time past unto the fathers by the prophets, 2 Hath in these last days spoken unto us by his Son, whom he hath appointed heir of all things, by whom also he made the worlds; 3 Who being the brightness of his glory, and the express image of his person, and upholding all things by the word of his power, when he had by himself purged our sins, sat down on the right hand of the Majesty on high; 4 Being made so much better than the angels, as he hath by inheritance obtained a more excellent name than they.

New Rendition

1 In many and various ways, God formerly spoke to our ancestors through the prophets. 2 In these latter days he has spoken to us through a Son, whom he appointed the heir of all things, and through whom he also made the worlds. 3 He is the reflection of God's glory and the exact appearance of his actual being, sustaining all things by his powerful word. After he, by himself, had made a purification of sins, he sat down on the right hand of the Majesty on high. 4 He became so much better than the angels as the name he has inherited is more excellent than theirs.

Translation Notes and Comments

Hebrews opens with a rather complex yet carefully crafted sentence that makes up verses 1–4. It begins with a participial phrase (1:1), followed by the main clause (1:2a) and two subordinate clauses (1:2b) where God is the subject. Next come two more subordinate clauses with the Son as the subject, each with additional participial phrases (1:3–4).[6] To communicate the author's thought as clearly as possible in English, our Rendition separates the whole into five sentences.

at sundry times and in divers manners / In many and various ways: This verse begins with two adverbs, πολυμερῶς (*polymerōs*) and πολυτρόπως (*polytropōs*). The adverb *polymerōs*, literally "in various parts" or "fragments," can mean "in various ways"[7] and therefore comes very close in the

6. Holzapfel and Wayment, *Making Sense,* 448–49.

7. Walter Bauer, *A Greek-English Lexicon of the New Testament and Other Early Christian Literature,* ed. F. W. Danker, 3d English ed. (Chicago: University of Chicago Press, 2000), 847 (hereafter cited as BDAG); LSJ, 978; Johannes P. Louw and Eugene A. Nida, *Greek-English Lexicon of the New Testament Based on Semantic Domains,* 2 vols. (New York: United Bible Societies, 1989), §89.81 (hereafter cited as Louw-Nida); C. A. J. Pillai, "In Many and Various Ways," *Bible Today* 21 (1965): 1385–89.

meaning to the adverb *polytropōs,* literally "in many ways."[8] Because of the close relationship between the meanings of these two words, scholars are divided in how to understand them. Some suggest that *polymerōs* refers to various parts or passages in the Old Testament and, thus, translate the word in its literal sense as "in various parts."[9] Others view the word more spaciously and, therefore, translate the word more idiomatically as "many/ sundry times."[10] Others take it as referring to the idea that God's revelations came in bits and pieces and, thus, translate it as "in a fragmentary manner."[11]

The Rendition follows those who consider that, in the phrase πολυμερῶς καὶ πολυτρόπως (*polymerōs kai polytropōs*), the two adverbs are used for stylistic effect and should be translated "in many and various ways."[12] This interpretation is reinforced by the fivefold alliteration "πολυμερῶς . . . πολυτρόπως . . . πάλαι . . . πατράσιν . . . προφήταις" (*polymerōs . . . polytropōs . . . palai . . . patrasin . . . prophētais*) that continues to the end of verse 1.

The various ways through which God spoke are well catalogued in the Old Testament. They include theophanies (for example, Gen. 3:9–21; 11:7; Isa. 6:1–3), dreams (Gen. 40–41; Dan. 2), visions (Ezek. 1:4–28; Dan. 7–12; Zech. 4–5), and revelations (Gen. 25:23–24; Jer. 1:4–10). The Lord also used instruments such as angels (for example, Gen. 16:11–14; Judg. 2:1–4; Zech. 1:11–14), seers (1 Sam. 9:9–19; Isa. 30:10), prophets (Ex. 7:1; Judg. 4:4; Amos 3:7), the Urim and Thummim (Ex. 28:30; Neh. 7:65), just the Urim (Num. 27:21; 1 Sam. 28:6), and dice or lots (Lev. 16:8–10; Joel 3:3).[13]

God . . . spake in time past / God formerly spoke: The word here, λαλήσας (*lalēsas*), is an aorist participle and translates literally as "God having spoken." It is, however, translated as a past tense verb in both the KJV and Rendition to better follow English usage. Though the aorist suggests a simple, one-time action completed in the past, namely during the Old Testament era, the author of Hebrews does not suggest that God had ceased to speak sometime in the past. Rather, he shows that Jesus has made

---

8. BDAG, 850; Louw-Nida, §§63.19; 67.11; 89.81.

9. BDAG, 847.

10. KJV, New International Version of the Bible (hereafter cited as NIV).

11. Louw-Nida, §63.19.

12. NRSV; Ellingworth, *Epistle to the Hebrews,* 91; Cockerill, *Epistle to the Hebrews,* 89.

13. See McConkie, *Doctrinal New Testament Commentary,* 3:137. The Book of Mormon shows the Lord revealing his word by using many of the same methods: theophanies (1 Ne. 1:9–10; Ether 3:13), visions (1 Ne. 8, 11–14; Alma 8:20), revelations (Jacob 1:6; Alma 9:21), persons such as angels (Jacob 7:5; 3 Ne. 7:18), seers (Mosiah 8:13; 28:16), and prophets (1 Ne. 22:2; Moro. 7:23), as well as instruments (Mosiah 8:13; Alma 37:21).

a new covenant and his apostles and prophets are still doing his work as evidenced by writing this Epistle. Indeed, even the Old Testament scriptures continue to carry his word and will and are, therefore, relevant for the author's contemporary audience.

The adverb πάλαι (*palai*) refers to a past point in time, that is, "long ago, in times past."[14] Its connotation is, however, more distant than near, and therefore, the Rendition uses "formerly,"[15] pointing to the Old Testament period.

unto the fathers by the prophets / to our ancestors through the prophets: The Greek noun πατήρ (*patēr*), especially when used in the plural as it is here, can refer not only to one's immediate father but also to one's ancestors, both male and female,[16] and is thus translated as "ancestors" in the Rendition. Although a couple of early papyri (𝔓[12] and 𝔓[46c]) include the possessive pronoun ἡμῶν (*hēmon*), "our," the reading without the pronoun—based on the majority of ancient texts—is undoubtedly correct. The use of the phrase οἱ πατέρες (*hoi pateres*) without the pronoun is uncommon—Christ uses it only in John 6:58 and 7:22. Paul also uses it when writing to the mixed Jewish and Gentile community in Rome (Rom. 9:5; 11:28; 15:8). That may be the reason why the form without the possessive pronoun is used here, although "our" could simply be implied or omitted to balance with ταῖς προφήταις (*tais prophētais*) or even to enhance the alliteration of the five words in this verse beginning with π—πολυμερῶς, πολυτρόπως, πάλαι, πατράσιν, and προφήταις (*polymerōs, polytropōs, palai, patrasin,* and *prophētais*).[17] In our Rendition, we have added "our," feeling that the pronoun is implied by the context.[18]

Those through whom God spoke were designated as *prophētēs,* "prophets." This is the Septuagint (abbreviated LXX) translation of the Hebrew נָבִיא (*nabî'*). The etymology of the Hebrew noun is uncertain. The word may be associated with the Akkadian verb *nabû*, "to name, call."[19] Based on this, taking the noun in its active voice, some scholars have argued that it designates

---

14. Louw-Nida, §67.24.

15. BDAG, 751.

16. BDAG, 786.

17. Ellingworth, *Epistle to the Hebrews,* 91.

18. The translators of NIV, New English Translation (hereafter cited as NET), and New Revised Standard Version (hereafter cited as NRSV) have all done the same.

19. L. Koehler, W. Baumgartner, and J. J. Stamm, *The Hebrew and Aramaic Lexicon of the Old Testament,* trans. and ed. M. E. J. Richardson, 5 vols. (Leiden, Neth.: E. J. Brill, 1994–2000), 661 (hereafter cited as *HAL*).

a person who calls out to others or, in religious terms, preaches.[20] Taking the noun in its passive voice, others have argued that it designates one who is called to perform a task, namely, that of speaking in behalf of others.[21] The need for such a person comes into play most notably in cases where estrangement has occurred and reconciliation is necessary. The latter interpretation seems to have the weight of evidence behind it.[22]

The Greek noun translated as "prophet" is a combination of the prefix προ- (*pro-*), meaning "before" (both spatially, "to stand before," and temporally, "to come earlier"), and the verb φημί (*phēme*), "to speak." It carries the nuance of both prediction and pronouncement. Over time it came to designate one who had authority to speak for a god; thereby, the word took on a very heavy religious nuance. When used by the early Christians, it carried more of the temporal sense of foretelling (for example, see Matt. 2:17, 23; 8:17; Acts 11:27–28; 21:10–11). Even so, the emphasis was on the divine authorization through which the individual spoke (for example, see Acts 3:18, 21).[23]

Hath in these last days spoken unto us by his Son / In these latter days he has spoken to us through a Son: In the expression ἐπ' ἐσχάτου τῶν ἡμερῶν (*ep' eschatou tōn hēmerōn*), "these latter days," the preposition *epi* with the genitive is taken temporally and points to a specific period of time.[24] The adjective ἔσχατος (*eschatos*) describes both something that follows a preceding item and the final item in a series. The KJV takes the phrase in the latter sense and translates it as "these last days."[25] The former definition, however, seems to be how the adjective is used here, and hence we translate

20. For discussion, see Hans-Joachim Kraus, *Worship in Israel: A Cultic History of the Old Testament* (Louisville, Ky.: John Knox Press, 1966), 102; and *HAL*, 661–62.

21. For example, see William Foxwell Albright, *From the Stone Age to Christianity: Monotheism and the Historical Process* (Baltimore: Johns Hopkins Press, 1990), 303–5; and *HAL*, 661–62.

22. Abraham is the first person the scriptures designate as a prophet, which occurred in connection with his reconciliation between God and Abimelech (Gen. 20). The first act that Moses performed after the Lord designated him as a prophet was to plead in behalf of his sister Miriam (Num. 12).

23. For discussion, see Moisés Silva, *New International Dictionary of New Testament Theology and Exegesis*, 4 vols. (Grand Rapids, Mich.: Zondervan, 2014), 4:161–73 (hereafter cited as *NID*).

24. Herbert Weir Smyth, *Greek Grammar* (Cambridge: Harvard University Press, 1956), §1689.

25. Louw-Nida, §61.13; BDAG, 397–98. Rather than following the usual plural form of ἐσχάτων (*eschatōn*) found in the LXX, the author uses the singular ἐσχάτου (*eschatou*), thus making it purposeful. See Cockerill, *Epistle to the Hebrews*, 90.

it as "these latter days" in our Rendition. This phrase goes all the way back to Genesis 49:1. The Hebrew אַחֲרִית הַיָּמִים (*aḥărît hayyāmîm*) is translated as ἐσχάτων τῶν ἡμερῶν (*eschatōn tōn hēmerōn*) in the LXX. The phrase "last days" in the Torah simply means "in the future," indicating no definite time frame. Over time, its use became more technical such that in prophetic literature it denotes *the* "end-time" (the *eschaton*), the period in which history would reach its full consummation and all of God's covenants and prophecies would find fulfillment.[26] The phrase thus focuses readers' attention on the conclusion and fulfillment of the Old Testament period. Its prophecies concerning the coming of the Lord have now come to pass. In that way, as the author of Hebrews stresses, the revelation of and through the Son is "the consummation of the age" (NR 9:26) of the law of Moses and of the old covenant.[27]

The fulfillment of the age, however, does not cause God to cease to speak through his instruments. Instead, a new dispensation has opened in which he speaks through his Son. The Greek here is instructive. The phrase ἐλάλησεν ἡμῖν ἐν υἱῷ (*elalēsen hemin in huiō*) translates literally as "has spoken to us in Son." The Greek noun has no definite article and, therefore, could be translated as "a Son."[28] However, that does not capture the nuance of the phrase. The article's absence stresses the quality of sonship, that is, God now speaks through the one who is nothing less than his full Son and is, thereby, divine. Therefore, his credentials are much greater than those of the prophets or even angels, as the author shows as he goes along.[29]

The preposition ἐν (*en*), "in," though often translated as "through," as in our Rendition, suggests the intimate nature of the relationship between God and his spokespersons. Though he is with them, he is more the driving force *in* them, and thus they commune together (see Jer. 8:18–9:3; 12:1–4; and Hosea 1:2–11). It is because God dwells in his Son that they share a oneness. As a result, the works and words of the Son are nothing less than those of the Father (see John 1:1–3; 5:19, 27; 14:11; 17:11, 21).[30] The author

---

26. See Nahum M. Sarna, *Genesis: The Traditional Hebrew Text with New JPS Translation,* vol. 1 of JPS Torah Commentary (Philadelphia: Jewish Publication Society, 1989), 332.

27. Cockerill, *Epistle to the Hebrews,* 90.

28. The definite article is often omitted in prepositional phrases and when speaking of unique and divine persons. See F. Blass and A. Debrunner, *A Greek Grammar of the New Testament and Other Early Christian Literature,* rev. ed. Robert W. Funk (Chicago: University of Chicago Press, 1961), §254.

29. Wallace, *Greek Grammar,* 245.

30. Though the idea of a divine indwelling is more Johannine and Pauline than what we find in Hebrews, the echo is still there. The Wisdom of Solomon 2:27, in the Old

stresses that in his day (the "latter days"), God's word has been magnified not just because it is current but because it comes from one who is divine.

whom he hath appointed heir of all things / whom he appointed the heir of all things: The aorist verb ἔθηκεν (*ethēken*; from τίθημι, *tithēmi*) in this context means to appoint someone to a task or function.[31] The tense suggests that the appointment of the Savior as heir was premortal. In the premortal world, God appointed the Savior as his κληρονόμος (*klēronomos*), "heir," over all that God has (see John 16:15).[32] That heirship also included God's power and priesthood. The connotation is, then, that Jesus was given authority, that is, kingly and priestly power, over all of God's kingdom and those who are in it. His Son therefore reigns as both king and priest.[33] As a result, all things are under his jurisdiction and he has full sovereignty.

by whom also he made the worlds / through whom he also made the worlds: The verb ποιέω (*poieō*), "to make, bring about," does not carry the nuance of making something from nothing, but rather of causing something to be organized, manufactured, or produced.[34]

The noun αἰών (*aiōn*) has the general sense of "a long period of time," without reference to beginning or end, but it can also refer to "a segment

---

Testament Apocrypha, describes how God's word, through the ages, has entered into the souls of holy people, making them not only the Father's friends but also prophets (compare *Barn.* 3:38). For discussion, see Ellingworth, *Epistle to the Hebrews,* 92.

31. BDAG, 1004; Maurer, *TDNT,* 8:157.

32. Inheritance was very important in the Roman world, and the laws governing it were carefully laid down. Heirs had all the rights and sovereignty of their benefactors. The writer of Hebrews assures his readers of the Son's authenticity by listing the ways he has become heir. See Simon Hornblower and Antony Spawforth, eds., *Oxford Classical Dictionary,* 3d ed. rev. (Oxford: Oxford University Press, 2003), s.v. "inheritance." The statement found in 1:2 strongly echoes Ps. 2:8, where God addresses the one who is anointed as his Son and details what he will receive. Bruce, *Epistle to the Hebrews,* 46. See also Andrew C. Skinner, "The Premortal Godhood of Christ: A Restoration Perspective," in *Jesus Christ, Son of God, Savior,* ed. Paul H. Peterson, Gary L. Hatch, and Laura Card (Provo, Utah: Religious Studies Center, Brigham Young University; Salt Lake City: Deseret Book, 2002), 50–78.

33. See Richard D. Draper and Michael D. Rhodes, *The Revelation of John the Apostle,* Brigham Young University New Testament Commentary Series (Provo, Utah: BYU Studies, 2013), 108–9. Daniel B. McKinlay, "Temple Imagery in the Epistles of Peter," in *Temples of the Ancient World: Ritual and Symbolism,* ed. Donald W. Parry (Salt Lake City: Deseret Book; Provo, Utah: Foundation for Ancient Research and Mormon Studies, 1994), 493, 498–99, notes that royal and priestly status were often combined in the psalms, which are believed to have been recited in the temple worship.

34. BDAG, 839–42. Some argue that the word in the plural refers to the universe as a whole. See for example, Bruce, *Epistle to the Hebrews,* 47.

of time as a particular unit of history, age."[35] In addition it can denote "the world" as a spatial concept. There is some disagreement between various dictionaries as to the meaning of the plural αἰῶνες (*aiōnes*). One maintains that both the singular and plural should be translated as a spatial concept, that is, "world."[36] Another states that the plural should be translated "universe."[37] Still another sees the plural as truly expressing a plural sense, that is, "worlds" or "spheres."[38] In our Rendition, based on Restoration scriptures, we have translated this noun in the plural sense.[39]

With the use of the plural form, the author of Hebrews shows that the Father has created not one world but many.[40] The author also shows that the executor is the Savior. As God explained to Moses, "Worlds without number have I created; and I also created them for mine own purpose; and by the Son I created them, which is mine Only Begotten" (Moses 1:33). Also, "the worlds were made by him; . . . all things were made by him, and through him, and of him" (D&C 93:10).

1:3 ***Who being the brightness of his glory / He is the reflection of God's glory:*** The noun ἀπαύγασμα (*apaugasma*) describes a radiance or efflux of light, either the direct radiance or a reflection of that radiance. The second sense seems to be used here.[41] Christ "reflects" the glory of God, his Father (NR).[42]

---

35. BDAG, 32–33; for discussion, see Sasse, *TDNT,* 1:197–209.

36. BDAG, 33, notes that the noun could also be understood as "a segment of time as a particular unit of history, age."

37. Louw-Nida, §1.2.

38. Sasse, *TDNT,* 1:204.

39. D&C 76:24; Moses 1:33; see also BDAG, 33; Sasse, *TDNT,* 1:203–4.

40. This idea was not foreign to many Jews. See the Midrash Gn. 3 on Gen. 1:5, which notes that Jehovah created other worlds. Specific citation in Genesis Rabbah 3:7, English translation in H. Freedman, *Genesis Rabbah,* vol. 1 in *Midrash Rabbah,* ed. J. Epstein (London: Soncino, 1983), 23–24.

41. BDAG, 99; LSJ, 181. Adjectives ending in -μα (*-ma*) regularly take the passive force. Blass and Debrunner, *Greek Grammar,* §109.

42. There is a strong echo here to the Jewish/middle Platonic apocryphal text Wisdom of Solomon 7:26, where "Wisdom" is personified and described as "the reflection of [God's] everlasting light" (*apaugasma gar esti phōtos aïdiou*). This is the only place in the LXX and New Testament outside of Heb. 1:3 where the word *apaugasma* is found. See Kenneth Schenck, *Understanding the Book of Hebrews: The Story behind the Sermon* (Louisville, Ky.: Westminster John Knox Press, 2003), 31. See also Hauk, *TDNT,* 3:137–38.

Abraham 3:24 states that in the premortal existence Jesus was "like unto God," suggesting that he shared to some extent the power and glory of the Father. However, as D&C 93:13 notes, "he received not of the fulness at first, but continued from grace to grace, until he received a fulness."

The semantic range of the noun δόξα (*doxa*), "glory," is very broad.[43] It includes, on the one hand, the idea of praise, majesty, honor, and greatness. These nuances in general look to the positive character and fame that a person receives for the excellence of his or her deeds or achievements. More specifically, the word connotes the renown, enthusiastic praise, and high honor that the righteous bestow upon God. That honor comes from the recognition of the supernal excellence of what the Father is and what he has done in behalf of his children.[44] On the other hand, the word points to the splendor and brightness associated with the very presence of God and denotes the intense visible manifestation of his power and intelligence.[45] Because of the broad range of meanings, context must be used to determine which should be applied. In this case, the noun includes both the majesty and power of the Divine.

the express image of his person / the exact appearance of his actual being: The Greek noun χαρακτήρ (*charaktēr*), as used here, describes

---

43. For the English word, see *Webster's New Dictionary of Synonyms* (Springfield, Mass.: Merriam-Webster, 1984), s.v. "glory, fame." For a more comprehensive study, see *NID,* s.v. "δόξα." In sum, the Greek term denotes the positive character and fame that a person receives for the excellence of his or her deeds or achievements. In the scriptures, it is most often associated with God. In one aspect it carries a strong sense of God's immense power as manifest in behalf of his children, a manifestation that brings to him fame, reverence, honor, and acclaim. Thus, the word also carries the idea of the renown, enthusiastic praise, and high honor that the righteous bestow upon God due to his concern and care for them. A number of Hebrew words are translated as "glory" in the LXX and stand behind the author's reference to God's glory. The most prominent are כָּבוֹד (*kāvôd*), "honor, reputation"; תִּפְאֶרֶת (*tip'eret*), "beauty, splendor, bravery"; and הוֹד (*hôd*), "majesty, dignity."

44. For the full semantic range, see Louw-Nida, §§1.15; 12.49; 14.49; 25.205; 33.357; 76.13; 79.18; 87.4, 23.

45. In the KJV, the Hebrew noun כָּבוֹד (*kābôd*) is translated as "glory," and it is likely that this is the nuance the author of Hebrews is seeking. See Marcus Jastrow, comp., *A Dictionary of the Targumim, the Talmud Babli, and Yerushalmi, and the Midrashic Literature,* 2 vols. (1943; New York: Judaica Press, 2004), s.v. "*Kabod.*" For the word's application in the New Testament, see Louw-Nida, §§12.6; 14.49; 79.18. In its visible manifestation, it appears as brilliant fire or extreme splendor. Its earthly manifestation is a sign of God's presence. That manifestation was often described as fire. The Jewish rabbis referred to this brilliant display of the divine presence as the *shekhinah* (שְׁכִינָה, *šĕkînāh*). The noun שְׁכִינָה (*šĕkînāh*) does not appear in the scriptures although the idea is there. The rabbis coined the noun from the verb שָׁכַן (*šākan*), "to dwell," to denote the brilliant manifestation of God's presence as he dwelt on the mortal plane. Because the *shekhinah* is manifested by radiance, both the Apocrypha and New Testament refer to it as δόξα (*doxa*), "glory," there being no other Greek word to catch the meaning. See Jacob Neusner, Alan J. Avery-Peck, and William Scott Green, *Encyclopedia of Judaism,* 5 vols. (Lieden, Neth.: Brill Publishers, 2004), s.v. "shekinah."

Christ's "outward appearance" or "form,"[46] which matches God's ὑπόστασις (*hypostasis*)—his "substantial nature, essence," or "actual being."[47] For both the author of Hebrews and his audience, "it probably went without saying that Jesus was distinguishable from God" but fully revealed him in both his glory and image.[48] Thus, Christ could explain to Philip that whosoever "hath seen me hath seen the Father" (John 14:8–9). His words suggest the exact resemblance between Father and Son. The nuance of the phrase, however, also includes the strong unity that exists between the two, the truth of which the author likely needed to remind his readers.[49]

upholding all things by the word of his power / sustaining all things by his powerful word: The verb φέρω (*pherō*) has the basic sense of "carry, bear," but in this case it has the extended meaning "to cause to continue in a state or condition" and so is translated as "sustain" in the Rendition.[50] The force of the present participle emphasizes Christ's continual preservation and maintenance of the created order.[51] The phrase τὰ πάντα (*ta*

---

46. BDAG, 1078.

47. BDAG, 1040; Holzapfel and Wayment, *Making Sense,* 449. Due to this passage and others, some suggest that the author was familiar with the first century BC Jewish work "The Wisdom of God" and freely used some of its images and descriptions. For a study, see R. G. Hamerton-Kelly, *Pre-existence, Wisdom, and the Son of Man: A Study of the Idea of Pre-existence in the New Testament,* vol. 21 of the Society for New Testament Studies Monograph Series (Cambridge: Cambridge University Press, 1983). See also Bruce, *Epistle to the Hebrews,* 49; and John P. Meier, "Symmetry and Theology in the Old Testament Citations of Heb 1,5–14," *Biblica* 66, no. 4 (1985): 524–28. Compare J. Rendel Harris, *The Origin of the Prologue to St. John's Gospel* (Cambridge: Cambridge University Press, 1917), 57–62. Mary Ann Beavis and HyeRan Kim-Cragg, *Hebrews,* ed. Linda Maloney, vol. 54 of Wisdom Commentary, ed. Barbara E. Reid (Collegeville, Minn.: Liturgical Press, 2015), bring a feminist interpretation to the work, highlighting the similarities between Hebrews and the book of Wisdom/Sophia. They show how both works share the same historical, ethical, cosmological, and sapiential themes, concluding that Hebrews is a submerged tradition of Wisdom/Sophia.

48. Cockerill, *Epistle to the Hebrews,* 94; Ellingworth, *Epistle to the Hebrews,* 100; see also R. E. Witt, "ΥΠΟΣΤΑΣΙΣ," in *Amicitiae Corolla: A Volume of Essays Presented to James Rendel Harris, D.Litt., on the Occasion of His Eightieth Birthday,* ed. H. G. Wood (London: University of London Press, 1933), 319–43.

49. Ellingworth, *Epistle to the Hebrews,* 100. Prov. 8:22–31, though referring to wisdom, uses similar language. Geneses Rabbah 1:1 notes that there was another with God in the beginning.

50. BDAG, 1051–52.

51. See S. C. Gayford, "The Aorist Participles in Hebrews 1:3; 7:27; 10:12," *Theology* 7 (1923): 282.

panta), "all things," is likely limited to those creations over which Elohim has jurisdiction (see Moses 1:32–33) and which the Son helped create (1:2).[52]

The noun ῥῆμα (*rhēma*), "word," can refer to anything that is uttered or spoken.[53] The LXX often uses the singular word *rhēma* in connection with God's spoken or revealed commands (see Ex. 19:6; Deut. 13:11; 1 Sam. 15:10; 1 Kgs. 17:2, 8; Jer. 1:1) and the plural, *rhēmata,* for the Ten Commandments (Ex. 34:1, 27–28), the contents of the *Shema* (Deut. 6:6), and the divine revelation at Sinai (Deut. 4:36). *Rhēma* has, then, a direct connection to God's will. The author of Hebrews connects *rhēma* to δύναμις (*dynamis*), "power," thus denoting "his powerful word." The phrase expresses the force by which the Son brings about and sustains his creations (11:3; Deut. 8:3).[54] The phrase shows that the Lord's word, that is, his will, has power in and of itself.[55] The Savior, then, acts as "the word of [God the Father's] power" in the creation process (Moses 1:32).

when he had by himself purged our sins / After he, by himself, had made a purification of sins: The phrase καθαρισμὸν . . . ποιησάμενος (*katharismon . . . poiēsamenos*), "made . . . purification," is an example of the middle voice of the verb ποιέω (*poieō*), "to make, cause," being used periphrastically (that is, in a roundabout way) to emphasize that Christ "of himself" had carried out this purification—he alone accomplished it without anyone else's help.[56] We have indicated this sense in our Rendition using the phrase "he, by himself, had made." Though the prepositional phrase δι' αὐτοῦ (*di' autou*), "by himself," is found in some early manuscripts, it is missing in others. It seems likely that it "was added in order to enhance the

52. Cockerill, *Epistle to the Hebrews,* 95; see also Bruce R. McConkie, *The Promised Messiah: The First Coming of Christ* (Salt Lake City: Deseret Book, 1978), 56.

53. BDAG, 905.

54. See *NID,* s.v. "ῥῆμα." That Hebrews uses *rhēma,* "word," in the two instances where the word is associated with creative power (1:3; 11:3) rather than *logos,* "word," is of note. The author may have chosen to not use the latter term to avoid the philosophical and theological nuances that the word carried, thus allowing him to concentrate specifically on the creative power exercised by the Lord. The Gospel of John 1:1–3, however, appears to use it because of all its philosophical and theological nuances. Where Hebrews does use the word *logos,* it is narrowly defined as that which God has spoken (2:2; 4:2; 5:13; 7:28; 12:19, 27; 13:7, 22).

55. This power is demonstrated in the account of the creation in Abr. 4, where it states that the Gods *order* various conditions to come about and then watch until they are obeyed. See Abr. 4:9–10, 18, 21, 25. See also Moses 7:13, where Enoch was able, by use of the power of the word of God, to move mountains and turn rivers out of their courses. Compare Morm. 8:24.

56. BDAG, 841; Smyth, *Greek Grammar,* §1722.

force of the middle voice of ποιησάμενος [*poiēsamenos*, 'having made']."[57] A few manuscripts also add the possessive pronoun ἡμῶν (*hēmōn*), "our," presumably to stop any speculation that the Savior may have died for his own sins (compare 5:3).[58]

The noun καθαρισμός (*katharismos*), "cleansing, purification," in the LXX generally referred to becoming clean from cultic impurity so that one could worship in the temple.[59] Hebrews, however, shows no concern for this nuance. Rather, it uses the term to refer to a cleansing from *inward* pollutions, those that darken and deform the soul and thereby estrange it from God.[60] That from which one must be cleansed is ἁμαρτία (*hamartia*), usually translated as "sin."[61] The noun denotes a deviation from moral behavior and is the generic term for all concrete wrongdoings. Its effect separates people from God because such persons choose a course in opposition to God's will, thus making themselves foreign not only to his ways but also to his nature.[62] The Savior's cleansing brings them back on course and thus bridges the gap that sin created.[63]

sat down on the right hand of the Majesty on high / he sat down on the right hand of the Majesty on high: In the phrase ἐν δεξιᾷ (*en dexia*), "on the right," the gender of the adjective *δέξιος* (*dexios*) is feminine because the noun *χειρός* (*cheiros*), "hand," though missing from the text, is understood.[64]

Because the right hand was a natural metaphor for power, to sit on God's right hand connoted a sharing in his power without limitation. The imagery used here does, however, suggest a subordinate role for the Son, for it is the Father who gives and the Son who receives the supreme status.[65] The

57. Metzger, *Textual Commentary*, 592. See also Ellingworth, *Epistle to the Hebrews*, 101.

58. Rom. 4:25; Gal. 1:4 make it clear the Lord died only for the sins of humankind. Ellingworth, *Epistle to the Hebrews*, 101.

59. The cultic idea of uncleanliness is found principally in Lev. 9–18 and includes contact with dead things, the flow of bodily fluids, skin diseases, sexual misconduct, idolatry, manslaughter, and a host of other acts. The whole is concerned with outward acts and appearances, not with inward motivation. See John Dunnill, *Covenant and Sacrifice in the Letter to the Hebrews*, vol. 75 of Society for New Testament Studies Monograph Series (Nashville: Society of Biblical Monograph Series, 1992), 69–111.

60. BDAG, 489; Delling, *TDNT*, 1:475–76.

61. BDAG, 50–51.

62. For discussion, see *NID*, s.v. "ἁμαρτία"; and Cockerill, *Epistle to the Hebrews*, 96.

63. For discussion, see Johnson, *Hebrews*, 71.

64. BDAG, 217.

65. Ellingworth, *Epistle to the Hebrews*, 103.

phrase "Majesty on high" is reverential and points to the Father's exaltation. It also serves to highlight the extreme greatness of the Son.

The noun μεγαλωσύνη (*megalōsynē*) denotes "a state of greatness or preeminence" and is used strictly in relation to and often as a periphrasis for the Divine.[66] The English word "majesty" catches the nuance.

1:4 ***Being made so much better than the angels / He became so much better than the angels:*** The verb γίνομαι (*ginomai*) means "to come into existence" but carries a wide range of nuances.[67] The one that applies best here is to "come into a certain state or to possess certain characteristics."[68] The force of the aorist participle used here, γενόμενος (*genomenos*), stresses the station at which the Son arrived and is, therefore, translated as "became" in the Rendition. The comparative adjective κρείττων (*kreittōn*) means to be of a higher rank or prominence than others and is often translated as "better." It does not carry the moral sense of being more righteous than someone else but of holding a higher position. This nuance should not be used to question the Lord's holiness but to emphasize his exalted station.

The noun ἄγγελος (*angelos*), "messenger, angel," as used in the scriptures most often refers to a semidivine being. The underlying force of the word, however, looks more to the message than the messenger.[69] This nuance emphasizes the office and function of these beings. They are, whether immortal or mortal, in a religious sense, God's messengers. Even so, they are beings of high rank.[70] The phrase τοσούτῳ κρείττων γενόμενος (*tosoutō*

---

66. Grundmann, *TDNT,* 4:544; BDAG, 623. See Sir. 44:2; Wis. 1:3; compare Mark 14:62.

67. For the semantic range, see Louw-Nida, §§13.3, 48, 80, 107; 15.1; 41.1; 57.2; 85.6, 7; 91.5.

68. BDAG, 196–99. Compare Anderson, *Understanding Paul,* 202.

69. Louw-Nida, §§12.28; 33.195 n. 38. "Latter-day Saints accept the reality of angels as messengers for the Lord" who are in form like human beings and wingless. Angels can be premortal, mortal, or postmortal beings. Some, like Enoch, Moses, and Elijah, are translated beings. "The angels who visit this earth are persons who have been assigned as messengers to this earth: 'There are no angels who minister to this earth but those who do belong or have belonged to it' (D&C 130:5)." Oscar W. McConkie, "Angels," in Ludlow, *Encyclopedia of Mormonism,* 1:40–41.

70. The intertestamental period was filled with interest in and speculation about angels. This interest carried over into the Christian era. In some instances, the factions' focus on angels threatened the centrality of the Savior in the salvation process. There was some speculation, perhaps based on LXX Deut. 32:8, that angels ruled over the nations and, therefore, had great power. See Cockerill, *Epistle to the Hebrews,* 115 n. 84. This issue, however, is of no concern for the author of Hebrews. Angels hold one position: as servants/messengers (1:7, 14). On angels, see Koester, *Hebrews,* 201; and Kittle, *TDNT,* 1:80–82. For references in Second Temple writings, see James H. Charlesworth, ed., *The Old Testament Pseudepigrapha,* 2 vols. (Garden City, N.Y.: Doubleday, 1983), 2:926–97.

kreittōn genomenos), "became so much better," stresses that, though the station of angels is very high, that of the Son is much higher.

as he hath by inheritance obtained a more excellent name than they / as the name he has inherited is more excellent than theirs: The noun ὄνομα (*onoma*), "name," though very often denoting the appellation by which a person is called, in many instances, such as here, connotes the rank, power, majesty, authority, and excellence of the person referred to. When speaking of members of the Godhead, it can refer to their very essence.[71]

The verb κληρονομέω (*klēronomeō*) means "to be an heir" and "to inherit." In the Roman culture, sons, heirs, and manumitted slaves usually took on the name of the person who was their benefactor. The result was participation in the dignity of the family.[72] The name Jesus inherited in Hebrews was simply "Son," meaning the "Son of God."[73]

Analysis and Summary

These verses serve as neither a thesis toward which the author builds his argument, nor a précis of points he wants to make, nor facts he wants to establish. Rather, they complement his style of interweaving themes to create the total picture he wishes to present.[74] In it he introduces the means by which the Father has and does reveal his will to his children. The author's witness is that God does speak to his children. He is not distant, unconcerned, or impassive but rather near, interested, and involved.[75] Elder Rich-

71. BDAG, 711–14; note particularly Dallin H. Oaks, *His Holy Name* (Salt Lake City: Bookcraft, 1998), 50.

72. Hornblower, *Classical Dictionary,* s.v. "names, personal, Roman."

73. Jesus often referred to himself as "the Son of man." For example, see Matt. 10:23; 12:8; 26:24. "With the definite article, *the* Son of Man described an expected apocalyptic heavenly figure, identified with the Messiah (Dan. 7:13). Jesus is the son of the archetypal Man, the perfect heavenly Man, the Eternal Father (Moses 6:57; 7:35). In this sense, 'Son of Man' equals 'Son of God' and conveys an intentional ambiguity, reflecting both Jesus' mortal and immortal parentage." Stephen E. Robinson, "Jesus Christ, Names and Titles of," in Ludlow, *Encyclopedia of Mormonism,* 2:740. This title has also been associated with the phrase "Son Ahman," found in D&C 78:20 and 95:17, where the term "Ahman" is believed to refer to the Father. See Edward J. Brandt, "Ahman," in Ludlow, *Encyclopedia of Mormonism,* 1:29.

74. Ellingworth, *Epistle to the Hebrews,* 90.

75. See D. Kelly Ogden and Andrew C. Skinner, *Verse by Verse: Acts through Revelation* (Salt Lake City: Deseret Book, 2006), 246. This same theme is also stressed in the book of Revelation, in which the Lord assures his Saints that he is well aware of their deeds and is responding to their needs. See Rev. 2:2, 9, 13, 19; 3:1, 8, 15.

ard L. Evans noted that all who desire it can know the Father "whom the scriptures testify is personal and approachable."[76]

The author of Hebrews emphasizes the important role the Son now plays as the means that God uses to communicate with his people. The author lists seven facts about the Son. Together, they stress one point: the revelations now coming through the Son carry the heaviest weight that can be given and therefore must be taken seriously.[77] In doing so, the author also reveals the superiority of the new covenant that the Son has now revealed. In the process, the author has reinforced and helped to preserve, for modern Saints, the understanding that the leadership of the early Church had of the Savior, his station, and his work.

Hebrews provides strong evidence that the idea held by some modern scholars—that the early Christians had a slowly evolving understanding of who and what Jesus was—is groundless.[78] Here, as in Paul's writings, we find a very full and very sophisticated Christology, consistent with the Restoration, that was so widely accepted by the ancient Church that the author could

---

76. Richard L. Evans, in CR, October 1954, 87.

77. Bruce, *Epistle to the Hebrews,* 46; Cockerill, *Epistle to the Hebrews,* 91.

78. The idea that Christians, under the influence of social and religious forces, slowly developed a high Christology was popularized by the *Religionsgeschichtliche Schule* during the late nineteenth and early twentieth centuries. Those who belonged to this school believed the Christian understanding of the Lord as divine developed gradually, not as the result from spiritual insight but as a product of historical forces. This thesis is exemplified by the work of Wilhelm Bousset, *Kyrios Christos: Geschichte des Christusglaubens von den Anfängen des Christentums bis Irenaus,* first published in Germany in 1913 but republished as *Kyrios Christos: A History of the Belief of Christ from the Beginnings of Christianity to Irenaus,* trans. John E. Steely (Nashville: Abingdon Press, 1970). Though few scholars today fully accept this school's premises, the thesis continues to have influence. For an example, see Kurt Rudolph, "Early Christianity as a Religious-Historical Phenomenon," in *The Future of Early Christianity: Essays in Honor of Helmut Koester,* ed. B. A. Pearson (Minneapolis: Fortress Press, 1991), 9–19. However, studies such as that of Larry W. Hurtado have shown it is very likely that "the truth of Jesus' messiahship and divinity was revealed by Jesus himself, and so naturally was taken up from the beginning in Christian beliefs and religious practice." See Hurtado, *Lord Jesus Christ,* 5. That is not to say, as Hurtado's work clearly shows (see particularly pp. 1–9, 496–518), that there was a perfect understanding from the beginning. It did take a little time, scripture study (that focused on many of the books that now comprise the Old Testament), critical thinking, and some revelation for an ever-more defined picture of the Lord to develop. Nonetheless, by the mid-first century, the Christian leadership was, by and large, clear about who they worshiped. A parallel may be found in the Restoration wherein the Lord revealed material "line upon line, precept upon precept" (D&C 98:12; 128:21) but nonetheless established early the core doctrines upon which the growing theology could be anchored.

ground his arguments on it. The Epistle shows no evidence of a doctrinal development. The whole is a sermonic exhortation that the author designed to reinforce what was already well known. He used the Christological elements to provide the reason for the behaviors he wanted his readers to emulate.[79] The weight of evidence in such statements as those found in John 1:1–4; 1 Corinthians 8:6; and Colossians 1:16, as well as those contained in Hebrews, all work to establish the understanding of the Lord held by these people. As one scholar noted, "Such statements about a historical human being who died a shameful death by crucifixion, not after centuries of reflection, but within two decades of his execution—ascribing to him a role in the shaping of the world!—are not to be attributed simply to a process of textual study, but above all to the impact of the resurrection experience, by which Jesus' followers experienced him after his death as the powerful life-giving [God]."[80]

In 1:2–3 the author has used three relative clauses to describe the greatness and grandeur of the Son as a means of establishing the magnitude of the new covenant he mediates.[81] The first clause focuses on his premortal appointment as heir over all that is God's and his role as creator (compare D&C 14:9; 76:24; 93:10); the second on his revelation of the glory, nature, and physical form of the Father; and the third on his continued sustaining power that keeps the cosmos in order.

The Son is in the brightness of the glory of his Father (1:3). The Father can bestow his glory upon others, which in turn brings them due honor and respect. Its bestowal, however, does more. It bequeaths to striving individuals power by which they can increase in obedience, ability, and understanding. It gives them access to an ever-greater comprehension of truth. Thus, the Lord has promised—to all whose eyes are single to his glory—that their bodies will be filled with the power of light. This endowment will enable them to comprehend all things (D&C 88:67). Great truths shall be available to them, and by living in accordance to these truths, they shall inherit eternal life.[82] The Son received the glory of the Father without measure and, thereby, became the brightness of the Father's glory.

---

79. Hurtado, *Lord Jesus Christ,* 497–98.

80. Johnson, *Hebrews,* 68.

81. Cockerill, *Epistle to the Hebrews,* 91.

82. For an in-depth study, see Richard D. Draper, "Light, Truth, and Grace: Three Themes of Salvation (D&C 93)," in *Sperry Symposium Classics: The Doctrine and Covenants,* ed. Craig K. Manscill (Provo, Utah: Religious Studies Center, Brigham Young University, 2004), 234–47.

The author of Hebrews describes the Son as having "exact appearance of [God's] actual being" (NR 1:3). The noun the author chose to express his point is telling: the Greek word χαρακτήρ (*charaktēr*) points to an "express image." The word denotes an "impressed stamp" or "engraved image"; by extension it connotes a "physical likeness" or "shared qualities." The text here is, therefore, the most vivid biblical comparison of the close resemblance between of the Father and Son. They possess a very similar "form" or "image" (see Philip. 2:5–7; Col. 1:13–15). The author parallels the terminology in Genesis 1:26–27 and in so doing shows that the Father, the Son, and humankind share the same physical "form" and "image."[83]

Elder Charles W. Penrose stated that when Jesus came to earth, "He represented [the Father]; for the Father was represented in Him, He being in the express image of the Father's person. He received the spirit of the Father, not by measure, but in its fullness. He came here [among other reasons] to represent the [Father] upon the earth that man might understand the Father, and to show a pattern to them that they might follow in his footsteps."[84] President Marion G. Romney stated, "One of the purposes of [Christ's] coming was to reveal himself and his Father. This he did in no uncertain manner,"[85] and Elder Bruce R. McConkie stated Christ was "the perfect revelation of God."[86]

The revelation of God found in this Epistle shows that he is aware, concerned, active, and, to some degree, knowable. "Much traditional religion assumes that only if God is 'utterly other,' that is, mysterious and unknowable, can he be properly reverenced. For Latter-day Saints, the foundation of worship is not the radical contrast but the intimate kinship of the Father and his children. Christ was near unto God because he was 'the brightness of his glory and the express image of his person' (Heb. 1:2). By keeping

83. Anderson, *Guide to Acts,* 87. A number of General Authorities use this verse, among others, as evidence that humankind is also in the image of the Father. For example, see Joseph F. Smith, in *Journal of Discourses,* 23:172–73; and Sterling W. Sill, in CR, October 1965, 58. The First Presidency in 1909 stated succinctly that Jesus saying, "He who hath seen me hath seen the father" (John 14:9) shows Christ was, as Hebrews states, in the "express image" of God's person (1:3), and "this alone ought to solve the problem [of whether or not man was literally created in God's image] to the satisfaction of every thoughtful, reverent mind." The First Presidency of the Church, "The Origin of Man," *Improvement Era* 13, no. 1 (November 1909): 77; see also Bruce R. McConkie, *A New Witness for the Articles of Faith* (Salt Lake City: Deseret Book, 1985), 67.

84. Charles W. Penrose, in *Journal of Discourses,* 25:331.

85. Marion G. Romney, in CR, April 1970, 68.

86. McConkie, *Doctrinal New Testament Commentary,* 3:137.

his commandments and walking in the way of his ordinances, every person walks in the path of the Master. In inspired worship, 'truth embraceth truth; virtue loveth virtue; light cleaveth unto light; mercy hath compassion on mercy' (D&C 88:40). The outcome for Christ was that he could pray, 'as thou, Father, art in me, and I in thee' (John 17:21)," and, of all his disciples both then and now, "that they all may be one; as thou, Father, art in me, and I in thee" (John 17:21). Such a relationship shows God not only to be close but also knowable.[87]

Latter-day scripture also makes it clear that the Father has given all power to his Son, who thereby acts as both creator and sustainer. To Moses the Father proclaimed, "By the word of my power, have I created [worlds], which is mine Only Begotten Son, who is full of grace and truth. And worlds without number have I created; and I also created them for mine own purpose; and by the Son I created them, which is mine Only Begotten" (Moses 1:32–33). The author of Hebrews refers to the Son's ability as "his powerful word" (1:3) and shows that it is the sustaining force of nature itself.[88]

Elder Neal A. Maxwell, citing 1:2–3, points out that Christ was the creator of many worlds besides this one but always under the Father's direction. Elder Maxwell notes that these worlds are intended for habitation by God's children as part of the glorious plan. Elder Maxwell remarks that "all this creating" has been done for the express purpose of "'bring[ing] to pass the immortality and eternal life of man' (Moses 1:39)."[89] He also notes that "it is interesting that some sincere Christians do not think of Christ in those, perhaps galactic, terms, thus ignoring this dimension of Jesus' divinity."[90]

The one grand personal act that the Savior did for those who would accept him and repent was purging them of all their sins. The author's understanding of sin accords well with that of many Jews at the time. Sin consists of acts that estrange both individuals and nations from Jehovah. Sin is both a falling away from a relationship of faithfulness toward God

87. Ludlow, *Jesus Christ,* 252.

88. Elder Orson Pratt notes that Jesus "had great knowledge before he was born into this world—sufficient to create the heavens and the earth, hence we read in the Hebrews that God, by his Son, made the worlds. This was before Jesus came here, and he must then have been the possessor of great knowledge to have been able to do that." Orson Pratt, in *Journal of Discourses,* 15:245. Some of these worlds are also inhabited by God's children. See Ludlow, *Jesus Christ,* 251.

89. Neal A. Maxwell, "Our Acceptance of Christ," *Ensign* 14, no. 6 (June 1984): 70. See also Neal A. Maxwell, "The New Testament—a Matchless Portrait of the Savior," *Ensign* 16, no. 12 (December 1986): 22; and McConkie, *Promised Messiah,* 55.

90. Maxwell, "Matchless Portrait," 22.

and disobedience to the commandments and manifests itself, among other ways, in neglect and lassitude (2:3; 5:11). In its extreme form, sin reveals itself in open rebellion against God's law (2:1–4; 3:7–9) and especially in apostasy (6:4–6; 10:26–31). Its keenest expression is in a willful and determined departure "from the order given by God" and the establishment "of oneself in one's own position and to go one's own way" (compare D&C 88:34–35).[91] The author's focus is, therefore, less on individual sin and more on general faithfulness.[92]

Hebrews shows that the Savior's sacrifice was necessary to make his people pure so they could enter into the new order he has established, an order that opened a way for them to have access to God as never possible under the Mosaic law. That access would come by continued obedience (10:1–18) and moral effort (12:1–4) on the part of those who brought themselves under his purifying power. Therefore, it was necessary for the author to give his readers a correct understanding of what purity consisted. Due to strong legalistic threads within ancient Judaism, impurity was more of an external than an internal condition. This misunderstanding allowed them to do egregious acts such as taking widows' houses (Matt. 23:14) and dishonoring parents (Mark 7:11–12). The Lord clearly countered this idea when he proclaimed, "Not that which goeth into the mouth defileth a man; but that which cometh out of the mouth, this defileth a man" (Matt. 15:11). He therefore castigated the Pharisees, saying, "Woe unto you, . . . for ye pay tithe of mint and anise and cummin, and have omitted the weightier matters of the law, judgment, mercy, and faith: these ought ye to have done, and not to leave the other undone" (Matt. 23:23). For that reason, he warned his disciples: "Do not ye after [the Pharisees'] works: for they say, and do not" (Matt. 23:3). His strong words reveal the problem of the legalistic tendencies among certain factions of the Jews that allowed them to reinterpret the law such that its original intent was broken.[93] It is not surprising then that the author of Hebrews focuses on the internal cleansing that the Lord, through his Atonement, brought about. In contrast to cultic rites that looked more

---

91. *NID,* 1:257.

92. The focus in the work as a whole is not on individual sin. Indeed, the only reference to individual sin is adultery and the love of money. See 13:4–5.

93. It is easy for a modern reader to view ancient Judaism as nearly monolithic and holistic when, in reality, it was in some cases bitterly divided with a number of crosscutting theological streams. See Daniel Boyarin, "Beyond Judaisms: Meṭaṭron and the Divine Polymorphy of Ancient Judaism," *Journal for the Study of Judaism* 41, no. 3 (2010): 323–65, who shows that there was not one Judaism but many aspects of this religious system.

at cleansing the body, the Epistle concentrates on the Savior's cleansing of the conscience (1:3). That means repentance is necessary, for "purifying actions are fully effective only when the conscience is cleansed, and cleansing the conscience takes place through faith" in Christ with repentance and obedience as its fruit (9:14; Ps. 51:17; Luke 3:3–8; Acts 3:19).[94]

Further, the author shows the Lord did not take his glorious station at the right hand of God until after Christ had taken care of what was necessary for the Father's children.[95] In short, his disciples' salvation came before his station. Indeed, it was the very means of his succession (9:11–14; 9:23–10:4; 10:11–14). With his resurrection and exaltation, he, at that point, became the heir of the Father, receiving immortal and eternal life (Philip. 2:6–9).

That Jesus sits at his Father's right hand signifies he shares without limitation the power, might, and majesty of the Divine, albeit in a subordinate role. At the moment of his enthronement, what he has been from the beginning in potential—the radiance of God's glory, the exact representation of his being, and the one who sustains all by his powerful word—came "to fruition and full expression in his exaltation and session."[96] Because he holds the Father's power, Jesus creates, controls, orchestrates, and oversees all that the Father has. His overall objective, however, is to direct his creations toward the Father's intended goal.[97]

In order to stress the Lord's greatness, the author notes that Christ has a better name than the angels. Besides denoting what a person is called, the nuance behind the word "name" (ὄνομα, *onoma*) can designate the reputation that a person has or the title he or she holds.[98] In this case, the author of Hebrews is likely referring not to the Lord's actual name (Jesus) but to his title as "Son" (1:2, 5–6). If that is the case, it could connote Jesus' title "Only Begotten," meaning the "Only Begotten of God in the flesh" (John 3:16; D&C 93:11; Moses 6:52).[99] The "name," therefore, would also suggest

---

94. Koester, *Hebrews,* 119.

95. The author expounds on this in 7:19–28. See Translation Notes with the associated Analysis for those verses.

96. Cockerill, *Epistle to the Hebrews,* 96.

97. Cockerill, *Epistle to the Hebrews,* 95; Meier, "Symmetry and Theology," 504–33; Graham Hughes, *Hebrews and Hermeneutics: The Epistle of Hebrews as a New Testament Example of Biblical Interpretation,* vol. 36 of Society for New Testament Studies Monograph Series, ed. Paul Trebilco (Cambridge: Cambridge University Press, 1979), 45 n. 22.

98. BDAG, 711–14.

99. Gerald Hansen Jr., "Only Begotten in the Flesh," in Ludlow, *Encyclopedia of Mormonism,* 2:729.

that the Savior, as God's Son, had the qualities of one who was divine. This would certainly give him a reputation and station above that of the angels.

One last point needs to be mentioned. There has been much discussion over the view that portions of verses 2 and 3 contain hymnic material older than Hebrews itself.[100] Whether or not that is the case, the doctrine taught here does have roots in the nascent Church. The author's words summarize the tradition that has come down to him but which he has recast in his own distinctive language.[101] His words certainly evidence the early knowledge that the Savior was with God from the beginning of the Savior's journey as Redeemer (see also Acts 2:34; Eph. 1:20; 1 Pet. 3:22) who came to earth to reveal the Father (John 1:18; 12:45; 14:5–14; 2 Cor. 4:4; Philip. 2:6; Col. 1:15). In sum, the passage "emphasizes that God has revealed himself completely, ultimately, and definitively in Jesus Christ who was 'appointed heir to all things' [1:2]. This idea is somewhat paradoxical because in antiquity the son became heir only after the father's death. In this case, the author states that the Son became heir after his own death."[102] Nonetheless, heir he was and heir he remains.

The Son Is Superior to the Angels (1:5–14)

This section contains a *catena* (a series or chain) of seven biblical passages that concentrate on the Savior's station as "Son" and is designed to verify that he is superior to the angels.[103] The writings of Second Temple Judaism show that

---

100. For discussion, see Koester, *Hebrews,* 178–79; Ellingworth, *Epistle to the Hebrews,* 96–97; Janusz Frankowski, "Early Christian Hymns Recorded in the New Testament: A Reconstruction of the Question in Light of Hebrews 1:3," *Biblische Zeitschrift* 27 (1983): 183–94; and Jack T. Sanders, *The New Testament Christological Hymns: Their Historical Religious Background,* vol. 15 of Society for New Testament Studies Monograph Series (Cambridge: Cambridge University Press, 1971).

101. F. F. Bruce, "The Kerygma of Hebrews," *Interpretation* 23, no. 1 (1969): 4. The doctrine is also found in such Christological hymns as Philip. 2:5–11; Col. 1:15–18.

102. Holzapfel and Wayment, *Making Sense,* 449; compare Cockerill, *Epistle to the Hebrews,* 94.

103. The author appeals primarily to the psalms (2 Sam. 7:15 and Deut. 32:43 being the exceptions). For a study, see Simon J. Kistemaker, *The Psalm Citations in the Epistle to the Hebrews* (Eugene, Ore.: Wipf and Stock, 2010). Each of the scriptures the author uses has its own Old Testament setting. Though that setting shows that some of the verses are definitely messianic, others are clearly not. In each case, however, there is

many Jews had a very high regard for angels. They primarily functioned as their Hebrew name, מַלְאָךְ (*mal'āk*), indicates, as messengers. Those holding this station could be either earthly or heavenly, and to distinguish the latter from the former, the biblical texts often used designations such as "the angel of the Lord" or "the angel of God" (for example, see Gen. 16:7–16; 31:11; Ex. 3:2). As superhuman entities, they could perform acts as Jehovah dictated. They were viewed, therefore, as beneficial and powerful but also dreadful and were therefore highly respected. Unfortunately, this respect opened the door to undue reverence that became a problem in both Judaism and Christianity.[104] The Epistle to the Hebrews, however, shows no concern for such a development. This section is not a polemic against angel worship but posits a high and respected place for them and in doing so emphasizes the greatness of the Son of God.[105]

The author takes his quotes from the Septuagint (LXX), a translation into Greek of the Hebrew Old Testament made between the fourth and second centuries BC. It became the preferred version of the biblical texts for Jews residing outside of Palestine, who spoke Greek and were no longer conversant in Hebrew. The author's use of this translation does not, therefore, attest to superiority of the LXX over the Hebrew text. The LXX was simply the text with which he and his readers were the most familiar.

Greek Text

5 Τίνι γὰρ εἶπέν ποτε τῶν ἀγγέλων· Υἱός μου εἶ σύ, ἐγὼ σήμερον γεγέννηκά σε, καὶ πάλιν· Ἐγὼ ἔσομαι αὐτῷ εἰς πατέρα, καὶ αὐτὸς ἔσται μοι εἰς υἱόν; 6 ὅταν δὲ πάλιν εἰσαγάγῃ τὸν πρωτότοκον εἰς τὴν οἰκουμένην, λέγει· Καὶ προσκυνησάτωσαν αὐτῷ πάντες ἄγγελοι θεοῦ. 7 καὶ πρὸς μὲν τοὺς ἀγγέλους λέγει· Ὁ ποιῶν τοὺς ἀγγέλους αὐτοῦ πνεύματα, καὶ τοὺς λειτουργοὺς αὐτοῦ πυρὸς φλόγα· 8 πρὸς δὲ τὸν υἱόν· Ὁ θρόνος σου ὁ θεὸς εἰς τὸν αἰῶνα τοῦ αἰῶνος, καὶ ἡ ῥάβδος τῆς εὐθύτητος ῥάβδος τῆς βασιλείας σου. 9 ἠγάπησας δικαιοσύνην καὶ ἐμίσησας ἀνομίαν· διὰ τοῦτο ἔχρισέν σε ὁ θεός, ὁ θεός σου, ἔλαιον ἀγαλλιάσεως παρὰ τοὺς μετόχους σου· 10 καί· Σὺ κατ' ἀρχάς, κύριε, τὴν γῆν ἐθεμελίωσας, καὶ ἔργα τῶν χειρῶν σού εἰσιν οἱ

a connection that allowed the author of Hebrews to justify his use of them as he did. Because the Old Testament context does not directly affect the use of the passages in Hebrews, we do not address them here. Nonetheless, see the discussion on "The Use of the Old Testament" in the introduction as well as the discussions in Bruce, *Epistle to the Hebrews,* 53–64; and Ellingworth, *Epistle to the Hebrews,* 110–32.

104. For discussion, see *Encyclopedia of Judaism,* s.v. "Angelology," http://jewishencyclopedia.com/articles/1521-angelology.

105. J. W. Thompson, "The Structure and Purpose of the Catena in Hebrews 1:5–13," *Catholic Biblical Quarterly* 38 (1976): 352–63.

οὐρανοί· 11 αὐτοὶ ἀπολοῦνται, σὺ δὲ διαμένεις· καὶ πάντες ὡς ἱμάτιον παλαιωθήσονται, 12 καὶ ὡσεὶ περιβόλαιον ἑλίξεις αὐτούς, ὡς ἱμάτιον καὶ ἀλλαγήσονται· σὺ δὲ ὁ αὐτὸς εἶ, καὶ τὰ ἔτη σου οὐκ ἐκλείψουσιν. 13 πρὸς τίνα δὲ τῶν ἀγγέλων εἴρηκέν ποτε· Κάθου ἐκ δεξιῶν μου ἕως ἂν θῶ τοὺς ἐχθρούς σου ὑποπόδιον τῶν ποδῶν σου; 14 οὐχὶ πάντες εἰσὶν λειτουργικὰ πνεύματα εἰς διακονίαν ἀποστελλόμενα διὰ τοὺς μέλλοντας κληρονομεῖν σωτηρίαν; [SBLGNT]

King James Version

5 For unto which of the angels said he at any time, Thou art my Son, this day have I begotten thee? And again, I will be to him a Father, and he shall be to me a Son? 6 And again, when he bringeth in the firstbegotten into the world, he saith, And let all the angels of God worship him. 7 And of the angels he saith, Who maketh his angels spirits, and his ministers a flame of fire. 8 But unto the Son he saith, Thy throne, O God, is for ever and ever: a sceptre of righteousness is the sceptre of thy kingdom. 9 Thou hast loved righteousness, and hated iniquity; therefore God, even thy God, hath anointed thee with the oil of gladness above thy fellows. 10 And, Thou, Lord, in the beginning hast laid the foundation of the earth; and the heavens are the works of thine hands: 11 They shall perish; but thou remainest; and they all shall wax old as doth a garment; 12 And as a vesture shalt thou fold them up, and they shall be changed: but thou art the same, and thy years shall not fail. 13 But to which of the angels said he at any time, Sit on my right hand, until I make thine enemies thy footstool? 14 Are they not all ministering spirits, sent forth to minister for them who shall be heirs of salvation?

New Rendition

5 For to which one of the angels has he ever said,

> "You are my son. Today I have fathered you"? [Ps. 2:7]

And also,

> "I will be a father to him, and he will be a son to me." [2 Sam. 7:14]

6 And also when he brings his firstborn into the world, he says:

> "Let all the angels of God worship him." [Ps. 97:7]

7 Referring to the angels he says:

> "He makes his angels as winds and his servants as flames of fire." [Ps. 104:4]

8 But about his Son he says:

> "Your throne, O God, is forever and ever, and a scepter of justice is the scepter of your kingdom. 9 You have loved righteousness and hated lawlessness. For this reason, O God, even your God, has anointed you with the oil of joy more than your companions." [Ps. 45:6–7]

10 And,

> "You, O Lord, in the beginning laid the foundations of the earth, and the heavens are the work of your hands. 11 They will perish, but you continue to exist forever. They will all wear out like clothing, 12 and like a cloak you will roll them up, and like clothing they will be changed. But you are the

same, and your years will never end." [Ps. 102:25–27]

13 But to which of his angels has he ever said,

"Sit down on my right until I have made your enemies as a footstool under your feet"? [Ps. 110:1]

14 Are not all angels ministering spirits who are sent forth to serve those who will inherit salvation?

Translation Notes and Comments

1:5 *For unto which of the angels said he at any time, Thou art my Son, this day have I begotten thee / For to which one of the angels has he ever said, "You are my son. Today I have fathered you":* The phrase is a quote from LXX Psalm 2:7.[106] On angels, see Translation Notes on 1:4 above and the Analysis below. Some Old Testament scriptures refer to angels as "sons of God" (LXX Gen. 6:2, 4; Deut. 32:43; Job 38:7; Ps. 28:1; 88:7), but the use is collective. No individual angel was ever given the title "son."[107] The author, therefore, uses this scripture not only to set Jesus apart from other divine beings but also to give him station above theirs. The way Jesus became "Son" is explicit: the verb γεννάω (*gennaō*) denotes the process of procreation, and therefore, in some divine way, God literally "fathered" Jesus (Matt. 1:16, 20; Luke 1:35).[108]

---

106. On the author's use of Old Testament passages, see the material under the heading "The Use of the Old Testament" in the introduction. The reference used by the author of Hebrews is quite implicit rather than explicit, but his methods show the importance of such verses. See McConkie, *Promised Messiah,* 80–81.

107. Again, the force of the words could be on the idea of Christ being "the Only Begotten Son in the flesh." See Translation Notes on 1:3 above.

108. BDAG, 193–94; compare G. B. Caird, "Son by Appointment," in *The New Testament Age: Essays in Honor of Bo Reicke,* ed. William C. Weinrich, 2 vols. (Macon, Ga.: Mercer University Press, 1984), 1:73–81. The scriptures make it clear that in some divine way, Jesus was conceived by the power of the Divine and was, thus, the literal son of God. See Joseph Fielding Smith, *Answers to Gospel Questions,* 5 vols. (Salt Lake City: Deseret Book, 1957–66), 5:33–35; and Gerald Hansen Jr., "Only Begotten in the Flesh," in Ludlow, *Encyclopedia of Mormonism,* 2:729. Compare Brigham Young, *Journal of Discourses,* 4:218; and Joseph F. Smith, *Box Elder News,* January 28, 1915, reprinted as "Jesus Christ, Literal Son of God, December 20, 1914," in *Messages of the First Presidency,* ed. James R. Clark, vol. 4 (Salt Lake City: Deseret Book, 1970), 327–32.

The adverb of time, σήμερον (*sēmeron*), "today," was used to denote any division of time marked by a clear beginning and ending but more specifically a particular day in which an event took place.[109] Just what day or time period the author of Hebrews had in mind is debated. Some scholars feel it pointed to the Lord's baptism, some to his resurrection, and others to his ascension.[110] The prophet Abinadi testified that he was "the Son, because of the flesh," having been conceived by the "power of God." Thus, the term "today" could point to Christ's entry into mortality at which time he became "the Only Begotten Son of God in the flesh"[111] (Mosiah 15:3; compare John 1:18; 3:16–18), a title of dignity and power possessed by no other person. The ancient and modern scriptures use the term to emphasize the unique relationship between the Father and the Son so far as the Savior's conception is concerned. According to Latter-day Saint theology, Jesus is literally the only begotten of God in the flesh (John 3:16; D&C 93:11; Moses 6:52). His mortal body was the offspring of his Eternal Father and his mortal mother, Mary (Luke 1:35; 1 Ne. 11:18), "not in violation of natural law but in accordance with a higher manifestation thereof."[112]

I will be to him a Father, and he shall be to me a Son / I will be a father to him, and he will be a son to me: The author used this quote from LXX 2 Samuel 7:14 to reinforce the point he made previously: on the one hand, God will take his position as the Son's Father seriously and will honor it fully, and, on the other, the Son will fully reciprocate.

1:6 ***And again, when he bringeth in the firstbegotten into the world / And also when he brings his firstborn into the world:*** The adverb πάλιν (*palin*), "also, again," is ambiguous. It can denote "a second time." If that is the case here, it would refer to a coming of the Lord after his mortal birth and, therefore, likely refer to his Second Coming. The word can also denote that which is second in a related list.[113] Since the author is listing a series of scripture to illustrate his points, this is likely his intent.[114] The word *palin* is, therefore, translated as "also" in the Rendition.

---

109. See *NID,* s.v. "σήμερον"; BDAG, 921.

110. For discussion, see Attridge, *Epistle to the Hebrews,* 54; and Ellingworth, *Epistle to the Hebrews,* 113–14.

111. See discussion in Translation Notes for 1:3 above.

112. James E. Talmage, *Jesus the Christ,* unabridged version (Salt Lake City: Deseret Book, 1982), 81.

113. BDAG, 752–53; Louw-Nida, §89.97.

114. For discussion, see Lane, *Hebrews 1–8,* 26; and Cockerill, *Epistle to the Hebrews,* 104 n. 22.

The temporal conjunction ὅταν *(hotan)* usually means "at the time that, whenever, when."[115] Here the text points to a specific time, but that time is ambiguous. It can be understood three ways. First, it could denote when Jesus comes into the world and takes upon himself the title of the "Only Begotten Son." At that moment, in the mortal realm where the drama of the Atonement must take place, Jesus becomes "Son," even the Son of God, and takes upon himself mortality, a condition essential to the Atonement. Second, it could point to the Second Coming, when Satan will be cast out and the earth "will be renewed and receive its paradisiacal glory" (A of F 10). Third, it could point to the Lord's enthronement, when he will sit "on the right hand of the Majesty on high" (1:3; see also D&C 66:12; 76:23).

The noun οἰκουμένη (*oikoumenē*), "world," can refer to both the inhabited earth or the celestial realm. Since 1:3 looks to the enthronement of Jesus and 2:5 references "the world to come," the context suggests that the term "world" as used here refers to the celestial realm.[116] That being the case, the scripture points to the Son's royal enthronement as the point when the angels worship him.[117]

Though the word πρωτότοκος (*prōtotokos*), "firstborn," is an adjective defining who the Son is, the definite article placed before it causes it to act as a noun in its own right.[118] The word denotes the first son born into a family. It connotes, however, the station, privileges, and responsibilities of that position. Used in that way, it is a "title of honor expressing priority of rank."[119] When it is related to the Savior, three meanings apply: first, he is the first born of all God's spirit children (12:23; Col. 1:15; Rev. 3:14; Moses 2:26; D&C 76:54, 94; 77:11; 93:21);[120] second, he is the Father's first and only Son born in the flesh (John 1:14, 18; 1 John 4:9; 2 Ne. 25:12; Jacob 4:5; Alma 5:48; D&C 20:21; 49:5); and third, his station is the first

---

115. BDAG, 730–3; see also Louw-Nida, §67.55.

116. See Cora Brady, "The World to Come in the Epistle to the Hebrews," *Worship* 39, no. 6 (1965): 329–39; George Johnston, "Οἰκουμένη and κόσμος in the New Testament," *New Testament Studies* 10 (1964): 352–54; and Cockerill, *Epistle to the Hebrews,* 104–5; and Attridge, *Epistle to the Hebrews,* 65–66.

117. For discussion, see Bruce, *Epistle to the Hebrews,* 56; and Ellingworth, *Epistle to the Hebrews,* 117–18.

118. Wallace, *Greek Grammar,* 233.

119. Lane, *Hebrews 1–8,* 26; see also BDAG, 894. For a study, see Larry R. Helyer, "The *Prōtotokos* Title in Hebrews," *Studies in Biblical Theology* 6 (1976): 7–9.

120. Ludlow, *Jesus Christ,* 262; compare John W. Welch and James V. Garrison, "The 'Hymn of the Pearl': An Ancient Counterpart to 'O My Father,'" *BYU Studies* 36, no. 1 (1996–97): 128–30.

of those entering into the new covenant and order he established (John 3:3–6; Rom. 8:29).

And let all the angels of God worship him / Let all the angels of God worship him: The source of this quote is unknown, but it combines themes from LXX Deuteronomy 32:43 and LXX Psalm 96:6.[121] The plural adjective πάντες (*pantes*), "all," shows that the Savior's station is above all of the angels. The plural imperative verb προσκυνησάτωσαν (*proskynēsatōsan*), "let . . . worship," expresses the "complete dependence on or submission to a high authority figure" that a person should show.[122] The root from which the word comes means to bend or prostrate oneself, thus suggesting the depth of the worshipful act. In the context here it emphasizes the reverence God expects the angelic host to show to his Son.[123]

There is a point of grammar worth noting here. In the phrase "worship him," the pronoun "him" is in the dative rather than the accusative case. Since the dative is used to indicate self-interest (that which benefits a party), the implication is that Jesus is a true God since the worshiper is benefited through his worship.[124] Conversely, the accusative case does not express self-interest and is, therefore, used with the worship of false gods since the worshiper derives no benefit therefrom.

1:7 ***And of the angels he saith, Who maketh his angels spirits, and his ministers a flame of fire / Referring to the angels he says: He makes his angels as winds and his servants as flames of fire:*** This verse is a quote from LXX Ps. 103:4.[125] The verb ποιέω (*poieō*), "to make," in this instance, points to divine activity in assigning the angels their station.[126] God does not, therefore, make them "spirits," but rather *messengers* to carry out

---

121. The LXX adds the phrase *προσκυνήσατε αὐτῷ, πάντες οἱ ἄγγελοι αὐτοῦ* (*proskynēsatōsan autō pantes hoi angeloi autou*), "let all his angels worship him." This phrase is not found in the KJV or Masoretic text. For LXX Ps. 96:7, see Ps. 97:7 in the Masoretic text and KJV.

122. BDAG, 882–83; Gareth Lee Cockerill, "Hebrews 1:6: Source and Significance," *Bulletin for Biblical Research* 9 (1999): 55–58.

123. The force of the imperative is very strong here. God is not just giving permission but is actually commanding the angels to worship the Son. Wallace, *Greek Grammar,* 486 n. 97.

124. Smyth, *Greek Grammar,* §1474.

125. In the Masoretic text and KJV, the passage is found at Ps. 104:4. The Hebrew text clearly differs from the translation in the LXX, stating that God "makes the winds his messengers and the flaming fire his ministers." Thus, the emphasis there is on the natural elements and not on angels as a class of supernatural beings.

126. BDAG, 39–42.

his will. The plural noun πνεύματα (*pneumata*), "spirits," can also denote "winds" and expresses the angels' wide-ranging nature.[127]

The noun λειτουργός (*leitourgos*), "servant, minister," points to a person of rank who engages in administrative or cultic practices. The point of the verse, as found in the LXX, is that Jehovah makes winds his messengers and fire his ministers.[128] Here the author's point is more that God makes his agents active and powerful as wind and fire,[129] but the emphasis is that, as great and powerful as angels are, they are still servants and do not come close to reaching the majesty and power of the Son.[130]

The JST changes the word order in verses 6 and 7 to read, "And again, when he bringeth in the first begotten into the world, he saith, And let all the angels of God worship him, *who maketh his ministers as a flame of fire.* And of the angels he saith, *Angels are ministering spirits.*"[131] The switch clarifies that God does not make his angels spirits, but rather that angels are ministers and spirits.[132]

In the context of Psalms and the KJV, this phrase looks to God's relationship with the natural elements. The "quotation . . . is concerned with the relation between God and the angels; it is not applied directly to the Son."[133] The JST, however, appears to state it is Christ, rather than God, who makes the ministers *as* a flame of fire. Since Christ and God are effectively one, this does not necessarily change much doctrinally, but it does serve to emphasize that it is the Savior who acts as their director. The JST statement that "angels are ministering spirits" clarifies the role of angels. Instead of just being spirits, they are spirits tasked with a specific purpose.[134] That it

---

127. Louw-Nida, §§12.33; 14.4.

128. Note particularly 4 Ezra 8:21–22 that says it is the angels' service that is as wind and fire. See Bruce, *Epistle to the Hebrews*, 58.

129. BDAG, 1060.

130. Koester, *Hebrews*, 194; Ellingworth, *Epistle to the Hebrews*, 121.

131. Italics signify changes from the KJV.

132. This doesn't mean that every angel is just a spirit. The angel Moroni, for instance, had a physical body when he appeared to Joseph Smith. JS–H 1:27–45. However, since the reference used here is from the Old Testament and because the Resurrection had not yet begun, the angels would have been ministering spirits. Compare D&C 129:1, 3.

133. Ellingworth, *Epistle to the Hebrews*, 120.

134. Joseph Smith made a distinction between angels and "ministering spirits," noting that the former were resurrected or translated beings while the latter were as yet unembodied spirits. "Minutes of a Conference of the Church of Jesus Christ of Latter Day Saints, Held in Nauvoo. Ill, Commencing Oct. 1st, 1841," *Times and Seasons* 2 (October 15, 1841): 577, online as "Discourse, 3 October 1841, as Reported by *Times and Seasons*," 577, Joseph Smith Papers, https://www.josephsmithpapers.org/paper-summary/

is Christ who directs them further emphasizes his high position within the kingdom of God.

1:8 ***Thy throne, O God, is for ever and ever / Your throne, O God, is forever and ever:*** The rest of verse 8 and all of verse 9 is a quote from LXX Psalm 44:7–8.[135] That 1:8 was theologically troubling for some scribes is evidenced by some variants that change Ὁ θρόνος σου ὁ θεὸς (*ho thronos sou, ho theos*), "your throne, O God," to Ὁ θρόνος αὐτοῦ ὁ θεὸς (*ho thronos autou ho theos*), "God is his throne."[136] The change seems to have been aimed at resolving the problem of the Davidic king being addressed as "God." With just a small adjustment in transcribing the text, a scribe makes Jehovah become the "throne"—the anchor or seat of the prince's power. This change of the Hebrew text, however, has little to support it.[137] In point of fact, the prince of David's line was the Messiah and as God's vice-regent would rule forever and could therefore be addressed as God.[138] Thus, the translation in the KJV is correct as it stands.[139] The author's point is, indeed, made by use of the vocative; Christ *is* God, the Son of God, whose rule will be εἰς τὸν αἰῶνα τοῦ αἰῶνος (*eis ton aiōna tou aiōnos*), "for ever and ever," a phrase stressing its eternal nature.[140]

a sceptre of righteousness is the sceptre of thy kingdom / a scepter of justice is the scepter of your kingdom: The ῥάβδος (*rhabdos*), literally

---

discourse-3-october-1841-as-reported-by-times-and-seasons/1. This definition, however, could only apply after the Resurrection because before that time only those who were translated (for example, Moses and Elijah) would have had bodies. The rest were either disembodied or unembodied spirits. See Bible Dictionary, s.v. "angels."

135. The reference is found in the KJV at Ps. 45:6–7 and in the Masoretic text at Ps. 45:7–8.

136. Ellingworth, *Epistle to the Hebrews*, 122–23; Metzger, *Textual Commentary*, 592–93.

137. Cockerill, *Epistle to the Hebrews*, 109 n. 53; Vincent Taylor, "Does the New Testament Call Jesus God?" *Expository Times* 73, no. 4 (1962): 116–18; see also Wallace, *Greek Grammar*, 59.

138. In Isa. 9:6, the title "Mighty God" is given to the coming king. For a study, see Benjamin Breckinridge Warfield, "The Divine Messiah in the Old Testament," in *Christology and Criticism* (New York: Oxford Press, 1929), 3–49; see also Murray J. Harris, "The Translation and Significance of ὁ θεός in Hebrews 1:8–9," *Tyndale Bulletin* 36 (1985): 129–62.

139. Johnson, *Hebrews*, 80; Wallace, *Greek Grammar*, 59; see also Blass and Debrunner, *Greek Grammar of the New Testament*, §147.

140. Louw-Nida, §67.95; Cockerill, *Epistle to the Hebrews*, 110 n. 56. Thompson, "Structure and Purpose," 358, notes that the phrase suggests immutability. See also McConkie, *Promised Messiah*, 107–8. On pages 81–82, he states that Ps. 45 is Messianic and therefore directed to the Son: "When words speak of one God who himself has a God, they are speaking of a Son who has a Father."

"a rod," was any stick put to use as a cane, staff, club, shepherd's crook, or scepter.[141] It is in the last sense that the noun is used here. The scepter was the symbol of a ruler's supreme excellence and power (Rev. 2:27; 12:5; 19:15).[142] Here it identifies the absolute sovereignty of the Son. The noun εὐθύτης (*euthytēs*), "righteousness, justice," denotes uprightness or strict adherence to what is proper according to divine law.[143] Taken together the symbol of the "scepter of justice" is that of the correctness and rightness that Christ will use to administer his eternal kingdom.

1:9 ***Thou hast loved righteousness, and hated iniquity / You have loved righteousness and hated lawlessness:*** In this phrase, two of the attributes that exemplify why Christ should have the throne forever are noted. The first is his love for δικαιοσύνη (*dikaiosynē*), "righteousness." The text uses the verb ἀγαπάω (*agapaō*), "love," to describe those feelings. The nuance behind the word is not only having affection for but also taking pleasure in something or someone.[144] The noun *dikaiosynē* denotes that which is correct, upright, and just and therefore conforms to divine law. Further, it carries a very active sense of not only standing against what is wrong but also in putting it right.[145]

The second attribute is the Lord's hatred for ἀνομία (*anomia*), "lawlessness, iniquity," the opposite of "righteousness."[146] The verb μισέω (*miseō*), "hate," means not only to have a strong aversion to something but also to detest it.[147] In this case, it describes the Savior's feelings toward the despising of God's law and the deliberate rebellion it produces.

A point of grammar is telling here. Both verbs are in the aorist tense and, thus, point to past action; it is because the Son has, from the beginning, loved righteousness and has, from the beginning, hated iniquity that he has been exalted.[148]

therefore God, even thy God, hath anointed thee with the oil of gladness above thy fellows / For this reason, O God, even your God, has

---

141. BDAG, 902; Louw-Nida, §6.218.

142. The use of the rod by Moses and Aaron also shows its importance as a symbol of power. Moses used the "rod of God" to do wonders (Ex. 4:17, 20). Aaron also used a rod to do miracles (Ex. 8:16–17). Further, it was the "rod of Levi" that budded showing Aaron was God's chosen priest (Num. 17:1–10).

143. BDAG, 406; Louw-Nida, §37.53.

144. BDAG, 5–6.

145. BDAG, 247–90; *NID*, s.v. "δικαιοσύνη."

146. BDAG, 85; see also Koester, *Hebrews*, 194.

147. BDAG, 652–53.

148. Cockerill, *Epistle to the Hebrews*, 111; compare Koester, *Hebrews*, 202.

anointed you with the oil of joy more than your companions: This part of the verse presents a problem with translation. In the phrase ὁ θεός, ὁ θεός σου (*ho theos ho theos sou*), literally "the God the God of you," both nouns appear to be in the nominative case. It could therefore be translated as "God, [who is] your God." But the noun *theos* with the definite article is very frequently used for the vocative,[149] as it in fact is in the previous verse (1:8) above. Thus it appears that the author is using this phrase to again affirm the sovereignty and dignity of the Son. Therefore, the Rendition takes the first noun as vocative and thus translates the phrase as "O God, even your God."[150] Taken this way, the author is emphasizing the station of the Savior as God.[151] The prepositional phrase διὰ τοῦτο (*dia touto*), literally "because of this," points to the reason why the Father has done what he has:[152] it is because the Son has continually exhibited the attributes noted.

The noun ἀγαλλίασις (*agalliasis*) denotes a piercing exclamation resulting from extreme joy.[153] The phrase ἔλαιον ἀγαλλιάσεως (*elaion agalliaseōs*), "oil of joy," refers to oil used by many Jews at the beginning of the great festivals.[154] Many anointed themselves in anticipation of the joy to come (see Isa. 61:3).[155] There is, however, another dimension to the word that seems at play. In ancient Israel, the verb χρίω (*chriō*), "to anoint," denoted the bequeathing upon a person the power of an office, especially that of king.[156] In this verse, it is the Father who anoints the Son with the "oil of joy" by which the Son's enthronement became complete.[157] By this means, Jesus

---

149. BDAG, 450.

150. Attridge, *Epistle to the Hebrews,* 59; Ellingworth, *Epistle to the Hebrews,* 124; Cockerill, *Epistle to the Hebrews,* 110.

151. Attridge, *Epistle to the Hebrews,* 59–60. The second ὁ θεός σου (*ho theos sou*), "your God," is here taken as the subject of the aorist verb ἔχρισεν (*echrisen*), "has anointed." See Blass and Debrunner, *Greek Grammar of the New Testament,* §147.

152. Johnson, *Hebrews,* 81.

153. Louw-Nida, §25.132.

154. Whether the oil produces the joy or is produced by the joy is an open question. See Wallace, *Greek Grammar,* 107.

155. BDAG, 4.

156. *NID,* 4:697–701.

157. Koester, *Hebrews,* 195; BDAG, 1991. Among the Jews, the "Anointed One" (in Hebrew, *Messiah*) was the title they used to designate the deliverer who would free them from worldly oppression. (At its core meaning, "messiah" is a title for the Judahite king and was so used long before "Judaism," as such, came on the world stage.) Seybold, *TDOT,* 9:43–54; see also Jacob Neusner, *Messiah in Context: Israel's History and Development in Formative Judaism* (Philadelphia: Fortress Press, 1984).

gained the epithet "the Christ." The Greek title ὁ Χριστός (*ho Christos*), literally "the Anointed," referenced a legitimate king. Because of its royal connotation, the title is very fitting for the Savior who rules as "King of kings" (Rev. 19:12–16).[158]

The nominalized adjective μέτοχος (*metochos*), "companion," connoted a person who was a partner or companion to another in a given business. Though some suggest the companions referred to here are angels, it seems more likely they are Jesus' disciples, those with whom he was engaged in the business of saving souls during and after his mortal ministry.[159] The phrase shows that his companions will find joy in the success of the work, but his will be even greater (compare D&C 18:13–15).

1:10–13 These verses are a direct quote from LXX Psalm 101:26–28.[160] The context of the psalm as a whole in both the Greek and Hebrew texts centers on an anonymous sufferer who cries to God for comfort in his wretched mortal state. He finds that comfort not from the easing of his condition but in sensing God's changelessness. In the verses cited by the author, the aggrieved one sees that the eternal purposes of God include the grief the sufferer now endures. He understands that it does not mean he is abandoned, like an old cloak or worn-out garment, but eventually his condition will be changed because of God's unchanging mercy toward his people.[161] The focus of the author of Hebrews is, however, exclusively on the changeless nature of Jesus.

1:10 ***And Thou, Lord, in the beginning hast laid the foundation of the earth; and the heavens are the works of thine hands / And "You, O Lord, in the beginning laid the foundations of the earth, and the heavens are the work of your hands:*** The simple conjunction καί (*kai*), "and," that introduces this scripture shows how seamlessly the thought in this psalm fits to the one before. Here the Son is referred to with the respectful vocative noun as κύριος (*kyrios*), "Lord."[162] In the Old Testament, as here, it is

158. The anointing of a king in ancient Israel denoted the inauguration of an intimate and exclusive relationship between the chosen person and Jehovah. Anointing also validated the person's appointment and signaled that he had the power to reign in God's name. For a discussion, see Marinus De Jorge, "Messiah," in Freedman, *Anchor Bible Dictionary,* 4:777–88.

159. Bruce, *Epistle to the Hebrews,* 61. For discussion, see Cockerill, *Epistle to the Hebrews,* 111.

160. In the KJV and Masoretic text, these are found in Ps. 102:25–27.

161. D. Guthrie and J. A. Motyer, eds., *The New Bible Commentary, Revised* (Grand Rapids, Mich.: Wm. B. Eerdmans, 1970), 514–15.

162. On the use of the vocative case here, see Wallace, *Greek Grammar,* 68.

one of Jehovah's titles. In its general sense, it denotes one who organizes, controls, and administers with authority.[163]

The phrase κατ' ἀρχάς (*kat' archas*), "in the beginning," appears to refer back to the point where the creation of this earth with its heaven was planned and then executed (Gen. 1:1–25; Moses 2:2–31; Abr. 4:1–25). The noun οὐρανοί (*ouranoi*), "heavens," though plural, does not refer to the sidereal sphere but to the firmament of the earth.[164] The noun χείρ (*cheir*), "hand," denotes both human and divine power that brings something about.[165] This verse emphasizes, as noted in 1:2, the Savior's creative power and his personal involvement in the creation of this earth and its firmament (see also D&C 14:9; 76:24; 93:10).

1:11 ***They shall perish; but thou remainest; and they all shall wax old as doth a garment / They will perish, but you continue to exist forever. They will all wear out like clothing:*** The verb ἀπόλλυμι (*apollymi*) in the middle voice as used here means "to perish, be ruined."[166] The nuance, however, does not mean to cease to exist. Though the Savior perished on the cross, he remains forever because he overcame death.[167] So, too, the earth will perish so far as its telestial nature is concerned but will move into an eternal celestial state (Rev. 21:1; D&C 77:1; 88:25–26). The passive of the verb παλαιόω (*palaioō*) means "to become old," thus "to wear out."[168] These two verbs are set in contrast to διαμένω (*diamenō*), "to remain," that is, "to continue to exist, to be permanent."[169] In contrast to ἀπολοῦνται (*apolountai*), "they will perish," which is in the future tense, διαμένεις (*diameneis*) means "you continue to exist." The present tense here is used "to express an action that is true for all time."[170] Hence the Rendition has "you continue to exist forever." The force behind the word points to an abiding stability that is impervious to both mutability and impermanence.[171]

1:12 ***as a vesture shalt thou fold them up, and they shall be changed / like a cloak you will roll them up, and like clothing they will be changed:*** The

---

163. *NID,* s.v. "κύριος"; Foerster, *TDNT,* 3:1088–94.

164. The noun οὐρανός (*ouranos*), "heaven," in Hebrews, is used most often in its plural form (4:14; 7:26; 8:1; 9:23; 12:23, 25), but when connected with τὴν γῆν (*tēn gēn*), "the earth," it refers to the atmosphere. Ellingworth, *Epistle to the Hebrews,* 127.

165. Lohse, *TDNT,* 9:429–32.

166. BDAG, 115–16.

167. Koester, *Hebrews,* 195.

168. BDAG, 751–52.

169. BDAG, 233; Louw-Nida, §13.89.

170. Smyth, *Greek Grammar,* §1877.

171. Lane, *Hebrews 1–8,* 31; see also Thompson, "Structure and Purpose," 260–61.

noun περιβόλαιον (*peribolaion*) referred to a garment that covered most of the body, thus "a cloak" or "robe,"[172] while ἱμάτιον (*himation*) denoted garments in general. The verb ἑλίσσω (*helissō*) denotes rolling up a garment for storage.[173] In contrast, the verb ἀλλάσσω (*allassō*) means "to change" from one outfit to another.[174] The phrase, then, emphasizes the continual exchanging of one article of clothing for another. Here the emphasis is on the work of the Son who changes one order of creation for another as easily as people change clothing (compare D&C 29:31–33).[175]

1:12 ***but thou art the same, and thy years shall not fail / But you are the same, and your years will never end:*** The phrase σὺ δὲ ὁ αὐτὸς εἶ (*su de ho autos ei*), "but you are the same," stresses the unchangeable nature of the Son, the present tense of the verb embracing both the past and the future.[176] That unchangeable nature, however, does not preclude his becoming mortal by taking upon himself the "form" of man (Mosiah 13:34; compare 2:14; Mosiah 3:7) or becoming immortal through the power of the Resurrection. Rather, it refers to his character and attributes.[177] The verb *ekleipō* means both "to die" and "to fail." The idea behind the phrase οὐκ ἐκλείψουσιν (*ouk ekeipsousin*), literally "never die," is that the Savior will never grow old and therefore live forever (compare D&C 76:4).[178]

1:13 ***But to which of the angels said he at any time, Sit on my right hand, until I make thine enemies thy footstool / But to which of his angels has he ever said, "Sit down on my right until I have made your enemies as a***

172. BDAG, 800.

173. BDAG, 317. Some variants of the LXX read ἀλλάξεις (*allaxeis*) as "to change" or "to exchange," which agrees with the indicative verb in the following clause. Metzger, *Textual Commentary,* 593. The word conveys the idea of changing clothes rather than storing them. Heb. 1:12 is reminiscent of LXX Isa. 34:4 and Rev. 6:14, which speak of the heavens being rolled up. In the Bible, the sky is viewed like a tent covering the earth that could be rolled up and removed.

174. BDAG, 45–46. The verb can also refer to making alterations to a piece of clothing, but that does not seem to be the context here.

175. Ellingworth, *Epistle to the Hebrews,* 128.

176. Koester, *Hebrews,* 104–5. For the unchangeable nature of God, see Dennis L. Largey, ed., *Book of Mormon Reference Companion* (Salt Lake City: Deseret Book, 2003), 297; and Rodney Turner, "The Imperative and Unchanging Nature of God," in *The Lectures on Faith in Historical Perspective,* ed. Larry E. Dahl and Charles D. Tate Jr. (Provo, Utah: Religious Studies Center, Brigham Young University, 1990), 199–220.

177. Dahl and Tate, *Lectures on Faith in Historical Perspective,* 67–70. These pages cover lecture 3:12–26.

178. Louw-Nida, §13.39; BDAG, 306. For discussion, see "Excursus on the Atonement: A View from Hebrews" in chapter 2 of this commentary.

footstool under your feet": This is a quote from LXX Psalm 109:1.[179] Though the original intent of the psalm was to reveal the divine ideal and pattern that the Davidic king was to follow,[180] the author repurposes it to stress its messianic emphasis and apply it to the Son.

The author's major purpose is to stress the difference between the Son and the angels. The author, following the rules of rhetoric, casts the question in such a way that the only correct answer is "none." By doing this, he puts himself and his readers in agreement on this point, thus allowing him to proceed with his argument.

The prepositional phrase ἐκ δεξιῶν (*ek dexiōn*) with the plural noun μερῶν (*merōn*), "parts," is used adverbially to refer to the right side of someone or something.[181] In a metaphorical sense it denotes the right hand (see Translation Notes on 1:3 above). The right side of a dignitary was the ultimate position of honor and power. Thus, the Son was to sit, that is, remain in that place—a place of both power and safety—until the Father had subdued the Son's enemies.[182]

The force of the noun ἐχθρός (*echthros*), "enemy," carries the idea of active hostility and hatred of one party towards another.[183] The context in the psalm points to no specific enemy and, therefore, the term likely refers to any and all who oppose the Lord.

A ὑποπόδιον (*hypopodion*) was a footstool. Often one was placed at the front of a throne. In a symbolic sense, when pertaining to people, it carried the idea of being in total subjugation.[184]

1:14 ***Are they not all ministering spirits / Are not all angels ministering spirits:*** The noun "angels" does not appear in the Greek text, but because the author has already noted in 1:7 that angels are both ministers and spirits, the word is used for clarity in the Rendition. That the phrase "ministering angels" can be found in other sources suggests the idea was in circulation (compare Moro. 10:14).[185] The question is so framed that a "yes" answer is demanded and, therefore, puts the reader in a state of agreement with the point made.

---

179. In the KJV and Masoretic text, this passage is found in Ps. 110:1.

180. Guthrie and Motyer, *New Bible Commentary,* 521.

181. BDAG, 217.

182. On the force of the aorist subjunctive θῶ (*thō*) from τίθημι (*tithēmi*), see Wallace, *Greek Grammar,* 479–80.

183. BDAG, 416; Louw-Nida, §39.10, 11.

184. BDAG, 1040; see Josh. 10:24; Bar. 4:25. Koester, *Hebrews,* 196.

185. See Philo, *Virtues* 74; *Mekilta* "Beshallaḥ" 3.98; compare Jub. 2:2; *T. Levi,* 3:5.

sent forth to minister for them who shall be heirs of salvation / who are sent forth to serve those who will inherit salvation: The noun διακονία (*diakonia*), "service," denotes, in this case, a specific kind of service "rendered in an intermediary capacity."[186] This idea is emphasized by the use of the passive participle ἀποστελλόμενα (*apostellomena*), "being sent forth." The word emphasized the appointment "of someone for the achievement of some objective."[187] The angels, whom the author of Hebrews has in mind, serve "those who will inherit salvation." This appears to be those who have made their calling and election sure, that is, those who have been sealed into heaven.[188]

Analysis and Summary

The author of Hebrews, in order to persuade his readers to not abandon the Savior, begins his reasoning by showing how much greater Jesus was than the angels. There was good reason he should start there. Angels played a very important role in the minds of many people, including Jews and Christians, who made up the Greco-Roman world during the New Testament period. Indeed, their universe was filled with spiritual forces that affected humankind and their destiny. The Greek culture, into which the Church was spreading, held high place for spiritual beings called δαιμόνια (*daimonia*), which could work both good and ill. For these people, the membrane between the spirit and physical worlds was very thin, thus allowing for easy access by spiritual beings into the human realm.[189]

Many felt that negotiations were possible. Indeed, there were certain divine beings (such as the god Hermes) who acted as messengers of the gods. These were called ἄγγελοι (*angeloi*), literally "messengers," and were powerful beings in their own right.[190] Augmenting this power was the authority of the divine being who sent them. As a result, they had full power to either bless or curse those to whom they were sent. Their appearance was, therefore, a cause for great anxiety.

---

186. BDAG, 230; see also Cockerill, *Epistle to the Hebrews*, 115.

187. BDAG, 120–21; Louw-Nida, §15.66, 67. D&C 7:6 refers to John the Revelator as a "ministering angel [who] shall be minister for those who shall be heirs of salvation who dwell on the earth."

188. For discussion, see McConkie, *Doctrinal New Testament Commentary*, 3:323–55.

189. See Plato, *Crat.* 407e. The *Metamorphoses* of Ovid shows example after example of the divine both molding and meddling in human affairs.

190. The title ἄγγελος (*angelos*) was used for the goddess Artemis at Syracuse and also for Zeus in Arabia. LSJ, 7.

The Jews and Christians were not immune from these same concerns. They were well aware of "the angel of the Lord" (ὁ ἄγγελος τοῦ κυρίου, *ho angelos tou kyriou*), who not only acted as Jehovah's messenger and agent (for example, see Ex. 14:19; 23:20; Num. 22:22; Judg. 6:11) but also represented him with full power and authority (for example, see Gen. 16:7; 21:17; 22:11; 31:11; Ex. 3:2; Judg. 2:1). They could also act as mediators between the mortal and divine spheres (for example, see Zech. 1:9, 12; 3:1).[191]

The Christians were especially aware of the appearance of angels acting as God's messengers (Matt. 1:20–24; 28:2; Luke 1:11; 2:9; 22:43; John 5:4; 12:29; 20:12; Acts 5:19; 8:26; 10:3; 12:7; 27:23) and believed that they would continue to play an important role in earthly events (Matt. 13:39, 41, 49; 22:30; 24:31; 27:23; 1 Cor. 4:9; 11:10), especially in the latter days and beyond (1 Cor. 6:3; 2 Thes. 1:7; Rev. 7:1–2; 8:2, 7, 10, 12; 9:13; 16:1–12; 20:1). In short, Christians knew that these heavenly beings held high position and great power.[192] The author of Hebrews skillfully uses his readers' understanding of them as his foil to showcase the greatness and supremacy of the Christ.[193]

To impress his readers with the importance, station, work, and power of Jesus, the author of Hebrews appealed to the Old Testament. He carefully selected and skillfully arranged seven scriptures to bolster his point.[194] For ease of reference, though the author used the LXX, the scripture notations here refer to the King James Bible verses.

The first scripture he used, quoted in 1:5, is found in Psalm 2:7. His purpose was to stress the Savior's relationship with God that no other being, including angels, shares, namely, that of Son. At first blush, this idea seems strange since all humankind, both physical and spiritual, are the Father's premortal children,[195] but in this case, "Son" is a title that nuances a special

---

191. Jewish literature of the period gives full play to the role and power of angels. For examples, see *1 En.* 9.3; 12.2; 71.1; *T. Levi* 18.5. Of special note is their power to bring blessings (2 Macc. 10:29; 4 Macc. 4:10; Tob. 5:4, 17, 20–21) or punishments (4 Macc. 7:11; Wis. 18:25). See also Joseph Fielding McConkie, *Witnesses of the Birth of Christ* (Salt Lake City: Bookcraft, 1998), 18.

192. Gabriel certainly flashed his authority when he told Zacharias that he stood "in the presence of God" (Luke 1:19).

193. For a study, see Johnson, *Hebrews,* 82–84; Meyer, *TDNT,* 4:215–25; and *NID,* s.v "λειτουργός."

194. It is of note that "seven," as with many numbers, carried both a quantitative and qualitative aspect. The latter denoted fulness or completeness, especially divine initiation and authority. See David E. Aune, *Revelation,* vol. 52 of Word Biblical Commentary, ed. Bruce M. Metzger, 3 vols. (Dallas: Word Book, 1997–98), 1:29. That nuance may be at play here.

195. Helen Lance Christianson, "Birth," in Ludlow, *Encyclopedia of Mormonism,* 1:115–16.

and unique relationship. It was a title that even the Savior did not have initially but received at a specific point in time. The concern with this idea is that other passages in Hebrews suggest that sonship was a permanent attribute of the Christ, not one that he obtained (1:2; 3:6; 5:8).[196] Further, there is no denying that Jesus is the Son of God and the first born of his creations (Col. 1:15; Rev. 3:14; Moses 4:2). Indeed, one of his titles is "Firstborn" (D&C 93:21). The solution is likely that the use of the word here is technical rather than general.

When Lucifer volunteered to save humankind, he said to God, "I will be thy son, and I will redeem all mankind" (Moses 4:1). Since he was already God's son,[197] what position was he volunteering for? Likely it was that of the "Only Begotten of God in the flesh." The duty that the one bearing this title required was the redemption of humankind (D&C 29:42, 46; 49:5; 138:57).[198] This may be the reason that Satan felt he needed that title.

Jesus filled that role (John 13:6; D&C 93:11; Moses 5:6–8; 6:52; see also 1 Ne. 11:18). Indeed, the Savior's glory was that "of the Only Begotten of the Father, full of grace and truth" (D&C 93:11). The Book of Mormon states that Jesus became "the Son, because of the flesh" (Mosiah 15:3).[199] The author of Hebrews has God saying to the one called "firstbegotten," (πρωτότοκος, *prōtotokos*), that "I will be to him a Father, and he shall be to me a Son" (1:5–6). It would appear, then, that the term is used in this technical sense and that the title "Son" referred to the Only Begotten Son of the Father in the flesh.[200] If that is the case, Jesus obtained the exalted name when he was born of Mary (1 Ne. 11:18–21), a name he alone holds and one that defines his nature and mission.[201]

---

196. See Ellingworth, *Epistle to the Hebrews,* 105–6.

197. Gayle Oblad Brown, "Premortal Life," in Ludlow, *Encyclopedia of Mormonism,* 3:1124.

198. Jeffrey R. Holland, "Atonement of Jesus Christ," in Ludlow, *Encyclopedia of Mormonism,* 1:84–85; Stephen E. Robinson, "Jesus Christ, Names and Titles of," in Ludlow, *Encyclopedia of Mormonism,* 2:742.

199. Largey, *Book of Mormon Reference Companion,* 27.

200. Gerald Hansen Jr., "Only Begotten in the Flesh," in Ludlow, *Encyclopedia of Mormonism,* 2:729; see also Meier, "Symmetry," 187; Lane, *Hebrews 1–8,* 17; Cockerill, *Epistle to the Hebrews,* 98 n. 60; and Ellingworth, *Epistle to the Hebrews,* 105–6. Note that other names have been suggested, but the weight of evidence in still on "Son." See also McConkie, *Promised Messiah,* 467–68.

201. According to Alma 7:10, the title "Son of God" came into play when Mary was overshadowed by the power of the Holy Ghost and conceived Jesus. It is of note that at the Lord's baptism (Matt. 3:17; Mark 1:11; Luke 3:22), the Father assured him he was his "beloved Son," and later, on the Mount of Transfiguration (Matt. 17:5: Mark 9:7), the Father again bore witness, this time to the disciples, that Jesus was his "beloved Son,"

The second scripture the author used, also quoted in 1:5, is found in 2 Samuel 7:14. It functioned to bolster and expand the idea contained in the first scripture. That one emphasized the relationship between Father and Son as a result of Jesus being "fathered" (γεννάω, *gennaō*) (Matt. 1:16, 20; Luke 1:33, 35) and, therefore, becoming the literal Son of God in the flesh.[202] By using this scripture, the author emphasized the result of that relationship: God will treat Jesus as a Son with all the love, care, and honor that is due him, and the Son will reciprocate in exactly the same way.

For the third scripture the author used, quoted in 1:6, there is no known source. It does, however, have elements found in Deuteronomy 32:43 and Psalm 97:6.[203] It served to show the reverence that the Father expects from the angels due to the station of the Son as the "first begotten" (*prōtotokos*). This title, translated as "Firstborn," applies to three time periods. The first was when Jesus was initially begotten as the "Firstborn" son of God in the premortal world (John 1:1–5, 14; Col. 1:15; Rev. 3:14; D&C 93:21; Moses 4:2).[204] The second was when Jesus came into mortality as the Son of Mary and of the Father as "the Firstborn Son of God in the flesh" (Matt. 1:16, 20; Luke 1:33, 35; 1 Ne. 11:18–21). The third was when Jesus was resurrected. At that time, he became the "firstborn" from the dead (Acts 26:23; 1 Cor. 15:32; Col. 1:18; Rev. 1:5). Each of these gave him station and reason to be reverenced.

The Father's proclamation that *all* the angels are to worship the Son is instructive. Every angel, as noted above, was a being of power, but some held higher rank than did others with the archangels being the highest.[205] The Father's proclamation excuses none; all, no matter their station,

---

adding they should listen to and follow him. God bore the same witness to Joseph Smith in his theophany. JS–H 1:17.

202. McConkie, *Doctrinal New Testament Commentary,* 3:140; McConkie, *Promised Messiah,* 143.

203. The LXX adds the phrase προσκυνήσατε αὐτῷ, πάντες οἱ ἄγγελοι αὐτοῦ (*proskynēsate auto, pantes hoi angeloi autou*), "let all his angels worship him." This phrase is not found in the KJV or Masoretic text. LXX Ps. 96:7 is found at Ps. 97:7 in the Masoretic text and KJV.

204. Jerry C. Giles, "Firstborn in the Spirit," in Ludlow, *Encyclopedia of Mormonism,* 2:728.

205. There is a priesthood order among the angels. "Discourse, between circa 26 June and circa 4 August 1839–A, as Reported by Willard Richards," 63, Joseph Smith Papers, https://www.josephsmithpapers.org/paper-summary/discourse-between-circa-26-june-and-circa-4-august-1839-a-as-reported-by-willard-richards/1; "History, 1838–1856, Volume C-1 [2 November 1838–31 July 1842]," 1307, Joseph Smith Papers, https://www.josephsmithpapers.org/paper-summary/history-1838-1856-volume-c-1-2-november-1838-31-july-1842/481. Some hold the highest rank of archangel. Among these are Michael and

were to worship the Son. The Greek word the author used, πορσκυνέω (*proskyneō*), in its Christian context expresses a special kind of worship—one that is deep, sincere, and heartfelt; one that should be directed only toward the Father and Son.[206]

The point in time when such worship took place could have been shortly after the Savior's resurrection when he finally ascended to his Father in heaven (see John 20:17). Then, when the Father brought him into the eternal world (1:6), he enthroned the Son and placed him on his right (1:3). At that time, having overcome all impediments to salvation, including death, Christ received both accolades and adoration from the angelic hosts. These acts of worship will not end there, however, but continue into eternity.[207]

The fourth scripture the author used, quoted in 1:7, is found in Psalm 104:4. Its purpose was to point out the place and ministry of angels and to show that they are lower than those of the Son. The Old Testament Psalm praises Jehovah for his power by which he is master over water, cloud, wind, and fire. All these he enlists to do his bidding.[208] The scripture equates angels with the winds and ministers with flames of fire—two forces that, when at full power, mortals cannot control yet God always can. But the point of the quote is that the job specifically assigned to angels is that of messengers, not creators or executors as is the Son.

The fifth scripture the author used, quoted in 1:8–9, is found in Psalm 45:6–7. Its purpose was to reinforce the fact of the high station of the Son and explain why he achieved that station. The first reason is that, though he is the Son, he is still God (Mosiah 3:5; 7:27). He holds the title, rank, dignity, and power of that office. Those who hold this office "have no end," thus are "from everlasting to everlasting." Further, "all things are subject unto them," and therefore they are "above all," such that even "the angels

---

Gabriel. On Gabriel, see Andrew C. Skinner, "Noah," in Ludlow, *Encyclopedia of Mormonism,* 3:1016–17; on Michael, see Arthur A. Bailey, "Adam," in Ludlow, *Encyclopedia of Mormonism,* 1:15–16; and Mark E. Petersen, "Adam, the Archangel," *Ensign* 10, no. 11 (November 1980): 16–18.

206. *NID,* s.v. "πορσκυνέω."

207. The book of Revelation has a number of scenes in which the Son is honored. See, for example, Rev. 5:11–14; 15:2–4.

208. The Hebrew text of the Old Testament is ambiguous and can also read "who makes the winds your messengers and the flames of fire your servants." This reading conforms to that found in Dead Sea Scroll 1QH 1:10–11. Attridge, *Epistle to the Hebrews,* 57 and n. 83.

are [also] subject unto them" (D&C 132:20).[209] Clearly, this station is superior to that of any of the angels.

A number of New Testament scriptures refer to Jesus as "God" (John 1:1, 18; 20:28; Rom. 9:5; Titus 3:4; 2 Pet. 1:1). The author of Hebrews, citing as he does this Old Testament psalm, deliberately puts scriptural authority behind this point. And he does something more: he ties the mortal Son to the deific office and, in that way, stresses that Jesus of Nazareth, though fully mortal, was also divine.[210]

The second implication of Jesus attaining the high position, as noted in 1:8, was that he would hold kingly power forever. The divine throne is his, and he will never step down or be forced therefrom.

The third implication of Jesus' honored position, as also shown in 1:8, is that symbolized in the imagery of the "righteous scepter." He will administer divine law over his kingdom with correctness and propriety. According to Psalm 45:2, his judgments will "be fairer than the children of men" because of "the grace"—that is, the compassion and favor for others—that he possesses.[211]

The fourth reason the Savior achieved his high station, as shown in 1:9, is because he has, from the beginning, loved righteousness. In the premortal world, all were given the opportunity to obey or disobey the words of God the Father and, thereby, gain or lose light and truth (Alma 13:3–5; D&C 93:29–33). The continual reception of light and truth gave one ever-greater abilities and power, eventually leading to exaltation. Disobedience, on the other hand, resulted in the loss of these elements, leading to damnation. The Savior's love of righteousness from the beginning expressed

---

209. There is much more to this office. For a study, see Robert L. Millet, "Jesus Christ, Fatherhood and Sonship of," in Ludlow, *Encyclopedia of Mormonism,* 2:739–40; and K. Codell Carter, "Godhood," in Ludlow, *Encyclopedia of Mormonism,* 2:553–55.

210. Johnson, *Hebrews,* 80. Because Latter-day Saints do not believe in the Trinity, the problem of subordinationism that so plagued the Christian community in the second and third centuries is not an issue. Jesus, as Son, is clearly subordinate to the Father as Jesus himself insisted. See Mark 10:18, 32; John 14:28. For a definition, see Angelo Di Berardino, ed., *Encyclopedia of the Early Church,* trans. Adrian Walford, 2 vols. (Oxford: Oxford University Press, 1992), s.v. "Subordinationism."

211. The Hebrew noun חֵן (*ḥēn*) used in this passage means "grace" or "favor." *HAL,* 332; Frances Brown, Samuel R. Driver, and Charles A. Briggs, *A Hebrew and English Lexicon of the Old Testament* (1952; rpt., Oxford: Clarendon Press, 1987), 336, page numbers hereafter are to the Clarendon edition (hereafter cited as BDB). In a sense, the Son's judgments could actually be unfair in that justice will be tempered with mercy, that is, a willingness to take extenuating circumstances into account thus mitigating against harshness and undue penalty.

itself in superior obedience. Part of that obedience included not just living God's law but also administering it and, very importantly, defending it (Rev. 19:19–20; Moses 4:2–3). As a result, he acquired power to the point that the Father ordained him to godhood with authority to create, redeem, and rule.[212]

The fifth reason Jesus achieved his high rank, as noted in 1:9, is because he "hated iniquity." The noun ἀνομία (*anomia*) has two shades of meaning, either "a state or condition of being disposed to what is lawless, lawlessness," or "the product of a lawless disposition, a lawless deed."[213] In most cases, the two senses cannot be sharply differentiated and are merely a difference in emphasis.[214] For the ever-obedient Son, acts of rebellion would have been especially odious because "that which breaketh a law, and abideth not by law, but seeketh to become a law unto itself, and willeth to abide in sin, and altogether abideth in sin, cannot be sanctified by law, neither by mercy, justice, nor judgment." It must, therefore, "remain filthy still" (D&C 88:35). Given that, it is little wonder that the Son hated lawlessness and promoted righteousness.

It was because of his superior love for and living according to righteousness—including standing up for what was right—that the Father anointed the Son with "the oil of joy more than [his] companions" (1:9). Indeed, that anointing gave him the title of Χριστός (*Christos*), "Christ," the Anointed One (מָשִׁיחַ, *māšîaḥ,* "Messiah" in Hebrew). The scripture highlights his anointing through which he gained royal status.[215]

The sixth scripture the author of Hebrews used, quoted in 1:10 (one that he designed to show the supremacy of Jesus over the angels), was Psalm 102:25–26. While all the other passages that the author has used up to this point emphasized Jesus' station as the Son of God and thereby heir of all things, this passage begins by focusing on his creative power. The psalm supports the point made in 1:2–3 that Jesus created all "the worlds" and "upholds all things by his powerful word." The emphasis is on a power he holds that no angel does. But there is more: in Latter-day Saint theology, as

212. See LaMar E. Garrard, "Jesus Is the Christ," in *Studies in Scripture, Volume Five: The Gospels,* ed. Kent P. Jackson and Robert L. Millet (Salt Lake City: Deseret Book, 1986), 321–44.

213. BDAG, 85.

214. W. Gutbrod and H. Kleinknecht, *TDNT,* 4:1085.

215. For a study, see Sungho Choi, *The Messianic Kingship of Jesus: A Study of Christology and Redemptive History in Matthew's Gospel with Special Reference to the Royal Enthronement Psalms* (Eugene, Ore.: Wipf and Stock, 2011).

the prime executor of God's will (John 1:1–3; Rev. 19:13; Jacob 4:9; Moses 1:32; 2:1), the Son became the Father of all creation and rules from that high rank.[216]

Apparently, the main reason the author chose to use this scripture, however, is not to stress the Lord's station but to emphasize one of his attributes: immutability (see 1:11–12). Though the definition of the word points to something that is "not capable or susceptible to change," Latter-day Saints agree with a more limited definition as it applies to the Savior that restricts his unchanging nature to his will, character, and fulfillment of covenantal promises (see, for example, 6:17–18; Num. 23:19; 1 Sam. 15:29; Ps. 102:26; Mal. 3:6; 2 Tim. 2:13; James 1:17; 3 Ne. 24:6; D&C 3:1–3; 35:1). Unlike some other religions, The Church of Jesus Christ of Latter-day Saints does not teach that immutability means Jesus cannot progress or be enlarged.[217] Nevertheless, it does mean that, so far as his character and attributes are concerned, he is "the same yesterday, today, and forever" (2 Ne. 27:23; 29:9; Alma 31:17; Morm. 9:9: Moro. 10:19).[218]

The author of Hebrews uses Psalm 102 to support not only this unchangeableness but also the abiding permanence of the Lord (1:11–12). Like clothes that are changed or wear out, the cosmos will also grow old and be put away (1:11–12), but the Son, ever fresh and ever alive, will ever remain.

The seventh and last scripture the author uses, Psalm 110:1, quoted in 1:13, is designed to forcefully stress the supremacy of Christ, bringing a well-calculated and climactic close to the catena. Its purpose is to recapitulate all the points made by the preceding quotes and drive home but one idea: Jesus really is far superior to the angels.[219] The focus here is twofold. The first is the station to which God has exalted Jesus. The Father has enthroned the Son on his right side, the position of prestige and power.[220] The second is God's promises to overcome all of his Son's enemies (see

216. See Hyrum L. Andrus, *God, Man, and the Universe* (Salt Lake City: Bookcraft, 1968), 223–25; and McConkie, *Mortal Messiah,* 35.

217. "Immutability of God," Theopedia, accessed December 2, 2015, https://www.theopedia.com/immutability-of-god. This source is an online conservative Christian encyclopedia. For LDS studies, see James R. Harris, "Eternal Progression and the Foreknowledge of God," *BYU Studies* 8, no. 1 (1967): 37–46; and Eugene England, "Perfection and Progression: Two Complimentary Ways to Talk about God," *BYU Studies* 29, no. 3 (1989): 31–47.

218. For discussion, see "Excursus on the Atonement: A View from Hebrews," in chapter 2 of this commentary.

219. Johnson, *Hebrews,* 31–32.

220. Thompson, "Structure and Purpose," 352–63.

Ps. 8:6). That the plural noun "enemies" (ἐχθρούς, *echthrous*) is not limited in the text suggests it refers to all beings who oppose the Lord. What must not be lost, as a nuance of the Greek word translated "enemies" shows, is the open and hostile hatred these people show toward the Lord. This hostility is the ground of their active opposition against him. Thus, they are his chief enemy. There is an echo here to the "sons of perdition," those beings who knowingly and willfully pervert the principles of righteousness and promote wickedness. Their great sin includes both covertly and openly fighting against God and his ways. These are they who would have willingly joined the crowd not only demanding but also rejoicing in the Savior's crucifixion.[221]

The author concludes in 1:14 with his own observation that the best the scriptures can say for angels is that they are God's ministers. His statement should not be taken to mean that he sees their station as lowly. It is not, for they are empowered to carry out God's dictates. Even so, they act as his servants and perform his will. Further, they are subject also to the Son (compare D&C 7:6; 76:88).[222]

Conclusion

A main intent of the author of Hebrews was to show to his readers the greatness of Christ in an effort to persuade them to not abandon their faith in him. Through the whole first chapter, the author keeps his readers focused on the Lord as the only being in whom to put their trust. The author uses angels—beings of immense power and authority—as his foil to show the greatness of the Son, stressing that they are but servants of the Most High while the Christ is his Son and heir.

---

221. Rodney Turner, "Sons of Perdition," in Ludlow, *Encyclopedia of Mormonism,* 3:1391.

222. Any being—spiritual, mortal, or resurrected—who is commissioned and empowered to do God's biding acts in the capacity of an angel. Joseph Smith referred to Enoch, a translated being, as a ministering angel to "terrestrial bodies" and to "heirs of salvation." "Instruction on Priesthood," 6. Angels will work as messengers and ministers of God in the heavens as well. In the afterlife, God will appoint certain inhabitants of the terrestrial kingdom to minister to those of the telestial. Thus, those in "the telestial receive [God's word by] the administering of angels who are appointed to minister for them, or [in other words] are appointed to be ministering spirits for them; for they [the telestial inhabitants] shall be heirs of salvation." D&C 76:86–88.

The author stresses the ascension of the eternal Son, the only one who sits on "the right hand of the Majesty on high" (1:3). The position makes it very clear that Christ is the one and only one who shares in divine splendor and power. That the Savior is seated stresses the finality of his position as Son and ruler. Even so, his role is subordinate to that of the Father.

Through the very skillful use and arrangement of the scriptures, the author is able to give clout to the points he makes as he lists the high position and accomplishments of the Son.[223] The result is a majestic, if brief, catalogue of the station, power, activities, and greatness of the Son.

But why this is important must not be overlooked. The Son is the Savior who "by himself purged our sins" (1:3). The author of Hebrews focuses on three critical aspects of Christ's saving ability. The first is his enthronement on the right hand of the Father and God's promise to subdue all of the Son's enemies (1:13). By this means, the Son's saving power is guaranteed and nothing can take it away. The second is his continuance. Though heaven and earth may pass away, the Savior ever remains (1:11). Therefore, his saving power will operate forever. The third is his immutability. He changes not but is "the same, and his years never fail" (1:12; see also D&C 76:4). As a result, he can be counted on to continue in his saving role. To those to whom the Epistle was written, the message should have been clear: for those who continue with faith in Christ, salvation is guaranteed.[224]

---

223. Attridge, *Epistle to the Hebrews,* 46 n. 140; Ellingworth, *Epistle to the Hebrews,* 103.

224. See Joshua W. Jipp, "The Son's Entrance into the Heavenly World: The Soteriological Necessity of the Scriptural Catena in Hebrews 1.5–14," *New Testament Studies* 56 (October 2010): 557–75.

Chapter 2

The Exalted Son

Introduction

The author of Hebrews, in the first four verses of this chapter, fires a hortative salvo designed to grab and hold his readers' attention.[1] It allows us to see why the author spent so much time and effort in the last chapter detailing the activities of the Son and defining the station he now holds with its attendant honors. In doing so, the author put real clout behind the strong admonition he ends with.

His words here expose the reason for his concern and reveal why he wrote with such earnestness and passion. His readers had become inattentive to the gospel principles revealed by and through the Son. Some appear to have gone so far as to disregard their covenantal relationship with him and, therefore, stood in danger of drifting off the course he had set.

The author makes no explicit mention as to what had distracted his readers from openly following the Savior, but the positive position he assigned to the angels in both chapters 1 and 2, along with his reverence for the Mosaic law (2:2), suggests that his audience continued to have spiritually unhealthy intellectual and emotional ties to certain aspects of Judaism and were slipping back into them, thus, leaving the gospel of Christ. As a result, they desperately needed to renew their appreciation for Christ and his example. To bring this about, they had to recommit to the message his representatives had delivered to them and once more anchor themselves to him.[2]

The author's admonition focuses on the spiritual and eternal consequences that would follow for losing faith in the Son and turning away from his gospel (2:1–4). To bolster his point, the author stresses the idea that God did not give supreme authority to any of the angels but only to the

1. Attridge, *Epistle to the Hebrews,* 63.
2. Koester, *Hebrews,* 208; Lane, *Hebrews 1–8,* 36.

Son (2:5–9) who, in turn, sanctified those who accepted him and brought them into oneness with him (2:10–13). The author then pointed out that, in order to fully understand humankind's challenges and trials, the Son himself became mortal and, as a result, is fully able to give both assistance and relief to the faithful. In that way, he became the trustworthy and faithful High Priest. The primary duty of those holding this office was to take care of the people. They were to do this by teaching them Jehovah's word (Num. 27:21) and making atonement for them (Ex. 30:10). These tasks Jesus performed fully and completely (2:14–18).[3]

Noteworthy is that, after he delivered his admonition, the author once again turned to scripture to cement his point. This break is very noticeable: in the first four verses, he not only abandons scriptural language but also uses idiomatic Hellenistic diction, likely "to confront the thought and life of his readers in a more arresting way than reliance upon familiar words and phrases would foster."[4] Nonetheless, he quickly returned to the scriptures—God's own voice[5]—to give authority to the ideas he was making.

In 2:5–18, the author skillfully completes his description of the exalted "Son of God." His emphasis is, however, not so much on the Lord's station as on how he got there. The Savior's condescension, mortality, suffering, death, and triumph are all duly noted. The focus is on the broad impact of his death—for all humankind (2:9)—and also on his conquest of Satan (2:14). Moreover, the author also offers glimpses into the Savior's important role as τὸν ἀρχηγὸν τῆς σωτηρίας αὐτων (*ton archēgon tēs sōtērias autōn*), "the founder of their salvation" (2:10).[6]

---

3. Attridge, *Epistle to the Hebrews,* 63. It is important to note, however, that though the Son has completed his work making eternal redemption possible, it awaits complete and final application and fulfillment in the lives of each individual dependent on their faithfulness. See Stephen S. Smalley, "The Atonement in the Epistle to the Hebrews," *Tyndale Bulletin* 7–8 (July 1961): 35, https://legacy.tyndalehouse.com/tynbul/Library/TynBull_1961_07_05_Smalley_AtonementInHebrews.pdf.

4. Lane, *Hebrews 1–8,* 35. Because of this switch in vocabulary, some have argued that this passage, and other hortatory passages like it, were later inserted into the text, thus disrupting the flow of the theological message originally being developed. For example, see F. C. Synge, *Hebrews and the Scriptures* (London: SPCK, 1959), 43–52. Most scholars today disagree with this analysis, seeing the hortatory sections as being the point of the theological developments. Attridge, *Epistle to the Hebrews,* 63 n. 8. For discussion, see Lane, *Hebrews 1–8,* 36.

5. The author's use of the Old Testament passages shows his firm belief that God continues to speak through the scriptures to the people of his day. For the author, every quote and reference he makes has equal weight because they are all God's active voice in history. Lane, *Hebrews 1–8,* cxvii.

6. The Greek word is translated as "captain" in the KJV. For development of this theme, see Translation Notes on 2:10 below.

The author also highlights another important reason that the Son became flesh. It was not just so he could conquer death through the power of the resurrection, it was also so he could empathize with those whose kind he had become (2:14–16). As a result, he is able to understand on a personal level weakness, infirmity, trials, and temptations (2:17–18). All these, plus pain and death, combine to make him the ideal High Priest (2:17).[7]

Warning Not to Drift Away (2:1–4)

Greek Text

1 Διὰ τοῦτο δεῖ περισσοτέρως προσέχειν ἡμᾶς τοῖς ἀκουσθεῖσιν, μήποτε παραρυῶμεν. 2 εἰ γὰρ ὁ δι᾽ ἀγγέλων λαληθεὶς λόγος ἐγένετο βέβαιος, καὶ πᾶσα παράβασις καὶ παρακοὴ ἔλαβεν ἔνδικον μισθαποδοσίαν, 3 πῶς ἡμεῖς ἐκφευξόμεθα τηλικαύτης ἀμελήσαντες σωτηρίας, ἥτις, ἀρχὴν λαβοῦσα λαλεῖσθαι διὰ τοῦ κυρίου, ὑπὸ τῶν ἀκουσάντων εἰς ἡμᾶς ἐβεβαιώθη, 4 συνεπιμαρτυροῦντος τοῦ θεοῦ σημείοις τε καὶ τέρασιν καὶ ποικίλαις δυνάμεσιν καὶ πνεύματος ἁγίου μερισμοῖς κατὰ τὴν αὐτοῦ θέλησιν. [SBLGNT]

King James Version

1 Therefore we ought to give the more earnest heed to the things which we have heard, lest at any time we should let them slip. 2 For if the word spoken by angels was steadfast, and every transgression and disobedience received a just recompence of reward; 3 How shall we escape, if we neglect so great salvation; which at the first began to be spoken by the Lord, and was confirmed unto us by them that heard him; 4 God also bearing them witness, both with signs and wonders, and with divers miracles, and gifts of the Holy Ghost, according to his own will?

New Rendition

1 Therefore we must pay much closer attention to what we have heard, so that we do not drift away. 2 For if the word spoken by angels proved to be valid, and every transgression and act of disobedience received just retribution, 3 how will we escape if we disregard so great a salvation? This salvation was first spoken by the Lord, and was confirmed to us by those who heard him. 4 God also testified with signs, wonders, and various miracles, and also with gifts of the Holy Spirit, according to his will.

---

7. Cockerill, *Epistle to the Hebrews,* 125.

Translation Notes and Comments

2:1 *Therefore we ought to give the more earnest heed to the things which we have heard / Therefore we must pay much closer attention to what we have heard:* The author is careful not to offend his hearers, so he includes himself in his admonition by using the first person plural "we."[8] Further, he likely felt that he too could do better. The phrase διὰ τοῦτο (*dia touto*), "for this reason, therefore," introduces the admonition and points to action that is needed. The verb δεῖ (*dei*) denotes both what must be done due to the gravity of a situation and what should be done because it is fitting.[9] Given the eternal consequences of disobedience, it seems the first nuance best fits the situation here and so is translated as "must" in our Rendition.[10]

The phrase περισσοτέρως προσέχειν (*perissoterōs prosechein*), "must pay much closer attention," stresses the ardent heed or attention that must be given to a situation. The present infinitive *prosechein,* "to heed, pay attention to,"[11] implies continual effort. With its use, the author avoids implying that his readers are not already paying attention. He also avoids offending them.[12]

The aorist passive participle ἀκουσθεῖσιν (*akoustheisin*), "the [things] heard," carries the nuance not simply of listening but of submissive acceptance of the message heard.[13] It most likely refers to the message both originally delivered by the Lord and then later by his servants.[14]

lest at any time we should let them slip / so that we do not drift away: The KJV here mistranslates the verb παραρρέω (*pararreō*), which has the basic sense "to flow beside, by, or past," not "to slip away." The term is actually nautical and, when used in a figurative sense, means "to drift from course" or "drift away."[15]

---

8. Wallace, *Greek Grammar,* 396–98, and n. 11, notes the possibility that the "we" points to two authors of the Epistle, but there is very little support for this view.

9. BDAG, 213–14; Louw-Nida, §71.21, 34.

10. Grundmann, *TDNT,* 2:21–25; Ellingworth, *Epistle to the Hebrews,* 135.

11. For a nautical nuance behind the word, see Earle Hilgert, *The Ship and Related Symbols in the New Testament* (Assen, Neth.: Royal Van Gorcum, 1962), 133–34; and Lane, *Hebrews 1–8,* 35. In this context, the word refers to anchoring a boat to a sea bed to keep it from floating away. The imagery suggests the author's readers need to remain anchored to what they have heard and thereby not be in danger of floating away.

12. Ellingworth, *Epistle to the Hebrews,* 136.

13. The verb ἀκούω (*akouō*) denotes not only hearing something but also paying attention to it with the implication of obeying what is heard. See Louw-Nida, §§24.52; 31.56; 36.14.

14. Ellingworth, *Epistle to the Hebrews,* 136.

15. LSJ, 1322; Louw-Nida, §31.69; BDAG 770. The idea that word denotes letting something of value slip away through lack of care is appealing (see Bruce, *Epistle to the Hebrews,*

2:2–4 These verses constitute one long sentence in the Greek manuscripts. For the sake of making the passage clearer in English, it is broken into three sentences in our Rendition.

2:2 ***if the word spoken by angels was steadfast / if the word spoken by angels proved to be valid:*** The conjunction εἰ (*ei*), "if," with the indicative of any tense designates a condition that is assumed to be true for the sake of argument.[16] The noun λόγος (*logos*), "word," likely refers to the law of Moses, which some Jews believed was given through angelic administration (Deut. 33:2).[17] The nuance of the aorist passive participle λαληθείς (*lalētheis*), "spoken," suggests that the author had a specific time and place in mind. Given the context of his work, it would appear that the author was referring to the time when Jehovah made his covenant with Israel at Sinai (12:18–19).

The adjective βέβαιος (*bebaios*), a legal term, has the basic meaning of "firm, steady," but here it is used in the extended sense of "sure, certain, valid" and implies the serious obligations the law placed upon the Israelites.[18] The word emphasizes the importance and legitimacy of the covenant and its requirements. The force of the aorist verb ἐγένετο (*egeneto*), "was, proved to be," strongly suggests the author saw that "the Law's validity belongs to the past."[19]

---

66), but the root word ῥέω (*rheō*), from which παραρέω (*pararreō*) comes, does not bear this out. See *NID,* s.v. "ῥέω."

16. Blass and Debrunner, *Greek Grammar of the New Testament,* §371; Wallace, *Greek Grammar,* 692–94.

17. Many of the ancient sources refer to the angelic ministration of the Law in order to stress its validity. See Acts 7:38, 53; *Jub.* 1:27, 29; 2:1; Josephus, *Ant.* 15.136. See also Cockerill, *Epistle to the Hebrews,* 118–19; and Ellingworth, *Epistle to the Hebrews,* 137–38. The idea of angelic administration was widely accepted among the Jews during the Second Temple period. Two important texts describing the angelic sphere are the Book of the Watchers (part of the book of Enoch) and the Jubilees, both of pre-Qumranic origin but found in several copies at Qumran. For examples, see CD II:17–21; 4Q180. One of the most important angels is the Angel of Presence, who mediates between God and humanity and particularly assists Moses. See 1QH XIV:13; 1Q28b IV:25–26; 4Q216 IV:6–V:1. This angel has a central role in the transmission of the law. The Qumranic material notes that angels are created by God but are subordinate to him in power and knowledge while being more wise and powerful than human beings. See 1QS IV:22; 4Q404; CD II:6; 1QM XII:1–9, XVII:6–9. However, in the Dead Sea Scrolls, there is no detailed description of the appearance of the angels. For a study, see Hanne von Wiessenberg, "Gods, Angels, and Demons in the Dead Sea Scrolls," accessed August 7, 2016, http://www.academia.edu/1499534/God_s_Angels_and_Demons_in_the_Dead_Sea_Scrolls.

18. LSJ, 312; BDAG, 172; Attridge, *Epistle to the Hebrews,* 65.

19. Ellingworth, *Epistle to the Hebrews,* 138.

every transgression and disobedience received a just recompence of reward / every transgression and act of disobedience received just retribution: The noun παράβασις (*parabasis*), "transgression," denotes an "act of deviating from an established boundary or norm, overstepping."[20] Moreover, in the New Testament, it specifically points to "acts of disobedience against the divine Law which were wittingly and willingly committed."[21]

The noun παρακοή (*parakoē*), "disobedience," connotes both the state of the mind and the will that led to sin. It strongly suggests a deliberate refusal to hear. Again, the emphasis is on the considered nature of the act, but the word looks more at a careless attitude (rather than the strong fervor implied in *parabasis*) that spawns the disobedience.[22]

The noun μισθαποδοσία (*misthapodosia*), literally "recompense," carries both a positive and negative aspect, initiated in response to a deed done. On the positive side, it denotes reward; on the negative, punishment.[23] Here not only is the negative aspect in mind but also the seriousness of the breach made against the law's obligations.[24] Thus, the word is translated as "retribution" in our Rendition.[25] That the noun is modified by the adjective ἔνδικος (*endikos*), "just, correct," underscores the idea that the punishment is fully deserved.[26]

2:3 ***How shall we escape, if we neglect so great salvation / how will we escape if we disregard so great a salvation:*** The question is designed to push the point introduced in the previous verse. The interrogative πῶς (*pōs*), "how," introduces a rhetorical question. Its negative force suggests that there is absolutely no way to escape.[27] The verb ἐκφεύγω (*ekpheugō*), "to escape," is key here. It denotes the avoiding of impending peril through flight.[28] The concern is expressed in the aorist participle ἀμελήσαντες (*amelēsantes*), "neglecting." The verb it is derived from, ἀμελέω (*ameleō*), "neglect, disregard," connotes making light of or disregarding something that should be taken with due seriousness.[29] The noun σωτηρία (*sōtēria*), "salvation," is here associated with the phrase

---

20. BDAG, 758.
21. Schneider, *TDNT,* 5:740.
22. BDAG, 766–67.
23. Louw-Nida, §38.17.
24. Attridge, *Epistle to the Hebrews,* 65.
25. BDAG, 653.
26. BDAG, 332.
27. Ellingworth, *Epistle to the Hebrews,* 139.
28. BDAG, 312.
29. BDAG, 52; Louw-Nida, §30.50; LSJ 80–81.

τοῖς ἀκουσθεῖσιν (*tois akoustheisin*), "to the things heard," in 1:1. In this context, it describes divine deliverance from physical and spiritual death that comes through the Atonement of Christ to those who repent and have faith in him.[30] It becomes, therefore, a synonym for the gospel. The kind of salvation the gospel brings "is not only a matter of being rescued from some negative worldly condition; it means participating in a higher order of reality."[31] Thus, the adjective modifying it, τηλικοῦτος (*tēlikoutos*), "so great," implies that the gospel was by many degrees greater than the law.[32]

which at the first began to be spoken by the Lord / This salvation was first spoken by the Lord: The Greek text transitions into the next thought using the relative pronoun ἥτις (*hētis*), "which." For clarity, our Rendition begins this phrase as a new sentence and, for that reason, translates *hētis* as "salvation," its antecedent. The phrase ἀρχὴν λαβοῦσα λαλεῖσθαι διὰ τοῦ κυρίου (*archēn labousa laleisthai dia tou kyriou*), literally "having taken a beginning to be spoken through the Lord," is translated as "was first spoken by the Lord" in our Rendition. "The Lord" here, of course, refers to Christ, who preached the gospel message of salvation during his earthly ministry.

was confirmed unto us by them that heard him / was confirmed to us by those who heard him: The aorist passive verb ἐβεβαιώθη (*ebebaiōthē*), "was confirmed," emphasizes the firmness or sureness of a given teaching. The aorist participial phrase τῶν ἀκουσάντων (*tōn akousantōn*), "those who heard," emphasizes the source of the teaching.[33] These persons, though unspecified, were nonetheless eyewitnesses and therefore fully able to confirm what Jesus had taught.[34]

2:4 ***God also bearing them witness / God also testified:*** The present participle συνεπιμαρτυροῦντος (*synepimartyrountos*) means "to join bearing witness with others." The two prefixes added to the root μαρτυρέω (*martyreō*), "witness"—συν- (*syn-*), "accompanied," and ἐπι- (*epi-*), "added

---

30. BDAG, 985–86; W. Foerster, *TDNT,* 7:996; see also Alma 12:33–34; 34:16; 42:13; and Moses 6:62. The meaning of the noun is very broad and, therefore, could include all forms of eschatological deliverance. See Attridge, *Epistle to the Hebrews,* 66–67.

31. Johnson, *Hebrews,* 90.

32. BDAG, 1001–2; Ellingworth, *Epistle to the Hebrews,* 139.

33. The verb ἀκούω (*akouō*), "to hear," carries the connotations of not just listening to but also of understanding and paying attention to and thus heeding something said. BDAG, 37–38.

34. Spencer W. Kimball, "The Privilege of Holding the Priesthood," *Ensign* 5, no. 11 (November 1975): 80. Whether or not these witnesses were still alive is not confirmed by the present tense since it can include a past act. See Blass and Debrunner, *Greek Grammar of the New Testament,* §339.

to"—must be given their weight. The force these prefixes give to the participle makes the items the author will mention next both accompany and add to the witness that came from the early leaders.[35]

signs and wonders: The evidence God uses to "confirm" the truth of the deliverance from spiritual death, as spoken by the Lord's leaders, is fourfold. The first confirmation is σημείοις (*sēmeiois*), "signs." The noun, in a theological context, denotes something seen or heard that acts to corroborate something else and appeals to one's understanding. It carries the nuance of an omen, that is, a foretoken of something coming.[36]

The second confirmation came through τέρασιν (*terasin*), "wonders," which is only found in combination with σημεῖα (*sēmeia*). It denotes, in a positive theological sense, events or deeds ascribed to "God's self-revelation as the Creator and the Governor of all events."[37]

divers miracles / various miracles: The third confirmation is through ποικίλαις δυνάμεσιν (*poikilais dynamesin*), literally "manifold powers."[38] Since the noun δύναμις (*dynamis*) can denote a deed done with divine power behind it, in its theological context, it is translated as "miracle."[39] The addition of the adjective ποικίλος (*poikilos*), "various, diversified," suggests not just one kind of miracle but many kinds.

gifts of the Holy Ghost / with gifts of the Holy Spirit: The fourth confirmation comes though πνεύματος ἁγίου μερισμοῖς (*pneumatos hagiou merismois*), literally "with distributions of the Holy Spirit." The noun μερισμός (*merismos*) refers to a "division" or a "distribution" of something[40] and is translated as "gifts" in both the KJV and our Rendition.[41]

according to his own will / according to his will: By using the noun θέλησις (*thelēsis*), "will," the author of Hebrews emphasizes that God determines all the means—signs, wonders, miracles, and gifts of the Holy Ghost—by which his doctrine will be established and confirmed.[42]

---

35. Ellingworth, *Epistle to the Hebrews,* 141. The nuance behind the noun μαρτυρέω (*martyreō*), "to witness," points to scripture. The threefold formula is based on Old Testament usage (see Deut. 4:34; 6:22; Neh. 9:10; Ps. 135:9; and Jer. 32:20–21) and is found in Acts 2:22; Rom. 15:19; 2 Cor. 12:12; and 2 Thes. 2:9.

36. Rengstorf, *TDNT,* 7:283–290; *NID,* s.v. "σημεῖον."

37. Rengstorf, *TDNT,* 8:124. See also BDAG, 999; and *NID,* s.v. "τέρας."

38. BDAG, 842, 262.

39. Grundmann, *TDNT,* 2:284–317.

40. BDAG, 633.

41. The Rendition sees πνεύματος ἁγιου (*pneumatos hagiou*) as an objective genitive and therefore denotes gifts proceeding from the Holy Spirit. See Bruce, *Epistle to the Hebrews,* 69 n. 7; and Ellingworth, *Epistle to the Hebrews,* 142.

42. BDAG, 447.

Analysis and Summary

It is with the first four verses of chapter 2 that the intensely pastoral and deeply practical side of this Epistle becomes evident.[43] The long question that makes up 2:2–4 does two things: first, it fleshes out and gives reason for the admonition in 2:1 to "pay much closer attention" to the word of salvation, and second, it emphasizes the urgency of an immediate response.[44]

In these verses, as well as in the chapter as a whole, the reason the author stresses the superiority of the Son over the angels becomes abundantly clear:[45] to make the distance between the Mosaic law and the "word" spoken by the Lord very apparent in order to emphasize the magnitude of the consequences of leaving the gospel law. It does this by pointing out how infractions against the Mosaic law demanded full and complete retribution from which there is no reprieve. When necessary, that includes the forfeiture of one's life.[46] Whether done through acts of outright rebellion (παράβασις, *parabasis*) or unwillingness to hear (παρακοή, *parakoē*), consequences followed (2:2). This old law, however, was administered through angels,[47] the servants of the Lord. The new law, identified as τηλικαύτης . . . σωτηρίας (*tēlikautēs . . . sōtērias*), "so great . . . a salvation," on the other hand, was delivered by none other than the Lord himself (2:3). The author makes his point by asking in essence, "If breaking the law administered by angels brought dire consequence, how much greater will be the consequences of breaking the new law administered by the Son?" To emphasize his point, the author uses a type of argument often employed by Jewish teachers during New Testament times. It is called *qal waḥomer,* meaning "from the light to the weighty." Using this technique, a writer or orator makes a statement about a "lighter" matter that then infers even greater weight to the "heavier" matter he mentions next.[48]

---

43. Johnson, *Hebrews,* 84.

44. Cockerill, *Epistle to the Hebrews,* 117.

45. Indeed, the author's whole thrust, as shown in his construction of this long conditional sentence (2:2–4), is to have his readers give assent to the points he is making and, thereby, accept his declaration that they must not leave the gospel behind. For details on how the author does this, see Johnson, *Hebrews,* 85, 87.

46. For example, see Num. 15:30.

47. The noun "salvation" used here is parallel to the "word spoken by angels" in 2:2.

48. Jesus also used this and other techniques. For example, see Matt. 12:9–14. For a study, see Linda King, "Jesus Argued Like a Jew," *Leaven* 19, no. 2 (2011): 74–79, accessed August 7, 2016, http://digitalcommons.pepperdine.edu/cgi/viewcontent.cgi?article=1116&context=leaven.

The Lord's coming into the world as "the Only Begotten Son" realizes the promises made by the prophets that a new covenant would be given (8:13; Isa. 55:3–5; Jer. 31:31–34; Ezek. 37:26–28). Its proclamation began when Jesus "came into the Galilee, preaching the gospel of the kingdom of God, and saying, The time is fulfilled, and the kingdom of God is at hand: repent ye, and believe the gospel" (Mark 1:14–15). It was further emphasized at the synagogue in Nazareth when he read the messianic passage from Isaiah 61:1–2, "The Spirit of the Lord is upon me, because he hath anointed me to preach the gospel to the poor; he hath sent me to heal the brokenhearted, to preach deliverance to the captives, and recovering of sight to the blind, to set at liberty them that are bruised, to preach the acceptable year of the Lord" (Luke 4:18–19), and then immediately declared, "This day is this scripture fulfilled in your ears" (Luke 4:21).[49]

Neither the author nor his readers seem to have heard the message directly from the Lord himself. Nonetheless, the doctrine had been vouchsafed by those who had heard him and were eyewitnesses to his ministry (2:3). But they are not the only witnesses. God himself confirms witnesses (βεβαιόω, *bebaioō*) in three additional ways (2:4). First, with signs and wonders (σημείοις τε καὶ τέρασιν, *sēmeiois te kai terasin*). Both words look at extraordinary events as well as portents or omens that act to corroborate that God's will is being done. The second is through various kinds of miracles (ποικίλαις δυνάμεσιν, *poikilais dynamesin*), that is, the power of God manifest through deeds.[50] The third and final way, and this is very important, is through the distribution of the gifts of the Spirit (πνεύματος ἁγίου μερισμοῖς, *pneumatos hagiou merismois*) that faithful men and women enjoyed and benefited from through possessing them and administering through them (see 1 Cor. 12–14).

That there are so many witnesses is an important point: the author of Hebrews is careful to meet the standards set down in Deuteronomy 19:15 that

49. Bruce, *Epistle to the Hebrews,* 68. These passages make it clear that this was at least one place where the gospel of salvation began to be preached. There was another: according to 1 Pet. 3:19–20; 4:6, the gospel of salvation was preached to the spirits in prison between the Lord's death and resurrection. See also D&C 138. The keys of this work were, however, restored to the earth on the Mount of Transfiguration when Peter received the binding and sealing keys (see Matt. 17). See Joseph Fielding Smith, *Doctrines of Salvation,* comp. Bruce R. McConkie, 3 vols. (Salt Lake City: Bookcraft,1954–56), 2:154–78; and Dale C. Mouritson, "Mount of Transfiguration," in Ludlow, *Encyclopedia of Mormonism,* 2:968–69.

50. Both Paul (Gal. 3:5) and Peter (1 Pet. 1:12) bore witness that the power of God was being displayed by mighty works of the Spirit. This power and confirming witness were manifest both by and for them.

in all matters pertaining to life and death "at the mouth of two witnesses, or at the mouth of three witnesses, shall the matter be established." All the acts the author lists are designed to confirm what was happening among the people to whom this Epistle is addressed. Indeed, if his audience is not experiencing these things, then his whole argument falls apart. But, his position stands because they are living witnesses to the reality of the manifestations of this spiritual power. The author can then cite the Father, the Son, those who heed him, and the divine displays by the Holy Spirit as confirmations of his point. His care to meet the standard of two or three witnesses acts as a tacit testimony to the gravity in which he sees the condition of his readers. These are matters of life and death, and they must not be trivialized.[51]

The author's point is that if disobedience to the lesser Mosaic law brought sure retribution, then disobedience to the superior law—the word of salvation—would be all that much greater "because the penalties for disobedience correspond to the magnitude of the gift being offered."[52]

Therefore, as he says in 2:1, his readers must pay much closer attention to the words of salvation that they have received lest they, like a ship that has lost its moorings, drift away (παραρρέω, *pararreō*) from safety.[53] The author's concern, as seen here, is that his readers were succumbing to the pressures—whether strong or weak, direct or indirect, pointed or subtle—that were being mounted against them.

The warning focuses on the consequences of "neglecting" (ἀμελέω, *ameleō*) the word of God. The nuance of the verb centers on not only taking something with less seriousness than it deserves but also making light of it. The result is its complete disregard.[54] Whether by inches or feet, the slow drift away from the gospel brings an ever-widening detachment that would, at first, diminish the importance of the gospel in the lives of his readers and, at last, lead to their full withdrawal from it. The author's point is clear: whether through rebellion or neglect, the plight of those who abandon the gospel would be perilous.[55]

---

51. Johnson, *Hebrews*, 88–89.

52. Johnson, *Hebrews*, 86.

53. Cockerill, *Epistle to the Hebrews*, 117.

54. Neglect is tantamount to a turning away from God and his purposes (see Jer. 4:17; 2 Macc. 4:14; Wis. 3:10; Matt. 22:5). See Cockerill, *Epistle to the Hebrews*, 120.

55. Bruce, *Epistle to the Hebrews*, 66–67. It is most likely that the people were slowly drifting away as shown by a reluctance to identify in public with the Christian community (10:25). This seems to have resulted more from moral and spiritual lethargy rather than outright rebellion. Cockerill, *Epistle to the Hebrews*, 118.

Jesus Was Made Like His Brothers (2:5–9)

Greek Text

5 Οὐ γὰρ ἀγγέλοις ὑπέταξεν τὴν οἰκουμένην τὴν μέλλουσαν, περὶ ἧς λαλοῦμεν· 6 διεμαρτύρατο δέ πού τις λέγων· Τί ἐστιν ἄνθρωπος ὅτι μιμνῄσκῃ αὐτοῦ, ἢ υἱὸς ἀνθρώπου ὅτι ἐπισκέπτῃ αὐτόν; 7 ἠλάττωσας αὐτὸν βραχύ τι παρ' ἀγγέλους, δόξῃ καὶ τιμῇ ἐστεφάνωσας αὐτόν, 8 πάντα ὑπέταξας ὑποκάτω τῶν ποδῶν αὐτοῦ· ἐν τῷ γὰρ ὑποτάξαι τὰ πάντα οὐδὲν ἀφῆκεν αὐτῷ ἀνυπότακτον. νῦν δὲ οὔπω ὁρῶμεν αὐτῷ τὰ πάντα ὑποτεταγμένα· 9 τὸν δὲ βραχύ τι παρ' ἀγγέλους ἠλαττωμένον βλέπομεν Ἰησοῦν διὰ τὸ πάθημα τοῦ θανάτου δόξῃ καὶ τιμῇ ἐστεφανωμένον, ὅπως χάριτι θεοῦ ὑπὲρ παντὸς γεύσηται θανάτου. [SBLGNT]

King James Version

5 For unto the angels hath he not put in subjection the world to come, whereof we speak. 6 But one in a certain place testified, saying, What is man, that thou art mindful of him? or the son of man, that thou visitest him? 7 Thou madest him a little lower than the angels; thou crownedst him with glory and honour, and didst set him over the works of thy hands: 8 Thou hast put all things in subjection under his feet. For in that he put all in subjection under him, he left nothing that is not put under him. But now we see not yet all things put under him. 9 But we see Jesus, who was made a little lower than the angels for the suffering of death, crowned with glory and honour; that he by the grace of God should taste death for every man.

New Rendition

5 For God did not put the world to come, about which we are talking, under the control of angels. 6 But somewhere someone testified saying,

> "What is man that you care for him, or the son of man that you are concerned about him? 7 You have made him a little less than angels. You have crowned him with glory and honor. 8 You have put all things under his feet" [Ps. 8:4–6].

So in putting all things under his control, he did not leave anything outside his control. But at present we do not yet see all things under his control. 9 But we see Jesus, who, for a little while, was made less than the angels, now crowned with glory and honor because he suffered death, so that by the grace of God he would experience death for the sake of everyone.

Translation Notes and Comments

2:5 ***For unto the angels hath he not put in subjection the world to come / For God did not put the world to come . . . under the control of angels:*** On angels, see the Translation Notes and Analysis for 1:4. The conjunction γάρ (*gar*), "for," can be a marker indicting cause, reason, or clarification. Here it likely points back to the reason why the author is so concerned about his readers abandoning "so great a salvation" as preached by the Lord. His point is that it would have consequences not only in this world but also the "world to come," for the Savior is also the master there.[56]

The verb ὑποτάσσω (*hypotassō*), "to subject, control," has military overtones pointing to both the organization and leadership of combat units. Due to its roots, it has come to denote two aspects of obedience. The first is negative. It looks to the domination of a conquered people and their involuntary situation.[57] The second is positive. It looks to the finer attributes expected of those in service, including a voluntary attitude of cooperation, responsibility, and commitment. In this positive sense, the word carries the idea of willing obedience and submission with no hint of coercion.[58] Only context can determine which nuance works.[59] In this instance, based on 2:8, it is the positive aspect that is in force. Therefore, to lessen the idea of subjugation, we translate the verb as "control" in our Rendition.

The "world to come," in the context of Hebrews, refers not just to the world of spirits but more to the eternities in which the Savior will rule (11:14–16, 40).[60] Even so, because of what the Lord has done and the position he now holds, that world has a present reality, and readers can therefore partake in mortality of some of the blessings they will receive in full in the next world.[61]

---

56. Johnson, *Hebrews,* 89. Therefore, translating it as "now"—as do Attridge, *Epistle to the Hebrews,* 69–70; and Lane, *Hebrews 1–8,* 42—misses the point. The word seems to be doing more than merely signaling that the author is picking up the thread he had dropped after 2:1. Compare Alan Mugridge, "Warnings in the Epistle to the Hebrews: An Exegetical and Theological Study," *Reformed Theological Review* 46 (1987): 74–82.

57. Louw-Nida, §37.31. The idea of compulsion can be seen in Luke 10:17, where the devils were subject to the disciples, and in Rom. 8:20, where creation itself, though against its will, must submit (ὑπετάγη, *hupetagē*) to futility.

58. For example, the youthful Jesus willingly submitted (ὑποτάσσω, *hypostassō*) himself to his parents (Luke 2:51). Also, Christian believers are to submit themselves voluntarily "to the Father of spirits" (Heb. 12:9).

59. BDAG, 1042; *NID,* s.v. "ὑποτάσσω"; Delling, *TDNT,* 8:27–48. Since the author of Hebrews constantly underscores the idea of self-sacrifice, his writings leave little room for a coercive nuance. Ellingworth, *Epistle to the Hebrews,* 145.

60. Compare D&C 130:19; and James P. Bell, "Purpose of Earth Life," in Ludlow, *Encyclopedia of Mormonism,* 3:1181. Note that the final consummation is associated with the "city that is to come" (13:14).

61. Koester, *Hebrews,* 213. Compare Thomas Kem Oberholtzer, "The Eschatological Salvation of Hebrews 1:5–2:5," *Bibliotheca Sacra* 145, no. 577 (1988): 83–97; and M. O.

2:6 ***But one in a certain place testified, saying / But somewhere someone testified saying:*** The place is Psalm 8:4–6. The author, to bolster his point, again turns to scripture. He may be vague about his source because his pattern is to cite only verses in which God is actually speaking, but that is not the case here: the Psalmist is asking the question. That may be the reason the author gives the source less, but not unimportant, authority.[62] The quote's significance is borne out by the author's use of the verb διαμαρτύρομαι (*diamartyromai*), "to solemnly testify," a word that emphasizes a serious response "to matters of extraordinary importance" to which one bears witness.[63]

What is man, that thou art mindful of him? / What is man that you care for him: This phrase begins a quote from Psalm 8:4–6.[64] The noun ἄνθρωπος (*anthrōpos*), "man," designates humankind in general.[65] Here it is a translation of the Hebrew אֱנוֹשׁ (*'ĕnôš*) of the Masoretic text of Psalm 8:5, which can be used either collectively, "all human beings," or individually, "a single human being," but the emphasis is on humanness of the subject or subjects.[66] The verb μιμνῄσκομαι (*mimnēskomai*), "to remember," means more than simply remembering; it is caring for or being concerned about.[67]

or the son of man, that thou visitest him? / or the son of man that you are concerned about him?: The verb ἐπισκέπτομαι (*episkeptomai*) means literally "to visit, inspect," but it connotes the helpful intent behind the act. It, therefore, has come to mean "to look after, be concerned about."[68] The verb in the Masoretic text of this psalm is פָּקַד (*pāqad*), which also has the same basic meaning of "to look at" but also the extended meaning of

---

Oyetade, "Eschatological Salvation in Hebrews 1:5–2:5," *Ilorin Journal of Religious Studies* 3, no. 1 (2013): 69–82, which show that the completion and consummation of Old Testament prophecies are essential to salvation. For that reason, the author warns his readers' against losing their future glory by careless inattention to the "great salvation" (2:3) as proclaimed by the Lord and vouchsafed by his death and return.

62. Philo used this expression even when he knew the source. See *Deus.* 74; *Ebr.* 61; *Plant.* 90. See also Koester, *Hebrews,* 213–14; Cockerill, *Epistle to the Hebrews,* 127, and n. 18.

63. BDAG, 233.

64. The author leaves out the phrase found in Ps. 8:6, "Thou madest him to have dominion over the works of thy hands." It is likely that the author left it out because its focus is clearly on Jehovah's placing the created world under the dominion of humankind rather than under the Son's, thus making the scripture harder to read in a messianic context. Attridge, *Epistle to the Hebrews,* 71.

65. BDAG, 81–82.

66. *HAL,* 70.

67. BDAG, 652; Louw-Nida, §29.16.

68. BDAG, 378.

"to be concerned for."[69] The writers of the New Testament often used the verb to describe "the loving and seeking care of God."[70]

The phrase υἱὸς ἀνθρώπου (*hyios anthrōpou*), "son of man," is a translation of the Hebrew בֶּן־אָדָם (*ben ʾādām*) of the Masoretic text of Psalm 8:5. The noun *ʾādām* is generally used collectively to describe "mankind," and *ben ʾādām* designates "an individual man."[71] As a proper name, it refers to Adam, the progenitor of the human race.[72] The equivalent Aramaic phrase occurs in Daniel 7:13, בַּר אֱנָשׁ (*bar ʾĕnāš*), with the same sense of "individual human being."[73] In Psalm 8:5, the use of *ʾĕnôš* and *ben ʾādām* is typical of the parallelistic structure of Hebrew poetry, where a thought is expressed twice with different wording. Thus *ʾĕnôš* and *ben ʾādām* are synonyms, both referring to a single individual.

The phrase *ben ʾādām,* "son of man," came to carry two quite different nuances during the New Testament period. One stressed the great divide between the mere human and the glorious divine. The other emphasized the closeness of the two. Expanding on the latter, in some Jewish and Christian circles, the term is used to describe a "transcendent eschatological agent of divine judgment and deliverance."[74] It is in that light that Jesus seems to have applied the term to himself.[75]

---

69. *HAL,* 956.

70. *NID,* s.v. "ἐπισκέπτομαι"; BDAG, 378.

71. *HAL,* 14.

72. *HAL,* 14.

73. *HAL,* 1819.

74. George W. E. Nickelsburg, "Son of Man," in Freedman, *Anchor Bible Dictionary,* 6:137. The phrase is most frequently found in Ezekiel. There is some debate as to whether it is used to stress the prophet's mere human status or to emphasize his lofty station as Jehovah's messenger. Given the usual positive use of the term, it is likely the latter. For discussion, see Nickelsburg, "Son of Man," 6:137–50; and Ellingworth, *Epistle to the Hebrews,* 150–51. As noted above, the Aramaic equivalent of the phrase also appears in Dan. 7:13 where a glorious messenger from God appears to the "Ancient of days," who, in Latter-day Saint theology, is Adam. Arthur A. Bailey, "Adam," in Ludlow, *Encyclopedia of Mormonism,* 1:15.

75. Bible Dictionary in the Latter-day Saint edition of the King James Version of the Bible, s.v. "Son of Man"; Attridge, *Epistle to the Hebrews,* 74. The concept of the Son of Man is part of a greater tradition of Second Temple Judaism. Its importance is suggested in the numerous Dead Sea Scrolls that mention the idea. See 4Q385 2, 5; 4Q385 3, 4; 4Q386 1 I, 4; 4Q386 1 II, 2; 4Q388 7, 7. For examples of Jesus applying the title to himself, see Matt. 8:20, 10:23; 12:8, 40; Mark 2:10; 8:31; 9:12, 31; Luke 6:5; 9:22, 26, 44, 58; and John 1:51; 3:13, 14; 6:27.

Which of the two nuances is at play here is unclear, but it is likely the former due to its association with the Savior.[76] Taken in that way, it sets up the paradox that God should be mindful of a mere human. According to the philosophical underpinnings of Stoicism and Platonism, the soul, or the eternal part of a person, originates in the invisible world of "Forms." This soul falls into the visible world of matter. The physical body is a hindrance to spiritual growth and enlightenment. Indeed, it can be the very entombment of the soul. The flesh, which so dominates each human, is the *ipso facto* source of all evil and separates humankind from the divine. Until humans free themselves from material things, the distance to the sacred is blocked, and they are little more than nothing.[77] The irony in Hebrews is that the human the author has in mind is Jesus. What the text makes clear is that the humanness of the Lord does not disqualify him from being in Elohim's care, having a personal relationship with him, and eventually being exalted. In Hebrews, the phrase indicates that the author also associates the term "Son of Man" with the Savior.

2:7 ***Thou madest him a little lower than the angels / You have made him less than angels:*** The MT for this verse reads וַתְּחַסְּרֵהוּ מְּעַט מֵאֱלֹהִים (*watĕḥassĕrēhû mĕʿaṭ mēʾĕlōhîm*), "you have made him a little less than God." The Hebrew word *ʾĕlōhîm* can be construed as a singular, "God," or as a plural, "gods," meaning other heavenly beings beside the Father.[78] The LXX, showing its theological preference for monotheism, solves the ambiguity by translating the word as ἄγγελοι (*angeloi*), "angels." On the phrases "a little lower than" and "less than," see the Translation Notes on 2:9 below.

thou crownedst him with glory and honour / You have crowned him with glory and honor: With this phrase, the author shows God's response to the humanness of Jesus. It is not off-putting but is the cause of his crowning. The verb στεφανόω (*stephanoō*), "to crown," connotes God's bestowal of honor and glory upon humankind due to their position as the Father's

---

76. Of the half-dozen times the phrase is used in John and over two dozen times used in Luke, the phrase refers to Jesus. It includes a definite article, thus "*the* Son of man" (see, for example, Luke 9:22, 26, 44, 58; John 3:13, 14; the only exception is John 5:27). Since the article is missing in the psalm's text and in Hebrews, it would suggest that the term refers to the mortal nature of its referents rather than to the eschatological vice-regent of God. See Attridge, *Epistle to the Hebrews,* 74–75; and Cockerill, *Epistle to the Hebrews,* 129–30.

77. Though the Jews and Christians had a much more positive view of humankind, the echo of Greek philosophy continued to have its influence. For discussion, see George Eldon Ladd, *The Pattern of New Testament Truth* (Grand Rapids, Mich.: Wm. B. Eerdmans Publishing, 1968), 13–40.

78. BDB, 43–44; *HAL,* 55.

supernal creation, but the author uses it to show God's response to Jesus' mortal mission.

On δόξα (*doxa*), "glory," see Translation Notes for 1:3. Here it carries the idea of the praise and commendation given by the Father for the work of the Son.

The noun τιμή (*timē*), "honor," denotes esteem or esteem one receives from others.[79] Here it looks to the respect the Father has for what the Son has done.

and didst set him over the works of thy hands: This phrase is found in both the MT and LXX of Psalm 8:6, but it is missing from some of the earliest copies of Hebrews. It is probable that it was an early scribal addition used to harmonize Hebrews with the psalm. It is, therefore, not surprising that many early Greek manuscripts include it as part of 2:7. Based on its exclusion from the earliest texts, our Rendition omits it.[80] It is possible the biblical scrolls the author knew did not have it, or since the phrase does contain true doctrine to which the author subscribes (see 1:2), he chose not to include it because it did not serve his present purpose.[81]

2:8 ***Thou hast put all things in subjection under his feet / You have put all things under his feet:*** This phrase finishes the author's quote of LXX Psalm 8:4–6 (KJV Ps. 8:4–6). The nominalized adjective πάντα (*panta*), "all things," is critical to his point and is meant to be all inclusive. See the Analysis below. For the verb ὑποτάσσω (*hypotassō*)—literally "to put under," that is, "to subject, control"—see Translation Notes for 2:5.

For in that he put all in subjection under him, he left nothing that is not put under him / So in putting all things under his control, he did not leave anything outside his control: As noted above, the author plays on the nominalized adjective πάντα (*panta*), "all things." For the verb ὑποτάσσω (*hypotassō*), "to put under, subject, control," see Translation Notes for 2:5. The adjective ἀνυπότακτος (*anhypotaktos*) means "not in subjection, without orders, independent."[82] The phrase οὐδὲν ἀφῆκεν (*ouden ophēken*), "he left nothing out," states the author's point—Jesus controls *everything.*

---

79. BDAG, 1005.

80. The earliest copy of this verse as found in 𝔓46 (c. AD 200), as well as the Codex Vaticanus and several other good manuscripts, supports leaving it out. Metzger, *Textual Commentary,* 593–94.

81. In the context of the Hebrew Bible, the psalm applies to humankind. The author is repurposing it to refer to Jesus, and this phrase and the verse that follows would detract from that emphasis. See Koester, *Hebrews,* 216.

82. BDAG, 91.

But now we see not yet all things put under him / But at present we do not yet see all things under his control: The author must now admit to a point: at the present time, Jesus does not have control of everything. Indeed, death and sin remain as well as all the vicissitudes of mortality. However, the adverb οὔπω (*oupō*), "not yet," is telling. Though, at present, the Father has "not yet" placed all things in subjection to the Son, he eventually will.

2:9 ***But we see Jesus, who was made a little lower than the angels / But we see Jesus, who, for a little while, was made less than the angels:*** On angels, see Translation Notes for 1:4 and the Analysis for that verse.

The phrase βραχύ τι (*brachy ti*) is ambiguous. Its basic sense is "a little something" and can mean either "a little (quantity/quality)" or "a little (time)."[83] The translation of the Hebrew מְעַט (*mĕʿaṭ*) has that same ambiguity.[84] In the previous citation from LXX Psalm 8:5–6 in 2:7 above, it is best understood in the sense of "a little less." In this verse, however, the author has used it in the temporal sense, "for a little while," and this is how we interpret it. Viewed in this way, it shows that the time Jesus spent as something "less than the angels" was of short duration, namely, his mortal life.

crowned with glory and honour / crowned with glory and honor: For a study of the term "glory," see Translation Notes for 1:3 with footnotes.

The noun τιμή (*timē*), "honor," when applied to people and divine beings, denotes the recognition that should be given due to the position, office, or wealth a person holds. The extent to which it should be given is based on the sphere of influence the person controls.[85] Honor, therefore, comes in ranks according to social order. A lower order must always give place to the higher. Though this custom was generally followed in the Church in that congregants were to be respectful of their leaders (Philip. 2:29; 1 Tim. 5:17), it was modified in that leaders were to show care for those under them. Indeed, even those in the lowest positions were to be shown special care and respect (1 Cor. 12:23–24). In its theological sense, "honor" denotes the reverence, obedience, and respect due to the Father and Son and expresses itself through sincere and heartfelt worship.[86]

---

83. The KJV follows the nuance of the Hebrew מְעַט (*mĕʾaṭ*) meaning "a little bit below" the Divine. Attridge, *Epistle to the Hebrews,* 75–76.

84. *HAL,* 511.

85. Because animals and slaves could not control their own destinies and were therefore insignificant, they were seen as having no honor (ἄτιμος, *atimos*). BDAG, 149. That, however, was modified in Christian circles where slaves were accepted as members of the community with standing (1 Cor. 7:22–23; 12:13; Eph. 6:9).

86. *NID,* s.v. "τιμή."

The perfect passive participle ἐστεφανωμένον (*estephanōmenon*), "having been crowned," has no political nuance. It denotes, rather, a wreathing of "someone's head with ornamental foliage" as a way of showing honor for a significant accomplishment that invites public recognition.[87] Here, the imagery is used metaphorically to suggest the respect God shows and wants others to show because of what the Son has done. As the phrase examined below shows, the Father bestows this honor on the Son because of his great sacrifice, a sacrifice that brought about the eternal Atonement.

for the suffering of death / because he suffered death: This simple yet profound phrase explains why God crowned Jesus with glory and honor. The key word here is the preposition διά (*dia*) that acts as a marker of cause and points to the reason Jesus was exalted,[88] identified by the noun πάθημα (*pathēma*), "suffering." The word carries the idea of bearing pain, insult, injury, and hardship, but also the idea of the mental anguish that such things can cause. It therefore carries a strong emotional undertone.[89] The author, however, has in mind but one act that is the *sine qua non* of what the Lord suffered, namely, death.

The noun θάνατος (*thanatos*), "death," in this context should be taken more as a theological term than a biological event. Many Jews and Christians saw death as the product of sin (Rom. 6:23). According to this view, everyone sins and therefore all bring death upon themselves. The result is not only separation of the body from the spirit but also of the self from Jehovah, "the source of life."[90] "Dying, therefore, is not primarily a biophysical process; it is the disintegration or ending of the life relationship with Yahweh,"[91] that is, in Latter-day Saint terms, "spiritual death" (see 2 Ne. 9:11–13). "'Spiritual' death and 'physical death,' inextricably bound up together, constitute the reality of a life in sin,"[92] which one can escape only through accepting the Lord (John 5:24; 8:51; 11:25). The term "death," then, denotes a twofold separation: one is physical (the spirit from the

87. BDAG, 944.

88. Louw-Nida, §89.26; BDAG, 225.

89. *NID*, s.v. "πάθημα."

90. The idea that Jehovah did not even remember the names of those in Hades (Ps. 6:5) lingered, but most accepted the idea that his domain included the underworld (Ps. 139:8); therefore confidence could be placed in him (Job 19:25; Ps. 73:24–25). For a study, see *NID*, 2:407.

91. *NID*, 1:153.

92. *NID*, 2:410.

body) and the other is spiritual (the person from God).[93] Jesus suffered both effects.

that he by the grace of God should taste death for every man / so that by the grace of God he would experience death for the sake of everyone: The subordinating conjunction ὅπως (*hopōs*), "so that," plays an important role here in that it emphasizes the purpose for the Savior's mortality.[94] It was so he could suffer death for humankind.

The term χάρις (*charis*), "grace," in this instance, denotes the beneficial disposition and kind benevolence that the Father shows for all his children.[95] It was God's will that the Savior should taste of death. The aorist verb *γεύσεται* (*geusetai*), "taste, partake of," in a metaphorical sense meant "to experience" something that was emotionally or cognitively bitter.[96] In this case it was death. In this context the preposition ὑπέρ (*hyper*) is telling. It indicates that an activity or event is in someone else's best interest[97] and is, therefore, translated as "for the sake of" in our Rendition. Also important is the adjective παντός (*pantos*), "everyone," that is, all humankind, for it emphasizes the inclusive nature of the Savior's Atonement.

This phrase has a significant textual variant. The reading found in the KJV, χάριτι θεοῦ (*chariti theou*), "the grace of God," is well supported by both the Alexandrian and Western text types.[98] This reading indicates that God was essential in Christ's Atonement by motivating and empowering the Savior. There are, however, a few New Testament manuscripts together with a number of early Church fathers, both Eastern and Western, where the passage reads χωρὶς θεοῦ (*chōris theou*), "without God."[99] This

---

93. BDAG, 442–43; Richard M. Romney, "Spiritual Death," in Ludlow, *Encyclopedia of Mormonism,* 3:1407–8.

94. BDAG, 718.

95. BDAG, 1079–81. For a study of grace from a Latter-day Saint perspective, see "Excursus on Grace" in Richard D. Draper and Michael D. Rhodes, *Paul's First Epistle to the Corinthians,* Brigham Young University New Testament Commentary Series (Provo, Utah: BYU Studies, 2017), 74–100.

96. Louw-Nida, §§24.72; 90.78; BDAG, 195; Attridge, *Epistle to the Hebrews,* 77.

97. BDAG, 1030–31.

98. For example, P^{46} ℵ A B C D.

99. For example, 1121b, 424c, 1739*. There is the possibility that an early scribe misread χάριτι (*chariti*), "by grace," and wrote instead χωρίς (*chōris*), "without." That, however, seems unlikely. The problem in ascertaining the correct reading is exacerbated by the fact that the adjective παντός (*pantos*), "all," is vague. It could be construed either as a masculine singular denoting "all people" or neuter singular denoting "all things," including people and God. A scribe may have been aware of Paul's statement that, when God placed all things in subjection to Christ, he did not include himself (1 Cor. 15:27). To make

reading can be taken to mean that Christ tasted death without the help or influence of God. This idea makes sense in light of the Lord's agonizing question, "My God, my God, why hast thou forsaken me?" (Mark 15:34, alluding to Ps. 22:1). Based on the textual evidence, however, it would appear that the phrase "without God" was a scribal gloss that was later introduced into the text.[100] For that reason, our Rendition follows the KJV in retaining the phrase "by the grace of God" but understanding it to refer to God's desire for Christ to suffer death for others but still allowing the Father to remove his assistance from the Son during his ordeal in Gethsemane. As Elder Richard G. Scott noted, "For reasons we do not fully know, while at the extremity of His capacity, at the time the Savior most needed succor, His Father allowed Him to shoulder the onerous responsibility with only His own strength and capacity."[101]

There is a grammatical nuance in this verse that is important. The author replaces the aorist verbs found in the psalm he quotes with the perfect passive participles ἠλαττωμένον (*ēlattōmenon*), "being made lower than," and ἐστεφανωμένον (*estephanōmenon*), "being crowned." In doing so, he changes the focus of the psalm from the activity of the Father to the situation of the Son (the author will, however, again place the focus back on the Father in 2:9). The point here is that the change from verbs to participles "enables the author to present Christ's humiliation and exaltation, not as a mere temporal succession, but as two complementary aspects of a single work."[102] In short, the condescension was necessary for the exaltation to occur.

---

sure a reader construed the passage to include this idea, it is possible that a scribe substituted *chōris,* "separate, apart from, without" (BAGD, 1095), for *chariti,* "by grace," thus allowing the text to read that Christ died for all "apart from," that is, not including, God.

The insertion of "without God," however, did not preclude other readings of the phrase. At least two others are possible. The first is that Jesus received no assistance from the Father as he went through the horrible hours leading to his death. The second is that he died without divine assistance, meaning that the Lord did not invoke his own divine powers to assist him in the atoning process. For discussion, see Ellingworth, *Epistle to the Hebrews,* 155–56; and Cockerill, *Epistle to the Hebrews,* 135 n. 47.

100. Metzger, *Textual Commentary,* 594. The motivation behind the change could have been to correct a wrong idea that a misreading of verse 8 could give. There it states that Father placed "all things" under the feet of the Son. Some may have feared that could be construed to include God.

101. Richard G. Scott, "He Lives! All Glory to His Name," *Ensign* 40, no. 5 (May 2010): 77.

102. Ellingworth, *Epistle to the Hebrews,* 154.

Analysis and Summary

In this pericope, the author continues to build his case as to why his readers should not abandon the Lord. He begins again by contrasting the rank, dignity, and station of the Son with that of the angels. He testifies that God gave no angel control (ὑποτάσσω, *hypotassō*) over "the world to come" but instead placed the whole under Christ's power (2:5).[103] The author's point was not only to assure his readers about the reality of the coming world but to convince his readers that the Savior is the master there. The author does so by building on the fact that Jesus' Resurrection and enthronement had been confirmed (βεβαιόω, *bebaioō*) by the many witnesses that the author cites (2:3–4). Thus, his readers can bank on its reality and the attendant reward or punishment.[104]

To further develop his argument, in 2:6–8, the author cites LXX Psalm 8:5–7: "What is man that you care for him, or the son of man that you are concerned about him? You have made him a little less than angels. You have crowned him with glory and honor. You have put all things under his feet" (NR 2:6–8).[105] In its Old Testament context, the scripture looks at the distance between Jehovah's power and majesty in contrast to humankind's weakness and inadequacy. It does so, however, not to belittle humankind but to highlight Jehovah's graciousness in caring for them. The author, however, uses it to describe the station of Jesus in mortality.

There is an aspect to the term "Son of Man" unique to Latter-day Saints that would also explain why holding this station, that is, being mortal, would not disqualify the Son from divine care. The Father identifies himself in scripture saying, "I am God; Man of Holiness is my name; Man of Counsel

103. There was a tradition among many in Second Temple Judaism concerning Enoch/Metatron that gave rise to the idea that the "angel of the Lord" was the "little YHWH." See Boyarin, "Beyond Judaisms," who notes that in the case of Divine Polymorphy, the Son would have godlike powers. See also Andrei A. Orlov, "Titles of Enoch-Metatron in 2 Enoch," *Journal for the Study of the Pseudepigrapha* 9, no. 18 (1998): 71–86, accessed August 7, 2016, http://www.marquette.edu/maqom/titles.html.

104. This idea will be more fully developed in 9:9–10, 14, 26–28, and kept in view in 10:19–20; 12:28. Attridge, *Epistle to the Hebrews,* 70.

105. Speaking of the dignity of each person, President John Taylor, in *Journal of Discourses,* 8:3–4, stated that each "is a God in embryo, and possesses within him a spark of that eternal flame which was struck from the blaze of God's eternal fire in the eternal world, and is placed here upon the earth that he may possess true intelligence, true light, true knowledge,—that he may know himself—that he may know God—that he may know something about what he was before he came here—that he may know something about what he is destined to enjoy in the eternal worlds."

is my name; and Endless and Eternal is my name, also" (Moses 7:35). That being the case, an angel commanded Adam to "teach it unto your children, that all men, everywhere, must repent, or they can in nowise inherit the kingdom of God, for no unclean thing can dwell there, or dwell in his presence; for, in the language of Adam, Man of Holiness is his name, and the name of his Only Begotten is the Son of Man, even Jesus Christ, a righteous Judge, who shall come in the meridian of time" (Moses 6:57). Thus, the nuance of the phrase shows the close, even paternal association, between the "Man of Holiness" and the "Son of Man," that is, the Son of God.

Further, the term "Son of Man" is the title by which he is known to the prophet Enoch, who reports that he "saw the day of the coming of the Son of Man, even in the flesh" (Moses 7:47). This vision so moved the prophet that he "cried unto the Lord, saying: When the Son of Man cometh in the flesh, shall the earth rest? I pray thee, show me these things. And the Lord said unto Enoch: Look, and he looked and beheld the Son of Man lifted up on the cross, after the manner of men" (Moses 7:54–55). Thus, it became obvious to the prophet that the earth's period of rest would not be synchronized with Christ's first coming. Nonetheless, there is hope, for the Lord assures Enoch, "As I live, even so will I come in the last days, in the days of wickedness and vengeance," at which time the earth would be purged of all iniquity (Moses 7:60). Thus, the term has an eschatological nuance. This nuance is picked up throughout the Doctrine and Covenants. For example, the signs that mark this era as the latter days are called "the signs of the coming of the Son of Man" (D&C 45:39; 58:65; 61:38; 63:53; 64:23; 68:12), and the Saints are instructed to "be prepared for the days to come, in the which the Son of Man shall come down in heaven" (D&C 65:5). At the time of his appearing, those in the graves "who shall hear the voice of the Son of Man . . . shall come forth . . . in the resurrection of the just" (D&C 76:16–17). The title, as developed in Latter-day Saint scripture, therefore, points to the eschatological aspect of the Lord's sonship. During his first coming, he brought to a close the law of Moses era and inaugurated the Christian era. At his Second Coming, he will inaugurate the paradisiacal era (A of F 10).[106]

---

106. According to Restoration scripture, this crowning is in the future. "When he [Christ] shall deliver up the kingdom, and present it unto the Father, spotless, saying: I have overcome and have trodden the wine-press alone, even the wine-press of the fierceness of the wrath of Almighty God. Then shall he be crowned with the crown of his glory, to sit on the throne of his power to reign forever and ever" (D&C 76:107–8).

It is clear that the author of Hebrews also saw in the term "Son of Man" messianic insights and therefore redirected its focus as noted above. No longer does the title refer to humankind as a whole but to a specific human, namely Jesus, the Son. In 2:9, the author states Jesus was "for a little while . . . made less than the angels" (NR 2:9). Thus, during his earthly ministry, he who was God voluntarily laid aside his majesty, glory, and station and condescended to become fully mortal.[107] The author carefully develops the Savior's threefold progression in the drama of redemption: the past condescension into mortality, the present enthronement at the right hand of God, and the future victory in which God will place "all things" under the Lord's feet.[108]

Taking 2:8–9 as a whole, the following insights become evident: the ministry of Jesus as "man"—that is, as one who was fully mortal just like all who come to earth—reveals humankind's true vocation. The trajectory of Jesus' life displays what the Father intended for all his children from the beginning. The idea that Jesus becoming mortal disqualifies him for enthronement and divine honor cannot be sustained. Indeed, the author insists that the Savior's debasement lasted "but a short time" and has already been replaced by divine glory, honor, and station.[109] Further, his condescension was necessary in order for him to accomplish the redemption of humankind.

Also, 2:9 underscores another idea that must not be missed. At this point in the narrative—where the emphasis is on the period of Jesus' condescension (being lower than the angels), that is, when he was fully human—the author, for the first time, mentions him by name. In doing so, he draws attention to the juxtaposition between the Lord's own subjugation and his triumph in overcoming death for all. Indeed, as 2:9 shows, the very purpose of his mortality was "so that" (ὅπως, *hopōs*) he could perform the Atonement. In this way, the author affirmed the terrible cost the Son had to pay for his place on the right hand of God.[110] As a direct result of accomplishing

---

107. It needs to be noted that, even though Jesus was fully mortal, he was still something more than human. In speaking about the Lord's coming into mortality, the Book of Mormon notes that he would "take upon him the form of man" but not actually be one (Mosiah 13:34). Indeed, he would suffer "more than man can suffer, except it be unto death" (Mosiah 3:7).

108. Lane, *Hebrews 1–8,* 48.

109. See Kistemaker, *Psalm Citations,* 106.

110. Cockerill, *Epistle to the Hebrews,* 132.

this, The Lord received his honor, glory, and station once more.[111] In this way, the author of Hebrews stresses the soteriological aspect of the Savior's act. He shows that the Lord's death was substitutionary in character, that is, he died on behalf of all humankind. Indeed, he was "the atoning sacrifice for our sins" (see, for example, 13:12; and 1 Pet. 2:21).[112]

In sum, 2:9 teaches one of the most important doctrines housed in the scriptures: the Lord's great suffering and death were not the mere fiat of history but were responses to divine necessity. According to some biblical passages, suffering was "seen to be the inherent result of an evil deed" (for example, see Prov. 26:27; and Ezek. 18:4, 10–13, 19–23).[113] Since, however, the Lord did no evil, the suffering he had to endure is all the more shocking and poignant.

The Doctrine and Covenants testifies to the depth of that suffering. Quoting the Lord himself, it reports that this "suffering caused myself, even God, the greatest of all, to tremble because of pain, and to bleed at every pore, and to suffer both body and spirit—and would that I might not drink the bitter cup, and shrink—Nevertheless, glory be to the Father, and I partook and finished my preparations unto the children of men" (D&C 19:18–19).

As Tad R. Callister stated, "Christ felt all pain—'the entire ocean of human affliction'—and did so without the shield of superhuman powers." He went on to say,

> The Savior's sacrifice required inexhaustible stamina in order to bear the consequences of our sins and weather the temptations of the Evil One. But his suffering must have been more than a resigned submissiveness or a fist-clenching "taking of the stripes." It must have been more than a defensive "holding of the fort" or raising of the shield to ward off the fiery darts of the Evil One. Part of the Savior's atoning quest must have included an element of conquering, an offensive struggle of sorts. There was a need for the Savior to voluntarily lay down his life so he could "[break] the bands of death" (Mosiah 15:8) and to "destroy him that had the power of death"

---

111. Lane, *Hebrew 1–8,* 48–49.

112. *NID,* s.v. "πάσχω."

113. *NID,* s.v. "πάσχω." The idea that Jesus died for others is well attested in the scriptures. For examples, see Mark 10:45; 14:24; Luke 22:20; John 6:51; 11:50–51; 1 Cor. 11:24; 15:3; Gal. 1:4; 2:20; and 1 Thes. 5:10; thus, the author is following and reiterating well-known material. Johnson, *Hebrews,* 92. The tie between sin and earthly divine punishment is at the heart of the repeated conflict between Job and his "friends" who insist he must have done something wrong in order to call down God's wrath. For a discussion, see Michael Austin, *Re-reading Job: Understanding the Ancient World's Greatest Poem* (Salt Lake City: Greg Kofford Books, 2014).

(Hebrews 2:14; see also 1 Corinthians 15:26). . . . This part of the battle may have necessitated an invasion of Satan's turf, perhaps even an intrepid trespass into the dark abyss of the Devil's domain.[114]

The result, as the author records in 2:8, is that the Father will put all things under the Son's control. The author admits that, for the time being, Jesus does not control all things. Nonetheless, through his redemptive act, the future has, indeed, been secured. The power of sin and death has, through the power of redemption, been nullified, thus opening the way for the faithful to receive the glory the Father intends for them.[115]

The Leader of Our Salvation (2:10–13)

Greek Text

10 Ἔπρεπεν γὰρ αὐτῷ, δι᾽ ὃν τὰ πάντα καὶ δι᾽ οὗ τὰ πάντα, πολλοὺς υἱοὺς εἰς δόξαν ἀγαγόντα τὸν ἀρχηγὸν τῆς σωτηρίας αὐτῶν διὰ παθημάτων τελειῶσαι. 11 ὅ τε γὰρ ἁγιάζων καὶ οἱ ἁγιαζόμενοι ἐξ ἑνὸς πάντες· δι᾽ ἣν αἰτίαν οὐκ ἐπαισχύνεται ἀδελφοὺς αὐτοὺς καλεῖν, 12 λέγων· Ἀπαγγελῶ τὸ ὄνομά σου τοῖς ἀδελφοῖς μου, ἐν μέσῳ ἐκκλησίας ὑμνήσω σε· 13 καὶ πάλιν· Ἐγὼ ἔσομαι πεποιθὼς ἐπ᾽ αὐτῷ· καὶ πάλιν· Ἰδοὺ ἐγὼ καὶ τὰ παιδία ἅ μοι ἔδωκεν ὁ θεός. [SBLGNT]

King James Version

10 For it became him, for whom are all things, and by whom are all things, in bringing many sons unto glory, to make the captain of their salvation perfect through sufferings. 11 For both he that sanctifieth and they who are sanctified are all of one: for which cause he is not ashamed to call them brethren, 12 Saying, I will declare thy name unto my brethren, in the midst of the church will I sing praise unto thee. 13 And again, I will put my trust in him. And again,

New Rendition

10 It was fitting for God, for whom and by whom all things exist, to make him perfect through suffering, who was the founder of their salvation and who had led many of God's children to glory. 11 Because both he who makes holy and those who are made holy are all of the same family. And for this reason he is not ashamed to call them brothers and sisters, 12 saying,

> "I will proclaim your name to my brothers and sisters, in the midst of the

114. Tad R. Callister, *The Infinite Atonement* (Salt Lake City: Deseret Book, 2000), 129. See also Erastus Snow, in *Journal of Discourses,* 7:355.

115. Lane, *Hebrews 1–8,* 50.

Behold I and the children which God hath given me.

assembly I will sing your praises." [LXX Ps. 21:23]

13 And again,

"I will trust in him." [Isa. 8:17]

And again,

"Here I am with the children that God has given to me." [Isa. 8:18]

Notes and Comments

2:10 ***For it became him, for whom are all things, and by whom are all things / It was fitting for God, for whom and by whom all things exist:*** The verb πρέπω (*prepō*) denotes that which is "fitting, proper," or "right" and, thus, carries heavy moral overtones.[116] The force of the imperfect tense suggests the continuing necessity of God's action. Though the noun "God" is not found in the Greek text, it is implied in the dative pronoun αὐτῷ (*autō*), "for him," and in the context of the rest of the verse.[117] We have thus supplied the words in our Rendition for clarification. The focus of the phrase is on the all-embracing creative power of God. Its tacit reminder is that even Christ's existence is due to an action of the Father.[118]

in bringing many sons unto glory / who had led many of God's children to glory: The aorist participle ἀγαγόντα (*agagonta*), "leading," as used in this context, means to guide someone to a moral or correct way.[119] Grammatically, the accusative participle *agagonta* could refer to either God or Christ, but its juxtaposition with the accusative noun ἀρχηγόν (*archēgon*) makes it more likely that it refers to Christ.

The text identifies those led as υἱοὺς (*hyious*), "sons." The broader context, however, would include not only God's sons but also his daughters, so the plural pronoun is translated as "children" in our Rendition. "God's" is not in the text but has been added for clarity. The phrase πολλοὺς υἱοὺς (*pollous hyious*), "many sons," implies that, though the Savior paves the way, not all will follow. The end of the path is δόξα (*doxa*), "glory," here connoting both honor and divine splendor.

---

116. Louw-Nida, §66.1; BDAG, 61.

117. Ellingworth, *Epistle to the Hebrews,* 159.

118. Of himself, the Savior testifies, "I was in the beginning with the Father, and am the Firstborn" (D&C 93:21).

119. BDAG, 16.

make . . . perfect through sufferings / to make him perfect through suffering: The verb τελειόω (*teleioō*) connotes that which is fully finished, completed, matured, and whole, thus made adequate for a necessary task.[120] In a cultic sense, it denotes a state of purification that makes one fit to perform temple functions.[121] That is likely the nuance here. In order for both the Savior and his mission to be "fully finished" and therefore perfected, it was necessary for him to suffer (see Translation Notes on 2:9 above). When the author of Hebrews uses the noun πάθημα (*pathēma*), "suffering," and its related verb πάσχω (*paschō*), "to suffer," in connection with the Lord, the author looks not only at Christ's death but everything that he experienced throughout his mortal life (2:9, 10, 18; 5:8; 13:12). It was all of these experiences, which culminated in his sufferings in Gethsemane and his death on the cross, that made him perfect in that nothing was left to be done. It seems that the author had all this in mind when he used the plural "sufferings" in this passage.

The preposition διά (*dia*) with the genitive expresses "means" and, thus, shows that the method of the Savior's perfection was sufferings.[122] It was through these sufferings of his mortal life and death that the Lord completed his mission and his personal preparation to receive—once more, and this time, fully—the glory of the Father.[123]

the captain of their salvation / the founder of their salvation: The text describes the Lord as ἀρχηγός (*archēgos*), that is, originator or founder. It carries the force of rule (one who initially sets up a kingdom and becomes its lawgiver) and therefore was translated in the KJV as "prince" (Acts 3:15; 5:31) and "captain" (2:10). But its strongest nuance is that of trailblazer, and therefore some prefer to translate the word as "pioneer."[124] The noun always refers to Jesus in his capacity as the one who pioneered the way to exaltation.[125] Another possible nuance here is that of author (as in 5:9). This word

---

120. Attridge, *Epistle to the Hebrews,* 83–84, and n. 52.

121. For Philo, τελειόω (*teleioō*) had a strong soteriological dimension (see *Leg.* 3.74, 100). With Plato, Philo saw in it a connection with the mystery cult initiation and, therefore, to temple worship and esoteric knowledge gained there. Philo, *Gig.* 54–55; *Vit. cont.* 25. In Plato's work, *Phaedr.* 249c, perfection is a state realized when one understands the mysteries.

122. Wallace, *Greek Grammar,* 368–69.

123. Ellingworth, *Epistle to the Hebrews,* 161–62, notes that the likely nuance here is that of bringing something to its goal, but he also feels that the cultic idea of qualifying something for worship likely applies. See also Ogden and Skinner, *Verse by Verse,* 247.

124. Louw-Nida, §§36.6; 68.2; BDAG, 138–39. Lane, *Hebrews 1–8,* 56, sees echoes of Greek heroes, such as Heracles, who earn their divinity through service to humankind.

125. Ellingworth, *Epistle to the Hebrews,* 160.

connotes one who originates and who is therefore the ultimate source of something.[126] In this case, it reveals Jesus as the source of eternal life.

What the Savior leads his people to is σωτηρία (*sōtēria*), "salvation." The basic meaning is "salvation from danger" but, in a theological context, it denotes being placed beyond the power of one's enemies—the greatest being death and hell.[127] In Hebrews, the author always looks to the Savior's redemptive power and to the hope grounded in the promise that "he is able, for all time, to save those who draw near unto God through him, since he always lives to make intercession for them" (NR 7:25).[128] In Latter-day Saint parlance, then, it may carry the idea of exaltation, that is, becoming like God in the ultimate sense.[129]

2:11 ***For both he that sanctifieth and they who are sanctified are all of one / Because both he who makes holy and those who are made holy are all of the same family:*** The conjunction γάρ (*gar*), "for, because," looks back at 2:10 and points to why the Lord can call those he saves "children," and thereby it does not so much draw a conclusion from that accomplishment as it deepens the insight.

The verb ἁγιάζω (*hagiazō*) means "to make holy" and thus "to sanctify," but in both of its forms in this passage it is used as a nominal participle. The nuances associated with this word, as the discussion to follow shows, are very broad. The root meaning of the verb suggests the idea of becoming separate from the common or mundane. The real force of the word, however, carries the idea of purity.[130] In its biblical setting, it does not have the force of either the English word "holiness" or "sanctity," both of which denote a state of spiritual perfection.[131]

A more complete understanding of its meaning is found in its use in the LXX, where it is translated from the Hebrew verb קִדֵּשׁ (*qiddēš*), "to set apart,

126. *Webster's New Dictionary of Synonyms,* s.v. "maker."

127. Alma P. Burton, "Salvation," in Ludlow, *Encyclopedia of Mormonism,* 3:1256–57. Joseph Smith taught, "Salvation is nothing more or less, than to triumph over all our enemies, and put them under our feet <and when we have power to put all enemies under our feet> in this world, and a knowledge to triumph over all evil Spirits in the world to come, then we are saved; as in the case of Jesus, who was to reign until he had put all enemies under his feet, and the last enemy was death." "History, 1838–1856, Volume D-1 [1 August 1842–1 July 1843]," 1549, Joseph Smith Papers, https://www.josephsmithpapers.org/paper-summary/history-1838-1856-volume-d-1-1-august-1842-1-july-1843/192.

128. *NID,* s.v. "σώζω."

129. Margaret McConkie Pope, "Exaltation," in Ludlow, *Encyclopedia of Mormonism,* 2:479.

130. *NID,* s.v. "ἁγιάζω"; Louw-Nida, §88.26.

131. *Webster's New Dictionary of Synonyms,* s.v. "holiness."

make holy or sacred."[132] The word refers to cultic functions and accoutrements which are dedicated to Jehovah and to him alone. This nuance ties it to rites of the tabernacle and, later, the temple and pertains to acts, instruments, and persons who serve him there. Hence, a strong meaning of "holiness" designates the state of one who has met the qualifications for and participates in sacred work.[133] Another nuance indicates "a wholehearted relationship to God."[134] In this aspect, it relates to τελείωσις (*teleiōsis*), "perfection." The emphasis of both words is on the "religious activity and observances which reflect one's dedication or consecration to God."[135] In its more restricted sense, it denotes a characteristic of a particular group of people. These are those who become part of the inner circle often referred to as "the sanctified," that is, those who are purified by the blood of Christ, are separated from the world, and have joined the family of God.[136] Thus, they can be referred to as "holy." The title the scriptures give these people is "Saint." The title strongly suggests that these people are godly. Indeed, one of the chief attributes of Jehovah is his holiness (Lev. 11:44–45; Ps. 99:9), and it is a state he demands of his children (Ex. 22:31). Therefore, those who attain to holiness are like him and are called "Saints."

Stressing the idea of unity and likeness, the author uses the phrase ἐξ ἑνὸς πάντες (*ex henos pantes*), "they are all one." Because the phrase is not specific, there is much debate concerning what the source of that oneness is.[137] If the source is God, then what makes Jesus and the children one is their now common divinity. If the source is Adam, then the oneness comes from their common humanity. But whatever the source, the author's point is Christ and his people share a bond so strong it makes them one. In our

---

132. *HAL*, 1072–75; BDB, 871–74.

133. Procksch, *TDNT*, 1:111–12.

134. For example, see Gen. 17:1; Deut. 18:13; and 1 Kgs. 8:61 where one is admonished to be perfect before God.

135. Louw-Nida, §53.44; BDAG, 997; Ellingworth, *Epistle to the Hebrews*, 164. The KJV uses the word "saint" to translate two different Hebrew words. The first is חָסִיד (*ḥāsîd*), which points to a person so touched by the divine as to be pious, merciful, and godly. *HAL*, 337; BDB, 339. The second is קָדוֹשׁ (*qādôš*), which denotes one who is dedicated to God and his ways and can function in cultic rites. *HAL*, 1066–67; BDB, 872. The Greek word translated as "saint" is ἅγιος (*hagios*) and carries much the same meaning as the two Hebrew words, that is, one who is separated from the world and is consecrated to do God's work. BDAG, 10–11.

136. BDAG, 9–10; *NID*, s.v. "ἅγιος."

137. See Ellingworth, *Epistle to the Hebrews*, 164–65; Cockerill, *Epistle to the Hebrews*, 142–43.

Rendition, in an attempt to emphasize this unity, we translate the phrase as "of the same family."[138]

The passage makes one more important point. It shows that the Savior is the sanctifying agent. In doing so, the text adds this role to those he played in both creation and final consummation of earth history (1:2, 8–12) as well as both supporting and rounding out his station and work as deity.

he is not ashamed to call them brethren / And for this reason he is not ashamed to call them brothers and sisters: The noun αἰτία (*aitia*) expresses the cause or reason why something is done. As used here, it looks more particularly at an "actual state of affairs" and points to why Jesus is not ashamed to be classed in the same family as his mortal kin.[139] Here, it is because of the sanctified condition they both share.

The noun ἀδελφοὺς (*adelphous*) in the plural, as it is here, can refer to both brothers and sisters and is translated as such in our Rendition.[140] It connotes the warm familial relationship that Christ has with these people. The verb καλέω (*kaleō*), "to call," in the present tense suggests that the Savior continues to call others as brothers and sisters.[141]

2:12 *I will declare thy name unto my brethren / I will proclaim your name to my brothers and sisters:* This quote is from LXX Ps. 21:23 (KJV Ps. 22:22).[142] It should be noted that in the Masoretic text of this verse (Ps. 22:23), the Hebrew אָח (*'āḥ*) only refers to males, even in the plural.[143] But it is clear that the author of Hebrews is using it in its broader Greek sense, and so our Rendition uses "brothers and sisters."

---

138. Here we follow the NIV Heb. 2:11. Whether the source is God or Adam, it is ultimately the same "family." As it says in the genealogy of Christ in Luke 3:38, Σὴθ τοῦ Ἀδὰμ τοῦ θεοῦ (*Sēth tou Adam tou theou*), "Seth [was] the son of Adam, [who was] the son of God" (NR). Since Adam was the son of God, we humans are all direct descendants of God through Adam. See also Joseph F. McConkie, "Jesus Christ, Symbolism, and Salvation," in *Studies in Scripture, Volume 6: Acts to Revelation,* ed. Robert L. Millet (Salt Lake City: Deseret Book, 1987), 194–95.

139. BDAG, 31; Ellingworth, *Epistle to the Hebrews,* 166; McConkie, "Symbolism, and Salvation," 194.

140. BDAG, 18. In two places in the scriptures, Jesus calls his disciples "brethren" (Matt. 28:10; John 20:17), but there is no known source where Jesus calls the Saints his brothers and sisters.

141. BDAG, 502–3; Koester, *Hebrews,* 238.

142. The author made a slight change in the quote from the LXX. He wrote, "I will declare thy name" (ἀπαγγέλλω, *apangellō*), thus suggesting praise, where the LXX has "I will recount [διηγήομαι, *diēgēomai*] thy name," suggesting describing or filling out something. See Koester, *Hebrews,* 230.

143. *HAL,* 29.

The verb ἀπαγγέλλω (*apangellō*) denotes proclaiming something publicly.[144] Here it carries the idea of great approval. The noun ὄνομα (*onoma*) denotes the name by which one is called. A nuance behind the word, however, points to the character or reputation, even the whole being, of the one named and therefore means "you" in the sense of the whole "you."[145] Here, it is the Father who is being extolled by the Son for the benefit and edification of the sanctified children.

in the midst of the church will I sing praise unto thee / in the midst of the assembly I will sing your praises: The noun ἐκκλησία (*ekklēsia*) denotes an assembly, gathering, or congregation. In the New Testament, the word points to both a specific congregation and to the community of believers as a whole.[146] The verb ὑμνέω (*hymneō*) denotes a hymn of praise. The whole phrase emphasizes the joy one person takes in publicly recognizing the sterling qualities in another. Again, it is the Father who is being praised.[147]

2:13 ***And again, I will put my trust in him / And again, I will trust in him:*** With the phrase καὶ πάλιν (*kai palin*), "and again," the author indicates he is quoting another passage of scripture. This quote is a fragment of Isaiah 8:17.[148] The focus here is expressed by the periphrastic future perfect ἔσομαι πεποιθώς (*esomai pepoithōs*), which carries the idea of being so convinced of the truthfulness of something that one puts his or her full trust in it.[149] The author sets Jesus up as the speaker to show the depth of his feelings for his Father.

And again, Behold I and the children which God hath given me / And again, Here I am with the children that God has given to me: With the phrase καὶ πάλιν (*kai palin*), "and again," the author indicates he is quoting yet another passage of scripture. The presentative particle ἰδού (*idou*), literally "look!" (translated "behold" in KJV), is here better translated as "here" with an appropriate form of the verb "to be,"[150] hence "Here I am" in our

144. BDAG, 95.

145. The noun, in its broad sense, points to something real, "a piece of the very nature of the personality whom it designates, expressing the person's qualities and power." BDAG, 711–14; Ellingworth, *Epistle to the Hebrews,* 168.

146. BDAG, 303–4.

147. Just when this praise will take or has taken place is not clear. It could be at Christ's enthronement, at the Second Coming, or at his final triumph. For views, see Cockerill, *Epistle to the Hebrews,* 143; and Attridge, *Epistle to the Hebrews,* 90.

148. See also 2 Sam. 22:3. The KJV translates the Masoretic Hebrew text, not the LXX Greek. The Hebrew has וְקִוֵּיתִי־לוֹ (*wĕqiwwîtî lô*), "and I will await/hope for him."

149. BDAG, 791–92.

150. BDAG, 468.

Rendition. The quote is a fragment of Isaiah 8:18. The plural noun παιδία (*paidia*), "children," designates a child usually below the age of puberty, albeit in a metaphorical nuance—it could be anyone whom a person cherishes as dearly as his or her own child.[151] The key to the verse is in the aorist phrase ἅ μοι ἔδωκεν ὁ θεός (*ha moi edōken ho theos*), "that God has given me." The children do not belong to Jesus but rather are his entrusted gifts from God.[152] Thus, they are all of great value.

Analysis and Summary

Verse 2:10 begins a new paragraph that ends with 2:17. In it the author develops the theme of the Savior's sharing in the trials and suffering of his mortal kin. These combine to show why he can lead them back to God. The author's tone is not apologetic, for he sees Christ's suffering as part of God's plan of redemption, a suffering that was fitting (πρέπω, *prepō*) given the honor and glory it would bring to the Lord.[153]

In 2:10, the author "boldly asserts his shocking thesis: it was 'appropriate' to the character and purposes of the sovereign God, the source, judge, and goal of 'all,' to use suffering to equip the Savior so that God could fulfill his purpose for his 'sons and daughters.' Christ's suffering was neither a logical necessity forced upon God nor a mere decision of his will, but an appropriate expression of the divine character."[154] This whole idea is underscored by the author's use of πρέπω (*prepō*), "to be fitting," rather than δεῖ (*dei*), "to be necessary." It was fitting for Jesus to be perfected through suffering because of what it would allow him to do and to be.[155]

The Greek verb τελειόω (*teleioō*), "to make perfect," does not carry the same force as the English word used to translate it. The latter reflects the ideal of being without flaw and having no defect, fault, or inefficacy of any kind. The Greek comes closer to the English word "whole" in its moral sense of completeness than to flawlessness.[156] The Greek word especially looks at the idea of being suitable to perform a task. Religiously it has various nuances, one

---

151. BDAG, 749; Louw-Nida, §§9.42, 46; 10.37; Cockerill, *Epistle to the Hebrews,* 145.

152. Ellingworth, *Epistle to the Hebrews,* 170.

153. The book of Revelation highlights the accolades that heaven pays to Christ for what he has done. See Rev. 5:9–10; 10:6–8.

154. Cockerill, *Epistle to the Hebrews,* 137.

155. See the discussions in Holzapfel and Wayment, *Making Sense,* 450; and Ogden and Skinner, *Verse by Verse,* 247.

156. *Webster's New Dictionary of Synonyms,* s.v. "perfect."

indicating "a wholehearted relationship to God,"[157] another being prepared for priestly duty,[158] and another, for mortal individuals, the completing of one's life-mission through death.[159] In the context of Hebrews, the Savior was made perfect, that is, "fit" and "complete," for his office of High Priest because of his suffering and death.

In the Greco-Roman context, *teleioō* was also used to describe being consecrated or initiated into one of the mystery religions.[160] As one scholar noted, "Through his suffering, Christ becomes the perfect model, who has learned obedience (5:8), and the perfect intercessor, merciful and faithful (2:17)." His perfection became complete when he entered into the honor and glory of his exaltation. His accomplishment serves as the promise that his followers can reach the same perfection. Further, this same scholar notes, "It is not through enlightenment or moral development [note, Christ was always sinless], but through the sonship characterized by faithful endurance that Christ attains 'perfection' and makes it possible for his 'perfected' followers to take the same route."[161]

The author makes it clear that Jesus was made perfect through suffering, suggesting it was by that means, and that means alone, that he was able to reach his goal of atoning for all. It also made him the perfect High Priest.[162] When both aspects are at play, then the point of Hebrews is that "by undergoing death, God accomplished his purpose whereby the Son would become a high priest [2:17], able to cleanse God's people from their sins, thus enabling them to approach God in true worship."[163]

It was by the means of the Savior's "sufferings" (παθηματα, *pathēmata*) that God perfected him so that he could lead the Father's sons and daughters to honor and glory. The plural "sufferings" (2:10) includes all the trials,

---

157. Compare Gen. 17:1, Deut. 18:13, 1 Kgs. 8:61, and Judg. 9:16, 19.

158. In the LXX, τελειόω (*teleioō*) is used to translate the Hebrew מִלֵּא יָד (*millē' yad*), literally "to fill the hand," meaning "to consecrate as a priest." *HAL,* 583–84. See LXX Ex. 29:9, 29, 33, 35; Lev. 8:33; 16:32; 21:10; and Num. 3:3.

159. Attridge, *Epistle to the Hebrews,* 85–86.

160. BDAG, 996. The author, however, does not show any influence upon his thought by Greek mystery cults. Fairhurst, "Hellenistic Influence in the Epistle to the Hebrews," 17–27.

161. Attridge, *Epistle to the Hebrews,* 87; see also Cockerill, *Epistle to the Hebrews,* 138–39; and Lane, *Hebrews 1–8,* 57–58.

162. It was the task of the Levitical high priest to present the offering that reconciled Israel with Jehovah (Ex. 30:10). Jesus did this, as the author shows, through offering his own blood (10:4–14).

163. Ellingworth, *Epistle to the Hebrews,* 163.

temptations, disappointments, and heartaches the Savior experienced as a mortal. It was both his willingness to suffer and his actual suffering of these vicissitudes that validated his perfect obedience (5:8–10; 10:5–10) and provided the flawless example of faithful endurance for the rest of God's children.[164]

Though it is true that Jesus eventually "ascended up on high," through his suffering he also "descended below all things, in that he comprehended all things" so "he might be in all and through all things, the light of truth" (D&C 88:6). This is "the light which is in all things, which giveth life to all things, which is the law by which all things are governed, even the power of God who sitteth upon his throne, who is in the bosom of eternity, who is in the midst of all things" (D&C 88:13). So terrible was the Lord's suffering compared to that of humankind that he could say, "The Son of Man hath descended below them all" (D&C 122:8).

Overcoming all these made him a fit "leader" for the exaltation of "many of [God's] children" (πολλοὺς υἱοὺς, *pollous hyious,* literally "sons," but used here in the more broad context to include all the faithful—both men and women).[165] That they are called "God's children" suggests they are a group separate from humanity as a whole and likely represent those who have been "born again" into Christ's kingdom (John 3:1–7), thus becoming his sons and daughters (Mosiah 5:7; 27:25; Alma 5:49; Ether 3:13–15; Moses 6:59), and are heirs not of general salvation but of exaltation.[166]

Along with the author of Hebrews (2:10), Peter testified that God lifted up Jesus to be not only the Savior but also the one to "lead the way" (ἀρχηγὸν καὶ σωτῆρα, *archēgon kai sōtēra*) to salvation (Acts 5:31). Peter also noted the irony that the leaders of the Jews killed the only one who could lead them to life (ἀρχηγὸν τῆς ζωῆς ἀπεκτείνατε, *archēgon tēs zōēs apekteinate*) (Acts 3:15). In this context, the noun ἀρχηγός (*archēgos*) carries the nuance of pioneer, founder, source, and author.[167] The idea of authorship is very applicable in 2:10, for Jesus is the one who brings about salvation for all humankind. But there is another nuance that needs to be stressed. Because

164. Johnson, *Hebrews,* 97; Cockerill, *Epistle to the Hebrews,* 138.

165. John 1:12 states that to those who accepted the Lord, God gave power to become the "children" (τέκνα, *tekna*) of God. See also Attridge, *Epistle to the Hebrews,* 78, who notes the term includes all members of the Christian community, both male and female.

166. Compare Ellingworth, *Epistle to the Hebrews,* 160; Hyrum L. Andrus, *Principles of Perfection* (Salt Lake City: Bookcraft, 1970), 170–80; Ed J. Pinegar, "Born of God," in Ludlow, *Encyclopedia of Mormonism,* 1:218–19.

167. *NID,* s.v. "ἀρχηγός."

Jesus not only paved the way to eternal life but also reached that goal, he became both the founder (*archēgos*) and perfecter (τελειωτής, *teleiōtēs*) of our faith (12:2) in that he not only shows us the way but makes it possible for us to get there if we will let him.[168]

With the phrase "the children that God has given to me" (NR 2:13), the author of Hebrews makes an important point: as a sacred trust, God has put into Christ's care his children's lives. The Savior perfectly understood his charge. With great desire he wished to be reunited with the Father in glory, but also to take with him those whom the Father had put in his trust. The Savior's intent is highlighted in his heartfelt prayer:

> O Father, glorify thou me with thine own self with the glory which I had with thee before the world was. . . . And all mine are thine, and thine are mine; and I am glorified in them. . . . Neither pray I for these alone, but for them also which shall believe on me through their word; that they all may be one; as thou, Father, art in me, and I in thee, that they also may be one in us: that the world may believe that thou hast sent me. And the glory which thou gavest me I have given them; that they may be one, even as we are one: I in them, and thou in me, that they may be made perfect in one; and that the world may know that thou hast sent me, and hast loved them, as thou hast loved me. Father, I will that they also, whom thou hast given me, be with me where I am; that they may behold my glory, which thou hast given me: for thou lovedst me before the foundation of the world. (John 17:5, 10, 20–24)

It is thus Jesus' intent that the faithful share in God's glory, that is, in his approbation and also in his power.

> Those who achieve this level of perfection will become joint-heirs with Christ: "For as many as are led by the Spirit of God, they are the sons of God. . . . And if children, then heirs; heirs of God, and joint-heirs with Christ; if so be that we suffer with him, that we may be also glorified together" (Rom. 8:14–17). "All that [the] Father hath" shall be given to them (D&C 84:37–38). In biblical terms, those who are worthy to share in all the power and glory that God himself has are called "gods": "Ye are gods; and all of you are children of the most High" (Ps. 82:6; John 10:34–38). Latter-day scriptures refer to several persons, including Abraham, Isaac, and Jacob, who once lived on earth and who are now resurrected beings and have become gods (D&C 132:37).[169]

---

168. The idea behind the word τελειωτής (*teleiōtēs*) is "one who brings something to a successful conclusion, perfecter" (BDAG, 997). It carries much the same nuance as a related word, τελείωσις (*teleiōsis*), which denotes "accomplishment, fulfillment, completion." LSJ, 1770; BDAG, 997.

169. K. Codell Carter, "Godhood," in Ludlow, *Encyclopedia of Mormonism,* 2:554.

People can be made holy, that is, sanctified. Indeed, it is one of the chief responsibilities of the Savior (10:10; 13:12; Ezek. 20:12; 1 Cor. 1:2, 30; Eph. 5:3, 26; D&C 20:31; 76:41; 84:23),[170] assisted by the Holy Ghost (Rom. 15:16; 1 Cor. 6:11; 2 Thes. 2:13; 1 Pet. 1:2; Alma 5:54; 13:12; 3 Ne. 27:20). Once perfected in him, people can "in nowise deny the power of God" (Moro. 10:32–33; compare Ether 12:27). In Latter-day Saint parlance,

> Sanctification is the process of becoming a saint, holy and spiritually clean and pure, by purging all sin from the soul. Latter-day Saint scriptures mention several factors that make sanctification possible.
>
> First is the Atonement of Jesus Christ (D&C 76:41–42; 88:18; Alma 13:11; Moro. 10:33). Christ's blood sanctifies God's repentant children by washing them clean in a way that extends beyond the remission of sins at baptism. This cleansing is given through grace to all who "love and serve God" (D&C 20:31). "For by the water ye keep the commandment; by the Spirit ye are justified, and by the blood ye are sanctified" (Moses 6:60; compare 1 John 5:8).
>
> Second is the power of the Holy Ghost, the agent that purifies the heart and gives an abhorrence of sin (Alma 13:12; 3 Ne. 27:20).
>
> Third is progression through personal righteousness (*see also* Justification). Faithful men and women fast; pray; repent of their sins; grow in humility, faith, joy, and consolation; and yield their hearts to God (Hel. 3:35). They also receive essential ordinances such as baptism (D&C 19:31) and, if necessary, endure chastening (D&C 101:5).[171]

The Son achieves sanctification for his people, as will be shown in chapter 10, by offering up his blood, through which they not only become holy but are also reconciled to the Father (10:10; 13:12). Thus, sanctification is a direct result of the Atonement,[172] but it comes through making and keeping covenants.[173]

The author makes an important point in 2:11 through the use of the generic phrase "from one [source]" (ἐξ ἑνός, *ex henos*). His point is that, whether one is sanctified or a sanctifier, there is a common font that makes them brothers and sisters. God is the Father of both Christ and the disciple,

---

170. The Old Testament notes that Jehovah is the sanctifying agent (Ex. 31:13; Lev. 20:8; 21:15; Ezek. 20:12; 37:28), but the duty of a priest, God's representative, is to do the same thing (Ex. 28:4; 29:33; 30:30; 40:13; Lev. 8:12; 1 Sam. 16:5).

171. C. Eric Ott, "Sanctification," in Ludlow, *Encyclopedia of Mormonism,* 3:1259–60.

172. Procksch, *TDNT,* 1:111–12.

173. David Peterson, *Hebrews and Perfection: An Examination of the Concept of Perfection in the "Epistle to the Hebrews"* (Cambridge: Cambridge University Press, 1982), stresses throughout his work that a proper understanding of sanctification cannot come without including the all-encompassing nature of the covenant motif.

albeit in differing but complementary ways. "The Son enters into the full exercise of his filial relationship through providing salvation and taking his seat at God's right hand (see 1:1–4). The 'sons and daughters' enter the fullness of their filial relationship through the provision of the Son. This correspondence reveals the fitting relationship between the Son and the 'sons and daughters,'" that is, they are all God's children and heirs of glory.[174] To all, including the Son, holiness comes extrinsically from the Father, who directly or indirectly makes them the same—they are godlike.[175] They are all separated from the world and devoted to the Father in carrying out his work of saving his other children (Eph. 6:6–8; Mosiah 2:17; Moses 1:29).

In 2:12–13, the author quotes twice from the Old Testament. The first scripture is found in Psalm 22:22. This passage has a certain poignancy about it since the psalm's beginning lines, "My God, my God, why hast thou forsaken me?" were quoted by the Savior while on the cross. Though the psalm starts out as a discouraged lament, it turns, with verse 22, into a song of trust and praise, stating, "I will declare thy name unto my brethren: in the midst of the congregation will I praise thee." Whether or not the author was playing on the psalm's connection with the cross is not known, but that echo remains clearly behind it.

The author of Hebrews then quotes two sentence fragments from LXX Isaiah 8:17–18. The first, "I will put my trust in him," and the second, "Behold I and the children God has given me," both combine to declare how the Savior, along with his children, will put their full trust in the Father. The author's point in doing so is to proclaim his praise to his Father for what the Father has done in the sanctification of Jesus and the children.

The quotes are a clear confession of Christ's brotherhood with the Father's other children and forcefully affirm his delight in accepting them on equal footing. The quotes also act as a clear invitation "for the sons and daughters to enjoy the benefits of their filial relationship with God now made available through their heavenly representative."[176] To the beleaguered audience to whom the author wrote, the mortal suffering of the Lord likely touched and strengthened them as they too had to endure hardship and rejection under very difficult circumstances (10:33–34). The suffering of

---

174. Cockerill, *Epistle to the Hebrews,* 141; see also Lane, *Hebrews 1–8,* 58.

175. It was the Father who sanctified the Son (John 10:36), likely when he was set apart and given the power to make the Atonement (Moses 4:2; Abr. 3:27), and the Son who sanctifies all others by calling them to the work and enabling them to do it.

176. Cockerill, *Epistle to the Hebrews,* 143.

Jesus—whom the author designates as their "pioneer" (*archēgos*)—would have inspired these people who did not yet see the world subordinated to him (2:8) to endure as he did to the same end.

The Merciful and Faithful High Priest (2:14–18)

Greek Text

14 Ἐπεὶ οὖν τὰ παιδία κεκοινώνηκεν αἵματος καὶ σαρκός, καὶ αὐτὸς παραπλησίως μετέσχεν τῶν αὐτῶν, ἵνα διὰ τοῦ θανάτου καταργήσῃ τὸν τὸ κράτος ἔχοντα τοῦ θανάτου, τοῦτ' ἔστι τὸν διάβολον, 15 καὶ ἀπαλλάξῃ τούτους, ὅσοι φόβῳ θανάτου διὰ παντὸς τοῦ ζῆν ἔνοχοι ἦσαν δουλείας. 16 οὐ γὰρ δήπου ἀγγέλων ἐπιλαμβάνεται, ἀλλὰ σπέρματος Ἀβραὰμ ἐπιλαμβάνεται. 17 ὅθεν ὤφειλεν κατὰ πάντα τοῖς ἀδελφοῖς ὁμοιωθῆναι, ἵνα ἐλεήμων γένηται καὶ πιστὸς ἀρχιερεὺς τὰ πρὸς τὸν θεόν, εἰς τὸ ἱλάσκεσθαι τὰς ἁμαρτίας τοῦ λαοῦ· 18 ἐν ᾧ γὰρ πέπονθεν αὐτὸς πειρασθείς, δύναται τοῖς πειραζομένοις βοηθῆσαι. [SBLGNT]

King James Version

14 Forasmuch then as the children are partakers of flesh and blood, he also himself likewise took part of the same; that through death he might destroy him that had the power of death, that is, the devil; 15 And deliver them who through fear of death were all their lifetime subject to bondage. 16 For verily he took not on him the nature of angels; but he took on him the seed of Abraham. 17 Wherefore in all things it behoved him to be made like unto his brethren, that he might be a merciful and faithful high priest in things pertaining to God, to make reconciliation for the sins of the people. 18 For in that he himself hath suffered being tempted, he is able to succour them that are tempted.

New Rendition

14 Now since the children share blood and flesh, he also in just the same way shared their humanity, so that through his death he might render the one who holds the power of death ineffective, that is, the devil, 15 and free them who through fear of death were in bondage their entire life. 16 For he is certainly not concerned about angels, but he is concerned about Abraham's descendants. 17 For this reason he had to be made like his brothers and sisters in every way, so that he could become a merciful and faithful high priest over the things relating to God, to atone for the sins of the people. 18 Because he himself has endured trials and temptations, he is able to help those who are tried and tempted.

Translation Notes and Comments

2:14 *Forasmuch then as the children are partakers of flesh and blood / Now since the children share blood and flesh:* The phrase ἐπεὶ οὖν (*epei oun*), "now since," gives the reason for why an action was done. Here, it refers to why Jesus took upon himself "flesh and blood."[177] The verb κοινωνέω (*koinōneō*) means to participate or share in something with the sense of equality or fulness.[178] The perfect tense here marks an enduring result of a completed action in the past and is best translated as a present tense.[179] The phrase "flesh and blood" denotes "the characteristics and nature of a human being" and connotes the full range of mortal experience.[180]

he also himself likewise took part of the same / he also in just the same way shared their humanity: The adverb παραπλησίως (*paraplēsiōs*) means "similarly, likewise," but in certain contexts it has the sense of "in just the same way,"[181] which is how we have translated it in our Rendition. In the phrase μετέσχεν τῶν αὐτῶν (*meteschen tōn autōn*), literally "he had a share in the same things," the "things" referred to are the "flesh and blood" mentioned earlier in the verse. Thus, for clarity, we translate it as "their humanity" in our Rendition. The author of Hebrews clearly sees the divine Lord taking upon himself a fully mortal body. The force of the aorist tense of the verb μετέσχεν (*meteschen*), "shared in," suggests the author understands that, though he once did, Christ no longer possesses a mortal nature.[182]

that through death he might destroy him that had the power of death, that is, the devil / so that through his death he might render the one who holds the power of death ineffective, that is, the devil: This phrase explains why the Savior had to die. The verb καταργέω (*katargeō*) means "to make ineffective" or "to incapacitate," as well as "to put something to an end." The various nuances, however, stop short of the idea of complete annihilation (compare Rom. 3:31; Eph. 2:15).[183] Since the devil, according to Latter-day Saint understanding, is a spirit being, he cannot be destroyed, but his power to promote death can be.

---

177. Cockerill, *Epistle to the Hebrews,* 147; Ellingworth, *Epistle to the Hebrews,* 170–71; see also Mosiah 7:27.

178. BDAG, 552.

179. Smyth, *Greek Grammar,* §1946.

180. Louw-Nida, §9.15; Bruce R. McConkie, *Mormon Doctrine,* 2d ed. (Salt Lake City: Bookcraft, 1966), 288.

181. BDAG, 770.

182. Ellingworth, *Epistle to the Hebrews,* 171.

183. BDAG, 525–26; Louw-Nida, §13.100, 163; Ellingworth, *Epistle to the Hebrews,* 173.

The noun διάβολος (*diabolos*), "devil," is one of the designations of Lucifer, the fallen "son of the morning" (D&C 76:25–27).[184] In Jewish and Christian literature, it carried the very strong nuance of a being of transcendent evil.[185] The noun κράτος (*kratos*) denotes "might," "power," or "sovereignty."[186] Here it connotes Satan's power to inflict death.

2:15 ***And deliver them who through fear of death were all their lifetime subject to bondage / and free them who through fear of death were in bondage their entire life:*** The verb ἀπαλλάσσω (*apallassō*) denotes being "set free from a controlling state or entity."[187] The noun δουλεία (*douleia*) denotes "slavery, servility," and, thereby, "bondage."[188] The sobering and potent "fear of death" has haunted humankind through the millennia. That fear has given a powerful coercive tool to some that they have used to intimidate others into bending to their will. Because that fear stops people from exercising their freedom, they are in bondage to it.[189]

2:16 ***For verily he took not on him the nature of angels; but he took on him the seed of Abraham / For he is certainly not concerned about angels, but he is concerned about Abraham's descendants:*** This is a difficult verse to translate because of the unclear use of the verb ἐπιλαμβάνομαι (*epilambanomai*), "to take hold of," which is used twice. In the New Testament, it is only used in the middle voice and has the basic meaning of physically taking hold of or grasping something.[190] A literal translation is, "He does not take hold of

---

184. Unlike the title "Satan," which carries the idea of slandering, διάβολος (*diabolos*) carries more of the idea of an embodiment of evil. See von Rad and Foerster, *TDNT*, 2:73–81.

185. BDAG, 226-27; Koester, *Hebrews*, 231.

186. BDAG, 565; Louw-Nida, §76.6.

187. BDAG, 96.

188. BDAG, 259. James Swetnam, "The Crux at Hebrews 2,9 in Its Context," *Biblica* 91, no. 1 (2010): 103–11, argues that 2:8–9 corresponds with 2:14–16, in which the author of Hebrews looks at Jesus as the sacrificial victim who died physically before his disciples and, in that way, helped them overcome their own fear of death. That seems partially correct but too narrow, for the death and resurrection of Jesus gives hope to all believers and thereby frees them from the fear of death.

189. Bruce, *Epistle to the Hebrews*, 86; Cockerill, *Epistle to the Hebrews*, 148. The author's words could show an influence of Stoic ideas applied to Jesus' redemption. Epictetus thought that "the epitome of all human evils stems from the fear of death, which often drives people to do wicked, shameful things. Stoics, in contrast, are liberated from the fear of death and so free to pursue good, happy lives fearlessly." See "William O. Stephens, Creighton University—Stoic Philosophy & Death," The Academic Minute, December 12, 2014, https://academicminute.org/2014/12/william-o-stephens-creighton-university-stoic-philosophy-death/.

190. BDAG, 373.

angels, but he takes hold of the seed of Abraham." In a more abstract sense, it seems to mean "to be concerned with/about Abraham's seed" or "to help Abraham's seed."[191] The early church fathers, both Greek and Latin, generally understood the phrase to refer to Christ's taking on human nature, and the KJV follows them.[192] However, there are compelling reasons for rejecting such an understanding. First of all, there is no parallel for this meaning in the Greek New Testament or anywhere else in Greek literature.[193] Second, both ἀγγέλων (*angelōn*), "of angels," and σπέρματος Ἀβρααμ (*spermatos Abraam*), "of seed of Abraham," are clearly more concrete than angelic or human nature. In addition, the use of the present tense, rather than the aorist—which is used in the preceding and following sentences—would be inappropriate as a reference to Christ's taking upon himself human nature since that had already occurred at his birth. Finally, if this were the sense of this verse, it would simply be repeating what was said in 2:14, and the causal particle γάρ (*gar*), "for," would be meaningless.[194] Thus, in our Rendition we have translated ἐπιλαμβάνομαι (*epilambanomai*) as "to be concerned about."

The JST changes this phrase to read, "He took not on him the likeness of angels." Just why Joseph Smith made the change from "nature" to "likeness" is unclear,[195] but the JST follows Hebrews in showing that the Savior became very much like righteous mortals.

There is no question that this translation emphasizes that the Savior's actions were motivated by his concern, not for the angels (who were in no need of it), but for a select group of people. There is some ambiguity as to whom the "seed" of Abraham is. In the most restricted sense, it could refer to the literal descendants of Abraham. Taking the nuance a little more broadly, the phrase could still point to a select group but include more than Abraham's literal descendants. In that case, it could refer to that group of people who have the right and responsibility to take the gospel to the world (Abr. 2:9, 11). Paul, however, extends the sense to refer to all who accepted the gospel of Jesus Christ (Rom. 9:6–7; Gal. 3:7, 16, 19). The book of Abraham supports this interpretation:

---

191. BDAG, 373; Louw-Nida, §35.1.

192. Ellingworth, *Epistle to the Hebrews,* 177.

193. BDAG, 373; LSJ, 642; Ellingworth, *Epistle to the Hebrews,* 177.

194. These arguments are set forth in Ellingworth, *Epistle to the Hebrews,* 177.

195. The phrase "nature of angels" denotes the essential qualities or the innate dispositions of these heavenly beings. Since Jesus was divine, he did not possess their "nature." As the author of Hebrews notes, he was "so much better than the angels" (1:4). He could, however, become "like" them, just as he became "like" mortals, but he did not do this. Instead, he chose to become fully mortal.

"As many as receive this Gospel shall be called after thy name, and shall be accounted thy seed, and shall rise up and bless thee, as their father" (Abr. 2:10).

2:17 ***Wherefore in all things it behoved him to be made like unto his brethren / For this reason he had to be made like his brothers and sisters in every way:*** The subordinating conjunction ὅθεν (*othen*), "for this reason," marks the basis for an action and, thereby, gives the reason for it.[196] In this case, it explains that what drove the Lord to become mortal was his care for Abraham's posterity.

The verb ὀφείλω (*ōpheilō*), "be obligated, must," denotes an indebtedness that puts one under obligation to pay. It connotes the need to pay a heavy moral or social obligation. In the context here, however, it carries the idea of being constrained by circumstances to do something and emphasizes its obligatory nature.[197] The imperfect tense is used here to "express past obligation" that carries into the present.[198]

The verb ὁμοιόω (*homoioō*) in the passive means "to be made like,"[199] and when coupled with κατὰ πάντα (*kata panta*), "in every way," the phrase expresses how fully the Savior became mortal. Indeed, becoming like his brothers and sisters bound him to them in history, in temptations, in trials, in suffering, in mortality, and in death.[200]

that he might be a merciful and faithful high priest in things pertaining to God / so that he could become a merciful and faithful high priest over the things relating to God: The conjunction ἵνα (*hina*), "so that," marks "a purpose, aim, or goal" and points to why Jesus had to become fully mortal.

The adjective ἐλεήμων (*eleēmōn*), "merciful," carries elements of both mercy and compassion. It connotes the feeling aroused when one sees another suffering from undeserved affliction. In the sense of compassion, it expresses an emotional sharing in the distress or misfortune of an equal. In the sense of mercy, it expresses a disinclination to be either rigorous or severe, especially toward an offending party.[201]

---

196. BDAG, 692–93.

197. BDAG, 743; Louw-Nida, §§57.221; 71.25. It can also mean to commit sin against another through which a heavy moral debt is incurred. Louw-Nida, §88.298.

198. Smyth, *Greek Grammar,* §1905.

199. BDAG, 707.

200. *NID,* s.v. "ὁμοιόω." The *only* exception was that Jesus never tasted of personal sin (4:15). See also McConkie, *Doctrinal New Testament Commentary,* 3:145–46.

201. BDAG, 316; Louw-Nida, §88.77; *NID,* s.v. "ἐλεήμων"; *Webster's New Dictionary of Synonyms,* s.vv. "sympathy," "forbearing."

The adjective πίστος (*pistos*) stresses "trustworthiness" or "faithfulness" to a cause or people.[202] As used here, the word suggests total faithfulness to God and his purposes. In the context of Jesus' ministry, this virtue is buttressed by the understanding he gained through experience of the importance of his responsibility toward those he served.[203]

The noun ἀρχιερεύς (*archiereus*) denotes *the* high priest in the Levitical system.[204] In Hebrews, however, the author uses the word more metaphorically to denote the high station the Savior holds over the priesthood. He uses it to showcase and expound on the Savior's saving acts toward his people.[205] For development, see "Excursus on the Atonement: A View from Hebrews" in this chapter.

to make reconciliation for the sins of the people / to atone for the sins of the people: The verb ἱλάσκομαι (*hilaskomai*), in its religious context, has the basic sense of reconciling a person to God.[206] The word carries the idea of showing "compassion and concern for someone in difficulty, despite that person's having committed a moral offense."[207] That concern drives the reconciling party to do what is necessary to restore the relationship.

The English verb "atone," used to translate ἱλάσκομαι (*hilaskomai*), denotes the restoration of balance between two parties lost due to an offensive action on the part of one. That balance is restored through some form of

---

202. BDAG, 820–21; *NID,* s.v. "πιστός." The whole family group focuses on that which either describes or evidences trust and faith. See Bultmann, *TDNT,* 6:174–228.

203. See Attridge, *Epistle to the Hebrews,* 95–96 nn. 189–90; Bruce, *Epistle to the Hebrews,* 88.

204. The term refers to the presiding priest whom God appointed to act only for a season. Once released, the individual no longer held that title. While this noun occurs only three times in the LXX (Lev. 4:3; Josh. 22:13; 24:33), it is found over forty times in the Greek Apocryphal texts as a reference to the high or chief priest of the Levitical Priesthood. For a study, see *NID,* 2:502–11. Joseph Smith equated the office with the Melchizedek Priesthood, noting, "Christ is the Great High Priest; Adam next." In doing so, the Prophet shows that the title, though not the authority, was common to both orders of the priesthood. "Discourse, between circa 26 June and circa 4 August 1839–A, as Reported by Willard Richards," 65.

205. The Gospels do not directly equate Jesus and the high priest, but they do show him doing priestly service. See David Rolph Seely and Jo Ann H. Seely, "Jesus the Messiah: Prophet, Priest, and King," in *Jesus Christ: Son of God, Savior,* ed. Paul H. Peterson, Gary L. Hatch, and Laura D. Card (Provo, Utah: Religious Studies Center, Brigham Young University, 2002), 259–64. Andrie du Toit, "Τὰ πρὸς τὸν θεόν in Romans and Hebrews: Towards Understanding an Enigmatic Phrase," *Zeitschrift für die Neutestamentliche Wissenschaft* 101, no. 2 (2010): 241–51, argues that the phrase is used in the cultic sense and, therefore, points to work done by a high priest in service at the tabernacle.

206. BDAG, 473–74.

207. Louw-Nida, §88.75.

compensation, usually "through acts that are good or meritorious."[208] In the Old Testament, "atonement" generally referred to those cultic activities of the priests that Jehovah designed to bring him and his people into oneness.[209] The focus of these activities was overcoming the offending and separating effects of sin.[210] The author of Hebrews appears to have Christ's passion in view, but the infinitive being in the present tense, "to atone," suggests "continuing application of the benefits of that sacrifice to God's people."[211]

The author of Hebrews emphasizes the role of Jesus as High Priest empowered to bring the Father's children into oneness with him through his own personal sacrifice. Noteworthy is that God is not the recipient of atonement. In the New Testament, the word always refers to God's action in relation to mankind.[212]

By becoming fully mortal and suffering its full effects, Jesus became "a merciful and faithful high priest" and, thus, one who could do what the office required, namely doing the service "with regard to God" (τὰ πρὸς τὸν θεόν, *ta pros ton theon*) in removing the sins of the people.[213]

2:18 ***For in that he himself hath suffered being tempted / Because he himself has endured trials and temptations:*** The verb πάσχω (*paschō*) denotes both undergoing and enduring something that is unpleasant.[214] The force of the perfect tense shows that, as far as the Savior is concerned,

208. *Webster's New Dictionary of Synonyms,* s.v. "expiation." The idea of reconciliation, due to religious controversies, has often taken a back seat to such ideas as appeasement, propitiation, and reparation, but it should never be lost sight of. For discussion of the issue, see *NID,* s.v. "ἱλάσκομαι."

209. For a discussion, see T. Benjamin Spackman, "The Israelite Roots of Atonement Terminology," *BYU Studies Quarterly* 55, no. 1 (2016): 39–64.

210. Louw-Nida, §40.9. Given the relative frequency of the word's appearance in the LXX, it is noteworthy that it only appears twice in the New Testament (2:17; Luke 18:13). The thrust of the New Testament, however, is more on reconciliation than expiation, and therefore the verb καταλλάσσω is favored. See, for example, Matt. 5:24; Rom. 5:10; 1 Cor. 7:11; and Col. 1:20–21.

211. Cockerill, *Epistle to the Hebrews,* 150. See also Jeffrey R. Holland's talk to those "who may feel they have somehow forfeited their place at the table of the Lord" and his promise of the merciful nature of the Divine. "'He Hath Filled the Hungry with Good Things,'" *Ensign* 27, no. 11 (November 1997): 65.

212. Friedrich Büchel, *TDNT,* 3:317.

213. Cockerill, *Epistle to the Hebrews,* 149. The phrase τὰ πρὸς τὸν θεόν (*ta pros ton theon*) is found in the LXX of the Pentateuch and points to the priests' responsibilities. For example, see Ex. 4:16; 18:19; Lane, *Hebrews 1–8,* 65.

214. Though πάσχω (*paschō*) can denote experiencing something pleasant, this nuance is used only once in the scriptures. See Gal. 3:4.

this kind of suffering is now in the past, left behind with his mortality. Even so, its effects in generating understanding, compassion, and mercy are still in full force.[215]

The verb πειράζω (*peirazō*) has a broader range of meaning than the English "tempt." Besides the sense "to tempt," it also includes "to try, attempt, make trial of, and put to the test."[216] Hence we have translated πέπονθεν αὐτὸς πειρασθείς (*peponthen autos peirastheis,* literally "he himself has endured, being tempted/tried") as "he himself has endured trials and temptations." The point is that during the Savior's life and ministry, he not only endured the temptations that all mortals experience, but he also experienced all the trials and tribulation associated with mortality (see Mosiah 15:5; Alma 7:11–13; and D&C 20:22).[217]

he is able to succour them that are tempted / he is able to help those who are tried and tempted: In our Rendition, we have used "those who are tried and tempted" to translate the nominalized present passive participle τοῖς πειραζομένοις (*tois perazomenois*). The verb βοηθέω (*boētheō*) means "to render assistance to someone in need, help, come to the aid of."[218] It points to the Savior's anxious willingness to supply whatever aid is necessary to sustain those in need.

Analysis and Summary

Having established the oneness between Christ and the other children of God—a oneness brought about through the power of sanctification—the author now turns to the great battle Jesus fought in order to deliver God's children from the forces of evil and death. The idea of the divine heroes fighting for and giving relief to the needy was well established in the Greco-Roman world.[219] Thus, the idea of the Savior's death and exaltation as battles fought and won to liberate his "brothers and sisters" fits well into the world of the community the author addressed.

---

215. Wallace, *Greek Grammar,* 574–76.

216. BDAG, 792–93.

217. McConkie, *Promised Messiah,* 499–501; see also Mosiah 3:7; 15:5.

218. BDAG, 180; Louw-Nida, §35.1. A pleasant nuance exists in the archaic English word "succour" used in the KJV. Taking its thrust from its Latin base (*succurrere,* "to run to the rescue"), "succour" implies a very dynamic movement to give aid.

219. Koester, *Hebrews,* 239; and Lane, *Hebrews 1–8,* 56, see a parallel in thought between the Savior's act and that of Heracles, whose conquests in the netherworld brought him deification and enabled him to help those in difficulty. See Homer, *Il.* 5.394–400; Euripides, *Alc.* 76, 843–44: Seneca, *Herc. fur.* 889–90.

The author's statements here suggest that the broad community of Christians accepted the idea that the Savior's death was central to God's plan. Indeed, it was the cornerstone of the early Christian witness of Christ (Acts 2:23; 10:39; 1 Cor. 15:3). This idea had become so broadly accepted the author felt no need either to defend or explain it. It would seem the Christian community by and large understood that because of sin, death entered the world (Rom. 5:12; 1 Cor. 15:56; 1 John 3:12) and that Jesus came to remove the effects of sin through his death (1 Cor. 15:3; Gal. 1:4).[220]

The author's argument is based on the unexplored assumption that the devil has the power of death. Given that Satan "is chief prosecutor in the heavenly court [Rev. 12:10], there is no difficulty in regarding him also as executioner-in-chief" (compare 1 Cor. 5:5).[221] Satan's power to inflict death actually comes not through his actions as tempter but through humankind's yielding thereto and sinning. It was a transgression of God's law that initiated the Fall and brought in the mortal condition of death (Gen. 2:17; Rom. 6:23; Moses 6:59).

Christ took on mortality that through the power of his own death, he could completely incapacitate (καταργέω, *katargeō*) the one who had power over death.[222] He did so by dying. The author of Hebrews leaves it at that and by so doing emphasizes the reason for the Savior's mortality and why he became like his "brothers and sisters." Playing in the background, however, is just how he was able to thwart Satan and undo his power. It was through the power of the keys of the resurrection which he held (1:3; Rev. 1:18; Alma 11:42; Hel. 14:17; Morm. 7:5).[223]

---

220. Ellingworth, *Epistle to the Hebrews,* 173.

221. Bruce, *Epistle to the Hebrews,* 86 n. 80.

222. The Greek text omits the personal pronoun "his own," but it is clear that the author is referring to Christ's death. By the way the author structured the phrase, he astutely emphasized that by his death, the Savior abolished the intimidating power of death. Cockerill, *Epistle to the Hebrews,* 147 n. 109.

223. McConkie, *Doctrinal New Testament Commentary,* 3:146; Smith, *Answers to Gospel Questions,* 1:165. The term "key" in connection with priesthood denotes the right to exercise the priesthood to perform tasks necessary for blessing, administration, or salvation. To "turn a key" means to inaugurate its use. See Alan K. Parrish, "Keys of the Priesthood," in Ludlow, *Encyclopedia of Mormonism,* 2:780–81. According to Church authority, "Priesthood keys are the authority God has given to priesthood [holders] to direct, control, and govern the use of His priesthood on earth." The Church of Jesus Christ of Latter-day Saints, *Handbook 2: Administering the Church* (Salt Lake City: The Church of Jesus Christ of Latter-day Saints, 2019), 2.1.1. For a discussion, see Dallin H. Oaks, "The Keys and Authority of the Priesthood," *Ensign* 44, no. 5 (May 2014): 49–52.

Both the idea and fact of death has haunted humankind from the beginning. This fear is very evident in the Greco-Roman world in which the community to which Hebrews was written.[224] In 2:15, the author explains how the Savior ended the "fear of death" for humankind. He did so by delivering them from its permanent effects and, thereby, bringing life and immortality to light (see 2 Tim. 1:10).[225] It was in entering into the spirit world that he opened its gates so that those within could escape from spiritual bondage. Indeed, even the gates of hell could not prevail against the keys he turned to initiate work for the dead (see Matt. 16:18–19). Ironically, even paradoxically, through the sin of those who killed him, he overthrew sin by opening the way to their repentance and return (see Acts 2:36–41; 3:12–26). And in being grasped by the grave, he was able to break its grip. Thus, by dying he slew death.[226]

Though the Savior did what he did for all humankind, there was one group for whom he had particular concern. The author identifies this group as "the seed of Abraham" (2:16). According the Pearl of Great Price, these are they who are charged to "bear this ministry and Priesthood unto all nations." Indeed, God promised Abraham that "this right shall continue in thee, and in thy seed after thee . . . [and by it] shall all the families of the earth be blessed" (Abr. 2:9, 11). Given their responsibility, it is little wonder the Savior would have special care for them. One of many positive effects of being delivered from the "fear of death" is these people could courageously carry out their mission no matter the cost.

In 2:17, the author of Hebrews shows that this is precisely the task Jesus, as High Priest, had to perform as to "things relating to God" (τὰ πρὸς τὸν θεόν, *ta pros ton theon*). That task was specifically one of reconciliation (ἱλάσκομαι, *hilaskomai*) between God and his children through expiation, that is, satisfying a wrong.[227] The idea of reconciliation as carried in the scriptures stands in marked contrast to the Greek idea of propitiation. Greek and Roman sacrifices were largely based on the notion that the world was an adversarial place, and the gods had powers, but they could

224. See Attridge, *Epistle to the Hebrews,* 93 nn. 165–66. The assurance the author gave would have had another positive effect, that of fortifying his readers against the fear of persecution. See Johnson, *Hebrews,* 100; Koester, *Hebrews,* 232.

225. Noteworthy is that, with one exception (13:20–21), the author of Hebrews never expressly mentions the Resurrection. Nonetheless, it is implied through the Lord's being raised to glory and enthroned by God (1:3).

226. Bruce, *Epistle to the Hebrews,* 86.

227. The verb usually translated as "reconcile" is καταλλάσσω (*katallassō*). See, for example, Matt. 5:24; Rom. 5:10; 1 Cor. 7:11; and Col. 1:20–21.

be placated to assist those in need.[228] Due to this view, propitiation—the process of averting anger and winning favor—was absolutely necessary and the main thrust of the sacrifices.

The KJV translation of 1 John 2:2 (see also 1 John 4:10) states that Jesus is "the propitiation for our sins." The Greek verb is ἱλάσκομαι (*hilaskomai*) and suggests Jesus did much more than assuage God's anger. In fact, the word is never used to describe any act on the part of a worshiper through which God is coaxed, bribed, cajoled, enticed, or forced into having a gracious disposition or favorable attitude toward him or her.[229] In short, the scriptures never speak of God as losing his love for a child even when he hates their actions. He is ever anxious to be reconciled to anyone who will turn to him, and the Father has done his part to make that happen. The scriptures do show it is the person who must be reconciled to God. Thus, any continuing resistance that exists is on the part of the person *alone.*[230]

That God ever loves and is ever open to reconciliation should not be taken to mean that he cannot be upset with both individuals and groups. Indeed, one of his attributes is divine "wrath" (*orgē*), and provoking it has consequences (for example, see Ex. 22:24; 32:10; 2 Kgs. 22:17; 2 Chr. 34:25; and D&C 63:33; 103:2). His anger is not uncontrolled rage but actually an expression of both his righteousness and holiness. As Elder Dallin H. Oaks noted, "God's anger and His wrath are not a *contradiction* of His love but an *evidence* of His love."[231] Nonetheless, the scriptures attest that an unprepared human will find that an encounter with that holiness can be quite dangerous (see Ex. 4:24–26; 19:9–13; and Isa. 6:5).

The Father's anger is provoked by disobedience, unfaithfulness, and apostasy. The author of Hebrews quotes the Lord as saying of the Israelites, "I sware in my wrath, They shall not enter into my rest" (3:11). By their rebellion they provoked the Father's wrath and, as a consequence, he excluded them from a celestial home (compare 4:3). His anger, however, need not last forever. The scriptural witness is that it "endureth but a moment" (Ps. 30:5; compare Isa. 26:20; 54:7–8). Standing behind the wrath, therefore, is the promise of redemption (compare 2 Sam. 24:16; Isa. 40:2; 51:22; 54:8–10;

---

228. *NID,* s.v. "ὀργή."

229. The related word ἱλασμός (*hilasmos*) is found only in 1 John 2:2 and 4:10, where it is wrongly translated as "propitiation" in the KJV. The RSV gets a little closer to its meaning by translating it as "expiation." The better translation as "atoning sacrifice" is found in the NIV and NRSV.

230. *NID,* s.v. "ὀργή."

231. Dallin H. Oaks, "Love and Law," *Ensign* 39, no. 11 (November 2009): 27.

and Hosea 14:4).[232] The author of Hebrews assures his readers "the Lord disciplines the one he loves, and chastises every child he accepts" and promises if they "endure these things for the sake of discipline, God is treating you as children. For what child is not disciplined by his father?" (NR 12:6–7; compare D&C 95:1). Further, he quotes the Lord as saying, "I will be merciful toward their iniquities and I will no longer remember their sins" (NR 8:12). Thus, reconciliation is completely possible. But for reconciliation to occur, someone must make expiation for guilt.

The reason guilt must be expiated lies in the character and nature of God. As noted above,[233] God is holy, a state which no mundane or sinful person wishes to tolerate or endure (Alma 5:22; 41:7). Thus, reconciliation is necessary "not because of some mechanistic view of the universe that requires an appropriate ritual as an antidote to nullify the effects of sin. It is because God himself is who he is and what he is."[234] For a person to wish to be near and remain with God, that person must also be holy. To make the condition possible, God both provides for and enjoins the reconciliation.

The means (as is explored in more detail in the "Excursus on the Atonement: A View from Hebrews" below) is through the Atonement of Jesus Christ. Here, however, it needs to be stressed that the reason there can be an atonement is because Jesus is the ἱλασμός (*hilasmos*), that is, the very means of obtaining forgiveness (1 John 2:2; 4:10). He is the one who satisfies justice and thereby releases a person from its demands (Rom. 3:23–25; Alma 42:15).

The atoning act, like that of repentance, does not change the Father's love toward an offending child but rather allows the Father to extend his mercy to the offender and bring him or her into oneness with himself. In sum, the force of ἱλάσκομαι (*hilaskomai*) dramatizes each individual's need to be reconciled to God, not God to him or her.

Having noted the above, there is a sense in which God is propitiated. It is "in the vindication of His holy and righteous character, whereby through the provision He has made in the vicarious and expiatory sacrifice of Christ, he has also dealt with sin so that He can show mercy to the believing sinner in the removal of his guilt and the remission of his sins."[235] The scriptures

---

232. *NID,* s.v. "ὀργή."

233. See Translation Notes for 2:11 with associated material in the Analysis dealing with holiness.

234. *NID,* s.v. "ἱλάσκομαι."

235. James Strong, "The New Strong's Expanded Dictionary of the Words in the Greek New Testament," in *The New Strong's Expanded Exhaustive Concordance of the Bible* (Nashville: Thomas Nelson Publishers, 2010), s.v. "ἱλάσκομαι."

show that saints and sinners alike ask God to be merciful (*hilaskomai,* "be propitious") toward them (for example, see Ps. 79:9 and Luke 18:13). The object of the request for that mercy is to restore a heartfelt desire for oneness that has been lost. The mercy comes, however, not because God changes his mind or attitude, but because the person, through repentance, comes under the power of the Atonement. In doing so, Christ takes away the uncleanliness, imputes righteousness, breaks down the barrier that sin erected, and places the person in a state of holiness, thus making reconciliation possible.[236]

The author, however, does not allow his readers to focus only on expiation (the removal of sin) or on propitiation (the assuaging of God's wrath).[237] Rather, he directs their attention to the work of the priest whose task it is to remove impurities. The old covenant, when properly understood and executed, removed the worshipers' outward uncleanliness and thus prepared them to enter God's service in the tabernacle and later in the temple. That preparation could then lead the worshiper to the deeper inner cleanliness required for a fuller communion with his or her God. As a result, as the Psalmist states, this person "shall receive the blessing from the Lord, and righteousness from the God of his salvation" (Ps. 24:5).

The target of the new covenant was deeper. It was also designed to remove the impurities of the human heart that prevent people from entering the eternal city (11:10; Rev. 21:2–3; D&C 76:66) and bring them into a position where they could more fully serve God. Thus, the author will tell his readers later in the Epistle that Jesus "will cleanse our conscience [συνείδησις, *syneidēsis*] from dead works to serve the living God" (NR 9:14).[238] Once the worshiper allows the Savior to remove the impurity, he or she enters into a state of holiness and is thus prepared to be at one with God.

The author's conclusion (2:18) is poignant. Because the Savior became fully mortal, he endured (πάσχω, *paschō*) all the pain, suffering, heartache,

---

236. *NID,* s.v. "ἱλάσκομαι"; see also Büchel, *TDNT,* 3:301–18; Jeffrey R. Holland, "Atonement of Jesus Christ," in Ludlow, *Encyclopedia of Mormonism,* 1:82–86; John Taylor, *The Mediation and Atonement* (Salt Lake City: Deseret News, 1882), 148–49; Hugh W. Nibley, "The Atonement of Jesus Christ," *Ensign* 20, no. 7 (July 1990): 18–23; no. 8 (August 1990): 30–34; no. 9 (September 1990): 22–26; no. 10 (October 1990): 26–31; and Ogden and Skinner, *Verse by Verse,* 247–48. For a study of mercy by a Latter-day Saint scholar, see W. Jeffrey Marsh, "The Living Reality of the Savior's Mercy," in Peterson, Hatch, and Card, *Jesus Christ: Son of God, Savior,* 152–75.

237. An element of propitiation exists in the Atonement in that Jesus took upon himself the sins of the people so God would remember those sins no more (10:17).

238. Cockerill, *Epistle to the Hebrews,* 151.

disappointments, and temptations that humankind faces. In addition, through the Atonement, he also experienced something he never knew as a mortal, namely, the crushing and excruciating power and pain of sin.[239] All these tried (πειράζω, *peirazō*) him to the core and in their wake left him with understanding, compassion, and mercifulness (see D&C 62:1). As a result, he not only willingly but also anxiously reaches out to assist his mortal brothers and sisters as they are tried.

These verses clearly teach that "the gospel is not an answer to the problem of suffering, nor a resolution, nor even a dissolution of it. The gospel is a *response* to suffering. It is the announcement that God has joined with us in our suffering (see Hebrews 5:8; and D&C 122). He has condescended to become like us, and because he has, he can offer us salvation. He does not offer a surcease of suffering in this life, but he can give us strength, a lightening of our burden (see Matthew 11:28–30), and the promise of salvation."[240]

---

239. W. Jeffrey Marsh, *His Final Hours* (Salt Lake City: Deseret Book, 2000), 48.

240. James E. Faulconer, *Romans 1: Notes and Reflections* (Provo, Utah: FARMS, Brigham Young University, 1999), 19, italics in original; see also Christie H. Frandsen, "Trials," in Ludlow, *Encyclopedia of Mormonism,* 4:1488; and Marsh, *His Final Hours*, 48.

Excursus on the Condescension of Jesus

According to the author of Hebrews, the Lord is very concerned "about Abraham's descendants" (2:16). The book of Abraham states that these would include more than the Patriarch's physical posterity, for "as many as receive this Gospel shall be called after thy name, and shall be accounted thy seed" (Abr. 2:10). To do the work the Father outlined for the Son, the author notes that "since the children [of God] share blood and flesh, he also in just the same way shared their humanity" (NR 2:14). Indeed, "he had to be made like his brothers and sisters in every way" (NR 2:17). Just what does the phrase "in every way" entail? Certainly, part of it was becoming fully mortal. "But we see Jesus, who, for a little while, was made less than the angels . . . so that by the grace of God he would experience death for the sake of everyone" (NR 2:9). But did being able to die constitute the whole of his likeness to his brothers and sisters? The author shares another dimension: "He himself has endured trials and temptations" (2:18). According to the author, "It was fitting for God . . . to make him perfect through suffering" (2:10). How is that the case? The Book of Mormon contains important insights into the nature of the mortal Christ including the necessity for him to take upon himself flesh and blood and to suffer trials and temptations in order to accomplish his mission. These insights round out the points the author of Hebrews makes.

For instance, the author of Hebrews testifies that Jesus "appeared to put away sin by the sacrifice of himself" (9:26). Further, the Savior was able to offer "one sacrifice for sins for ever" (10:12). The Book of Mormon refers to this as the "great and last sacrifice" that would make atonement for humankind eternally. Speaking of that sacrifice, the text states that it shall not be "a sacrifice of man, neither of beast, neither of any manner of fowl; for it shall not be a human sacrifice; but it must be an infinite and eternal sacrifice. . . . And behold, this is the whole meaning of the law, every whit pointing to that great and last sacrifice; and that great and last sacrifice will be the Son of God, yea, infinite and eternal" (Alma 34:10, 14).[241]

The Book of Mormon witnesses that the being who would make the great and last sacrifice was someone special, someone unique. Even so, he

241. This excursus, with some modification, is taken from Richard D. Draper, "The First Coming of the Lord to the Jews: A Book of Mormon Perspective," in *The Book of Mormon: The Foundation of Our Faith, the 28th Annual Sidney B. Sperry Symposium* (Salt Lake City: Deseret Book, 1999), 73–86.

was still mortal. Indeed, his mortality was an essential element in being able to perform the Atonement. And yet, he was different from all his mortal kin in that he was never man and he was never human. The term "man" designates one who is descended from Adam, "the first man of all men" (Moses 1:34). The term "human," as an adjective, describes that which relates to or is characteristic of man. Taken together, the terms seem to define that which is not yet God. As the Psalmist said, "What is man, that thou art mindful of him? and the son of man, that thou visitest him? For thou hast made him a little lower than the angels [Heb. אֱלֹהִים, *ĕlōhîm*], and hast crowned him with glory and honour" (Ps. 8:4–5). Certainly, humans are not second-class citizens of the cosmos, but neither are they God. The Savior, however, even as a mortal, was God.[242]

In highlighting this fact, the Book of Mormon presents aspects of his life and ministry not found in the other standard works. It stresses his uniqueness by emphasizing that he was God on Earth, fully divine while being fully mortal.

No Book of Mormon prophet ever knew the mortal Lord before his appearance in 3 Nephi. All the information they received concerning that aspect of his ministry came through revelation. But what they did know is noteworthy. As one examines the revelations which deal with the mortal ministry, that material which God saw necessary to give the Nephites, two points become clear: first, there were certain elements the Nephites needed to know in order to have faith in Christ; and second, those elements concerned the nature of his person, character, and ministry.

The revelations carry the burning witness that the mortal Christ was the ever-living, omnipotent Lord. King Benjamin expressed his understanding by saying, "The time cometh, and is not far distant, that with power, the Lord Omnipotent who reigneth, who was, and is from all eternity to all eternity, shall come down from heaven among the children of men, and shall dwell in a tabernacle of clay" (Mosiah 3:5; compare Alma 7:10). The prophet's words focus on the eternal nature of the mortal Christ. His mortal nature and ministry must be understood in terms of his eternal nature and ministry. His mortality was, however, neither adjunct nor ancillary to his eternal nature but absolutely essential. Indeed, the focus of all the faith that came before and all the confirmation that came after centered on what he was and did in mortality. Conversely, at no point did his mortality restrain his divinity. He never ceased being God, the Eternal God, at any moment. Further, the whole thrust of his mortal ministry focused on eternity and on

242. Compare McConkie, *Doctrinal New Testament Commentary,* 3:143.

eternal lives. His actions and teachings were not calculated to bring women and men into terrestrial or telestial glory but into everlasting life.

The testimony that Amulek bore against the antagonistic Zeezrom shows this point. Their dialogue goes as follows:

> And Zeezrom said unto him: Thou sayest there is a true and living God?
> And Amulek said: Yea, there is a true and living God.
> Now Zeezrom said: Is there more than one God?
> And he answered, No.
> Now Zeezrom said unto him again: How knowest thou these things?
> And he said: An angel hath made them known unto me.
> And Zeezrom said again: Who is he that shall come? Is it the Son of God?
> And he said unto him, Yea. . . .
> Now Zeezrom saith again unto him, Is the Son of God the very Eternal Father?
> And Amulek said unto him: Yea, he is the very Eternal Father of heaven and of earth, and all things which in them are; he is the beginning and the end, the first and the last; And he shall come into the world to redeem his people; and he shall take upon him the transgressions of those who believe on his name; and these are they that shall have eternal life, and salvation cometh to none else. (Alma 11:26–33, 38–40)

The Savior came into mortality as the Eternal Father, bequeathing eternal life to those who believed on him. The greatest work he did, that which brought meaning to all he accomplished as a premortal God and his power as a postmortal God, was grounded in his mortal ministry. The Book of Mormon witness is that the Savior possessed the qualities of being infinite and eternal. He received this dimension of his being as the divine physical Son of Elohim. Thus, he was unlike any other mortal because he did not receive his physical life, as all others do, through Adam. An angel instructed Nephi that the Savior would not be conceived as other mortals are. Nephi beheld his mortal mother, Mary, in a vision. As he did so, an angel said to him, "Behold, the virgin whom thou seest is the mother of the Son of God, after the manner of the flesh. . . . And I looked and beheld the virgin again, bearing a child in her arms. And the angel said unto me: Behold the Lamb of God, yea, even the Son of the Eternal Father [meaning Elohim in this case]" (1 Ne. 11:18, 20–21; compare Alma 7:10). The point is that although Jesus was born after "the manner of the flesh," the way all babies are born, his father was not a son of Adam but the Father of Adam, even God (following Luke 3:38; and Moses 6:22).[243]

243. See also First Presidency of the Church, "Origin of Man," 75–81.

The Book of Mormon reveals other ways in which Jesus was distinct. Abinadi taught, "God himself should come down among the children of men, and take upon him the form of man, and go forth in mighty power upon the face of the earth" (Mosiah 13:34). Note that Abinadi did not say Jesus would be a man but rather he would have "the form of man." He insisted that "Christ was the God, the Father of all things, and said that he should take upon him the image of man, and it should be the image after which man was created in the beginning; or in other words, he said that man was created after the image of God, and that God should come down among the children of men, and take upon him flesh and blood, and go forth upon the face of the earth" (Mosiah 7:27).[244]

His point is that humankind was created in the image of God, not the other way around. Thus, the Savior appears to look like man, but in reality, it is man who looks like him. He set the pattern; man is, however, an excellent copy. Thus, the Savior is distinct, being the perfect model from which the image of humankind is derived. Speaking of his mortal form, the Book of Mormon teaches another point. Though he had a fine physical body, it was similar to that of many of the sons of Adam and Eve and therefore the Lord did not physically stand out. According to Mosiah 14:2 (compare Isa. 53:2), "he hath no form nor comeliness; and when we shall see him there is no beauty that we should desire him." There was no radiance, no angelic glory, no overpowering attractiveness, no unusual handsomeness nor manliness which made him really different. Mankind is created in the image of God, and the likeness is a good one.

But the Savior, aside from his image or form, was still God. This allowed him to fulfill his responsibilities and duties. According to King Benjamin, "he shall suffer temptations, and pain of body, hunger, thirst, and fatigue, even more than man can suffer, except it be unto death" (Mosiah 3:7). Note that the hunger, thirst, or fatigue he endured would kill a human. That Benjamin lists the Lord's temptations along with these pains suggests their extreme nature. Yet, in spite of all these more-than-human deeds, those unto whom he would come would "consider him a man, and say that he hath a devil, and scourge him, and crucify him" (Mosiah 3:9).

---

244. When the Lord appeared to the brother of Jared, he declared, "Behold, this body, which ye now behold, is the body of my spirit; and man have I created after the body of my spirit; and even as I appear unto thee to be in the spirit will I appear unto my people in the flesh" (Ether 3:16).

An angel asked the prophet Nephi a poignant question: "Knowest thou the condescension of God?" Nephi answered, "I know that he loveth his children; nevertheless, I do not know the meaning of all things" (1 Ne. 11:16–17). The angel then revealed to Nephi not only the condescension of God, but the love on which it was grounded. The term "condescension" means to descend from a higher to a lower state, to willingly waive the privileges of one's rank or dignity.[245] That God, the Son, came to the earth as fully mortal, giving up for a time his honor, glory, and power, and took upon himself all the weaknesses, shortcomings, and challenges emphasizes how far his condescension reached.

Further, the God Jesus would condescend to be baptized by the mortal man, John. As the angel said, "Behold the condescension of God! And I [Nephi] looked and beheld the Redeemer of the world, of whom my father had spoken; and I also beheld the prophet who should prepare the way before him. And the Lamb of God went forth and was baptized of him" (1 Ne. 11:26–27). Through this condescension, the Savior showed the way for all men and women no matter how high or low born (2 Ne. 31:4–10). Through his submission he humbled his flesh to the will of the Father and fulfilled his promise that he would show unto the children of men the way to eternal life.

Christ's love manifested itself in many ways during his mortal ministry. We will consider just three of those ways here. The first was in his service to others. Alma bears record, saying, "The Son of God shall come in his glory; and his glory shall be the glory of the Only Begotten of the Father, full of grace, equity, and truth, full of patience, mercy, and long-suffering, quick to hear the cries of his people and to answer their prayers. And behold, he cometh to redeem those who will be baptized unto repentance, through faith on his name" (Alma 9:26–27). These verses clearly detail the attributes which the mortal Messiah would manifest during his ministry. The scripture stresses the redeeming nature of his work. Nephi testifies of the Lord's love as he saw

> the Son of God going forth among the children of men; and I saw many fall down at his feet and worship him. . . . And I beheld that he went forth ministering unto the people, in power and great glory; and the multitudes

245. Byron R. Merrill, "Condescension of God," in Ludlow, *Encyclopedia of Mormonism,* 1:305, notes that "the condescension of God" has two possible interpretations: the first is that God the Father condescended to be the actual and perfect father of a mortal being; the second is that Christ condescended to experience the pains of mortal life.

> were gathered together to hear him. . . . And I beheld multitudes of people who were sick, and who were afflicted with all manner of diseases, and with the devils and the unclean spirits; and the angel spake and showed all these things unto me. And they were healed by the power of the Lamb of God; and devils and unclean spirits were cast out. (1 Ne. 11:24, 28, 31)

Through his love, the Lord manifests his power not only over the natural world but also over the demonic.

The second way that the Savior manifested his love was by suppressing his divine power so that he felt the full weight of mortality. As Alma states, "And he shall go forth, suffering pains and afflictions and temptations of every kind; and this that the word might be fulfilled which saith he will take upon him the pains and the sicknesses of his people. And he will take upon him death, that he may loose the bands of death which bind his people; and he will take upon him their infirmities, that his bowels may be filled with mercy, according to the flesh, that he may know according to the flesh how to succor his people according to their infirmities" (Alma 7:11–12). Alma reveals an important aspect of the Lord's mortal ministry that should not be overlooked. The Savior suffered affliction and pain and was not absolved from temptations of any kind so that he might fully understand his people. There is a popular notion that good people know little if anything about the power of temptation. This is patently false. It is the wicked who know little of its allure, seducing force, and punishing power because they never resist. How do they know what it is like to have to be strong for an hour, a day, or a year? The Savior never gave in. He stands alone as the one who never fell captive to the enticements of sin for a lifetime. He knows more about the power of temptation than any.[246] For this reason, he can "succor his people according to their infirmities."

He had to take upon himself the pains and afflictions of those whom he healed or forgave. When he healed and forgave sins, it took power out of him (see Luke 6:19; 8:46).[247] His love often pushed him to the point of physical and spiritual exhaustion. It was for this reason that he had to escape from the multitudes from time to time to find renewal in his Father or in desperately needed rest.

---

246. C. S. Lewis, *Mere Christianity: An Anniversary Edition of the Three Books The Case for Christianity, Christian Behavior, and Beyond Personality* (New York: Macmillan, 1981), 120.

247. Though the KJV translates the Greek as "virtue," the word is *dynamis*, "power."

Finally, the third way the Savior manifested his love was by not only being strong enough to endure the pain of healing and sin but also strong enough to overcome the excruciating pain of death and hell. As Nephi saw, the multitudes "cast him out from among them" and "the Son of the everlasting God was judged of the world." "And I, Nephi, saw that he was lifted up upon the cross and slain for the sins of the world" (1 Ne. 11:28, 32–33). Indeed, those who believed that he was but a man scourged and crucified him (Mosiah 3:9). Nephi reveals the basis of the Savior's willingness to endure both the pain and the humiliation:

> And the world, because of their iniquity, shall judge him to be a thing of naught; wherefore they scourge him, and he suffereth it; and they smite him, and he suffereth it. Yea, they spit upon him, and he suffereth it, because of his loving kindness and his long-suffering towards the children of men. And the God of our fathers, who were led out of Egypt, out of bondage, and also were preserved in the wilderness by him, yea, the God of Abraham, and of Isaac, and the God of Jacob, yieldeth himself, according to the words of the angel, as a man, into the hands of wicked men, to be lifted up, according to the words of Zenock, and to be crucified, according to the words of Neum. (1 Ne. 19:9–10)

It was in enduring these horrible deeds that the mortal God made manifest his long-suffering and loving kindness.

All this, the Book of Mormon prophets knew, was toward a divine end. As the Lord himself testifies,

> And my Father sent me that I might be lifted up upon the cross; and after that I had been lifted up upon the cross, that I might draw all men unto me, that as I have been lifted up by men even so should men be lifted up by the Father, to stand before me, to be judged of their works, whether they be good or whether they be evil—And for this cause have I been lifted up; therefore, according to the power of the Father I will draw all men unto me, that they may be judged according to their works. And it shall come to pass, that whoso repenteth and is baptized in my name shall be filled; and if he endureth to the end, behold, him will I hold guiltless before my Father at that day when I shall stand to judge the world. (3 Ne. 27:14–16)

The Book of Mormon acts as a second witness to the one in Hebrews 2:7–9, 17–18, that we worship a God who can be touched with both our strivings and failures, for he was indeed tried, tempted, and in this way filled with mercy and compassion. Thus, the author could say that Jesus "could become a merciful and faithful high priest over the things relating to God" (NR 2:17). "Because he himself has endured trials and temptations," the author testifies, "he is able to help those who are tried and tempted" (NR 2:18). As the author also testifies, "For we do not have a high priest who is unable to sympathize with our weaknesses, but . . . was tried and tempted in every way just like us" (NR 4:15). Because he is ever God and yet fully human, he knows mortality and loves mortals, perfectly understanding them because of his own personal experience.[248] The author's admonition ever applies: "So let us approach the throne of grace with confidence, so that we may receive mercy and find grace to help in time of need" (NR 4:16).

248. See S. Brent Farley, "The Baptism and Temptations of Jesus," in Jackson and Millet, *Studies in Scripture, Volume 5*, 175–87.

Excursus on the Atonement: A View from Hebrews

Christ as the Great High Priest

The author of Hebrews carefully explains his view of how the process of atonement operates. He does so by looking at the work of Christ through two lenses: first, that of High Priest, and second, that of the sacrifice. His view of Christ's atonement draws upon prevailing images from the religious heritage of his readers. The author's study of the role of Jesus has made a solid contribution to a more complete understanding of Jesus and his saving work.

The author sets the groundwork by revealing that the earthly priests were but types or shadows of the true priest, Jesus (8:5), but also that they were legitimately ordained to do the services of "things pertaining to God." They were especially authorized to make offerings and sacrifices for sin (5:1). Based on those ideas, the author validates the Lord's authority to perform priesthood acts. He shows the Lord's priesthood is greater than that of Aaron, for his was after the higher order of Melchizedek (5:6–7). Further, unlike that of the Levitical priests, his was established by a divine oath (7:21) that made it permanent (ἀπαράβατος, *aparabartos*) (7:24). The author of Hebrews went on to explain that Jesus became fully mortal in order to experience all the vicissitudes of life. That experience assured he would be a merciful and faithful high priest as he served his people.

One of the major tasks of the Levitical high priest was to intercede in behalf of the children of Israel by making an atonement for them (for example, see Ex. 30:16; Lev. 1:4; 4:20, 26, 31, 35; and many references throughout chapters 5, 9, 14, 16). This Jesus did by interceding for his people (Heb. 7:25) and making reconciliation for sin (2:17). The author of Hebrews witnesses that Jesus was totally faithful to this charge (3:2).

It is of special note that it was Jehovah who instituted the sacrificial system. He designed it to do two things: first, to allow a substitute to take the place of the offending party as the means through which sin could be covered over and thereby Jehovah's anger mitigated. Second, to provide a ransom that satisfied Jehovah's demands for some kind of satisfaction. Neither layman nor priest could determine what these atoning offerings would be. Jehovah made it clear that he and he alone could define them.[249] There was

249. BDB, 497–98, shows only Jehovah determines what is sufficient and satisfactory for the individual to sacrifice. The whole of the book of Leviticus details Jehovah's

good reason. As will be shown below, they were types of the sacrifice of the Son and, therefore, had to be precise in what they were intended to reveal.

The paradox must be noted and its implications understood. It was the offended party, Jehovah himself, who was the one who not only determined how the sin could be covered over, the breach crossed, and atonement made, but also who supplied the means (for example, see 1 Chr. 15:13; but also Lev. 4:20, 26; 5:10). Therefore, sacrifices were not essentially, albeit necessarily, a person's action. They were, rather, Jehovah's own act initiated by his own pardoning mercy.[250] Therefore, he designed them to give deep and poignant insight to those with eyes to see.

Jesus as the Great and Last Sacrifice

The author of Hebrews presents Jesus not just as High Priest but also as the consummate sacrifice. The law demanded blood be shed—the symbol of death—for expiation to be achieved (Lev. 16:11, 15–16; 17:11). This is because the effects of sin—the distancing from God, the harming of the soul, and the arousal of God's anger—must be dealt with and abrogated.[251] But, and this is important to note, that is the Savior's concern. It is his task to plead for the individual who has returned. To these souls, the Lord can say, "Listen to him who is the advocate with the Father, who is pleading your cause before him—Saying: Father, behold the sufferings and death of him who did no sin, in whom thou wast well pleased; behold the blood of thy Son which was shed, the blood of him whom thou gavest that thyself might be glorified; wherefore, Father, spare these my brethren that believe on my name, that they may come unto me and have everlasting life" (D&C 45:3–5). The Lord does not approach the Father on the merits of the one he pleads for but on his own. Thus, the person does not have to worry about this aspect of the process, knowing that the Son has acted as the advocate, the Father has already been satisfied, and the price of union has been paid.

The way Jesus put away the sin was by sacrificing himself for many (9:26, 28; 10:19; 13:12). The qualifier is of note. Though he overcame physical

---

instructions dealing with even minute aspects of the life of his people. That book, along with its companions Exodus and Deuteronomy, underscores Jehovah's refusal to allow humans to determine how to live in accordance to his will and more especially how to regain his favor.

250. BDB, 497–98.

251. S. Erlandsson, "The Wrath of YHWH," *Tyndale Bulletin* 23 (1972): 111–16, accessed March 14, 2016, https://legacy.tyndalehouse.com/tynbul/Library/TynBull_1972_23_07_Erlandsson_WrathOfGod.pdf.

death for all, he did not do so as far as spiritual death caused by individual disobedience was concerned.[252] It was limited in breadth to those willing to come under his atoning power. Nonetheless, in giving his life, he purged their sins and, thereby, cleansed these recipients from moral impurity (1:3; 9:14). This he did once for all (7:27) and, thereby, earned eternal redemption for all (9:12). In sum, the Savior paid the wage of sin with his own blood, dying so that all people might live. Through the Savior's expiation, he paid the wage of sin and made good the injury, thus removing all obstacles so that unity between the Father and his children could occur.

Immutability of God

The author of Hebrews, to teach an important point about the Lord, quoted Psalm 102:25–27: "Of old hast thou laid the foundation of the earth: and the heavens are the work of thy hands. They shall perish, but thou shalt endure: yea, all of them shall wax old like a garment; as a vesture shalt thou change them, and they shall be changed: But thou art the same, and thy years shall have no end." The author apparently chose this scripture not so much to stress the Lord's station but to emphasize one of his attributes, that of immutability. This term is found only in 6:17–18 as the translation of the Greek ἀμετάθετος (*ametathetos*). In that context, it denotes the unchangeable nature of Jehovah's counsel, oaths, and promises.

Theologians, however, have adopted the term to describe the very nature of God himself. Based on scriptures such as Exodus 3:14, where God says of himself, "I am that I am," and Psalm 90:2, which describes Jehovah as being "from everlasting to everlasting," theologians argue that God cannot change and is, thereby, immutable (see also Num. 23:19; 1 Sam. 15:29; Ps. 102:26; Mal. 3:6; 2 Tim. 2:13; James 1:17; Alma 7:20; Moro. 8:18; 9:10; and D&C 3:2; 20:17). Nearly all Christians agree with the definition found in Hebrews 1:12 and 13:8 that God is unchangeable in his character, will, and covenantal promises (see also 6:17–18; compare D&C 104:2).

Misunderstanding comes when these ideas are interpreted through the lens of Greek philosophy. Classical philosophers from Plato to Plotinus and Christian theologians from Augustine through Thomas Aquinas and into the modern era have all agreed that whatever is worthwhile and true is unchanging and must therefore be immaterial. "Things made of matter are

252. The first source of spiritual death is the fall of Adam wherein all his progeny were cut off from the presence of God (Hel. 14:16). This death, as well as the physical, was overcome by Christ for all.

constrained by time and place, and while there are truths about contingent things, which we call facts, metaphysical truths pertain to the way things have to be in order to be at all, regardless of their location or history. If this higher form of truth cannot be found in material things, then it must be looked for in the ideas and concepts that belong to logic and metaphysics. Truth, beauty, and goodness, it follows, lie beyond this world of fleeting appearances."[253] And that includes God. He is "the being of all that exists, but in such a way that God's own being is utterly beyond everything that we can know in this world. The world is knowable only in light of an essentially mysterious and absolutely 'other' deity."[254]

Theologians also insist that Jehovah's immutability defines all of his other attributes. He cannot gain knowledge since he knows all things eternally and infinitely. Further, he is all wise, fully merciful, good, and gracious. Because of that, he does not feel negative emotions such as anger, jealousy, or disappointment. Though the scriptures are full of such references, they are but anthropomorphisms that ascribe to Deity human emotions.[255]

Some theologians realized there was a problem with this view of an utterly unchangeable God because he did change from immaterial to material due to the incarnation. To resolve this problem, these theologians introduced the idea of variance. Though God could not change, he could vary. Because of this ability, his attitude could change toward a person from negative to positive based on his or her acceptance of God and his ways.[256] Even so, God never has nor ever will feel anger or distress over the acts of his children. Since his feelings cannot change, and because he is pure love, those scriptures that suggest he feels anger or jealousy do not describe reality but are a mere model used to motivate humans to do his will.

Restoration Insights: A God Who Feels

The Restoration has freed Latter-day Saint doctrine from those pieces of Platonic philosophy that contributed to the Nicene Creed and its conception of a mysterious, unknowable God. The Restoration made "personality ontologically basic" and as a result made "God more like us and thus more

253. Stephen H. Webb, *Mormon Christianity: What Other Christians Can Learn from the Latter-day Saints* (Oxford: Oxford University Press, 2013), 28–29.

254. Stephen H. Webb, "Toward a Mormon Systematic Theology: Essay on *Wrestling the Angel* by Terryl L. Givens," *BYU Studies Quarterly* 54, no. 1 (2015): 142.

255. James Strong, "New Strong's Expanded Dictionary . . . Hebrew," s.v. "אַף."

256. "Immutability of God," Theopedia.

intelligible."[257] Due to that freedom, it can be said that God's immutability, or unchangeableness, "does not preclude enlargement in his kingdom, nor, perhaps, new thoughts, new vistas, and new experiences."[258] According to Elder B. H. Roberts,

> [God's] immutability should be regarded as stability, adherence to principle. . . . But God's immutability should not be so understood as to exclude the idea of advancement or progress of God. Thus, for example: God's kingdom and glory may be enlarged, as more and more redeemed souls are added to his kingdom: as worlds and world-systems are multiplied and redeemed and enrolled with celestial spheres, so God's kingdom is enlarged and his glory increased. . . . An absolute immutability would require eternal immobility—which would reduce God to a condition eternally static, which, from the nature of things, would bar him from participating in that enlargement of kingdom and increasing glory that comes from redemption and progress of men. And is it too bold a thought, that with this progress, even for the Mightiest, new thoughts, and new vistas may appear, inviting to new adventures and enterprises that will yield new experiences, advancement, and enlargement even for the Most High?[259]

This also means that those scriptures which ascribe passions to God are not anthropomorphism but actual descriptions of his feelings. Attributing love, mercy, and kindness to him is correct but so is attributing to him jealousy and anger. The point is God can be offended, which is where the Atonement comes in. It is necessary because sin arouses God's anger.[260] The Father's intense displeasure would better be understood by the word "indignation." Where "anger" denotes a strong but undirected feeling of displeasure, "indignation" points to a more intense and deep feeling associated

---

257. Webb, "Systematic Theology," 142.

258. Alan K. Parrish, "Doctrine and Covenants Section 76 and the Visions of Resurrected Life in the Teachings of Elder John A. Widtsoe," in *Doctrines for Exaltation: The 1989 Sperry Symposium on the Doctrine and Covenants* (Salt Lake City: Deseret Book, 1989), 219.

259. B. H. Roberts, "Fourth Year, the Atonement," in *The Seventy's Course in Theology,* 2 vols. (Salt Lake City: Deseret News, 1907–12), 2, no. 4:66–67.

260. The English word "anger" is translated from the Hebrew word אַף (*'ap*). The noun denotes "nostril" or "nose" (Gen. 24:47), but it has come to connote anger in the sense of the "nostrils becoming hot, burning" as happens when one is angry (Gen. 30:2). The noun is often translated in a divine context as "his anger was kindled" or "his anger burned" (Ex. 4:14). Well before New Testament times, אַף (*'ap*) came to denote "anger" itself. Gen. 27:45; *HAL,* 76–77; BDB, 60. The phrase "to provoke to anger" is a translation of the word כָּעַס (*kā'as*). *HAL,* 491; BDB, 494. Both indicate God's response to the deliberate breaking of his laws.

with offended righteousness aroused by acts that are mean, shameful, or otherwise unworthy.[261]

Implications of a God Who Feels

The author of Hebrews is well aware that God sees that justice is served, for "every transgression and disobedience received a just recompence of reward" (2:2). This applied particularly to those who came out of Egypt. About them God said, "I was grieved with that generation, and said, They do alway err in their heart; and they have not known my ways. So I sware in my wrath, They shall not enter into my rest" (3:10–11). As noted above, one of God's attributes is divine wrath. Even the Savior is not above negative feelings. One of the reasons he received his high station was because he "hated iniquity" (1:9).

There is a very positive side to the idea that God can have negative emotions. It suggests the depth of his love for humankind. It gives answer to the question, "What is man, that thou art mindful of him? and the son of man, that thou visitest him?" (Ps. 8:4; compare Job 7:17). It is because God sets "his heart upon humankind" that he can be hurt. Enoch saw God's tears coming down as "rain upon the mountains" as the Father looked upon the abuses of humankind against humankind (Moses 7:28). Enoch saw that "it is not their wickedness, but their 'misery,' not their disobedience, but their 'suffering,' that elicits the God of Heaven's tears."[262]

But Enoch also saw something else. Humankind's wickedness triggered more than sorrow. The Lord explained to Enoch that he had given humankind a "commandment, that they should love one another, and that they should choose me, their Father; but behold, they are without affection, and they hate their own blood; and the fire of mine indignation is kindled against them; and in my hot displeasure will I send in the floods upon them" (Moses 7:33–34; see also Deut. 4:25; 6:15; 29:28; Ps. 7:11; Isa. 1:4; 34:2; Jer. 32:30; Eph. 5:3–7; Col. 3:6; Alma 12:36; and D&C 29:17; 35:14; 43:26; 56:1; 87:6).

The scripture clearly shows that sin evokes God's indignation. The noun ἁμαρτία (*hamartia*), "sin," originally meant "missing the mark," suggesting

261. *Webster's New Dictionary of Synonyms,* s.v. "anger."

262. Terryl Givens and Fiona Givens, *The God Who Weeps: How Mormonism Makes Sense of Life* (Salt Lake City: Ensign Peak, 2012), 25. Givens and Givens note that God's love for humankind "means responsibility, sacrifice, vulnerability" on his part. He has chosen to love "even at, necessarily at, the price of vulnerability." Indeed, "his freely made choice to inaugurate and sustain costly loving relationships *is* the very core of his identity." Givens and Givens, *God Who Weeps,* 24.

going beyond what is proper or good.[263] By New Testament times this idea had faded and the word had come to denote a moral deviation that consisted of two parts: unfaithfulness to God and disobedience to his law.[264] It connoted any act that distanced a person from God and more especially the determination of a person to be a law unto him or herself (10:16–31, 39; see also D&C 88:35).

Though God is loving, that he feels indignation means that sin will not happen without impunity.[265] As Elder Dallin H. Oaks stated,

> Some seem to value God's love because of their hope that His love is so great and so unconditional that it will mercifully excuse them from obeying His laws. In contrast, those who understand God's plan for His children know that God's laws are invariable, which is another great evidence of His love for His children. Mercy cannot rob justice, and those who obtain mercy are "they who have kept the covenant and observed the commandment" (D&C 54:6).
>
> We read again and again in the Bible and in modern scriptures of God's anger with the wicked and of His acting in His wrath against those who violate His laws. How are anger and wrath evidence of His love? Joseph Smith taught that God "institute[d] laws whereby [the spirits that He would send into the world] could have a privilege to advance like himself." God's love is so perfect that He lovingly requires us to obey His commandments because He knows that only through obedience to His laws can we

---

263. For discussion, see Paul Y. Hoskisson, "Looking beyond the Mark," in *A Witness for the Restoration: Essays in Honor of Robert J. Matthews,* ed. Kent P. Jackson and Andrew C. Skinner (Provo, Utah: Religious Studies Center, Brigham Young University, 2007), 149–64.

264. *NID,* s.v. "ἁμαρτία"; compare D&C 88:21, 35.

265. The Lord clearly makes this point in his earliest biblical description of himself. There he states, "Thou shalt worship no other god: for the Lord, whose name is Jealous, is a jealous God" (Ex. 34:14). The Hebrew word translated as "jealousy," קַנָּא (*qannā'*), can also be translated as "intense zeal," and "strong ardor." It describes the emotion which causes one to act to safeguard a valued object or possession. To one who would turn against him, the Lord warns, "The Lord will not spare him, but then [when the person turns away] the anger of the Lord and his jealousy shall smoke against that man" (Deut. 29:20). Here, Jehovah ties his anger and his jealousy together. The point is this: God's judgments are a reflection of his jealousy and are motivated by his indignation. Thus, the judgments of God do not reflect a blind, aloof, and mechanically operative force. They reflect neither *karma* nor fate. The judgments of God come from an "absolute and totally personal Creator" whose judgment "operates within the context of His love and hate, His grace towards his people and His wrath towards His enemies." Rousas John Rushdoony, *The Institutes of Biblical Law* (n.p.: Presbyterian and Reformed Publishing, 1973), 24. God's jealousy is the total assurance that no one is going to *ultimately* get away with anything.

become perfect, as He is. For this reason, God's anger and His wrath are not a *contradiction* of His love but an *evidence* of His love.[266]

Paul fully understood the universal truth that the "wages of sin is death" (Rom. 6:23). A sterling example, as the author of Hebrews shows, is the consequence of the rebellion of the children of Israel in the wilderness (3:16–19). Though death refers to both a physical condition (the separation of the body from the spirit) and a spiritual one (the separation of a person from God), since the Savior overcame both physical death and the first spiritual death unconditionally for all (Alma 40:11, 26), it is only spiritual death caused by a person's disobedience that is in view here.[267]

The Need for Atonement

The scriptures are replete with statements about the Savior's Atonement. There is, however, much that is lacking. A case in point is the treatment in Hebrews, which focuses on only two aspects of the Lord's work. As a result of the lack of a comprehensive study in the Bible, a number of theories have been put forth to explain why the Atonement was needed and how it worked.[268] They are all a response to the perceived nature of sin. Sin is, at the least, "a violation of a moral norm and . . . the effects are more extensive than a guilty conscience."[269] Though repentance requires a verbal acknowledgement of regret and restitution to the degree possible, that does not militate fully against sin's enduring legacy. A fateful act creates a situation that must be removed, not simply ignored or brushed aside. The act of sin creates a condition described scripturally by means of a number of metaphors, including the breaking of a soul, the soiling of the hands or garments, the placing of a heavy weight on the shoulders, and the gaining of a substantial debt. Removal of the consequences of sin, therefore, entails someone healing the soul, cleansing the hands, lifting the burden,

---

266. Oaks, "Love and Law," 26–27, italics in original.

267. For a comprehensive review for that portion of the Lord's work that was universally efficacious, see David L. Paulsen, "The Redemption of the Dead: A Latter-day Saint Perspective on the Fate of the Unevangelized," in *Salvation in Christ: Comparative Christian Views,* ed. Roger R. Keller and Robert L. Millet (Provo, Utah: Religious Studies Center, Brigham Young University, 2005), 263–98.

268. Because a discussion of these theories lies outside the parameters of this study, they are not developed here. For a brief overview, see Leon Morris, "Theories of the Atonement," Monergism.com, accessed March 15, 2016, http://www.monergism.com/thethreshold/articles/onsite/atonementmorris2.html.

269. Gary A. Anderson, *Sin: A History* (New Haven, Conn.: Yale University Press, 2010), 3.

and paying the debt.[270] The point of agreement is that the cure comes from outside the self. But it must be kept in mind that the consequence of sin, no matter what the metaphor, is estrangement of the person from God.

The author of Hebrews views the Savior's work as that cure. Jesus' death was to make reconciliation (ἱλάσκομαι, *hilaskomai*) between the Saint and God (2:17). The particular metaphor the author uses for sin is that of soiling the individual, which then necessitates a cleansing from moral impurity (1:3; 9:12–14). Such cleansing is necessary if the individual is to return to God. God's indignation for sin is genuine, but so is the constancy of his mercy, and where the latter never dissipates, the former can (Ps. 85:4; 103:9; Isa. 48:9; 2 Ne. 20:25; D&C 98:47–48). Indeed, it is because of the everlasting nature of his mercy and the transitory nature of his indignation that the Lord provides the means by which his anger can be mitigated. In the Old Testament, forgiveness came through ritual—albeit hopefully based on repentance—primarily through an elaborate system of sacrifices. It is the imagery of those sacrifices taking place on the Day of Atonement that the author keeps before his readers (9:1–28). Once forgiveness came, atonement was possible.

The Hebrew verb כִּפֵּר (*kipper*), translated "to atone for sin,"[271] carries the root meaning of "to cover over" but not in the sense of hiding something as much as preventing its negative effects. The word is used most often in connection with sacrificial rites, where the spiritual consequences of sin had to be covered over in order for its penalty—in this case, the loss of Jehovah's favor and the execution of his indignation—to be annulled. The covering acted as the purification.

In that light, *kipper* denotes an act to make an offended party willing to forgive (Ps. 32:5) or to appease his or her wrath (Prov. 16:14). But when Jehovah is the subject, *kipper* takes on the sense "to purge, to make expiation" or "to forgive" (Ps. 65:3; 78:38). Its result is a cleansing from sin.

---

270. Anderson, *Sin,* x, notes that the primary metaphor for the effect of sin across the scriptures is that of stain, but he traces how sin, viewed initially as weight that must be lifted and carried away, was replaced by the idea of debt that can only be satisfied by repayment, forgiveness, or punishment. This idea of sin as debt stands behind the New Testament idea that the Savior's Atonement paid the debt of sin and he can, therefore, forgive the sinner. See particularly pp. 3–5 in this work.

271. In the KJV, the *pi'el* form of the verb was translated various ways to represent some form of atonement: "atone" more than seventy times, "purge" or "purge away" nine times, "reconcile" or "reconciliation" seven times, "forgive" three times, "pacify" two times, "merciful" two times, "cleanse" two times, and "disannul," "appease," "put off," and "pardon" one time each. Strong, "New Strong's Expanded Dictionary . . . Hebrew," s.v. "כָּפַר."

Because of his grace, Jehovah expiates guilt by withdrawing his anger and purging the sin. If Jehovah does not atone or make expiation, the sinner must die (Isa. 22:14; Jer. 18:23), but if Jehovah does so, the person lives (Ps. 118:17–18). Jehovah's purpose is clearly stated in the instructions for the sin offering: "The priest shall make an atonement for them, and it shall be forgiven them" (Lev. 4:20, 26, 31, 35).[272]

The KJV translation of 1:3 states that Jesus "purged our sins." The noun καθαρισμός (*katharismos*), "purge," refers to cleansing or purifying an object. Though the LXX generally uses this term to refer to becoming clean from cultic impurity so that one can worship in the temple,[273] the author stresses a cleansing from *inward* pollutions, those that stain and corrupt the soul and thereby estrange it from God.[274] Even so, he is aware of the importance of the external ritual washings in the salvation process, admonishing his readers, "Approach the sanctuary with a true heart in full assurance of faith, having our hearts cleansed from a consciousness of evil and having our bodies washed with pure water" (10:22). He may be alluding to baptism,[275] but he seems to have preparation for temple worship in mind.[276] This would be in keeping with his Old Testament imagery, looking at the need for the high priest to wash himself before entering into the Most Holy Place (Lev. 16:4). Jehovah did promise his people that he would "sprinkle clean water" upon them through which they would receive a "new heart" and a "new spirit." The result of the outward ordinance would give his people the ability to keep and administer his statutes (Ezek. 36:25–27).[277]

---

272. The Book of Mormon puts an additional twist on the matter by introducing the idea of satisfying not just God but the demands of the law. "And if there was no law given, if men sinned what could justice do, or mercy either, for they would have no claim upon the creature? But there is a law given, and a punishment affixed, and a repentance granted; which repentance, mercy claimeth; otherwise, justice claimeth the creature and executeth the law, and the law inflicteth the punishment; if not so, the works of justice would be destroyed, and God would cease to be God" (Alma 42:21–22). This passage does not suggest the law operates independent of God, for it is "given," but it does make the punishment less personal on God's part. See also Spackman, "Israelite Roots of Atonement Terminology," 39–64.

273. For a study, see Dunnill, *Covenant and Sacrifice*, 69–111.

274. BDAG, 489; Delling, *TDNT*, 1:475–76.

275. William L. Lane, *Hebrews 9–13*, vol 47b of Word Biblical Commentary, ed. David A. Hubbard and Glenn W. Barker (Dallas: Word Book Publisher, 1991), 287; Anderson, *Understanding Paul*, 218–19.

276. O'Brien, *Letter to the Hebrews*, 367–68; Cockerill, *Epistle to the Hebrews*, 475.

277. Though the context suggests an outward washing, the effect is an inward cleansing. See Bruce, *Epistle to the Hebrews*, 255.

As the great High Priest, Jesus offered himself as the eternal atoning sacrifice with power to cleanse both conscience and soul (1:3; 9:14). He became

> the mediator of this new and better covenant (Heb. 8:6), putting the law of God into the hearts of his people (Heb. 8:10; 10:16). The old law (of Moses), with its performances and sacrifices, had been fulfilled. Through the new covenant, God promised to remember the sins of the repentant no more (Heb. 10:17), and each Saint was challenged to enter into "a new and living way" through the blood of Christ (Heb. 10:15–20). Those who were willing to do so in patience and faith would be justified [that is, become free of sin] and receive the promise (Heb. 10:35–38).[278]

All this Jesus did once for everyone (7:27) and thereby earned eternal redemption for all (9:12).

The Sacrificial System as Prophecy by Ordinance

The author of Hebrews uses the imagery of the Old Testament priests and procedures to great advantage (see particularly chapters 9–10). He sees them as types and shadows (8:5) that help the individual understand more fully the role of Christ as both sacrifice and High Priest. God placed the types and shadows there from the inception of the law of sacrifice. Through revelation, the righteous knew that salvation would come through the sacrifice of the Son. The law of sacrifice was instituted in the days of Adam to emphasize this point. Indeed, as an angel explained to Adam, "This thing is a similitude of the sacrifice of the Only Begotten of the Father, which is full of grace and truth. Wherefore, thou shalt do all that thou doest in the name of the Son, and thou shalt repent and call upon God in the name of the Son forevermore" (Moses 5:7–8; see also Jacob 4:4–5; and Mosiah 3:15). Even the elaborate system revealed to Moses was, at its base, both symbolic and prophetic, looking as it did to the future atoning act of the Son. This system of prophecy through ordinance was designed to point the soul to Christ, and "for this cause it [was] sanctified unto [the believers] for righteousness" (Jacob 4:5).[279]

However, even though the Savior has expiated all taint of sin, oneness with the Father has not yet been achieved. Though the Savior has set up all the conditions to make that possible, the last move is on the part of the

278. Draper, "Hebrews, Epistle to the," 1:581–82.

279. For a study, see Julie M. Smith, "Point Our Souls to Christ: Lessons from Leviticus," in *Studies in the Bible and Antiquity* 1 (2009): 67–82, accessed March 13, 2016, https://scholarsarchive.byu.edu/cgi/viewcontent.cgi?article=1010&context=sba.

person. God will not force a person to heaven. Though all may be set in order, their return must be an act of will on their part. In short, the person themself must decide if they want to live with God—and that requires living his kind of life, that is, being holy as he is holy. As the author of Hebrews states, the end of all is so "that we might be partakers of his holiness" (12:10).

Mortal life, as designed by God, is meant to be transformative (10:10, 22–25). It is a preparatory state wherein a person puts off the "natural man" and becomes "a child" of God (Mosiah 3:19–20; Alma 42:10), walking in all holiness before the Lord (D&C 21:4). The author of Hebrews notes that the reason the Mosaic system did not work was because it did not purge the conscience of sin (10:2–4). Even so, it did show the way, for even under the new covenant, the heart had to be "sprinkled from an evil conscience, and our bodies washed with pure water" (10:22). Through the double preparation of both soul and body, God could write his word on the heart and, thereby, transform the person's life (8:10–12). As a result, God will be merciful toward sins. Indeed, he will remember them no more (8:12).

The Role of Repentance

A major drive for the author of Hebrews was to warn his readers of the consequence of sin, especially that of faithlessness, and to encourage them not to let the promise of eternal life drift away (2:1). To continue on a path of unfaithfulness would bring "a just recompence" (2:2). Indeed, those who fell away would find it hard to come to repentance that would renew them again (6:4–6). To make his point, he appealed to the Mosaic law.

Though the law of performances and ordinances, focused as it was on outward conformance, led to a legalistic interpretation of the law of Moses, the real purpose of that law was the transformation of the human heart. Indeed, as more than one prophet made clear, hundreds of sacrifices without rendering such a change would not satisfy Jehovah's righteousness (Ps. 50:7–15; Micah 6:7) and therefore had no merit. Through Isaiah the Lord declared,

> To what purpose is the multitude of your sacrifices unto me? saith the Lord: I am full of the burnt offerings of rams, and the fat of fed beasts; and I delight not in the blood of bullocks, or of lambs, or of he goats. When ye come to appear before me, who hath required this at your hand, to tread my courts? Bring no more vain oblations; incense is an abomination unto me; the new moons and sabbaths, the calling of assemblies, I cannot away with; it is iniquity, even the solemn meeting. Your new moons and your

> appointed feasts my soul hateth: they are a trouble unto me; I am weary to bear them. And when ye spread forth your hands, I will hide mine eyes from you: yea, when ye make many prayers, I will not hear: your hands are full of blood. (Isa. 1:11–15)

Thus, it was not attending meetings, honoring holidays, or performing rituals—including participating in sacrificial rites—that satisfied Jehovah's righteousness and mitigated his anger. Rather, it was repentance that counted.

In the KJV, two Hebrew words are translated as "to repent." The first, נִחַם (*niḥam*), denotes both "to be sorry, regret, repent" and "to be comforted." The verb carries the idea of making a strong turn from a wrong course of action to a correct one through which a person finds, at last, comfort.[280] The stress of the word is on the visible change that takes place in the repentant person's actions and its result, namely returning to God and the feeling of well-being that brings.[281]

The second word, שׁוּב (*šûb*), denotes "a turning back" or a coming back to a position one formerly held. It also implies a cessation of wrong action. At its heart, then, this verb, like the word *niḥam,* connotes a returning to the relationship one originally had with God. It also implies conversion—a change of disposition and character—that results from the action.[282]

What is missing from the thrust of both verbs is the negative view of repentance that colors so much of Christian, including Latter-day Saint, misunderstanding of the principle. Neither word looks at the process as some kind of punishment, nor do they suggest it is something by which an individual escapes pain and punishment, though that is indeed the case. Their focus is not so much on sin as it is on return. In sum, it is the correcting of one's course that ultimately leads to comfort from a restored relationship with the Father and the Son that counts.

There are, then, two stages in the process of forgiveness. The Old Testament refers to these as, first, the covering over of the sin (כִּפֵּר, *kipper,* "to appease, make amends, make atonement"),[283] and second, the cleansing of

---

280. The English word "comfort" is derived from Latin *com-,* "with," and *fortis,* "strength," suggesting that in the process of repentance a person exerts strength leading to a change of course and action. *Merriam-Webster's Collegiate Dictionary,* 11 ed. (2008), s.v. "comfort."

281. BDB, 636; *HAL,* 688; R. Laird Harris, Gleason L. Archer Jr., and Bruce K. Waltke, eds., *Theological Wordbook of the Old Testament,* 2 vols. (Chicago: Moody Press, 1980), 1344 (hereafter cited as *TWOT* with the word's reference number following).

282. BDB, 996, 1000, 1117; *HAL,* 1429–32; *TWOT,* 2340.

283. *HAL,* 484.

its effects (טָהֵר, *ṭihar,* "to cleanse, purify, pronounce clean").[284] In the context of the New Testament, the noun ἱλασμός (*hilasmos*) is used to indicate the setting aside of sin as guilt against God.[285] Such expiation denotes the expunging of the guilt, the cleansing of the individual, and his or her reconciliation to God—in a word, "atonement." This was an important point for the author of Hebrews (2:17). In this setting, reconciliation does not imply any propitiation of God. Reconciliation refers instead to the purpose which God himself has fulfilled by sending his Son to intercede for the individual. Hence, the force of the word emphasizes God's graciousness and expresses his love.

The Indignation of God

The author of Hebrews is well aware of the reality of the indignation of the Father. Indeed, rebellion can bring out the full measure of God's wrath (3:11; 4:3). The author assures his readers the Father is acutely aware of all that goes on and none can escape him (4:12–13). Those who continue in faithlessness will find that they have lost their chance of salvation (4:1). The author, therefore, warns his readers to take heed "lest there be in any of you an evil heart of unbelief, in departing from the living God" (3:12). Indeed, his readers must not be "slothful, but followers of them who through faith and patience inherit the promises" (6:12). The righteous, however, need not be concerned with God's indignation. Due to the Atonement of the Savior and through their own repentance, the Father remembers the sins of the faithful no more (8:12).

That is not, however, the case with the recalcitrant sinner. The author of Hebrews is well aware

> it is impossible, concerning those who have once been enlightened, who have tasted the heavenly gift, who have become partakers of the Holy Ghost, and who have tasted the good word of God and the wonders of the world to come, if they should fall into apostasy, to restore them again to repentance. Because they crucify the Son of God again for themselves and hold him up to contempt. For if soil soaks up the rain that often falls upon it and produces useful vegetation for those on whose account the

---

284. *HAL,* 369–70.

285. Herrmann, *TDNT,* 3:301–10; Büchel, *TDNT,* 3:310–18. The word ἱλασμός only appears twice in the New Testament, in 4:10 and 1 John 2:2. Its cognate ἱλαστήριον also only appears twice—at Rom. 3:25, where it denotes the "means of expiation," and Heb. 9:5, where it refers to the mercy seat in the tabernacle.

> land is tilled, it receives a blessing from God. But if it produces thorns and thistles, it is worthless and is going to be cursed. In the end it will be burned. (NR 6:4–8)

Having refused to repent before the final judgment, those who refuse God's ways will feel the full weight of his indignation.

The Restoration provides plenty of details on what happens to these people. As God told Enoch, "I will shut them up; a prison have I prepared for them . . . [and] they shall be in torment" (Moses 7:38–39). The prison is hell and these souls will feel its full effects (Isa. 66:24; Mark 9:43; Mosiah 2:38; D&C 43:33). The scriptures describe the torment as burning in "a lake of fire and brimstone" (for example, see 2 Ne. 9:16; Jacob 3:11; Mosiah 3:27; and D&C 63:17; 76:36–37). The imagery is figurative, but the pain it suggests is real. Joseph Smith taught that "man is his own tormentor, and is his own condemner,"[286] and each will feel a fire of conscience set ablaze by a remorseful realization of the pain and agony their sins caused (Mosiah 2:38; Alma 36:12–16).

Concerning the work of hell, one scholar noted that even here (and perhaps especially here) God's mercy is extended, allowing—if not forcing—sinners to be "cleansed through suffering that would have been obviated by the Atonement of Christ had they repented during mortality (D&C 19:15–20; Alma 40:13–14). At the last resurrection . . . hell will give up [these] captive spirits. Many of these spirits will enter into the telestial kingdom in their resurrected state (2 Ne. 9:10–12; D&C 76:84–89, 106; Rev. 20:13). . . . [They] will be cleansed, will cease to experience the fiery torment of mind, and will be resurrected with their physical bodies."[287]

The reason why they will cease to feel such racking pain, however, must be noted. These people will eventually repent, reach to Christ, and be blessed by his Atonement. As the Father explained to Enoch, he whom "I have chosen hath pled before my face. Wherefore, he suffereth for their sins; [and] inasmuch as they will repent in the day that my Chosen shall return unto me" they will become free (Moses 7:39).

The experience of Alma the Younger is telling. He states that, due to his own willful rebellion, he was for "three days and three nights in the

286. "Conference Minutes," *Times and Seasons* 5 (August 15, 1844): 616, online as "Discourse, 7 April 1844, as Reported by *Times and Seasons*," Joseph Smith Papers, https://www.josephsmithpapers.org/paper-summary/discourse-7-april-1844-as-reported-by-times-and-seasons/5.

287. M. Catherine Thomas, "Hell," in Ludlow, *Encyclopedia of Mormonism*, 2:585–86.

most bitter pain and anguish of soul" (Alma 38:8). He also reported, "I was racked with eternal torment, for my soul was harrowed up to the greatest degree and racked with all my sins. Yea, I did remember all my sins and iniquities, for which I was tormented with the pains of hell" (Alma 36:12–13). However, the suffering did stop. He reports that eventually "I did cry out unto the Lord Jesus Christ for mercy, . . . and I did find peace to my soul." Not only did he find peace, but also he received "a remission of my sins" (Alma 38:8).

It should be noted that Alma's suffering moved him to Christ, and as a result, as he testifies, "My soul was filled with joy as exceeding as was my pain" (Alma 36:20). Further, a vision was opened to him and he saw God "sitting upon his throne, . . . and my soul did long to be there" (Alma 36:22). Through the work of the Savior, Alma had become holy. As a result, he yearned to be with God.

What is critical is Alma's suffering changed the heart of neither the Father nor the Son. It did not cause God to move closer to him. The Father was always there. He had given his Only Begotten Son to make expiation for Alma. When Alma accepted what the Savior had done, he received the mercy he sought. But even the mercy was already there. Alma just had to reach out and get it. Reconciliation came when Alma, not God, finally moved.

Knowing that reconciliation was possible, the author of Hebrews assures his readers, "Regarding you we are confident of better things that pertain to salvation. For God is not unjust so as to overlook your labor and love that you have demonstrated for his name by having served the saints and continuing to do so. Now we desire that each of you demonstrate the same earnestness toward the full assurance of your hope until the end, so that you do not become lazy, but emulators of those who through faith and patience inherit the promises" (NR 6:9–12).

Grace in Hebrews

The author is very aware of the role grace plays in the salvation process. It is worth mentioning, however, that Paul concentrates on grace and justification (for example, see Rom. 3:24–26) while the author of Hebrews concentrates on expiation and sanctification. Even so, the idea of unearned divine assistance is definitely there. It was through God's grace that Jesus suffered death for all (2:9), a heart (the very soul of the individual) is secured (13:9), and a person can properly serve God (12:28). One can lose God's grace by deliberate and especially spiteful disobedience (12:15, 29). These passages show that the author is very aware of the importance of grace, but he apparently assumes his readers' acceptance of this doctrine and, therefore, does not focus on it as did Paul.

The Restoration backs up Hebrews on the importance of grace in the salvation process. The term "grace" denotes the positive predisposition that God has for his children and its absolute necessity in the salvation process. According to the Book of Mormon, "It is only in and through the grace of God that ye are saved" (2 Ne. 10:24). Further, "We know that it is by grace that we are saved, after all we can do" (2 Ne. 25:23).[288] Though individuals must do their part, "redemption cometh in and through the Holy Messiah; for he is full of grace and truth" (2 Ne. 2:6). The prophet Jacob testified that "the Lord God showeth us our weakness that we may know that it is by his grace, and his great condescensions unto the children of men, that we have power to do these things" (Jacob 4:7). Further, Moroni testified that it is by the grace of God that one becomes perfect in Christ (Moro. 10:32–33). And the Lord assures his readers, "My grace is sufficient for all men that humble themselves before me; for if they humble themselves before me, and have faith in me, then will I make weak things become strong unto them" (Ether 12:27).

Summary

It is the Father who designed the means by which a returning party could, once again, come to oneness with him. The author of Hebrews shows how the rituals and history of the Old Testament era all point to the willingness of God to bring his people back to him. He, the offended party, provided both the way (repentance) and the means (the sacrifice of his Son) for that oneness to occur. But the heart of the Savor's salvific work was not the placation of God but to bring reconciliation. Since the Father is the one who instituted the means by which reconciliation could be met, the sacrifices and other acts he designed were neither to placate nor to mollify him nor even to gain his favor. As the Apostle John noted, "Herein is love, not that we loved God, but that he loved us, and sent his Son to be the propitiation

288. Some aspects of the Atonement are unearned and unmerited. They are acts of sheer grace. Other aspects do require a response from the Saint. Even here, however, the degree to which the reception of grace is merited can be questioned. Jeffrey R. Holland, "Atonement of Jesus Christ," in Ludlow, *Encyclopedia of Mormonism,* 1:82–86. For other studies on grace, see Stephen E. Robinson, *Believing Christ: The Parable of the Bicycle and Other Good News* (Salt Lake City: Deseret Book, 1992); Robert L. Millet, *Grace Works* (Salt Lake City: Deseret Book, 2003); and Sheri Dew, *Amazed by Grace* (Salt Lake City: Deseret Book, 2015).

for our sins" (1 John 4:10; see also 1 John 2:2).[289] His indignation toward sinful acts and those who perpetuate them does not suppress let alone extinguish his love. The fact that he set up both the way and the means by which a sinner can find holiness and thereby oneness with him demonstrates that reconciliation is not of God toward humankind, but of humankind toward God.[290] He is the one who reaches out to us in order to make it possible for us to be united with him. Therefore, we, with the readers of Hebrews, can take heart, and "since we have a great high priest who has passed through the heavens, even Jesus the Son of God, let us hold firmly to our confessed allegiance to him. For we do not have a high priest who is unable to sympathize with our weaknesses, but although he was tried and tempted in every way just like us, he was without sin. So let us approach the throne of grace with confidence, so that we may receive mercy and find grace to help in time of need" (NR 4:14–16).

289. John twice describes Christ as ἱλασμός ... περὶ τῶν ἁμαρτιῶν ἡμῶν (*hilasmos ... peri tōn hamartiōn hēmōn*) (1 John 2:2 and 4:10). This can either be translated as "an expiation (KJV propitiation) for our sins" or "a sin-offering for our sins." BDAG, 474. Paul, in Rom. 3:25, calls Christ a ἱλαστήριον (*hilastērion*), a "means of expiation."

290. TDNT, 3:317.

Chapter 3

Come Out of the Wilderness "Today"

Introduction

With this chapter, the author of Hebrews begins the second major division of his treatment of Jesus as divine Son and High Priest. His discussion will run through 5:10. He begins by building on the two characteristics that make Jesus attractive as priest: his mercifulness and faithfulness (2:17). The author develops them, however, in reverse order from the sequence in which he introduced them. He begins with a study of Jesus' faithfulness (3:1–6) and then contrasts that with the faithlessness of Israel's forebearers. He next admonishes his readers to take a lesson from the senseless tragedy of the loss of divine favor that overtook these hard-hearted and rebellious souls (3:7–4:14). Finally, he gives his readers hope by focusing on the compassion of the Savior, who fulfills his role as the merciful High Priest in the service of his God (4:15–5:10).[1]

In the first section (3:1–6), the author clearly states the lesson he wants his readers to get from what he has told them about the Lord. That lesson is strong and poignant. He stresses the need for his readers not to abandon the Lord but rather to imitate his faithfulness. To make his point, the author contrasts Jesus with Moses. Doing so discloses his genius. Moses was revered second only to Abraham by most Jews.[2] Moses was "the unique agent of revelation and divinely chosen leader" who established the house

---

1. Lane, *Hebrews 1–8,* 68.

2. For example, Philo refers to Moses as both "high priest" (*Her.* 82; *Sacr.* 130; *Mos.* 1.334, 2.2–7, 66–70, 153, 187, 275) and, of interest, "god" (*Mos.* 1.158; *Somn.* 2.189), coming from the Lord's statement "I have made thee god to Pharaoh" (Ex. 7:1). See also Jeremias, *TDNT,* 4:849, who notes that Moses was viewed as higher than the angels and as the central figure in Jewish salvation history. Latter-day Saints also hold him in high regard. See McConkie, *Promised Messiah,* 441–42.

of Israel.[3] The author takes nothing away from the prophet's greatness but heightens that of the Savior by contrasting Moses' station as the builder of the house of Israel with that of Jesus, who is its ruler.

In the second section (3:7–19), the author gives his readers a stiff warning. They are not to follow after the disobedience of their ancestors, who had been given every opportunity to enter into the promised land where they could find rest but instead rebelled. Using LXX Psalm 94:7b–11 as his scriptural text (3:7–11), the author emphasizes that through their lack of faith, they lost everything (3:19). Showing the results of history, the author assures his readers that the same could happen to them (3:11–12). His point is that they are fully accountable to the word of God as now revealed, not through prophets such as Moses but by the Father's own Son.[4] Therefore, they must pay heed lest they let the reward "drift away" (2:1) and they find themselves, like their ancestors, cut off from the "rest" of the Lord (3:18–19).

Jesus Greater than Moses (3:1–6)

Greek Text

1 Ὅθεν, ἀδελφοὶ ἅγιοι, κλήσεως ἐπουρανίου μέτοχοι, κατανοήσατε τὸν ἀπόστολον καὶ ἀρχιερέα τῆς ὁμολογίας ἡμῶν Ἰησοῦν, 2 πιστὸν ὄντα τῷ ποιήσαντι αὐτὸν ὡς καὶ Μωϋσῆς ἐν τῷ οἴκῳ αὐτοῦ. 3 πλείονος γὰρ οὗτος δόξης παρὰ Μωϋσῆν ἠξίωται καθ' ὅσον πλείονα τιμὴν ἔχει τοῦ οἴκου ὁ κατασκευάσας αὐτόν· 4 πᾶς γὰρ οἶκος κατασκευάζεται ὑπό τινος, ὁ δὲ πάντα κατασκευάσας θεός. 5 καὶ Μωϋσῆς μὲν πιστὸς ἐν ὅλῳ τῷ οἴκῳ αὐτοῦ ὡς θεράπων εἰς μαρτύριον τῶν λαληθησομένων, 6 Χριστὸς δὲ ὡς υἱὸς ἐπὶ τὸν οἶκον αὐτοῦ· ὅς οἶκός ἐσμεν ἡμεῖς, ἐὰν τὴν παρρησίαν καὶ τὸ καύχημα τῆς ἐλπίδος κατάσχωμεν. [SBLGNT]

King James Version

1 Wherefore, holy brethren, partakers of the heavenly calling, consider the Apostle and High Priest of our profession, Christ Jesus; 2 Who was faithful to

New Rendition

1 Therefore, holy brothers and sisters, partners in a heavenly calling, carefully consider Jesus, the apostle and high priest whom we confess. 2 He was

---

3. Cockerill, *Epistle to the Hebrews,* 153.

4. Clyde J. Williams, "Whoso Treasureth Up My Word Shall Not Be Deceived," in Jackson and Skinner, eds., *Witness for the Restoration,* 129–47, who, in his careful analysis, investigates the power, meaning, and purpose of God's "word," especially as revealed through the Book of Mormon.

him that appointed him, as also Moses was faithful in all his house. 3 For this man was counted worthy of more glory than Moses, inasmuch as he who hath builded the house hath more honour than the house. 4 For every house is builded by some man; but he that built all things is God. 5 And Moses verily was faithful in all his house, as a servant, for a testimony of those things which were to be spoken after; 6 But Christ as a son over his own house; whose house are we, if we hold fast the confidence and the rejoicing of the hope firm unto the end.

faithful to the one who appointed him, just like Moses was in all God's household. 3 For Jesus has been found to be worthy of greater glory than Moses, just as the builder of a house has greater honor than the house itself. 4 For every house is built by someone, but the builder of all things is God. 5 Now Moses was faithful as a servant in all God's household, to testify of the things that were going to be said. 6 But Christ is faithful as a son over God's household, whose household we are, if we hold firmly to our confidence and the hope we are proud of.

Translation Notes and Comments

3:1 *holy brethren / holy brothers and sisters:* For the plural noun ἀδελφος (*adelphos*) being translated as "brothers and sisters," see Translation Notes for 2:17.[5] That the author uses the adjective "holy" to define the state of his readers is telling.[6] The Savior, as sanctifier (2:11; 10:10, 14), has made them holy so that they can partner with him in their "heavenly calling."

partakers of the heavenly calling / partners in a heavenly calling: The nominalized adjective μέτοχος (*metochos*), "partner," is commonly used to describe a business associate of equal rank, that is, someone who shares in both the work of the business and in the profits made by that business.[7] The author has already used this term in 1:9 and 2:14, showing the importance of the relationship the word nuances.

The phrase κλήσεως ἐπουρανίου (*klēseōs epouraniou*), "heavenly calling," is ambiguous. It could refer to either a call to heaven or a call from heaven. Both work, and they are not mutually exclusive. The context, however, suggests the author has in mind the latter because he was "partnered" with

5. BDAG, 18.

6. The adjective ἅγιοι (*hagioi*) could be translated with the next phrase as "holy partakers of the heavenly calling." Either way, it reveals the author's feelings that his readers have not yet lost their position under the grace of the Lord. James Hope Moulton and George Milligan, *The Vocabulary of the Greek New Testament: Illustrated from the Papyri and Other Non-literary Sources* (Grand Rapids, Mich.: Wm. B. Eerdmans, 1952), 4. See also Cockerill, *Epistle to the Hebrews,* 158 n. 3.

7. BDAG, 642.

his readers in some enterprise. Likely that enterprise was their combined responsibility to further the work of the kingdom.[8]

consider the Apostle and High Priest of our profession, Christ Jesus / carefully consider Jesus, the apostle and high priest whom we confess: All of the earliest and best manuscripts omit "Christ," and so it was left out in our Rendition.

The verb κατανοέω (*katanoeō*) is an intensified form of the verb *νοέω* (*noeō*), "to comprehend." As such, it means "to consider carefully" or "to reflect on."[9] The object of that reflection was to be Jesus in light of two of his offices, apostle and high priest.

Only here, in all the scriptures, is Jesus referred to as an ἀπόστολος (*apostolos*), "apostle," but the appellation certainly applies. The verb on which the word is derived, ἀποστέλλω (*apostellō*), means "to send forth" but carries with it the idea of bequeathed authority to carry out a specific mission.[10] Jesus referred to himself as a "sent one" (Matt. 10:40; John 17:3) and in turn sent forth others to carry on his work (Mark 6:7; Luke 6:13; 9:10). To these he gave the very fitting title "apostles" and, in that way, stressed the authority standing behind the message that they preached.[11] Since the word designates anyone who was "sent forth," holding that title did not necessarily mean that a person was one of the Twelve Apostles.[12] The Savior certainly was not, and yet he was fully empowered to act as God's envoy and to

8. Joseph Smith (perhaps with others) wrote that Paul and others operated under their heavenly calling to declare the gospel. *Times and Seasons,* September 1, 1842, 905. Brigham Young, in *Journal of Discourses,* 9:364, and John Taylor, in *Journal of Discourses,* 1:24, also equated the phrase with preaching the gospel. McConkie, *Doctrinal New Testament Commentary,* 3:147, felt it was receiving the Melchizedek Priesthood, as did Joseph L. Wirthlin, Conference Report, October 1953, 14.

9. BDAG, 522–23; Louw-Nida, §30.3.

10. Daniel H. Ludlow, *A Companion to Your Study of the New Testament* (Salt Lake City: Deseret Book, 1982), 78.

11. Moulton and Milligan, *Vocabulary,* 69, notes that it carries the nuance of being commissioned. See also Rengstorf, *TDNT,* 1:407–47. S. Kent Brown, "Apostle," in Ludlow, *Encyclopedia of Mormonism,* 1:59–61, notes that the office applies to one who is sent forth to represent another and, in a religious context, designates a "divinely chosen envoy."

12. In addition to the original Twelve, the scriptures show Matthias was added to their number (Acts 1:26). Paul (Rom. 1:1; 1 Cor. 1:1; 2 Cor. 1:1) and Barnabas (Acts 14:4, 14) are also called "apostles," and Paul's statements in 1 Cor. 9:1–6 strongly imply that he and Barnabas had the same rights and privileges as the other members of the Twelve. Some scholars, based on Rom. 16:7, suggest Andronicus and Junias/Junia were also called apostles, but the text is ambiguous and can also be understood as simply saying these two individuals were known *to* the Apostles. Thorpe B. Isaacson and Alvin R. Dyer were sustained as modern Apostles but were never part of the Twelve.

carry out his assigned mission. Indeed, he was sent not only to reveal God's word, but also to reveal God himself (see 1:1–2 in light of John 14:8–14).

Jesus was also ἀρχιερεύς (*archiereus*), "high priest." The term designated the chief priest who had authority to oversee all the functions of the temple and other religious rites. For discussion, see both the Translation Notes for 2:17 with associated Analysis and also the section on "Jesus as High Priest" in "Excursus on the Condescension of Jesus" found at the end of chapter 2. The point being made here is that the Savior, as the high priest, provided the means for the "great salvation" of the people (2:3).[13]

The noun ὁμολογία (*homologia*), literally "speaking the same thing," carries the idea of common assent. In addition, it means "confessing" something or "professing" someone. Behind it stands the idea of speaking out, that is, openly proclaiming what one knows to be true (as an example, see 1 Tim. 6:12),[14] thus, in Latter-day Saint parlance, "bearing testimony."

The phrase τῆς ὁμολογίας ἡμῶν (*tēs homologias hēmōn*), "of our confession," connotes that to which a person outwardly expresses allegiance. It is unclear if this phrase is pointing to a set formula or confessional or to witnessing faith in the Lord himself.[15] That the former is the case is very doubtful. First, it is unlikely that full-scale creedal formulations had been developed this early,[16] and second, the context itself suggests that the witness is to the reality of Jesus as Son of God, Apostle, and High Priest who presides over the Church.[17] Because a literal translation of this whole phrase would be awkward in English and we wanted to put emphasis on its nuance, we phrased our Rendition to make it clear that the confession centers on Jesus.

3:2 *Who was faithful to him that appointed him / He was faithful to the one who appointed him:* The emphasis in this phrase is expressed by the adjective πιστός (*pistos*), "faithful." Here it connotes doing fully and continually all that God commands (10:7).[18] For discussion, see Translation Notes for 2:17.

---

13. Cockerill, *Epistle to the Hebrews,* 160.

14. BDAG, 708–9; *NID*, s.v. "*ὁμολογέω*."

15. O'Brien, *Letter to the Hebrews,* 130; Ellingworth, *Epistle to the Hebrews,* 199. For a study, see J. N. D. Kelly, *Early Christian Creeds,* 3d ed. (London: Bloomsbury Academic, 2006).

16. It is possible that the beginning of creedal or confessional formulas was being laid down at this time. On this, see Anthony C. Thiselton, *The First Epistle to the Corinthians: A Commentary on the Greek Text,* New International Greek Testament Commentary (Grand Rapids, Mich.: Wm. B. Eerdmans, 2000), 631–32, 918, 1187.

17. Cockerill, *Epistle to the Hebrews,* 161. The difference between the act of confessing and the truth confessed are virtually impossible to separate. Louw-Nida, §33.274; BDAG, 709.

18. John Taylor, in *Journal of Discourses,* 21:370, observed that the reason Jesus held these high positions was because he honored his birthright and was, therefore, anointed

The verb ποιέω (*poieō*) has the root sense of "to make" with the extended meanings "to cause, bring about, accomplish, prepare," and even "appoint,"[19] the sense that it has here. Hence the articular aorist participle τῷ ποιήσαντι (*tō poiēsanti*) is translated as "the one who appointed" in our Rendition and refers to God. It carries the same sense in LXX 1 Sam. 12:6, κύριος ὁ ποιήσας τὸν Μωυσῆν καὶ τὸν Ααρων (*kyrios ho poiēsas ton Mōysēn kai ton Aarōn*), "the Lord who appointed Moses and Aaron."

In sum, the word refers to God as the one who prepared and appointed Jesus for his mission. The context of the whole phrase suggests the subordinate role the Savior plays. The author uses that subordination as the base point for comparing and contrasting Moses with Jesus. Here it sets them both on the same plane, allowing them to be compared. From here on, however, the author will contrast them.

in all his house / in all God's household: The noun οἶκος (*oikos*), like the Hebrew בַּיִת (*bayit*), means not only "house" in the sense of "dwelling place," including the temple as God's dwelling place, but also the inhabitants of a house as in "household, family."[20]

In the phrase τῷ οἴκῳ αὐτοῦ (*tō oikō autou*), "his house," the possessive pronoun is ambiguous. It could refer to Moses, Jesus, or God. However, since this is a paraphrase of Numbers 12:7, which reads in the Masoretic text עַבְדִּי מֹשֶׁה בְּכָל־בֵּיתִי נֶאֱמָן הוּא (*'abdî mōšeh běkōl bêtî ne'ěmān hû'*), "my servant Moses is faithful in all my house(hold)," it is clear this refers God's house, not Moses'.[21] God declares that Moses is noted for his faithfulness in God's family. For clarity, our Rendition translates the phrase as "God's household."[22]

---

above his fellows. See also Cockerill, *Epistle to the Hebrews,* 162. For the stress on the nuance of "reliability" (that which gives the same results in successive trials) rather than on "fidelity" (strict compliance to an obligation), see Attridge, *Epistle to the Hebrews,* 109 n. 52.

19. BDAG, 839–42; Louw-Nida, §§13.9; 42.29; LSJ, 1428; Johnson, *Hebrews,* 107.

20. BDAG, 698–99; *HAL,* 124–25.

21. The LXX reads, ὁ θεράπων μου Μωυσῆς, ἐν ὅλῳ τῷ οἴκῳ μου πιστός ἐστιν (*ho therapōn mou Mōysēs, en holō tō oikō mou pistos estin*), "my servant Moses, in my entire house he is faithful" (authors' translation).

22. The lack of clarity of the pronouns used in verses 1–5 has caused a great deal of discussion. For example, see Ellingworth, *Epistle to the Hebrews,* 195–96; and Cockerill, *Epistle to the Hebrews,* 165–66. Since in Latter-day Saint theology Jehovah and Jesus are one and the same, it was Jesus, as Jehovah, who established the house of Israel and who also established the covenant community during the Old Testament era. Since, however, the foundation of both is divine, and the Father is the one who ultimately establishes all

3:3 ***For this man was counted worthy of more glory than Moses / For Jesus has been found to be worthy of greater glory than Moses:*** The vague pronoun οὗτος (*houtos*), "this one," is translated as "Jesus" in our Rendition for clarity.

The allusion is to Numbers 12:7 (which the author will actually quote in 3:5). The verb ἀξιόω (*axioō*) means "to consider worthy, deserving" and in the passive, as here, "to be considered worthy" and carries the idea of receiving recognition or reward based on merit.[23] In this context, it applies to Jesus and sets him apart from Moses, who, though very faithful, did not merit the glory that the Lord did. The force of the perfect tense emphasizes the ever continuing validity of this value judgment.[24] To catch the force of the passive voice and perfect tense, our Rendition translates it as "has been found to be worthy."

The noun δόξα (*doxa*), "glory," in this context, refers to the honor a person deserves due to unusual merit, exemplary deed, or the high office he or she holds. It applies particularly to Christ for his efforts in behalf of the Father's children. The author's words show that the Savior's "glory" is greater than Moses' in both degree and kind.[25]

inasmuch as he who hath builded the house hath more honour than the house / just as the builder of a house has greater honor than the house itself: The verb κατασκευάζω (*kataskeuazō*) means "to build."[26] Here, the active, aorist participle of the verb, nominalized by using the definite article, literally "the building one," is translated in our Rendition as "the builder."

On οἶκος (*oikos*), "house," see Translation Notes for 3:2.

In this verse, the author has changed the focus from δόξα (*doxa*), "glory," to τιμή (*timē*), "honor," which denotes the relative value or esteem something has. Here it points specifically toward the outward manifestation, that is, the acknowledgment, of that esteem.[27] In this case, it connotes the

---

things, it is fitting to see God as the referent of the pronoun. Therefore, the Rendition consistently translates the vague possessive pronoun αὐτοῦ (*autou*), "his," as "God's."

23. BDAG, 94; Louw-Nida, §§65.17; 66.6. In Matt. 10:10; Luke 10:7; and 1 Tim. 5:17, the word denotes work that merits pay. Since the emphasis in much of the New Testament is on God's grace as the means of salvation, the word gives balance, showing that people can be counted worthy of sharing in God's work and becoming part of his realm. Luke 20:35; Acts 5:41; 2 Thes. 1:11; see also *NID*, s.v. "*ἄξιος*."

24. Koester, *Hebrews*, 244.

25. Cockerill, *Epistle to the Hebrews*, 164.

26. BDAG, 526–27.

27. BDAG, 1005.

high regard that the architect/constructor receives for the execution of a well-done design.

3:4 ***For every house is builded by some man; but he that built all things is God / For every house is built by someone, but the builder of all things is God:*** In this verse, the author states the obvious (houses do not build themselves), but does so to make his point: God is the creator and architect of everything. He is the ultimate builder and he continues to be so.

3:5 ***And Moses verily was faithful in all his house, as a servant / Now Moses was faithful as a servant in all God's household:*** On the adjective πιστός (*pistos*), "faithful," see Translation Notes for 2:17 and 3:2. As also in 3:2, the text has τῷ οἴκῳ αὐτοῦ (*tō oikō autou*), "his house," but in our Rendition we changed this to "God's household" for clarity.

The noun θεράπων (*therapōn*), "attendant, aide, servant," denotes a person who renders devoted service more especially in a cultic setting. It connotes a great deal of trust in the person.[28] Behind the word also stands the authority through which the trusted operates.[29] The *therapōn* held a higher social position than the δοῦλος (*doulos*), "slave." Even so, the *therapōn* was under both the master of the house and the master's wife and children.[30]

for a testimony of those things which were to be spoken after / to testify of the things that were going to be said: This phrase is vague, making it difficult to translate. The problem lies with the future passive participial phrase τῶν λαληθησομένων (*tōn lalēthēsomenōn*) from the verb λαλέω (*laleō*), "to speak." The phrase translates literally as "of the things that will be said." Since the future tense in Greek is often used to express purpose, the idea here could refer to "the things that should be spoken." The author is likely saying that Moses' purpose was to testify of Christ. Translating the phrase as we have admittedly leaves open such questions as who was going to speak and when these things were (or are) going to be spoken of (that is, either talked about or revealed). Fortunately, it is clearer just what the things to be discussed are and thereby easier to make an educated guess as to what the author has in mind. It is certain that Moses was faithful

---

28. BDAG, 453; *NID*, s.v. "θεραπεύω."

29. In the New Testament, the noun appears only here. In the LXX, it is used as the translation of the Hebrew עֶבֶד (*'eved*) and refers, very often, to those under a ruler who hold official authority. HAL, 774; BDB, 713. Thus, the Old Testament uses this term to refer to both Moses (for example, Ex. 14:31 and Num. 12:7–8) and, significantly, the Messiah (Isa. 42:1–7; 49:1–7; 50:4–10; 52:13–53:12).

30. Bruce, *Epistle to the Hebrews*, 92–93.

in revealing God's law to his people and also in testifying of the Messiah. That law was filled with types and shadows of things to come (Mosiah 3:15; 16:14). More specifically, it was designed to disclose the work and ministry of the Son (2 Ne. 11:4; Jacob 4:5; Alma 25:15; Moses 5:6–8; Gal. 3:24). In chapters 8–10, the author bears witness to the high priesthood and atoning sacrifice of the Son as revealed through the types of the Old Testament.[31] That to which Moses testified appears to have been the work of the Redeemer.

One aspect of that work, and one which the author of Hebrews emphasizes, is the fuller revelation, in his day, of the gospel through the Son (1:1–2) and, more especially, of the Son's salvific work (1:3). Thus, when Moses spoke of the "blood of the covenant" (NR 9:20), his testimony foreshadowed the new covenant Jesus would establish through his death. Indeed, what God had spoken through Moses revealed various aspects of the Lord's nature and mission. This is what made the old law such a good type; it was filled with foreshadowings of what the Savior would do and would bring about.[32] Thus, it would appear that it was these things that were, at some time in the future, to be spoken of. That being the case, the author is here doing just that and had divine backing to do it.[33]

To take all of this into consideration and to better help the reader, our Rendition changes the prepositional phrase εἰς μαρτύριον (*eis martyrion*), "for a testimony," to the more concrete "to testify," and the articular future passive participle τῶν λαληθησομένων (*tōn lalēthēsomenōn*), "things to be spoken after," to "the things that were going to be said."

3:6 *But Christ as a son over his own house / But Christ is faithful as a son over God's household:* The adjective πιστός (*pistos*), "faithful," used in the Rendition, is not found in the Greek text. The conjunction δέ (*de*), "but," however, acts as a marker of comparison between Moses and Jesus, and since the point of comparison is faithfulness, the word is added to make the comparison clear. Though both were faithful, that is where the comparison ends. Moses was servant; Jesus is Son.

As in 3:2 and 4, the Greek text has "his house," but we changed this in the Rendition to "God's household" for clarity.

---

31. Cockerill, *Epistle to the Hebrews,* 169, and n. 56. Paul noted that God preserved the record of Israel's rebellion as a warning for Christians to not follow their ways. He then lists explicit examples. 1 Cor. 10:6–10; see also Jude 1:5.

32. Koester, *Hebrews,* 246; Cockerill, *Epistle to the Hebrews,* 169 with n. 56.

33. For a discussion of the problem, see Ellingworth, *Epistle to the Hebrews,* 207–9.

whose house are we / whose household we are: A variant reading exists of the relative pronoun in this phrase. The reading ὅς (*hos*), "which," is most likely a scribal modification of οὗ (*hou*), "whose," to clarify that Christians are of God's house, not Christ's house.[34] The SBLGNT text chose the reading ὅς (*hos*), whereas the Nestle-Aland 28th edition chose οὗ (*hou*). We have followed the Nestle-Aland text in our Rendition.

The point the author is making is that those who have taken advantage of Christ's Atonement have become part of God's family. As Paul taught the Ephesians, God has "foreordained us for adoption through Jesus Christ as his children" (Eph. 1:5, our translation). He also taught the Romans, "For everyone who is led by the Spirit of God are God's children. For you have not received a spirit of slavery leading again to fear, but you have received a spirit of adoption in which we cry out 'Abba,' father. This same Spirit testifies to our spirit that we are God's children. And if we are children, we are also heirs, heirs of God" (Rom. 8:14–17, our translation).

if we hold fast the confidence and the rejoicing of the hope firm unto the end / if we hold firmly to our confidence and the hope we are proud of: The verb κατέχω (*katechō*), "hold fast," means "to adhere firmly to" something. Here it refers to the traditions and teachings that these Saints had received. The emphasis is on the needed force or tightness of the grip.[35]

The noun παρρησία (*parrēsia*) describes "a state of boldness and confidence."[36]

The noun ἐλπίς (*elpis*), "hope," means "looking forward to something with some reason for confidence respecting fulfillment."[37] It is the power that supports and drives faith.[38] The noun καύχημα (*kauchēma*), "proud," denotes that which one is pleased or delighted with. It nuances such delight in something that one both rejoices and glories in it.[39] The distinction the word carries, however, stands in stark contrast to φυσίωσις (*physiōsis*), "swell-headedness, pride, conceit." This word connotes an "exaggerated

34. Metzger, *Textual Commentary,* 595.

35. BDAG, 532–33. The prefix κατα- (*kata-*) often has an intensive force. Smyth, *Greek Grammar,* §1691.3.

36. Louw-Nida, §25.158; BDAG, 781–82. Josephus, *Ant.* 18.1.6 §24, notes that it is the underlying resoluteness of either a martyr or soldier who is in a fearful situation. That would especially include death.

37. BDAG, 319–20.

38. For a study, see Bultmann and Rengstorf, *TDNT,* 2:517–35; and *NID,* s.v. "ἐλπίς." The implications of this word and its relationship to faith are discussed more completely in chapter 11.

39. BDAG, 536–37; Louw-Nida, §§25.203; 33.368, 371, 372.

self-conception," a kind of self-conceit that drives one to compete with others.[40] Its source is inward. The source of *kauchēma,* on the other hand, is outward. In this case, it looks to the Savior, expressing the joy that a testimony of his reality and work brings, connoting a boastful hope.

The phrase τὸ καύχημα τῆς ἐλπίδος (*to kauchēma tēs elpidos*), literally "the pride/boasting of the hope," is awkward in English and has been rephrased in our Rendition for better understanding as "the hope we are proud of."

Several early manuscripts add the phrase μέχρι τέλους βεβαίαν (*mechri telous bebaian*), "firm until the end."[41] The phrase is most likely an interpolation added to make this verse parallel with verse 14.[42] Hence, the phrase is omitted in our Rendition.

Analysis and Summary

In this section, as he builds his case, the author uses an episodic rather than a linear development of thought. Using Numbers 12:7 as his text, he makes a series of observations that allows him to emphasize the supremacy of Jesus over Moses. Note the author takes nothing away from the prophet. Indeed, the comparison between Jesus and Moses serves to support the author's argument. The higher the status of Moses, the higher that of the Lord. Therefore, this section should not be viewed as a polemic against Moses.[43]

The segment acts as a midrash (that is, an examination and explanation) on Numbers 12:7, focusing particularly on being "faithful" (πιστός, *pistos*).[44] The Old Testament context of this verse (Num. 12:3–13) actually extols the faith of Moses and its result. Because of the prophet's total willingness to do as Jehovah commands, he speaks to Moses in ways different from other prophets. The other prophets receive Jehovah's word in visions and in dreams, but with Moses "will I speak mouth to mouth" (Num. 12:8). The setting certainly showcases the high respect Jehovah had for his prophet and forewarns of consequences that will fall on any who dishonor him.

---

40. BDAG, 1069. For a study, see Lewis, *Mere Christianity,* 117–27.

41. These include the very important א, A, C, and D. Metzger, *Textual Commentary,* 595.

42. An important disqualifier is based on the rules of Greek grammar. The adjective βεβαίαν (*bebaian*) is feminine but the noun it modifies, τὸ καύχημα (*to kauchēma*), is neuter. The lack of coordination suggests that *bebaian* was not part of the original work.

43. Attridge, *Epistle to the Hebrews,* 105.

44. Ellingworth, *Epistle to the Hebrews,* 194; Attridge, *Epistle to the Hebrews,* 109 n. 53. For a discussion and definition of "midrash" with bibliography, see Avram R. Shannon, "Mormons and Midrash: On the Composition of Expansive Interpretation in *Genesis Rabbah* and the Book of Moses," *BYU Studies Quarterly* 54, no. 2 (2015): 19–21.

Laying this comparison as his foundation, the author of Hebrews then uses it to show how much higher Jesus is than Moses.[45] In 3:2 the author simply equates them (they are both fully faithful to God), but in 3:3 he subordinates Moses, saying that Jesus was worthy of greater glory than Moses. In 3:5–6 the author further subordinates Moses, stating that he is but God's servant (θεράπων, *therapōn*) in the household while Jesus is God's Son set over God's household.[46]

The author's intent is to further persuade his readers not to abandon Jesus. He calls them "holy" (ἅγιος, *hagios*), suggesting that they remain under the cleansing power of the Atonement. Because of this blessed condition, they are "partakers of the heavenly calling" (3:1). The calling is both from and to heaven. In the first instance, they have received their call from heaven through the Son (1:1–3; 2:3). It can be realized as they partner with him in the work of salvation. In the second instance, they have received their call to heaven, and it can be realized only as they hold fast to their testimonies and publicly (ὁμολογέω, *homologeō*) stand as witness for who and what Christ is: Son of God, High Priest, and Apostle (3:1).[47]

By focusing on two of the Lord's offices, those of Apostle and (Israelite) High Priest (3:1), the author emphasizes the divine authority through which the Savior operated. An apostle (ἀπόστολος, *apostolos*) was one empowered and sent out (ἀποστέλλω, *apostellō*) to do a task in behalf of another. Behind the title stood the authority of the one who made the assignment.[48] In this case, it was the Father. Thus, the title witnessed that Jesus operated under divine authority. This verse gives evidence that the Savior organized his Church and that it continued to function under divine authority and apostolic leadership.

The office of high priest in the Aaronic order was that of chief administrator. During the period of the priest's service, he was authorized to make

---

45. One of Moses' chief duties was acting as an intermediary between Israel and Jehovah. This parallels the duty of Jesus as mediator between humanity and God. Attridge, *Epistle to the Hebrews,* 105. The text does not disclose whether or not the author has this in mind, but the idea likely played in the background. Certainly, the role of both as revelators is clearly transparent in the passage. Cockerill, *Epistle to the Hebrews,* 163–64, and n. 29.

46. The author may also have been influenced by LXX 1 Chr. 17:11–15. In these verses Jehovah declares that he will honor the heir of David by setting him over the Father's house and kingdom forever. See Lane, *Hebrews 1–8,* 72, but Lane's text mistakenly cites 1 Chr. 7 instead of 17.

47. Attridge, *Epistle to the Hebrews,* 108. It would appear that these Saints have received the "call" but have not yet made it "sure."

48. BDAG, 120–121, 122; *NID,* s.v. "ἀποστέλλω."

expiation for the sins of Israel[49] and, having done that, bring them into association with the Divine as God's own people (Ex. 19:5; 29:44–46; Lev. 16:3–28). This imagery, therefore, looks not at the Lord's power but what he was to do with that power—cleanse the people (that is, justify them), make them holy (that is, sanctify them), and bring them to God.

The author states that Jesus was considered "worthy" or "deserving" (ἄξιος, *axios,* "to be held in highest esteem"[50]) of the glory he received (3:3). The force of the verb, here a divine passive, tacitly shows that it was the very Father who considered the Lord worthy. What made the Son worthy was his fulfilling of his twofold responsibility as Apostle and High Priest.[51]

A notable theme in this section is that identified by the noun οἶκος (*oikos*), used in 3:2–6, which, like its Hebrew counterpart בַּיִת (*bayit*) in its basic sense, means "a dwelling, house." The noun can also be used metaphorically to describe the members of a household, that is, "family," or even a whole group of people descended from a common ancestor, that is, "nation."[52] *Oikos* is used six times in 3:2–6. The sense is "house" in 3:3 and 4, where it is used with the verb κατασκευάζω (*kataskeuazō*), "to build." The sense of "family" applies in 3:2, 5, and 6. The author contrasts Moses, who "was faithful as a servant *in* all God's household" (NR 3:5, italics added) with Christ, who "is faithful as a son *over* God's household, whose household we are" (NR 3:6, italics added). This highlights a common topic in the scriptures, namely that those who acknowledge Christ as their Savior and strive to keep his commandments become members of God's family with God as their Father and Christ as his firstborn son.[53]

Christ's followers, however, had to meet a twofold requirement in order to remain as God's household (3:6). First, they had to "hold fast" (κατέχω, *katechō*), that is, adhere firmly, to the traditions and teachings they had received and do so with a cheerful confidence (παρρησία, *parrēsia*) in what

49. For a list of the high priest's duties, see Ex. 28:6–42; 29:6; 39:27–29; and Lev. 6:19–23; 21:10. For Latter-day Saints, the office of high priest belongs to the Melchizedek order of the priesthood. See A. L. Richards, "High Priest," in Ludlow, *Encyclopedia of Mormonism,* 2:587–88.

50. BDAG, 93–94.

51. This also included being the complete and full revelation of Deity and fulfilling all that Moses prophesied he would do. See Cockerill, *Epistle to the Hebrews,* 165.

52. BDAG, 698; *HAL,* 124–25.

53. For example, Hos. 1:10; John 1:12; Rom. 8:14; 2 Cor. 6:18; Gal. 4:5, 7; 6:10; Eph. 2:19; Philip. 2:15; 1 Pet. 4:17; 1 John 3:2; Mosiah 27:25; Ether 3:14; D&C 34:3; 76:24, 58; and Moses 6:68; 8:13.

they knew to be true.[54] Second, they had to "hold fast" to the "hope [they were] proud of," that is, the favorable and confident expectation they had in Christ and the delight (καύχημα, *kauchēma*) that caused them to both rejoice and glory in him (3:6).[55] In order to do so, the Saint would need to live a life filled with "a robust faith in God's future reward rather than [one] in pursuit of the temporal, visible rewards offered by the present world."[56] If they did these things—centering their faith in Christ—they would be in no danger of losing their reward.

Warning against Unbelief (3:7–19)

Greek Text

7 Διό, καθὼς λέγει τὸ πνεῦμα τὸ ἅγιον· Σήμερον ἐὰν τῆς φωνῆς αὐτοῦ ἀκούσητε, 8 μὴ σκληρύνητε τὰς καρδίας ὑμῶν ὡς ἐν τῷ παραπικρασμῷ, κατὰ τὴν ἡμέραν τοῦ πειρασμοῦ ἐν τῇ ἐρήμῳ, 9 οὗ ἐπείρασαν οἱ πατέρες ὑμῶν ἐν δοκιμασίᾳ καὶ εἶδον τὰ ἔργα μου 10 τεσσεράκοντα ἔτη· διὸ προσώχθισα τῇ γενεᾷ ταύτῃ καὶ εἶπον· Ἀεὶ πλανῶνται τῇ καρδίᾳ· αὐτοὶ δὲ οὐκ ἔγνωσαν τὰς ὁδούς μου· 11 ὡς ὤμοσα ἐν τῇ ὀργῇ μου· Εἰ εἰσελεύσονται εἰς τὴν κατάπαυσίν μου. 12 βλέπετε, ἀδελφοί, μήποτε ἔσται ἔν τινι ὑμῶν καρδία πονηρὰ ἀπιστίας ἐν τῷ ἀποστῆναι ἀπὸ θεοῦ ζῶντος, 13 ἀλλὰ παρακαλεῖτε ἑαυτοὺς καθ' ἑκάστην ἡμέραν, ἄχρις οὗ τὸ Σήμερον καλεῖται, ἵνα μὴ σκληρυνθῇ τις ἐξ ὑμῶν ἀπάτῃ τῆς ἁμαρτίας· 14 μέτοχοι γὰρ τοῦ Χριστοῦ γεγόναμεν, ἐάνπερ τὴν ἀρχὴν τῆς ὑποστάσεως μέχρι τέλους βεβαίαν κατάσχωμεν. 15 ἐν τῷ λέγεσθαι· Σήμερον ἐὰν τῆς φωνῆς αὐτοῦ ἀκούσητε, Μὴ σκληρύνητε τὰς καρδίας ὑμῶν ὡς ἐν τῷ παραπικρασμῷ. 16 τίνες γὰρ ἀκούσαντες παρεπίκραναν; ἀλλ' οὐ πάντες οἱ ἐξελθόντες ἐξ Αἰγύπτου διὰ Μωϋσέως; 17 τίσιν δὲ προσώχθισεν τεσσεράκοντα ἔτη; οὐχὶ τοῖς ἁμαρτήσασιν, ὧν τὰ κῶλα ἔπεσεν ἐν τῇ ἐρήμῳ; 18 τίσιν δὲ ὤμοσεν μὴ εἰσελεύσεσθαι εἰς τὴν κατάπαυσιν αὐτοῦ εἰ μὴ τοῖς ἀπειθήσασιν; 19 καὶ βλέπομεν ὅτι οὐκ ἠδυνήθησαν εἰσελθεῖν δι' ἀπιστίαν. [SBLGNT]

---

54. Louw-Nida, §25.158; BDAG, 781–82. Andrew J. Wilson, "Hebrews 3:6b and 3:14 Revisited," *Tyndale Bulletin* 62, no. 2 (2011): 247–67, argues that in both Hebrews 3:6b and 3:14 the author is using an evidence-to-inference conditional alongside a warning. Wilson points out that evidence that one has partnered with Christ is holding fast one's confidence, which will preserve the individual in righteousness as they continue to exercise faith in him. Such faithfulness is essential to inheriting eternal life. Wilson concludes that, in both instances, the statements should be treated as genuine admonitions with two purposes: first, to exhort the readers to persevere in faith, and second, to encourage them to do so by stressing the danger of apostasy.

55. BDAG, 536–37; Louw-Nida, §§25.203; 33.368, 371, 372; Johnson, *Hebrews,* 110–11.

56. Cockerill, *Epistle to the Hebrews,* 173.

King James Version

7 Wherefore (as the Holy Ghost saith, To day if ye will hear his voice, 8 Harden not your hearts, as in the provocation, in the day of temptation in the wilderness: 9 When your fathers tempted me, proved me, and saw my works forty years. 10 Wherefore I was grieved with that generation, and said, They do alway err in their heart; and they have not known my ways. 11 So I sware in my wrath, They shall not enter into my rest.) 12 Take heed, brethren, lest there be in any of you an evil heart of unbelief, in departing from the living God. 13 But exhort one another daily, while it is called To day; lest any of you be hardened through the deceitfulness of sin. 14 For we are made partakers of Christ, if we hold the beginning of our confidence steadfast unto the end; 15 While it is said, To day if ye will hear his voice, harden not your hearts, as in the provocation. 16 For some, when they had heard, did provoke: howbeit not all that came out of Egypt by Moses. 17 But with whom was he grieved forty years? was it not with them that had sinned, whose carcases fell in the wilderness? 18 And to whom sware he that they should not enter into his rest, but to them that believed not? 19 So we see that they could not enter in because of unbelief.

New Rendition

7 Therefore, as the Holy Spirit says,

> "Today, if you would listen to his voice, 8 do not harden your hearts as in the rebellion, during the day of testing in the wilderness, 9 when your ancestors tried and tested me and saw my works for forty years. 10 For this reason I was very angry with that generation and said, 'They are always going astray in their hearts and they have not understood my ways.' 11 So I swore an oath in my anger, 'They will certainly not enter into my rest.'" [LXX Ps. 94:8–11]

12 Brothers and sisters, beware that none of you have an evil, unbelieving heart so that you rebel against the living God. 13 Rather encourage each other daily while it is still called "Today," so that none of you will become hardened by the deception of sin. 14 For we have become partners with Christ, if indeed we hold fast to our initial resolve until the end. 15 As quoted above,

> "Today, if only you would listen to his voice. Do not harden your hearts as in the rebellion." [LXX Ps. 94:8]

16 For who heard and rebelled? Was it not everyone who came out of Egypt led by Moses? 17 And with whom was God angry for forty years? Was it not those who sinned, whose dead bodies fell in the wilderness? 18 And to whom did he swear that they would not enter into his rest if it was not those who were disobedient? 19 And so we see that they were not able to enter because of unbelief.

Translation Notes and Comments

3:7–11 The author begins this section by quoting LXX Psalm 94:8–11.[57] He then uses it as the basis for his admonition that follows.

3:7 ***Wherefore (as the Holy Ghost saith, To day if ye will hear his voice / Therefore, as the Holy Spirit says, "Today, if you would listen to his voice:*** With the coordinating conjunction διό (*dio*), "therefore," the author signals that he is now going to back up the point he has just made. Following his pattern of quoting scriptures in which the Divine speaks, he picks this scripture to build his case. However, he only obliquely attributes the source as God the Father, using instead a reference to the "Holy Spirit."

The adverb σήμερον (*sēmeron*), "today," designates a specific and short period of time, but not necessarily one of twenty-four hours. Rather, it denotes a space of time when something must be completed or else the result would be either compromised or forfeited.[58] The use of the word "suggests a sense of continuing and open-ended revelation by God: God speaks 'today' (Heb 1:1)."[59]

The force of this phrase is in the verb ἀκούω (*akouō*), "to hear, listen." It can also mean not only to listen to something but also to give careful attention to, heed.[60] The subjunctive mood of the verb with the conditional particle ἐάν (*ean*) introduces a third-class condition that can range "in meaning from more probable future to mere hypothetical situation. The context is determinative"[61] and here suggests mere possibility. Thus we translate the phrase as "if you would listen" in our Rendition.

The noun φωνή (*phōnē*), "voice," in a theological sense connotes the expression of God's will no matter how it comes (compare Jer. 7:21–28; and D&C 1:38; 18:33–36; 21:5). In the present context, it likely points to Jehovah's instructions to Israel when he gave them his law (Deut. 4:11–13).[62]

3:8 ***Harden not your hearts, as in the provocation, in the day of temptation in the wilderness / do not harden your hearts as in the rebellion, during the day of testing in the wilderness:*** The concern in this verse is with the καρδία (*kardia*), "heart." The author uses it in its metaphorical sense,

---

57. This is Ps. 95:8–11 in the KJV.

58. Fuchs, *TDNT,* 7:269–75; BDAG, 921; Draper, "Hebrews, Epistle to the," 2:582.

59. Johnson, *Hebrews,* 114. Ellingworth, *Epistle to the Hebrews,* 224, notes that the period is "as long as God continues to offer the opportunity of entering his promised resting-place." *Sēmeron* is one of the words that the "midrash" in Hebrews focuses on. For a discussion, see "Developmental Process" in the book's introduction.

60. BDAG, 37–38.

61. Wallace, *Greek Grammar,* 712.

62. BDAG, 1071–72; *NID,* s.v. "φωνή."

connoting the entire spectrum of mental and emotional activities, including all rational elements. The idea also involves both a person's moral decisions, including both vices and virtues (Matt. 15:19–20), and the dwelling place of heavenly powers (Acts 15:9; Rom. 2:15).[63]

The verb σκληρύνω (*sklērynō*), "make hard," denotes that process of making something rigid or unyielding.[64] In a theological sense, it connotes conditions that create a stubborn and recreant resistance to the word of God. The imagery of a hard heart suggests both the depth and obdurate nature of a person's opposition to the Divine.[65] It is little wonder the Father is anxious to keep his children from yielding to such a condition and demands correction if they do.[66]

Verse 8 in LXX Psalm 94 uses the noun παραπικρασμός (*parapikrasmos*) to describe the result of hard-heartedness. The word denotes revolt and rebellion.[67] It carries the nuance of an action so reprehensible that it not only embitters its target but also provokes him or her to anger.[68] The setting of this action in the Old Testament was the outrageous rebellion of the children of Israel against Jehovah during their stay at the oasis Kadesh-Barnea (Ex. 15:23; 17:7; Num. 14:1–45; 20:2–5).[69]

---

63. BDAG, 508–9; *NID,* s.v. "καρδία"; Johnson, *Hebrews,* 115.

64. BDAG, 930.

65. The verb σκληρύνω (*sklērynō*) is translated from the Hebrew word קָשָׁה (*qāšāh*), "to be hard, difficult, stubborn." BDB, 903. A hard heart and stiff neck make it impossible for a person to yield to God, and, thus, they come to destruction. Prov. 28:14; 29:1; see also Zipor, *TDOT,* 13:190–92.

66. The phrase to not harden one's heart was often used by later prophets to warn the Israelites to not repeat the sins of the forebearers. See 2 Chr. 30:8; Neh. 9:16–17, 29; Jer. 7:26; Acts 19:9; see also Koester, *Hebrews,* 255.

67. BDAG, 770.

68. The noun is related to the verb πικραίνω (*pikrainō*), which, in the active voice, means "to be bitter" and, in the passive, "to embitter" or "to irritate." The addition of the prefix παρα- (*para-*) strengthens the idea giving it the sense of willfully provoking someone to the point of anger. See Michaelis, *TDNT,* 6:122–27; and *NID,* s.v. "πικρός." Thus, the verb παραπικραίνω (*parapikrainō*) means to make someone either severely embittered or very angry.

69. The MT puts the rebellion at Meribah and Massah. See Ps. 95:7–9. See also Cockerill, *Epistle to the Hebrews,* 176, and n. 11. For a good study of Israel's rebellion and its ramifications on its history, see G. W. Coats, *Rebellion in the Wilderness: The Murmuring Motif in the Wilderness Traditions of the Old Testament* (Nashville: Abingdon Press, 1968). One must, however, allow the idea that the author could have in mind the whole forty-year period as the time during which the Hebrews successively saw Jehovah's works, rebelled, and were punished. Cockerill, *Epistle to the Hebrews,* 180–81.

The text uses the phrase τὴν ἡμέραν τοῦ πειρασμοῦ (*tēn hēmeron tou peirasmou*), "the day of testing," to describe this period. The phrase is a good one because it gives, from Jehovah's perspective, what these people were doing. The noun πειρασμός (*peirasmos*), "test, trial, temptation,"[70] carries both a positive and negative nuance. Positively, it denotes the act of putting someone on trial to determine his or her mettle. On the negative side, it points to the act of tempting someone to do something wrong.[71] The positive side seems to be at play here, and therefore we translated it as "testing" in our Rendition. Israel was continually testing Jehovah's mettle. They learned a harsh lesson when wrath was his response.

The related verb πειράζω (*peirazō*) also carries two different nuances. On the positive side, it connotes broadly the attempt to try something and, more narrowly, the determination "to learn the nature or character of someone or something by submitting such to a thorough and extensive testing."[72] On the negative side, as here, the word picks up a more distinct Hebrew connotation. It is used as a translation for the word נִסָּה (*nissāh*), "to put to the test, to try," pointing to an action motived by skepticism to find out the truth, value, or worth of something.[73] In the context of both Numbers and Psalms, it describes Israel's actions that expose their groundless distrust of Jehovah and underscores the enormity of their faithless defiance of him.[74] Jehovah had proved his power over both earth and people when he freed the Hebrews from Egyptian bondage. To deny that power just a short time later, as Israel did at Kadesh-Barnea, was the height of faithlessness, arrogance, and insolence. To keep testing Jehovah for forty more years was unconscionable.

3:9 ***When your fathers tempted me, proved me, and saw my works forty years / when your ancestors tried and tested me and saw my works for forty years:*** The Psalmist separates himself from his readers by referring to the rebellious souls as "your ancestors." For the verb πειράζω (*peirazō*), "to test, try," see Translation Notes on 3:8. The phrase ἐπείρασαν οἱ πατέρες ὑμῶν ἐν δοκιμασίᾳ (*epeirasan hoi pateres hymōn en dokimasia*) is literally "your

70. BDAG, 793.

71. Louw-Nida, §27.46. The scriptures repeatedly use this nuance to describe the work of both Satan and some Pharisees who "tempted" the Lord. See Matt. 4:1; 16:1; 19:3; 22:35; Mark 8:11; 10:2; Luke 11:16; John 8:6. Louw-Nida, §§27.31, 46; 68.58; 88.308; see also BDAG, 792–93. For a study, see *NID*, s.v. "πειράζω."

72. BDAG, 792–93.

73. *HAL*, 701; BDB, 650; *TWOT*, 1373.

74. BDAG, 793. For a study, see Helfmeyer, *TDOT*, 9:443–55.

ancestors tried [me] with testing." In our Rendition, we have translated this as "tried and tested." We have translated πατέρες (*pateres,* literally "fathers") as "ancestors."

The noun δοκιμασία (*dokimasia*), "testing, examination," carries the meaning of putting something to the test to determine its genuineness.[75] It does not carry the negative nuance of tempting someone or trying to put them in a bad light, and, thus, in that much it stands in contrast to πειρασμός (*peirasmos*). People can try God "by complaining against him or by challenging him in unbelief (compare Ex. 17:1–7; 1 Cor. 10:9), by defying him in disobedience (Heb. 3:8), or by demanding signs or miracles from him for an unworthy motive, such as to exalt themselves or to satisfy their curiosity (Matt. 12:39)."[76]

The phrase τεσσαράκοντα ἔτη (*tessarakonta etē*), "forty years," is placed at the beginning of 3:10 rather than at the end of 3:9. However, since both versification and punctuation are later additions to the text, it is ambiguous to which phrase "forty years" refers. It could be either the period of Israel's trying and testing the Lord in the wilderness or of his anger with Israel. The author seems to prefer the first sense because he inserted the conjunction διό (*dio*), "therefore," between "forty years" and "I was very angry."[77] Our Rendition follows this interpretation.

3:10 *Wherefore I was grieved with that generation, and said, They do alway err in their heart; and they have not known my ways / For this reason I was very angry with that generation and said, "They are always going astray in their hearts and they have not understood my ways":* The author uses the subordinating conjunction διό (*dio*), "wherefore, for that reason," to emphasize why the action he will next address happened.[78] That action was Jehovah's determination that the rebellious Israelites would

75. BDAG, 256. The MT uses the word בָּחַן (*bāḥan*), which means "to test, try, or prove" something. The word's thrust is that of seeking knowledge through testing or trying something. *HAL,* 119; BDB, 103; *TWOT,* 230. The Hebrews were wrong in doing this because Jehovah had already proven himself in freeing them. For a study, see Tsevat, *TDOT,* 2:69–71.

76. Ludlow, *Selections,* 454.

77. The term may have had special meaning for the author and his readers since the belief was current that there would be another probationary period of forty years at the end-time. See *b. Sanh.* 110b. If Hebrews was written shortly after the fall of Jerusalem, the period marked nearly forty years since the Savior's death and suggested trials were about to begin in earnest. See Bruce, *Epistle to the Hebrews,* 99.

78. BDAG, 250. The conjunction does not appear in the LXX. By adding it, the author more closely connects Jehovah's anger with the rebellion. Cockerill, *Epistle to the Hebrews,* 179–80; compare Attridge, *Epistle to the Hebrews,* 115; and Lane, *Hebrews 1–8,* 86.

not enter in to his "rest" (for development, see below). The text uses the verb προσοχθίζω (*prosochthizō*) to describe the emotion that led Jehovah to make this decision. The word means "to feel strong irritation for what someone has done,"[79] but its various connotations help get a better feel for the force of the word. They include being very upset, highly provoked, intensely angry, and wrath filled.[80] The emphasis in the nuances is that of the depth of the displeasure. In sum, *prosochthizō* is much stronger than the usual verb translated "to be angry," ὀργίζω (*orgizō*).

On καρδία (*kardia*), "heart," see Translation Notes for 3:8 above. The verb πλανάω (*planaō*) has two nuances. First, it means "to go astray" or to "wander about aimlessly." Second, it means "to mislead, deceive," and "seduce."[81] In its passive voice, as found here, it means to be led astray or misguided.[82] The second nuance informs the first. It gives the reason why a person is off the path—he or she has been misguided, deceived, seduced. Here the use of the accompanying adverb ἀεί (*aei*), "always," is telling. It shows that the Israelites were continually being deceived and points to the source of their deception as their own hearts.

The verb γινώσκω (*ginōskō*) means "to know" but can carry the nuance of having a close, even intimate, relationship with another.[83] In this case, it is Jehovah who is the object of the knowledge. The Old Testament makes it clear that people can know him. This knowledge comes primarily through his self-revelation, especially in the saving acts he performs (for example, see Ex. 6:7; 7:4–5; 10:1–2; 18:8–11; 31:13; Ezek. 20:12–20). To know him means to enter into a personal relationship with him and to do what he required (for example, see Jer. 22:15–16; 2 Ne. 31:14). Refusing to know him leads to sin, especially the worship of false gods (Judg. 2:10–11; Hosea 4:1–5; 6:6–7; Titus 1:16). Israel should have known Jehovah especially through the display of his divine power in Egypt and at Sinai as well as through his various saving acts. They, in spite of all the evidence, refused and rebelled (Isa. 45:4; Jer. 4:22).[84]

The noun ὁδός (*hodos*), "way," denotes a path or road, but also a manner of behavior. It connotes more especially actions that reveal the depth of a

79. Louw-Nida, §88.72.

80. BDAG, 884; LSJ, 1522.

81. BDAG, 821–22.

82. Louw-Nida, §31.8, and n. 2. In Rev. 12:9, the definite article is combined with the present participle to give Satan the designation of the deceiver.

83. BDAG, 199–200.

84. *NID*, s.v. "γινώσκω."

person's commitment to a certain highly moral and spiritual existence.[85] This is especially true when Jehovah commands his people to walk in his way (Gen. 18:19; 1 Kgs. 2:3; 8:58; Ps. 119:1–6). The sin of Israel is that they refused to know God's ways and, therefore, were off the path (LXX Ps. 94:10).[86]

3:11 ***So I sware in my wrath, They shall not enter into my rest) / So I swore an oath in my anger, 'They will certainly not enter into my rest':*** The psalm expressed the result of the depth of the Lord's displeasure with Israel's rebellion with the verb ὀμνύω (*omnyō*), "to swear an oath."[87] This act was the strongest way of assuring something would be done. Israel would not get away with their rebellion; God's oath, driven by his anger, would assure it.[88]

The phrase εἰ εἰσελεύσονται (*ei eiseleusontai*) consists of the conditional particle εἰ (*ei*) followed by the verb εἰσέρχομαι (*eiserchomai*) in the future tense. It translates literally as "if they will enter." This is a Hebraism where the particle אִם (*'im*) is used in an oath formula to express a strong negation.[89] Thus, we translate the phrase as "they will certainly not enter" in our Rendition.

The noun κατάπαυσις (*katapausis*) means "cessation of work or activity, rest."[90] It is a translation for the Hebrew מְנוּחָה (*mĕnûḥāh*), "resting place, place of quiet."[91] In its spiritual sense, it connotes a state of peace set on the assurance of God's goodwill and protection. In its setting in the Old Testament, it denoted not only Israel's possession of the promised land but also the divine protection and care that would accompany it, a care that assured them of peace and plenty. It was also used in the typological sense

85. BDAG, 691–92; Michaelis, *TDNT,* 5:43–48. The concept holds an important place in the idea of the "two ways"—one of progression and one of retrogression; one toward God, the other away from him; one toward eternal life and one toward spiritual death. *NID,* s.v. "ὁδός."

86. Noteworthy is that in the New Testament, the gospel was referred to simply as "the way." See Luke 1:76; Acts 2:28; 9:2; 13:10; Rom. 11:33; 1 Cor. 4:17.

87. BDAG, 705–6. The verb also implied punishment if what was sworn to was found to be untrue.

88. Johnson, *Hebrews,* 116; Cockerill, *Epistle to the Hebrews,* 181–82. The Book of Mormon prophets Jacob and Alma were certainly concerned that their people might also rebel and miss entering into the rest of the Lord. See Jacob 1:7; 6:6; Alma 12:34, 35; 13:13. The idea of the divine oath is another one of the words that the "midrash" of Hebrews focuses on. For a discussion, see "Developmental Process" in the book's introduction.

89. BDAG, 278; *HAL,* 60.

90. BDAG, 523–24. For discussion, see Translation Notes for 4:1 with associated Analysis.

91. *HAL,* 600.

of entering into the heavenly realm.[92] It is this sense the author of Hebrews uses when he applies the term to his readers.

3:12 ***Take heed, brethren, lest there be in any of you an evil heart of unbelief / Brothers and sisters, beware that none of you have an evil, unbelieving heart:*** The verb βλέπω (*blepō*) means "to see" and, in its command form, "see to it" and connotes the need to pay attention due to the whereabouts of something hazardous or life threatening; thus, "take heed." We thus translate it with the strong "beware"[93] in our Rendition.

For "brothers and sisters," see Translation Notes for 2:11. Here the author's use of the noun brings him and his readers together as members of God's family.[94]

In the phrase καρδία πονηρὰ ἀπιστίας (*kardia ponēra apistias*), the noun ἀπιστία (*apistia*), "unbelief," is a genitive of reference[95] and thus is translated literally as "a heart evil with reference to unbelief." Such a literal translation is rather awkward, so we have rendered it as "an evil, unbelieving heart."[96] It equates to the "hard heart" in the psalm, but the author, at this point, chooses to focus more on the heart's faithlessness than its hardness. In so doing, he is able to keep his theme—the importance of maintaining faith in the Lord—ever before the eyes of his readers.

in departing from the living God / so that you rebel against the living God: The verb ἀφίστημι (*aphistēmi*) in the second aorist form, as found here, means to withdraw or separate oneself from someone and "to fall away, revolt."[97] The noun ἀποστασία (*apostasia*), from which the English "apostasy" derives, is related to it. Thus, it betrays the author's fear that his readers' ἀπιστία (apistia), "unfaithfulness," would lead to actual rebellion.

The phrase ἐν τῷ ἀποστῆναι (*en tō apostēnai*) is an articular infinitive in the dative case governed by the preposition ἐν (*en*), which expresses

92. BDAG, 523–24; for discussion, see *NID*, s.v. "ἀναπαύω"; and Cockerill, *Epistle to the Hebrews*, 194, and n. 100.

93. BDAG, 178–79.

94. Cockerill, *Epistle to the Hebrews*, 182.

95. Wallace, *Greek Grammar*, 127–28.

96. Moulton and Milligan, *Vocabulary*, 58, note that it also carries the nuance of "incredulous," the refusal to accept what is proffered as true. See also Ellingworth, *Epistle to the Hebrews*, 222.

97. BDAG, 157–58; Louw-Nida, §39.41. The unbelieving heart is evidenced by the falling away. O'Brien, *Letter to the Hebrews*, 146. At 146 n. 122, O'Brien also notes that the similarity in sound between "unbelief" (*apistias*) and "falling away" (*apostēnai*) as evidence for this connection.

result[98]; thus, literally "in the rebelling from God." Due to its awkwardness, we render the phrase as "so that you rebel" in our Rendition. In that way, it shows the result of an unbelieving heart; namely, rebellion.

The last phrase, θεοῦ ζῶντος (*theou zōntos*), the "living God," is important to the author's theme. God remains ever active and ever speaking because he is ever living. Thus, his ability to bless or punish never ceases.

3:13 ***But exhort one another daily, while it is called To day / Rather encourage each other daily while it is still called "Today":*** The author expresses the antidote to rebellion with the verb παρακαλέω (*parakaleō*). In the context here, it means "to make a strong request" and thus "to urge, encourage" someone to do something. It also carries the nuance of instilling someone with hope.[99] This admonition was timely given the pull of society against the believers and the promise of growing persecution. Mutual encouragement would act as a break to apostasy.[100]

To stress his point, the author uses the phrase καθ' ἑκάστην ἡμέραν (*kath ekastēn hēmeran*), "day by day," or, in short, "daily." His exhortation suggests that the pressure upon his readers warranted constant, even daily, support, and that the needed support could be gained through the efforts of the community as a whole.[101] Tacitly the author shows his support for and understanding of the value of the community of the Saints.

On the adverb σήμερον (*sēmeron*), "today," see Translation Notes for 3:7.

lest any of you be hardened through the deceitfulness of sin / so that none of you will become hardened by the deception of sin: The phrase is a passive of permission warning the readers against allowing themselves to be led astray.[102] The phrase shows that a person's agency is involved here. On "hardened," see Translation Notes for 3:8.

The noun ἁμαρτία (*hamartia*), "sin," originally denoted "missing the mark," suggesting going beyond what is proper or good.[103] By New Testament times this idea had faded and the word had come to denote a moral

98. Wallace, *Greek Grammar,* 593 n. 12.

99. BDAG, 764–65. The work instills hope by showing what God has made possible for his people. See Richard J. Ounsworth, "On the Threshold of the Promised Land–Psalm 95 in the Letter to the Hebrews," *Religious Life Review* 50 (2011): 69–78.

100. Bruce, *Epistle to the Hebrews,* 100. The force of the phrase looks more to community support than self-examination. Ellingworth, *Epistle to the Hebrews,* 220–21; see also Schmitz, *TDNT,* 5:773–99.

101. Cockerill, *Epistle to the Hebrews,* 185, and n. 51.

102. Cockerill, *Epistle to the Hebrews,* 187.

103. For discussion, see Hoskisson, "Looking beyond the Mark," 149–64.

deviation that consisted of two parts: unfaithfulness to God and disobedience to his law.[104] It connoted any act that distanced a person from the Father and more especially the determination of a person to be a law unto him- or herself (10:16–31, 39; see also D&C 88:35).

The noun ἀπάτη (*apatē*) denotes both "deception" and "deceitfulness." The nuance behind it is telling. It looks to the pleasure "that involves one in sin."[105] The author is realistic enough to know that sin has a draw. It is seductive. The word "deception" implies the use of tricks, especially illusion, to get what one wants, while "deceitfulness" looks at working through the credulity of an individual by dishonest means to obscure or hide one's real intent.[106] Here, the author makes sin an agent and thereby is better able to denote its ability to deceive people by its allure, which can result in a hardened heart.

3:14 ***For we are made partakers of Christ / For we have become partners with Christ:*** On the adjective μέτοχος (*metochos*), "partner," see Translation Notes for 3:1. As a substantive, the noun denotes not only any close companionship between two or more people but more especially between business partners.[107] As used here, it points to a very close relationship between Christ and his disciples.[108] They all participate together not only in spreading the gospel message but also in sharing his divine power. The phrase, as used by the author, strongly hints that an intimate bond between Lord and the Hebrew brothers and sisters still existed but was in danger of being lost.[109]

---

104. *NID,* s.v. "ἁμαρτία"; compare D&C 88:21, 35.

105. BDAG, 99.

106. *Webster's New Dictionary of Synonyms,* s.v. "deception" and "deceitful." The author's use of the term follows that of scripture in general (see, for example, Rom. 7:11; 2 Thes. 2:10; compare 2 Cor. 11:3 with its allusion to Gen. 3:13), and therefore, speculation on the nature of the sin's deceit is unnecessary. Attridge, *Epistle to the Hebrews,* 117.

107. BDAG, 643; Lane, *Hebrews 1–8,* 87. In Jewish literature, the noun also denoted those who would be fellows with God or his heavenly host (*1 En.* 104:6; *Ep. Apos.,* 19) or with the Messiah (2 Esd. 7:28; 14:9), a fitting term for Jesus. In this light, see John 13:8, where Jesus warns Peter that the disciple would have "no part with me," meaning "no companionship with me" (οὐκ ἔχεις μέρος μετ' ἐμοῦ, *ouk echeis meros met emou*).

108. The phrase could be easily tied to the idea that disciples individually can share in the divine nature (12:10; 2 Pet. 1:4; 1 John 3:2) or that the Church as a body is the place the spirit of God is found (1 Cor. 3:16; 12:27; Eph. 4:15–16). The KJV follows this idea. See Attridge, *Epistle to the Hebrews,* 117–18. It is more likely, however, that, given the context of Hebrews, the author means to convey the idea that there is unity between the Lord as High Priest and his disciples. Ellingworth, *Epistle to the Hebrews,* 227.

109. Cockerill, *Epistle to the Hebrews,* 188–89.

if we hold the beginning of our confidence steadfast unto the end / if indeed we hold fast to our initial resolve until the end: The author's use of the intensive particle ἐάνπερ (*eanper*), "if indeed," emphasizes the conditional quality of the relationship his readers have with the Savior and, therefore, serves as a clear warning.[110]

The noun ὑπόστασις (*hypostasis*) has a broad range of meanings, including the essential or basic structure/nature of an entity with its substantial essence, actual being, and reality (Latin *substantia*). In addition, it can refer to "a support; deposit; sediment," or "a plan that one devises for an action, project, undertaking, or endeavor." It also denotes "a steadfast commitment to a professed obligation" and "a situation, condition, or frame of mind." Finally, it points to "the guarantee of ownership or entitlement based on a title, deed, or lease."[111] The meaning here seems to be pointing to the original commitment each new convert to the gospel makes at the time of his or her baptism, namely to be "willing to take upon them the name of Jesus Christ, having a determination to serve him to the end" (D&C 20:37). To best capture that idea, in our Rendition we translate it as "our initial resolve." The KJV's translation of the term as "confidence" has no support.[112]

On βέβαιος (*bebaios*), "steadfast, unwavering," see Translation Notes for 2:2. Here the word stresses the strength that needs to be applied to accomplish a deed. Some debate exists as to what the author means with his admonition to μέχρι τέλους βεβαίαν κατάσχωμεν (*mechri telous bebaian kataschōmen*), "hold fast [to our initial resolve] until the end." No doubt many in the nascent Church believed that the Lord's return to set up his kingdom was near (Acts 1:6; 1 Cor. 1:7; 15:52; 1 Thes. 2:19–20; 3:13; 4:13–18; 2 Pet. 3:13–14).[113] They were also well aware that there would be a preceding apostasy and restoration (Matt. 13:25; 24:9–12; Acts 3:19–21; 20:28–31; 1 Cor. 11:18; 2 Thes. 2:3–4). As a result, the author of Hebrews could be admonishing his readers to stay true until the Second Coming or to stay true unto death.[114] Given that the

---

110. BDAG, 267–68; Moulton and Milligan, *Vocabulary,* 177. It is the suffix "*-per*" that acts as the intensifier.

111. BDAG, 1040–41. See also Moulton and Milligan, *Vocabulary,* 659–60; and Köster, *TDNT,* 8:572–89. That the latter article runs for sixteen pages suggests the breadth of nuances this word carries.

112. BDAG, 1040–41.

113. Brigham Young, in *Journal of Discourses,* 12:65, noted that many in the New Testament Church "were mistaken with regard to the time of the winding up scene, thinking it was much nearer than it really was, and they might have made mistakes in other respects."

114. Attridge, *Epistle to the Hebrews,* 118; on the idea that the Saints were anticipating the coming of Christ, see Ellingworth, *Epistle to the Hebrews,* 224.

New Testament suggests the Church leaders were very aware of the rapidly approaching apostasy (Gal. 1:6; 3:1; 1 Tim. 1:6; 4:1; 2 Tim. 1:15; 4:4; 2 Pet. 2:1; 3:17; 1 John 2:18; 4:1; Rev. 2:2), the author is likely encouraging his readers to stay faithful for the duration of their mortal lives.[115]

3:15 ***While it is said, To day if ye will hear his voice, harden not your hearts, as in the provocation / As quoted above, "Today, if only you would listen to his voice. Do not harden your hearts as in the rebellion":*** For discussion of this scripture, see Translation Notes for 3:7 and 8 above. The author repeats this verse to emphasize the admonition and warning he will next give.

3:16 ***For some, when they had heard, did provoke: howbeit not all that came out of Egypt by Moses / For who heard and rebelled? Was it not everyone who came out of Egypt led by Moses?:*** This verse begins with the first two of five rhetorical questions that the author asks and then answers. Because the Greek translation of the psalm makes the Hebrew original quite vague, the author's questions give the Greek text both context and focus by stating who rebelled, when, and under whose leadership.[116]

The purpose of these two questions is to stress that the *entire* rebellious generation had heard Moses' witness and seen Jehovah's mighty works that so humbled the Egyptians. In spite of this, the Hebrews remained faithless.[117] Their action is described as παραπικρασμός (*parapikrasmos*), "revolt, rebellion."[118] For development, see Translation Notes for 3:8 above. The idea here is that, even though the whole assembly heard Jehovah's word, the entire lot rebelled. Having personally and directly heard his word made their act all the more grievous and anger provoking.[119]

---

115. See Draper and Rhodes, *Paul's First Epistle to the Corinthians,* 395–96. The same applies even today. See John M. Madsen, "Enduring to the End," in Ludlow, *Encyclopedia of Mormonism,* 2:456–57.

116. Vanhoye, *Letter to the Hebrews,* 89–90.

117. The only exceptions were Caleb and Joshua. Num. 26:65; 32:12; Deut. 1:36–38. That τίνες (*tines*) can be taken as "some," see Ellingworth, *Epistle to the Hebrews,* 229–30. That translation would allow for the exception of Caleb and Joshua. However, the weight of evidence for "all those" is strongest. Note Num. 14:2, 5, 7, 10, 22, which state all of Israel were in rebellion. See also Attridge, *Epistle to the Hebrews,* 120, and n. 92; and Cockerill, *Epistle to the Hebrews,* 191.

118. BDAG, 770.

119. Lane, *Hebrews 1–8,* 88. Though the term is found only here in the New Testament, it is found more frequently in the Old (Deut. 31:27; 32:16; LXX Ps. 77:17, 40, 46; 105:7; Ezek. 2:3, 5–8) and in each case suggests an act that is extremely provocative. Attridge, *Epistle to the Hebrews,* 120 n. 91.

In the phrase διὰ Μωϋσέως (*dia Mōyseōs*), literally "through Moses," the preposition διά (*dia*), as used here, expresses the agent by which something is done.[120] For clarity we have expanded the phrase to read "led by Moses" in our Rendition.

3:17 ***But with whom was he grieved forty years? was it not with them that had sinned, whose carcases fell in the wilderness? / And with whom was God angry for forty years? Was it not those who sinned, whose dead bodies fell in the wilderness?:*** The author follows the first two rhetorical questions with two more to again stress the point he wants to make. This set identifies how long Jehovah was vexed and with whom. His feelings are described as προσοχθίζω (*prosochthizō*), "to be angry." For development, see Translation Notes for 3:8 above. For the phrase τεσσεράκοντα ἔτη (*tesserakona etē*), "forty years," see Translation Notes for 3:9 above.[121]

The author here alludes to Numbers 14:20–35. The verb ἁμαρτάνω (*hamartanō*) means "to sin." For development, see Translation Notes for 3:13 above. The noun κῶλον (*kōlon*) refers to a dead body.[122] Here it points to the end result of rebellion. These people died in the wilderness physically. Jehovah allowed that to happen because they were already spiritually dead.

3:18 ***And to whom sware he that they should not enter into his rest, but to them that believed not? / And to whom did he swear that they would not enter into his rest if it was not those who were disobedient?:*** The author here asks and answers the last of his rhetorical questions. On both the verb ὀμνύω (*omnuō*), "to swear an oath," and the noun κατάπαυσις (*katapausis*), "rest," seeTranslation Notes for 3:11 above.

The verb ἀπειθέω (*apeitheō*), "to disobey, be disobedient," in the New Testament always describes disobedience toward God.[123] It expresses itself outwardly in disobedience. The seat of Israel's rebellion was this stubborn refusal to be persuaded no matter what Jehovah did. In face of the unmistakable and irrefutable evidence of his existence and power, such rebellion was unconscionable. The verb reinforces the picture that the Old Testament paints of these people (for example, see Ezek. 20:5–24). Their hearts were so diamond-hard that nothing could penetrate them. No force could turn them to Jehovah.

---

120. BDAG, 223–26.

121. The term definitely refers to those who had seen the marvelous work of Jehovah in freeing them from Egypt as well as Jehovah's disclosure at Sinai. Bruce, *Epistle to the Hebrews,* 102.

122. BDAG, 579.

123. BDAG, 99; Louw-Nida, §31.07; 36.23; Bultmann, *TDNT,* 6:10–11.

3:19 ***So we see that they could not enter in because of unbelief / And so we see that they were not able to enter because of unbelief:*** With the phrase καὶ βλέπομεν (*kai blepomen*), "and so we see," the author draws his conclusion. With acute insight, he exposes the seat of Israel's rebellion and its resultant curse. It was ἀπιστία (*apistia*), "disbelief." For development, see Translation Notes for 3:12 above. The result of disbelief is a lack of trust.[124] Because the Hebrews did not trust God, they would not follow his ways. Since his ways lead to his "rest," they never found it and therefore forfeited eternal life.[125]

Analysis and Summary

The author of Hebrews, in order to forcefully develop his thesis, draws upon the continuity of God's people. He does not, however, at this point mention the blessings that can accrue through that relationship. Instead, he draws a negative lesson from the past by focusing on the consequences of faithlessness (3:19, drawn from Num. 14). To emphasize his point, he quotes from Psalm 95:7–11, where the Psalmist castigates Israel's faithlessness.[126]

The inspired Old Testament poet clearly sets out the problem by quoting Jehovah as saying, "They are always going astray in their hearts and they have not understood my ways" (Ps. 95:10; NR Heb. 3:10). With these words, the poet reveals both the cause and the effect of Israel's rebellion. The cause was the condition of the Hebrews' hearts, referring to their complete moral and mental center.[127] The effect was that this condition kept them from understanding and following God's ways.[128] And why? Because of deception. The Hebrews took something false as true—their perceived good situation under Egyptian rule and their belief in the power of the Egyptians gods (Ex. 17:3; Ezek. 20:8, 16; see also Num. 14:2–5; 20:3–5).[129]

---

124. Louw-Nida, §31.40, 98; see also Johnson, *Hebrews,* 115–16, 119; and Cockerill, *Epistle to the Hebrews,* 183.

125. The Prophet Joseph Smith noted that a person is "never damned for believing too much, but they are damned for unbelief." "History, 1838–1856, Volume F-1 [1 May 1844–8 August 1844]," 103–4, Joseph Smith Papers, https://www.josephsmithpapers.org/paper-summary/history-1838-1856-volume-f-1-1-may-1844-8-august-1844/109.

126. Faithlessness here is not a passive or lethargic disbelief, but an active resistance to the will of God. Attridge, *Epistle to the Hebrews,* 116–17.

127. Strong, "New Strong's Expanded Dictionary . . . Greek," s.v. καρδία.

128. Louw-Nida, §31.8, and n. 2. In Rev. 12:9, the definite article is combined with the present participle to give Satan the designation of "the Deceiver."

129. A careful reading of the Exodus story shows that the Israelites were of two minds in Egypt. They were under the heavy burden of slavery and resented, even cried against it,

What made their rebellion so particularly onerous was that Jehovah's power was fully revealed in Egypt and at Sinai. Even if the Egyptian gods actually existed, his display of power proved them impotent before his omnipotence.[130] Even so, these hardened people refused to be persuaded by it and accept him as their God (Ezek. 20:7–8). President Brigham Young noted, "If they had been sanctified and holy, the children of Israel would not have travelled one year with Moses before they would have received their endowments and the Melchisedec Priesthood."[131]

As the text shows (3:10), the driving force behind their obdurate stubbornness was their hearts (καρδία, *kardia*). As used here, the imagery connotes not simply emotions, as it does in English, but also the full spectrum of a person's mental and emotional activities. It also points to the very depths of their soul, that which determines who and what they are.[132] It was here, at their very center, where the Israelites were deceived.

The problem with their hearts was that they were hard (σκληρύνω, *sklērynō*).[133] The imagery points to the very depths of their character and shows its rigid stubbornness, an obdurate nature that continually resisted the word of God. It made them unwilling, if not unable, to repent, that is, to abandon their seductive idolatry and return (שׁוּב, *šûb*) to Jehovah.[134] It was for this reason, according to the Old Testament, that Jehovah threatened on more than one occasion to destroy them (Ex. 32:9–10; Deut. 9:13–14).

---

but they also enjoyed a good deal of security. Noteworthy is that when Jehovah assigned Moses his task of freeing Israel, the prophet's first fear was that the Hebrews would not believe him. For that reason, the first set of signs God gave Moses were to convince the stubborn-hearted Hebrews he was indeed Jehovah's prophet. Ex. 4:1–9. Ezekiel exposed fully the folly of these Hebrews, noting that they refused to give up their idolatry and deliberately rebelled against Jehovah. Thus, they forfeited their blessing of entering into the holy land. Ezek. 20:5–9; see also Johnson, *Hebrews,* 116.

130. For those with eyes to see, Jehovah's plagues challenged the power of a number of Egyptian gods and proved them defenseless if not nonexistent. For a study, see John J. Davis, *Moses and the Gods of Egypt: Studies in Exodus* (Grand Rapids, Mich.: Baker Book House, 1986).

131. Brigham Young, in *Journal of Discourses,* 6:100.

132. See Behm, *TDNT,* 3:605–9.

133. BDAG, 930.

134. Their descendants suffered from the same malady. The Lord told Isaiah that his people "draw near me with their mouth, . . . but have removed their heart far from me" (Isa. 29:13–14), and as a consequence, their wisdom and understanding would fail. When the heart is wrong, the things of God cannot be known. When they are unknown, God is unknown. Thus, the Savior warned that even though there were those who would do good deeds, because these did not bring them to know him, they were working iniquity. As a result, he would say to them, "ye never knew me, depart from me" (JST Matt. 7:22–23).

The imagery of the hard heart is often associated with that of a stiff neck when describing these people (see 1 Ne. 2:11; Jacob 4:14; Alma 9:5, 31, for examples of being stiff necked). The two work together nicely. Though both define a stubborn disobedience, the hard heart looks to the soul of the individual while stiff neck looks to the actions.[135] The result of both is the same: an inability to understand the things of God (1 Ne. 7:8; 2 Ne. 25:28; 32:7; Enos 1:22).[136] The Book of Mormon describes the state of such a person as being "past feeling" (1 Ne. 17:45; Moro. 9:20; see also Eph. 4:19).[137] The imagery works. Since God reveals his will through the mind and heart (D&C 8:2; compare D&C 9:7–9; 64:34), feelings are part of the revelatory process. When one cannot feel the Lord's words, he or she cannot understand them. As a result, such people constantly resisted the Spirit of God (Acts 7:51; Jarom 1:3–4).

In Israel's case, sin deceived and blinded their hearts such that they could not see, let alone walk, the path Jehovah had set for them. However, it took energy to not know the path. Indeed, the revelation at Sinai described it in detail (Ex. 6:4; Deut. 4:13; 5:2). Further, they had covenanted to stay on it (Ex. 19:1–8; see also Josh. 24:27). Because of the clarity with which Jehovah had revealed both himself and his law, the Israelites' rejection of them constituted the most grievous of sins.[138] The result was distressing—they did not know (γινώσκω, *ginōskō*) Jehovah.[139] That condition precluded them not only from receiving his ultimate blessing, but also from partaking of his mercy (Isa. 27:11).

In sum, the imagery of a hard heart connotes the obdurate nature of a person's soul. The author of Hebrews uses Israel's history as a warning that if not corrected, faithlessness leads not only to the abandonment of God but also to a rebellion against his ways (3:10). The prophet Alma, interpreting Psalm 92 in the same way as the author of Hebrews, warned his people,

> If ye will harden your hearts ye shall not enter into the rest of the Lord; therefore your iniquity provoketh him that he sendeth down his wrath

---

135. The conditions most often arise when one is reproved and reacts against it. Prov. 29:1; see also Neh. 9:16, 17, 29; and Jer. 7:26; 19:15. The same Hebrew verb, קָשָׁה (*qāšāh*), used in each of these instances is the same one that describes the condition of Pharaoh's heart in Ex. 7:3.

136. Largey, *Book of Mormon Reference Companion,* 319, 744.

137. Largey, *Book of Mormon Reference Companion,* 631–32.

138. To describe Israel's sin, Moses used the verb הִמְרָה (*himrāh*), "to behave rebelliously." Deut. 1:26, 43; 9:23; *HAL,* 633; BDB, 598.

139. *NID,* s.v. "γινώσκω." This condition continued to plague them. See Isa. 1:3; Jer. 2:8; 5:21; 8:7; and Hos. 5:4; 6:6. The result was that they forfeited Jehovah's mercy. Isa. 27:11.

> upon you as in the first provocation, yea, according to his word in the last provocation as well as the first, to the everlasting destruction of your souls; therefore, according to his word, unto the last death, as well as the first. And now, my brethren, seeing we know these things, and they are true, let us repent, and harden not our hearts, that we provoke not the Lord our God to pull down his wrath upon us in these his second commandments which he has given unto us; but let us enter into the rest of God, which is prepared according to his word. (Alma 12:36–37; see also Alma 13:13)

In order for people so affected to get on the path, they must first see through sin's deceptions to the true God and then sacrifice the evil heart—"sacrifice" being an excellent symbol of faith and trust—that developed because of their initial blindness.[140]

For a person to sacrifice such a heart—and given the power of sin's hold, such a sacrifice is extremely difficult to make—thrills God. But the real sacrifice is not of giving the heart away but of setting it right. The only way to do that is to break it. It is in this light that the Psalmist states that "the sacrifices of God are a broken spirit, [that is, metaphorically] a broken and a contrite heart" (Ps. 51:17) and promises that "the Lord is nigh unto them that are of a broken heart; and saveth such as be of a contrite spirit" (Ps. 34:18). The poet was also acutely aware of the amazing consequences of such a great sacrifice. Indeed, Jehovah "healeth the broken in heart, and bindeth up their wounds" (Ps. 147:3), thus making the person spiritually whole and well.

To make such a sacrifice demands that individuals "rend that veil of unbelief which doth cause [them] to remain in [their] awful state of wickedness, and hardness of heart, and blindness of mind." The reward for doing this is wondrous. To these softened souls, those "great and marvelous things which have been hid up from the foundation of the world" will be revealed unto them (Ether 4:15; see also Jacob 1:7; and 3 Ne. 12:19).[141]

None of those who came out of Egypt received such a blessing because of their faithlessness. But there was another and even more severe result of Israel's revolt. The author describes it as "rebellion" (παραπικρασμός, *parapikrasmos*)

---

140. See Johnson, *Hebrews,* 117–18.

141. The same is true today. The Lord has commanded his modern disciples, "Thou shalt offer a sacrifice unto the Lord thy God in righteousness, even that of a broken heart and a contrite spirit" (D&C 59:8). For those who have been formerly hardened, the Lord has made such a sacrifice as a condition of being baptized (D&C 20:37; see also 3 Ne. 9:20). It is these also for whom the Savior "offereth himself a sacrifice for sin" (2 Ne. 2:7).

(3:8). The word denotes a state of affairs that provokes a person to intense anger.[142] In this case, what Israel did was incite Jehovah's wrath (3:10). And it is little wonder—these people were so brazen as to continually put Jehovah on trial (3:9). The Psalmist used two words to describe what they did: a verb meaning "to make trial of, put to the test" (πειράζω, *peirazō*)[143] and a noun meaning "test, examination" (δοκιμασία, *dokimasia*).[144] Together these words suggest the wearing and exasperating character of Jehovah's experience with these people as he dealt with them over the forty-year period. And although Jehovah came through in every instance, they were unrelenting in their distrust of him.

The result was that Jehovah would not allow these rebellious souls to enter into his "rest" (κατάπαυσις, *katapausis*). The term has two meanings. One denotes the conditions that the faithful would find in the promised land. There they would experience ease under Jehovah's care. The other more typological meaning connotes God's heavenly realm.[145] These rebellious souls would have access to neither. Because of their hard hearts, they "could not endure [God's] presence; therefore, the Lord in his wrath . . . took Moses out of their midst, and the Holy Priesthood also," but in his mercy, the Lord allowed "the lesser priesthood" to continue (D&C 84:23–24).[146]

The word "wrath" stresses the frightening response of Jehovah to Israel's rebellion (and that of any other people). Because the exclusive power of the higher priesthood is to minister the fulness of the gospel and to hold "the key of the mysteries of the kingdom, even the key of the knowledge of God," and because only through it is "the power of godliness manifest" (D&C 84:19–20), its loss meant there would be no direct access between Israel and Jehovah.[147]

---

142. BDAG, 770; *NID,* s.v." πικρός."

143. BDAG, 792–93; *NID,* s.v. "πειράζω"; see also Johnson, *Hebrews,* 115.

144. BDAG, 256.

145. *NID,* s.v. "ἀναπαύω."

146. Douglas H. Parker and Ze'ev W. Falk, "Law of Moses," in Ludlow, *Encyclopedia of Mormonism,* 2:810–12; see also McConkie, *Promised Messiah,* 406.

147. The Hebrews used the phrase אֶרֶךְ אַפַּיִם (*'erek 'appayim*), meaning "slow to anger," to describe one of the attributes of Jehovah. The phrase is consistently translated in the LXX with "μακρόθυμος," denoting that which is self-controlled, patient, and forbearing. BDAG, 613. This attribute, however, did not preclude God swelling with anger when certain sins were committed. His ire often expressed itself in his leaving the rebellious to face the consequences of their actions.

It is very important to note that though these Israelites through their continual rebellion rejected Jehovah, he never rejected them. Instead, year after taxing year, he worked with them, lifted them, and protected them. That is not to say that he intervened in every trial. At times he attempted to let them learn from their own mistakes. Even so, when push came to shove, he was there for them.

There are at least two reasons why. First, though filled with anger, his mercy kept it in abeyance. Indeed, one of his traits that drew people to him was his mercy expressed as loving kindness (albeit undergirded with a touch of steel) (Ps. 89:1; 106:7, 45; 117:2; Isa. 57:1; Lam. 3:22, 32).[148] The second reason was that, according to Ezekiel, mercy was for the sake of Jehovah's name, "that it should not be polluted before the heathen, among whom they [the Hebrews] were" (Ezek. 20:9). He had made a covenant with their forefathers, Abraham, Isaac, and Jacob, that he would watch over their posterity such that they would become plentiful.

Though the vast majority of Hebrews were astonishingly unable to see it, they were on the brink of destruction as a people in Egypt—the killing of male babies a sure attestation. As threatening as their physical demise was, their spiritual demise was even greater. According to Ezekiel, so wicked had they become that Jehovah determined that he would "pour out [his] fury upon them, to accomplish [his] anger against them in the midst of the land of Egypt" (Ezek. 20:8). However, even though greatly upset, as a God who keeps covenants, he forestalled the move (Ezek. 20:9). Unfortunately, the Hebrews did not respond to his mercy. The show of his power, from their point of view, did little more than drive them away from their comforts. As a result, they first murmured and then rebelled against him.[149] Although Jehovah went out of his way to sustain them, his unrelenting ire never abated until the last of that generation finally fell in the wilderness (3:17). But during the journey, a new and, it was hoped, more pliant generation matured ready to receive the land and enjoy God's rest (Deut. 4:20–24; 6:3–9; 11:1–9).

---

148. The Hebrew word חֶסֶד (*ḥesed*), often translated as "mercy," combines the traits of love, strength, and steadfastness. It is one of the most important words in Old Testament ethic and theology. It nuances covenant relationships, especially that between Jehovah and Israel, and connotes the reciprocal rights and obligations between them. The translation of the word as "loving kindness" is good, but too soft. One needs to feel behind it the firmness conveyed in such words as constancy and toughness.

149. One cannot help but think of Laman and Lemuel, who continually murmured against God because, like Israel, they were blinded by the seduction of sin. Compare Ex. 15:24; 17:3; Num. 14:2; 16:41; and 1 Ne. 2:11; 3:31; 17:17.

The rebellion of the Israelites at Kadesh-Barnea was, then, the culmination of all Israel's apostasy and, therefore, served as the perfect example for the author of Hebrews.[150] He used that history, which clearly showed the consequences of faithlessness, to forcefully warn his readers what would happen if they followed their ancestors' path.

Behind the author's use of the scripture is a tacit insistence that the potential for great blessings also leads to the potential for great cursings. But, it should be noted, he does not use the delinquent ancient Israelites as a type of the new Israel.[151] Indeed, "both groups are part of the one people of God called by his word to the same kind of faith and obedience in anticipation of the same 'rest.' Thus the wilderness generation's loss of God's 'rest' poses the sternest warning to contemporary believers. On the basis of this continuity the [author] urges his hearers to separate themselves from their predecessors by persevering in faithful obedience."[152]

The specific Kadesh-like trial the author's readers were facing, the text does not reveal. Many scholars accept the idea that the Christians were suffering from social unacceptance and were worried that more severe persecutions were looming in the near future.[153] Whatever else his concern, the author is worried with his readers' reaction thereto. The possible rejection of the new covenant placed readers in a situation as precarious as that of ancient Israel. His desire was to awaken within them the awful consequences of their current tendency to "neglect so great salvation" (2:3) and let it "drift away" (NR 2:1). They must hold fast to the end or, like their forebearers, lose all.[154] Indeed, "a relapse from Christianity into Judaism would be comparable to the action of the Israelites when they 'turned back in their hearts to Egypt' [compare Acts 7:39]; it would not be a mere return

150. Cockerill, *Epistle to the Hebrews,* 155–56; compare Koester, *Hebrews,* 264 n. 124.

151. To see ancient Israel as a "type" is misleading because it suggests the two are not both "God's people" sharing in one long history. On this, see Jon Laansma, *"I Will Give You Rest": The Rest Motif in the New Testament with Special Reference to Mt 11 and Heb 3–4* (Tübingen: Mohr Siebeck, 1997), 275; compare Ellingworth, *Epistle to the Hebrews,* 216.

152. Cockerill, *Epistle to the Hebrews,* 154–55. Kimball, "Privilege of Holding the Priesthood," 80, notes that resting is not relaxing or sitting around: "It is he who is the most dynamic, the one who works the hardest, puts in the longest hours, and lives the closest to his Heavenly Father who is rested—rested from his labors, but not put away from his work."

153. For review, see Lane, *Hebrews 1–8,* 90.

154. Cockerill, *Epistle to the Hebrews,* 156.

to a position previously occupied, but a gesture of outright apostasy, a complete break with God."[155]

To give punch to what he says, the author not only uses scripture but makes it relevant to his hearers through his emphasis on the word "today" (σήμερον, *sēmeron*). The term designates a specific and short period of time during which something must be completed or the result would be either compromised or forfeited.[156] At stake here is eternal life. We find this same usage in the Doctrine and Covenants, where the Lord gives the Latter-day Saints much the same warning: this period is one of "sacrifice, and a day for the tithing of my people" and that "after today cometh the burning" (D&C 45:6). Indeed, "tomorrow all the proud and they that do wickedly shall be as stubble" (D&C 64:22–24; compare John 9:4; and Jacob 6:6).[157]

The author, playing off this idea, stresses the need for his readers to hear (ἀκούω, *akouō*) God's voice. Since they are free to pay attention or not,[158] he is anxious they do not miss the opportunity (3:7, 13). To do so would cost them their eternal lives, thus his insistence that they hear "today" before it is too late. All should be warned that it is possible for anyone to "procrastinate the day of [their] repentance until the end," for then "cometh the night of darkness wherein there can be no labor performed" (Alma 34:33).

The admonition "do not harden your heats" (NR 3:8, 15) is instructive. It shows that it is the person who makes the heart hard. How does the person do that? He or she must have access to God's word and then deliberately resist it. But why the resistance? It is because of the enticements, the initial intoxication, and the deception of sin. When a person yields to those enticements, the hardening process begins and continues until the person's heart becomes so hard it resists both the influence and power of the Spirit to soften it.

155. Bruce, *Epistle to the Hebrews,* 100; compare D. H. Tongue, "The Concept of Apostasy in the Epistle to the Hebrews," *Tyndale Bulletin* 5–6 (1960): 19–26, who suggests that the readers were Jewish Christians who were tempted to return to some form of Judaism instead of advancing to Christian perfection.

156. Fuchs, *TDNT,* 7:269–75; BDAG, 921.

157. Each person's lifetime may be termed "today," for it is specifically designed as the period in which to prepare for eternal life. Alma 12:24; 34:32; 42:10–13. The sense of the word is that of God's continual and open-ended revelation to his people (Heb. 1:1). Johnson, *Hebrews,* 114. Thus, "it is called today until the coming of the Son of Man" (D&C 64:23).

158. BDAG, 37–38.

The irony is that even though sin becomes a very hard, demanding master—one that will all too often brutalize the soul—it is still a binding one that the person no longer has the will to escape. Even though the individual cannot break sin's grip, there is a power that can, but they tragically will not reach for it. Indeed, God is ever willing to help, but that cannot happen to these people because their hearts have become too hard and unyielding to the influence of the Spirit of God.

In reality, sin is not an agent; it is a deed. Nonetheless, there is a real and active agent out there, and the scriptures clearly reveal his work, desires, and aims. He is Lucifer, son of the morning, the angel who rebelled against God (D&C 76:25–27; Moses 4:1–4) and became Satan (Rev. 12:7–9). Being miserable, he now seeks the misery of all humankind (2 Ne. 2:18, 27).

It is of note that, in the battle between him and God, they both seek the same objective: the hearts of the children of men. Indeed, Satan must first get hold of people's hearts so they will not yield to the truth (Alma 10:25; Hel. 6:31; D&C 10:20, 32; 78:10). When people do not listen—and the first move is the person's—Satan is able to blind their eyes so that they cannot understand God's word. Truly it becomes "a foolish and a vain thing" to them (3 Ne. 2:2; see also Alma 10:25). Thus, we see that he is indeed the great deceiver (D&C 50:3; 52:14).

To accomplish his goals, Satan often sends forth "lyings . . . to harden [people's] hearts, to the intent that they might not believe" (3 Ne. 1:22). He also stirs up "people to do all manner of iniquity, and to the puffing them up with pride, tempting them to seek for power, and authority, and riches, and the vain things of the world" (3 Ne. 6:15). But his whole thrust in stirring them up to rebel is to "lead their souls to destruction" (D&C 10:22, 27; 64:17).

He is subtle. At first, he binds them with nonchafing, almost comfortable "flaxen cord[s]" (2 Ne. 26:22), but eventually, he switches to hard, chafing chains (Alma 12:6) from which they cannot escape. Indeed, at this point he has "sealed [them] his" (Alma 34:35). When they can no longer escape from him, "he having subjected them according to his will" (Alma 12:17), he unleashes his full fury upon them with the intent of making them as miserable as possible for as long as possible. What he does is called "the buffetings of Satan" (D&C 78:12; 82:21; 104:9–10; 132:26). The word describes a pitiless attack accomplished by repeated and hard blows.

It must be remembered that all this misery happens because these people yielded to the blandishments of sin that turned their hearts hard. Thus, did they yield themselves to the power of Satan (compare 3 Ne. 7:5).

But what needs to be kept in mind is Christ will destroy Satan and his works "at the end of the world" (D&C 19:3). One way Christ will accomplish this is, ironically, through the brutality of hell. What heaven cannot accomplish, Hades will. Here, when their "soul [is] racked with eternal torment" (Mosiah 27:29), these people's hard hearts will finally break. When they do, these people's spirits will also be contrite. Then they will, at last, reach to their Savior for release and redemption (compare Alma 26:6–19). And he will respond. As one General Authority noted, "Through paying the debt of sin for each of us, Jesus brings us, if we desire," to life.[159] Through his mercy and grace, he will bring even these once hardened souls, finally, to a place of rest and peace.[160]

---

159. David B. Haight, *A Light unto the World* (Salt Lake City: Deseret Book, 1997), 128.

160. As a Latter-day Saint scholar observed, "Some of us have the naive opinion that Jesus merely pays the debt of sin for man and resurrects us, and from there we must work out our salvation by our works. Those who hold this view should read and understand Section 93 of the Doctrine and Covenants. We are to be glorified by grace." Hyrum L. Andrus, *The Glory of God and Man's Relation to Deity* (Provo, Utah: Extension Publications, Brigham Young University, 1964), 31. It should also be noted that, because of their rebellion, these people cannot receive celestial glory and be reunited with the Father (D&C 76:98–112; 88:21–24). Nonetheless, they are resurrected and go to a kingdom of glory, a place of happiness. There they receive some association with the Divine through the administration of the Holy Spirit (D&C 76:81–86). The only ones who actually receive eternal punishment with the devil and his angels are those whose hearts are so hard that even the immense pressure of hell cannot break them. These are Perdition's sons and suffer his fate (D&C 76:43–49). For Latter-day Saint studies on grace, see Gerald N. Lund, "The Grace and Mercy of Christ," in Peterson, Hatch, and Card, *Jesus Christ: Son of God, Savior,* 18–49; Robinson, *Believing Christ,* 57–108; Draper and Rhodes, *Paul's First Epistle to the Corinthians,* 74–100; Brent J. Schmidt, *Relational Grace: The Reciprocal and Binding Covenant of* Charis (Provo, Utah: BYU Studies, 2015); Robert L. Millet, *Grace Works (*Salt Lake City: Deseret Book, 2003); and Sheri Dew, *Amazed by Grace* (Salt Lake City: Deseret Book, 2015).

Chapter 4

The Promise of Divine Rest through Jesus, the Great High Priest

Introduction

Having examined the seat of ancient Israel's rebellion against Jehovah and its disastrous results, in this chapter the author states the lessons he wants his readers to learn (4:1–3, 14–16). He admonishes them not to be faithless as their ancestors were, having a faithlessness that cost them the great blessing of entering the "rest of the Lord" (4:4–13). As he builds his case, the author uses subtle and, with a superficial reading, what appear to be somewhat illusive arguments. The seat of his case centers on the force of the richly nuanced noun "rest" (κατάπαυσις, *katapausis*), which he introduced in chapter 3. Up to this point, however, he has not provided a clue as to how he wants it understood. A reason may be that he did not want his readers distracted from his main point: the ancients lost their reward due to faithlessness and its final manifestation, outright rebellion. Now, through the development of a skillful, exegetical argument, the author at last discloses what he understands as "God's 'rest.'"[1]

The author stresses to his readers that although the previous recipients of the opportunity of entering into Jehovah's rest failed to achieve it (4:2), God has appointed another period during which the promise can be realized: it is "to day" (4:7). Because this term connotes a short and specific interval, it gives urgency to realizing the promised blessing lest it be lost once again. That urgency gives force to the admonitions the author makes (4:1, 11).[2]

1. Attridge, *Epistle to the Hebrews,* 123; Cockerill, *Epistle to the Hebrews,* 196.
2. Attridge, *Epistle to the Hebrews,* 123.

The author develops his argument by interweaving three scriptures. The first, LXX Psalm 94:11 (4:3b),[3] recounts Jehovah's oath that none of the rebellious Israelites will enter into his "rest." The second passage, Genesis 2:2 (4:4), recounts God's declaration that he will "rest" on the seventh day of creation. The author uses this passage to establish the fact that God prepared a celestial "rest" from the foundation of the earth, a "rest" that some will enter at some later point. His third scripture, LXX Psalm 94:7 (4:11), contains the invitation for believers to enter God's "rest." The author uses it to show that the rebellious children of Israel's failure to enter into God's rest does not mean the opportunity is closed for all time. Indeed, the opportunity was not spent. One can still enter into it as long as they do so "to day."[4]

The author then assures his readers that not only can they enter into God's rest, but they will find divine help in doing so (4:14–16). That help will come from their great High Priest, who, having borne the whole of mortal experience, can sympathize with their weaknesses and commiserate with their challenges. They can therefore approach him in confidence (4:16).

The Rest That God Promises (4:1–13)

Greek Text

1 Φοβηθῶμεν οὖν μήποτε καταλειπομένης ἐπαγγελίας εἰσελθεῖν εἰς τὴν κατάπαυσιν αὐτοῦ δοκῇ τις ἐξ ὑμῶν ὑστερηκέναι· 2 καὶ γάρ ἐσμεν εὐηγγελισμένοι καθάπερ κἀκεῖνοι, ἀλλ' οὐκ ὠφέλησεν ὁ λόγος τῆς ἀκοῆς ἐκείνους, μὴ συγκεκερασμένους τῇ πίστει τοῖς ἀκούσασιν. 3 εἰσερχόμεθα γὰρ εἰς κατάπαυσιν οἱ πιστεύσαντες, καθὼς εἴρηκεν· Ὡς ὤμοσα ἐν τῇ ὀργῇ μου, Εἰ εἰσελεύσονται εἰς τὴν κατάπαυσίν μου, καίτοι τῶν ἔργων ἀπὸ καταβολῆς κόσμου γενηθέντων, 4 εἴρηκεν γάρ που περὶ τῆς ἑβδόμης οὕτως· Καὶ κατέπαυσεν ὁ θεὸς ἐν τῇ ἡμέρᾳ τῇ ἑβδόμῃ ἀπὸ πάντων τῶν ἔργων αὐτοῦ, 5 καὶ ἐν τούτῳ πάλιν· Εἰ εἰσελεύσονται εἰς τὴν κατάπαυσίν μου. 6 ἐπεὶ οὖν ἀπολείπεται τινὰς εἰσελθεῖν εἰς αὐτήν, καὶ οἱ πρότερον εὐαγγελισθέντες οὐκ εἰσῆλθον δι' ἀπείθειαν, 7 πάλιν τινὰ ὁρίζει ἡμέραν, Σήμερον, ἐν Δαυὶδ λέγων μετὰ τοσοῦτον χρόνον, καθὼς προείρηται, Σήμερον ἐὰν τῆς φωνῆς αὐτοῦ ἀκούσητε, μὴ σκληρύνητε τὰς καρδίας ὑμῶν· 8 εἰ γὰρ αὐτοὺς Ἰησοῦς κατέπαυσεν, οὐκ ἂν περὶ ἄλλης ἐλάλει μετὰ ταῦτα ἡμέρας. 9 ἄρα ἀπολείπεται σαββατισμὸς τῷ λαῷ

---

3. This is Psalm 95 in the MT, the KJV, and most English Bibles.
4. Cockerill, *Epistle to the Hebrews,* 197.

τοῦ θεοῦ· 10 ὁ γὰρ εἰσελθὼν εἰς τὴν κατάπαυσιν αὐτοῦ καὶ αὐτὸς κατέπαυσεν ἀπὸ τῶν ἔργων αὐτοῦ ὥσπερ ἀπὸ τῶν ἰδίων ὁ θεός. 11 σπουδάσωμεν οὖν εἰσελθεῖν εἰς ἐκείνην τὴν κατάπαυσιν, ἵνα μὴ ἐν τῷ αὐτῷ τις ὑποδείγματι πέσῃ τῆς ἀπειθείας.

12 Ζῶν γὰρ ὁ λόγος τοῦ θεοῦ καὶ ἐνεργὴς καὶ τομώτερος ὑπὲρ πᾶσαν μάχαιραν δίστομον καὶ διϊκνούμενος ἄχρι μερισμοῦ ψυχῆς καὶ πνεύματος, ἁρμῶν τε καὶ μυελῶν, καὶ κριτικὸς ἐνθυμήσεων καὶ ἐννοιῶν καρδίας· 13 καὶ οὐκ ἔστιν κτίσις ἀφανὴς ἐνώπιον αὐτοῦ, πάντα δὲ γυμνὰ καὶ τετραχηλισμένα τοῖς ὀφθαλμοῖς αὐτοῦ, πρὸς ὃν ἡμῖν ὁ λόγος. [SBLGNT]

King James Version

1 Let us therefore fear, lest, a promise being left us of entering into his rest, any of you should seem to come short of it. 2 For unto us was the gospel preached, as well as unto them: but the word preached did not profit them, not being mixed with faith in them that heard it. 3 For we which have believed do enter into rest, as he said, As I have sworn in my wrath, if they shall enter into my rest: although the works were finished from the foundation of the world. 4 For he spake in a certain place of the seventh day on this wise, And God did rest the seventh day from all his works. 5 And in this place again, If they shall enter into my rest. 6 Seeing therefore it remaineth that some must enter therein, and they to whom it was first preached entered not in because of unbelief: 7 Again, he limiteth a certain day, saying in David, To day, after so long a time; as it is said, To day if ye will hear his voice, harden not your hearts. 8 For if Jesus had given them rest, then would he not afterward have spoken of another day. 9 There remaineth therefore a rest to the people of God. 10 For he that is entered into his rest, he also hath ceased from his own works, as God did from his. 11 Let us labour therefore to enter into that rest, lest

New Rendition

1 Therefore let us be concerned, while the promise of entering into his rest still stands, that none of you should be found to have failed to reach it. 2 For we have also had the gospel preached to us even as they did, but the message they heard did not benefit them, because they were not united with those who listened in faith. 3 For we who have believed enter into that rest, as he has said:

> "So I swore an oath in my anger, 'They will certainly not enter into my rest'" [LXX Ps. 94:11],

although God's works have been finished since the founding of the world. 4 For somewhere he has spoken about the seventh day as follows:

> "And God rested on the seventh day from all of his works." [LXX Gen. 2:2]

5 And as cited earlier,

> "They will certainly not enter into my rest." [LXX Ps. 94:11]

6 Now since it remains for some to enter into that rest, and those who formerly had the gospel preached to them did not enter in because of disobedience, 7 God again appoints a certain day, "Today," speaking much later through David, as has been previously cited,

any man fall after the same example of unbelief. 12 For the word of God is quick, and powerful, and sharper than any twoedged sword, piercing even to the dividing asunder of soul and spirit, and of the joints and marrow, and is a discerner of the thoughts and intents of the heart. 13 Neither is there any creature that is not manifest in his sight: but all things are naked and opened unto the eyes of him with whom we have to do.

"Today, if only you would listen to his voice! Do not harden your hearts." [LXX Ps. 94:7]

8 For if Joshua had given them rest, God would not have spoken later of another day. 9 Consequently a Sabbath rest remains for the people of God. 10 For anyone who enters into God's rest, he also rests from his works just as God rested from his own works. 11 Therefore, let us strive to enter into that rest, so that no one will fall into that same pattern of disobedience. 12 For the word of God is living and active, sharper than any double-edged sword that penetrates until it separates soul and spirit, joint and marrow, and is able to discern the thoughts and intentions of the heart. 13 No one is hidden from his sight, but everything is open and laid bare to the eyes of him to whom we must give an accounting.

Translation Notes and Comments

4:1 ***Let us therefore fear / Therefore let us be concerned:*** The author uses the subordinating conjunction οὖν (*oun*), "therefore," to signal his readers that he is now making his point. The Greek verb φοβέομαι (*phobeomai*) carries the meaning of being "apprehensive" or "afraid."[5] In our Rendition, we felt that "concern" rather than "fear" best conveyed the sense of the word in modern English. By using the first-person plural hortatory subjunctive form of the verb, "let *us* be concerned" (emphasis added), the author ties himself to his readers and softens any antagonism his admonition might generate.[6] The phrase should also force his readers to consider the matter at hand with more gravity and circumspection than they have in the past.[7]

5. BDAG, 1060.
6. See Johnson, *Hebrews,* 124; and Cockerill, *Epistle to the Hebrews,* 200.
7. Cockerill, *Epistle to the Hebrews,* 201.

a promise being left us of entering into his rest / while the promise of entering into his rest still stands: The noun κατάπαυσις (*katapausis*), "rest," as used by the author, looks primarily to the place where God's rest can be found. The noun is used in the LXX as a translation of the Hebrew מְנוּחָה (*mĕnûḥāh*), "resting place, place of quiet."[8] Just as the promised land was a real place of rest, so too the Father, through the Son, has prepared another real place of rest, this one eternal and where his children can be with him forever.

The author chooses not to use another noun, ἀνάπαυσις (*anapausis*), "rest," which denotes the *result* of rest: refreshment, recuperation, and rejuvenation. Therefore, he shies away from the connotation of the peace or repose one finds in unity with God, one that brings respite from the vicissitudes of life.[9] In mortality, such a state is found only in part, when one has a firm testimony that the gospel is true and that his or her life is pleasing to God.[10] There is little doubt that this idea stands behind the author's imagery, but the challenges and heartaches of mortality remain as long as one is here. Thus, it is to the celestial city, with its mansions for the righteous, that the author looks (11:10; 12:22; see also Matt. 5:5; and D&C 59:2; 98:18. The place's beauty is compellingly symbolized in Rev. 21:10–22:5).[11]

The noun ἐπαγγελία (*epangelia*), "promise," denotes an announcement openly or publicly proclaimed concerning something that will or must be done. Because it also carries the force of obligation, it is often appropriately translated as "promise," as in the KJV and NR. When the noun deals with God, the echo of sacred covenant stands behind it.[12]

The verb καταλείπω (*kataleipō*), "to stand," carries two nuances: one is to leave something behind, and the other is to leave something in existence.[13] It is the latter at play here. The verb's use shows the promised blessing is

---

8. *HAL*, 600. The word denotes "eternal rest" in 4Q525 14 II, 14, and is connected with the Day of Atonement in 1QpHab XI 6–8. It has temple significance in contemporary rabbinic literature and shows up in Tosefta Zevahin 13:9.

9. *NID*, s.v. "ἀναπαύω"; compare Christie H. Frandsen, "Trials," in Ludlow, *Encyclopedia of Mormonism*, 4:1488.

10. Joseph F. Smith, *Gospel Doctrine*, 11th ed. (Salt Lake City: Deseret Book, 1959), 58. He further notes on page 126 that "rest" does not refer to cessation of physical labor, but to "spiritual rest and peace which are born from a settled conviction of the truth in the minds of men."

11. For development, see Analysis below.

12. BDAG, 355–56; *NID*, s.v. "ἐπαγγελία."

13. BDAG, 520–21. Louw-Nida, §§15.57; 85.65 point to the first nuance while §13.92 points to the second.

still open, but the intimation behind the word suggests that condition will not be the case for long.

lest . . . any of you should seem to come short of it / that none of you should be found to have failed to reach it: The verb δοκέω (*dokeō*) means "to think" or "suppose." It also means "to seem" and by extension takes on a forensic nuance of "to be found out" or "judged."[14] This nuance is likely at play here. If this is the case, then it stands as a warning that these people, the author's target audience, be not found or judged to have fallen short of their goal.[15]

The verb ὑστερέω (*hystereō*) means "to fail to attain an object due to one's own neglect." It also carries a sense of being inferior to others or deficient in some virtue.[16] Another nuance is that of a success lost only by inches, thus "to fall short."[17] A feeling of shame, therefore, shades the word, connoting that with only a little more effort, a person could have obtained a goal.

4:2 ***unto us was the gospel preached / we have also had the gospel preached to us:*** This phrase is rendered by a single periphrastic verb in Greek, ἐσμεν εὐηγγελισμένοι (*esmen euēngelismenoi*). It uses the perfect passive of εὐαγγελίζω (*euangelizō*), meaning "to announce good news" and in its Christian context denotes "the gospel."[18] The noun form of this verb, εὐαγγέλιον (*euangelion*), refers generally to any kind of "good news," but in the New Testament, it more specifically applies to the proclamation of salvation through the ministry and Atonement of the Lord.[19] A result of the Lord's salvific act is divine "rest" for the righteous. In the case of the children

---

14. Lane, *Hebrews 1–8,* 93 note d; Attridge, *Epistle to the Hebrews,* 124. Louw-Nida, §30.96, nuances it as making "a choice based on something being better or superior."

15. Cockerill, *Epistle to the Hebrews,* 201.

16. *NID,* s.v. "ὕστερος."

17. BDAG, 1043–44. This is the same Greek word Matthew uses in stating the question that the rich young man asked Jesus, "What do I still lack?" (Matt 19:20), and the same word Mark uses in Jesus' reply, "You lack one thing: . . . sell whatever you have and give it to the poor" (Mark 10:21).

18. BDAG, 402. Joseph Smith took this to mean that the ancient Israelites, after they left Egypt, had the gospel preached to them. See "The Elders of the Church in Kirtland, to Their Brethren Abroad," *Evening and Morning Star* 2, no. 18 (March 1834): 143, noted in *Joseph Smith's Commentary on the Bible,* comp. and ed. Kent P. Jackson (Salt Lake City: Deseret Book, 1994), 186. McConkie, *Doctrinal New Testament Commentary,* 3:149, states that Moses preached the "fulness of the Gospel" as well as offered the Israelites the higher priesthood. See also D&C 84:23–27.

19. BDAG, 402–3. That is not to say, when applied to the Israelites, there was no Christian content. Likely the "good news" also included all that could be apprehended in

of Israel, this act allows Jehovah to invite them to enter into his rest or, as the author calls it, "so great salvation" (2:3). Putting the author's point in its context, he notes that there is a precise parallel between ancient Israel and his readers, and, therefore, they had better take note.[20]

the word preached did not profit them / the message they heard did not benefit them: The phrase ὁ λόγος τῆς ἀκοῆς (*ho logos tēs akoēs*), literally "the word of hearing," is very compact in Greek.[21] In our Rendition, we have translated it simply as "the message they heard" to make the sense clearer in English.

The verb ὠφελέω (*ōpheleō*) means to "help, aid, benefit, be of use (to)" but carries the nuance of being successful in accomplishing some goal.[22] In the case of rebellious Israel, God's word, delivered with force at Sinai, did not benefit them at all. In fact, it did just the opposite: it proved the source of their cursing. The author's warning is clear: his readers must distance themselves from the same response of faithlessness or suffer the same fate.[23]

not being mixed with faith in them that heard it / because they were not united with those who listened in faith: There are a number of Greek variants to this phrase, all dealing with how to understand the perfect passive participle of the verb συγκεράννυμι (*syngkerannymi*), "to blend, unite." The reading that best explains the other variants is συγκεκερασμένους (*syngkekerasmenous*), a masculine plural accusative agreeing with ἐκείνους (*ekeinous*), "those ones," which referrs to the previous phrase and thus grammatically fits the best.[24] Therefore, unlike the KJV, our Rendition unites the phrase τῇ πίστει (*tē pistei*), "with faith," to the following substantive participle τοῖς ἀκούσασιν (*tois akousasin*), "to those who heard," rather than to the previous participle "having joined themselves."[25] Doing so shifts the thrust of the entire clause. The KJV emphasizes God's "word" not benefitting the Israelites because it was not mixed with faith. Our Rendition, on the other hand, emphasizes the "word" not benefiting the

---

the writings of the prophets and, more especially, of Moses about the Savior before his incarnation. Ellingworth, *Epistle to the Hebrews,* 241.

20. Bruce, *Epistle to the Hebrews,* 105; Laansma, *"I Will Give You Rest,"* 285; Ellingworth, *Epistle to the Hebrews,* 255.

21. The phrase is taken here as a descriptive genitive. Attridge, *Epistle to the Hebrews,* 125.

22. BDAG, 1107–8.

23. Ellingworth, *Epistle to the Hebrews,* 254.

24. For discussion, see Metzger, *Textual Commentary,* 595.

25. Here we follow Attridge, *Epistle to the Hebrews,* 125–26; and Cockerill, *Epistle to the Hebrews,* 203 n. 30. See also Ellingworth, *Epistle to the Hebrews,* 243; and James Swetnam, "The Meaning of τοῖς ἀκούσασιν at Hebrews 4:2," *Biblica* 93, no. 4 (2012): 601–8.

Israelites because they separated themselves from those who had faith—namely, Moses, Caleb, and Joshua. Because these men all had faith and that faith greatly benefited them (the latter two even entering into the promised land; see Num. 26:65; 32:12; and Deut. 1:36), the Israelites' separation left them in an even more damnable position.[26]

4:3 ***For we which have believed do enter into rest, as he said, As I have sworn in my wrath, if they shall enter into my rest / For we who have believed enter into that rest, as he has said: "So I swore an oath in my anger, 'They will certainly not enter into my rest'":*** The plural verb εἰσερχόμεθα (*eiserchometha*), "we enter," though in the present tense, carries the force of a future event. That is not to say that a person cannot enjoy a sense of spiritual peace and rest in mortality, but the full realization of the "rest of God" will be in the future.[27] On the noun κατάπαυσις (*katapausis*), "rest," see Translation Notes for 4:1 with the accompanying Analysis.

The quote comes from LXX Psalm 94:11[28] and was previously quoted in 3:11. For insights, see Translation Notes for that verse. For the author's purposes, the important word in the quote is the pronoun "they," implied in the plural indicative future verb εἰσελεύσονται (*eiseleusontai*). It shows that the oath barring some from entering God's rest applied only to those faithless people. With the phrase οἱ πιστεύσαντες (*hoi pisteusantes*), "who have believed," the author sets up the contrast between the believing Christian and the faithless Israelite who suffered the consequences of Jehovah's anger. The author's point is that the Christian faithful—not being guilty of provoking God's wrath—can enter into the Father's rest.[29]

The JST makes the following modifications to this clause: "If they *harden their hearts they shall not enter into my rest; also, I have sworn, If they will not harden their hearts,* they shall enter into my rest" (italics indicate the added words). The quote from the Psalm is actually quite oblique to the author's point. The psalm focuses on God's oath that the rebellious shall not enter into his rest. The author uses it to show, *by implication,* that the righteous

26. Attridge, *Epistle to the Hebrews,* 125–26.

27. Koester, *Hebrews,* 270.

28. Ps. 95:11 in the MT and the KJV. The author weaves Ps. 95 and Gen. 2 together in an impressive chiastic pattern.

29. Bruce, *Epistle to the Hebrews,* 106. A variant uses the hortatory εἰσερχώμεθα, "let us enter into [his] rest," instead of the present indicative εἰσερχόμεθα, "we enter into [his] rest." See Metzger, *Textual Commentary,* 596. While there is not much difference, the preferred reading "we enter into [his] rest" seems more doctrinally confirming because it means that those who believe can enter into God's rest (compare D&C 19:9).

can enter into that rest. Because the author's point is only implied, the scripture's use creates tension. The change in the JST resolves that tension by having God swear not that the rebellious shall not enter into his rest but that the faithful will. It is of note that the JST does not make a correlating change to the KJV Psalm 95:11, likely because in that setting there is no tension that needs resolution.

although the works were finished from the foundation of the world / although God's works have been finished since the founding of the world: The noun "God" is not in the Greek text but is added to our Rendition for clarity.[30]

The concessive conjunction καίτοι (*kaitoi*), "although," is used to create tension and grab readers' interest. In this case, it highlights the tension between the two scriptures the author is using to make his point. In one, God refuses to let rebellious Israel enter into his rest (4:3), and in the other, God has already entered therein (4:4). As a result, it could be considered closed to anyone else.

The noun ἔργον (*ergon*), "work, deed," denotes that which displays itself in any kind of activity.[31] In this case, it refers to certain works that were completed when the world was founded. The JST modifies this phrase to read, "Although the works *of God* were *prepared, (or, finished,)* from the foundation of the world" (italics indicate the added words). The change makes it clear that the "works" referred to are those of God. What is not clear is why the JST adds the word "prepared." Since the verb "prepare" can also mean to make or create something so that it is ready for use, the JST's change could be emphasizing the preparation of the Earth during the creation for its purpose as a place where God's children could be tested "to see if they will do all things whatsoever the Lord their God shall command them" (Abr. 3:25).

4:4 ***For he spake in a certain place of the seventh day on this wise, And God did rest the seventh day from all his work / For somewhere he has spoken about the seventh day as follows: "And God rested on the seventh day from all of his works":*** The quote is from Genesis 2:2. The author breaks here from his usual pattern of citing passages where God speaks. Because the Genesis 2 account does not have God speaking but rather

30. The change is based on the JST of 4:3, the Greek inference, and the idea that all scripture is God's word anyway. See D&C 1:38. See also Lane, *Hebrews 1–8,* 100; and Johnson, *Hebrews,* 127.

31. BDAG, 390–91.

reports what he did, the author is vague about his source.[32] However, he does not refrain from appealing to scriptural authority to further his argument. Here he lays the foundation for his next argument by connecting "rest" with "work" and the "seventh day." In doing so, he begins a verbal analogy in which he uses one passage of scripture to illuminate another.[33] On the noun κατάπαυσις (*katapausis*), "rest," seeTranslation Notes for 4:1 with the corresponding Analysis below.

The Genesis quote could create confusion in the minds of the original audience. It could be read to suggest that God, having finished his work, entered into his rest, and, therefore, he has ceased all activity. If that is the case, then he no longer speaks or acts and is little more than a passive retiree.[34] By implication, God's rest is closed and no one else can enter therein. The author resolves any confusion in 4:6–10 by showing that, at the end of the creation period, God "began" to rest, implying that divine rest yet remains open and, therefore, others can enter therein.[35]

The author further resolves any confusion in another way. He uses the perfect tense of the verb εἴρηκεν (*eirēken,* from εἶπον [*eipon*], "to speak," with which he introduced the quotes in both 4:3 and 4) to indicate that God has never ceased to speak, and therefore, his word is ongoing.[36]

4:5 ***And in this place again, If they shall enter into my rest / And as cited earlier, "They will certainly not enter into my rest":*** In the phrase καὶ ἐν τούτῳ πάλιν (*kai en toutō palin*), literally "and in this again," the antecedent of the neuter pronoun *toutō,* "this," is the passage from LXX Psalm 94:11 cited in 4:3.[37] The phrase, therefore, refers the reader back to that citation,

32. This same treatment is found at 3:6.

33. Under rabbinic influence, this method would later be codified and become known as *gezerah shawah.* For discussion, see the section "Development Process" in the introduction. In sum, the basis of this methodology is the rabbinical belief that "all of Scripture is meaningful and indeed has a single author, so that the occurrence of a word in one passage can be used to illuminate the use of the word in another passage. The two passages, indeed, can stand as mutually interpretive." Johnson, *Hebrews,* 175.

34. Johnson, *Hebrews,* 128; Cockerill, *Epistle to the Hebrews,* 207.

35. John Walton, *Genesis 1 as Ancient Cosmology* (State College, Penn.: Eisenbrauns, 2011), 179–83, argues that ancient Near Eastern readers would understand that deity rests only in temples. Thus, on the seventh day, God took up his "rest" in the heavenly temple. If the author's readers were aware of this connection, then the imagery would point to the temple as the place they would find divine rest.

36. This tense describes an event whose effect, though completed in the past, is ongoing. Wallace, *Greek Grammar,* 573; Cockerill, *Epistle to the Hebrews,* 206.

37. Wallace, *Greek Grammar,* 333–34.

which we indicate with the rendering "in this place."[38] The author repeats this quote so he can more easily address the tension between it and Genesis 2:2. His point is that God's rest must have remained open even after the creation since God gave the Israelites a chance to enter it.

4:6 *Seeing therefore it remaineth that some must enter therein / Now since it remains for some to enter into that rest:* With the phrase ἐπεὶ οὖν (*epei oun*), "now since," the author signals his readers he is about to conclude his point and resolve any tension created by the sources he has quoted. That point is not stated, however, until 4:7.

The passive of the verb ἀπολείπω (*apoleipō*) denotes "to remain."[39] In this case, it is God's "rest" that remains open. The phrase, then, shows that as God's rest was open to the children of Israel, it still remains open to the Christians. In the phrase εἰς αὐτήν (*eis autēn*), literally "into it," the feminine pronoun *autēn* refers back to κατάπαυσις (*katapausis*), "rest." In our Rendition, we have translated this as "into that rest" for clarity.

they to whom it was first preached entered not in because of unbelief / those who formerly had the gospel preached to them did not enter in because of disobedience: This long phrase interrupts the author's signal that he is going to make his point, delaying it until 4:7.

For the ease of reading, the aorist passive participle εὐαγγελίζω (*euangelizō*), literally "having the good news preached," is translated as a relative clause in our Rendition.[40]

The noun ἀπείθεια (*apeithia*) means "disobedience." In the New Testament, the word's emphasis is on a movement away from Christian belief while in the Old Testament, emphasis is on the act of willful noncompliance.[41] Since the phrase points to an Old Testament event, we use the latter nuance in our Rendition. Its use forces the author's readers to face the reality and gravity of their forebearers' loss.

In sum, the assumption on which the author bases his argument is that God established his rest when he laid the foundation of the world and then invited ancient Israel into it. Thus, he never intended for that rest to be his alone. Though the rebellious Israelites did not make it, that did not mean others could not. But the Christian generation must not do as the ancients

---

38. Ellingworth, *Epistle to the Hebrews*, 252.

39. BDAG, 115; Louw-Nida, §85.65.

40. The aorist passive participle here expresses the simple past in contrast to the perfect passive participle used in 4:2, where the present result of a past action is stressed.

41. BDAG, 99; Louw-Nida, §§31.107; 36.23.

(4:11). They must, instead, respond in faith to the "good news" preached to them by continuing in all diligence.[42]

4:7 *Again, he limiteth a certain day / God again appoints a certain day:* With this phrase, the author makes his point. The semantic range of the verb ὁρίζω (*horizō*) includes both "to set limits to" and "to determine" or "appoint."[43] Because God officially set up a day of rest, the second sense best fits the context and is, therefore, used in our Rendition. The adverb πάλιν (*palin*), "again," is important here because it shows that an action has been repeated. In this case, a period of rest is again being appointed.

saying in David, To day, after so long a time; as it is said / speaking much later through David, as has been previously cited: The Greek prepositional phrase μετὰ τοσοῦτον χρόνον (*meta tosouton chronon*), literally "after so much time," is translated simply as "much later" in our Rendition. The author's point is that, though Israel rebelled centuries before King David's reign, God gave a telling insight through this inspired poet.

That Jehovah spoke ἐν Δαυίδ (*en Dauid*), "in David," does not mean that God spoke through the writings of David (that is, the Psalms). Rather, in keeping with the author's thesis that God spoke and speaks through his prophets, the author notes that God spoke through the man David.[44]

The rest of the verse, not reproduced here, is from LXX Psalm 94:7–8,[45] which the author already cited in 3:7 and alluded to in 3:13, 15. The author does modify the quote by cutting out the phrase "as in the rebellion," likely because he has already developed that theme (3:11–12). Its absence also suggests that he expected better things of his readers.[46]

Using the scripture as his proof text, the author now develops the theme of "to day" that he introduced in 3:13. Here again is an example of the author using verbal analogy as a tool of interpretation.[47] The term, as explained in the Translation Notes for 3:7, connotes a short period of time when something can be done. The author uses it to motivate his readers to obtain the rest God has now opened to them.

harden not your hearts / Do not harden your hearts: See Translation Notes for 3:8.

---

42. Cockerill, *Epistle to the Hebrews,* 208–9.
43. BGAD, 723.
44. Attridge, *Epistle to the Hebrews,* 130 and n. 95.
45. Psalm 95:7–8 in the KJV.
46. Cockerill, *Epistle to the Hebrews,* 209.
47. This hermeneutical methodology is call *gezerah shawah.* See note 33 in this chapter.

4:8 ***For if Jesus had given them rest / For if Joshua had given them rest:*** Having relieved the tension created in his juxtaposition of LXX Psalm 94:7 to Genesis 2:2, in this verse, the author moves to defuse another potential problem (see below).

In the LXX, the Hebrew name יְהוֹשֻׁעַ (*Yehôšûaʿ*), "Joshua" (meaning "Jehovah is salvation"), is rendered Ἰησοῦς (*Iēsous*), "Jesus," in Greek. In the Old Testament, it is the name of Moses' assistant and successor,[48] and therefore in this passage it references Joshua, not Jesus as the KJV has it.

On the noun κατάπαυσις (*katapausis*), "rest," see Translation Notes for 4:1 above with correlating Analysis below.

then would he not afterward have spoken of another day / God would not have spoken later of another day: In our Rendition, we have replaced "he" with "God" to make it clear that it is God, not Joshua, who spoke of another day.

This whole clause, together with the if-clause that precedes it, forms a Greek past contrary-to-fact condition. That condition is based on the assumption of a false position for the sake of argument.[49] The author's argument is as follows: If Israel, under Joshua, had entered into God's rest (which did not happen), God would not have spoken of a later date when someone else could do so. But God did so speak, and, therefore, there is a future day when entering into that rest will be possible.

The author's use of the contrary-to-fact condition allows him to blunt the position of anyone insisting that since Israel did enter the promised land with Joshua, the promise was fulfilled.

4:9 ***There remaineth therefore a rest to the people of God / Consequently a Sabbath rest remains for the people of God:*** The conjunction ἄρα (*ara*), "therefore, consequently," indicates that the author is now making his point.

The noun σαββατισμός (*sabbatismos*), translated as "rest" in the KJV, designates not just any period of relaxation and refreshment but a Sabbath rest or observance.[50] It stands in contrast to the noun σάββατον (*sabbaton*), which simply refers to the seventh day of the week, although, for the

48. This is the same name "an angel" told Joseph to name the son that Mary would bear, "for he shall save his people from their sins" (Matt. 1:21). Earlier, Gabriel had given Mary the same command (Luke 1:31). The author does not appear to be developing any Joshua/Jesus typology but rather uses Joshua in a historical capacity. For discussion, see Cockerill, *Epistle to the Hebrews,* 209 and n. 49.

49. Wallace, *Greek Grammar,* 694–96; the condition is called "unreal" in Smyth, *Greek Grammar,* §§2302–30.

50. BDAG, 909.

Jews, that was a day of rest.[51] The author uses the noun very deliberately to stress his point: God's rest—a Sabbath celebration—is yet open for faithful Christians. For these people, most of whom "could hardly escape from the tyranny of work, the *Sabbath*, or 'rest,' was a physical relief and a spiritual blessing" (see Isa. 56:2, 4–7; 58:13–14).[52] To consider living eternally in such a state would have had an immense appeal.

The author gives his readers a sense of the peace, joy, and festal atmosphere they can expect in the Father's kingdom, provided that they do not abandon their Lord.[53] In essence, he is promising them that, as hard as times then were, the world to come will more than compensate for it. As surely as God rested at the end of his creative period, so too the Saints can rest from theirs.[54]

4:10 ***For he that is entered into his rest / For anyone who enters into God's rest:*** In this verse, in contrast to the previous one, it is the noun κατάπαυσις (*katapausis*) that is translated as "rest." In our Rendition we have changed "his" to "God's" to make it clear that it is God's rest that is meant.[55]

The implied pronoun "he" is vague, and, therefore, some scholars have argued that it applies to Christ. The context, however, strongly suggests that the author has his readers in mind.[56] They are experiencing a rough time that promises to get even worse. The counter-promise is that upon the successful completion of this very intense period of toil and worry, *every* person who faithfully endures will find celestial rest.

he also hath ceased from his own works, as God did from his / he also rests from his works just as God rested from his own works: The phrase καὶ αὐτός (*kai autos*), "he also," is emphatic, thus stressing that it is the person himself or herself who will be, at last, freed from the heavy toil and constant grind of mortality. On the noun "works," see Translation Notes for 4:3 above. Freed from such heavy work—the crucible in which a son

51. BDAG, 909. For a recent study, see Erhard Gallos, "Κατάπαυς and Σαββατισμός in Hebrews 4," *Andrews University Seminary Studies* 50 (Spring 2012): 67–68.

52. Ralph Gower, *The New Manners and Customs of Bible Times* (Chicago: Moody Press, 1987), 354.

53. The noun σαββατισμός carries a sense of rest and peace—an escape from the toils and trials of mortality—and especially the joyous worship of the Father and Son in the eternal realm. The author will more fully develop this theme in 12:22–23. Lane, *Hebrews 1–8,* 102; Laansma, *"I Will Give You Rest,"* 278–79.

54. Cockerill, *Epistle to the Hebrews,* 210–11.

55. Bruce, *Epistle to the Hebrews,* 109 and n. 32.

56. For discussion, see Attridge, *Epistle to the Hebrews,* 131; and Cockerill, *Epistle to the Hebrews,* 211.

and daughter of the Father is made—each faithful individual will enter godly rest.

4:11 ***Let us labour therefore to enter into that rest / Therefore, let us strive to enter into that rest:*** The conjunction οὖν (*oun*), "therefore," points back to the earlier warning that God's rest can be lost.

The verb σπουδάσωμεν (*spoudasōmen*) is an aorist subjunctive functioning in a hortatory capacity, "let us."[57] Again, the author includes himself to allay any antagonism his admonition may have aroused.

The verb σπουδάζω (*spoudazō*) means to be especially conscious of the need to quickly discharge an obligation or fulfill a duty. Thus, it carries the sense of making every effort or of striving zealously to obtain a goal. Behind it stands a sense of urgency.[58] The author's plea is not simply to remain faithful but to put instant and continuous effort into gaining the reward that potentially awaits them.[59]

lest any man fall after the same example of unbelief / so that no one will fall into that same pattern of disobedience: The structure of this clause is important. The author puts the phrase ἵνα μὴ . . . τις (*hina mē . . . tis*), "lest" or "so that no one," right up front, making it emphatic. In doing so he stresses his fear for the spiritual lives of his readers.[60]

The punch of this verse is, however, in the verb πίπτω (*piptō*), "to fall." Though it carries the primary meaning of falling down, closely behind it is the idea of being destroyed.[61] The noun ὑπόδειγμα (*hypodeigma*) describes "an example of behavior used for purposes of moral instruction, [that is, as] an example, model, [or] pattern."[62] It suggests the idea of repeated activity and can be either negative (as in the case with Sodom and Gomorrah; see 2 Pet. 2:6) or positive (as in the case of temple activities; see 8:5; 9:23).[63]

There is a significant manuscript variant for this phrase. Later manuscripts, including the Textus Receptus (which the KJV follows), have

57. Cockerill, *Epistle to the Hebrews,* 212 nn. 59, 60; compare Harold W. Attridge, "'Let Us Strive to Enter That Rest': The Logic of Hebrews 4:1–11," *Harvard Theological Review* 73 (1980): 279–88.

58. BDAG, 939; Louw-Nida, §§25.74; 68.79.

59. See Lane, *Hebrews 1–8,* 94.

60. Ellingworth, *Epistle to the Hebrews,* 258; compare O'Brien, *Letter to the Hebrews,* 160; and Joseph McConkie, "Jesus Christ, Symbolism, and Salvation," 199–201.

61. BDAG, 815–16; Louw-Nida, §§13.97; 20.60.

62. BDAG, 1037.

63. Koester, *Hebrews,* 273.

ἀπιστίας (*apistias*), "unbelief."[64] Earlier manuscripts have ἀπειθείας (*apeitheias*), "disobedience."[65] Our Rendition follows the latter for two reasons: first, it is found in the early manuscripts, and second, it conforms to the idea that, though the Israelites were indeed faithless, the focus in this section of Hebrews is on the outward expression of that faithlessness—namely, disobedience (4:6).[66]

The warning expressed here, however, is not only against faithlessness or disobedience per se but also against their ultimate consequence: falling into destruction.[67] Given the author's focus on the sad but telling effect of Israel's constant rebellion—one destructive disaster after another until an entire generation passed away—his concern for the state of his readers is clear. Due to his strong admonition and example, his readers should take his words seriously.

4:12 ***For the word of God is quick, and powerful / For the word of God is living and active:*** The author imputes to the noun λόγος (*logos*), "word," a dynamic quality in order to push his agenda. The present participle ζῶν (*zōn*), "living," is used in the metaphorical sense of being active or alive,[68] describing the functioning, vigorous quality of God's "word" (compare Acts 7:38, 1 Cor. 1:18; and 2 Cor. 6:7, where Paul also associates the "word" with God's power).

The adjective ἐνεργής (*energēs*) denotes what is "effective, active," and "powerful."[69] While the KJV legitimately focuses on the might of God's word, our Rendition focuses on its activity, thus emphasizing its dynamic, current nature. This is in keeping with the author's thesis that God's word is not dormant. The Father has spoken *and* continues to speak. His words count because they don't just exist, they have vigor and yield practical results.

The author's imagery in this verse is intense, vivid, and forceful, but not original, coming as it does from the Old Testament.[70] The coordinating

---

64. See particularly P[46], ℵ*, lat. sysh. See Ellingworth, *Epistle to the Hebrews,* 259.

65. Ellingworth, *Epistle to the Hebrews,* 259; Attridge, *Epistle to the Hebrews,* 123.

66. The distinction is somewhat artificial, and the overall concern is with both. Attridge, *Epistle to the Hebrews,* 132.

67. BDAG, 1037; see also O'Brien, *Letter to the Hebrews,* 174.

68. BDAG, 426. In KJV English, "quick" meant "alive," not "fast" as in modern English.

69. BDAG, 335.

70. This phrase's creative force can be seen in Gen. 1:3; Ps. 33:9; Isa. 55:11; and such apocryphal works as Sir. 42:15 and Wis. 9:1. Its forensic aspect can be seen in Jer. 7:13 and Amos 1:2; and, as imaged by a sword, Isa. 34:5–6; 66:16. In Prov. 5:4, the imagery expresses severe judgment against immorality. The phrase first appears in the description

conjunction γάρ (*gar*), "for," is causal. The author uses it to explain why no one will get away with unbelief, even if they try to hide it. Sincerity in the striving for God's rest is all important.

and sharper than any twoedged sword / sharper than any double-edged sword: The adjective δίστομος (*distomos*), literally "two-mouthed," combined with the noun μάχαιρα (*machaira*) primarily designates a short sword or dagger, as opposed to a saber or dueling sword.[71] The phrase τομώτερος ὑπὲρ (*tomōteros hyper*) stresses the "word's" sharpness, it is "sharper than" any sword. The emphasis, however, is not on the word's likeness to a sword but on its distinction from it. It is sharper than any sword can be; therefore, it can do work that no sword can. It can cut cleaner, deeper, and more thoroughly.[72]

piercing even to the dividing asunder of soul and spirit, and of the joints and marrow / that penetrates until it separates soul and spirit, joint and marrow: The verb διϊκνέομαι (*diikneomai*) denotes piercing or penetrating something.[73]

---

of Ehud's dagger with which he executed God's judgment against King Eglon. See Jud. 3:16. In Eph. 6:17, Paul uses the sword as a metaphor for God's word. The imagery of the sharp two-edged sword as God's word is particularly highlighted in the book of Revelation. In powerful and telling apocalyptic images, John sees in vision the Savior and states that "out of his mouth continually issued a sharp two-edged sword" (Rev. 1:16). The force of the present active participle ἐκπορευομένη (*ekporeuomenē*), "going out, exiting, issuing," expresses the continual nature of the issuance. The point of the imagery is that Christ's word is ever active and ever judicial. See also Rev. 2:12 and 19:15, which show that the two-edged sword represents the Lord's executive power.

71. BDAG, 622. Earlier in Greek literature, this sword differed from the ῥομφαία (*rhomphaia*), a broad sword used in battle. The noun μάχαιρα (*machaira*) nuanced a smaller instrument used for precise cutting, such as a scalpel. By New Testament times, however, the distinction had largely disappeared. See Attridge, *Epistle to the Hebrews,* 134–35 and nn. 17, 30.

Even so, the author's use of the term suggests an instrument, though having two edges, that does a surgical procedure. See Gene R. Smillie, "'Ο Λογοσ Του Θεου' in Hebrews 4:12–13," *Novum Testamentum* 46, no. 4 (2004): 348–49.

72. The metaphorical imagery of the sword is found in both ancient and modern scriptures, denoting both God's word and his spirit. See, for example, Prov. 5:4; Isa. 49:2; Eph. 6:17; Alma 60:29; Hel. 13:5; 3 Ne. 29:4; and D&C 6:2; 33:1. For a discussion, see Largey, *Book of Mormon Reference Companion,* 635–36. The Old Testament imagery was used frequently in the early sections of the Doctrine and Covenants (see 6:2; 11:2; 12:2; 14:2; 27:1; 33:1). The use of this phrase in the early days of the Restoration likely reflected the idea that the word of God is not dormant and that the Father continues to speak in this dispensation.

73. BDAG, 245.

The JST changes "soul" to "body," thus marking a distinction between the soul (the temporal being) and the spirit (the eternal being).[74]

The phrase ἄχρι μερισμοῦ (*achri merismou*), literally "as far as the separation,"[75] denotes the objective of the "word's" cut: not to kill, but to separate for further work. The depth is extreme; not only does God's "word" separate spirit from body but also joint from joint. It even cuts open the bone, exposing the marrow.[76] The imagery suggests the depth of God's investigation: he overlooks nothing.

and is a discerner of the thoughts and intents of the heart / and is able to discern the thoughts and intentions of the heart: The adjective κριτικός (*kritikos*), "discern," denotes the ability to make proper judgments. It also nuances the authority which makes the judgment binding.[77] The English word "discern," meaning the ability to accurately see below the surface and understand "what is not evident to the average mind,"[78] is an excellent translation.

The noun καρδία (*kardia*), "heart," is important here, for it connotes the very core of the individual, including the intellectual, emotional, and spiritual dimensions.[79] For a more detailed study, see Translation Notes for 3:8 with associated Analysis.

---

74. The problem with this verse is that the two elements (body or soul/spirit and joint/marrow) are not parallel. Marrow does not stand opposite joint. The meaning of this phrase has therefore generated a good deal of discussion. See Koester, *Hebrews,* 274; and Cockerill, *Epistle to the Hebrews,* 216. Noteworthy is that Joseph Smith was not consistent in his definition of "soul." On one hand, D&C 88:15 defines the soul as the spirit and the body, likely referring to a person's total self. In Abr. 2:24–25, "soul" refers to the physical nature, while in 5:7 it refers to the whole person. Joseph Smith also used it to describe the best of a person (Joseph Smith and Frederick G. Williams to John S. Carter, April 13, 1833, retained copy, in Joseph Smith Letterbook 1:32); a person's moral nature ("History, 1838–1856, Volume A-1 [23 December 1805–30 August 1834]," 425, Joseph Smith Papers, https://www.josephsmithpapers.org/paper-summary/history-1838-1856-volume-a-1-23-december-1805-30-august-1834/431; "History, 1838–1856, Volume D-1," 1535); and a person's self ("History, 1838–1856, Volume C-1 Addenda," 75, Joseph Smith Papers, https://www.josephsmithpapers.org/paper-summary/history-1838-1856-volume-c-1-addenda/75).

75. BDAG, 161.

76. Smillie, "'Ο Λογοσ Του Θεου' in Hebrews 4:12–13," 343; O'Brien, *Letter to the Hebrews,* 175.

77. BDAG, 570; Louw-Nida, §56.23.

78. *Webster's New Dictionary of Synonyms,* s.v. "discernment"; see also Ogden and Skinner, *Verse by Verse,* 249. Leon R. Hartshorn, "Discernment, Gift of," in Ludlow, *Encyclopedia of Mormonism,* 1:384, notes that individuals upon whom the spirit of God rests can also receive the gift of discernment.

79. In modern culture, the heart is tied more directly to the emotional side of a person while the brain or head is tied to the conscious or rational side. Such was not the case in the world of the Bible.

This clause lists two items that the "word" is able to discern. Though the two items are close in meaning, their differences are important. The first is ἐνθύμησις (*enthymēsis*). This noun denotes the content of what is thought—the actual ideas and considerations. As used here it describes "the unexpressed and hidden thing in man which God's omniscience sees and judges."[80] The second is ἔννοια (*ennoia*), which denotes the act of deliberation and consideration, that is, the process of one's inner reasoning. It nuances that which influences what one believes and how one acts—things which are often deliberately hidden from others. Therefore, its tone is generally negative, describing "the morally questionable thoughts in the hidden innermost part of man" (see Matt. 9:4; 12:25; and Acts 17:29).[81] Taken together, these two terms describe "all that goes on in the human 'heart.'"[82]

4:13 *Neither is there any creature that is not manifest in his sight / No one is hidden from his sight:* At this point, the author drops his metaphor and references instead the eventual reality that all people will encounter as they stand in the presence of the all-seeing Father to be judged.

The noun κτίσις (*ktisis*) refers primarily to the act of creation but also denotes that which is created, thus "creature," meaning "a living thing."[83] But in the scriptures, more often than not it denotes all of humankind (Mark 16:15; Rom. 1:25; 8:19–21; Gal. 6:15). On a higher spiritual level, it particularly denotes "the creative act of God, whereby a [person] is introduced into the blessing of salvation" and, by accepting it, becomes a "new creature"—a new creation—through Christ (Rom. 8:18–25; 2 Cor. 5:17; Gal. 6:15; Col. 1:15, 23).[84] It is likely that both of these latter two definitions apply here. We have, therefore, rendered the phrase οὐκ ἔστιν κτίσις (*ouk estin ktisis*) as "no one is."

The adjective ἀφανής (*aphanēs*) means "to be hidden, unseen" or "invisible,"[85] while the adverb ἐνώπιον (*enōpion*) means "in the sight of"[86] with the overtone of being "in the presence of" (for example, Gen. 16:13; Ex. 33:11; Lev. 4:4; 24:3; and Deut. 31:11). Taken together, these words stress

80. Büchel, *TDNT,* 3:172; BDAG, 336; Louw-Nida, §30.15.

81. Behm, *TDNT,* 969–71; BDAG, 337; Louw-Nida, §30.5.

82. O'Brien, *Letter to the Hebrews,* 177 n. 138; Cockerill, *Epistle to the Hebrews,* 217. Johnson, *Hebrews,* 135, notes that the ability to discern between these two words "is the more impressive because the difference between them is so slight and unavailable to human perception" that only God can do it. Compare Alma 12:7; 18:32; and 3 Ne. 11:3.

83. BDAG, 146. This broad definition includes humans and both domestic and wild animals. In Rev. 5:13 and 8:9, John calls the celestial animals he sees by the related noun κτίσμα (*ktisma*), "created things."

84. BDAG, 572-3; *NID,* s.v. "κτίζω."

85. BDAG, 154.

86. BDAG, 342.

that nothing is or can be hidden from the sight of God. In this case, the focus is primarily on humankind and specifically on the author's readers.

but all things are naked and opened unto the eyes of him with whom we have to do / but everything is open and laid bare to the eyes of him to whom we must give an accounting: The operative word in this clause is the adjective πάντα (*panta*), "all things" or "everything," showing the inclusive nature of the effect of an act—in this case, the ability of God to detect all that goes on in each individual.[87]

To stress the extent of the Father's ability to discern an individual's core moral values, the author uses two terms. The first is the adjective γυμνός (*gymnos*), "naked, uncovered, bare."[88] The second is the perfect passive participle τετραχηλισμένα (*tetrachēlismena*), "to be laid bare."[89] Taken together, they emphasize that nothing can be hidden from God.[90]

In the last phrase, the Greek is very compact, πρὸς ὃν ἡμῖν ὁ λόγος (*pros hon hēmin ho logos*), literally "to whom for us the accounting." The dative pronoun ἡμῖν (*hemin*), "us," can be translated as a dative of reference, thus meaning "to whom the word must be given [in reference] to us," or as a dative of instrument, meaning "to whom the word [must be given] by us."[91] Because the force of the phrase is judicial and therefore points to a personal accounting, the latter expression seems the best and is used in our Rendition.[92] The noun λόγος (*logos*), usually translated as "word," is used here in the special sense of "accounting" or "reckoning"[93] and is so translated in our Rendition.

---

87. Louw-Nida, §§59.23; 63.2; 78.44. See 2 Ne. 9:20; Alma 18:32; and D&C 1:1; 6:16; 15:3; 67:1.

88. BDAG, 208. D&C 6:16 states, "there is none else save God that knowest thy thoughts and the intents of thy heart."

89. The participle is derived from the verb *τραχηλίζω* (*trachēlizō*), "to lay bare." BDAG, 1014; Smillie, "'O Λογοσ Του Θεου' in Hebrews 4:12–13," 347–48; Cockerill, *Epistle to the Hebrews,* 218. The term *τραχηλίζω* (*trachēlizō*) is found only here in the New Testament. In secular literature, the term is used in sports for seizing someone by the neck, in medicine for pulling back the neck for an operation, and in a judicial setting for exposing a person's gullet for execution. In this case, it denotes the full disclosure of a person's thoughts and intents.

90. This idea is fundamental to both Jewish and Christian theology. For example, see Gen. 6:5; 1 Sam. 16:7; 1 Chr. 28:9; and 1 Cor. 3:20, which all show that Jehovah knows people's thoughts and intents. For additional references, see Attridge, *Epistle to the Hebrews,* 136 and nn. 48, 49; and Lane, *Hebrews 1–8,* 103. In Latter-day Saint theology, God is said to "know all things." See 2 Ne. 2:24; 27:26; Morm. 8:17; D&C 38:2; 127:2; and Moses 1:6.

91. Cockerill, *Epistle to the Hebrews,* 218 n. 21.

92. Koester, *Hebrews,* 275.

93. BDAG, 600; see also Gene R. Smillie, "'The Other Λόγος' at the End of Heb. 4:13," *Novum Testamentum* 47, no. 1 (2005): 19–25.

Analysis and Summary

The author's focus in this section is on God's "rest" (κατάπαυσις, *katapausis*) and the importance of obtaining it. He uses as his introductory text LXX Psalm 94:11 (4:3), which speaks of those whom Jehovah swore "in [his] wrath that they should not enter into [his] rest" because of their faithless disobedience. The author strongly warns his readers the same could happen to them and, therefore, they must act now (4:1–2).

The author begins his admonition (4:1) by noting that ancient Israel's entrance into the promised land did not mean that Jehovah's promise of rest had been exhausted. Indeed, the author's generation also had the promise of entering into God's rest. In fact, they had access to a better spiritual rest than did their ancestors. Entrance, however, was not guaranteed. Therefore, readers should have a genuine fear that they too might miss it (ὑστερέω, *hystereō*, "to fall short"). The parallel between the two peoples was similar enough that a comparable disaster could overtake them (4:2), for both had the same "word" preached to them.

The author does not place his stress on the result of rest (ἀνάπαυσις, *anapausis*, meaning rejuvenation, refreshment, and relaxation) but on the place where it is found (κατάπαυσις, *katapausis*, denoting a place where one finds security, peace, and happiness). Given the threatening climate in which they were living, this emphasis would have been the real draw to the Hebrew brothers and sisters.

Having introduced the theme of "rest," the author next defines its nature and assures his readers that it is yet available. He does this in two parts: 4:3–5 and 4:6–11.[94] In the first part, he begins by introducing another scripture, Genesis 2:2: "And God did rest the seventh day from all his works" (4:4). This verse defines the term "rest" as something the Divine does and therefore is ultimately celestial. Thus, the author contrasts it with and sets it apart from its Old Testament definition. His development follows his usual use of verbal analogy to connect disparate ideas and bring out new meaning.[95] In the Old Testament, the word referred to Jehovah's promise that he would give Israel "rest" by providing a promised land. The "rest" would come through two stages. The first was by Israel's conquest of their enemies

94. Vanhoye, *Letter to the Hebrews*, 90–93.

95. Though not as developed as the rabbinic hermeneutical principal of *gezerah shawah* would become, the author does feel free to connect two passages of scripture that use the same word (here "rest" from Ps. 95 and Gen. 2) and allow them to inform one another. On the author's methodology, see the section "How the Author Developed His Message" in the introduction.

through which they would secure the land (Deut. 3:20; 12:10; 25:19; Josh. 1:13, 15; 21:44). The second was by being able to live securely and in peace, enjoying the produce from vineyards and orchards (1 Kgs. 4:25).

By tying this concept to the activity of the Divine, the author moves it from the temporal and immediate to the spiritual and eternal. He further draws out the implication of this insight. Since there is a divine "rest," some must enter therein (4:6). To bolster his case, he quotes LXX Psalm 94:7: "To day if ye will hear his voice, harden not your hearts" (4:7). From this phrase, he draws two conclusions. First, God's rest is yet open (4:9), and second, the requirement for entering into it is to safeguard the heart against disbelief and disobedience (4:6, 11).

To give his readers a feel and a hope for what is in store for them, in 4:9 he introduces the Sabbath rest (σαββατισμός, *sabbatismos*).[96] The impetus for the author's appeal is likely his readers' discomfort in the present. They are not enjoying a state of rest to any noticeable degree. He wants them to realize, however, that even though they are not enjoying it at present, it does belong to them as a future inheritance.[97]

"Entering" into divine rest suggests it is not just a state but also a location. There is a place of rest, and that is where the Father dwells. It is the place of the eternal Sabbath celebration (4:4–5) where the righteous cease from the toils and struggles of this mortal life (4:10) and enter into a fulness of joy.[98]

---

96. BDAG, 909. For the Jewish background on Sabbath rest, see Attridge, *Epistle to the Hebrews,* 130–31; and Michael J. Graetz and others, "Sabbath," in *Encyclopaedia Judaica,* 2d ed., vol. 17, ed. Michael Berenbaum and Fred Skolnik (Detroit: Macmillan Reference, 2007), 616–22. For Latter-day Saint understanding, see McConkie, *Doctrinal New Testament Commentary,* 3:151; and Smith, *Gospel Questions,* 1:99–107; see also Ezra Taft Benson, *God, Family, Country: Our Three Great Loyalties* (Salt Lake City: Deseret Book, 1974), 97–107; and Gordon B. Hinckley, *Teachings of Gordon B. Hinckley* (Salt Lake City: Deseret Book, 1997), 558–60.

97. Bruce, *Epistle to the Hebrews,* 110; for a study, see also C. K. Barrett, "The Eschatology of the Epistles to the Hebrews," in *The Background to the New Testament and Its Eschatology,* ed. W. D. Davis and D. Daube (Cambridge: Cambridge University Press, 1956), 363–92.

98. It is for this end that humankind was created (2 Ne. 2:25). Those who are worthy servants will enter into the joy of their Lord (Matt. 25:20–25), and when they sit down with the Father, they will experience a fulness of that joy (3 Ne. 28:10). Indeed, those "who have believed in the Holy One of Israel . . . [and] endured the crosses of the world, and despised the shame of it, they shall inherit the kingdom of God, which was prepared for them from the foundation of the world, and their joy shall be full forever" (2 Ne. 9:18).

Though definitely oriented toward the future, the author does not state when exactly the period of divine rest begins. Is it at death or after the resurrection? From a particular Latter-day Saint perspective, it begins for the righteous immediately after death.[99] As the Lord explained, those who die "shall rest from all their labors here, and shall continue their works" in the world of spirits (D&C 124:86). He noted further that those who "die shall rest from all their labors, and their works shall follow them; and they shall [eventually] receive a crown in the mansions of my Father, which I have prepared for them" (D&C 59:2). The Book of Mormon is more expressive, stating that between death and resurrection, "the spirits of all men, whether they be good or evil, are taken home to that God who gave them life. And then shall it come to pass, that the spirits of those who are righteous are received into a state of happiness, which is called paradise, a state of rest, a state of peace, where they shall rest from all their troubles and from all care, and sorrow" (Alma 40:11–12; see also Alma 60:13).

That is not to say that a person cannot enter into a state of rest in mortality. The Book of Mormon makes it clear that one reason for preaching the gospel is so that people can enter into that rest (Alma 13:6). It goes on to state that "after being sanctified by the Holy Ghost, . . . there were many, exceedingly great many, who were made pure and entered into the rest of the Lord their God" (Alma 13:12). Therefore, one can indeed enjoy a

> state of peace that comes with redemption; spiritual enjoyment resulting from the power or presence of the Lord. Divine rest in this life begins with humbling oneself, repenting (Alma 13:12–13), having one's garments washed in the Savior's blood through faith and repentance (3 Ne. 27:19)—that is, obtaining the remission of sins (Alma 12:34; 13:16)—and coming unto Christ (Jacob 1:7; Alma 16:17). Personal revelation brings rest to the soul (Enos 1:17). Those who are meek and lowly of heart find rest to their souls (Alma 37:34). Even in the midst of trials one can experience a degree of rest, bearing one's afflictions with patience and a firm hope of rest one day from all affliction. (Alma 34:41)[100]

---

99. The Book of Mormon makes it very clear that "whosoever repenteth, and hardeneth not his heart, he shall have claim on mercy through mine Only Begotten Son, unto a remission of his sins; and these shall enter into my rest" (Alma 12:34). However, so far as the hard-hearted are concerned, God has sworn "in [his] wrath that [they] shall not enter into [his] rest" (Alma 12:35).

100. Largey, *Book of Mormon Reference Companion,* 679; see also McConkie, *Doctrinal New Testament Commentary,* 3:151–52.

One aspect of the Savior's appeal to people was he would give them rest (Matt. 11:28–29). In his case, it was from an overly strict interpretation and application of the Mosaic law, a strictness that made it at best heavy and at worst painful. Over and over, Jesus showed he was the one who properly interpreted and applied the law and, therefore, could bring them rest in the security that they were one with God.[101]

However, the highest type of divine rest connotes a person's receiving "the fulness of his [God's] glory" (D&C 84:24). Though the author of Hebrews does not say so specifically, a tacit assumption is shared between him and his readers that the goal of human existence is a share in God's own "glory" (δόξα, *doxa*). "It is stated explicitly in 2:10 that God is leading many sons [and daughters] to glory, and we saw in that place that 'glory' must mean a share in God's own way of existing, a participation in God's own presence and power"[102] and therein to find peace and rest.

Speaking on this, one scholar noted, "Prophets labor diligently to persuade their people to enter into this rest (Jacob 1:7; cf. Alma 13:6; D&C 84:23–24). The Book of Mormon refers to three degrees of divine rest: the rest available in mortality, in paradise, and in the kingdom of God after resurrection."[103] For the author of Hebrews, the primary focus seems to be on the latter. He is interested in the place where people enter into God's rest, in the reality of God's kingdom. He expresses this view in his references to a homeland (11:13–16) and a "city which hath foundations, whose builder and maker is God" (11:9–10; 12:22). For Latter-day Saints, all these are symbols of the celestial kingdom.[104]

These references to a concrete reality stand in contrast to the metaphor of the "most holy place" (which the author develops in 4:14–10:25). The author uses this metaphor as a means of encouraging his readers to

101. For studies, see *NID*, s.v. "ἀναπαύω"; and Bauernfeind, *TDNT*, 3:627–28.

102. Johnson, *Hebrews*, 130.

103. Largey, *Book of Mormon Reference Companion*, 679: see also Dennis L. Largey and Larry H. Dahl, *Doctrine and Covenants Reference Companion* (Salt Lake City: Deseret Book, 2012), 542–43.

104. Here too the emphasis is on the place, not the state. The place is the glorified and sanctified earth (Ether 13:9; D&C 63:21; 77:1; 88:18–20) that the Saints will inherit (Matt. 5:5; D&C 45:58; 56:20; 63:20; 103:7). The state is described as "everlasting life" or "eternal life" (Hel. 12:26; 3 Ne. 5:13; 26:5; D&C 29:43; 68:12; 75:5; 138:51), and more particularly as "eternal lives" (D&C 132:24; see Shirley S. Ricks, "Eternal Lives, Eternal Increase," in Ludlow, *Encyclopedia of Mormonism*, 1:465). God's work and glory is getting people to enter this state (Moses 1:39) where they will enjoy the delight of celestial society (D&C 130:2).

continued faithfulness in the present. It represents, as this study will show, the condition in which enabling grace is found leading to unity with the Father. Through his priesthood, Christ has now opened this place, allowing the righteous to enter therein.[105]

The reason the author stressed the place rather than the state of rest may be because his readers, feeling the pressures and threats of this world, needed the assurance that an actual place above and beyond this one existed—a location with concrete reality. Though there may be times when the abstract and ethereal have their place, this was not one of them. These people needed to be assured that an actual celestial place awaited them where they would be free from the cares, concerns, and pressures of mortality, a place where "God shall wipe away all tears" and there shall be "no . . . sorrow, nor crying, neither shall there be any more pain: for the former things are passed away" (Rev. 21:4). In short, a place of rest.

To give even more force to his exhortation, the author uses bold and forceful imagery that gives to God's "word" (λόγος, *logos*) a dynamic and energetic quality expressed in four aspects (4:12–13).[106] First, it is living. As with God's works, there is no end to God's words (Moses 1:38). They are ever in force. Whether spoken by the prophets, Apostles, or his Son, the Father's word continues to show the way to his rest.[107]

Second, God's word is active and powerful (ἐνεργής, *energēs*). Consider both of these aspects in the creation accounts when, with a word, God brought chaos into order.[108] With the noun *energēs,* the author stresses the word's continuing dynamic quality. What the "word" has done before, it continues to do and, therefore, cannot be ignored or discounted.

---

105. For discussion, see O'Brien, *Letter to the Hebrews,* 165–66; Cockerill, *Epistle to the Hebrews,* 63–70, 197–200; and Laansma, *"I Will Give You Rest,"* 278–79.

106. The echo of Ps. 95:7, "Today, if you will hear his voice . . ." (our translation), reverberates through this last section. Lane, *Hebrews 1–8,* 96; Attridge, *Epistle to the Hebrews,* 133. The author's focus seems to be less on the "word" as a call to fidelity and more as "a dimension of God's creating and judging power." Johnson, *Hebrews,* 136.

107. Cockerill, *Epistle to the Hebrews,* 215.

108. The idea is expressed in Hebrew by the phrase וַיֹּאמֶר אֱלֹהִים (*wayyō'mer 'ĕlōhîm*), "and God said." Note Gen. 1:3, 6, 9, 14, 24, 26, 29; compare Moses 2:3–25. In Abr. 4:3–20, the "word" of the gods expresses both creative force and intent. With a word they created light and darkness and the expanse of heaven (Abr. 4:4, 6). They also "ordered" the waters and lands to be separated as well as other items to be created (Abr. 4:7). And in all this, "the Gods watched those things which they had ordered until they obeyed" (Abr. 4:18).

Third, God's word is razor sharp. Because of this it can penetrate and separate spirit and body, joint and marrow (4:12).[109] The first two elements look at the two aspects of each person, their spiritual and physical natures. The second two elements focus on elements of their physical being.[110] Both sets of images, however, are to be taken metaphorically and make the same point: nothing, no matter how deeply concealed, can be hidden from God (4:13).

Fourth, God's word is able to discern (κριτικός, *kriticos*) the thoughts and intents generated at the very depths of every individual (4:13). To stress his point, the author again brings in the imagery of the heart, assuring his readers that God never ceases to gaze upon it (4:12).[111] Echoes of the warning against letting their hearts harden reverberate through this section (3:8, 15). The author's message is clear: every heart, no matter how hard, will yield to God's scalpel, and its deepest desires will be revealed.

The author's point is that a person's thoughts, motives, and intents are perfectly clear to God. Even a person's thought processes (ἔννοια, *ennoia*) are known to him. All will be taken into consideration on judgment day. As President John Taylor noted, "We may succeed in hiding our affairs from men; but it is written that for every word and every secret thought we shall have to give an account in the day when accounts have to be rendered before God, when hypocrisy and fraud of any kind will not avail us; for by our words and by our works we shall be justified, or by them we shall be condemned."[112]

In sum, the imagery of God's "word" takes on a judicial quality as it executes his intents.[113] However, to fit his purposes, the author reverses the usual order of a judicial process. These usually proceed through the stages of inquiry, judgment, and sentencing. Here, on the contrary, "the author speaks first of the sword ready to carry out the sentence; then he talks about judgment, and at the end has some reflection on the capacity to make

---

109. This clause is quoted in D&C 33:1 with portions also quoted in D&C 6:2; 11:2; and 14:2, where it carries the same force as in Hebrews.

110. Koester, *Hebrews*, 274.

111. Koester, *Hebrews*, 274.

112. John Taylor, in *Journal of Discourses*, 24:232.

113. The imagery of God's word having both the martial and forensic characteristics was well known in Jewish circles. For example, in Wis. 18:16, God's word is personified as a "slashing warrior" whose sword represents "the irrevocable decree" of Jehovah that "fills the earth with death."

an inquiry."[114] This arrangement reveals the author's great rhetorical skill which he uses to "produce a strong dissuasive effect on the hearers."[115]

At 4:13, the author drops his metaphor and looks at the Father's omniscience. This power is so all pervading and penetrating that nothing is invisible or hidden from it, especially sin. Indeed, by this power everything is uncovered (γυμνά, *gymna*) and laid bare (τετραχηλισμένα, *tetrachēlismena*). All desires and intents are known to him and will be fully disclosed to others (Luke 12:3; D&C 1:3; 88:108–10) unless repentance intervenes (Ps. 25:7; Isa. 43:18, 25; Ezek. 18:22)[116] Indeed, God "knoweth all things, and there is not anything save he knows it" (2 Ne. 9:20; compare Morm. 8:17), including "all the thoughts and intents of the heart" (Alma 18:32) and even all works of darkness, no matter how well hidden they may be (2 Ne. 27:27).

Thus, the focus of this passage is not on the act of the executioner's sword but on the exposing power of God's word. In nonmetaphorical terms, this passage is about the futility of trying to hide anything from the Divine. By extension, it is about being honest with self and God. The Hebrew brethren and sisters were going through a dark time, one that might tempt them to turn from the Savior. This they cannot do without losing "so great salvation" (2:3) and forfeiting entering into God's rest. As Elder Oaks witnessed, "he who presides over [the] Eternal Tribunal knows our secret acts, and he is 'a discerner of the thoughts and intents of the heart.'"[117] These Christians, therefore, must stay true to their God and be faithful to their core. Only then can they be judged fit for the Sabbath rest.[118]

Such exacting and forceful words were doubtlessly worrisome for many of the author's readers. But he knew exactly what he was doing and deliberately built up the tension. In doing so, he did more than hold the interest of his readers; he also laid the ground work for their acceptance of the hope he would now give them.

---

114. Vanhoye, *Letter to the Hebrews,* 95.

115. Vanhoye, *Letter to the Hebrews,* 95.

116. Cockerill, *Epistle to the Hebrews,* 217.

117. Dallin H. Oaks, "My Brother's Keeper," *Ensign* 16, no. 11 (November 1986): 20.

118. See Cockerill, *Epistle to the Hebrews,* 217 n. 14; see also Smillie, "'Ο Λογοσ Του Θεου' in Hebrews 4:12–13," 338–59; Lane, *Hebrews 1–8,* 102; and Arthur A. Bailey, "A Message of Judgment from the Olivet Sermon," in *The Lord of the Gospels: The 1990 Sperry Symposium on the New Testament,* ed. Bruce A. Van Orden and Brent L. Top (Salt Lake City: Deseret Book, 1991), 10.

Jesus the Great High Priest (4:14–16)

Greek Text

14 Ἔχοντες οὖν ἀρχιερέα μέγαν διεληλυθότα τοὺς οὐρανούς, Ἰησοῦν τὸν υἱὸν τοῦ θεοῦ, κρατῶμεν τῆς ὁμολογίας. 15 οὐ γὰρ ἔχομεν ἀρχιερέα μὴ δυνάμενον συμπαθῆσαι ταῖς ἀσθενείαις ἡμῶν, πεπειρασμένον δὲ κατὰ πάντα καθ' ὁμοιότητα χωρὶς ἁμαρτίας. 16 προσερχώμεθα οὖν μετὰ παρρησίας τῷ θρόνῳ τῆς χάριτος, ἵνα λάβωμεν ἔλεος καὶ χάριν εὕρωμεν εἰς εὔκαιρον βοήθειαν. [SBLGNT]

King James Version

14 Seeing then that we have a great high priest, that is passed into the heavens, Jesus the Son of God, let us hold fast our profession. 15 For we have not an high priest which cannot be touched with the feeling of our infirmities; but was in all points tempted like as we are, yet without sin. 16 Let us therefore come boldly unto the throne of grace, that we may obtain mercy, and find grace to help in time of need.

New Rendition

14 Therefore, since we have a great high priest who has passed through the heavens, even Jesus the Son of God, let us hold firmly to our confessed allegiance to him. 15 For we do not have a high priest who is unable to sympathize with our weaknesses, but although he was tried and tempted in every way just like us, he was without sin. 16 So let us approach the throne of grace with confidence, so that we may receive mercy and find grace to help in time of need.

Translation Notes and Comments

4:14 *Seeing then that we have a great high priest, that is passed into the heavens / Therefore, since we have a great high priest who has passed through the heavens:* Again the author uses the conjunction οὖν (oun), "therefore, consequently," to signal he is now ready to make his point. That point rests on one fact: "we have a great high priest." On this imagery, see Translation Notes for 2:17 with associated Analysis.[119]

The verb διέρχομαι (*dierchomai*), "to pass through," means in this instance to move into or through an area or place.[120] That place is τοὺς

119. See also the section on "Jesus as High Priest" in "Excursus on the Atonement: A View from Hebrews" found at the end of chapter 2. On the typological aspects of the priest, see McConkie, *Doctrinal New Testament Commentary,* 1:718–24.

120. BDAG, 244.

οὐρανούς (*tous ouranous*), "the heavens." With Paul, the author of Hebrews sees the celestial realm as multilevel (2 Cor. 12:2).[121] To stress the Lord's ascendancy, these witnesses state he passed *through* them (Eph. 4:10) and now presides over them (7:26; 8:1). The author uses the perfect, active participle διεληλυθότα (*dielēlythota*) to express Jesus' movement through the heavens to show Jesus has entered his station above them and still remains there. The author's point is that since the Lord's ascension, this is the place from which he continues to administer all heavenly and earthly affairs (9:24; Rom. 8:34).

even Jesus the Son of God / Jesus the Son of God: With this phrase, the author again equates Jesus of Nazareth with the Son of God, emphasizing they are the same.

let us hold fast our profession / let us hold firmly to our confessed allegiance to him: The verb *κρατέω* (*krateō*) means "to adhere to something strongly" with an emphasis on the firmness of the grip.[122] The force of its subjunctive mood, as found here, is hortatory: "let us hold." It also shows they already possess a testimony. All he wants them to do is grip it as firmly as they can.[123] By using the first-person plural, the author includes himself and thereby softens any antagonism his exhortation may arouse.

The noun ὁμολογία (*homologia*) in this instance is a "statement of allegiance, as a content of an action," and, therefore, the word connotes an open—that is, public—confession or acknowledgement.[124] For further study, see Translation Notes for 3:1. In our Rendition, we have expanded "confession" to "confessed allegiance to him" both to capture the full nuance of the word and to add clarity.

4:15 ***For we have not a high priest which cannot be touched with the feeling of our infirmities / For we do not have a high priest who is unable to sympathize with our weaknesses:*** On the term "high priest," see Translation Notes for 2:17.

---

121. It is unlikely that the author is influenced by rabbinic, Hellenistic, or even gnostic views of the celestial realm being composed of a two-, three-, or seven-layered heaven. Even so, the idea of a multilayered cosmos and heaven would not have seemed strange to those living at the time. The author's point, however, is that Jesus ascended through however many there were to finally reach the dwelling place of the Father. Cockerill, *Epistle to the Hebrews,* 224 n. 10.

122. BDAG, 564.

123. Cockerill, *Epistle to the Hebrews,* 224 n. 15.

124. BDAG, 709.

The verb συμπαθέω (*sympatheō*) means literally "to suffer together with," that is, "to sympathize with."[125] The term connotes an emotional identification with another "often accompanied by deep tenderness."[126] In addition, "it always includes the element of active help."[127] And it needs to be stressed it does not bear in the slightest degree the air of pity sometimes associated with the English word "sympathy." To take it otherwise would violate the author's point that Jesus entered fully into mortality with all its weaknesses and suffering.[128]

The noun ἀσθένεια (*astheneia*), though denoting a full range of limitations and inabilities from mere timidity to severe illness, is best understood as "weakness." We felt that this word choice is best because it addresses a deficiency or inferiority of mind, will, or body that mortals have.[129]

but was in all points tempted as are we / he was tried and tempted in every way just like us: The verb πειράζω (*peirazō*) has a broader range of meaning in Greek than the English verb "to tempt." It also encompasses both "to test" or "to try."[130] Hence, in our Rendition, we have translated the perfect passive participle πεπειρασμένον (*pepeirasmenon*) as "tried and tempted." The force of that perfect is instructive, showing that "Jesus endured temptation through his entire life until its completion at/in his death (see Luke 22:28, 31), when he 'resisted to the point of shedding' his own blood (12:4)."[131] Now, having overcome temptation, he is in a position to also enable his people to do the same.[132]

The phrase κατὰ πάντα (*kata panta*), "in all points, in every way," stresses the breadth of the Lord's trials. During his mortal sojourn, he was spared from nothing. Thus, there is nothing a person goes through, including grief, loss, pain, and sorrow, that Jesus cannot empathize with.[133]

---

125. LSJ, 1680; BDAG, 958. The English word "sympathize" is a direct borrowing from the Greek. See also Holzapfel and Wayment, *Making Sense,* 452.

126. *Webster's New Dictionary of Synonyms,* s.v. "sympathy."

127. Lane, *Hebrews 1–8,* 114; compare 10:34; 4 Macc. 4:25; 13:23; *T. Sim.* 3:6; and *T. Ben.* 4:4.

128. Johnson, *Hebrews,* 140.

129. BDAG, 142; Louw-Nida, §§23.143; 25.269; 74.23.

130. BDAG, 792–93. Ogden and Skinner, *Verse by Verse,* 249, notes that "righteous living does not protect us from temptation but it does protect us from succumbing to temptation."

131. Cockerill, *Epistle to the Hebrews,* 226.

132. See Lane, *Hebrews 1–8,* 114.

133. Bruce, *Epistle to the Hebrews,* 115–16, and n. 65. On the Lord's ability to be tempted, see McConkie, *Promised Messiah,* 1:273–74; 498–500; see also Alma 7:11.

In the prepositional phrase καθ' ὁμοιότητα (*kath' homoiotēta*), "in the same way,"[134] the pronoun "us" is not present in the Greek but is understood. For clarity, we have translated this as "just like us." The KJV similarly renders this "as are we." This understanding reinforces the point that Christ has quite literally experienced all that any mortal ever has.

yet without sin / he was without sin: With this phrase, the author makes a major distinction between humankind and our Lord. Jesus never yielded to temptation, never committed a sin.

4:16 *Let us therefore come boldly unto the throne of grace / So let us approach the throne of grace with confidence:* Again, the subordinating conjunction οὖν (*oun*), "so, therefore," draws the readers' attention to the author's conclusion. In this context, it means "for this reason," pointing back to the fact that the Christians have a compassionate, sympathetic High Priest ready to accept them and minister to them. It also underscores the reason for the hortatory subjunctive mood of the verb προσέρχομαι (*proserchomai*), "let us approach." This same phrase is often used in the LXX with covenantal overtones.[135] It is in temple worship that the participant approaches God confidently in most solemn worship because he or she has been prepared to meet him.

The noun παρρησία (*parrēsia*) carries a range of meanings, including fearlessness, boldness, and confidence. The term is especially apropos when it comes to the feeling of confidence a person should have when approaching someone of high rank whom they know is on their side.[136]

The phrase τῷ θρόνῳ τῆς χάριτος (*tō thronō tēs charitos*), "the throne of grace," can refer to either the royal seat to which the Son has ascended (1:3, 8, 13; 10:12) or, more likely, based on 8:1; 12:2, to the Father's throne. Either way, the nuance is to the power, authority, and respect that symbol represents.[137] In reality, based on 2 Nephi 9:41, it is the Son whom the person actually approaches. Of importance is the noun that describes the throne, τῆς χάριτος (*tēs charitos*), "of grace." On the implications of this word, see below.

This passage echoes a portion of the rites of *Yom Kippur* or "Day of Atonement," the only fast commanded by Jehovah during Moses' administration (Lev. 16:23, 26–32; compare Ex. 30:10; and Num. 29:7–11). The

134. BDAG, 707.

135. See Attridge, *Epistle to the Hebrews,* 141.

136. BDAG, 781–82; LXX Job 22:26; 27:9–10. In the Apocrypha, the righteous will stand "with great confidence" (ἐν παρρησίᾳ πολλῇ, *en parrēsia pollē*) before the judgment tribunal. Wis. 5:1; compare 2 Esd. 7:98.

137. Koester, *Hebrews,* 282–84.

Jewish and perhaps many of the gentile Christians in the author's audience would have been very aware of the nature and importance of the ordinances performed that day.

The Lord set this day apart from all others as the most holy. Its rites were designed to bring Israel as a people and the Israelites as individuals into oneness with Jehovah. On this day as part of an elaborate ritual, the high priest entered the Holy of Holies, the most sacred room in the tabernacle and later the temple, and there before God's throne (called the "mercy seat") made a blood offering to atone for his sins and those of the people. As the author will develop in later chapters, Jesus as the new High Priest will himself make an offering of his own blood to accomplish what the old order was unable to do. See Translation Notes with their associated Analyses in chapters 9 and 10.

that we may obtain mercy / so that we may receive mercy: The conjunction ἵνα (*hina*), "so that," is important here because it points to the purpose of approaching the throne. That purpose is twofold. The first, as expressed in this phrase, is to "receive mercy." The semantic range of the noun ἔλεος (*eleos*), "mercy," is rather broad. It includes compassion, clemency, kindness, and pity.[138]

In the present context, the noun looks to God's concern and kindness for his children expressed as compassion, sympathy, and even clemency.[139] It particularly connotes the willing assistance the Father gives to a child due to his love. It is often tied to the idea of covenant and God's outreach to those under covenant to assist them. It expresses itself most fully in God's willingness to forgive sins and thereby elevate the misery such evils bring.

and find grace to help in time of need / and find grace to help in time of need: In this clause, the author states the second reason why his readers should approach "the throne of grace." It is to χάριν εὕρωμεν (*charin heurōmen*), "find grace."

The noun χάρις (*charis*), "grace," in the present context designates the Father's favorable predisposition toward his children expressing itself in

---

138. BDAG, 316. The range of meanings, in Jewish circles, that the Greek noun took on may have been a result of its use to translate primarily the Hebrew חֶסֶד (*ḥesed*), "favor, grace," (HAL, 336–37) but also חֵן (*ḥēn*), "favor, grace," and רַחֲמִים (*raḥămîm*), "mercy" (HAL, 1218). The noun חֶסֶד (*ḥesed*) connotes the force which lay behind covenant keeping and therefore was tied to love, respect, and care. It also expresses one's drive to assist another in need. *NID*, s.v. "ἔλεος"; BDB, 338–39; Zobel, *TDOT*, 5:44–64. Though the word touches in meaning the word ἱλάσκομαι (*hilaskomai*) in that both contain an aspect of mercy, it does not carry the idea of appeasing, propitiating, or reconciling estranged persons. See BDAG, 473–74; for discussion, see the Translation Notes for 2:17 with associated Analysis.

139. BDAG, 316.

compassion and understanding. The term nuances the outreach of his divine love as revealed through the ministry of the Son. It looks more particularly to the enabling gift the Father freely and lovingly gives to those who strive to do his will. This gift empowers them to do what they could not otherwise do.[140]

The noun βοήθεια (*boētheia*) denotes "help" or "assistance" that is offered to meet a need.[141] The stress of the word is in its outreach. It is expressed when a person, seeing a need, willingly responds to meet it. The author couples the noun with the adjective εὔκαιρος (*eukairos*), "well-timed, opportune," or "convenient."[142] The sense of the phrase is that divine help can surely be received in the Lord's due time and season.

Analysis and Summary

The author has used considerable care and great skill to prepare his listeners for the point he wants to emphasize. He has based his appeal on the tragic history of the Israelites' wilderness rebellion and its severe consequences. His appeal also meant that his readers, sensing what could befall them, would better appreciate what the Son, their High Priest, has done for them.

The author has also carefully developed his case to emphasize not only his readers' need for continued faithfulness to the Son of God but also for the obligation that rests upon them to make a bold, public declaration (ὁμολογία, *homologia*) of their belief.[143] With the authority of scripture behind him, the author has shown them that nothing is hidden from the eyes of the Divine (4:13). All will answer to him—not just for what they have done but also for what they have thought and intended. None can escape the reckoning (λόγος, *logos*) demanded by "the all-penetrating 'word' of the all-knowing God" (see 4:13).[144] The author's intent is for his readers to feel the full weight of the responsibility that now lies upon them.

Using the anxiety he has created, the author now turns to assure his readers that they can make a more than adequate response to God's demands. More importantly, they will have divine help in doing so.[145] This assurance is grounded on the reality of the Son's enthronement (4:14). He now sits

140. BDAG, 1079–81. For further study, see Translation Notes for 2:9 with accompanying documentation.

141. BDAG, 180.

142. BDAG, 407.

143. BDAG, 709.

144. Cockerill, *Epistle to the Hebrews,* 218.

145. Cockerill, *Epistle to the Hebrews,* 218–19.

at the seat of power. In addition, he is also the great High Priest who has already purified his people from sin (1:3).

Now comes the point. Given who the Savior is and what he has done for them, there is no reason for them not to "hold fast" to their "confessed allegiance [ὁμολογία, *homologia*] to him" (4:14).

In case that incentive is not enough, the author presents another reason for them to not abandon their faith in the Son or hesitate in bearing their witness of him. This Son of God, this great High Priest, can sympathize with his people. Why? Because he has been tried and tempted (πειράζω, *peirazō*) in the same ways they have (4:15).[146] Indeed, he has suffered "in every way" (κατὰ πάντα, *kata panta*) possible.

The author's teaching suggests the Savior not only experienced all of the temptations that mortals face but also all the trials of mortality, including hunger, thirst, sickness, and pain of body, as well as the mental and emotional anguish caused by others. As the prophet Alma explained so eloquently, "He shall go forth, suffering pains and afflictions and temptations of every kind; and this that the word might be fulfilled which saith he will take upon him the pains and the sicknesses of his people. And he will take upon him death, that he may loose the bands of death which bind his people; and he will take upon him their infirmities, that his bowels may be filled with mercy, according to the flesh, that he may know according to the flesh how to succor his people according to their infirmities" (Alma 7:11–12; compare D&C 62:1; 101:2).[147]

Explaining and expanding on this idea, Elder Bruce R. McConkie asked, "Why does Christ intercede for his erring brethren with such infinite compassion? Because he knows by experience the anguish and pain of mortal suffering and the severity of Lucifer's temptations; because he can put himself in the position of feeble man and then feel the infinite joy of the soul who overcomes the world and feels himself reconciled to Him who is perfect and Almighty."[148]

Though tempted on every point and tried in every way, the Master never yielded to sin (4:15). Elder Howard W. Hunter noted,

> It is important to remember that Jesus was capable of sinning, that he could have succumbed, that the plan of life and salvation could have been

146. BDAG, 792–93.

147. See also McConkie, *Doctrinal New Testament Commentary,* 3:154. Farley, "Temptations of Jesus," 181, notes that, though the Gospels record specifically the Lord's temptations in the wilderness, they were not the only ones he endured.

148. McConkie, *Doctrinal New Testament Commentary,* 3:154. See also J. Devan Cornish, "Learning How the Atonement Can Change You," *Ensign* 32, no. 4 (April 2002): 20–23.

> foiled, but that he remained true. Had there been no possibility of his yielding to the enticement of Satan, there would have been no real test, no genuine victory in the result. If he had been stripped of the faculty to sin, he would have been stripped of his very agency. It was he who had come to safeguard and ensure the agency of man. He had to retain the capacity and ability to sin had he willed so to do. As Paul wrote, "Though he were a Son, yet learned he obedience by the things which he suffered" (Heb. 5:8); and he "was in all points tempted like as we are, yet without sin" (Heb. 4:15). He was perfect and sinless, not because he had to be, but rather because he clearly and determinedly wanted to be. As the Doctrine and Covenants records, "He suffered temptations but gave no heed unto them." (D&C 20:22.)[149]

Throughout his ministry, he remained pure and holy in thought, emotion, and deed. There were certain ramifications for the rest of humankind for his doing so. According to Joseph Smith, Jesus "kept the law of God, and remained without sin, showing thereby that it is in the power of man to keep the law and remain also without sin; and also, that by him a righteous judgment might come upon all flesh, and that all who walk not in the law of God may justly be condemned by the law, and have no excuse for their sins. And he being the Only Begotten of the Father, full of grace and truth, and having overcome, received a fullness of the glory of the Father."[150] The statement that a person can live without sin should likely be taken with a caveat. Jesus revealed that it was indeed possible but only under a certain condition. Joseph Smith pointed out this condition, stating, "None ever were perfect but Jesus, and why was he perfect? because he was the son of God, and had the fulness of the Spirit, and greater power than any man."[151] Thus, being enabled by being God's Son and having a fulness of the Spirit, the Lord possessed powers that others must grow into. Having a "fulness of the Spirit" gave the Lord the unique ability to resist sin. The Prophet's words suggest that when others obtain the "fulness of the Spirit" they too will be able to do in practice what was otherwise impossible. At one time,

---

149. Hunter, "Temptations of Christ," 17–19.

150. W. Jeffrey Marsh, *His Final Hours* (Salt Lake City: Deseret Book, 2000), 37–38, quoted in Robin Scott Jensen, Richard E. Turley Jr., and Riley M. Lorimer, eds., *Revelations and Translations, Volume 2: Published Revelations,* The Joseph Smith Papers (Salt Lake City: Church Historian's Press, 2011), 2:52–54.

151. *Times and Seasons* 2 (June 1, 1841): 429–30, online as "Discourse, 16 May 1841, as Reported by *Times and Seasons,*" Joseph Smith Papers, https://www.josephsmithpapers.org/paper-summary/discourse-16may-1841-as-reported-by-times-and-seasons/1. See also Rodney Turner, "Grace, Mysteries, and Exaltation," in Millet, *Studies in Scripture, Volume 6,* 119.

he prayed that those who participate in temple worship "may grow up in thee, and receive a fulness of the Holy Ghost" (D&C 109:14–15), suggesting that gaining this helpful and necessary power is possible.

That Jesus was perfect, however, should not be construed to mean that Jesus did not feel the press of mortality with all its burdens and temptations. But by resisting—by never yielding to the pangs of hunger or thirst or pain of body or of spirit, by never giving into temptation or seduction no matter how strong—he felt their full and crushing weight as no mortal ever has. And as he endured the crucible of Gethsemane where he prayed—no, begged—the Father not to make him drink the bitter cup, he learned the full cost of obedience. Thus, he can sympathize fully and completely with all his fellows.[152]

As a result, as one scholar clearly noted, "the High Priest of our Christian profession is not an absentee Master, not a distant Deity, not one who 'cannot be touched with the feeling of our infirmities'—because he too has known the perils and pains of mortality and the anguish of alienation—he knows our needs, he fully understands. Because of the intercession of Christ, we are entitled to 'come boldly unto the throne of grace.'"[153]

The operative word here is "boldly" (παρρησίᾳ, *parrēsia,* or "with confidence"). Because of what the Savior has done—because of how he can sympathize with those who suffer under the plague of weaknesses and flaws—those who stay true to him need have no fear in approaching either him or the Father (4:16). Indeed, he is their advocate (παράκλητος, *paraklētos*; 1 John 2:1; see also Isa. 51:22; 2 Ne. 2:9; Jacob 3:1; Moro. 7:28; D&C 29:5; 32:3; 45:3).[154]

But what does it mean to approach "the throne of grace"? Two aspects are possible. The first is prayer, in which the person comes before the Father in supplication or thanksgiving (LXX Jer. 7:16). In ancient times, it was before the royal throne where people appeared to plead for relief or assistance and where mercy could be found.[155] Both Christians and Jews believed God had two thrones. One was in heaven (8:1; Ps. 11:4; 103:19; Isa. 6:1; Rev. 4:1–2, 9; 7:10–12; 19:4) and the other on the earth. The latter was in the temple and known as the "mercy seat" (9:5; Ex. 25:17–22;

---

152. Lane, *Hebrews 1–8,* 114; Bruce, *Epistle to the Hebrews,* 116, and n. 65; compare O'Brien, *Letter to the Hebrews,* 184.

153. Robert L. Millet, *Jesus Christ, the Only Sure Foundation* (Salt Lake City: Bookcraft, 1999), viii.

154. For development, see Translation Notes for 2:17 with associated Analysis.

155. For example, see Dio Cassius, *Roman History* 59.6.3; and Josephus, *Ant.* 18.107.

2 Kgs. 19:15; Ps. 80:1; 99:1). Before Christ finished his ministry, that throne could be approached only by the high priest and then only on an annual basis (this ceremony is detailed in Lev. 16). As the author will later explain (9:6–10), the symbolism behind the ritual showed that direct access to the Divine was closed as long as the Levitical order was in place. But through the Atonement, that throne (that is, direct access to the Father) had now become open to all (10:19).

The second aspect of approaching the throne is judgment, in which righteous people come to God in order to receive their reward (Ps. 58:11; Rev. 3:21; 2 Ne. 9:15–18; Alma 5:15–16; 12:12; 41:14). Though the prospect of standing before the throne of God "striketh the wicked with awful dread and fear," for the righteous it is "the pleasing bar of God" (Jacob 6:13; compare Moro. 10:34). That being the case, it is little wonder that the righteous should feel a great deal of confidence as they approach it.

What is the purpose of approaching the throne of grace? The author gives two reasons (4:16). The first is so the faithful may obtain mercy (ἔλεος, *eleos*). The noun connotes compassion and sympathy grounded in love that the Father has for his children.[156] It expresses itself most clearly as the Father's forgiveness of sin, resulting in the cessation of the misery that evil brings. The second is so the contrite may find the power of grace in their time of need.[157] The noun "grace" (χάρις, *charis*) denotes the enabling power that flows from the Father and the Son because of their love and kind benevolence to faithful individuals. By means of this gift, the faithful are enabled to do what they could not do on their own.[158] As Elder Bruce C. Hafen stated,

> The Savior's grace can bless us, beyond its compensation for our sins, in our quest for divine perfection. While much of the perfection process involves a healing from sin and bitterness, the process involves an additional, affirmative dimension through which we may acquire a Christlike nature, becoming even as the Father and Son are.
>
> In his own development toward perfection, the Savior received *the Father's* grace. He "received not of the fulness at the first, but received grace for grace . . . until he received a fulness." (D&C 93:12–13.) His life

156. BDAG, 316.

157. See Gene R. Cook, "Receiving Divine Assistance through the Grace of the Lord," *Ensign* 23, no. 5 (May 1993): 81.

158. BDAG, 1079–81. For studies on grace from a Latter-day Saint perspective, see Dew, *Amazed by Grace*; Millet, *Grace Works*; and Draper and Rhodes, *Paul's First Epistle to the Corinthians*, 146–82.

> was sinless; hence, he received grace not to compensate for his sins, but to empower his personal growth: "Though he were a Son, yet learned he obedience by the things which he suffered; And *being made perfect,* he became the author of eternal salvation." (Heb. 5:8–9; italics added.)[159]

The same is true of the faithful Saint. The Lord promised that those who strive to keep his commandments "shall receive of his fulness, and be glorified in me as I am in the Father; therefore, I say unto you, you shall receive grace for grace" (D&C 93:20). Receiving the Savior's grace means becoming not only sin-free but also righteous. When the soul feels that happen and accepts it, all feelings of guilt are left behind. As the two blessings of mercy and grace are taken together, we see the power that comes from approaching the throne. Through grace, all guilt is removed; through mercy, all misery is removed.

The point is this: through the Savior's obedient sacrifice, the sins of the faithful have been "purged" and their conscience cleansed "from dead works" (9:14). Feeling the joy and assurance these bring, the son or daughter can approach the Father in full confidence (4:16). This confidence transcends feeling. It is also grounded on the sureness that they have been authorized to enter the Father's presence.[160]

In sum, the author ends this hortatory section by not only recalling his doctrinal theme but also enriching it. He does so by declaring "we have a living high priest" who has gone "through the heavens" and is "*the* Son of God" (4:14, italics added). In short, Christ has accomplished his mission. For that reason, the author admonishes his readers to "hold fast" to their testimonies (4:14). The Greek verb translated as "hold fast" (κρατέω, *krateō*) is related to the noun κράτος (*kratos*), "strength," and emphasizes the force needed to accomplish a task. This last phrase, "hold fast to the confession" (that is, "testimony"), is expressed in just three words in the Greek text (κρατῶμεν τῆς ὁμολογίας, *kratōmen tēs homologias*), and one of them is a definite article. The severe brevity greatly enhances the force of the author's heartfelt desire and allows him to bring this section of work to a close with a resounding bang.[161]

159. Bruce C. Hafen, "Beauty for Ashes: The Atonement of Jesus Christ," *Ensign* 30, no. 5 (May 1990): 7–13, italics in original.

160. Cockerill, *Epistle to the Hebrews,* 228.

161. Vanhoye, *Letter to the Hebrews,* 95.

Chapter 5

A Priest Forever

Introduction

At the conclusion of the last chapter, the author successfully admonished his readers not only to hold tightly to their testimonies but also to take advantage of what their faithfulness could bring them. By pushing forward, they could obtain the hope, mercy, and grace the ministry of the Great High Priest opened for all (4:14–16). The author, in this chapter, continues to develop this theme by expanding his consideration of Christ's high-priestly office and what flows out of it. In doing so, he answers two questions that many of his readers may have had concerning the Lord's priesthood. First, "if [Christ] is the kind of High Priest intimated in these verses, how does he relate to the God-established Aaronic Priesthood?" and second, "What biblical authority does he [the author] have for Christ's priesthood in light of the perpetual character attributed to that earlier priesthood instituted by Moses at God's direction?"[1]

By comparing and contrasting the new High Priest with his old counterparts, the author very successfully answers these questions. The author develops his answers by introducing the qualities and work that the office of the Aaronic high priest required. He does this in three stages. First, he looks at its function (5:1); second, at the personal qualities one must have to hold the office (5:2–3); and third, at the divine authorization necessary for the priest to properly officiate (5:4).[2]

1. Cockerill, *Epistle to the Hebrews,* 229.

2. Attridge, *Epistle to the Hebrews,* 138. Each point of comparison yields to a point of contrast and, in each case, underscores the superiority of the new high priest. Albert Vanhoye, *Old Testament Priests and the New Priest According to the New Testament,* new ed., trans. J. Bernard Orchard (Leominster, Eng.: Gracewing, 2009), 133–37.

Next, the author applies these to Christ but in reverse order. First, the author cites from scripture the divine call the Savior received to be both the Father's Son and his priestly representative (5:5–6). Second, he notes the Savior's sympathetic qualities that he learned through the suffering that obedience caused (5:7–8). And, third, he emphasizes the Lord's salvific powers that rest upon and are assured by his "perfection" and priestly office (5:9–10). The author will use this material as the foundation on which he will build his study of the priesthood "after the order of Melchisedek" (7:17) in chapter 7 and on the salvific function of the Savior's priestly act of Atonement in chapters 8–10.[3]

The author, dramatically switching tone, ends this pericope (5:11–14) by chastening his readers for their slowness to learn and understand the doctrine, a malaise growing primarily out of their continued and shameful spiritual immaturity.

Jesus the Great High Priest (5:1–10)

Greek Text

1 Πᾶς γὰρ ἀρχιερεὺς ἐξ ἀνθρώπων λαμβανόμενος ὑπὲρ ἀνθρώπων καθίσταται τὰ πρὸς τὸν θεόν, ἵνα προσφέρῃ δῶρά τε καὶ θυσίας ὑπὲρ ἁμαρτιῶν, 2 μετριοπαθεῖν δυνάμενος τοῖς ἀγνοοῦσι καὶ πλανωμένοις ἐπεὶ καὶ αὐτὸς περίκειται ἀσθένειαν, 3 καὶ δι' αὐτὴν ὀφείλει, καθὼς περὶ τοῦ λαοῦ, οὕτως καὶ περὶ αὑτοῦ προσφέρειν περὶ ἁμαρτιῶν. 4 καὶ οὐχ ἑαυτῷ τις λαμβάνει τὴν τιμήν, ἀλλὰ καλούμενος ὑπὸ τοῦ θεοῦ, καθώσπερ καὶ Ἀαρών. 5 Οὕτως καὶ ὁ Χριστὸς οὐχ ἑαυτὸν ἐδόξασεν γενηθῆναι ἀρχιερέα, ἀλλ' ὁ λαλήσας πρὸς αὐτόν· Υἱός μου εἶ σύ, ἐγὼ σήμερον γεγέννηκά σε· 6 καθὼς καὶ ἐν ἑτέρῳ λέγει· Σὺ ἱερεὺς εἰς τὸν αἰῶνα κατὰ τὴν τάξιν Μελχισέδεκ, 7 ὃς ἐν ταῖς ἡμέραις τῆς σαρκὸς αὐτοῦ δεήσεις τε καὶ ἱκετηρίας πρὸς τὸν δυνάμενον σῴζειν αὐτὸν ἐκ θανάτου μετὰ κραυγῆς ἰσχυρᾶς καὶ δακρύων προσενέγκας καὶ εἰσακουσθεὶς ἀπὸ τῆς εὐλαβείας, 8 καίπερ ὢν υἱός, ἔμαθεν ἀφ' ὧν ἔπαθεν τὴν ὑπακοήν, 9 καὶ τελειωθεὶς ἐγένετο πᾶσιν τοῖς ὑπακούουσιν αὐτῷ αἴτιος σωτηρίας αἰωνίου, 10 προσαγορευθεὶς ὑπὸ τοῦ θεοῦ ἀρχιερεὺς κατὰ τὴν τάξιν Μελχισέδεκ. [SBLGNT]

---

3. Attridge, *Epistle to the Hebrews,* 138. For a study, see James Kurianal, *Jesus Our High Priest: Ps 110,4 as the Substructure of Heb 5,1–7,28* (Frankfurt am Main: Peter Lang, 2000), especially 49–83.

King James Version

1 For every high priest taken from among men is ordained for men in things pertaining to God, that he may offer both gifts and sacrifices for sins: 2 Who can have compassion on the ignorant, and on them that are out of the way; for that he himself also is compassed with infirmity. 3 And by reason hereof he ought, as for the people, so also for himself, to offer for sins. 4 And no man taketh this honour unto himself, but he that is called of God, as was Aaron. 5 So also Christ glorified not himself to be made an high priest; but he that said unto him, Thou art my Son, to day have I begotten thee. 6 As he saith also in another place, Thou art a priest for ever after the order of Melchisedec. 7 Who in the days of his flesh, when he had offered up prayers and supplications with strong crying and tears unto him that was able to save him from death, and was heard in that he feared; 8 Though he were a Son, yet learned he obedience by the things which he suffered; 9 And being made perfect, he became the author of eternal salvation unto all them that obey him; 10 Called of God an high priest after the order of Melchisedec.

New Rendition

1 Now every high priest who is chosen from among mankind is put in charge of matters pertaining to God in their behalf, to offer gifts and sacrifices for sins. 2 He is able to deal gently with the ignorant and those who have gone astray, since he himself is beset with weakness. 3 And because of this, he must make sin offerings for himself as well as for the people. 4 Now no one takes this honor for himself, on the contrary, he is called by God, just like Aaron. 5 Thus Christ also did not glorify himself in becoming a high priest, rather he was glorified by the one who said to him,

> "You are my son. Today I have begotten you." [LXX Ps. 2:7]

6 As he also said in another place,

> "You are a priest forever according to the order of Melchizedek." [LXX Ps. 109:4]

7 During his mortal life, Christ offered prayers and supplications, with loud cries and tears, to the one who was able to save him from death, and he was heard because of his reverent devotion to God. 8 And although he was a son, he learned obedience through the things that he suffered. 9 And having become perfect, he became the source of eternal salvation for all those who obey him, 10 and he was designated by God to be a high priest according to the order of Melchizedek.

Translation Notes and Comments

5:1 *For every high priest taken from among men / Now every high priest who is chosen from among mankind:* The conjunction γάρ (*gar*), "for, now, in fact," plays an important role here by emphasizing that the premises the author rests his case on are beyond dispute and, therefore, the conclusions he draws therefrom are sound.[4]

The verb λαμβάνω (*lambanō*), found here as a present middle or passive participle, has the basic sense in the middle voice of "taking hold (of something)" but with the extended sense of "choosing (someone)."[5] Our Rendition has the latter translation with attributive force, thus, "who is chosen."[6] Though the author states that every high priest "is chosen from among mankind," technically the person was chosen from the Levitical tribe, for only they had the right to priestly office. That restriction, however, did not apply to the Lord because he was not a descendent of Aaron. To make his thesis work, however, the author leaves the field from which priests were chosen very broad. By doing so, he could show that Jesus was not only among mankind, he was also one with them. As a result, the Lord's call conformed to the requirement of being "chosen from among mankind" even though he was yet God.[7]

is ordained for men in things pertaining to God / is put in charge of matters pertaining to God in their behalf: The verb καθίστημι (*kathistēmi*), used here in its present, passive, third-person singular form, means literally "to set down." It carries the extended sense of appointing someone to a position of authority and, thereby, putting them "in charge" of seeing a task gets completed.[8]

The preposition ὑπὲρ (*hyper*) when followed by the genitive has the sense of "over" and "for, in behalf of, for the sake of (someone or something)."[9] In the present context, it explains why the high priest was chosen—to serve the people in sacred matters. Though he shared in common with his fellow priests the authority to instruct the people in the basic principles of the Mosaic law, to determine whether a person was or was not ritually clean, and to offer sacrifices for thanksgiving and other purposes, he stood apart as the only priest authorized to enter the Holy of Holies and make expiation in behalf of all Israel.[10]

---

4. Vanhoye, *Letter to the Hebrews,* 98; Smyth, *Greek Grammar,* §2803.
5. BDAG, 583–85; Louw-Nida, §§18.1; 30.86.
6. The KJV takes it with adverbial force, but it flows better with the attributive. Either way, it does not change the sense of the phrase. Cockerill, *Epistle to the Hebrews,* 232 n. 12.
7. Cockerill, *Epistle to the Hebrews,* 232–33.
8. LSJ, 854–55; BDAG, 492–93. Its use here is a divine passive showing that what "has been established" was by God. Cockerill, *Epistle to the Hebrews,* 237 n. 38.
9. BDAG, 1030–31. In this case, it carries the nuance of benefaction. Louw-Nida, §90.36.
10. Koester, *Hebrews,* 120.

that he may offer both gifts and sacrifices for sins / to offer gifts and sacrifices for sins: The subordinating conjunction ἵνα (*hina*), "so that," expresses purpose by pointing to the specific activity the high priest was "put in charge" of.

The verb προσφέρω (*prospherō*), "to offer," is a cultic term meaning "to accomplish sacrifice."[11] Though the high priest had many duties, none surpassed in importance making sacrifices in behalf of the Israelites.[12]

The phrase δῶρά τε καὶ θυσίας (*dora te kai thysias*), "gifts and sacrifices," is a fixed formula denoting sacrifices in general and thus making it artificial and unnecessary to distinguish between the two nouns.[13] The preposition ὑπὲρ (*hyper*), unlike its use in the phrase just above, gives the reason for an action. In this case, that action was "to remove," that is, "to purge," sin.[14]

5:2 ***Who can have compassion on / He is able to deal gently with:*** The verb μετριοπαθέω (*metriopatheō*) has the basic sense of moderating one's feelings toward another and is here best translated as "deal gently with."[15] The whole phrase focuses on why it is essential that the high priest be taken from among the people: he is just like them and, therefore, Jehovah expects him not only to restrain his anger against them but also to be temperate toward them.[16]

the ignorant, and on them that are out of the way / the ignorant and those who have gone astray: The verb ἀγνοέω (*agnoeō*), "to be ignorant," in participle form denotes specifically one who sins unintentionally due to failure of knowing the law.[17] The participle form of the verb πλανάω (*planaō*) means "to lead astray, cause to wander" but in the passive voice, as here, "to go astray, wander off,"[18] hence translated in our Rendition as "those who

---

11. BDAG, 886; Weiss, *TDNT,* 9:67; Attridge, *Epistle to the Hebrews,* 143 n. 84.

12. BDAG, 886. Though the sacrifices on the Day of Atonement may have stood behind this verse (see 9:11–14), it does not have to be in view since the high priest offered sins in behalf of himself on other occasions. See Lev. 4:3–12; 9:7–14; 16:6, 11, 24; Ellingworth, *Epistle to the Hebrews,* 277; and Cockerill, *Epistle to the Hebrews,* 236.

13. Ellingworth, *Epistle to the Hebrews,* 274–75; Attridge, *Epistle to the Hebrews,* 143, and n. 85.

14. See Lane, *Hebrews 1–8,* 116; and Louw-Nida, §89.38.

15. BDAG, 643; Louw-Nida, §88.65; LSJ 1122. This is the only occurrence of this word in the New Testament, but it was very important for Stoics. Plutarch thought that the true sage should not be too "*pathetic*" (*apathes*) but should be "compassionate" (*metriopathes*). See Plutarch, *Virt. Mor.* 7.

16. Lane, *Hebrews 1–8,* 116–17; Cockerill, *Epistle to the Hebrews,* 234.

17. BDAG, 12–13.

18. BDAG, 821–22; LSJ, 1411.

have gone astray." The participle expresses that the person did indeed know the law but allowed himself or herself to be enticed to break it.[19]

Taken altogether, the phrase shows that, either through ignorance or misunderstanding, the person broke the law and, therefore, stood under its penalty of either reprimand or punishment. However, the high priest was to administer with understanding and kindness toward these people. That was not to be the case with all sinners, however. The verbs *agnoeō* ("ignorant") and *planaō* ("astray") stand in contrast to the nouns παράβασις (*parabasis*), "transgression," and παρακοή (*parakoē*), "disobedience," both of which connote a deliberate, willful, calculated deviation from the law—the two sins Israel was most guilty of.[20] For these, only a sincere confession coupled with a specific and heavy sacrifice would find expiation (see Lev. 5:6–19).

for that he himself also is compassed with infirmity / since he himself is beset with weakness: The verb περίκειμαι (*perikeimai*), when used with an accusative direct object, means "to have around oneself, wear, be clothed in." The wearing included items such as clothing, garlands, and even chains (see Acts 28:20).[21] We felt that "beset with" best conveyed in English the sense of being surrounded, when used with the abstract noun ἀσθένεια (*astheneia*), "weakness."[22] The latter word denotes incapacity or limitation inherent in a person. In general, it refers to the full range of frailties to which all humans are heirs, including those physical, psychological, emotional, and moral.[23]

5:3 ***by reason hereof / because of this:*** The phrase καὶ δι' αὐτὴν (*kai di' autēn*), "because of this," is important here because it points back to the

19. The phrase could be taken to refer to only one set of sinners—those who, through whatever means, have broken the law due to a lack of knowledge. See Bruce, *Epistle to the Hebrews,* 120. The καί (*kai*), "and," seems rather to be marking a list and therefore suggests separation. See Ellingworth, *Epistle to the Hebrews,* 276. Whichever is the case, the phrase does not suggest willful and deliberate rebellion.

20. For discussion, see Translation Notes for 2:2 with associated Analysis.

21. LSJ, 1376; BDAG, 801–2; Büchel, *TDNT,* 3:656. When associated with something heavy, it connotes a burden. See Mark 9:42; Acts 28:20; and Ellingworth, *Epistle to the Hebrews,* 277.

22. Merriam-Webster, s.v. "beset," https://www.merriam-webster.com/dictionary/beset.

23. BDAG, 142. Though the Old Testament and other sources describe in detail the beautiful robes the high priest wore to accentuate his authority and separate him from other priests (see Ex. 28; Sir. 45:6–13; Philo, *Mos.* 2.109–35; and Josephus, *Ant.* 3.151–87), Hebrews shows that, from the eyes of the Divine, he like all mortals wears "weakness" and therefore does not stand separate from them but among them. Koester, *Hebrews,* 286–87; see also Vanhoye, *Old Testament Priests,* 139.

inherent weakness of the high priest. But the thrust of the whole verse is not on the weakness itself but what grows out of it, that is, yielding to sin.[24]

he ought, as for the people, so also for himself, to offer for sins / he must make sin offerings for himself as well as for the people: The verb ὀφείλω (*opheilō*), "must," denotes being constrained by obligation to do something.[25] In this case, it emphasizes the absolute necessity of the high priest to include himself in the sin offering in order to receive forgiveness. The necessity laid upon him was due to his own weakness and, by extension, sinfulness. Together they evidence his insufficiency and hint at the need for a greater High Priest who does not have to sacrifice for himself.[26]

5:4 ***no man taketh this honour unto himself / no one takes this honor for himself:*** The verb λαμβάνω (*lambanō*), "to take, receive," in the present context means "to take as one's possession."[27] The phrase οὐχ ἑαυτῷ τις λαμβάνει (*ouch heautō tis lambanei*) is emphatic—absolutely no one takes priesthood authority upon himself. It can only be received as a call from God.[28]

The noun τιμή (*timē*), "honor," denotes the respect or esteem that people hold for a deserving person or for an office or position.[29] In the present context, it also carries the idea of a "right that is especially conferred," pointing to priestly office.[30]

but he that is called of God, as was Aaron / on the contrary, he is called by God, just like Aaron: The adversative particle ἀλλά (*alla*), "but," after a negative, as here, carries the force of "on the contrary."[31] The verb καλέω (*kaleō*), meaning "to call," is found here as a passive participle and connotes being chosen "for receipt of a special benefit or experience."[32] It also

24. Cockerill, *Epistle to the Hebrews,* 235, and n. 28.

25. BDAG, 743.

26. Cockerill, *Epistle to the Hebrews,* 236–37. The necessity also shows that, ironically, the mediator needs mediation.

27. BDAG, 583–85; Louw-Nida, §57.55, 125.

28. Lane, *Hebrews 1–8,* 117; see also Koester, *Hebrews,* 297.

29. BDAG, 1005. The word does not carry the nuances of fame, notoriety, or éclat as found in English. For the full range semantic domains see Louw-Nida, §§57.161, 167; 65.1; 87.4.

30. BDAG, 1005; Attridge, *Epistle to the Hebrews,* 144–45, and n. 108; Josephus, *Ant.* 12.42; Philo, *Mos.* 2.225. No one can assume such an honor; it must be conferred by God. See Vanhoye, *Old Testament Priests,* 120.

31. BDAG, 44–45.

32. BDAG, 502–4; see also McConkie, *Doctrinal New Testament Commentary,* 3:156. Bruce A. Van Orden, "The Pastoral Epistles," in Millet, *Studies in Scripture, Volume 6,* 181,

implies the establishment of a new and closer relationship between the one calling and the one called.[33]

The conjunction καθώσπερ (*kathōsper*) means "just as" or "in the same way as"[34] and looks to Jehovah's call of Aaron as the model that the author insists must be followed in order for any person to exercise authentic priestly authority (see Ex. 4:10–16, 27–31; 5:1–12:50; and especially Ex. 28:1–4; 29; and D&C 84:18, 26–27).[35]

5:5 ***So also Christ glorified not himself to be made an high priest / Thus Christ also did not glorify himself in becoming a high priest:*** The adverb οὕτως (*houtōs*), "thus, also," points back to what was done and stresses the sameness with something that has happened.[36] It serves here as a point of comparison between the Lord and his Aaronic priestly counterpart.[37] The verb δοξάζω (*doxazō*), "glory," carries the nuance of influencing another's opinion of oneself as a means of enhancing one's reputation.[38] This deed the Savior did not do.

but he that said unto him, Thou art my Son, to day have I begotten thee / rather he was glorified by the one who said to him, "You are my son. Today I have begotten you": This passage is found in Psalm 2:7, which the author has already quoted in 1:5. For discussion, see Translation Notes for that verse. The author's point is that Jesus received his divine commission directly from his Father.

5:6 ***As he saith also in another place, Thou art a priest for ever after the order of Melchisedec / As he also said in another place, "You are a priest forever according to the order of Melchizedek":*** The quote is from LXX Psalm 109:4.[39] The adverb καθώς (*kathōs*), "as," points to the accuracy of what is about to be quoted.

The operative phrase here is the εἰς τὸν αἰῶνα (*eis ton aiōna*), "forever," referencing and emphasizing the eternal nature of the Son's appointment to priestly office.

---

notes that men like Titus and Timothy were responsible to commission church leaders who, like today, need no prior or formal training.

33. See Louw-Nida, §33.312.

34. The adverb is parallel to καθώς (*kathōs*) but looks only at the similarity between items, thus, "just as." BDAG, 493–94.

35. One can hear an echo to Korah's attempt to usurp priesthood authority from Moses. See Num. 16:5; and Ellingworth, *Epistle to the Hebrews,* 280.

36. BDAG, 741–42.

37. Cockerill, *Epistle to the Hebrews,* 237.

38. BDAG, 258.

39. This is Ps. 110 in the KJV.

The noun τάξις (*taxis*), "order," is also important, referencing as it does an arrangement of people into specific task groups. It also carries the idea that each group has its own responsibility and aims, but these fit the objectives of the whole.[40] The author's readers would have been familiar with the various orders within the Levitical Priesthood that divided Levites from priests and priests from the high priest. With the phrase κατὰ τὴν τάξιν Μελχισέδεκ (*kata tēn taxin Melchisedek*), "according to the order of Melchizedek," the author reveals there is yet another divinely appointed order outside those of the Aaronic Priesthood. The implication of his statement is that this other order had a function that differed from that of the sons of Levi but also consisted of priestly offices.[41]

5:7–10 In the Greek manuscript, these three verses comprise a single extended relative clause designed to showcase the Savior's total sufficiency in executing his office of High Priest. For ease of reading, our Rendition breaks the clause into three sentences using finite verbs to translate the participles in the original.[42]

5:7 ***Who in the days of his flesh / During his mortal life:*** The author begins this phrase with the pronoun *hos* (ὃς), "who." Throughout his work, though the phrase is grammatically subordinate, the author uses it to signal he is about to emphasize some characteristic about the passion or exaltation of the Savior (see 1:2; 12:2) or his high priestly office (7:27; 8:1; compare 7:16; 9:14).[43] In this context, the pronoun focuses on the whole spectrum of the Lord's lifelong suffering that culminated with his passion in Gethsemane.

The noun σάρξ (*sarks*), literally "flesh," also nuances a person's "mortal nature."[44] We have, therefore, rendered the phrase ἐν ταῖς ἡμέραις τῆς

40. BDAG, 989; Louw-Nida, §61.3; compare Luke 1:8.

41. Louw-Nida, §58.21. Jehovah instituted the lesser but no less functioning priesthood of Aaron due to Israel's rebellion. In doing so, he took "away the [higher order of the] priesthood out of their midst; therefore," he declared, "my holy order, and the ordinances thereof, shall not go before them" (JST Ex. 24:1). Even so, "the lesser priesthood continued, which priesthood holdeth the key of the ministering of angels and the preparatory gospel; Which gospel is the gospel of repentance and of baptism, and the remission of sins, and the law of carnal commandments" (D&C 84:26–27). For a study of Melchizedek, see Translation Notes for 7:1 with associated Analysis.

42. Some authorities suggest that these verses capture an early Christian hymn. Since, however, the context follows all the themes the author has advanced, that seems unlikely. But for discussion, see Ellingworth, *Epistle to the Hebrews,* 284–85.

43. Ellingworth, *Epistle to the Hebrews,* 286–87.

44. BDAG, 914–16.

σαρκὸς αὐτοῦ (*en tais hēmerais tēs sarkos autou*), literally "in the days of his flesh," as "during his mortal life" because it marks the period when the Savior experienced all the limitations and frailties of all mortals.[45]

offered up prayers and supplications with strong crying and tears / Christ offered prayers and supplications, with loud cries and tears: The Greek text has the phrase σαρκὸς αὐτοῦ (*sarkos autou*), "his mortal life," which leaves the possessive pronoun *autou*, "his," vague. In the Rendition, we end the previous clause with this and begin a new sentence, inserting the noun "Christ" to make it clear that this passage is referring to the Savior, not to Melchizedek.

The noun δέησις (*deēsis*), "prayer," refers to a petition to the Divine for a specific benefit and appeals to God's graciousness or favor in order to get it.[46] It stands in contrast to προσευχή (*proseuchē*), the term generally used for prayer, although this noun can be used more specifically for those used in praise and worship.[47]

The noun ἱκτηρία (*hiktēria*), "supplication," carries the idea of approaching someone for a great favor. The word connotes the intensity and fervor of the one making the plea, an intensity heightened due to concern that the request will be met with resistance.[48] The noun is attached to the phrase "loud cries and tears," which deepens its force and betrays the extreme distress behind the person's plea.

The clause seems to focus especially on Christ's experience in the Garden of Gethsemane and on the cross, but it could also refer to his heartfelt appeal for divine assistance during the whole of his ministry. Even so, it's clear that his suffering climaxed in the garden and on the cross.[49]

unto him that was able to save him from death / to the one who was able to save him from death: The phrase σῴζειν αὐτὸν ἐκ θανάτου (*sōzein auton ek thanatou*), "save him from death," suggests the idea of not only being saved from the experience of dying but also of being saved "out of"

45. Vanhoye, *Old Testament Priests,* 124.

46. *NID,* s.v. δέομαι; Greeven, *TDNT,* 2:40–42. In the LXX, the verb is used most often as the translation of the Hebrew חָנַן (*ḥānan*), meaning "to show favor to" or "to act through grace." It connotes an attribute held exclusively by the Divine and looks to Jehovah's merciful response to the cry of the vexed. BDB, 336–37.

47. Greeven, *TDNT,* 2:807–8; BDAG, 878–79.

48. The word means literally "an olive branch." It refers more specifically to one borne by a supplicant to induce favor from one in power. By extension, it came to denote the supplication itself. Büchel, *TDNT,* 3:296–97.

49. See Vanhoye, *Old Testament Priests,* 124–25; Cockerill, *Epistle to the Hebrews,* 243; and McConkie, *Doctrinal New Testament Commentary,* 3:158.

or "from" the realm of death.[50] The author's view seems to carry the idea that the Savior's heartfelt petition to the God of life was not just to preserve him from dying but also to work against the power of death lest it keep him bound should he die. Even so, the emphasis is on Christ's hope of being preserved from the agony that will lead to his death.[51]

and was heard in that he feared / and he was heard because of his reverent devotion to God: The verb εἰσακούω (*eisakouō*), "to hear," is important here because it means not only to hear someone but to respond to their request.[52] Throughout his life, the Savior's prayers went neither unheard nor unanswered, although they were answered in the Father's own way.

In this passage, the challenge is to correctly interpret the noun εὐλάβεια (*eulabeia*), "devotion." Both the noun and the related verb and adjective (εὐλαβέομαι, *eulabeomai,* and εὐλαβής, *eulabēs*) focus on a sense of caution or prudence. When used in reference to Deity, the noun connotes a feeling of reverence, devotion, and piety.[53] It stands in contrast to the noun φόβος (*phobos*), which could describe both "fear" and "reverence."[54] In our Rendition, we have tried to capture the full sense of the word by translating it as "reverent devotion to God."

5:8 *Though he were a Son, yet learned he obedience by the things which he suffered / And although he was a son, he learned obedience through the things that he suffered:* The coordinating conjunction καίπερ (*kaiper*), "although,"[55] plays an important role here by stressing that the Lord's sonship did not help him in any way. In spite of the fact he was *the* Son of God,

---

50. The phrase for being saved from dying would be σῴζειν ἀπὸ θανάτου (*sōzein apo thanatou*). See Attridge, *Epistle to the Hebrews,* 150. McConkie, *Doctrinal New Testament Commentary,* 3:158, notes, "these words mean our Lord himself was saved from eternal death through the atonement, which salvation is also the common inheritance of all men."

51. Cockerill, *Epistle to the Hebrews,* 243–44.

52. BDAG, 293.

53. BDAG, 409; LSJ, 720; Louw-Nida, §53.7; Bultmann, *TDNT,* 2:751–54. For discussion, see Koester, *Hebrews,* 289–90; and Johnson, *Hebrews,* 146–47.

54. BDAG, 1062. In secular Greek literature, the noun initially referred to a condition that caused flight but soon came to nuance the feeling that engendered the action. The translators of the LXX used it to render a number of Hebrew words, most dealing with the negative emotion of fright. It was, however, often used to translate the noun יָרֵא (*yārēʾ*). That noun denoted human reaction to immense power and thereby became associated with the positive ideas of awe and reverence. *TWOT,* 6:290–315; BDB, 431–32. In New Testament times, it continued to carry both the negative and positive connotations. *NID,* s.v. "φόβος."

55. BDAG, 497.

he was not precluded from learning through tough experience.[56] The verb μανθάνω (*manthanō*), "to learn," carries, in this context, the realizing or understanding of something less through instruction than actual experience and practice.[57]

The verb πάσχω (*paschō*), "to suffer," denotes experiencing any strong sensation or impression. Though this does not disallow a positive nuance, the negative dominates. The term, therefore, refers to experiencing some kind of discomfort, be it physical, psychological, emotional, or spiritual. The force of the verb is generally toward the heavier and severer nature of the discomfort.[58]

The author expresses what Jesus came to understand through his suffering by using the noun ὑπακοή (*hypakoē*), "obedience."[59] The meaning of the related verb ὑπακούω (*hypakouō*), "to answer a call or summons," is instructive in understanding the noun. It carries the nuance of carrying out instructions.[60] Jesus carried out the instructions in his summons from God even to the point of dying through the ignominious and excruciating suffering of the cross (Philip. 2:8). The reported idea that the passage suggests Jesus learned the value of obedience through the stinging consequence that disobedience caused is clearly false. Rather, the word denotes the Savior's personal experience growing out of his constant obedience and his understanding that "became richer with each act of obedience culminating in the cross."[61] In short, by firsthand experience, he learned through what he suffered—lifelong submission, including death—to make obedience his own trait.[62]

The JST contains a note stating that "the 7th and 8th verses of this chapter are a parenthesis alluding to Melchizedek and not to Christ." The switch of emphasis from Christ to Melchizedek resolves a number of issues

---

56. No definite article is attached to the noun "son," and the phrase carries the idea that "Son of God though he was" he still had to suffer. Bruce, *Epistle to the Hebrews,* 130; see also Lane, *Hebrews 1–8,* 120–21.

57. BDAG, 615; Louw-Nida, §27.15. The focus of the domain to which the verb belongs points not so much to the capacity to learn as it does to the process by which the learning comes. Louw-Nida, §38.1 n. 5.

58. Louw-Nida, §§24.78; 90.66; BDAG, 785–86.

59. The noun denotes, among other things, the compliance or submission that is expected of a slave to his master's will. BDAG, 1028. Vanhoye, *Old Testament Priests,* 126–30, carefully distinguishes between the obedience he "learned," noted in 5:8, and his complete submission to the will of the Father in 5:7.

60. *NID,* s.v. "ὑπακούω."

61. Cockerill, *Epistle to the Hebrews,* 248.

62. Attridge, *Epistle to the Hebrews,* 152–53.

raised due to the Prophet's understanding of these verses. These issues are, among others, first, the persons offering up strong and tearful cries "to the one who could save him from death"; second, that he was heard "because he feared" implying that he feared for his life; and third, that he learned obedience apparently through suffering the consequences of disobedience. Since none of these conditions seemed to apply to the Savior, the solution was that they must apply to Melchizedek. As the above comments show, when properly understood, each of these conditions (but not the conclusions) did apply to the Lord. However, that does not preclude Melchizedek from experiencing similar conditions and behaving in similar ways, things that being a type of Christ would demand.[63] Even so, the Greek text suggests the author had the Savior in mind.

5:9 ***And being made perfect / And having become perfect:*** This phrase is the translation of τελειωθείς (*teleiōtheis*), the aorist passive participle of τελειόω (*teleioō*), which carries the basic meaning of "to complete, bring to an end, finish, and accomplish." The verb also refers to that which is mature, fully developed, and fully successful. Some even viewed death positively when seen as the moment when a good person's life was fully complete.[64] By extension, the passive force takes the sense of "making or becoming whole, complete, or perfect."[65]

Note that most of the nuances of this word do not refer to mortal perfection. The passage here is such a case. The word points to the fact that Jesus, having completed his mission on earth and having taken his place beside his Father, has become fully successful in his role as Savior.[66] Everything he was commissioned to do, he did. As a result, "he received all power, both in heaven and on earth, and the glory of the Father was with him" (D&C 93:17; see also 1:1–3; Matt. 28:18; 1 Cor. 15:27; and 1 Pet. 3:22). He has, therefore, reached a state of perfection or completeness from which he can now forever minister his saving powers.

---

63. Ogden and Skinner, *Verse by Verse,* 249–50; Holzapfel and Wayment, *Making Sense,* 453; Robert J. Matthews, "I Have a Question," *Ensign* 17, no. 8 (August 1987): 21. McConkie, *Doctrinal New Testament Commentary,* 3:157, points out that these items "apply with equal and perhaps even greater force to the life and ministry of him through whom all the promises made to Melchizedek were fulfilled."

64. For discussion, see *NID,* s.v. "τέλος."

65. BDAG, 996; Louw-Nida, §§9.10; 68.22, 23, 31; 88.36, 38. This is the same verb that Christ used on the cross just before he died, when he said, "It is finished" (τετέλεσται, *tetelestai,* third-person singular of the perfect tense in John 19:30). Christ uses the related adjective τέλειος (*teleios*) in his Sermon on the Mount when he commanded, "Be ye therefore perfect" (Matt. 5:48).

66. Ellingworth, *Epistle to the Hebrews,* 294.

he became the author of eternal salvation unto all them that obey him / he became the source of eternal salvation for all those who obey him: The nominalized adjective αἴτιος (*aitios*), "cause, source," denotes that which, in whole or in part, produces a result or effect.[67] In this case it points to the Savior's salvific powers.[68]

The basic nuance of the verb ὑπακούω (*hypakouō*) is "to follow instructions" and thus "obey, follow, be subject to."[69]

The phrase σωτηρία αἰωνίου (*sōtēris aiōniou*), "eternal salvation," in Latter-day Saint parlance refers to eternal life or exaltation in the celestial kingdom.[70] Though Christ brought universal salvation from physical death, that is not true of the second spiritual death. He saves people from this death on the basis of their faith, trust, and obedience to him (James 2:14–22; 1 Ne. 15:32; Mosiah 3:24; Alma 9:28).[71] The author's point in this verse is that Jesus is both the antecedent and determinate of salvation. He alone is the "source" of this wondrous gift.[72]

5:10 ***Called of God an high priest after the order of Melchisedec / and he was designated by God to be a high priest according to the order of Melchizedek:*** The verb προσαγορεύω (*prosagoreuō*) means to address or call someone by name or some other appellation.[73] Here it refers to God addressing Jesus as "High Priest." Since the English word "designate" carries the sense of declaring "one's choice for incumbency of an office, position, post or benefice," we use it in our Rendition.[74] For a study of Melchizedek, see Translation Notes for 7:1 with associated Analysis.

---

67. BDAG, 31.

68. Nephi states that he and his people "talk of Christ, we rejoice in Christ, we preach of Christ, we prophesy of Christ, and we write according to our prophecies, that our children may know to what source they may look for a remission of their sins" (2 Ne. 25:26).

69. BDAG, 1028.

70. For discussion, see Larry E. Dahl, "Degrees of Glory," in Ludlow, *Encyclopedia of Mormonism,* 1:367–69. See also Arthur A. Bailey, "Elect of God," in Ludlow, *Encyclopedia of Mormonism,* 2:448; Draper, "Hebrews, Epistle to the," 2:581; and James K. Lyon, "Repentance," in Ludlow, *Encyclopedia of Mormonism,* 3:1217.

71. This is not to say that the author is unconscious of the role grace plays in the salvation process (see the subsection "Grace in Hebrews" in "Excursus on the Atonement: A View from Hebrews," found in chapter 2). He seems very aware of it, but that is not his emphasis in this Epistle.

72. See Johnson, *Hebrews,* 148. McConkie, *Doctrinal New Testament Commentary,* 3:158, focusing only on the concept of the source of salvation as "authorship," notes that God the Father is actually the author of salvation, but that Jesus, by adopting it, "made it his own, in the sense that through his atoning sacrifice he caused its terms and conditions to have eternal efficacy."

73. BDAG, 875; Louw-Nida, §33.127; Ellingworth, *Epistle to the Hebrews,* 296.

74. *Webster's New Dictionary of Synonyms,* s.v. "designate."

Analysis and Summary

Following his exhortation in the last chapter, the author here resumes his explication, this time focusing on the implications of the office and duties of the Levitical high priest that shed light on the work of the Son as the eternal Melchizedek High Priest. Noteworthy is that the author's thrust, at this point, is not on the priest as the servant of God but as the servant of humankind.

The author emphasizes the weakness, that is, the humanity, of those who hold that office, not to put them down but to show it is because of this that they should know how to relate and minister to those whom they are called to serve.[75] The Savior shares this condition. The author, however, uses his comparison between the Eternal High Priest and the mortal high priest to dramatically emphasize the superiority of the Savior's priesthood and service.

The author emphasizes this point in this pericope through the use of a chiastic structure that can be diagramed as follows.[76]

Old High Priest	Category of Comparison/Contrast	New High Priest
2a He is able to deal gently with the ignorant and those who have gone astray,	*Effectiveness*	9 And having become perfect, he became the source of eternal salvation for all those who obey him.
2b since he himself is beset with weakness.	*Humanity*	8 And although he was a son, he learned obedience through the things that he suffered.
3 And because of this, he must make sin offerings for himself as well as for the people.	*Sacrifice*	7 Christ offered prayers and supplications, with loud cries and tears, to the one who was able to save him from death, and he was heard because of his reverent devotion to God.

75. Only after establishing the first point does the author acknowledge that the high priest is ordained to serve God in his sanctuary (5:1; 8:1–2). Vanhoye, *Letter to the Hebrews*, 98.

76. For discussion, see Cockerill, *Epistle to the Hebrews*, 230–32, and nn. 5–6. The amount of discussion over the nuance of the chiastic structure suggests a need to be cautious drawing too much from it. See Ellingworth, *Epistle to the Hebrews*, 271.

By using this structure, the author highlights the importance of authority for any person to hold this office and showcases the additional power held by the Lord. For example, while the Aaronic high priest could but "deal gently" (μετριοπαθέω, *metriopatheō*) with those in need (5:2a), the Melchizedek High Priest could save them (5:9). Thus, this chiastic formula is integral to the author's point and allows him to stress the superiority of the new order over the old.[77]

In addition, the author also shows that the Lord met the full criteria of the priesthood office as set down by the Torah.[78] There were four conditions: first, every high priest was selected from humankind and served in the office for their sake; second, he was to represent the people "in matters pertaining to God"; third, he had to be appointed (καθίστημι, *kathistēmi*) from on high; and fourth, his major task was to offer "gifts and sacrifices for sin" (5:1). As the author points out, the Savior came short in none of these.[79]

To obtain the priesthood, the author insists on the necessity of following the divine pattern (5:5). All must be called "in the same way" (καθώσπερ, *kathōsper*) as was Aaron. The author maintains that the dignity and authority of priesthood office cannot be realized by self-appointment (5:4). It comes only from divine authorization. The author has already pointed this out in 5:1 where he noted that "every high priest" was appointed by Jehovah.[80] Even though Jesus was the Son of God, he "did not thrust himself into priestly office but waited for the summons of his Father" (compare D&C 27:8).[81]

The author turns to scripture to bolster his point. He had already introduced Jesus as "Son" in 1:1–3 and as "the great high priest" in 2:17–18. Now in 5:5–6 the author uses LXX Psalm 2:7 with LXX Psalm 109:4 to join the two ideas. His point is that the same Divine Being who made Jesus "Son"

---

77. Cockerill, *Epistle to the Hebrews,* 230–32.

78. The Hebrew word "Torah" generally refers to the first five books of the Old Testament but can refer to entire Hebrew Bible. The author, admittedly, develops his thesis on the basis of his own criteria but does hit the major points. For a study, see William Horbury, "The Aaronic Priesthood in the Epistle to the Hebrews," *Journal for the Study of the New Testament* 19 (1983): 43–71. For the concept of the Old Testament priesthood in general, see Ryan Bonfiglio, "Priests and Priesthood in the Hebrew Bible," Oxford Biblical Studies Online, accessed February 8, 2016, http://www.oxfordbiblicalstudies.com/resource/priests.xhtml.

79. Johnson, *Hebrews,* 142–43.

80. That verse uses the divine passive of καθίστημι (*kathistēmi*). Cockerill, *Epistle to the Hebrews,* 237 n. 38.

81. Lane, *Hebrews 1–8,* 118; see also Holzapfel and Wayment, *Making Sense,* 452–53; and Ogden and Skinner, *Verse by Verse,* 249.

is the same one who declared him "Priest." By wedding these two scriptures, the author of Hebrews shows that the Lord's right to preside over the Melchizedek order of the priesthood was because he was the Son of God, receiving the Father's power and authority by right.

Highlighting the nuance of these verses, one scholar noted that "despite the Protestant theory of 'priesthood of the believers,' both Testaments show an operating priesthood authority based on authoritative ordination."[82]

Joseph Smith taught, "No man can administer salvation through the gospel to the souls of men, in the name of Jesus Christ, except he is authorized from God, by revelation, or by being ordained by some one whom God hath sent by revelation. . . . And I would ask, how was Aaron called, but by revelation?"[83] The Prophet also taught, "The priesthood is an everlasting principle and existed with God from Eternity and will to Eternity, without beginning of days or end of years."[84] He noted further that Jesus held and exercised this authority before he was born and then again on earth. Commenting on this, Elder Bruce R. McConkie stated, "As pertaining to his mortal ministry, Christ our Lord received the Melchizedek Priesthood here on earth, and was ordained to the office of a high priest therein, thus setting an example for others and being in all things the Prototype of salvation."[85]

Joseph Smith taught that all priesthood is Melchizedek. In fact, anciently the priesthood was called "the Holy Priesthood, after the order of the Son of God," but was later, "out of respect or reverence to the name of the Supreme Being, to avoid the too frequent repetition of his name, they, the church, in ancient days, called that priesthood after Melchizedek" (D&C 107:3–4). The reference is to the great priest who was a contemporary with Abraham. Some translate the priest's name as "King of Righteousness" and see him as a

---

82. Anderson, *Guide to Acts,* 91.

83. "Copy of a Letter from J. Smith Jr. to Mr. [Isaac] Galland," March 22, 1839, published in *Times and Seasons* 1, no. 4 (February 1840): 54, online as "Letter to Isaac Galland, 22 March 1839," Joseph Smith Papers, https://www.josephsmithpapers.org/paper-summary/letter-to-isaac-galland-22-march-1839/4; see also A of F 5 and McConkie, *Doctrinal New Testament Commentary,* 3:155. D&C 27:8 confirms that Joseph Smith was so called.

84. "History, 1838–1856, Volume C-1," 11 [addenda]. The Prophet's language comes from Hebrews.

85. McConkie, *Doctrinal New Testament Commentary,* 3:157. The idea is also implied in Joseph Smith's statement, "If a man gets a fulness of the Priesthood of God he has to get it in the same way that Jesus Christ obtained it, and that was by keeping all the commandments and obeying all the ordinances of the house of the Lord." "History, 1838–1856, Volume D-1," 1572.

type of Christ (see Translation Notes with related Analysis for of 7:2). If that is a correct translation, then the priesthood is the "Priesthood of the King of Righteousness."

The Prophet also explained that "there are different portions or degrees of it."[86] These he identified as priesthood orders, of which there are three: the Melchizedek, Patriarchal, and Levitical.[87] He also noted that the Patriarchal and Levitical (Aaronic) orders of the priesthood were subsumed in the Melchizedek order (D&C 107:1–8). In sum, God arranged the priesthood in various grades—or better, orders—grouped according to their preassigned duties and bound by the keys of authority they held. In this way, God eliminated possible confusion and arranged the aggregate to work efficiently to fulfill their various responsibilities and objectives, always for the good and aims of the whole.

The author of Hebrews laments that "we have much to say about this that is difficult to explain, since you have become hard of hearing. For although you should already have become teachers by this time, you need someone to again teach you" (NR 5:11–12). Joseph Smith appears to have been able to elaborate on the nature of priesthood and teach the Saints important truths that the author of Hebrews may only have had in mind.

The Prophet taught that the Melchizedek Priesthood "is the channel through which all knowledge, doctrine, the plan of salvation and every important truth is revealed from heaven."[88] He also explained that those holding the fulness of this priesthood "are kings and priests to the most high God, holding the keys of power and blessings. In fact, that Priesthood is a perfect law of Theocracy, and stands as God, to give laws to the people, administering endless lives to the sons and daughters of Adam." The Prophet went on to say, "the Melchizedek Priesthood holds the right from the Eternal God, and not by descent from father or mother; and that priesthood is [as] eternal as God himself, having neither beginning of days nor end of life."[89]

---

86. "Account of Meeting and Discourse, 5 January 1841, as Reported by William Clayton," 5, Joseph Smith Papers, https://www.josephsmithpapers.org/paper-summary/account-of-meeting-and-discourse-5-january-1841-as-reported-by-william-clayton/2.

87. "Journal, December 1842–June 1844; Book 3, 15 July 1843–29 February 1844," [71]–[74], Joseph Smith Papers, https://www.josephsmithpapers.org/paper-summary/journal-december-1842-june-1844-book-3-15-july-1843-29-february-1844/78; "History, 1838–1856, Volume E-1," 1708; see also D&C 107:1–8.

88. "Instruction on Priesthood," 1.

89. "History, 1838–1856, Volume E-1," 1708. For a brief discussion of the Melchizedek order of the priesthood as it ministers today, see Jae R. Ballif, "Powers and Offices in the Melchizedek Priesthood," in Ludlow, *Encyclopedia of Mormonism,* 2:882–85.

During the Levitical administration, not all ordinances were available (D&C 84:23–27). The author of Hebrews notes this lack in the way he constructed 5:1–3, stressing the insufficiency of the Levitical high priest and pointing to the need of another who is fully sufficient, namely, the great High Priest.[90] The contrast between the two priests is arresting. The Aaronic high priest is chosen from among men (5:1),[91] namely, the Aaronites, while the Son of God is selected from the whole of humanity. The high priest is beset with weakness (5:2) and thus must make offerings for himself as well as for others (5:3), where the new High Priest shares in the common weakness but never succumbs thereto and thus has no need to make a sin offering in behalf of himself.[92] While the high priest can deal gently with sinners (5:2), the High Priest can save them (5:9).

Though the idea of authority marks this entire pericope (5:1–10), standing beside it is the notice of the Savior's compassion introduced in 2:17–18 and repeated in 4:15–16. This virtue he shares in common with his Aaronic priestly counterpart. This capacity to feel with others, as it pertains to the Aaronic high priest, has two dimensions. First, because the high priest is "beset with weakness" (μετριοπαθεῖν δυνάμενος, *metriopathein dynamenos*), he is able to "deal gently" (μετριοπαθέω, *metriopatheō*) with those who are "ignorant and those who have gone astray" (NR 5:2). Second, he must offer sacrifices not only for them but for himself (5:3).[93] For these reasons, he is in a position to be neither high-handed nor haughty toward those whom he serves.[94]

Of particular note is that, for the first time in the Epistle to the Hebrews, the Savior's ministry is linked with sacrificial vocabulary. Indeed, the primary duty of the high priest is "to offer gifts and sacrifices" (5:1), and the repeated use of the verb "to offer" (προσφέρω, *prosphereō*) stresses the point (5:3, 7).[95]

---

90. Cockerill, *Epistle to the Hebrews,* 232–37; Vanhoye, *Old Testament Priests,* 142.

91. Though the text reads ἐξ ἀνθρώπων λαμβανόμενος (*eks anthrōpōn lambanomenos*), "was taken from among men," the biblical setting makes it clear that the selection was among the Aaronites only. See "Bible Dictionary," s.v. "High Priest."

92. Some push the parallel too far, suggesting Jesus had to offer sacrifices for himself due to his shared weakness with humankind, but they do not catch the nuance that the weakness associated with the Aaronic high priest points to that person yielding to it, something Jesus never did (4:15). See Cockerill, *Epistle to the Hebrews,* 236 n. 36.

93. The author repeats this requirement in 7:27; 9:7. It is found in Lev. 9:7. In the case of the Savior, he did not have to offer a sacrifice due to his own weaknesses because he never yielded to them. His need was, rather, based on keeping the covenant he had made with his Father to act as Redeemer and bring him glory (Luke 22:42; 2 Ne. 31:6–7; D&C 19:18–19; Moses 4:2; 7:39; Abr. 3:27).

94. Johnson, *Hebrews,* 143.

95. Vanhoye, *Letter to the Hebrews,* 98.

Though the Old Testament focuses on the unique position of the high priest and all that sets him apart from other priests and more especially apart from the people,[96] the author of Hebrews stresses the high priest's commonality with them: he is "chosen from among men," he is put "in charge of matters in their behalf," he shares their "weaknesses" and therefore must make offerings also for himself (NR 5:1–3). Even so, the author does note one very important difference: he is "in charge of matters [καθίστημι, *kathistēmi*] pertaining to God in their behalf, to offer gifts and sacrifices for sins" (NR 5:1).

The author brings out an important lesson when he notes that the high priest's sacrifices are to cover two kinds of sins (5:2). First are those done in ignorance (ἀγνοέω, *agnoeō*), a case where a person, due to no neglect on his or her own, did not know the law and unintentionally violated it.[97] Second are those done due to weakness (ἀσθένεια, *astheneia*), a case where a person, due to his or her own vulnerability, was drawn to sin due to the actions of another.[98] In both cases, the person did not initiate the move but was led astray. For both, the high priest was to "deal gently" (μετριοπαθέω, *metriopatheō*) (NR 5:2).

Of importance is that the sacrifice designed to bring expiation was a type of the sacrifice of the Savior, whose "blood atoneth for the sins of those who have fallen by the transgression of Adam, who have died not knowing the will of God concerning them, or who have ignorantly sinned" (Mosiah 3:11).

But what of those who deliberately sinned, especially where the sinner recruited others to sin as well? These did not warrant a gentle hand, and the sacrifice required was hefty and included, in addition to the trespass or guilt offering made at the temple, full restitution to the offended party plus an additional twenty percent.[99] Again, the sacrifice had a typological aspect, teaching that sins deliberately committed require deep and thorough repentance designed to requite, so far as possible, the suffering of the victim.[100]

The author does not become hortatory at this point, but his message is clear. In 5:8, he presents the Savior as one who learned the joy of obedience (ὑπακοή, *hypakoē*) through suffering because that is what the author

---

96. For those items which set the high priest apart, see Ex. 28:6–42; 29:6; 39:27–29; Lev. 6:19–23; 21:10; and Num. 27:21.

97. *NID*, s.v. "ἀγνοέω."

98. *NID*, s.v. "ἀσθένεια."

99. Many offences required such a sacrifice. See Lev. 5:6–19; 6:2–6, 17; 7:1–7; 14:12–28; 19:21–22. See also Hans-Josef Klauk, "Sacrifice and Sacrificial Offerings," trans. Reginald N. Fuller, in Freedman, *Anchor Bible Dictionary*, 5:870–91.

100. Andrew Jukes, *The Law of the Offerings* (Grand Rapids, Mich.: Kregel Publications, 1976), 172–88.

is calling on his readers to do. Jesus understands firsthand (μανθάνω, *manthanō*) the full cost of obedience since he was fully obedient not only throughout his life but even into death and beyond. As a result, he can be fully sympathetic in understanding the toll that obedience takes. He can, therefore, be moved to make divine intercession on behalf of his people.[101]

A very important lesson can be learned here: "The gospel is not an answer to the problem of suffering, nor a resolution, nor even a dissolution of it. The gospel is a *response* to suffering. It is the announcement that God has joined with us in our suffering. . . . He has condescended to become like us, and because he has, he can offer us salvation. He does not offer a surcease of suffering in this life, but he can give us strength, a lightening of our burden (see Matthew 11:28–30), and the promise of salvation."[102]

The result of the Lord's obedience was "to become perfect" (τελειόω, *teleioō*), the word referring to the completion of his mission, including both dying and overcoming death (5:9). To emphasize the point, Jesus' perfection was one of vocation, not of moral excellence.[103] In the realm of obedience and adherence to the will of the Father, Jesus was always without flaw. He did not become complete "through a process of growth in moral perfection, but he did achieve it through consistent obedience of his earthly life."[104]

---

101. Attridge, *Epistle to the Hebrews,* 152–53. For a study, see Johnson, *Hebrews,* 149–52, where he presents an excellent excursus on "Suffering and the Obedience of Faith." See also Monte J. Brough, "Between Two Gardens: The Law of Sacrifice," in *Speeches: Brigham Young University 1995–96* (Provo, Utah: Brigham Young University Press, 1996), 160, https://speeches.byu.edu/wp-content/uploads/pdf/Brough_Monte_1996_02.pdf. The author of Hebrews says obedience is an important element of the law of sacrifice and notes that Jesus himself learned obedience and was obedient to the ultimate degree. Compare Adney Y. Komatsu, "Looking to the Savior," *Ensign* 17, no. 5 (May 1987): 78–79.

102. Faulconer, *Romans 1: Notes and Reflecions,* 19, italics in original.

103. Cockerill, *Epistle to the Hebrews,* 249. See also Lane, *Hebrews 1–8,* 122; and Vanhoye, *Old Testament Priests,* 133, who both note, significantly, that in the LXX version of the Pentateuch, the verb τελειόω (*teleioō*) is used exclusively to denote the consecration of a priest. With the author's rich acquaintance with the Old Testament, Vanhoye points out, there is little doubt he would have missed this nuance.

104. Cockerill, *Epistle to the Hebrews,* 249. Compare McConkie, *Promised Messiah,* 198, 456, who notes that though Jesus was God, he still had to work out his salvation though obedience in the mortal sphere and thus become perfect. McConkie notes further that his perfection was like unto God's. The word's use in the mystery religions, as noted above, seems to suggest that it had a general meaning relating to the final consummation in various religious and philosophical systems in the ancient world. According to David A. DeSilva, *Perseverance in Gratitude: A Socio-rhetorical Commentary on the Epistle "to the Hebrews"* (Grand Rapids, Mich.: Wm. B. Eerdmans, 2000), 195, in the Greco-Roman sphere, the adjective τελειός (teleios) was used "in philosophical texts to refer to those who had attained the goal of the philosophy (whether contemplation of the realm

That the Savior was "made perfect" is of special note. The passive force of the participle used in 5:9 (τελειωθείς, *teleiōtheis*, "being made perfect") points to the work of God. It tacitly reveals the Lord's total dependence on his Father both to show him the way and give him the power (John 5:19, 20, 30; see also John 14:24; 1 Cor. 15:28; and Col. 1:19). Here, too, the Lord is the exemplar. He declared that the Father "gave me of his fulness" (D&C 93:4).[105] Indeed, "power [was] given unto him from the Father to redeem [his people] from their sins" (Hel. 5:11). No one, including Jesus, was ever meant to go alone.[106] Even so, salvation is only for those who obey him (5:9).[107]

What the author has only alluded to (4:16), and will later more fully develop (12:25–29), is the Savior provides the means by which the faithful can, with confidence, approach his divine throne for aid and spiritual sustenance. He is most willing to extend his mercy and provide his grace to the degree necessary for those who strive to do his will to successfully complete their mission on earth.[108]

We add here that this is the sense in which Jesus commanded his people to be "perfect" (Matt. 5:48; 3 Ne. 12:48). His was not a command to moral perfection but, rather, an admonition to do as he had done—to successfully complete the assigned mortal mission. In that, Jesus and the Father are the archetype or pattern. They have set up the ideal they wish their people to follow. Those who impose a moral reading of the word "perfect" in the commands in Matthew and 3 Nephi are misunderstanding. Further, those who use 1 Nephi 3:7 as a proof text that moral perfection in mortality is possible are setting up the impossible as a standard. Being battered against this reef, more than one soul has perished. To push the point, note that Jesus was not "made perfect" until after his resurrection. Only then had he fulfilled every jot and tittle of the law. He fully realized his perfection only when he received the full glory of the Father, sat upon the divine throne (1:3–4), and began to administer completely his divine

---

of ideas in Plato, or the realization of every virtue in Stoic authors)." The idea of obtaining a goal or completely meeting a requirement seems to be the general sense in which the author of Hebrews uses the word.

105. McConkie, *Witness of the Birth,* 55, notes that "Christ obtained the fulness of his Father by going from one grace to a greater grace [see D&C 93:12–13], in so doing marking a path that all who choose may follow."

106. The exception is in the Lord's passion when the Father withdrew his spirit from his Son. On this see Brigham Young, in *Journal of Discourses,* 3:205–6.

107. Bruce, *Epistle to the Hebrews,* 132–33; compare Carol Lee Hawkins, "Perfection," in Ludlow, *Encyclopedia of Mormonism,* 3:1074–75.

108. Cockerill, *Epistle to the Hebrews,* 250.

saving power.[109] Elder Russell M. Nelson, after studying the Greek word translated as "perfection" (*teleios*), concluded that the nuance of the New Testament word "perfect" means "'to reach a distant end, to be fully developed, to consummate, or to finish.'" He went on to say, "Please note that the word does not imply 'freedom from error'; it implies 'achieving a distant objective.'"[110] President Ezra Taft Benson noted, "We must be careful, as we seek to become more and more godlike, that we do not become discouraged and lose hope. Becoming Christlike is a lifetime pursuit and very often involves growth and change that is slow, almost imperceptible."[111] It is by not giving in but by ever reaching to fully obey that each Saint will reach celestial glory, that is, perfection.

This brings us back to the Lord's own obedience—that is, his suffering to do his Father's will. His submission could only be completed by his going onto the cross and coming out of the tomb.[112] As a result of his perfect suffering, Jesus became not only the "source" (αἴτιος, *aitios*) of eternal life for all others but also their sustaining power.[113] He can perfect them because he has, indeed, become perfect himself. Through the power of his Atonement, he can cleanse them and make them whole, clean, and complete, thus perfect (see Moro. 10:32–33, but compare 7:18–19; 10:14).

The author's focus is therefore on mediation. He looks initially at the activities of the Levitical high priest through which the strained relationship between Jehovah and his people was overcome and unity restored.[114] The high priest is able to mediate through the authorized offering he makes. Of special note is that his offering has two aspects: "on the one hand, it is an act of worship made to God; on the other hand, it is at the same time

109. McConkie, *Doctrinal New Testament Commentary,* 3:158.

110. Russell M. Nelson, "Perfection Pending," *Ensign* 25, no. 11 (November 1995): 86.

111. Ezra Taft Benson, "A Mighty Change of Heart," *Ensign* 19, no. 10 (October 1989): 5.

112. Therefore, his perfection should not be limited to his death, Resurrection, or enthronement. The term denotes his complete obedience to God throughout his entire life. See Attridge, *Epistle to the Hebrews,* 86–87; Craig Allen Hill, "The Use of Perfection Language in Hebrews 5:14 and 6:1 and the Contextual Interpretation of 5:11–6:3," *Journal of the Evangelical Theological Seminary* 57, no. 4 (2014): 727–42, accessed February 13, 2016, https://www.etsjets.org/files/JETS-PDFs/57/57-4/JETS_57-4_727-42_Hill.pdf. For a formal study, see the whole of Peterson, *Hebrews and Perfection.*

113. D&C 88:11–13.

114. Jeffrey R. Holland, "Atonement of Jesus Christ," in Ludlow, *Encyclopedia of Mormonism,* 1:82–86. On Aaron's mediation on behalf of the Hebrews, see Num. 14:5; 16:47–48; and Ps. 106:16; see also Bruce, *Epistle to the Hebrews,* 120.

an act of mercy on behalf of sinners."[115] These two aspects give insight into the Savior's ministry, focusing first on his relationship with humankind and second on his relationship with his Father in their behalf. Indeed, this twofold idea is the cement that holds this section tightly together (4:15–5:10) and becomes the foundation upon which the author will build the rest of his argument (chapters 7–10).

A Castigation on Unwillingness to Learn and Spiritual Immaturity (5:11–14)

Greek Text

11 Περὶ οὗ πολὺς ἡμῖν ὁ λόγος καὶ δυσερμήνευτος λέγειν, ἐπεὶ νωθροὶ γεγόνατε ταῖς ἀκοαῖς· 12 καὶ γὰρ ὀφείλοντες εἶναι διδάσκαλοι διὰ τὸν χρόνον, πάλιν χρείαν ἔχετε τοῦ διδάσκειν ὑμᾶς τινὰ τὰ στοιχεῖα τῆς ἀρχῆς τῶν λογίων τοῦ θεοῦ, καὶ γεγόνατε χρείαν ἔχοντες γάλακτος, οὐ στερεᾶς τροφῆς. 13 πᾶς γὰρ ὁ μετέχων γάλακτος ἄπειρος λόγου δικαιοσύνης, νήπιος γάρ ἐστιν· 14 τελείων δέ ἐστιν ἡ στερεὰ τροφή, τῶν διὰ τὴν ἕξιν τὰ αἰσθητήρια γεγυμνασμένα ἐχόντων πρὸς διάκρισιν καλοῦ τε καὶ κακοῦ. [SBLGNT]

King James Version

11 Of whom we have many things to say, and hard to be uttered, seeing ye are dull of hearing. 12 For when for the time ye ought to be teachers, ye have need that one teach you again which be the first principles of the oracles of God; and are become such as have need of milk, and not of strong meat. 13 For every one that useth milk is unskilful in the word of righteousness: for he is a babe. 14 But strong meat belongeth to them that are of full age, even those who by reason of use have their senses exercised to discern both good and evil.

New Rendition

11 We have much to say about this that is difficult to explain, since you have become hard of hearing. 12 For although you should already have become teachers by this time, you need someone to again teach you the fundamental principles that God has spoken. You have gone back to needing milk, not solid food. 13 For anyone who drinks only milk, being still an infant, is unacquainted with the teachings of righteousness. 14 But solid food is for the mature, who because of their maturity have their faculties trained to distinguish between good and evil.

115. Vanhoye, *Letter to the Hebrews,* 100.

Translation Notes and Comments

5:11 ***Of whom we have many things to say, and hard to be uttered / We have much to say about this that is difficult to explain:*** The relative masculine pronoun οὗ (*hou*), "this," could be taken as a referent to either Christ or Melchizedek, but the context suggests it is best taken in a neutral sense which would reference the Lord's priesthood and the activities it drove.[116] It is therefore translated as "this," meaning "about this subject," in our Rendition.

The adjective δυσερμήνευτος (*dysermēneutos*) denotes any concept that is hard to understand.[117] Its nuance suggests that the reason is not so much the fault of the person as it is of the complexity of the material itself.[118] In the author's view, however, his readers have no excuse not to comprehend it. The force of the present tense of this phrase shows that the author is going to move ahead with his teachings even though his readers are ill prepared to hear it.

seeing ye are dull of hearing / since you have become hard of hearing: The subordinate conjunction ἐπεί (*epei*), "since," identifies why the concept mentioned above is difficult to understand. The adjective νωθρός (*nōthros*) refers primarily to that which is "lazy" but also to that which is "dull" in the sense of being slow in perception or "sluggish" in response, that is, "hard of hearing."[119] These people have difficulty hearing not because the concepts are too difficult but because they will not put forth the effort. Admittedly, the doctrine is advanced and takes real effort to understand and implement. But the problem was not, at its base, with the doctrine but with these Saints' receptivity.[120] In this context, *nōthros* connotes moral blame. The author's readers have made themselves "dull of hearing" and thereby could very easily forfeit the greater knowledge available to them.[121]

The force of the perfect voice of the verb γίνομαι (*ginomai*), "to become," shows their state of dullness is nothing new. Its seat was in the past, but it has continued right into the present.[122]

---

116. See Lane, *Hebrews 1–8,* 136; and Cockerill, *Epistle to the Hebrews,* 254.

117. BDAG, 265.

118. Lane, *Hebrews 1–8,* 135–36, notes that the phrase was used in many writings to designate an item the author or speaker felt was of particular importance. See also Cockerill, *Epistle to the Hebrews,* 254–55.

119. BDAG, 683. Louw-Nida, §32.47, translates the phrase as "slow to understand," but the prime root is laziness. See also §88.249.

120. Preisker, *TDNT,* 4:1126.

121. Lane, *Hebrews 1–8,* 136.

122. Cockerill, *Epistle to the Hebrews,* 257.

5:12 For when for the time ye ought to be teachers, ye have need that one teach you again / For although you should already have become teachers by this time, you need someone to again teach you: The verb ὀφείλω (*opheilō*), "ought to be, should have become," found here in the form of a present participle, denotes the need to meet certain social or moral obligations.[123] In this case, it was becoming διδάσκαλοι (*didaskaloi*), "teachers." In its Christian context, the noun carried the nuance of one who has the authority to instruct others in the things of God (Acts 13:1; 1 Cor. 12:28–29; Eph. 4:11).[124] The related verb διδάσκω (*didaskō*) means "to cause to learn" or "to teach."[125] In the New Testament, it points to the truths Jesus taught (see, for example, Matt. 4:23; 9:35; Rom. 12:7; 1 Cor. 4:17; and 1 Tim. 4:11).[126]

The noun χρόνος (*chronos*) designates "an indefinite period of time during which some activity or event takes place, time, period of time." [127] Unlike the noun καιρός (*kairos*) that denotes a limited period specifically suited for an act and thus has the feel of quality, *chronos* refers to time in general, pointing to a broad period in which many things can be accomplished. It thus has the feel of quantity. Here it connotes the idea that these people had plenty of time to learn, but they were just too lazy to bother.[128]

which be the first principles of the oracles of God / the fundamental principles that God has spoken: The phrase τὰ στοιχεῖα τῆς ἀρχῆς τῶν λογίων τοῦ θεοῦ (*ta stoicheia tēs archēs tōn logiōn tou theou*) consists of the plural noun *stoicheia,* which refers to the "basic components" of anything,[129] followed by three nouns in the genitive: *archēs,* "beginning"[130]; *logiōn,* "sayings"[131]; and *theou,* "God." The whole phrase we have translated as "the fundamental principles that God has spoken." The phrase shows the author's irritation with these people, accusing them of needing to go back to gospel basics.

123. BDAG, 743.

124. BDAG, 241; Rengstorf, *TDNT,* 2:157–58. *Didaskalos* is often translated as "master" in the KJV (see, for example, Matt. 10:24–25; and Luke 6:40). This was the title people used the most often to address Jesus (see, for example, Matt. 8:19; 12:38; 19:16; 22:36; Mark 4:38; 9:5; Luke 5:5; 7:40; and John 8:4; 13:13).

125. BDAG, 241.

126. BDAG, 241.

127. BDAG, 1092.

128. Ellingworth, *Epistle to the Hebrews,* 302–5.

129. BDAG, 946.

130. BDAG, 137.

131. BDAG, 598.

and are become such as have need of milk, and not of strong meat / You have gone back to needing milk, not solid food: The force of the perfect active form of the verb γίνομαι (*ginomai*), "to be, become,"[132] as used here, is important. It points to a retrogression in these people's spiritual maturity and is thus translated as "have gone back" in our Rendition.[133] They have regressed to the state of spiritual infancy.

The noun γάλα (*gala*), "milk," in this context refers "to elementary gospel instruction."[134] The phrase στερεᾶς τροφῆς (*stereas trophēs*) denotes solid food, but in this case spiritual nourishment.[135] This whole clause is particularly biting because it suggests they once had a capability that through willful laziness they have now lost.

5:13 ***For every one that useth milk is unskilful in the word of righteousness: for he is a babe / For anyone who drinks only milk, being still an infant, is unacquainted with the teachings of righteousness:*** The noun ἄπειρος (*apeiros*) denotes a lack of skill due to being either unacquainted with or unaccustomed to something. We have chosen "unacquainted" in our Rendition because it suggests the lack of personal or firsthand knowledge of a subject and thus has a certain unpleasant rub to it. These people should have been well acquainted with the doctrinal points the author is making but have not put forth the effort.

The very broad noun λόγος (*logos*), "word,"[136] is here translated as "teaching" to keep it parallel with the noun διδάσκαλος (*didaskalos*), "teacher."

In the phrase λόγος δικαιοσύνης (*logos dikaiosynēs*), "teaching of righteousness," the noun *dikaiosynē*, "righteousness," has a wide range of nuances, including all that conforms to the revealed will of God as well as the sum total of his requirements for the faithful.[137] The author, however, appears to be using the phrase in the more narrow sense of understanding the role of the Savior, and particularly the use of his priesthood, in the salvation process.[138]

---

132. BDAG, 196–99.

133. Ellingworth, *Epistle to the Hebrews,* 301; Lane, *Hebrews 1–8,* 136–37.

134. BDAG, 186.

135. BDAG, 1017.

136. BDAG, 598–601. The author uses the word *logos* to denote that which God has spoken (2:2; 4:2; 5:13; 7:28; 12:19, 27; 13:7, 22).

137. Strong, "New Strong's Expanded Dictionary . . . Greek," s.v. "*δικαιοσύνη*"; BDAG, 247–48.

138. For the range of meanings the phrase λόγου δικαιοσύης (*logou dikaiosynēs*) can have, see Ellingworth, *Epistle to the Hebrews,* 306–7. He concludes that the best understanding is to take in the context of the whole Epistle as looking to the work and ministry

5:14 ***But strong meat belongeth to them that are of full age / But solid food is for the mature:*** Here again we have the adjective τέλειος (*teleios*) referred to in 5:9. In the present context, it means "fully grown, mature."[139] Moreover, the word was also used as a technical term of the Greco-Roman mystery religions to refer to someone who had been initiated into their mystic rites,[140] and as such the word here may also be subtly referring to those who have experienced the Christian rites of baptism, confirmation, and possibly even the endowment and eternal marriage.[141]

even those who by reason of use have their senses exercised to discern both good and evil / who because of their maturity have their faculties trained to distinguish between good and evil: This is the only use of the noun ἕξις (*hexis*) in the Greek New Testament, making it somewhat hard to translate, but in this context, it seems best to take it as "a state of maturity."[142]

The abstract noun αἰσθητήριον (*aisthētērion*), literally "organ of sense," is often used figuratively for the capacity for discernment. By extension it connotes those faculties that make discernment possible.[143] It is found here in the plural and modified by the perfect passive participle of γυμνάζω (*gymnazō*), "to exercise, train." Thus, our translation is "faculties trained" in the Rendition.

The nominalized adjective καλός (*kalos*), "good," in the present context denotes not just anything that is morally fit but particularly those teachings and ideas that are pleasing to God because they contribute to salvation.[144] The nominalized adjective κακός (*kakos*), "evil," on the other hand, denotes teachings and ideas that are not just morally reprehensible

---

of the Savior. See also Cockerill, *Epistle to the Hebrews,* 258–59, who also notes these teachings point to the Savior and his high priesthood.

139. BDAG, 995–96.

140. BDAG, 995–96.

141. The noun τελειότης (*teleiotēs*) carries the meaning of being mature and perfected as well as "being complete." It is likely that the word in Philip. 3:15 and Col. 1:26–28 was used in that sense. BDAG, 995–96. Given that the author is very interested in Old Testament temple worship, there may be an echo of this nuance in his writings.

142. BDAG, 350; O'Brien, *Letter to the Hebrews,* 210. John A. L. Lee, "Hebrews 5:14 and ΕΞΙΣ: A History of Misunderstanding," *Novum Testamentum* 39, no. 2 (1997): 151–76, has shown convincingly that the KJV translation of the term as "exercise" is wrong; it denotes rather a "state" or "condition."

143. BDAG, 29.

144. The term the author chooses to use is καλός (*kalos*), not ἀγαθός (*agathos*), "good." The two terms are very similar in meaning and are often used interchangeably, although *kalos* tends to have a more moralistic aspect. BDAG, 504–5. See also Cockerill, *Epistle to the Hebrews,* 259, and n. 26.

but which are also spiritually dangerous.[145] Mature disciples, because their spiritual faculties are well honed, can tell the difference between the two.

Analysis and Summary

These verses mark a transition from instruction to admonition and even censure. Thus, they contain a sudden and dramatic shift in tone. Though he has gently chided his readers before (see 2:1–4; 4:1–3), there his tone had been conciliatory (see 2:1; 4:1, where he includes himself in the admonition). Here it is strongly condemnatory with no hint of apology. He knows, however, what he is doing: he is pricking his hearers' conscience for their laziness. By doing so, he is forcing them to evaluate their current state in light of their forsaken responsibilities. He deliberately uses an overstatement (at 6:12 he notes he is writing so that his readers will not be lazy or slothful in their faith) to grab their attention.[146] He needs them to be fully attentive, he warns (5:11), because he is about to broach "teaching difficult to explain" (λόγος δυσερμήνευτος, *logos . . . dysermēneutos*).[147]

The author forcefully points out their problem (5:11). He uses a phrase that translates literally as "you have become lazy (dull or sluggish) in hearing" (νωθροὶ γεγόνατε ταῖς ἀκοαῖς, *nōthroi gegonate tais akoais*). The adjective "lazy, sluggish"[148] (νωθρός, *nōthros*) in this context takes on a biting force connoting not simple intellectual inertia, which would have been bad enough, but an active resistance to God's message.[149] It strongly echoes conditions that brought on Israel's wilderness rebellion (see Ex. 32:7–14). Through resistance to hearing Jehovah's word, those people had hardened their hearts and lost all.

The author really castigates his readers, pointing out that "by this time" (διὰ τὸν χρόνον, *dia ton chronon*) they should be teaching this material, not needing to be taught it (5:12). These were not new converts but seasoned

---

145. BDAG, 501.

146. Johnson, *Hebrews,* 154, notes that altering rhythm and focus was a way ancient rhetoricians kept the attention of their audience.

147. Compare Vanhoye, *Letter to the Hebrews,* 110. Jesus admonished his early disciples not to share sacred teachings and moments until after the Resurrection. Even then, they were to be guarded. See Hugh Nibley, "Baptism for the Dead in Ancient Times," in *Mormonism and Early Christianity,* ed. Todd M. Compton and Stephen D. Ricks (Provo, Utah: Foundation for Ancient Research and Mormon Studies, 1987), 113. Such is not the case here, for the author clearly goes forward with his teachings.

148. BDAG, 683.

149. Johnson, *Hebrews,* 155.

members who should have long since learned the doctrine. He concludes that there is only one reason for their failure: they are spiritual infants (*nēpios*) unable to stomach solid spiritual food (στερεᾶς τροφῆς, *stereas trophēs*). Being restricted to milk, they have prepared themselves only to receive the rudiments (στοιχεῖα, *stoikeia*) of the gospel (5:12–13).[150]

The author's use of physical food to symbolize doctrinal themes (5:12–14) is not unique. Paul did the same thing and to make the same point (see 1 Cor. 3:2). Both authors note that only the mature can handle solid food; babes can stomach only milk. Those who are not adults in their faith simply cannot comprehend the profound realities that undergird and overarch Christian doctrine. The point of both writers is that if their audiences cannot handle the doctrine of the kingdom, they must be spiritual infants—to their shame.[151] But on the part of the author of Hebrews, he is not going to let their immaturity stop him from delivering his message. They had better grow up fast, because he is about to hit them with hard doctrine.

---

150. Just what the author had in mind as rudiments is unclear, and any guesses are only speculative or misleading. Cockerill, *Epistle to the Hebrews,* 256.

151. Vanhoye, *Letter to the Hebrews,* 110–11; Lane, *Hebrews 1–8,* 135.

Chapter 6

"Let Us Go On unto Perfection"

Introduction

At the conclusion of chapter 5, the author of Hebrews contrasted the less spiritually mature, whose senses were so undeveloped that they could only stomach the milk of the gospel, with the more spiritually mature, whose senses were developed to the point that they could digest solid spiritual food. The lives of the latter group had been continually exercised in the gospel of faith and a reliance upon the Father and the Son. They were motivated by their hope in the promises available to them through the priestly Atonement of the Savior. As a result, they were moving to full spiritual maturity that brings eventual perfection.[1]

Because of their spiritual development, they could discern not only what was morally right but more particularly the finer shades of what was the most pleasing to the Father and Son.[2] Through this sensitivity, they were able to avoid, even spurn, anything that would slow their spiritual progress. But unfortunately there were some who, although they had begun the journey, had to their shame regressed into a state of spiritual immaturity (5:11–13). Knowing it takes solid food to wean babes from milk, the author begins feeding his readers the gospel—the "great salvation" (2:3)—straight and pure.[3]

---

1. The adjective (used as a noun in 5:14) τέλειος (*teleios*) could be translated as "perfect" since the author used the verb form to refer to the Savior's own perfecting in 2:10 and 5:9 and will refer to the Lord's perfecting of the Saints in 10:14; 11:40; and 12:23, but see Translation Notes for 6:1.

2. The adjectives καλός (*kalos*), "useful," and ἀγαθός (*agathos*), "good," imply "not only what is morally right but what is appropriate in God's sight." Cockerill, *Epistle to the Hebrews,* 259 n. 26. Compare Dallin H. Oaks, "Good, Better, Best," *Ensign* 37, no. 11 (November 2007): 104–7.

3. Cockerill, *Epistle to the Hebrews,* 259–60. Note also the phrase καλὸς κ'ἀγαθός used by classical Greek writers describes "the chivalrous ideal of the complete human personality, harmonious in mind and body, foursquare in battle and speech, song and action."

He begins this chapter by admonishing his readers to strive for further spiritual maturity by advancing beyond the elementary teachings of the gospel (6:1–3). He then gives them a stiff warning that turning away from the gospel after having been enlightened by its power would bring severe and eternal consequences (6:4–8). He assures them, however, that he really does expect better things of them. Indeed, the Father is well aware of their sacrifices and service. The author assures them that all he wants is that they continue exhibiting such a degree of faith "unto the end" so they can inherit all the promises given to the faithful (6:9–12). This leads him into a declaration of how serious God is in keeping the promises he has made to his trusting followers. The Father has even gone so far as to swear an unbreakable oath upon which the Saints can put their full trust (6:13–18). If that were not enough, the author assures his readers, Jesus has himself ascended up on high where he works in their behalf as the great High Priest after the order of Melchizedek (6:19–20). All this can be for them like a firm and certain anchor they can rely on (6:19).

Not Laying Down Again the Foundation (6:1–3)

Greek Text

1 Διὸ ἀφέντες τὸν τῆς ἀρχῆς τοῦ Χριστοῦ λόγον ἐπὶ τὴν τελειότητα φερώμεθα, μὴ πάλιν θεμέλιον καταβαλλόμενοι μετανοίας ἀπὸ νεκρῶν ἔργων, καὶ πίστεως ἐπὶ θεόν, 2 βαπτισμῶν διδαχὴν ἐπιθέσεώς τε χειρῶν, ἀναστάσεώς τε νεκρῶν καὶ κρίματος αἰωνίου. 3 καὶ τοῦτο ποιήσομεν ἐάνπερ ἐπιτρέπῃ ὁ θεός. [SBLGNT]

King James Version

1 Therefore leaving the principles of the doctrine of Christ, let us go on unto perfection; not laying again the foundation of repentance from dead works, and of faith toward God, 2 Of the doctrine of baptisms, and of laying on of hands, and of resurrection of the dead, and of eternal judgment. 3 And this will we do, if God permit.

New Rendition

1 Therefore let us advance beyond the elementary principles of Christ's teachings and go on to full maturity and not lay down again the foundation of repentance from dead works and of faith in God, 2 of the teachings of baptisms and the laying on of hands, of the resurrection of the dead, and of eternal judgment. 3 And we will do this, if God permits.

Translation Notes and Comments

6:1 *Therefore leaving the principles of the doctrine of Christ / Therefore let us advance beyond the elementary principles of Christ's teachings:* The author once again includes himself in his admonition and so joins with his fellow Saints, defusing any antagonism.

The phrase τὸν τῆς ἀρχῆς τοῦ Χριστοῦ λόγον (*ton tēs archēs tou Christou logon*), literally "the beginning word of Christ," clearly refers back to τὰ στοιχεῖα τῆς ἀρχῆς τῶν λογίων τοῦ θεοῦ (*ta stoicheia tēs archēs tōn logiōn tou theou*), "the fundamental principles that God had spoken," of the previous chapter (NR 5:12).

The verb ἀφίημι (*aphiēmi*) has the general sense of causing someone or something to undergo separation.[4] Here the idea is not to abandon but simply to "leave (behind), to go on to something else,"[5] hence "advance beyond" in our Rendition. The phrase, therefore, should not be taken to mean that the elements he lists (see below) of faith, repentance, and so on are to be abandoned but rather to stand as the foundation upon which he wishes others to build.[6] It needs to be stressed that the author is not denigrating these principles. Indeed, he sees these principles as the foundation of his readers' understanding upon which they should be building a loftier understanding of the ways of the Divine. The problem was that these fundamentals had to be revisited over and over again.

To make certain that the importance of the first principles were not undercut by the mistranslation of the KJV, the JST changes the verse to read, "Therefore *not* leaving the principles of the doctrine of Christ. . . ."[7]

let us go on unto perfection / let us . . . go on to full maturity: The verb φέρω (*pherō*), "to bear, carry" or "go on to," is found here in its hortatory, subjunctive passive form and therefore connotes the idea of being carried toward an objective.[8] Used as a divine passive, it is a tacit witness that it is God who does the carrying and thereby emphasizes one's need to rely on him.[9]

---

4. BDAG, 156.

5. BDAG, 156.

6. Koester, *Hebrews,* 303; Attridge, *Epistle to the Hebrews,* 162. John W. Welch, *An Epistle from the New Testament Apostles: The Letters of Peter, Paul, John, James, and Jude, Arranged by Themes, with Readings from the Greek and the Joseph Smith Translation* (Salt Lake City: Bookcraft, 1999), 8, notes that those principles mentioned in 6:1–3 show a particular affinity to the teachings of the Lord's disciples.

7. Ogden and Skinner, *Verse by Verse,* 250.

8. BDAG, 1051–52; Cockerill, *Epistle to the Hebrews,* 262.

9. Wallace, *Greek Grammar,* 437–38.

The noun τελειότης (*teleiotēs*), "perfection, completeness," can also refer to "maturity" in the sense of reaching a state of full development.[10] The nuance of the word in the present context is therefore not the flawless excellence and holiness of a person but rather the quality of the fully and finished state at which they need to arrive. The phrase "full maturity" in our Rendition best carries this idea.

not laying again the foundation / and not lay down again the foundation: The noun θεμέλιος (*themelios*), "foundation," denotes the supporting structure on which something stands.[11] The verb καταβάλλω (*kataballō*), "lay down," connotes the idea of anchoring something so securely that it becomes permanent.[12] The two words show that the foundational principles are never to be abandoned but form the strata upon which the rest of the gospel rests. But it is noteworthy that to continually lay down the foundation precludes any further progress on the structure.[13]

of repentance from dead works: The noun μετάνοια (*metanoia*), "repentance," connotes a change of mind.[14] In its moral sense, it normally denotes the process of turning from sin to righteousness with the nuance of conversion—actual change—strongly attached. The word also carries the idea of commitment to a person and their ideals.[15] Therefore, repentance is a call to discipleship. Let us emphasize that the word suggests that it is not enough to give up sin; it must be replaced by good works.[16]

---

10. BDAG, 996. Vanhoye, *Letter to the Hebrews,* 111, notes that the author is playing on the double meaning of τέλειος (*teleios*) as both perfect and adulthood, thus suggesting the completeness found in maturity. See also Johnson, *Hebrews,* 166–67.

11. BDAG, 448–49.

12. BDAG, 514.

13. The structure of 6:1–2 can be read such that it separates the foundational principles of repentance and faith from the teachings of baptism, laying on of hands, judgment, and resurrection. For discussion, see Koester, *Hebrews,* 310–11; Lane, *Hebrews 1–8,* 140; Cockerill, *Epistle to the Hebrews,* 263–64 n. 41. It is clear, however, that the author includes all of these as foundational principles.

14. BDAG, 640. The verb, μετανοέω (*metanoeō*), from which the noun μετανοῖα (*metanoia*) is derived, is a compound of the prefix μετά (*meta*), which indicates an alteration or change (see Smyth, *Greek Grammar,* §§1691, 1694), and the verb νοέω (*noeo*), which has the basic sense of "to grasp or comprehend something on the basis of careful thought." BDAG, 674. Thus *metanoia* is "a change of mind," a "conversion." BDAG, 640. In the New Testament, the noun and the verb refer to the process of religious and moral conversion. Behm and Würthwein, *TDNT,* 4:999–1000; *NID,* s.v. "μετανοέω."

15. Seen in this light, faith, repentance, conversion, and discipleship are all interrelated steps involved in the same process. See *NID,* s.v. "μετανοέω."

16. The Savior made this point very clearly in his parable of the unclean spirit, which, being exorcised from his old habitat, returned to find it "swept and garnished" but empty. His reaction to all that free space was to find "seven other spirits more wicked than

The author's phrase νεκρῶν ἔργων (*nekrōn ergon*), "dead works," carries three possible meanings. It could refer to the works of the Jewish law. In that case, the author would be warning his readers of the danger of returning to their former religion and taking upon themselves once more the entire and unnecessary weight of the Mosaic law. The problem in doing so would be that, having been fulfilled by the Lord, the law was no longer a living system, and following it would not just be a waste of time but also a loss of salvation.[17] The author likely had this in mind (it was definitely a problem faced by both Paul and John), but there are other possibilities.[18]

The phrase could also refer to sinful works, those that defile the conscience, make a person spiritually unclean, and put her or him on the road to death (Prov. 9:14; 10:2–3). Those who do not repent are "immoral" (12:16–17), and impending judgment awaits them (Prov. 3:14). Indeed, the wages of sin is death (Rom. 6:23).[19]

Finally, the phrase could refer to the sin of idolatry. Any devotion to an idol, since it is dead (Ps. 106:28; Isa. 44:9–20; Jer. 10:5; Dan. 5:32), is a dead work, because no blessings can come therefrom. In Christian thinking, conversion to the Savior meant turning from idolatry and accepting the "living God" (Acts 14:15; 2 Cor. 6:16; 1 Thes. 1:9).[20] Accepting this position would be based on the idea that the author's main audience were Gentiles, but again, the context suggests otherwise.

Of the three, the last seems to be the least likely. The scriptures reference "dead works" four times (6:1–2; 9:13–14; Moro. 8:23; D&C 22:1–4). Taking them together, they refer to ordinances that either never did or no longer have value. There are two main reasons why they are dead. First, the faithless have not lived up to the requirements of the law and sensed the value of its ordinances for themselves. Their lack of faith has made their works dead. Such was the case with many in Israel whose unworthiness made their offerings hypocritical and thereby abominable before God (for example, see Isa. 1:13). Second, the ordinances of the old law have been superseded

himself" who all entered and "dwell there." The Savior concluded that "the last state of that man is worse than the first" (Luke 11:24–26).

17. D&C 22 ties "dead works" both to the Mosaic law and to baptisms performed before the Church was organized.

18. See Lane, *Hebrews 1–8,* 140. On the Judaizers (those who taught Christianity was a subset of Judaism and the law of Moses remained valid), see James W. Aageson, "Judaizing," in Freedman, *Anchor Bible Dictionary,* 3:1089.

19. Koester, *Hebrews,* 305; Cockerill, *Epistle to the Hebrews,* 265 n. 47; Bruce, *Epistle to the Hebrews,* 139–40.

20. Cockerill, *Epistle to the Hebrews,* 265.

by the new law. Once the new law has come, practicing the ordinances of the old law is no longer valid and becomes "dead works." Such was the case with the Mosaic law. Though its ordinances were once valid, under the new law, their practice is a dead work.

faith toward God / faith in God: The author's use of the noun πίστις (*pistis*), "faith," is consistent. It centers in the Divine and points to the outcome of a hope that brings an absolute assurance that the promises of Christ will be fully realized at some future time. The word includes, however, an additional assurance that the Lord's power also operates in the present, through which the Saint can find peace and progression.[21] For a fuller treatment, see Translation Notes along with the associated Analysis for 11:1–3.

6:2 ***the doctrine of baptisms / the teachings of baptisms:*** The noun βαπτισμός (*baptismos*) means "baptism, washing, ablution."[22] The variety of definitions plus its plural form, as found here, make it unclear exactly what the author had in mind. Further, the normal term for the Christian ordinance itself is βάπτισμα (*baptisma*). Though *baptismos* could refer to various Jewish cleansing rituals (9:10; Mark 7:4), given the context, the word more likely referred to some Christian practice. That the author considers the teaching a foundational doctrine, and because it is closely connoted to the practice of laying on of hands, it would appear that he does have the ordinance of baptism in mind.[23]

laying on of hands / the laying on of hands: In the present context, the phrase seems to point to the procedure through which the bestowing the gift of the Holy Ghost was given (Acts 8:17–18; 9:7–18; 19:5–6). However, the practice of laying on hands for healing (Mark 1:41; 6:5), blessing (Mark 10:13–16), or setting apart (Acts 6:6; 13:3; 1 Tim. 4:14; 5:22; 2 Tim. 1:6) cannot be excluded.

---

21. For discussion, see *NID,* s.v. "πιστεύω," particularly the portion dealing with Hebrews.

22. BDAG, 165.

23. William E. Berrett, *Blessed Are They Who Come unto Me* (Provo, Utah: Ensign Publishing, 1979), 16, sees this phrase as one of several examples illustrating an emphasis on the necessity of baptism for the living and dead. That the same word (*baptismos*) is used in Col. 2:12 and for the ordinance performed by John the Baptist (Josephus, *Ant.* 18.117) also suggests that it is the rite of baptism that is meant here. It is possible that a member could have gone through three baptisms: that of a Jewish proselyte, then that of John the Baptist, and that of Christ. Cockerill, *Epistle to the Hebrews,* 266 n. 49; but see also Koester, *Hebrews,* 305; and Ellingworth, *Epistle to the Hebrews,* 315.

resurrection of the dead / the resurrection of the dead: The noun ἀνάστασις (*anastasis*), literally "a rising up," was used by the Christians to refer to the resurrection instituted by the Lord.[24]

eternal judgment: The force of the phrase κρίματος αἰωνίου (*krimatos aiōniou*), "eternal judgment," as used here, is positive. It refers to the final pronouncement by Jesus that the person who perseveres in righteousness is one with him and has obtained eternal life (11:6; Matt. 5:12; Luke 6:35; Col. 3:24; D&C 127:4).[25]

6:3 *And this will we do, if God permit / And we will do this, if God permits:* The verb ποιέω (*poieō*) means "to do" or "to make something happen."[26] In this case, it refers to the process of going beyond the rudiments of the gospel in at least two ways: first, gaining an understanding of the higher doctrines, more especially the role of Christ as the great High Priest in the salvation process; and second, partaking of the power that he can give. In this way, one progresses toward spiritual maturity and the completeness it will bring. That the form of the word is plural shows that the author (as in 6:1) includes himself and thus identifies with his readers.

The verb ἐπιτρέπω (*epitrepō*), "permit," denotes allowing something to be done.[27] The force of the word in the present context stresses that the move to maturity is not done without divine assistance, direction, and allowance. One does not simply take this course of action upon oneself. To attempt to do so would be the height of arrogance and folly. To both understand and obtain the blessings that come through the high priestly authority of the Lord is beyond any mortal's means. Divine permission must be granted and help extended.[28]

---

24. BDAG, 71–72.

25. Joseph Smith taught that "the doctrine of the resurrection of the dead and eternal judgment are necessary to preach among the first principles of the Gospel of Jesus Christ." "History, 1838–1856, Volume C-1," 8 [addenda]. The six gospel principles the author lists show the continuity of the Christian message from its beginning. Each of these concepts can be found in the sermons of the Savior and his Apostles. For example, faith and repentance (Matt. 3:1–3; Mark 1:15; Acts 2:38; 20:21), baptism (Acts 2:41; 9:18; Rom. 6:3–4; Gal. 3:27; 1 Pet. 3:21), the laying on of hands (Matt. 9:18; Mark 10:13, 16; Luke 4:40; Acts 6:6; 8:14–17; 9:12, 17; 13:3; 19:1–7; 28:8; 1 Tim. 4:14; 5:22; 2 Tim. 1:6; James 5:14–16), and resurrection and judgment (Matt. 10:15; 12:36; Mark 12:18–27; Acts 17:31; Rom. 2:16; 1 John 4:17).

26. BDAG, 839–42.

27. BDAG, 384–85.

28. Though the phrase "God willing" was common among Jews and Christians (Acts 18:21; Rom. 1:10; 1 Cor. 4:19; James 4:15; Josephus, *Ant.* 20.267), the emphasis in this verse is more forceful than usual. See Attridge, *Epistle to the Hebrews,* 165; Koester, *Hebrews,* 306; and Cockerill, *Epistle to the Hebrews,* 267.

Analysis and Summary

The author's plea to his readers is for them to not "lay down again the foundation of repentance from dead works" (NR 6:1). He is calling them to refrain from those activities that would lead them away from oneness with the Lord. The means is through repentance. The readers of the Epistle would have understood the noun differently than modern readers because those people were not exposed to the false doctrine of original sin and the depravity of man. Jewish readers would have understood the term in light of two Hebrew verbs. The first verb is the root נחם (*nḥm*), which has several senses depending on the verbal form. In the niphal, נִחַם (*niḥam*), it means "to regret," "to be sorry," and "to console oneself"; in the piel, נִחַם (*niḥam*), it means "to comfort"; in the pual, נֻחַם (*nuḥam*), "to become consoled"; and in the hithpael, הִתְנַחֵם (*hitnaḥēm*), "to plot revenge, be grieved by, and allow oneself to be comforted."[29] In the KJV, the niphal, נִחַם (*niḥam*), is translated as "to repent" forty-one times, and the piel, נִחַם (*niḥam*), "to comfort," fifty-seven times.[30] The second verb is שׁוּב (šûb), with the basic meaning "to turn back, return," especially in a theological sense "to turn back to God and be devoted to him," and it can also mean "to turn away from, abandon."[31]

The author's Greek readers would have understood the term in light of the verb "to repent" (μετανοέω, *metanoeō*), which means literally "to change one's mind." Its two components are μετά (*meta*), which denotes an alteration or change, and νοέω (*noeo*), "to grasp or comprehend something on the basis of careful thought." The word points to a new and better perception due to a clearer understanding resulting in a change of mind for the better.[32] Importantly, it also implies an attendant change in behavior.

None of the Hebrew and Greek words נִחַם (*niḥam*), שׁוּב (*šûb*), μετανοῖα (*metanoia*), and μετανοέω (*metanoeō*) necessarily implied a direct moral nuance or association with sin connected to the idea of repentance. Therefore, the Old Testament writers had no qualms in reporting that God "repented" of certain actions (for examples, see Gen. 6:6; Ex. 32:14; and Judg. 2:18). However in the New Testament period, the Greek term did gain the nuance

29. *HAL*, 688–89.

30. Strong, "New Strong's Expanded Dictionary . . . Hebrew," s.v. "נחם."

31. *HAL*, 1429–30.

32. Thus *metanoia* is "a change of mind," a "conversion." BDAG, 640. In the New Testament, the noun and the verb refer to the process of religious and moral conversion. Behm and Würthwein, *TDNT*, 4:999–1000.

of turning from sin to righteousness with the idea of conversion—actual change—strongly attached. It also carried the idea of commitment to a person and their ideals.[33] Therefore, repentance is a call to discipleship. Let us emphasize that the word suggests that it is not enough to give up sin; it must be replaced by good works.

Speaking on the subject of repentance, Elder Theodor M. Burton asked, "Just what *is* repentance? Actually, in some ways it is easier to understand what repentance is *not* than to understand what it *is.*" He then answered:

> As a General Authority, I have prepared information for the First Presidency to use in considering applications to readmit repentant transgressors into the Church and to restore priesthood and temple blessings. Many times a bishop will write, "I feel he has suffered enough!" But suffering is not repentance. Suffering comes from *lack* of complete repentance. A stake president will write, "I feel he has been punished enough!" But punishment is not repentance. Punishment *follows* disobedience and *precedes* repentance. A husband will write, "My wife has confessed everything!" But confession is not repentance. Confession is an admission of guilt that occurs as repentance begins. A wife will write, "My husband is filled with remorse!" But remorse is not repentance. Remorse and sorrow continue because a person has *not* yet fully repented. Suffering, punishment, confession, remorse, and sorrow may sometimes accompany repentance, but they are not repentance. What, then, *is* repentance?
>
> To find the answer to this question, we must go to the Old Testament. The Old Testament was originally written in Hebrew, and the word used in it to refer to the concept of repentance is *shube.* We can better understand what *shube* means by reading a passage from Ezekiel and inserting the word *shube,* along with its English translation. To the "watchmen" appointed to warn Israel, the Lord says:
>
> "When I say unto the wicked, O wicked man, thou shalt surely die; if thou dost not speak to warn the wicked from his way, that wicked man shall die in his iniquity; but his blood will I require at thine hand.
>
> "Nevertheless, if thou warn the wicked of his way to turn from [*shube*] it; if he do not turn from [*shube*] his way, he shall die in his iniquity; but thou hast delivered thy soul. . . .
>
> "Say unto them, As I live, saith the Lord God, I have no pleasure in the death of the wicked; but that the wicked turn from [*shube*] his way and live" (Ezek. 33:8–11).

---

33. Seen in this light, faith, repentance, conversion, and discipleship are all interrelated steps involved in the same process. See *NID,* s.v. "μετανοέω."

> I know of no kinder, sweeter passage in the Old Testament than those beautiful lines. In reading them, can you think of a kind, wise, gentle, loving Father in Heaven pleading with you to *shube,* or turn back to him—to leave unhappiness, sorrow, regret, and despair behind and turn back to your Father's family, where you can find happiness, joy, and acceptance among his other children?
>
> That is the message of the Old Testament. Prophet after prophet writes of *shube*—that turning back to the Lord, where we can be received with joy and rejoicing. The Old Testament teaches time and again that we must turn from evil and do instead that which is noble and good. This means that we must not only change our ways, we must change our very thoughts, which control our actions.
>
> The concept of *shube* is also found in the New Testament, which was written in Greek. The Greek writers used the Greek word *metaneoeo* to refer to repentance. *Metaneoeo* is a compound word. The first part, *meta-*, is used as a prefix in our English vocabulary. It refers to change. The second part of the word *metaneoeo* . . . can mean . . . the mind, thought, thinking, or spirit—depending on how it is used.
>
> In the context in which *meta-* and *-neoeo* are used in the New Testament, the word *metaneoeo* means a change of mind, thought, or thinking so powerful that it changes one's very way of life. I think the Greek word *metaneoeo* is an excellent synonym for the Hebrew word *shube.* Both words mean thoroughly changing or turning from evil to God and righteousness.[34]

The message of this section of Hebrews, however, does not center on repentance but hinges on the meaning of the noun τελειότης (*teleiotēs*). Its semantic range includes being complete, finished, accomplished, mature, and perfect.[35] Since the author used the word to contrast spiritual babes and adults in the preceding chapter, in the present context, it most likely denotes that maturity of practice, insight, and understanding exhibited by the spiritually advanced Saints among the author's audience. It does not, therefore, nuance directly a state of moral excellence and flawlessness but rather the state of completeness and spiritual maturity that the priestly ministry of the Savior is meant to provide (7:11; 10:14).

---

34. Theodore M. Burton, "The Meaning of Repentance," *Ensign* 18, no. 8 (August 1988): 7–8, italics in original.

35. BDAG, 996; see also Louw-Nida, §1.243, where the semantic range for the verb τελειόω (*teleioō*) and the noun τέλειος (*telieos*) are given.

A connection, however, does exist "between the maturity (τελειότης) that the addressees are urged to attain and the perfection (τελείωσις) that Christ affords."[36] This is exposed in the careful and subtle wordplay of the author. Christian maturity follows the desirable path of leaving behind the "milk" of the gospel and partaking of its "solid food" (NR 5:12, a reference to the doctrines the author is teaching), then yielding to what Christ, as the enthroned High Priest, demands to perfect his people. This perfection is made possible through sanctification by Christ's sacrifice (10:10), which cleanses the faithful, makes their souls righteous, and unites them with the Father.[37]

This means that in mortality there is an unrealized or future dimension to the Saints' blessings which demands that, in the present, they "follow faithfully their forerunner and leader to the perfection of heavenly glory (2:10; 6:20). The mature Christian is expected not only to 'ingest' the solid food but also to follow Christ on the path to final perfection, whatever the cost."[38] Becoming fully mature in the gospel requires continual perseverance to the faith with total reliance upon the Lord.[39] Though salvation and perfection

---

36. Attridge, *Epistle to the Hebrews,* 162–63. The strongest nuance of the noun *teleiōsis,* as found in Hebrews, is that of fulfillment, completion, or, in short, achieving spiritual maturity. In the next chapter, the author will note that such "perfection," or maturity, simply could not come through the Levitical law (7:11). The author's point is not that the Levitical law prevented people from drawing near to God through its performances and ordinances. In fact, it both encouraged and made it possible for them to do so (note 10:1; 11:6). Indeed, there is nothing intrinsically wrong with the old law. The problem is when people do not see it for what it was—a type or shadow anticipating a reality (Mosiah 16:14). That reality is not the antithesis of the shadow but its fulfillment. Fulfillment is what "perfection" denotes—the coming to full maturity through the high priestly work of Christ. Lane, *Hebrews 1–8,* 181. For the author of Hebrews, "perfection is a matter of human transformation rather than cultic transaction. It combines elements of maturity and moral growth (see 5:14)." Johnson, *Hebrews,* 185. The glory and promise of the new law was that it brought in a "better hope," making the process of moral growth and spiritual maturation surer, stronger, and more complete (6:19). Lane, *Hebrews 1–8,* 181. For a study, see Kevin B. McCruden, "The Concept of Perfection in the Epistle to the Hebrews," in Mason and McCruden, *Reading the Epistle to the Hebrews,* 209–29, who concludes that Jesus' perfection was defined in large part by his faithfulness to his Father's will even unto dying. For believers, perfection comes ultimately when they inherit a place in God's presence, having completed their mission. They can, however, reach perfection in mortality when they have experienced deep communion with God, a communion made possible through the sacrifice of the great High Priest, Jesus the Christ.

37. For a study, see Translation Notes with its associated Analysis for 10:10.

38. Attridge, *Epistle to the Hebrews,* 163.

39. David A. deSilva, "Hebrews 6:4–8: A Socio-rhetorical Investigation (Part 1)," *Tyndale Bulletin* 50, no. 1 (1999): 33–57, argues that the author of Hebrews's desire for total

are the destination, as the author stresses, the process that leads to these necessitates the help and power of Christ every step of the way (6:3).

In order to move ahead, the author's readers must get beyond their preoccupation with the basic teachings (6:1–2). Continually relaying these foundational principles as the only necessities for salvation is fruitless because it brings no progression. Instead, his readers must attend to those teachings that are not only for the more mature but that actually produce full maturation. The problem with the fundamentals is not that they are false or even harmful. Indeed, they are the very foundation upon which all else rests. Their problem is that they cannot produce the faith necessary for perseverance because they do not reveal the full necessity of the Savior in the salvation process and what he ultimately requires. Further, they do not emphasize the blessings both in mortality and immortality such faith brings.[40] Therefore, to lay again and again this foundation "is an exercise in futility."[41] It is through the advanced doctrines that an understanding of the indispensable role of the Savior comes. It is through these that one not only becomes spiritually mature but also able to persevere in faith doing all that is necessary until one gains the "perfection" (*teleiōsis*) that only Christ can give.[42]

In sum, the author of Hebrews urges his readers to "go on unto perfection" because they have "tarried too long in the foothills of spiritual experience. Having 'tasted of the heavenly gift, . . . the good word of God, and the powers of the world to come' (Hebrews 6:4–6), they could no longer delay resuming the climb lest they lose the *promise*."[43] The author warns, "Be not slothful, but followers of them who through faith and patience inherit [or, are inheriting] the promises" (6:12). The promises that the author refers to

---

commitment to Jesus and their fellow Saints on the part of his readers was based on the social mores of patronage obligations. In that system, perseverance was not only the just but also the expedient course of action; it alone was the means that met the obligation of gratitude.

40. Cockerill, *Epistle to the Hebrews,* 261–62.

41. Johnson, *Hebrews,* 158.

42. Cockerill, *Epistle to the Hebrews,* 262. Elder Boyd K. Packer taught that "our behavior is not totally controlled by natural impulses. Behavior begins with belief as well. Beliefs are born of philosophies, of doctrines. Doctrines can be spiritual or secular, wholesome or destructive, true or false. . . . True doctrine, understood, changes attitudes and behavior. The study of the doctrines of the gospel will improve behavior quicker than a study of behavior will improve behavior. Preoccupation with unworthy behavior can lead to unworthy behavior. That is why we stress so forcefully the study of the doctrines of the gospel." Boyd K. Packer, "Little Children," *Ensign* 16, no. 11 (November 1986), 17.

43. M. Catherine Thomas, "Hebrews: To Ascend to the Holy Mount," in *Temples of the Ancient World: Ritual and Symbolism,* ed. Donald W. Parry (Salt Lake City: Deseret Book; Provo, Utah: FARMS, 1994), 479, ellipses and italics in original.

are likely reflected in God's promise to the faithful in this our day: "Therefore, sanctify yourselves that your minds become single to God, and the days will come that you shall see him; for he will unveil his face unto you, and it shall be in his own time, and in his own way, and according to his own will. Remember the great and last promise which I have made unto you" (D&C 88:68–69).

The author of Hebrews

> uses several different terms . . . for the experiences associated with this promise: for example, *obtaining a good report* (11:39), *entering into the Lord's rest* (4:3, 10), *going on to perfection* (6:1), *entering into the holiest* (10:19), *being made a high priest forever* (7:17), *knowing the Lord* (8:11; D&C 84:98), *pleasing God* (Hebrews 11:5), *obtaining a witness of being righteous* (11:4), and *having the law written in the heart* (8:10; 10:16; Jeremiah 31:31–34). He speaks of boldly pursuing the fulfillment of the promise: Grasp, he says, the hope that is set before you, which enters behind the veil, where Jesus, as a forerunner, has already entered (see Hebrews 6:18–20, NIV).[44]

The teachings of the author of Hebrews dovetail nicely with those found in the Lectures on Faith that were partially based on Hebrews. According to the lectures, persevering in righteousness and doing all that God commands

> requires more than mere belief, or supposition that he is doing the will of God, but actual knowledge: realizing, that when these sufferings are ended he will enter into eternal rest; and be a partaker of the glory of God.
>
> . . . When he has this knowledge, and most assuredly knows that he is doing the will of God, his confidence can be equally strong that he will be a partaker of the glory of God.
>
> . . . A religion that does not require the sacrifice of all things, never has power sufficient to produce the faith necessary unto life and salvation; for from the first existence of man, the faith necessary unto the enjoyment of life and salvation never could be obtained without the sacrifice of all earthly things: it was through this sacrifice, and this only, that God has ordained that men should enjoy eternal life; and it is through the medium of the sacrifice of all earthly things, that men do actually know that they are doing the things that are well pleasing in the sight of God. When a man has offered in sacrifice all that he has, for the truth's sake, not even withholding his life, and believing before God that he has been called to make this sacrifice, because he seeks to do his will, he does know, most assuredly, that God does and will accept his sacrifice & offering, & that he has

---

44. Thomas, "Hebrews: To Ascend to the Holy Mount," 480, italics in original.

> not nor will not seek his face in vain. Under these circumstances, then, he can obtain the faith necessary for him to lay hold on eternal life.[45]

Herein lie some of the advanced doctrines of the modern kingdom. In Latter-day Saint vernacular, many of these doctrines and practices are referred to as the "mysteries of God" (see, for example, 1 Ne. 2:16; Alma 12:9; and D&C 8:11; 11:7). While the author of Hebrews never uses the term "mystery," Paul does (1 Cor. 4:1; 14:2; Eph. 1:9; Col. 2:2; 1 Tim. 3:16).[46] And though the author does not use the term, it would appear that he is referring to much of the same material. In the New Testament, the Greek word μυστήριον (*mystērion*) describes "that which transcends normal understanding," consisting of those teachings, doctrines, and practices that can only come by revelation.[47] These contain material

> revealed only to the faithful but not given to the "world" or to the uninitiated. (Matt. 13:11; 1 Cor. 2:7; Eph. 3:1–7; 1 Ne. 10:11; D&C 42:61, 65). . . . In latter-day scripture the word "mysteries" typically has three interrelated meanings. First, the mysteries consist of significant truths about God and his works. Second, faithful, obedient members of the Church will be given this sacred knowledge through revelation. Finally, those who are not made partakers of this special understanding will not attain the same glory as those who are. Understanding the mysteries of God is a gospel privilege for the reverent who serve God faithfully (D&C 76:1–10; cf. 1 Ne. 10:17–19; Moses 1:5).[48]

Noteworthy is one additional dimension, namely that the mysteries of godliness are also associated with temple worship. In this inference, we see a connection with a term dear to the author of Hebrews: τελειότης (*teleiotēs*). Though the word carries the meaning of being mature and perfected, it also means "being complete," and the adjective τέλειος (*teleios*) was used to refer to a person who had been initiated into one of the mystery religions.[49] Given that the author is very interested in Old Testament temple worship, there may be an echo of this nuance in his writings.

---

45. "Lecture Sixth. Of Faith," in *Doctrine and Covenants of the Church of the Latter-Day Saints,* comp. Joseph Smith and others (Kirtland, Ohio: F. G. Williams, 1835), 60–61, photoreproduced in Jensen, Turley, and Lorimer, *Revelations and Translations, Volume 2,* 370–71. For discussions of the *Lectures on Faith* and their origin, authorship, and message, see Dahl and Tate, *Lectures on Faith in Historical Perspective.*

46. For a discussion of the use of the word μυστήριον (*mystērion*) by Paul, see Draper and Rhodes, *Paul's First Epistle to the Corinthians,* 147–48, 161–62, 172–73, 229–30.

47. BDAG, 661–62; Bornkamm, *TDNT,* 4:821.

48. Clark D. Webb, "Mysteries of God," in Ludlow, *Encyclopedia of Mormonism,* 2:977.

49. The word in Philip. 3:15 and Col. 1:26–28 was likely used in that same sense. BDAG, 995–96.

The Peril of Falling Away (6:4–8)

Greek Text

4 Ἀδύνατον γὰρ τοὺς ἅπαξ φωτισθέντας γευσαμένους τε τῆς δωρεᾶς τῆς ἐπουρανίου καὶ μετόχους γενηθέντας πνεύματος ἁγίου 5 καὶ καλὸν γευσαμένους θεοῦ ῥῆμα δυνάμεις τε μέλλοντος αἰῶνος, 6 καὶ παραπεσόντας, πάλιν ἀνακαινίζειν εἰς μετάνοιαν, ἀνασταυροῦντας ἑαυτοῖς τὸν υἱὸν τοῦ θεοῦ καὶ παραδειγματίζοντας. 7 γῆ γὰρ ἡ πιοῦσα τὸν ἐπ' αὐτῆς ἐρχόμενον πολλάκις ὑετόν, καὶ τίκτουσα βοτάνην εὔθετο ν ἐκείνοις δι' οὓς καὶ γεωργεῖται, μεταλαμβάνει εὐλογίας ἀπὸ τοῦ θεοῦ· 8 ἐκφέρουσα δὲ ἀκάνθας καὶ τριβόλους ἀδόκιμος καὶ κατάρας ἐγγύς, ἧς τὸ τέλος εἰς καῦσιν. [SBLGNT]

King James Version

4 For it is impossible for those who were once enlightened, and have tasted of the heavenly gift, and were made partakers of the Holy Ghost, 5 And have tasted the good word of God, and the powers of the world to come, 6 If they shall fall away, to renew them again unto repentance; seeing they crucify to themselves the Son of God afresh, and put him to an open shame. 7 For the earth which drinketh in the rain that cometh oft upon it, and bringeth forth herbs meet for them by whom it is dressed, receiveth blessing from God: 8 But that which beareth thorns and briers is rejected, and is nigh unto cursing; whose end is to be burned.

New Rendition

4 Now it is impossible, concerning those who have once been enlightened, who have tasted the heavenly gift, who have become partakers of the Holy Ghost, 5 and who have tasted the good word of God and the wonders of the world to come, 6 if they should fall into apostasy, to restore them again to repentance. Because they crucify the Son of God again for themselves and hold him up to contempt. 7 For if soil soaks up the rain that often falls upon it and produces useful vegetation for those on whose account the land is tilled, it receives a blessing from God. 8 But if it produces thorns and thistles, it is worthless and is going to be cursed. In the end it will be burned.

Translation Notes and Comments

6:4–8 These verses consist of one long sentence composed of five clauses each governed by a participle. For ease of reading and understanding, we have broken these clauses down into sentences and have translated the participles as finite verbs in our Rendition. The last two clauses, describing what the postapostate life consists of (recrucifying the Savior and holding him in contempt), use present active participles. Some construe these as temporal, thus giving the two clauses the sense of "so long as they are recrucifying the Lord and holding him contempt," they cannot be "renewed to repentance."[50] According to Restoration scriptures, however, such a construal is incorrect. D&C 76:35–37 states that these people, "having denied the Holy Spirit after having received it, and having denied the Only Begotten Son of the Father, having crucified him unto themselves and put him to an open shame, . . . are they who shall go away into the lake of fire and brimstone, with the devil and his angels—And the only ones on whom the second death shall have any power." Taking this into account, the Rendition construes the participles as causal. These people cannot be moved to repentance *because* of the deeds they have done and are continually doing and *because* God is not willing to make an exception for them. They will come under the firm hand of justice. Though this gives a very harsh cast to the author's message, mollifying the text does a disservice because doing so would soften the eschatological magnitude of what these souls reject and the seriousness of their sin. Our Rendition, then, follows both the feel of the Greek text and current doctrine.[51]

6:4 *For it is impossible for those who were once enlightened / Now it is impossible, concerning those who have once been enlightened:* The adjective ἀδύνατος (*adynatos*) denotes that which is absolutely incapable of happening: "impossible."[52] In 6:6, the author will clarify exactly what is impossible.

The adverb ἅπαξ (*hapax*), "once," plays a key role here because it sets down the rules. Once an event has taken place, there is no going back, no undoing of what has been done. Thus, the word carries the force of finality.[53]

The verb φοτίζω (*phōtizō*), "to enlighten,"[54] found here in the form of a passive participle, refers to that which is fully known due to its being revealed clearly and completely. The noun φῶς (*phōs*), "light," connotes

50. For discussion, see Bruce, *Epistle to the Hebrews,* 149.

51. See the arrangement in Vanhoye, *Letter to the Hebrews,* 108. McConkie, *Doctrinal New Testament Commentary,* 3:160–62, devotes space not to an analysis of the text but to a discussion on Lucifer and the sons of perdition. Though it is possible the author of Hebrews was using the rhetorical strategy δείνωσις (*deinōsis*), "exaggeration," to get the audience's attention, both the context and Restoration scriptures suggest that is not the case. The author's views did not, however, unite the early Christians to just one stance on repentance. For example, the Shepherd of Hermas states that repentance is only possible once for a grievous sin committed after baptism (6:4–5; 30:2–31:7; 61–63; 103:6).

52. BDAG, 22.

53. See BDAG, 97, where the word is translated "once and for all"; see also Johnson, *Hebrews,* 162; and Stählin, *TDNT,* 1:382.

54. BDAG, 1074; Louw-Nida, §28.36. Some early authorities associated enlightenment with baptism (see Ellingworth, *Epistle to the Hebrews,* 319), but these reflect an

first, the force that both reveals knowledge of transcendent matters, and second, the power that touches and transforms the inner life of the soul. Its source is divine.[55] Since the author uses a divine passive (in which God's action is hidden behind the passive voice),[56] it suggests the operation of the Father or Son in bringing the soul to enlightenment.

The JST makes an important change to this phrase: "for *he* hath made it impossible" (italics added to show change). The pronoun refers to Deity. In making the change, the text points to conditions laid down by God that preclude certain acts from being pardoned.[57]

have tasted of the heavenly gift / who have tasted the heavenly gift: The verb γεύομαι (*geuomai*), "to taste," metaphorically refers to experiencing something cognitively or emotionally.[58] The emphasis is on the deep and personal nature of the experience.[59]

Though the author does not define what he means by the phrase τῆς δωρεᾶς τῆς ἐπουρανίου (*tēs dōreas tēs epouraniou*), "the heavenly gift," context suggests it is the "great salvation" (2:3), that is, the redemption that comes through the Lord.[60]

made partakers of the Holy Ghost / become partakers of the Holy Ghost: The nominalized adjective μέτοχος (*metochos*), "partaker," carries the meanings of both having companionship with and participating in. The latter nuance dominates here suggesting partaking of the blessings of the Spirit.[61]

---

understanding from the second and third century rather than the first. See Cockerill, *Epistle to the Hebrews,* 269 n. 4.

55. *NID,* s.v. "φῶς," notes that *phōs,* "light," very early in Greek literature, became associated with the sphere of ethical good and moral understanding. As a power, it played a role in the redemption of the sinner. The Old Testament makes it an attribute of Jehovah and a visible sign of his presence and of deliverance. In the New Testament, Jesus is the light and uses this power to transform men and women into the children of God (John 1:5, 9; 8:12; 9:5; 12:46). The person, however, must open his or her heart in order to partake of this transforming and saving power. See Alma 19:6 for the role light played in the conversion of Lamoni. For an extended study, see Conzelmann, *TDNT,* 9:310–58; and from a Latter-day Saint perspective, Draper, "Light, Truth, and Grace," 234–47.

56. Wallace, *Greek Grammar,* 437–38.

57. Bailey, "Message of Judgment," 20. Callister, *Infinite Atonement,* 98–100, notes that the impossibility of the sons of perdition being redeemed is not a deficiency in the Atonement but a result of the fact that these people have deliberately rejected it.

58. BDAG, 195.

59. Louw-Nida, §90.78; Ellingworth, *Epistle to the Hebrews,* 320; Lane, *Hebrews 1–8,* 141.

60. Given the brevity of the reference, care must be taken to not get too specific. Lane, *Hebrews 1–8,* 141; Attridge, *Epistle to the Hebrews,* 170, and n. 51.

61. BDAG, 643; Ellingworth, *Epistle to the Hebrews,* 321; Koester, *Hebrews,* 314; Bruce, *Epistle to the Hebrews,* 146.

6:5 have tasted the good word of God / who have tasted the good word of God: On the verb "taste," see 6:4 above. The phrase καλὸν . . . θεοῦ ῥῆμα (*kalon . . . theou rhēma*), "good word of God," likely refers to the content of the gospel and particularly the witness of salvation through Christ Jesus. That adjective καλός (*kalos*), "good," being placed at the front of the sentence (just after the connective καί, *kai*) stresses the quality of the Father's word. The adjective denotes what is beautiful and pleasing and more particularly useful.[62] That the author used the noun ῥῆμα (*rhema*),"word," here rather than his usual *logos* (see 2:2; 4:2, 12; 5:13) means little since both refer to the living word of God.[63]

The idea of the living word is particularly at play here, since the "good word" brings with it the great temporal and spiritual blessings that are so useful in acquiring eternal life.

the powers of the world to come / the wonders of the world to come: The noun δύναμις (*dynamis*), "power," in this context, looks to the capabilities of those who are exalted.[64] In mortality, one gets a taste of this power through at least two means: first, by possessing and exercising spiritual gifts, and second, by performing operations through the authority of the priesthood.

6:6 If they shall fall away / if they should fall into apostasy: The verb παραπίπτω (*parapiptō*), literally "to fall beside," which is only found once in the New Testament in this passage, has the sense "to fail to follow through on a commitment, fall away, commit apostasy."[65] The force of the word is on the extent of the moving away; that is, it suggests a total break from the relationship. In a religious context, what the individual breaks is likely the covenantal bond with the Lord.[66] *Parapiptō* can, therefore, be translated as "fall into apostasy."[67] Its form here as an aorist participle

---

62. BDAG, 504–5; Louw-Nida, §§65.43; 79.9; 88.4. Καλός (*kalos*) stands in contrast to ἀγαθός (*agathos*), "good," in that the latter does not carry the nuance of benefaction or usefulness. See Louw-Nida, §§65.20; 88.1.

63. Attridge, *Epistle to the Hebrews,* 170; Ellingworth, *Epistle to the Hebrews,* 321. Philo used the words as synonyms in *Fug.* 137; *Leg.* 3.169, 174–75.

64. BDAG, 262–63.

65. Louw-Nida, §34.26.

66. BDAG, 770. In the LXX, the verb παραπίπτω (*parapiptō*) and the related noun παράπτωμα (*paraptōma*) are used as translations for the words related to the verb מָעַל (*ma'al*), "to be untrue, violate one's legal obligations," in the Hebrew Bible. HAL, 612–13; see also LXX Ezek. 14:13; 15:8; 18:24; 20:27; *TWOT,* 1230.

67. BDAG, 770.

reinforces the idea of the completeness of the apostasy with its sundering of all connections with the Father and Son.[68]

to renew them again unto repentance / to restore them again to repentance: With this phrase, the author finally notes what it is that is impossible for a once-enlightened person to be. The verb ἀνακαινίζω (*anakainizō*) means "to restore" in the sense of returning something to a previous state. On the noun μετάνοια (*metanoia*), "repentance," see 6:1 above. Here, with the use of the preposition εἰς (*eis*), "to, into," it connotes entering into a state of rightness with God.[69]

The way the author constructs this section leaves open the question, For whom is it impossible to make restoration to repentance? There are three possibilities. First, it could refer to members or leaders in the congregation who simply lack the power or influence to repent. Second, it could refer to God's unwillingness to forgive the recalcitrant and rebellious soul. Admittedly, the Father has the ability to forgive any and all, but he has made it clear that he will forgive whom and only whom he chooses (D&C 64:10; compare Rom. 9:18; and D&C 56:14). For example, the wilderness generation so provoked him that he barred them from entrance into the Holy Land (3:7–4:13). Further, Esau, having sold his birthright, though his remorse was great, found that God would not allow the birthright to be restored (12:17). So too those who abuse the Son will find the Father barring heaven against them. Third, this section could refer to the person himself who has become hate filled and hardened to the point where repentance is impossible. The continual rebellion and hard-heartedness of the wilderness generation cost them entrance into the Holy Land. Under no circumstances would they yield to God. It is the same with those whom the author has in mind. Their hard-heartedness will not allow them under any circumstance to accept any divine help. It is the definitiveness of their rejection that makes repentance impossible. By repudiating the Lord, they

68. Cockerill, *Epistle to the Hebrews,* 274–75.

69. As a marker of a goal involving an affective aspect, the word connotes an entry into a state of being, in this case righteousness. BDAG, 290. This idea has generated a good deal of scholarly discussion. See, for example, D. Barnhart, "The Life of No Retreat: An Exegetical Study of Hebrews 6:1–12," *Central Biblical Quarterly* 19 (1976): 16–31; P. E. Hughes, "Hebrews 6:4–6 and the Peril of Apostasy," *Westminster Theological Journal* 35 (Winter 1973): 137–55; and I. H. Marshall, "The Problem of Apostasy in New Testament Theology," *Perspectives in Religious Studies* 14, no. 4 (1987): 65–80. For a summary, see Koester, *Hebrews,* 319–23. For a Latter-day Saint view, see "Excursus on Unforgivable and Unpardonable Sins" below.

have rejected his plan. Since there is no other means or way to salvation—and reliance and unity with Christ are demanded—repentance is impossible for these souls.[70] Though the second and third possibilities both have merit, insights from the Restoration suggest it is the latter of these two that best fits. For discussion, see "Excursus on Unforgivable and Unpardonable Sins" below.[71]

seeing they crucify to themselves the Son of God afresh / Because they crucify the Son of God again for themselves: With this awful imagery, the author begins to present the conditions that exclude an apostate from repentance. The verb ἀνασταυρόω (*anastauroō*), "to crucify again,"[72] refers to one of the most cruel and sadistic means of death devised by sick minds.[73] Crucifixion was a method that combined maximum pain with the greatest duration of time. Further, because the victims were generally displayed naked to the public, it was also humiliating. Since the Romans usually restricted this form of execution to the most severe crimes against the state, crucifixion carried an additional weight of ignominy.[74]

---

70. For discussion, see Koester, *Hebrews,* 312–13; Lane, *Hebrews 1–8,* 142; Attridge, *Epistle to the Hebrews,* 169; and Cockerill, *Epistle to the Hebrews,* 275. J. Reuben Clark, "I Am the Resurrection and the Life," *Improvement Era* 46 (January 1943): 63, noted that all who deny Christ *after* they have received the light are open to the full condemnation allotted by the scriptures. Right from the beginning, God made it clear that only through his Son's name, which is "the only name which shall be given under heaven, salvation shall come unto the children of men" (Moses 6:52; compare Mosiah 5:8–10).

71. Whether or not a person could be forgiven of serious postbaptismal sins was a major point of contention between the western and eastern Christian churches and was also one of the reasons the western church was not fond of Hebrews. For a synopsis, see David Brattston, "The Forgiveness of Post-baptismal Sin in Ancient Christianity," *Churchman* 105, no. 4 (1991): 332–49, accessed August 10, 2016, https://biblicalstudies.org.uk/pdf/churchman/105-04_332.pdf.

72. The noun σταυρός (*stauros*) denotes a stake or cross used for execution. BDAG, 941. The verb form is σταυρόω (*stauroō*). Here, however, the author uses the unique verb ἀνασταυρόω (*anastauroō*). BDAG, 72. The prefix ἀνά (*ana*) originally referred to an upward direction and therefore could give the verb the nuance of one being lifted up on a cross. BDAG, 57. Some ancient and modern commentators, however, see the word as meaning "again." See Origin, *Fr. Jo.* 20.12; Chrysostom, in *PG,* 63:79; and BDAG, 72; for discussion, see Ellingworth, *Epistle to the Hebrews,* 324; and Cockerill, *Epistle to the Hebrews,* 274.

73. Cicero, *Verr.* 2.5.165, 168, referred to crucifixion as the *summum supplicium,* "most extreme," form of punishment. The top three, in order of increased severity, were beheading, burning, and crucifixion.

74. For discussion, see Gerald G. O'Collins, "Crucifixion," in Freedman, *Anchor Bible Dictionary,* 1:1207–10.

The depth of these people's apostasy is shown in that they figuratively put to death the Savior ἑαυτοῖς (*heautois*), "for themselves." Their act is personal. They crucify him by rejecting all that he is and stands for, the "equivalent to participating in his state execution."[75] Thereby, they stand shoulder to shoulder with those who did the actual deed. And more. Along with their guilty companions, they seek to destroy the effect of all he did and stands for.

and put him to an open shame / and hold him up to contempt: The verb παραδειγματίζω (*paradeigmatizō*) denotes disgracing someone publicly. In the present context, it also carries the added weight of holding someone in contempt not just due to a lack of respect but because of the disdain in which one person holds another.[76] The force of the verb is on the openness and public nature of these people's opposition to the Lord. They are recruiters to their cause.

6:7 ***For the earth which drinketh in the rain that cometh oft upon it / For if soil soaks up the rain that often falls upon it:*** To drive his point home, the author uses an example from nature and agriculture. The noun γῆ (*gē*), literally "earth, soil," given the context of this and the next verse, looks to an area of land rather than the whole globe as the example the author wishes to focus on.[77] The verb πίνω (*pinō*) denotes taking in any liquid and means both to "drink" and to "soak up."[78] Figuratively, these images represent the downpouring of God's Spirit upon the individual.

and bringeth forth herbs meet for them by whom it is dressed / and produces useful vegetation for those on whose account the land is tilled: The verb τίκτω (*tiktō*) means to bring something into the world, hence, "to produce."[79] The adjective εὔθετος (*euthetos*) means "fit" or "useful" and, when modifying βοτάνη (*botanē*), "plant, vegetation,"[80] looks to items that are edible for both humans and animals.[81] The verb γεωργέω (*geōrgeō*) means "to till, cultivate,"[82] and the whole phrase looks to a bountiful harvest from field, garden, orchard, and vineyard.

75. Johnson, *Hebrews,* 161; see also Ogden and Skinner, *Verse by Verse,* 250.
76. BDAG, 761.
77. Ellingworth, *Epistle to the Hebrews,* 326.
78. BDAG, 814.
79. BDAG, 1004.
80. Louw-Nida, §3.14; BDAG, 181.
81. Ellingworth, *Epistle to the Hebrews,* 327.
82. BDAG, 195.

receiveth blessing from God / it receives a blessing from God: The noun εὐλογία (*eulogia*), "blessing," carries the nuance of a bounteous gift. The idea of this phrase is that by doing as it was designed, the field "receives rich blessing from God," with emphasis on the blessing's abundance.[83]

This verse contains a number of significant modifications in the JST. First, the intent changes from a parable to a statement about the Second Coming and the state of those dwelling on the earth at that time, looking to "the day that cometh" when the earth will bring forth plenty for all "who dwelleth thereon." Further, those who at that point in time bask in God's blessings "shall be cleansed by fire."

6:8 *But that which beareth thorns and briers is rejected / But if it produces thorns and thistles, it is worthless:* On "produce," see 6:7 above. The nouns ἄκανθα (*akantha*), "a thorny plant,"[84] and τρίβολος (*tribolos*), "a thistle,"[85] stand in contrast to the βοτάνη εὔθετος (*botanē euthetos*), "useful edible plants," referred to above. The author's image is not of weeds in general but those that, due to their spines and thorns, offer the greatest threat to removal. Since they provide no sustenance, they are ἀδόκιμος (*adokimos*), "worthless."[86]

Again the JST refocuses this verse as it did the one above by changing the thrust from a parable to a statement about the last days, stating, "they who bring not forth good fruits, shall be cast into the fire." Note that while the righteous in 6:7 are "cleansed by fire," the wicked in this verse are destroyed by it.

and is nigh unto cursing / and is going to be cursed: The phrase here is very compact: καὶ κατάρας ἐγγύς (*kai kataras engus*), literally "and [is] close to a curse." Its thrust points to the sureness of what will happen to the field because it received rain in abundance but did not produce what it was tilled for. The noun κατάρα (*katara*) denotes "a curse" and carries the idea of a destruction that cannot be avoided.[87] The opposite of blessings,

83. BDAG, 408–9.

84. BDAG, 34.

85. BDAG, 1015.

86. BDAG, 21. Compare Ogden and Skinner, *Verse by Verse,* 250–51. The author of Hebrews uses generic terms, so the exact plants he has in mind, if any, are unknown. See Gen. 3:18, where Elohim uses the phrase to describe some of the earthly conditions Adam and Eve will face. See also Matt. 7:16.

87. Many in the Greco-Roman world continued to be influenced by an ancient belief that the words of a curse (ἀρά, *ara*) took on an intrinsic and independent power once released by an imprecation. Thus, words of malediction were seen as more than mere wishes but as operative powers that continued to work until their energy was spent. *NID,*

cursings were an inherent part of the covenant concept and common to various settings in the biblical world.

whose end is to be burned / In the end it will be burned: The noun καῦσις (*kausis*), literally "burning,"[88] denotes the effect of the curse referred to in the previous phrase. The clause has only an implied verb, which, due to the force of the earlier phrase, we cast as a future prophetic tense, "will be," in our Rendition.

Analysis and Summary

The author's forceful use of the laden words "to fall away, commit apostasy" (παραπίπτω, *parapiptō*)[89] gives a shocking description of what these once fully and thoroughly converted persons have done (6:6). Theirs is not a matter of faults or errors but of deliberate abandonment of principles and covenants, a willful walking away from the gifts and powers of the Spirit they once enjoyed.[90]

According to the text, in order to belong to this group, these souls must meet certain criteria (6:4–5). First, they must have been enlightened (φοτίζω, *phōtizō*)—that is, have had a very clear and inspired understanding of the gospel. Second, they must have tasted (γεύομαι, *geuomai*) of the heavenly gift—that is, they have personally felt the promise of the redemption that comes through the Lord. Third, they must have personally partaken of the powers of the Holy Spirit—that is, they have had spiritual gifts manifest in their lives. Fourth, they must have tasted the good word of God—that is, they have an understanding of the content of the gospel and particularly the witness of salvation through Christ Jesus. They also must know personally of the gospel's usefulness. And fifth, they must have tasted of the powers of the world to come—that is, they have possessed and used the gifts of the Spirit and performed operations through the authority of the priesthood.

The aorist tense of the participle translated as "to fall away" (παραπίπτω, *parapiptō*), as found here, gives an important insight. These apostates are

---

s.v. "ἀρά." Among the Jews, the words themselves did not have independent force but, when expressed in a religious context, exposed the intent of the Divine. Usually, once pronounced, divine curses were irrevocable unless Jehovah intervened (usually because some condition had been met). For discussion, see Büchel, *TDNT,* 1:449–51; and Scharbert, *TDOT,* 13:37–44.

88. BDAG, 536.

89. BDAG, 770.

90. Johnson, *Hebrews,* 161; compare Holzapfel and Wayment, *Making Sense,* 453–54.

not rejecting mere instruction (λόγος, *logos*) but actual experience: "They *were* once for all enlightened, they *did* taste, they *had* been made partakers! The 'falling away' is not from an external teaching but from the experience that the [readers] have themselves had."[91] There is an important lesson here: deep and sure spiritual experiences are no guarantee against failure. Having experienced all that they did, certain Hebrew brethren still fell into apostasy (6:6). Brigham Young explained:

> Is there a reason for men and women being exposed more constantly and more powerfully, to the power of the enemy, by having visions than by not having them? There is and it is simply this—God never bestows upon his people, or upon an individual, superior blessings without a severe trial to prove them, to prove that individual, or that people, to see whether they will keep their covenants with him, and keep in remembrance what he has shown them. Then the greater the vision, the greater the display of the power of the enemy. . . . So when individuals are blessed with visions, revelations, and great manifestations, look out, then the Devil is nigh you, and you will be tempted in proportion to the vision, revelation, or manifestation you have received.[92]

In the activities of the apostate life, we see expressed the full depth of the rancor these people feel (6:6). First, they recrucify (ἀνασταυρόω, *anastauroō*) Christ for themselves (ἑαυτοῖς, *eautois*); that is, they work to the same ends the original perpetrators did—to secure personal station and gain. Second, due to their despiteful disposition toward him, they hold the Savior publicly in contempt (παραδειγματίζω, *paradeigmatizō*). They have come to believe that he has no value and that his life and teachings are worthless. The prophet Nephi knew that "there are many that harden their hearts against the Holy Spirit, that it hath no place in them; wherefore, they cast many things away which are written and esteem them as things of naught" (2 Ne. 33:2). The effect is spiritual blindness that, according to the prophet Jacob, "came by looking beyond the mark" (Jacob 4:14). In other words, these people either hoped to find salvation in something beyond Christ or rejected the idea of salvation altogether.[93] The result is that "they must needs fall; for God hath taken away his plainness from them" (Jacob 4:14). This point is arresting. Due to their determined recalcitrance, the Lord removes

---

91. Johnson, *Hebrews,* 162, italics in original.

92. Brigham Young, in *Journal of Discourses,* 3:205–6.

93. For examples, see the teachings of Sherem (Jacob 7:1–9), Nehor (Alma 1:1–4), and Korihor (Alma 30:12–18).

his spirit, and they can no longer see what, to the faithful, is evident and clear. Thus, as Isaiah witnessed, "They have not known nor understood: for he [God] hath shut their eyes, that they cannot see; and their hearts, that they cannot understand" (Isa. 44:18). Being spiritually blind, these souls work actively, forcefully, and openly against the Savior and his Church, driven by a deep but false belief that they can destroy his work.

There is another revealing and telling aspect of their rebellion brought out by the grammar in Hebrews. In the text, the words "recrucify" (*anastauroō*) and "hold in contempt" (*paradeigmatizō*) are both present active participles. The tense shows the postapostate life consists of a continual recrucifying of the Savior coupled with an incessant and public contempt of him. These souls never rest. They continually work against the Master's cause. However, since he is essentially unreachable and so cannot be stopped or even hurt directly, they spend their time working against his Church and his people. Being so driven, apostates are unable to either seek repentance or want it.[94] In addition, the Holy Spirit will no longer strive with them to assist them to repent. As a result, "it is impossible for those who were once enlightened" to repent (6:4).[95]

The author wisely chose to use the third-person plural "they" so as not to accuse his readers of so serious an evil. Even so, his is a strong warning for them not to fall into such a damnable condition. His requirements needed to make such a dramatic fall reveal the depth of these once-converted souls and the profundity of their willful acts of not only abandoning but also spurning the Lord.

To make his point, the author uses a parable drawn from agriculture (6:7–8). He uses the image of a field to symbolize the person, an abundant and beneficial downpour of rain to symbolize the richness of Spirit the person enjoyed, the production of edible plants as a symbol of the proper response to this gift, and noxious weeds for an improper response. The result of a proper response—the use of spiritual strength to nourish others—brings additional blessings from God. On the other hand, an improper response—the production of noxious attitudes and spiritually harmful activities—brings a cursing that eventually expresses itself as a fiery destruction.[96]

---

94. Cockerill, *Epistle to the Hebrews*, 276.

95. See James A. Cullimore, "The Importance of a Personal Testimony," *Ensign* 2, no. 7 (July 1972): 57.

96. See Vanhoye, *Letter to the Hebrews*, 112; compare D&C 104:3.

The Nephite prophet Jacob stands as a second witness to this teaching. To those among his own people who have tasted of the good word of life, Jacob asks,

> Today, if ye will hear [God's] voice, harden not your hearts; for why will ye die? For behold, after ye have been nourished by the good word of God all the day long, will ye bring forth evil fruit, that ye must be hewn down and cast into the fire? Behold, will ye reject these words? Will ye reject the words of the prophets; and will ye reject all the words which have been spoken concerning Christ, after so many have spoken concerning him; and deny the good word of Christ, and the power of God, and the gift of the Holy Ghost, and quench the Holy Spirit, and make a mock of the great plan of redemption, which hath been laid for you? (Jacob 6:6–8)

For those who do so, Jacob witnesses, "According to the power of justice, for justice cannot be denied, ye must go away into that lake of fire and brimstone, whose flames are unquenchable, and whose smoke ascendeth up forever and ever, which lake of fire and brimstone is endless torment" (Jacob 6:10).

There is an important lesson here.[97] Some sins are more than a yielding to weakness or inadequacy. There are some that are simply a strong and abiding refusal to do right and a rejection of Jesus and his Atonement. These kinds of sin comes from partaking of the effects of true spiritual conversion and then rejecting them and their source. Therefore, further conversion is no longer possible since the ground of that conversion has been rejected.[98]

---

97. See Bruce, *Epistle to the Hebrews,* 147–49.
98. Johnson, *Hebrews,* 163.

Excursus on Unforgivable and Unpardonable Sins[99]

Are there sins that are not covered by the Atonement? That is a question raised when the author of Hebrews states that there is a certain group of people who being "once enlightened, . . . if they shall fall away" cannot be renewed "again unto repentance" (6:4, 6). The question is particularly acute since a cursory reading may suggest that anyone who felt the influence of the Holy Ghost or had a semblance of a testimony could not repent if they decided to leave the Church. Doubtlessly such feelings would cause heartache for someone who sees a loved one stray from the true principles of the gospel. However, it is clear that many people who have left the Church or who have even been excommunicated have successfully repented and been brought back into full fellowship. Clearly, whatever sins the author of Hebrews is referencing, it must be something extremely serious.

The Book of Mormon and the Doctrine and Covenants offer some additional insight into what makes a sin so bad that those who commit it cannot be renewed "again unto repentance," or in other words, what makes a sin unforgivable.[100] According to these texts, there are two sins that fall into this category, namely murder and blasphemy against the Holy Ghost. Concerning the former, the scripture states, "He that kills shall not have forgiveness in this world, nor in the world to come" (D&C 42:18). Likewise, those who commit blasphemy against the Holy Ghost, the scripture states, "shall not be forgiven in the world nor out of the world" (D&C 132:27). It seems fairly explicit from these verses that both murder and blasphemy carry the same penalty, namely being unforgiveable.

There have been attempts to differentiate between an "unpardonable" and an "unforgiveable" sin. This appears to be influenced by the Book of Mormon where only blasphemy against the Holy Ghost, not murder, is stated to be "unpardonable" (Jacob 7:19; Alma 39:6). This distinction between unforgivable and unpardonable sins is used to explain why some murderers can receive full redemption, some only an inheritance in the

99. Much of this essay was taken from an unpublished paper by Nathaniel Pribil, in possession of the authors.

100. While there may be a different nuance between an unpardonable and an unforgiveable sin, for the purposes of brevity and consistency, the sin(s) for which there is no repentance are here referred to as unforgiveable.

telestial kingdom, and some the full weight of the eternally damned.[101] Tension arises because the Doctrine and Covenants, as noted above, spells out the same penalty for both murder and blasphemy against the Holy Ghost.

The distinction between unforgivable and unpardonable sins is artificial since there is no mention of a sin being unpardonable in the Doctrine and Covenants, and likewise there is no unforgivable sin mentioned in the Book of Mormon. Both terms seem to point to the same idea, that some sins simply cannot be forgiven. But which ones? Murder is definitely included but, it need be emphasized, only on certain conditions. Alma 39:6 explains that while forgiveness for murder is not easily obtained, it does not preclude the possibility of full forgiveness. In addition, scriptures listing sins for which repentance is granted include murder (Alma 54:7; Hel. 8:26; 3 Ne. 30:2). One particular example in the Book of Mormon is that of the people of Anti-Nephi-Lehi who repented of the murders they had committed and received full pardon (Alma 24:10–16). To be sure, their repentance was very difficult and required a lot from these people, but forgiveness did come.

We conclude, therefore, that there must be a difference in the kind of murder noted in the Book of Mormon and the one condemned in the Doctrine and Covenants. The difference is the amount of light and knowledge received by the one committing the murder. Orson Pratt explained this distinction:

> If two persons were each to commit a murder—shed innocent blood—and one had a full knowledge of the revealed law of God, and the other was in entire ignorance of it, there would be a distinction in judging these two characters. We would say at once that he who had sinned against knowledge should receive a heavier punishment than he who had not this knowledge. Suppose that Saints, who have not only heard the law of God, but have embraced the Gospel of the Son of God, have been renewed in their minds by the power of the Holy Ghost and have tasted the good word of God and the powers of the world to come, should be so far overcome as to shed innocent blood, would there be any forgiveness for them? Not at all. . . . Such a person commits the unpardonable sin.[102]

---

101. These are the sons of perdition. For a study of these sins, see H. Dean Garrett, "The Three Most Abominable Sins," in *The Book of Mormon: Alma, the Testimony of the Word,* ed. Monte S. Nyman and Charles D. Tate Jr. (Provo, Utah: Religious Studies Center, Brigham Young University, 1992), 157–71.

102. Orson Pratt, in *Journal of Discourses,* 15:314–15.

This explains why the Anti-Nephi-Lehites found forgiveness. They were ignorant of the will and law of God before their conversion. Likewise, the other scriptures that demand repentance for murder appear to be applicable to individuals who also lacked full knowledge of God's will. In fact, it seems that forgiveness is only impossible for those who are members of the Church and attain unto a certain spiritual height. It's safe to say that the vast majority of murderers do not meet the qualifications for becoming sons of perdition. Yet some do. But before we can determine which ones qualify and which do not, we must explore another concept.

There is one sin that whoever commits it will find no forgiveness ever. The Savior stated that "all sins shall be forgiven unto the sons of men, and blasphemies wherewith soever they shall blaspheme: But he that shall blaspheme against the Holy Ghost hath never forgiveness" (Mark 3:28–29). In the Book of Mormon, Alma states that "once [the Holy Ghost] has had place in you, and ye know that ye deny it, behold, this is a sin which is unpardonable" (Alma 39:6). Neither of these scriptures details just what it means to deny or blaspheme against the Holy Ghost. Fortunately, Joseph Smith explained: "What must a man do to commit the unpardonable sin? He must receive the Holy Ghost, [and] have the heavens opened unto him, and know God, and then sin against Him; . . . He has got to say that the sun does not shine while he sees it—he has got to deny Jesus Christ when the heavens have been opened unto him, and to deny the plan of salvation with his eyes open to the truth of it."[103]

Further, in D&C 76:31, the Lord describes the sons of perdition as those who "know my power, and have been made partakers thereof, and suffered themselves through the power of the devil to be overcome, and to deny the truth and defy my power." Furthermore, D&C 84:41 explains that "whoso breaketh this [oath and covenant of the priesthood] after he hath received it, and altogether turneth therefrom, shall not have forgiveness of sins in this world nor in the world to come."

Given these criteria, it becomes clear that few apostates from the church could qualify as sons of perdition. They simply have never had the high level of knowledge that such requires. As Brigham Young put it, "How much does it take to prepare a man, or woman, or any being, to become angels to the devil, to suffer with him to all eternity? Just as much as it does to prepare a man to go into the celestial kingdom."[104] It appears that one

---

103. "History, 1838–1856, Volume E-1," 1976.
104. Brigham Young, in *Journal of Discourses,* 3:93.

must deliberately and consciously choose to sin against the Savior and reject him completely with full knowledge of what he or she is doing.

This is where the sin of murder comes in. D&C 132:27 states, "The blasphemy against the Holy Ghost, which shall not be forgiven in the world nor out of the world, is in that ye commit murder wherein ye shed innocent blood, and assent unto my death, after ye have received my new and everlasting covenant, saith the Lord God."[105] It would appear that in this context "innocent blood" refers to the Savior's blood. "To shed his innocent blood is to 'assent unto [his] death' and is 'blasphemy against the Holy Ghost.'"[106]

The passage in the Doctrine and Covenants could then mean that, after entering into the new and everlasting covenant, if a person has become so fallen as to agree with the murder of the Savior, he or she commits spiritual murder. However, given the penalties for murder in the Doctrine and Covenants, it also seems likely that after one has received all the ordinances of the gospel, culminating in the marriage covenant, and then has the spiritual blackness to commit premeditated murder, then that one has sinned so far against the light and knowledge received that redemption is also impossible.

This idea is corroborated by Joseph Smith's description of those who commit the unpardonable sin. He stated, "When a man begins to be an enemy to this work, he hunts me—he seeks to kill me, and never ceases to thirst for my blood. He gets the spirit of the devil—the same spirit that they had who crucified the Lord of life—the same spirit that sins against the Holy Ghost."[107] So it seems that, whether or not a murder is actually committed, the sin considered blasphemy against the Holy Ghost and shedding innocent blood is to desire and seek the death of God's chosen vessels.

For such wanton and willful sins, there is no forgiveness. Joseph Smith explained why. He set his explanation in the context of the contention among certain other Christians concerning the effects of grace. Some

---

105. The scriptures give the term "innocent blood" rather broad meaning. It is used in the Book of Mormon "in reference to Abinadi (Mosiah 17:10), king Lamoni (Alma 20:18–19), and the believing women and children of Ammonihah (Alma 14:11)" and "might be thought of as the blood of those persons without guile, or of little ones who have not sinned." In some scriptural contexts, to shed innocent blood simply means to take life unjustly or against God's will (for example, Deut. 19:10–13; 1 Kgs. 2:31; Jer. 22:3). The D&C refers to the "innocent blood" of Joseph and Hyrum Smith with the same meaning (D&C 135:4, 7; 136:36). Largey, *Book of Mormon Reference Companion,* 339.

106. Largey, *Book of Mormon Reference Companion,* 339.

107. "History, 1838–1856, Volume E-1," 1976.

contended that once a person had partaken of God's grace and fallen away, they could never be restored to it. Others contended that one could have grace at one point in time then fall from it and then, at another point in time, receive it again, and that this could be done repeatedly. The Prophet noted that both positions were wrong. Truth, he said, lay between them, "for according to the scriptures, if men have received the good word of God, and tasted of the powers of the world to come, if they shall fall away, it is impossible to renew them again, seeing they have crucified the son of God afresh, and put him to an open shame, so there is a possibility of falling away, you could not be renewed again, and the power of Elijah cannot seal against this sin, for this is a reserve made in the seals and powers of the Priesthood."[108]

Seen in this light, murder and blasphemy against the Holy Ghost are two sides of the same coin. The type of murder one has to commit to qualify as a son of perdition requires the same mindset as denying the Holy Ghost. Likewise, one who denies the Holy Ghost must be entirely willing to shed innocent blood even if they do not actually do so.

The enormity of this sin is reflected in the penalty inflicted on those who commit it. According to the Doctrine and Covenants, these people "are vessels of wrath, doomed to suffer the wrath of God, with the devil and his angels in eternity. . . . These are they who shall go away into the lake of fire and brimstone, with the devil and his angels—And the only ones on whom the second death shall have any power; Yea, verily, the only ones who shall not be redeemed in the due time of the Lord, after the sufferings of his wrath" (D&C 76:33–38). The actual details of their punishment have never been revealed fully to any others. The Lord has shared a glimpse of it with a few prophets, but the height, breadth, and depth thereof will be known only to those who will suffer it (D&C 76:45–48). All others will be redeemed into some kingdom of glory, whether that is the telestial, terrestrial, or celestial.[109]

---

108. "History, 1838–1856, Volume E-1," 1921. The Prophet also noted that there was a way to safeguard oneself against this sin. He stated, "Until we have perfect love we are liable to fall [from grace, but] when we have a testimony that our names are sealed in the Lamb's Book of life we have perfect love & then it is impossible for false Christs to decieve us." Minutes, Orange Township, Cuyahoga Co., Ohio, October 25–26, 1831, 13, in "Minute Book 2," Joseph Smith Papers, https://www.josephsmithpapers.org/paper-summary/minute-book-2/15.

109. See D&C 76 for full details on what qualifies individuals for a particular kingdom. The severity of committing murder when one is under covenant gave rise to the

There is no doubt that the Atonement of Christ satisfied divine law and therefore covered all sins. However, that does not mean automatic forgiveness for any and all transgressions.[110] The Father and the Son will forgive only on condition of repentance. Repentance means a person changing his or her behavior from destructive to constructive. To forgive one who insists on being destructive—on thwarting God and working against his plan even to the point of willingly cutting down the Lord or his servants—would prove harmful in that it would encourage these hardened apostates in their activities. The two sins of shedding innocent blood and denying the Holy Ghost are continuous and outward manifestations of an inward condition. That condition is a refusal to repent no matter the cost. Therefore, because such a person refuses to repent, the Lord refuses to forgive him or her (see Mosiah 2:36–39).

---

teachings popularly referred to as "blood atonement." A discussion of this topic lies outside of the sphere of this commentary. For a brief analysis, see Lowell M. Snow, "Blood Atonement," in Ludlow, *Encyclopedia of Mormonism,* 1:131; for extended treatments, see Smith, *Answers to Gospel Questions,* 1:180–91; and Charles W. Penrose, *Blood Atonement, as Taught by Leading Elders of The Church of Jesus Christ of Latter-day Saints* (Salt Lake City: Deseret News, 1916), accessed March 5, 2016, https://babel.hathitrust.org/cgi/pt?id=njp.32101078192455&view=1up.

110. Automatic forgiveness seems to have been the position taken by the Nephite Nehor and his followers who "testified unto the people that all mankind should be saved at the last day, and that they need not fear nor tremble, but that they might lift up their heads and rejoice; for the Lord had created all men, and had also redeemed all men; and, in the end, all men should have eternal life" (Alma 1:4).

Do Not Become Apathetic (6:9–12)

Greek Text

9 Πεπείσμεθα δὲ περὶ ὑμῶν, ἀγαπητοί, τὰ κρείσσονα καὶ ἐχόμενα σωτηρίας, εἰ καὶ οὕτως λαλοῦμεν· 10 οὐ γὰρ ἄδικος ὁ θεὸς ἐπιλαθέσθαι τοῦ ἔργου ὑμῶν καὶ τῆς ἀγάπης ἧς ἐνεδείξασθε εἰς τὸ ὄνομα αὐτοῦ, διακονήσαντες τοῖς ἁγίοις καὶ διακονοῦντες. 11 ἐπιθυμοῦμεν δὲ ἕκαστον ὑμῶν τὴν αὐτὴν ἐνδείκνυσθαι σπουδὴν πρὸς τὴν πληροφορίαν τῆς ἐλπίδος ἄχρι τέλους, 12 ἵνα μὴ νωθροὶ γένησθε, μιμηταὶ δὲ τῶν διὰ πίστεως καὶ μακροθυμίας κληρονομούντων τὰς ἐπαγγελίας. [SBLGNT]

King James Version

9 But, beloved, we are persuaded better things of you, and things that accompany salvation, though we thus speak. 10 For God is not unrighteous to forget your work and labour of love, which ye have shewed toward his name, in that ye have ministered to the saints, and do minister. 11 And we desire that every one of you do shew the same diligence to the full assurance of hope unto the end: 12 That ye be not slothful, but followers of them who through faith and patience inherit the promises.

New Rendition

9 Now although we speak in this way, dear friends, regarding you we are confident of better things that pertain to salvation. 10 For God is not unjust so as to overlook your labor and love that you have demonstrated for his name by having served the saints and continuing to do so. 11 Now we desire that each of you demonstrate the same earnestness toward the full assurance of your hope until the end, 12 so that you do not become lazy, but emulators of those who through faith and patience inherit the promises.

Translation Notes and Comments

6:9 *But, beloved, we are persuaded better things of you, and things that accompany salvation / Now . . . dear friends, regarding you we are confident of better things that pertain to salvation:* This section begins with a marked difference in the author's tone. With the use of the warm plural adjective ἀγαπητοι (*agapētoi*), "beloved [ones]" or "dear friends," the author reaches out to his readers with assurance. This feeling is reinforced by the author's use of the verb πείθω (*peithō*), "to persuade, have confidence in." It suggests a conviction so strong that a person is willing to put his or her full trust in the matter or person.[111]

111. BDAG, 791–72; Ellingworth, *Epistle to the Hebrews*, 329.

On the plural pronoun "we," see Translation Notes for 5:11. The nominalized comparative adjective κρείσσονα (*kreissona*), "better things," points to a more advantageous position or understanding.[112] Here it seems to refer to the author's belief that his readers are far from falling into apostasy and will, like the good field he had mentioned, be blessed of God. He strengthens this conviction with his reference to σοτηρία (*sōtēria*), "salvation," suggesting he fully believes his readers will achieve it.[113]

though we thus speak / although we speak in this way: The verb λαλέω (*laleō*), "to speak,"[114] coupled with the adverb οὕτως (*houtōs*), "thus, so," points back to the warning the author has just given.[115] The phrase εἰ καί (*ei kai*), literally "even if," has concessive force meaning "in spite of the fact that" and is therefore translated as "although" in our Rendition. The author uses the whole phrase to soften, by way of apology, the clear but harsh warning he had given.[116]

6:10 *For God is not unrighteous to forget your work and labour of love / For God is not unjust so as to overlook your labor and love:* The conjunction γάρ (*gar*), "for," is causal and explains why the author has faith that his readers will be saved. It is based on his understanding of the nature of God. The adjective ἄδικος (*adikos*), "unjust," denotes that which is contrary to what is proper or right.[117] That it is coupled with the negative οὐ (*ou*), "not," strengthens its force and therefore carries the idea that there is absolutely no way God could be so unjust as to overlook a person's good works.[118]

The verb ἐπιλανθάνομαι (*epilanthanomai*) means both "to forget" something and also "to be inattentive" such that it is overlooked.[119] The context suggests the latter nuance, so it is used in our Rendition.

---

112. BDAG, 566. The text uses the term "better" to reference the "absolute excellence of the eternal destiny God has for the faithful" and the provisions he has set in place so they can obtain it. Cockerill, *Epistle to the Hebrews,* 280.

113. Lane, *Hebrews 1–8,* 143–44; Ellingworth, *Epistle to the Hebrews,* 329.

114. BDAG, 582–83.

115. BDAG, 741–42.

116. We are reminded of the prophet Jacob in the Book of Mormon, who felt the weight of inflicting pain on the innocent as he warned his own people of their sins and even broached the same subject of committing sins that lead one to hell. See Jacob 2–3.

117. The noun ἀδικία (*adikia*) and the verb ἀδικέω (*adikeō*) refer to any deviance from what is correct. The semantic range reaches from pettiness to outright treachery, but the shared nuance is always the unjustness of an act. Therefore, it is an attribute never shared by Deity. BDAG, 21; Schrenk, *TDNT,* 1:161–63.

118. Ellingworth, *Epistle to the Hebrews,* 330.

119. Thus, to both forget and neglect. Louw-Nida, §29.14, 17. The idea is that God would never forget. Just the opposite is implied: in his righteousness, he remembers (see Gen. 8:1; 9:15–16; Ex. 2:24; 6:5). Johnson, *Hebrews,* 165.

The nouns ἔργον (*ergon*), "work, labor,"[120] and ἀγάπη (*agape*), "love,"[121] qualify each other; the labor is motivated by the love and the love is expressed through the labor. *Agapē* denotes a very inclusive and unwearying kind of love that most fully manifests itself in continual service.[122]

which ye have shewed toward his name / that you have demonstrated for his name: The verb ἐνδείκνυμι (*endeikymi*) denotes showing attention to a cause, thus "to show" or "demonstrate."[123] The preposition εἰς (*eis*), "toward, for," in this context is a marker of reference pointing to God.[124]

The noun ὄνομα (*onoma*), "name,"[125] stands for Deity himself. To do something in his name usually means to do so by his authority, but here the phrase more likely refers to what lay behind and motivated the loving service these Saints continually render, that is, their love for the Father.[126] As King Benjamin testified, though he had spent much time in serving his people, in reality he had "only been in the service of God." He went on to tell his audience that he mentioned "these things that ye may learn wisdom; that ye may learn that when ye are in the service of your fellow beings ye are only in the service of your God" (Mosiah 2:16–17). What King Benjamin says here should not be taken to mean that the object of love is exclusively God and not the people served. That is indeed not the case. The pureness of the love manifest in selfless service and care for others does seem to be gifted by God and also exercised for his good.[127]

in that ye have ministered to the saints, and do minister / by having served the saints and continuing to do so: The verb διακονέω (*diakoneō*) has a wide range of nuances including performing obligated service, carrying out official duties, and meeting immediate needs. The latter likely is meant here, so the verb is translated as "serve" in our Rendition. That the verb is found both as an aorist participle, "having served," expressing a simple past aspect, and as a present active participle, "continuing to serve," underscores the continual nature of the service these Saints have and are rendering to one another. The noun ἅγιος (*hagios*), "saint,"

120. BDAG, 390–91.

121. BDAG, 6.

122. See Johnson, *Hebrews,* 165–66; compare Hel. 10:4.

123. BDAG, 331–32.

124. Louw-Nida, §90.41; BDAG, 288–93.

125. BDAG, 711–14.

126. The phrase means "with regard to him" or "to his account." See Moulton and Milligan, *Vocabulary,* 451; and Ellingworth, *Epistle to the Hebrews,* 331.

127. On this idea, see 2 Ne. 9:40; Mosiah 2:4; 23:15; Moro. 7:13, 48; 8:17; and D&C 42:29, 45; 88:40.

denotes members of the Christian community (for example, see Acts 9:32, 41; 26:10; Rom. 1:7; 1 Cor. 1:2; 2 Cor. 1:1; Eph. 1:1; Philip. 1:1; Col. 1:2; Jude 1:3; and Rev. 11:18).

6:11 ***And we desire that every one of you do shew the same diligence / Now we desire that each of you demonstrate the same earnestness:*** The verb ἐπιθυμέω (*epithymeō*) means "to long for" or "to greatly desire" something.[128] Here it shows the depth of feeling the author has for his fellow Saints. On the verb "demonstrate," see 6:10 above.

The noun σπουδή (*spoudē*), "diligence, earnestness," denotes the depth and strength of a civic or religious commitment. That commitment is entwined with a "personal moral excellence or optimum devotion to the interest of others" and therefore carries the idea of a zealousness for their good.[129] Because the English word "earnest" carries the idea of a serious and, often, enthusiastic and zealous devotion for a cause, we have used it in our Rendition.[130]

to the full assurance of hope unto the end / towards the full assurance of your hope until the end: The preposition πρός (*pros*) in this context acts as a marker of movement "toward" an objective. The noun πληροφορία (*plērophoria*) denotes "a state of complete certainty" and therefore of "full assurance" of something often due to the witness of the Holy Ghost (10:22),[131] while the noun ἔλπις (*elpis*), "hope," carries the very positive expectation of realizing a greatly desired object.[132] The word connotes, therefore, not a "theoretical knowledge of some vague future salvation." In the author's context, hope denotes a confident, even sure, expectation of the reception of the salvation the Father has promised and spiritually confirmed.[133]

The phrase expresses the author's great desire for his readers to realize a spiritual witness that they will gain eternal life. This witness will then be the foundation of their hope that will fuel their faith. Being thus fueled, faith will move them to persevere ἄχρι τέλους (*achri telous*), "until the end."

---

128. The prefix ἐπί (*epi*), "on," intensifies the force of θυμός (*thymos*), "desire, passion," thus denoting a very strong feeling. Smyth, *Greek Grammar,* §1687.2; BDAG, 371–72; Louw-Nida, §25.12, 20.

129. BDAG, 939–40.

130. *Webster's New Dictionary of Synonyms,* s.v. "serious."

131. Though the cognates of the word, especially in non–New Testament Greek, carry the idea of fulness, in the New Testament context, the word denotes a "full conviction" in gaining an objective. Koester, *Hebrews,* 317; Delling, *TDNT,* 6:310–11; Moulton and Milligan, *Vocabulary,* 519–20.

132. BDAG, 319–20.

133. *NID,* s.v. "ἔλπις."

It is likely that the "end" the author refers to is τὰς ἐπαγγελίας (*tas apangelias*), "the promises [of eternal life]," which he will mention in 6:12 below.[134]

6:12 *That ye be not slothful / so that you do not become lazy:* The phrase ἵνα μή (*hina mē*), literally "that not," expresses the reason or cause for something. In this case, it is the author's fear that his readers may become νωθρός (*nōthros*), "slothful, lazy." For development, see Translation Notes for 5:11. Here the word stands opposite ἐπιθυμέω (*epithymeō*), "to earnestly desire," found in 6:11 and suggests a lazy, half-hearted approach to living the gospel.[135]

but followers of them who through faith and patience inherit the promises / but emulators of those who through faith and patience inherit the promises: The noun μιμητής (*mimētēs*) denotes an "imitator, model."[136] As used here, the word does not denote following the external activities of the one to be imitated but rather having the same attitude toward God and determination to follow his ways that the model did.[137] "Emulator" best catches the sense of the word in English, and we have translated it thus in our Rendition. The word suggests a way of life derived from an understanding of the personal consequences of the ministry and Atonement of Christ—forgiveness and access to grace and the Holy Spirit. Imitation is not then so much pious achievement as it is an attitude of thankfulness, acceptance of the promises the Father has made, and perseverance in serving him.[138]

The two chief virtues of such people are πίστις (*pistis*), "faith," and μακροθυμία (*makrothymia*), "patience." For a full development of "faith," see Translation Notes for 11:1–2 below with the corresponding Analysis. For the present, we need only note that "faith" denotes the assuredness of a promised blessing. The noun *makrothymia* denotes both a "state of being tranquil while awaiting an outcome" and "of being able to bear up under provocation."[139] Though both nuances apply here, the former seems to

134. Ellingworth, *Epistle to the Hebrews,* 332.

135. BDAG, 683; Preisker, *TDNT,* 4:1126.

136. BDAG, 652.

137. Ellingworth, *Epistle to the Hebrews,* 333.

138. The model (6:13–18; 11:4–31) looks to the patriarchs whose lives were those of faith and trust in Jehovah. Thus, the model is more of a mindset than a performance. When Paul asks his readers to imitate him, it is only after he has declared his own personal weaknesses (1 Cor. 4:9–16; Philip. 3:8–17). Thus, it is total trust in Christ, not an individual prophet's behavior, that the author is asking readers to imitate. See Michaelis, *TDNT,* 4:659–74.

139. BDAG, 612–13.

carry the greater weight. As the context shows (see below), it connotes a calm willingness to wait for God to fulfill the promised blessings.

The verb κληρονομέω (*klēronomeō*), translated "to inherit," also means "to obtain" or "to come by a possession" through any rightful means. Here it points to τὰς ἐπαγγελίας (*tas epangelias*), "the promises." Chief among those promises are those made to Abraham, as the very next verse notes. The Apostle Paul explained the connection between the gospel of Jesus Christ and the promises made to Abraham in his Epistle to the Galatian Saints: "Now if you are Christ's, then you are Abraham's seed, heirs according to the promise" (Gal. 3:18, our translation), and "so you are no longer a slave, but a son, and if a son, you are also an heir through God" (Gal. 4:7, our translation). That the noun is plural looks to more than one promise. Since, as the Old Testament shows, God's promises are rich and manifold, the phrase likely points to blessings both in mortality and beyond. The scriptures are replete with examples, but the author likely points to those that compose the "great salvation" (2:3) he is anxious that his readers reach for.

A grammatical point is worth noting: *klēronomeō,* as found in this verse, is a present active participle and suggests the author is pointing to the way in which all the faithful throughout the generations have obtained and will obtain these promises for themselves.[140]

Analysis and Summary

Having given his readers a very strict warning that likely caused them some deep reflection, the author now greatly softens his tone. Hopefully, his clear, if harsh, warning—that they must stop their spiritual regression or suffer possibly dire consequences (5:11–6:3)—has placed them in a mood for the counsel and assurance he now turns to give them.

He encourages them with the warm address "beloved friends" (ἀγαπητοι, *agapētoi*) and assures them that he is very much persuaded that they will achieve "better things that pertain to salvation" (NR 6:9). His positive assurance stands in contrast to the negative assurance of damnation that he gave to the apostates (6:8). The author assures his readers that he will not back down from his conviction of the good their works have done, even though he used some forceful language (6:9). The point he wishes to make is actually enhanced by setting up his argument in this way, since they have

140. Ellingworth, *Epistle to the Hebrews,* 333; Cockerill, *Epistle to the Hebrews,* 284.

now hopefully (as noted above) grasped the desperate consequences that their backsliding could cause and are very willing to change.[141]

In 6:10, the author expresses the ground for the assurance he has for his fellow Saints' success. It is based on two of his favorite themes: God's faithfulness to his people and his people's faithfulness to their God. Using an emphatic double negative (ου . . . ἄδικος, *ou . . . adikos*), "by no means unjust," the author assures them there is absolutely no way the Father would be so unjust as to overlook their deeds motivated by love. These were services done on the Father's account and in response to the immediate need of their fellow Saints (6:10). The readers' love was particularly evident, as the author later reveals, in their outreach to those who had felt the bitter and heavy hand of persecution. Indeed, these serving Saints had put their own reputation—and perhaps even their lives—in danger in doing so (10:33–34). Further, they have not let this discourage them from continued service.[142]

That the author does not directly bring in his favorite themes of faithfulness and obedience is noteworthy. But by mentioning loving service in lieu of these, he can focus on and confirm the sincerity of what the Saints have done and his faith in what their actions will yield. Nonetheless, they yet lack a foothold on important doctrines that will sustain them in persevering in their actions—faith in the reality of what God has in store for them coupled with the assurance that he has already provided a means for their success. The author begins at this point to more fully develop these doctrines.[143] This will take him through chapter 12.

The author begins (6:11) by expressing his strong desire that his readers will continually show their earnestness—expressed in an enthusiastic and unremitting zeal to their cause—until they receive the full assurance of their hope (ἔλπις, *elpis*). In this context, hope carries the idea of a confident expectation, grounded in spiritual confirmation, that they will receive the salvation the Father has promised. The author states that he wants them to reach this state of hopefulness, knowing that it will be a hedge against slothfulness, sluggishness, or apathy in their duty to the Lord (6:12). Indeed, he wishes them to show the same zeal in their moving forward in faith as they have in service to one another.[144]

---

141. Cockerill, *Epistle to the Hebrews,* 280–81.

142. Lane, *Hebrews 1–8,* 144; Koester, *Hebrews,* 317.

143. Cockerill, *Epistle to the Hebrews,* 281–82.

144. Johnson, *Hebrews,* 166.

Further, he expresses his desire that they imitate (μιμητής, *mimētēs*) those who have inherited, that is, received, the promises (6:12). That imitation does not point to external behavior but to a firm inner belief. It expresses a way of life based on accepting the Savior and his offer of forgiveness and grace with its attendant power of the Spirit that assures one that eternal life is waiting. In short, the author asks readers to take Christ at his word.

The author witnesses that many have done this and received the reward (6:12). This is an important point because he shows his readers that the goal can be realized and that many have done so (he will develop this theme through the rest of the Epistle). The virtues that make this possible are faith (πίστις, *pistis*) and patience (μακροθυμία, *makrothymia*). The former denotes assuredness, again through a witness of the Spirit, that the promised blessings will be given. The second denotes a tranquil waiting, undisturbed by doubts or events, for the promises to be realized. The author stresses that this "faithful perseverance"[145] is the assurance that his readers will receive "the kingdom that cannot be removed" (NR 12:28).[146] As long as they put forth such faith, the objective is guaranteed. Nothing can stop them from obtaining it.

The phrase "inheriting the promises" (6:12) is charged with nuances. Many of these relate to covenants and God's dealing with ancient Israel.[147] But behind all these stands something else that enlightens the word "inherit." The author wants his readers to push forward to make their "hope sure." He now turns to show them how.

The Certainty of God's Promise (6:13–20)

Greek Text

13 Τῷ γὰρ Ἀβραὰμ ἐπαγγειλάμενος ὁ θεός, ἐπεὶ κατ' οὐδενὸς εἶχεν μείζονος ὀμόσαι, ὤμοσεν καθ' ἑαυτοῦ, 14 λέγων· Εἰ μὴν εὐλογῶν εὐλογήσω σε καὶ πληθύνων

145. The phrase τὴν πληροφορίαν τῆς ἐλπίδος (*tēs plērophorian tēs elpidos*) is likely a hendiadys (one by means of two) where the first word acts as an adjective defining the last one.

146. See Attridge, *Epistle to the Hebrews*, 176–77; and Koester, *Hebrews*, 318.

147. Cockerill, *Epistle to the Hebrews*, 284.

πληθυνῶ σε· 15 καὶ οὕτως μακροθυμήσας ἐπέτυχεν τῆς ἐπαγγελίας. 16 ἄνθρωποι γὰρ κατὰ τοῦ μείζονος ὀμνύουσιν, καὶ πάσης αὐτοῖς ἀντιλογίας πέρας εἰς βεβαίωσιν ὁ ὅρκος· 17 ἐν ᾧ περισσότερον βουλόμενος ὁ θεὸς ἐπιδεῖξαι τοῖς κληρονόμοις τῆς ἐπαγγελίας τὸ ἀμετάθετον τῆς βουλῆς αὐτοῦ ἐμεσίτευσεν ὅρκῳ, 18 ἵνα διὰ δύο πραγμάτων ἀμεταθέτων, ἐν οἷς ἀδύνατον ψεύσασθαι θεόν, ἰσχυρὰν παράκλησιν ἔχωμεν οἱ καταφυγόντες κρατῆσαι τῆς προκειμένης ἐλπίδος· 19 ἣν ὡς ἄγκυραν ἔχομεν τῆς ψυχῆς, ἀσφαλῆ τε καὶ βεβαίαν καὶ εἰσερχομένην εἰς τὸ ἐσώτερον τοῦ καταπετάσματος, 20 ὅπου πρόδρομος ὑπὲρ ἡμῶν εἰσῆλθεν Ἰησοῦς, κατὰ τὴν τάξιν Μελχισέδεκ ἀρχιερεὺς γενόμενος εἰς τὸν αἰῶνα. [SBLGNT]

King James Version

13 For when God made promise to Abraham, because he could swear by no greater, he sware by himself, 14 Saying, Surely blessing I will bless thee, and multiplying I will multiply thee. 15 And so, after he had patiently endured, he obtained the promise. 16 For men verily swear by the greater: and an oath for confirmation is to them an end of all strife. 17 Wherein God, willing more abundantly to shew unto the heirs of promise the immutability of his counsel, confirmed it by an oath: 18 That by two immutable things, in which it was impossible for God to lie, we might have a strong consolation, who have fled for refuge to lay hold upon the hope set before us: 19 Which hope we have as an anchor of the soul, both sure and steadfast, and which entereth into that within the veil; 20 Whither the forerunner is for us entered, even Jesus, made an high priest for ever after the order of Melchisedec.

New Rendition

13 For when God made a promise to Abraham, since he did not have anyone greater to swear by, he swore by himself, 14 saying,

> "I will surely bless you and multiply you." [LXX Gen. 22:17]

15 And thus because Abraham waited patiently, he received the promise. 16 For people swear by something greater, and an oath provides a confirmation that brings an end to their entire dispute. 17 In regard to this, because God desired to show more clearly to the heirs of the promises the unchangeable nature of his purpose, he guaranteed it with an oath, 18 so that by these two unchangeable things, in which it is impossible for God to lie, we who have taken refuge, might have strong encouragement to seize the hope that is placed before us. 19 This hope we have as an anchor for our souls, that is firm and reliable, that enters into the inner sanctuary behind the veil. 20 There Jesus, who ran before us, went in on our behalf, because he had become

> "a high priest forever after the order of Melchizedek" [LXX Ps. 109:4].

Translation Notes and Comments

6:13 ***For when God made promise to Abraham, because he could swear by no greater, he sware by himself / For when God made a promise to Abraham, since he did not have anyone greater to swear by, he swore by himself:*** On the promises, see 6:14 below. The force of the author's argument hangs on the verb ὀμνύω (*omnyō*), "to swear an oath." This constitutes an act of affirming "the veracity of one's statement by invoking a transcendent entity." It carries the tacit force of punishment if one were found to have used the oath to deceive.[148] Since an oath requires invoking a superior power, and there is none greater than God, he can only swear upon himself.[149]

6:14 ***Surely blessing I will bless thee, and multiplying I will multiply thee / "I will surely bless you and multiply you":*** This is a quote from LXX Genesis 22:17, with modification. In the Genesis text, what Jehovah promises to multiply is not Abraham but τὸ σπέρμα σου (*to sperma sou*), "your seed." The author, however, focuses more specifically on Abraham and God's promise to bless him. The verb εὐλογέω (*eulogeō*), "to bless," means "to provide with divine benefits," including a bestowal of God's gracious power.[150] The verb πληθύνω (*plēthynō*) in this context means "to grow or increase" in general. In the Genesis context, it means "to be increased in number," thus pointing to Abraham's posterity.[151]

The scripture the author refers to uses the Hebrew infinitive absolute construction.[152] To translate, as literally as possible, the nuance of the grammar into Greek, the author uses the combination εὐλογῶν εὐλογήσω (*eulogōn eulogēsō*), "in blessing I will bless," and πληθύνων πληθυνῶ

---

148. Deception in the form of a lie is particularly at the forefront. See BDAG, 705–6.

149. This is likely an allusion to Gen. 22:16; for a study, see Blane Conklin, *Oath Formulas in Biblical Hebrew* (Warsaw, Ind.: Eisenbrauns, 2011).

150. BDAG, 407–8. The same scripture is used in James 2:21–22 to stress that faith is demonstrated by actions.

151. BDAG, 826. Jehovah's blessing consisted of two parts: Abraham would have a great posterity, and they would inhabit the promised land (Gen. 12:7; 13:14–15; Abr. 2:6–9). The lack of reference to the latter promise may be due to the author's desire to have his readers not look at the temporal promise but the eternal one, that is, the one that looked to the divine city (11:10). Attridge, *Epistle to the Hebrews,* 178–79; Koester, *Hebrews,* 328; and Ellingworth, *Epistle to the Hebrews,* 335, convincingly argue that "the promise" actually includes all the promises Jehovah made to Abraham but climaxes in the oath made after Abraham's sacrifice of Isaac.

152. In the New Testament, this construction is only found in quotations from the LXX. Ellingworth, *Epistle to the Hebrews,* 337.

(*plēthynōn plēthynō*), "in multiplying I will multiply." Since the use of this construction is to emphasize the sureness of what is promised, we have translated the entire phrase as "I will *surely* bless and multiply you" in our Rendition (italics added).

6:15 ***And so, after he had patiently endured, he obtained the promise / And thus because Abraham waited patiently, he received the promise:*** The circumstantial aorist participle μακροθυμήσας (*makrothymēsas*), literally "having waited patiently," is best understood in a causative sense rather than a temporal (as the KJV does) and is thus translated as "because Abraham waited patiently" in our Rendition. For the verb μακροθυμέω (*makrothymeō*), "wait patiently," see 6:12 above. In its context here, the word stresses the quality of the wait. It was not one of heavy endurance but of persistent faithfulness throughout.

The verb ἐπιτυγχάνω (*epitynchanō*) denotes "to achieve or gain one's goal."[153] In this case, that goal is τῆς ἐπαγγελίας (*tēs epangelias*), "the promise." The fact that Abraham obtained the promise acts as a bona fides of Jehovah's faithfulness in fulfilling his word.[154]

6:16 ***For men verily swear by the greater / For people swear by something greater:*** Here the author states the obvious, but it helps him make his point. On the verb ὀμνύω (*omnyō*), "to swear an oath," see 6:13 above. An oath, by its very nature, appeals to a transcendent power as surety of what is being said or promised.

an oath for confirmation is to them an end of all strife / an oath provides a confirmation that brings an end to their entire dispute: The Greek syntax here is quite foreign to English structure. The phrase is translated literally as "of all, for them, dispute an end for confirmation [is] an oath." We have attempted to modify it in our Rendition to give better clarity while still retaining the sense of the Greek.

The noun βεβαίωσις (*bebaiōsis*), "confirmation," looks at the process by which a promise or statement is validated or confirmed.[155] The process involves ὁ ὅρκος (*ho horkos*), "the oath," that is, the formal pronouncement itself.[156] The result is ἀντιλογίας πέρας (*antilogias peras*), "an end to dispute,"

---

153. BDAG, 385.

154. In this case, the promise was not possessing the promised land but having a son through whom Abraham's great posterity was guaranteed. Koester, *Hebrews,* 326; Cockerill, *Epistle to the Hebrews,* 285–86; compare O'Brien, *Letter to the Hebrews,* 236.

155. BDAG, 173.

156. *NID*, s.v. "ὅρκος"; BDAG, 723.

where *antilogias* denotes both contradiction and disputation. The phrase carries the idea of a complete resolution of any conflict.[157]

6:17 ***Wherein God, willing more abundantly to shew unto the heirs of promise the immutability of his counsel / In regard to this, because God desired to show more clearly to the heirs of the promises the unchangeable nature of his purpose:*** The beginning phrase ἐν ᾧ (*en hō*), "in regard to which," points back to the oath and underscores its significance so far as its use by Jehovah.[158]

The verb ἐπιδείκνυμι (*epideiknymi*), "to show," carries the nuance of demonstrating that something is true beyond dispute and is often associated with divine revelation.[159] The comparative adverb περισσότερον (*perissoteron*), "even more," modifies *epideiknymi* with the sense "more clearly."[160] Those whom Jehovah wanted to assure were the κληρονόμοις (*klēronomois*), "heirs." The author, likely to hold interest, does not designate who the heirs are until 6:18.[161]

The nominalized adjective ἀμετάθετον (*ametatheton*) means "unchangeableness."[162] The noun βουλή (*boulē*) denotes "a plan" or intended "purpose."[163] It can also refer to a resolution or decision that often carries the idea of "divine will." In this context, the phrase points to the unalterable nature of what Jehovah has resolved to do.[164] Taken all together, the clause shows that with unusual, even over-abundant desire, Jehovah wished to affirm that his promises to Abraham—and by inference to all others under covenant—would stand unchanged and unaltered forever.

confirmed it by an oath / he guaranteed it with an oath: The verb μεσιτεύω (*mesiteuō*) means "to mediate, act as a surety," and in a derived

---

157. The noun is quite strong, carrying the nuance of both hostility and rebellion and points to the heat behind a dispute. BDAG, 89; Louw-Nida, §§33.445, 446; 39.35. That an oath can mollify these feelings shows its strength. On the power of the oath to settle arguments in court, see Philo, *Somn.* 1.12; *Abr.* 273; compare Cicero, *Top.* 77.

158. Cockerill, *Epistle to the Hebrews,* 287 n. 8.

159. BDAG, 370; Louw-Nida, §72.5; Ellingworth, *Epistle to the Hebrews,* 341.

160. BDAG, 806.

161. Attridge, *Epistle to the Hebrews,* 181.

162. BDAG, 53. This is the only use of this noun in the New Testament, making it somewhat difficult to determine the exact nuance to be taken here, but the force of "unchangeable nature" seems to hold. See Cockerill, *Epistle to the Hebrews,* 288 n. 11.

163. Louw-Nida, §72.5.

164. BDAG, 181–82. In the Old Testament, there is a direct connection between Jehovah's word and oath and his word and plan. Both rely heavily on the fidelity of his covenantal promises. Lane, *Hebrews 1–8,* 152.

sense "to guarantee,"[165] as in our Rendition. The ὅρκος (*horkos*), "oath"—actually, the formal pronouncement of the oath—is how God affixed his guarantee to the promise. In the Old Testament, all oaths were to be sworn in the name of Jehovah (Deut. 6:13; 10:20). To lie, then, was seen as breaking the third commandment (Ex. 20:7; Deut. 5:11; Zech. 5:3–4).

6:18 *That by two immutable things / so that by these two unchangeable things:* The noun πρᾶγμα (*pragma*) denotes anything that is done, thus, "event, deed, or thing."[166] The two things noted are most likely the promise (Gen. 22:17) and the oath (Ps. 110:4).[167] On the adjective ἀμετάθετον (*ametatheton*), "unchangeable, unalterable," see 6:17 above. Here the adjective shows the timeless, unchangeable, and unalterable nature of the promise Jehovah guaranteed by the oath. The author's point is that "because God is faithful to his own purposes, the readers should remain faithful to their hope of sharing in what he has promised them."[168]

in which it was impossible for God to lie / in which it is impossible for God to lie: The adjective ἀδύνατος (*adynatos*) denotes anything incapable of being done, thus "impossible."[169] The verb ψεύδομαι (*pseudomai*) denotes any kind of deception or falsehood, particularly the telling of a lie.[170]

who have fled for refuge / we who have taken refuge: The verb καταφεύγω (*katapheugō*) means both to flee to some place and to take refuge there.[171] It appears here as a nominalized active aorist participle, which is best rendered in English as the relative clause "who have taken refuge."[172]

---

165. BDAG, 634. This is the only place the word is found in scripture, thus making its full nuance difficult to ascertain, but the idea of assuring something will be done holds. See Ellingworth, *Epistle to the Hebrews,* 342; and Cockerill, *Epistle to the Hebrews,* 287 n. 10.

166. BDAG, 858–86.

167. Lane, *Hebrews 1–8,* 152; Attridge, *Epistle to the Hebrews,* 181–82; Philo, *Abr.* 273.

168. Ellingworth, *Epistle to the Hebrews,* 342.

169. BDAG, 22.

170. BDAG, 1096–97. The idea of God securing his word with an oath did hold a potential and dangerous misunderstanding. It opened the door to the idea that God could, under other circumstances, lie. The first-century Jewish scholar Philo picked up on this nuance. Even though the Old Testament is clear that Jehovah cannot lie (1 Sam. 15:29; Job 36:4; LXX Num. 23:19; KJV Ps. 33:11; Isa. 46:10–11), Philo wanted to make sure his audience understood the oath was used only to bolster the faith of the recipient of the promise and not because Jehovah actually had to use it to secure his word. See Philo, *Sacr.* 91–94; *Abr.* 273; compare *Leg.* 3.204. Ellingworth, *Epistle to the Hebrews,* 343; Attridge, *Epistle to the Hebrews,* 180.

171. BDAG, 529.

172. The aorist participle expresses a simple occurrence of an action that is usually antecedent to the main verb. Smyth, *Greek Grammar,* §1872c; Wallace, *Greek Grammar,* 614–15.

The context of Hebrews suggests the flight is from a spiritually dangerous and physically hostile world. The shelter or protection from the world is the gospel in general and the promises of God in particular. The author's admonitions that readers stay faithful "unto the end" (6:11) remind them that although they have found refuge, they must continue to press toward the final rest of the Lord (4:1, 11),[173] the ultimate place of refuge.

we might have a strong consolation / might have strong encouragement: The noun παράκλησις (*paraklēsis*) denotes an act that emboldens others to act or believe; thus, it is translated as "encouragement" in our Rendition.[174] The adjective ἰσχυρός (*ischyros*), "strong," points to both physical and spiritual strength,[175] but here it emphasizes the acme of encouragement brought by knowing that God's promises can be fully realized.

to lay hold upon the hope set before us / to seize the hope that is placed before us: The verb κρατέω (*krateō*) means "to grasp, seize, or adhere strongly" to something.[176]

On ἔλπις (*elpis*), "hope," see 6:11 above and the Analysis below. The verb πρόκειμαι (*prokeimai*) carries the sense of something being "set" or "placed before" someone.[177] The aorist infinitive form of the verb κρατέω (*krateō*) leaves open whether or not these Saints have actually obtained the hope or if it still lies ahead. Very likely, it is the realization of the hope that lies ahead. The hope itself they already possess or can get.[178]

6:19 ***Which hope we have as an anchor of the soul, both sure and steadfast / This hope we have as an anchor for our souls, that is firm and reliable:*** The noun ἔλπις (*elpis*), "hope," is the antecedent referred to by the relative pronoun ἣν (*hēn*), "which" or "that." Our Rendition follows the KJV for clarity.[179]

The author uses an analogy to emphasize the value of hope. The noun ἄγκυρα (*angkyra*) denotes a ship's anchor. Like an anchor, hope has two

---

173. The author also uses the imagery of "a better country" and the city of God (11:10, 16). Note that the objective is the *place* of refuge and peace; the result is the *state* of rest.

174. BDAG, 766.

175. BDAG, 483–84.

176. BDAG, 564–65.

177. BDAG, 871.

178. For discussion, see Ellingworth, *Epistle to the Hebrews,* 344; Attridge, *Epistle to the Hebrews,* 183; Lane, *Hebrews 1–8,* 153.

179. We take the relative pronoun ἣν (*hēn*), "that," as modifying the participle εἰσερχομένην (*eiserchomenēn*), "entering into," showing that it refers back to the noun ἔλπις (*elpis*), the last word in the preceding verse. Doing this safeguards the imagery so it is not the anchor but the hope that penetrates the veil. See Ellingworth, *Epistle to the Hebrews,* 345; and O'Brien, *Letter to the Hebrews,* 241.

characteristics. The first is defined by the adjective ἀσφαλής (*asphalēs*), which refers to something that is stable and firm.[180] The nuance is to something that cannot be moved out of its place. The second is defined by the adjective βέβαιος (*bebaiōs*), which refers to "something that can be relied on not to cause disappointment" and so is "reliable."[181] What hope anchors is the ψυχή (*psyche*), "soul"—in this context, the center or inner life of the individual Saint.[182]

which entereth into that within the veil / that enters into the inner sanctuary behind the veil: The nominalized adjective τὸ ἐσώτερον (*to esōteron*), literally "the inner part of," refers to what is on the other side of something. In this case, that something is the καταπέτασμα (*katapetasma*). The noun in general refers to a curtain, but in this case, it is the veil of the tabernacle or temple. What is on the other side is the "inner sanctuary" or Holy of Holies that represents heaven.[183] The Greek text does not have the noun "sanctuary," but we have added it to our Rendition for clarity. The author gives hope a dynamic quality by placing it in the Holy of Holies or, less symbolically, in heaven. In this way, he stresses that since one's hope has already arrived there, then so too can the individual who possesses it.

6:20 ***Whither the forerunner is for us entered, even Jesus / There Jesus, who ran before us, went in on our behalf:*** The noun πρόδρομος (*prodromos*) denotes a person who goes ahead or before, that is, "a forerunner."[184] In our Rendition, we have translated it as a relative clause to better express the sense of the word. To clinch his point, the author notes that not only

---

180. It also denotes that which is in a person's best interest, therefore, what is safe and secure. BDAG, 147.

181. BDAG, 172. For a study, see Charles A. Kennedy, "Early Christians and the Anchor," *Biblical Archaeologist* 38, no. 3/4 (1975): 115–24.

182. BDAG, 1098–1100. The noun connotes the essence of the person and that portion of selfhood that is eternal, transcending even death (10:39; 13:17); see also Cockerill, *Epistle to the Hebrews,* 290.

183. In LXX Ex. 26:33 and Lev. 16:2, 12, 15, the phrase ἐσώτερον τοῦ καταπετάσματος *(esōteron tou katapetasmatos)*, "inside the veil," denotes the resting place of the ark of the covenant and the place that only the high priest could enter. For studies, see Norman H. Young, "'Where Jesus Has Gone as a Forerunner on Our Behalf' (Hebrews 6:20)," *Andrews University Seminary Studies* 39, no. 2 (Autumn 2001): 165–73; and Norman H. Young, "The Day of Dedication or the Day of Atonement? The Old Testament Background to Hebrews 6:19–20 Revisited," *Andrews University Seminary Studies* 40, no. 1 (Spring 2002): 61–68. Richard M. Davidson, "Christ's Entry 'Within the Veil' in Hebrews 6:19–20: The Old Testament Background," *Andrews University Seminary Studies* 39, no. 2 (Autumn 2001): 175–90, suggests that the phrase could be used to refer to the whole of the tabernacle and specifically to the inauguration of the structure for the Lord's purposes.

184. BDAG, 867. Compare Ether 12:4.

has hope successfully entered the "inner sanctuary," but so has Christ, showing the possibility of that happening to others. The preposition ὑπέρ (*hyper*) plays an important role here, denoting that which is done for or in behalf of others. It shows one reason for the Lord's ministry: to prepare the way for his disciples to follow.

made an high priest for ever after the order of Melchisedec / because he had become "a high priest forever after the order of Melchizedek": The circumstantial aorist participle γενόμενος (*genomenos*) is taken here as expressing causation, hence "because he had become" in our Rendition. The phrase is a citation from LXX Psalm 109:4, which the author already referred to in 5:6, 10. For discussion, see Translation Notes with the associated Analysis found there.

Analysis and Summary

The author again reaches to the Old Testament to find examples upon which to establish and illustrate his point. He also again uses verbal analogy, that of oath-swearing, as his link. He chooses, with little wonder, Abraham as his focus, which allows the author to highlight the motif of swearing an oath as well as showcasing the idea that as Abraham received Jehovah's blessings (6:15; see also Abr. 1:18–19; 2:8–11), so too his readers could receive them. These blessings would come through the Savior's ministry as High Priest (6:19–20). However, like Abraham's response, the reward would come only through faithful perseverance (6:15).

To strongly stress his point, the author goes to great lengths to show how far Jehovah was willing to go to assure his people that his promises were absolutely reliable and immutable. He did this by swearing an oath. "Although God's integrity was beyond question, he condescended to use an oath, the means by which unreliable human beings affirm their truthfulness."[185] His willingness to set aside his dignity was motivated by his desire to convince Israel that they could fully trust him (6:17). By implication, that same desire was true in behalf of the author's readers. Thus, God's promises remained under guarantee, for they were bound by his personal integrity, his promise, and his oath. Nothing could make their realization more sure (6:18).

The author's purpose in appealing to scripture was to stress the importance and nature of God's oath in order to encourage his fellow Saints to persevere in faith. The promise coupled with the oath provided two

185. Cockerill, *Epistle to the Hebrews*, 287.

unbreakable and unchangeable aspects of the one covenant that substantiated the absolute sureness of God's plan of salvation. The author is not exaggerating when he witnesses that such an assurance is a "*strong* encouragement" for faithful perseverance (NR 6:18, italics added).[186] The same assurance is there for the Saints living during any period of time.[187]

Here, Abraham sets the example as one who took Jehovah at his vouchsafed word. Though the author does not refer to the binding of Isaac (Gen. 22:1–12) directly (he will later), there is a strong echo to it. The significance of that sacrifice, and the seat of the author's point, rests on Abraham's unshakable reliance on Jehovah's promise that "in Isaac shall thy seed be called" (Gen. 21:12). Knowing that Jehovah could not lie, Abraham, not knowing how God would fulfill the oath, went forward with the sacrifice and secured the promises.[188]

The promise operates for and the plan applies to those whom the author states "have fled for refuge" (6:18). In his context, that would refer to those who have refused to yield to the unfaithfulness to which Israel's wilderness generation was so prone and also to the rebellion of those who had apostatized from the Church.[189] Using today's metaphor, these are they who have followed the Lord's command to flee "from Babylon, from the midst of wickedness, which is spiritual Babylon" (D&C 133:14). And there is good reason for flight—"Babylon the great . . . shall fall" (D&C 1:16). Therefore, the Lord warns, "For after today cometh the burning—this is speaking after the manner of the Lord—for verily I say, tomorrow all the proud and they that do wickedly shall be as stubble; and I will burn them up, for I am the Lord of Hosts; and I will not spare any that remain in Babylon" (D&C 64:24).[190]

The author admonished his readers "to seize the hope that is placed before us" (NR 6:18). As used in the New Testament, the noun "hope" (ἔλπις, *elpis*) has three aspects.[191] First and most frequently, it denotes a confidence in obtaining an objective, mainly God's promises to their "fathers" (Acts 26:6),[192] but more particularly eternal life, "which God,

186. Cockerill, *Epistle to the Hebrews,* 288.

187. Cockerill, *Epistle to the Hebrews,* 288.

188. Attridge, *Epistle to the Hebrews,* 179; Bruce, *Epistle to the Hebrews,* 152–53. The author will revisit this event and more fully explain its significance at 11:17.

189. Cockerill, *Epistle to the Hebrews,* 289.

190. For a study, see Dennis A. Wright, "Great and Abominable Church," in Ludlow, *Encyclopedia of Mormonism,* 2:568–69.

191. BDAG, 319–20; Louw-Nida, §25.59, 61, 62.

192. It also includes the assurance expressed by the fathers. For instance, of Abraham, Paul states that he "against hope believed in hope, that he might become the father of

that cannot lie, promised before the world began" (Titus 1:2; compare Titus 3:7). This confidence is based on a spiritual confirmation. Indeed, the Saints "abound in hope, through the power of the Holy Ghost" (Rom. 15:13; compare Rom. 5:5). It is important to keep this point in mind. Confirmation looks to the Holy Ghost, who testifies "to them that are sanctified" (10:14–15) and allows them to "draw near with a true heart in full assurance of faith" (10:22). By yielding to this hope, they obtain the "better things that pertain to salvation" (NR 6:9), moving them "toward the full assurance of [that] hope" (NR 6:11) "to inherit the promises" (6:12). Note also, hope comes by the grace of Christ (2 Thes. 2:16) as his free gift to sustain those who are striving to do his will.[193]

In this aspect, hope is most clearly joined with faith. As faith encompasses the steps one takes to reach an objective, hope is what fuels and propels one to take those steps. Successfully taking those steps, furthermore, brings reward. On the basis of the reward realized, hope grows ever more certain until it reaches "a perfect brightness" (2 Ne. 31:20) that propels faith to its completion.[194]

Second, hope denotes the basis or ground on which the person's confidence lies. This can include the faithfulness of the Christian community (1 Thes. 2:19), but more particularly the "Lord Jesus Christ, who is our hope" (1 Tim. 1:1, our translation; compare Col. 1:27), and, of course, also the Father (Rom. 15:13).

Third, hope defines what that object is. This includes such things as the Resurrection (1 Cor. 15:52–56; compare Acts 23:6; 24:15), the coming of the Lord (Titus 2:13), becoming one with Christ (Col. 1:27; 1 John 3:2–3), and, ultimately, the reward in heaven (Col. 1:5; 1 Thes. 5:8).

A key attribute of hope is that it is not egocentric. It places faith and reliance not on the individual but on God and Christ. Its center is the Atonement and the power of grace that flows from it, a power that the Saints not only can but do tap into. Realizing that power—in the form of inspiration,

---

many nations" (Rom. 4:18). In other words, with all evidence to the contrary, Abraham kept his confidence in God and thereby realized the promise.

193. For some excellent studies on the importance and power of hope, see Neal A. Maxwell, "Hope through the Atonement of Jesus Christ," *Ensign* 28, no. 11 (November 1998): 61–63; and Neal A. Maxwell, "'Brightness of Hope,'" *Ensign* 24, no. 11 (November 1994): 34–36.

194. For a detailed discussion of faith and its relationship with hope, see Translation Notes with the related Analysis for of all of chapter 11.

revelation, witness from the Spirit, and the possession and use of its gifts—is the sure foundation on which hope rests.[195]

> The concept of hope plays a vital role in Latter-day Saint thought. Firmly centered in Christ and his resurrection, it is the "hope of eternal life" (Titus 1:2) repeatedly alluded to by Paul. It is the opposite of the despair found among those who are "without Christ, having no hope, and without God in the world" (Eph. 2:12). As the Book of Mormon prophet Moroni writes, "If ye have no hope, ye must needs be in despair" (Moro. 10:22). For those, however, who accept Christ's Atonement and resurrection, there comes a "brightness of hope" (2 Ne. 31:20) through which all who believe in God "might with surety hope for a better world" (Ether 12:4). . . . [It is] the confidence or trust in God that springs from knowledge that mankind is saved through the Atonement ("for we are saved by hope," Rom. 8:15). Hence, hope is inseparably connected with faith.[196]

The author uses an anchor as a symbol of a hope that is grounded on a witness of the Spirit (6:19). The imagery allows him to stress two aspects of this kind of hope: firmness and certainty. Due to these two qualities, it acts as a safeguard to the very soul of the faithful Saint.[197] Joseph Smith tied the imagery to the assurance that comes from receiving the "more sure word of prophecy," a revelation by which a person knows that his or her calling and election to a heavenly station has been secured.[198] This is the assurance that the sealing power of the Holy Spirit of Promise has, in fact, taken effect and guaranteed the person's reward.[199] The Prophet declared, "Having this promise sealed unto them, it was as an anchor to the Soul sure and steadfast, though the thunders might roll, and lightnings flash, and earthquakes bellow, and war gather thick around, yet this hope and knowledge would support the soul in every hour of trial, trouble and tribulation. Then

---

195. Compare *NID,* s.v. "ἔλπις."

196. James K. Lyon, "Hope," in Ludlow, *Encyclopedia of Mormonism,* 2:656–57.

197. Bruce, *Epistle to the Hebrews,* 154–55.

198. For discussion, see Roy W. Doxey, "Calling and Election," in Ludlow, *Encyclopedia of Mormonism,* 1:248; and Largey, *Book of Mormon Reference Companion,* 176–77; for expanded treatments, see Marion G. Romney, in CR, October 1965, 20–23; McConkie, *Doctrinal New Testament Commentary,* 3:325–50; and Andrus, *Principles of Perfection,* 323–55.

199. Lawrence R. Flake, "Holy Spirit of Promise," in Ludlow, *Encyclopedia of Mormonism,* 2:651–52; for extended studies, see McConkie, *Doctrinal New Testament Commentary,* 2:493–94; Marion G. Romney, *Look to God and Live* (Salt Lake City: Deseret Book, 1971), 125–31; and James E. Faust, *Reach Up for the Light* (Salt Lake City: Deseret Book, 1990), 116–23.

knowledge through our Lord and Savior Jesus Christ is the grand key that unlocks the glories and mysteries of the kingdom of heaven."[200]

In the final two verses, the author focuses on the object of that hope, namely Jesus Christ, who, the author notes, is the forerunner, the one who has already traversed the necessary distance and shown not only that it can be done but also how (6:20). Finally, the author looks at the tabernacle with its imposing veil, a once-impenetrable barrier to all but the high priest, now opened to all by the great High Priest whose authority lasts forever. In the Greek text, the author places the prepositional phrase εἰς τὸν αἰῶνα (*eis ton aiōna*), "forever," last in this section of his work, giving it final force. In doing so, he emphasizes that the saving and mediating work of Christ will never end.[201] Being grounded on this fact, the author notes that the Saints' hope has, as it were, already entered into the inner sanctuary, tacitly showing that as one holds onto this Spirit-inspired and -assured hope, nothing can keep the faithful Saint from the heavenly reward.[202]

---

200. "History, 1838–1856, Volume D-1," 1549.
201. Attridge, *Epistle to the Hebrews,* 185; Cockerill, *Epistle to the Hebrews,* 292–93.
202. Bruce, *Epistle to the Hebrews,* 155.

Chapter 7

The Priesthood Order of Melchizedek

INTRODUCTION

Following his transitioning pattern, the author once again uses the last topic mentioned in the previous discussion as the introduction to this one.[1] In this case, it is Jesus as High Priest and forerunner who breached "the veil" and by so doing prepared the way for the faithful to enter heaven (6:19–20). The image of "entering inside the veil" evokes the Day of Atonement ritual, when the Levite high priest entered the Holy of Holies and performed the annual rite for the redemption of Israel. Only the high priest was ever allowed in the room, a proscription beginning with Aaron, the first Levitical high priest. That Jesus entered beyond the veil (6:19), as the forerunner showing the way for the rest of the faithful, the author insists, made him superior to Aaron (7:11).

In this way, the author sets the stage for his further development of the theme he left off at 5:10, namely (as stated in LXX Ps. 109:4) that God declared the Son to be a priest after the order of Melchizedek.[2] The author uses his exposition of the psalm here as the foundation on which he builds a beautiful monument celebrating the Son's divine and eternal authority.[3]

---

1. In doing so, the author follows Semitic rhetorical rules rather than those of the Greco-Romans. Vanhoye, *Letter to the Hebrews,* 115.

2. Cockerill, *Epistle to the Hebrews,* 292. For a study, see Robert L. Millet, "The Holy Order of God," in Nyman and Tate, *Book of Mormon: Alma, the Testimony of the Word,* 61–88.

3. Cockerill, *Epistle to the Hebrews,* 292–93. The title of "high priest" is ascribed neither to Melchizedek nor to the scion of David in Ps. 110:4. In both cases, the individuals are called "priests." The title "high priest" (ἀρχιερεύς, *archiereus*) was a later development among the Jews. However, to emphasize the Savior's superior position, the author refers to him as the great High Priest from 2:17 on. Vanhoye, *Letter to the Hebrews,* 126.

In this chapter, the author develops the significance of the Savior being the Melchizedek High Priest forever, while in chapters 8 through 10 he develops the implications of the great High Priest entering into the holy celestial realm as the forerunner.

Through his use of verbal analogy and this critical exposition of the psalm, the author provides an authoritative scriptural confirmation of the superiority and preeminence of Christ's priesthood. The psalm further substantiates the eternity of the Lord's power and thereby promotes the idea that it will be efficacious forever.[4]

The author ties this section together by contrasting the Melchizedek high priest with his Aaronic counterpart. His argument is convincing, admittedly, only for those who share his premises, but that likely would have included most—if not all—the audience to whom the document is addressed.[5]

In 7:1–3, the author recalls Melchizedek's meeting with Abraham after the patriarch had rescued his nephew Lot from captivity and defeated the armies of four kings in the process (Gen. 14:14–24). In 7:4–10, the author uses this incident to emphasize the greatness of this high priest, showing him to be superior even to Abraham and, by implication, Levi and Aaron. In 7:11–25, the author arranges his argument around the phrases in LXX Psalm 109:4. In 7:11–19, he looks at the ramifications for Jesus' position in the Melchizedek order of the priesthood. In 7:20–22, he looks at the implications of God's declaration that he has sworn an oath concerning his Son's authority from which he will not repent. And in 7:23–25, the author looks at the salvific consequences of Jesus being a high priest forever.

In the JST, Joseph Smith made significant modifications to some of the verses in this chapter and in doing so addressed some of the more confusing statements therein. His primary focus was on Melchizedek and the order of the priesthood he belonged to.

---

4. Cockerill, *Epistle to the Hebrews,* 292–93. The author continues to use verbal analogy. For discussion, see note 33 in chapter 4.

5. Johnson, *Hebrews,* 174.

The Greatness of Melchizedek, the "Priest of the Most High God" (7:1–10)

Greek Text

1 Οὗτος γὰρ ὁ Μελχισέδεκ, βασιλεὺς Σαλήμ, ἱερεὺς τοῦ θεοῦ τοῦ ὑψίστου, ὁ συναντήσας Ἀβραὰμ ὑποστρέφοντι ἀπὸ τῆς κοπῆς τῶν βασιλέων καὶ εὐλογήσας αὐτόν, 2 ᾧ καὶ δεκάτην ἀπὸ πάντων ἐμέρισεν Ἀβραάμ, πρῶτον μὲν ἑρμηνευόμενος βασιλεὺς δικαιοσύνης ἔπειτα δὲ καὶ βασιλεὺς Σαλήμ, ὅ ἐστιν βασιλεὺς εἰρήνης, 3 ἀπάτωρ, ἀμήτωρ, ἀγενεαλόγητος, μήτε ἀρχὴν ἡμερῶν μήτε ζωῆς τέλος ἔχων, ἀφωμοιωμένος δὲ τῷ υἱῷ τοῦ θεοῦ, μένει ἱερεὺς εἰς τὸ διηνεκές.

4 Θεωρεῖτε δὲ πηλίκος οὗτος ᾧ δεκάτην Ἀβραὰμ ἔδωκεν ἐκ τῶν ἀκροθινίων ὁ πατριάρχης. 5 καὶ οἱ μὲν ἐκ τῶν υἱῶν Λευὶ τὴν ἱερατείαν λαμβάνοντες ἐντολὴν ἔχουσιν ἀποδεκατοῦν τὸν λαὸν κατὰ τὸν νόμον, τοῦτ' ἔστιν τοὺς ἀδελφοὺς αὐτῶν, καίπερ ἐξεληλυθότας ἐκ τῆς ὀσφύος Ἀβραάμ· 6 ὁ δὲ μὴ γενεαλογούμενος ἐξ αὐτῶν δεδεκάτωκεν Ἀβραάμ, καὶ τὸν ἔχοντα τὰς ἐπαγγελίας εὐλόγηκεν. 7 χωρὶς δὲ πάσης ἀντιλογίας τὸ ἔλαττον ὑπὸ τοῦ κρείττονος εὐλογεῖται. 8 καὶ ὧδε μὲν δεκάτας ἀποθνῄσκοντες ἄνθρωποι λαμβάνουσιν, ἐκεῖ δὲ μαρτυρούμενος ὅτι ζῇ. 9 καὶ ὡς ἔπος εἰπεῖν, δι' Ἀβραὰμ καὶ Λευὶ ὁ δεκάτας λαμβάνων δεδεκάτωται, 10 ἔτι γὰρ ἐν τῇ ὀσφύϊ τοῦ πατρὸς ἦν ὅτε συνήντησεν αὐτῷ Μελχισέδεκ. [SBLGNT]

King James Version

1 For this Melchisedec, king of Salem, priest of the most high God, who met Abraham returning from the slaughter of the kings, and blessed him; 2 To whom also Abraham gave a tenth part of all; first being by interpretation King of righteousness, and after that also King of Salem, which is, King of peace; 3 Without father, without mother, without descent, having neither beginning of days, nor end of life; but made like unto the Son of God; abideth a priest continually. 4 Now consider how great this man was, unto whom even the patriarch Abraham gave the tenth of the spoils. 5 And verily they that are of the sons of Levi, who receive the office of the priesthood, have a commandment to take

New Rendition

1 Now this Melchizedek, a king of Salem, a priest of the Most High God, met Abraham as he was returning from the defeat of the kings, and he blessed him. 2 Abraham also apportioned to him one tenth of everything. First, the name Melchizedek means "King of Righteousness," but he was also King of Salem, that is "King of Peace." 3 Without father or mother, without a genealogy, having neither beginning of days nor end of life, being like the Son of God, he remains a priest for all time. 4 But look how great he was! Abraham the patriarch gave him a tenth of his plunder. 5 Indeed the sons of Levi who have received the priesthood have a mandate, according to the law, to collect tithes from the people, that is, from their brothers,

tithes of the people according to the law, that is, of their brethren, though they come out of the loins of Abraham: 6 But he whose descent is not counted from them received tithes of Abraham, and blessed him that had the promises. 7 And without all contradiction the less is blessed of the better. 8 And here men that die receive tithes; but there he receiveth them, of whom it is witnessed that he liveth. 9 And as I may so say, Levi also, who receiveth tithes, payed tithes in Abraham. 10 For he was yet in the loins of his father, when Melchisedec met him.

even though they are also descendants of Abraham. 6 But Melchizedek, who was not of the same ancestry as the Levites, has collected tithes from Abraham and has blessed him who had the promise. 7 Now beyond all doubt, an inferior person is blessed by one who is higher in rank. 8 And in one case tithes are received by mortal men, but in the other case by one who is declared to be alive. 9 Indeed, one might say that Levi, who receives tithes, paid tithes through Abraham, 10 for he was still in the loins of his ancestor when Melchizedek met him.

Translation Notes and Comments

7:1–3 In the Greek text, these three verses constitute one long complex sentence. For the sake of easier reading and understanding, our Rendition breaks these into separate sentences necessitating the change of some participles into finite verbs.

7:1 ***For this Melchisedec, king of Salem / Now this Melchizedek, a king of Salem:*** This phrase has reference to Genesis 14:18–19. The spelling "Melchisedec" is the KJV rendering of the Old Testament "Melchizedek." Since the Church uses the Old Testament spelling, we use it in our Rendition. On the priest and Salem, see Analysis for 7:2 as well as the "Excursus on Melchizedek" below.

priest of the most high God / a priest of the Most High God: The adjective ὕψιστος (*hypsistos*) is a superlative meaning "most high" and is often found in the LXX in combination with θεός (*theos*), "God," and rendered in English as "the most high God." There was a Canaanite deity whose name title was עֶלְיוֹן (*ʿelyôn*), "Most High," and on that basis, some scholars have speculated that Melchizedek officiated for this god.[6] However, in Genesis 14:22, Abraham identifies the "most high God" with Jehovah, stating, "I have lifted up my hand before Jehovah, the most high God" (Gen. 14:22, our translation). The title was certainly used by the Israelites for Jehovah (Deut. 32:8–9; 2 Sam. 22:14; Ps. 7:17; 97:9). Further, based on information

6. See Cross, *TDOT,* 1:255–56.

in the Book of Mormon (Alma 13:14–18) and the Doctrine and Covenants (D&C 68:15, 19; 84:14; 107:1–3), it is clear that Melchizedek worshiped Jehovah and administered under his name.[7]

who met Abraham returning from the slaughter of the kings / met Abraham as he was returning from the defeat of the kings: The story is told in Genesis 14. At this point in the Old Testament history, Jehovah had not yet bequeathed to Abram his new name. The author, however, is not concerned with this technicality and so refers to the patriarch as "Abraham."

and blessed him / and he blessed him: The content of this blessing is not recorded in any of the accounts dealing with this incident, including the JST, though that account mentions this blessing twice (see JST Gen. 14:25, 37). Joseph Smith, however, did comment on it, stating that the faithful priest bestowed upon the patriarch "the last law, or a fulness of the law or priesthood, which constituted him a king and priest after the order of Melchesideck, or an endless life."[8]

The account provides a hint as to the blessing's impetus. This was Abraham's faith in Jehovah and his open vow that he would keep none of the spoils (Gen. 14:22–23) from the war. Through this covenant, Abraham was able to witness to all that Jehovah, and Jehovah alone, was the source of Abraham's wealth (JST Gen. 14:40).

7:2 ***To whom also Abraham gave a tenth part of all / Abraham also apportioned to him one tenth of everything:*** This phrase in the KJV is a paraphrase from Genesis 14:20. The nominalized adjective δεκάτη (*dekatē*), "a tenth," denoted a tenth of something given for a specific purpose.[9] It is in this account that the idea of the tithe is first introduced in the scriptures. Just how this fraction became associated with the Lord's portion is unknown, but the tradition was carried forward by Jacob. After his theophany at Bethel, in which he received a personal confirmation that the promises of his grandfather, Abraham, would be his, Jacob vowed to donate to Jehovah a tenth of everything he would ever receive (Gen. 28:18–22). The

---

7. See Mark E. Petersen, *Abraham: Friend of God* (Salt Lake City: Deseret Book, 1976), 91–95.

8. Joseph Smith, discourse, recorded by James Burgess, August 27, 1843, in Andrew F. Ehat and Lyndon W. Cook, *The Words of Joseph Smith: The Contemporary Accounts of the Nauvoo Discourses of the Prophet Joseph* (Provo, Utah: Religious Studies Center, Brigham Young University, 1980), 245–46.

9. BDAG, 216–17.

Mosaic law cemented the practice and made it a requirement for all of God's people (see Deut. 12; 14; 26).[10]

The verb μερίζω (*merizō*) means "to divide, deal out," and "apportion."[11] The best translation here is "apportion" because it means "to make a proportionate division or distribution of" something.[12] In this case, it refers to Abraham's welfare offering to the faithful priest. According to the JST version of Genesis 14:38, the reason Abraham made the offering was because "God had appointed [Melchizedek] to receive tithes for the poor." Further, it notes that Abraham was most generous because he gave "of all his riches which he possessed, which God had given him more than that which he had need" (JST Gen. 14:39).

first being by interpretation King of righteousness / First, the name Melchizedek means "King of Righteousness": "The name Melchizedek" is not in the Greek text but is added in our Rendition for clarity. The Hebrew מַלְכִּי־צֶדֶק (*malkîṣedeq*) consists of two nouns, מֶלֶךְ (*melek*), "king," plus צֶדֶק (*ṣedeq*) "righteousness." The name can also be understood to mean "Righteous King."[13] For further discussion, see "Excursus on Melchizedek" below.

also King of Salem, which is, King of peace / but he was also King of Salem, that is "King of Peace": The Hebrew place name שָׁלֵם (*šālēm*) may be a shortened form of יְרוּשָׁלַיִם (*yĕrûšālayyîm*), "Jerusalem."[14] The adjective שָׁלֵם (*šālēm*), "complete, perfect, whole,"[15] is cognate with the noun שָׁלוֹם (*šālôm*), which, among other things, means "peace."[16] As is often the case in the Bible, the etymologies applied are not strictly and linguistically precise but were often used to serve the need of the person doing the analysis.

---

10. See J. Christian Wilson, "Tithe," in Freedman, *Anchor Bible Dictionary,* 6:578–80. It is of note that the Lord returned his tenth to the Levites as a means of sustaining both them and their families no matter where they lived in the Holy Land (Num. 18:21).

11. BDAG, 631–32; Louw-Nida, §§57.89, 90; 63.23.

12. *Collegiate Dictionary,* s.v. "apportion." The LXX as well as other references to the account uses the verb δίδωμι (*didōmi*), "to give." See Attridge, *Epistle to the Hebrews,* 188 n. 28. The author of Hebrews probably used μερίζω (*merizō*) to emphasize that a tithe or offering was paid by Abraham. Cockerill, *Epistle to the Hebrews,* 296–97 n. 5.

13. *HAL,* 593. On this title from a first-century Jewish perspective, see Josephus, *Ant.* 1.180; and Philo, *Alleg. Interp.* 3.79–82; see also *Tg. Neof.* Gen. 14. For a study, see Martin McNamara, "Melchizedek: Genesis 14, 17–20 in the Targums, in Rabbinic and Early Christian Literature," *Biblica* 81 (2000): 1–31, http://contentdm.lib.byu.edu/cdm/ref/collection/rsc/id/40997. Compare Ogden and Skinner, *Verse by Verse,* 251–52.

14. *HAL,* 1539. Philo, *Alleg. Interp.* 3.79–82, interprets the phrase this way.

15. *HAL,* 1528. In this respect, it has a close affinity to the Greek τελείωσις (*teleiōsis*).

16. *HAL,* 1506–10.

7:3 ***Without father, without mother, without descent / Without father or mother, without a genealogy:*** The adjectives ἀπάτωρ (*apatōr*), "without father," and ἀμήτωρ (*amētōr*), "without mother," in secular documents denote a person who was either illegitimate or orphaned.[17] That is not the case in a religious setting where they are used to describe a characteristic of the eternal gods.[18] The adjective ἀγενεαλόγητος (*agenealogētos*) means "without genealogy or pedigree."[19]

This phrase has been taken in two ways. First, it can be a description of Melchizedek himself, making him thus a divine or angelic figure. Some Jews contemporary with the New Testament thought of Melchizedek as quasi-divine and immortal.[20] This idea may have influenced the author since he shared a similar worldview with his readers. Such a view would work well for him because of his desire to tie Melchizedek to the Savior as a type. Second, it can be a reference to the priest's lack of a biblical genealogy, thus making his relationship to other biblical personalities unknown.[21] This, too, would serve the author well, since he contrasts the genealogically bound Levitical order of the priesthood with that of the nongenealogically bound order of the Melchizedek.

The JST solution is to refocus the subject from the faithful priest to his priesthood. It prefaces this verse with, "For this Melchizedek was ordained a priest after the order of the Son of God, which order was without father" (JST 7:3). This idea conforms well with the author's desire to show that the higher priesthood held by both Melchizedek and Jesus was untied to the linage restrictions of the Levitical order.[22]

---

17. Koester, *Hebrews,* 342–44; Schrenk, *TDNT,* 5:1019–21.

18. Attridge, *Epistle to the Hebrews,* 190 with n. 51.

19. BDAG, 9. It is found biblically only here, making its precise meaning unclear. See Louw-Nida, §10.25; and Moulton and Milligan, *Vocabulary,* 3. Some have speculated, due to the exalted language, that the author is actually quoting a hymn to the high priest. See Attridge, *Epistle to the Hebrews,* 189–90; and Koester, *Hebrews,* 349–50. Since, however, the author has proved himself capable of such elevated language, there is no need to believe he is using an unknown source. Cockerill, *Epistle to the Hebrews,* 298.

20. See Dead Sea Scroll 11Q13 on Melchizedek.

21. Bruce, *Epistle to the Hebrews,* 159–60; Johnson, *Hebrews,* 176; Cockerill, *Epistle to the Hebrews,* 298 nn. 13, 14.

22. O'Brien, *Letter to the Hebrews,* 248–53; Cockerill, *Epistle to the Hebrews,* 300. Moshe Reiss, "The Melchizedek Traditions," *Scandinavian Journal of the Old Testament* 26, no. 2 (2012): 259–65, shows that, among the Jews, there seems to have been two different Melchizedeks. One is the human who blessed Abraham after the battle of the kings (Gen. 14). The other is an eschatological heavenly being (perhaps even semidivine) who will announce Messiah ben Joseph just as Elijah will announce Messiah ben

having neither beginning of days, nor end of life / having neither beginning of days nor end of life: This phrase, if applied to Melchizedek, would show his divine or eternal nature. Again, the JST changes the phrase so that it refers not to the priest but to his priesthood (JST 7:3).

made like unto the Son of God / being like the Son of God: The verb ἀφομοιόω (*aphomoioō*) means to make one thing like or similar to another. With passive force, as found in this phrase, it means "to be like or resemble" another thing.[23] If allied to Melchizedek, it emphasizes his excellence as a type for Christ, being like God's Son. Again, the JST changes the focus from the faithful priest himself to those who, like him, receive the higher priesthood. It states that "all those who are ordained unto this priesthood are made like unto the Son of God" (JST 7:3).[24]

abideth a priest continually / he remains a priest for all time: The verb μένω (*menō*), "stay, remain, abide," carries the idea of "a steady continuance in a state."[25] Because it also carries the nuance of living in a specific extended condition, it describes well the possession of the priesthood.

The adjective διηνεκής (*diēnekēs*) denotes that which continues without interruption and therefore pertains to "all time."[26] As a reference to Melchizedek, the phrase shows the eternality of his priesthood. This characteristic, when applied to Melchizedek, would serve well the author's desire to show he was an excellent type of Christ.

The JST, however, changes the focus from the faithful priest to the Savior, thus showing that he is the one who has and does abide as a priest forever (JST 7:3).[27]

7:4 ***Now consider how great this man was, unto whom even the patriarch Abraham gave the tenth of the spoils / But look how great he was! Abraham the patriarch gave him a tenth of his plunder:*** This verse holds the heart of the author's argument. He has carefully used the Genesis account to make this one point: as great as Abraham was, Melchizedek

---

David prior to the millennial era of peace. The author of Hebrews uses the figure, Reiss concludes, to show that Melchizedek was greater than Abraham and that Jesus held the Melchizedek Priesthood.

23. BDAG, 158.

24. See also *DNTC,* 3:167.

25. BDAG, 630–31.

26. BDAG, 245; Koester, *Hebrews,* 343.

27. This attribute separates him somewhat from Melchizedek, whom the author does not describe as being a priest "forever" (εἰς τὸν αἰῶνα, *eis ton aiōna*) as he does the Son (7:17, 21) but as a priest "in perpetuity" (εἰς τὸ διηνεκές, *eis to diēnekes,* 7:3). The reason is likely that as a matter of scriptural foreshadowing the type does not "have the same degree of reality as its accomplishment." Vanhoye, *Letter to the Hebrews,* 118.

was even greater. How does the scripture show this? By stating that it was Abraham who paid the tithes *to* the high priest.

To draw attention to his point, the author uses the imperative form of the verb θεωρέω (*theōrō*), "to observe, play close attention to."[28] The adjective πηλίκος (*pēlikos*), "how great," is used here with exclamatory force as in our Rendition.[29] It highlights the faithful priest's extraordinary importance.[30]

The author also gives Abraham the title πατριάρχης (*patriarchēs*), "patriarch," important as a reminder that the prophet was the direct ancestor of Levi and Aaron.

The noun ἀκροθίνιον (*akrothinion*), "spoil, plunder," denotes literally the topmost or best part of a heap and carries the nuance of "first fruits," that which is reserved for a divinity. In the sense used in this verse, however, it probably has the general sense of the loot or plunder taken after a victorious battle.[31] Though the account here notes that Abraham gave only a tenth, albeit the best tenth, of the war plunder, the JST account states that "Abraham paid unto him tithes of all that he had, of all the riches which he possessed" (JST Gen. 14:39).

7:5 ***they that are of the sons of Levi, who receive the office of the priesthood / the sons of Levi who have received the priesthood:*** As the price for redeeming the children of Israel from Egyptian bondage, Jehovah asked for the firstborn son in each family to serve him (Ex. 13:2; 22:29; Num. 3:13). He provided a way, however, for this son's redemption from his service (Ex. 34:20; Num. 3:12–13). The families were to pay the Lord a price that then freed the firstborn from his service, and in their place Jehovah took the tribe of Levi (Num. 3:44–51). From that time forth, only those of the tribe of Levi could hold the priesthood.[32] The preposition ἐκ (*ek*), "from, of," in the phrase "they that are of" can be taken as derivative and, thereby, refer to those descendants of Levi whom the Lord later called to hold priesthood office.[33]

---

28. BDAG, 454.

29. Ellingworth, *Epistle to the Hebrews,* 360.

30. BDAG, 811.

31. BDAG, 40. The LXX of Gen. 14:20 states that Abraham gave him δεκάτην ἀπὸ πάντων (*dekatēn apo pantōn*), "tithes of all."

32. Merlin D. Rehm, "Levites and Priests," in Freedman, *Anchor Bible Dictionary,* 4:297–310.

33. It is unlikely that the force of the preposition is partitive because that would suggest only some of the Levites received the priesthood in Moses' day. Such was not the case. See Ellingworth, *Epistle to the Hebrews,* 362; and Cockerill, *Epistle to the Hebrews,* 308 n. 56.

The noun ἱερατεία (*hierateia*) denoted both "priestly office" and its service.[34] It is translated as "priesthood" in the KJV. It is here that the word is used for the first time in the New Testament.[35] The root meaning came from ἱερός (*hieros*), "sacred," which in turn was derived from ἱερόν (*hieron*), "temple." In the Near Eastern world, the idea of priesthood was inseparably connected to the temple and the work that went on there.[36]

have a commandment to take tithes of the people according to the law / have a mandate, according to the law, to take tithes of the people: The noun ἐντολή (*entolē*) means "a commandment" or "mandate."[37] Though both words nuance a dictate that must or should be obeyed, the word "mandate" carries a strong implication of imperativeness because it is issued from the highest of authorities[38]—in this case, the Mosaic law. For that reason, it is used in our Rendition.

The Levites are able to carry out their mandate by virtue of holding priesthood authority. The noun ἱερατεία (*hierateia*), as noted above, denotes both the priestly office and the service it is designed to render.[39] The authority accompanying the mandate was not to be questioned because it was established by divine law.[40]

that is, of their brethren / that is, from their brothers: The noun ἀδελφός (*adelphos*) denotes a brother or a near kinsman or anyone joined to another in a common cause.[41] The author uses the term to stress that even though the Levites are part of a brotherhood of Israel, they still hold authority to which the others must accede. Nonetheless, they are all still "brothers," and by use of the term, the author does diminish the distance between priest and people. At the same time, he lays the groundwork to subordinate all of Abraham's descendants below the authority of Melchizedek.[42]

though they come out of the loins of Abraham / even though they are also descendants of Abraham: The noun ὀσφῦς (*osphys*) denotes the loins or reproductive organs, but metaphorically it means to be a descendant of

34. BDAG, 469.
35. The term "priesthood" is found only in 7:5, 11, 12, 14, 24, and 1 Pet. 2:5, 9.
36. For discussion, see Schrenk, *TDNT,* 3:247–52.
37. BDAG, 340.
38. *Webster's New Dictionary of Synonyms,* s.v. "command"; see Lane, *Hebrews 1–8,* 168.
39. BDAG, 469.
40. For a discussion of the sacerdotal order and its connection to the temple, see Schrenk, *TDNT,* 3:221–83; and Dommershausen, *TDOT,* 7:66–75.
41. BDAG, 18.
42. Cockerill, *Epistle to the Hebrews,* 309.

another.[43] The author's point is that though genealogically all the tribes should be considered equal, that was not the case. The Levites held Jehovah's authority and thus a place of honor and deference.

7:6 ***he whose descent is not counted from them / Melchizedek, who was not of the same ancestry as the Levites:*** The noun "Melchizedek" is not found in the Greek text but is added to our Rendition for clarity. The verb γενεαλογέω (*genealogeō*) means to trace one's ancestry.[44] It is found in this phrase as a passive participle and, with μή (*mē*), "not," a marker of negation.[45] It thus denotes one who is not of the same ancestry as another. The author's point is that, unlike the blood tie between Levi and the other tribes, there was no such tie between the faithful priest and the patriarch, making Abraham's deference to Melchizedek all the more imposing.

received tithes of Abraham, and blessed him that had the promise / has collected tithes from Abraham and has blessed him who had the promise: This verse is a paraphrase of Genesis 14:19–20. The verbs δεκατόω (*dekatoō*), "to collect a tithe," and εὐλογέω (*eulogeō*), "to bless," are both in the perfect tense. This tense was often used by some New Testament–period Jews to refer to an Old Testament event to emphasize its allegorical value, a usage that is rare in the New Testament but one that "the author of Hebrews is particularly fond of."[46]

The noun ἐπαγγελία (*epangelia*), "promise," denotes in this case Jehovah's declaration to bless Abraham with its attendant obligation on God's part (noted in 6:13–15).[47] The author likely wanted to keep these in the forefront so he could contrast them with the lesser blessing that came through the Mosaic law and also to show the promise did not stop Melchizedek from bestowing additional blessings and assurances.[48] In that way, the author aligns the priest with Jehovah as a giver of blessings and therefore a person of great importance.[49] This act, again, shows Melchizedek's superiority over Abraham.

7:7 ***And without all contradiction the less is blessed of the better / Now beyond all doubt, an inferior person is blessed by one who is higher in rank:*** The phrase χωρὶς δὲ πάσης ἀντιλογίας (*chōris de pasēs antilogias*)

---

43. BDAG, 730; Louw-Nida, §8.42, 43.
44. BDAG, 192.
45. BDAG, 644–46.
46. Wallace, *Greek Grammar,* 581–82; see also Attridge, *Epistle to the Hebrews,* 196 n. 128.
47. BDAG, 355–56.
48. Attridge, *Epistle to the Hebrews,* 196.
49. Cockerill, *Epistle to the Hebrews,* 310.

connotes a fact beyond dispute or doubt. Actually, the author's point is not always accurate. There are many scriptural examples where one of lesser station blessed one of greater (for example, 2 Sam. 14:22; 1 Kgs. 1:47; Job 31:20).[50] Within his context, however, the author's reasoning is sound enough, and he is not overly exaggerating a position to bolster the point that Melchizedek's blessing Abraham makes the faithful priest the superior to the patriarch and, by implication, to Levi.[51]

7:8 ***here men that die receive tithes; but there he receiveth them, of whom it is witnessed that he liveth / in one case tithes are received by mortal men, but in the other case by one who is declared to be alive:*** The phrases ὧδε μὲν . . . ἐκεῖ δὲ (*hōde men . . . ekei de*), "and here . . . but there," marks an emphatic opposition that the author uses to stress the great difference between the Levites and Melchizedek.[52]

The verb ἀποθνήσκω (*apothnēskō*), "to die," points to the mortality of all priests and stands in contrast to μαρτυρούμενος ὅτι ζῇ (*martyroumenos hoti zē*), "[he who] is declared to be alive," that is, Melchizedek.[53] Again the author is stressing the superiority of the faithful priest over the lesser priests and in doing so foreshadows the superiority of the Lord, who, unlike the mortal priests, needs no one to succeed him in office.[54]

7:9 ***And as I may so say, Levi also, who receiveth tithes, payed tithes in Abraham / Indeed, one might say that Levi, who receives tithes, paid tithes through Abraham:*** With the phrase καὶ ὡς ἔπος εἰπεῖν (*kai hōs epos eipein*), "as one might say," the author signals that he is now moving to his conclusions and that he is doing so through the use of a figure of speech.[55] His

50. O'Brien, *Letter to the Hebrews,* 253, contends that the distinction between εὐλογέω (*eulogeō*) meaning "to bless" and meaning "to praise" (BDAG, 407–8) must be kept in mind. Though an inferior may "praise" a superior, it is the superior who "blesses" the inferior.

51. Ellingworth, *Epistle to the Hebrews,* 366; Attridge, *Epistle to the Hebrews,* 196; Cockerill, *Epistle to the Hebrews,* 310.

52. Cockerill, *Epistle to the Hebrews,* 306 n. 48.

53. The author describes the Levites not simply as "mortals" but as "dying human beings." In this way, the author makes another connection between priest and God, giving Melchizedek even more cachet. Here human effort is futile. Cockerill, *Epistle to the Hebrews,* 311, citing Moulton and Milligan, *Vocabulary,* 38; Ellingworth, *Epistle to the Hebrews,* 367.

54. Attridge, *Epistle to the Hebrews,* 196. The godly qualities the author ascribes to Melchizedek are important to his case for they make him an excellent type of the Lord.

55. Though the phrase is found in Jewish literature (for example, see Philo, *Opif.* 13; *Plant.* 158; *Ebr.* 51; Josephus, *Ant.* 15.387), it is unique here in the Bible. It suggests that the author is acknowledging that the point he is making goes beyond the evidence but nevertheless should be taken seriously. Vanhoye, *Letter to the Hebrews,* 120; Koester, *Hebrews,* 345.

proposition allows him to state his thesis clearly: the Levitical Priesthood is inferior to that of Melchizedek as shown by Abraham—and by implication, Levi—paying tithes to the faithful priest.

7:10 ***For he was yet in the loins of his father, when Melchisedec met him / for he was still in the loins of his ancestor when Melchizedek met him:*** The phrase explains just how Levi, the tither, could have paid tithes. It was through the vicarious act of his progenitor.[56]

Analysis and Summary

For the points the author of Hebrews wishes to make, Melchizedek and the priesthood he held play a key role. In three different chapters, the author brings them to the forefront (5:6, 10; 6:20; 7:1, 10–11, 15, 17, 21). One of the important reasons for this was to show that the faithful priest was an excellent type of the Savior and therefore a figure who could more fully reveal the Son. The biblical account plus Restoration insights supports the author's point.

He begins his argument by appealing to scripture, namely, the story recorded in Genesis dealing with the Jews' own highly revered ancestor, Abraham, meeting the faithful priest (7:1–3; Gen. 14:17–20). After the patriarch had defeated the armies of the kings who had kidnapped his nephew Lot, other rulers who had been routed by these armies came to meet and likely congratulate him. Among these were Bera, king of Sodom, and some of his associates. He wanted but one thing: "Give me the persons," he said, "and take the goods to thyself" (Gen. 14:21). Abraham, willingly freeing the captives, refused the additional offer, stating, "I will not take from a thread even to a shoelatchet, and that I will not take any thing that is thine, lest thou shouldest say, I have made Abram rich" (Gen. 14:23). Apparently, the king's reputation had preceded him, and Abraham wanted as little to do with him as possible. That was not true of another king then present.

This was Melchizedek, the king of Salem. Of the event, the scriptures state only that he "brought forth bread and wine: and he was the priest of the most high God. And he blessed him, and said, Blessed be Abram of the most high God, possessor of heaven and earth: And blessed be the most high God, which hath delivered thine enemies into thy hand. And he gave him tithes of all" (Gen. 14:18–20).

---

56. The Christians had no doubt that Abraham was the "father" of all Israel, including Levi and their own spiritual head. Matt. 3:9; Luke 1:73; 3:8; 16:24; John 8:39, 53, 56; Acts 7:2; Rom. 4:1; James 2:21.

With the exception of a brief mention of his name in LXX Psalm 109:4, Melchizedek does not show up again in scripture until our author brings him to the fore. Even in the author's treatment, there is little information about the man because the author uses the passage primarily to provide exegesis on the Old Testament account.

The author's take on the text is arresting because he does not actually quote fully the story in Genesis but only those portions that serve his purpose. Further, he makes significant extrapolations from what it does not say.

Since Genesis gives no genealogy of the faithful priest, the author describes him as without father, mother, or genealogy and therefore "having neither beginning of days nor end of life" (7:3).[57] The author may have wanted to emphasize this because, according to the Mosaic law, it was critical that a man be able to prove his priestly ancestry in order to be considered legitimate (Num. 3:10, 38). The proscription was taken with such seriousness that when the Jews returned to Jerusalem from Babylon (c. 530 BC), only those who could prove their descent from Levi and Aaron were allowed to enter into the priesthood ranks (Ezra 2:61–63). The author uses this requisite to make a contrast with the higher priesthood, which requires no lineage in order to hold it.[58] The author does his work well. Though the scripture suggests a strong resemblance between the ancient faithful priest and the Savior, it is the author's "conscious selecting and shaping of the Scripture text that makes the resemblance impressive."[59]

Reading the text as it stands, the description of Melchizedek gives him divine qualities and makes his priesthood eternal. Indeed, through the development of his exegetical argument, the author clarifies what he means by the phrase he quotes from LXX Psalm 109:4: "You are a priest forever according to the order of Melchizedek" (our translation). "It is now seen to reinforce 'forever,' because to be a priest of this fashion or order is to be, as Gen 14:17–20 shows, an eternal priest."[60] Further, Melchizedek was "made like unto the Son of God" (7:3). These conditions make him an excellent type of Christ.

---

57. The author is apparently following the interpretive principle *non in tora non in mundo* ("not in the Torah, not in the world"), which is an argument from silence. The position is that if something is not mentioned in the text, it never existed at all. In this case, since the scriptures mention no genealogy for Melchizedek, he never had one, thus showing he possessed an element of the divine. Johnson, *Hebrews,* 177; Attridge, *Epistle to the Hebrews,* 190 with n. 49.

58. Vanhoye, *Letter to the Hebrews,* 117–18.

59. Johnson, *Hebrews,* 178.

60. Attridge, *Epistle to the Hebrews,* 191.

It was important for the author's purposes to show that Melchizedek was greater than Abraham because of his unlimited life and the eternal nature of his priesthood. It was these that made him an excellent type of the Son. The author's take on the ancient faithful priest, however, does not appear to be unique. Indeed, he seems to be building upon then-current ideas and speculations about that figure and so would have had little trouble with the audience buying into his thesis.[61]

The rub for Latter-day Saints is that in Latter-day Saint scripture, Melchizedek is not seen as an angelic or divine figure but as a very worthy, albeit fully mortal, man (see JST Gen. 14:25–40; Alma 13:14–19; D&C 107:1–4). The JST solution is to refocus most of the phrases found in 7:3 so that they apply to the priesthood held by both the righteous priest and the Savior. It is the Melchizedek Priesthood that has no basis in parenthood or genealogy and has no beginning of days or end of years, and all those who hold it are "made like the Son of God." It is this—an everlasting power—that is eternal and stretches from the ancient past into the glorious future without lapse.

What we must not overlook, however, is that the author's main point is legitimate: Abraham did hold Melchizedek in honor and showed him deference, thus illustrating that the great faithful priest held a higher position in the priesthood than did the patriarch. The point is explicitly made by Abraham's honoring Melchizedek by paying tithes to him and receiving a blessing at his hand (7:5, 7). By using the title "patriarch," the author reminds his readers that Abraham is the direct progenitor of Levi and Aaron and thereby sets up the proof of his argument that Melchizedek and his priesthood are superior to them and theirs.[62]

Joseph Smith, commenting on these verses, stated that the author of Hebrews was referring to three different orders of priesthood, "namely the priesthood of Aron, Abraham, and Melchizedeck. Abraham's priesthood was of greater power than Levi's and Melchizedeck's was of greater power than that of Abraham."[63] By introducing another order of the priesthood, the Prophet added to the dualistic priesthood categories of Levitical or Aaronic and Melchizedek that the author of Hebrews likely had in mind. The introduction of an additional order suggests that the Prophet's

---

61. Attridge, *Epistle to the Hebrews,* 191–92 with n. 74; Cockerill, *Epistle to the Hebrews,* 298 with nn. 13–15.

62. Attridge, *Epistle to the Hebrews,* 195. For a summary, see Holzapfel and Wayment, *Making Sense,* 454.

63. Joseph Smith, discourse, recorded by James Burgess, August 27, 1843, in Ehat and Cook, *Words of Joseph Smith,* 245–46.

understanding of the nature of priesthood was still advancing, especially as he came to see aspects of it in a more temple-centric way.

Speaking of the Levitical order of the priesthood, Joseph Smith noted there was no "sealing power attending this priesthood that would admit a man into the presence of God." The priesthood of Abraham, or the patriarchal order of the priesthood, he noted, had a "more exalted power" that enabled the holder to "talk and walk with God." But it was the Melchizedek order of the priesthood that held the fulness of power. When Melchizedek blessed Abraham, the priest gave the patriarch "the last law or a fulness of the law or priesthood which constituted him a king and priest after the order of Melchesideck or an endless life."[64] Joseph Smith emphasized that "the power of the Melchisek P'd [Priesthood] was to have the power of an 'endless lives.'"[65] This order of the priesthood was not "the power of a Prophet nor apostle nor Patriarch only," the Prophet stated, "but of [a] King & Priest to God to open the windows of Heaven and pour out the peace & Law of endless Life to man & No man can attain to the joint heirship with Jesus Christ with out being administered to by one having the same power & Authority of Melchisedec."[66]

Before moving on, we feel one more point is in order. By use of his exegesis of the Old Testament text, the author shows that the relatively new Christian faith actually had an ancient antecedent so far as the power through which it operated was concerned. He was, through that means, able to make a direct connection to the past that suggested the Christian movement itself was superior to that of the Jewish.

---

64. Joseph Smith, discourse, recorded by James Burgess, August 27, 1843, in Ehat and Cook, *Words of Joseph Smith,* 245–46. See also Richard G. Ellsworth and Melvin J. Luthy, "Priesthood," in Ludlow, *Encyclopedia of Mormonism,* 3:1133–38.

65. Joseph Smith, discourse, recorded by William Clayton, August 27, 1843, in Ehat and Cook, *Words of Joseph Smith,* 247. Ogden and Skinner, *Verse by Verse,* 252, notes that "the Melchizedek Priesthood is the power of endless life and lives because it administers the ordinances that bring endless posterity (D&C 132:19–24)." See also McConkie, *Doctrinal New Testament Commentary,* 3:171–72.

66. Joseph Smith, discourse, recorded by Franklin D. Richards, August 27, 1843, in Ehat and Cook, *Words of Joseph Smith,* 245.

Excursus on Melchizedek[67]

The figure of Melchizedek has intrigued both Jews and Christians for millennia.[68] The author of Hebrews was able to capitalize on and exploit this interest. Even today there are those who have tried to discover more about this ancient and enigmatic figure. Their studies are, however, shaded by theological nuance. As one scholar pointed out, "People have said of Melchizedek primarily what their theologies required. . . . The orientation is dictated by the theological framework within which each interpretation of the basic Old Testament texts was made."[69] In short, those who have focused on Melchizedek were influenced by their theology but also used it to advance their cause. The same could be said for Latter-day Saints for whom the ancient faithful priest has an important place in theology. Many are aware of him mostly because his name is associated with the highest order of the priesthood (D&C 107:1–3).

On the other hand, the Restoration has given to Latter-day Saints some additional material that provides more information about the man Melchizedek and his importance. For example, the Hebrew noun מַלְכִּי־צֶדֶק (*malki-ṣedeq*), "Melchizedek," can be interpreted as a proper name, a title, or an epithet.[70] The word has been split into two parts, *malki* and *ṣedeq,* in an attempt to tease out what it means. Multiple Latter-day Saint interpretations have been offered, among them, "my king is righteous," "the King is

67. Much of this excursus was taken from an unpublished paper by Nathaniel Pribil, in possession of the authors.

68. Reiss, "Melchizedek Traditions," 259–65, provides a look at the Melchizedek traditions circulating at the time Hebrews was written. He discusses many issues and points of view, concluding that there appear to be two different ideas concerning the high priest in that era: one a historical figure and the other a heavenly being. See also Joseph A. Fitzmyer, "'Now This Melchizedek . . .' (Heb 7,1)," *Catholic Biblical Quarterly* 25, no. 3 (July 1963): 305–21; and Joseph A. Fitzmyer, review of *The Melchizedek Tradition: A Critical Examination of the Sources to the Fifth Century A.D. and in the Epistle to the Hebrews,* by Fred L. Horton Jr., *Catholic Biblical Quarterly* 39, no. 3 (July 1977): 436–38.

69. John W. Welch, "The Melchizedek Material in Alma 13:13–19," in *By Study and Also by Faith: Essays in Honor of Hugh W. Nibley on the Occasion of His Eightieth Birthday, 27 March 1990,* ed. John M. Lundquist and Stephen D. Ricks, vol. 2 (Salt Lake City: Deseret Book; Provo, Utah: Foundation for Ancient Research and Mormon Studies, 1990), 254. Two examples would be Attridge, *Epistle to the Hebrews,* 192–95, and Johnson, *Hebrews,* 181–83.

70. Ann Nicholls Madsen, "Melchizedek, the Man and the Tradition" (master's thesis, Brigham Young University, 1975), 35.

Legitimate," "Righteousness is King," or even "My Lord is Sedeq."[71] Since other kings in the area and time had names similar to this one, it is also a possibility that the term "Melchizedek" functioned like the title "Pharaoh" and was the title given to whoever held the kingship over a certain city or region.[72]

The author of Hebrews uses it as a proper name and interprets it as "king of righteousness" (7:2). His position seems solid especially since he uses the ancient king as a type of Christ who can be considered *the* king of righteousness.[73] Latter-day Saint theology also seems to support this interpretation since the name "Melchizedek Priesthood" would then mean "priesthood of the king of righteousness," a strong echo to the Lord himself.

A theory that circulated among some Latter-day Saints concerning Melchizedek was that he was Shem, the son of Noah.[74] Early Jewish sources also held this view and may have influenced this idea among some Latter-day Saints. The Jewish accounts are very late, being created around AD 130.[75] For the most part, both members of the Church and other scholars have discounted them, feeling that the reason certain Jews propounded the idea was to counter the Christians' insistence on using Melchizedek as a type of Christ.[76]

Giving credence to discounting the idea is D&C 84:14, which states Melchizedek "received [the priesthood] through the lineage of his fathers, even till Noah."[77] This indicates that there were multiple generations separating Noah from Melchizedek, thereby ruling out Melchizedek as being Shem.

---

71. Vanhoye, *Letter to the Hebrews,* 117; Welch, "Melchizedek Material," 245; Madsen, "Melchizedek," 34; Johnson, *Hebrews,* 176–77.

72. Madsen, "Melchizedek," 35. Certain Jews believed that Satan's specific name was *Melkiresha,* "My king is wicked." See 4Q286–7 in G. Vermes, *The Dead Sea Scrolls in English,* 3d ed. (London: Penguin Books, 1987), 161.

73. See Cockerill, *Epistle to the Hebrews,* 297.

74. For the earliest published mention of this idea, see "Ancient Ruins," *Times and Seasons* 5 (December 15, 1844): 746, likely written by John Taylor. This position is still being held by some scholars. See, for example, Alvin R. Dyer, *Who Am I?* (Salt Lake City: Deseret Book, 1966), 400.

75. Madsen, "Melchizedek," 49.

76. Madsen, "Melchizedek," 58. There is some circumstantial evidence that does connect Melchizedek with Shem, but it is weak. See Alma E. Gygi, "Is It Possible That Shem and Melchizedek Are the Same Person?" in "I Have a Question," *Ensign* 3, no. 11 (November 1973): 15–16.

77. See, for example, Charles W. Penrose, in *Journal of Discourses,* 24:305; John Taylor, in *Journal of Discourses,* 21:244; and Charles E. Haggarty, "Melchizedek . . . King of Salem," *Improvement Era* 55, no. 7 (July 1952): 512–14.

What Restoration material does say about Melchizedek is arresting. He was evidently born a prince, for he reigned "under his father" (Alma 13:18). Though he lived among people who "waxed strong in iniquity and abominations" (Alma 13:17), even as a child he was remarkably faithful, even stopping the mouth of lions and quenching the violence of fire (JST Gen. 14:26). It is not surprising, then, that at some point, he "took upon him the high priesthood forever" (Alma 13:14).

As an adult, he ruled over his people as both king and priest. That authority, along with his remarkable faith, gave him such cachet with the people that he was able to convert them and bring them into covenant with Jehovah (Alma 13:18).

"As high priest, some of his functions were keeping 'the storehouse of God' where the 'tithes for the poor' were held (JST Gen. 14:37–38), giving blessings to individuals such as Abraham (JST Gen. 14:18, 25, 37), preaching repentance (Alma 13:18; cf. [Alma] 5:49), and administering ordinances 'after this manner, that thereby the people might look forward on the Son of God . . . for a remission of their sins, that they might enter into the rest of the Lord' (Alma 13:16; JST Gen. 14:17)."[78]

According to the Genesis account, he was the king of Salem. It is unclear precisely what city the document refers to. Jewish tradition holds that Salem is the ancient name of Jerusalem.[79] However, other places have been offered as possible contenders. For instance, in Genesis 33:18 there is a city "Shalem" in Shechem, about forty miles north of Jerusalem. This spot is a strong contender due to its centrality, which afforded it a natural place for a priest-king to rule over the surrounding region.[80] There is even a chance that "Salem" could be a figurative name since, as the author of Hebrews points out, it means "peace" (7:2). The king of Salem could, therefore, just signify that he brought peace to the land, whatever land that may be.[81]

Latter-day scripture, however, seems to corroborate that there was an actual place called Salem. According to the Book of Mormon, "Melchizedek was a king over the land of Salem," where he established "peace in the

---

78. Bruce Satterfield, "Melchizedek," in Ludlow, *Encyclopedia of Mormonism,* 2:879, ellipses in original.

79. Madsen, "Melchizedek," 36; Ellingworth, *Epistle to the Hebrews,* 355.

80. Madsen, "Melchizedek," 38–40; George Wesley Buchanan, *To the Hebrews,* vol. 36 of the Anchor Bible (New York: Doubleday, 1972), 118.

81. Joseph Smith stated that Melchizedek did not reign over any particular city or area. He was king of "shaloam" meaning the "king of peace or righteousness and not of any country or nation." Ehat and Cook, *Words of Joseph Smith,* 246.

land in his days; therefore he was called the prince of peace, for he was the king of Salem" (Alma 13:17–18; see also JST Gen. 14:33). These details suggest a double irony since Melchizedek was not only the king of a land called "peace" but actually brought peace to the land.

As the KJV text reads, Melchizedek is described as being "without father, without mother, without descent, having neither beginning of days, nor end of life" (7:3). This reading implies that Melchizedek was some sort of godlike eternal figure. Most scholars, however, interpret this as a reference to the lack of a preserved genealogy in the biblical text.[82] The JST makes it clear, however, that the subject of the phrase is not Melchizedek but his priesthood. It is this that has eternal qualities (7:3). Outside of the JST, this interpretation seems to fit the intent of the author of Hebrews since he is showing that the priesthood which Melchizedek and Christ hold is not dependent, as is the Levitical Priesthood, on lineage or a priestly line. Instead it is given by God to those who are found worthy, Melchizedek being a perfect example.[83]

Given all this, it is not surprising that the great high priest became a prototype of Jesus Christ (7:15).[84] According to the Book of Mormon, "There were many [high priests] before him, and also there were many afterwards, but none were greater" (Alma 13:19). The Doctrine and Covenants states that this faithful ruler was "such a great high priest" that the holy priesthood became associated with his name. "Before his day it was called *the Holy Priesthood, after the Order of the Son of God.* But out of respect or reverence to the name of the Supreme Being, to avoid the too frequent repetition of his name, they, the church, in the ancient days, called that priesthood after Melchizedek, or the Melchizedek Priesthood" (D&C 107:2–4; italics in original).

The brief Genesis account suggests that some ritual took place when Abraham and Melchizedek met after the battle of the kings. Just what happened has been interpreted quite differently depending on various

---

82. Lane, *Hebrews 1–8*, 157; Ellingworth. *Epistle to the Hebrews,* 358.

83. The author's intent may have been to cast the priesthood net rather wide to include those not of Levitical descent, of which most of the members of the Church would have been. This move would have bolstered the idea that their access to the priesthood was legitimate with evidence that predated the Aaronic era. The author does address the Lord's non-Levitical lineage in 7:14.

84. See McConkie, *Doctrinal New Testament Commentary,* 3:166. The Bible does not refer to Melchizedek as a "high priest" but rather as "the priest of the most high God" (Gen. 14:18).

religious beliefs. The fact that the king brought with him bread and wine is of interest. Various Christian denominations have taken this as a precursor to the ordinance Jesus initiated at the last supper, namely, the sacrament. This view can be seen in the Eucharist as early as the third century and in modern Catholic mass services that still make reference to Melchizedek.[85] Other commentators, however, see Melchizedek doing no more than following a hospitality custom that carried no theological symbolism or meaning.[86] Alma makes no mention of the wine and bread, and that may be because he saw no significance to it. The author of Hebrews seems to follow suit.[87] Had there been some kind of tie, since the author makes direct ties between king and Savior, we would think he would have mentioned it. Some feel that JST changes to Genesis 14:18 stating Melchizedek "brake bread and blest it; and he blest the wine" support a sacramental idea.[88] Though it does suggest that there was a religious component to the meal, the high priest's act may have been nothing more than expressing gratitude to Jehovah for the victory during its celebration.

It is of note that at this encounter, the Bible uses the term "priest" for the first time and also that Melchizedek was a priest of "the most high God" (Gen. 14:17).[89] Whatever the specific functions of Melchizedek's interaction with Abraham, latter-day scriptures make it clear that Melchizedek held the high priesthood of God. Further, he was the one who gave it to Abraham (D&C 84:14; compare Abr. 1:1–4).[90]

---

85. Madsen, "Melchizedek," 71, 76. There is evidence from the early Iron Age that some societies struck loyalty oaths, made covenants, and renewed friendships through a ritual meal involving wine and bread. See James B. Pritchard, *Ancient Near Eastern Texts Relating to the Old Testament with Supplement,* 3d ed. (Princeton: Princeton University Press, 1969), 539.

86. Madsen, "Melchizedek," 90.

87. The author may have chosen to leave it out because it suggested that Melchizedek was in a subordinate position to Abraham. Vanhoye, *Letter to the Hebrews,* 117.

88. For example, see Bruce R. McConkie, *Promised Messiah,* 384.

89. That is not to say Melchizedek was the first of all priests. Alma 13:19 makes it clear he was not. Even so, he did give the office special quality. Some commentators argue that Melchizedek was actually a priest of a local Canaanite divinity and not actually a priest of the God of Abraham. Servants of other deities have been found with similar epithets. Madsen, "Melchizedek," 44. The author of Hebrews, however, believed Melchizedek worshiped Jehovah as the only true God. Also, both Alma and the JST clearly state that Melchizedek was a holder of the true and legitimate high priesthood of God (Alma 13:14, JST Gen. 14:27–28).

90. Alma and the JST are the only sources in any scripture or apocryphal accounts to call Melchizedek a "high priest" of God. See the excellent study by Welch, "Melchizedek

The biblical accounts are so brief that it is impossible to know just when Abraham received his ordination. The Restoration does provide, however, a suggestion. According to the book of Abraham, while the prophet was still in Ur, the Lord promised him, "I will take thee, to put upon thee my name, even the Priesthood of thy father, and my power shall be over thee" (Abr. 1:18). Sometime later, as the prophet was living in Haran, Jehovah again spoke to him, saying, "I have purposed to take thee away out of Haran, and to make thee a minister to bear my name in a strange land" (Abr. 2:6). Indeed, Abraham and his posterity were to "bear this ministry and Priesthood unto all nations" (Abr. 2:9). This took place when Abraham was sixty-two years old (Abr. 2:14). On the basis of these verses, it would appear that Abraham was ordained to the priesthood before he left Haran. That being the case, he would have held the priesthood decades before his battle with the four kings and his meeting Melchizedek. Since it was Melchizedek who ordained Abraham to the priesthood (D&C 84:14), it would appear that they had known each other years before the meeting recorded in Genesis.

The question could then be asked, to what did Melchizedek bless Abraham after the encounter with the kings? Joseph Smith's insight, noted above, suggests it was the fulness of the Melchizedek order of the priesthood through which the patriarch became a king and priest over his posterity.[91] Given that God promised Abraham eternal increase, having this power was essential to receiving the fulness of the covenantal blessing. The patriarch was ordained to the highest order of the priesthood and partook of its fulness in preparation for the birth of both Ishmael and Isaac.

Material," 238–78, who argues that "Alma's discourse on how man comes to know and participate in the plan of redemption (Alma 12:9–13:30) contains a noteworthy use of the material about Melchizedek in Genesis 14:17–24 and in other sources available to him" but which have been lost today (238).

Melchizedek gained some attention among certain Jews beginning in the first century BC. Among the Dead Sea Scrolls, 11QMel (c. 100 BC) focuses on his role as an end-time redeemer who will, among other things, save the elect. For a study, see James A. Sanders, "Cave 11 Surprises and the Question of Canon," in *New Directions in Biblical Archaeology,* ed. David Noel Freedman and Jonas C. Greenfield (Garden City, N.Y.: Doubleday, 1971), 113–30. Philo, the first-century AD Jewish scholar, viewed Melchizedek in metaphorical terms as the divine *logos,* the thought of God that formed the pattern on which all things were based. *Abr.* 235; *Leg.* 3.79–82; *Congr.* 89.

91. Joseph Smith, discourse, recorded by James Burgess, August 27, 1843, in Ehat and Cook, *Words of Joseph Smith,* 245–46. For a study on the concept of the fulness of the priesthood, see Draper and Rhodes, *Revelation of John the Apostle,* 45–52.

To what degree the author of Hebrews was privy to all this is unknown. What is certain is that he understood the importance of the Melchizedek order of the priesthood and used the great high priest as a means to showcase its importance and its superiority to the Levitical order. In this way, he continued his mission of discouraging his audience from forsaking the Lord. The argument he made here laid the foundation for the points he would next develop. In short, he ably allowed his readers to see the need for a higher or more full priesthood, one that provided what the old order could not, a surer promise of eternal life.

Christ and the Melchizedek Priesthood (7:11–17)

Greek Text

11 Εἰ μὲν οὖν τελείωσις διὰ τῆς Λευιτικῆς ἱερωσύνης ἦν, ὁ λαὸς γὰρ ἐπ' αὐτῆς νενομοθέτηται, τίς ἔτι χρεία κατὰ τὴν τάξιν Μελχισέδεκ ἕτερον ἀνίστασθαι ἱερέα καὶ οὐ κατὰ τὴν τάξιν Ἀαρὼν λέγεσθαι; 12 μετατιθεμένης γὰρ τῆς ἱερωσύνης ἐξ ἀνάγκης καὶ νόμου μετάθεσις γίνεται. 13 ἐφ' ὃν γὰρ λέγεται ταῦτα φυλῆς ἑτέρας μετέσχηκεν, ἀφ' ἧς οὐδεὶς προσέσχηκεν τῷ θυσιαστηρίῳ· 14 πρόδηλον γὰρ ὅτι ἐξ Ἰούδα ἀνατέταλκεν ὁ κύριος ἡμῶν, εἰς ἣν φυλὴν περὶ ἱερέων οὐδὲν Μωϋσῆς ἐλάλησεν. 15 Καὶ περισσότερον ἔτι κατάδηλόν ἐστιν, εἰ κατὰ τὴν ὁμοιότητα Μελχισέδεκ ἀνίσταται ἱερεὺς ἕτερος, 16 ὃς οὐ κατὰ νόμον ἐντολῆς σαρκίνης γέγονεν ἀλλὰ κατὰ δύναμιν ζωῆς ἀκαταλύτου, 17 μαρτυρεῖται γὰρ ὅτι Σὺ ἱερεὺς εἰς τὸν αἰῶνα κατὰ τὴν τάξιν Μελχισέδεκ. [SBLGNT]

King James Version

11 If therefore perfection were by the Levitical priesthood, (for under it the people received the law,) what further need was there that another priest should rise after the order of Melchisedec, and not be called after the order of Aaron? 12 For the priesthood being changed, there is made of necessity a change also of the law. 13 For he of whom these things are spoken pertaineth to another tribe, of which no man gave attendance at the altar. 14 For it is evident that our Lord sprang out of Juda; of which tribe Moses spake nothing concerning priesthood. 15 And it is yet far more evident: for that after the similitude of Melchisedec there ariseth another priest, 16 Who is made, not after the law of a carnal commandment, but after the power of an endless life. 17 For he testifieth, Thou art a priest for ever after the order of Melchisedec.

New Rendition

11 Therefore, if perfection had been possible through the Levitical priesthood, for based on it, the people received the law, then what further need would there have been to speak of a different kind of priest arising according to the order of Melchizedek rather than according to the order of Aaron? 12 For if the priesthood is changed, then there must also be a change in the law. 13 For the one, about whom these things are said, belongs to another tribe from which no one has ever officiated at the altar. 14 For it is clear that our Lord arose from Judah, and Moses said nothing about priests from that tribe. 15 And it is still more clear if another priest arises in the same way as Melchizedek, 16 who has become a priest not according to a legal requirement with regard to his ancestry, but according to the power of an indestructible life. 17 For it is declared,

> "You are a priest forever according to the order of Melchizedek." [Ps. 110:4]

Translation Notes and Comments

7:11 ***If therefore perfection were by the Levitical priesthood . . . / Therefore, if perfection had been possible through the Levitical Priesthood . . . :*** This is a contrary-to-fact condition that indicates "the assumption of an untruth (for the sake of argument)."[92] For the noun τελείωσις (*teleiōsis*), "perfection," see Translation Notes for 6:1 with its associated Analysis. In the present context, *teleiōsis* denotes a state necessary for salvation, specifically to be in the right relationship with the Divine.[93] The idea of flawless excellence associated with the English word, though present, takes on secondary force and is more the result of *teleiōsis* than a description of it.[94]

The author's focus is on the Λευιτικὴ ἱερωσύνη (*Leuitikē hierōsynē*), "the Levitical Priesthood," and specifically on its limitation in bringing about Jehovah's designs, namely *teleiōsis*. He also uses the term τάξις Ἀαρών (*taxis Aarōn*), "order of Aaron" (see below), and makes no distinction between Levites and priests.[95] Understanding this idea is important because it speaks to how the author understood the Israelite/Jewish cultic system. All members of it were regarded as having authority. Though he notes the priesthood's lack of power, nonetheless it should be kept in mind that it was through this divinely appointed and legitimate authority that the Mosaic law operated.

for under it the people received the law / for based on it, the people received the law: The phrase looks back to Exodus 19–24, where Jehovah established his law with the children of Israel and they accepted it.

The phrase is parenthetical. The author uses it to establish the basis or ground upon which the law of Moses rested. He uses the phrase ἐπ' αὐτῆς

92. This is despite it missing the usual marker ἄν (*an*) that the author normally employs. Wallace, *Greek Grammar,* 694; see also Blass and Debrunner, *Greek Grammar of the New Testament,* §360.

93. Koester, *Hebrews,* 353.

94. BDAG, 996. Vanhoye, *Letter to the Hebrews,* 111, notes that the author is playing on the double meaning of τέλειος (*teleios* as both completeness and adulthood), the word thus suggesting the completeness found in maturity. See also Johnson, *Hebrews,* 166–67. For a fuller treatment, see Translation Notes for 2:10, 12, and 5:9 with the respective Analyses.

95. Ellingworth, *Epistle to the Hebrews,* 371. The phrase is found nowhere else in scripture, and it is possible the author coined it. Cockerill, *Epistle to the Hebrews,* 314 n. 3. The word *taxis,* "order," does not mean commandment but rather "disposition" or "category." Vanhoye, *Letter to the Hebrews,* 121.

(*ep' autēs*), "based on it," emphasizing that the priesthood is fundamental and essential to the law.[96]

The verb νομοθετέω (*nomotheteō*), "to receive," looks to the authority through which a law is initiated and sanctioned and thus carries the idea of founding or ordaining a law.[97] It is in the perfect tense, thus emphasizing an event that was completed in the past but has results continuing to the present time.[98] The author's point is that the Levitical order of the priesthood stood as the authorizing agent of the Mosaic law.[99] Because the priesthood established the law, the functioning of the required ordinances was legitimized. That also meant that living under that law necessitated the perpetual administration of priesthood ordinances that it required. To do away with the ordinances was tantamount to doing away with the priesthood.[100] Further, doing away with the priesthood meant doing away with the law.

what further need was there that another priest should rise after the order of Melchisedec, and not be called after the order of Aaron? / then what further need would there have been to speak of a different kind of priest arising according to the order of Melchizedek rather than according to the order of Aaron?: The important word in this phrase is the noun χρεία (*chreia*), "need." It stresses the absolute necessity of something being done.[101] In this case, it was ἕτερον ἀνίστασθαι ἱερέα (*heteron anistasthai hierea*), the "arising of a different kind of priest." The verb ἀνίστημι (*anistēmi*), found

---

96. BDAG, 363–67. The preposition can be taken three ways. First, the law was given "on the basis of" the Levitical Priesthood, meaning that the law drew its authority from the priesthood. Second, the law was given "about" the Levitical Priesthood, meaning its intent was to disclose the priesthood and show how it was to function. And third, the law was received "under" or during the ministry of the Levitical Priesthood. The latter idea seems the weakest because Jehovah actually gave the law before he set up the Levitical order of the priesthood. See Koester, *Hebrews,* 353. Using the events of the Restoration as a model, it would appear that the priesthood preceded the giving of the law since Joseph Smith and Oliver Cowdery received both the Aaronic and Melchizedek Priesthoods before the Church was even organized. See D&C 13:1; 27:7–8; JS–H 1:68–72; and *Saints: The Story of the Church of Jesus Christ in the Latter Days,* vol. 1, *The Standard of Truth, 1815–1846* (Salt Lake City: The Church of Jesus Christ of Latter-day Saints, 2018), 67, 84.

97. BDAG, 676; Louw-Nida, §33.340.

98. Wallace, *Greek Grammar,* 573.

99. Though the prepositional phrase ἐπ' αὐτῆς (*ep' autēs*) is somewhat vague, most translators see it as referring to the Levitical Priesthood. See Johnson, *Hebrews,* 185; Attridge, *Epistle to the Hebrews,* 200 n. 30; and Ellingworth, *Epistle to the Hebrews,* 372.

100. Ellingworth, *Epistle to the Hebrews,* 372; Cockerill, *Epistle to the Hebrews,* 316; compare O'Brien, *Letter to the Hebrews,* 258.

101. BDAG, 1088.

here as a present middle infinitive, "to arise," denotes the coming forth of a person to take up an office or function.[102]

The adjective ἕτερον (*heteron*) in the phrase ἕτερον . . . ἱερέα (*heteron . . . hierea*) can mean either "another" or a "different" priest. The latter nuance means "of a dissimilar in kind."[103] It is this nuance that is at play here,[104] hence our Rendition uses the phrase "a different kind of priest." The author has not yet identified precisely who he has in mind, but the reference is clearly to the Savior, who was a different kind of priest from the old ones. As noted above, he was neither weak nor flawed, and the ordinances that come through his system are eternal in their effect.

7:12 ***For the priesthood being changed / For if the priesthood is changed:*** The verb μετατίθημι (*metatithēmi*), "to change," found in this passage as a genitive absolute participial, we translated circumstantially in a conditional sense using "if."[105] The verb means to transfer an office from one person to another and also to change or alter a decree or law.[106] It is the latter nuance that is at play here. By tying it to the noun ἀθέτησις (*athetēsis*), "annulment,"[107] in 7:18, the author shows just how extreme the change will be.[108]

there is made of necessity a change also of the law / then there must also be a change in the law: The prepositional phrase ἐξ ἀνάγκης (*ex anangkēs*), "out of necessity, necessarily,"[109] emphasizes that a change in priesthood logically requires a change in the law and is thus translated "must" in our Rendition. Since, from a Latter-day Saint perspective, each priesthood order administers specific ordinances and oversees certain laws and

---

102. BDAG, 83. The verb is also used to describe the Savior's rising from the dead (Matt. 17:9; 20:19; Luke 18:33; Acts 17:3; Rom. 6:9; 1 Thes. 4:14). That the author associates it with Jesus receiving the power of "indestructible life" (NR 7:16) suggests he may have been playing on the polyvalent potential of the word: "Jesus is priest above all because of his resurrection and exaltation to God's right hand." Johnson, *Hebrews,* 187.

103. BDAG, 399; Bruce, *Epistle to the Hebrews,* 165 n. 45.

104. Cockerill, *Epistle to the Hebrews,* 315–16.

105. Wallace, *Greek Grammar,* 632–33.

106. BDAG, 642.

107. BDAG, 24.

108. Attridge, *Epistle to the Hebrews,* 200–201. See also McConkie, *Doctrinal New Testament Commentary,* 3:170–71. The idea of changing the priesthood ran against the notion that it was permanent and therefore no change could be made to it (Ex. 40:15; Num. 18:19; 25:13). The argument of the author is that the change is not within the Levitical Priesthood but a change to a new order of priesthood. Koester, *Hebrews,* 354.

109. BDAG, 60–61. This is a strong word as its nuances "constraint" and "torture" show.

doctrines according to the keys it holds,[110] a change in priesthood means that there will be some modification or alterations of the laws and practices it controls. The move from the Levitical to the Melchizedek order of the priesthood meant profound changes to the Mosaic law. Some of these changes—such as the cessation of blood sacrifices and much of the Levitical temple rites—were sweeping.

7:13 ***For he of whom these things are spoken pertaineth to another tribe, of which no man gave attendance at the altar / For the one about whom these things are said belongs to another tribe from which no one has ever officiated at the altar:*** In the phrase ἐφ' ὃν γὰρ (*eph hon gar*), literally "for in respect to whom," an antecedent needs to be supplied. Our Rendition uses "the one," meaning the priest who will arise of the Melchizedek order.[111] The demonstrative pronoun ταῦτα (*tauta*), "these things," refers to what the author has been saying about this one's priesthood.

The verbs μετέχω (*metechō*), "to share in" or "to belong to,"[112] and προσέχω (*prosechō*), "apply oneself to" or "to officiate at,"[113] are both found here in the perfect tense. The use of this tense highlights the fact that never has one from another tribe ever officiated in Levitical sacrifices. The author makes this point to stress that a different kind of priest must arise, totally unlike those serving in Levitical capacity.

The problem the author is addressing here is whether Jesus, born into the tribe of Judah, possessed any priesthood at all, let alone a superior one. According to the Mosaic law, only those of the tribe of Levi could hold the priesthood (Gen. 49:5–7; Ex. 28:1–4; Num. 1:47–54). Taking the biblical statements as found in Exodus 30:21 and Leviticus 6:18, 22; 7:34–36, many Jews understood that the Levitical Priesthood would stand forever.[114] Therefore, in their view, Jesus had no claim on priesthood authority. The

---

110. See Richard G. Ellsworth and Melvin J. Luthy, "Priesthood," in Ludlow, *Encyclopedia of Mormonism,* 3:1133; and Allen K. Parrish, "Keys of the Priesthood," in Ludlow, *Encyclopedia of Mormonism,* 2:780–81.

111. A. T. Robertson, *A Grammar of the Greek New Testament in the Light of Historical Research,* 4th ed. (Nashville: Broadman Press, 1934), 721, notes that οὗτος (*houtos*), "he" or "one," is implied in the phrase.

112. BDAG, 642.

113. BDAG, 879–80.

114. For a discussion of how the Jews at the time of Christ viewed the law and priesthood, see Barry Joslin, *Hebrews, Christ, and the Law: The Theology of the Mosaic Law in Hebrews 7:1–10:18* (Milton Keynes, U.K.: Paternoster, 2008), 23–90; and Sidney G. Sowers, *Hermeneutics of Philo and Hebrews: A Comparison of Interpretation* (Richmond: John Knox Press, 1965), 98–99 n. 27.

author of Hebrews picks up on this and, in this section, seeks to justify the Christian position.

7:14 ***For it is evident that our Lord sprang out of Juda; of which tribe Moses spake nothing concerning priesthood / For it is clear that our Lord arose from Judah, and Moses said nothing about priests from that tribe:*** The adjective πρόδηλος (*prodēlos*) points to something that is quite clear or evident[115] and acts as the author's concession to the rule found in the Mosaic law. There is not so much as a whisper there that anyone from another tribe, including one as prominent as Judah, would ever hold the Levitical Priesthood.[116]

The verb ἀνατέλλω (*anatellō*), "to spring up, arise,"[117] found here in the perfect tense, points to the Savior's tie to the tribe of Judah. The author's use of the verb is telling. His objective is to show that "the Lord" is a different kind of priest and even his mortal ancestry is different. The other priests *descended* from Levi, but Jesus *arose* from Judah.[118] The author's imagery may be based on Isaiah 4:2; 11:1–5, and Jeremiah 23:5–6, which speak of the arising of a "righteous branch" that shall come to rule in equity and justice.[119] The idea also echoes LXX Numbers 24:17, where Balaam prophesied that "a star shall rise (*anatellō*) from Jacob."[120] The focus of both sets of Old Testament images is on the figures arising to great heights.

The perfect tense is significant. It infers that though Jesus arose at a specific time and place, his rise is still in effect; he has, indeed, arisen from mortal birth to eternal life and there ever remains.[121]

7:15 ***And it is yet far more evident: for that after the similitude of Melchisedec there ariseth another priest / And it is still more clear if another priest arises in the same way as Melchizedek:*** The sentence (7:15–16) is

115. BDAG, 867.

116. Ogden and Skinner, *Verse by Verse,* 252, notes that "Jesus was not from the tribe of Levi; his priesthood was greater."

117. BDAG, 73.

118. Though a number of Bibles translate the verb as "descended" (for example, NIV, RSV, NRSV), that meaning, though found in BDAG, 73, is not attested in any passages in the LXX or other Greek literature. See LSJ, 123; and Moulton and Milligan, *Vocabulary,* 38.

119. *NID,* s.v. "ἀνατελλω."

120. Attridge, *Epistle to the Hebrews,* 201; Cockerill, *Epistle to the Hebrews,* 320. This verb, like ἀνίστημι (*anistēmi*), "to arise," also echoes the idea of resurrection and exaltation of the Lord. The author may have been playing on this to add depth of understanding to what the Lord did. Johnson, *Hebrews,* 187; Koester, *Hebrews,* 355.

121. Bruce, *Epistle to the Hebrews,* 165–66 nn. 42, 46; O'Brien, *Letter to the Hebrews,* 260–61.

constructed as a condition of fact. Its purpose is to gain the assent of the author's readers.[122] The use of "if" does not question that such a priest will arise but indicates that when he does arise, he will have certain characteristics or attributes.

The adjective κατάδηλος (*katadēlos*) denotes that which is very clear or plain.[123] The author uses it in contrast to πρόδηλος (*prodēlos*), found in the previous verse, denoting that which is rather clear or plain. To heighten the contrast, the author adds the comparative adverb περισσότερον (*perissoteron*), "more, even more."[124]

The prepositional phrase κατὰ τὴν ὁμοιότητα (*kata tēn homoiotēta*), literally "according to the likeness of," has the sense "in the same way as," and it is so translated in our Rendition.

7:16 ***Who is made, not after the law of a carnal commandment / who has become a priest not according to a legal requirement with regard to his ancestry:*** The verb γίνομαι (*ginomai*), "become," in the present context, does not mean to be produced or made but to "come into a certain state,"[125] hence we have used "has become" in our Rendition. It is found here in the perfect tense, implying that "our Lord" (7:14) has already become a high priest and that he will continue in that capacity for eternity.[126]

The noun "a priest" is not found in the Greek text but is added for clarity. The phrase νόμον ἐντολῆς σαρκίνης (*nomon entolēs sarkinēs*), literally "the fleshly commandments of the law," refers to the genealogical restrictions the Mosaic law imposed on holding the Levitical Priesthood.[127] The author's point is that "our Lord" (7:14) did not have to follow that dictum. He did, however, as the next phrase shows, have to follow another.

but after the power of an endless life / but according to the power of an indestructible life: The preposition κατά (*kata*), "in accordance with" or "according to,"[128] carries the idea of reaching a state because of meeting certain demands or requirements. In this case, becoming a Melchizedek priest comes by virtue of a specific power, having an "indestructible life."

---

122. According to Wallace, *Greek Grammar,* 450, this condition indicates an "*assumption of truth for the sake of argument*" (italics in original). See also Cockerill, *Epistle to the Hebrews,* 321.

123. BDAG, 516.

124. BDAG, 806.

125. BDAG, 196–99.

126. Cockerill, *Epistle to the Hebrews,* 322 n. 42.

127. Lane, *Hebrews 1–8,* 183; Ellingworth, *Epistle to the Hebrews,* 378–79; Johnson, *Hebrews,* 188.

128. BDAG, 511–13.

The adjective ἀκατάλυτος (*akatalytos*), "indestructible,"[129] plays an important role in understanding what the author is telling his audience. Various nuances of the word include "indissoluble" and "endless." Of these, "indestructible" gives the best thrust to the author's point: that which cannot be destroyed is neither dependent on nor subject to anything for its existence. It therefore lasts forever. By extension, everything associated with it also has an eternal quality. Further, no power or authority can take away, lessen, or in any way alter it or anything associated with it. Thus, an indestructible life describes the quality of life possessed by the Divine.[130]

Only death can destroy life. But Jesus overcame death and in so doing made his life indestructible. On the basis of his possessing that quality of life, God gave him priesthood power that operates eternally.[131] Thus, Christ will hold this office forever.

The question arises, when did Jesus receive his priesthood ordination? Here the author of Hebrews ties it to Jesus' receiving the powers of an indestructible life. Since he died, it could be argued that he received the priesthood at the time of or shortly after the Resurrection. However, Jesus was never subject to death in the same way mortals are. Indeed, he came into mortality with the power to overcome death and was, therefore, never actually subject to it. As he said, "As the Father hath life in himself; so hath he given to the Son to have life in himself" (John 5:26). He stated further that his Father loved him "because I lay down my life, that I might take it again. No man taketh it from me, but I lay it down of myself. I have power to lay it down, and I have power to take it again" (John 10:17–18). He also proclaimed that he possessed "the keys of hell and death" (Rev. 1:18). In sum, he ever mastered death. Therefore, it would appear he did not need to wait until the Resurrection to meet the necessary requirements of having an indestructible life. He held this power at some point in the premortal existence and likely received the power of the priesthood at the same time. Thus, John could proclaim Jesus was God before he entered the world (John 1:1–3), and the author of Hebrews could witness that the Lord upheld "all things by the word of his power" (1:3). For this reason, it is easy to understand that, as early as the beginning of human history, the priesthood was called "the Holy Priesthood, after the Order of the Son of God" (D&C 107:3; compare D&C 76:57).

---

129. BDAG, 35; Louw-Nida, §13.47.

130. Büchel, *TDNT,* 4:338.

131. Ellingworth, *Epistle to the Hebrews,* 378–79.

Having noted that, there was a moment during the Savior's mortality when he did receive a divine endowment of power that could have included that of the priesthood. According to D&C 93:15–17, at his baptism, "the Holy Ghost descended upon him in the form of a dove, and sat upon him, and there came a voice out of heaven saying: This is my beloved Son, . . . [and] he received a fulness of the glory of the Father; And he received all power, both in heaven and on earth, and the glory of the Father was with him, for he dwelt in him." Clearly, from at least this point on, the mortal Savior had a fulness of divine power.

Through the Lord's exercise of the keys associated with priesthood power—that is, the authority to preside over, use, and delegate it[132]—the fundamental principles, government, and doctrine of God's kingdom can be revealed, instituted, and administered.[133] The author's point is that the Lord's priesthood, with all its benefits, will function eternally. One of its greatest benefits for the faithful is also receiving an indestructible life and, with it, eternal priesthood authority.

7:17 ***For he testifieth, Thou art a priest for ever after the order of Melchisedec / For it is declared, "You are a priest forever according to the order of Melchizedek":*** The verb μαρτυρέω (*martyreō*), found here in a passive tense, means to affirm something in a supportive manner, thus "to declare" it.[134] The author again appeals to LXX Psalm 109:4 for that support. The point is that "the most fundamental difference in the priesthood of Jesus is not his earthly origin but his heavenly destination" where he will preside as High Priest forever more.[135]

Analysis and Summary

This section focuses on the means by which "perfection" (τελείωσις, *teleiōsis*) is attained. In some places, the Bible uses the word in a rather restricted cultic sense wherein it is tied to temple worship and the authority to perform its ordinances. It is through these that both priest and people can draw nearer to Jehovah. In this context, then, perfection is reached when one is united with God on earth through priesthood ordinances. This unity

132. Allen K. Parrish, "Keys of the Priesthood," in Ludlow, *Encyclopedia of Mormonism,* 2:780–81.

133. "History, 1838–1856, Volume A-1," 285.

134. BDAG, 617–18.

135. Johnson, *Hebrews,* 189.

and type of earthly perfection paves the way for total unity (oneness with the Father and Son) and ultimate perfection in heaven.[136]

However, the author argues, the old system did not bring about unity with God on earth. The problem was that the sacrifices were actually impotent, having no continuous means of cleansing the people and keeping them clean, thereby bringing them closer to God and thus to perfection (compare 9:9; 10:1). The problem could clearly be seen in the case of the priests themselves. They suffered from human weaknesses and were burdened with sin (see 5:1–3; 7:11–14; 9:1–10).[137] The author highlighted their impotency by citing LXX Psalm 109:4, showing the need for another kind of priest to arise who was affected by neither of these debilitating problems.[138]

The author's argument that perfection could not come through the lesser priesthood and its ordinances (7:11) has only some legitimacy. To give credit, the author never claims absolutely that the Israelites could not have drawn near to Jehovah, thus gaining perfection through the work of the law and its temple rituals (see 10:1; 11:6). In point of fact, other scriptures suggest that under the right circumstances, they could. Jehovah established a revision of the Mosaic law due to Israel's rebellion at Sinai (see Ex. 32). He gave it because the Israelites had "hardened their hearts and could not endure his presence. . . . Therefore, he took Moses out of their midst, and the Holy Priesthood also" (D&C 84:24–25; see also 3:16–19; Mosiah 3:14).[139] Though they had forfeited access to the fulness of the gospel and the higher priesthood, in his mercy Jehovah gave them a preparatory gospel designed to be a "schoolmaster to bring us unto Christ" and eventually to the fulness of his gospel (Gal. 3:24; compare Jacob 4:5; and Alma 34:14).[140]

Concerning this law, the Book of Mormon teaches "that it was expedient that there should be a law given to the children of Israel, yea, even a very strict law; for they were a stiffnecked people, quick to do iniquity, and slow to remember the Lord their God." Therefore, Jehovah gave them "a law of performances and of ordinances, a law which they were to observe strictly

136. For a fuller treatment, see Comments for 2:10, 12; 5:9 with their associated Analysis. It is of note that the higher priesthood holds the "key of the mysteries of the kingdom, even the key of the knowledge of God." It is through the ordinances thereof, specifically temple worship, that "the power of godliness is manifest" which prepares each person to "see the face of God, even the Father, and live" (D&C 84:19–22).

137. Cockerill, *Epistle to the Hebrews,* 315.

138. See Delling, *TDNT,* 8:79–86; Lane, *Hebrews 1–8,* 180.

139. See also "History, 1838–1856, Volume A-1," 230.

140. Parker and Falk, "Law of Moses," 2:812, italics removed.

from day to day, to keep them in remembrance of God and their duty towards him." Nonetheless, the text notes, "all these things were types of things to come" (Mosiah 13:29–31). This sacred volume reveals that Jehovah so filled the law with types and shadows that, for those who could and would see, it revealed much about the nature and ministry of Christ and thereby engendered faith in him. Indeed, the book states it was "for this end hath the law of Moses been given . . . of God . . . [for] the typifying of [Christ]" (2 Ne. 11:4). Thus, because they had eyes to see, the faithful "did look forward to the coming of Christ, considering that the law of Moses was a type of his coming, and believing that they must keep those outward performances until the time that he should be revealed unto them" (Alma 25:15). As a result, "the law of Moses [pointed their] souls to him; and for this cause it [was] sanctified unto [them] for righteousness" (Jacob 4:5).

Thus, for those who saw it for what it was, the law was not impotent. Admittedly, like all ordinances, in and of itself it had no efficacy. But as it brought—through revelation—understanding and faith in the Savior, it functioned exactly as Jehovah designed it to and thereby proved a means of salvation. Therefore, the law—with its temple rituals and the Levitical Priesthood that supported it—was authentic and functional. Through it a person really could be drawn to God and reach perfection (*teleiōsis*) in the cultic sense. Even so, its authority extended only to lesser things, such as the law of carnal commandments and baptism (D&C 84:26–27) and therefore could not fully function to make the people perfect in the ultimate sense.[141]

The reason the old law did not fully work was not because it was powerless or had "anything intrinsically wrong with it, but because in the divine arrangement it was designed as a shadow, anticipating the substance. The substance, therefore, far from opposing the shadow, is its *fulfillment—this is perfection.*"[142] The term "perfection" in the context of Hebrews looks at the Son's fulfillment of the promises he has made in the new covenant as High Priest. The realization of these promises, made possible through his

---

141. The noun τελείωσις (*teleiōsis*), used in the LXX, does not denote the quality of perfection but rather describes an action, that of "making something perfect," and refers specifically to the consecration of a priest. He becomes "perfect," that is, whole, complete, upon his anointing. The problem was that the act did not necessarily bring him to a higher state of righteousness. Thus, there was a need for the introduction of another order of the priesthood that had the power of transformation. Vanhoye, *Letter to the Hebrews,* 121.

142. Moises Silva, "Perfection and Eschatology in Hebrews," *Westminster Theological Journal* 39, no. 1 (1976): 68, italics in original.

priestly service, makes access to the Father possible in more sure ways than the old covenant could.[143] The significant difference, then, between the old covenant and the new was the "better hope" through which the Christian could draw even nearer to God (7:19).

In sum, the Savior's restoration of the fulness of the gospel with its attendant knowledge, priesthood power, hope, and grace opened wonderful possibilities. It made much stronger, more certain, and fully complete the realization of drawing nearer to their Father, thus, obtaining perfection.[144] What the Mosaic law could do only in part, the law of the gospel could do in full.[145] Through its sacrifices, the old law could make the faithful clean for a season but not ultimately. It could bring them closer to Jehovah but not keep them there. Thus, it lacked the power in and of itself to perfect them.

Seen in this light, "perfection," as the author uses it, includes not only the fulfillment and completion of the right relationship with God but adds the dimension of sinlessness.[146] And more: it also connotes sanctification, that deep and abiding spiritual cleansing that made the soul pure and holy (2:11; 9:13; 10:11–14; compare Lev. 11:45; Rom. 8:1–4; Mosiah 5:2; and Alma 5:14; 13:12).

In addition, the definition implies a transformation through which the Saint became like Christ (compare 1 John 3:1–2). This transformation the old covenant simply could not accomplish. Higher ordinances, covenants, and priesthood powers were required. All these came through Christ and were the means that enabled him to bring ultimate perfection to the individual. Thus, though an individual may deny himself of ungodliness and love God, it is only through the Father's grace and sufficiency that a person is perfected. Indeed, as the Book of Mormon teaches, it is because of God's grace that "ye may be perfect in Christ; and if by the grace of God

---

143. Lane, *Hebrews 1–8,* 181.

144. Preisker, *TDNT,* 2:331.

145. An important aspect of perfection is tied to the idea of holiness. This word denotes in large part separation from the world. The more one distances himself or herself from the world, the closer to God and perfection he or she becomes. To assist the Saint in doing this, the Lord restored the law of the gospel. James E. Talmage, *The Vitality of Mormonism* (Boston: n.p., 1919), 169, noted that this law "is a perfect law and the sure effect of full obedience thereto is perfection" (quoted in Elouise M. Bell, "Holiness," in Ludlow, *Encyclopedia of Mormonism,* 2:648). The Savior's sermons both in the Holy Land (Matt. 5–7) and at the temple at Bountiful in America (3 Ne. 12–14) were directed to those who were to live the law of the gospel and to making sure it was clearly understood. See Thomas W. Mackay, "Beatitudes," in Ludlow, *Encyclopedia of Mormonism,* 1:98.

146. Lane, *Hebrews 1–8,* 181; Cockerill, *Epistle to the Hebrews,* 315.

ye are perfect in Christ, ye can in nowise deny the power of God." The result is that "ye [are] sanctified in Christ by the grace of God, through the shedding of the blood of Christ, which is in the covenant of the Father unto the remission of your sins, that ye become holy, without spot" (Moro. 10:32–33).

The emphasis in Hebrews, however, is not on this ultimate aspect of perfection (though it does stand behind it) but on oneness and unity with the Father and Son and the glory and rest that unity will bring.[147]

It is on the strength of LXX Psalm 109:4, where the Father decrees that his Son will be a "priest for ever," that the author builds his case. The author contrasts the Levitical law and Melchizedek power, between that which has its basis in the flesh and that which has its basis in an indestructible life (7:16–17). In this centers the entire superiority of Jesus, the High Priest after the order of Melchizedek, over his Aaronic counterpart. Jesus is High Priest *forever.*[148]

The author uses God's statement to emphasize the need of another order of priesthood that could do what the Levitical one could not. That divine injunction did demand that the Aaronic Priesthood order be "changed" and another order reestablished (7:12). This reestablished order differed from the Levitical in a number of ways. First and foremost, it made unity with God more sure than the old system (7:11). Second, it was neither restricted by genealogy nor administered by flawed human beings but by the flawless and eternal Son of God. Third, it was not bound by lesser ordinances. Fourth, all the righteous had access to it. And finally, it administered all necessary ordinances to unite one fully with the Father. In short, the new order of priesthood overcame the insufficiency of the old one.[149]

Beginning in 7:13, the author addresses a problem many of his readers would have been aware of. According to the law, the priesthood belonged exclusively to the Levitical tribe. Further, many Jews believed, based on Leviticus 6:18–22; 7:34–36; and Exodus 30:21, that privilege and obligation were everlasting and thus nontransferable, and therefore the ordinances

---

147. See Ellingworth, *Epistle to the Hebrews,* 371; Koester, *Hebrews,* 353; compare O'Brien, *Letter to the Hebrews,* 257.

148. Büchel, *TDNT,* 4:338–39.

149. The change in priesthood orders from Levitical to Melchizedek brought with it sweeping changes. Though it is true that the cultic sacrifices and temple rituals were all done away, so too there was an elevation in the moral law, as the Savior made very clear in the Sermon on the Mount (Matt. 5–7). Cockerill, *Epistle to the Hebrews,* 317 n. 20. Compare Ogden and Skinner, *Verse by Verse,* 252.

assigned to it could only be executed by the Levites.[150] In 7:14 the author readily admits that the scriptures are quite clear on this subject and that Jesus was from the tribe of Judah, and there was not a breath anywhere in the scriptures that suggested one from that tribe would ever have the priesthood. The tacit question was, then, how could Jesus lay claim to it? This question the author answers in 7:15. He notes that it is even more clear, based on LXX Psalm 109:4 (which he does not quote here but tacitly points back to), that another kind of priest would arise like Melchizedek. The author then elucidates just what this means. The priesthood of this new priest would be neither tied to the regulations of the Mosaic law nor bound by its genealogical restrictions (7:16). The author had already made it abundantly clear (7:12) that a change in priesthood meant that the strictures of the old law would no longer apply. A new order of priesthood would bring in a fulness of laws and ordinances. That another priest would arise from Judah only clinches his point.[151]

Jesus was like Melchizedek, not Aaron. That the Son became a priest "according to the power of an indestructible life" shows how superior his priesthood was. To emphasize his point, the author sets up a series of contrasts: "'Power' contrasts with 'law'; 'live,' with 'ordinance'; and 'indestructible,' with 'fleshly.' This new priesthood is based on nothing less than the power of God."[152]

A Better Hope by Which We Draw Near to God (7:18–28)

Greek Text

18 ἀθέτησις μὲν γὰρ γίνεται προαγούσης ἐντολῆς διὰ τὸ αὐτῆς ἀσθενὲς καὶ ἀνωφελές, 19 οὐδὲν γὰρ ἐτελείωσεν ὁ νόμος, ἐπεισαγωγὴ δὲ κρείττονος ἐλπίδος, δι' ἧς ἐγγίζομεν τῷ θεῷ. 20 Καὶ καθ' ὅσον οὐ χωρὶς ὁρκωμοσίας (οἱ μὲν γὰρ χωρὶς ὁρκωμοσίας εἰσὶν ἱερεῖς γεγονότες, 21 ὁ δὲ μετὰ ὁρκωμοσίας διὰ τοῦ λέγοντος πρὸς αὐτόν· Ὤμοσεν κύριος, καὶ οὐ μεταμεληθήσεται, Σὺ ἱερεὺς εἰς τὸν αἰῶνα), 22 κατὰ τοσοῦτο κρείττονος διαθήκης γέγονεν ἔγγυος Ἰησοῦς. 23 Καὶ οἱ μὲν

150. See note 98 in this chapter.

151. Cockerill, *Epistle to the Hebrews,* 321. Though the tribe of Judah was associated primarily with kingship, the *Testament of Levi* 8.14 speaks of a descendent of Judah who will establish a new priesthood associated with the Gentiles.

152. Cockerill, *Epistle to the Hebrews,* 323.

πλείονές εἰσιν γεγονότες ἱερεῖς διὰ τὸ θανάτῳ κωλύεσθαι παραμένειν· 24 ὁ δὲ διὰ τὸ μένειν αὐτὸν εἰς τὸν αἰῶνα ἀπαράβατον ἔχει τὴν ἱερωσύνην· 25 ὅθεν καὶ σῴζειν εἰς τὸ παντελὲς δύναται τοὺς προσερχομένους δι' αὐτοῦ τῷ θεῷ, πάντοτε ζῶν εἰς τὸ ἐντυγχάνειν ὑπὲρ αὐτῶν. 26 Τοιοῦτος γὰρ ἡμῖν καὶ ἔπρεπεν ἀρχιερεύς, ὅσιος, ἄκακος, ἀμίαντος, κεχωρισμένος ἀπὸ τῶν ἁμαρτωλῶν, καὶ ὑψηλότερος τῶν οὐρανῶν γενόμενος· 27 ὃς οὐκ ἔχει καθ' ἡμέραν ἀνάγκην, ὥσπερ οἱ ἀρχιερεῖς, πρότερον ὑπὲρ τῶν ἰδίων ἁμαρτιῶν θυσίας ἀναφέρειν, ἔπειτα τῶν τοῦ λαοῦ (τοῦτο γὰρ ἐποίησεν ἐφάπαξ ἑαυτὸν ἀνενέγκας)· 28 ὁ νόμος γὰρ ἀνθρώπους καθίστησιν ἀρχιερεῖς ἔχοντας ἀσθένειαν, ὁ λόγος δὲ τῆς ὁρκωμοσίας τῆς μετὰ τὸν νόμον υἱόν, εἰς τὸν αἰῶνα τετελειωμένον. [SBLGNT]

King James Version

18 For there is verily a disannulling of the commandment going before for the weakness and unprofitableness thereof. 19 For the law made nothing perfect, but the bringing in of a better hope did; by the which we draw nigh unto God. 20 And inasmuch as not without an oath he was made priest: 21 (For those priests were made without an oath; but this with an oath by him that said unto him, The Lord sware and will not repent, Thou art a priest for ever after the order of Melchisedec:) 22 By so much was Jesus made a surety of a better testament. 23 And they truly were many priests, because they were not suffered to continue by reason of death: 24 But this man, because he continueth ever, hath an unchangeable priesthood. 25 Wherefore he is able also to save them to the uttermost that come unto God by him, seeing he ever liveth to make intercession for them. 26 For such an high priest became us, who is holy, harmless, undefiled, separate from sinners, and made higher than the heavens; 27 Who needeth not daily, as those high priests, to offer up sacrifice, first for his own sins, and then for the people's: for this he did once, when

New Rendition

18 For there is an abrogation of the former commandment because of its weakness and uselessness 19 (for the law made nothing perfect) but there is now a better hope by which we draw near to God. 20 And it was not without an oath (for some have become priests without an oath). 21 But Jesus did become a priest with an oath sworn by him who said to him,

> "The Lord swore and will not change his mind, 'you are a priest forever.'" [Ps. 110:4]

22 For that reason Jesus has become the guarantee of a better covenant. 23 Now there were many who became priests because they were prevented by death from continuing in their priestly office, 24 but Jesus, because he continues to live forever, has a permanent priesthood. 25 Therefore, he can also completely and eternally save those who come to God through him, since he always lives to make intercession for them. 26 For it was indeed fitting that we should have such a high priest, holy, innocent, undefiled, having been separated from sinners, and exalted higher than the heavens. 27 One who does not on a daily basis need to first offer

he offered up himself. 28 For the law maketh men high priests which have infirmity; but the word of the oath, which was since the law, maketh the Son, who is consecrated for evermore.

sacrifices for his sins, and then for the sins of the people, as the other high priests did, because he did this once for all when he offered himself. 28 For the law appoints as high priests men who have weakness, but the word of the oath that came after the law appoints a son who has been made perfect forever.

Translation Notes and Comments

7:18 ***For there is verily a disannulling of the commandment going before for the weakness and unprofitableness thereof / For there is an abrogation of the former commandment because of its weakness and uselessness:*** The noun ἐντολή (*entolē*), "commandment," does not refer to just one segment of the Mosaic law but to the whole.[153]

The noun ἀθέτησις (*athetēsis*) denotes not only setting something aside but also canceling or repealing it.[154] Because the English noun "abrogation" denotes effectively dispensing with or abolishing a law or statute,[155] we use it in our Rendition. This use of the word is important. The law was at one time valid and therefore had to be obeyed, or unwanted consequences followed (2:2). Once the governing priesthood was changed, however, God abrogated the old law, and it became invalid as a means of drawing people closer to Jehovah.

The adjective ἀσθενής (*asthenēs*), "weak, powerless," denotes something that is ineffective because of its inherent limitations or deficiencies.[156] The adjective ἀνωφελής (*anōphelēs*), "useless," denotes something that has absolutely no value.[157] Both of these adjectives we translate as neuter nouns, yielding "weakness and uselessness." The author is using very strong and perhaps even exaggerated ideas here to make his point. "With the inauguration of Christ's priesthood comes not simply as an amendment of the Law, but its definitive 'abrogation' (ἀθέτησις, *athetēsis*)."[158]

153. Ellingworth, *Epistle to the Hebrews,* 381.

154. Ellingworth, *Epistle to the Hebrews,* 380; BDAG, 24; Louw-Nida, §§13.36; 76.24.

155. *Webster's New Dictionary of Synonyms,* s.v. "annul"; "nullify."

156. BDAG, 142–43.

157. BDAG, 92–93.

158. Koester, *Hebrews,* 355–56; Attridge, *Epistle to the Hebrews,* 203. It should be noted, however, that the author views the Mosaic law as both prior to the implementation of the priesthood of the Lord and also foreshadowing it (9:9–10; 10:1). The Mosaic law is "weak" and "useless" because the coming of the greater power has now abrogated

7:19 ***For the law made nothing perfect / (for the law made nothing perfect):*** This phrase constitutes a parenthetical expression. The subordinate conjunction γάρ (*gar*), "for," is important here because it has causal force, showing the reason why God annulled the law. It was weak and useless because it could bring nothing to perfection.[159] On the verb τελειόω (*teleioō*), "perfection," see Translation Notes on the related noun τελείωσις (*teleiōsis*) for 7:11 with the associated Analysis.

The JST of 7:19 notes that the old law suffered from an additional weakness. Not only did it not make anything perfect, it "was administered without an oath" (compare D&C 84:40–41). The change makes this verse parallel with 7:21 in contrasting the old law with the new.

but the bringing in of a better hope did; by the which we draw nigh unto God / but a better hope is introduced by which we draw near to God: The phrase ἐπεισαγωγὴ δὲ κρείττονος ἐλπίδος (*epeisagōgē de kreittonos elpidos*), literally "but an introduction of a better hope," is quite compact in Greek. In our Rendition, we have expanded it to "but a better hope is introduced" to better express the idea in the original text.

The "better hope," given the context, does not mean that God has made the Saints more hopeful, but that he has given them a hope for something better. In 7:22 he defines what that something is (see below).[160]

The verb ἐγγίζω (*engizō*) means "to draw near" and is used often in describing the approach by mortals to divine beings.[161] The nuance of the

---

it, but that does not suggest a relative inferiority. It was, after all, God's law. The abrogation, rather, points to the law's fundamental inability, due to its essential human ("fleshly," σάρκινος, *sarkinos*) foundation, to bring about permanent unity between God and humankind.

159. From the perspective of a Levitical priest, the idea that the law with its sacrifices was useless would appear blatantly false, for the priesthood accomplished its purpose in keeping the covenant between Jehovah and Israel. On the other hand, from the viewpoint of the author of Hebrews, the law was useless because it could not bring about that perfection necessary for a godlike life. Johnson, *Hebrews,* 189. Both the Apostle Paul and the author of Hebrews denigrate the law. The Apostle does it on the basis that it lacked the power to make people just; the author of Hebrews does it because it could not establish "a good mediator between the people and God." Vanhoye, *Letter to the Hebrews,* 122.

160. Ellingworth, *Epistle to the Hebrews,* 382. According to Ogden and Skinner, *Verse by Verse,* 252, "the 'better hope' is the gospel covenant with its attendant Melchizedek Priesthood blessings."

161. BDAG, 270. People can draw near to God in three ways. The first is through prayer and worship (Gen. 18:23; Ps. 148:14; Isa. 29:13; 58:2). The priests drew near to Jehovah as they entered the temple courtyard and went into the sanctuary (Ex. 19:22; Lev. 10:3;

verb suggests close association without contact. The verb suggests that a person approaches God but is not yet actually at one with him. To do that, one more step is necessary (see 13:12 below). Nonetheless, the new covenant gives the Saints a vision of what is to come.

The JST treats the old law more gently than does the KJV. It notes the old law "*was only* the bringing of a better hope, by the which we draw nigh to God" (italics highlight the addition). Although the addition does limit the old law, showing that it did little more than bring with it hope of salvation, it nevertheless did bring hope. For those who understood it as a type and shadow of the nature, ministry, and saving power of the Lord and saw through its symbolism his salvation, it did give hope (for discussion, see Analysis above).

7:20–22 These verses constitute a very complex syntactical sentence in Greek that presents a number of translation challenges as is indicated below. The author so constructs the sentence to stress how vastly God's oath—that the Son would be a high priest forever—separates Jesus from his counterparts among the Aaronites. The author does this with the use of two key phrases. The first is καθ' ὅσον (*kath hoson*), "to the degree that" (at the beginning of 7:20), and the second is κατὰ τοσοῦτο (*kata tosouto*), "to that same degree" (at the introduction of 7:22). His point is that to the low degree that a Levitical priest received his office with no promise it would continue forever, to that same degree—albeit in the opposite direction—Jesus received his office with an oath that his priesthood would continue forever. As a result, he could be what no Levitical priest ever could, a "guarantee of a better covenant" (NR 7:22). Due to how cumbersome a more literal translation of the Greek of these verses would be, we have been less precise in following the text but have still tried to capture the full range of nuances the author intended to convey.

7:20 ***And inasmuch as not without an oath / And it was not without an oath:*** The noun "it" is implied by the third-person singular form of the verb and refers back to the "better hope" (7:19) that the new priesthood made possible. What the author is emphasizing is that the better hope came because of the oath. For discussion on ὁρκωμοσία (*horkōmosia*), "oath," see Translation Notes for ὅρκος (*horkos*), "oath," for 6:17 with the associated Analysis.

21:21). The second is through faith, that is, by following God's commandments (Hos. 12:6; Zeph. 3:2; James. 4:8). The third is by entering into God's eternal rest (Heb. 4:3–5; Jacob 1:7; Alma 12:27). See Koester, *Hebrews,* 356.

And inasmuch as not without an oath he was made priest / (for some have become priests without an oath): The phrase "he was made priest" is not found in the Greek text and was added by the KJV's translators in an attempt to make sense of a difficult passage. This phrase is parenthetical and the author uses it to emphasize his point that Levitical priests received office with no oath of confirmation.

7:21 ***The Lord sware and will not repent, Thou art a priest for ever after the order of Melchisedec / "The Lord swore and will not change his mind, 'you are a priest forever'":*** Once again the author quotes LXX Psalm 109:4 for proof of his position. The verb μεταμέλομαι (*metamelomai*) means to change one's mind.[162] With the addition of the negative particle οὐ (*ou*), "not," the phrase οὐ μεταμεληθήσεται (*ou metmelēthēsetai*) stresses the impossibility that God would ever change his mind.

7:22 ***By so much was Jesus made a surety of a better testament / For that reason Jesus has become the guarantee of a better covenant:*** The phrase κατὰ τοσοῦτο (*kata tosouto*) means "to that same degree" and stresses the high degree to which God made the Savior the sureness of the benefits of the new covenant.

The adjective ἔγγυος (*engyos*) denotes that which assures the fulfillment of a pledge, promise, or covenant.[163] Under God's plan, this is Jesus. Through him and his eternal life and priesthood, God assures or guarantees that the terms of the new and better covenant will be fulfilled.

The comparative adjective κρείττων (*kreittōn*) denotes what is "more advantageous" or "better."[164] The noun διαθήκη (*diathēkē*), "covenant," carries two nuances. On the religious plane, it points to an agreement between an individual and the Divine.[165] On the mortal plane, it denotes an agreement or contract between equal parties[166] as well as a "last will and testament," that is, a legal document in which a person's wishes were administered and properties distributed after his or her death. The LXX used this term for the translation of the Hebrew בְּרִית (*bĕrît*), "covenant."

---

162. BDAG, 639.

163. Preisker, *TDNT,* 2:329. People took the responsibility of becoming a "surety" very seriously. Proverbs 17:18 and 22:26 even caution against it. There is little wonder since a person was fully liable for any defaul, which could lead to bankruptcy and serving jail time. In the most severe cases, it could even mean death. Koester, *Hebrews,* 363–64.

164. BDAG, 566.

165. This would have fallen under the suzerain-vassal category, which includes not only covenants between gods and people but also between greater and lesser kings.

166. For example, see 2 Sam. 3:13, where David and Abner make a parity covenant or agreement (*berit/diatheke*) between themselves.

One nuance is important here: the decree was initiated and dictated by a single person. It was not the result of any kind of negotiation or settlement between parties. In Judeo-Christian terms, Jehovah alone set all conditions of the agreement between him and others. They were free to either accept or reject the agreement. They were not, however, free to suggest let alone make any modifications to the agreement, nor were they free of the consequences of their choices.[167] As President Joseph Fielding Smith noted,

> The gospel covenant is the promise of God to grant to man, through man's obedience and acceptance of the ordinances and principles of the gospel, the glory and exaltation of eternal life. It is the Father in Heaven who stipulates the terms of the covenant. Man has no say in the matter or right to alter or annul any provision of the covenant. His duty is to accept on the terms which are presented to him from the Almighty, in full faith and obedience, without complaint or desire because of personal weakness to alter or annul, what the Father offers for man's salvation.[168]

7:23 ***And they truly were many priests, because they were not suffered to continue by reason of death / Now there were many who became priests because they were prevented by death from continuing in their priestly office:*** In this verse, the author states the obvious to push his point. The verb παραμένω (*paramenō*) means "to continue in an office or calling."[169] The verb κωλύω (*kōlyō*) means "to stop, hinder," or "prevent" something from happening. In this case, it was θάνατος (*thanatos*), "death," that caused the need to constantly replace Levitical priests. The verb γίνομαι (*ginomai*), "become,"[170] is found here as a perfect participle, the perfect tense emphasizing why there was a need to constantly and continually replace the priests.

7:24 ***But this man, because he continueth ever, hath an unchangeable priesthood / but Jesus, because he continues to live forever, has a permanent priesthood:*** Though the text has ὁ (*ho*), "he," we have translated it as "Jesus" in our Rendition for clarity. The verb μένω (*menō*), "to stay, remain," or "continue," when associated with life, suggests its persistent character.[171]

167. BDAG, 228–29; Koester, *Hebrews,* 364. The author of Hebrews uses the word both as "will" and as "covenant," and, therefore, context must determine which meaning to apply. Ellingworth, *Epistle to the Hebrews,* 388; Johnson, *Hebrews,* 192. For development, see "Excursus on the 'Better Covenant' in Hebrews" below.

168. Smith, *Doctrines of Salvation,* 1:162.

169. BDAG, 769.

170. BDAG, 196–99.

171. BDAG, 630–31.

In this case, that persistence is defined by the prepositional phrase εἰς τὸν αἰῶνα (*eis ton aiōna*), "forever."

The adjective ἀπαράβατος (*aparabatos*) denotes that which is "permanent and unchangeable,"[172] the idea being that the effect, force, and potency of the Lord's priesthood will last eternally.

7:25 ***Wherefore he is able also to save them to the uttermost / Therefore he can also completely and eternally save those:*** The coordinating conjunction ὅθεν (*hothen*), "therefore," explains why Jesus is able to fully save his people. It is because his priesthood and life are eternal.[173]

The verb σῴζω (*sōzō*) means "to save" and in the present context refers to the spiritual and eternal salvation promised by God to the faithful.[174] The prepositional phrase εἰς τὸ παντελὲς (*eis to panteles*), literally "to the entire," has two possible interpretations, either "completely" or "forever."[175] The former sense is used by the KJV, but the ancient Vulgate, Syriac, and Coptic translations use the latter. Modern translations are divided.[176] We assume that the author understood this dual sense of the phrase and purposely used it to convey both ideas, and so we translated it as "completely and eternally" in our Rendition.[177]

that come unto God by him / who come to God through him: The verb προσέρχομαι (*proserchomai*) means "to come before" or "approach" another and is often used to describe a person's motivation in worship.[178] In the present context, it refers to that point when the righteous soul is united once more with the Father. The phrase δι' αὐτοῦ (*di' autou*), "through him," likely refers to the Savior's atoning power and the grace that flows therefrom that enables the faithful to come to the Father and be saved. The whole verse looks back to the "better hope" provided by the new covenant (7:19).

---

172. Louw-Nida, §13.61. Some translators have given the word the meaning of "nontransferable" and "without a successor." The motivation seems to be to lessen if not eliminate the need for the continuance of priesthood authority as such on the earth. See Anderson, *Guide to Acts,* 96–98; and S. Kent Brown, "The Dead Sea Scrolls: A Mormon Perspective," *BYU Studies* 23, no. 1 (Winter 1983): 49–66. But such an idea is not associated with the word in any classical or Koine Greek text. See BDAG, 97; LSJ, 178; and Moulton and Milligan, *Vocabulary,* 53.

173. BDAG, 692–93; Koester, *Hebrews,* 364.

174. BDAG, 982–83; see also Translation Notes for 2:10.

175. BDAG, 754. See also Holzapfel and Wayment, *Making Sense,* 454–55; and McConkie, *Doctrinal New Testament Commentary,* 3:175.

176. NET "completely," NIV84 "completely" with footnote "or forever," and NRSV "for all time" with footnote "or completely."

177. See also Ellingworth, *Epistle to the Hebrews,* 391. One thing is clear: "the salvation provided by Christ is everlasting precisely because it is complete." Koester, *Hebrews,* 365.

178. BDAG, 878; Cockerill, *Epistle to the Hebrews,* 335.

seeing he ever liveth to make intercession for them / since he always lives to make intercession for them: This phrase explains why the Saints will enjoy eternal life. The circumstantial present active participle ζῶν *(zōn)*, "living," is used causally and translated "since he . . . lives" in our Rendition.[179] The verb ἐντυγχάνω (*entyngchanō*) means "to petition or make appeal in behalf of another" and, therefore, "to intercede."[180] The phrase should not be read to mean that Jesus lives exclusively to make intercession for others or that the Saints need constant intercession. Rather, it means that because he lives forever, he will always be able to make such intercession when necessary.[181] The author's point is that Christ is always there for his people (9:24; see also 1 John 2:1; 2 Ne. 2:9; Mosiah 15:8; Moro. 7:28; and D&C 29:5; 32:3; 45:3; 62:1; 110:4).

7:26 ***For such an high priest became us / For it was indeed fitting that we should have such a high priest:*** The verb πρέπω (*prepō*) "denotes what is fitting or proper in the light of certain circumstances or a particular relationship; with regard to the position or nature of the persons involved."[182] The circumstances that warranted this specific kind of high priest was the people's need for salvation. The particular relationship was that they had entered into the gospel covenant through which they had become once again the children of God. Because of both the need and the Saints' response, it was altogether proper for God to provide a high priest specifically fitted for the task that needed to be done.

who is holy, harmless, undefiled, separate from sinners / holy, innocent, undefiled, having been separated from sinners: The author lists the characteristics of "such a high priest." The adjective ὅσιος (*hosios*) describes "being without fault relative to deity, devout, pious, pleasing to God, holy."[183] The adjective notes the Lord's *religious* qualifications.[184]

---

179. Ellingworth, *Epistle to the Hebrews,* 392 n. 5; Robertson, *Grammar,* 300.

180. BDAG, 341; *NID,* s.v. "ἐντυγχάνω." The responsibility of intercession was primarily that of the priest. Attridge, *Epistle to the Hebrews,* 210–11; Johnson, *Hebrews,* 194. The word carried two aspects. One was a plea for assistance when one needed help or was wronged; the other was a plea for forgiveness when one transgressed against another. Both work in this instance. Koester, *Hebrews,* 366.

181. Cockerill, *Epistle to the Hebrews,* 336. On Jesus' role as intercessor and advocate, see the subsection "Jesus as the Great and Last Sacrifice" in "Excursus on the Atonement: A View from Hebrews" in chapter 2.

182. Cockerill, *Epistle to the Hebrews,* 339 n. 5; see also Moulton and Milligan, *Vocabulary,* 534; and BDAG, 861.

183. BDAG, 728; *NID,* s.v. "ὅσιος." The common Greek word for "holy" is ἅγιος (*hagios*), which the LXX uses as the translation of the Hebrew קָדוֹשׁ (*qādôš*). Conversely, ὅσιος (*hosios*) is normally used in the LXX as the translation of חָסִיד (*ḥāsîd*), meaning "devout, faithful," or "pious."

184. Grundmann, *TDNT,* 3:482.

The adjective ἄκακος (*akakos*), literally "not bad," has two senses in Greek: it can denote a person who does no evil and a person who is not touched by evil.[185] Thus, it carries the nuances of guilelessness and innocence.[186] The adjective denotes the Lord's *moral* qualifications.

The adjective ἀμίαντος (*amiantos*) denotes that which is unsoiled or undefiled.[187] In the New Testament, it is only used figuratively as "pure" in a religious or moral sense.[188] It stands in contrast to and derives its nuance from its antonym μιαντός (*miantos*), which denotes that which is polluted or unclean in a cultic sense.[189] The adjective highlights the Savior's *cultic* qualifications.

The phrase κεχωρισμένος ἀπὸ τῶν ἁμαρτωλῶν (*kechōrismenos apo tōn hamartōlōn*), literally "having been separated from those who sin," shows not just that he is different from sinners but that he has actually been separated from them by his exaltation. The verb χωρίζω (*chorizo*), "to separate," is found here in the form of a perfect passive participle, the voice suggesting that the separation was due to divine action and also that the separation does and will continue to exist.[190]

made higher than the heavens / exalted higher than the heavens: The comparative adjective ὑψηλότερος (*hypsēloteros*) denotes that which is higher than something else.[191] The noun οὐρανός (*ouranos*), "heaven," is found here in the plural and can denote the firmament, the starry sky, or the abode of Deity.[192] The author likely pulled the phrase from Psalms 57:5, 11 and 108:5, in which the Psalmist praises Jehovah and declares his wish that his God be exalted above the heavens. In that context, even though the noun is plural, it refers to the firmament rather than the abode of Deity.[193]

---

185. Grundmann, *TDNT,* 3:482.

186. BDAG, 34; LSJ, 47; *NID,* s.v. "κακός"; see also Attridge, *Epistle to the Hebrews,* 213.

187. BDAG, 54. Though the word can mean "blameless" in general, it more specifically applied to the temple. See 2 Macc. 14:26; 15:34; and Josephus, *J.W.* 6.99.

188. BDAG, 54.

189. *NID,* s.v. "μιαίνω."

190. Cockerill, *Epistle to the Hebrews,* 341; Wallace, *Greek Grammar,* 437–38.

191. BDAG, 1044–45; compare Louw-Nida, §83.50.

192. BDAG, 737–39.

193. The Semitic people did believe in multiple heavens, and Paul spoke of a "third heaven" along with paradise (2 Cor. 12:2). The same word, however, even in the plural, also applied to earth's sky. *NID,* s.v. "οὐρανός"; for an extended study see Traub, *TDNT,* 5:497–543.

The verb γίνομαι (*ginomai*), "to become," in the present context means "to come into a certain state" and therefore together with the adjective ὑψηλότερος (*hypsēloteros*) connotes being "raised up" or "exalted."[194]

JST 7:25 replaces "higher than the heavens" with "ruler over the heavens." It appears the text takes the noun "heavens" as referring to the abode of Deity. By changing the emphasis from location to presiding authority, it negates any idea that there is a place above the celestial realm.

7:27 ***Who needeth not daily, as those high priests, to offer up sacrifice, first for his own sins, and then for the people's / One who does not on a daily basis need to first offer sacrifices for his sins, and then for the sins of the people as the other high priests did:*** The author seems to be referencing the תָּמִיד (*tāmîd*), that is, the daily ritual of the burnt offering (Lev. 1:3–17). It is possible, however, that he is conflating that with part of the ritual on the Day of Atonement in which the high priest first made expiation for his sins before making it for the people as a whole (see Lev. 16:23; 26–33; compare Ex. 30:10; and Num. 29:7–11). The operative word here is the noun ἀνάνκη (*anangkē*), "necessity." It denotes the constraint inherent in the sacrifices because they could empower neither priest nor participant to live sin free.[195] As a result, the high priest had to perform the ritual annually on the tenth day of the seventh month and include a sacrifice for himself. There was no other option if their relationship with Jehovah was to continue intact.

for this he did once, when he offered up himself / because he did this once for all when he offered himself: The author here refers to the Lord's crucifixion. His stress is twofold: first, on the voluntary nature of the sacrifice—Jesus offered himself (Luke 22:19; John 6:51; 10:15); and second, on the sufficiency of sacrifice—it needed to be done only once.

The verb ἀναφέρω (*anapherō*), "to offer up," pertains to making a sacrificial offering.[196] It is found here in the form of an aorist participle. We have translated this as instrumental, thus showing Jesus did not make the offering "for himself" but for others. The aorist tense also emphasizes the "once for all" nature of the act.[197] Its permanent effect made any repetition unnecessary. This idea the author emphasizes with the adverb ἐφάπαξ (*ephapax*),

---

194. BDAG, 196–99. In other places, the author refers to Jesus entering into heaven (9:24) and being seated by God in heaven (8:1).

195. BDAG, 60–61.

196. BDAG, 74–75.

197. Cockerill, *Epistle to the Hebrews,* 343 n. 28.

denoting an act taking place at one time and eliminating the need for any further recurrence; thus it is translated as "once for all."[198]

The author's use of this past tense of the verb ἀναφέρω (*anapherō*) contrasts with his use of the present tense in the previous phrase when describing the Levitical high priest's acts. By using it, the author is able to highlight the continuing necessity (and by extension, insufficiency) of the Levitical sacrifices.

The JST of this verse reads, "*And not* as those high priests, *who offered* up sacrifice *daily,* first for *their* own sins, and then for the *sins of the people;* for *he needed not offer sacrifice for his own sins, for he knew no sins; but for the sins of the people. And* this he did once, when he offered up himself" (italics used to show the changes). The modifications make the verse read more smoothly in English, and they explain why the Savior did not have to make a sacrifice for himself. As the KJV reads, the pronoun τοῦτο (*touto*), "this," in 7:27 is vague and could be interpreted to refer to the need for Jesus, like the high priest, to offer a sacrifice first for his own sins. The change in the JST clears up the ambiguity.

7:28 ***For the law maketh men high priests which have infirmity / For the law appoints as high priests men who have weakness:*** The verb καθίστημι (*kathistēmi*) means "to appoint someone to a position or to put him or her in charge of something."[199] In this case, the priest was put in charge of making sacrifices and was appointed to that position on the basis of the Levitical Priesthood.

The noun ἀσθένεια (*astheneia*), "weakness,"[200] refers to the constraints inherent within the realm in which the Mosaic law functioned. Those constraints were twofold: first, they limited the priesthood genealogically, and second, they appointed flawed and imperfect human beings to the high position. For discussion, see Translation Notes for 5:2–3.

but the word of the oath, which was since the law, maketh the Son, who is consecrated for evermore / but the word of the oath that came after the law appoints a son who has been made perfect forever: The phrase ὁ λόγος δὲ τῆς ὁρκωμοσίας (*ho logos de tēs horkōmosias*), "the word of the oath," refers to LXX Psalm 109:4, in which God proclaimed the Son's eternal high-priestly station. The weight of the author's point is in the noun ὁρκωμοσία (*horkōmosia*), "oath," an act through which God binds himself

---

198. BDAG, 417.
199. BDAG, 492; Louw-Nida, §37.104.
200. BDAG, 142.

to a people and course of action that makes a pronouncement certain.[201] For discussion, see Translation Notes for 6:13, 16–18.

The preposition μετά (*meta*), "after," marks "a previous point in time in relation to an act."[202] In this case, the author uses it to stress that God's oath to his Son came after the establishment of the law of Moses and therefore was not disannulled by it. That unbreakable oath appointed (καθίστημι, *kathistēmi*) the Son to his position. Through the use of the word, the author tacitly shows "the living God continues to reveal his will."[203] He is in charge and can make changes at any time. Therefore, revelation is ongoing and its need will never be set aside.

The verb τελειόω (*teleioō*), "to finish, complete, fulfill, make perfect," stresses the eternal nature of the Son. Here the word is found in the form of a perfect passive participle. The voice shows that it took divine action to make the Son "perfect." For discussion, see Translation Notes with the related Analysis for 6:1. In the present context, the word stands in contrast to the "weakness" of the priests appointed by the law. Therefore, it stresses the Savior's reception of the full powers and attributes of the Divine that made him strong and fit for the task (Col. 1:18–19; 2:9; D&C 93:17). By nuance it also shows the eternal degree and quality of his perfection.[204]

That the author concludes this section with the perfect passive participle τετελειωμένον (*teteleiōmenon*), "having been perfected," illustrates his skill as a writer. In addition to forcefully concluding the section, the word serves two more purposes. It recalls the first affirmation of the subject of perfection the author introduced in 5:9–10, and it signals his readers that he is now going to more fully develop that affirmation.[205]

Analysis and Summary

In 7:18–25, the author continues to contrast the Levitical with the Melchizedek order of the priesthood. He has shown that the former was established by a "fleshly ordinance," that is, on the basis of genealogical descent. He now shows how the restrictions based on "law," "ordinance," and "fleshly" imply an inadequacy of the old order. Mere ordinance cannot compete with a divine oath (7:21–22); the promise of the law cannot compete with

201. BDAG, 723.

202. BDAG, 636–38; see also McConkie, *Doctrinal New Testament Commentary*, 3:175.

203. Johnson, *Hebrews*, 196.

204. Cockerill, *Epistle to the Hebrews*, 344–45.

205. Vanhoye, *Letter to the Hebrews*, 127.

a "better hope" (7:19) or the "better covenant" (NR 7:22) that God has given through his Son; a priesthood based on mortal descent (implied by "fleshly") cannot compete with one based on an "indestructible life" (7:16, 24). The problem with the old order, the author shows, was that its priesthood rested upon human weakness and was limited by human frailty (see 5:1–3) without providing power to overcome both.[206]

Having elucidated for his readers the great benefits that befall those who are ever true to the great High Priest, the author now breaks into a grand description of all the ways that Jesus is exactly what his people need. In 7:26–28, the author ties insights from LXX Psalm 109:4 with the themes he introduced in 2:17–18; 4:14–16; and 5:1–10 and will further develop in 8:1–10:18. In these verses, he combines summary and announcement that skillfully highlight the truths he wants to proclaim. His skill calls his readers to engage with their great High Priest who has made himself so suitable for their specific needs. In doing so, he lays the groundwork on which he will further develop the Lord's effectiveness. The author's intent seems to be motivating his readers to reach for aid and find the means to persevere through the power of the great High Priest.

To make his point, in 7:26, the author lists the attributes that make the Savior exactly what the people need. He first states that the Savior is "holy," here carrying the force of being religiously observant to every moral obligation. The author uses the word to denote the Lord's moral qualifications.[207] He next states the Lord is "innocent," denoting blamelessness and impeccability in working with people.[208] The author uses it to denote the Lord's social qualifications. He next states the Savior is "undefiled," the adjective denoting that which is unsoiled and clean in every respect but also carrying the idea of being ritually clean and therefore able to perform priestly temple service, more especially a sacrificial offering.[209] The author uses it to highlight the Savior's cultic qualifications. He next states the Savior is "separated from those who sin," the phrase highlighting not just that the Son is different from sinners but that he is actually separated from them by his exaltation.[210] The author uses this to highlight the Savior's eternal

---

206. Cockerill, *Epistle to the Hebrews,* 322–23. On the importance of the oath and covenant to the Melchizedek Priesthood today, see McConkie, *Doctrinal New Testament Commentary,* 3:173–74.

207. Grundmann, *TDNT,* 3:482.

208. BDAG, 34; *NID,* s.v. "κακός"; see also Attridge, *Epistle to the Hebrews,* 213.

209. BDAG, 54.

210. Cockerill, *Epistle to the Hebrews,* 341; Wallace, *Greek Grammar,* 437–38.

qualifications. Finally, the author states the Savior is "exalted higher than the heavens," here most likely meaning he inhabits a realm beyond the firmament or earthly sky.[211] This exalted position is the end result of his having met all the necessary qualifications.

Only after having assured his readers of the Son's qualifications and exalted state does the author turn to the sacrifice that those required. He has been building up to this supernal act through his entire Epistle. Continually raising his readers' anticipation and expectation, he has described the Son as having "purged our sins" (1:3), tasting "death for every man" (2:9), and offering "up prayers and supplications with strong crying and tears" (5:7). By placing the gracious, sinless, eternal, and exalted High Priest before his readers, the author has put them in a position to grasp the significance, importance, and result of the Lord's self-sacrifice.

It is by contrasting this effective self-sacrifice, inherent in the new covenant, with the ineffective sacrificial rituals of the old that the author is able to emphasize what the Savior has done (7:27). He appeals to the ritual of the Day of Atonement and sets up a double contrast. The first is to the work of the Levitical high priest who—due to moral weakness—must make a sacrifice for his own sins before he can do the same for his people. This act stands in contrast to the work of the Son who—being full of moral strength—did not have to sacrifice for himself. The second contrast is to the annual performance of the Levitical sacrifices. The continual practice was tacit evidence that the system really did not work. The repeated nature of these sacrifices stands in contrast to the sacrifice of the Son that needed to be done but once to have full effect. The singularity of the act was tacit evidence that it did work once for all.[212]

Having laid this groundwork here, the author will make the Lord's self-sacrifice the central theme in each of the three sections he will now develop (8:1–13; 9:1–22; 9:23–10:18). Throughout these sections, the author will bring into ever sharper focus what the Savior has done for his people.[213]

Verse 7:28 serves as an excellent summary of all that the author wants to say about the divine High Priest. The author skillfully contrasts the ordinance of the Mosaic law that appointed weak men to the temporary if high

---

211. This is based on Ps. 57:5, 11; 108:5, wherein Jehovah is praised by the wish that he be exalted above the heavens.

212. Cockerill, *Epistle to the Hebrews,* 342. See also Holzapfel and Wayment, *Making Sense,* 455.

213. Cockerill, *Epistle to the Hebrews,* 342.

position to God's oath that appointed the new and perfected High Priest to an eternal position. The former appointment was based on genealogy (7:3–14), the latter "on the power of an indestructible life" (7:15–19, 23–25). The former appointment ordained many "human beings" to be priests, while the latter ordained only the Son to be the High Priest forevermore. The former appointment gave position to sin-prone men (5:1–3) that necessitated making sacrifices for both them and the people, while the latter appointment gave position to the perfect Son who needed not make sacrifice for himself, being sinless, but for the people only (JST 7:26). Through this act, he became perfect, meaning he completed all the Father asked him to do. The righteous Son achieved this state through a sacrifice he did not need to make in behalf of himself, one he did, however, need to make in obedience to God (4:15; 5:8–9; 10:5–10).

The Father, on account of the Son's selfless sacrifice, consecrated him to his exalted position over the priesthood. Through this power, based on his atoning sacrifice, he is able to cleanse and perfect his people, seal them into eternal life, and lead them into the rest of the Father to dwell with him forever. In this way, the Savior fulfilled the responsibilities that befell him as the Son of God. At the same time, he provided the ultimate revelation of God for humankind (1:1–4; John 14:6–11). The author's phrase "a Son made perfect forever" affirms the Savior's eternal Sonship gained by his flawless work during his mortal ministry, his obedience to all the Father asked him to do, and his self-sacrifice on Golgotha. On these rest his exaltation and present position on the right hand of God. Here he sits as the sole "source of eternal salvation" for everyone (NR 5:9). It is because of all this that he is exactly suited to meet his people's needs.[214]

The Son's perfection and holiness is built upon his fulfilling the law through which the ordinances of the Levitical temple rites were set aside as the sign of dedication to Jehovah. The Savior's model reveals that perfection "demands the total dedication of the human spirit to God and the progressive openness of human freedom to the will of God. Such transformation is possible for other humans because it has been accomplished first through Christ the priest. Only the one who has become perfect in this way can make others perfect in this way. By thus becoming 'perfect,' Jesus has in turn become 'the cause of eternal salvation' to those who obey him (5:9)."[215]

214. Cockerill, *Epistle to the Hebrews,* 344–45.
215. Johnson, *Hebrews,* 186.

Excursus on the "Better Covenant" in Hebrews

The idea of covenant (διαθήκη, *diathēkē*) serves a central purpose in the Epistle to the Hebrews. The author develops the theme of a new and better covenant established by God and guaranteed by Jesus "more fully than any other N[ew] T[estament] writer, the epistle accounting for just over half of the occurrences of *diathēkē* in the N[ew] T[estament]."[216] Even so, it shows a close affinity to other treatments in the holy book and more especially Paul, suggesting that the doctrine's theological roots reach into the earliest Christian traditions. Because the author's use of the word, though distinctive, is neither obtuse nor technical, determining its depth and breadth as understood by the Christian leadership and propounded under their authority is not difficult. Further, it rests on ancient biblical foundations but adds an additional dimension to them. Understanding those foundations helps disclose the importance of "covenant" in the Epistle to the Hebrews and for early Christian theology generally.

God's Use of Covenants

As scholars and theologians have sought for the "thematic center" of the Bible, it is not surprising that they have returned repeatedly to the idea of covenant. The reason is that it is *the* religious metaphor for the relationship between people and God. The word "metaphor," however, should not be taken to mean that the concept of "covenant" began as a mere idea initially embraced in the ancient mind that eventually came to define the center of orthodoxy for the believing community and that, over time, evolved into ritual. The earliest records instead suggest that the ancient Israelites and their Hebrew forebearers saw covenant from its genesis as "enacted reality" that defined proper behavior and relationships. For them particularly it was the degree to which they kept these positive values that determined the extent of Jehovah's rule and protective power over them.

Further, as will be shown below, the covenant people did not see these values as something God gave exclusively to the children of Israel and their descendants. It would appear that they understood that these moral laws introduced by covenant were something God designed as a means of transcending culturally bound norms and politically enforced laws and as a

216. Ellingworth, *Epistle to the Hebrews*, 386.

means of bringing all under his benevolent rule.[217] From the first time the practice of covenant is introduced in the scriptures, we see that making covenants is one of Jehovah's major devices for communicating divine values that define and dictate human relationships. All of these Jehovah designed to proceed along a moral plane that transcended coercive force.[218]

These ideals were important to the author of Hebrews, and, as will be shown both below and in the commentary, they play an important part in understanding the ideas he was communicating.

The Force of Covenants

Outside of the Old Testament in Greek culture, the root of the Greek noun διαθήκη (*diathēkē*) means "to dispose of and bequeath property or other goods." By the sixth century BC, its meaning narrowed to "a will or testament." It began to connote a written document and thereby took on a more concrete aspect of a legal text. As a result, its meaning began to merge with συνθήκη (*sunthēkē*), an actual "agreement, compact, or treaty."[219]

Covenants could be made between two main groups—person to person or person to a god. The use of the former was very prevalent throughout the ancient Near East. Though it is possible that other Near Eastern cultures had the idea that a covenantal relationship could be established between themselves and their gods, the evidence is largely inferential.[220] Not so with the children of Israel. In this culture, the reality of a covenantal relationship with their God came anciently and deeply and marked a special characteristic of their religion. Its salient feature across time was that it demanded exclusive loyalty to but one God, thus precluding dual- or multiple-tiered loyalties that marked so many of the other religions of the ancient Near East.[221]

Even when a covenant did not transcend the human plane, those cultures that employed them understood that they were not to be taken lightly or

---

217. See George E. Mendenhall, "Covenants," in Freedman, *Anchor Bible Dictionary,* 1:1201.

218. Mendenhall, "Covenants," in Freedman, *Anchor Bible Dictionary,* 1:1201; compare Ringgren, *TDOT,* 1:273–75.

219. *NID,* s.v. "διαθήκη."

220. Certain Moabites were called the "people of Chemosh" (Num. 21:29), just as the Israelites were called "the people of the Lord" (Judg. 5:11), suggesting they have both had a similar covenantal bond with the deity they worshiped. Outside of these few inferences, no other evidence exists to date.

221. J. A. Thompson, *The Ancient Near Eastern Treaties and the Old Testament* (London: Tyndale Press, 1964), 26–27, accessed March 26, 2016, https://biblicalstudies.org.uk/pdf/tp/treaties_thompson.pdf; Weinfeld, *TDOT,* 2:278.

toyed with. Covenants were sealed by oaths that called upon the gods as witnesses. Thus, they were considered sacral and binding. To break one, since they were backed by the gods, threatened severe consequences.[222] Religious oaths, such as those the Israelites practiced, also worked on the human plane, for they followed the format of judicial proceedings and strictures. In that way they took on a cast that gave them an earthly legal status.[223] Thus religious oaths (that is, between a person or a people and a god) and secular oaths (that is, between people of equal rank or between people of higher rank and those of a lower) had both an earthly and a heavenly aspect.

Old Testament Covenants

In the LXX, διαθήκη (*diathēkē*) was used as the translation of בְּרִית (*berît*), "agreement, covenant" (for example, see Gen. 15:18).[224] The phrase looked primarily at agreements between Jehovah and his people.[225] Studying the inception of covenants reveals that they constituted divine promises in which the recipient of the blessings contributed nothing to the arrangement or its details. All was unilateral, both being begun and dictated by Jehovah. Though the Old Testament continues to use *berît* to designate agreements between equals, there was, in the Jewish use of the term, a move that separated the word from συνθήκη (*sunthēkē*), which nearly always suggested negotiation and compromise.[226]

---

222. Weinfeld, *TDOT,* 2:256.

223. Quell, *TDNT,* 2:109–10.

224. The etymology of the Hebrew noun בְּרִית (*berît*), "covenant," is uncertain, but in the Old Testament, it implied not so much an agreement between parties as it denoted an imposition or obligation one party put upon another. For example, see Ex. 24:3–8, which notes that "the laws of the covenant" describe the obligations the Hebrews took upon themselves as imposed by Jehovah. Weinfeld, *TDOT,* 2:255.

225. Gen. 21:27; 31:44; 1 Kgs. 5:12; 2 Sam. 3:13; and Jer. 34:8 all provide examples of covenants or agreements made between equals. Jehovah, however, was invoked as the legitimating and enforcing authority.

226. In a secular sense, even in the Bible, the word was sometimes used to describe a "parity treaty" among equals (for example, between friends such as those described in 1 Sam. 18:3; 20:8 and between rulers as in Gen. 21:27, 32), although even these secular agreements carried the religious overtone in that God was the chief witness (for example, see Gen. 31:44–50; compare 1 Kgs. 5:12).

Scholars have tried to determine if there was an ancient original and unambiguous understanding of covenant on which the others stood and drew their force. To date, though some interesting theories have been put forth, all efforts have been unsuccessful. See Mendenhall, "Covenants," in Freedman, *Anchor Bible Dictionary,* 1:1180–81. For discussion, see *NID,* s.v. "διαθήκη." On more solid ground is understanding the purpose of covenants. Broadly speaking across time and culture in the ancient Near East, people of various ranks

Jehovah's covenant with Noah (Gen. 6:18), the patriarchs (2 Kgs. 13:23), and David (Ps. 89:3) was not theirs alone; it extended to their posterity (Gen. 9:8–9; 15:18; Moses 7:52; compare 2 Sam. 7:12–16). This is especially noticeable in God's covenant with Abraham (Gen. 17:7), which extended to all Israel across time (Ex. 6:4–5).[227] Jehovah's covenant, combining as it did both religious and legal elements, formed the basis of "rightly ordered relationships" on the earthly plane for every generation that volunteered to come under it. It also defined the elements necessary for a divinely instituted fellowship between Jehovah and his people and drew heavily on his redeeming them.[228] A major draw for the people was the promise of protection by the all-powerful Jehovah.[229]

---

and ethnic groups used them to describe acceptable behavior, and parameters of social interaction and to define limits of activities, influence, and rule. It was the formal covenant that stated precisely what these were, made them binding, and stipulated the benefits for keeping the bond and the curses for not. It was here the covenant took on its religious aspect with the gods, who were expected to bring retribution upon the covenant breaker. Mendenhall, "Covenants," in Freedman, *Anchor Bible Dictionary,* 1:1181–83.

The ongoing scholarly debate on the root of biblical covenants is of little importance for most Latter-day Saints. This is because the debate hinges on whether the Pentateuch was a pious fiction created during the period of the monarchy or whether it had a historical basis reaching into Israel's past. Though Latter-day Saints recognize the Bible has its difficulties and inaccuracies (A of F 8), documents of the Restoration (for example, see Moses, Abraham, and the JST) show that the story line sits solidly on a historical foundation. Therefore, the concept of making and keeping divine covenants reaches back to the genesis of humankind's interaction with the Divine.

On the basis of the historical accuracy of the Pentateuch, some scholars see a direct relationship between the Mosaic covenant and the suzerain treaties found in a number of Near Eastern cultures. For an analysis of these, see Michael D. Coogan, *A Brief Introduction to the Old Testament* (Oxford: Oxford University Press, 2009), 100–103. That all the elements to greater or lesser degree are found in the Mosaic covenant seems more than coincidental and, therefore, suggests a connection. One point that seems very clear is that the importance and use of covenants is of great age. For studies, see W. Beyerlin, *Origins and History of the Oldest Sinaitic Traditions,* trans. S. Rudman (Oxford: Basil Blackwell, 1965). This work, though dated, continues to have relevance. See also William J. Dumbrell, *Covenant and Creation: A Theology of the Old Testament Covenants,* 2d ed. (Milton Keynes, Eng.: Paternoster, 2002); and Meredith G. Kline, "Canon and Covenant," *Westminster Theological Journal* 32 (1969): 49–67, accessed March 3, 2016, https://meredithkline.com/files/articles/Canon-and-Covenant-1.pdf.

227. *NID,* s.v. "διαθήκη."

228. Rushdoony, *Institutes of Biblical Law,* 8; Beyer, *TDNT,* 2:702–4. The importance of redemption underlies much of the covenant motif and is central to that of Abraham. For a study, see Janet Lane, "The Redemption of Abraham," in *Astronomy, Papyrus, and Covenant,* ed. John Gee and Brian M. Hauglid (Provo, Utah: Foundation for Ancient Research and Mormon Studies, Brigham Young University, 2005), 167–74.

229. Cross, *TDOT,* 1:256.

> There is no firmer guarantee of legal security, peace or personal loyalty than the covenant. Regard for the institution is made a religious duty by means of the oath taken at its establishment. Those who enter into the covenant know that [Jehovah] Himself keeps strict watch over the sworn fellowship and its order. Violation or deprecation of the accepted duty is recognised to be sin in the strictest possible sense of disregard for the will of [Jehovah]. To forget the covenant of brethren is to awaken the wrath of [Jehovah] (Am[os] 1:9). The covenant thus implies the unconditional validity of law surrounded by sacral assurances. It means legitimate order as opposed to caprice, uncertainty and animosity.[230]

The covenant, therefore, set up the rules of the theocracy in which Israel was to dwell with Jehovah as their king.[231] The period of the judges emphasizes this point. During much of this time, both the prophets and judges resisted any move toward human kingship, seeing such as an affront to their only and true sovereign if not an act of rebellion against him.[232] When Israel did finally get its king, it came as an act of compromise. Jehovah was still *the* King and therefore he would appoint all others to their post. They were to rule under his authority and according to his law. Thus, both human kings and their subjects remained as vassals to the true king (1 Sam. 12:14, 24–25; 2 Kgs. 11:17).

The idea of fellowship imparted to "covenant" the feeling of friendship, good will, and even love. The latter idea was expressed by the Hebrew noun חֶסֶד (*ḥesed*), denoting "covenantal loyalty" and "steadfast love," the noncoercive but certain power that kept both parties bound to the agreement.[233] The Israelites were therefore admonished to honor the covenant as stressed by such expressions as "with all their heart and with all their soul" (see 2 Kgs. 23:3; compare Deut. 6:5). The outflow on God's part for those of his people who strove to keep covenants was grace.

---

230. Quell, *TDNT,* 2:115.

231. For a time, the popular belief was that this idea came to the fore during the period of the monarchy and was then imposed on the more ancient text during periods of redaction. Over time it has become increasingly apparent that the idea of sacral kingship is one of the most ancient and genuine aspects of the Israelite religion. See Mendenhall, "Covenants," in Freedman, *Anchor Bible Dictionary,* 1:1180; and Ringgren, *TDOT,* 1:275.

232. For example, note Gideon's reply to those who wished to make him king (Judg. 8:22–23) and Samuel's explicit warnings about the drawbacks of having a human rather than a divine king (1 Sam. 8:6–7; 10:17–25; 12:17). The role of the prophets through much of the Old Testament was to remind the people of and bring them back under the covenant. Johnson, *Ancient Near Eastern Treaties,* 29–30.

233. Weinfeld, *TDOT,* 2:258–9.

The Covenant before Sinai[234]

The author of Hebrews refers to Jehovah's covenant made at Sinai as "the first covenant" (9:1, 15). It is likely that the author had in mind that this was God's first covenant specifically with the Israelites. The Old Testament shows that God had made covenants with many people before that time. Neither the Genesis text nor the account in the book of Moses specifically mention God making a covenant with Adam and Eve. That Adam was baptized suggests some form of the covenant was known to him (Moses 6:64–65). Further, God commanded that Adam worship him and live the law of sacrifice (Moses 5:5). God further demanded repentance with the promise that "as thou hast fallen thou mayest be redeemed, and all mankind, even as many as will" (Moses 5:9). The text is clear that the gospel was preached from the beginning and all things connected therewith God confirmed "by an holy ordinance" (Moses 5:59). This statement makes it clear that, from some point, Jehovah had established a God-ordered way of life for his children.

Further, no mention is made of Jehovah establishing a covenant with any of the patriarchs until Enoch. This prophet's work suggests that the idea of covenant may have been playing in the background, for he preached the gospel and demanded that people repent and be baptized so that they could "enjoy the words of eternal life in this world, and eternal life in the world to come" (Moses 6:59). At some point, Jehovah did establish a covenant with him. It was unusual in the breadth of the power it gave to its recipients. It included the power "to break mountains, to divide the seas, to dry up waters, and to turn them out of their course." It extended "to put[ting] at defiance the armies of nations" and "subdu[ing] principalities and powers," but more especially "stand[ing] in the presence of God" and "do[ing] all things according to his will" (JST Gen. 14:30–31; see also D&C 76:57).

That covenant, at least in part, was then reestablished with Noah (JST Gen. 9:21–25) but contained an additional element that made it unique from all other covenants Jehovah would make; it included not only Noah and his descendants but also "every living creature." It housed an assurance that never again would life, especially innocent life, be taken again on such a massive scale.[235] To assure its validity, God gave the rainbow as its token

234. In his work *Priesthood and Church Government* (Salt Lake City: Deseret Book, 1939), 1–30, Elder John A. Widtsoe traces the advance of priesthood over the ages and includes its connection with covenants.

235. This portion of the covenant rested on God's oath to Enoch that he would stay the floods and call upon the children of Noah. It also included the promise that there would always remain a remnant of Enoch's descendants on the earth. See Moses 7:51–52.

(Gen. 9:9–17). The covenant Jehovah made with Enoch was also extended to Melchizedek, and he was "ordained an high priest after the order of the covenant which God made with Enoch" (JST Gen. 14:27).

Jehovah next established his covenant with Abram. It consisted of three parts: the promise that Abram's seed would grow to national proportions, that his name would become great, and that Jehovah would bless his friends and allies and curse his enemies. It included the notice that somehow all the families of the earth would be blessed because of him (Gen. 12:2–3). It is of note that it was instituted as a means of reassuring Abram that what Jehovah promised would be realized. When the patriarch questioned, "Whereby shall I know that I shall inherit [the land]?" (Gen. 15:7–8), Jehovah instituted the covenant.[236] This account shows Jehovah's willingness, even condescension, to assuage Abram's concerns through the use of the common means known to Abram of securing a promise, that is, through making a covenant.

Due to the amount of information that has come through the Restoration, we have a large window through which to see how this covenant worked. Jehovah established it by a theophany, for the "Lord appeared unto" Abraham (Abr. 2:6). The basis of the covenant and the assurance of the realization of its blessing rested upon Jehovah's sovereignty over the earth, his omnipotence (Abr. 2:7), and his omniscience (Abr. 2:8). According to the Genesis account, the covenant consisted of three elements: that Abraham would have a great posterity, that they would inherit a specific land, and that Jehovah would be his children's God and they would be his people (Gen. 17:1–9).[237] The token of the covenant was circumcision (Gen. 17:10–14).

The account in the book of Abraham, however, has a different stress. There the text emphasizes two items: the greatness of Abraham's future reputation among the nations and the right to the priesthood among his posterity through all generations of mortal time. That blessing came, however, with a price: the covenant stipulated the obligation Abraham's posterity had of carrying the gospel to all the world. This information fills in the missing material in Genesis, specifying how Abraham would be a

236. The way the scriptures lay out the story, it would appear that this is a royal grant covenant with Jehovah being the one who performed the necessary oath ritual.

237. We need to point out that women were also involved in the covenant since the center of most of them is eternal family life. For a good study of this aspect, see Janet Hovorka, "Sarah and Hagar: Ancient Women of the Abrahamic Covenant," in Gee and Hauglid, *Astronomy, Papyrus, and Covenant,* 147–66.

blessing to future generations.[238] This covenant was later renewed and then extended to Isaac and his posterity (Gen. 17:21). Due to sin,[239] the covenant was broken at some point during the centuries when the children of Israel were in Egypt[240] and therefore had to be renewed.

The Mosaic Covenant

The institution of the Mosaic covenant reveals the strong unilateral thrust of divine covenants. It was Jehovah who re-called the children of Israel to be his own people and who instituted and defined the content, obligations, and limitations of the covenant. Indeed, it was through the covenant that they became his kin.[241] Central to the covenant and the basis of its appeal was Jehovah's promise that faithfulness to him would result in peace and salvation. Further, the promise, being based on and deriving force from its Abrahamic precedent, could not be revoked due to Israel's disobedience

---

238. The text additionally notes all those who accept the gospel would be counted as Abraham's posterity (Abr. 2:10).

239. According to Ezek. 20:5–9, the Hebrews became idolatrous in Egypt. Though Jehovah reached out to them, they would not abandon their idols. This aroused his anger, but for his name's sake, he spared them and raised up Moses to bring them out of a both spiritually and physically deadly environment.

240. The scriptures give different lengths of time for the Hebrews' stay in Egypt. Some state it was for 400 years (Gen. 15:13; Acts 7:6) and others for 430 years (Ex. 12:40–41; Gal. 3:16–17). A few modern researches have suggested it was more like 215 years. Their reasoning is based on Paul's statement that the Mosaic law was given 430 years after Jehovah established his covenant with Abraham (Gal. 3:16–17). They discount the statement in Ex. 12:40–41 that the Hebrews were in Egypt for the full 430 years and instead suggest the period of persecution actually began in Abraham's day when Ishmael despised Isaac, which happened 30 years after God established his initial covenant with Abraham (Gen. 12:1–3; 21:8–9; Gal. 4:29). The despising was 400 years before Israel escaped from Egypt. That would put the Hebrews' moving into Egypt 215 years before Moses delivered them. One of the earliest commentators to propound this view was Henry Ainsworth, *Annotations on the Pentateuch or the Five Books of Moses; the Psalms of David and the Song of Solomon* (Glasgow: Blackie and Son, 1843), 83, as noted in David Wright, "How Long Were the Israelites in Egypt," Answers in Genesis, July 5, 2010, https://answersingenesis.org/bible-questions/how-long-were-the-israelites-in-egypt/.

241. Echoes of this idea can be found in King Benjamin's sermon where he states that "because of the covenant which [his people had made, they] shall be called the children of Christ, his sons, and his daughters; for behold, this day he [had] spiritually begotten [them]" (Mosiah 5:7). The Lord explained to the brother of Jared that to those who believed on his name, he would give eternal life. Indeed, through their redemption, they would become his sons and daughters (Ether 3:13–14). See also Spackman, "Israelite Roots of Atonement Terminology," 53–57.

(Isa. 54:10; 55:3). The covenant, therefore, bound God to Israel in such a way that precluded all arbitrariness.

That is not to say that there was ever any indication that the sinful or rebellious would receive the blessings of the covenant promised. Indeed, they would not, but the covenant still bound Jehovah to the Israelite people even during periods of rebellion and apostasy. He, therefore, was duty bound to work to bring them back, seen through much of the book of Exodus[242] and also in the former and latter-day promises to restore the ten tribes and gather Israel (for example, see Deut. 30:3; Ps. 107:3; Isa. 5:26; 6:13; 11:11; 45:5; Jer. 29:14; 32:37; Ezek. 20:41; 36:34; Jacob 6:2; 3 Ne. 20:29; D&C 29:7; 45:25; and A of F 10).

At Sinai, Jehovah sought to renew the covenant and keep his oath to Abraham, calling again the children of Israel to be his people, and they in turn accepted him to be their God. The covenant was anchored securely in the reality of the historical event of the Exodus wherein Jehovah manifested his great power. For the author of Hebrews and his readers, as certain as was the history, so certain was the covenant.

Through the use of the covenant, the responsibilities of all parties were clearly defined and agreed to, thus leaving no room for doubt or ambiguity. It also bound both parties equally to one another. In addition, since Jehovah would never break a covenant, it put Israel in control of her relationship with him. If she violated the clearly agreed-upon principles outlined in the law, Jehovah was no longer bound to act as her God and to grant her favor or make her the chief of all nations.[243] When she lost prestige and influence, she had only herself to blame. On the other hand, the result of covenant keeping would allow her to live in a state of salvation because the Israelites' temporal fellowship with God, being both perfect and assured, foreshadowed their eternal relationship with him.

Unfortunately, that high state was never reached. Due to Israel's rebellion, Jehovah gave them a lesser law as the basis for the covenant (JST Ex. 34:1–2; D&C 84:19–26). Paul fully understood the Mosaic covenant was "added because of transgression" and would stay in effect until "the seed [that is, Jesus] should come to whom the promises were made" (Gal. 3:19). The amended covenant was not without power or hope. Indeed, it held "the key to the ministering of angels and the preparatory gospel" (D&C 84:26).

---

242. *NID,* s.v. "διαθήκη."
243. Hauck, *TDNT,* 1:122.

The covenant was formally established, according to Exodus 24:3–8. All the necessary elements are found there. Moses read "out of the book of the covenant" all of Jehovah's stipulations. All the people verbally agree to them. Then Moses splashed "the blood of the covenant" from the sacrificed animal on the people as a simile curse for what would happen to them if they violated the covenant.

Of particular note is Jehovah's willingness to accept these very weak and very human individuals as one with him. Jehovah had invited them into his presence and they had accepted the invitation. In response, they entered into the presence of the Divine—a being of unimaginable power and majesty. Often such encounters have been met with fear. Even the unusual faith of the brother of Jared did not stop him from being "struck with fear" when he encountered Jehovah (see Ether 3:6–8), and Moses, during his first encounter, feared "to look upon God" (Ex. 3:6). At one point, Jehovah invited Moses and seventy-three of the elders of Israel to climb Sinai and enter his presence (Ex. 24:9–11). These seventy-four men that day stood in the grip of the *numen tremendum*—the full power of the supernatural—but God chose to not terrify or even overwhelm them. Instead he chose to make league with them. God's acceptance would likely have impressed on them that they were not dealing with the beings of dread worshiped by others—beings who had to be pacified, mollified, and appeased. Far different was this God from those the Egyptians and others worshiped. Exodus suggests that from their first encounter with the true God, the children of Israel had to start learning afresh nearly everything they thought they knew about Deity.[244]

Though established under the hands of majesty, some of the prophets understood that this covenant was not designed to last forever. Indeed, they witnessed Jehovah would establish a new covenant—even a covenant of peace—not written on stone tablets but on the hearts and in the minds of its receivers. The basis of the new covenant was anchored to the core principle that formed the center of the old, namely those who agreed to abide by it would be Jehovah's people and he would be their God. But there was more; he would make them clean, remembering their sins no more (Jer. 31:31–34; Ezek. 34:25; 36:24–28; 37:26). On this idea rests the understanding of the covenant as found in the New Testament.

---

244. Hauck, *TDNT,* 1:122. When Gideon saw the angel of Jehovah in a vision, he feared for his life, but Jehovah reassured him he was not in danger: "Peace be unto thee; fear not: thou shalt not die." In response, the judge built an altar and named it "Jehovah-shalom," indicating peace, not fear, came from interacting with God and his angels (Judg. 6:22–24).

Covenant in the New Testament

During the third to first centuries before Christ, some factions of Judaism began building their "fence" around the Torah, rationalizing the process by appealing to the need to define and protect covenantal law. The process accelerated during the early Christian era. Rabbinic Judaism viewed "covenant" primarily as a formal system. They designed it to give meaning mainly to those who belonged to their ethnicity as well as to provide a base for solidarity and cohesion. The rabbis designed the "fence" to uphold the values and ways of behavior as they interpreted Torah.[245] The result made most forms of Judaism exceptionally legalistic but also protected it from outsiders and gave support to their ethnic group.[246]

Conversely, the Christian leadership viewed "covenant" as "a socially enacted historical reality that accompanied sufficient functional changes in old patterns of behavior so as to rupture old ethical and political bases of social solidarity and cohesion, and to replace these with a larger vision of human community." Jesus himself began the process.[247] In doing so, the Christian movement restored "covenant" to the ideological matrix at play when Jehovah established it with Abraham and later with Moses and as it was upheld and promoted by Israel's prophets. In sum, Jehovah designed "covenant" to create "a religious community that cut across old parochialisms." His aim was a societal system that was "not defined by legal norms and backed up by coercive power. The basis of the society was the complete internalization ethic of the rule of God, ideally envisioned (but imperfectly realized) in the Sinai suzerainty treaty."[248]

Paul counted the covenant as one of the great advantages ancient Israel had over other nations, which, even as a Jewish Christian, Paul continued to value (Rom. 9:4). As critical as he was of the old law (see Rom. 3:4–18), he still understood that it came from the same God as the new covenant (see Rom. 3:7, where Paul calls it "the truth of God"), and therefore it had value.

---

245. *M. Avot* 1:1.

246. Mendenhall, "Covenants," in Freedman, *Anchor Bible Dictionary,* 1:1201.

247. Mendenhall, "Covenants," in Freedman, *Anchor Bible Dictionary,* 1:1201. Jesus pushed against what some considered to be "proper" social and religious boundaries by eating and drinking with "sinners" (Matt. 9:19–13) and by challenging the rules of Sabbath observance (Matt. 12:10; Mark 2:23–27), eating conventions (Mark 7:1–5), and other "traditions" favored and promulgated by the Pharisees that the Lord knew took people away from the intent of the Law (Matt. 15:1–6).

248. Mendenhall, "Covenants," in Freedman, *Anchor Bible Dictionary,* 1:1201. For a brief but well-done study, see Weinfeld, *TDOT,* 2:266–70; for an extended one, see Thompson, *Ancient Near Eastern Treaties,* 7–23.

Paul and the author of Hebrews use the word "covenant" both in the Hellenistic sense of a set of binding agreements and in the Hebrew sense of defining right relations with Jehovah. Context must be used to tell the difference. Each writer moves between the two definitions as suits his purpose. The link that joins the two concepts is that of a will. After the death of the testator,[249] the agreement cannot be annulled or changed in any way. So too God's laws, set down by covenant, are unalterable, inviolable, and of absolute validity (Gal. 3:15–18). But here the link ends since God can never die.

Staying in covenant therefore assures the faithful of their reward. The reason is that the new covenant comes with power. God promised that a Deliverer would arise in Zion through whom the ungodliness of Jacob would be overcome and turned away, "for this is my covenant unto them, when I shall take away their sins" (Rom. 11:26–27).[250] The major problem with the old covenant was that Israel could not meet its provisional requirements. It lacked the necessary power by which they could gain the strength to overmaster themselves and live according to its strictures. For that reason, it had to be abolished (καταργέω, *katargeō*) and another instituted that came with the necessary power (Rom. 1:16; 15:13; 16:25; 2 Cor. 12:9; Col. 1:10–11). Thus, as the author of Hebrews states, Christ is the guarantor of the new covenant (9:11–15) through which the faithful can be given power to overcome "the natural man," be cleansed from sin, and enter into the eternal rest of the Lord (4:11).[251]

With the coming of Jesus, as the author of Hebrews shows, came a "better hope" based on the "new covenant." That hope was founded not only on a vision of what God had set in opening the door to his "rest" but also the acquiring of power through his grace so that the person could achieve it. Indeed, the work of the Savior was to bring humankind into a position not of covenant breaking but of covenant keeping. He freed those who would follow him "from the law of sin and death" (Rom. 8:2) "that the righteousness of the law might be fulfilled in [them]" (Rom. 8:4). The purpose of the Atonement is, then, to allow grace to operate in the lives of the disciples. This aspect was woven into the Mosaic law, the giving of which was in itself an act of divine grace. Through its rituals, a properly repentant Israelite found forgiveness of sin and unity with Jehovah and received his grace.[252]

---

249. For discussion on the role of the testator, see Translation Notes for 9:16–17 below with the corresponding Analysis.

250. *NID,* s.v. "διαθήκη."

251. Schmidt, *TDNT,* 1:130.

252. The faithful Nephites, though living under the Mosaic law, were well aware that they operated under divine grace. Indeed, they were thankful for "the wisdom of

The Divine, however, never intended that grace should set aside that law but that grace would fulfill it and enable humankind to live it.[253] The author of Hebrews seems to have seen grace as "a free manifestation of divine love," the objective of which was to make men and women "live in communion with God," who imparts "to them the treasure of grace and the heavenly inheritance."[254] Further, it embraced all who would come under it. What therefore the old covenant could only do in part, the new covenant could do fully.[255]

God, his mercy and grace" (2 Ne. 9:8) and believed that "only in and through the grace of God" people were saved (2 Ne. 10:24). The Lord showed these people their weakness so that they would know that it was by his grace that they received revelation and prophecy (Jacob 4:6–7). They, therefore, felt the need to continue supplicating for the Lord's grace (Alma 7:3). They understood that through repentance people could be restored to grace (Hel. 12:14) and that people could come to perfection only through those means (Moro. 10:22–23). Even so, as Nephi stated, "Notwithstanding we believe in Christ, we keep the law of Moses, and look forward with steadfastness unto Christ, until the law shall be fulfilled. For, for this end was the law given; wherefore the law hath become dead unto us, and we are made alive in Christ because of our faith; yet we keep the law because of the commandments." Even so, Nephi continued to preach of Christ so the "children may know to what source they may look for a remission of their sins" and therefore of "the deadness of the law"; and they, by knowing the deadness of the law, "may look forward unto that life which is in Christ, and know for what end the law was given. And after the law is fulfilled in Christ, that they need not harden their hearts against him when the law ought to be done away." Though that was the case, his people must "keep the performances and ordinances of God until the law shall be fulfilled which was given unto Moses" (2 Ne. 25:23–30).

253. Rushdoony, *Institutes of Biblical Law,* 3–4.

254. Ellingworth, *Epistle to the Hebrews,* 388.

255. The Latter-day Saint view of covenants fits nicely with that of the author of Hebrews. For Latter-day Saints, covenant making and keeping play a critical role in the salvation process. See Wouter Van Beek, "Covenants," in Ludlow, *Encyclopedia of Mormonism,* 1:331–33.

Chapter 8

A New Covenant with the House of Israel

Introduction

With chapter 8, the author of Hebrews begins the central portion of his Epistle. He will bring it to a close at 10:18. In the various sections that compose this portion, we find the heart of the author's Christological exposition as he more fully develops his explication of Christ.[1] In doing so, he will release the tension he has been deliberately creating up to this point. He has stressed that Jesus has become the one and only effective High Priest by offering himself once for all as the fully sufficient sacrifice for sin,[2] who "can also completely and eternally save those who come to God through him" (NR 7:25). Building upon this foundation—a foundation the author has so carefully laid in the forepart of his Epistle—he now discusses in detail the long-awaited theme of the significance and ramifications of the Savior's self-sacrifice. He lays out his thesis so well that he satisfies the curiosity of all who want to know. In sum, he states that "by his sacrifice the Son has atoned for sin, entered the heavenly Sanctuary as High Priest, and established the New Covenant. Thus, [the author] uses the themes of sanctuary, covenant, and sacrifice to disclose the full magnitude of the Son's self-offering."[3]

The author links this section with the preceding one by the use of the image of the high priest, noting that God's oath—which succeeded the Mosaic law with its Levitical Priesthood—appointed the Son to the high priesthood. He

1. Attridge, *Epistle to the Hebrews*, 216.
2. Cockerill, *Epistle to the Hebrews*, 346.
3. Cockerill, *Epistle to the Hebrews*, 346.

is the one whom the Father "made perfect forever" (NR 7:28). Thus, the subject announced in 5:9—Christ having been "made perfect" is the only source of eternal salvation—and recalled in 7:28 is the thesis of this entire section (8:1–10:18).[4]

The unparalleled artistry of the author comes out clearly here. He develops his argument "like a symphony in three movements (8:1–13; 9:1–22; 9:23–10:18)." In each movement, he develops the themes of sanctuary, sacrifice, and covenant. "Each movement begins with the theme of sanctuary (8:1–2; 9:1–10; 9:23–24) and ends with covenant (8:7–13; 9:16–22; 10:15–18). At the center of each is the everexpanding theme of sacrifice (8:3–6; 9:11–15; 9:25–10:14)."[5]

The structure of the first and second movements (8:1–13 and 9:1–28) is concentric.

> Six subdivisions are distinguishable that correspond to one another in the order ABCC'B'A'. To the first subdivision (8:3–6), which criticizes the former worship that has been established at an early level, is opposed the last subdivision (9:24–28), in which Christ reaches the heavenly level. The second subdivision (8:7–13), which uses the oracle of the new covenant to criticize the first covenant, is completed by the penultimate subdivision (9:15–23), which presents Christ as "mediator of a new covenant" and shows the relation of the latter with the first covenant. The two central subdivisions (9:1–10 and 9:11–14) correspond to each other by opposing each other; the first describes and criticizes the worship of the Old Testament; the second describes the liturgical action of Christ and proclaims its efficacy. At the central point (9:11), the name of *Christ* is proclaimed, with his title of *high priest.*[6]

In the third movement, the author stresses the unique quality of the Lord's sacrifice that, unlike that of the high priest, had to be done but once (9:24–28). This movement ends declaring the efficacy of Christ's oblation that prepares the way for God to establish the new covenant in which, as he

4. Vanhoye, *Letter to the Hebrews,* 127; Cockerill, *Epistle to the Hebrews,* 345. There is some disagreement between authorities as to where the structural units actually break, but most agree that 8:1–10:18 compose a single and progressive development. For discussion, see Cockerill, *Epistle to the Hebrews,* 346 n. 5. What is important is that, however the units are divided, that division does not stand in the way of seeing the brilliant and powerful witness of the nature, work, and importance of the Savior that the author gives.

5. Cockerill, *Epistle to the Hebrews,* 346–47.

6. Vanhoye, *Letter to the Hebrews,* 128–29, italics in original.

declares, "I will make with them after those days, says the Lord, I will put my laws on their hearts and I will write them on their minds" (NR 10:16).

In the initial section under study here (8:1–6), the author is most anxious that his readers "grasp the implications of who this High Priest *now* is—the sum of what he has always been and what he has now become. He is the eternal Son who through his obedient, incarnate life offered himself in death and is now seated at God's right hand fully able to meet their deepest need."[7] This point rests on the inadequacy of the old law, on which the author has already dwelt and to which he will refer again (8:7, 13). Though the law had validity during its tenure, it has now been superseded by a new law and covenant.

The common element in both the Levitical and the new dispensation is the operation of the priesthood presided over by a high priest. The problem with the earlier dispensation was the administrators were weak, suffering from sickness and death. The new dispensation, however, brought Christ, strong, immortal, and exalted forever. That is not to say he was untried. Indeed, the author does not shy away from the Lord's own humanity (2:10–18) and weakness (5:2).[8] These, however, were necessary in order for the Savior to empathize with his people and to suffer death on their behalf. By these means, he has been empowered to bring all who will to realize perfection, that is, completeness, and eternal oneness with the Father (10:14; 11:40; 12:23). As such, Christ has become the consummate high priest who has offered the acceptable sacrifice for all.

In the beginning lines of chapter 8, the author summarizes the point he has been making by noting that Jesus, the categorical high priest, now presides in heaven and is the minister of the heavenly tabernacle set up by God (8:1–2). The author next describes the nature of the Lord's ministry: it is sacrificial (8:3). He admits that the Lord would not have been able to offer an acceptable sacrifice through the Aaronic order since he was not of Levitical descent but is quick to note that the earthly priests actually served as but shadows and types of the eternal order of things (8:4–5). Jesus, on the other hand, obtained the "more excellent ministry" because he is the "mediator [or guarantor] of a better covenant," one legally established on the ground of a better promise (8:6). The author goes on to show, by quoting LXX Jeremiah 38:31–34 (31:31–34 in the KJV), that God had

7. Cockerill, *Epistle to the Hebrews,* 345–46.
8. Ellingworth, *Epistle to the Hebrews,* 397.

already made provisions for this new covenant when he revealed to that prophet that he would indeed establish it. By its means, he would bring people to know the Lord (8:8–12). He concludes that if the old covenant had worked, there would have been no need for a new one to replace it and emphasizes that the old covenant has now become obsolete and is about to pass away (8:13).

Priests Serve as an Example and Shadow of Heavenly Things (8:1–6)

Greek Text

1 Κεφάλαιον δὲ ἐπὶ τοῖς λεγομένοις, τοιοῦτον ἔχομεν ἀρχιερέα, ὃς ἐκάθισεν ἐν δεξιᾷ τοῦ θρόνου τῆς μεγαλωσύνης ἐν τοῖς οὐρανοῖς, 2 τῶν ἁγίων λειτουργὸς καὶ τῆς σκηνῆς τῆς ἀληθινῆς, ἣν ἔπηξεν ὁ κύριος, οὐκ ἄνθρωπος. 3 πᾶς γὰρ ἀρχιερεὺς εἰς τὸ προσφέρειν δῶρά τε καὶ θυσίας καθίσταται· ὅθεν ἀναγκαῖον ἔχειν τι καὶ τοῦτον ὃ προσενέγκῃ. 4 εἰ μὲν οὖν ἦν ἐπὶ γῆς, οὐδ᾽ ἂν ἦν ἱερεύς, ὄντων τῶν προσφερόντων κατὰ νόμον τὰ δῶρα· 5 (οἵτινες ὑποδείγματι καὶ σκιᾷ λατρεύουσιν τῶν ἐπουρανίων, καθὼς κεχρημάτισται Μωϋσῆς μέλλων ἐπιτελεῖν τὴν σκηνήν, Ὅρα γάρ, φησίν, ποιήσεις πάντα κατὰ τὸν τύπον τὸν δειχθέντα σοι ἐν τῷ ὄρει). 6 νυνὶ δὲ διαφορωτέρας τέτυχεν λειτουργίας, ὅσῳ καὶ κρείττονός ἐστιν διαθήκης μεσίτης, ἥτις ἐπὶ κρείττοσιν ἐπαγγελίαις νενομοθέτηται. [SBLGNT]

King James Version

1 Now of the things which we have spoken this is the sum: We have such an high priest, who is set on the right hand of the throne of the Majesty in the heavens; 2 A minister of the sanctuary, and of the true tabernacle, which the Lord pitched, and not man. 3 For every high priest is ordained to offer gifts and sacrifices: wherefore it is of necessity that this man have somewhat also to offer. 4 For if he were on earth, he should not be a priest, seeing that there are priests that offer gifts according to the law: 5 Who serve unto the

New Rendition

1 Now the main point in what is being said is this: we have such a high priest who sat down at the right hand of the throne of the Majesty in the heavens. 2 He is a minister of the sanctuary, even the true tabernacle, which the Lord, not man, set up. 3 Now every high priest is appointed to offer gifts and sacrifices, therefore it is necessary that this high priest also have something to offer. 4 So if he were on earth, he would not even be a priest, since there are already priests who offer gifts according to the law. 5 These priests serve as an example

example and shadow of heavenly things, as Moses was admonished of God when he was about to make the tabernacle: for, See, saith he, that thou make all things according to the pattern shewed to thee in the mount. 6 But now hath he obtained a more excellent ministry, by how much also he is the mediator of a better covenant, which was established upon better promises.

and shadow of heavenly things, as Moses was warned as he was about to erect the tabernacle, for God said,

> "See that you make everything according to the pattern that was shown to you on the mountain." [Ex. 25:40]

6 But as it is, Jesus has obtained a more excellent ministry, to the extent that he is also a guarantor of a better covenant that has been legally enacted on better promises.

Translation Notes and Comments

8:1 *Now of the things which we have spoken this is the sum / Now the main point in what is being said is this:* The noun κεφάλαιον (*kephalaion*), literally "little head," refers to "a brief statement concerning some topic or subject," hence "main point"[9] as in our Rendition.

The author's use of the present passive participle λεγομένοις (*legomenois*), "what is being said,"[10] stresses not only what he has said but more especially what he is saying and will say about the Savior's priesthood and sacrifice. Thus, taken as a whole, this sentence summarizes the points he will make in the next section of his letter (running from 8:7–10:18). His transition is smooth. Note that by the end of the paragraph (8:6), he has refocused his readers' attention from Christ's priesthood to his sacrifice, and in that way introduces his upcoming major theme.[11]

We have such an high priest / we have such a high priest: The phrase looks back to 7:27–28, stressing first the total sufficiency of the Lord's atoning sacrifice made in behalf of all and second his perfection (NR 7:28). This is the kind of high priest they have: one who has been "made perfect" and now presides in the heavens.[12] The passage also looks forward to 8:2,

9. BDAG, 541; Koester, *Hebrews,* 374–75. See also Ronald Williamson, *Philo and the Epistle to the Hebrews* (Leiden, Neth.: E. J. Brill, 1970), 127–29, who notes that the "main point" is the transitional "crown" between what the author has said and what he will say about the Lord.

10. BDAG, 588–90.

11. Ellingworth, *Epistle to the Hebrews,* 400.

12. Vanhoye, *Letter to the Hebrews,* 128.

showing that he is now "the ministering priest in the heavenly sanctuary."[13] The phrase opens the way for the author to make a fuller elaboration of the distinctive character of the Savior's priesthood, "which has to do not only with who he is but also with what he offers, namely himself."[14]

who is set on the right hand of the throne of the Majesty in the heavens / who sat down at the right hand of the throne of the Majesty in the heavens: This phrase is an allusion to LXX Psalm 109:1, which the author previously cited (1:3, 13). The adjective δεξιός (*dexios*) denotes the right side of something. The feminine form, found here, was often used symbolically to reference a person's right hand and more especially, when used with God, to represent his divine power.[15] The noun θρόνος (*thronos*), "throne," in this instance, acts as a periphrasis (that is, a roundabout way of referring to someone) for God himself.[16] For that reason, in our Rendition, we translate the phrase as "right hand" rather than "right side." The position is one of power and prestige that the author uses to stress the Lord's high station.[17] The noun μεγαλωσύνη (*megalōsynē*), "greatness, majesty," is used only of God in the New Testament, and in this case, it is a periphrasis for God the Father himself.[18] Thus, we have translated it as "the Majesty" in our Rendition.

8:2 ***A minister of the sanctuary, and of the true tabernacle / He is a minister of the sanctuary, even the true tabernacle:*** In Greek society, the λειτουργός (*leitourgos*), "minister," was a public servant and benefactor often responsible to put on public festivals and devotions to the gods. In the New Testament, the term identified one who was engaged in administering the various temple performances and ordinances.[19] The idea of public service, however, even though of a sacred nature, should not be

---

13. Lane, *Hebrews 1–8,* 204.

14. Johnson, *Hebrews,* 196.

15. BDAG, 217–18; Louw-Nida, §§82.8; 8.32; 76.4.

16. Even so, it does admit to a standard feature that Jewish scholars attributed to the temple in heaven. Attridge, *Epistle to the Hebrews,* 217. The idea that the earthly sanctuary had a certain correspondence to the heavenly one was current during this period among many Jews and found particularly in Jewish and rabbinic apocalyptic literature. See Aelred Cody, *Heavenly Sanctuary and Liturgy in the Epistle to the Hebrews: The Achievement of Salvation in the Epistle's Perspectives* (St. Meinrad, Ind.: Grail Publications, 1960), 9–46, whose premise is that the origin of the idea of a heavenly sanctuary is Semitic.

17. Though the primary allusion here is to Ps. 110:1, there is an echo of LXX Zech. 6:13, where the prophet refers to an anointed priest who sits on God's right side.

18. BDAG, 623.

19. BDAG, 591–92; Johnson, *Hebrews,* 198; Cockerill, *Epistle to the Hebrews,* 352.

dismissed since the Lord's teachings and work were generally very public, being intended for all who would listen (see John 18:19–21).[20]

The plural noun ἅγια (*hagia*), literally "holy things," is often translated as "sanctuary" and as such referred to the Jewish temple, but it here designates its heavenly counterpart.[21] The noun σκηνή (*skēnē*), literally "tent," referred to the tabernacle used by the Israelites from the time of the Exodus to the completion of Solomon's temple.[22] But here, like *hagia,* it refers to the "true" heavenly temple. The author's use of the adjective ἀληθινός (*alēthinos*), "true," to describe it should not be construed to mean that anything about the Mosaic tabernacle was false, especially since it was Jehovah who commanded its building and revealed its ordinances. It means, rather, that the tabernacle was but a pattern or a type of the "true," or real, eternal heavenly realm.[23]

Some authorities see the author's use of the words τῶν ἁγίων (*tōn hagiōn*), "the sanctuary," and τῆς σκηνῆς (*tēs skēnēs*), "the tabernacle," as indicating the inner room (holy of holies) and outer room (holy place) in

---

20. There were occasions when he did ask his disciples and others to not disclose his doings, but that was to protect the work of the ministry. For example, see Mark 1:43–45; 8:29–30.

21. BDAG, 11–12. There was an idea among some ancient Near Eastern cultures that there was a mystical analogical relationship that tied the celestial and terrestrial spheres together. Thus, earthly temples had their heavenly counterpart. Goppelt, *TDNT,* 8:256–57. Truman G. Madsen, *The Temple: Where Heaven and Earth Meet* (Salt Lake City: Deseret Book, 2015), 95–96, noted that "only in the temple are you placed in covenant-harmony with divine powers."

22. BDAG, 928. In the LXX historical books and Psalms, σκηνή (*skēnē*), "the tent," and especially σκηνὴ τοῦ μαρτυρίου (*skēnē tou martyriou*), "the tent of witness," referred to the Mosaic tabernacle. For example, see Ex. 28:43; 29:4, 10, 11; 30:20; Lev. 1:3, 5; Num. 1:1, 50; and Josh. 18:1; 19:51.

23. Ellingworth, *Epistle to the Hebrews,* 401; Cockerill, *Epistle to the Hebrews,* 356. Compare Philip Edgcumbe Hughes, "The Blood of Jesus and His Heavenly Priesthood in Hebrews: Part III, The Meaning of 'The True Tent' and 'The Greater and More Perfect Tent,'" *Bibliotheca Sacra* 130 (October 1973): 305–14. G. W. MacRae, "Heavenly Temple and Eschatology in the Letter to the Hebrews," *Semeia* 12 (1978): 179–99, posits that the author of Hebrews held a realized eschatological view of the temple. According to this view, the temple models how the universe itself is oriented; the Holy of Holies is to the temple what heaven is to the universe. Many of the author's readers, however, probably held a futurist eschatology. According to that view, the earthly temple is a model of an "actual" temple in heaven. The author did not attempt to argue with this view but rather shored it up using his own position. It is because the author has mixed two different eschatological positions that there are different views of the "true temple" in Hebrews.

the bipartitioned edifice.[24] It is more likely, given how the author develops this theme in the rest of the Epistle, that the two terms should be construed as a hendiadys (that is, the expression of a single idea by two words connected with "and"), thus both pointing to the same reality—representing heaven itself.[25] We have therefore translated the phrase as "the sanctuary, even the true tabernacle" in our Rendition.

which the Lord pitched, and not man / which the Lord, not man, set up: The verb πήγνυμι (*pēgnymi*) means to set up or construct an object, thus, to pitch or set up a tent.[26] The phrase echoes LXX Numbers 24:6, where Balaam refers to God's pitching tents, a metaphor for his establishing the house of Israel and, therefore, tacitly hinting at its eternal nature. The author seems to be emphasizing the same idea, albeit having the Savior as the facilitator. In this way, the author subtly shows that the "true tent" is superior to the one Moses had set up and which had long since disappeared.

8:3 ***For every high priest is ordained to offer gifts and sacrifices / Now every high priest is appointed to offer gifts and sacrifices:*** For "high priest," see Translation Notes for 5:1 and the associated Analysis. One of the major tasks of the Levitical priest was to offer gifts and sacrifices to Jehovah in behalf of a person or the people (Lev. 1–5). The ἀρχιερεύς (*archiereus*), "high priest," not only oversaw that these tasks were properly done but could also do them himself.

The power for a priest to legitimately perform service came from being appointed (καθίστημι, *kathistēmi,* "to appoint"), the verb denoting the act of assigning someone to a position of authority.[27]

wherefore it is of necessity that this man have somewhat also to offer / therefore it is necessary that this high priest also have something to offer: The coordinating conjunction ὅθεν (*hothen*), "therefore," marks "the basis for an action"[28] and here emphasizes the reason for that action. The neuter

---

24. Attridge, *Epistle to the Hebrews,* 218, 222; for a discussion, see Lane, *Hebrews 1–8,* 200–201 note e; and Johnson, *Hebrews,* 199. That the idea was current among some Jews can be seen from *1 En.* 14:10–20; *T. Levi* 3:2–4.

25. This translates καί (*kai*) as epexegetical (that is, it acts to give additional information), and thus it is rendered as "that is." For discussion, see Cockerill, *Epistle to the Hebrews,* 354–55; Johnson, *Hebrews,* 199; and Koester, *Hebrews,* 376. Based on their understanding of the scriptures, some Jews viewed the earthly temple as a model of the universe. For a study, see G. K. Beale, *The Temple and the Church's Mission: A Biblical Theology of the Dwelling Place of God* (Downers Grove, Ill.: InterVarsity Press, 2004), 31–60.

26. BDAG, 811.

27. BDAG, 492.

28. BDAG, 692–93. Wallace, *Greek Grammar,* 664–65, notes that this relative adverb indicates the result of the action.

adjective ἀναγκαῖον (*anangkaion*) with ἐστιν (*estin*) means "it is necessary to" and denotes an action that must be done.[29] In this case, it refers to having a sacrificial offering. The idea expressed in the phrase is that since the purpose of the appointment of priests is to make sacrificial offerings for the people, Christ's appointment held no exception. The author does not specify what that offering is here but has already done so in 7:27. He will do so again in 9:14.

The noun "high priest" is not in the Greek text but is intimated by the accusative pronoun τοῦτον (*touton*), "this one," and therefore is inserted in our Rendition for clarity.

Noteworthy is a point from grammar. The author, in describing the offerings of the Levitical priests, uses the present infinitive προσφέρειν (*prospherein*), "to make offerings," showing the continuing nature of their work, but when he refers to the Savior's offering, he uses the aorist tense προσενέγκῃ (*prosenengkē*), "made an offering," showing that the Savior's offering was singular, sufficient, and definitive. Further, the priests offer θυσίας (*thysias*), "sacrifices"—note the plural—where the Savior offers τι (*ti*), "something," in the indefinite singular: himself, once for all.[30]

8:4 ***For if he were on earth, he should not be a priest / So if he were on earth, he would not even be a priest:*** The author states the obvious; since Jesus was from the tribe of Judah, the Mosaic law disqualified him from holding the priesthood, let alone being a high priest. The grammatical construction here, however, is telling. The author couches the phrase as contrary to fact, that is, the assuming of an untruth for the sake of argument.[31] From that, we can extrapolate that he is saying, "If [this high priest] were on earth (but he is not), he would not be a priest (although in fact he is a priest)."[32]

seeing that there are priests that offer gifts according to the law / since there are already priests who offer gifts according to the law: This phrase explains why Jesus was not needed as a Levitical priest; namely, this very

---

29. BDAG, 60–61; LSJ, 100. Here, as is often the case in Greek, the verb ἐστίν (*estin*) is omitted but understood. Smyth, *Greek Grammar,* §944.

30. Koester, *Hebrews,* 377. The author's use of the present tense here does not necessarily imply that the temple was currently functioning. He is, rather, arguing on the basis of "general principles founded on the timeless legislation of the Torah." Attridge, *Epistle to the Hebrews,* 219 n. 36.

31. Wallace, *Greek Grammar,* 694–96.

32. Koester, *Hebrews,* 377. The author in this verse does not restrict his focus to just the high priest but broadens it to include the whole of priests. Even so, the singular verb ἦν (*ēn*), "was" (translated as "were," an English subjunctive, because it is in a contrary-to-fact condition), points back to Jesus as high priest (8:3b). Ellingworth, *Epistle to the Hebrews,* 405.

legitimate and necessary job was already being filled by members of the Levitical order.

8:5 *Who serve unto the example and shadow of heavenly things / These priests serve as an example and shadow of heavenly things:* For the sake of clarity, we have broken the long Greek sentence into a separate one at this point. With this phrase, the author lays the groundwork for the argument he will next present. The Levitical priests, and by inference their duties, he describes as being, first, ὑπόδειγμα (*hypodeigma*), an "outline, example, sketch, pattern, or model."[33] The noun usually denotes a moral example,[34] but in this instance, the author uses it to indicate something that serves to illuminate something larger, in this case the system of salvation as determined by God. Thus, the word connotes that the Levitical priests with their service were an earthly outline or sketch of heavenly realities.[35] More specifically, their service and work served as an example of the future work of the Savior.[36] Second, they are σκιά (*skia*), "a shadow," a silhouette of something real.[37] The religious aspect of the noun denotes that which is bound to and dependent on heavenly realities but gives only an outline.[38] The author's point is that his readers must not see the Levitical temple service as the full expression of priestly authority and activity. Nonetheless, since the earthly priests do present a shadow of the heavenly reality, much can be learned from their station and service.[39]

as Moses was admonished of God / as Moses was warned: The author now turns to scripture to bolster his point. The verb χρηματίζω (*chrēmatizō*) denotes a divine injunction or warning.[40] The author's word choice stresses the importance of Jehovah's stern instructions that Moses do exactly as told.

---

33. BDAG, 1037; see also Schlier, *TDNT,* 2:32–33. On the word's connection with middle Platonism, see the introduction pages 22–24.

34. BDAG, 1037.

35. Ellingworth, *Epistle to the Hebrews,* 406.

36. BDAG, 1037.

37. BDAG, 929–30.

38. Ellingworth, *Epistle to the Hebrews,* 406.

39. Compare Harold W. Attridge, "The Uses of Antithesis in Hebrews 8–10," *Harvard Theological Review* 79, nos. 1–3 (1986): 5–9. If the phrase is taken as a hendiadys, then the words can be translated as "a shadowy outline." Lane, *Hebrews 1–8,* 201 note i. Such a translation would downplay the value of the Mosaic law and its rituals, making it little more than a suggestion or a glimpse of the real thing. On this idea, see E. Kenneth Lee, "Words Denoting 'Pattern' in the New Testament," *New Testament Studies* 8, no. 2 (1962): 168.

40. BDAG, 1089.

See, saith he, that thou make all things according to the pattern shewed to thee in the mount / for God said, "Look, you will make everything according to the pattern that was shown to you on the mountain": This is a quote from LXX Exodus 25:40. The word "God" is not in the Greek text, but we have added it in our Rendition for clarity. The quote stresses Jehovah's insistence that great care be taken in making the details and the accompanying instructions on the structure and service of the tabernacle as given in the vision a reality.

The noun τύπος (*typos*), usually translated as "pattern," connotes, as used here, the archetype of the tabernacle on which the copy was based.[41] What Moses saw was the "original," and his tabernacle and its associated priestly ministry were the ὑπόδειγμα (*hypodeigma*), "example,"[42] and σκιά (*skia*), "shadow."[43] Due to Moses and his artisans' care, the tabernacle and its service were nonetheless authentic representations.[44] But because they were made from earthly elements, even though they were counterparts of the heavenly reality, they acted more as an image or shadowy reflections and not a perfect duplication of the same.

The purpose of the *hypodeigma* and *skia* were to make the reality better known or understood. Thus, Jehovah stressed the need for Moses to "make

41. BDAG, 1019–20. The MT uses the noun תַּבְנִית (*tabnît*) to denote a pattern or model, but the word carries the nuance of "first copy" or "prototype" of which the product is an approximate replica. BDB, 125; Wagner, *TDOT*, 2:179–80. Though τύπος *(typos)* often denotes a signet's impress in a wax seal, the author redefines the term by pairing *typos* with ἀντίτυπος (*antitypos*), "copy," in 9:24. In so doing, he makes *typos* analogous to the pattern in the signet and the *antitypos* to the impression in the wax. Lane, *Hebrews,* 201, note m. Over the history of its use, *typos* developed a wide range of meanings, some of which are hard to define. In the case of Hebrews, however, it is clear that the word denotes the heavenly original upon which the plan of the tabernacle was based. Goppelt, *TDNT,* 8:246–59; *NID,* s.v. "τύπος."

42. BDAG, 1037; Lee, "Words Denoting 'Pattern,'" 168, notes that ὑπόδειγμα (*hypodeigma*) is an example by means of suggestion rather than direct comparison. Hence the author of Hebrews used it to show how the temple rites were suggestive of the true heaven rather than a concrete direct copy or example. The Mosaic law was not a copy of the true covenant but merely suggestive of it.

43. Both words denote "the mere representation" of something real. BDAG, 929–30.

44. The building of the first temple in this dispensation was preceded by a vision received by the First Presidency (Joseph Smith, Sidney Rigdon, and Fredrick G. Williams) on June 3 or 4, 1833. In this vision, they were shown the pattern of the temple in great detail. Truman O. Angell, Journal, cited in Elwin C. Robison, *The First Mormon Temple: Design, Construction, and Historic Context of the Kirtland Temple* (Provo, Utah: Brigham Young University Press, 1997), 8. In this connection, see D&C 94:2; 95:3–6; 97:10; 115:14–16.

everything according to the pattern [*typos*]" (NR) he was shown. Every detail counted, for each revealed, in symbolic terms, some aspect of the divine environment and intent. Thus, the example and shadow worked to point to that heavenly reality and even reveal some of its secrets. From the author's point of view, through the lens of Christianity, the ancient Israelite cultus was a type or foreshadowing of Christ and his ministry.[45]

8:6 ***But now hath he obtained a more excellent ministry / But as it is Jesus has obtained a more excellent ministry:*** "Jesus" is not in the text, but we have added it to the Rendition for clarity.

The author at this point concludes his argument by means of contrasting this statement with the one he made in 8:4: if Jesus were on the earth, he would not be a Levitical priest. The opening phrase, νυνὶ δέ (*nyni de*), "but now," signals the current condition, one in which the Son has risen in life and station, indeed, to that of being the heavenly High Priest. For that reason, we have translated the phrase "but as it is."[46]

The verb τυγχάνω (*tynchanō*), "obtain," denotes reaching, attaining, or obtaining a goal or station, but here it connotes the Lord's "achievement, success, and victory" in overcoming all enemies and gaining the post of eternal High Priest.[47] That the author uses the perfect tense τέτυχεν (*tetychen*), "has obtained," shows that what the Lord achieved is complete, needing no further work.

To describe that achievement, the author used the phrase διαφορωτέρας ... λειτουργίας (*diaphorōteras ... lietourgias*), "a more excellent ministry." The adjective διάφορος (*diaphoros*) points to that which is different from other items in its class in quality and excellence.[48] The noun λειτουργία (*leitourgia*) denotes public service, and in the case of the Lord, it points to his ministration as the eternal High Priest who, having made the ultimate sacrifice in giving his own blood, has made it possible for all—the entire public—to be reconciled to the Father and partake of immortal life.[49] The phrase emphasizes the height of the Lord's ministry over that of his Levitical counterpart.

---

45. Schlier, *TDNT,* 2:33. See also McConkie, *Doctrinal New Testament Commentary,* 3:176.

46. BDAG, 682. The δέ (*de*) in this verse is inferential, pointing back to the μέν (*men*) in 8:4, and in this way connects the two. See Lane, *Hebrews 1–8,* 208; and Ellingworth, *Epistle to the Hebrews,* 408.

47. Cockerill, *Epistle to the Hebrews,* 352, 362–63.

48. BDAG, 239–40. The author introduces the second half of a *qal waḥomer* comparison in order to stress the height of the Lord's "more excellent ministry" above that of the Levitical priest. Ellingworth, *Epistle to the Hebrews,* 410.

49. Cockerill, *Epistle to the Hebrews,* 362.

by how much also he is the mediator of a better covenant / to the extent that he is also a guarantor of a better covenant: With this phrase, the author once again reveals the superiority of the Lord's ministry over that of his Levitical counterpart. The result of his achievement is that he has become the mediator or guarantor of a better covenant.[50] Variations of this phrase are also found in 9:15, διαθήκης καινῆς μεσίτης ἐστίν (*diathēkēs kainēs mesitēs estin*), "he is the guarantor of the new covenant," and 12:24, διαθήκης νέας μεσίτῃ Ἰησοῦ (*diathēkēs neas mesitē Iēsou*), "to Jesus, the mediator of the new covenant."

The noun μεσίτης (*mesitēs*), derived from the adjective μέσος (*mesos*), "middle," has the basic sense of "one who mediates between two parties to remove a disagreement or reach a common goal," thus one who acts as a "mediator" or "arbitrator."[51] But it was also used in a legal context to describe a witness to a legal transaction who would guarantee that the terms of the agreement would be carried out, that is, a "guarantor."

That it has this added nuance in this passage is supported by two other passages in Hebrews. The first is in 7:22, where we read κρείττονος διαθήκης γέγονεν ἔγγυος Ἰησοῦς (*kreittonos diathēkēs gegonen engyos Iēsous*), "Jesus has become the guarantee [ἔγγυος, *enguos*] of a better covenant" (NR). This is quite similar to the passage here in 8:6. It is clear that the author considers the two nouns *engyos* and *mesitēs* to be closely related in meaning. The other passage is in 6:17, where to stress "the unchangeable nature of his purpose, [God] guaranteed [μεσιτεύω, *mesiteuō*] it with an oath" (NR). This is the only place in the NT where this verb is used. It is derived from *mesitēs* and has the basic meaning "to mediate"[52] but also has the derived sense "to guarantee,"[53] which is clearly its meaning here.

One scholar, in a well-developed discussion of *mesitēs,* summarized the usage of the term in the New Testament: "Since the basic meaning is still mediator, *μεσίτης* is in fact more than *ἔγγυος*. The latter simply stresses the guaranteeing of salvation, the former its accomplishment, which also

---

50. For a study, see Walter C. Kaiser Jr., "The Old Promise and the New Covenant: Jeremiah 31:31–34," *Journal of the Evangelical Theological Society* 15 (Winter 1972): 11–23.

51. BDAG, 634. The problem with using the common nuance of the noun μεσίτης (*mesitēss*) as "mediator," or go-between, is that it makes God the one who must be placated, the one whose mind must be changed, the one whose wrath must be assuaged. The scriptures are clear, however, that the plan of salvation originated with God, who put all the elements in place, including giving his Only Begotten Son so all who believed on him would have eternal life (John 3:16), and who is ever on the side of his children.

52. LSJ, 1106.

53. BDAG, 634.

entails mediatorial death."[54] Christ's role as mediator does differ from that of someone mediating between two parties who disagree but need to make compromises to come to agreement. In our becoming reconciled with God, God does not need to change, but we do. It is Christ's atoning sacrifice that enables each of us to overcome our sins, to change the fallen natural man into a saint, and to become reconciled with our Father. A passage from the Doctrine and Covenants poignantly describes Christ carrying out this role: "Listen to him who is the advocate with the Father, who is pleading your cause before him—Saying: Father, behold the sufferings and death of him who did no sin, in whom thou wast well pleased; behold the blood of thy Son which was shed, the blood of him whom thou gavest that thyself might be glorified; Wherefore, Father, spare these my brethren that believe on my name, that they may come unto me and have everlasting life" (D&C 45:3–5).

which was established upon better promises / that has been legally enacted on better promises: This phrase explains why the Lord's new covenant is better than that of Moses. The verb νομοθετέω (*nomotheteō*) denotes the enacting of a law or, in this case, the initiation of a new covenant. The author's choice of word does give weight to the legal aspect of establishing the covenant and thereby stresses its legitimate nature.[55] Its enactment is based on κρείττοσιν ἐπαγγελίαις (*kreittosin epangeliais*), "better promises," than that of the old covenant. These "better promises" the author will soon define by turning to the scriptures. The passive voice of the verb *nomotheteō,* as found here, translates as "has been legally enacted" and is likely a divine passive, suggesting that God is the νομλθέτης (*nomothetēs*), that is, the one who enacted the law.[56]

Analysis and Summary

In this unit (chapters 8–10), the author brings his readers to the heart of his Christological development. With this section (chapter 8), he begins "to explain the climatic and pivotal significance of the exalted Son's self-offering through which he became the 'Source of eternal salvation' (5:9) to all who heed him."[57] The author's witness is that this is the kind of high priest that they have (8:1), one who has been made perfect, has been victorious over all his enemies, and now sits in power on the right hand of God

54. Oepke, *TDNT,* 4:598–624, quote on 620.
55. BDAG, 676; Louw-Nida, §33.339.
56. Lane, *Hebrews 1–8,* 201, note q; Wallace, *Greek Grammar,* 437–38.
57. Cockerill, *Epistle to the Hebrews,* 351.

(see D&C 76:23; Moro. 7:27), able to minister eternal life to all those who accept him and live in faith.

To bolster his readers' faith, the author stresses the present reality of the Son's station. He does so to assure them of a full reward for enduring to the end. His intent is also to warn them away from the faithlessness he described in 3:7–4:11. At the same time, he lays the groundwork to encourage them to model the faithful endurance of those he will eulogize in 11:1–40.[58]

In 8:1–2, the author sets the foundation on which he will build both his minor and major premises. The foundational ground is that the Son has ascended to the heavenly throne where he acts as the minister (λειτουργός, *leitourgos*) of the "heavenly tabernacle" or, in other words, of the divine sphere. The author's first minor premise, based on LXX Psalm 109:1, 4 (along with his readers' understanding of the role of the high priesthood, see 5:1), is that "every high priest is appointed to offer gifts and sacrifices" (NR 8:3) in behalf of the people. With the phrase "therefore it is necessary" (ἀναγκαῖον ἔχειν, *anankaion echein*) (NR 8:3), the author introduces the first of two conclusions. The first he states in 8:3b: the Son, as High Priest, must also have something to offer, identified by the simple indefinite pronoun τις (*tis*), "something." He seems to be deliberately leaving the description of the offering vague so that he can pick up the idea later (9:25–10:4) and more fully develop it.[59]

In 8:4–5, he develops his second conclusion. It begins with the obvious statement that if Jesus were on the earth instead of ministering in heaven, he would not be a priest at all because the Levitical Priesthood's various functions and responsibilities had already been assigned to others.[60] That did not prevent him, however, from holding a higher order of the priesthood and from ministering it in and from heaven. In fact, since no one ever before had been appointed to this specific and needful duty, it became all the more necessary for him to do so. By these means, the author subtly shows the superiority of the heavenly High Priest over his earthly counterparts.

To push his point even further, in 8:5 the author defines the tabernacle, including the role of the Levitical Priesthood, as but an example or a mere shadow of the eternal order of reality. As a proof text, he quotes from LXX Exodus 25:40. There Jehovah tells Moses to make sure, in building

58. Cockerill, *Epistle to the Hebrews*, 350.

59. Cockerill, *Epistle to the Hebrews*, 357–58.

60. Cockerill, *Epistle to the Hebrews*, 358–59; Koester, *Hebrews*, 377.

the tabernacle, to give great care to follow the "design" (τύπος, *typos*) as revealed to him. From this the author concludes that the earthly sanctuary, with its various accoutrements, functions, and functionaries, though an authorized counterpart, is still but a copy of the heavenly original (9:11).[61] Thus, the earthly priests are but precursors of the heavenly High Priest, who ministers not as they do in a temporal and temporary sanctuary set up by mortal man but in the eternal one set up by God (8:2). Again, the author here lays down the foundation on which he will build later (9:1–10). There he will showcase the importance of the Lord's work by again contrasting its full sufficiency with that of the inefficiency of the Levitical Priesthood.

The author has already introduced the idea of Christ passing through the veil and entering into the heavenly Holy of Holies. That imagery anticipates "the great imaginative leap of this composition: picturing heaven as the true sanctuary. The logic is impeccable. If what defines a sanctuary is the presence of God, where God essentially and eternally exists must be the real 'holy place.' All of the subsequent argument flows from this simple imaginative premise."[62] It is in this light that Jesus should be understood as minister of the sanctuary pitched by God and not man (8:2).

Note the author is not against the Levitical order of the priesthood, for it did serve an important purpose. The tabernacle with its ordinances relates to the heavenly as a shadow does to the object that casts it (8:5). In other words, there is a strong and direct connection between the two such that much can be learned about the real by studying and understanding its silhouette. Thus, his words affirm the positive function of the old order. Just as an outline or blueprint of an original source reveals much about it, so too do the tabernacle and the rituals performed therein, along with those who perform them, reveal much about the Lord and his ministry.[63] In sum,

61. Goppelt, *TDNT,* 8:257–58. See also Gert J. Steyn, "'On Earth as It Is in Heaven. . . .' The Heavenly Sanctuary Motif in Hebrews 8:5 and Its Textual Connection with the 'Shadowy Copy' [*hypodeigmati kai skia*] of LXX Exodus 25:40," *HTS Teologiese Studies / Theological Studies* 67, no. 1 (2011), accessed November 17, 2016, https://hts.org.za/index.php/HTS/article/view/885/1634. Steyn argues that the reference to the tabernacle as a type or shadow of the true is not referencing Platonism. The concept of the heavenly tabernacle is found in other Jewish texts such as the Wisdom of Solomon and the *Testament of Levi.* Though Hebrews is the only New Testament text that explicitly references a heavenly tabernacle, the concept of it can be found in other books, such as Rev. 4–5 and Col. 2:17. The author could have been influenced by Philo in quoting Ex. 25:40, but it is more likely that both were influenced by the same Jewish tradition.

62. Johnson, *Hebrews,* 198.

63. Cockerill, *Epistle to the Hebrews,* 359–60.

Jehovah gave the Levitical rites as anticipatory to and revelatory of the mission of Christ, and therefore, as the author shows over and over, it both testifies of and discloses the Lord and his salvific work. Though the Mosaic ordinances were but an approximate reminiscence, God designed them not only to "suggest the idea of the original [but also] to train the people of God to appreciate eventually the heavenly reality itself."[64] But, as the author insists, the Levitical Priesthood must be taken neither as the full nor the eternal order of sacred things.

The Book of Mormon complements and rounds out what the author says about the Mosaic law being a type and shadow prefiguring the work of the Savior. According to King Benjamin, God appointed to the Israelites "a law, even the law of Moses. And many . . . types, and shadows showed he unto them concerning [Christ's] coming" (Mosiah 3:14–15). Indeed, as Abinadi stated, "The law of Moses . . . is a shadow of those things which are to come" (Mosiah 16:14). He also testified, "Salvation doth not come by the law alone . . . [which law was designed] to keep [the Israelites] in remembrance of God and their duty towards him. But . . . all these things were types of things to come" (Mosiah 13:28, 30–31). For the faithful among the Nephites, the law worked to that end, for "they did look forward to the coming of Christ, considering that the law of Moses was a type of his coming." Thus, "the law of Moses did serve to strengthen their faith in Christ; and thus, they did retain a hope through faith, unto eternal salvation" (Alma 25:15, 16).

Some scholars see the reference to a divine "archetype" (τύπος, *typos*) in 8:5 as supporting the notion that the author was drawing heavily on Platonic ideas in this section.[65] They see the "true tent" as the author's view of a heavenly reality (8:2) and the tabernacle as but an earthly "copy" and "shadow" of the real thing. If such were the case, the idea would strongly echo the Platonic notion of "Forms."[66] The problem with this view is it

64. Lane, *Hebrews 1–8,* 106. Elder John Taylor, in *Journal of Discourses,* 17:375, stated that "the things which exist in the Church of God here are patterns of those which exist in the heavens. God said to Moses—'See that thou make all things according to the pattern that I showed thee in the mount.' The pattern that we have is a pattern of that which exists in the heavens, the organization of the Priesthood that will exist throughout eternity."

65. For a study, see Thompson, "Middle Platonism," 31–52.

66. Plato, *Rep.* 7.514–17. Philo viewed Ex. 20:40 in Platonic terms. See *Mos.* 2.71–75; *Leg.* 3.100–103; *QE,* 2.52; *Plant.* 26–27. For general discussions, see R. M. Dancy, *Plato's Introduction of Forms* (Cambridge: Cambridge University Press, 2004); and Gail Fine, *Plato on Knowledge and Forms: Selected Essays* (Oxford: Clarendon Press, 2003). Williamson, *Philo and the Epistle,* 157–59, argues that while some may be tempted to say that

demands that what the author refers to is either an eternal ideal (the εἶδος, *eidos,* that is, the Platonic "Form"[67]) or some timeless ministry performed in an everlasting sanctuary.[68] Rather, for the author, the "example" and "shadow" were derived from and anticipated both the earthly and heavenly ministry of the Son whose teachings, actions, and succession to the heavenly throne made salvation possible for God's people.[69] Thus, the tabernacle "prefigured the 'place' of God's presence that Christ entered and the heavenly high-priestly ministry upon which he embarked."[70] As is noted in the introduction to this volume, the author's writings suggest he possessed a rather light knowledge of Platonism and demonstrate he had little belief in its major tenets. Even so, like later Christian theologians of this early era, he does employ some Platonic assumptions and ideas current in the greater culture to explain and promote his theses, but he clearly did not rely upon them or necessarily promote them.[71]

In 7:11–19, the author linked priesthood and covenant such that the change in one necessitates a change in the other. Therefore, a change in priesthood meant a change in ministry. He readdresses that point in 8:6, but this time, rather than focusing on the superiority of Jesus' sacrificial gift over that of the Levitical high priest, he stresses the result—Jesus has obtained a better ministry commensurate to the superiority of the new covenant over the old. The author describes the Lord's higher ministry with the noun μεσίτης (*mesitēs*). Though the word usually refers to one who helps two parties become reconciled, in this case the author's focus is not on that aspect of the Savior's work. Instead, he looks to Christ's relationship to the new covenant now enacted by God. The Savior is the one

---

8:5 shows Platonic or "Philonism" tendencies, that is not the case. The temple is not a copy of an eternal temple in heaven that has existed for all eternity. Instead the temple foreshadowed the future kingdom in heaven that Christ's physical death on Earth inaugurated. In order for it to be Platonic, Christ's heavenly kingdom would have to precede the tabernacle, which is not the case.

67. LSJ, 482. The author of Hebrews never uses the Platonic term εἶδος (*eidos*), "Form," but rather τύπος (*typos*), "example" or "pattern."

68. Hurst, *Epistle to the Hebrews,* 13–17, notes that ὑπόδειγμα (*hypodeigma*) should not be translated as "copy" in Hebrews. Rather, it refers to a basis for likeness or imitation. It is an outline or pattern, a starting point from which to build. Treating it like a copy Platonizes the text without basis. The author's use of σκιά (*skia*) also points that the temple is a pattern of a future realization rather than a copy of a current heavenly model.

69. Williamson, *Philo and the Epistle,* 157–59; Hurst, *Epistle to the Hebrews,* 13–17.

70. Cockerill, *Epistle to the Hebrews,* 362.

71. Thompson, "Middle Platonism," 51; see also Johnson, *Hebrews,* 201–2. For more on this issue, see the introduction, pages 22–24.

who is both bona fides of the law and acts as guarantee of its success.[72] In sum, as the eternal High Priest, whose sacrifice he has formerly offered and which God has now accepted—thus his blood becoming the surety of the new covenant—Jesus is the guarantee that the blessing promised will be realized by all those who enter into it and endure in faith to the end.

Up to this point, the author has not explained how the covenant that God has now enacted is either new or better than the old one, but by use of a verb νομοθετέω (*nomotheteō*), "to enact a law," the author does stress its legality and legitimacy.[73] The new covenant is an expression of God's will just as was the old one, and so it too is valid, but by inference, it has superiority because it is God's latest word (1:1–2; 2:1). That Jesus is the chief minister of the new law points up his superiority over his Levitical kin and the old covenant.

With 8:3–6, the author prepares his readers for the further development of his argument. Having established that Jesus currently serves in and administers from the "true tent" (8:3), the author then refers to the Levitical cult as an "example" (ὑπόδειγμα, *hypodeigma*) and "shadow" (σκιά, *skia*) of this reality (8:5). He then expresses the superiority of the Lord's priesthood and the new covenant he administers over the old (8:6). Each of these points he will develop more fully in the following chapters, but he will do so in reverse order. He will examine the new covenant in 8:7–13; the typological character of the worship performed under the old covenant and its sanctuary in 9:1–10. And finally, he will define the nature of Christ's self-sacrifice in 9:11–10:18.[74]

The First Covenant Is Now Obsolete (8:7–13)

Greek Text

7 Εἰ γὰρ ἡ πρώτη ἐκείνη ἦν ἄμεμπτος, οὐκ ἂν δευτέρας ἐζητεῖτο τόπος· 8 μεμφόμενος γὰρ αὐτοὺς λέγει· Ἰδοὺ ἡμέραι ἔρχονται, λέγει κύριος, καὶ συντελέσω ἐπὶ τὸν οἶκον Ἰσραὴλ καὶ ἐπὶ τὸν οἶκον Ἰούδα διαθήκην καινήν, 9 οὐ κατὰ τὴν διαθήκην

72. Ellingworth, *Epistle to the Hebrews,* 342, 410; Cockerill, *Epistle to the Hebrews,* 287 n. 10.

73. Though the author does not specifically state that God was the initiator of the new covenant, he does imply it by using the divine passive. See Wallace, *Greek Grammar,* 437–38.

74. Johnson, *Hebrews,* 199–200.

ἣν ἐποίησα τοῖς πατράσιν αὐτῶν ἐν ἡμέρᾳ ἐπιλαβομένου μου τῆς χειρὸς αὐτῶν ἐξαγαγεῖν αὐτοὺς ἐκ γῆς Αἰγύπτου, ὅτι αὐτοὶ οὐκ ἐνέμειναν ἐν τῇ διαθήκῃ μου, κἀγὼ ἠμέλησα αὐτῶν, λέγει κύριος. 10 ὅτι αὕτη ἡ διαθήκη ἣν διαθήσομαι τῷ οἴκῳ Ἰσραὴλ μετὰ τὰς ἡμέρας ἐκείνας, λέγει κύριος, διδοὺς νόμους μου εἰς τὴν διάνοιαν αὐτῶν, καὶ ἐπὶ καρδίας αὐτῶν ἐπιγράψω αὐτούς, καὶ ἔσομαι αὐτοῖς εἰς θεόν καὶ αὐτοὶ ἔσονταί μοι εἰς λαόν. 11 καὶ οὐ μὴ διδάξωσιν ἕκαστος τὸν πολίτην αὐτοῦ καὶ ἕκαστος τὸν ἀδελφὸν αὐτοῦ, λέγων· Γνῶθι τὸν κύριον, ὅτι πάντες εἰδήσουσίν με ἀπὸ μικροῦ ἕως μεγάλου αὐτῶν. 12 ὅτι ἵλεως ἔσομαι ταῖς ἀδικίαις αὐτῶν, καὶ τῶν ἁμαρτιῶν αὐτῶν οὐ μὴ μνησθῶ ἔτι. 13 ἐν τῷ λέγειν Καινὴν πεπαλαίωκεν τὴν πρώτην, τὸ δὲ παλαιούμενον καὶ γηράσκον ἐγγὺς ἀφανισμοῦ. [SBLGNT]

King James Version

7 For if that first covenant had been faultless, then should no place have been sought for the second. 8 For finding fault with them, he saith, Behold, the days come, saith the Lord, when I will make a new covenant with the house of Israel and with the house of Judah: 9 Not according to the covenant that I made with their fathers in the day when I took them by the hand to lead them out of the land of Egypt; because they continued not in my covenant, and I regarded them not, saith the Lord. 10 For this is the covenant that I will make with the house of Israel after those days, saith the Lord; I will put my laws into their mind, and write them in their hearts: and I will be to them a God, and they shall be to me a people: 11 And they shall not teach every man his neighbour, and every man his brother, saying, Know the Lord: for all shall know me, from the least to the greatest. 12 For I will be merciful to their unrighteousness, and their sins and their iniquities will I remember no more. 13 In that he saith, A new covenant, he hath made the first old. Now that which decayeth and waxeth old is ready to vanish away.

New Rendition

7 For if that first covenant had been faultless, there would have been no occasion sought for a second one. 8 For finding fault with the people he says:

> "Look, days are coming, says the Lord, when I will establish a new covenant with the house of Israel and with the house of Judah. 9 Not according to the covenant that I made with their ancestors in the day that I took them by their hand to lead them out of the land of Egypt, because they did not continue in my covenant, and I ceased to be concerned with them, says the Lord. 10 For this is the covenant that I will make with the house of Israel after those days, says the Lord, I will put my laws in their minds and write them on their hearts. I will be their God and they will be my people. 11 And no one will teach his fellow citizen and no one will teach his brother saying, 'Know the Lord,' because everyone will know me from the least to the greatest. 12 For I will be merciful toward their unrighteous deeds and I will no longer remember their sins." [LXX Jer. 38:31–34]

13 By saying "new," God has declared the first covenant obsolete, and what becomes obsolete and grows old will soon vanish.

Translation Notes and Comments

8:7 ***For if that first covenant had been faultless, then should no place have been sought for the second / For if that first covenant had been faultless, there would have been no occasion sought for a second one:*** The author once again uses a contrary-to-fact condition to make his point.[75] The Greek text does not have the word "covenant" in it, but it is inferred in the phrase ἡ πρώτη (*hē prōtē*), "the first," in which the definite article and the adjective are feminine gender and therefore refer back to διαθήκης (*diathēkēs*) in 8:6, and so "covenant" is supplied in both the KJV and our Rendition. The phrase refers to the Mosaic law, which, however, was certainly not the first covenant Jehovah established with people. But given the author's demonstrable knowledge of the scriptures, it is safe to assume he knew that. The Mosaic law was, however, the first covenant God established with the Israelites as a people, and that is likely what the author had in mind.[76]

The alpha privative adjective ἄμεμπτος (*amemptos*), "faultless," denotes something that is irreproachable because it has no flaws.[77] Such the old covenant was not. Its failure was not a weakness in the covenant itself but, as the author has already shown, with the Levitical Priesthood, which was insufficient in producing perfection in the people (7:11, 18). See Translation Notes for 8:8. Even so, the weakness of the old system, based on the old covenant, required its replacement with a new.[78]

Because the old covenant was not faultless, it gave occasion for seeking another. The author uses the noun τόπος (*topos*), "place," in a nonliteral sense, giving it the meaning of "occasion,"[79] that is, providing the reason why a new covenant had to be sought.

8:8–12 These verses are a direct quote from LXX Jer. 38:31–34 (31:31–34 in the KJV).

8:8 ***finding fault with them / finding fault with the people:*** The noun "people" is not found in the Greek text but is implied by the plural pronoun *autous,* "them," and added to our Rendition for clarity. The author's words bolster the point that he had already made that God found fault with the wilderness generation.[80] They failed to live up to the covenant as expressed

75. See examples at 4:8; 7:11; 8:4; 10:2; 11:15.

76. Vanhoye, *Letter to the Hebrews,* 133.

77. BDAG, 52.

78. Compare Vanhoye, *Letter to the Hebrews,* 133.

79. BDAG, 1011–12.

80. See Johannes L. P. Wolmarans, "The Text and Translation of Hebrews 8:8," *Zeitschrift für die neutestamentliche Wissenschaft* 75 (1984): 139–44, who argues that the problem

through their disbelief and attendant rebellion against Jehovah and his law. It is their failure that evidences the weakness of the first covenant. To stress the point, it was not that these people were incapable of obeying the law—they were capable[81]—but their refusal to do so demonstrated the insufficiency in the old covenant. It never transformed their hearts. For this reason, a new and more spiritually powerful one was needed.[82]

Behold, the days come, saith the Lord, when I will make a new covenant / "Look, days are coming, says the Lord, when I will establish a new covenant: The particle ἰδού (*idou*), "behold, look," is used to draw attention to what is going to be said next and highlights its importance.[83] Here it signals a prophetic promise.

The verb συντελέω (*synteleō*), "carry out, accomplish, establish,"[84] denotes bringing into reality something that has been either promised or expected and is used here to indicate God's intent of accomplishing his desire to bring in a new covenant devoid of the weaknesses of the old one. In this phrase, the author alters the LXX use of διατίθημι (*diatithēmi*), "to make a formal arrangement,"[85] by replacing it with *synteleō*. The change is likely more than stylistic. Though the verb is not synonymous with τελειόω (*teleioō*), it still echoes "the prominent motif of Christ's perfection, and one of the effects of the new covenant and its sacrifice will be the perfection of believers."[86]

8:9 ***Not according to the covenant that I made with their fathers / Not according to the covenant that I made with their ancestors:*** This phrase emphasizes the distance between the old and new covenants. Only a slight resemblance would exist between the two. As with 8:8, the author again does not precisely quote the LXX. He changes the verb διατίθημι (*diatithēmi*) to ποιέω (*poieō*), that is, from making a significant agreement to simply making something. Again the reason may be more than stylistic.

---

was with the covenant, but his thesis is weakened because it is built on a manuscript variant that replaces accusative pronoun αὐτούς (*autous*), "them," with the dative αὐτοῖς (*autois*), "to them." See Metzger, *Textual Commentary*, 597; Ellingworth, *Epistle to the Hebrews*, 415; and Attridge, *Epistle to the Hebrews*, 225 n. 2.

81. The author's reference to the obedience of the faithful in 11:1–38 clearly shows that long before Jesus came with his transforming power, people were not only capable of obeying but often did obey God's laws.

82. Cockerill, *Epistle to the Hebrews*, 366.

83. BDAG, 468; Louw-Nida, §91.13.

84. BDAG, 975.

85. BDAG, 238.

86. Attridge, *Epistle to the Hebrews*, 227. The gospel is the everlasting covenant, but its revelation after a period of apostasy makes it new to the generation that receives it. See McConkie, *Doctrinal New Testament Commentary*, 3:178.

The author may be suggesting that "God's actions in establishing the two covenants are of a different order," and he will "make" (*poieō*) the new one "in a more profound and effective way."[87]

The plural noun πατέρες (*pateres*) denotes "revered deceased persons with whom one shares beliefs or traditions."[88] The English word "ancestor" connotes specifically a "lineal descent though one's father or mother" while "forefather" looks more at the "strength of family feeling or of persistence of a family in one locality."[89] "Ancestor" seem to have more of the feel here and is therefore used in our Rendition.[90]

because they continued not in my covenant, and I regarded them not / because they did not continue in my covenant, and I ceased to be concerned with them: The LXX, which the author follows, has οὐκ ἐνέμειναν ἐν τῇ διαθήκῃ μου (*ouk enemeinan en tē diathēkē mou*), "they did not continue in my covenant." The Masoretic text is much more condemning; it states, הֵפֵרוּ אֶת־בְּרִיתִי (*hēpērû 'et bĕrîtî*), "they broke (or destroyed) my covenant."

The author follows LXX Jeremiah 38:32, which has ἠμέλησα αὐτῶν (*ēmelēsa autōn*), "I was not concerned with them."[91] The verb ἀμελέω (*ameleō*) means "to neglect, to be unconcerned" about someone or something. The point of the phrase is that because these people cared nothing for God's sacred covenant, he ceased to concern himself with them.

8:10 *For this is the covenant that I will make with the house of Israel / For this is the covenant that I will make with the house of Israel:* The verb διατίθημι (*diatithēmi*), which shares the same root as *διαθήκη* (*diathēkē*), "covenant," denotes a formal arrangement to have something done, thus "to decree" or "ordain."[92] In the middle voice, as found here, it connotes specifically the making of a covenant.[93] The phrase can be construed as God saying, "I will covenant a covenant with them," the force of the repeated words giving weight to the uncompromising nature of both the agreement the people will make and to the agreement itself.

87. Attridge, *Epistle to the Hebrews,* 227.

88. The noun also denoted belonging and status in patriarchal Mediterranean societies. BDAG, 786–88; *NID,* s.v. "πατήρ"; Schrenk, *TDNT,* 5:945–1022.

89. *Webster's New Dictionary of Synonyms,* s.v. "ancestor."

90. For the range of meanings, see Louw-Nida, §1.190, and specifically §10.20.

91. The chapter numbering is different in the LXX where the Jeremiah material is found in 38:31–34 instead of 31:31–34 as in the KJV. The Masoretic text has וְאָנֹכִי בָּעַלְתִּי בָם (*wĕānōkî bāʿaltî bām*), "and I was a husband to them" (Jer. 31:32).

92. BDAG, 228–29.

93. *NID,* s.v. "διαθήκη"; Louw-Nida, §34.43.

I will put my laws into their mind, and write them in their hearts / I will put my laws in their minds and write them on their hearts: The preposition ἐπί (*epi*), "on, upon," is found before καρδίας (*kardias*), "hearts," and so we have translated it "on" in our Rendition rather than "in" as does the KJV. Also, the Masoretic text has נָתַתִּי אֶת־תּוֹרָתִי בְּקִרְבָּם וְעַל־לִבָּם אֶכְתֲּבֶנָּה (*nātattî et tôrātî bĕqirbām wĕʿal libbām ʾektăbennāh*), "I will put my law in their inward parts and upon their heart I will write it."

8:11 ***And they shall not teach every man his neighbour / And no one will teach his fellow citizen:*** The noun πολίτης (*politēs*), "fellow citizen,"[94] is used in the LXX as the translation of the Hebrew רֵעַ (*rēʿa*), "neighbor,"[95] found in the Masoretic text.[96] The author, as nearly always, follows the LXX, and our Rendition does as well, but the point in both LXX and MT is the same: due to the power of the new covenant, there will be no need for a person to teach another. And why? Because all will know the Lord through the intimate and transforming power of the Spirit.

8:12 ***For I will be merciful to their unrighteousness, and their sins and their iniquities[97] will I remember no more / For I will be merciful toward their unrighteous deeds and I will no longer remember their sins":*** The adjective ἵλεως (*hileōs*), "merciful," means not only to be favorably disposed toward someone but also implies the "overcoming of obstacles that are unfavorable to a relationship."[98] The author's words therefore imply a positive and deliberate act on the part of God toward the person who has entered into the new covenant with him.

The noun ἀδικία (*adikia*) denotes "acts that violate standards of right conduct" but more particularly deeds that are unjust and therefore particularly grievous.[99] The noun ἁμαρτία (*hamartia*) denotes a "departure from either human or divine standards of uprightness" and can connote any wrongful act from an involuntary error to a deliberate and grave sin against deity.[100] The two terms taken together show that God will be merciful

94. BDAG, 846.

95. *HAL*, 1254.

96. Ellingworth, *Epistle to the Hebrews*, 417.

97. The phrase in the KJV "and their iniquities" (καὶ τῶν ἀνομιῶν, *kai tōn anomiōn*) is an addition found in the Textus Receptus and appears to have been assimilated from 10:17. The phrase, however, is not found in the best manuscripts and is, therefore, not included in the Rendition. Ellingworth, *Epistle to the Hebrews*, 417.

98. BDAG, 474.

99. BDAG, 20–21; Louw-Nida, §88.21.

100. BDAG, 50–51.

toward all sins from inadvertent to deliberate and from small to great. That mercy extends to God's even forgetting that the sins were ever committed. The author signals the completeness of that forgetting by using the strongest form of negation in Greek, οὐ μή (*ou mē*),[101] translated as "no longer" in our Rendition. The phrase rules out any possibility that God will ever remember the misdeeds.

This verse gives the reason why no one will need to be taught about the Lord. They will know him personally and intimately because they have partaken of his cleansing power through which their sins have been purged and their consciences made free (1:3; 9:14).

8:13 ***In that he saith, A new covenant, he hath made the first old / By saying "new," God has declared the first covenant obsolete:*** "God" is not in the Greek text, but we have supplied it in our Rendition for clarity. The verb παλαιόω (*palaioō*), found here in the perfect tense, means "make old, declare/treat as obsolete."[102] The nuance is that the covenant at Sinai has become unserviceable and outmoded. The author is careful to note that it is God who canceled its validity and thereby abrogated it.[103] Further, the author's use of the perfect tense stresses the idea that the effect is to be considered permanent.[104] The inference is that the new covenant is completely serviceable, effective, and now in force.

Now that which decayeth and waxeth old is ready to vanish away / and what becomes obsolete and grows old will soon vanish: For emphasis the author again uses the verb παλαιόω (*palaioō*) in a passive participial form. In doing so, he stresses the obsoleteness of the old covenant and, for further emphasis, adds another dimension using the aorist active participle of the verb γηράσκω (*gēraskō*), meaning "to grow old."[105] The covenant made at Sinai has not only become obsolete but, like old age, its condition cannot be reversed. The author describes the result with the noun ἀφανισμός (*aphanismos*), "the condition of being no longer visible." But the word

101. Wallace, *Greek Grammar,* 468.

102. BDAG, 751.

103. Lane, *Hebrews 1–8,* 210; Seesemann, *TDNT,* 5:720. See Moulton and Milligan, *Vocabulary,* 475, for the sense of abrogation. For a study, see David Peterson, "The Prophecy of the New Covenant in the Argument of Hebrews," *Reformed Theological Review* 38, no. 3 (September–December 1979): 74–81, who posits that the old covenant was from its inception but a copy of the "real" or eternal one and therefore always needed to be replaced. Its ordinances did foreshadow the blood and sacrifice of the Lord and therefore pointed toward him.

104. Ellingworth, *Epistle to the Hebrews,* 418.

105. BDAG, 196.

often has the transferred sense of "destruction."[106] The imagery is that of one tottering on the edge of the grave.

Note the author does not say the old law has actually vanished. His use of the preposition ἐγγύς (*engys*), "near,"[107] shows that at the time when Jeremiah's prophecy will be fulfilled—which was then happening—the death knell of the old covenant was being sounded.

Analysis and Summary

To bolster and expand his point on the reality, need, and value of a new covenant, the author of Hebrews again appeals to scripture. He bases his argument on the faultiness of the first covenant. He uses LXX Jeremiah 38:31–34 (KJV Jer. 31:31–34) to show what that fault was, its result, and what God intended as its remedy.

Though the author does not point it out, it is nonetheless noteworthy that God was not initiating the new covenant with the Jews. There was good reason. According to Joseph Smith, "Christ, in the days of his flesh, proposed to make a covenant with them, but they rejected him and his proposals, and in consequence thereof, they were broken off, and no covenant was made with them." For this reason, "the heralds of salvation [the Apostles] said to them 'lo we turn unto the Gentiles,' and the Gentiles received the covenant, and were grafted in from whence the chosen family were broken off."[108]

Three times Jeremiah assures his audience that these words come straight from God (LXX Jer. 38:31, 32, 33; KJV Jer. 31:31, 32, 33). The triple repetition stresses that it was God himself who found fault with the old covenant and promised a new one.[109] The author uses this scripture to drive this point home.

---

106. BDAG, 155; Ellingworth, *Epistle to the Hebrews,* 419. The phrase εἰς ἀφανισμόν (*eis aphanismon*) is used very often in judgment formulas (for example, see in LXX 3 Kgs. 9:7; Micah 1:7; Joel 1:7; Jer. 9:11; Ezek. 6:14) and echoes that idea here.

107. BDAG, 271.

108. The Prophet went on to observe that, unfortunately, the Gentiles also failed to receive the blessings, and therefore the fulfillment of the promise has had to wait until the latter days. "History, 1838–1856, Volume A-1," 259. See also McConkie, *Doctrinal New Testament Commentary,* 3:178–79. It will be during this era that the Jews will also, once more, find a place in the covenant. See Kaiser, "Old Promise and the New Covenant," 22–23.

109. Cockerill, *Epistle to the Hebrews,* 364. This scripture is important to the author's point and dominates this section of his argument. See O'Brien, *Letter to the Hebrews,* 287. But it is Christ's willingness to do the Father's will (Ps. 40:6–8) that is the overall theme on which the author builds. See Cockerill, *Epistle to the Hebrews,* 348 n. 8.

That the author attaches blame to the covenant itself is somewhat puzzling, especially in light of 8:8, which specifically states the fault was with the people. In point of fact,

> the failure of people to keep a covenant does not by itself condemn the terms of the covenant or require a new framework for the relationship. But however illogical, that is the line our author follows. It is important to remember that for the author, it is precisely the failure of the people to keep it that reveals the inadequacy of the first covenant. Why? Here we again see the author's conviction that the worth of a covenant is measured by its efficacy in perfecting persons. Their failure to be perfected is a failure of the covenant as such.[110]

Some have interpreted the new covenant as having abolished priestly prerogatives and thereby opening the way for a "priesthood of all believers."[111] The text of Jeremiah, however, is clear that the covenant is with the "house of Israel and . . . Judah." It belongs to the people and, therefore, does not abolish the need for a priestly order. The author of Hebrews never describes the community as a priesthood, but rather as a community that must meet together for mutual support and encouragement (10:24–25), suggesting the need for priesthood officers to preside at such gatherings.[112]

Verse 8:9 presents a very paternal picture of Jehovah intervening in behalf of the Hebrews and leading them out of Egyptian bondage "by the hand." This caring act makes their rejection of his covenant all the more scandalous because it highlights the ungrateful nature of the people that clearly expresses their infidelity.[113]

In 8:10, the author shows that a major feature of the new covenant is where it will be recorded. Moses' law, though produced by the finger of God, was written on stone tablets (Ex. 24:12; 31:18; 34:1; Deut. 4:13; compare 2 Cor. 3:3). It never made its way into the minds and hearts of the people. The result was twofold: the people remained in their sins and they

---

110. Johnson, *Hebrew,* 205.

111. For a discussion, see "Priesthood of All Believers," Theopedia, accessed November 24, 2016, https://www.theopedia.com/priesthood-of-all-believers; and Timothy J. Wengert, "The Priesthood of All Believers and Other Pious Myths," in *Saying and Doing the Gospel Today: Mass, Ministry, Mission,* ed. Rhoda Schuler, Institute of Liturgical Studies Occasional Papers no. 12 (Valparaiso, Ind.: Institute of Liturgical Studies, 2007), 92–115, accessed November 24, 2016, https://scholar.valpo.edu/cgi/viewcontent.cgi?referer=&httpsredir=1&article=1118&context=ils_papers.

112. Ellingworth, *Epistle to the Hebrews,* 414.

113. Vanhoye, *Letter to the Hebrews,* 133.

never came to know God, the former being the major contributor to the latter. As the author shows, that will not be the case with the new covenant. It will be written in the minds and on the hearts of the people. The phrase does not refer to memorization[114] but to implementation. Jeremiah's words suggest a spiritual transformation in the very depths of the people who willingly enter into the new covenant. Through its power, they will gain a transformed mind and a transformed heart.[115] These will come as their consciences are purged of sin (1:3; 9:14) and will result in empowerment through which deep and true spiritual worship will be maintained.[116]

The author's point is that the Lord will help his people understand the new law both intellectually, "in their minds," and spiritually, "on their hearts." This is clarified by the Lord's words to Oliver Cowdery: "Yea, behold, I will tell you in your mind and in your heart, by the Holy Ghost, which shall come upon you and which shall dwell in your heart. Now, behold, this is the spirit of revelation; behold, this is the spirit by which Moses brought the children of Israel through the Red Sea on dry ground" (D&C 8:2–3). We understand the things of God through revelation, which we often grasp with both our intellectual faculties and our spiritual faculties.

The new covenant, thereby, overcomes the fault of the old one by providing a way for people to overcome sin and come to know God. Verses 10–12 detail the "better promises" of the new covenant. They show that these are fourfold: first, the people will accept Jehovah as their God; second, he will accept them as his people; third, the entire community will come to know God; and finally, God will be merciful to them and remember their sins no more.

These "better promises" support the point the author made in 8:6 that Jesus has "obtained a more excellent ministry" than any former high priest. He is the minister of the new covenant and more. His blood acts as the covenant's surety, which allows him to be the guarantee of its effectiveness.[117]

---

114. Bruce, *Epistle to the Hebrews,* 189.

115. Note that Ezekiel, a contemporary of Jeremiah, also speaks of this transformation in which God will replace the people's "stony heart" with a new one that will allow them to "walk in [God's] statutes, and keep [his] ordinances and do them" (Ezek. 11:19–20).

116. Bruce, *Epistle to the Hebrews,* 190; Attridge, *Epistle to the Hebrews,* 227.

117. The two English words denote that which ensures that a promise or obligation will be realized. The "guarantee" is the person who accepts—especially under a contractual (or in a religious sense, a covenantal) agreement—that responsibility. He or she acts to ensure that another will receive "the possession or enjoyment of a right, privilege, or prerogative." The "surety" is the provision for protection of the person against the loss of the promise. On these terms, see *Webster's New Dictionary of Synonyms,* s.v. "guarantee." Together, these words describe the Savior's covenantal relationship between God and his

Those who enter into it in faith are ensured that the blessings will be realized because the High Priest is already serving in the "true tabernacle" to their good.

As the new covenant is highly superior to the old one, to that same extent is the Savior's high priestly ministry. In sum, the verses from Jeremiah "illuminate the superiority of the New Covenant and thus the fathomless magnitude of Christ's high-priestly ministry in the heavenly dwelling place of God."[118]

Interestingly, God presents the result of the new covenant in the exact words he used to present the old one: "I will be to them a God, and they shall be to me a people" (8:10; see Ex. 6:7; Lev. 26:12; Duet. 26:17–19; and Ezek. 37:27). What is different is not the intent of the law—to create the spiritual family of God—but, as 8:11 shows, its result. This time the people will come to know him and receive fully of his mercy and grace.

None of this works, however, unless the people come under the new covenant. The author is most anxious therefore that his readers realize the foolishness of returning to the old one. He makes his point in 8:13. He uses the verb πεπαλαίωκεν (*pepalaiōken*), "he has made old," referring to a direct act of God. Note that the author does not base his argument only on an exegetical conclusion drawn from his use of LXX Jeremiah 38 (KJV Jer. 31). The new covenant is not simply or only a question of definition. It is rather a new and wonderful act of God as borne witness by the scriptures. It is in the author's further development of his argument that the importance of this foundational point becomes ever clearer. Though the Jeremiah passage is not Christological nor does the author interpret it as such, as he will show (9:11–14), its full significance can only be understood in light of the Atonement from which the new covenant draws its substance, meaning, and power (9:15).[119]

A thrilling aspect of the new covenant is that God will remember no more the sins of those who accept it. Angels keep books of judgment in heaven (Rev. 20:12), but what the books contain is what God chooses to remember, *not* what he chooses to forget, and what "God forgives, he also forgets; and what God forgets is blotted for ever from the record."[120] What could be a better promise?

---

people. Jesus himself is the "guarantee" and his blood the "surety" that the faithful will realize the full blessing of the new covenant.

118. Cockerill, *Epistle to the Hebrews,* 365.

119. Ellingworth, *Epistle to the Hebrews,* 417–18.

120. G. B. Caird, *A Commentary on the Revelation of St. John the Divine* (Peabody, Mass.: Hendrickson Publishers, 1966), 224.

Chapter 9

Christ, a High Priest of Good Things to Come

Introduction

To see the relationship of this section to the development of the author's total argument, see the introduction to chapter 8.

The author begins this section with a more complete development of what was but a minor theme in the previous one. There he focused primarily on "sanctuary" (8:1–2) and "covenant" (8:7–13) with just a nod to "sacrifice" (8:3–6). His intent was to highlight Christ as the "guarantor" of the new covenant who stood as "minister" in the heavenly tabernacle. When it came to the subject of the Lord's sacrifice, the author did little more than deny it was different from those administered "according to the law." He explained that these sacrifices were but a type and shadow of the true (8:3–6). In this section, the theme of the Savior's offering stands center stage while those of sanctuary and covenant take a minor but supportive role. The author discusses the Mosaic tabernacle (9:1–10) and Jehovah's establishment of the old covenant (9:16–22) only to fully expose and stress their insufficient if preparatory character. With this as his foil, he "vigorously affirms the unfathomable efficacy of Christ's sacrifice offered 'according to the eternal Spirit' and thus able to 'cleanse the conscience' (9:11–15)."[1] The flow of this section goes as follows:

In the first paragraph, the author begins by introducing the sanctuary and its regulations through which the old covenant operated (9:1). He then describes, in some detail, the sanctuary in terms of the Old Testament tabernacle and its arrangement and equipment (9:2–5). He notes the

1. Cockerill, *Epistle to the Hebrews*, 370.

different ceremonies that took place in the sanctuary and Holy of Holies. He contrasts the daily services performed by the priests with the annual sacrifice performed by the high priest alone on the Day of Atonement (9:6–7). The author then makes his point by translating what the ceremony taught: "The limited access to the inner sanctuary indicates that the sacrifices offered under the old covenant did not have an interior effect on the conscience of human worshipers (8–9), but only concerned fleshly externals (10)."[2]

In the next paragraph, the author contrasts the old system and its weaknesses and limitations with the new covenant established by the Lord. He stresses that the Savior's sacrifice was performed in the heavenly perfect tabernacle (9:11) and not with animal blood but with his own (9:12). The author then makes his point, using a *qal waḥomer* or an *a fortiori* argument, that if animal sacrifices purified the flesh of the worshipers, how much more does the blood of Christ cleanse their consciences, putting them in a position to fully serve their God (9:13–14)?[3]

In the next paragraph—pivotal to the author's work as he looks back at LXX Jeremiah 38 (Jer. 31 in the KJV) and the promise of a new covenant—he makes explicit the thesis he has hinted at earlier: Jesus is the mediator or testator of the new covenant (9:15). However, to make the covenant effective, for a testator must die before his will has effect, Jesus had to die (9:16–17). Through the shedding of the blood of the sacrificial animals, even the first covenant made this clear (9:18–19), for Moses sprinkled the people, the tabernacle, and its furnishing with the "blood of the covenant" to initiate it (NR 9:20–21). The author concludes that there is no cleansing or remission of sin without blood being shed (9:22).

Having made the connection between the new covenant and the purifying death that established it, in the last paragraph, the author again turns his readers' attention to the ritual of the Day of Atonement and applies it to the Savior's own death. However, the Lord's death was very much different than that of animals. First, his blood was offered in the heavenly or real tabernacle (9:23–24), and second, he had to offer it only once for all (9:25–26). The author concludes that since all die but once and then stand for judgment, so too the Savior died once for the sins of many, and he will return in judgment and bring salvation to all who await him (9:27–28).

---

2. Attridge, *Epistle to the Hebrews,* 231.

3. On the nature and use of the *qal waḥomer* or *a fortiori* argument, see discussion in the introduction on page 30.

A Worldly Sanctuary (9:1–10)

Greek Text

1 Εἶχε μὲν οὖν ἡ πρώτη δικαιώματα λατρείας τό τε ἅγιον κοσμικόν. 2 σκηνὴ γὰρ κατεσκευάσθη ἡ πρώτη ἐν ᾗ ἥ τε λυχνία καὶ ἡ τράπεζα καὶ ἡ πρόθεσις τῶν ἄρτων, ἥτις λέγεται Ἅγια· 3 μετὰ δὲ τὸ δεύτερον καταπέτασμα σκηνὴ ἡ λεγομένη Ἅγια Ἁγίων, 4 χρυσοῦν ἔχουσα θυμιατήριον καὶ τὴν κιβωτὸν τῆς διαθήκης περικεκαλυμμένην πάντοθεν χρυσίῳ, ἐν ᾗ στάμνος χρυσῆ ἔχουσα τὸ μάννα καὶ ἡ ῥάβδος Ἀαρὼν ἡ βλαστήσασα καὶ αἱ πλάκες τῆς διαθήκης, 5 ὑπεράνω δὲ αὐτῆς Χερουβὶν δόξης κατασκιάζοντα τὸ ἱλαστήριον· περὶ ὧν οὐκ ἔστιν νῦν λέγειν κατὰ μέρος.

6 Τούτων δὲ οὕτως κατεσκευασμένων, εἰς μὲν τὴν πρώτην σκηνὴν διὰ παντὸς εἰσίασιν οἱ ἱερεῖς τὰς λατρείας ἐπιτελοῦντες, 7 εἰς δὲ τὴν δευτέραν ἅπαξ τοῦ ἐνιαυτοῦ μόνος ὁ ἀρχιερεύς, οὐ χωρὶς αἵματος, ὃ προσφέρει ὑπὲρ ἑαυτοῦ καὶ τῶν τοῦ λαοῦ ἀγνοημάτων, 8 τοῦτο δηλοῦντος τοῦ πνεύματος τοῦ ἁγίου, μήπω πεφανερῶσθαι τὴν τῶν ἁγίων ὁδὸν ἔτι τῆς πρώτης σκηνῆς ἐχούσης στάσιν, 9 ἥτις παραβολὴ εἰς τὸν καιρὸν τὸν ἐνεστηκότα, καθ' ἣν δῶρά τε καὶ θυσίαι προσφέρονται μὴ δυνάμεναι κατὰ συνείδησιν τελειῶσαι τὸν λατρεύοντα, 10 μόνον ἐπὶ βρώμασιν καὶ πόμασιν καὶ διαφόροις βαπτισμοῖς, δικαιώματα σαρκὸς μέχρι καιροῦ διορθώσεως ἐπικείμενα. [SBLGNT]

King James Version

1 Then verily the first covenant had also ordinances of divine service, and a worldly sanctuary. 2 For there was a tabernacle made; the first, wherein was the candlestick, and the table, and the shewbread; which is called the sanctuary. 3 And after the second veil, the tabernacle which is called the Holiest of all; 4 Which had the golden censer, and the ark of the covenant overlaid round about with gold, wherein was the golden pot that had manna, and Aaron's rod that budded, and the tables of the covenant; 5 And over it the cherubims of glory shadowing the mercyseat; of which we cannot now speak particularly. 6 Now when these things were thus ordained, the priests went always into the first tabernacle, accomplishing

New Rendition

1 So the first covenant had requirements for worship as well as an earthly sanctuary. 2 For a tent was set up, and in the front section were the lamp stand, table, and presentation of the loaves. This section is called the Holy Place. 3 And after the second curtain there was another section called the Most Holy Place. 4 Within it were the golden incense altar and the ark of the covenant that was completely overlaid with gold, in which were the golden jar containing the manna, Aaron's staff that had budded, and the tablets of the covenant. 5 Above the ark were the cherubim of glory overshadowing the mercy seat. Now is not the time to speak of these things in more detail. 6 After these things had been prepared in this manner, the priests were

the service of God. 7 But into the second went the high priest alone once every year, not without blood, which he offered for himself, and for the errors of the people: 8 The Holy Ghost this signifying, that the way into the holiest of all was not yet made manifest, while as the first tabernacle was yet standing: 9 Which was a figure for the time then present, in which were offered both gifts and sacrifices, that could not make him that did the service perfect, as pertaining to the conscience; 10 Which stood only in meats and drinks, and divers washings, and carnal ordinances, imposed on them until the time of reformation.

continually entering into the outer section of the tent performing worship services. 7 But only the high priest entered into the inner section of the tent, once a year, and not without bringing the blood that he offered for his own sins and the sins of the people. 8 By this the Holy Spirit was making it clear that the way into the Most Holy Place had not yet been revealed while the outer section of the tent still existed. 9 This was a symbol pointing to the then-present time, indicating that the gifts and sacrifices they were offering could not perfect the worshiper with respect to his conscience, 10 since they are only concerned with food, drink, various washings, and external regulations imposed until the time of reformation.

Translation Notes and Comments

9:1 *the first covenant had also ordinances of divine service / the first covenant had requirements for worship:* Here the author refers to the law of Moses. For "first covenant," see Translation Notes for 8:1.[4] With the law came the rites and regulations through which its priesthood authority would be expressed and the people blessed. The noun δικαίωμα (*dikaiōma*) designates "a regulation relating to just or right action."[5] It is modified by the noun λατρεία (*latreia*), which is used to describe cultic service or worship of God.[6] Thus the phrase δικαιώματα λατρείας (*dikaiōmata latreias*) denotes "regulations, requirements, and commandments" associated with cultic worship and therefore includes the design, contents, functions, and ordinances of the tabernacle.

a worldly sanctuary / an earthly sanctuary: The neuter noun ἅγιον (*hagion*), literally "that which is holy," most often refers to the sanctuary of a temple.[7] In its adjectival form, as used here, it denotes the Mosaic tabernacle,[8]

---

4. Here the superlative πρῶτος (*prōtos*) is used as a comparative since only two things are compared, the old and the new covenants. See Wallace, *Greek Grammar,* 303.

5. BDAG, 249–50.

6. BDAG, 249–50, 587; *NID,* s.v. "λατρεύω"; Ellingworth, *Epistle to the Hebrews,* 421.

7. BDAG, 10–11.

8. BDAG, 10–11.

a portable temple. Its features are described in Exodus 26. According to most commentators, it was 30 cubits long (about 45 feet) and 10 cubits wide and high (about 15 feet). Its exterior on the back and sides was composed of 46 trellises made of acacia wood and fitted with golden rings so that each piece could be attached to its neighbor. All were overlaid with gold. Serving as an inner lining and suspended over the whole was a richly embroidered linen fabric of blue, purple, and scarlet. Figures of the cherubim were embroidered upon it. The interior was separated into two chambers by a curtain. Over this structure a tent was spread. The opening of the tabernacle was toward the east and closed from the general view by a screen or curtain.[9]

The author identifies the nature of the structure with the adjective κοσμικός (*kosmikos*), "earthly, worldly."[10] The adjective does not, in the present context, carry the pejorative nuance of that which is morally reprehensible or at enmity with God. Rather, it stresses location, that is, what is on the earth.[11] This sets it apart from its heavenly archetype. For this reason, the word is translated as "earthly" in our Rendition. The nuance of the word does, however, stress the rather severe limitations of the tabernacle because it was part of the temporary created order as opposed to the heavenly eternal order, the one Christ entered and from which he ministers. By implication, this earthly sanctuary was not the abode of God.[12] Indeed, the author never mentions God in association with the earthly tabernacle or its rites. In doing so, he tacitly relativizes both. Even so, he does recognize that they do have importance as prefigurations of the Lord and his ministry.[13]

9:2–5 These verses form a chiasmus:

A Content of the outer chamber (9:2a)
  B Name of the outer chamber (9:2b)
    C The veil separating the inner and outer chambers (9:3a)
  B′ Name of the inner chamber (9:3b)
A′ Content of the inner chamber (9:4–5)

Through this arrangement the author stresses the significance of the veil and lays the ground work for his later argument.[14]

---

9. "Bible Dictionary," s.v. "Tabernacle"; Richard Elliot Freidman, "Tabernacle," in Freedman, *Anchor Bible Dictionary,* 6:292–300.

10. BDAG, 560–61.

11. BDAG, 560–61. The idea does contain a negative or pejorative cast hinting that the tabernacle was not really Jehovah's dwelling place. Vanhoye, *Letter to the Hebrews,* 137.

12. Cockerill, *Epistle to the Hebrews,* 372–73; Vanhoye, *Letter to the Hebrews,* 137.

13. Vanhoye, *Letter to the Hebrews,* 139.

14. Ellingworth, *Epistle to the Hebrews,* 422.

9:2 there was a tabernacle made / a tent was set up: The noun σκηνή (*skēnē*) describes a temporary shelter like a tent or hut.[15] In the LXX, it was translated from the Hebrew מִשְׁכָּן (*miškān*), "dwelling place,"[16] and אֹהֶל (*ʾōhel*), "tent,"[17] both of which were used to refer to the portable sanctuary the Israelites carried with them during the Exodus.[18] Although there was only a single tent, the author uses the noun *skēnē* to describe both the first section and the second section of the tabernacle, which were separated by a curtain.[19]

The verb κατασκευάζω (*kataskeuazō*), "to set up," can denote all stages of making something ready for use including its building, furnishing, and equipping.[20] The nuance of the word is that Moses put every detail into place so that the first chamber could function fully as directed by the Lord.

the first / the front section: The feminine singular adjective πρώτη (*prōtē*), "first,"[21] modifying the noun σκήνη (*skēnē*), "tent," designates the first section a priest would enter when coming into the tabernacle. Hence it is translated as "the front section" in our Rendition to distinguish it from the outer courtyard, where a number of rituals were performed, and the inner section or Holy of Holies, where only specific rites were performed.

the candlestick / the lamp stand: The KJV contains the mistranslation of λυχνία (*lychnia*) as "candlestick." The noun actually refers to the menorah, a stand with seven branches, the top of each holding an oil lamp (see Ex. 25:31–37; 37:17–24).[22] Of all the furnishings of the Holy Place, it was the most elaborate and richly ornamented. Its primary purpose was to supply light for the Holy Place, its second to represent the presence and glory of God.[23] It stood on the south side of the first chamber of the tabernacle and later temple.

---

15. BDAG, 928.

16. *HAL,* 646–47.

17. *HAL,* 19.

18. The Israelites continued to use the tabernacle after settling in Palestine until the temple of Solomon was built. Though set up at some place in the temple precincts, it was no longer used for worship purposes. It was apparently destroyed with the temple by the Babylonians in 589 BC. Freidman, "Tabernacle," in Freedman, *Anchor Bible Dictionary,* 6:292–300. The Vulgate translates the Hebrew מִשְׁכָּן (*miškān*), "tent," as the Latin *tabernaculum,* "tent." Charlton T. Lewis and Charles Short, *A New Latin Dictionary* (Oxford: Oxford University Press, 1958), 1931. The English word "tabernacle" found in the KJV is derived from this source.

19. For discussion, see Michaelis, *TDNT,* 7:368–94.

20. BDAG, 526–27. The LSJ, s.v. "κατασκευάζω," notes that the word, when referring to a building, means "fully furnished."

21. BDAG, 892–94.

22. BDAG, 606.

23. Cyrus Adler and Judah David Eisenstein, "Menorah," *Jewish Encyclopedia,* accessed October 1, 2016, http://www.jewishencyclopedia.com/articles/10685-menorah. For studies,

The table / table: The author used the noun τράπεζα (*trapeza*), "table," to designate the four-legged stand on which the "shewbread" was placed. It was made of acacia wood overlaid with gold and had a double crown or border around the top. It was two cubits wide (approximately 36 inches), one cubit deep (about 18 inches), and one and a half cubits high (about 27 inches). On each of its feet were rings through which poles could be passed for transport. It was placed on the north side of the Holy Place (Ex. 25:23–28).

Shewbread / the presentation of the loaves: In the KJV, "shewbread" is the translation of ἡ πρόθεσις τῶν ἄρτων (*hē prothesis tôn artōn*), literally "the presentation of the loaves of bread," which in turn was translated from the Hebrew לֶחֶם הַפָּנִים (*leḥem happānîm*), literally "the bread of the face," meaning the bread placed before the face of Jehovah.[24] The phrase refers to the twelve loaves of bread that were placed on the table in the first room of the tabernacle (and later also in the temple) as an offering to God. A possible translation could be "presence bread" since Exodus 25:30 states that these loaves were to be ever present before the Lord. The noun "shewbread" came into English in the sixteenth century as a translation of the German *Schaubrot* that denoted these sacred loaves.[25]

According to 1 Chronicles 9:32, the priestly clan of Kohathites had the responsibility of preparing the loaves.[26] The loaves were made from two omers of fine flour (about 4.9 pounds), to which no leaven was added, and then baked (Lev. 24:5–6). Fresh loaves were placed in two rows on the table each Sabbath, and the old loaves were eaten by the priests (see Ex. 25:30; Lev. 2:11; Num. 4:7–8; and 1 Sam. 21:4–6; compare Matt. 12:4; and Luke 6:4).[27]

the sanctuary / the Holy Place: At this point, the author mentions the name of the first chamber, Ἅγια (*Hagia*), that is, "Holy." This is a translation of the Hebrew קֹדֶשׁ (*qōdeš*), "holiness," from the Masoretic text.[28] The author does not modify the adjective with a definite article. The gender of the adjective is, however, feminine, thus modifying the feminine noun σκηνή (*skēnē*), "tent," found in the previous phrase but not brought

---

see Henry W. Soltau, *The Holy Vessels and Furniture of the Tabernacle* (1851; Grand Rapids, Mich.: Kregel Publications, 1975), 73–83; and James Strong, *The Tabernacle of Israel: Its Structure and Symbolism* (Grand Rapids, Mich.: Kregel Publications, 1987), 67–72.

24. *TWOT*, 1782a; BDB, 542.

25. *Collegiate Dictionary*, s.v. "shewbread." The spelling "shew" is a British variant of the word "show."

26. This was one of the three Levitical divisions, the other two being the Gershonites and Merarites (Num. 3:14–21).

27. See Strong, *Tabernacle of Israel*, 63–64; and Soltau, *Holy Vessels*, 49–52.

28. *HAL*, 1077. For examples, see Ex. 26:33; 35:19.

forward.[29] The author called this space simply "holy," but we have supplied the noun "place" in our Rendition to give the adjective a more concrete cast.[30] Though there is some debate as to its proportions,[31] the chamber appears to have been ten cubits wide and high (about 15 feet) and twenty long (about 30 feet). Appointed priests entered it at least twice daily to perform prescribed ordinances.

9:3 *after the second veil / after the second curtain:* The second curtain is generally believed to be a curtain or veil separating the first part of the sanctuary, "the Holy Place," from the rear chamber, "the Most Holy Place."[32]

---

29. The various manuscripts are divided as to how this noun is accented. Accented Ἅγια, the adjective is a neuter plural, but accented Ἁγία, it is a feminine singular. In the earliest manuscripts, no accents were written. The Masoretic text has קֹדֶשׁ (*qodesh*), which is a masculine noun, "holiness," rather than an adjective. LXX Ex. 26:33 has τοῦ ἁγίου (*tou hagiou*), which could be either masculine or neuter singular. In our Rendition, we have chosen to treat it as a feminine singular agreeing with σκήνη (*skēnē*).

30. It is possible that the adjective should be construed as a proper name, thus, "The Holy." See Ellingworth, *Epistle to the Hebrews,* 423. A number of textual variants exist that change these verses so they more closely follow the description of the interior of the tabernacle as found in Ex. 26:33, where the Holy Place and the Most Holy Place are mentioned together. Vanhoye, *Letter to the Hebrews,* 137.

31. For discussion, see Freidman, "Tabernacle," in Freedman, *Anchor Bible Dictionary,* 6:292–300.

32. "Bible Dictionary," s.v. "Tabernacle." There is some confusion in the scriptures about this veil as well as some of the other items associated with the tabernacle. The problem arises with the Pentateuch itself. The descriptions of the tabernacle and its furnishings found in Exodus, Leviticus, and Numbers are, in some details, ambiguous at best and inconsistent at worst. Complicating the issue, the LXX differs in some instances from the MT in describing the tabernacle and its furnishings. Johnson, *Hebrews,* 217.

In fact, there is no direct evidence in the biblical texts that there was a "second curtain" in the Tabernacle. Though the פָּרֹכֶת (*pārōket*), "covering," is described in Ex. 26:31–33, 36–37, both the MT and the LXX for these verses are unclear as to the fabric's function. It is definitely a covering, but the question is whether it was suspended over the ark of the covenant on a wooden frame or in front of the ark on a shaft. The view affects how one understands the position of the incense altar. In the former case, it stood "before the ark," making it part of the Holy of Holies; in the latter, it was "before the veil" and therefore in the Holy Place. For discussions, see Ellingworth, *Epistle to the Hebrews,* 423–27; Cockerill, *Epistle to the Hebrews,* 375–76; Freidman, "Tabernacle," in Freedman, *Anchor Bible Dictionary,* 6:292–300; and Gane and Milgrom, *TDOT,* 12:95–97.

In an attempt to harmonize the various biblical descriptions, ancient Jewish scribes (whose accuracy is questionable) developed the traditional view of the tabernacle. Attridge, *Epistle to the Hebrews,* 234. The author may have followed these somewhat clearer sources in his description of the tabernacle and its rituals, but what seems most likely is that he was not overly concerned with the exact details of the furnishings but with the separation between the Holy Place and the Holy of Holies. See Ellingworth, *Epistle to the Hebrews,* 427. Supporting this idea is that even the author's description of the activities of the high priest on the Day of

The first curtain, which is not mentioned in Hebrews, was the one that covered the entrance to the sacred tent.

the tabernacle which is called the Holiest of all / another section called the Most Holy Place: The back section or, using the author's model, the second "tent" was partitioned off by a curtain. In the Masoretic text, this section is called קֹדֶשׁ הַקֳּדָשִׁים (*qōdeš haqqŏdāšîm*), literally "holy of holies" (Ex. 26:33, 34), which is the Hebrew way of rendering a superlative since Hebrew did not have a separate grammatical form for the comparative. The Greek rendering of this is literally Ἅγια Ἁγίων (*hagia hagiōn*), "holy of holies." We have translated the phrase as "the Most Holy Place" in our Rendition to best catch the sense in modern English.[33]

This chamber was ten cubits high, wide, and broad (about 15 feet cubed) and covered by the same fabric as the Holy Place. The author's reference to this section as a "second tent" may have been to accentuate, for the sake of argument, the difficulty of moving from one tent to the other.[34]

9:4 ***the golden censer / the golden incense altar:*** There is a problem with the term the author uses to describe this item of furniture. The LXX consistently uses the noun θυσιαστήριον (*thysiastērion*) to denote the incense altar. The author, however, uses the term θυμιατήριον (*thymiatērion*), which generally refers not to the altar but to an incense burner—a shallow pan on which incense was placed and burned.[35] Given that the author describes the furnishings of the tabernacle and not any specific vessels used therein and that the text on which he draws (the LXX) does not refer to an incense pan at this point (Ex. 30:1–6), he is most likely referring to the altar.[36] Contemporary

---

Atonement do not fully correlate with the biblical texts. Rather, the author seems to simplify them so that he can move to his point. What is important, however, is that the author's inaccuracies do not detract from his message. We should rather accept the author's determining of these things as a means of understanding his view on the postmortal ministry of the Lord. Johnson, *Hebrews,* 217–18. By placing the altar of incense in the Holy of Holies, the author enhances the chamber's beauty and necessity in the expiation ritual and also enriches the chamber's symbolism of the heavenly realm where the Lord reigns.

33. This phrase represents a subset of the genitive of subordination and points to both the main noun and genitive noun as having the same *lexeme,* that is, of emphasizing the par excellence of the item noted. Wallace, *Greek Grammar,* 103 n. 84, 298.

34. Ellingworth, *Epistle to the Hebrews,* 424.

35. Vanhoye, *Letter to the Hebrews,* 137–38. See also Moulton and Milligan, *Vocabulary,* 294.

36. BDAG, 461. For discussion, see Bruce, *Epistle to the Hebrews,* 200–202; and Ellingworth, *Epistle to the Hebrews,* 425–27. That Ex. 30:1–6 coupled with Lev. 16:12, 18 has Aaron bring incense into the Most Holy Place and then go out to burn it on the incense altar confirms the placement of the altar in the Holy Place. Most recent commentators agree. See Cockerill, *Epistle to the Hebrews,* 376–77; and O'Brien, *Letter to the Hebrews,* 308–9.

Jewish writers also referred to the altar by this term, suggesting this position is correct.[37]

The MT is unclear as to where the incense altar actually stood,[38] and this causes a problem with the author's description. The altar was most likely in front of the curtain separating the Holy Place from the Most Holy Place. It was a cubit on each side (about 18 inches) and two cubits tall (about 36 inches). It had a projection (קֶרֶן, *qeren,* "horn") on each of the top four corners, and the top was encircled by a crown. The whole was gilded. On two of its sides under the "horns" were rings through which rods could be inserted when the altar needed to be transported (Ex. 30:1–10).

the ark of the covenant / the ark of the covenant: The noun κιβωτός (*kibōtos*) denoted a "box, chest."[39] The word is the translation of the Hebrew אָרוֹן (*'ărôn*), "chest," that designated the box in which the tablets of the Mosaic law were stored (Ex. 25:10, 21).[40] The chest was two and a half cubits long (about three and a half feet) by one and a half cubits wide and high (about 27 inches) and made of acacia wood. Rings were placed on its long axis through which poles could be inserted for transport.

The author calls the chest the κιβωτὸς τῆς διαθήκης (*kibōtos tēs diathēkēs*), most often translated as "ark of the covenant." The addition of διαθήκη (*diathēkē*), "covenant," properly describes the vessel since it contained the stone tablets on which the Ten Commandments were inscribed that formed the basis of the Mosaic covenant. In LXX Exodus 25:16, these tablets are called τὰ μαρτύρια (*ta martyria*), "the testimonies," and in LXX Exodus 25:10, the ark is called the κιβωτὸς μαρτυρίου (*kibōtos martyriou*), "the chest of the testimony." Both share the idea that the tablets were direct witnesses or testimonies of God's acceptance of Israel as his people.

The designation of the holy vessel by the English word "ark" came from the Latin noun *arca* denoting a chest,[41] although the Greek κιβωτός (*kibōtos*), in addition to meaning "a chest," also denoted a sea-faring vessel such as Noah built.[42]

the golden pot that had manna / the golden jar containing the manna: The noun στάμνος (*stamnos*), "pot, jar," denoted a wide-mouthed earthen

37. Philo, *Mos.* 2.94, 101, 105; *Her.* 226–7; *Spec.* 1.231. Josephus used both terms. For θυματήριον (*thymatērion*), see *Ant.* 4.32, 34, 57; for θυσιαστήριον (*thysiastērion*), see *Ant.* 4.147, 193, 198.

38. Freidman, "Tabernacle," in Freedman, *Anchor Bible Dictionary,* 6:292–300.

39. BDAG, 544.

40. *HAL,* 85.

41. *Collegiate Dictionary,* s.v. "ark."

42. BDAG, 544.

vessel used to hold foodstuffs.[43] The noun μάννα (*manna*) is a borrowing from the Hebrew מָן (*mān*), the word spoken by the Israelites when they awoke one morning to find this substance covering the ground that translates roughly as "what is it?"[44] Moses identified it as "bread" from Jehovah that would be continually given to the people for sustenance while on their journey (see Ex. 16:11–26). Moses commanded Aaron to fill an *omer*-sized gilded jar (about one liter[45]) with this substance and place it *before* the ark of the covenant (Ex. 16:34–35) as a testimony of God's care for his people. The author takes some liberty with the text here by placing the jar inside the ark.

Aaron's rod that budded / Aaron's staff that had budded: The noun ῥάβδος (*rhabdos*) denotes a rod or staff.[46] The story of Aaron's staff is found in Numbers 17:6–10: because of rebellion among the people over priesthood authority, the Lord instructed Moses to have each tribe supply him with a staff on which their tribal name was inscribed. These he placed before the ark in the tabernacle. The next day he brought the whole out. All remained barren except Aaron's, which had not only budded but also bore almonds. Jehovah's point was to show the rebellious Israelites that his power was with the Levites and especially Aaron. Jehovah commanded Moses to place this rod, along with the jar of manna, *before* the ark (Num. 17:10). Again, the author takes liberty with the text by placing the rod inside the ark of the covenant.

the tables of the covenant / the tablets of the covenant: The noun πλάξ (*plax*) denoted a thin flat stone on which something could be written.[47] The phrase αἱ πλάκες τῆς διαθήκης (*hai plakes tēs diathēkēs*), "the tablets of the covenant," refers to the second set of stone tables on which Moses inscribed the Decalogue (see Ex. 34:1–28).[48] The first set, written by the hand of God, Moses destroyed after seeing the Israelites worshiping the golden calf (see Ex. 32:1–19).[49] Jehovah commanded him to place the new set in the ark of the covenant (Ex. 25:16).

---

43. BDAG, 940.

44. BDAG, 577.

45. Biblical dry measures can only be approximated. The Bible identifies an *omer* as a day's ration of bread (Ex. 16:15, 22, 32), which translates in today's terms as about one liter. Marvin A. Powell, "Weights and Measures," in Freedman, *Anchor Bible Dictionary,* 6:897–908.

46. BDAG, 902.

47. BDAG, 822.

48. Though God, in Ex. 34:1, states that he will write upon the tablets, 34:27–28 makes it clear that Moses actually did the inscribing. According to JST Ex. 34:1–2, the tablets contained much more than just the Decalogue: a rather complete recording of the covenantal requirements and associated items.

49. The JST of Ex. 34:1–2 notes that God instructed Moses to make a second set of tablets upon which the Lord wrote. The material however would not be identical to the

9:5 ***And over it the cherubims of glory shadowing the mercyseat / Above the ark were the cherubim of glory overshadowing the mercy seat:*** The cherubim were two carved and gilded winged figures that sat on the lid of the ark of the covenant (Ex. 25:22).[50] The noun is a transliteration of the Hebrew כְּרוּבִים (*kĕrûbîm*), the plural of כְּרוּב (*kĕrûb*). The term appears over ninety times in Old Testament but only here in the New. These creatures always have a sacral context, but other than being fanciful winged creatures, there is little known about them. From what can be gathered in their scriptural context, they seem to be guardians of sacred items and act as steeds for Jehovah's chariot and as protectors of his holiness.[51]

The author adds the noun δόξα (*doxa*), "glory," to describe them (for a study of "glory," see Translation Notes for 1:3), but that word is not associated with the cherubim in Exodus 25. Verse 22 in that chapter, however, does suggests a meaning: Jehovah will meet with the people between the cherubim; thus the word *doxa* suggests the presence of God.[52] The phrase then points not to the glory of the cherubim but to the glory of God that dwells between them.[53]

The verb κατασκιάζω (*kataskiazō*), "overshadow,"[54] suggests that the two wings of each cherub stretched toward the other cherub, casting a shadow over the lid of the mercy seat (see Ex. 25:20).

---

former because, as Jehovah explained, "I will take away the priesthood out of their midst; therefore, my holy order, and the ordinances thereof, shall not go before them." Instead, the Lord substituted the law of "carnal" commandments.

50. BDAG, 1084.

51. In Ezek. 1:4–14, they pulled God's chariot. They were also the assigned guardians of the tree of life (Gen. 3:24) and Jehovah's throne (1 Sam. 4:4; Ps. 80:1; Isa. 37:16). In *1 En.* 71:7, they are described as "those who sleep not" but "guard the throne of God's glory." For discussion, see Carol Meyers, "Cherubim," in Freedman, *Anchor Bible Dictionary,* 1:899–900; and *NID,* s.v. "Χερούβ." In the MT, they show up most often in association with the tabernacle and temple. For a study of the role of the cherubim as guardians as well as the nature of sacred space in the Jerusalem temple, see Avram R. Shannon, "'Come Near unto Me': Guarded Space and Its Mediators in the Jerusalem Temple," in *Ascending the Mountain of the Lord: Temple, Praise, and Worship in the Old Testament,* ed. David Rolph Seely, Jeffrey R. Chadwick, and Matthew J. Grey (Provo, Utah: Religious Studies Center, Brigham Young University; Salt Lake City: Deseret Book, 2013), 66–84.

52. Ezek. 9:3; 10:1–20; 11:22 tie God's glory to the cherubim as Isa. 6:1–3 does to the seraphim. Ellingworth, *Epistle to the Hebrews,* 430. For a study of δόξα (*doxa*), "glory," see F. Raurell, "Certain Affinities between Ez-LXX and the Epistle to the Hebrews with regard to the 'Doxa' and 'the Cherubins,'" *Estudios Franciscanos* 86 (1985): 209–32.

53. Koester, *Hebrews,* 396.

54. BDAG, 527.

The mercy seat, Greek ἱλαστήριον (*hilastērion*), "place of propitiation,"[55] translates from the Hebrew כַּפֹּרֶת (*kappōret*), meaning probably "atonement" or "instrument of atonement," and designated the lid of the ark of the covenant.[56] Further, on the Day of Atonement, the high priest sprinkled the blood offerings upon and before the seat to make atonement for the people (Lev. 16:14–15). Thus, the mercy seat was the place where Israel's sins, both corporate and individual, were forgiven. For these reasons, the Israelites viewed it as the most holy item among all their sacred objects.

of which we cannot now speak particularly / Now is not the time to speak of these things in more detail: With these words, the author signals that, though much more could be said about all the items,[57] he intends to move on.

9:6 ***when these things were thus ordained / After these things had been prepared in this manner:*** On the verb κατασκευάζω (*kataskeuazō*), "to prepare," see Translation Notes for 9:2. The phrase shows the author was well aware that the rituals of the tabernacle did not commence until after everything had been set in place. All must be exactly right in dealing with such sacred worship.

the priests went always into the first tabernacle, accomplishing the service of God / the priests were continually entering into the outer section of the tent performing worship services: The author focuses on the daily activities associated with the Holy Place. The author describes the priests' duties as τὰς λατρείας ἐπιτελοῦντες (*tas latreias epitelountes*), "performing worship services." The phrase uses strictly cultic terms. According to the Mosaic law, a selected priest entered the Holy Place multiple times to carry out the services of offering incense at the time of both morning and evening prayers, filling the menorah lamps with oil, relighting them (Ex. 27:20–21), and, when necessary, changing the loaves of shewbread (Ex. 40:22–23).[58]

The two verbs εἴσειμι (*eiseimi*), "to enter," and ἐπιτελέω (*epiteleō*), "to perform," are both iterative presents and thereby emphasize the repetitive nature of the priests' services.[59] To further stress this point, in order to contrast these services with those performed by the high priest on the Day of Atonement, the author uses the phrase διὰ παντός (*dia pantos*), "at

55. BDAG, 474. The LSJ, s.v. "ἱλαστήριον," also includes as a definition a monument indicating an act that was done but once and remembered thereafter.

56. *HAL*, 495.

57. Philo, *Mos.* 2:97–100, is an example of an extended discussion.

58. See Soltau, *Holy Vessels*, 55–57, 82–83, 99.

59. Smyth, *Greek Grammar*, §§1790–94; Cockerill, *Epistle to the Hebrews*, 379.

all times, or continually,"[60] thus emphasizing that these services took place over and over again.

The author makes another rather subtle point by using a different word for Christ's entering into the "true tabernacle" (εἰσέρχομαμι, *eiserchomai,* rather than εἴσειμι, *eiseimi*; see 9:12, 25; compare 6:19–20) and in that way stresses the difference between the two acts.[61] Continuing his subtle approach, he uses the verb "perform" (ἐπιτελέω, *epiteleō*) with a soft irony. Greek regularly uses the term to describe the execution of cultic rituals and particularly the bringing the rite to completion.[62] The author however shows that the Levitical priests are never able to bring their rituals to completion, for they could never go further than the first tent. "They never achieve even symbolic access into the divine Presence. Thus, the [author] lays a firm foundation for demonstrating the ineffectiveness of the ministry on which the First Covenant was established."[63]

9:7 ***into the second went the high priest alone / only the high priest entered into the inner section of the tent:*** In this verse, the author looks at the ritual executed in the Most Holy Place on the Day of Atonement as prescribed in Leviticus 16:3–32 (see also Ex. 30:10; and Num. 29:7–11). For a description of the ordinances associated with this fast, see "Excursus on the Ritual of the Day of Atonement" below.

once every year / once a year: The fast was celebrated on the tenth day of the seventh month of each year (Lev. 23:27). The law dictated that only on this day was anyone allowed inside the Most Holy Place, and that person was exclusively the high priest.

not without blood / not without bringing the blood: The law required that the high priest sprinkle seven times before the mercy seat the blood of both the sacrificial bullock and the he-goat in order for an atonement to take place (Lev. 16:18).

he offered for himself, and for the errors of the people / that he offered for his own sins and the sins of the people: The author's use of the verb προσφέρω (*prospherō*), "to offer," to describe the high priest's blood offering is telling, for there is no Old Testament precedent that associates this word

---

60. Louw-Nida, §67.15, 86. See also Dennis Hamm, "Praying 'Regularly' (not 'Constantly'): A Note on the Cultic Background of *dia pantos* at Luke 24:53, Acts 10:2 and Hebrews 9:6, 13:15," *Expository Times* 116, no. 2 (November 2004): 50–52.

61. Ellingworth, *Epistle to the Hebrews,* 433.

62. BDAG, 383; Herodotus, *Hist.* 2.63; 4.26; Philo, *Dreams* 1.214–15; Josephus, *Ant.* 4.123; 9.273.

63. Cockerill, *Epistle to the Hebrews,* 379.

with the sacrificial offerings.[64] The author is tying the high priest's act to the atoning sacrifice of the Lord (9:14, 25, 28; 10:12; see also the use of the cognate noun προσφορά [*prosphora*] in 10:10, 14). In doing so, he subtly presents a contrast between the repeated blood sprinklings under the old covenant to the once-for-all self-offering of the Lord's blood under the new covenant.[65]

This whole phrase is important because it shows that, for all his holiness, the high priest himself was not without sin and therefore in need of expiation. Note that up to this point, the author has emphasized the distinction of the high priest vis-à-vis the other priests because he is a type of Christ. At this point, where the author wants to stress the ineffectiveness of the old covenant, he not only matches the high priest with other priests but also with the people as a whole. In this way, the author begins to widen the gulf between this priest and the Lord.[66]

The noun ἀγνόημα (*agnoēma*) often denotes sins committed unintentionally,[67] but Leviticus 16:16 makes clear that all sin is in focus.[68] In a number of instances in ancient writings, the term *agnoēma* merges in meaning with that of *hamartia*, that is, sin in general.[69] It would appear, then, that so far as the author is concerned, there was little difference between sins

64. The connection is made only in the New Testament. Cockerill, *Epistle to the Hebrews,* 380 n. 42. The verb's general use simply means to bring or present something to another. BDAG, 886. In Matt. 5:23; 8:4, it does take on the religious nuance of a sacrificial offering. It is the author of Hebrews, however, who really ties the two concepts together. On the other hand, the noun προσφορά (*prosphora*), "a voluntary offering," does have strong religious overtones. Both Acts 21:25 and Eph. 5:2 tie the word directly to the Savior's act of giving himself as an offering for others. BDAG, 887. But, again, it is the author of Hebrews who most strongly ties the two concepts together.

65. Note the difference between the phrase ἅπαξ τοῦ ἐνιαυτοῦ (*hapax tou eniautou*), "once a year," used here and ἐφάπαξ (*ephapax*), "once for all," in 9:12. See also Norman H. Young, "The Gospel according to Hebrews 9," *New Testament Studies* 27, no. 2 (1981): 207–9.

66. Ellingworth, *Epistle to the Hebrews,* 435.

67. BDAG, 13; Louw-Nida, §88.302. If taken in this light, the noun suggests one more difference between the work of the high priest through which only unintentional sins could be forgiven and that of Christ whereby all sins can be forgiven. Ellingworth, *Epistle to the Hebrews,* 435; Robert P. Gordon, *Hebrews,* 2d ed., Readings: A New Biblical Commentary, ed. John Jarick (Sheffield, Eng.: Sheffield Phoenix Press, 2008), 117–18.

68. The LXX reads πασῶν τῶν ἁμαρτιῶν αὐτῶν (*pasōn tōn hamartiōn autōn*), "for the trespass of all their sins," and the MT reads וּמִפִּשְׁעֵיהֶם לְכָל־חַטֹּאתָם (*ûmippišʿêhem lekol ḥaṭṭōʾtām*), "because of the transgression of all their sins." Both sources indicate that all of Israel's sins were to be remitted.

69. BDAG, 50–51.

committed in ignorance and those committed knowingly.[70] It is possible, however, the author is focusing not so much on sins as upon "failings," or to be more true to the Greek, "ignorances," for he fully believes it is "impossible to remove sins by the blood of bulls and goats" (NR 10:4).[71]

9:8 *The Holy Ghost this signifying / By this the Holy Spirit was making it clear:* The author's note follows his pattern of authenticating his argument by an appeal to the divine inspiration undergirding the scriptures.[72] Here the author's point is that it is the Spirit who reveals the inadequacy of the old covenant.

The verb δηλόω (*dēloō*), "to make clear," carries the nuance of not only making something very clear but also of making something known that was previously unknown.[73] With this word, the author shows, under the influence of the Spirit, he is presenting an idea his audience had not understood or realized before even though it was clearly in the scriptures.[74]

that the way into the holiest of all was not yet made manifest, while as the first tabernacle was yet standing / that the way into the Most Holy Place had not yet been revealed while the outer section of the tent still existed: The startling information was that the old covenant, symbolized by the first tent,[75] did not show the way to God as symbolized by the Most Holy Place[76] and would not as long as it stood. The verb φανερόω (*phaneroō*) denotes revealing or making something known,[77] a power the old covenant simply did not have. Thus, it becomes clear why the author states that the way into the heavenly Most Holy Place could not be "made known" under the old covenant. If the rituals of the first "tent" could not even provide a way into the second "tent," how could they possibly reveal (*phaneroō*) a way into heaven itself?[78]

---

70. In the LXX of Judg. 5:20 and in the apocryphal works Tob. 3:3; Sir. 23.2; 1 Macc. 13:39, both terms are found together suggesting that the difference in meaning, if any, was slight. Thus, Cockerill, *Epistle to the Hebrews,* 380 with n. 43, argues that the author was referring to sins in general because, as the author clearly states, the work of the high priest brought only a ceremonial physical cleansing, while Christ cleansed the conscience (that is, metaphorically, the heart or inner core of the individual). See Translation Notes for 9:13–14 below.

71. Vanhoye, *Letter to the Hebrews,* 140.

72. Bruce, *Epistle to the Hebrews,* 208; Vanhoye, *Old Testament Priests,* 186.

73. BDAG, 222; Louw-Nida, §§28.42; 33.152.

74. Koester, *Hebrews,* 397; Attridge, *Epistle to the Hebrews,* 240.

75. Attridge, *Epistle to the Hebrews,* 240; Ellingworth, *Epistle to the Hebrews,* 437.

76. Cockerill, *Epistle to the Hebrews,* 381–82.

77. BDAG, 1048.

78. Vanhoye, *Letter to the Hebrews,* 140; Cockerill, *Epistle to the Hebrews,* 382.

9:9 *Which was a figure for the time then present / This was a symbol pointing to the then-present time:* The noun παραβολή (*parabolē,* from which the English term "parable" comes) denotes something that serves as a model, example, or symbol for something else.[79] Literally it means to set two things side by side and to then compare them as a symbol. Here it points to the nature of the Holy Place as the symbol of the Levitical period. The phrase εἰς τὸν καιρὸν τὸν ἐνεστηκότα (*eis ton kairon ton enestēkota*), literally "to the time the present," is vague, but since the author is contrasting the old covenant vis-à-vis the new, it more likely refers to the period in which the old covenant was in force.[80] This interpretation is indicated in our Rendition by the word "then."[81]

in which were offered both gifts and sacrifices, that could not make him that did the service perfect, as pertaining to the conscience / indicating that the gifts and sacrifices they were offering could not perfect the worshiper with respect to his conscience: The author uses the phrase δῶρά τε καὶ θυσίαι (*dōra te kai thysiai*), "gifts and also sacrifices," to point to the sacrificial rites of the Mosaic period (5:1; 8:3) and here states their deficiency: the sacrificial rites failed to "perfect" the consciences of those who came to worship.

---

79. BDAG, 759–60.

80. The phrase εἰς τὸν καιρὸν τὸν ἐνεστηκότα (*eis ton kairon ton enestēkota*), literally "to the time the present," is vague and therefore has led to much debate. For a discussion on the contested points in this verse, see Ellingworth, *Epistle to the Hebrews,* 439–41. On his part, Ellingworth takes εἰς (*eis*) as "until" rather than "before" and καιρόν (*kairon*) as an adverbial accusative of extent of time. By doing so, he concludes that the phrase means "until the present time." By doing so, he is able to exclude the period of the Savior's ministry as when the old covenant was fulfilled. Agreeing is Martin Emmrich, "*Pneuma* in Hebrews: Prophet and Interpreter," *Westminster Theological Journal* 64, no. 1 (Spring 2002): 55–71, who argues that the phrase points exclusively to the author's period where this truth is for the first time fully disclosed. With others, we take the simpler and more direct view that the parable denotes the whole time when the old covenant was in force that ended with the resurrection of the Lord. This approach seems best since the author himself defines the term as meaning when Mosaic sacrifices and gifts were offered (9:10). Cockerill, *Epistle to the Hebrews,* 383–84; Bruce, *Epistle to the Hebrews,* 209.

81. R. L. Omanson, "A Superior Covenant: Hebrews 8:1–10:18," *Review and Expositor* 82, no. 3 (1985): 361–73, basing his analysis on Heb. 8:1–10:18, argues that the author of Hebrews insists that Christ established a covenant superior to that of Sinai. Even so, the author repeatedly makes connections to sacrificial imagery that, though it was no longer directly relevant to his audience (since the new covenant no longer required animal sacrifices), it was what they were familiar with and, therefore, made it easier for him to make his point.

On the noun "perfect," see Translation Notes for 2:10 and the associated Analysis. In the present context, it is important to keep in mind that the noun τελειόω (*teleioō*), "perfect," comes closer to the English word "whole" in its moral sense of completeness rather than to the more common idea of flawlessness. The Greek word especially looked at the idea of being suitable to perform a task, which is, in this case, entering into God's presence.

The problem with the rites of the old covenant was that they never prepared the participants to enter into the Father's glory because they did not have the power to change the conscience of the individuals. The noun συνείδησις (*syneidēsis*), "conscience," as used here, denotes "the inward faculty of distinguishing right and wrong" and connotes a heightened "moral sensitivity" with an accompanying purity of mind.[82] The author emphasizes that the participants in the sacrificial rituals went away still somewhat troubled in the conscience because they sensed the ritual, having to be done over and over, had brought no real change in their lives.

9:10 ***Which stood only in meats and drinks, and divers washings / they are only concerned with foods, drinks, various washings:*** The JST changes the KJV from "stood" to "consisted," which better fits modern English. The Greek phrase has no verb, but to give a feeling of the sense, we have added "they are" in our Rendition. The preposition ἐπί (*epi*) seems best taken as a marker of perspective,[83] and we have translated it as "concerned" in our Rendition.[84]

Here the author defines the narrow focus of the Mosaic ordinances. The author's use of μόνον (*monon*), "only," is emphatic. These ordinances could *only* produce the kind of external purity that came from such washings and oblations.[85] They consisted of three sets. The first was βρῶμα (*brōma*), the noun denoting food in general, that is, all that is nourishing.[86] The author however uses the term to denote the various sacrifices the priests offered during worship service that included not only sacrificial animals but also the offering of "firstfruits" consisting of properly prepared grains, bread

82. BDAG, 967–68; Louw-Nida, §26.13; Bertram, *TDNT,* 7:898–925.

83. BDAG, 365.

84. The author's meaning for the preposition ἐπί (*epi*) is not clear. Its range of definitions includes "on, about, concerning, on the basis of, in addition to, connected with," among others. For discussion, see Ellingworth, *Epistle to the Hebrews,* 443. Of these options, its use as a marker of perspective seems best translated as "concerning," as noted above.

85. Cockerill, *Epistle to the Hebrews,* 385.

86. BDAG, 184.

stuffs, and the products of field, orchard, and vineyard.[87] The second was πόμα (*poma*), the noun pointing to any beverage that satisfies thirst,[88] but the author uses it for the "drink offering," consisting of one-quarter *hin* of wine (about 1.5 U.S. gallons) offered at the tabernacle with the sacrificial victim (Lev. 23:13, 18, 37).[89] The third was βαπτισμός (*baptismos*), the noun referring specifically to the ceremonial washing of dishes to continue ritual purity but also of persons preparing for worship services. This Greek term generally implies dipping and immersing things to cleanse them.[90]

carnal ordinances / external regulations: The phrase δικαιώματα σαρκός (*dikaiōmata sarkos*), literally "ordinances of the flesh," is used by the author to refer to those cultic activities that were limited to humankind's mortal or earthly existence. The noun σάρξ (*sarx*), in the present context, denotes "the outward side of life" and is therefore translated as "external" in our Rendition.[91] The noun δικαίωμα (*dikaiōma*) refers to requirements and commandments necessary for right or just actions.[92] We have translated the plural as "regulations" in our Rendition because it connotes a "prescription by authority for the control or management of an organization or system,"[93] in this case the rituals associated with the old covenant.

imposed on them until the time of reformation / imposed until the time of reformation: The verb ἐπίκειμαι (*epikeimai*), here in participial form,

---

87. The KJV uses "firstfruits" as the translation for two different Hebrew nouns. The first and more common is בִּכּוּרִים (*bikûrîm*), denoting all offerings made at the tabernacle that were not animals or libations. See Ex. 23:16, 19; 34:22, 26; Lev. 23:17; Num. 28:26; *TWOT,* 244; BDB, 114; *HAL,* 130. The second noun is רֵאשִׁית (*rēʾšît*), denoting that which is of first rank in goodness and value or the best of a group. See Num. 18:12; Deut. 26:2, 10; *TWOT,* 2097; BDB, 912; *HAL,* 1170. Firstfruits were presented at the tabernacle but were not offered upon the altar as were the blood sacrifices. For a study of all the sacrifices, see Jukes, *Law of the Offerings.*

88. BDAG, 850.

89. The Hebrew נֶסֶךְ (*nesek*) denoted a wide range of intoxicating beverages used for cultic purposes. Their use was connected closely with mystery religions and their temple rites. The purpose of the *nesek* was to "effect sacramental communion with the redeemer god and its destiny." Goppelt, *TDNT,* 6:137. For the Hebrews, it served to effect a fellowship with Jehovah and was part of, but never in lieu of, a covenant meal. Goppelt, *TDNT,* 6:145; *TWOT,* 1375; BDB, 651.

90. For the covenantal baptismal rite, the Christians used the term βαπτίσμα (*baptisma*). BDAG, 165.

91. BDAG, 914–16; see also Koester, *Hebrews,* 399–400.

92. BDAG, 249–50.

93. *Webster's New Dictionary of Synonyms,* s.v. "law."

carries the idea of something imposed through force or pressure.[94] The author's use of the word reveals his bias not only on the obligatory but also the suppressive nature of the old covenant.[95]

His use of the preposition μέχρι (*mechri*), "until," is important to his argument because it suggests the limited duration that Jehovah intended for the old covenant. It was to hold force only until a set time was reached. The author describes that time as διόρθωσις (*diorthōsis*). This noun denotes first, the process that leads to a time when conditions will be set right, and second, to the results of that process.[96] It connotes the point at which things that were wrong or needed improvement were rectified, thus a period of reformation or even complete renewal. In this case, it looked to the correction of the law that concerned itself only with the external things of the body and not the internal well-being of spirit where the heart was transformed.[97]

Analysis and Summary

There are three anomalies between the author's description of the tabernacle in 9:2–4 and how the structure is traditionally viewed: the designation of two tents rather than one (9:2–3), the order of the furnishings (9:2, 4), and the side of the veil on which the incense altar stood (9:4).

Taking these items in reverse order, the MT and the LXX are somewhat vague concerning the placement of the second veil, but it was most likely a separating curtain between the Holy Place and the Most Holy Place (see Translation Notes for 9:2–3 above). That being the case, then the placement of the altar of incense is immediately before the veil in the Holy Place. The author, however, places the altar before the veil in the Most Holy Place. In doing so, he creates a problem with the spatial axis of his model. The question arises of why he placed the altar in the Holy of Holies. Exacerbating the problem is that the author also places the pot of manna and rod of Aaron inside the ark of the covenant rather than before it as the MT dictates.[98]

---

94. BDAG, 373–74; Louw-Nida, §§85.4; 19.43; 76.17.

95. Though the word is somewhat neutral, since patristic times, there has been an emphasis on its nuance to suggest the burdens imposed by the old covenant and especially the pharisaical elaboration of its demands. Moulton and Milligan, *Vocabulary,* 240, allows for the harsh nuance "oppress." See Ellingworth, *Epistle to the Hebrews,* 444.

96. Louw-Nida, §62.5, 6; BDAG, 251. For the term emphasizing the idea of correction, see Attridge, *Epistle to the Hebrews,* 243 and n. 165.

97. Attridge, *Epistle to the Hebrews,* 231.

98. Kuhn, *TDNT,* 1:3–4.

Because of these things, the spatial axis of the author's model is somewhat confusing. Even so, the idea of movement from the more holy to the most holy is clear, an idea very important to the author's point: the old order, though holy, could not do its job and therefore that inadequacy necessitated a move to the most holy to get the job done. But to stress the law's inadequacy, the author omits a point made in the biblical text. This room housed the mercy seat, the lid to the ark of the covenant, before and upon which the high priest sprinkled blood on the Day of Atonement. Upon it sat the "cherubims of glory" (9:5). According to Exodus 25:22 (see also Lev. 16:2), these acted as "the throne of God." Indeed, the Lord "dwelleth between the cherubims" (1 Sam. 4:4; 2 Sam. 6:2).[99] But in all of the author's descriptions of the Most Holy Place, the author never mentions God. The same is true of the tabernacle's rites (9:6–7). By doing so, "the author relativizes the worth of the former sanctuary and its rites. He recognizes, however, that they did have a certain value as prefigurations that help to express the mystery of Christ."[100]

Unfortunately, the temporal axis the author develops is also somewhat complex. The author contrasts not only the past (the old covenant) with the present (the new covenant) but also—with Platonic overtones—the temporal (the realm of materiality and change) with the eternal (the realm of spirituality and changelessness). As one scholar noted, "the 'outer tent' therefore can stand for *both* earthly, temporal worship *and* for the worship of the first covenant. Likewise, the 'inner tent' corresponds *both* to the new covenant *and* to heaven/the eternal/God's presence. It is a small wonder," he concludes, "given these two kinds of difficulties, that Hebrews sometimes grows obscure, and readers sometimes get confused."[101]

We can only speculate, but the author was likely not overly concerned about the details of the tabernacle and passed over these with a little imprecision and simplification in order to get to his main point, that of the acute separation between the two chambers.[102]

In 9:5, the author moves from his description of the furniture in the Holy Place to that of the Most Holy Place. In doing so, he focuses his readers' attention on the place of atonement, the mercy seat. Here, under the

---

99. Jehovah was addressed as the God who sits upon or dwells between the cherubim. See 2 Kings 19:15; Ps. 99:1.

100. Vanhoye, *Letter to the Hebrews,* 139.

101. Johnson, *Hebrews,* 218.

102. Ellingworth, *Epistle to the Hebrews,* 426–27.

Mosaic law, expiation actually took place through the sprinkling of the blood of the sacrificial victims. All this was a type anticipating the sacrifice of the Lord. As High Priest, the Savior made atonement for all and now governs from his divine throne. His act allows all who will accept him to enter with him into the true tabernacle, that is, into celestial glory where he and the Father dwell. By doing so, his throne becomes a "throne of grace" (4:16) and a true "mercy seat" for his people. Thus, the ritual of the Day of Atonement was, like other sacrifices, full of foreshadowings that anticipated the all-sufficient power in Christ.[103]

Up to this point, the author has distinguished the holiness and duties of the high priest over that of his fellow priests as he acts as a type of the Savior. In 9:7 that changes. To emphasize the ineffectiveness of the old covenant, the author stresses the inadequacy of the ordinances performed even by the high priest. He can enter the Most Holy Place only once a year; he must do so with blood and that blood is shed not only for the sins of the people but also for himself. Further, the ordinance must be done every year. The author's point is that all these items show how ineffective the system was.

A major point of the author's description of the nature and service of the old system is the impossibility of approaching the Divine through such an "earthly sanctuary" (NR 9:1). The author uses the daily rituals performed in the sanctuary as evidence that the old law simply did not work, because its ordinances had to be done over and over, thus evidencing their lack of effectiveness (9:6). "The details used in describing this 'earthly sanctuary' keep [the author's readers] from forgetting its earthly, and therefore limited, character."[104]

The center piece of this pericope is the impenetrable boundary of the veil separating the Holy Place from the Holy of Holies. As 9:8 shows, the Holy Place, as long as it stood, was a graphic reminder that access to the most holy things of God was not possible until Christ came. The annual entrance of the high priest into that sacred space was "the exception that proves the rule."[105] The author's point is that though the first covenant "might have been oriented toward the Most Holy Place, . . . it was confined to the Holy Place. This very fact showed its inability to bring people into God's presence

103. Cockerill, *Epistle to the Hebrews,* 378.
104. Cockerill, *Epistle to the Hebrews,* 372.
105. Attridge, *Epistle to the Hebrews,* 240.

and its nature as foreshadowing a fulfillment to come. By contrast, the New Covenant has no Holy Place but only the Most Holy Place that is 'heaven itself' (9:24)."[106]

The author's purpose in describing in detail the majesty of the Holy of Holies (9:3–4) seems to be to emphasize that its ritual was designed to foreshadow the Savior's entrance onto the heavenly realm (see 9:11–14).[107] Indeed, the Savior actually did what the Levitical high priest on the Day of Atonement only foreshadowed (see Lev. 16): the Lord, as true high priest, with his own blood, entered the heavenly Holy of Holies and made expiation for the people, every one of them.[108]

Noteworthy is that, though the author of Hebrews does highlight the differences between the old covenant and the new with emphasis on the failure of the former, he still has respect for it and its institutions because it presented a powerful shadow and sketch of the real. He did not stand alone. The idea of a shadow temple on earth and a true temple in heaven was current in Judaism. Many saw the earthly sanctuary as defective and needing either correction or replacement.[109] As a result, the author's "distinction between an earthly and heavenly sanctuary, the first ineffective and the second effective, is far from being a rejection of contemporary Jewish sensibility. Indeed, it fits comfortably within a multifaceted spirit of longing within Judaism for a presence of God more powerful than that mediated by the cult of animal sacrifice. What distinguishes Hebrews in this, as in its language about covenant, is the author's conviction that [God's] presence has been realized in the death and exaltation of Jesus."[110]

---

106. Cockerill, *Epistle to the Hebrews,* 382.

107. Cockerill, *Epistle to the Hebrews,* 372; see also Ogden and Skinner, *Verse by Verse,* 256.

108. Goppelt, *TDNT,* 8:256–57; compare McConkie, *Doctrinal New Testament Commentary,* 3:183. Charles W. Penrose, in *Journal of Discourses,* 24:97, noted that "we read that 'without the shedding of blood there is no remission of sins.' Not my blood or your blood is to be shed for the remission of our sins; but He who was without sin allowed His blood to be shed as a sacrifice for our sins."

109. For a study, see Cody, *Heavenly Sanctuary,* 9–46. Solomon eventually replaced the Mosaic tent/tabernacle with a permanent and beautifully constructed temple. But the replacement of the old structure itself symbolized an eventual need for further fulfillment even of the existing new one.

110. Johnson, *Hebrews,* 232. For studies, see Johnson, *Hebrews,* 227–32; and Philip Church, "The Temple in the Apocalypse of Weeks and in Hebrews" *Tyndale Bulletin* 64, no. 1 (2013): 109–28, accessed November 16, 2016, https://legacy.tyndalehouse.com/Bulletin/64=2013/06_Church-20.pdf.

Even so, as the author states, the old system was "imposed" (ἐπίκειμαι, *epikeimai*) upon Israel (9:10), but only for a certain period of time—it was never designed to be everlasting. Indeed, a "time of correction" (καιροῦ διορθώσεως, *kairou diorthōseōs*) would come in which the weaknesses of the old law would be set right (9:10).[111] As 9:11–15 reveal, the author has in mind the ministry of the Lord, who fulfilled the old law and established the new covenant.

The intrinsic relationship between the old law's inability to spiritually cleanse a person and, as a result, the inability of that person to enter into the presence of the Father must not be overlooked or downplayed. The author's point is that only those who have been cleansed from sin and who then continue to live in faithfulness are enabled to enjoy celestial glory. As the author has already pointed out, it had been the Father's intent, even from the time he first established the Mosaic law, to replace it with one written on the hearts of the people (8:8–12).

The author's purpose in this section is twofold. The first is to fully expose the insufficient nature of the sacrifices of the old covenant to make a change in the worshiper's "conscience" (συνείδησις, *syneidēsis*). The word denotes a sense of moral awareness. In the broader Greek culture of the time, the word carried the nuance of the pain a person sensed when they knowingly broke a moral law. The author plays on that nuance. Though each person could be ritually cleansed by participating in the cultic worship services, the cleansing of the conscience did not take place. An inward uncleanliness remained that caused discomfort among the participants and acted as a barrier between the worshiper and God.[112]

111. Even from the institution of the sacrificial system, forgiveness came not through the actual act of sacrificing, but because of the people's faith in Christ that the sacrifice represented. Mosiah 3:18 states, "Salvation was, and is, and is to come, in and through the atoning blood of Christ, the Lord Omnipotent." See McConkie, *Doctrinal New Testament Commentary,* 3:181.

112. See *NID,* s.v. "συνείδησις." G. S. Selby, "The Meaning and Function of Συνείδησις in Hebrews 9 and 10," *Restoration Quarterly* 28 (1985–86): 145–54, argues that the contextual use of the word *syneidēsis* suggests a conscience that serves to continually remind people of their defilement by sin. This internal feeling of guilt is separate from external or ritual defilement and is the true barrier separating people from God. Christ's sacrifice is thus superior to the old covenant since he can cleanse the inner conscience. By cleansing the inner reminder of guilt, God's people can now have confidence in their relationship with him. James Thompson, "Hebrews 9 and Hellenistic Concepts of Sacrifice," *Journal of Biblical Literature* 98, no. 4 (1979): 567–78, shows that not just Christians rejected the idea that material sacrifices had power to cleanse the soul; a number of sources show that some Greco-Roman writers also shared this view.

The second purpose is to stress that by the Lord's obedient sacrifice, he made the all-sufficient sacrifice through which the believer's conscience is fully cleansed, providing the way for her or him to gain access to the transforming power of grace. By that means, the disciple is prepared to enter into God's glory. In sum, "Christ's obedience empowers the faithful to live in obedience and in fellowship with God (see 10:5–10). [Each disciple comes] through him to God's 'throne' in order to find grace for living this life of faithfulness (4:14–16; 10:19–25)."[113]

According to Elder McConkie, these Hebrew Saints had "a working knowledge of the Lord's dealings with ancient Israel." Because of that, the author of Hebrews was able to "show them that the whole system of Mosaic laws, ordinances, and performances was so designed and ordained to typify and bear record of Christ. Speaking similarly to his Nephite brethren, Abinadi says, 'that all these things were types of things to come' (Mosiah 13:31)." He went on to note, "For more than 1400 years the Lord required Israel to perform rites and ordinances in such a way as to point attention forward to Christ and his atonement. Thus, to a people indoctrinated with the performances of the past, their fulfillment in Christ was the consummation of a glorious hope."[114]

---

113. Cockerill, *Epistle to the Hebrews,* 386.
114. McConkie, *Doctrinal New Testament Commentary,* 3:180.

Excursus on the Ritual of the Day of Atonement[115]

Although there were a number of festival days called for under the Mosaic law, the most solemn and important was the Day of Atonement, known in Hebrew to this day as Yom Kippur. The rites associated with the holy day are detailed in Leviticus 16. The sole purpose of the offerings, sacrifices, and ordinances executed on this day was for the expiation of all sins committed by the Israelites during that year, except for blasphemy.[116] In marked contrast to the other festival days, which had feasts and rejoicing, the Israelites fasted and solemnly sought God's forgiveness.[117] This was the only day of the year that the high priest was allowed into the Holy of Holies, the inner room of the tabernacle or temple. The specific steps the law required mark the importance and uniqueness of this event. On the importance of this ritual, Elder Bruce R. McConkie stated,

> The atonement of the Lord Jesus Christ . . . is what the law of Moses is all about. The law itself was given so that men might believe in Christ and know that salvation comes in and through his atoning sacrifice and in no other way. Every principle, every precept, every doctrinal teaching, every rite, ordinance, and performance, every word and act—all that appertained to, was revealed in, and grew out of the ministry of Moses, and all the prophets who followed him—all of it was designed and prepared to enable men to believe in Christ, to submit to his laws, and to gain the full blessings of that atonement which he alone could accomplish. And the chief symbolisms, the most perfect similitudes, the types and shadows without peer, were displayed before all the people once each year, on the Day of Atonement.[118]

The fast was celebrated on the tenth day of the seventh month of each year. Instead of wearing his richly embroidered and ornamented robes, the high priest wore white garments that, though similar to a regular priest's attire, were made of pure linen and served to symbolically mark his entrance into

115. Much of this material comes from an unpublished paper by Nathaniel Pribil, in possession of the authors.

116. Walter C. Kaiser Jr., "The Book of Leviticus," in *The New Interpreter's Bible* (Nashville: Abingdon Press, 1994), 1:1009–10; see also John E. Hartley, *Leviticus,* vol. 4 of Word Biblical Commentary (Dallas: Word Books, 1992), lxx–lxii; Jacob Milgrom, *Leviticus 1–16,* vol. 3 of the Anchor Bible (New York: Doubleday, 1991), 175–76.

117. Hartly, *Leviticus,* 243.

118. McConkie, *Promised Messiah,* 435.

the heavenly court.[119] The fast began with the high priest taking "a bullock as a sin offering and a ram as a burnt offering for himself and his house; and two he-goats as a sin offering and a ram as a burnt offering for the congregation of Israel. He presented the bullock and the two goats before the door of the tabernacle. He then cast lots upon the two goats. One was to be for the Lord for a sin offering. The other was for Azazel (the completely separate one, the evil spirit regarded as dwelling in the desert), to be sent away alive into the wilderness."[120] One scholar, exploring the importance of this part of the ritual, stated,

> Every drama must have a conflict, and nothing is more impressive than the manner in which the problem of evil was treated in the temple. The showdown is of course between good and evil; and these, following the usual temple practice, are represented figuratively or by proxy. Before the altar in Jerusalem all the sins and vices of the people were shifted to the figure of a scapegoat, which thereby became an object of utter loathing, a *pharmakos* ["sorcerer"], an embodiment of all evil, driven out into the wilderness to perish, taking all the sins of the people with him. . . . In the scapegoat, Israel recognized that the enemy they were driving with stones and curses was the evil that was in themselves. They were the bad guys.[121]

The rules dictated that the high priest enter the Holy of Holies three times: first with a censer and incense that he burned to set up smoke, ostensibly in order to hide himself from the divine presence as a means of protecting himself (Lev. 16:12–13)[122]; next with the blood of the sacrificial bull that he sprinkled seven times before the mercy seat (Lev. 16:14); and finally with the blood of the sacrificial goat that he also sprinkled before the mercy seat (Lev. 16:15).

Returning to the courtyard of the tabernacle, he laid both hands on the second goat, known as the "scapegoat," and, by that means, put all the sins of Israel on it. The goat was then driven into the wilderness to die and in that way symbolically removed all the iniquities of the people. Once that was done, the blood and remains of both the sacrificial bull and goat were burned outside of the camp. Then the high priest changed back into his regular vestment and closed the ritual by making a burnt offering for himself and for the people. Through these means, Jehovah declared that the sins of Israel would be removed and their negative effects nullified.[123]

---

119. Milgrom, *Leviticus 1–16,* 1016.
120. "Bible Dictionary," s.v. "Fasts."
121. Hugh Nibley, *Temple and Cosmos,* ed. Don E. Norton (Salt Lake City: Deseret Book, 1992), 74–75.
122. Kaiser, "Book of Leviticus," 1:1111.
123. Hartly, *Leviticus,* 244.

He Offered Himself without Spot to God (9:11–14)

Greek Text

11 Χριστὸς δὲ παραγενόμενος ἀρχιερεὺς τῶν γενομένων ἀγαθῶν διὰ τῆς μείζονος καὶ τελειοτέρας σκηνῆς οὐ χειροποιήτου, τοῦτ᾽ ἔστιν οὐ ταύτης τῆς κτίσεως, 12 οὐδὲ δι᾽ αἵματος τράγων καὶ μόσχων διὰ δὲ τοῦ ἰδίου αἵματος, εἰσῆλθεν ἐφάπαξ εἰς τὰ ἅγια, αἰωνίαν λύτρωσιν εὑράμενος. 13 εἰ γὰρ τὸ αἷμα τράγων καὶ ταύρων καὶ σποδὸς δαμάλεως ῥαντίζουσα τοὺς κεκοινωμένους ἁγιάζει πρὸς τὴν τῆς σαρκὸς καθαρότητα, 14 πόσῳ μᾶλλον τὸ αἷμα τοῦ Χριστοῦ, ὃς διὰ πνεύματος αἰωνίου ἑαυτὸν προσήνεγκεν ἄμωμον τῷ θεῷ, καθαριεῖ τὴν συνείδησιν ἡμῶν ἀπὸ νεκρῶν ἔργων εἰς τὸ λατρεύειν θεῷ ζῶντι. [SBLGNT]

King James Version

11 But Christ being come an high priest of good things to come, by a greater and more perfect tabernacle, not made with hands, that is to say, not of this building; 12 Neither by the blood of goats and calves, but by his own blood he entered in once into the holy place, having obtained eternal redemption for us. 13 For if the blood of bulls and of goats, and the ashes of an heifer sprinkling the unclean, sanctifieth to the purifying of the flesh: 14 How much more shall the blood of Christ, who through the eternal Spirit offered himself without spot to God, purge your conscience from dead works to serve the living God?

New Rendition

11 But when Christ came, a high priest of good things that have come, he passed through the greater and more perfect tent that was not made by human hands, that is not of this creation. 12 And it was not by the blood of goats and calves, but by his own blood that he entered once for all into the Holy Place after he, by himself, had obtained eternal redemption. 13 For if the blood of goats and bulls, and the ashes of a heifer sprinkled on those who are impure sanctifies them so that their bodies are cleansed, 14 how much more does the blood of Christ, who through the eternal Spirit offered himself as an unblemished offering to God, cleanse our conscience from dead works to worship the living God.

Translation Notes and Comments

9:11–12 These verses constitute one long sentence that is somewhat hard to follow. We have broken it into two sentences based on the following reasoning. Though the aorist participle παραγενόμενος (*paragenomenos*), translated as "when [Christ] came," is technically dependent on the main verb of verse 12, εἰσῆλθεν (*eisēlthen*), "he entered," the author's forceful affirmation that contrasts Christ's sacrifice with that of the Mosaic covenant suggests that the participle be taken as a coordinate of the main verb. That being the case, we have translated the participle as a finite verb and made verse 11 its own sentence.[124]

9:11 ***Christ being come an high priest of good things to come / But when Christ came, a high priest of good things that have come:*** That the author begins this section of his argument with the noun Χριστός (*Christos*), "Christ," is important;[125] it draws attention to and puts focus on the title that the Savior bore. The Greek noun is a translation of the Hebrew מָשִׁיחַ (*māšîaḥ*), "Messiah," derived from the trilateral root משח (*msḥ*), meaning "to anoint." In the Israelite culture, an anointing set one apart from others in such positions as king and priest. The title gained a more focused meaning during the postexilic period. Some Jews viewed the title as designating a future high priest or royal figure anointed by God to raise the Jewish nation to a position of power and authority.[126] Though the author of Hebrews shows no interest in Jesus as a temporal king or earthly priest, he uses the nuances of the title that brought the two offices together to his advantage. He however changed the focus from earth to heaven and from temporal salvation to eternal.[127]

The adversative particle δέ (*de*), "but," acts as the complement of μὲν οὖν (*men oun*) in 9:1. The two act together to emphasize the point being made. The nuance of the former is "on the one hand" while the latter means "on the other hand."[128]

The verb παραγίνομαι (*paraginomai*), "to come" or "arrive," found here as an aorist middle participle, is used circumstantially and is thus translated as "when . . . [he] came."[129] In this case, the author apparently had heaven in mind.[130] When the Savior arrived there, he did so in his position as High Priest.[131] The verb emphasizes that Jesus did not usurp this authority upon entering heaven but was given it before he arrived.[132]

---

124. Cockerill, *Epistle to the Hebrews,* 389.

125. Vanhoye, *Letter to the Hebrews,* 142.

126. On the anointed priest, see 11Q13 18; 1QS 9:11; 1Q28a 2:14, 20; and as a royal figure, see CD 12:23–24; 14:19; 19:10–11. In Christian apocryphal sources, see *2 Bar.* 29:3; 30:1; 72:2; *4 Ezra* 12:32.

127. Due to the influence of late first- and second-century Christian thinkers, there developed in the community the idea that the Jews expected a delivering Messiah. That view of the future "anointed one," however, was never very strong among the majority of Jews. For analysis, see Jorge, "Messiah," in Freedman, *Anchor Bible Dictionary,* 4:777–88.

128. Wallace, *Greek Grammar,* 672; Lane, *Hebrews 9–13,* 229 note a.

129. BDAG, 760–61.

130. Koester, *Hebrews,* 407; Attridge, *Epistle to the Hebrews,* 245.

131. Ellingworth, *Epistle to the Hebrews,* 449.

132. Koester, *Hebrews,* 412.

The adjective ἀγαθός (*agathos*) acts here as a substantive and as such denotes "good things,"[133] meaning, in this case, Christ's self-offering in behalf of his people that brought them a personal and present cleansing from sin.[134]

by a greater and more perfect tabernacle / he passed through the greater and more perfect tent: There is some disagreement concerning what this passage says about the author's cosmology, particularly if he views heaven as having various levels or degrees.[135] Taking the passage as it stands, the author is apparently not making a statement about the nature of heaven, but about Christ and the result of his Atonement, namely entering into the heavenly realm as High Priest and Savior.

The preposition διά (*dia*) can act as a marker for either an extension through an area ("to pass through") or of instrumentality or circumstances by which something happens ("by means of, via, through").[136] While the KJV takes the latter view, our Rendition takes the former because the "tent" was not the means by which the "good things" came about, but the Savior's Atonement was. In fact, the author makes clear that it is *through* Christ's blood that cleaning comes.[137]

As noted at 8:2, the "greater and more perfect tent" (σκηνή, *skēnē*) is heaven through which the Lord passed to take up his divine position on the right hand of God. That is not to say that he passed from one heaven to get to another, but rather he passed through heaven as a king may have to pass through his throne room to get to his throne.[138] The comparative

---

133. BDAG, 3–4.

134. This interpretation is based on accepting the reading of those manuscripts that have τῶν γενομένων ἀγαθων (*tōn genomenōn agathōn*), "good things that have come," rather than those that read τῶν μελλόντων ἀγαθῶν (*tōn mellontōn agathōn*), "good things about to come." The former look to the Atonement of the Lord and what grows out of it, the latter to the promise of eternal life which he affords. The manuscript tradition is about equally split, but because of the author's emphasis on the accomplished fact of the Lord's Atonement and because the former manuscripts are slightly better for this reading, we have followed them in our Rendition. We need to note, however, that the two ideas are so interconnected that only technically can they be separated. See also Cockerill, *Epistle to the Hebrews,* 390. See Metzger, *Textual Commentary,* 598. Hughes, "Blood of Jesus and His Heavenly Priesthood," 313–14, argues that, on the basis of the Savior's work, there is no celestial "Holy Place" distinct from the "Most Holy Place."

135. For discussion, see Ellingworth, *Epistle to the Hebrews,* 445–47.

136. BDAG, 223–26.

137. See Translation Notes and Analysis on 9:14; Vanhoye, *Letter to the Hebrews,* 145.

138. Some scholars have suggested that Jesus passed through the heavens, meaning the sky, to get to the realm where the Father dwells. This does not work because "the

μείζονος (*meizonos*), "greater," connotes dignity and grandeur rather than dimension.[139]

not made with hands, that is to say, not of this building / that was not made by human hands, that is not of this creation: The noun κτίσις (*ktisis*) denotes something created and often refers to the work of God.[140] Here it refers to the σκηνή (*skēnē*), "tent," which represents heaven. Some commentators, however, see the *skēnē* as representing the body of Christ.[141] Since, however, the author is clear that he is referring to something not of earthly creation, it seems likely that he is referring not to the Savior's body but to the heavenly realm through which the Savior passed to take his place at the Father's side. Others have put forward the idea that there is a close correspondence between earth and heaven such that there is a heavenly tabernacle, that is, an intermediary heaven through which Christ passed. This idea falls short because such would be of the temporal order and therefore "of this creation" and pass away when it does.[142]

9:12 ***Neither by the blood of goats and calves / it was not by the blood of goats and calves:*** The author uses this phrase to capture all of the Mosaic sacrifices. He is careful to put an emphasis on the presentation of the victims' blood in order to highlight the point he wishes to make.

by his own blood he entered in once into the holy place / by his own blood that he entered once for all into the Holy Place: With this phrase and the one that follows, the author makes the point not only of this section of his argument but of the whole chapter. Two ideas need to be stressed. The first is caught in the phrase διὰ . . . τοῦ ἰδίου αἵματος (*dia . . . tou idiou haimatos*), literally "by his own blood." The author is careful to not to intimate that Jesus carried blood into the next realm, but rather the author emphasizes that by the means of Jesus' blood—that is, the effects of his

---

heavens" are part of the created order, and the author is clear that the heaven he is referring to is.not. Others have proposed that there is an intermediary heaven between earth and the celestial realm. For a study, see Cody, *Heavenly Sanctuary,* 77–107. Both ideas are superfluous to the author's point. His description of the place as "true" and "greater and more perfect" suggests he has the dwelling place of God in mind. See Cockerill, *Epistle to the Hebrews,* 392.

139. Johnson, *Hebrews,* 235. Note that the author uses the term to implicitly denote God and his reward in 6:13, 16.

140. BDAG, 572–73.

141. For discussion, see Vanhoye, *Letter to the Hebrews,* 145–47; Ellingworth, *Epistle to the Hebrews,* 447–48. Hughes, "Blood of Jesus and His Heavenly Priesthood," 305–9, surveys the various theories on how the "tent" is the symbol of Christ's body.

142. Vanhoye, *Letter to the Hebrews,* 145.

Atonement—he entered the heavenly realm. The author's emphasis here is Jesus did not offer the blood of vicarious sacrifices, as did the high priest, but gave his *own* blood.[143]

The second idea is caught in the phrase εἰσῆλθεν ἐφάπαξ (*eisēlthen ephapax*), "entered once for all." The adverb *ephapax* denotes an action "taking place once and to the exclusion of any further occurrence."[144] Through this statement, the author stresses that the Lord's Atonement was fully sufficient, thus never having to be performed again, and therefore he had a permanent place in God's presence.

The author states the Savior entered τὰ ἅγια (*ta hagia*), "the Holy Place."[145] Up to this point, the author has used this phrase to denote the "first tent" or first section of the Mosaic tabernacle. Here, he uses it to denote the heavenly realm that is in reality *the* Holy Place of which the tabernacle as a whole was but a model.

having obtained eternal redemption for us / after he, by himself, had obtained eternal redemption: This phrase is critical to the author's point. The verb εὑρίσκω (*heuriskō*) denotes the obtaining or securing of something sought for,[146] in this case αἰωνίαν λύτρωσιν (*aiōnian lytrōsin*), "eternal redemption." The verb is found here as a circumstantial aorist participle in the middle voice used in a temporal sense. The voice is often used to indicate that the subject acts *for* or *by* him- or herself.[147] Thus, we have translated the phrase, "after he, by himself, had obtained eternal redemption." That is to say, he did not enter and *thus* obtain eternal redemption, but he entered *after* he had obtained that redemption. He obtained it in Gethsemane and on Golgotha.[148] The adjective αἰώνιος (*aiōnios*), "eternal," is important because it underscores not just the quality but also the quantity of the deliverance that God grants; never will sin or death have any hold on the redeemed.

---

143. Cockerill, *Epistle to the Hebrews,* 393.

144. BDAG, 417.

145. This is in fact a neuter plural in form but singular in sense. BDAG, 11.

146. Louw-Nida, §13.17; BDAG, 411–12.

147. Wallace, *Greek Grammar,* 418–19.

148. Though some scholars have suggested on the basis of the Day of Atonement ritual that Jesus brought his own blood into heaven, this simply pushes the typology of the ritual too far. For discussion, see Bruce, *Epistle to the Hebrews,* 213–14; Cockerill, *Epistle to the Hebrews,* 394–95; O'Brien, *Letter to the Hebrews,* 321 n. 89; Vanhoye, *Letter to the Hebrews,* 143. Of note is that Jesus does plead with the Father in behalf of his people, saying, "Behold the blood of thy Son which was shed, the blood of him whom thou gavest that thyself might be glorified" (D&C 45:4), but this does not necessitate the blood being actually present, only remembered.

The noun λύτρωσις (*lytrōsis*), "redemption," in general, denotes the "experience of being liberated from an oppressive situation."[149] It is related to the noun λύτρον (*lytron*), "a ransom"—that is, the price demanded to free someone from captivity or punishment—and to the verb λυτρόω (*lytroō*)—to free someone by paying the demanded ransom.[150] In a religious context, *lytrōsis* refers to the Savior's deliverance of the repentant soul from guilt, sin, and death by his offering a commensurate expenditure, in this case, his blood. The noun ἀπολύτρωσις (*apolytrōsis*), "release, deliverance," expresses the result (see Luke 21:28; Rom. 3:24; 8:23; Eph. 1:7; 4:30; and Col. 1:14) but also carries the idea that the demanded ransom has been fully paid.[151]

The phrase "for us," as found in the KJV, is not supported by any Greek manuscripts and is therefore left out of our Rendition.

9:13 *For if the blood . . . and the ashes . . . sanctifieth to the purifying of the flesh / For if the blood . . . and the ashes . . . sanctifies them so that their bodies are cleansed:* The author here admits that the Mosaic rituals had their effect: they sanctified. The verb ἁγιάζω (*hagiazō*), "to sanctify," denotes the act of setting something apart so that it can be properly used for ritual purposes. So far as people are concerned, it denotes the act of eliminating any cultic impurities so that a person can be included in holy services or moral associations.[152] Here the verb connotes the preparation of the Israelite for worship at the tabernacle and continued membership in the community at large.

Jehovah gave the sacrifices of the Mosaic law to achieve this state, and they worked, but only up to a point. Their focus was on the σάρξ (*sarks*), "flesh," the noun here connoting conformance to outward standards of morality.[153] By performing the sacrifices dictated by the law, the worshiper was purified or cleansed from physical contamination. In sum, the preparation resulted in the achievement of a state of καθαρότης (*katharotēs*), "cultic purity."[154]

149. BDAG, 606; Johnson, *Hebrews,* 236; Ellingworth, *Epistle to the Hebrews,* 453. The only other place the word appears in the New Testament is in Luke 2:38. Louw-Nida, §37.128, translates the word as "liberation." The LXX uses the verb in reference to Jehovah's freeing Israel from Egyptian bondage. See Ex. 6:6; 13:15; 15:13; and Deut. 7:8; 9:26; 13:5.

150. BDAG, 606.

151. BDAG, 117; Louw-Nida, §37.128. For discussion, see Johnson, *Hebrews,* 236.

152. BDAG, 9–10; Vanhoye, *Letter to the Hebrews,* 147–48.

153. Louw-Nida, §26.7; BDAG, 915–16.

154. BDAG, 490.

9:14 ***How much more:*** With the phrase πόσῳ μᾶλλον (*posō mallon*), "by how much more," the author concludes the *qal waḥomer* or the *a fortiori* argument begun in 9:13.[155] The phrase's force serves to stress the vast difference between what the Mosaic offerings did and what Christ has done.

who through the eternal Spirit offered himself without spot to God / who through the eternal Spirit offered himself as an unblemished offering to God: The phrase διὰ πνεύματος αἰωνίου (*dia pneumatos aiōniou*) is translated as "through the eternal spirit."[156] The meaning of the phrase is very difficult to determine. The preposition διὰ (*dia*), "through," serves here as a marker of either instrumentality or agency by which an act is accomplished.[157] The question is whether the author has in mind either the Holy Spirit or Christ's spirit as the active agent or instrument. Did he offer himself up through the agency of his own spirit or through the instrumentality of the Holy Ghost?[158] The text gives no clear answer to the problem, but the author is clear on his main point: Jesus offered himself as a spotless sacrifice.

The adjective ἄμωμος (*amōmos*) denotes that which is without defect, blemish, or fault[159] and was a requirement of animals used for sacrifices under the Mosaic law.[160] The cultic nuance is carried over here (as it is in 1 Pet. 1:19) and emphasizes the typological nature of the Levitical sacrifices

---

155. On the nature and use of the *qal waḥomer* or *a fortiori* argument, see discussion in the introduction on page 30. This formulation, later codified by the rabbis, was designed to draw a conclusion that is inferred to be even more certain than another and to emphasize the distance between the consequences of two actions. For discussion, see Analysis for 2:1–4; and Johnson, *Hebrews,* 238.

156. A number of Greek texts do have πνεύματος ἁγίου (*pneumatos hagiou*), "Holy Spirit," of which the Textus Receptus (followed by the KJV translators) is one, but the majority read πνεύματος αἰωνίου (*pneumatos aiōniou*), "eternal Spirit." Those texts which have changed the wording likely show that the copyist understood "eternal Spirit" as a periphrasis of "Holy Spirit." Metzger, *Textual Commentary,* 598–99.

157. BDAG, 223–26. For arguments that the phrase refers to the Holy Spirit, see Bruce, *Epistle to the Hebrews,* 217; Vanhoye, *Letter to the Hebrews,* 149; and Büchel, *TDNT,* 4:339. For those who opt for Christ's spirit, see Geerhardus Vos, "The Priesthood of Christ in the Epistle to the Hebrews," *Princeton Theological Review* 5, no. 3 (1907): 423–47; and Schweizer, *TDNT,* 6:446. For analysis, see Cockerill, *Epistle to the Hebrews,* 397–98 with n. 53, who notes that the debate over whether the word refers to Jesus' spirit or the Holy Ghost detracts from the author's point that, one way or another, the Savior's atoning work was based on the power of God.

158. For discussion, see Johnson, *Hebrews,* 236.

159. BDAG, 56; Moulton and Milligan, *Vocabulary,* 28–29.

160. See Lev. 3–5; and Num. 28–29; compare Ezek. 43:22–25. It is used in the LXX to translate the Hebrew תָּמִים (*tāmîm*), which carried the nuances of "complete, undamaged, blameless, and perfect." BDB, 1070–71; *HAL,* 1748.

as prefiguring the qualifications of the Lord as *the* unblemished offering.[161] The word does not refer to some timeless holiness on the part of the Savior but specifically to the blamelessness that he achieved during his mortal mission and retains as the heavenly High Priest. His continual state of blamelessness while yet mortal is the basis for God's fully accepting the Lord's self-offering when the time came.[162]

the blood of Christ . . . purge your conscience / the blood of Christ . . . cleanse our conscience: There are important variants to this phrase. Whether this phrase reads "your [ὑμῶν, *hymōn*] conscience" or "our [ἡμῶν, *hēmōn*] conscience" is nearly equally divided among the ancient manuscripts. Because the author generally uses the second-person plural *hymōn* only in hortatory sections (which this is not), we have used *hēmōn* in our Rendition.[163] It seems very likely that the author would include himself as a beneficiary of the effects of the Lord's Atonement, showing he has first-hand knowledge of its healing effects.

On "conscience" (συνείδησις, *syneidēsis*), see 9:9 above with the associated Analysis. The verb καθαρίζω (*katharizō*), in the Old Testament sense of the word, denotes the process of ritual cleansing in order for a person to worship at the tabernacle, but the author uses the verb in the sense of cleansing from inward pollution, that is, to denote a purification from sin.[164] The nuance the author puts on the word, however, is the consciousness of the recipient of the cleansing effect of the Atonement in his or her life. They experience a clear conscience because faith in the Atonement has purged any feelings of guilt.

from dead works to serve the living God / from dead works to worship the living God: For a discussion of the phrase "dead works," see the Translation Notes for 6:1. Here we note the reference could be taken in either of two ways. First, it could refer to the ordinances of the Mosaic law that have now been superseded by those of the new covenant and thereby have become not only ineffective but also useless. As such they amount to little more than "dead works." Or second, it could refer to the results of a faithless nature that makes any ordinance a dead work because it is not efficacious for the sinful individual. Both ideas could be at play here.

161. See Lane, *Hebrews 9–13,* 240; and Johnson, *Hebrews,* 238.

162. This was a state he achieved and maintained in mortality and that has continued with him in heaven. Lane, *Hebrews 9–13,* 240; Ellingworth, *Epistle to the Hebrews,* 458; Cockerill, *Epistle to the Hebrews,* 400.

163. Metzger, *Textual Commentary,* 599.

164. BDAG, 488–89.

The verb λατρεύω (*latreuō*), "to serve" or "to worship," in a religious sense usually denotes cultic service, but the author of Hebrews uses it to describe not only the service of the priest but that of all of God's people (note 9:9; 10:1; 12:28).[165] The author here identifies a major reason the Savior did what he did: to put people in a position where, like him, they could effectively serve the Father through sincere worship.

Analysis and Summary

The author's use of the phrase "but . . . Christ" presents a sharp contrast between the focus of 9:1–10 and that of 9:11–14. He has shown the Holy Place provided no access to heaven, "but Christ" has now opened the way. The emphasis in the former section is on the tabernacle itself (although in 9:9b–10, the author does note that the insufficiency of the sacrifices of the old covenant was the reason access to God could not be obtained) while that of the latter is on the full sufficiency of the Lord's sacrifice that provides complete access to God. In this section, the author provides his most thorough analysis of the Savior's fulfillment of the typological sacrificial rites established by the Mosaic covenant. Throughout, the author emphasizes "blood," "self-sacrifice," and "cleansing." The author makes it clear in 9:12–14 the Savior was able to enter the heavenly realm and make way for others to do so because he did what the old covenant failed to do: he purged sins and cleansed the conscience of the worshiper. The author is careful to help his readers see that the whole of the Levitical system was restricted exclusively to external purification. The best it could do was point to that internal purification so necessary to enter the presence of God.[166]

From an Old Testament perspective, it was the victims' blood that contained a vital force capable of opposing and subduing evil and quashing spiritual death. In instituting the Mosaic rites, Jehovah explained that "the life of the flesh is in the blood, and I have given it to you on the altar to make atonement for your souls; for its blood shall make atonement for the soul" (Lev. 17:11, our translation; compare Deut. 12:23). "But in the sacrifice of Christ, the relation between blood and sacrifice is reversed: whereas

165. BDAG, 587; Moulton and Milligan, *Vocabulary,* 371; Strathmann, *TDNT,* 4:58–65; Attridge, *Epistle to the Hebrews,* 252; Cockerill, *Epistle to the Hebrews,* 401 n. 71.

166. Cockerill, *Epistle to the Hebrews,* 397; compare Ogden and Skinner, *Verse by Verse,* 257.

in the Old Testament it was the blood that gave value to the sacrifices, in the case of Christ, it is his sacrifice that gave value to his blood."[167]

Evidencing the fully sufficient work of Christ is the author's note in 9:11–12 that the Savior entered heaven "once for all" (ἐφάπαξ, *ephapax*), "a term that excludes both the necessity and the possibility of repetition."[168] The Savior's redeeming work was full, complete, and final, requiring nothing more, forever.[169]

In 9:14, the author clearly states the benefits of Christ's Atonement. The author first describes what it cleanses: "our conscience" (συνείδησις, *syneidēsis*). When God established his covenant with Israel, he also gave them his law. In doing so, he laid down the standard he expected his people to follow. At the same time, he created a condition in which the individual conscience had a standard external to itself. That meant a person did not decide what was right and what was wrong; the law did. The person, however, could choose to conform to the law or not. The result of choosing not to conform was identified by the noun "transgression" (παράβασις, *parabasis*).[170] Such an act was a heavy sin because the person knew the law and the consequences of breaking it and yet chose to do so. Even so, the Atonement of the Lord is so strong it can reach even those who have broken the law in this manner and redeem them if they will but repent and follow him.

The effect of the Lord's self-sacrifice was directed not at an outward cleansing as was the old covenant. Instead, it focused on the inward cleansing of "the conscience." The Atonement also had the effect of purifying it. Both cleansing and purifying refer to the same reality. Cleansing "emphasizes the removal of sinful pollutions," while purifying refers to "the readiness of the cleansed heart to approach God."[171] Taken together they denote the "moral transformation of the worshipper."[172]

---

167. Vanhoye, *Letter to the Hebrews,* 148. Noteworthy is that in D&C 45:4, the Savior pleads with the Father for his people on the basis of the blood he has shed. Compare McConkie, *Doctrinal New Testament Commentary,* 3:184–85; and Anderson, *Understanding Paul,* 215–19.

168. Lane, *Hebrews 9–13,* 239.

169. Stählin, *TDNT,* 1:383–84.

170. For a study, see Schneider, *TDNT,* 5:739–40.

171. Cockerill, *Epistle to the Hebrews,* 401.

172. Johnson, *Hebrews,* 238.

The term "conscience," as used by the author, carries much of the same nuance as does the term "heart" (καρδία, *kardia*).[173] Both refer to the center of a person's religious life that embraces "the whole person in relationship to God" and where each individual confronts God's holiness.[174] On the basis of the conscience and the heart, a person decides for himself or herself if they want to remain with the Father and Son in the heavenly realm (2 Ne. 9:46; Alma 5:15–25; 34:33–34).[175]

The author next states what the conscience is cleansed from, namely "dead works" (νεκρῶν ἔργων, *nekrōn ergon*). His reference is likely to the works of the Mosaic law. God instituted that law with its performances and ordinances to keep the Israelites "in remembrance of [him] and their duty towards him" (Mosiah 13:30). Paul referred to it as "a schoolmaster to bring us unto Christ" (Gal. 3:24), but seeing the Lord in the rituals of the law required an eye of faith. That was the intent from its institution. God designed the law to point the faith-filled to Christ. The lack of faith in the Savior on Israel's part made the law and its ordinances ineffective. As a result, even when the sacrifices were offered, they could not instill an inner state of purity and left an "evil, unbelieving heart" (NR 3:12) that became the seat for faithlessness, disobedience, and outright rebellion (3:7–4:11). As a result, the worshiper was not freed from propensities that led to misdeeds and the threat of spiritual death.

Finally, the author indicates the Atonement's positive result, namely the worshipers' ability to "serve the living God." With the sinful pollutions removed from the conscience, it is cleansed and the barrier between it and God is removed. This cleansing not only delivers the soul from the wrath of God but also enables it to enter the Holy Place, God's true sanctuary. But the Atonement does more; it acts in mortality to empower the worshiper to follow God's ways and have fellowship with him.[176] Thus, having realized the promise of the Atonement, they are not only prepared but also anxious to serve him in his way.

---

173. See Translation Notes on 4:12 with the associated Analysis. Though the word denotes the entire range of a person's mental and emotional condition, it connotes the hidden springs of a person's life. If that seat is impure, it shapes and therefore defiles all he or she does (Matt. 15:19, 20). On the other hand, if it is pure, it sanctifies all a person does. The heart is *the* sphere of divine influence (Rom. 2:15), having the same properties as the conscience in Acts 2:37 and 1 John 3:20. See Behm, *TDNT,* 3:611–14; and *NID,* s.v. "καρδία."

174. Lane, *Hebrews 9–13,* 240–41.

175. Cody, *Heavenly Sanctuary,* 151–55.

176. O'Brien, *Letter to the Hebrews,* 326.

Without the Shedding of Blood There Is No Forgiveness (9:15–22)

Greek Text

15 Καὶ διὰ τοῦτο διαθήκης καινῆς μεσίτης ἐστίν, ὅπως θανάτου γενομένου εἰς ἀπολύτρωσιν τῶν ἐπὶ τῇ πρώτῃ διαθήκῃ παραβάσεων τὴν ἐπαγγελίαν λάβωσιν οἱ κεκλημένοι τῆς αἰωνίου κληρονομίας. 16 ὅπου γὰρ διαθήκη, θάνατον ἀνάγκη φέρεσθαι τοῦ διαθεμένου· 17 διαθήκη γὰρ ἐπὶ νεκροῖς βεβαία, ἐπεὶ μήποτε ἰσχύει ὅτε ζῇ ὁ διαθέμενος. 18 ὅθεν οὐδὲ ἡ πρώτη χωρὶς αἵματος ἐγκεκαίνισται· 19 λαληθείσης γὰρ πάσης ἐντολῆς κατὰ τὸν νόμον ὑπὸ Μωϋσέως παντὶ τῷ λαῷ, λαβὼν τὸ αἷμα τῶν μόσχων μετὰ ὕδατος καὶ ἐρίου κοκκίνου καὶ ὑσσώπου αὐτό τε τὸ βιβλίον καὶ πάντα τὸν λαὸν ἐράντισεν, 20 λέγων· Τοῦτο τὸ αἷμα τῆς διαθήκης ἧς ἐνετείλατο πρὸς ὑμᾶς ὁ θεός· 21 καὶ τὴν σκηνὴν δὲ καὶ πάντα τὰ σκεύη τῆς λειτουργίας τῷ αἵματι ὁμοίως ἐράντισεν. 22 καὶ σχεδὸν ἐν αἵματι πάντα καθαρίζεται κατὰ τὸν νόμον, καὶ χωρὶς αἱματεκχυσίας οὐ γίνεται ἄφεσις. [SBLGNT]

King James Version

15 And for this cause he is the mediator of the new testament, that by means of death, for the redemption of the transgressions that were under the first testament, they which are called might receive the promise of eternal inheritance. 16 For where a testament is, there must also of necessity be the death of the testator. 17 For a testament is of force after men are dead: otherwise it is of no strength at all while the testator liveth. 18 Whereupon neither the first testament was dedicated without blood. 19 For when Moses had spoken every precept to all the people according to the law, he took the blood of calves and of goats, with water, and scarlet wool, and hyssop, and sprinkled both the book, and all the people, 20 Saying, This is the blood of the testament which God hath enjoined unto you. 21 Moreover he sprinkled with blood both the tabernacle, and all the vessels of the ministry.

New Rendition

15 And for this reason, Christ is the guarantor of a new covenant, so that those who have been called might receive the promise of an eternal inheritance through his death by which he redeemed them from the transgressions under the first covenant. 16 Now where there is a testamentary covenant, the testator's death must be established. 17 For a testamentary covenant is valid only with respect to dead people, since it is never in force while the testator is alive. 18 For this reason not even the first covenant was inaugurated without blood. 19 For after every commandment of the law had been declared to all the people by Moses, he took the blood of calves and of goats, with water, scarlet wool, and hyssop and sprinkled the scroll itself and all the people, 20 saying,

> "This is the blood of the covenant that God has commanded you to keep" [Ex. 24:8].

22 And almost all things are by the law purged with blood; and without shedding of blood is no remission.

21 He also sprinkled the tent and all of the things used in the worship service with blood. 22 Indeed almost everything is purified with blood according to the law, and without the shedding of blood there is no forgiveness.

Translation Notes and Comments

9:15 for this cause he is the mediator of the new testament / for this reason, Christ is the guarantor of a new covenant:[177] The phrase διὰ τοῦτο (*dia touto*), "on account of this" or "for this reason," points to the effective sacrifice of the Lord in 9:14. For the noun μεσίτης (*mesitēs*), "guarantor, mediator," see Translation Notes for 8:6. The importance of the word here is that it emphasizes the Savior's role as the one who guarantees that the promises of the new covenant will be fully realized by the faithful. For the phrase διαθήκης καινῆς (*diathēkēs kainēs*), "new covenant," see Translation Notes for 8:6 and 8:8 with the related Analysis.

that by means of death, for the redemption of the transgressions that were under the first testament, they which are called might receive the promise of eternal inheritance / so that those who have been called might receive the promise of an eternal inheritance through his death by which he redeemed them from the transgressions under the first covenant: This is a very complex sentence in Greek. A somewhat literal translation is, "so that, a death having occurred for the redemption of the transgressions under the first covenant, they who have been called might receive the promise of the eternal inheritance." In our Rendition, we have reordered the sentence and made some additions to make the sense clear in English. On "redemption," see Translation Notes for 9:12 above. On "transgression," see Translation Notes for 2:3.

In the present context, it is important to understand that the noun παράβασις (*parabasis*) denotes stepping over or transgressing against established bounds and in particular doing so with full knowledge that

177. There is some disagreement as to whether 9:15 should complete the argument presented in 9:11–14 or introduce that in 9:16–22. See Holzapfel and Wayment, *Making Sense,* 455; and Cockerill, *Epistle to the Hebrews,* 387–88. Because the phrase καὶ διὰ τοῦτο (*kai dia touto*), "and on account of this," points to the mediation of the Savior, it seemed best to us that the phrase should conclude this section. See Lane, *Hebrews 9–13,* 241; Johnson, *Hebrews,* 239; and O'Brien, *Letter to the Hebrews,* 327.

it is wrong.[178] Transgression is never inadvertent. It is the result of a willful and knowing choice to break a divine law.[179] The author of Hebrews has focused on Israel's rebellion against God due to their faithlessness. Yet he assures his readers that all who have broken the law from Moses' time to the present are not without hope. The sacrifice of Christ can still redeem them.[180] The author explains how redemption can come even to those whose sins amount to the weight of transgression. The Savior's self-sacrifice is simply that strong. The author does put a caveat on the breadth of the Lord's saving act. He does so with his use of the subjunctive aorist verb λάβωσιν (*labōsin*), "might receive." The subjunctive is the mood of probability but not certainty.[181] Here it indicates that there is a condition that must be met in order for salvation to occur. People must be numbered among οἱ κεκλημένοι (*hoi keklēmenoi*), "those who have been called."[182] These include all those who across time have responded or will respond to the voice of the Master and come unto him. The perfect passive participle found in this phrase gives an additional nuance to the author's words. Not only does it suggest current faithfulness but also carries the idea of continuous perseverance in the service of the Master.[183]

The author described the result with the words αἰωνίου κληρονομίας (*aiōniou klēronomias*), "an eternal inheritance." The noun κληρονομία (*klēronomia*) denotes an inheritance, something that is bequeathed to an heir due to the good wishes of the benefactor. Inheritances are unearned. By adding the adjective αἰώνιος (*aiōnios*), "eternal," the phrase points to transcendent salvation in the celestial kingdom.[184]

---

178. BDAG, 758; Schneider, TDNT, 5:739–40.

179. For a study, see *NID*, s.v. "παράβασις"; and Schneider, *TDNT*, 5:736–44.

180. B. J. Ribbens, "Forensic-Retributive Justification in Romans 3:21–26: Paul's Doctrine of Justification in Dialogue with Hebrews," *Catholic Biblical Quarterly* 74, no. 3 (2012): 548–67, argues that both Paul (Rom. 3:24–26) and the author of Hebrews (ch. 9–10) establish an early Jewish-Christian tradition of a retributive context for God's justification of his people. It is on this basis that those who respond to God's word will find themselves forgiven.

181. Wallace, *Greek Grammar*, 461–63.

182. The passive voice of verb καλέω (*kaleō*) means "to be called" or "invited." In a scriptural sense, it carries the nuance of being called or summoned as a witness. BDAG, 502–3; Moulton and Milligan, *Vocabulary*, 318. If that is the case here, then those who receive God's blessing are those who were not only summoned to bear witness of him and his Son but also fulfilled that task.

183. Cockerill, *Epistle to the Hebrews*, 403.

184. BDAG, 547–48; *NID*, s.v. "κλῆρος"; McConkie, *Doctrinal New Testament Commentary*, 3:184.

9:16–17 ***For where a testament is, there must also of necessity be the death of the testator. For a testament is of force after men are dead: otherwise it is of no strength at all while the testator liveth / Now where there is a testamentary covenant, the testator's death must be established, for a testamentary covenant is valid only with respect to dead people, since it is never in force while the testator is alive:*** Due to the complexity of the issues these two verses create, we analyze them together.

Just what the author intended in these verses has caused a good deal of discussion. The problem centers on how the noun διαθήκη (*diathēkē*) is interpreted. The Greek word denotes "a last will and testament," "a contract," and "a covenant."[185] In secular Greek from the fifth century BC into the New Testament period, the noun uniformly referred to a last will and testament and nothing else. Analyses show that the noun pointed to an "'arrangement' made by one party with plenary power, which the other party may accept or reject, but cannot alter."[186] A last will and testament is the primary example. The Jewish translators of the LXX, however, were not bound by Greek constraints. They saw in the word a close enough parallel to the Hebrew בְּרִית (*bĕrît*), "covenant," to use it as their translation of the noun. What seems to have appealed to them was that a covenant between God and man was not a "compact," that is, a negotiated agreement between equals. The standards of any covenant are set by God and him alone.[187] The unilateral aspect of the word *diathēkē* proved to be exactly the nuance the translators needed for an agreement between Jehovah and Israel, and they used the word consistently to denote that kind of covenant.[188]

The question arises, which of these two nuances, "will" or "covenant," was at play among the Christians during the New Testament period? For Diaspora Jews (those who resided outside of Palestine) such as Paul and the author of Hebrews, the two nuances could have easily and freely mingled. Though the idea of covenant likely dominated, the idea of will was not

---

185. BDAG, 228; see also McConkie, *Doctrinal New Testament Commentary,* 3:183. Compare Ogden and Skinner, *Verse by Verse,* 257.

186. Moulton and Milligan, *Vocabulary,* 148–49.

187. The LXX does use the term for "parity treaties" between equals (for example, see Gen. 21:27; and 1 Sam. 18:3), secular agreements of which Jehovah was called upon as witness (for example, see Gen. 31:44–50), arrangements between a superior with those in his charge (for example, see Jer. 34:8), and of a conqueror's agreement with a subjugated people (for example, see Josh. 9:11–15).

188. Moulton and Milligan, *Vocabulary,* 148–49.

far distant and therefore influenced them.[189] In 9:16–17, as translated in the KJV, we can see a possible intermingling of ideas, and that intermingling does lend itself to a certain inconsistency on the author's part, for everywhere else in his work, *diathēkē* means "covenant."[190] Even so, that the author, who is very skilled in the Greek language, uses the middle voice with the aorist participle of *diatithēmi* seems to bear out that he knew of his inconsistent use here. The verb means to "arrange for the disposition of property after one's death."[191] The middle voice shows that the person is performing this act for and in behalf of himself.[192] If the author had used the passive voice, then the phrase would show that someone or something else was performing an act for the person. That would make a strong argument that the death needed to activate the agreement was that of a sacrificial animal. The author, however, did not use the passive voice here. Thus, grammar rules out the idea of the sacrificial offering being the one that gives its life to initiate the agreement. Something or someone else must do it.

The JST 9:16–18 shows that Joseph Smith recognized the inconsistency in the KJV and gave the idea of covenant full billing. It reads, "For where a covenant is, there must also of necessity be the death of the [sacrificial] victim. For a covenant is of force after the victim is dead; otherwise it is of no strength at all while the victim liveth. Wherefore neither first covenant was dedicated without blood." The change from the emphasis in the KJV

---

189. In Gal. 3:15–17, Paul speaks of "a man's agreement" (*diathēkē,* translated as "covenant" in the KJV) that, once attested, could not be changed or annulled. He goes on to state that the Mosaic covenant was the same way. Once it was confirmed, it, too, could not be changed or annulled. That is the reason Jesus did not replace or in any way abrogate the old covenant but fulfilled it by satisfying all of its requirements (Matt. 5:17–19).

190. Moulton and Milligan, *Vocabulary,* 148–49. Most commentators accept this view believing that the author is "deliberately and for a limited purpose, comparing two different institutions (divine covenant and human wills) insofar as death happens to be associated with both." See *NID,* s.v. "διαθήκη," and especially 1:700. Compare Ellingworth, *Epistle to the Hebrews,* 462–63. Noteworthy is that the author certainly does not try to equate the Mosaic covenant with a human will. That there were sacrifices associated with divine covenant stresses that the author saw it as very different from human wills. Even so, there could have been some overlapping in the early Christians' understanding of the concept.

Wilford Woodruff, in *Journal of Discourses,* 21:194; and B. H. Roberts, in *Journal of Discourses,* 25:143, used the idea that a testament requires the death of the testator to explain that the deaths of Joseph and Hyrum Smith, along with other martyrs, were necessary in order to put a seal on and witness to the work of this dispensation.

191. BDAG, 238.

192. Wallace, *Greek Grammar,* 414–15.

suggests that Joseph Smith understood the covenant ritual. A covenant was not in force until the covenant-victim had been sacrificed, its shed blood initiating, ratifying, and sealing the covenant. Thus, the JST places the initiation of the covenant on the death of the covenant-victim.

Though a good argument can be made for understanding *diathēkē,* in the present context, either as "will" or as "covenant,"[193] we felt that "will," due to grammatical considerations, the arguments of a number of scholars, the nearly universal translation of *diathēkē* as "will" in various translations of this verse, and the weight of the JST, made for the stronger case. In doing so, we recognize the unusual inconsistency in the author's presentation, but we can see why he is doing it. As one authority asked, "What is the necessary connection between the death of Christ and the new διαθήκη?" and then rejoined, "The author answers in v. 16 f., not with a material argument as in v. 11 ff., but with a formal *argumentum ad hominem.* . . . If a διαθήκη is to come into force, death is presupposed. In light of the external similarity that there is both death and a διαθήκη, he jumps from the religious to the current legal sense of διαθήκη, even at the risk of involving himself in contradictions which show there is no real parallel."[194] But we must admit that, when all is said and done, there is no real theological importance whichever choice is made. That being said, it needs to be kept in mind that a will is a type of covenant. Thus, we have used the phrase "testamentary covenant" for *diathēkē* in our Rendition.[195]

9:18 *Whereupon neither the first testament was dedicated without blood / For this reason not even the first covenant was inaugurated without blood:* The conjunction ὅθεν (*othen*), "for this reason," acts as a marker for the basis of an action.[196] Here it puts stress on the need for blood to both inaugurate and ratify the Mosaic covenant. The verb ἐγκαινίζω (*engkainizō*) denotes those aspects. It means "to cause something to come

---

193. For examples of those scholars who view *diathēkē* as "covenant," see John Hughes, "Hebrews IX 15ff. and Galatians III 15ff.: A Study in Covenant Practice and Procedure," *Novum Testamentum* 21, no. 1 (1979): 27–96; Scott W. Hahn, "A Broken Covenant and the Curse of Death: A Study of Hebrews 9:15–22," *Catholic Biblical Quarterly* 66, no. 3 (2004): 416–36; and Cockerill, *Epistle to the Hebrews,* 405–7. For those examples of those who view it as "will," see Behm, *TDNT,* 2:131–32; Moulton and Milligan, *Vocabulary,* 148–49; and Ellingworth, *Epistle to the Hebrews,* 462–64.

194. Behm, *TDNT,* 2:131. For Behm's entire treatment on the subject of διαθήκη, see pp. 104–34.

195. Following Bruce, *Epistle to the Hebrews,* 219 and n. 100.

196. BDAG, 692–93.

into being" or "to take effect."[197] The emphasis is on the newness of the thing being established and therefore points to not only the law's inauguration but also to its ratification. The initial shedding of the blood and then its administration inaugurated the first covenant and thereafter acted to ratify it before the Israelites. Not until this action had taken place was the covenantal law valid and effective.[198] Once the act was done, however, the law was in full force and the penalty for breaking it could be imposed. Further, the continued practice of blood-offerings made effective the objective—specifically expiation—of the varied rituals of the Mosaic law.

9:19 ***For when Moses had spoken every precept to all the people according to the law / For after every commandment of the law had been declared to all the people by Moses:*** The conjunction γάρ (*gar*), "for," signals that the author is now going to verify his point. To do so, he appeals to scripture (Ex. 24:3–8). He shows that there was an order in which the covenant was inaugurated and ratified. The first step was the declaration of the law before those upon whom it would take effect. The phrase πάσης ἐντολῆς (*pasēs entolēs*), "every commandment," connotes that Moses declared before the people the full extent of the law. The phrase παντὶ τῷ λαῷ (*panti tō laō*), "all the people," points out that no one who would be affected by the law was left out. Even though the author does not mention that the people also accepted it, such is implied.

he took the blood of calves and of goats, with water, and scarlet wool, and hyssop, and sprinkled both the book, and all the people / he took the blood of calves and of goats, with water, scarlet wool, and hyssop and sprinkled the scroll itself and all the people: The second step in the law's ratification was the administration of the blood. The noun βιβλίον (*biblion*) denotes a "scroll"[199] (books would not come into common use until the late second century AD). In preparation for the ratification ceremony, Moses recorded the full law on a scroll and then set it before the congregation of Israel (Ex. 24:4). He then placed a solution consisting of water and the blood of calves and goats into a bowl.[200] He also made an aspergillum (a liturgical brush) by binding stocks of the herb hyssop with a red woolen

---

197. Louw-Nida, §13.85; BDAG, 272; Attridge, *Epistle to the Hebrews,* 257 with n. 39.

198. BDAG, 272; Louw-Nida, §13.84.

199. BDAG, 176.

200. A number of Greek texts do not include the phrase καὶ τῶν τράγων (*kai tōn tragōn*), "and of goats." As it stands, it is parallel to the phrase in 9:12, and we have therefore left it in our Rendition. See Metzger, *Textual Commentary,* 599.

cord or strip of cloth. Using this instrument, he sprinkled the blood on the people and the scroll. By doing so, he symbolically bound the people and the law together.

The author actually supplies more information about this ceremony than is found in either the MT or the LXX biblical text. There it mentions only the sacrifice of an ox, used as a peace offering, whose blood was used in the ceremony. The text says nothing of calves or goats. It also does not mention the use of the aspergillum. The author may have had additional sources at his command or, to make his point, he added details of his own extrapolated from his knowledge of the law.[201]

9:20 ***This is the blood of the testament which God hath enjoined unto you / "this is the blood of the covenant that God has commanded you to keep":*** This verse describes that last step in the inauguration of the Mosaic law. The author quotes Exodus 24:8. The verb ἐντέλλομαι (*entellomai*) means to give instructions, orders, or commands. The nuance behind the word is that of the official sanction and authority on which the law rests.[202] His use of the word is telling. The LXX actually uses an aorist middle form of the verb διατίθημι (*diatithēmi*), which denotes the making of a formal agreement between parties.[203] The word in the MT is כָּרַת (*kārat*), literally "to cut," but when used together with בְּרִית (*bĕrît*), "covenant," it means "to make a covenant,"[204] and thus the Old Testament phrase can be translated as "the covenant Jehovah has made (or cut) with you." By replacing that verb with the stronger *entellomai,* the author is able to stress the official nature of the agreement and the divine authority that upholds it.

9:21 ***Moreover he sprinkled with blood both the tabernacle, and all the vessels of the ministry / He also sprinkled the tent and all of the things used in the worship service with blood:*** There is no biblical passage that states that this ritual took place. Again, the author may have had access to sources no longer available, or based on the law as a whole, he may have assumed this rite happened. The phrase does, however, help him set up the point that he makes in the next verse.

---

201. For example, water was used for the purification of cult officials, the people, and lepers (Num. 19:7–10; Lev. 14:5–9). According to Lev. 14:6, scarlet and hyssop along with cedar wood were used to make an aspergillum for the cleaning of the leper. For discussion, see Ellingworth, *Epistle to the Hebrews,* 468.

202. Louw-Nida, §33.329; BDAG, 339.

203. BDAG, 238.

204. BDB, 503–4. The cutting refers to the customary cutting of a sacrificial animal when making a covenant. *HAL,* 500.

9:22 ***And almost all things are by the law purged with blood / Indeed almost everything is purified with blood according to the law:*** In this phrase, the author is careful not to overstate his case. He uses the adverb σχεδόν (*schedon*) advisedly. It means "nearly" or "almost." Some aspects of ritual cleansing required water, not blood.[205] Even so, blood was the usual means of achieving purification and particularly expiation. As noted in 9:13, the verb καθαρίζω (*katharizō*), "cleanse, purify," in the Mosaic sense, denotes the process of ritual cleansing needed for participation in the worship at the tabernacle.[206] Here the idea is expanded to include the means of sanctifying by which the building and its accouterments were made ready for holy service.

and without shedding of blood is no remission / and without the shedding of blood there is no forgiveness: The noun αἱματεκχυσία (*haimatekchysia*) denotes "the shedding or pouring out of blood,"[207] but the author uses it to describe the blood offerings at the altar of the tabernacle as well as the atoning blood shed by the Lord.[208] The author's emphasis is on the effect of the administration of the blood, namely ἄφεσις (*aphesis*), which had two senses, the first being "freeing and liberating from something that confines, release" for example from captivity, and the second "freeing from an obligation, guilt, or punishment, pardon, cancellation."[209] It is in the second sense that it is used here with the emphasis on forgiveness or pardon from sins.

The author's sentence is vague because he specifies neither the kind of blood that needs to be shed nor what sin or sins are forgiven. However, many in the Greco-Roman world believed that blood sacrifices were

---

205. Cleansing agents included water (Lev. 15:10) and fire (Num. 31:23).

206. BDAG, 488–89. It is also associated with Greek mystery religions the nature of whose rites only the initiates could know. See Moulton and Milligan, *Vocabulary,* 311.

207. BDAG, 27.

208. Because the word is found nowhere else in the Greek biblical manuscripts, some have suggested it was coined by the author. See T. C. G. Thornton, "The Meaning of αἱματεκχυσία in Heb. IX. 22," *Journal of Theological Studies* 15, no. 1 (April 1964): 63–65. See also William G. Johnsson, "The Cultus of Hebrews in Twentieth-Century Scholarship," *Expository Times* 89, no. 4 (1978): 104–8, who argues that the word points specifically to the administering of the blood via sprinkling or pouring. See also Norman H. Young, "Αἱματεκχυσία: A Comment," *Expository Times* 90, no. 6 (1979): 180, who argues that Hebrews's use of the word is not intended to tie the meaning back to the sacrifices required under the old covenant but to emphasize how Christ's death involved the full-scale shedding of his blood. In that way, the Savior offered a superior method of redemption.

209. BDAG, 155.

necessary for purification. The context here suggests that the author, on the basis of the law, had sacrificial blood in mind.[210]

Analysis and Summary

In 9:15, the author clearly points out how Christ became the mediator (that is, the guarantor) of the new covenant: his blameless life made his self-offering acceptable to God. As a result, the Savior was able to redeem those who transgressed because of the weakness inherent in the first covenant. His sacrifice brought to an end all Mosaic sacrifices that could only cleanse "the flesh" (9:13). "Thus, by establishing an effective way of approaching God, [the Savior] terminated the Old Covenant as a way of salvation and inaugurated the New that it typified."[211] His sacrifice was, then, one of covenant inauguration. Of its new promise he became the mediator. His work in that capacity is not, however, that of a mere go-between, but that of the guarantee of the fulfillment of all promises that his Atonement makes possible.[212]

The author stresses in 9:15 that a major aspect of the Lord's sacrifice was to redeem those who were guilty of transgressing the first covenant. He focuses here on former transgressions committed under the Mosaic law because the Israelites' redemption from those sins laid the foundation that made the new covenant necessary. Their repentance made it necessary for Jehovah to write the new law on their hearts because they were justified through his forgiveness and could, thereby, receive the influence and power of the Holy Ghost (8:10; 10:16; Jer. 31:33).[213]

Note the Lord's sacrifice was retroactive, reaching back to all people of all ages. An angel declared to King Benjamin that Christ's "blood atoneth for the sins of those who have fallen by the transgression of Adam." He went on to say that those who lived before the coming of the Lord who believed "that Christ should come, the same might receive remission of their sins, and rejoice with exceedingly great joy, even as though he had already come among them" (Mosiah 3:11, 13).[214]

---

210. The idea that the shedding of a criminal's blood, especially for the sin of murder (Gen. 9:6), cannot be ruled out as a component in the author's thought. Vanhoye, *Letter to the Hebrews,* 155.

211. Cockerill, *Epistle to the Hebrews,* 402.

212. For a study of Christ's role as mediator, priest, guarantee, and minister, see Jerome H. Neyrey, "Jesus as Broker in Hebrews: Insights from the Social Sciences," in Mason and McCruden, *Reading the Epistle to the Hebrews,* 145–70.

213. Vanhoye, *Letter to the Hebrews,* 152.

214. It appears that the Atonement not only included sins committed from the beginning of human history but also those committed in the premortal existence. According

The author refers to those whose consciences have been cleansed as "those who have been called" (οἱ κεκλημένοι, *hoi keklēmenoi*). This group is composed not only of those whose lives are directed by faith and the resultant obedience but also who continually persevere in the service of the Master.[215] Notably, the author's words do not exclude those who rebelled during the Mosaic era.[216] There is a subtle hint here of vicarious work for the dead through which even those rebellious souls can become "the called" and, with the living, receive the promise of an eternal inheritance (see 1 Pet. 3:18–20; 4:6; compare Moses 7:37–39; D&C 76:73).

The author's words reveal both the breadth and width of the Lord's Atonement. Its breadth is vast, covering all those who throughout the entire history of the world come to him. Its width is very narrow, for it excludes all those who do not. The Lord himself made abundantly clear all must enter "at the strait gate: for wide is the gate, and broad is the way, that leadeth to destruction, and many there be which go in thereat: Because strait is the gate, and narrow is the way, which leadeth unto life, and few there be that find it" (Matt. 7:13–14; see also 2 Ne. 31:18; 33:9; 3 Ne. 27:33; and D&C 132:22).

Noteworthy is that the author's point, so carefully but briefly made in 9:12–15, is only an introduction to the theme. He will more fully develop the significance of the Mosaic sacrificial typology in 10:5–10 and reveal completely "the ultimate secret of Christ's effective self-offering."[217] Even so, the author is clear that redemption comes to all only by the means of the Savior's death (9:15). John Taylor stated,

---

to Alma 13:3, there was a "preparatory redemption" made for those who "in the first place" exercised faith in Christ and did "good works." The Atonement also allowed all to become innocent again in their infant state (D&C 93:38). See John W. Welch, "The Temple in the Book of Mormon: The Temples at the Cities of Nephi, Zarahemla, and Bountiful," in Parry, *Temples of the Ancient World,* 366; and Hyrum L. Andrus, *Doctrinal Commentary on the Pearl of Great Price,* rev. ed. (Salt Lake City: Deseret Book, 1967), 206.

215. Cockerill, *Epistle to the Hebrews,* 403. Those who composed this group may have roots that go back to the premortal existence. See Orson F. Whitney, *Saturday Night Thoughts: A Series of Dissertations on Spiritual, Historical, and Philosophic Themes* (Salt Lake City: Deseret Book, 1921), 129–30. This applies to those who are called to priesthood authority. As the author of Hebrews states, people do not take this honor upon themselves, but they must be called of God (5:4). Some of those to whom the author wrote were members of this group (3:1). In modern history, the Lord has noted that "many are called" but do not remain part of this group due to unfaithfulness (D&C 121:40; compare Matt. 24:14).

216. Johnson, *Hebrews,* 240.

217. Cockerill, *Epistle to the Hebrews,* 387.

> In some mysterious, incomprehensible way, Jesus assumed the responsibility which naturally would have devolved upon Adam; but which could only be accomplished through the mediation of Himself, and by taking upon Himself their sorrows, assuming their responsibilities, and bearing their transgressions or sins. In a manner to us incomprehensible and inexplicable, he bore the weight of the sins of the whole world; not only of Adam, but of his posterity; and in doing that, opened the kingdom of heaven, not only to all believers and all who obeyed the law of God, but to more than one-half of the human family who die before they come to years of maturity, as well as to the heathen, who, having died without law, will, through His mediation, be resurrected without law, and be judged without law, and thus participate, according to their capacity, works and worth, in the blessings of His atonement.[218]

As we look at the ransom model of the Atonement accepted by the author of Hebrews, the question naturally arises why God would demand the suffering and death of Jesus as the means of removing the consequences of sin from the Father's other children. Was there no other way the Father could free them except through such a brutal and torturous means? Neither in Hebrews nor in the New Testament as a whole and specifically in the recorded words of Jesus is this question ever addressed. The Savior made it clear that "the Son of Man came not to be served but to serve, and to give his life as a ransom for many" (Mark 10:45, our translation). These words are revealing because they show the voluntary nature of the self-sacrifice effected by the Lord. To stress the point, the Savior's words emphasize that his Atonement was a deliberate, willful act of obedience to God that allowed for a substitution in which one life could be given for others. That life paid the ransom that freed, potentially, all others from the consequences of sin and spiritual death. The scripture makes clear that the ransom is paid to God, allowing him to free others from the demands of justice and, if they will, let them come under the power of his mercy (see also 2 Ne. 9:26; and Alma 42:13–28).

The author of Hebrews takes this idea for granted. It was fitting that Christ should suffer and die to redeem his people and make them perfect, in respect to conscience (2:9–10; 9:9). Thus, the author never asks the question of why it was necessary for the Father to demand of the Son such a brutal death. The author is satisfied to understand it was simply necessary for the Savior to bow to the will of God by giving himself as the ransom.

218. Taylor, *Mediation and Atonement,* 148–49.

The author, therefore, leaves unexplored the reason behind the divine will (as do the other New Testament writers; compare Matt. 11:25–26; Mark 13:32; 14:35–36; 15:34). We can say that the

> complete subjection to God's will is an integral part of the service which Jesus renders to God. For Jesus, God does not owe anyone, not even the Son, a manifestation of His reasons, let alone a justification of His acts and demands. What God wills and does, He does for reasons which are holy, just and wise. But this does not mean that He will disclose the reasons. There is a purpose behind God's will; it is not caprice. But man can know this purpose only if and in so far as God reveals it to him. What is here revealed to man is that the death of Jesus is service to God, and that it is a vicarious death for many in virtue of which they find freedom from sin.[219]

Whatever else the case, Jesus serves as the model for devotion to God. Therefore, what he requires of the rest of us is no more than what he has given. His obedience is the essence, ground, and revelation of the law of sacrifice we as Christians are asked to follow.

In 9:15, the author clearly states the two goals of the Savior's death. The first was for the redemption of those who transgressed under the first covenant and looks specifically at those transgressions committed against the Mosaic law. The second goal was "so that those who [are] called might receive the promise of an eternal inheritance" (NR 9:15; compare Rom. 3:24–26). The phrase prefigures the promises Jehovah made with Abraham (1:8–16) and thereby designates eternal lives (see D&C 132:30–31).[220]

---

219. Büschel, *TDNT,* 4:344. Alma 42:22–23 states that "there is a law given" to which both a reward for keeping it and a punishment for breaking it were affixed. He also notes that due to the Atonement of Christ, "mercy claimeth the penitent" by satisfying the demands of the law. The scripture does not however identify who the giver or givers of the law were. According to D&C 132:8–12, God's house is a house of order and that order is based on the law that the Father and Son "ordained unto you, before the world was." These verses suggest that these two are the lawgivers. The scriptures clearly state, "All kingdoms have a law given" and "unto every law there are certain bounds also and conditions." Further, "that which is governed by law is also preserved by law and perfected and sanctified by the same" (D&C 84:34–38). Unfortunately, these facts do not explain why the law was such that the Son had to die. They do show God's demands are neither capricious nor absurd but based on law. All understood and agreed to these conditions before coming to this earth. Gerald N. Lund, "Plan of Salvation, Plan of Redemption," in Ludlow, *Encyclopedia of Mormonism,* 3:1088; Andrus, *God, Man, and the Universe,* 279–80. The one fact the Savior makes very clear is "no man shall come unto the Father but by me or by my word, which is my law" (D&C 132:12). Until God gives more information, the reason why he demanded a ransom in blood must rest there.

220. Johnson, *Hebrews,* 240.

In 9:18, the author make his point: as with most covenants, the Mosaic law was inaugurated and ratified by the death of the sacrificial victim and the administration of its blood.[221] To validate his point, in 9:19–20, the author appeals to Exodus 24:3–8. There the steps necessary to establish the covenant are recorded: Moses copied the law onto a scroll, he read its contents to the people, they covenanted to live the law, Moses inaugurated and ratified the covenant by sacrificing the required animals and sprinkling a solution of the sacrificial blood and water upon the scroll and people thus binding them together, and finally the prophet declared the law was then binding upon the people. To make his point, the author notes only that Moses read the law, inaugurated it by the sprinkling of blood, and declared its established validity.[222]

There is an insightful parallel between the Exodus account of the establishment of the Mosaic law and that of Matthew's account of Christ's inaugurating the new covenant at the Last Supper. "Moses 'took' the 'blood' and 'sprinkled' the people, saying, 'this is the blood of the covenant.' Christ 'took' the 'cup' and 'gave to his disciples saying, . . . for this is my blood of the [new] covenant.' Furthermore, 'without the shedding of blood there is no release' (v. 22) may echo the blood 'which is poured out for many for the forgiveness of sins' in Matt 26:28."[223] To what extent the author's readers would have been attuned to this nuance is unknown, but the close parallel suggests the author saw a connection between the establishment of the old covenant and the new.[224]

Having validated his position, the author makes his point: blood, and only blood, brings forgiveness. The author's appeal is to Jehovah's statement in Leviticus 17:11 that he has given to Israel the blood "upon the altar to make an atonement for your souls: for it is the [sacrifice's] blood that maketh an atonement for the soul."[225] The Hebrew verb translated "to atone" is כִּפֶּר (*kipper*). Its basic meaning is to "cover over" with the extended sense of "atone, make amends."[226] The purpose of such covering is to put a barrier between

221. See McConkie, *Doctrinal New Testament Commentary,* 3:183.

222. For discussion, see Johnson, *Hebrews,* 242.

223. Cockerill, *Epistle to the Hebrews,* 409.

224. Cockerill, *Epistle to the Hebrews,* 409; see also Ellingworth, *Epistle to the Hebrews,* 469.

225. In the LXX, the verb translated as "to atone" is ἐξιλάσκομαι (*exilaskomai*) and means "to appease." BDAG, 350. In its religious but broader context, it portrays the idea that sin causes the gods to become angry, and this can bring upon the offending party divine wrath. To appease them, a gift had to be given or an action completed. When such were offered and accepted, then gods were appeased and good relations restored.

226. BDB, 497–98.

a wrongful deed and its ill effects. When such a deed broke the relationship between persons, the purpose of the *kipper* was to expiate the wrongdoing and propitiate or placate the offended party. By this means, the offense was covered over and a good relationship restored.

The purpose of the Mosaic sacrifices was to atone for sin and thus bring about a reconciliation between the offender and Jehovah.[227] According to the view of sin during the Mosaic period, committing a transgression could not simply be forgotten and walked away from. The only way sin could be forgiven was by one of the expiatory rituals defined in the law. Jehovah allowed for the transgression to be passed onto a sacrificial animal and, with its death, the guilt to be removed from the person (Lev. 16:20–22; compare 17:11). The act emphasizes that God alone can forgive sins, but this requires an act of atonement that required something of the sinner.

However, some of Israel's prophets were well aware that a multitude of sacrifices would not satisfy God's offended righteousness (see Micah 6:7; and Ps. 50:7–15). In fact, only God could provide an acceptable atonement for sin that would act to assuage his wrath. This meant that his righteousness was neither implacable nor capricious because he was not only willing to but actually did provide a satisfactory substitute in place of the sinner. The priest at the altar, then, acted as a type for God who brought forth the requisite offering. This act emphasized that it was not so much the person's actions, though important, but God's that brought pardoning mercy. As the Christians saw it, the sacrifices of the Mosaic ritual covered over the sins of the people until Christ came and took them all away (see 10:4; and John 1:29).

Isaiah understood that God would lay the sins of Israel (and other nations for that matter) on the coming Servant of God (55:6–13). This holy being's administration would "bring about an all-embracing atonement and forgiveness of sin."[228] The New Testament description of the work of the Lord builds on this. The central focus is on total forgiveness for sin through the death of Christ as the sacrificial Lamb and the expiation it brings. His act not only makes of no account the sin that has been committed but it also allows for the full acceptance of the sinner back into the family of God. To emphasize, the Atonement not only makes the person sin-free but also changes his or her status from sinner to saint, from one estranged to one in full fellowship, from one tainted with sin to one pure of all sin—in sum, from unrighteous to fully righteous. Such forgiveness of sin and the imputation of

227. BDB, 497–98; *TWOT,* 1023.

228. *NID,* s.v. "ἀφίημι."

righteousness,[229] however, does not come except through repentance and confession (6:1, 6; see also Mark 1:15; Acts 2:38; 5:31; James 5:16; and 1 John 1:9). To denote the effect of pardoned sin, the author of Hebrews uses the noun "forgiveness" (ἄφεσις, *aphesis*), meaning "the act of freeing someone from an obligation, guilt, or punishment."[230] As one scholar noted, "Though our efforts to be righteous are necessary, they will forevermore be insufficient. Paul teaches a profound truth [in 2 Cor. 5:21]—that as we come unto Christ by the covenant of faith, our Lord's righteousness becomes our righteousness. He justifies us in the sense that he *imputes*—meaning, he reckons to our account—his goodness and takes our sins. This is the *great exchange.*"[231]

The author emphasizes that, on the basis of the Mosaic law, no forgiveness could be achieved without the shedding of blood. This fact becomes the ground on which he will next make his case for the necessity of the Lord's sacrifice.

He Now Appears in the Presence of God for Us (9:23–28)

Greek Text

23 Ἀνάγκη οὖν τὰ μὲν ὑποδείγματα τῶν ἐν τοῖς οὐρανοῖς τούτοις καθαρίζεσθαι, αὐτὰ δὲ τὰ ἐπουράνια κρείττοσι θυσίαις παρὰ ταύτας. 24 οὐ γὰρ εἰς χειροποίητα εἰσῆλθεν ἅγια Χριστός, ἀντίτυπα τῶν ἀληθινῶν, ἀλλ' εἰς αὐτὸν τὸν οὐρανόν, νῦν ἐμφανισθῆναι τῷ προσώπῳ τοῦ θεοῦ ὑπὲρ ἡμῶν· 25 οὐδ' ἵνα πολλάκις προσφέρῃ ἑαυτόν, ὥσπερ ὁ ἀρχιε ρεὺς εἰσέρχεται εἰς τὰ ἅγια κατ' ἐνιαυτὸν ἐν αἵματι ἀλλοτρίῳ, 26 ἐπεὶ ἔδει αὐτὸν πολλάκις παθεῖν ἀπὸ καταβολῆς κόσμου· νυνὶ δὲ ἅπαξ ἐπὶ συντελείᾳ τῶν αἰώνων εἰς ἀθέτησιν ἁμαρτίας διὰ τῆς θυσίας αὐτοῦ πεφανέρωται. 27 καὶ καθ' ὅσον ἀπόκειται τοῖς ἀνθρώποις ἅπαξ ἀποθανεῖν, μετὰ δὲ τοῦτο κρίσις, 28 οὕτως καὶ ὁ Χριστός, ἅπαξ προσενεχθεὶς εἰς τὸ πολλῶν ἀνενεγκεῖν ἁμαρτίας, ἐκ δευτέρου χωρὶς ἁμαρτίας ὀφθήσεται τοῖς αὐτὸν ἀπεκδεχομένοις εἰς σωτηρίαν. [SBLGNT]

---

229. In Rom. 4:11–24, Paul stresses the idea that through a person's faith, the Atonement allows for righteousness to be imputed to the individual. The verb λογίζομαι (*logizomai*) means "to impute, reckon." In a theological sense, it refers to God's reckoning to a person's account a degree of righteousness that a person does not actually possess, at least not initially. What the Father reckons is the full righteousness of Christ. As a result, each individual who comes under the Father's favor is judged and responded to as if he or she were fully righteous. For discussion, see Heidland, *TDNT,* 4:284–92.

230. BDAG, 155; *NID*, s.v. "*ἀφίημι.*"

231. Robert L. Millet, *Selected Writings of Robert L. Millet,* Gospel Scholars Series (Salt Lake City: Deseret Book, 2000), 73, emphasis added.

King James Version

23 It was therefore necessary that the patterns of things in the heavens should be purified with these; but the heavenly things themselves with better sacrifices than these. 24 For Christ is not entered into the holy places made with hands, which are the figures of the true; but into heaven itself, now to appear in the presence of God for us: 25 Nor yet that he should offer himself often, as the high priest entereth into the holy place every year with blood of others; 26 For then must he often have suffered since the foundation of the world: but now once in the end of the world hath he appeared to put away sin by the sacrifice of himself. 27 And as it is appointed unto men once to die, but after this the judgment: 28 So Christ was once offered to bear the sins of many; and unto them that look for him shall he appear the second time without sin unto salvation.

New Rendition

23 Therefore, it was necessary that the models of these heavenly things be purified with these sacrifices, but the heavenly things themselves need better sacrifices than these. 24 For Christ did not enter a sanctuary made by human hands, a copy of the true one, but he entered into heaven itself, to now appear in God's presence on our behalf, 25 nor to offer himself again and again, like the high priest enters the sanctuary every year with blood that is not his own, 26 for otherwise he would have had to suffer many times since the foundation of the world. But now he has appeared once for all at the close of the present age to take away sin by his sacrifice. 27 And just as human beings are destined to die once, and then afterwards face judgment, 28 so also Christ, after he was once offered up to bear the sins of many, will also appear a second time to those who eagerly wait for him, not to bear sin, but to bring salvation.

Translation Notes and Comments

9:23 *It was therefore necessary that the patterns of things in the heavens should be purified with these / Therefore, it was necessary that the models of these heavenly things be purified with these sacrifices:* The author's use of the phrase ἀνάγκη οὖν (*anangkē oun*), "it was therefore necessary," is important here because it signals the conclusion he wishes to draw from his discussion thus far. The noun ἀνάγκη (*anangkē*) denotes a necessity. The nuances it carries reveal the strength of the word. These are "complete obligation, compulsion," and even "inevitability."[232]

For the term "model" (ὑπόδειγμα, *hypodeigma*), see Translation Notes for 8:5 with the associated Analysis. For our purposes here, we need only

232. In Greek mythology, Ananke (Anance) was the goddess of inevitability. Among Greek thinkers, ἀνάγκη (*anangkē*) was the force that dominated and governed the universe. BDAG, 60–61; Louw-Nida, §71.30, 38; *NID*, s.v. "ἀνάγκη."

note that the term refers to the earthly tabernacle that is simply a model or copy of the heavenly tabernacle, that is, heaven itself.

For the term "purify," see Translation Notes for 9:22. In the present context, the term refers to the action necessary to prepare a structure of divine worship. The noun "sacrifices" is not found in the Greek text, but because the demonstrative pronoun τούτοις (*toutois*), "these," is vague, we have added it in our Rendition for clarity.

but the heavenly things themselves with better sacrifices / but the heavenly things themselves need better sacrifices than these: The phrase αὐτὰ δὲ τὰ ἐπουράνια (*auta de ta epourania*), "but the heavenly things themselves," points to "the spiritual and 'heavenly' sanctuary and 'true tabernacle' and all that appertains thereto in relation to Christ and His sacrifice as antitypical of the earthly tabernacle and sacrifices under the Law."[233] In sum, this phrase refers to the heavenly realm, the very seat of God.

The comparative adjective κρείττων (*kreittōn*), in the phrase κρείττοσιν θυσίαις (*kreittosin thysiais*), "better sacrifices," denotes that which is more useful or more advantageous than something else.[234] In this case, the author's point is that earthly sacrifices simply would not prepare heavenly things for acceptation. Indeed, a far greater sacrifice would be necessary to sanctify the heavenly original than the earthly copy. By his use of the plural for the noun, "sacrifices," he equates both the Lord's suffering and death with that of the sacrificial animals.

9:24 ***For Christ is not entered into the holy places made with hands / For Christ did not enter a sanctuary made by human hands:*** The author makes a shift in imagery here. Earlier he used the noun ἅγια (*hagia*), "holy place," to denote what he called the "first tent," that is, the first chamber of the tabernacle. Here he uses it to denote the heavenly realm.[235] The author contrasts the reality with its earthly counterpart, the tabernacle, which was made through human effort. See Translation Notes for 8:2 with associated Analysis.

which are the figures of the true / a copy of the true one: On "copy," see Translation Notes for 8:5 with the associated Analysis. The author uses the noun ἀντίτυπα (*antitypa*), literally "copy, representation," to describe

---

233. Strong, "New Strong's Expanded Dictionary . . . Greek," s.v. "ἐπουράνος"; see also BDAG, 388.

234. BDAG, 566.

235. The author uses the term in the present context to denote the Most Holy Place, which stood as a representation of heaven. See Young, "Gospel according to Hebrews 9," 199–200.

the Mosaic tabernacle and its furnishings, and the term could be rendered "counter-pattern" or "corresponding pattern." The idea is that the earthly pattern or copy corresponds to the heavenly original as a symbol or shadow corresponds to its reality.[236]

but into heaven itself / but he entered into heaven itself: With this phrase, the author points to that to which the type of the tabernacle actually pointed.

now to appear in the presence of God for us / to now appear in God's presence on our behalf: Here the author states the reason why Jesus entered heaven, which is summed up in the simple phrase ὑπὲρ ἡμῶν (*hyper hēmōn*), "in our behalf." The preposition is instructive because it indicates an activity is done not only in someone's behalf but also in his or her best interest.[237]

9:25 ***Nor yet that he should offer himself often, as the high priest entereth into the holy place every year with blood of others / nor to offer himself again and again, like the high priest enters the sanctuary every year with blood that is not his own:*** This sentence stresses the difference between the activities of the earthly high priest and that of Christ. The conjunction οὐδέ (*oude*), "nor,"[238] introduces the contrast.

The author's use of the present active verb προσφέρω (*prospherō*), "to bring, present," has caused considerable discussion among scholars. The author uses the word to contrast the sprinkling of sacrificial blood done by the high priest with the offering made by Christ himself. Since the sprinkling and therefore expiation was done after the animal was sacrificed, some have concluded that the author is saying that Christ continues to make his Atonement even after his ascension.[239] Such, however, is likely not the case. Taking the statement in context, it is clear the author's point is that the "presentation" (*prospherō*) of the high priestly offering is no longer in force, being replaced by the once and only "offering" (προσφορά, *prosphora*) of Christ upon the cross.[240]

---

236. BDAG, 90–91; Bruce, *Epistle to the Hebrews,* 230 n. 156. For a study of the heavenly temple, see Jay A. Parry and Donald W. Parry, "The Temple in Heaven: Its Description and Significance," in Parry, *Temples of the Ancient World,* 515–32.

237. BDAG, 1030–31.

238. LSJ, 1268; BDAG, 734–35.

239. For this view, see David J. MacLeod, "The Cleansing of the True Tabernacle," *Bibliotheca Sacra* 152 (January–March 1995): 60–71.

240. BDAG, 887; Young, "Gospel according to Hebrews 9," 207–9; see also Wilfrid Stott, "The Conception of 'Offering' in the Epistle to the Hebrews," *New Testament Studies* 9, no. 1 (1962): 62–67.

The pronoun ἑαυτόν (*heauton*), "himself," is important here because it continues the author's contrast between Jesus and the high priest. The high priest offered something other than himself, namely, the victim's blood. The Lord offered himself totally and completely.

The adverb πολλάκις (*pollakis*) means "many times, frequently."[241] Here it points to the annual activity that fell to the high priest on the Day of Atonement. Given that there were periods, some rather long, during which the Israelite priest was unable to perform this ritual, it still took place well over a thousand times between its inauguration and the time of the Savior. We have tried to catch the author's nuance by translating the adjective as "again and again" in our Rendition.

The author points to another striking difference between Jesus and the high priest with the phrase ἐν αἵματι ἀλλοτρίῳ (*en haimati allotriō*), literally "with blood belonging to others."[242] Because the phrase "of others" is somewhat vague, we have translated it as "not his own" in our Rendition.

9:26 ***For then must he often have suffered since the foundation of the world / for otherwise he would have had to suffer many times since the foundation of the world:*** The conjunction ἐπεί (*epei*) gives the reason or cause for an act to happen, often elliptically "for (if it were different), for otherwise,"[243] as we have translated it in our Rendition.

The verb δεῖ (*dei*), "must, have to," is important here because it denotes necessity borne by the compulsion of law[244] and shows the heavy consequences if the Savior's act had not been "once for all." That consequence the author notes with the adverb πολλάκις (*pollakis*) that means "many times, frequently."[245] It stands in contrast to the author's use the adverb ἐφάπαξ (*ephapax*) in 9:12, which denotes an action "taking place once and to the exclusion of any further occurrence."[246] Through this statement, the

241. BDAG, 846.

242. The phrase carries a strong negative quality. The idea of blood "not his own," (ἀλλοτρίῳ, *allotriō*) echoes the LXX Old Testament phrase "gods not their own" (ἀλλότριοι, *allotrioi*). The phrase is sometimes translated as "strange gods" (for example, see LXX Gen. 35:2, 4; Deut. 31:16, 18, 20; Josh. 24:14, 20, 23; and Judg. 10:16), and that idea could carry over here—the blood was "strange" and therefore unable to have any cleansing effect. See Cockerill, *Epistle to the Hebrews,* 421 n. 10.

243. BDAG, 360. The author is presenting a contrary-to-fact condition albeit without signaling it with the usual particle *an.* The phrase "otherwise he would have had to suffer" acts as the counterfactual point showing the need that the Savoir would have otherwise had to suffer continually if his Atonement had not been fully sufficient. Lane, *Hebrews 9–13,* 233 note kk.

244. BDAG, 213–14; Grundmann, *TDNT,* 2:21–25.

245. BDAG, 846.

246. BDAG, 417.

author stresses that the Lord's Atonement was fully sufficient and therefore fulfilled all requirements. As a result, the Savior gained a permanent place in God's presence.

but now once in the end of the world hath he appeared to put away sin by the sacrifice of himself / But now he has appeared once for all at the close of the present age to take away sin by his sacrifice: The noun αἰών (*aiōn*) denotes an age or era,[247] while the noun συντέλεια (*synteleia*) denotes its closing or completion.[248] Here the author has reference to his own period, not to the end of the world.[249]

The position of the verb φανερόω (*phaneroō*), "to appear," is important. It is the last word in the sentence and comes after the phrase "by his sacrifice." This position gives a double nuance to the whole expression. The first is that of "doing away with sin" through Christ, and second is that through his sacrifice Christ "was manifested." Both nuances are true.[250] The verb often refers to the revelation or disclosure of Jesus as divine and acts as a reminder that he, as Savior and High Priest, reveals the Father (1:1–3; see also John 14:6–14) and by that means accomplished a major duty of his work as Son. Further, his appearance accomplished what the old covenant could not—a way to God.[251]

In this phrase, the author emphasizes another purpose of that appearing—to take away sin.[252] With telling force, the author uses the perfect tense of the verb πεφανέρωται (*pephanerōtai*), "he has appeared," to emphasize the permanent effect of the Savior's self-offering at his first appearing.[253]

The key word in the author's argument is the adverb ἅπαξ (*hapax*), "once."[254] Jesus' sacrifice was fully efficient and, therefore, like his appearance as a mortal, had to occur only once.

---

247. BDAG, 32–33.

248. BDAG, 974–75; Sasse, *TDNT,* 1:203.

249. The phrase is a variant denoting the end of time or the close of earth's history at the time of the Second Coming, but here the author's use of the plural αἰώνων (*aiōnōn*), "ages," suggests that he is not referring to the end time but to the climatic event of the ages, that is, the Atonement of Christ. Bruce, *Epistle to the Hebrews,* 231; Delling, *TDNT,* 8:64–66.

250. Vanhoye, *Letter to the Hebrews,* 157.

251. Cockerill, *Epistle to the Hebrews,* 425.

252. This appearing is, then, not that before the Father after the Atonement but to Jesus' people during his mortal ministry. Koester, *Hebrews,* 422. Even so, the author ever keeps before the eyes of his readers the whole work of the Savior that includes his self-sacrifice through his present intercession in their behalf. Cockerill, *Epistle to the Hebrews,* 424 n. 27.

253. Cockerill, *Epistle to the Hebrews,* 425; Ellingworth, *Epistle to the Hebrews,* 484.

254. Though the simple form is used, it carries the same emphatic meaning as ἐφάπαξ (*ephapax*) in 9:12. Bruce, *Epistle to the Hebrews,* 231 n. 159.

That the author uses the singular "sin," in the phrase ἀθέτησιν ἁμαρτίας (*athetēsin hamartias*), "the annulment of sin," stresses the idea that sin is the negative principle and force that effects one's separation from God. The noun ἀθέτησις (*athetēsis*) denotes the removal of something,[255] but the nuance in this case is much stronger. It carries more of the force of an annulment, that is, of the reduction of something to nothing.[256] In the present context, the noun suggests the compete obliteration of the effects of sin.

The phrase διὰ τῆς θυσίας αὐτοῦ (*dia tēs thysias autou*), "through his sacrifice," is emphatic and therefore stresses the idea that Jesus took away sin by sacrificing *himself.*[257] With the use of the phrase, the author hits at the central work that Jesus did as both sacrifice—the offering—and as High Priest—the offeror—to fulfill the will of God (10:5–7). Because the law could not take sin away, Christ had to. But he did more; he completely obliterated sin and its effects.[258]

9:27 ***as it is appointed unto men once to die, but after this the judgment / just as human beings are destined to die once, and then afterwards face judgment:*** The impersonal middle deponent verb ἀπόκειται (*apokeitai*), "destined," points to that which is "unavoidable due to inevitable circumstances," particularly death.[259] The noun κρίσις (*krisis*), "judgment," denotes, in this instance, the final judgment. The author does not have the resurrection in view; to make his point, he skips right to the final judgment that will determine the ultimate state of the soul.[260]

9:28 ***Christ was once offered to bear the sins of many / so also Christ, after he was once offered up to bear the sins of many:*** There is a correlation between this phrase and the one above that should not be overlooked. The author brings this out by beginning the full sentence with καθ' ὅσον (*kath hoson*), "just as," and beginning this phrase with οὕτως καί (*houtōs kai*), "so also." The point the correlation makes is that "just as men were appointed to die once," "even so" Christ was appointed to be sacrificed once. The author's point is that "the validity of Christ's work is substantiated by its correspondence to the human situation."[261]

---

255. Louw-Nida, §13.36.

256. Louw-Nida, §76.24; BDAG, 24; Moulton and Milligan, *Vocabulary,* 12; *NID,* s.v. "ἀθετέω."

257. Ellingworth, *Epistle to the Hebrews,* 483.

258. Johnson, *Hebrews,* 245.

259. BDAG, 113.

260. The idea was current among the Greeks (for example, see Plato, *Rep.* 10.614b–621d) and the Jews (for example, see Dan. 7:26; 2 Macc. 6:26; 7:17, 19; and *1 En.* 1:7; 5:6, 50, 53–56).

261. Cockerill, *Epistle to the Hebrews,* 425 n. 29.

In 9:25, the author notes that the Savior "offered" (προσφέρω, *prospherō*) himself. Here the author uses the aorist passive participle προσενεχθεὶς (*prosenextheis*) of the same verb and states the Lord "was offered." Likely the passive voice, as happens so often in the New Testament, acts as a "divine passive," hiding the direct action of God.[262] The phrase ἀνενεγκεῖν ἁμαρτίας (*anenengkein hamartias*), "to bear sins," states the purpose for which the Father offered his Son (compare John 3:16). This phrase echoes strongly the prophecy of Isaiah that the "suffering servant" whom Jehovah "gave . . . up for our sins" would bear "the sins of many" and be delivered to death "because of their iniquities" (LXX Isa. 53:6, 12, our translation).[263]

The adjective πολλῶν (*pollōn*), "of many," shows that some aspects of this offering will not be inclusive. The author, in the phrase studied below, identifies those upon whom the full blessing of the Savior's offering will apply. Even so, the "many" includes a number so vast it is hard to imagine (see Rev. 7:9).

unto them that look for him shall he appear the second time without sin unto salvation / will also appear a second time to those who eagerly wait for him, not to bear sin, but to bring salvation: The verb ἀπεκδέχομαι (*apekdechomai*) means "to await eagerly"[264] and connotes the positive, even anxious, expectation and desire on the part of the Saints for further and closer association with their Lord, and the expected realization of the promises he has made.[265] The appearance to which the author refers is the Second Coming, at which time he will bring his full reward to the faithful.[266]

In the phrase χωρὶς ἁμαρτίας (*chōris hamartias*), literally "without sin," the nuance of the preposition, in this instance, does not mean "lacking sin" but rather "without relationship to sin."[267] The phrase does not mean that the Savior's return will verify or confirm his sinlessness (the author has already established the Lord's sinless nature) but rather that the focus

262. Wallace, *Greek Grammar,* 437–38; Ellingworth, *Epistle to the Hebrews,* 486–87.

263. In this case, the second aorist active infinitive ἀνενέγκειν (*anenenkein*) of ἀναφέρω (*anapherō*) carries the nuance of taking upon oneself the burden of another. BDAG, 75; Ellingworth, *Epistle to the Hebrews,* 487.

264. BDAG, 100.

265. Ellingworth, *Epistle to the Hebrews,* 487.

266. The last phrase εἰς σωτηρίαν (*eis sōtērian*), "for salvation," is somewhat vague and can be construed, if one takes εἰς (*eis*) with ἀπεκδεχομένοις (*apekdechomenois*), to mean that God's people will be waiting for God's salvation. Such a construction is, however, rather awkward. It is less awkward to take εἰς (*eis*) with ὀφθήσεται (*ophthēsetai*) thus meaning people are waiting for the Savior's promise of salvation to be fulfilled in their behalf. See Ellingworth, *Epistle to the Hebrews,* 488.

267. BDAG, 1095; Louw-Nida, §89.120.

of this coming will be different. His first coming focused on the Atonement and the removal of sin from others; his second coming will focus on the reward for the faithful.[268] Thus, we translate the phrase "not to bear sin" in the Rendition.

Analysis and Summary

At this point, the author begins his more complete exposition on the Savior's sacrificial death. He has carefully shown that both purification and redemption were associated with the covenant's inauguration. Both required the death of the sacrificial victim. In 9:23–28, the author stresses the finality of the Lord's once-for-all cleansing at the time when he inaugurated and put in force the new covenant (9:12) by contrasting it with both the initiation of the old covenant and the ritual of the Day of Atonement. On the basis of his model, he insists that since earthly things associated with the first covenant had to be cleansed by sacrificial means, so too did all corresponding "heavenly things."[269]

The author's exposition divides into three sections.[270] In the one addressed here, he presents his definitive evidence for the full effectiveness of the Lord's sacrifice. He leaves behind his concerns with covenant and blood and concentrates on "heavenly things." He boldly affirms the High Priest has entered into the "Holy Place," that is, heaven itself, and daringly proclaims that the all-sufficient sacrifice of the Lord has also procured for disciples an entrance into heaven (9:23–24). The author now turns to the task of describing in detail the supernal nature of this sacrifice that he will not conclude until 10:14.

Extrapolating based on tabernacle typology, in 9:23 the author uses both the necessity and the method of purification of the tabernacle to explain why there had to be an Atonement. As the earthly tabernacle with its furnishings had to be purified and dedicated through the administration of blood, so too did the heavenly.[271] He stresses, however, that such a

268. Ellingworth, *Epistle to the Hebrews,* 487.

269. Cynthia Long Westfall, *A Discourse Analysis of the Letter to the Hebrews: The Relationship between Form and Meaning* (London: T&T Clark International, 2005), 210–11.

270. These are 9:25–10:4; 10:5–10; and 10:11–14. Ellingworth, *Epistle to the Hebrews,* 489, begins the author's development of the theme with 10:1, while Cockerill, *Epistle to the Hebrews,* 419, begins it with 9:25. We follow Cockerill here because 9:25 introduces and lays down the framework for the author's development.

271. If middle-Platonic ideas are at play here, then the Holy Place is to be taken not as metaphor but as the ideal. See Attridge, *Epistle to the Hebrews,* 260–62. Any connection between the author's analogy and Plato's ideals, however, is very unlikely. For a thorough discussion of the whole issue, see Thompson, "Middle Platonism," 31–52.

purification would require far more than that of mere fleshly sacrifices that worked for the temporal order (9:23). Due to necessity, the Savior did not appear in heaven without the obligatory offering. Both his appearance and his offering were made in behalf of the believers' interest (9:24).

The author's comments that "heavenly things themselves" need to be cleansed and that what Christ offered were "better sacrifices" brings two questions to mind. First, how is it that "heavenly things" must be cleansed and second, why does the author denote the Savior's offering as "sacrifices"?[272]

To answer the second question first and thus to lay down the basis to answer the first, the author uses the plural "sacrifices" to equate what the Savior did with that of the continual offerings the high priest had to administer annually on the Day of Atonement. He states clearly that the very necessary purification associated with the earthly tabernacle typifies the need for the same to be done to the true "heavenly things" themselves. His point is that, by analogy, the way the sacrificial offering cleansed "the pattern," so Christ cleanses the heavenly. Furthermore, since cleansing the tabernacle was a prerequisite to its entrance, the cleansing of the "true" was necessary to enter it. This the Savior accomplished by his "once for all" (9:12) sacrifice that allowed him, as the eternal High Priest, to enter heaven.[273]

So far as the first question is concerned, what polluted the earthly tabernacle was not its place but the sins of the people (Ex. 30:10; Lev. 16:16, 19). Preexilic Judaism looked at sin as a deliberate offense toward God. In later Judaism, sin became more oriented toward the Mosaic law and defined as transgression against any of its parts, including both "cultic violations and errors, and criminal offenses."[274] Many rejected the idea of communal sin and saw it as strictly individual.

Hebrews looks at sin as both universal and individual. It views iniquity through the lens of the high-priestly ministry with its sacrificial system in making atonement for sin. Christ is both the High Priest and the sacrifice that takes away sin. He does this through his atoning sacrifice that needed to

272. The idea of a heavenly tabernacle or that heaven itself would need cleaning has caused no little discussion. For examples, see Buchanan, *To the Hebrews,* 162; James Swetnam, "On the Imagery and Significance of Hebrews 9,9–10," *Catholic Biblical Quarterly* 28, no. 2 (1966): 163–65; and Moffatt, *Critical and Exegetical Commentary,* 132. For a comprehensive discussion of the various ideas concerning the meaning of the cleansing, see Ellingworth, *Epistle to the Hebrews,* 476–77; and Bruce, *Epistle to the Hebrews,* 228 n. 152. For the reason the author may have used the plural "sacrifices," see Johnson, *Hebrews,* 242–45; and Bruce, *Epistle to the Hebrews,* 228 nn. 150, 151.

273. Cockerill, *Epistle to the Hebrews,* 416.

274. Stählin and Grundmann, *TDNT,* 1:289.

be offered but once for all (9:26–28). He has thus inaugurated the messianic age in which the Saints can stand sinless.[275] But until that happened, "sins formed a barrier that prevented them from coming into God's presence and exposed them to his wrath." Once again, using a *qal waḥomer* argument,[276] the author of Hebrews, to paraphrase, asks, "If sin erected a barrier forbidding entrance into the sanctuary that was a 'pattern,' how much more did it bar the way into the 'true' Sanctuary in which God dwells."[277] Thus, such defilement was an objective impediment to entrance into God's presence and had to be cleansed.[278] In sum, the imagery of need for a cleansing of the heavenly Holy Place is likely a metaphor for human intransigence that produces an impregnable barrier and threatens the soul with eternal recompense. The cleansing represents the Savior's removal of that barrier so the repentant can enter heaven, making genuine fellowship with God possible.[279] Furthermore, we must stress, a rite of the purification does not necessarily imply the object was previously impure any more than a rededication of a holy site means the first dedication did not work.[280] There is no doubt, however, that Christ's act was one of consecration and inauguration.

The author points out clearly to his readers that Jesus died in their behalf (9:24). On the basis of the author's cultic imagery, entrance into the "true" Holy Place involved not only its consecration but also the purification of those who would enter. In this way, the author expresses both the subjective and objective significance of the Lord's sacrificial act.[281] The subjects are the individuals within the Christian community, and the object is to bring them eternal life by preparing the way.

In 9:25, the author points out the vast difference between the works of the Levitical high priest and Christ. In doing so, the author sets the stage to showcase the grandeur of the sacrifice appropriate for the Lord's cleansing of "heavenly things." He shows there were three differences: first, the Lord presents himself as the sacrifice while the high priest did not; second, he

---

275. Grundmann, *TDNT,* 1:314.

276. On the nature and use of the *qal waḥomer* or *a fortiori* argument, see discussion in the introduction on page 30.

277. Cockerill, *Epistle to the Hebrews,* 416.

278. Lane, *Hebrews 9–13,* 247; Koester, *Hebrews,* 421; Cockerill, *Epistle to the Hebrews,* 416.

279. Cockerill, *Epistle to the Hebrews,* 416–17. Vanhoye, *Letter to the Hebrews,* 155, notes that the phrase is a general statement of "the need for sacrifices that find their completion in heaven."

280. Ellingworth, *Epistle to the Hebrews,* 477.

281. See N. A. Dahl, "A New and Living Way: The Approach to God according to Hebrews 10:19–25," *Interpretation* 5, no. 4 (1951): 404.

does not have to do it over and over as did the high priest; and third, he uses his own blood and not that of some sacrificial animal as the high priest did to make the necessary offering.

In 9:26, the author shows that through his sacrifice, the Savior did more than merely weaken or restrain the effects of sin; he brought about its abolishment (ἀθέτησις, *athetēsis*) once for all (ἐφάπαξ, *ephapax*). He took the entire weight of the consequence of sin—not just the believers' deserved punishment—and bore it away.[282] In doing so, he was able to deliver people from its demands. In sum, the Savior did more than deliver his people from the consequences of sin. He also delivered them from its pollutions and domination and thus made way for their total liberation from its demands.[283] Through his self-sacrifice, he annulled the effects of sin, reducing those effects to nothingness. As a result, sin will never be able to regain its destructive power—Christ vanquished it once for all. Through that act, he inaugurated the purification of the cosmos (8:10–12). Thus, his Atonement, inaugurated in Gethsemane and climaxed on Golgotha, dominates all history from the beginning to the end of time.[284]

In 9:27–28, the author makes an interesting contrast between the consequences of people dying and Christ dying. "Men and women die once, by divine appointment, and in their case, death is followed by judgment. Christ died once, by divine appointment, and his death is followed by salvation for all his people. This is so because in his death he bore the 'sins of many,' offering up his life to God as an atonement in their behalf."[285]

---

282. Cockerill, *Epistle to the Hebrews,* 427. The singular here stands in contrast to the plural "sins" used in 1:3; 2:17; 9:28; 10:11 and thereby connotes with emphasis "sin" as *the* principle force that stands between the individual and God. Cockerill, *Epistle to the Hebrews,* 423.

283. Bruce, *Epistle to the Hebrews,* 232. See also Ogden and Skinner, *Verse by Verse,* 257.

284. Cockerill, *Epistle to the Hebrews,* 423 n. 22. The cosmic nature of the Lord's Atonement is revealed in D&C 76:23–24: "We heard the voice bearing record that he is the Only Begotten of the Father—That by him, and through him, and of him, the worlds are and were created, and the inhabitants thereof are begotten sons and daughters of God." The statement is made even more emphatic and plain in the poetic rendering of this verse: "And I heard a great voice, bearing record from heaven—He's the Savior and only begotten of God: By him, of him, and through him the worlds were all made, Even all that career in the heavens so broad; Whose inhabitants, too, from the first to the last, Are saved by the very same Savior as ours; And, of course, are begotten God's daughters and sons, By the very same truths and the very same powers." Joseph Smith, "To W. W. Phelps, Esq.: A Vision," *Millennial Star* 20 (September 18, 1858): 599, https://contentdm.lib.byu.edu/digital/collection/MStar/id/21456.

285. Bruce, *Epistle to the Hebrews,* 231–32.

In doing so, the Savior provided for humankind the perfect antidote for what has been called "the universal human predicament." All face the pall of death, and whether they know it or not, they will also face judgment. The latter will become appallingly clear to the ignorant, the denier, and the wicked upon the moment of death. If death has its sting, so much more will be the fear of judgment (Jacob 6:13; Alma 40:11–14; Moses 7:1). Since judgment was a well-known principle among the author's readers (6:2; compare Alma 12:27), his words would have rung abundantly clear.

Jesus was the Father's offering "to bear the sins of many" (9:28; compare D&C 76:41). The Savior's return will confirm the Father's faith in that offering. The focus of the Son's first coming was on the Atonement with the objective of obliterating sin. And the Atonement worked for all those who had and would have faith in him. Because of his work, sin no longer has force and therefore cannot determine the final state of its once-victims. That work having been accomplished, the Savior can move to the work of his Second Coming. To those "that look for him he shall appear" for their vindication and to bequeath their reward.[286]

---

286. For a study, see Draper and Rhodes, *Revelation of John the Apostle,* especially 264, 268, 784–94.

Chapter 10

A New and Living Way

Introduction

To see the relationship of this section to the development of the author's total argument, see the introduction to chapter 8. Here he continues the themes developed in chapter 9. As a result, there is some repetition of subjects, but here he completes his arguments such that chapter 10 is a critical and integral part of his work.

In chapter 9, the author cited and expanded on the definitive evidence for the sole effectiveness of the Savior's sacrifice. In the forepart of this chapter (10:1–10), he expands on that theme, thus tackling the most critical part of his argument. In these verses, the author reiterates the weakness of the Mosaic law and gives the reason why Christ's sacrifice was fully sufficient for the salvation of all: it was accomplished by the "blameless" (NR 9:14), fully mortal, absolutely obedient, divine Son of God. In order to give legitimacy to his point, the author appeals to LXX Psalm 39:7–9 (Ps. 40:6–8 in the KJV), using it to show that the Savior's willingness and determination to do the Father's will was foreknown.

In the next section (10:11–18), the author articulates both the station that the Lord has achieved and the benefit his sacrifice has brought to the faithful. The author appeals for the fifth time to LXX Psalm 109:1, 4,[1] to provide evidence that Jesus has already ascended to heaven and waits for his enemies to become his footstool. The author again appeals to LXX Jeremiah 38:33–34 (31:33–4 in the KJV) to remind his readers that God had decreed there would be a new law given, one inscribed in the hearts of the believers. The result will be a total forgiveness of their sins.

1. See 1:3, 13; 5:5–6; 6:20; 7:1–25; 8:1–2.

In the final section (10:19–39), the author turns to hortatory both admonishing and wheedling his readers to continue in faithfulness—a condition not foreign to them. This section breaks down into four parts. The first (10:19–25) speaks to the specific situation in which the Saints find themselves and the attitude of faith, hope, and charity they must engender in one another. The second (10:26–31) consists of a stern warning against faithlessness and apostasy. The third (10:32–35) focuses on the past faithfulness and generosity this people have exhibited and asks them to continue in such good works. The final section (10:38–39) focuses on the need for faith and endurance and acts to introduce chapter 11.

This section reveals the author's great anxiety as he reminds his readers in very strong language that eternal punishment awaits should they fall away. He asks them to exercise the same faith they had already expressed when they stood their ground during a time of severe opposition. He admonishes them not to throw away their confidence. Rather, they must remain firm to their confession of hope so that they can be among the faithful who will be saved.

The Blood of Goats and Bulls Contrasted with That of Christ (10:1–10)

Greek Text

1 Σκιὰν γὰρ ἔχων ὁ νόμος τῶν μελλόντων ἀγαθῶν, οὐκ αὐτὴν τὴν εἰκόνα τῶν πραγμάτων, κατ᾽ ἐνιαυτὸν ταῖς αὐταῖς θυσίαις ἃς προσφέρουσιν εἰς τὸ διηνεκὲς οὐδέποτε δύναται τοὺς προσερχομένους τελειῶσαι· 2 ἐπεὶ οὐκ ἂν ἐπαύσαντο προσφερόμεναι, διὰ τὸ μηδεμίαν ἔχειν ἔτι συνείδησιν ἁμαρτιῶν τοὺς λατρεύοντας ἅπαξ κεκαθαρισμένους; 3 ἀλλ᾽ ἐν αὐταῖς ἀνάμνησις ἁμαρτιῶν κατ᾽ ἐνιαυτόν, 4 ἀδύνατον γὰρ αἷμα ταύρων καὶ τράγων ἀφαιρεῖν ἁμαρτίας. 5 διὸ εἰσερχόμενος εἰς τὸν κόσμον λέγει· Θυσίαν καὶ προσφορὰν οὐκ ἠθέλησας, σῶμα δὲ κατηρτίσω μοι· 6 ὁλοκαυτώματα καὶ περὶ ἁμαρτίας οὐκ εὐδόκησας. 7 τότε εἶπον· Ἰδοὺ ἥκω, ἐν κεφαλίδι βιβλίου γέγραπται περὶ ἐμοῦ, τοῦ ποιῆσαι, ὁ θεός, τὸ θέλημά σου. 8 ἀνώτερον λέγων ὅτι Θυσίας καὶ προσφορὰς καὶ ὁλοκαυτώματα καὶ περὶ ἁμαρτίας οὐκ ἠθέλησας οὐδὲ εὐδόκησας, αἵτινες κατὰ νόμον προσφέρονται, 9 τότε εἴρηκεν· Ἰδοὺ ἥκω τοῦ ποιῆσαι τὸ θέλημά σου· ἀναιρεῖ τὸ πρῶτον ἵνα τὸ δεύτερον στήσῃ. 10 ἐν ᾧ θελήματι ἡγιασμένοι ἐσμὲν διὰ τῆς προσφορᾶς τοῦ σώματος Ἰησοῦ Χριστοῦ ἐφάπαξ. [SBLGNT]

King James Version

1 For the law having a shadow of good things to come, and not the very image of the things, can never with those sacrifices which they offered year by year continually make the comers thereunto perfect. 2 For then would they not have ceased to be offered? because that the worshippers once purged should have had no more conscience of sins. 3 But in those sacrifices there is a remembrance again made of sins every year. 4 For it is not possible that the blood of bulls and of goats should take away sins. 5 Wherefore when he cometh into the world, he saith, Sacrifice and offering thou wouldest not, but a body hast thou prepared me: 6 In burnt offerings and sacrifices for sin thou hast had no pleasure. 7 Then said I, Lo, I come (in the volume of the book it is written of me,) to do thy will, O God. 8 Above when he said, Sacrifice and offering and burnt offerings and offering for sin thou wouldest not, neither hadst pleasure therein; which are offered by the law; 9 Then said he, Lo, I come to do thy will, O God. He taketh away the first, that he may establish the second. 10 By the which will we are sanctified through the offering of the body of Jesus Christ once for all.

New Rendition

1 Now since the law is but a shadow of good things to come and not the actual form of these things, it can never, by the same sacrifices continually offered year after year, perfect those who come to worship. 2 Otherwise would not the sacrifices have ceased being made? For the worshipers would have no longer had a consciousness of their sins, having been cleansed once for all. 3 On the contrary, in those sacrifices there was a yearly reminder of their sins, 4 because it is impossible to remove sins by the blood of bulls and goats. 5 So when Christ came into the world, he said,

> "You did not want a sacrifice and an offering, but you prepared a body for me. 6 You did not delight in burnt offerings and sin offerings. 7 Then I said, 'See, I have come—in a papyrus scroll it has been written about me—to do your will, O God.'" [LXX Ps. 39:7–9; KJV Ps. 40:6–8]

8 When he said above, "Sacrifices and offerings and burnt offerings and sin offerings you did not want nor did you delight in them" (which are offered according to the law), 9 he then said, "See, I have come to do your will," he abolishes the first so that he can establish the second. 10 It is by his will that we are sanctified through the offering of the body of Jesus Christ once for all.

Translation Notes and Comments

10:1 ***For the law having a shadow of good things to come, and not the very image of the things / Now since the law is but a shadow of good things to come and not the actual form of these things:*** The opening participial phrase is causal and emphasizes the reason why a statement is true.[2] Its point is because the law is but a shadow, it has no real power.

The author uses the ὁ νόμος (*ho nomos*), "the law," as a broad reference to the entire corpus of Mosaic rituals, ordinances, and regulations. He now refers to it as the σκία (*skia*), "shadow," to describe the law's relationship with his present circumstances, but this time he teams it up with the noun εἰκών (*eikōn*), "image, form." This noun denotes something that represents something "else in terms of basic form and features."[3] He points out the "law" does not have the quality of concrete reality. In doing so, he shows it did not possess the essential and substantial nature of the higher law with its ordinances and therefore suffered weakness to the degree that even obedience to its requirements left the worshiper spiritually lacking. Even so, like a shadow, the law did have a link to a reality, and that reality was the promise of "good things to come," namely salvation though Christ.[4]

can never with those sacrifices which they offered year by year continually make the comers thereunto perfect / it can never, by the same sacrifices continually offered year after year, perfect those who come to worship: The phrase οὐδέποτε δύναται (*oudepote dynatai*), "never can," is very forceful and coupled with εἰς τὸ διηνεκὲς (*eis to diēnekes*), "without interruption, continually,"[5] shows the insufficiency of the Mosaic sacrifices—no matter the number given, the long period during which the sacrifices were offered, or the sincerity of the worshiper—in making a person fully righteous.[6]

On the the verb τελειόω (*teleioō*), "to be whole, complete," see Translation Notes for 2:10–11 with the associated Analysis. Noteworthy is that the word, though often translated as "perfection," does not carry the idea of

2. Cockerill, *Epistle to the Hebrews,* 429.

3. BDAG, 281–82. In concrete terms, the noun can refer to a statue, painting, or bust. Figuratively, it connotes a close representation of a prototype or architype. See Kittel, von Rad, and Kleinknecht, *TDNT,* 2:381–97.

4. The present participle in the phrase τῶν μελλόντων ἀγαθῶν (*tōn mellontōn agathōn*), "good things to come," denotes what will come to pass, and therefore the whole looks to the future and the reward that awaits the faithful. Koester, *Hebrews,* 430–31; Cockerill, *Epistle to the Hebrews,* 428–29.

5. BDAG, 245. This interpretation takes εἰς τὸ διηνεκὲς (*eis to diēnekes*) as qualifying the previous προσφέρουσιν (*prospherousin*), "to offer" (as in 7:3), rather than the following verb δύναται (*dynatai*), "is able." This interpretation makes it clear that it is the sacrifices that "can never . . . perfect," rather than the law. For discussion see, Ellingworth, *Epistle to the Hebrews,* 490–91.

6. See Ogden and Skinner, *Verse by Verse,* 258.

total flawlessness and faultlessness as it does in English. Rather it stresses the idea of wholeness, completeness, and spiritual maturity.[7] In the Greek system, "to perfect" something was to bring it to its intended goal. In the context of Hebrews, the goal of the law was to make the Israelites free of sin (as shown in 10:2) and bring them into the presence of Jehovah. That the sacrifices had to be done repeatedly showed the law as it was did not and would not work, no matter how long it was practiced.[8]

The verb προσέρχομαι (*proserchomai*), "to come to, approach,"[9] is here used in a cultic sense of approaching God to make him an offering in worship; hence, we have translated it as "come to worship" in our Rendition.

10:2 *For then would they not have ceased to be offered? / Otherwise would not the sacrifices have ceased being made?:* The conjunction ἐπεί (*epei*) is used elliptically in the sense "for (if it were different), otherwise,"[10] thus forming the "if-clause" of a contrary-to-fact condition, the "then-clause" being οὐκ ἂν ἐπαύσαντο προσφερόμεναι (*ouk an epausanto prospheromenai*), "would not they have ceased being made?" In our Rendition, we have added "the sacrifices" for clarity. The author's point is that if the sacrifices actually worked to make one whole, their repeal would have been unnecessary.

because that the worshippers once purged should have had no more conscience of sins / For the worshipers would have no longer had a consciousness of their sins, having been cleansed once for all: In our Rendition, we give a rather free rendering of the Greek articular infinitive phrase διὰ τὸ μηδεμίαν ἔχειν ἔτι συνείδησιν ἁμαρτιῶν τοὺς λατρεύοντας (*dia to mēdemian echein eti syneidēsin hamartiōn tous latreuontas*), more literally "because of the worshippers no longer having consciousness of sins." Though it is tempting to translate the noun συνείδησις (*syneidēsis*) as "conscience" (as in 9:14 and the KJV) as a contrast with "remembrance" in 10:3, the usual meaning of "consciousness" fits better.[11] Thus we have taken the following ἁμαρτιῶν (*hamartiōn*), "sins," as an objective genitive.

On "conscience," see Translation Notes for 9:9 with associated Analysis. The noun συνείδησις (*syneidēsis*) denotes a personal knowledge of right from wrong that, when violated, gives one a sense of guilt, that is, a

7. BDAG, 996; Delling, *TDNT,* 8:67–87.

8. Cockerill, *Epistle to the Hebrews,* 430.

9. BDAG, 878; Schneider, *TDNT,* 2:683–84; Carol Lee Hawkins, "Perfection," in Ludlow, *Encyclopedia of Mormonism,* 3:1074–75.

10. BDAG, 360.

11. Cockerill, *Epistle to the Hebrews,* 431.

consciousness of blame before God.[12] The author's point is that when a person has been cleansed of sin, then any feeling of guilt should no longer be in his or her conscious mind.

On "purged, cleansed," see Translation Notes for 9:14 with associated Analysis. The author's use of the perfect participle of the verb καθαρίζω (*katharizō*), "having been cleansed," suggests that he sees the act of Christ resulting in a complete, even exhaustive and perpetual purification of each faithful soul.[13]

10:3 ***But in those sacrifices there is a remembrance again made of sins every year / On the contrary, in those sacrifices there was a yearly reminder of their sins:*** The author unabashedly looks to a negative but important effect of the elaborate ritual on the Day of Atonement. The noun ἀνάμνησις (*anamnesis*) denotes a remembrance or reminder of the past.[14] In this case, the whole focus of the yearly fast is on the consciousness of sin held by priest and people. The ordinance was designed to rid all of sin but instead brought to full consciousness the weakness and sins of the people.[15] Thus the ritual was a tacit witness the law had no power to change them.

If they actually worked, then the sacrifices would no longer be necessary because the worshiper would have been cleansed once for all and would no longer feel guilty for sins. The sacrifices served not as a witness that sins were overcome but that they continued. Such sacrifices had the power neither to cleanse nor change the soul. On the other hand, the blood of Christ did.

10:4 ***For it is not possible that the blood of bulls and of goats should take away sins / because it is impossible to remove sins by the blood of bulls and goats:*** Here the author identifies what the problem was. The

12. Fitzer, *TNDT,* 7:956–59; Ellingworth, *Epistle to the Hebrews,* 494; Lane, *Hebrews 9–13,* 255 note j. According to President Spencer W. Kimball, "'Conscience is a celestial spark which God has put into every man for the purpose of saving his soul.' Certainly it is the instrument which awakens the soul to consciousness of sin, spurs a person to make up his mind to adjust, to convict himself of the transgression without soft-pedaling or minimizing the error, to be willing to face facts, meet the issue, and pay necessary penalties—and until the person is in this frame of mind he has not begun to repent." Spencer W. Kimball, *The Teachings of Spencer W. Kimball,* ed. Edward L. Kimball (Salt Lake City: Bookcraft, 1982), 86.

13. Lane, *Hebrews 9–13,* 255 note i.

14. BDAG, 68.

15. Bruce, *Epistle to the Hebrews,* 236–37. Philo, *Mos.* 2.107; *Spec.* 1.215, notes that the sacrifices brought a reminder of guilt to the wayward person, and in *Plant.* 108, he notes that the sacrifices also brought the sins to God's remembrance.

conjunction γὰρ (*gar*), "for, because," is causal, introducing an explanation of why something is the way it is. The author's use of the adjective ἀδύνατος (*adynatos*) is telling. The word denotes something that is incapable of happening because it is impossible.[16] Here it refers specifically to the efficacy of blood sacrifices to remove sin.

10:5–7 These verses are a quote from LXX Psalm 39:7–9 (Ps. 40:6–8 in the KJV). The author uses this scripture to substantiate the point made above and to provide a position from which to elaborate that point below.[17]

10:5 *Wherefore when he cometh into the world, he saith / So when Christ came into the world, he said:* In our Rendition, we have added "Christ" as the subject of the clause for clarity, although it is not until 10:10 that the author explicitly refers to "Jesus Christ" by name.

The conjunction διό (*dio*), "therefore, so," is referential, giving the reason for something to happen. Here the author uses it to explain the Lord's understanding of his mission.

The verb εἰσέρχομαι (*eiserchomai*), "to come into," found here in the form of a present active participle, points to the time when Christ was either coming or about to come into the world. Either way, the idea is that at that point, he knew what his mission was. The participle shows that his very act of taking upon himself the form of man was an act of obedience that would climax on the cross.[18] The author uses the phrase to denote just when the Lord spoke the words the author quotes next.

The verb λέγει (*legei*) is a historical present and is thus translated as "he said" in our Rendition.

Sacrifices and offerings thou wouldest not / "You did not want a sacrifice and an offering: The aorist phrase οὐκ ἠθέλησας (*ouk ēthelēsas*), literally "you did not want," carries the nuance of not wishing for something to happen and certainly taking no pleasure or delight in it when it did.[19]

16. BDAG, 22.

17. For a study, see Walter C. Kaiser Jr., "The Abolition of the Old Order and Establishment of the New: Psalm 40:6–8 and Hebrews 10:5–10," in *Tradition and Testament: Essays in Honor of Charles Lee Feinberg*, ed. John S. Feinberg and Paul D. Feinberg (Chicago: Moody Press, 1981), 19–37.

18. Cockerill, *Epistle to the Hebrews*, 434.

19. The verb θέλω (*thelō*) denotes a desire for something to happen that benefits oneself because it promises to be pleasurable or delightful. BDAG, 447–48; Louw-Nida, §25.1, 102. The particle οὐκ (*ouk*), "not," changes the nuance from pleasure and delight to displeasure and vexation.

but a body hast thou prepared me / but you prepared a body for me:[20] The particle δὲ (*de*), "but," acts here as a marker of contrast.[21] The verb καταρτίζω (*katartizō*) means to prepare something for a specific purpose. In this context, it points to a specific reason God prepared a mortal body for his Son, which was to be the acceptable sacrifice for sin that none of the blood offerings were.

There is significant variance between the LXX and the MT in this scripture, and it becomes easy to see why the author preferred the LXX.[22] The central difference is the MT states God "opened my ears" where the LXX states God "prepared a body for me." The differences between the two are difficult to explain, but for the author of Hebrews, the idea that God prepared a body exactly right for the sacrifice that was needed "once for all" had great appeal.[23]

10:6 *In burnt offerings and sacrifices for sin thou has had no pleasure / You did not delight in burnt offerings and sin offerings:* This phrase parallels the one in the previous verse and gives it force. The aorist phrase οὐκ εὐδόκησας (*ouk eudokēsas*) means to be dissatisfied and, when looking at action, to be displeased and unapproving of it.[24]

10:7 *Then said I, Lo, I come (in the volume of the book it is written of me,) to do thy will, O God / Then I said, 'See, I have come—in a papyrus scroll it has been written about me—to do your will, O God'":* This phrase points to an unknown but prerecorded prophecy. The noun βιβλίον (*biblion*) denotes a papyrus scroll. The author likely had the Pentateuch in

20. This phrase, as noted above, comes from the LXX version of Ps. 39:6. The corresponding MT (Ps. 40:7) reads אָזְנַיִם כָּרִיתָ לִּי (*'oznayim kārîtā lî*), "you have hollowed out ears for me," which may mean something like "you have made it plain to me." This is another case where the author's interpretation of an OT passage is dependent on the LXX rather than the MT. Jared M. Compton, "The Origin of Σῶμα in Heb. 10:5: Another Look at a Recent Proposal," *Trinity Journal* 32, no. 1 (Spring 2011): 19–29.

21. BDAG, 213; Louw-Nida, §89.124.

22. First, the MT states "You [Jehovah] have opened my ears" rather than the LXX "You have prepared a body for me." Second, the MT at the beginning of 10:6 states God did not want a "whole burnt offering" where the LXX uses the plural "whole burnt offerings." Third, the MT has "you requested not [sacrifices]" where the LXX has "you are not pleased" with these sacrifices. Finally, the MT has "to do your will, O my God, I have resolved," where the LXX puts "O my God" before "to do your will" and ends without noting "I have resolved."

23. Compare McConkie, *Doctrinal New Testament Commentary,* 3:187–88. For a discussion, see Compton, "Origin of Σῶμα," 19–29.

24. The verb εὐδόκησας (*eudokēsas*) points to a state of being satisfied and taking good pleasure in something. BDAG, 404. The particle οὐκ (*ouk*), "not," changes the nuance to that which is dissatisfying and more especially unpleasant.

mind but could have thought in terms specific to the scroll comprising Deuteronomy, since it contained the laws governing kingship.[25]

The particle ἰδού (*idou*), "behold, lo, see," is used to draw attention to what follows. Here it emphasizes the Lord's determination to do the Father's will no matter the cost.

10:8 ***Above when he said, Sacrifice and offering . . . / When he said above, "Sacrifices and offerings . . . ":*** With this phrase, the author draws his readers' minds back to the quote to reinforce the Lord's lack of delight in the blood offerings.

which are offered by the law / (which are offered according to the law): Here the author states the obvious but does so for a reason. He attaches law and sacrifice together to show that as the sacrifices were defective in producing the desired state of purity, so too was the law.

10:9 ***Then said he, Lo, I come to do thy will, O God. He taketh away the first, that he may establish the second / he then said, "See, I have come to do your will," he abolishes the first so that he can establish the second:*** The author not only draws his readers' attention to the scripture but also states its implication. However, he modifies the text to suit his point. Where both the LXX and MT read, "then I said,"[26] the author rephrases as "then he said" and in doing so rivets his readers attention on the Savior's affirmation that he came strictly to do the Father's will.[27]

By doing the Father's will, the Lord adversely affected Israel's understanding of what the old covenant was supposed to do. The verb ἀναιρέω (*anaireō*), "to take away, abolish,"[28] carries the nuance of destroying something utterly.[29] It is an emphatic word and reveals the author's distain for the inadequacy of the old law.

The verb ἵστημι (*histēmi*), found here as an aorist subjunctive, primarily means "to establish" but carries the nuance of not only putting something in force but also of making it firm and enduring.[30] The word stresses the lasting power the new covenant will have.

---

25. Attridge, *Epistle to the Hebrews,* 275.

26. LXX Ps. 39:7; MT Ps. 40:7.

27. Cockerill, *Epistle to the Hebrews,* 440.

28. BDAG, 64.

29. The verb carries the idea of taking something away through violence and is usually associated with killing it. Strong, "New Strong's Expanded Dictionary . . . Greek," s.v. "ἀναιρέω." According to McConkie, *Doctrinal New Testament Commentary,* 3:188, the Savior did away with the old system "that he might establish the pre-eminence of his own atoning sacrifice."

30. BDAG, 482–83; Louw-Nida, §§13.29, 90; 85.8. McConkie, *Doctrinal New Testament Commentary,* 3:187, notes that the Psalm shows that when Christ comes in the flesh,

10:10 *By the which will we are sanctified through the offering of the body of Jesus Christ once for all / It is by his will that we are sanctified through the offering of the body of Jesus Christ once for all:* On "sanctified," see Translation Notes for 2:11 with the associated Analysis. Here the verb's nuance is to be made holy and, thus, to be like God. The form of the verb here is a perfect passive participle, the perfect tense showing that the author's readers "have been made holy." It affirms "the definitive nature and abiding effectiveness of the purification from sin that Christ has provided through his obedience."[31] The act does not bring about the mere legal standing of sin-freeness that "justification" denotes or the flawlessness that "perfection" suggests. Rather, it connotes the Savior's act of setting the people apart for God's service by cleansing them from both the dominion and pollution of sin (9:14).[32] The present context suggests a state that the disciples have achieved, but one that is not yet permanent and therefore remains a task to be completed fully through faithful endurance.[33] This act enables them to feel comfortable if not eager to enter the divine presence. These sanctified souls can fearlessly "approach the throne of grace with confidence, so that [they] may receive mercy and find grace to help in time of need" (NR 4:16).

That condition has come about in only one way. To describe it, the author uses the noun προσφορά (*prosphora*). It denotes an offering made to Jehovah but connotes one voluntarily given.[34] In this case, it points specifically to the Savior's offering his own body, his act of supreme willingness.

The phrase ἐν ᾧ θελήματι (*en hō thelēmati*), "by which will," connotes the Father's will as accomplished by the Son.[35] The whole sentence reveals why the Father willed the Son to die. It was to bring about the state of sanctification to the true worshiper.

A telling word in the author's argument is the adverb ἐφάπαξ (*ephapax*), "once for all" (see Translation Notes for 7:27; 9:12), which stresses the idea of the permanent nature of an act that precludes any need for repetition.[36] The author concludes this sentence with it to give emphatic force.

---

sacrifices will be done away. In the Book of Mormon, the Lord declares, "Ye shall offer up unto me no more the shedding of blood; yea, your sacrifices and your burnt offerings shall be done away, for I will accept none of your sacrifices and your burnt offerings. And ye shall offer for a sacrifice unto me a broken heart and a contrite spirit" (3 Ne. 9:19–20).

31. Cockerill, *Epistle to the Hebrews,* 443.

32. Cockerill, *Epistle to the Hebrews,* 443. Vanhoye, *Letter to the Hebrews,* 167, notes it is equivalent to a priestly consecration.

33. Ellingworth, *Epistle to the Hebrews,* 511.

34. BDAG, 887; Weiss, *TDNT,* 9:68.

35. Ellingworth, *Epistle to the Hebrews,* 505.

36. BDAG, 417.

Analysis and Summary

This portion of the author's argument falls into three parts: 10:1–4, 5–10, and 11–18. In the first, the author repeats his criticism on the ineffectiveness of the old system. In the second, he "explains why the blood of Christ succeeded where animal blood failed."[37] In the third, he returns to the topic of Christ as the great High Priest, the mediator and source of grace and salvation.

In this first section, the author recapitulates the foundation on which his criticism of the old covenant rests, but where in chapters 8 and 9 he focused on the ordinances of the tabernacle, he looks, this time, specifically at the Mosaic law. His is a rather bold if not radical critique of what many held as sacred and some inviolable. But his objective is to persuade his audience to not return to the law, and therefore, he emphasizes that the problem rests with the very law itself, not just with its cultic practices. He admits that the law has its place as a shadow (σκία, *skia*) of "good things to come," but it should not be taken as having power in and of itself to make one fit for entrance into God's kingdom.[38]

He stresses that the continual need to make offerings clearly betrays the inadequacy of the law to perfect the people and cleanse their conscience (10:2). Indeed, the repetition was clear proof that the people were really not changing for the better (10:3). Further, no matter how long the sacrifices were performed and the law administered, it could never provide the completeness necessary for the people to enter God's presence.[39]

A Jew could well object to the author's point, insisting that the object of the Day of Atonement was the annual *removal* of sins.[40] But the author's point is that even though that is the case, the public consciousness that each Israelite had sinned (including the high priest himself) and kept sinning was at the forefront of the day's activities and could not be ignored or dismissed because of some hope that such sins had been removed. Further, there was no record that suggested that because of these activities, God would forget the sins. On the other hand, it was on record that in consequence of the effect of the new covenant, God would forget them (8:12; 10:17).[41]

---

37. Cockerill, *Epistle to the Hebrews,* 433.

38. Vanhoye, *Letter to the Hebrews,* 158–59.

39. Only by a full and definitive cleansing from sin could the people as a whole be prepared and authorized to enter the divine presence. Peterson, *Hebrews and Perfection,* 146–47.

40. This is the view of the Torah, the Mosaic law itself, and therefore, the position had plenty of backing. The author, however, rejects this position based on the prophetic scriptures he quotes, all of which come from outside the Torah.

41. Bruce, *Epistle to the Hebrews,* 237–38.

The author points out that, like the tabernacle, the law itself was but a "shadow." Even so, it silhouetted "good things to come" (10:1; also 8:5). For that very reason the law had its place.[42] Though the system it generated could not bring salvation, it could and did "anticipate the future by being its opposite and thus by showing the need of what was to come."[43] The Mosaic law was, thus, "not a somewhat deceptive reflection of the eternal but a divinely ordained, though imperfect, anticipation and foreshadowing of God's full salvation to come."[44] The author's point, tacitly made, is that for those with faith to see, the law prefigured the work and ministry of the Messiah from whom an actual cleansing of the conscience could come.[45]

Such a cleaning is necessary, as one scholar pointed out, because

> just as a man, conscious of having injured his neighbor, cannot be comfortable in his neighbor's presence, so a man conscious of having broken the laws of God cannot endure His presence. As all mankind are guilty of sin in some degree, none could return to the presence of God, and joy in that presence, save a way should be provided whereby this consciousness of sin should be removed. That was provided for in the gospel plan. The Son of God was commissioned of the Father to reveal Himself to man, to urge man to have faith in the Father, and eventually to win man's love by giving His life in man's behalf. Having awakened in man a knowledge of God and a consciousness of sin, man was called upon to repent, with the promise that upon sincere repentance God will forgive man his sins and man can stand unashamed in the Father's presence.[46]

The key in understanding the author's point in this regard lies in a correct interpretation of the phrase "a consciousness of their sins" (NR 10:2). A false reading would be that if a person has received forgiveness of sin, then he or she would no longer have any recollection of it. That however is not the case. The author's position is that once cleansed, the faithful should not be plagued by the false notion that some taint of sin remains. In short, they should no longer feel any guilt.[47] Giving up such a feeling

---

42. Attridge, *Epistle to the Hebrews,* 268.

43. Cockerill, *Epistle to the Hebrews,* 428.

44. Cockerill, *Epistle to the Hebrews,* 428–29; see also Ellingworth, *Epistle to the Hebrews,* 490–91; and Lane, *Hebrews 9–13,* 253–54, 259.

45. See McConkie, *Doctrinal New Testament Commentary,* 3:187.

46. William E. Berrett, *The Restored Church* (Salt Lake City: Deseret Book, 1953), 560.

47. The noun συνείδησις (*syneidēsis*) denotes the pain people feel when they do something wrong. Reflecting this view, the NIV translation of 10:2 is "the worshipers would have been cleansed once for all, and would no longer have felt guilty for their sins." Bruce, *Epistle to the Hebrews,* 234, translates the phrase as "they would no longer have

takes faith on the part of the Saint. That faith rests on the belief in the total effectiveness of the Atonement of Christ expressed through the process of repentance. Such faith brings about the necessary condition of a clear conscience as assurance comes. According to Spencer W. Kimball, "Sometimes a guilty consciousness overpowers a person with such a heaviness that when a repentant one looks back and sees the ugliness, the loathsomeness of the transgression, he is almost overwhelmed and wonders, 'Can the Lord ever forgive me? Can I ever forgive myself?' But when one reaches the depths of despondency and feels the hopelessness of his position, and when he cries out to God for mercy in helplessness but in faith, there comes a still, small, but penetrating voice whispering to his soul, 'Thy sins are forgiven thee.'"[48]

The aim of worship, as the author sees it, is to gain access to God. This can be achieved only by a cleansing of the conscience, not simply by a display of outward piety that the misunderstanding of the Mosaic law had popularized.[49] Through the cleansing work of the Savior comes comfort in close association with the Divine. The result is the soul—freed from feelings of guilt—is drawn to the holiness of the Father and the Son rather than being repelled by it.

The problem with the sacrifices of the old covenant is that by themselves, it was impossible for the offerings to cleanse anyone from sin because they consisted of nothing more than the blood of goats and bulls. The author pushes this point by placing the adjective ἀδύνατος (*adynatos*), "impossible," as the first word in 10:4. Though many had condemned the offerings of hypocrites as having no force, the prophets still felt the offerings had great value.[50] The author, with the use of the verb "abolish, destroy" (ἀναιρέω, *anaireō*, 10:9), clearly, forcefully, and even pitilessly rejects the whole system standing alone as having any efficacy.[51] As he has shown, he fully accepts the need for the shedding of blood that sin may be removed and an atonement be made (9:22), but it is utterly impossible for the blood of bulls and goats to do so. But as the means of coming to understand the

---

any conscience of sins," meaning that they, having been cleansed through the process of proper worship, would no longer feel guilty.

48. Spencer W. Kimball, *The Miracle of Forgiveness* (Salt Lake City: Bookcraft, 1969), 344.

49. Johnson, *Hebrews,* 246.

50. 1 Sam. 15:22–23; Ps. 40:7–10; Isa. 1:10–12; Jer. 6:20; 7:21–23; Hosea 6:6; Micah 6:6–9. For Hellenistic Judaism, see *Let. Aris.* 234; Philo, *Plant.* 107–8; *Mos.* 2.108; *Spec. Laws* 1.271–72; and Josephus, *Ant.* 6.141–43.

51. Cockerill, *Epistle to the Hebrews,* 432.

work and ministry of the Lord through the law's typology, the offerings held an important place. They witnessed that nothing short of the blood of Christ offered once for all (ἐφάπαξ, *ephapax*) would do (9:12, 14, 26; 10:10).

According to the Book of Mormon, it was expedient "that there should be a great and last sacrifice; yea, not a sacrifice of man, neither of beast, neither of any manner of fowl; for it shall not be a human sacrifice" (Alma 34:10). The reason is that the sacrifice of neither man nor animal can atone for sin (Alma 34:11–12). This made the great and last sacrifice expedient. Indeed, "the whole meaning of the law [pointed to] that great and last sacrifice; and that great and last sacrifice will be the Son of God, yea, infinite and eternal" (Alma 34:14).

The author's view correlates with that of the prophet Amulek who testified,

> it is expedient that there should be a great and last sacrifice, and then shall there be, or it is expedient there should be, a stop to the shedding of blood; then shall the law of Moses be fulfilled; yea, it shall be all fulfilled, every jot and tittle, and none shall have passed away. And behold, this is the whole meaning of the law, every whit pointing to that great and last sacrifice; and that great and last sacrifice will be the Son of God, yea, infinite and eternal. And thus he shall bring salvation to all those who shall believe on his name; this being the intent of this last sacrifice, to bring about the bowels of mercy, which overpowereth justice, and bringeth about means unto men that they may have faith unto repentance. (Alma 34:13–15)

To drive home his point, the author first quotes from LXX Psalm 39:7–9 (KJV Ps. 40:6–8) in 10:5–7 and then requotes certain phrases in 10:8–9. In doing so, he appeals to the Old Testament itself as the basis for his harsh critique of the law. These scriptures clearly state that Jehovah did not want any of the sacrifices or oblations Israel was offering. The idea was not novel. A number of prophets had stated the same thing (see LXX Ps. 50:18; Isa. 11:1; Jer. 6:20; Hosea 6:6; and Amos 5:22), but with skill, the author chose exactly the right one to help make his case. There were at least four good reasons: "first, it lists several kinds of sacrifice to be rejected; second, it offered a replacement solution, the personal availability to do the will of God; third, an allusion to the incarnation of the Son of God could be seen in this text, and therefore it could be put into the mouth of Christ at the time of his entry into the world; fourth, the attitude of availability expressed in the psalm ('Behold, I have come, O God, to do your will') is the attitude taken by Jesus in the Gospels."[52]

---

52. Vanhoye, *Letter to the Hebrews,* 161. For the Savior's attitude of submission to the Father's will, see Matt. 26:39, 42; Mark 14:36; Luke 22:42; and John 4:34; 5:30; 6:38.

Using the psalm, the author is able to note what has been abolished, that is, "sacrifices and offerings,"[53] and then what has been established, namely, Christ's willing sacrifice. The author uses the scripture to push his point that with the coming of the Savior, God has rejected the old system—not because it was wrong but because it was weak. By itself, it simply could not remove sin and transform the soul. Its ability to foreshadow and typify the real power that was to come, however, gave it purpose and kept it in place *until* the Type arrived. At that point, the law had fulfilled its purposes and could be replaced. Thus, the author states that through the obedience of Christ, the first was abolished that the second might stand (10:9).

What exactly did the obedience of Jesus abolish, and what exactly did it establish? Two points need to be noted because the exact language of the author is important. First, the author is not saying that Jehovah's covenant with Israel had been nullified and replaced by another made exclusively with the Christians. The author nowhere intimates that God has become disinterested in the Jewish people. From the author's point of view, God's promise to Abraham continues in effect. Second, the author does not reject divine law as such. He insists, as one scholar has noted, that "God's will can be expressed by the scroll of the book [10:7] as well as in the heart [10:16]." What the author opposes, as this scholar points out, is the false notion that either the Mosaic law or the rites of the tabernacle provided complete access to God. Access is achieved only by faithful obedience exemplified in the life and ministry of the Son. The author thus takes his place among those prophets who denied the "efficacy of ritual when the deeper covenantal obligations [were] being neglected."[54]

The question is, does the author's use of the very strong verb "to take away, abolish, destroy" (ἀναιρέω, *anaireō*)[55] stand in contradiction to the Savior's own statement that he came not "to destroy [καταλύω, *katalyō*] the law and the prophets" but "to fulfill [πληρόω, *plēroō*] them" (Matt. 5:17–18, authors' translation)?[56] A key to the answer is in understanding the

53. The author notes specifically θυσίας (*thysias*), "sacrifices"; προσφοράς (*prosphoras*), "offerings"; ὁλοκαυτώματα (*holokautōmata*), "burnt offerings"; and ἁμαρτίας (*hamartias*), "sin offerings," and in doing so includes the entire gambit of those sacrifices the law demanded for atonement and gratitude. For studies, see Ellingworth, *Epistle to the Hebrews,* 502; and Attridge, *Epistle to the Hebrews,* 274.

54. Johnson, *Hebrews,* 253.

55. Koester, *Hebrews,* 434; Ellingworth, *Epistle to the Hebrews,* 504.

56. The verb translated "abolish" is καταλύω (*kataluō*). It means to invalidate the effect or force of something but carries the nuance of destroying it. BDAG, 521–22.

verb *plēroō,* which means both to complete something and also to bring it to an end generally by meeting all its requirements.[57] By doing so, though an object is put away, neither its purpose nor intent is done away. Thus, the Lord did put away the Mosaic law with all its offerings. To his American disciples he declared, "By me redemption cometh, and in me is the law of Moses fulfilled." Therefore, "ye shall offer up unto me no more the shedding of blood; yea, your sacrifices and your burnt offerings shall be done away, for I will accept none of your sacrifices and your burnt offerings." Instead, "ye shall offer for a sacrifice unto me a broken heart and a contrite spirit" (3 Ne. 9:17, 19–20; Christ is here paraphrasing Ps. 51:17).[58] His doing so shows Jesus does not reject the law of sacrifice in general, only the Mosaic expression of that law.[59]

Here, concerning the cultic aspects of the law, the intent of the author of Hebrews and the Savior align. The Lord did not do away with its ethical teachings but did raise them to a higher level (see Matt. 5–7).[60] He did, however, do away with the cultic section of the law. And why? Because his coming completed its purpose as foreshadowing his life and ministry. As the author states repeatedly, what the law could not do, Jesus did. One additional task the author completed was to destroy or abolish the false interpretation and understanding of the law as the foundation on which the new law would be permanently placed (ἵστημι, *histēmi*).

The heart of the matter is stated in 10:10. In sum, the mortal Savior's obedience to the Father's "will" in both depth and breadth is the exclusive source of the Saint's sanctification.[61] The author stresses this point in four ways. First, for the first time since 8:1, he uses the first person plural

57. BDAG, 827–28; Louw-Nida, §§35.33; 59.33, 37; 68.26.

58. For a discussion of Christ's fulfilling the law of Moses, see Bruce R. McConkie, *The Mortal Messiah: From Bethlehem to Calvary,* 4 vols. (Salt Lake City: Deseret Book, 1954–56), 1:124–57; 2:131–44.

59. Cockerill, *Epistle to the Hebrews,* 441 n. 41.

60. For a discussion, see Holzapfel and Wayment, *Making Sense,* 51–52.

61. In a number of scriptures, God has commanded his people to sanctify themselves (see Lev. 11:44; 1 Sam. 16:5; 1 Chr. 15:12; and D&C 43:11; 133:4). As each of these scriptures show, the command does not mean it is possible for a person to become self-sanctified. On the negative side, the phrase means to either guard against or rid oneself of anything that would put distance between oneself and God. On the positive side, it denotes participating in certain practices that would bring one closer to God. As the Lord said to his Kirtland, Ohio, Saints, "Assemble yourselves together, and organize yourselves, and prepare yourselves, and sanctify yourselves; yea, purify your hearts, and cleanse your hands and your feet before me, that I may make you clean" (D&C 88:74). Note that in this case the person does external and preparatory tasks that an inner cleansing may come from Christ.

pronoun.[62] In doing so, he makes all—writer and reader—one and brings himself with the rest of his audience under the power of God's grace. Thus, he can say that "we" have now all become holy. In 10:22, he will state the result, specifically that we can draw near unto God with complete confidence.[63]

The author clearly states the twofold efficacy the self-sacrifice of Christ accomplished for the believer. It could do what the "blood of bulls and of goats" could not do, that is, take away sin (9:13). It could add the high spiritual dimension of sanctification through which the individual could take on a level of holiness associated with God.[64]

Second, the author uses the perfect tense to describe what the Savior has done for his people: "we have been made holy" (ἡγιασμένοι ἐσμέν, *hagiasmenoi esmen*), "to be sanctified, to be made holy."[65] With the use of this tense, the author affirms the "definitive nature and abiding effectiveness of the purification from sin that Christ has provided through his obedience."[66] The Savior's obedience has made it possible for the Saints to be set apart for God's ends because they are free from sin and worldly pollutions. Thus, they are fully prepared not only to come into his presence but also to do his work and receive their reward. As one scholar noted, such a "transformation is only given to humans through the intervention of a mediator who bears within him both divine life and human mortality. The author therefore declares not that we have sanctified ourselves, but rather that 'we have been sanctified' by means of that 'will of God' (*thelēma theou*) of which the psalmist spoke. . . . The offering of Jesus was complete,

62. The author consistently uses the first person plural in this section of his argument (8:1–10:18) to stress and affirm the benefits received by the Saints through the benevolent and loving act of the Savior.

63. Cockerill, *Epistle to the Hebrews,* 442.

64. Vanhoye, *Letter to the Hebrews,* 162.

65. The verb ἁγιάζω (*hagiazō*) carries much the same nuance as καθαρίζω (*katharizō*), "to cleanse, purify" (BDAG, 488–89). It is the Savior who makes people "holy" by cleansing them from sin (NR 2:11). Thus, by coming under the power of his blood, they become "saints" of God (compare 6:10; 13:24). The act necessitates a change from a carnal and fallen state "to a state of righteousness" by being "redeemed of God, becoming his sons and daughters" once more. In this way, those under the Atonement's power become "new creatures" and "unless they do this, they can in nowise inherit the kingdom of God" (Mosiah 27:25–26). As the prophet and king Benjamin noted, "The natural man is an enemy to God, and has been from the fall of Adam, and will be, forever and ever, unless he yields to the enticings of the Holy Spirit, and putteth off the natural man and becometh a saint through the atonement of Christ the Lord" (Mosiah 3:19).

66. Cockerill, *Epistle to the Hebrews,* 443; see also Attridge, *Epistle to the Hebrews,* 279.

involving his entire somatic existence. Therefore, the 'cleansing' accomplished by Jesus was complete."[67]

According to Elder McConkie,

> The atonement of Christ is the rock foundation upon which all things rest which pertain to salvation and eternal life. Hence the Lord said to Adam: "By the blood ye are sanctified" (Moses 6:60), although the usual scriptural pronouncement is that men are "sanctified by the reception of the Holy Ghost." (3 Ne. 27:20.) The meaning is that although men are sanctified by the power of the Holy Ghost, such sanctifying process is effective and operative because of the shedding of the blood of Christ. Thus Moroni says that the faithful saints are "sanctified in Christ by the grace of God, through the shedding of the blood of Christ, which is in the covenant of the Father unto the remission" of their sins, that they become holy and without spot. (Moro. 10:33.)[68]

Third, the author emphasizes the extent of Christ's obedience by stating he fulfilled the Father's will even unto death. Indeed, the Father had prepared the Son's body for just such an end (10:5). For Latter-day Saints, the death of the Lord would include surrendering his soul to spiritual death and his body to physical.[69] This total submission was the supernal and consummate act of obedience.[70]

Fourth, the author closes this portion of his discussion with the very powerful "once for all" (ἐφάπαξ, *ephapax*), referring to an act so fully done it precludes the need for any other such action.[71] The adverb does not just mean "once for all people." That idea greatly shortchanges and limits the idea it carries. The author uses the term to show the definitive nature of the Savior's act (compare Rom. 6:10)[72] and uses it to bring to a climatic close his point. The adverb teaches that the Lord's Atonement is so full, so complete, so effective, and so broad that it was done once for all time, once for all eternity, and once for all the spheres over which the Lord presides.

---

67. Johnson, *Hebrews,* 253.

68. McConkie, *Doctrinal New Testament Commentary,* 3:188.

69. Being perfect, Christ was not subject to that spiritual death caused by sin. In Gethsemane and on the cross, he suffered sin's full effects. On spiritual death, see Richard M. Romney, "Spiritual Death," in Ludlow, *Encyclopedia of Mormonism,* 3:1407–8; and Jeffrey R. Holland, "Atonement of Jesus Christ," in Ludlow, *Encyclopedia of Mormonism,* 1:82–86.

70. Cockerill, *Epistle to the Hebrews,* 443–44.

71. BDAG, 417.

72. *NID,* s.v. "ἅπαξ."

Thus, so far as the salvation of humankind is concerned, nothing needed or could to be added to it forever. By means of his obedience even unto death, Jesus secured for all the faithful a place in the heavenly realm.[73]

Using the idea of "once for all," the author lays down the foundation for the next level of his argument. He will return to the idea of the inefficacy of the old rituals to emphasize the indisputable fact that Christ's offering was not only unique but also perfectly and fully efficacious for those who receive sanctification (10:14).[74]

No Longer an Offering for Sin (10:11–18)

Greek Text

11 Καὶ πᾶς μὲν ἱερεὺς ἕστηκεν καθ' ἡμέραν λειτουργῶν καὶ τὰς αὐτὰς πολλάκις προσφέρων θυσίας, αἵτινες οὐδέποτε δύνανται περιελεῖν ἁμαρτίας. 12 οὗτος δὲ μίαν ὑπὲρ ἁμαρτιῶν προσενέγκας θυσίαν εἰς τὸ διηνεκὲς ἐκάθισεν ἐν δεξιᾷ τοῦ θεοῦ, 13 τὸ λοιπὸν ἐκδεχόμενος ἕως τεθῶσιν οἱ ἐχθροὶ αὐτοῦ ὑποπόδιον τῶν ποδῶν αὐτοῦ, 14 μιᾷ γὰρ προσφορᾷ τετελείωκεν εἰς τὸ διηνεκὲς τοὺς ἁγιαζομένους. 15 μαρτυρεῖ δὲ ἡμῖν καὶ τὸ πνεῦμα τὸ ἅγιον, μετὰ γὰρ τὸ εἰρηκέναι· 16 Αὕτη ἡ διαθήκη ἣν διαθήσομαι πρὸς αὐτοὺς μετὰ τὰς ἡμέρας ἐκείνας, λέγει κύριος, διδοὺς νόμους μου ἐπὶ καρδίας αὐτῶν, καὶ ἐπὶ τὴν διάνοιαν αὐτῶν ἐπιγράψω αὐτούς, 17 καὶ τῶν ἁμαρτιῶν αὐτῶν καὶ τῶν ἀνομιῶν αὐτῶν οὐ μὴ μνησθήσομαι ἔτι· 18 ὅπου δὲ ἄφεσις τούτων, οὐκέτι προσφορὰ περὶ ἁμαρτίας. [SBLGNT]

King James Version

11 And every priest standeth daily ministering and offering oftentimes the same sacrifices, which can never take away sins: 12 But this man, after he had offered one sacrifice for sins for ever, sat down on the right hand of God; 13 From henceforth expecting till his enemies be made his footstool. 14 For by one offering he hath perfected for ever them that are sanctified.

New Rendition

11 And every priest stands daily serving and frequently offering sacrifices that are never able to remove sins. 12 But Christ, after he had offered for all time a single sacrifice for sin, sat down on the right hand of God, 13 then waiting until his enemies are placed as a footstool under his feet. 14 Indeed, by a single offering he has forever perfected those who are sanctified. 15 And the

---

73. Cockerill, *Epistle to the Hebrews,* 444.

74. Vanhoye, *Letter to the Hebrews,* 162.

15 Whereof the Holy Ghost also is a witness to us: for after that he had said before, 16 This is the covenant that I will make with them after those days, saith the Lord, I will put my laws into their hearts, and in their minds will I write them; 17 And their sins and iniquities will I remember no more. 18 Now where remission of these is, there is no more offering for sin.

Holy Spirit also testifies to us, for after having said,

> 16 "This is the covenant I will make with them after those days, says the Lord, I will put my laws on their hearts and I will write them on their minds" [Jer. 31:33],

17 he also says,

> "I will no longer remember their sins and transgressions." [Jer. 31:34]

18 Now where there is forgiveness for these, there is no longer any offering for sin.

Translation Notes and Comments

10:11 ***And every priest standeth daily ministering and offering oftentimes the same sacrifices, which can never take away sins / And every priest stands daily serving and frequently offering sacrifices that are never able to remove sins:*** In this new pericope, the author really drives home his thesis. Again, choosing his words carefully, he reminds his readers of the ineffective nature of the Mosaic sacrifices. The phrase πᾶς μὲν ἱερεύς (*pas men hiereus*), "every priest," includes not just the high priest, the author's primary target up to this point, but every authorized minister.

Though offered on a frequent, even daily basis, their sacrifices had no power to remove sins. The author stresses this point by the use of the phrase οὐδέποτε δύνανται (*oudepote dynantai*), "never able," reflecting the sacrifices' total impotency.

10:12 ***But this man, after he had offered one sacrifice for sins for ever, sat down on the right hand of God / But Christ, after he had offered for all time a single sacrifice for sin, sat down on the right hand of God:*** This phrase uses the demonstrative pronoun οὗτος (*houtos*), "this [one]," rather than a noun as the subject of the sentence. We have added "Christ" to our Rendition for clarity. The author uses the pronoun to refer to Jesus as High Priest in order to contrast his offering against the myriads performed by his fellow priests. His was μίαν . . . θυσίαν (*mian . . . thysian*), "a single sacrifice."

The author's emphasis is not, however, on the sacrifice but on its result. He paraphrases LXX Psalm 109:1 (Ps. 110:1, which he also paraphrases in 1:13). The adjective διηνεκής (*diēnekēs*) is telling. It carries the primary meaning of something being "continuous, without interruption, perpetual," but it often carries a "particular focus upon the future" and therefore can mean "always, forever."[75] Its position in this phrase allows it to be taken two ways. If it is taken with the preceding phrase, it can be translated as "having offered one sacrifice forever." If it is taken with the phrase that follows, it can be translated as "he sat down forever at God's right hand."[76] Though the author's style is fluid enough to accommodate variation, because he has used the phrase ἐν δεξιᾷ (*en dexia*), "on the right hand," with what has preceded it before (7:3; 10:1, and again in 10:14), we have followed that model in our Rendition.[77]

The author underscores the result of the Lord's sacrifice by using the aorist tense of the verb καθίζω (*kathizō*), "to sit." In that way he marks the finality of the enthronement of the Lord that resulted from his sacrifice for sins.[78]

10:13 ***From henceforth expecting till his enemies be made his footstool / then waiting until his enemies are placed as a footstool under his feet:*** The author again paraphrases LXX Psalm 109:1 (Ps. 110:1). The JST changes the vague phrase "expecting till" found in the KJV to the more concrete "to reign until." The verb in the Greek text, ἐκδέχομαι (*ekdechoma*), found here in the form of a present participle, means "to await" and also "to expect." It carries the connotation of "an eager expectation" or anxious waiting for something good.[79] As it stands, the participle refers to the Savior's waiting for his final triumph when all his enemies will be overcome. That does not mean, however, that in the meantime he is doing nothing. The JST corrects any such idea showing that he has already taken up the work of reigning.

10:14 ***For by one offering he hath perfected for ever them that are sanctified / Indeed, by a single offering he has forever perfected those who are sanctified:*** The conjunction γάρ (*gar*) is important here, acting as it does as a maker of inference.[80] In this case, it denotes a self-evident conclusion and thus can be translated as "indeed" and "certainly." Because it nuances the idea of being free from doubt, we have used the former in our Rendition.

---

75. Louw-Nida, §67.95; BDAG, 245.

76. Ellingworth, *Epistle to the Hebrews,* 509.

77. For discussion, see Bruce, *Epistle to the Hebrews,* 244 n. 57; Lane, *Hebrews 9–13,* 256 note z; and Ellingworth, *Epistle to the Hebrews,* 509–10.

78. The aorist, in this case, has a constative value. Wallace, *Greek Grammar,* 557–58.

79. Ellingworth, *Epistle to the Hebrews,* 510.

80. BDAG, 189–90.

For the term "sanctified," see Translation Notes for 10:10 above with its accompanying Analysis. For the sense of the verb τελειόω (*teleioō*), here in the perfect active form, "he has perfected," see Translation Notes for 10:1 above and 2:10–11 with the associated Analysis. Here we need only note that the connotation is that of the fulfillment of all that is necessary for the disciple to have access to God.[81]

The author's emphasis is on the once-for-all sacrifice the Lord made for the believer. Note that the author states perfection comes after sanctification (see Analysis below). Further, he denotes its effect with the adverbial phrase εἰς τὸ διηνεκές (*eis to diēnekes*), "forever" (see Translation Notes for 10:12), emphasizing the full and eternal sufficiency of the Lord's self-sacrifice in behalf of the disciple.

10:15 ***Whereof the Holy Ghost also is a witness to us / And the Holy Spirit also testifies to us:*** The author now returns to scripture to bolster his thesis, but as is his practice, he quotes a passage in which Deity speaks. The phrase τὸ πνεῦμα τὸ ἅγιον (*to pneuma to hagion*) refers to the Holy Spirit that the author sees as the inspiring principle and authoritative force behind the scriptures.[82] To describe its work, he uses the verb μαρτυρέω (*martyreō*), "to witness, testify," to the truthfulness of something.[83] The author likely has the third member of the Godhead in mind.

10:16 ***This is the covenant that I will make with them after those days, saith the Lord / "This is the covenant I will make with them after those days, says the Lord:*** The author once again quotes LXX Jeremiah 38:33 (Jer. 31:33 in the JST). For discussion, see Translation Notes for 8:10. The author does make a significant change in his rephrasing. Where the original (which he quotes in 8:10) states that God will make the covenant with "the house of Israel," the author makes it more applicable to his audience by changing the wording to "with them" and thereby including his readers. The change he makes reveals his view that his Christian audience is the direct spiritual descendants of those with whom the original covenant was made. God spoke to these former people "by the prophets," and he now speaks to this group through the Son (1:1), but the important point is that it is still God who does the speaking. In doing so, he constitutes the Hebrew Saints as members of his continued work of salvation through Christ Jesus.[84]

81. Ellingworth, *Epistle to the Hebrews,* 511. See Alma 34:13–15.
82. O'Brien, *Letter to the Hebrews,* 358.
83. BDAG, 617–18.
84. Cockerill, *Epistle to the Hebrews,* 456.

I will put my laws into their hearts, and in their minds will I write them / I will put my laws on their hearts and I will write them on their minds": This phrase is a continuation of the quote from LXX Jeremiah 38:33 (Jer. 31:33 in the JST). For discussion, see Translation Notes for 8:10–12 with associated Analysis.

Though in 8:10 the author quotes Jeremiah precisely, in this rephrasing he makes two significant changes. First, he reverses the order, placing "heart" before "mind," and second, he changes its preceding preposition "into" (εἰς, *eis*) to "upon" (ἐπί, *epi*), thus having God's laws written *upon* both the heart and mind. By placing such emphasis on the heart, the author highlights the transformation of the very core of the individual.

10:17 ***And their sins and iniquities will I remember no more / "I will no longer remember their sins and transgressions":*** This verse is the conclusion of the material found in LXX Jeremiah 38:34. Again, the author makes some changes from the original to stress his point. In the LXX version, the text reads καὶ τῶν ἁμαρτιῶν αὐτῶν οὐ μὴ μνησθῶ ἔτι (*kai tōn hamartiōn ou mē mnēsthō eti*), "and their sins I will remember no more" (our translation). Here the author of Hebrews retains ἁμαρτιῶν (*hamartiōn*) but adds a second noun, ἀνομιῶν (*anomiōn*) "transgressions, lawless deeds."[85] The change likely reflects a look back at the breaking of the first covenant that resulted from the Israelites unwillingness to be guided by Jehovah's laws.[86] The change emphasizes that even such flagrant acts will find full forgiveness.

Thus, God will definitely remember forever neither the sins nor the lawless deeds of those who come under the power of the Son's mercy. It is noteworthy that the author uses the statement to identify the effect of Christ's atoning act on God. Once the Savior has paid for the sin and the person thereby is cleansed, the Father remembers it no more. For discussion, see Translation Notes for 8:12 with the associated Analysis.

10:18 ***Now where remission of these is, there is no more offering for sin / Now where there is forgiveness for these, there is no longer any offering for sin:*** This sentence concludes the author's argument for the section that began in 8:1 and also serves as a summary of his thesis. For discussion on ἄφεσις (*aphesis*), "remission, forgiveness," see Translation Notes for 9:22 with associated Analysis.

---

85. BDAG, 85.
86. Ellingworth, *Epistle to the Hebrews,* 514.

Analysis and Summary

Though repeating points he has made earlier, this portion of the author's argument is not a mere résumé of what he has said. Rather, it serves as a climatic description and summary of all the Savior has done and all he has become through his self-offering, resulting in his ability to empower his Saints to persevere during the present trials. The reason is because the Lord has now realized his Father's invitation to "sit at my right hand" (10:12) and can from there minister to his disciples' needs. Thus, this closing section (10:11–18) brings to mind the full impact of all that has been said about the greatness of Christ and what he has done and is doing for his people.[87]

In this part of his treatise, the author emphasizes the total effectiveness of Christ's sacrifice. The author has set the stage by noting Christ offered "his own blood" (9:12) in perfect obedience to the Father's will. The author now more fully explains "what Christ has become through his once-for-all sacrifice and the benefits made available therefrom for his people."[88]

The author appeals to LXX Psalm 39:7–9 (Ps. 40:6–8 in the KJV) to show that God never intended for propitiation to come through animal sacrifices but through the body of his Son. As the author interprets this scripture, he sees that one cultic principle of sacrifice (and all that was built upon it) was to be abolished (ἀναιρέω, *anaireō*) through the force of another. The new principle, as shown in the prophetic critique of the Psalmist, is the self-sacrifice of the Son (see Alma 34:13–15). The author attributes the words in the psalm to the Lord himself, spoken upon his divine enthronement, to show the Savior acknowledged that God's sacrifice was the Son's own body (σῶμα, *sōma*) given in death. Yet the quality of the sacrifice was not its mere physical component. The reason his giving of himself had effect was because of his total obedience to the will of God. The author's assessment of the meaning of the scripture in 10:10 captures completely his understanding of what the Savior did: "it is by his [God's] will that we are sanctified through the offering of the body of Jesus Christ once for all" (NR).[89]

In 10:11, to drive home his point, the author again reminds his readers that the Levitical priests—not just the high priest, his primary focus up to this point—had to make sacrifices "day after day" but to no avail since the

87. Cockerill, *Epistle to the Hebrews,* 446–47.
88. Cockerill, *Epistle to the Hebrews,* 445–46.
89. Attridge, *Epistle to the Hebrews,* 269.

blood of the offerings could "never take away sins" and thereby sanctify and perfect the worshiper. Therefore, the author describes their condition as continually standing (ἵστημι, *histēmi*). They can never sit because their job was never done.[90]

That is not the case with those who come under the power of the Atonement. Speaking of the Lord's reconciliation between God and his people, one scholar noted,

> *Concilio* is a seating together in a *council.* Our word *council* comes from that. *Reconciliation* is to be called back to the council and sit down again. You are called to sit down with Abraham, Isaac, and Jacob—to return. Every term, every translation, every equivalent of *atonement* has the idea of *coming back. Redemption* means you will be *brought back again.* . . .
>
> . . . These words from the Latin that begin with *re* always imply *going back to a former state, returning home again.* And, of course, the Hebrew word for it is *tᵉshûvāh* and then *yᵉshîvāh.* The *tᵉshûvāh* is *return home*; the *yᵉshîvāh* is *sit down when you get home.* We repeatedly have the formula in the Book of Mormon, "Will you have place with us?"[91] Come in and have place to sit down with Abraham, Isaac, and Jacob. . . . It's the Atonement that reconciles you; it's the *at-one-ment* that brings you back home to sit down in the company of the whole family.[92]

In 10:12, the author contrasts the ineffective if perpetual work of the priests with the one saving act of the Lord. The author does this by introducing the subject with an aorist participial instrumental phrase that shows Christ "offered for all time a single sacrifice for sin" (NR). But the author's focus is not on the sacrifice, but its result: the Savior "sat down on the right hand of God" (NR). This singular act stands as visual witness that the Lord's sacrifice worked. While the author's image of the priests leaves them ever standing because their work is never done, that of the Son shows him sitting because his work is finished, total, and complete.[93]

---

90. To push his point, the author uses the perfect tense ἕστηκεν (*hestēken*) of the verb ἵστημι (*histēmi*), which is intransitive and present in meaning, thus, "he stands," that is, he had set himself but is now standing, whereas the present tense is transitive, "he set."

91. For example, see Alma 7:25; and Hel. 3:30.

92. "Lecture 24, Jacob 3–4: Filthiness and the Atonement," in Hugh Nibley, *Teachings of the Book of Mormon, Semester 1: Transcripts of Lectures Presented to an Honors Book of Mormon Class at Brigham Young University, 1988–1990* (Provo, Utah: Foundation for Ancient Research and Mormon Studies, 2004), 311, 312–13, https://scholarsarchive.byu.edu/cgi/viewcontent.cgi?article=1070&context=mi, italics in original.

93. The author uses the aorist tense of the verb καθίζω (*kathizō*), thereby emphasizing the finality of the Lord's secession. The phrase became a center piece of the Apostles' and

In 10:13–17, the author returns to the theme he developed in 8:1–6, where he used the imagery of a "shadow" to describe the earthly counterpart of a heavenly reality. Now he shifts from a vertical to a horizontal plane to show that the "shadow" of good things that have come (10:1) describes a temporal reality—Christ's self-sacrifice has "by a single offering . . . forever perfected those who are sanctified" (NR 10:14). This idea is important to the author's overall reason for writing. He is stressing the present reality of the Savior's station as a minister already empowered in heaven who can be reached for assistance (4:16). Thus, the author reassures his audience they will find help to persevere in faith.

Note perfection comes after sanctification. As noted earlier in this work (see Translation Notes for 2:10 with associated Analysis), the verb "perfect" (τελειόω, *teleioō*) connotes that which is fully finished, completed, matured, and whole, thus made adequate for a necessary task.[94] Though the author uses it primarily to denote consecration by which priests were made ready for cultic service, he also uses it for the state of the Saints that prepares them for eternal life.[95] To enter this state, the disciple must first become sanctified (ἁγιάζω, *hagiazō*). For discussion, see Translation Notes for 2:11 with the associated Analysis. In sum, the word means "holy" and designates the state of one who has met the qualifications for and participates in sacred work.[96] Both verbs connote an enabling cleansing from sin and pollution that prepares the Saint to enter God's presence. Here "perfect" may point to the direct, personal, and everlasting association between God and the person, while "sanctified" refers to the sinless state that makes the association possible.[97]

The author uses the perfect tense to describe the nature of the perfection, putting emphasis on its lasting effect—a condition that faithlessness can destroy, but which faithfulness will preserve. The author's words show that, from his point of view, his readers have already entered into this state and need only to maintain it.

---

disciples' witness of the final triumph of the Lord. See Mark 16:19; and Col. 3:1. In vision, Stephen saw the glorified Savior as he sat beside God (Acts 7:55–56), and Peter witnesses that from that position, the Lord ruled over angels, powers, and authorities (1 Pet. 3:22). Compare D&C 76:23.

94. Attridge, *Epistle to the Hebrews,* 83–84, and n. 52.

95. *NID*, s.v. "τέλος."

96. Procksch, *TDNT,* 1:111–12.

97. Peterson, *Hebrews and Perfection,* 151–52.

Because they have come to Christ in faith, he has both cleansed and perfected them. The author's emphasis is that these conditions, if maintained, will need neither supplementation nor renewal any more than the Savior's ascension will need repeating. Given this understanding, it is little wonder the author is most anxious his readers persevere in righteousness. To fall away would destroy the holy state in which they find themselves and cut them off from the only source of mercy, grace, and power they so desperately need and can call upon.[98]

In 10:15–17, the author reiterates part of his earlier quotation of LXX Jeremiah 38:31–34 (in 8:8–12) that touches on the new law God will establish. However, he uses the scripture to make a different point by focusing on the results of the placement of the law: it will be written on the disciples' hearts and minds, suggesting their total assimilation of the laws, and as a result, they show the same willful obedience that their Savior did.[99] But as grand as that is, the next phrase is the heart of matter: God will remember their sins no more. Because of this, the author concludes, where sin has been fully forgiven and forgotten, there is no further need for a sacrifice for sin (10:18). Thus, the all sufficient work of Christ has done away with any need for any portion, let alone the whole, of the sacrificial system.

In sum, in this section, the author "shows how it is that Christ's sacrificial death is an appropriate one, indeed a sufficient condition for the establishment of a new covenant (9:15–22), the covenant of interior renewal promised by Jeremiah."[100] The result, as the author restates in 10:17 (see 8:12 and KJV Jer. 31:34), is that God remembers the sin no more. Once the Savior has paid for the sin and the faithful one is fully cleansed, the work of the Atonement, so typified in the offerings of the Mosaic law, has completed its work. Through his faithful and full obedience, the Savior has become the mediator of the new covenant as the consummate High Priest. As a result, he can provide for his people not only forgiveness of sins but also the power to overcome the weakness from which the sin arose (see Ether 12:27). The author's point is that Jesus' Atonement is not only the only source of grace, but it is also the only necessary one.[101]

---

98. Ellingworth, *Epistle to the Hebrews,* 452.
99. Attridge, *Epistle to the Hebrews,* 281.
100. Attridge, *Epistle to the Hebrews,* 269.
101. Cockerill, *Epistle to the Hebrews,* 446.

Drawing Near to God in Enduring Faith (10:19–25)

Greek Text

19 Ἔχοντες οὖν, ἀδελφοί, παρρησίαν εἰς τὴν εἴσοδον τῶν ἁγίων ἐν τῷ αἵματι Ἰησοῦ, 20 ἣν ἐνεκαίνισεν ἡμῖν ὁδὸν πρόσφατον καὶ ζῶσαν διὰ τοῦ καταπετάσματος, τοῦτ' ἔστιν τῆς σαρκὸς αὐτοῦ, 21 καὶ ἱερέα μέγαν ἐπὶ τὸν οἶκον τοῦ θεοῦ, 22 προσερχώμεθα μετὰ ἀληθινῆς καρδίας ἐν πληροφορίᾳ πίστεως, ῥεραντισμένοι τὰς καρδίας ἀπὸ συνειδήσεως πονηρᾶς καὶ λελουσμένοι τὸ σῶμα ὕδατι καθαρῷ· 23 κατέχωμεν τὴν ὁμολογίαν τῆς ἐλπίδος ἀκλινῆ, πιστὸς γὰρ ὁ ἐπαγγειλάμενος· 24 καὶ κατανοῶμεν ἀλλήλους εἰς παροξυσμὸν ἀγάπης καὶ καλῶν ἔργων, 25 μὴ ἐγκαταλείποντες τὴν ἐπισυναγωγὴν ἑαυτῶν, καθὼς ἔθος τισίν, ἀλλὰ παρακαλοῦντες, καὶ τοσούτῳ μᾶλλον ὅσῳ βλέπετε ἐγγίζουσαν τὴν ἡμέραν. [SBLGNT]

King James Version

19 Having therefore, brethren, boldness to enter into the holiest by the blood of Jesus, 20 By a new and living way, which he hath consecrated for us, through the veil, that is to say, his flesh; 21 And having an high priest over the house of God; 22 Let us draw near with a true heart in full assurance of faith, having our hearts sprinkled from an evil conscience, and our bodies washed with pure water. 23 Let us hold fast the profession of our faith without wavering; (for he is faithful that promised;) 24 And let us consider one another to provoke unto love and to good works: 25 Not forsaking the assembling of ourselves together, as the manner of some is; but exhorting one another: and so much the more, as ye see the day approaching.

New Rendition

19 Therefore, brothers and sisters, since we have confidence to enter the sanctuary by the blood of Jesus, 20 which opens up to us a new and living way through the veil, that is, through his body, 21 and since we have a great priest over the house of God, 22 let us approach the sanctuary with a true heart in full assurance of faith, having our hearts cleansed from a consciousness of evil and having our body washed with pure water. 23 Let us hold firmly to our confession of hope without wavering, for the one who made the promise is trustworthy. 24 Let us consider how we can urge each other to love and good works 25 and not neglect our own meetings, as some are in the habit of doing, but encourage each other all the more since you see the Day drawing near.

Translation Notes and Comments

10:19–25 These verses constitute one long and involved periodic sentence. We break it into two in our Rendition in consideration of English style and to give better understanding and flow.

10:19 *Therefore:* This conjunction is important because it signals that the author is now moving to his conclusion of the material he began to develop 10:10, where he noted that by the Father's will all are sanctified through the Savior's self-offering.[102]

brethren / brothers and sisters: As noted previously, the plural noun ἀδελφοί (*adelphoi*) can include both men and women,[103] so we have translated it "brothers and sisters" in our Rendition. By introducing this new section with this plural noun, the author subtly reminds his readers of their station as members of the household of God and affirms their common heritage in the same divine family (2:10–18; 3:1, 12). Further, the Savior is in no way ashamed to be identified with them (2:11).[104]

Having . . . boldness to enter into the holiest by the blood of Jesus / since we have confidence to enter the sanctuary by the blood of Jesus: The author refers back to the admonition and encouragement he made earlier (see 4:16).

The circumstantial participle ἔχοντες (*echontes*), translated "having" in the KJV, is important. It is causal in sense and can be translated as "because" or "since we have" like in our Rendition. It introduces the effect Christ's sacrifice should have on each believer.[105] That is, because of what the Savior has accomplished, the author's readers should feel fully confident in approaching God.

The author chose the noun παρρησία (*parrēsia*), "boldness, confidence," to show what his readers' attitude should be. The word carries the idea of an absolute fearlessness in approaching a task that might otherwise be intimidating.[106] Further, it also holds the nuance of a person being authorized to do something. This nuance gives a more complete expression to just exactly what the Lord accomplished for his people.[107] They not only can approach God with confidence, but they are also authorized to do so. This confidence is derived from and based on "the blood of Jesus," that is, on faith in the effects of his Atonement. It is therefore a gift from God.

---

102. It can be argued that the conclusion could also rest upon material the author presented as far back as 7:1. See Vanhoye, *Letter to the Hebrews,* 166.

103. BDAG, 18.

104. Cockerill, *Epistle to the Hebrews,* 466.

105. Ellingworth, *Epistle to the Hebrews,* 517.

106. BDAG, 781–82; Louw-Nida, §25.158.

107. *NID,* s.v. "παρρησία"; Cockerill, *Epistle to the Hebrews,* 466; Lane, *Hebrews 9–13,* 274 note b.

The author uses the nominalized, genitive, neuter plural adjective τῶν ἁγιῶν (*tōn hagiōn*), literally "of holies" (translated as "sanctuary" in the Rendition), to symbolize the divine realm and to keep a tie to the work of the high priest on the Day of Atonement.

10:20 ***By a new and living way, which he hath consecrated for us, through the veil / which opens up to us a new and living way through the veil:*** This phrase presents a translation challenge. A literal rendering would be "which he inaugurated for us, a new and living way through the veil."[108] The problem is to what the relative pronoun ἥν (*ēn*), "which," refers. If it refers to the noun εἴσοδον (*eishodon*), "entrance," the phrase would read, "which [entrance] he inaugurated for us through the veil in a new and living way." If the pronoun is taken with the present participle ἔχοντες (*echontes*), "having," at the beginning of the sentence, then the phrase would read, "Having . . . a new and living way which he inaugurated for us through the veil."[109] Either way, the point is that Jesus did something never done before: he inaugurated *the* way into heaven.

The author reassures his readers that they can succeed in their quest because, at last, a unique and successful means has been prepared. The verb ἐγκαινίζω (*engkainizō*), "to open up, inaugurate," denotes a condition that has been recently achieved that allows something to happen or to go into effect.[110] Under the law of Moses, access to the "Holy of Holies," referred to in the previous verse, was restricted to the high priest, who could enter it but once a year on the Day of Atonement. The author's point is that Christ's Atonement opens up a way through the veil into the presence of God. The caveat however is that those who so enter can do so only by accepting Christ as their Savior and being obedient to his commandments. The use of the adjective πρόσφατος (*prosphatos*), which denotes "new, recent" and carries the extended sense of "not previously existing" (which seems to be the sense in this passage), bears this out.[111] The present, active participle of the verb ζάω (*zaō*), "to live,"[112] helps clarify what this "new and living way" is. The Savior did not merely open up the way; he actually is "the way, the truth, and the light. No one comes to the Father except through [him]" (John 14:6, our translation).

---

108. The Greek reads, ἣν ἐνεκαίνισεν ἡμῖν ὁδὸν πρόσφατον καὶ ζῶσαν (*hēn enekainisen hēmin hodon prosphaton kie zōsan*).

109. Vanhoye, *Letter to the Hebrews,* 166.

110. BDAG, 272; Louw-Nida, §13.84.

111. BDAG, 886.

112. BDAG, 424–25.

In sum, the author again plays on the imagery of the veil of the tabernacle that separated the people from the Most Holy Place, using the veil to symbolize the inability of the people to become pure enough to enter God's presence (for discussion, see Translation Notes for 6:19 and 9:3 with associated Analyses). However, all is not lost. There is another "way." The Savior's Atonement, along with the gospel standards, provides the means for a person to become pure enough to enter into eternal life.[113] "The way"—that is, the Savior—is able to do what the old covenant could not, that is, penetrate the veil by making the faithful pure.

his flesh / through his body: What made the passage possible, that is, what opened the way for all to enter God's presence, the author describes by the noun σάρξ (*sarx*), "flesh, body."[114] The word connotes the Savior's mortality, that is, his physical life that he gave up for all in order to open the way to God. His death did this by allowing his mercy, grace, and power to flow into the lives of all those who would follow him, bringing to them forgiveness and the ability to live acceptably before the Father.

Due to the complexity of this sentence (10:21–22), there is some ambiguity whether "flesh" should be construed with "veil" or "way." If taken with "way," the author is saying that through the way of the Lord's flesh—that is, his full obedience—he has opened the veil for access to God.[115] If taken with "veil," the author is saying that through the veil—that is, the Lord's mortal body given in death—he has opened the way to God.[116] Based on grammatical considerations, we have opted for the latter translation in our Rendition, though the former is also valid.[117] Either way, the point is that due to his sacrifice, Christ has done something no high priest had ever done before: he has opened the portal to heaven.

---

113. BDAG, 691–92; Ellingworth, *Epistle to the Hebrews,* 519. For a study, see Maurer, *TDNT,* 6:766–67.

114. BDAG, 914–16.

115. For discussion, see Ellingworth, *Epistle to the Hebrews,* 519–20.

116. See Lane, *Hebrews 9–13,* 284–85; and Attridge, *Epistle to the Hebrews,* 285–87.

117. This passage has caused a great deal of debate. For discussion, see Ellingworth, *Epistle to the Hebrews,* 519; and Cockerill, *Epistle to the Hebrews,* 468–69. Concerning grammatical considerations, the first is word order, where καταπετάσματος (*katapetasmatos*) is closer to σαρκός (*sarkos*) than ὁδόν (*hodon*). The second is case, because τοῦτ' ἔστιν (*tout' estin*) normally links items of the same case and this matches *katapetasmatos* with *sarkos,* which are both in the genitive case. It must be admitted, however, that the author seems to have redefined the symbol of the veil. Up to this point, it has been the impenetrable curtain separating people from God. Here the author makes it Christ's flesh and thereby gives it power to no longer separate the person from God but to gain access to him. The shift is quite remarkable. See Bruce, *Epistle to the Hebrews,* 251–53, who sees no problem with the transition.

10:21 ***And having an high priest over the house of God / since we have a great priest over the house of God:*** The Greek text does not have the words "having" or "since we have." They are inserted for clarity. Also, the insertion helps emphasize the author's focus on the benefits that come to the saint from the Savior's station at the head of the priesthood.

The author breaks from his practice of denoting the high priest as ἀρχιερεύς (*archiereus*)[118] and instead refers to him as ἱερέα μέγαν (*hiera megan*), "great priest." The use follows the LXX, which refers to the high priest as ὁ ἱερεὺς ὁ μέγας (*ho hiereus ho megas*).[119] A passage from LXX Leviticus 21:10 may have informed the author's choice. It mentions "the great priest . . . on whose head the oil of anointing is poured and who has been consecrated to wear the priestly garments" (our translation).[120]

This Old Testament passage is alive with terms dear to the author. Here he juxtaposes the noun ὁ ἱερεὺς ὁ μέγας (*ho hiereus ho megas*), "the great priest," the adjective χριστός (*christos*), "anointed" (the noun Χριστός, *Christos,* denoting "the anointed one"), and the perfect passive participle of τελειόω (*teleioō*), "perfected, consecrated," a verb that is used nine times in Hebrews, twice in this chapter (10:1, 14). In sum, the author connects an anointing with the Great Priest and his consecration or perfection that gives him the right to wear the priestly attire.

The phrase τὸν οἶκον τοῦ θεοῦ (*ton oikon tou theou*), "the house of God," echoes the idea of both tabernacle and heaven. The verse stresses the high position that the Lord holds in both the earthly and heavenly spheres in which the Father presides. The phrase also calls the readers' attention to their own position as members of this prestigious and eternal house.[121] On this basis—that of having such a Great Priest—the reader can have full confidence, even boldness, in approaching Deity.[122]

10:22 ***Let us draw near / let us approach the sanctuary:*** This is the first of the author's three admonitions based on Christ's position as the presiding heavenly Priest.

---

118. This term he uses nineteen times elsewhere in Hebrews.

119. This is the translation of the Hebrew הַכֹּהֵן הַגָּדוֹל (*hakkōhēn haggādôl*), literally "the great priest." See McConkie, *Doctrinal New Testament Commentary,* 3:191.

120. The Greek is ὁ ἱερεὺς ὁ μέγας . . . τοῦ ἐπικεχυμένου ἐπὶ τὴν κεφαλὴν τοῦ ἐλαίου τοῦ χριστοῦ καὶ τετελειωμένου ἐνδύσασθαι τὰ ἱμάτια (*ho hiereus ho megas . . . tou epikechymenou epi tēn kephalēn tou elaiou tou christou kai teteleiōmenou endysasthai ta himatia*).

121. Koester, *Hebrews,* 449.

122. O'Brien, *Letter to the Hebrews,* 362–63.

The word "sanctuary" is not in the Greek text but is understood from the admonition to "enter the sanctuary" in NR 10:19 above, so we have added it in our Rendition for clarity. Here it stands for the Father.

The verb προσέρχομαι (*proserchomai*), "approach," can carry the nuance of entering into the presence of the Divine,[123] a condition which Jesus has now made possible.

with a true heart in full assurance of faith: The adjective ἀληθινός (*alēthinos*), "true," connotes such ideas as "trustworthy, authentic, genuine" and carries the idea of being all that something should be.[124]

On καρδία *(kardia)*, see Translation Notes on 3:8. Here we need but note that the word carries the idea of those inner motives, desires, and feelings that dictate a person's life. Thus, a true heart is one freed of guile, deceit, or hypocrisy; one that has been transformed through the purifying power of the Savior. It is a heart upon which the new covenant not only can be but also has been inscribed (Jer. 31:33).

The noun πληροφορία (*plērophoria*) denotes a "state of complete certainty, full assurance."[125] Here it is anchored to the witness of a profound change of heart that has resulted through one's faith in Christ and puts away any fear of approaching God. The transformation has proven the Lord fully faithful to his promise and should result in the person's fully surrendering himself or herself in obedience to the Father.[126]

having our hearts sprinkled from an evil conscience / having our hearts cleansed from a consciousness of evil: This phrase explains what constitutes a "true heart." The verb ῥαντίζω (*rantizō*) generally denotes sprinkling something with a liquid but here designates the act of cleansing oneself from ritual uncleanliness and from sin.[127] In this passage the word is found in the form of a perfect passive participle, used circumstantially that indicates the completion of an act that has permanent results.[128] On συνείδησις (*syneidēsis*), "consciousness," see Translation Notes on 9:9.

our bodies washed with pure water / having our body washed with pure water: The verb λούω (*louō*), "to wash," is found here in the form of a perfect passive participle.[129] This may be an oblique reference to

---

123. BDAG, 878.
124. BDAG, 43; Louw-Nida, §§70.3; 72.1; 73.2.
125. BDAG, 827.
126. Lane, *Hebrews 9–13,* 286.
127. BDAG, 903; Vanhoye, *Letter to the Hebrews,* 168.
128. Smyth, *Greek Grammar,* §1872.
129. BDAG, 603–604; *NID,* s.v. "λούω."

baptism, *the* rite of covenant acceptance.[130] In keeping with the author's Old Testament imagery, the phrase does bring to mind the need that the high priest had of thoroughly washing himself before entering the Most Holy Place (Lev. 16:4). More particularly, it reflects Jehovah's promise that he will "sprinkle clean water" upon the faithful through which they will receive a "new heart" and a "new spirit." Receiving these will result in the person having the Father's spirit within them such that they will be able to keep and administer his statutes (Ezek. 36:25–27).[131]

10:23 ***Let us hold fast the profession of our faith without wavering / Let us hold firmly to our confession of hope without wavering:*** This is the second of the author's admonitions that can be realized because of the Savior's high position as Great Priest. The verb κατέχω (*katechō*) means "to adhere firmly to traditions, convictions, or beliefs."[132]

On ὁμολογία (*homologia*), "confession," see Translation Notes for 3:1; 4:14. As used here, the noun denotes the public act of expressing a conviction for and allegiance to a person or cause.[133] It connotes a depth of belief that motivates one to push for a particular outcome.[134] The outward manifestation, in Latter-day Saint parlance, is bearing testimony. In this case, the confession consists of the "hope" the Saint has in a full salvation because of his or her faith in Christ.

The noun ἔλπις (*elpis*), "hope," means "the looking forward to something with some reason for confidence respecting fulfillment, hope, expectation."[135] In the New Testament, though the idea of receiving a future blessing remains, it is augmented by a belief that the hope generated by the Old Testament witness has, through the coming of the Messiah, now been realized. "What was previously future has now become present for believers: justification, a personal relationship with God as his child, the indwelling of the Holy Spirit, and a new people of God comprising believers from Israel and the

---

130. Lane, *Hebrews 9–13,* 287; Bruce, *Epistle to the Hebrews,* 255; Attridge, *Epistle to the Hebrews,* 288–89; Ellingworth, *Epistle to the Hebrews,* 523–24; Vanhoye, *Letter to the Hebrews,* 168–69; Anderson, *Understanding Paul,* 218–19. It is more likely, however, that the author is keeping with his tabernacle imagery. See O'Brien, *Letter to the Hebrews,* 367–68; Cockerill, *Epistle to the Hebrews,* 475.

131. Though the context suggests an outward washing, the effect is an inward cleansing. See Bruce, *Epistle to the Hebrews,* 255.

132. BDAG, 532–33.

133. BDAG, 709.

134. Michel, *TDNT,* 5:199–220; *NID,* s.v. ὁμολογέω (*homologeō*).

135. BDAG, 219–20.

nations."[136] The word points to the energy that stands behind a willingness to publicly acknowledge one's steadfastness to Christ based on the blessing he is giving and will give as the Great Priest. The phrase τῆς ἐλπίδος (*tēs elpidos*), "the hope," is an objective genitive and as such indicates not a hopeful confession but a confession that centers on a specific hope.[137]

The author stresses this idea with the adjective ἀκλινῆ (*aklinē*), "unwavering,"[138] that modifies τὴν ὁμολογίαν (*tēn homologian*), "the confession." The adjective is in a predicate position.[139] As such it is often used where English would employ an adverb.[140] Therefore, in our Rendition, we have translated it as an adverbial phrase, "without wavering," as does the KJV and many modern translations.[141]

(for he is faithful that promised) / for the one who made the promise is trustworthy: With this phrase, the author identifies what stands behind his admonition. The conjunction γὰρ (*gar*), "for," is important here because it precedes the reason for the requested act.

As noted in the Translation Notes for 4:1, the noun ἐπαγγελία (*epangelia*), "promise," denotes an announcement openly or publicly proclaimed concerning something that will or must be done. More than intention stands behind it. Rather, it connotes the concrete determination that assures that what is proclaimed will be realized. Because it also carries the force of obligation, it is often appropriately translated as "promise" as in the KJV and Rendition. When dealing with God, the echo of sacred covenant stands behind it.[142]

On πιστός (*pistos*), "faithful, trustworthy," see Translation Notes for 6:1. Here the stress is on the word's place and effect as one of the Father's primary virtues and the trust one can have in him because of it.[143] The Savior confirmed his Father's trust through his life of total obedience coupled with its results (his enthronement) and by so doing has proved the Father's integrity and reliability. Those acts should earn his children's complete confidence.

---

136. *NID*, s.v. "ἔλπις."

137. Lane, *Hebrews 9–13,* 276 note q; compare Ellingworth, *Epistle to the Hebrews,* 525; and Vanhoye, *Letter to the Hebrews,* 169.

138. BDAG, 36.

139. If it were in an attributive position, it would clearly have adjectival force. Smyth, *Greek Grammar,* §§910b, 911, 912.The word is separated from the noun it modifies by the genitive phrase τῆς ἐλπίδος (*tēs elpidos*), "of the hope," for emphasis.

140. Smyth, *Greek Grammar,* §§1042–43.

141. NRSV, NIV84, NET.

142. BDAG, 355–56; *NID,* s.v. "ἐπαγγελία."

143. Louw-Nida, §31.88.

10:24 ***And let us consider one another to provoke unto love and to good works / Let us consider how we can urge each other to love and good works:*** This is the last of the author's three admonitions based on the result of the Lord's station as the Great Priest.

The Greek phrase is translated literally as "Let us consider each other with reference to urging of love and of good works."[144] The KJV has a rather literal translation that, unfortunately, doesn't work well in English. In our Rendition, we have tried to give the sense in a more easily understood way.

The verb κατανοέω (*katanoeō*), "consider," connotes the idea of seeing beyond the surface. It carries the idea of seeing into the soul of the individual, of an understanding that is spirit to spirit.[145]

The noun παροξυσμός (*paroxysmos*) means "rousing to activity" and can be translated as "stirring up, provoking, encouraging, urging."[146] Because the word "urge" means to press or incite someone toward a definite end,[147] we have used it in our Rendition.

The object of the urging is twofold: to increase ἀγάπη (*agapē*), "love," and καλῶν ἔργων (*kalōn ergōn*), "good works." On these see Translation Notes for 6:10 with associated Analysis. In the present context, the noun *agapē* denotes a very inclusive and unwearying love that most fully manifests itself in continual service toward the best for a loved one.[148] Because of the loving nature in which it is rendered, that service can be defined as "good works," the noun ἔργον (*ergōn*) denoting "work, labor"[149] and the adjective καλός (*kalos*) denoting that which is good and useful but carrying the idea of that which contributes to a person's salvation.[150]

10:25 ***Not forsaking the assembling of ourselves together, as the manner of some is / And not neglect our own meetings, as some are in the habit of doing:*** The verb ἐγκαταλείπω (*engkataleipō*) means "to forsake, abandon, or neglect" something and emphasizes a deliberate and uncaring attitude that is totally willing to leave others in the lurch.[151]

---

144. The Greek reads, κατανοῶμεν ἀλλήλους εἰς παροξυσμὸν ἀγάπης καὶ καλῶν ἔργων (*katanoōmen allēlous eis paroxysmon agapēs kai kalōn ergōn*).

145. BDAG, 522–23; Louw-Nida, §§30.4, 43; 32.12; Lane, *Hebrews 9–13,* 276 note r.

146. BDAG, 780; Louw-Nida, §90.55; Lane, *Hebrews 9–13,* 276 note s. The word's force can be seen in its more usual negative nuances such as a pointed and even heated disagreement or a sharp argument. Louw-Nida, §33.451; Koester, *Hebrews,* 445.

147. *Webster's New Dictionary of Synonyms,* s.v. "urge."

148. BDAG, 6. See Johnson, *Hebrews,* 165–66; and Vanhoye, *Letter to the Hebrews,* 169; compare Hel. 10:4.

149. BDAG, 390–91.

150. BDAG, 504–5; Louw-Nida, §§65.43; 88.4; 87.25.

151. BDAG, 273; Johnson, *Hebrews,* 261.

The noun ἐπισυναγωγή (*episynagōgē*) denotes an ingathering, that is, a meeting or assemblage.[152] Apparently, church attendance had been dropping off. The noun ἔθος (*ethos*), "habit," describes a customary manner of behavior and suggests that some Christians had abandoned the Church for quite a period of time. The genitive pronoun ἑαυτῶν (*heautōn*), "our," in association with "meetings" could suggest some of the members had abandoned the Christian assemblies and returned to Jewish worship or moved into heretical circles.[153] The context however suggests the move was into inactivity.[154]

but exhorting one another / but encourage each other: The verb παρακαλέω (*parakaleō*) carries the idea of strongly urging someone to a course of action.[155] Here it refers to staying strong to the hope that the covenantal promises and the Lord's station as exalted Great Priest should give each Saint.

and so much the more as ye see the day approaching / all the more since you see the Day drawing near: The phrase καὶ τοσούτῳ μᾶλλον (*kai tosoutō mallon*), "and all the more," stresses the urgency that stands behind the need for the encouragement and points to the nearness of a singular event. Here it references an event the author's readers see approaching. It is unlikely, though possible, that the author has the day of a person's death in mind. The context (see 10:36–38) suggests however that the author is referring to a "Day" that all will experience together.[156] We have capitalized "Day" since it is often used in the New Testament as a technical term referring to Christ's Second Coming.[157] In the present context, however, the word's emphasizes is more on what follows, that is, the pleasant "Day of Judgment" wherein the author's readers can at last enjoy fully the realization of blessings of the new covenant that they now enjoy only in part (compare Jacob 6:13; and Moro. 10:34).

---

152. BDAG, 382. The related Jewish word "synagogue" also means "assembly" and was used by Apostolic and post-Apostolic authors to refer to Christian meetings. Further, the noun used in this passage, along with its related verb, was used both in the scriptures and other sacral writings to denote the assembly or assembling of God's people at the final judgment. See 2 Macc. 2:7; Matt. 23:37; Mark 13:27; 2 Thes. 2:1. For an extended study, see Schrage, *TDNT,* 7:841–43.

153. Koester, *Hebrews,* 446.

154. Bruce, *Epistle to the Hebrews,* 257–58; Ellingworth, *Epistle to the Hebrews,* 529.

155. BDAG, 764–65.

156. Cockerill, *Epistle to the Hebrews,* 480 and n. 68. Based on 1:13; 2:5–10; 9:27–28; 10:38–39, the coming "Day" does not appear to refer to the time of death but to the Day of Judgment.

157. Lane, *Hebrews 9–13,* 277 note x. See 1 Thes. 5:2; and 2 Thes. 2:2. See also McConkie, *Doctrinal New Testament Commentary,* 3:191.

Analysis and Summary

The author has been feeding his readers the "solid food" of the gospel (NR 5:14) and in so doing has prepared them for the banquet of which this portion of his Epistle consists. By now they should have gained a profound understanding of and a deep appreciation for who Christ is and his example. Further, they should be fully prepared to take advantage of what he offers.

This stage being set, the author now gives them a comprehensive view of the expectations that they should realize because of what Christ has done. The author lists these in the form of a series of admonitions that he introduces with the phrase "since we have"[158] (10:19, which the Rendition repeats at the beginning of 10:21).

He shows them that, because of what Christ has done, they now have free access to the inner sanctuary or, less symbolically, to heaven itself. Jesus, through his self-offering, that is, "his body" (NR 10:20), has done what a myriad of high priests could not do. "He gained access by a new way to the living God, not only for himself, but for all who through him will share God's life."[159] In sum, the author is saying that since his readers have this Great Priest, they have gained three things: an ability to penetrate the veil, a method to do it, and a priest who will take them through.[160]

The author's phrase "having our hearts cleansed from a consciousness of evil and having our body washed with pure water" (NR 10:22) points to that work of the Saint that was made possible because of the Great Priest. Salvation is a cooperative effort. Therefore, each faithful person has to take advantage of what Jesus has made possible by repenting and accepting that the Atonement is sufficient. Further, he or she must be willing to purify the body as well. Elder Bruce R. McConkie notes that this act is "an apparent allusion to those ordinances whereby the saints of the new covenant are made clean through conformity to the Lord's law (D. & C. 88:74–75; 124:37–40), even as Aaron and his sons were washed in the days of the old covenant (Ex. 29:4)."[161] Here the emphasis is on the present state of the author's readers and stresses the current effect of what Christ has done. That both phrases contain a perfect participle indicates that not

---

158. This idea is expressed by the causal, circumstantial participle ἔρχοντες (*erchontes*).

159. Ellingworth, *Epistle to the Hebrews,* 521. Compare McConkie, *Doctrinal New Testament Commentary,* 3:190–91; and Ogden and Skinner, *Verse by Verse,* 258.

160. Vanhoye, *Letter to the Hebrews,* 167.

161. McConkie, *Doctrinal New Testament Commentary,* 3:191.

only have these people been cleansed, they continue to be so through the effective work of their High Priest.[162]

Based on the Atonement and the confidence that should grow out of it, the author makes a threefold admonition: first, to approach the sanctuary (that is, the heavenly realm) with true hearts in a fulness of faith (10:22); second, to exercise the confession of their hope without wavering (10:23); and third, to urge each other to love and good works (10:24). Note that by enjoining the three virtues—hope, faith, and love—the author has encompassed the whole of Christian life and at the same time introduced the themes he will develop in the next three chapters.[163]

The first admonition takes its force from the power growing out of what Christ has done. It now allows the people of faith to approach God by drawing continually near to him through prayer and worship (10:22). The emphasis is on the need to keep drawing near to God. Being close to him is not a matter of "once and done" but of living in such a way that the distance between the self and the Father continually grows more narrow. Thus, the act comprehends the entire compass of the life of faith.[164] Being near God is essential to a person's spiritual wellbeing and the very essence of her or his station as a Saint—one of God's own people (4:16; 7:25).[165] Further, their continued drawing close to their God will be the means by which they will be preserved from their present and future trials until they enter his divine presence (12:25–29).

Tied directly to the first admonition is the second, to hold tight to the confession of the firm hope they now enjoy (10:23). Because Jesus has opened the way, the faithful are able to continually draw near to him. They must, however, not slide back but firmly hold to the hope that their testimonies have brought. The author's referral to the confession of hope (ὁμολογία, *homologia*) likely encompasses not just one's private assent to Christian ways but more importantly to the public witness of Christ's Sonship and the salvation that comes only through him. It is in such active persevering that one acquires all that God has promised.

The author confirms for his readers that their hope (ἔλπις, *elpis*) will be fully rewarded because the one who made the promise can be fully trusted

162. Cockerill, *Epistle to the Hebrews,* 475.

163. Lane, *Hebrews 9–13,* 280.

164. Cockerill, *Epistle to the Hebrews,* 472, 475–76.

165. Compare Lane, *Hebrews 9–13,* 286–87.

(πιστός, *pistos*) to fulfill it (10:23). The hope is specific. It is the reception of full access to God, the bona fides of which the readers are now realizing in their increasingly close relationship with him.

Tied directly to the second admonitions is the third, to help one another to keep the faith (10:24). The author's focus is on each individual and the help he or she can render to the community of the Saints. The author uses the noun "urging" (παροξυμός, *paroxsymos*) to stress the energy each person should put into helping the others. The object of the urging is toward two objectives: greater love and more good works. The noun "love" (ἀγάπη, *agapē*) denotes "the quality of warm regard for and interest in another, esteem, affection, regard, love."[166] As described by the author of Hebrews, it goes well beyond mere sentimentality but connotes a heart oriented toward appropriate action.[167] As such it provides not only the energy but also the direction for selfless caregiving. The phrase "good works" stands opposite that of "dead works" (9:14) from which the Savior has cleansed the believer. Good works both benefit and please the receiver and also God. "In 13:1–6 the [author] will describe these works as deeds of brotherly love, hospitality, concern for the suffering, sexual purity, and generosity. The [author's] hearers have practiced such conduct in the past (6:10). He would have them continue to encourage one another in this behavior, for it is the full expression of the community life appropriate for God's people."[168]

The author gives two ways in which his readers can realize his admonitions (10:25). First, they are to continue to attend meetings, where they can find mutual support and help when needed. Second, they are to urge one another (παρακαλέω, *parakaleō*) to keep the faith and rely on the firm hope they have in God's promises that can be realized both in the present and in the future.

The author's admonition serves as a window, giving a peek at the ongoing and relentless nature of the persecution these people are facing. Some have abandoned the Church altogether and by so doing have deprived their fellow Saints of much needed support.[169] As the author has pointed out earlier, the abandonment has arisen in part because of the passage

---

166. BDAG, 6.

167. Cockerill, *Epistle to the Hebrews,* 478.

168. Cockerill, *Epistle to the Hebrews,* 479; Compare Vanhoye, *Letter to the Hebrews,* 169. Note Moro. 6:4–6 on the importance of Church attendance and urging one another to faithfulness.

169. Johnson, *Hebrews,* 261.

of time in which the converts' initial enthusiasm for the gospel has died down. Some became lazy (νωθρός, *nōthros*; see 5:11–14),[170] and this initially paved the way to inactivity and finally to complete abandonment of the Christian cause (4:1–3; 6:4–6). As the author will point out in the next section (10:26–31), these people are in grave danger. Here his emphasis is on the promised blessings. It is Christ, the all-sufficient "Great Priest," who has provided the resources "of escaping the fate of the unfaithful and joining the victorious faithful. The urgency of obedience is all the clearer because the 'word' of God that the hearers have received is nothing less than the astounding revelation of Christ's full sufficiency to save."[171] All they have to do is take advantage of it, and a large part of that is holding firm to their confession to the end.

The urgency to obedience and faithfulness is enhanced because the "Day" is approaching (10:25). From the beginning of his Epistle, the author has reminded his readers that they must encourage one another while "it is called To day" (3:7–15) and prepare themselves to "enter into God's rest" (4:11). "Today" does not last forever, and when it is over, there is no time for repentance. A new "Day" comes, and that day is *the* Day of Judgment.

A Warning against Sin (10:26–31)

Greek Text

26 Ἑκουσίως γὰρ ἁμαρτανόντων ἡμῶν μετὰ τὸ λαβεῖν τὴν ἐπίγνωσιν τῆς ἀληθείας, οὐκέτι περὶ ἁμαρτιῶν ἀπολείπεται θυσία, 27 φοβερὰ δέ τις ἐκδοχὴ κρίσεως καὶ πυρὸς ζῆλος ἐσθίειν μέλλοντος τοὺς ὑπεναντίους. 28 ἀθετήσας τις νόμον Μωϋσέως χωρὶς οἰκτιρμῶν ἐπὶ δυσὶν ἢ τρισὶν μάρτυσιν ἀποθνῄσκει· 29 πόσῳ δοκεῖτε χείρονος ἀξιωθήσεται τιμωρίας ὁ τὸν υἱὸν τοῦ θεοῦ καταπατήσας, καὶ τὸ αἷμα τῆς διαθήκης κοινὸν ἡγησάμενος ἐν ᾧ ἡγιάσθη, καὶ τὸ πνεῦμα τῆς χάριτος ἐνυβρίσας. 30 οἴδαμεν γὰρ τὸν εἰπόντα· Ἐμοὶ ἐκδίκησις, ἐγὼ ἀνταποδώσω· καὶ πάλιν· Κρινεῖ κύριος τὸν λαὸν αὐτοῦ. 31 φοβερὸν τὸ ἐμπεσεῖν εἰς χεῖρας θεοῦ ζῶντος. [SBLGNT]

---

170. BDAG, 683. Louw-Nida, §32.47, translates the phrase as "slow to understand," but the prime root is laziness. See §88.249.

171. Cockerill, *Epistle to the Hebrews*, 463.

King James Version

26 For if we sin wilfully after that we have received the knowledge of the truth, there remaineth no more sacrifice for sins, 27 But a certain fearful looking for of judgment and fiery indignation, which shall devour the adversaries. 28 He that despised Moses' law died without mercy under two or three witnesses: 29 Of how much sorer punishment, suppose ye, shall he be thought worthy, who hath trodden under foot the Son of God, and hath counted the blood of the covenant, wherewith he was sanctified, an unholy thing, and hath done despite unto the Spirit of grace? 30 For we know him that hath said, Vengeance belongeth unto me, I will recompense, saith the Lord. And again, The Lord shall judge his people. 31 It is a fearful thing to fall into the hands of the living God.

New Rendition

26 For if we intentionally sin after we have received a knowledge of the truth, there no longer remains any sacrifice for sins, 27 but only a certain fearful expectation of judgment and a consuming ardor of fire that will devour God's adversaries. 28 Anyone who rejected the law of Moses dies without mercy

> "on the testimony of two or three witnesses." [Deut. 17:6]

29 How much greater punishment do you think someone deserves who has treated the Son of God with disdain, and who has profaned the blood of the covenant by which he was sanctified, and who has outraged the Spirit of grace? 30 For we know the one who said,

> "Vengeance is mine; I will repay!" [Deut. 32:35]

and also

> "The Lord will judge his people." [Deut. 32:36]

31 It is a frightening thing to fall into the hands of the living God.

Translation Notes and Comments

10:26 *For if we sin wilfully after that we have received the knowledge of the truth / For if we intentionally sin after we have received a knowledge of the truth:* The adverb ἑκουσίως (*ekousiōs*) means "willingly, deliberately, intentionally" and emphasizes the purposeful and persistent nature of the intent behind an act.[172] The author gives the word force by placing it at the beginning of his sentence.

The author identifies the act with the verb ἁμαρτάνω (*hamartanō*), "to sin," found here as a plural, present participle, thus hinting at a specific category of wickedness, that of the rebellious. The present tense suggests

172. BDAG, 307; Louw-Nida, §§25.65; 30.64; Cockerill, *Epistle to the Hebrews,* 483.

the persistence of the disobedience.[173] In this instance, the heavy sin the author is referring to, as the context shows (see below), is not merely that of abandoning the Church or forsaking God and Christ or even breaking the new covenant. Rather, it denotes not only rebelling against them but also reaching out to others to do the same.

The preposition μετά (*meta*), "after," is important here for it gives the parameters in which an action takes place, indicating that only after certain conditions are met will the objective be realized.

That condition is gaining ἐπίγνωσις (*epignōsis*), "knowledge." The noun denotes becoming fully acquainted with something known before (γνῶσις, *gnōsis*) that leads to an expanded and often an exact understanding of that thing. It suggests such a depth of participation between the "knower" and the thing known that it has a powerful influence on the former. In the New Testament, that which can be known to this degree is limited to transcendent and moral matters. The word also carries a strong connotation of a tender, deep, and abiding relationship with God.[174]

What is known is ἀλήθεια (*alētheia*), "truth." The Greek noun only lightly touches on the idea of that which conforms to reality, having no distortion or amplification. The word stands in contrast to that which is false or deceitful and connotes the idea of what can be relied upon and, in that sense, is closely tied to the word of God. In addition, it carries echoes of faithfulness and of Jehovah's binding himself through covenant to do as he promised.[175] It also connotes that which is revealed and suggests correct doctrine. In the present context, the emphasis seems to be on the gospel and particularly on the absoluteness and finality of the Christian message.[176]

there remaineth no more sacrifice for sins / there no longer remains any sacrifice for sins: The verb ἀπολείπω (*apoleipō*), "to remain," here denotes that which is reserved for future enactment.[177] The author stresses the idea that when a person has sinned against a "knowledge of the truth," there is no expiation, "no further sacrifice to take away sin,"[178] and as result, the person must face the full reproach of not only his or her rebellion against the truth but also encouraging others to do the same. For a

---

173. Koester, *Hebrews,* 451; Ellingworth, *Epistle to the Hebrews,* 532.

174. BDAG, 369; Louw-Nida, §28.18; Bultmann, *TDNT,* 1:689–719; Strong, "New Strong's Expanded Dictionary . . . Greek," s.v. "ἐπίγνωσις."

175. BDAG, 42–43.

176. *NID,* s.v. "ἀλήθεια"; Bultmann, *TDNT,* 1:232–51.

177. BDAG, 115.

178. Ellingworth, *Epistle to the Hebrews,* 533.

study, see the excursus on "Unforgivable and Unpardonable Sins" found in chapter 6.

10:27 ***But a certain fearful looking for of judgment and fiery indignation, which shall devour the adversaries / but only a certain fearful expectation of judgment and a consuming ardor of fire that will devour God's adversaries:*** To strengthen his point, the author paraphrases LXX Isaiah 26:11.[179] The author uses the pronoun τὶς (*tis*), "a certain," to heighten his emphasis on the kind of fear that those who rebel against "a knowledge of truth" can expect.[180]

The noun ἐκδοκή (*ekdochē*) denotes an expectation of something in the future that can be for good or bad.[181] The adjective φοβερός (*phoberos*), "fearful,"[182] designates something very bad, indeed a fear amounting to terror brought on by the power and force of the intimidating agency.[183] In this case, that agent is the omnipotence of God. The feeling of terror is likely realized at the time of death (see Alma 40:12–14), although some may experience that condition before then (for example, see Jacob 7:19).

The paraphrase from Isaiah identifies three things: the source of the fear, those who will face it, and what will happen to them. The source is the πυρὸς ζῆλος (*pyros zēlos*), literally "zeal of fire." The noun ζῆλος (*zēlos*) denotes "intense positive interest in something, zeal, ardor" as well as "intense negative feelings [such as] jealousy, envy."[184] In this case, fire seems to be personified with the human emotion of zeal or ardor.[185] Thus the idea is best expressed in English as "the consuming ardor of fire" as in our Rendition. This word in the scriptures often connotes the exacting nature of a punishment inflicted by deity.[186]

---

179. Though it is possible the author is quoting a source, the difference between this passage and the known passages from the LXX are sufficiently different to suggest he is paraphrasing. The LXX reads, καὶ νῦν πῦρ τοὺς ὑπεναντίους ἔδεται (*kai nyn pyr tous hypenantious edetai*), "and now fire shall devour the adversaries."

180. Ellingworth, *Epistle to the Hebrews,* 534. It is God's "fiery indignation" that moves him to protect "the weak things of the world, those who are unlearned and despised" who take up the Lord's defense (D&C 35:13–14).

181. BDAG, 1060–62.

182. BDAG, 1060.

183. *NID,* s.v. "φόβος"; Balz and Wenke, *TDNT,* 9:189–219.

184. BDAG, 417; Louw-Nida, §78.25; BDAG, 427.

185. Stumpff, *TDNT,* 2:882–83.

186. BDAG, 898–99. It is possible to take phrase "of fire" as a genitive of apposition and therefore mean "the zeal that is fire." Ellingworth, *Epistle to the Hebrews,* 535.

The author describes those who will face such fiery fierceness as ὑπεναντίους (*hypenantious*), "opponents, adversaries, or enemies."[187] The Greek word suggests the strong opposition and deep hostility that lies behind these people's mutiny against God and his truth,[188] which helps explain his strong judgment upon them.

10:28 *He that despised Moses' law died without mercy under two or three witnesses / Anyone who rejected the law of Moses dies without mercy "on the testimony of two or three witnesses":* To further push his point, the author quotes a portion of Deuteronomy 17:6. The verb ἀθετέω (*atheteō*) means to reject something, believing it to be worthless or invalid.[189] In the Old Testament context, the word emphasized the action taken by an individual to both discount and impede God's work, thus committing sacrilege.

The result was death χωρὶς οἰκτιρμῶν (*chōris oiktirmōn*), "without mercy." The noun οἰκτιρμός (*oiktirmos*) connotes "concern over another's misfortune, pity, mercy, compassion."[190] The preposition χωρίς (*chōris*), "without,"[191] negates any feelings of compassion, thereby prohibiting any help or assistance whatsoever to the flagrant sinner.

Under the Mosaic law, the death penalty required more than one witness against the accused person to assure that spite, anger, or greed were not the motivating forces behind the charge of sacrilege (Num. 35:30; Deut. 17:6; 19:15).

10:29 *Of how much sorer punishment, suppose ye, shall he be thought worthy, who hath trodden under foot the Son of God / How much greater punishment do you think someone deserves who has treated the Son of God with disdain:* In this verse, the author defines the exact nature of the sin he has warned his readers against.

This verse presents translation difficulties because ancient Greek did not use any punctuation marks. Thus, various biblical versions have translated the verse differently. Some treat it as an exclamation,[192] others as a statement,[193] and others as a question.[194] We have chosen to follow the last

187. Ellingworth, *Epistle to the Hebrews,* 535.

188. BDAG, 1030; compare the adjective ἐναντίος (*enantios*) in BDAG, 330–31. See Joshua 1:18.

189. BDAG, 24; Maurer, *TDNT,* 8:158–61.

190. *NID*, s.v. "οἰκτιρμός"; BDAG, 700.

191. BDAG, 1095.

192. For example, see Revised English Bible and Today's English Version.

193. For example, Jerusalem Bible and New Jerusalem Bible.

194. For example, KJV, NRSV, NIV, and Jerusalem Bible.

option, treating the phrase as an interrogative,[195] because we see the author designing the question, given the severity of breaking certain Mosaic laws, to cause his readers serious reflection as he identifies the consequence of the sin against the new covenant.

The noun τιμωρία (*timōria*), "punishment," in the New Testament always denotes punishment inflicted by God.[196] Unlike other kinds of divine punishment, this kind has no corrective basis.[197] In other words, it is not meant to reform. It is rather an expression of vengeance upon those who willfully and deliberately sin against the Father, his Son, his people, and his covenant. It is designed to satisfy God's sense of outraged justice and to defend his honor and that of the law the person violated.[198]

The egregious act consists of three aspects, and in this phrase, the author identifies the first. The verb καταπατέω (*katapateō*) in its literal sense means to deliberately trample something hard enough to cause it injury. In a metaphorical sense, it means to despise something and treat it with the utmost disdain.[199] In all cases, the nuance of intended injury should be remembered. Such actions show scorn for the Atonement and spurn Jesus and his loving self-sacrifice.

and hath counted the blood of the covenant, wherewith he was sanctified, an unholy thing / and who has profaned the blood of the covenant by which he was sanctified: This phrase identifies the second aspect of the sin. With the words τὸ αἷμα τῆς διαθήκης (*to haima tēs diathēkēs*), "the blood of the covenant," the author seems to be echoing Exodus 24:8 and the inauguration of Jehovah's covenant with Israel, which continued among the Christians (albeit with modifications) because of the Atonement of the Lord.[200]

Due to the power of the "blood," the participant became ἡγιάσθη (*hagiasthē*), "sanctified," and a member of a choice inner circle consisting of those whom the Savior had cleansed.[201] These are they who have been moved into the divine holy sphere and thereby were separated from the common, mundane, and impure.[202]

---

195. For discussion, see Ellingworth, *Epistle to the Hebrews,* 538.
196. BDAG, 1006.
197. LSJ, 1795.
198. Johnson, *Hebrews,* 264.
199. BDAG, 523; Louw-Nida, §§19.52; 88.196.
200. Ellingworth, *Epistle to the Hebrews,* 540.
201. BDAG, 9–10.
202. *NID,* s.v. "ἅγιος."

The participial phrase κοινὸν ἡγησάμενος (*koinon hēgēsamenos*), "who has regarded as profane," stands opposite in meaning to the word ἡγιάσθη (*hagiasthē*). The phrase denotes treating something as ordinary and common. In a negative sense, it indicates that which is impure, contaminating, and even defiling.[203] When it comes to the actions of people, it points more specifically to that which profanes in the sense of treating the sacred with irreverence and even contempt. It therefore carries the idea of defiling what is holy.[204]

hath done despite unto the Spirit of grace? / who has outraged the Spirit of grace?: Here the author identifies the last aspect of this egregious sin. The verb ἐνυβρίζω (*enybrizō*), "insult, outrage," means to treat something or someone, because of feelings of superiority, with acute disdain. It connotes the acts of a person who insolently and wantonly humiliates, shames, and especially outrages another.[205]

The phrase τὸ πνεῦμα τῆς χάριτος (*to pneuma tēs charitos*), "the spirit of grace," is vague. The only other place it shows up in the scriptures is in LXX Zechariah 12:9, where Jehovah promises to send a spirit of grace upon the king and inhabitants of Jerusalem so their spiritual eyes would be opened "and they shall look upon [their Lord] whom they have pierced, and they shall mourn . . . and be in bitterness" because of what they have done to him. The author gives no clue if he has this passage in mind, but it does fit his warning. On the other hand, he has noted that the Lord offered himself as the perfect sacrifice "through the eternal Spirit" (9:14), a pure act of grace. To spurn the Spirit and the grace that flows from it would be very detrimental to the soul. Paul warned his readers, "Do not frustrate the grace of God" by looking for some other source of righteousness than the Lord and thus make vain his death (Gal. 2:21). However the author intended the phrase, it seems to be an oblique reference to the Savior's Atonement.

---

203. BDAG, 551–52; Ellingworth, *Epistle to the Hebrews,* 540–41.

204. BDAG, 552; Louw-Nida, §53.33; compare §53.39; and *NID,* s.v. "κοινός." For a more broad treatment, see Hauck, *TDNT,* 3:789–97. C. E. Carlston, "The Things That Defile (Mark VII. 14) and the Law in Matthew and Mark," *New Testament Studies* 15, no. 1 (1968–69): 75–96, argues that nothing outside a man can defile him but only that which is within can do so. Further, Jesus not only set aside the "traditions of the elders" but also the binding force of the Mosaic covenant. Understanding what is profane gives a better grasp of what is holy and vice versa, an essential ability in religion. The contrast places greater emphasis on those actions that are necessary and proper to achieve holiness.

205. The word is not found anywhere else in the New Testament and, therefore, its meaning is supplied by its use in secular sources. BDAG, 342.

10:30 ***For we know him that hath said, Vengeance belongeth unto me, I will recompense, saith the Lord / For we know the one who said, "Vengeance is mine; I will repay!":*** In order to buttress his point, the author refers to Deuteronomy 32:35. His exact wording is found in neither the MT nor the LXX, but it is attested in Romans 12:19 and some Targums.[206]

Though he does not mention God directly, the author does force his readers to remember who made the statement and therefore to take seriously the divine warning. His focus is on ἐκδίκησις (*ekdikēsis*), "vengeance," the noun denoting an act of divine justice meted out against those who spurn God and willfully break his commandments (see 2 Thes. 1:8).[207]

The result is ἀνταποδίδωμι (*antapodidōmi*), the verb meaning to repay an equivalent.[208] In the LXX, it indicates Jehovah's "paying back" the rebellious with exacting punishment, but rewards the righteous (LXX Lev. 18:25; Deut. 32:41, 43; Judg. 1:7; Ps. 30:23; 40:10). The verb is used in this case to describe the retribution God will inflict upon the recalcitrant (compare Rom. 12:19).[209]

And again, The Lord shall judge his people / and also, "The Lord will judge his people": The author again reaches to scripture to support his point. This time he quotes from Deuteronomy 32:36. The author's use of the phrase καὶ πάλιν (*kai palin*), "and again" / "and also," is important here because it allows him to give added force to the second scripture and thereby give it the punch he desires it to have.[210]

Though the verb κρίνω (*krinō*) can mean "to rule," it usually means "to judge" in the forensic sense.[211] More broadly, it can mean both "to condemn" and "to vindicate." For that reason, the author could be using the scripture to make one of two points. He could be using it as a warning against those who have apostatized from the Church and are seeking its hurt. In such a case, having once been God's people, they will find that they come

---

206. See the Targums *Onqelos*; *Neofiti*; and *Pseudo-Jonathan*. Though this exact wording cannot be found in any extant manuscript, it may have been in one known to the author and his audience.

207. BDAG, 301. For a discussion, see J. Proctor, "Judgement or Vindication? Deuteronomy 32 in Hebrews 10:30," *Tyndale Bulletin* 55, no. 1 (2004): 65–80.

208. BDAG, 87.

209. Johnson, *Hebrews,* 266.

210. Ellingworth, *Epistle to the Hebrews,* 542, but the author also uses it to good rhetorical effect. James W. Thompson, *Hebrews,* Paideia: Commentaries on the New Testament. (Grand Rapids, Mich.: Baker Academic, 2008), 209.

211. BDAG, 567–69; Louw-Nida, §56.20, 30.

under very acute punishment.[212] Or the author could be using the scripture to bolster the steadfastness of the faithful. God's righteous judgments are designed to help his people, including taking vengeance upon those who either harm or try to harm them. The context in both Deuteronomy and here appears to be one of avenging the faithful by moving against those who are unfaithful.[213] That would suggest the author is using the scripture as reassurance to the faithful that God will not ultimately let the work of the apostates harm his people or his work.

The noun κύριος (*kyrios*), "Lord," in this case specifically refers to God the Father, the final judge who presides over the highest court of appeal but also who acts to avenge his people.

10:31 ***It is a fearful thing to fall into the hands of the living God / It is a frightening thing to fall into the hands of the living God:*** On φόβερος (*phoberos*), "fearful, frightening," see Translation Notes on 10:27 above. The English adjective "fearful" focuses on something that makes one afraid or alarmed, resulting in a deep and emotional loss of courage, while "frightful" denotes that which throws one into alarm or consternation. It carries the idea of such an outrageous or shocking quality as to cause temporary paralysis.[214] It is the latter nuance that seemed to us to best carry the force of the Greek and is therefore used in our Rendition.

Analysis and Comments

The warning the author gives in these verses stresses the importance of his readers following through with the admonition he gave in 10:25. He has already given them such a notice (see 6:4–8), but earlier his intent was to rouse his readers from their spiritual lethargy by seeing clearly the power of their Lord and realizing the importance of his high priesthood and the role it now plays in their lives. Here the author's focus is on the full sufficiency of Christ and his past and current work as their enthroned High Priest. Because of the clear and careful layout of the author's teaching about the Savior (indeed, the solid food for the spiritually mature, see 5:12, 14), his

---

212. Vanhoye, *Letter to the Hebrews,* 173.

213. In the following scriptures, the idea of understanding κρίνω (*krinō*) to mean "avenge" stands out: LXX Ps. 134:14; Prov. 31:8, 9; and Isa. 51:22. In all these, it carries the idea of deliverance from evil and of salvation for the righteous oppressed. Indeed, the vindication and salvation of the righteous are the end results of God's judgment. For studies, see Büchel and Herntrich, *TDNT,* 3:921–54; *NID,* s.v. "κρίνω"; Proctor, "Judgement or Vindication?" 71–73; and James Swetnam, "Hebrews 10,30–31: A Suggestion," *Biblica* 75, no. 3 (1994): 388–94.

214. *Webster's New Dictionary of Synonyms,* s.v. "fearful."

readers are in a precarious position if they neglect—and especially if they abandon—the work. Thus, he raises the alarm lest his readers reject the clearly explained and carefully arranged exposition on the salvation that comes only through Christ and his Atonement. "The urgency of his concern has increased in direct proportion to the way in which the magnitude of this provision has become clear: there is no other way of salvation if one abandons the all-sufficient sacrifice of Christ."[215]

To further the force of his admonition, in 10:26 the author exchanges the impersonal speech he used earlier (see 6:4–8, "if they shall fall away") with the fully personal speech ("if we sin willfully") found in these verses. If anyone, including himself, should fall away through persistent willful sinning after gaining the knowledge they have along with the degree of the Lord's power they have enjoyed, there is no forgiveness (see "Excursus on Unforgivable and Unpardonable Sins" in chapter 6). Such a result for those who have experienced such spiritual highs would be tragic, and the author does not want this to happen.

In an attempt to not increase the anxiety among the overly sensitive faithful among his readers, he details specifically the aspects of such a gross sin that falling away entails. Such sin is "intentional, persistent, and informed."[216] It is grounded on having had a knowledge (ἐπίγνωσις, *epignosis*) that is specific, full, and personal.[217] That knowledge is of the truth (ἀλήθεια, *alētheia*).[218] Such knowledge consists of information coming largely through revelation and confirmation of the Spirit.[219] In the present context, the emphasis seems to be on the gospel, particularly on the absoluteness and finality of the Christian message.[220] Through coming to recognize and know the truth, one enters the community defined by the living God.[221]

---

215. Cockerill, *Epistle to the Hebrews,* 482.

216. The Mosaic law, as well as non-Jewish counterparts (see Koester, *Hebrews,* 451, for sources), distinguished between intentional and unintentional sins and the punishment that should befall the perpetrator. See Num. 15:22–31; and Deut. 17:12–13. The author of Hebrews may be playing on this theme, but it is unlikely he has this in mind since he is looking specifically at sin against the new covenant. For discussion, see Cockerill, *Epistle to the Hebrews,* 483–84.

217. BDAG, 369; Louw-Nida, §28.18.

218. The phrase "knowledge of the truth" would have been well known to those Christians familiar with Paul's writings. See 1 Tim. 2:4; 2 Tim. 2:25; 3:7; and Titus 1:1. Many would have been well aware of the responsibility such a knowledge carried.

219. BDAG, 42–43; *NID,* s.v. "ἀλήθεια."

220. Bultmann, *TDNT,* 1:232–51.

221. Johnson, *Hebrews,* 261.

The author states very specifically the result of deliberately abandoning and working against such truth: "there no longer remains any sacrifice for sins" (NR 10:26). After knowing the Lord and then rejecting and fighting against him and his cause, such people are left to themselves without hope, recourse, or remedy for their actions.[222] For a study, see Translation Notes for 6:4–8 along with the associated Analysis.

The author has already noted that, because of the Savior's actions, the faithful should fear neither approaching the throne of grace (4:16) nor the final judgment (2:15) and the Son will assure them of their joyful place in the city of their God (12:22–29). In 10:27, the author contrasts their reward with the fate of the willfully rebellious. These, repudiating the Atonement, have traded the blessing of hope for the terrible prospect of the Father's "fiery fierceness" (πυρὸς ζῆλος, *pyros zēlos*) upon them. They have spurned the Atonement and have sought to defame the Father's glorious Son and his mission. In short, they have become not only the Savior's but also God's enemies (ὑπεναντίους, *hypenantious*) and therefore will feel the full weight of God's wrath when they stand before him (1:13; 10:27).[223]

To stress his point, the author once again applies what has become known as the *qal waḥomer* argument; that is, he emphasizes the greater by contrasting it with the lesser. In 10:28, he notes that those who broke certain aspects of the Mosaic law were put to death without pity (Deut. 13:8; 17:2–6; 19:13, 21).[224] By committing certain sins, they forfeited their physical lives. How much greater should the penalty be, he asks in 10:29, for those who have repudiated Christ? Through the question, he appeals to his readers' sense of justice and fair play as a means of having them side with God's action in taking vengeance (ἐκδίκησις, *ekdikēsis*) on the sinner (10:30).

At the end of 10:29, the author skillfully and clearly describes the egregious sin the rebellious have committed. It has three aspects. The first is treating the Son of God with disdain, the Greek word καταπατέω

222. Cockerill, *Epistle to the Hebrews,* 485.

223. Johnson, *Hebrews,* 262.

224. On the nature and use of the *qal waḥomer* or *a fortiori* argument, see discussion in the introduction on page 30. The author's focus seems to be on Deut. 7:2–6, which required the death penalty for idolatry, that is, the turning away from the Mosaic covenant. See Attridge, *Epistle to the Hebrews,* 295; and Johnson, *Hebrews,* 264. In such cases, the idolater was to be put to death. No exceptions. See Ellingworth, *Epistle to the Hebrews,* 537; and Lane, *Hebrews 9–13,* 277 note dd. Such willful rebellion against Jehovah would parallel the willful rebellion of the Christian apostate but bring about a spiritual rather than a physical retribution.

(*katapateō*) suggesting trampling someone with the intent to cause injury[225] and thus exposing the purpose of the rebellion: to hurt the Lord and mock his Atonement. As the author noted in 6:6, they crucify the Son of God again (compare 1 Ne. 19:7; and D&C 76:35).

The next aspect points specifically to their attitude about the Lord's self-sacrifice. They have profaned (κοινάω, *koinaō*) the blood of the covenant, referring to the sacrifice that made the new covenant possible. This very blood, at one time, had made them holy, but in spite of that, they now claim it to be ordinary and therefore of no effect. In doing so, they have, without shame, desecrated it.[226]

The final aspect looks to the climaxing insult, one toward the Spirit of grace. The author has already noted that these people have partaken of the Holy Spirit (6:4, compare 2:4). Having done so has left them open to a condemnation spoken by the Lord when he stated, "All sins shall be forgiven unto the sons of men, and blasphemies wherewith soever they shall blaspheme: But he that shall blaspheme against the Holy Ghost hath never forgiveness, but is in danger of eternal damnation" (Mark 3:28–29; compare Matt. 12:31–32; and Luke 12:10). The reason is that a witness from the Holy Ghost comes with divine authority and testifies with revelatory power to the person, resulting in a sure knowledge (ἐπίγνωσις, *epignosis*). Those who have such a knowledge and "then link themselves with Lucifer and come out in open rebellion, also become sons of perdition," and for these there is no forgiveness.[227] Indeed, the author warns against those who "draw back unto perdition" (10:39). The repudiation of the Spirit of grace is most serious because doing so is nothing short of rejecting the presence of God in their lives.[228]

The author clearly shows this sin is no minor transgression but rather an expression of full-blown apostasy—a turning away from the truth with intent to destroy it (compare 3:12–19). Here is revealed the shocking

225. BDAG, 523; Johnson, *Hebrews,* 264; compare Thompson, *Hebrews,* 209.

226. Cockerill, *Epistle to the Hebrews,* 489 and n. 35.

227. McConkie, *Doctrinal New Testament Commentary,* 1:273; see also Holzapfel and Wayment, *Making Sense,* 96–97; 2 Pet. 2:20–22; 2 Ne. 9:14–16; and D&C 29:27–30; 76:32–49. For a study of the scripture in context, see Donald A. Hagner, *Matthew 1–13,* vol. 33a of Word Biblical Commentary (Dallas: Word Books, 1993), 345–48. Since Paul was aware of various degrees of glory (see 1 Cor. 15:40–42; and 2 Cor. 12:1–4), there is a possibility the author of Hebrews may also have been aware of this idea. The author, in his context, is more likely looking at a person's forfeiture of salvation from heaven.

228. Cockerill, *Epistle to the Hebrews,* 490–91; see also Vanhoye, *Letter to the Hebrews,* 172.

character of these people's rebellion. It shows the apostate has not only fallen from grace but also mocks the giver of that grace.[229] As in 6:4–8, such a one cannot return because she or he is denying the very basis on which such a return rests.[230] As a result, they face the fiery indignation (πυρὸς ζῆλος, *pyros zēlos*) of a just God. Such is the nature of retributive punishment (τιμωρία, *timōria*).[231]

Such a judgment upon the willfully rebellious, as the author suggests in 10:30, is in keeping with the scriptural record of God's dealings with such people. The author draws his support from Deuteronomy 32:35: "To me belongeth vengeance, and recompence." In this scripture, God affirms both his right to judge the rebellious and his intent to do so. The term "vengeance" (ἐκδίκησις, *ekdikēsis*), as applied to God, denotes neither retaliation nor revenge. It is rather the judicial act of avenging unjust and persistent misdeeds directed toward one of the Father's own. Its purpose is to vindicate that person's faith and steadfastness. The nature and extent of this retributive punishment is up to God alone (see Ex. 7:4; 12:12; Num. 31:2; 33:4; Judg. 11:36; 2 Sam. 4:8; Ps. 17:4–7; 94:1; Luke 18:7–9; and Acts 7:24). The promise is, as the scripture the author refers to states, such punishment will come; God will "pay back" (ἀναποδίδωμι, *anapodidōmi*) the rebellious for their sins but on his own terms and in his own way (see Lev. 18:25; Deut. 32:6, 41, 43; Judg. 1:7; LXX Ps. 7:4; 30:23; 40:10).[232] For the believer, faith is in letting God handle the hurt caused by the misdeed (see D&C 64:11).

In 10:30, the author quotes a portion of Deuteronomy 32:36: "The Lord shall judge his people" (see also Ps. 135:14). In this context, the verb "judge" (κρίνω, *krinō*) likely takes on the positive aspect of vindication against those hostile to God's own.[233] The author appears to be using the scripture as a necessary corollary to the judgment that he sees coming against the unfaithful. God will repay these for their rebellion and, by doing so, will vindicate the faith of the steadfast. By making this point, the author lays the foundation for the words of comfort and the admonition he will make in the next section (10:32–39).[234]

---

229. Johnson, *Hebrews,* 264.
230. Johnson, *Hebrews,* 265.
231. Johnson, *Hebrews,* 264.
232. Johnson, *Hebrews,* 266.
233. Proctor, "Judgment or Vindication," 71–73; Swetnam, "Hebrews 10,30–31," 388–94.
234. For discussion, see Cockerill, *Epistle to the Hebrews,* 492–93.

The author concludes this section (10:31) with a solemn and alarming observation: "It is a fearful thing to fall into the hands of the living God." The words express the author's "deep conviction of the awesome holiness of the divine majesty" of an ever-living God whose judgment never fails against the rebellious and ungodly.[235] According to the Book of Mormon, the willfully rebellious should

> fear, and tremble before God . . . for the Lord redeemeth none such that rebel against him and die in their sins; yea, even all those that have perished in their sins ever since the world began, that have wilfully rebelled against God, that have known the commandments of God, and would not keep them; these are they that have no part in the first resurrection. . . . Salvation cometh to none such; for the Lord hath redeemed none such; yea, neither can the Lord redeem such; for he cannot deny himself; for he cannot deny justice when it has its claim. (Mosiah 15:26–27)

Indeed, God's commandments

> shall stand as a bright testimony against [these] people, at the judgment day [and being evil] they are consigned to an awful view of their own guilt and abominations, which doth cause them to shrink from the presence of the Lord into a state of misery and endless torment, from whence they can no more return; therefore they have drunk damnation to their own souls. Therefore, they have drunk out of the cup of the wrath of God, which justice could no more deny unto them . . . therefore, mercy could have claim on them no more forever. And their torment is as a lake of fire and brimstone, whose flames are unquenchable, and whose smoke ascendeth up forever and ever. (Mosiah 3:24–27)

As one authority noted, "The living God is fearsome precisely because, like his own word, he sees deeply and truly into the heart of his own creatures, and demands of them a truth commensurate with his own. It is not a game. It is the most ultimate reality, and therefore, quite properly, 'fearful.'"[236]

---

235. Bruce, *Epistle to the Hebrews,* 265; compare Lane, *Hebrews 9–13,* 295–96.
236. Johnson, *Hebrews,* 266–67.

An Admonition to Not Abandon One's Confidence in God (10:32–39)

Greek Text

32 Ἀναμιμνῄσκεσθε δὲ τὰς πρότερον ἡμέρας, ἐν αἷς φωτισθέντες πολλὴν ἄθλησιν ὑπεμείνατε παθημάτων, 33 τοῦτο μὲν ὀνειδισμοῖς τε καὶ θλίψεσιν θεατριζόμενοι, τοῦτο δὲ κοινωνοὶ τῶν οὕτως ἀναστρεφομένων γενηθέντες· 34 καὶ γὰρ τοῖς δεσμίοις συνεπαθήσατε, καὶ τὴν ἁρπαγὴν τῶν ὑπαρχόντων ὑμῶν μετὰ χαρᾶς προσεδέξασθε, γινώσκοντες ἔχειν ἑαυτοὺς κρείττονα ὕπαρξιν καὶ μένουσαν. 35 μὴ ἀποβάλητε οὖν τὴν παρρησίαν ὑμῶν, ἥτις ἔχει μεγάλην μισθαποδοσίαν, 36 ὑπομονῆς γὰρ ἔχετε χρείαν ἵνα τὸ θέλημα τοῦ θεοῦ ποιήσαντες κομίσησθε τὴν ἐπαγγελίαν· 37 ἔτι γὰρ μικρὸν ὅσον ὅσον, ὁ ἐρχόμενος ἥξει καὶ οὐ χρονίσει· 38 ὁ δὲ δίκαιός μου ἐκ πίστεως ζήσεται, καὶ ἐὰν ὑποστείληται, οὐκ εὐδοκεῖ ἡ ψυχή μου ἐν αὐτῷ. 39 ἡμεῖς δὲ οὐκ ἐσμὲν ὑποστολῆς εἰς ἀπώλειαν, ἀλλὰ πίστεως εἰς περιποίησιν ψυχῆς. [SBLGNT]

King James Version

32 But call to remembrance the former days, in which, after ye were illuminated, ye endured a great fight of afflictions; 33 Partly, whilst ye were made a gazingstock both by reproaches and afflictions; and partly, whilst ye became companions of them that were so used. 34 For ye had compassion of me in my bonds, and took joyfully the spoiling of your goods, knowing in yourselves that ye have in heaven a better and an enduring substance. 35 Cast not away therefore your confidence, which hath great recompence of reward. 36 For ye have need of patience, that, after ye have done the will of God, ye might receive the promise. 37 For yet a little while, and he that shall come will come, and will not tarry. 38 Now the just shall live by faith: but if any man draw back, my soul shall have no pleasure in him. 39 But we are not of them who draw back unto perdition; but of them that believe to the saving of the soul.

New Rendition

32 But remember the former days in which you endured a great struggle with suffering after you had been enlightened. 33 Sometimes you were publicly exposed to insults and afflictions, at other times you were partners with those who were so treated. 34 For you indeed had compassion on prisoners, and you cheerfully accepted the seizure of your possessions, recognizing that you yourselves have a better and enduring possession. 35 So do not abandon your confidence; it has a great reward. 36 For you need endurance so that after you have accomplished God's will, you will receive the promise. 37 For

> "just a little longer" [Isa. 26:20],

and

> "he who is coming will arrive and he will not delay." [Hab. 2:3]

> 38 "But my righteous one will live by faith, and if he hesitates to act, my soul will not be pleased with him." [Hab. 2:4]

39 But we are not the kind of people who hesitate to act, which results in destruction, but we are the kind of people who believe, which results in preserving the soul.

Translation Notes and Comments

10:32 ***But call to remembrance the former days, in which, after ye were illuminated, ye endured a great fight of afflictions / But remember the former days in which you endured a great struggle with suffering after you had been enlightened:*** The author sees the hope of the present in having his readers remember their former strength.[237] He asks them to focus on two elements. The first he mentions in this phrase. It is centered on what the author describes as πολλὴν ἄθλησιν (*pollēn athlēsin*), "the great struggle," suggesting a former period in which persecution was particularly active and strong.

At this point, the author introduces for the first time the virtue of ὑπομένω (*hypomenō*), which means "to maintain a belief or course of action in the face of opposition, stand one's ground, hold out, endure." [238] Such endurance is active rather than passive, expressing as it does a strong resistance by holding one's ground. The author ties this virtue to hope in Christ when he admonishes his readers in 10:23 to maintain "*without wavering*" their confession of hope (italics added; see also 1 Thes. 1:3).

The noun ἄθλησις (*athlēsis*) denotes the effort put forth in an athletic contest both in preparation and execution.[239] Athletics held an important place in Greek culture where emphasis was placed not just on the mind but also on the body. Philosophers likened the virtuous life to an athletic contest that required discipline, endurance, and suffering in order to succeed.[240]

---

237. Paul also uses this same strategy to encourage his readers to remain steadfast. See 1 Cor. 4:4–9; 2 Cor. 7:15; Philip. 1:3–11; 1 Thes. 1–3; 2 Tim. 1:6.

238. BDAG, 1039; Louw-Nida, §39.20.

239. The word sometimes carries a connection to combat and in that case connotes both a struggle against an opposition that seeks dominance by the use of force or intimidation and also remaining on the battlefield rather than deserting it. Ellingworth, *Epistle to the Hebrews,* 545–46; Louw-Nida, §§50.3; 74.13; *NID,* s.v. "ἄθλησις." Paul, in Philip. 1:27; 4:3, used the word ἄθλησις (*athlēsis*), "contest, struggle," to describe the communal conflict for the gospel cause endured by the Christians. The author of Hebrews seems to be using it exclusively in an athletic context. Vanhoye, *Letter to the Hebrews,* 174.

240. See also Paul's teachings in Philip. 3:13–14 and 1 Cor. 9:23–25. Cockerill, *Epistle to the Hebrews,* 497. For a study, see N. C. Cory, *Endurance in Suffering: Hebrews 12:1–13*

The adjective πολύς (*polys*) denotes something "large in quantity or measure," thus, "great" or "mighty."[241] The author's use of the word stresses the height of the difficulty of the affliction these Saints had endured.

The verb φωτίζω (*phōtizō*), "enlightened," found here as an aorist passive participle, means to have something made known concerning transcendent or deeply spiritual matters and connotes that which is made known or very plain via revelation.[242] The force of the aorist tense suggests a single experience in the past. Likely this was at baptism with its confirmation that bestows the gift of the Holy Ghost through whose power witness, knowledge, and ratification come.[243] The verse suggests that it was on account of their enlightenment that these Saints were able to endure the period of struggle and suffering.

10:33 ***Partly, whilst ye were made a gazingstock both by reproaches and afflictions; and partly, whilst ye became companions of them that were so used / Sometimes you were publicly exposed to insults and afflictions, at other times you were partners with those who were so treated:*** The words "sometimes" and "at other times" are our translation of the correlative or paired conjunctions μέν (*men*) and δέ (*de*). These are often used, as in this instance, to emphasize a contrast and are often translated as "on the one hand . . . on the other hand. . . ."[244]

The author exposes the bite in what these Saints have had to endure by using the verb θεατρίζω (*theatrizō*), found in the text as a present passive participle. As such, it means to be exposed to public ridicule and made a community spectacle.[245]

The nouns ὀνειδισμός (*oneidismos*), "insult," and θλίψσις (*thlipsis*), "affliction," capture the result of the public exposure. The former describes "an act of disparagement that results in disgrace" that can lead to reviling.[246] The latter denotes "trouble that leads to distress" that also includes affliction.[247]

in Its Rhetorical, Religious, and Philosophical Context (Cambridge: Cambridge University Press, 1998).

241. BDAG, 847–50.

242. BDAG, 1074; Louw-Nida, §28.36.

243. Ellingworth, *Epistle to the Hebrews,* 545; see also Bruce Douglas Porter, "Gift of the Holy Ghost," in Ludlow, *Encyclopedia of Mormonism,* 2:543–44.

244. Wallace, *Greek Grammar,* 672; Lane, *Hebrews 9–13,* 277 note mm.

245. BDAG, 446; Bertram, *TDNT*, 3:27–43.

246. BDAG, 710.

247. BDAG, 457. The noun θλίψσις (*thlipsis*) has strong physical overtones suggesting abuse. Johnson, *Hebrews,* 269.

Together the words cover both verbal and physical abuse.[248] That both words are found in the plural suggests the breadth of hardship these people had gone through.

The noun κοινωνός (*koinōnos*), "partner," denotes the depth of an experience that two people or a community share together.[249] The author's statement shows that the persecution these people experienced was universal. It did, however, hit some harder than others, but all seem to have been afflicted. Those less affected, however, did not hide or draw back from helping but rather stepped forward, partnering in the burden of their fellow Christians.

10:34 ***For ye had compassion of me in my bonds / For you indeed had compassion on prisoners:*** There are two main variant readings of this phrase. Some look at Saints being compassionate to the author of the Epistle while in bonds (as in the KJV) while others look at Saints being compassionate to Christian prisoners (as in our Rendition). The KJV follows the Textus Receptus reading δεσμοῖς μου (*desmois mou*), "my bonds." The largest number of manuscripts, however, have τοῖς δεσμίοις (*tois desmiois*), "toward the prisoners."[250] It is not hard to see how the variant found in the Textus Receptus came to be. A scribe would simply and mistakenly omit the first iota in the word δεσμίοις (*desmiois*), "prisoners," leaving δεσμοῖς (*desmois*) "bonds." Then another scribe, trying to improve the sense, would need but add a personal pronoun, either αὐτων (*autōn*), "their," referring to those mentioned in previous verse, or μου (*mou*), "my," referring to the author (the addition may have seemed logical and proper because it imitates passages in Philip. 1:7, 13, 14, 16; and Col. 4:18).[251] As noted, the weight of evidence is that the phrase is referring to prisoners.

The verb συμπαθέω (*sympatheō*) means "to have/show sympathy with."[252] The word leaves the impression that these people did not avoid or shun those Christians who found themselves prisoners of the state but aided them as best they could.

took joyfully the spoiling of your goods / you cheerfully accepted the seizure of your possessions: The noun χαρά (*chara*) denotes the experience of gladness and by extension to enter into a state of joyfulness.[253] The virtue

248. Attridge, *Epistle to the Hebrews*, 298.
249. BDAG, 553–54; Johnson, *Hebrews*, 270.
250. Metzger, *Textual Commentary*, 600–601.
251. Metzger, *Textual Commentary*, 600–601.
252. BDAG, 958.
253. BDAG, 1077; Louw-Nida, §15.123, 124.

"joy" is more than an emotion. "It is a moral disposition. Unlike happiness, for example, which is dependent on positive circumstances, joy is a moral disposition of contentment/receptivity even in the midst of suffering."[254] Because the English word "cheerful" carries the idea of "a strong and, often, a spontaneous flow of good spirits either as a result of feeling glad or happy or as a result of an equable disposition or of a naturally sanguine temperament,"[255] it is used in our Rendition.

The noun ἁρπαγή (*harpagē*) denotes both robbery and plunder.[256] Since, however, in this instance, the act seems to have been initiated by the state (although mob violence cannot be ruled out), the word is translated as "seizure" in our Rendition, but "confiscation" would also work.[257]

The verb προσδέχομαι (*prosdechomai*) means not only to accept something but also to anticipate it.[258] The word is telling because it suggests that even when these Saints' goods were not taken, they still held the attitude that should it happen, all would be well.[259]

knowing in yourselves that ye have in heaven a better and an enduring substance / recognizing that you yourselves have a better and enduring possession: The verb γινώσκω (*ginōskō*), found here as a present active participle, means not only "to know about something" but also to comprehend or grasp its significance. More specifically, as in this instance, it acts as an indicator of what one does surely know, thus, "to recognize," which we use in our Rendition.[260]

The noun ὕπαρξις (*hyparxis*), "possession,"[261] normally refers to earthly property, but in this context, it likely connotes heavenly substance (and perhaps even a state of being) that is far superior to anything the earth can offer.[262] The adjective κρείττων (*kreittōn*), "better," the first of two words the author uses to describe the possession, denotes that which is more advantageous than something else and suggests the notion of that

254. Johnson, *Hebrews,* 271.

255. *Webster's New Dictionary of Synonyms,* s.v. "glad."

256. BDAG, 133.

257. See Johnson, *Hebrews,* 271, including sources; and Attridge, *Epistle to the Hebrews,* 299 nn. 31–32.

258. BDAG, 877.

259. In this they followed the Savior's counsel when facing tribulation. See Matt. 5:12; and Luke 6:22; see also Acts 5:41; Rom. 5:3; 2 Cor. 11:21–30; and 1 Pet. 4:13.

260. BDAG, 199–201.

261. BDAG, 1029.

262. Attridge, *Epistle to the Hebrews,* 300.

thing being truly superior.[263] The verb μένω (*menō*), "to remain, endure, continue," the second word used to describe the possession, denotes that which continues to exist.[264] It is found here as a present active participle and suggests the enduring nature of the possession it modifies. Taken together, the two descriptive words suggest that the possession is the redemption that comes through the Savior.[265]

The phrase "in heaven" is not found in the best Greek manuscripts and is therefore left out of our Rendition.[266] There is little doubt, however, that the author is referring to the eternal reward that awaits the righteous.

10:35 ***Cast not away therefore your confidence, which hath great recompense of reward / So do not abandon your confidence; it has a great reward:*** The conjunction οὖν (*oun*), "therefore, so," plays an important role here because it introduces the reason why the author's readers should respond to his admonition.

The imperative force of the verb ἀποβάλλω (*apoballō*) denotes getting rid of something viewed as substandard or undesirable, thus, "to throw off, reject, abandon, do away with."[267] As the sentence stands, it is impossible to know if the action described is a vigorous thrust or a more passive letting go.[268] Since the author shows concern that his readers are slowly drifting away from the truth, the English word "abandon" catches that nuance and is therefore used in our Rendition.

For the noun παρρησία (*parrēsia*), "confidence," see Translation Notes for 10:19 above. Here it denotes a state of boldness, confidence, or fearlessness—a divinely given attribute (according to 10:19)—that the author's readers had enjoyed and exhibited in the past. Based on the earlier experience they had successfully gone through, they should have seen its value and realized its reward and therefore, under the present circumstances, resisted losing it even though it now had become their task.[269]

The noun μισθαποδοσία (*misthopdosia*), "reward," denotes, in this case, a highly favorable recompense for service rendered.[270] The author's

263. BDAG, 566; Louw-Nida, §65.21.

264. BDAG, 630–31.

265. Cockerill, *Epistle to the Hebrews,* 503.

266. Ellingworth, *Epistle to the Hebrews,* 550.

267. BDAG, 107; Louw-Nida, §§13.45; 49.19.

268. Ellingworth, *Epistle to the Hebrews,* 550–51.

269. Lane, *Hebrews 9–13,* 278 note ss. Bruce, *Epistle to the Hebrews,* 271, notes that the word is used both for the confidence the Christian should have in approaching God (4:16; 10:19) and the boldness needed to stand up to unbelievers.

270. The noun can be construed negatively and denote a punishment that exactly balances the offense. BDAG, 653.

coupling it with the adjective μέγας (*megas*), "great, large,"[271] heightens its worth. Based on 10:36, the phrase appears to refer to the result of doing the will of God and through that receiving the promises of the new covenant.

10:36 *For ye have need of patience, that, after ye have done the will of God, ye might receive the promise / For you need endurance so that after you have accomplished God's will, you will receive the promise:* To the attribute of παρρησία (*parrēsia*),"confidence, courage," the author adds ὑπομονή (*hypomonē*), "patience, endurance." He stresses its importance by placing it as the first word in his sentence. For analysis, see Translation Notes for 10:32. Here we need note only that the noun denotes "the capacity to hold out or bear up in the face of difficulty"[272] and carries the force of steadfastness to a cause. This trait many in the Greco-Roman world viewed as one of the noblest of human values.[273] Though the English noun "patience" works denoting as it does a calm and composed capacity to withstand suffering and provocation while awaiting a promised outcome,[274] the noun "endurance" in this context seems better. It denotes a resistance especially to destructive forces or agencies that exceeds what is normal or expected.[275] We have therefore used this in our Rendition. The Greek word stands in contrast to ὑποστολή (*hypostolē*), "hesitancy, timidity" (10:39), and seems to be anchored to the covenant relationship and the hope in the promise that undergirds it.[276]

The verb ποιέω (*poieō*), found here in the form of an active aorist participle, means "to undertake or do something that brings about an event, state, or condition" and therefore refers to accomplishing a task to achieve a specific end.[277] In this case, that task is to accomplish τὸ θέλημα τοῦ θεοῦ (*to thelēma tou theou*), "the will of God." The phrase likely pertains less to any given set of commandments and more to faithful endurance and steadfastness to the gospel cause and its center, Jesus Christ.[278]

The author clearly states the purpose and the result that comes from endurance. It is to "receive the promise." The noun ἐπαγγελία (*epangelia*),

---

271. BDAG, 623–24.

272. BDAG, 1039–40. The noun refers to a temper that refuses to succumb under social pressure no matter how strong. At 6:12, the author called on his readers to exercise patience. The word he used there, μακροθυμία (*makrothymia*), denotes the self-restraint that resists "hastily retaliating a wrong" and is opposed to wrath and revenge.

273. *NID*, s.v. "υπομονή."

274. *Webster's New Dictionary of Synonyms,* s.v. "patience."

275. Louw-Nida, §§25.174; 29.20; *Webster's New Dictionary of Synonyms,* s.v. "continue."

276. *NID*, s.v. "ὑπομένω."

277. BDAG, 839–40.

278. Ellingworth, *Epistle to the Hebrews,* 553.

"promise,"[279] as used by the author, maintains a strong echo of Jehovah's covenant with Abraham, Isaac, and Jacob as well as Israel as a whole (4:1; 6:13–17), namely, that they would come to possess the holy land and enter into his rest, both symbols of eternal life.

10:37 ***For yet a little while, and he that shall come will come, and will not tarry / Because "just a little longer," and "he who is coming will arrive and he will not delay":*** In order to bolster his point, the author stitches two scriptures together. The phrase μικρὸν ὅσον ὅσον (*micron hoson hoson*), "just a little longer,"[280] comes from LXX Isaiah 26:20, where the prophet instructs the Jews to hide themselves for safety reasons a little while longer while the Lord's anger against idolaters becomes spent. The emphasis there is on the shortness of the time they will need to wait. The rest of the phrase comes from LXX Habakkuk 2:3. There the Old Testament prophet instructs his people to be patient for the one who is coming and will not long delay. Some Jews, like the Christians, read this passage with Messianic overtones.[281]

Two items are noteworthy. First, there is little doubt that the author takes the passage as God's word, yet he breaks from his usual pattern by not signaling his readers that he is referring to scripture. Just why he did not do so is unknown.[282] Second, the author or his source has rearranged the text more freely than usual; however, the new arrangement does allow the author to better make his point.[283]

The verb ἥκω (*hēkō*), "to come, arrive," is often used in the LXX as God coming either to judge or save his people.[284] In this instance, it is likely that the author is referring to Christ and his Second Coming. In 10:25, the author has mentioned that Judgment Day is approaching. Here he notes the time is short.[285]

---

279. BDAG, 355–56.

280. The phrase translates literally as "a little how much, how much" and means "a little bit longer." Vanhoye, *Letter to the Hebrews,* 176.

281. O'Brien, *Letter to the Hebrews,* 389; Bruce, *Epistle to the Hebrews,* 273; Lane, *Hebrews 9–13,* 304–5.

282. Some speculate that the phrases were so well known or formulaic that they needed no such introduction, but that should have applied to the other scriptures the author quoted. For discussion, see Cockerill, *Epistle to the Hebrews,* 506 and n. 44.

283. For discussion, see Cockerill, *Epistle to the Hebrews,* 506–7; 509 n. 52.

284. Ellingworth, *Epistle to the Hebrews,* 556.

285. Since the author makes no comment on the passage concerning how soon he sees the end coming, drawing conclusions on how near he felt the Parousia was is mere speculation. Ellingworth, *Epistle to the Hebrews,* 555. On the view of the nearness of the Second

The verb χρονίζω (*chronizō*), "tarry, delay," echoes Isaiah 13:22, where the prophet speaks of a coming judgment. The author uses the word to stress the shortness of the period of suffering and therefore the need not to give up.

10:38 ***Now the just shall live by faith / "But my righteous one will live by faith:*** This verse is taken from LXX Habakkuk 2:4. In the ancient manuscripts containing this portion of Hebrews, there are textual variations. They all differ in their treatment of the genitive pronoun μου (*mou*), "my." Some texts place it after ὁ δίκαιος (*ho dikaios*), "the righteous one," so that the phrase translates as "my righteous one will live by faith." Others place it after πίστεως (*pisteōs*), "faith," translating it as "the righteous one will live by faith in me." Some manuscripts leave it out. A translation would be "the righteous will live by faith." Due to the support of early and reliable texts, the weight of evidence suggests the first reading is the more likely, and we follow it in our Rendition.[286]

The phrase ὁ δὲ δίκαιός μου (*ho de dikaios mou*), "my righteous one," refers to a person who has been made righteous or just through the power of the Lord and who has, thereby, become one of the Savior's own.[287] The context of Hebrews suggests the author has the individual Saint in view. Having gained this station, however, does not guarantee eternal life. This idea likely lies behind the author's admonition that each person must persevere in living the good life ever depending on God's promise and power.[288]

but if any man draw back, my soul shall have no pleasure in him / and if he hesitates to act, my soul will not be pleased with him": This phrase is also from Habakkuk 2:4. The verb ὑποστέλλω (*hypostellō*) means "to draw back, avoid, or hesitate from doing something."[289] In the present context, it suggests reticence in proclaiming or defending the gospel (compare Acts 20:20, 27) and of defecting from its cause.[290] The phrase ἡ ψυχή μου (*hē psyche mou*), "my soul," suggests the very depth of a person—"I myself"—and suggests the seriousness with which the Lord takes a person's unwillingness

---

Coming in Hebrews, see the subsection "The Degree of the Influence of Apocalyptic Thought and Expectations of the Parousia" in the introduction of this volume.

286. Metzger, *Textual Commentary,* 601.

287. The word refers not only to one who shows the highest standards of rectitude but also to one who has been made that way through Christ. BDAG, 246–47; Louw-Nida, §§88.12; 34.47.

288. Lane, *Hebrews 9–13,* 307.

289. BDAG, 1041.

290. Vanhoye, *Letter to the Hebrews,* 176.

to stand up for what is right. The result, as the phrase suggests, amounts to God's rejection of the one who hesitates in expressing her or his faith and defects from the cause after having once been made righteous.[291]

10:39 ***But we are not of them who draw back unto perdition; but of them that believe to the saving of the soul / But we are not the kind of people who hesitate to act, which results in destruction, but we are the kind of people who believe, which results in preserving the soul:*** This is a very condensed sentence in Greek, which could be literally translated as "But we are not of hesitancy to destruction but of faith to preservation of soul." The genitive nouns ὑποστολῆς (*hypostolēs*), "of hesitancy," and πίστεως (*pisteōs*), "of faith," can be construed as either genitives of quality,[292] that is, "We are the kind of people who . . . ," or membership in a group,[293] that is, "We belong to those who . . . ." Based on textual evidence, we have chosen the former as the more likely and used it in our Rendition.

The noun ἀπώλεια (*apōleia*), "punishment," carries the strong denotation of ruin but carries the nuance of the eternal punishment that besets the wicked.[294] The noun περιποίησις (*peripoiēsis*), "preserving," expresses a sense of security and safety.[295] The noun ψυχή (*psyche*), "soul," denotes "the seat and center of human life."[296]

In the two prepositional phrases εἰς ἀπώλειαν (*eis apōleian*) and εἰς περιποίησιν ψυχῆς (*eis peripoiēsin psychēs*), the preposition εἰς (*eis*) indicates "the result of an action or condition,"[297] thus "resulting in destruction" and "resulting in preserving the soul" in our Rendition.[298]

---

291. Lane, *Hebrews 9–13,* 278, notes bbb, ccc; Schrenk, *TDNT,* 2:738–51; Vanhoye, *Letter to the Hebrews,* 176.

292. Smyth, *Greek Grammar,* §1320; Ellingworth, *Epistle to the Hebrews,* 557.

293. Ellingworth, *Epistle to the Hebrews,* 557; BDAG, 285.

294. BDAG, 127.

295. BDAG, 804.

296. BDAG, 1098–2000.

297. BDAG, 290.

298. J. T. Dennison Jr., "Chiastic Homoioptoton in Hebrews 10:39 and 11:1," *Kerux: The Journal of Northwest Theological Seminary* 26, no. 3 (2011): 16–19, shows that the author of Hebrews ties the idea of the heavenly possession in chapter 10 to that in chapter 11 by using a literary technique called *homoioptoton* in 10:39 and 11:1. This technique uses similar case endings that are repeated in series. Dennison also shows that not only is this technique used—similar case endings patterned "s" to "n" in 10:39 and "n" to "s" in 11:1—but also that the sequence is chiastic.

Analysis and Summary

Having served his readers with a stern warning, the author now turns to an admonition that centers on the continued blessings his audience will receive if they endure through faith. In doing so, he provides the modern reader with a window through which to view the hardships that these early Saints had gone through. The author acknowledges their great struggle (πολλὴν ἄφλησιν, *pollēn aphlēsin*). Using words that focus on arena and theater, he appeals to the status the public gives to successful athletes in the hopes of encouraging this suffering minority to act in faith and endure their difficult hardships. By doing so, the author promises they can turn their present poor circumstances into a contest through which they can achieve the victor's crown.[299] He recognizes that they have gone through a period characterized with sufferings, tribulations, and reproaches (10:32–33).[300] During that time, some had endured open humiliations, often being made public spectacles, perhaps even being denounced in the theaters if not publicly beaten.[301] With courage, those not directly targeted at the moment willingly stepped forward to assist those being derided. The faithful even openly cared for those imprisoned.[302] But the big show of faith was that they accepted the seizure of their property with good will (10:34). Just how this happened the author does not state, but this disfavored minority were likely all too often the victims of

299. The account seems to point to a particular period of rather intense persecution rather than the more common disregard and disrespect the Christians had to constantly endure. Koester, *Hebrews*, 464; Bruce, *Epistle to the Hebrews*, 267–68. The "crown" (στέφανος, *stephanos*) was a wreath placed on the head of an athletic champions and successful warrior. It represented both triumph and public honor. BDAG, 943–44.

300. That these were characteristic of what the early Saints had to endure, see Matt. 5:11–12; James 1:2, 12; and 1 Pet. 1:6.

301. Koester, *Hebrews*, 459. The noun θέατρον (*theatron*) denotes both the "theater" and the spectacles that were put on there. BDAG, 446. These arenas were sometimes places of public outcry. Such happened to some of Paul's companions. See Acts 19:24–41. Even the uncondemned could be flogged at the whim of a magistrate. For example, see Acts 16:19–24, and on the general suffering of the Christians, see Rom. 5:3; 8:35; 12:12; and 2 Cor. 1:4, 8; 2:4; 4:17; 6:4–5; 7:4; 8:13.

302. All seemed to have been treated poorly at one point or another, none being free from the tribulation. Cockerill, *Epistle to the Hebrews*, 488; Ellingworth, *Epistle to the Hebrews*, 546. For examples of Christians caring for their imprisoned fellows, see Philip. 4:15; 4:14–18; Ignatius, *Eph.* 1:2; *Magn.* 1:1; *Trall.* 1:2; Lucian, *Peregr.* 12–13; and Tertullian, *Mart.* 1.

greedy and covetous officials, who were not uncommon in the Greco-Roman world.[303] This often left the person or family destitute, and the family situation became even harder if the head of the household was banished or imprisoned.

The author highlights the past strength of these people with the word "partner" or "fellow sharer" (κοινωνός, *koinōnos*). During the tough period, they did not shy away from either their own or the suffering of others but instead supported and sustained one another through it all—and they survived. That they did so is rather remarkable given the view held by many people in the Greco-Roman world and the number of leaders who were willing to put pressure on the Christian community. Romans liked very old and traditional religions and practices (*mos maiorum*), and they were innately suspicious of most Eastern religions, perceiving them as a seedbed of disloyalty toward the cult of the emperor. Christianity particularly was viewed as a new, unpatriotic, and disloyal Eastern religion that worshiped a crucified God (the typical punishment prescribed to those who led slave revolts). The general attitude toward the Christians was captured by the Roman historian Tacitus, writing toward the end of the first and into the second century. He described Christianity as "a most mischievous superstition" and claimed its people had a deep "hatred against mankind."[304] Since the view seems to have been rather widespread, the divine hand can be seen in that Christianity survived at all, let alone thrived.[305]

In 10:34, the author notes what sustained these early Christians. They had a deep witness that there was an enduring, even eternal, possession awaiting them. This stand confirmed that they already possessed that attribute of faith that the author will focus on in the next chapter—an attribute that allowed them to see the hidden reality beyond earthy horizons where a treasure both "superior" (κρείττονα, *kreittona*) and "enduring" (μένουσαν, *menousan*) awaited them.

---

303. For studies, see Craig R. Koester, "Conversion, Persecution, and Malaise: Life in the Community for Which Hebrews Was Written," *HTS Teologiese Studies / Theological Studies* 61, nos. 1–2 (2005): 231–51, accessed January 24, 1017, https://hts.org.za/index.php/hts/article/view/444/343; and Brian Rapske, *The Book of Acts and Paul in Roman Custody* (Grand Rapids, Mich.: Wm. B. Eerdmans, 1994), 10–20. It is possible they were subject to mob action and lost property through group theft. For examples, see Eusebius, *Hist. eccl.* 3.17; and Attridge, *Epistle to the Hebrews*, 299.

304. Tacitus, *Ann.* 15.44.

305. For a study, see Robert L. Wilken, *The Christians as the Romans Saw Them* (New Haven, N.J.: Yale University Press, 1984).

The author hints at what gave them this sight in 10:32, noting they had been "enlightened" (φωτίζω, *phōtizō*) likely through the power and gift of the Holy Ghost. Such enlightenment, according to President Lorenzo Snow, comes from "a complete baptism—a tangible immersion in the heavenly principle or element, the Holy Ghost; and even more real and physical in its effects upon every part of [the] system [that is, the whole soul] than the immersion by water; dispelling forever, so long as reason and memory last, all possibility of doubt or fear."[306]

Based on their faithful past performance and its result, the author rests the admonition he now makes (10:35). Through the rest of the paragraph, his focus is on three key attributes he wishes his readers to inculcate: "confidence" (παρρησία, *parrēsia*) in standing up for Christian ideals, "endurance" (ὑπομονή, *hyponone*) during times of trial, and "faith" (πίστις, *pistis*) in the promises of the covenant.[307]

In 10:35, he cautions his readers against abandoning (ἀποβάλητε, *apobalēte*) their confident boldness in the Lord. The nuance of the admonition is that they continue to be bold in both living and proclaiming their Christianity. Such courageous acts would show that their spiritual center focuses on the eternal, not the transitory. He wants them to keep up this attitude. They must be willing to pass over present ease for the heavenly "great reward" (μεγάλην μισθαποδοσίαν, *megalēn misthapodosian*) he assures them they will receive.

But, as he notes in 10:36, they will need more than confidence; they will also need endurance to get through their present distress. By the power of this virtue, they will accomplish the will of God in standing up for what they believe, no matter the cost. Here we find a strong echo to 10:7–10 and the Savior's personal self-sacrifice that he made to fulfill the Father's will. The author promises his readers that through endurance they will receive the fulness of the promise of the new covenant (see 4:1, 8; 6:12, 17; 8:6; compare James 1:4; and 1 Pet. 4:19).[308]

---

306. Eliza R. Snow Smith, *Biography and Family Record of Lorenzo Snow* (Salt Lake City: Deseret News, 1884), 8.

307. Attridge, *Epistle to the Hebrews,* 300.

308. Vanhoye, *Letter to the Hebrews,* 176. It is of note that the author uses the verb κομίζω (*komizō*), "to receive," to indicate the action his readers can expect concerning their reward while he uses the verb ἐπιτυγχάνω (*epityngchanō*), "to achieve, obtain," to describe that of the Old Testament heroes (6:15; 11:33; compare Rom. 11:7). Likely this was to highlight the difference between the rewards of the two sets of people. The Old

The author's admonition "has been crafted to encourage endurance and forestall discouragement engendered by opposition or by the dulling effect of time. Those who endure persist in a life of faith and obedience despite opposition from the unbelieving world. Thus, the [author] can describe the person who has endured to the end as one who has 'done the will of God.'"[309]

To bolster his point, in 10:37–38, the author appeals to scripture. Coupling Isaiah 26:20 with LXX Habakkuk 2:3–4, he shows the coming of the Lord is not long off; therefore, those who are righteous will need to endure for but a short time longer. Any desire to hold back in giving their all will bring upon them the Lord's displeasure. The author closes the pericope (10:39) by assuring his readers that they, himself included, are not the kind of people who would hesitate to act (ὑποστολῆς, *hypostolēs,* the word denoting all signs of timidity, shrinking back, or hesitation[310]), which would lead to destruction of the soul, but rather they are the kind who, through trust in making and keeping covenants with God, preserve the soul.[311]

Testament group did not "receive" the promises while in this life. Nonetheless, they did "achieve" much, and therefore their reward came after death. On the other hand, the author's readers can expect "to receive" the promise in the near future as part of the eschatological rewards for the faithful. See 2 Cor. 5:10; Eph. 6:8; Col. 3:25; and 1 Pet. 1:9; 5:4.

309. Cockerill, *Epistle to the Hebrews,* 505.

310. BDAG, 1041.

311. Attridge, *Epistle to the Hebrews,* 301–2. For a study of the importance of not hesitating to do righteousness but of acting in faith to preserve the soul as found in Hebrews, see Matthew C. Easter, *Faith and the Faithfulness of Jesus in Hebrews,* vol. 160 of Society for New Testament Studies Monograph Series (Cambridge: Cambridge University Press, 2014), 132–64.

Chapter 11

The Power of Faith

Introduction

The eleventh chapter of the Epistle to the Hebrews is one of the most famous passages of the entire book (and in many cases of the entire New Testament). In this section, the author of Hebrews uses examples and allusions from the Old Testament to illustrate the importance of faith in his theological argument. He begins with a description of faith, briefly discusses the "elders," that is, those faithful Old Testament progenitors whom he will use as his examples, then shows how the activities and blessings of the various named individuals, beginning with Abel and ending with "the prophets," demonstrates the manifold ways they expressed their faith.

The illustrations are of interest for at least two reasons. The first is the accounts often include details not available in the biblical record as we currently have it. Whether these are interpretive additions or represent traditions available to the author of Hebrews, we do not know. The second is the author's ability to make the Old Testament relevant to the needs of his readers.

For modern readers, the central issue and real importance of this section of the Epistle is how to understand the author's description of faith (πίστις, *pistis*).[1] The author appeals to historical events, suggesting that he views "faith" in its temporal context. For instance, in 11:1 he makes a somewhat vague reference to "things not seen," but in 11:7 he refers to "things not seen as yet." The addition of the term "yet" clarifies the former statement, showing his first remark is not to things invisible in and of themselves (at

1. For a discussion of whether or not the author's emphasis is on the Hebraic/temporal or the Greek/spatial, see Ellingworth, *Epistle to the Hebrews,* 562. Based on the evidence from the text itself, the Hebraic/temporal has the best support, and therefore we follow that here.

least so far as this world is concerned) but to things not yet made visible or wholly clear to those moving through this transitory period that demands walking by faith. Thus, the patriarchs saw Jehovah's promises "from afar," that is, they were not yet clear. Even Abraham when he "went out" did not yet know where God would lead him (11:8). The patriarchs dwelt in tents even though they were promised they would eventually live in a city for which God had both laid the foundation and built the superstructure (11:10) but which was invisible to the worldly. But these patriarchs, through the power of faith, "saw" what was invisible to those without faith (namely, God's realities) and accordingly persevered in covenant keeping.[2] So it is with all the other examples of faith the author lists.

In setting up his next argument, the author has already noted the relationship among endurance, obedience, and faith (10:35–39). He now turns to show how faith (11:1–40) and endurance (12:1–11) are the hallmarks of the way of life he wants for his readers. The author has already shown the detrimental effects of unbelief and disobedience and what they cost the wilderness generation (3:7–4:11). He now emphasizes the positive counterpart to these two sins with the expression "by [or through] faith." The essence of faith is belief; obedience is the expression of faith. Where there is no obedience, there is no faith. Where obedience is slow in coming or grudgingly given, faith is weak. Where obedience is willfully and fully given, faith is strong.

Throughout this chapter, the author describes what it means to "live by faith." As one scholar noted, the author shows that faith "is to live as if God's promise of future reward is sure and his power for present victory is real." In doing so, the author stresses that faith is more than a mental act but rather a way of life that encompasses obedience. He goes on to show "'endurance' is persistence in this life of faith despite hardship and persecution." In sum, "the life of faith is a life of endurance through reliance on God. Those who lived 'by faith' according to 11:1–40 exemplified the 'endurance' enjoined in 12:1–13."[3]

The author of Hebrews uses the dative πίστει (*pistei*) of the noun, "with/through faith," very skillfully to vary the pace of his discourse and thus emphasize the importance of his various points. "The absence of πίστει from vv. 10 and 12 slows the pace in preparation for the extended comment

---

2. Ellingworth, *Epistle to the Hebrews,* 562–63.

3. Cockerill, *Epistle to the Hebrews,* 505.

of vv. 13–16. Conversely, the frequent repetition of πίστει in vv. 27–31 increases the pace in preparation for the even more rapid summary of vv. 32–38, within which still further acceleration can be discerned."[4]

The author's development breaks down into two long sections. The first (11:1–7) includes a description of faith, a statement of its value in being able to understand history from the creation onward, and examples from the earliest period of biblical history as expressed by Abel, Enoch, and Noah. He then moves to his second section, which has four parts. The first deals with the faith of the patriarchs Abraham, Isaac, Jacob, and Joseph (11:8–22); the second with the faith of Moses highlighted with examples from his ministry (11:23–31); the third with a general overview of the victories of the faithful and a catalog of all they had to endure; and the fourth with the result of faithful living for them and also for the authors' readers (11:32–40).[5]

A Description of Faith (11:1–3)

Greek Text

1 Ἔστιν δὲ πίστις ἐλπιζομένων ὑπόστασις, πραγμάτων ἔλεγχος οὐ βλεπομένων· 2 ἐν ταύτῃ γὰρ ἐμαρτυρήθησαν οἱ πρεσβύτεροι. 3 πίστει νοοῦμεν κατηρτίσθαι τοὺς αἰῶνας ῥήματι θεοῦ, εἰς τὸ μὴ ἐκ φαινομένων τὸ βλεπόμενον γεγονέναι. [SBLGNT]

King James Version

1 Now faith is the substance of things hoped for, the evidence of things not seen. 2 For by it the elders obtained a good report. 3 Through faith we understand that the worlds were framed by the word of God, so that things which are seen were not made of things which do appear.

New Rendition

1 Now faith deals with the reality of things that are hoped for, the evaluation of the truth of things that are not seen. 2 For by it our ancestors were commended by God. 3 By our faith we understand that the worlds were organized by the word of God, so that what is visible was made by what is invisible.

4. Ellingworth, *Epistle to the Hebrews,* 561.
5. Vanhoye, *Letter to the Hebrews,* 177–78.

Translation Notes and Comments

11:1 ***Now faith is the substance of things hoped for, the evidence of things not seen / Now faith deals with the reality of things that are hoped for, the evaluation of the truth of things that are not seen:*** Although the noun πίστις (*pistis*), "faith," appears early in this phrase, in order to place it in the author's context, those words the author uses to describe it are investigated briefly here and then more fully in the Analysis section. There and in the "Excursus on Faith" the noun is defined.

The noun ὑπόστασις (*hypostasis*) is cognate with the Latin *substantia,* from which the English noun "substance" is derived.[6] It means literally "that which stands under" and therefore something that supports what is above it. The word can also describe "the essential or basic structure/nature of an entity, substantial nature, essence, actual being."[7] It stresses the sure reality of its object "often in contrast to what merely seems to be."[8] In 1:3, the same word is used describing Christ as χαρακτὴρ τῆς ὑποστάσεως αὐτοῦ (*charactēr tēs hypostaseōs autou*), "the exact appearance of his [God's] actual being." In our Rendition, we have translated it as "reality," which seems to best catch the sense in this passage.[9] If we have faith in Jesus Christ and his teachings, then we assume the reality of the things for which we hope, such as forgiveness of our sins, our sanctification, and our ultimate exaltation in the celestial kingdom. This in turn motivates us to conform our lives to principles of Christ's gospel in the hope that through his infinite Atonement we can obtain these blessings.

The JST replaces "substance" with "assurance" and in doing so takes the objective nuance and replaces it with a subjective one. The noun is parallel with "confidence" in that both stress a trust in their object, be it a person, idea, or purpose. "Assurance," however, implies such a commitment to that

---

6. The Vulgate translates ὑπόστασις (*hypostasis*) as *substantia*, "that of which a thing consists, the being, essence, contents, material, substance." Lewis and Short, *New Latin Dictionary,* 1782. The Latin noun *substantia* never had the sense "confidence, assurance."

7. BDAG, 1040–41.

8. BDAG, 1040–41.

9. BDAG, 1040, states, "Among the meanings that can be authenticated for [Heb. 11:1] a strong claim can be made for realization of a plan." Köster, *TDNT,* 8:587–88, states, "It is plain, then, that in [Hebrews] ὑπόστασις always denotes the 'reality' of God which stands contrasted with the corruptible, shadowy, and merely prototypical character of the world but which is paradoxically present in Jesus and is the possession of the community as faith."

person, idea, or purpose that it replaces doubt with a never-questioning confidence in what the person says or does or what the idea or purpose requires.[10] It was likely this nuance that appealed to Joseph Smith.[11]

The problem with translating the noun ὑπόστασις (*hypostasis*) as either "confidence" or "assurance" is that not a single example of the word with these nuances can be found in ancient texts.[12] Further, the author uses the noun πληροφορία (*plērophoria*), which means "full assurance, certainty,"[13] in 6:11; 10:22. If he wanted to give πίστις (*pistis*) either of these nuances, he would likely have chosen *plērophoria.*

The noun ἔλεγχος (*elengchos*) describes "the act of presenting evidence for the truth of something."[14] In Latter-day Saint theology, it is the Holy Spirit that gives proof of the reality of the gospel truths. As Moroni stated, "By the power of the Holy Ghost ye may know the truth of all things" (Moro. 10:5). In the context of Hebrews, that knowledge would be the sureness of the promised blessings.

The noun πράγμα (*pragma*), "thing," denotes any kind of concern or matter and also any kind of deed, undertaking, or event. The author uses the plural form but does not explain what "things" he has in mind.[15] The best understanding of the phrase likely comes from the author's statement in 10:39 that faith brings to everyone what is necessary to preserve the soul. In that context, "all things" would include having the grace and power of God active in readers' lives, knowing they are commended by God and will receive the promise. By their very nature, these "things" are οὐ βλεπομένων (*ou blepomenōn*), "not seen." This phrase marks those items that are spiritual in contrast to those that are temporal. The author's thrust is that we should place our confidence in the former, not the latter.[16]

---

10. *Webster's New Dictionary of Synonyms,* s.v. "confidence."

11. This is the nuance found in the German Bible, which by at least 1844, Joseph Smith felt was the most nearly correct translation. "Conference Minutes," *Times and Seasons* 5 (August 15, 1844): 614. For discussion on this nuance of ὑπόστασις (*hypostasis*), see Analysis below.

12. Moulton and Milligan, *Vocabulary,* 659–60.

13. BDAG, 827.

14. BDAG, 315; Büchel, *TDNT,* 2:476. The Vulgate translates it as *argumentum,* "the means by which an assertion or assumption may be made clear, proved, an argument, evidence, proof (and in particular, that which rests upon facts, while *ratio* is that which depends upon reasoning)." Lewis and Short, *New Latin Dictionary,* 159.

15. BDAG, 858–59.

16. BDAG, 315.

11:2 ***For by it the elders obtained a good report / For by it our ancestors were commended by God:*** The phrase ἐν ταύτῃ (*en tautē*), "by it," is instrumental and refers to the kind of faith the author has just described and which he now attributes to the Old Testament faithful.[17]

The nominalized adjective οἱ πρεσβύτερος (*hoi presbyteros*) is used here to designate "the men of old," a term that referred to "ancestors."[18] While not all of the readers of Hebrews may have been physical descendants of the Old Testament people subsequently described, they could certainly be described as spiritual descendants.

The verb μαρτυρέω (*martyreō*), here in the aorist passive,[19] means "to be well spoken of, approved, or commended."[20] Because the word "commend" carries the nuance not only of warm approval but also of calling attention to the merits of an individual,[21] we use it in our Rendition. Verses 11:4 and 11:5 make it clear this commendation comes from God, and so for clarity, we have added "by God" in our Rendition.

11:3 ***Through faith we understand that the worlds were framed by the word of God / By our faith we understand that the worlds were organized by the word of God:*** The author uses the first person plural of the verb νοέω (*noeō*), "we know," to identify himself with his readers—the power of faith brings them into the company of the faithful together. The verb denotes comprehending or grasping something based on careful thought and analysis, thus, "to understand." It also carries the nuance of heeding something with the intent of appropriately acting upon it.[22]

This passage as it reads in the KJV can be interpreted to refer to the faith of either God or the believers. However, reading the dative noun πίστει (*pistei*), "by faith," as modifying the infinitive κατηρτίσθαι (*karērtisthai*), "to be organized," rather than the verb νοοῦμεν (*nooumen*), "we understand," does not work here.[23] Nowhere else in Hebrews does the author

17. Cockerill, *Epistle to the Hebrews*, 522 n. 13.

18. BDAG, 862.

19. Μαρτυρέω (*martyreō*) acts as a cumulative aorist and as such connotes the approbation God gave to all the faithful people the author will list. Lane, *Hebrews 9–13*, 326 note g, 330. The English word "martyr" comes from this Greek word.

20. BDAG, 617–18; LSJ, 1018; Strathmann, *TDNT*, 4:497.

21. *Webster's New Dictionary of Synonyms*, s.v. "commend."

22. BDAG, 674–75; Louw-Nida, §§30.3; 32.2.

23. This is, however, the way the *Lectures on Faith* takes the phrase. No doubt this is because the *Lectures* author (likely Sidney Rigdon) unquestionably relied on the verse as found in the KJV. See Lecture 1:14–19.

say or even imply that God does things by faith;[24] moreover, such an interpretation would render ῥήματι θεοῦ (*rhēmati theou*), "by God's word," redundant.[25] Therefore, grammatically speaking, the author is emphasizing yet again the breadth of vision that faith gives to the believer. Hence in our Rendition, we have inserted the possessive pronoun "our" to make it clear that understanding comes by our faith.

The verb καταρτίζω (*katartizō*) here has the sense "to put in order, organize."[26] Compare this with the creation account in the book of Abraham where "the Gods, organized and formed the heavens and the earth" (Abr. 4:1).

The noun ῥῆμα (*rhēma*), "word," denotes a statement of any kind, but "primarily focuses on the content of the communication."[27] It therefore connotes especially a command of God.[28] The idea behind a divine command is not restricted to statements of moral instruction but includes any decree made by godly authority. Thus, God's instructions to the elements during the creation period constituted orders or commands (see Gen. 1; Moses 2).[29]

so that things which are seen were not made of things which do appear / so that what is visible was made by what is invisible: This phrase is grammatically rather complex. It uses a negated articular infinitive phrase, εἰς τὸ μή (*eis to mē*), "so that not,"[30] which modifies the perfect active infinitive γεγονέναι (*gegonenai*), rendered as "was made." The two are, however, separated by a phrase consisting of two participles used nominally: ἐκ φαινομένων (*ek phainomenōn*), "from things that appear," and τὸ

---

24. Moreover, Alma's statement that "faith is not to have a perfect knowledge of things; therefore if ye have faith ye hope for things which are not seen, which are true" (Alma 32:21; compare Ether 12:6) would seem to preclude God having faith, since he has a perfect knowledge of all things.

25. Ellingworth, *Epistle to the Hebrews,* 568. For further discussion, see Analysis below.

26. Delling, *TDNT,* 1:476; LSJ, 910; BDAG, 526.

27. Louw-Nida, §33.98.

28. BDAG, 905.

29. Note in Abraham 4:7–11, 18, the Gods are said to have "ordered" the physical material to do their will.

30. The problem is what μή (*mē*), "not," modifies. The KJV has it modify ἐκ φαινομένων (*ek phainomenōn*), "from things that appear." Not surprisingly the NKJV follows this understanding. So too does the NIV. Lane, *Hebrews 9–13,* 326–27 note k, feels this is the more natural reading. However, these do not take into account the chiastic structure of the sentence.

βλεπόμενον (*to blepomenon*), "that which is seen." Separating the negation from its object is very unusual word order, but the author constructed it so as to form a chiasmus that emphasizes his point:

a κατηρτίσθαι—organized
  b τοὺς αἰώνας—the worlds
    c ῥήματι θεοῦ—the word of God
    c' μὴ ἐκ φαινομένων—not from things visible
  b' τὸ βλεπόμενον—that which is seen
a' γεγονέναι—made

Thus, the unusual word order emphasizes that the phrase "not from things visible" refers to God's commanding word.[31] We have rendered that phrase as "what is invisible."

Analysis and Summary

The author begins this chapter with a description of faith (πίστις, *pistis*). The noun can be translated as "trust, confidence, faith,"[32] with "faith" being used by most biblical translators. Although the first readers of Hebrews probably understood this definition, that is not necessarily the case today. The different translations of this verse in the various modern translations as well as differing interpretations in scholarly commentaries and papers witness to the difficulty in properly understanding the definition. The author's objective, however, seems clear: he has crafted his first sentence such that it would stimulate his readers into a life of obedience to God.

The difficulty centers on whether the two nouns ὑπόστασις (*hypostasis*) and ἔλεγχος (*elengchos*) should be understood objectively as "reality" and "evaluating the truth" or subjectively as "assurance" and "conviction."[33]

The writers of the KJV chose to translate ὑπόστασις (*hypostasis*) as "substance," a borrowing from the Latin *substantia,* "that of which a thing consists, the being, essence, contents, material, substance,"[34] which is cognate with the Greek *hypostasis.* During the era of the KJV translation, the term

31. This passage has led some to read into the text Platonic overtones of reality. See, for example, Attridge, *Epistle to the Hebrews,* 316; and Thompson, *Hebrews,* 232. The connection is tenuous at best. Koester, *Hebrews,* 474, and Cockerill, *Epistle to the Hebrews,* 524 n. 24, have correctly noted, "Hebrews fails to consistently posit the connectedness between heavenly patterns and earthly realities that we would expect from a document rooted in Platonic dualism."

32. BDAG, 818.

33. Ellingworth, *Epistle to the Hebrews,* 564–65.

34. Lewis and Short, *New Latin Dictionary,* 1782.

carried deep theological overtones. In certain circles, it came to have two main meanings. The first was "that which exists by itself" and therefore depends on nothing else. By that definition, God was pure substance. However, the second was a derivative definition: items that require only the existence of God in order to be.[35] Because faith is neither an abstraction nor mere concept, it has an actual reality or existence of its own, and therefore it has "substance."[36] The question is whether the author of Hebrews saw it in this light.

The basic meaning of ὑπόστασις (*hypostasis*) is "that which stands under," thus denoting in an objective sense a "support" or "foundation." It could also connote "the essence or basic nature of an entity" and was used by the philosophers to separate mere "appearance" from "reality."[37] It can be used for "a plan that one devises for action, plan, project, undertaking, endeavor," also a "situation, condition," and a "guarantee of ownership/entitlement, title deed."[38] Although both Martin Luther and Philip Melanchthon, as they wrestled with the problem, preferred the sense of "confidence, assurance," and several modern translations follow their lead, there is no firm support for that sense.[39] In contrast, 3:14 states, "We have become partners with Christ, if indeed we hold fast to our initial resolve until the end" (our translation), where ὑπόστασις (*hypostasis*) is translated "resolve."

Compare this definition of faith with that given by Alma: "Faith is not to have a perfect knowledge of things; therefore if ye have faith ye hope for things which are not seen, which are true" (Alma 32:21). This adds a clarifying dimension; *true* faith must be based in truth. One can have belief

---

35. Though very dated, the following study is still informative: T. B. Strong, "The History of the Theological Term 'Substance,'" *Journal of Theological Studies* 2 (January 1901): 224–35; 3 (October 1901): 22–40; 4 (October 1902): 28–45; see also Jean-Luc Marion, "The Essential Incoherence of Descartes' Definition of Divinity," trans. Frederick P. Van de Pitte, in *Essays on Descartes' Meditations,* ed. Amélie Oksenberg Rorty (Berkley: University of California Press, 1986), 303–5.

36. The word "substance" has kept a good deal of that meaning up to this time, although it has largely lost the theological overtones. It denotes three things: first, the essential, fundamental characteristic or attribute that makes up its object, that is, it points to the object's essence; second, the ultimate reality whether seen or unseen that underlies all outward manifestations; and third, the material from which something is made. *Collegiate Dictionary,* s.v. "substance."

37. BDAG, 1040–41; O'Brien, *Letter to the Hebrews,* 399; Attridge, *Epistle to the Hebrews,* 307–8.

38. BDAG, 1040–41.

39. BDAG, 1040–41. On Luther's position, see the "Excursus on Faith" below.

but not faith in that which is false. The reason is that the "things hoped for" actually exist independent of a person's faith, but because they have not yet been fully experienced they are not perfectly known in the present but will be. That is not true of what is false. No matter how hard a person believes and works to its ends, falseness has no independent existence and can therefore never be realized.

In a very detailed and exhaustive study of ὑπόστασις (*hypostasis*), one scholar concluded, "It is plain, then, that in [Hebrews], ὑπόστασις always denotes the 'reality' of God which stands contrasted with the corruptible, shadowy, and merely prototypical character of the world but which is paradoxically present in Jesus and is the possession of the community as faith."[40] Therefore, we have translated the word as "reality" in our Rendition.[41]

How is faith the reality of "things hoped for"? Again, the examples the author presents are helpful. Because faith is expressed in enduring obedience—a trait required for attaining eternal life—anyone who exercises faithful obedience will ultimately obtain all the promised blessings.

The question naturally arises, how did πίστις (*pistis*) take on the strong subjective nuance found in the KJV and other biblical translations? The answer is through the work of Luther's colleague Melanchthon, who, influenced by his background in liberal arts and the classics, developed a humanistic mode of thought that informed his theology. Over time he developed a combination of humanistic and Christian ideals that he wove into his theological essays and lectures. These ideals supplied his strong belief in human free will. Reacting to some of the theological arguments of the day that denied free will and made conversion to Christ strictly a matter of divine fiat, he desired to put the individual back on the stage as an active participant. That necessitated giving faith a subjective cast. To do so, he reinterpreted faith, dividing it into knowledge, assent, and trust, which made the participation of the individual critical in the conversion process. Based on this belief, he influenced Luther to translate the Greek word *hypostasis* as "confidence" (*Zuversicht*) in the reformer's translation of the Bible.[42] From there the subjective nuance spread quickly among the various branches of Protestantism.

---

40. BDAG, 1040. "Among the meanings that can be authenticated for [11:1,] a strong claim can be made for realization of a plan." For a study, see Köster, *TDNT,* 8:572–89.

41. Ellingworth, *Epistle to the Hebrews,* 565.

42. For a study, see John Schofield, *Philip Melanchthon and the English Reformation* (Farnham, Eng.: Ashgate Publishing, 2006).

On the other hand, seeing faith as the perseverance and endurance that walking in the Lord's way entails is also supported by the second word the author uses to describe it, namely ἔλεγχος (*elengchos*). Translating this noun presents a special challenge. In the general literature, it almost always denotes reproof, correction, and punishment.[43] None of these definitions apply in this context. Therefore, the word's meaning must be taken from its current setting, which gives it a positive rather than a negative sense. In this light, the verb describes the act of presenting evidence, thus, "to bring to light, to expose, to demonstrate, to prove," and "to convince."[44] Based on this, the meaning of the noun ranges from "the act of presenting evidence for the truth of something, proof, proving," through "the act of charging a person with wrongdoing, accusation," to "expression of strong disapproval, reproof, censure."[45] The context suggests that "absence of doubt," or even "evidence," does not really work. Rather, the word connotes "the presenting of evidence" to establish the truthfulness or reality of "things unseen."[46]

The author categorizes "things" in two ways. The first is ἐλπιζομένων (*elpizomenōn*), the neuter passive participle denoting "things that are hoped for," and the second is πραγμάτων . . . οὐ βλεπομένων (*pragmata . . . ou blepomenōn*), "things not seen." The absence of *kai,* "and," suggests the two clauses are parallel, with each element informing the other, making both that which is hoped for and is as yet unseen. The verb βλέπω (*blepō*), "to see," denotes not only the ability to see but also to understand and perceive.[47] Therefore, something can be manifest but because it is not understood or perceived can remain "unseen."

Taking the whole sentence together, it appears that the "things hoped for" already exist and are therefore an unseen reality. From the context of the chapter, they consist of such things as God's acceptance, receiving his blessings and power in this life, and eventually eternal life. These are "hoped for" primarily because their full attainment is reserved for the future. What the author seems to have in mind by the phrase "things not seen" is that the power of God is available to his people while yet in the present and is a power not perceived or understood by those without faith. Thus, the author's admonition to "draw near" is for the reception of the

43. Büchel, *TDNT,* 2:476.
44. BDAG, 315.
45. BDAG, 315.
46. BDAG, 315.
47. BDAG, 178–79; Louw-Nida, §§24.411; 32.11.

benefits available here and now (4:16; 10:22) while his counsel to "hold fast" pertains to the final salvation in the future (4:14; 10:23).[48]

"How does faith 'prove' the unseen reality of God, his power and faithfulness?" asks one scholar. The examples the author gives reveal the answer: "Through trust in God the faithful experience his power in their lives and receive his approval. Thus, they confirm his reality."[49] It is noteworthy that because of their faith, these biblical heroes received divine commendation (μαρτυρέω, *martyreō*), the word connoting not only warm approval but also a desire to call attention to the merits of the individual (11:2).[50]

In sum, "faith is oriented toward both the future, hoped-for realization of God's promised reward [11:9, 11, 13, 26, 39–40] and the present but unseen reality of God's existence, providence [11:6], fidelity [11:11] and power [11:19]."[51]

In 11:3, the author states that faith enables the believer to understand that God created entire worlds through the operation of his "word." The author of Hebrews has already noted that it was the Son "by whom [God] made the worlds" (1:2). Compare this with what God said to Moses: "By the word of my power, have I created [worlds without number], which is mine Only Begotten Son. . . . I also created them for mine own purpose; and by the Son I created them, which is mine Only Begotten" (Moses 1:32–33). Also, in the beginning of the Gospel of John we read, "In the beginning was the Word, and the Word was with God. . . . All things were made by him" (John 1:1–3). Note that John uses the Greek noun λόγος (*logos*), "word," whereas the author of Hebrews uses ῥῆμα (*rhēma*), "word," in this passage. They do overlap in meaning, but *logos* has a much broader range of meaning, including not only "a communication whereby the mind finds expression" and thus "word, speech, statement, instruction, teaching, message, subject, matter," but also "computation, reckoning, reason, motive, respect, regard."[52] *Rhēma* has a more restricted semantic domain that includes "that which is said," thus "word, saying, expression of any kind" and "something that can be spoken about," such as "an object, matter,

48. Cockerill, *Epistle to the Hebrews,* 520 n. 2.

49. Cockerill, *Epistle to the Hebrews,* 521.

50. *Webster's New Dictionary of Synonyms,* s.v. "commend."

51. Cockerill, *Epistle to the Hebrews,* 520. Though some maintain that the idea of "things not seen" hints at Platonic dualism, the idea of God's expressing his power and faithfulness to his people in unseen but definite ways was consonant with those who relied on the Old Testament.

52. BDAG, 598–601.

or event."[53] The author may use this term because it more forcefully suggested a decree made by godly authority.

In 11:3, the author emphasizes that through the power of invisible things—namely the word and power of God but also such things as his fidelity, providence, and love for his children—the visible world came into being.[54] The author's point here stresses his thesis about faith. "It is not the visible world of daily experience," noted one scholar, "but God and his word that constitute ultimate reality. His word is ultimate because it is the means of creation. Thus, it is also the means of redemption . . . and final judgment. . . . To live 'by faith' then, is from beginning to end to live in accord with the word of God."[55]

53. BDAG, 905.
54. Attridge, *Epistle to the Hebrews,* 311.
55. Cockerill, *Epistle to the Hebrews,* 524.

Excursus on Faith

This excursus introduces the concept of "faith" (πίστις, *pistis*) as an indispensable principle in the salvation process and locates the word within its historical context. This excursus then looks at the biblical meanings of those words frequently translated by the English term.[56] Finally, the excursus examines the principle through the lens of the Restoration. This section's primary focus, however, is on faith as used in the Epistle to the Hebrews, making brief references to the concept as found in the Old Testament, the Gospels, some of Paul's writings, and the Epistle of James.

The author of Hebrews stresses the need for faith as *the* key element in gaining the promises of God in this life and eternal life in the world to come (6:12; 10:22–23, 38; 11:1–39; 13:7). "Faith," as used by him and other gospel writers, is a concept peculiar to emerging Christianity in that it linked belief with fidelity.

The modern problem with understanding faith in its biblical context arises primarily from the attempts of certain Christian theologians to codify and define its meaning in harmony with "the emerging philosophical language of the scholastics."[57] Eventually it came to mean, among the orthodox Christians, "the act of the intellect when it assents to divine truth under the influence and will moved by God through grace."[58] Because this definition reduced the power of faith to an intellectual exercise, some Protestant reformers sought a definition based more on biblical sources. Unfortunately, nowhere in the Bible was the concept of faith so fully articulated that the reformers could agree on exactly what it was. In actuality, the Bible in neither its Hebrew nor Greek texts has a word that exactly translates into the English word "faith."[59] Though the Greek noun πίστις (*pistis*)

56. For studies, see Bultmann, *TDNT,* 6:174–228; *NID,* s.v. "πιστεύω"; and J. E. Botha, "The Meaning of *pisteúō* in the Greek New Testament: A Semantic-Lexicographical Study," *Neotestamentica* 21, no. 2 (1987): 225–40. For Latter-day Saint sources, see Dahl and Tate, *Lectures on Faith in Historical Perspective*; Spencer W. Kimball, *Faith Precedes the Miracle* (Salt Lake City: Deseret Book, 1972); Douglas E. Brinley, "Faith in Jesus Christ," in Ludlow, *Encyclopedia of Mormonism,* 2:483–85; and "Faith in Jesus Christ," Gospel Topics, The Church of Jesus Christ of Latter-day Saints, accessed January 31, 2017, https://www.churchofjesuschrist.org/study/manual/gospel-topics/faith-in-jesus-christ.

57. Dieter Lührmann, "Faith," trans. Frank Witt Hughes, in Freedman, *Anchor Bible Dictionary,* 2:744, but see also 749–58.

58. Thomas Aquinas, *Summa Theologica* 2.2.q2.a.9.

59. The English word comes from the Latin root *fidere,* "to trust." In the thirteenth century, it came to denote faithfulness to a trust or promise and loyalty to a person. By

approximates the sense of faith as "assent," it and the other biblical words translated as "faith" are much more broad and fluid.

In the Hebrew Bible, the closest we can come to the concept of faith is that of "faithfulness." The Hebrew Bible expresses the thought with the root אמן (*'mn*). This trilateral root yields to a wide range of meanings, including "to support, foster" and "to be firm, faithful, and true." It also carries the idea of believing in a person or idea to the point of full trust in them or it.[60]

In its passive stem, the Hebrew word denotes that which lasts or endures. A person with this quality is one who fulfills his obligations and could, therefore, be trusted. In this context, it is easy to see that the word had two connotations, that of faithfulness and also of trustworthiness. A person who has been "faithful" (אָמוּן, *'āmûn*) in the past can be counted on to be "trustworthy" (אָמוּן, *'āmûn*) in the future.[61] Note that these ideas are expressed by the same Hebrew word.

In its causative stem, the Hebrew word means "to stand fast, to be fixed to a spot." Out of this grew the idea of trust and confidence especially when it came to dealings with Jehovah. When a person, such as Abraham, developed an abiding, deep, and personal relationship with God, she or he could express faith, that is, have total confidence in him. God's people could also have such a relationship that faithfulness was enjoined upon them.[62]

On the Greek side, the noun πίστις (*pistis*) and the verb πιστεύω (*pisteuō*) range in meaning from mere belief through credence to full confidence and complete trust.[63] These nuances carry the idea of a steadfast reliance upon others that also includes fidelity to their cause. Further, they carry the idea that faith is the guarantee that assures a person that something will be done. In this vein, they are connected to oaths and explain the trust biblical people placed in them. Finally, they denote the proof of a statement or

---

the fourteenth century, it included an assent of mind to the truth of a statement for which there was incomplete evidence. From that time forward, it began to look more singly to religious matters and was used most generally to nuance both Christian beliefs and those of other religious persuasions. It also took on the idea of fidelity to family, church, and God. Eventually, it began to connote confidence in a principle or person, especially God and Christ, because of the belief in their truthfulness or reliability. See Online Etymology Dictionary, s.v. "faith," accessed January 31, 2017, https://www.etymonline.com/word/faith.

60. BDB, 52–53; *TWOT,* 116.

61. BDB, 52–53; *TWOT,* 116.

62. BDB, 52–53. For more complete studies, see Jepsen, *TDOT,* 1:292–323; and *TWOT,* 2584–85.

63. BDAG, 818–20.

claim. People in the Greco-Roman world viewed the trait very positively. It was a highly respected characteristic that allowed others to rely on the person who possessed this virtue.[64]

In a religious context, the LXX consistently translates the Hebrew אֵמוּן (*ʾēmûn*) into the Greek πίστις (*pistis*) and thereby brings the double idea of faithfulness and trustworthiness into the world of the Jewish diaspora and earliest Christianity. Due to the influence of the LXX upon the early Church, these nuances continued in Christian circles. But there was another influence at play. Due to the book of Ecclesiasticus (also known as Ben Sira), a work widely circulated between 200 and 175 BC, *pistis* became more closely associated with one's relationship to the Mosaic law as an instrument that expressed Jehovah's will. In this way, the word came to nuance one who took upon himself God's law. The Jewish thinkers referred to those who did so as "the people of faith" as well as "the faithful." It was by taking upon themselves fully and completely God's law that both Abraham and Moses became models of faith.[65] Over time, more and more Jews in the broader community used the term as self-referential; they were the "people of faith"—the ones under God's law.[66]

In the New Testament, the range of meanings narrows somewhat. Concretely, *pistis* denotes a conviction to gospel truths that commits the believer to God and Christ and suggests full reliance upon them. In its more abstract mode, it points to consistency and constancy in what the Christian professes including moral living, gospel truths, and fidelity to the Father and Son. It expresses itself in trust and confidence in them, but most strongly in obedience to their will. The phrase ἡ πίστις (*hē pistis*), "the faith," came to denote the entire range of Christian doctrine.[67]

Because of trouble with the Jews arising due to resentment with the Christians using the term "the faithful" for themselves, the Christian writers began to emphasize the more traditional Greek religious meanings of the word in their later epistles, including Hebrews. Even so, though no one

64. Lührmann, "Faith," in Freedman, *Anchor Bible Dictionary,* 2:749–58.

65. Sir. 44:20; 45:4.

66. The faith of Israel became more centered on their relationship between community and God. Being a person of faith was no longer tied to a "conversion" experience that developed faith, but to the inclusion in the covenant community by which they became the people of Jehvoah. See Lührmann, "Faith," in Freedman, *Anchor Bible Dictionary,* 2:748.

67. BDAG, 816–20. For more complete studies, see Lührmann, "Faith," in Freedman, *Anchor Bible Dictionary,* 2:749–58; Bultmann, *TDNT,* 6:174–228; and *NID,* s.v. "πιστεύω."

meaning became attached to the word, at its center it connoted the different ways through which salvation was accomplished in Christ.[68]

In the writings of Paul, *pistis* took on the meaning of turning away from the Mosaic law and turning or being converted to Christ and his teachings. It came to be associated with conversion since faith had to be present in the act of accepting the Christian proclamation. In this way *pistis* came to carry the heavy Old Testament nuance of "faithfulness." It is through the expression of faithfulness that a person found himself or herself justified—freed from the blight of sin with an accompanying imputation of righteousness. To emphasize this point, Paul appealed to the faith of Abraham that led to God declaring him "righteous" a full 430 years before Moses received the law (see Rom. 4), thus showing the law was not needed in the salvation process. The Apostle also connects faith with hope and love as the cardinal virtues on which salvation rests (see Rom. 5:1–5; 1 Cor. 13:13; and 1 Thes. 1:3; 5:8).[69]

Interestingly, given how much the author's doctrine parallels that of Paul in so many instances, the author of Hebrews shows no Pauline influence in this area.[70] The author never uses the term in the same Christological context as Paul does. Rather, for the author, it marks "the way" that those who are faithful to the Great High Priest must follow. In short, it is the force that expresses itself in obedience. This concept of faith comes very close to the idea found in James. "Works," that is, obedience to the gospel and its associated laws, are how one expresses faith. Without those "works," faith is not living but dead (James 2:14–20). The focus of faith in James is as a virtue that needs to be proven and tested. In his Epistle, faith and obedience are "indissolubly linked." Indeed, "faith understood merely as trust and confession is not able to save."[71]

Neither James nor Paul ever expressly define what faith is, but does the author of Hebrews do so? The first verse in chapter 11 does address what faith is, but the verse does not work well for a full "Christian" definition because it makes no reference to Christ and little to God as the objects

68. Lührmann, "Faith," in Freedman, *Anchor Bible Dictionary,* 2:749–58.

69. Lührmann, "Faith," in Freedman, *Anchor Bible Dictionary,* 2:749–58; *NID,* s.v. "πιστεύω."

70. Also, there could be no influence of later dogmatics on him and appealing to those sources is, therefore, not helpful in determining the author's intent.

71. *NID,* s.v. "πιστεύω."

of faith.[72] Note the author's description is not specifically religious and applies to relations not only with God but also between humans.[73]

The author's statement can, however, be seen as a partial definition and one in harmony with the view of faith presented in the whole of the author's work. The objective view that "faith can guarantee the blessings that we hope for, or prove the existence of realities that are [yet] unseen" emphasizes faith's function rather than its nature. The statement "accords well with the rest of the chapter," which focuses on how faith causes one to act, especially in times of trial.[74] The verse definitely highlights essential characteristics of faith important to the author's readers, designed to lift and motivate these persecuted people.[75] The most natural view of what the author is doing in the first verse is to see it as "a summary of what faith does" or accomplishes. "Faith binds the believer securely to the reality of what he does not (yet) see, but for which he hopes."[76]

All the examples underscore the author's temporal, forward-looking orientation that emphasizes endurance in order to get the reward. Though none of his examples look specifically to the person or ministry of Christ, his work as High Priest, author, and mediator stands behind them. What is more in the fore is God's faithfulness that can and must be relied upon to support the Saints during mortal trials. All the blessings noted by the author—entering God's resting place (4:3) and receiving God's promises (6:12; 10:36–39)—are dependent on "hold[ing] fast" to the faith (10:23–25).[77]

The author's statement, as translated in the KJV, that "faith is the substance [ὑπόστασις, *hypostasis*] of things hoped for" (11:1) could give the impression that faith creates, that is, gives reality to, those "things." In point of fact, the "things hoped for" exist independent of any person's faith. Examples would be God's saving grace, the coming of Christ, the Resurrection, and salvation in the celestial kingdom. Understanding *hypostasis* as "reality" works because behind the word stands the certainty of things that have an objective reality. Faith makes possible the acquisition of the reality on which hope is based.

---

72. Richard Ounsworth, "Faith in the Epistle to the Hebrews," *Scripture Bulletin* 43, no. 1 (January 2013): 22–32, convincingly shows that the way the author frames his argument in chapter 11 reveals an understanding of faith that is profoundly Christological even though he is subdued in his examples.

73. Vanhoye, *Letter to the Hebrews,* 179.

74. Ellingworth, *Epistle to the Hebrews,* 566.

75. Cockerill, *Epistle to the Hebrews,* 520 n. 1; *NID,* s.v. "πιστεύω."

76. Ellingworth, *Epistle to the Hebrews,* 566.

77. Ellingworth, *Epistle to the Hebrews,* 563.

Even though salvation has an objective reality, *our* obtaining that reality is not necessarily certain. To make it sure *for us* takes faith. Thus, faith makes real (or gives substance or reality to) *our* obtaining salvation. It is *our* faith in Jesus Christ that causes the things we hope for—forgiveness of our sins, our sanctification, and our ultimate exaltation—to become reality. Faith brings the future promise into the present and in so doing makes it a reality *for us.*[78] Faith empowers the individual to both "see" in mortality and realize in the afterlife that reality, even though that reality is invisible to and therefore beyond the reach of the faithless.

Thus, "it is true that such a life of faith does not bring the future, hoped-for salvation into existence. It is, however, the means the [author] would have his [readers] pursue in order that this final salvation might become a reality for them. Perseverance in such faith is also the guarantee of future enjoyment. Thus, this understanding of the opening [sentence in chapter 11] is in perfect accord with the author's pastoral concern that his hearers live by faith in order to receive what God has promised."[79]

In sum, Hebrews links faith with fidelity, trust, and obedience. The depth of one's faith is revealed in the degree of his or her conformity to gospel standards and reaches its greatest expression in enduring compliance. Thus, faith is expressed through deeds of obedience. Such steadfastness to God guarantees one will receive eternal life. Thus, faith is the realization of things hoped for because the promises of the future are, through continued obedience, made sure in the present.

An intriguing and insightful parallel to chapter 11 is found in Ether 12:6–22, where Moroni also promotes faithfulness by showcasing the acts of those who had come before. Paralleling the description given by the author of Hebrews, Moroni states that faith is "things which are hoped for and not seen" (Ether 12:6, 8–9). His development of this theme does not have quite the strong structural organization as does Hebrews, but there are definitely literary and structural elements present. For example, Moroni's discussions of the individuals who possessed faith are introduced with the formula "Behold it was by faith that X did Y." Thus, in Ether 12:11, it is Moses receiving the law (see Ex. 20–23); in Ether 12:13, it is Alma and Amulek's escaping from prison (see Alma 14:28); in Ether 12:14, it is Nephi and Lehi's

78. In this light it is easy to see that steadfast faith is the ground on which making one's calling and election sure sits. On this doctrine, see Doxey, "Calling and Election," in Ludlow, *Encyclopedia of Mormonism,* 1:248; and McConkie, *Doctrinal New Testament Commentary,* 3:323–53.

79. Cockerill, *Epistle to the Hebrews,* 521.

preaching to the Lamanites (see Hel. 5:23); in Ether 12:15, it is Ammon converting the Lamanites (see Alma 17–27); in Ether 12:17, it is the three disciples postponing death till the Lord comes (see 3 Ne. 28:4–10); and in Ether 12:20–21, it is the brother of Jared seeing the finger of the Lord and then "all the inhabitants of the earth which had been, and also all that would be; and [the Lord withholding nothing] from his sight, even unto the ends of the earth" (Ether 3:25).

Moroni is not the only Book of Mormon prophet to address the principle of faith. Alma also broached the subject. In his discourse he taught the people that faith is "not [to have] a perfect knowledge—even so it is with my words. Ye cannot know of their surety at first, unto perfection, any more than faith is a perfect knowledge." By "perfect knowledge" he means to know perfectly that his words are true, that is, to have proof the gospel is authentic. On that basis he asks his hearers to exercise a modicum of faith and experiment upon his words. He asks them to plant, as it were, a seed and to nourish it through obedience. He promises them that "if ye do not cast it out by your unbelief, that ye will resist the Spirit of the Lord," they will find that "it beginneth to enlighten my understanding, yea, it beginneth to be delicious to me." They will then have to admit "that this is a good seed, or that the word is good." He then asks, "Would not this increase your faith? I say unto you, Yea; nevertheless it hath not grown up to a perfect knowledge." In other words, even though they have found delight in God's word, they still do not have a "perfect knowledge," or a full assurance, that can come. To get that they must continue to act in obedience.

Alma warns against those who say, "If thou wilt show unto us a sign from heaven, then we shall know of a surety; then we shall believe" (Alma 32:17), who demand they skip the faith-obedience stage and go straight to the "faith-power" stage. Alma explains that such simply would not bring a "perfect knowledge" (Alma 32:21). An outward sign is no internal proof that the word is true. Rather, people must, based on the results of their planting the seed, "nourish it with great care, that it may get root, that it may grow up, and bring forth fruit" (Alma 32:37). He promises them, "If ye will nourish the word, yea, nourish the tree as it beginneth to grow, by your faith with great diligence, and with patience, looking forward to the fruit thereof, it shall take root; and behold it shall be a tree springing up unto everlasting life" (Alma 32:41) and "by and by ye shall pluck the fruit thereof, which is most precious" and "feast upon [it] even until ye are filled" (Alma 32:42). Only when that happens will they have a "perfect knowledge." The point is that once they have the power of the God in their life, then their knowledge is perfect. Their faith-obedience, as promised, has brought them to faith-power and a "perfect knowledge," or sure proof that the gospel is true.

In sum, for Alma, faith is expressed by doing what is necessary to reach a goal, in this case, the assurance the gospel is true. Once that assurance has come, then the exercise of faith in that area will cease because the promise has been realized. Alma's expression is "faith is dormant." That does not mean faith-obedience can be set aside, for there are yet other promises that can be realized. But the investigator-level of faith has served its purpose; its goal has been realized, and therefore faith on that level need no longer be exercised.

This leads us to one more aspect of faith. Not only is it an expression of obedience, it is also an expression of power—Godly power. Indeed, the *Lectures on Faith* state that faith is not only a principle of action but also "*the* principle of power."[80] As the author of Hebrews notes, by possessing such faith, people "conquered kingdoms, . . . shut the mouth of lions, quenched the power of fire, . . . were made mighty in battle, caused enemy armies to retreat, . . . [and] received their dead raised again to life" (NR 11:33–35). Indeed, miracles were and are wrought through faith. This kind of faith—faith-power as separate from faith-obedience but a manifestation and confirmation of the latter—is a gift of the Spirit. In short, this is a divine endowment that the Book of Mormon refers to as "exceedingly great faith" (Moro. 10:11). Faith-power allows its holder to do the miraculous works of God. The Lord promised that "signs"—an expression of faith-power—would follow those who exercised faith-obedience (Mark 16:17; see also Morm. 9:24; Ether 4:18; and D&C 58:64; 84:65–72; 124:98–99). Such power, as the scriptures teach, comes as evidence of possessing this gift of the Holy Ghost (Acts 1:8; compare Heb. 2:4; 1 Cor. 12:9). Such power, we must stress, is dependent on faith-obedience, which must precede it. Thus, the visible signs of miracles are initially "things which are hoped for and not seen; wherefore, dispute not," cautions Moroni, "because ye see not, for ye receive no witness until after the trial of your faith" (Ether 12:6). In sum, only after one has shown continued faith-obedience is faith-power manifested in his or her life with signs.

---

80. Lecture 1:15, italics added. For a study, see lecture 1 in Dahl and Tate, *Lectures on Faith in Historical Perspective,* 33–34, 36–37, lecture 7 in Dahl and Tate, *Lectures on Faith in Historical Perspective,* 95, 96; and Dennis F. Rasmussen, "What Faith Is," in Dahl and Tate, *Lectures on Faith in Historical Perspective,* 166, 169.

The *Lectures on Faith* explains the importance of the sacrificial aspect of obedience in obtaining faith-power:

> A religion that does not require the sacrifice of all things never has power sufficient to produce the faith necessary unto life and salvation; for from the first existence of man, the faith necessary unto the enjoyment of life and salvation never could be obtained without the sacrifice of all earthly things. It was through this sacrifice, and this only, that God has ordained that men should enjoy eternal life; and it is through the medium of the sacrifice of all earthly things that men do actually know that they are doing the things that are well pleasing in the sight of God. When a man has offered in sacrifice all that he has for the truth's sake, not even withholding his life, and believing before God that he has been called to make this sacrifice because he seeks to do his will, he does know, most assuredly, that God does and will accept his sacrifice and offering, and that he has not sought nor will he seek His face in vain. Under these circumstances, then, he can obtain the faith necessary for him to lay hold on eternal life.[81]

This brings us to the last aspect of faith we wish to consider here: the faith of Christ. The term as we are using it does not mean faith *in* Christ, but rather the faith the Savior possesses and exemplifies. As Heavenly Father requires of all, Jesus, too, had to express his faith through obedience, and that included sacrifice—deep, meaningful, and difficult sacrifice. Indeed, no one knows the cost of obedience more completely than he does, for it cost him tremendous suffering, ending in giving his life. He gave it not because *he* willed to do so but because the Father did. In fact, Jesus really did not want to (see Matt. 26:39–42; Mark 14:36; and Luke 22:42). He confessed the "suffering caused myself, even God, the greatest of all, to tremble because of pain, and to bleed at every pore, and to suffer both body and spirit—and would that I might not drink the bitter cup, and shrink—Nevertheless, glory be to the Father, and I partook and finished my preparations unto the children of men" (D&C 19:18–19). And what was the result? As the author of Hebrews states, "He became the source of eternal salvation for all those who obey him" (NR 5:9).

One point we would like to make clear is that faithfulness, due to the faith of Christ, does not imply perfection. As the author of Hebrews shows, the Lord worked with flawed people. One, Rahab, was even a prostitute. Despite their flaws, he exercised both mercy and grace toward

81. Lecture 6:7. See also Robert J. Matthews, "Great Faith Obtained Only through Personal Sacrifices," in Dahl and Tate, *Lectures on Faith in Historical Perspective,* 243, 244, 247–61.

them. Indeed, the scriptures show how willing the Lord was to extend his "arm of mercy toward those who trust in him rather than in the arm of flesh (2 Ne. 4:34; Mosiah 23:22; 29:20)."[82] These scriptures hold promise for those who feel less than adequate in their faith. As the author of Hebrews shows, flawed people can still exercise sufficient righteousness to receive God's blessings in this life—including his approbation, the gifts of the Spirit, and the assurance that they are doing his will—and eternal life in the world to come. Admittedly, these come in consequence of his grace, but they nevertheless come. Further, those who strive can be assured of being strengthened by the grace of Christ. In this light, Paul could say salvation rests on the faith of Jesus. The Apostle stresses that salvation "might be by grace; to the end the promise might be sure to all the [faithful]" (Rom. 4:16). The Apostle understood well that "by grace are ye saved through faith; and that not of yourselves: it is the gift of God" (Eph. 2:8). Thus, he insists, "Ye are all the children of God by faith in Christ Jesus" (Gal. 3:26). According to the Book of Mormon, God's people are able to come to him through "relying wholly upon the merits of him who is mighty to save" (2 Ne. 31:19). One of the reasons for God's people to be nourished "by the good word of God" is "to keep them in the right way . . . relying alone upon the merits of Christ, who was the author and the finisher of their faith" (Moro. 6:4). The book emphasizes the need to have "perfect faith" ("meaning, presumably, a wholehearted belief in, a complete trust in, and a total reliance upon the cleansing power of Christ's redeeming blood"[83]) anchored in "the Holy one of Israel" in order to be saved in God's kingdom (2 Ne. 9:23).

Thus, drawing out the message about faith from Hebrews shows that faith-obedience should not be equated with perfection. Rather, faith is continued endurance that relies on Christ in spite of weakness. It is expressed in "developmental repentance" and seeking to become the kind of person Christ wants his people to be.[84] The Lord is very merciful, for he states that those who are *willing* to keep his commandments are eligible to have his spirit always (D&C 20:77). All are dependent on grace, for when grace comes into one's life, it opens the way for greater faith given as a gift of the

82. Largey, *Book of Mormon Reference Companion,* 260.

83. Largey, *Book of Mormon Reference Companion,* 260.

84. The phrase comes from Elder Neal A. Maxwell, "Applying the Atoning Blood of Christ," *Ensign* 27, no. 11 (November 1997): 22, who noted that the "process of developmental repentance occurs when we truly take His yoke upon us, thus finally qualifying for God's greatest gift—eternal life (see Matt. 11:29; D&C 6:13; D&C 14:7)."

Spirit and with it the ability to give even greater obedience. The combination of our faithful endurance in Christ and his saving grace brings all that is necessary for us to receive the promises.

Thus, it can be seen that the Restoration perspective on faith covers the aspects of faith explored above.[85] Faith is the first principle of the gospel (A of F 4; see also 3 Ne. 27:16–21) that makes all other blessings possible. In a general sense, it is a "trust, confidence, and belief, based on evidence, in someone or something that motivates one to resolve to act," and from the religious standpoint, it is "trust and confidence in and reliance upon the merits, mercy, and grace of Jesus Christ that leads to repentance and a continual willingness and striving to keep his commandments."[86]

In summary, faith can be viewed through two lenses. If we choose to view it through the subjective lens, then faith is an inward feeling of confidence, even sureness, that "things hoped for"—namely, that the individual will dwell in the eternal city with the Father and the Son—will be realized. If we choose the objective lens, then faith results in and proves the reality of those "things hoped for." Due to the influence of the Protestant background, from which many early converts to the Church came, the subjective view has prevailed in the modern Church. A good example of this can be seen in a discussion of faith presented by President Dieter F. Uchtdorf:

> Faith is a strong conviction about something we believe—a conviction so strong that it moves us to do things that we otherwise might not do. "Faith is being sure of what we hope for and certain of what we do not see."
>
> While this makes sense to believing people, it is often confusing to nonbelievers. They shake their heads and ask, "How can anyone be certain of what they cannot see?" To them, this is evidence of the irrationality of religion.
>
> What they fail to understand is that there are more ways to see than with our eyes, more ways to feel than with our hands, more ways to hear than with our ears. . . .
>
> . . . The Apostle Paul encourages us to seek the voice that speaks to our spirit, not just to our ears. He taught, "The person without the Spirit does not accept the things that come from the Spirit of God but considers them foolishness, and cannot understand them because they are discerned only through the Spirit." Or perhaps we should consider the words

85. For a brief discussion of faith as viewed by the Latter-day Saints in comparison with how it is viewed by many Protestants, see Anderson, *Understanding Paul,* 219–20.

86. See Largey, *Book of Mormon Reference Companion,* 260–64; and Largey and Dahl, *Doctrine and Covenants Reference Companion,* 202–3.

> of Saint-Exupéry's Little Prince, who said: "One sees clearly only with the heart. Anything essential is invisible to the eyes." . . .
>
> Faith *is* powerful, and often it does result in miracles. But no matter how much faith we have, there are two things faith cannot do. For one, it cannot violate another person's agency. . . .
>
> The second thing faith cannot do is force our will upon God. We cannot force God to comply with our desires—no matter how right we think we are or how sincerely we pray. Consider the experience of Paul, who pleaded with the Lord multiple times for relief from a personal trial—what he called "a thorn in the flesh." But that was not God's will. Eventually, Paul realized that his trial was a blessing, and he thanked God for not answering his prayers the way he had hoped. . . .
>
> No, the purpose of faith is not to *change* God's will but to empower us to *act on* God's will. Faith is trust—trust that God sees what we cannot and that He knows what we do not. Sometimes, trusting our own vision and judgment is not enough.[87]

Both the subjective and objective views of faith are doctrinally sound. Further, they are not mutually exclusive. Like other aspects of the gospel, faith is progressive. Initially, it is expressed as faith-obedience. On the investigator level, faith opens the eyes to the possibilities of the vast realities that lie beyond earthly horizons and brings hope that, through belief in Christ, they can be obtained. Motivated by this vision, the investigator expresses the next level of faith by entering into a covenantal relationship with the Lord. This opens the door to the powers of the gift of the Holy Ghost and the whisperings of the Spirit. Based on this confirmation, the testimony of the new member grows and hope increases. The person then expresses greater faith by striving to live the Lord's commandments. The result of this level of faith manifests itself in expressions of divine power in the person's life that is faith-power. Love increases and the gifts of the Spirit become more prevalent. The grace of Christ abounds assisting the individual not only to desire greater righteousness but also to have the power to live better. Thus, this greater obedience results in aspects of the promised blessings, specifically that of divine power, being realized in the present. It is on this level, the power level, that faith comes as a gift of the Spirit.

Experiencing this power acts as proof of the actuality of all the other promises and that they too will be realized, among them having a place in the eternal city. This proof becomes the foundation in which the highest level of faith sits. It expresses itself as continued and enduring trust,

87. Uchtdorf, "Fourth Floor, Last Door," 16, 17, italics in original.

obedience, and service. This level of faith becomes the seal or realization of all future blessings, for they are secured or made sure to the individual *in the present.*

To the author of Hebrews, faith allows the person to see unseen heavenly realities and acts as the guarantee that they will be achieved. The faithful understand these to be more real, or rather, more desirable and enduring, than anything the earth can offer and, thus, are willing to sacrifice all earthly things to get them. Faith also brings into the present the powers of the divine that then acts as proof not only that all promised blessings can be realized but actually are.

The Examples of Abel, Enoch, and Noah (11:4–7)

Greek Text

4 Πίστει πλείονα θυσίαν Ἅβελ παρὰ Κάϊν προσήνεγκεν τῷ θεῷ, δι᾽ ἧς ἐμαρτυρήθη εἶναι δίκαιος, μαρτυροῦντος ἐπὶ τοῖς δώροις αὐτοῦ τοῦ θεοῦ, καὶ δι᾽ αὐτῆς ἀποθανὼν ἔτι λαλεῖ. 5 Πίστει Ἑνὼχ μετετέθη τοῦ μὴ ἰδεῖν θάνατον, καὶ οὐχ ηὑρίσκετο διότι μετέθηκεν αὐτὸν ὁ θεός· πρὸ γὰρ τῆς μεταθέσεως μεμαρτύρηται εὐαρεστηκέναι τῷ θεῷ, 6 χωρὶς δὲ πίστεως ἀδύνατον εὐαρεστῆσαι, πιστεῦσαι γὰρ δεῖ τὸν προσερχόμενον τῷ θεῷ ὅτι ἔστιν καὶ τοῖς ἐκζητοῦσιν αὐτὸν μισθαποδότης γίνεται. 7 πίστει χρηματισθεὶς Νῶε περὶ τῶν μηδέπω βλεπομένων εὐλαβηθεὶς κατεσκεύασεν κιβωτὸν εἰς σωτηρίαν τοῦ οἴκου αὐτοῦ, δι᾽ ἧς κατέκρινεν τὸν κόσμον, καὶ τῆς κατὰ πίστιν δικαιοσύνης ἐγένετο κληρονόμος. [SBLGNT]

King James Version

4 By faith Abel offered unto God a more excellent sacrifice than Cain, by which he obtained witness that he was righteous, God testifying of his gifts: and by it he being dead yet speaketh. 5 By faith Enoch was translated that he should not see death; and was not found, because God had translated him: for before his translation he had this testimony, that he pleased God. 6 But without faith it is impossible to please him: for he that cometh to God must believe that he is, and that he is a rewarder of them that diligently seek him. 7 By faith Noah, being warned of God of things not seen as yet, moved with fear, prepared an ark to the saving of his house; by the which he condemned the world, and became heir of the righteousness which is by faith.

New Rendition

4 By faith Abel offered a greater sacrifice to God than Cain, for which he was commended as righteous, God himself commending him for the gifts; moreover, by faith, although he has died, he still continues to speak. 5 By faith Enoch was taken up so that he did not experience death,

> "and he was not found because God took him up." [Gen. 5:24]

Before his being taken up, he was commended for

> "having pleased God." [Gen. 5:22, 24]

6 Now without faith it is impossible to please God, for one who approaches God must believe that he is and that he rewards those who seek him. 7 By faith Noah, after he had received a divine warning about things not yet seen, out of reverent regard, built an ark to save his family. By faith he condemned the world and became an heir of righteousness in accordance with his faith.

Translation Notes and Comments

11:4 ***By faith Abel offered unto God a more excellent sacrifice than Cain / By faith Abel offered a greater sacrifice to God than Cain:*** The author now begins a section in which he selects examples of people in the Old Testament who accomplished great things through acting on their faith. He regularly begins each account with πίστει (*pistei*), the dative singular of πίστις (*pistis*), used instrumentally, "by the means of faith." The account of Abel and Cain is found in Genesis 4:1–16 and Moses 5:16–41. The biblical account does not say what the problem with Cain's sacrifice was. The Genesis text leaves one to wonder if it was because it was not an animal. However, at least in Mosaic times, the "firstfruits" of the ground were deemed acceptable (Ex. 23:16, 19). The author describes Abel's sacrifice with the comparative adjective πλείονα (*pleiona*), which does not usually carry the meaning of quality but of quantity, thus, "much, many, great, plenteous."[88] This suggests the author views the problem of Cain's sacrifice is that it is paltry in nature.

by which he obtained witness that he was righteous / for which he was commended as righteous: The verb μαρτυρέω (*martyreō*) generally means "to be witness" to something but here suggests the idea of being "well-spoken of."[89] To emphasize this idea, we have translated it as "commend" in our Rendition.

The adjective δίκαιος (*dikaios*), "righteous," suggests one who is careful in keeping divine law.[90] The phrase above shows the care came because of Abel's faith. It was the condition of his heart that motivated him to keep God's commandment in God's way and thus earn the epithet "righteous."

God testifying of his gifts / God himself commending him for the gifts: In this phrase, the pronoun αὐτοῦ (*autou*), "his, himself," can be understood in two ways. It can be taken to modify τοῖς δώροις (*tois dōrois*), "his [Abel's] gifts," which the KJV does, or τοῦ θεοῦ (*tou theou*), "God himself." We felt that the second interpretation fits the context better because God commends people for their faith of which gifts are but an evidence.[91] Thus, we follow this idea in our Rendition.

---

88. BDAG, 847–50. That is not to say that the idea of "more worthy" is not present, but it is only as a nuance. Thus, πλείονα (*pleiona*) could be understood to mean "of greater value." Ellingworth, *Epistle to the Hebrews,* 571. For references to possible scriptures that use *pleiona* in a qualitative sense, see Lane, *Hebrews 9–13,* 327 note m.

89. BDAG, 617–18; Louw-Nida, §33.262, 263.

90. BDAG, 246–47; *NID,* s.v. δικαιοσύνη.

91. Lane, *Hebrews 9–13,* 327 note n. For discussion, see Bruce, *Epistle to the Hebrews,* 282–83; and Ellingworth, *Epistle to the Hebrews,* 572.

The plural noun δώροις (*dōrois*), "gifts,"[92] supports the idea of the plentiful nature of Abel's sacrifice compared with the skimpy one of Cain.

and by it he being dead yet speaketh / moreover, by faith, although he has died, he still continues to speak: The way the KJV reads, "by it" could be taken to refer to the gifts Abel offered. The phrase δι' αὐτῆς (*di autēs*), "by it," however, because of the feminine gender of the pronoun, clearly refers to his faith. To make this clear, we have translated *autos,* "it," as "faith" in our Rendition.

The verb ἀποθενῄσκω (*apothenēskō*), "to die," can carry the nuance of dying by violent means.[93] Death, however, did not stop Abel's ability "to speak" through his example of faith to the readers of this Epistle. The author seems to be alluding to Genesis 4:10, which states Abel's innocent blood cries to God from the ground. The author makes an implicit connection between the innocent blood of Abel and that of Christ, which the author makes explicitly clear in 12:24, where he states that his readers have association with Jesus as mediator of the new covenant and thereby come under "the blood of sprinkling, that speaketh better things than that of Abel."[94]

11:5 *By faith Enoch was translated that he should not see death; and was not found, because God had translated him / By faith Enoch was taken up so that he did not experience death, "and he was not found because God took him up":* The author is referring to LXX Genesis 5:24. The forepart is a paraphrase while the ending is a direct quote.[95] The verb εὑρίσκω (*heuriskō*), meaning "to find, discover," is found here in the passive mood and has the sense of "can no longer be found despite a thorough search," thus, "to disappear."[96] It is translated from the MT אֵינֶנּוּ (*'ênennû*), "he is/was not," which often means "is/has vanished."[97]

The verb μετατίθημι (*metatithēmi*), "taken up," means "to convey from one place to another, to transfer" and "to effect a change in state or condition," thus, "to change, alter."[98] It is translated from the MT לָקַח (*lāqaḥ*),

---

92. BDAG, 267.

93. BDAG, 111.

94. Vanhoye, *Letter to the Hebrews,* 180.

95. It reads καὶ οὐχ ηὑρίσκετο, ὅτι μετέθηκεν αὐτὸν ὁ θεός (*kai ouch hēurisketo, hoti metethēken auton ho theos*), "and he was not found, because God took him up." The author did change the conjunction ὅτι (*hoti*) to the more emphatic form διότι (*dioti*), both meaning "that."

96. BDAG, 411.

97. BDB, 24.

98. BDAG, 642.

"to take up, take and go away with,"[99] the implication being that God took Enoch up into heaven with him. The KJV uses the verb "translate," which is derived from the passive perfect participle *translatus,* of the Latin *transfero,* "to convey over, transport, transfer."[100]

Though only a connotation in the Greek, in Latter-day Saint usage, "translation" refers to the process of changing someone who is mortal to a state in which they are no longer subject to pain and sickness but remain alive until the Second Coming of Christ, at which time they will be instantly changed to an immortal, resurrected state (see 3 Ne. 28:1–9, 36–40).[101] These include Enoch and all the inhabitants of his city, Zion; the Apostle John; three of the Nephite twelve Apostles; Elijah; and possibly Moses and Alma the younger. There may be others as well that the scriptures do not mention (see D&C 49:8).

for before his translation he had this testimony, that he pleased God / Before his being taken up, he was commended for "having pleased God": This is a modified quote from LXX Genesis 5:22 and 24. There, as here, the text refers to Enoch as εὐαρεστέω (*euaresteō*), the verb referring to one who pleases another because of acts they have performed.[102]

This is another example of the author using the LXX reading of the Old Testament to bolster his reasoning, one which the MT does not support. The Hebrew text simply notes that Enoch "walked with God," saying nothing about the prophet pleasing him.[103]

11:6 *But without faith it is impossible to please him / Now without faith it is impossible to please God:* The author uses this phrase to justify his statement that Enoch had faith. The Old Testament says nothing about his faith, although it is implied. The author brings the implication to the fore, assuring his readers that the only way Enoch could have pleased God was through the exercise of faith. The adjective ἀδύνατος (*adynatos*),

99. *HAL,* 534.

100. Lewis and Short, *New Latin Dictionary,* 1889.

101. McConkie, *Doctrinal New Testament Commentary,* 3:219; Mark L. McConkie, "Translated Beings," in Ludlow, *Encyclopedia of Mormonism,* 4:1485–86. One nuance of the verb is "change of state or condition." BDAG, 642.

102. Louw-Nida, §25.93, notes that it also means to be well-disposed toward another and connotes the cause behind the disposition.

103. The passage in the LXX reads καὶ εὐηρέστησεν Ενωχ τῷ θεῷ (*kai euērestēsen Enōch tō theō*), "and Enoch pleased God," which differs from the MT that reads וַיִּתְהַלֵּךְ חֲנוֹךְ אֶת־הָאֱלֹהִים (*wayyithallēk ḥănôk et hā'ĕlōhîm*), "and Enoch walked with God." This is an example of the tendency of the translators of the LXX to modify passages that referred to God with anthropomorphic language. Ellingworth, *Epistle to the Hebrews,* 576.

"impossible," is important here, for it emphasizes the author's point that faith stands behind everything that pleases God.

The Greek here is very compact, literally translated as "now without faith impossible to please." In our Rendition, we have added "it is" and "God" to make the sense of the passage clear in English.

for he that cometh to God must believe that he is, and that he is a rewarder of them that diligently seek him / for one who approaches God must believe that he is and that he rewards those who seek him: In this clause, the author identifies certain conditions of true worship. The verb ἐκζητέω (*ekzēteō*), "to seek out, search for," found here as a present participle, denotes either looking for something with the intent of securing it or seeking out persons with the hope of developing a relationship with them. Behind it stands the idea of the considerable effort put forth by the seeker.[104]

The verb πιστεύω (*pisteuō*), "to believe," is often translated as "to have faith," but because the context here looks to a person's spiritual condition early on, "believe" is the best translation.

In the phrase ὅτι ἔστιν (*hoti estin*), "that he [God] is," the verb is emphatic and as such emphasizes the need for the person to believe in the actual existence of God.[105]

The noun μισθαποδότης (*misthapodotēs*), literally "paymaster," as used here, refers to one who delivers a reward or recompense.[106] Both testaments use the idea of reward as the means by which God motivates people to faithfulness.[107] The author does not disclose here what exactly the reward is, but it becomes increasingly clear as he develops his thesis.

As the phrase stands, it is possible that two of the components, belief that God exists and belief that he rewards, are not correlative but consequential: God exists and therefore he rewards.[108]

11:7 ***By faith Noah, being warned of God / By faith Noah, after he had received a divine warning:*** The biblical account of Noah is found in Genesis 6–9. As with Enoch, there is no explicit mention in the biblical account of Noah having faith nor is there in the book of Moses. There it does say, "Noah and his sons hearkened unto the Lord," and that "Noah was a just man, and perfect in his generation; and he walked with God" (Moses 8:13, 27).

---

104. BDAG, 302.

105. Ellingworth, *Epistle to the Hebrews,* 576–77.

106. Louw-Nida, §38.18; BDAG, 653. For the sake of flow, we have translated the noun as a verb in our Rendition.

107. Preisker, *TDNT,* 4:695–728.

108. Ellingworth, *Epistle to the Hebrews,* 577.

Extrabiblical sources do explicitly mention Noah's faith. Clement of Rome stated that Noah had been "faithful through his ministry."[109] Since Clement was familiar with the Epistle to the Hebrews, he may have derived this point from it. The Sibylline Oracles also mention the faithfulness of Noah and that he "cared deeply concerning good works."[110]

The verb χρηματίζω (*chrēmatizō*), here used in the passive voice, means "to receive a divine message or warning."[111] Though there is little doubt that the message included a warning, it could have been much broader, including instructions on what to preach and how to build an ark.[112]

of things not seen as yet, moved with fear, prepared an ark to the saving of his house / about things not yet seen, out of reverent regard, built an ark to save his family: With this phrase, the author again stresses one of his major themes: faith is an expression of assurance in the reality of "things not seen"—in this case, it was in God's judgment upon the world in the form of the flood.

The verb εὐλαβέομαι (*eulabeomai*) denotes not only caring for a matter but also giving it attentive, even reverent regard. The nuance behind it is one of a deep awe that promotes obedience.[113]

he condemned the world, and became heir of the righteousness which is by faith / he condemned the world and became an heir of righteousness in accordance with his faith: The verb κατακρίνω (*katakrinō*), "condemn," denotes the act of "pronouncing a sentence after determination of guilt."[114] Though the phrase does not preclude the more positive idea that Noah's condemnation came due to his righteousness in contrast to his contemporaries' wickedness,[115] scriptural evidence suggests a more active

---

109. 1 Clem. 9:4 reads, Νῶε πιστὸς εὑεθεὶς διὰ τῆς λειτουργίας αὐτοῦ παλιγγενεσίαν κόσμῳ ἐκήρυξεν (*Nōe pistos euetheis dia tēs leitourgias autou palingenesian kosmō ekēryxen*), "Noah, having been found faithful through his ministry, proclaimed a rebirth of the world."

110. *Sib. Or.* 1.136 states, ἦν Νῶε, πιστότατος, καλοῖς τ' ἔργοισι μεμηλώς (*ēn Nōe, pistotatos, kalois t'ergoisi memēlōs*), "Noah was very faithful and cared deeply, concerned about good works."

111. BDAG, 1089; Louw-Nida, §28.39; Reicke, *TDNT,* 9:480–82.

112. Ellingworth, *Epistle to the Hebrews,* 578.

113. BDAG, 407; Louw-Nida, §53.7. An alternate translation construes "concerning events not yet seen" with "regard." Doing so places the emphasis on "Noah's state of mind, which was full of dread in the face of an imminent catastrophe, when he responded to God in faith." Lane, *Hebrews 9–13,* 327 note u. Noah manifested this aspect of faith by moving into the ark a full week before the rains came. Gen. 7:10.

114. BDAG, 519.

115. *1 Clem.* 9:4 stresses the positive aspect of Noah's teaching.

pronouncement of guilt. According to Moses 8:14–30, he preached gospel truths as well as a severe warning against their rejection.

The Greek of the last phrase in this clause is quite condensed, making it difficult to clearly sense the author's intent. It reads literally "and became heir according to righteousness of the faith." The verb γίνομαι (*ginomai*), "to become," found here in aorist form, thus "became," also means "to be made" and implies divine action. The noun κληρονόμος (*klēronomos*), "heir," denotes one who receives something as a personal possession; although "heir" certainly works, the word is not confined thereto. The noun δικαιοσύνη (*dikaiosynē*), "righteousness," denotes that which is proper and in accordance with divine law. Further, it carries a very active sense of not only standing against what is wrong but also fighting for what is right.[116] The preposition κατά (*kata*), "in accordance with," here carries the nuance of being consistent, in harmony, and in conformity with something else.[117] The author makes the acquisition of righteousness a corresponding reward for faith.

If it was Noah's righteousness that commended him to God in the first place, how then did he become an heir of righteousness (the phrase even hinting at an action by God) when he already possessed this virtue? This problem is compounded by the author's use of κληρονόμος (*klēronomos*), which denotes the reception of any gift, including an inheritance. How was righteousness a divine gift? The resolution may be that the righteousness spoken of here came from God, "the rewarder," as a recompense for Noah's earlier faithfulness and is a higher order of righteousness. It may be because of this amplified righteousness that God could entrust Noah as the new master of the created order and parent of the human race.[118] His faith exhibited by his righteousness would allow God to trust him with such a great responsibility.

Analysis and Summary

In this section, the author begins his list of Old Testament heroes and heroines.[119] Giving unity to the whole is the author's repeated use of the phrase "by faith" (πίστει, *pistei*), which he uses to introduce each illustration. The multiple uses of the word serve to emphasize the point.

---

116. BDAG, 247–49; *NID*, s.v. δικαιοσύνη.

117. BDAG, 511–13.

118. As Ellingworth, *Epistle to the Hebrews*, 580, notes, "The parallels between Gn. 1:28–30 and 9:1–3 are close."

119. Much of the material in this and the following analyses is taken from an unpublished paper by Nathaniel Pribil.

In 11:4, the author begins his illustrations. The first biblical figure he mentions is Abel (Gen. 4:2–9; see also Moses 5:17–20). It is intriguing that the author's account of the faithful in Old Testament times begins with this figure rather than with his father, Adam. There are a number of possibilities as to why. Rhetorically, the purpose of this part of the discourse is to illustrate to the author's readers the various ways in which their ancestors have exercised faith. In Genesis, as it is currently constituted, there is not much to suggest that Adam exercised faith.[120] Rhetorically, then, this chapter's point is better served by focusing on Abel rather than his father.

Within the confines of the narrative in Genesis, Abel is primarily known for being the first victim of a murder, having been killed by his brother Cain.[121] The emphasis in Hebrews, however, is not on Abel's murder but instead on his sacrificial offering. The author focuses on the nature of the sacrifice Abel willingly brought to God—described as "plenteous" (πλείων, *pleiōn*) in nature and fully acceptable to God. According to the account in Moses 5:20, Abel brought the "firstlings of his flock, and of the fat thereof." The first description suggests the quantity; the second, quality. By implication it would seem the problem with Cain's sacrifice was not that it was the fruit of the field as much as its measly nature. According to the account in Moses 5:18, another problem was Cain's offering was instigated not at the request of God but by Satan.[122] Additionally, through Adam and Eve's teachings, both Cain and Abel would have been taught that sacrifices were in similitude of the future sacrifice of the Lord (Moses 5:6–12). The two defects in Cain's offering show not only an utter lack of faith in God but also a disrespect to Christ.[123] On the other hand, Abel's plenteous sacrifice

---

120. The portions of Joseph Smith's New Translation of the Bible dealing with Adam and Eve after the Fall show that they indeed exercised great faith. See Moses 5:3–9.

121. Abel's name is an example of symbolic names within the scriptural record. In Hebrew, Abel's name is *Hebel,* which means "fleetingness" and references the fact that Abel's life was cut short. There are hints in JST Gen 17:7 that Abel had more significance in some people's minds during the days of Abraham: "And [they] have said that the blood of the righteous Abel was shed for sins; and have not known wherein they are accountable before me." On the falseness of this idea, see Bruce R. McConkie, "The Salvation of Little Children," *Ensign* 7, no. 4 (April 1977): 3–7.

122. This same idea appears in the apocryphal work *Apoc. Ab.* 24.5.

123. According to Joseph Smith, Cain had the proper authority to offer sacrifices, but three problems made his work unacceptable: it was instigated by Satan, it was not a blood sacrifice, and it showed no faith in God or Christ. See "The Elders of the Church in Kirtland, to Their Brethren Abroad," 143; and "History, 1838–1856, Volume C-1," 17 [addenda]. For a study, see Andrus, *Doctrinal Commentary,* 332–37.

demonstrated the depth of his faith. He took the best and sacrificed it. He saw no need to use these as breeding stock to make his herds better or his flocks stronger. Because of faith, he saw that God was the real strength of his herd and flock. Further, Abel evidenced his vision of the pure nature and grand character of Christ, of whom his sacrifices were performed in similitude.

Another insight comes from a statement made by Joseph Smith. He asked, "How did [the author of Hebrews][124] know so much about Abel, and why should he talk about his speaking after he was dead?" The Prophet answered that Abel speaking "after he was dead must be, by being sent down out of heaven, to administer."[125] At another time, Joseph said, "He magnified the Priesthood which was conferred upon him and died a righteous man, and therefore has become an Angel of God by receiving his body from the dead, therefore holding still the keys of his dispensation and was sent down from heaven unto [the author] to minister consoling words and to commit unto him a knowledge of the mysteries of Godliness."[126] For Joseph Smith then, the author of Hebrews had additional knowledge about Abel because he had firsthand interactions with Abel through heavenly ministration. Thus, the author's interaction with and knowledge about Abel would have served as his impetus to begin these examples with this faithful being.

The next individual the author focuses on, Enoch, resonates well in Latter-day Saint thought as well as in the worldview of the Epistle to the Hebrews. This figure, who is mentioned in only four sparse verses in Genesis 5:21–24, was important in some strands of the Judaism of the Second Temple period. As with Melchizedek, the all-too-brief verses found in the Bible about Enoch beg for further information. Interest is heightened especially because of the statement that he "walked with God" (Gen. 5:22) and further the fact that, according to the English translation of the Masoretic text, instead of dying, "[Enoch] was not; for God took him" (Gen. 5:24).[127] Hebrews follows the LXX, which states, in addition to what is in the MT,

---

124. The word in the original is "Paul." The Prophet followed the popular belief of his day and never seems to have questioned it. For discussion, see the introduction to this volume.

125. "Instruction on Priesthood," 5.

126. "History, 1838–1856, Volume C-1," 17 [addenda].

127. The LXX replaces the Hebrew לָקַח (*lāqaḥ*), "to take away," with the Greek μετατίθημι (*metatithēmi*) meaning "to convey from one place to another; to effect a change in state or condition." BDAG, 642.

that "Enoch was well-pleasing to God, and was not found, because God translated him" and thereby underscores the author's view of Enoch as a very righteous figure.

The positive figure of Enoch is by no means a required reading of Genesis. There is, in fact, a large and complex body of literature from the ancient world related to him and his connection to the heavenly realm,[128] and Second Temple Judaism is deeply ambivalent about Enoch. On the one hand, God's walk with Enoch is sometimes interpreted as the result of God wanting to support a somewhat inconsistent friend rather than a statement of Enoch's high spiritual status.[129] On the other hand, some writings associate him with the angel Metatron—the scribe of God—and sometimes with the "angel of the presence," both very powerful figures in Jewish mythology.[130] The author of Hebrews comes down very strongly on the side of Enoch being a positive figure. Indeed, "before [Enoch's] translation, he had this testimony, that he pleased God" (11:5). There is, in Hebrews, no ambiguity on Enoch's faithfulness—not only had he pleased God, he knew he had done so. This recognition provided the groundwork for his faith, if not amplifying it (11:6).

At this point, the author makes an aside to justify how he can use Enoch as an example of faith when the scriptures do not mention it: anyone who understands how God works would know that faith must stand behind any commendation he gives, for it would be impossible (ἀδύνατος, *adynatos*) to please God, no matter the action, without faith (11:6).

In making his declaration, the author reveals three conditions necessary for people to truly worship deity (11:6): first, they must believe (πιστεύω, *pisteuō*) God exists; second, they must exert considerable and sincere

---

128. For a book-length discussion of the importance of the Enoch tradition in Latter-day Saint thinking, see Hugh Nibley, *Enoch the Prophet,* ed. Stephen D. Ricks, vol. 2 of The Collected Works of Hugh Nibley (Salt Lake City: Deseret Book; Provo, Utah: Foundation for Ancient Research and Mormon Studies, 1986). More recently on the same topic, see Jeffrey M. Bradshaw and David J. Larsen, *In God's Image and Likeness 2: Enoch, Noah, and the Tower of Babel* ([Salt Lake City]: Interpreter Foundation and Eborn Books, 2010), 33–196.

129. See Genesis Rabbah 25:1. On this topic, Philip Alexander has observed, "It is well known that classic rabbinic sources have very little to say about Enoch: he is not mentioned even once in the two Talmuds or the tannaitic Midrashim . . . ; the references to him in GenR are generally denigratory." Phillip Alexander, "3 (Hebrew Apocalypse of) Enoch," in Charlesworth, *Old Testament Pseudepigrapha,* 1:232 n. 28.

130. The literature on this point is immense. A useful starting point is Boyarin, "Beyond Judaisms," 323–65.

effort (ἐκζητέω, *ekzēteō*) in coming to him with the intent of forming a bonding relationship; and third, they must believe he rewards (he is the μισθαποδότης, *misthapodotēs,* "paymaster"[131]) those who make the effort. Having made this assertion, the author continues to give scriptural examples to show its truth.

Following Enoch, the author highlights Noah, the famous builder of the ark. Noah is given much more coverage in the Old Testament than either Abel or Enoch. Noah's story runs from Genesis 6:5 through 9:29. Noah illustrates faith in "things as not yet seen" (NR 11:7), thus illustrating the author's thought in 11:1. The nonvisual aspect of faith is a major point in the definition of faith the author builds up in this chapter (see 11:6, 16, 39–40), and Noah is an example without equal, for he built the ark without having seen rain, let alone a flood. Because of this, Noah "condemned the world, and became heir of the righteousness which is by faith" (11:7).[132] Thus, in addition to highlighting the nonvisual aspect of faith, Noah represents the reward that is inevitable for the faithful.[133]

The Faith of Abraham (11:8–22)

Greek Text

8 Πίστει καλούμενος Ἀβραὰμ ὑπήκουσεν ἐξελθεῖν εἰς τόπον ὃν ἤμελλεν λαμβάνειν εἰς κληρονομίαν, καὶ ἐξῆλθεν μὴ ἐπιστάμενος ποῦ ἔρχεται. 9 πίστει παρῴκησεν εἰς γῆν τῆς ἐπαγγελίας ὡς ἀλλοτρίαν, ἐν σκηναῖς κατοικήσας μετὰ Ἰσαὰκ καὶ Ἰακὼβ τῶν συγκληρονόμων τῆς ἐπαγγελίας τῆς αὐτῆς· 10 ἐξεδέχετο γὰρ τὴν τοὺς θεμελίους ἔχουσαν πόλιν, ἧς τεχνίτης καὶ δημιουργὸς ὁ θεός. 11 πίστει καὶ αὐτῇ Σάρρᾳ δύναμιν εἰς καταβολὴν σπέρματος ἔλαβεν καὶ παρὰ καιρὸν ἡλικίας, ἐπεὶ

---

131. Louw-Nida, §38.18; BDAG, 653.

132. Vanhoye, *Letter to the Hebrews,* 181.

133. Joseph Smith taught that Noah was the angel Gabriel who appeared in Daniel 8:16 and 9:21 and who has a major role in the birth narratives of John the Baptist and Jesus Christ in the early chapters of Luke's Gospel. Joseph Smith said of Noah/Gabriel, "Then to Noah who is Gabriel he stands next in authority to Adam, in the priesthood, he was called of God to this office. & was the father of all living, in this day, & to him was given the dominion." "Discourse, between circa 26 June and circa 4 August 1839–A, as Reported by Unknown Scribe," [2], Joseph Smith Papers, accessed October 12, 2015, https://www.josephsmithpapers.org/paper-summary/discourse-between-circa-26-june-and-circa-4-august-1839-a-as-reported-by-unknown-scribe/1.

πιστὸν ἡγήσατο τὸν ἐπαγγειλάμενον· 12 διὸ καὶ ἀφ' ἑνὸς ἐγεννήθησαν, καὶ ταῦτα νενεκρωμένου, καθὼς τὰ ἄστρα τοῦ οὐρανοῦ τῷ πλήθει καὶ ὡς ἡ ἄμμος ἡ παρὰ τὸ χεῖλος τῆς θαλάσσης ἡ ἀναρίθμητος.

13 Κατὰ πίστιν ἀπέθανον οὗτοι πάντες, μὴ λαβόντες τὰς ἐπαγγελίας, ἀλλὰ πόρρωθεν αὐτὰς ἰδόντες καὶ ἀσπασάμενοι, καὶ ὁμολογήσαντες ὅτι ξένοι καὶ παρεπίδημοί εἰσιν ἐπὶ τῆς γῆς. 14 οἱ γὰρ τοιαῦτα λέγοντες ἐμφανίζουσιν ὅτι πατρίδα ἐπιζητοῦσιν. 15 καὶ εἰ μὲν ἐκείνης μνημονεύουσιν ἀφ' ἧς ἐξέβησαν, εἶχον ἂν καιρὸν ἀνακάμψαι· 16 νῦν δὲ κρείττονος ὀρέγονται, τοῦτ' ἔστιν ἐπουρανίου. διὸ οὐκ ἐπαισχύνεται αὐτοὺς ὁ θεὸς θεὸς ἐπικαλεῖσθαι αὐτῶν, ἡτοίμασεν γὰρ αὐτοῖς πόλιν.

17 Πίστει προσενήνοχεν Ἀβραὰμ τὸν Ἰσαὰκ πειραζόμενος, καὶ τὸν μονογενῆ προσέφερεν ὁ τὰς ἐπαγγελίας ἀναδεξάμενος, 18 πρὸς ὃν ἐλαλήθη ὅτι Ἐν Ἰσαὰκ κληθήσεταί σοι σπέρμα, 19 λογισάμενος ὅτι καὶ ἐκ νεκρῶν ἐγείρειν δυνατὸς ὁ θεός· ὅθεν αὐτὸν καὶ ἐν παραβολῇ ἐκομίσατο. 20 Πίστει καὶ περὶ μελλόντων εὐλόγησεν Ἰσαὰκ τὸν Ἰακὼβ καὶ τὸν Ἠσαῦ. 21 πίστει Ἰακὼβ ἀποθνῄσκων ἕκαστον τῶν υἱῶν Ἰωσὴφ εὐλόγησεν, καὶ προσεκύνησεν ἐπὶ τὸ ἄκρον τῆς ῥάβδου αὐτοῦ. 22 πίστει Ἰωσὴφ τελευτῶν περὶ τῆς ἐξόδου τῶν υἱῶν Ἰσραὴλ ἐμνημόνευσεν, καὶ περὶ τῶν ὀστέων αὐτοῦ ἐνετείλατο. [SBLGNT]

King James Version

8 By faith Abraham, when he was called to go out into a place which he should after receive for an inheritance, obeyed; and he went out, not knowing whither he went. 9 By faith he sojourned in the land of promise, as in a strange country, dwelling in tabernacles with Isaac and Jacob, the heirs with him of the same promise: 10 For he looked for a city which hath foundations, whose builder and maker is God. 11 Through faith also Sara herself received strength to conceive seed, and was delivered of a child when she was past age, because she judged him faithful who had promised. 12 Therefore sprang there even of one, and him as good as dead, so many as the stars of the sky in multitude, and as the sand which is by the sea shore innumerable. 13 These all died in faith, not having received the promises, but having seen them afar off, and were persuaded of them, and embraced

New Rendition

8 By faith Abraham obeyed when he was called to go out to a place which he would receive as an inheritance, and he went out without knowing where he was going. 9 By faith he dwelt as a foreigner in the land of promise, living in tents with Isaac and Jacob, who were joint heirs of this same promise. 10 For he was looking forward to a city that had firm foundations, whose architect and builder was God. 11 By faith Abraham, although he was advanced in years, received the capability to father a child together with Sarah, since he considered the one who made the promise to be trustworthy. 12 Therefore from one man, although he had become impotent, there arose posterity

> "as numerous as the stars of heaven
> and as innumerable as the sand on the
> seashore." [Gen. 22:17]

13 All these people died, true to their faith, without having received those

them, and confessed that they were strangers and pilgrims on the earth. 14 For they that say such things declare plainly that they seek a country. 15 And truly, if they had been mindful of that country from whence they came out, they might have had opportunity to have returned. 16 But now they desire a better country, that is, an heavenly: wherefore God is not ashamed to be called their God: for he hath prepared for them a city. 17 By faith Abraham, when he was tried, offered up Isaac: and he that had received the promises offered up his only begotten son, 18 Of whom it was said, That in Isaac shall thy seed be called: 19 Accounting that God was able to raise him up, even from the dead; from whence also he received him in a figure. 20 By faith Isaac blessed Jacob and Esau concerning things to come. 21 By faith Jacob, when he was a dying, blessed both the sons of Joseph; and worshipped, leaning upon the top of his staff. 22 By faith Joseph, when he died, made mention of the departing of the children of Israel; and gave commandment concerning his bones.

things that were promised but saw them in the distance and welcomed them and acknowledged that they were strangers and sojourners on this earth. 14 For those who say such things make it clear that they are seeking a homeland. 15 And if they had been thinking of that country they had come from, they would have had an opportunity to return to it. 16 But in fact, they long for a better homeland, that is, a heavenly one. Therefore God is not ashamed to be called their God, because he prepared a city for them. 17 By faith Abraham, when he was tested, offered Isaac as a sacrifice. He who had received the promises was about to sacrifice even his only son, 18 concerning whom he was told,

> "through Isaac your posterity will be called." [Gen. 21:12]

19 He reasoned that God could even raise someone from the dead, and figuratively speaking, he did receive him back from there. 20 By faith Isaac also blessed Jacob and Esau concerning future things. 21 By faith Jacob, being about to die, blessed each of Joseph's sons and

> "worshiped as he leaned on his staff." [LXX Gen. 47:31]

22 By faith Joseph near the end of his life mentioned the exodus of the children of Israel and gave instructions concerning his bones.

Translation Notes and Comments

11:8 ***By faith Abraham, when he was called to go out into a place which he should after receive for an inheritance, obeyed / By faith Abraham obeyed when he was called to go out to a place which he would receive as an inheritance:*** Here we see Abraham as an excellent example of obedience as an expression of forward-looking faith. The story is told in

Genesis 12:1–5, although the author omits the material in Genesis 12:1–3. These contain Jehovah's promises to the prophet. Since they are not the subject of the author's theme, he leaves them to concentrate on his central point.[134] In this first phrase, it is Abraham's obedience.

The verb καλέω (*kaleō*), "to call," is found here as a present passive participle and, in this instance, carries the idea of a summons and stresses its divine nature. It also carries the nuance that the person being summoned has been chosen for a special benefit.[135] The present participle suggests no lapse in time between call and response—Abraham immediately obeyed.[136] The author identifies Abraham's faith as the reason for the benefit and in doing so aligns with James 2:21–23 in seeing Abraham's faith as a meritorious achievement rewarded by God.[137]

The verb ὑπακούω (*hypakouō*), "to obey," denotes not only following instructions but also nuances a willingness to be subject to the one who calls.[138] The LXX also uses it as a reference to Abraham's obedience (Gen. 22:18; 26:5).[139]

The verb μέλλω (*mellō*),[140] "to be about to," followed by an infinitive can denote an event that will definitely happen in the near or certain future,[141] and in this case it points to the sureness of the possession of the promised land by Abraham's posterity. It also highlights the irony, as noted below, of Abraham's living there as a sojourner with no claim to the smallest part of the land and therefore being forced to buy a piece of his God-given land for the burial of Sarah. It further highlights his forward-looking faith and thereby his willingness to abide by God's timing in fulfilling the blessing.

and he went out, not knowing whither he went / and he went out without knowing where he was going: This is the critical phrase in the author's example. The Lord made it clear that he was sending Abraham to a promised land, but Abraham had no idea where it was. In the previous phrase, the author referred to it as simply τόπος (*topos*), "a place."

11:9 ***By faith he sojourned in the land of promise, as in a strange country / By faith he dwelt as a foreigner in the land of promise:*** The verb παροικέω

134. Ellingworth, *Epistle to the Hebrews,* 580–81.
135. BDAG, 502–4.
136. Lane, *Hebrews 9–13,* 343 note a.
137. Ellingworth, *Epistle to the Hebrews,* 581.
138. BDAG, 1028–29.
139. BDAG, 1028–29; Cockerill, *Epistle to the Hebrews,* 538.
140. BDAG, 627–28.
141. BDAG, 628.

(*paroikeō*) denotes “to inhabit a place as a foreigner.”[142] The irony of Abraham’s situation is highlighted by the phrase ὡς ἀλλοτρίαν (*hōs allotrian*), literally “as a foreign [land],”[143] which we have translated as “a foreigner” in our Rendition to follow English idiom (see Gen. 23:4). Due to Jehovah’s command, the patriarch moved to the land he was promised as an inheritance, but all his days he acted as if it were not his.[144]

dwelling in tabernacles with Isaac and Jacob, the heirs with him of the same promise / living in tents with Isaac and Jacob, who were joint heirs of this same promise: The phrase ἐν σκηναῖς κατοικήσας (*en skēnais katoikēsas*), “living in tents,” continues the irony because a σκηνή (*skēnē*), “tent,” is usually a temporary dwelling place.[145] Naming the other two patriarchs and noting they were συνκληρονόμοι (*syngklēronomoi*), “joint heirs,”[146] to the promise magnifies the irony.

The preposition μετά (*meta*), “with,” creates a problem, suggesting that Abraham and Jacob lived together although they did not. The author, however, unconcerned with chronology, is following a long tradition that groups these three together.[147]

11:10 ***For he looked for a city which hath foundations, whose builder and maker is God / For he was looking forward to a city that had firm foundations, whose architect and builder was God:*** The noun πόλις (*polis*), “city,” here refers to the heavenly city, the imagery consistent with the time period when heaven was viewed as a divine city (see Rev. 3:12; 21:2–22:5).[148]

This verse explains why the patriarchs were willing to remain strangers in the land of promise. The verb ἐκδέχομαι (*ekdechomai*), “to look forward to” something,[149] found here in the imperfect tense, connotes that Abraham lived in a continual state of anticipation. Because his view always looked to the future, the promised land was never his objective.

The noun θεμέλιος (*themelios*), “foundation stone,” is found here in the plural since anciently the foundation structure of a building was made up of multiple stones. In our Rendition, we have translated it as “firm

142. BDAG, 779; Michel, *TDNT,* 5:153–55.

143. BDAG, 47–48.

144. Ellingworth, *Epistle to the Hebrews,* 583.

145. For discussion, see Michaelis, *TDNT,* 7:368–81.

146. BDAG, 952.

147. Ellingworth, *Epistle to the Hebrews,* 583.

148. See also 2 Esdr. 10:27; compare 2 Esdr. 10:42, 44. For a study, see Strathmann, *TDNT,* 6:516–35.

149. BDAG, 300.

foundations" to emphasize the solidity and permanence of the city. The nuance is one of permanency; the imagery stands in contrast to a tent that has no foundation and is therefore impermanent.[150]

The two nouns τεχνίτης (*technitēs*), "craftsman, designer" but here "architect,"[151] and δημιουργός (*dēmiourgos*), "builder,"[152] emphasize that the heavenly city was both envisioned and built by God, the phrase stressing its divine origin from inception to completion. Behind the expression stands the idea of permanence that gives the city a reality beyond anything earthly. It appears to have been both its permanence and holiness that gave it the power to eclipse all things temporal so far as the desires of the patriarchs were concerned. Because of faith they were enabled to see this heavenly city and wait expectantly to inherit it.

11:11 ***Through faith also Sara herself received strength to conceive seed, and was delivered of a child when she was past age / By faith Abraham, although he was advanced in years, received the capability to father a child together with Sarah:*** The phrase καταβολὴν σπέρματος (*katabolēn spermatos*), literally "throwing down of seed," is a technical term for "the sowing of seed" and in particular of the sexual function of a male, "begetting."[153] The Talmud teaches, "His father emits the white seed. . . . His mother emits the red seed. . . . The Holy One, Blessed be He, inserts into him a spirit, the soul."[154] However, in this context, it is clear that Abraham is the subject of the third person aorist verb ἔλαβεν (*elaben*), "he received," because in 11:12 both the pronoun ἑνός (*henos*), "one [man]," and the perfect passive participle νενεκρωμένου (*nenekrōmenou*), "having become as if dead" (that is, in this case, "impotent"), are masculine gender in form, and so the phrase could not be referring to Sarah.

This is one of the more problematic verses in Hebrews because there are two major variants in the early manuscripts: αὐτὴ Σάρρα στεῖρα (*autē Sarra steira*), "Sarah herself, [who was] sterile," and καὶ αὐτὴ Σάρρα (*kai autē Sarra*), "and Sarah herself,"[155] only suggesting she was infertile. A third possibility is to read the phrase as in the dative case since in the early uncial manuscripts, the iota subscript was regularly not written: καὶ αὐτῇ Σάρρᾳ (*kai autē Sarra*), "and with Sarah herself,"[156] suggesting that she, along with Abraham, was beyond childbearing years. Other scholars consider

150. Ellingworth, *Epistle to the Hebrews*, 584.
151. BDAG, 1001.
152. BDAG, 223.
153. LSJ, 885; BDAG, 515; Schrenk, *TDNT*, 3:621–23.
154. *B. Niddah*, 31b.
155. Metzger, *Textual Commentary*, 602.
156. Metzger, *Textual Commentary*, 602; Schrenk, *TDNT*, 3:621–23.

the whole phrase as an early gloss. That the idea is found in one form or another in all the manuscripts suggests something was originally there but has become corrupted.[157] The KJV takes Sarah as the subject. We have chosen to take the phrase in the dative case and translate it as "together with Sarah" in our Rendition because it works better given the overall setting.[158]

because she judged him faithful who had promised / since he considered the one who made the promise to be trustworthy: For whether the subject of this phrase is Sarah or Abraham, see the discussion above.

The subordinate conjunction ἐπεί (*epei*), "since, because," is causal and used by the author to show that "Abraham's faith is a response to God's faithfulness."[159]

The verb ἡγέομαι (*hēgeomai*), "to consider," denotes engaging in mental activity and implies taking something or someone seriously.[160] In this case, it is Jehovah. The adjective *pistis* here takes on the nuance of "trustworthy" because what God promised had not yet been realized.

11:12 ***Therefore sprang there even of one / Therefore from one man . . . there arose posterity:*** The conjunction διό (*dio*), "therefore," acts to further the author's conclusion that Abraham's posterity was a direct result of the godly power given him due to his faithfulness.[161]

There is an echo here to Isaiah 51:2, noting Abraham was "alone" when he was called and stressing there were none other at the time, indicating that all that happened did so through this one man (compare Deut. 26:5).

The verb γεννάω (*gennaō*) means "to become the parent of, beget, or give birth to," of either a father or a mother, and in the passive voice, as found here, it means "to be born."[162] For better clarity in modern English, we have translated it in our Rendition as "there arose posterity."

and him as good as dead / although he had become impotent: The phrase καὶ ταῦτα (*kai tauta*) is used adverbially, "and at that" taking on the sense of "although,"[163] which is how we translated it in our Rendition. The perfect

---

157. Metzger, *Textual Commentary,* 602; Schrenk, *TDNT,* 3:621–23.

158. As does Bruce, *Epistle to the Hebrews,* 294–96; Attridge, *Epistle to the Hebrews,* 324–26; Ellingworth, *Epistle to the Hebrews,* 586–89; and others. This position is also taken in the NIV. On the other hand, Cockerill, *Epistle to the Hebrews,* 542–45; Johnson, *Hebrews,* 291–92; and others take Sarah as the subject, as does the KJV.

159. Ellingworth, *Epistle to the Hebrews,* 589.

160. BDAG, 434.

161. Ellingworth, *Epistle to the Hebrews,* 590.

162. BDAG, 193–94.

163. BDAG, 741; Smyth, *Greek Grammar,* §1251. This is the only use of the plural ταῦτα (*tauta*) in the NT, it being a classical usage; for example, see Josephus, *Ant.* 2.266. The singular τοῦτο (*touto*) is used elsewhere. Wallace, *Greek Grammar,* 335 n. 56.

passive participle νενεκρωμένου (*nenekrōmenou*), literally "to have become dead," is here used in the sense "worn out, impotent" of a person whose physical capabilities have failed.[164] Thus we have translated it "he had become impotent" in our Rendition.

so many as the stars of the sky in multitude, and as the sand which is by the sea shore innumerable / "as numerous as the stars of heaven and as innumerable as the sand on the seashore": Jehovah used the imagery in both phrases to express the innumerable posterity that Abraham will engender.[165]

11:13 ***These all died in faith, not having received the promises, but having seen them afar off, and were persuaded of them, and embraced them / All these people died, true to their faith, without having received those things that were promised but saw them in the distance and welcomed them:*** This sentence begins with the prepositional phrase κατὰ πίστιν (*kata pistin*), "with respect to faith." The author does break his rhythmic repetition of "by faith" to give the phrase, as we see it, a different nuance. "It is not that they died because of their faith or by means of their faith, but that they died as people who had lived faithfully, despite the fact that they did not receive the fulfillment of the promises."[166] We have translated this as "true to their faith" to best catch its sense in English.

The verb ἀσπάζομαι (*aspazomai*), "to welcome," carries the nuance of the happiness associated with the arrival of something or someone that has been highly anticipated.[167] The force of the word here suggests the patriarchs, though seeing the promises yet future, by faith happily welcomed them as a present reality.

and confessed that they were strangers and pilgrims on the earth / and acknowledged that they were strangers and sojourners on this earth: The verb ὁμολογέω (*homologeō*) means "to confess, acknowledge." The problem with both English words is they come close to the idea expressed by the Greek word but can carry a negative connotation of disclosing something against one's will. "Confession" often suggests giving deference to the opinion of others while "acknowledgment" suggests making something known that could have been kept back.[168] That is not the case with *homologeō*; it

164. BDAG, 667–68.

165. Compare Deut. 1:10; 10:22, where Moses uses the imagery in the first phrase to describe Israel and show that God had fulfilled his promise to Abraham.

166. Johnson, *Hebrews,* 292.

167. BDAG, 144.

168. *Webster's New Dictionary of Synonyms,* s.v. "acknowledgement."

carries the idea of openly proclaiming one's opinion or position on a given issue, in short, to make one's stand known.[169] Despite the possible negative nuance, given that "acknowledge" carries the idea of making something known, we have used it in our Rendition.

Though the author does not say to whom the patriarchs made their acknowledgement, he does state what that acknowledgement was: the noun ξένος (*xenos*), "stranger," denoted not only someone passing through an area but also the resident alien.[170] Though Jehovah promised Abraham the land of Canaan, he also said Abraham and his children would dwell as strangers (גֵּר, *gêr*; see Gen. 17:8). The Hebrew word also denotes both a foreigner passing through an area and also a resident alien. When taking on the second nuance, it denoted someone who was protected by the law but could not or was not allowed to have part in certain activities and could not hold land or certain offices (for examples, see Ex. 12:43; 29:33; and Num. 3:10; 18:4).[171] These exclusions protected both the civil and religious institutions as well as the land from foreign control.

The adjective παρεπίδημος (*parepidēmos*), when used as a substantive, means a "sojourner," that is, one who is residing temporarily in a place away from the homeland.[172] It describes one who is in a more temporary and dependent circumstance than the ξένος (*xenos*), although the scriptures use both terms together, heightening the idea of the impermanence of the person's attachment to the area and people.[173] In the New Testament, the two terms stressed the idea of the Saints being virtual visitors to this earth due to their relationship with the Lord and his promise of a permanent place in his kingdom.

11:14 ***For they that say such things declare plainly that they seek a country / For those who say such things make it clear that they are seeking a homeland:*** The author here states the implication of what the patriarchs

---

169. BDAG, 708. The noun ὁμολογία (*homologia*) denotes more than agreement with others. Rather, it indicates not only a sincere consent to a cause that is felt to be valid but also taking action to promote it. *NID,* s.v. "ὁμολογέω."

170. BDAG, 684.

171. BDB, 158; *TWOT,* 330.

172. BDAG, 775.

173. Abraham referred to himself as a "sojourner" (תּוֹשָׁב, *tôshāb*) when he bargained with the sons of Heth for the burial place for Sarah (Gen. 23:4). DBD, 444; *TWOT,* 922. Attridge, *Epistle to the Hebrews,* 330, suggests ξένος (*xenos*), "alien," is a bit stronger than πάροικος (*paroikos*), "resident alien." It is of note that the author is not playing off some earthly alienation engendered in the author's mind by being exposed to Platonic dualism. Cockerill, *Epistle to the Hebrews,* 551.

acknowledged. The verb λέγω (*legō*), "to say, speak," refers to the patriarchs' acknowledgement that they were strangers and sojourners.

The verb ἐμφανίζω (*emphanizō*), "make clear," carries the nuance of more than making a mere verbal statement but of testifying "to matters of transcendent physical sight."[174] Those who so speak do not stand back or answer with timidity but openly and often officially declare their stand.[175]

The verb ἐπιζητέω (*epizēteō*), "to seek,"[176] suggests diligence in looking for what one wants. Its position as the last word in the sentence gives it even more punch—"the path pursued 'by faith' is no course of passive indolence. Because these heroes who lived 'by faith' were aliens on earth, most anxious to reach their home, they 'diligently sought' it by persevering in the life of faith and obedience" and were not ashamed to show it.[177]

The noun πατρίς (*patris*) denotes one's homeland as well as one's hometown. It carries the warm nuance of familial connections. In a religious sense, it refers to the heavenly home the Father promises his faithful.[178]

11:15 ***if they had been mindful of that country from whence they came out / if they had been thinking of that country they had come from:*** The author, in this verse, makes it clear that, in their acknowledgement, the patriarchs were not thinking about the land Abraham came from. The author emphasizes his point by casting the sentence as an unreal condition expressing a hypothetical situation.[179]

The verb μνημονεύω (*mnēmoneuō*), "be mindful, remember," found here in the imperfect tense, denotes a state of continual consciousness about the object remembered, albeit stopping short of being obsessed with the thought.[180] The patriarchs' thoughts did not dwell on Abraham's former home in Ur, which, at least for Abraham, could clearly be remembered. Rather, they looked to another one.

The noun "country" is not found in the Greek text but is implied by the demonstrative pronoun ἐκείνης (*ekeinēs*), "of that," referring to the

174. BDAG, 325–26.

175. Ellingworth, *Epistle to the Hebrews,* 595.

176. BDAG, 371; Louw-Nida, §25.9.

177. Cockerill, *Epistle to the Hebrews,* 552.

178. BDAG, 788–89.

179. Wallace, *Greek Grammar,* 694–95. The contrary-to-fact condition assumes an untruth for the sake of argument.

180. BDAG, 655; Louw-Nida, §29.7, 8. Ellingworth, *Epistle to the Hebrews,* 597, suggests "meant" as a good nuance of word as used here.

country from which Abraham had come, and is supplied in both the KJV and our Rendition.

they might have had opportunity to have returned / they would have had an opportunity to return to it: This phrase contains the author's proof of the point he is making. The author's use of the noun καιρός (*kairos*), "opportunity," means that the possibility of returning to Ur was ever present with the patriarchs but, because that was not their objective, they never took it.

11:16 ***But now / But in fact:*** Since the phrase νῦν δέ (*nyn de*) contrasts a real state of affairs with the unreal condition in the previous verse,[181] we have translated it "but in fact" in our Rendition.

they desire a better country, that is, an heavenly / they long for a better homeland, that is, a heavenly one: The verb ὀρέγομαι (*oregomai*), "desire, long for," denotes both aspiring to and striving for a goal and nuances the energy put behind trying to achieve it.[182] Due to Stoic usage, the verb acquired the religious nuance of striving for a heavenly goal.[183] For the patriarchs, obtaining the heavenly city was more than a passing fancy. They worked for the day.

The adjective κρείτων (*kreitōn*), "better," denotes something that is of a higher rank or more prominent than something else,[184] suggesting why Ur held no appeal to them.

The noun πατρίς (*patris*), "country, homeland" (for a definition, see Translation Notes for 11:14), is not found in the Greek text but is implied by the adjective *kreitōn* and is therefore added in both the KJV and our Rendition. The grammatical comparative suggests such a contrast between the present, temporal, transient, worldly order and that of the eternal, stable, heavenly one that, for the patriarchs, the former lost all its appeal.[185]

wherefore God is not ashamed to be called their God / Therefore God is not ashamed to be called their God: The verb ἐπαισχύνομαι (*epaischynomai*), "to be ashamed," means to feel pain due to a threat of loss of status.[186] Jehovah had no worries about this given the faith of these people. The subordinating conjunction διό (*dio*), "therefore," serves to introduce the reason God was not ashamed to be called their God. They would never

181. BDAG, 681; LSJ, 1185.

182. BDAG, 721; Louw-Nida, §25.15, suggests "eagerly long for."

183. Ellingworth, *Epistle to the Hebrews,* 598. Philo, *Virt.* 218, used the word to denote a striving for a relationship with God.

184. BDAG, 566.

185. Ellingworth, *Epistle to the Hebrews,* 598.

186. BDAG, 357.

diminish his reputation or demean his character, let alone abandon him (compare Ex. 3:6, 15, 16; 4:5).[187]

he hath prepared for them a city / he prepared a city for them: This phrase shows how God showers his approval upon them. The verb ἑτοιμάζω (*hetoimazō*), "to prepare," is found here in the aorist tense, suggesting God did not wait until they demonstrated their righteousness before building them a city. Thus, his promise is not an "empty accolade" but a concrete if spiritual reality.[188]

11:17 ***By faith Abraham, when he was tried / By faith Abraham, when he was tested:*** The verb πειράζω (*peirazō*), found here as a present passive participle, has a broad range of meanings, including "to attempt to do something," "to put someone or something to the test," and "to tempt."[189] The second sense is to be understood in this passage. The participle acts as a circumstantial clause and translates as "when he was tested." By using the passive voice, the author was able to keep to his point without distraction, but the connotation of the work of the divine is only slightly masked.

offered up Isaac / offered Isaac as a sacrifice: The verb προσφέρω (*prospherō*), literally "to bring to," found here in the perfect tense, is used in the technical sense of making an offering or sacrifice.[190] The author's use of the tense could indicate either that he viewed the event "in terms of its allegorical or applicational value" as referring to the Atonement[191] or that Abraham's mindset of the sacrifice of Isaac was that it was a done deal, having lasting consequences.[192]

he that had received the promises offered up his only begotten son / He who had received the promises was about to sacrifice even his only son: The verb ἀναδέχομαι (*anadechomai*), "to receive, accept," is quite strong and carries three nuances: receiving something with confidence, undertaking something, or assuming responsibility for something.[193] Here the word suggests Abraham accepted the covenantal promises and assumed responsibility for them.

---

187. In reality, God can never lose prestige or power. It is only in the perception that others hold of him that such a loss can occur.

188. Cockerill, *Epistle to the Hebrews,* 554.

189. BDAG, 792–93.

190. BDAG, 886.

191. Wallace, *Greek Grammar,* 581–82. See also *BDF,* §342.5.

192. Lane, *Hebrews 9–13,* 346 note jj.

193. BDAG, 62; Moulton and Milligan, *Vocabulary,* 32; Lane, *Hebrews 9–13,* 346 note ll.

The promises refer to the covenant that God made with Abraham in Genesis 13:14–17 and confirmed in Genesis 15:4–18 and 22:17–18, which included the blessing of a numerous posterity mentioned in 11:12 above.

The verb προσφέρω (*prospherō*), "to sacrifice," is repeated but in the imperfect tense, stressing the fact that Abraham was about to sacrifice his son but did not actually follow through.

The adjective μονογενής (*monogenēs*) means "only [son]."[194] Abraham had other sons besides Isaac, including Ishmael, his son through Sarah's maidservant, Hagar. Isaac is described, however, by this term because he alone was designated as the heir of the covenant that God had made with Abraham. The next verse makes this clear. With the use of the adjective, the author may have wanted to bring in Messianic overtones (Jesus was referred to by this same term; see John 1:14, 18; 3:16, 18; and 1 John 4:9) and thereby subtly connect Abraham and Isaac with God and Christ.

11:18 *Of whom it was said, That in Isaac shall thy seed be called / concerning whom he was told, "through Isaac your posterity will be called":* The setting for Jehovah's pronouncement was when Sarah insisted Hagar and Ishmael be sent away for mocking her. God's words assured Abraham that the covenant was still intact even though Ishmael was no longer an heir, for that particular promise would be realized in Isaac.

The noun σπέρμα (*sperma*), "posterity," in this instance does not carry the often-used meaning of either semen or seed but that of descendant.[195]

The noun καλέω (*kaleō*), "to call, summon," here carries the nuance of calling someone to a task; in this case, it is that of Isaac to produce Abraham's posterity. The phrase could therefore have the sense "through Isaac you will have your posterity."[196]

11:19 *Accounting that God was able to raise him up, even from the dead / He reasoned that God could even raise someone from the dead:* With the middle verb λογίζομαι (*logizomai*), "to reason, give careful thought to a matter,"[197] the author describes Abraham's mindset as the author understands it at the time the patriarch offered up Isaac.

The verb ἐγείρω (*egeirō*), "to raise," found here as a present infinitive, in a general sense means to go from a lower to a higher position and so "to arise, stand," but in this context, the phrase ἐκ νεκρῶν (*ek nekrōn*), "from

---

194. BDAG, 658.

195. BDAG, 937; Ellingworth, *Epistle to the Hebrews,* 602.

196. BDAG, 502–504; Louw-Nida, §33.312.

197. BDAG, 597–98.

the dead," shows it means to be restored to life.[198] Just where the author got this idea is unknown, but it offers an elegant solution to an age-old problem (see Analysis below). Abraham reasoned that even if he did sacrifice Isaac, God, who cannot lie, would restore him to life.

from whence also he received him in a figure / figuratively speaking, he did receive him back from there: The verb *komizō* means to get back what is one's own[199] and suggests the bond between Isaac and Abraham.

The noun παραβολή (*parabolē*), "figure, type," denotes something that serves as a model or example.[200] In this case, it refers to Isaac's near sacrifice. Though his death did not actually happen, in a sense God did release Isaac from death, not through direct divine power but through the use of a substitute—the ram in the thicket. Here, the author brings in an echo of the resurrection. Though this echo could look at the specific Resurrection of the Lord, which would make Isaac a type of Jesus, the context of the chapter suggests the author is looking at the general resurrection, to which his readers, through faithfulness, could look forward.[201]

11:20 ***By faith Isaac blessed Jacob and Esau concerning things to come / By faith Isaac also blessed Jacob and Esau concerning future things:*** The author refers to events recorded in Genesis 27:27–39. The verb εὐλογέω (*eulogeō*), "to bless," means "to provide with divine benefits," including a bestowal of God's gracious power through which the blessing can be realized.[202]

The verb μέλλω (*mellō*), found here as plural, neuter, present participle and translated as "future things" in our Rendition, denotes that which is inevitable (see Translation Notes for 11:8) and confirms the inspiration behind the blessings, for only God knows the future.

The word καί (*kai*) usually acts as a conjunction and is translated as "and." Here, however, it acts as an adverb and is translated as "also" in our Rendition. As such, it makes Isaac's faith equivalent to Abraham's. It also goes with *mellō* and shows that Isaac's faith, like that of the other patriarchs, had a definite forward orientation.[203] Note the author says nothing about the content of those blessings, likely because they are ancillary to his focus on the future-looking aspect of faith.

---

198. BDAG, 271–72. It does not, unlike ἀνάσταις (*anastasis*), connote resurrection.
199. BDAG, 557.
200. BDAG, 759–60.
201. Ellingworth, *Epistle to the Hebrews,* 604; O'Brien, *Letter to the Hebrews,* 425.
202. BDAG, 407–8.
203. Ellingworth, *Epistle to the Hebrews,* 604.

11:21 ***By faith Jacob, when he was a dying, blessed both the sons of Joseph / By faith Jacob, being about to die, blessed each of Joseph's sons:*** The author refers here to events recorded in Genesis 48:15–22. The verb ἀποθνήσκω (*apothnēskō*) means not only "to die" but also "to be about to die," which is its sense here.[204] Jacob's blessing of his sons is described in Genesis 47:29–49:33. The author again does not mention the content of the blessings even though they pertain to the future, likely because they were not the focus of his message.

and worshipped, leaning upon the top of his staff / and "worshiped as he leaned on his staff": There is a conflation here between events in Genesis 48 (the blessing of Joseph's sons) and those of Genesis 47:29–31 (the promise of Joseph to bury Jacob's bones in the promised land). The LXX differs from the KJV in stating what happened. The latter states that after the promise of Joseph, Jacob "bowed himself upon the bed's head" (Gen. 47:31) while the former states that "Israel did reverence, leaning on the top of his staff" (LXX Gen. 47:31).[205] Context suggests the LXX is correct.

The verb προσκυνεύω (*proskyneuō*), "to worship," connotes an expression of dependence on or submission to a higher authority and often expressed itself in acts ranging from a polite acknowledgement to full prostration.[206] Here it could refer to either Jacob's grateful acknowledgement of his dependence on Joseph to carry out his promise not to bury Jacob in Egypt or his expression of faith that God would indeed give Jacob's descendants the promised land where Joseph would bury his bones (see Gen. 50:7–13).

The verbs "leaning, leaned" are not found in the Greek text, which is literally translated as "Jacob . . . did reverence on the tip of the rod of him." Both the KJV and our Rendition supply the words to clarify that Jacob was not using the rod as an object of worship but of support.[207] The imagery suggests Jacob's dependence on his staff because of his advanced age.

11:22 ***By faith Joseph, when he died, made mention of the departing of the children of Israel / By faith Joseph near the end of his life mentioned***

---

204. BDAG, 111.

205. The MT has the noun מִטָּה (*miṭṭāh*), "bed," while the LXX, assuming a different voweling, has מַטֶּה (*maṭṭeh*), "staff." See Bruce, *Epistle to the Hebrews,* 306; Ellingworth, *Epistle to the Hebrews,* 606.

206. BDAG, 882–83.

207. The Vulgate does make Jacob worship the top of his staff. For discussion, see Bruce, *Epistle to the Hebrews,* 306 and nn. 159, 160; Lane, *Hebrews 9–13,* 347 note yy; and Ellingworth, *Epistle to the Hebrews,* 606.

the exodus of the children of Israel: This phrase alludes to Genesis 50:24–25. The verb τελευτάω (*teleutaō*) means "to come to an end" and was a euphemism for death.[208] Here it is found as a present participle connoting that Joseph was near death.

The verb μνημονεύω (*mnēmoneuō*) means "to remember, recall," but here the nuance rather than looking backward looks forward to the Exodus and so is translated as "mention" in both the KJV and our Rendition.[209]

gave commandment concerning his bones / gave instructions concerning his bones: The verb ἐντέλλω (*entellō*) means "to give instructions" and by extension "commandments."[210] The instructions associated with Joseph mentioning the Exodus expresses his faith that the sojourn of the Hebrews in Egypt would come to an end and that they would possess the promised land.

Analysis and Summary

Like the Bible itself, the author jumps from Noah to Abraham. Because this prophet is one of the two most important Old Testament biblical figures (the other being Moses) to the Jewish congregation to which the Epistle, in large part, was directed, the author gives him a good deal of attention. Abraham's willingness to leave his homeland "not knowing whither he went" (11:8) provides the author with a chance to highlight two of his major themes. First, faith expresses itself in trustful obedience to God's commands even when the objective or result of that command is not yet known. Such is not, however, blind faith. Obedience to commands is based on an assurance that God always works to the believer's good. Sometimes faith is, admittedly, a step into the dark, but one based on the success of trusting God in the past.[211] Nephi proclaimed his faith in God, stating, "I will go and do the things which the Lord hath commanded, for I know that the Lord giveth no commandments unto the children of men, save he shall prepare a way for them that they may accomplish the thing which he commandeth them" (1 Ne. 3:7). This assurance came from seeing how God had operated in the past. Even so, when the time came, Nephi had to prove the sincerity of his faith by stepping literally into the darkness and was rewarded for doing so (1 Ne. 4:4–6).

208. BDAG, 997.

209. BDAG, 655.

210. BDAG, 339.

211. Much of the material in this analysis is taken from an unpublished paper by Nathaniel Pribil, in possession of the authors.

There is a difference between blind confidence and the faith the author of Hebrews has in mind. Learning the difference between the two is one of the reasons we were sent to earth. To illustrate this point, one scholar asked,

> What is the difference between a workable or fanciful plan in business or engineering? As it unfolds, there are indications and trends. In religious faith, the Holy Ghost is the source of spiritual confirmations, and the Savior promised finding by seeking (Matt. 7:7–8). Blind confidence in an untruth is shown by the Book of Mormon analogy of the infertile seed that no amount of good treatment can make grow (Alma 32:21–43). Operational faith is the focus of the scriptures—knowing the plan of salvation to prepare for an eternal future. Thus, faith is not primarily an intellectual but a creative process. [The author] signals that at the outset of Hebrews 11 by an example of the divine use of faith: "Through faith we understand that the worlds were framed by the word of God, so that things which are seen were not made of things which do appear" (Heb. 11:3). A bridge or a building is drawn in detail before a beam or board is erected. Reality comes after creative vision. So faith lies behind all action, linking the inner image with working power to bring it about.[212]

The second theme the author highlights using Abraham as his model is the discontent with this world felt by the followers of Christ. Even though Abraham lived, albeit as a sojourner, in a promised land, it was for him a "strange country" (11:9). The word translated as "strange" in the KJV is ἀλλότριος (*allotrios*), "that which belongs to another," but carries the nuance of that which is foreign or alien and therefore strange. When pushed, it can even refer to that which is hostile to one's well-being.[213] The tension arose because Abraham with the other patriarchs looked "forward to a city that had firm foundations, whose architect and builder was God (NR 11:10). This is significant especially in reference to 11:13–16, where the author extends the migration of Abraham and the sojourn of the patriarchs into an anticipation of living in God's country.

With 11:13–16, the author breaks the flow of his narrative to make a point—faith's ability to open the eyes of the righteous so they can see the ultimate reality and respond thereto—that fits well with the patriarchal generation, and more explicitly with Abraham than with his son and grandson, whose

---

212. Anderson, *Understanding Paul,* 221–22; see also Kimball, *Teachings,* 56; Neal A. Maxwell, *We Talk of Christ, We Rejoice in Christ* (Salt Lake City: Deseret Book, 1984), 87; Boyd K. Packer, *The Holy Temple* (Salt Lake City: Bookcraft, 1980), 184–85; and Boyd K. Packer, *"That All May Be Edified"* (Salt Lake City: Bookcraft, 1982), 340.

213. BDAG, 47–48; Louw-Nida, §§39.12; 92.20.

stories he uses as a bridge to get to Moses. A counterpoint can most certainly be drawn from the wilderness generation, who never had the faith to see that they could possess the promised land, let alone the eternal city. Not so for the patriarchs.[214]

In this section, the author emphasizes the nomadic aspects of the patriarchs' lives, stating that because of their faith they "confessed that they were strangers and pilgrims on the earth" (11:13). He emphasizes they could have had it differently but refused (11:15). This is all part of his lead-up to one of the most important verses in this section: "But now they desire a better country, that is, an heavenly" (11:16). Thus, the attitude of Abraham (and his descendants) becomes an example of the one the Saints should have toward the things of the world. The patriarchs' feelings also reveal the longings of the righteous for their heavenly home.

In this context, the author brings in Sarah (one of two women mentioned in this section). Her role is secondary but essential, for the focus remains on Abraham's faith in God's promise that he would sire a son through Sarah. It was, according to our reading, Abraham who "judged him faithful who had promised" (11:11). This verse is important because it provides focus on another aspect of faith the author is developing: righteous people's response to God's faithfulness. The focus of the adjective "faithful" is on trustworthiness and dependability[215] and ties to the idea of "the substance of things hoped for" (11:1) that faithful people have in the promises of God. As noted in 11:6, the reason people can express faith in God is because of their trust in him to do as he says. Abraham's response to God's promise amply illustrates this aspect of faith.

Indeed, the birth of Isaac was the sign that God's promise of an innumerable posterity was being realized. The author uses the example to prove to his readers that God was and is faithful, because they knew of its literal fulfillment—the rest of the chapter focusing as it does on Abraham's trusting and very large posterity. The author has already brought his readers into the picture as the final proof that the promise has been realized fully in their day through Christ acting as he did, as an anchor sure and steadfast (6:19–20).[216]

In 11:17–19, the author discusses the attempted sacrifice of Isaac as recorded in Genesis 22.[217] The importance of the illustration used here,

214. Ellingworth, *Epistle to the Hebrews,* 592.

215. BDAG, 820–21.

216. Cockerill, *Epistle to the Hebrews,* 546.

217. The *Aqedah* or "The Binding of Isaac" has caused much debate and discussion in Jewish, Muslim, and Christian circles primarily because of the statement in Genesis

as with the one above, is that faith reveals itself in complete confidence in God's trustworthiness. This particular trial of faith was based on the incongruity between God's promise that through Isaac would Abraham's large posterity come and God's demand that Abraham sacrifice his son.

The author's focus is on *why* Abraham was willing to sacrifice Isaac. The author has already stressed that God keeps covenants (6:13–20), and it was possible for God to keep this one, Abraham accounted, because God was fully able to raise Isaac up from the dead (11:19). The Greek word translated as "accounted" is the aorist participle λογισάμενος (*logisamenos*) that carries the meaning of evaluating or considering an idea very carefully and fully.[218] The use of the word indicates that Abraham had been most careful in developing his faith in God and on that basis could, at this point, take God at his word that Isaac would be the source of Abraham's posterity, even though it flew in the face of what God now demanded. The lesson learned from this incident is relevant for God's people living in any time. As Jesus said, the Saints "must needs be chastened and tried, even as Abraham, who was commanded to offer up his only son. For all those who will not endure chastening, but deny me, cannot be sanctified" (D&C 101:4–5). The Lord commands, "Go ye, therefore, and do the works of Abraham; enter ye into my law and ye shall be saved. But if ye enter not into my law ye cannot receive the promise of my Father, which he made unto Abraham" (D&C 132:32–33). The scripture suggests the trial associated with the promise is very real and very deep and one which no one can escape.

President John Taylor once stated he "heard the Prophet Joseph [Smith] say, in speaking to the Twelve on one occasion: 'You will have all kinds of trials to pass through. And it is quite as necessary for you to be tried as it was for Abraham and other men of God, and (said he) God will feel after

---

wherein God stopped Abraham from sacrificing his son, saying, "For now I know that thou fearest God, seeing thou hast not withheld thy son, thine only son from me" (Gen. 22:12). The rub with this quote is that it suggests God is less than all-knowing and that he put Abraham though this horrible ordeal for God's own, not Abraham's, sake. The debates and discussion are well beyond the parameters of this commentary, and because the author of Hebrews does not give the problem a nod, we have chosen not to develop it. For brief but very good discussions, see Johnson, *Hebrews,* 294–95; Hugh Nibley, *Nibley on the Timely and Timeless,* vol. 1 of Religious Studies Monograph Series (Provo, Utah: Religious Studies Center, 1978), 130–44; and Andrew C. Skinner, *Prophets, Priests, and Kings: Old Testament Figures Who Symbolize Christ* (Salt Lake City: Deseret Book, 2005), 33–44. For a comprehensive overview, see Mishael Caspi and John T. Greene, *Unbinding the Binding of Isaac* (Lanham, Md.: University Press of America, 2007).

218. BDAG, 597–98.

you, and He will take hold of you and wrench your very heart strings, and if you cannot stand it you will not be fit for an inheritance in the Celestial Kingdom of God.'"[219]

Speaking also of the test given to Abraham, President George Q. Cannon said,

> Why did the Lord ask such things of Abraham? Because, knowing what his future would be and that he would be the father of an innumerable posterity, He was determined to test him. God did not do this for His own sake for He knew by His foreknowledge what Abraham would do; but the purpose was to impress upon Abraham a lesson and to enable him to attain unto knowledge that he could not obtain in any other way. That is why God tries all of us. It is not for His own knowledge for He knows all things beforehand. He knows all your lives and everything you will do. But He tries us for our own good that we may know ourselves; for it is most important that a man should know himself.
>
> He required Abraham to submit to this trial because He intended to give him glory, exaltation and honor; He intended to make him a king and a priest, to share with Himself the glory, power and dominion which He exercised. And was this trial any more than God himself had passed through?[220]

President Cannon's referring to Abraham's sacrifice of Isaac as a type of the trial that the Father himself had to go through follows the idea of other Christian writers. In the view of the author, this idea, if present at all, is somewhat distant. Instead, he shows that the test of Abraham is not so much to see if a person is willing to sacrifice all as it is a test to see if a person will continue to exercise faith in God—expressed in trustful obedience—even when God appears to have reneged on the promise. From the author's point of view, for all appearances to the contrary, Abraham knew God would not break his word, and therefore the patriarch never intended to return to Sarah without his son.[221]

---

219. John Taylor, in *Journal of Discourses,* 24:197.

220. George Q. Cannon, *Gospel Truth: Discourses and Writings of George Q. Cannon,* ed. Jerreld L. Newquist (Salt Lake City: Deseret Book, 1987), 89. For a general discussion of the Latter-day Saint view for the need for personal sacrifice, see Robert J. Matthews, "Great Faith Obtained Only through Personal Sacrifice," in Dahl and Tate, *Lectures on Faith in Historical Perspective,* 241–62.

221. Abraham's words to his servant, "I and the lad will go yonder and worship, and come again to you" (Gen. 22:5), suggest he fully intended to come back with Isaac.

Thus, Abraham's willingness to make the sacrifice was specifically derived from two aspects of his faith. The first was in God's immediate power over life and death.[222] The second was in God's trustworthiness to fulfill all he had promised. Through this example, the author of Hebrews highlights Abraham's faith in the full trustworthiness of God.

The author next focuses on each of the patriarchs in turn, although not with equal coverage. Isaac, although important in the above discussion, receives only a brief mention that focuses on his prophetic ability revealed in his blessings to his children (11:20; see Gen. 27). Intriguingly, there is no reference to the wrangling between Jacob and Esau. Given the generally negative valence that Esau/Edom had in Jewish writings of the Second Temple period, the omission is noteworthy but that detail is likely left out because it did not demonstrate an aspect of faith the author needed.[223]

Like Isaac, Jacob is included in this section and, like his father, the focus is on his prophetic ability as demonstrated in his blessings upon the heads of Joseph's sons (11:21). The focus is intriguing because it leaves out the example of faith of Israel's blessing on his other sons (see Gen. 49). Also omitted are some of the more dramatic stories, such as his vision of the ladder into heaven at Bethel or wrestling with the angel at Penuel. The pattern continues with Joseph, who prophesied that the Hebrews would return to the promised land (11:22). The author does not use any of the events in Joseph's life that definitively show his faithfulness to God and God's response to him (for example, refusing Potiphar's wife or interpreting dreams). These patriarchs are used to highlight but one aspect of faith: that of seeing the future—the reality that had not yet been realized.

---

222. It is unlikely that this passage has echoes of the Resurrection. Though the prophet Jacob stated that Abraham's "offering up his son Isaac [was] a similitude of God and his Only Begotten Son" (Jacob 4:5), the emphasis is not on the Resurrection but on the willingness of the Father to give his Son for others. It would make little sense for God to promise Abraham that his posterity would come through Isaac and then wait for nearly two millennia to have it fulfilled.

223. This is especially true in light of 12:16, where Esau is held up as a negative example for Christians to avoid. In Rabbinic thinking, Esau is associated with Rome and from there with the Roman Church. See Solomon Zeitlin, "The Origin of the Term Edom for Rome and the Roman Church," *Jewish Quarterly Review* 60, no. 3 (1970): 262–63; and Mirielle Hadas-Lebel, "Jacob et Esaü ou Israël et Rome dans le Talmud et le Midrash," *Revue l'Histoire des Religions* 201, no. 4 (1984): 369–92.

The Faith of Moses (11:23–28)

Greek Text

23 Πίστει Μωϋσῆς γεννηθεὶς ἐκρύβη τρίμηνον ὑπὸ τῶν πατέρων αὐτοῦ, διότι εἶδον ἀστεῖον τὸ παιδίον καὶ οὐκ ἐφοβήθησαν τὸ διάταγμα τοῦ βασιλέως. 24 πίστει Μωϋσῆς μέγας γενόμενος ἠρνήσατο λέγεσθαι υἱὸς θυγατρὸς Φαραώ, 25 μᾶλλον ἑλόμενος συγκακουχεῖσθαι τῷ λαῷ τοῦ θεοῦ ἢ πρόσκαιρον ἔχειν ἁμαρτίας ἀπόλαυσιν, 26 μείζονα πλοῦτον ἡγησάμενος τῶν Αἰγύπτου θησαυρῶν τὸν ὀνειδισμὸν τοῦ Χριστοῦ, ἀπέβλεπεν γὰρ εἰς τὴν μισθαποδοσίαν. 27 πίστει κατέλιπεν Αἴγυπτον, μὴ φοβηθεὶς τὸν θυμὸν τοῦ βασιλέως, τὸν γὰρ ἀόρατον ὡς ὁρῶν ἐκαρτέρησεν. 28 πίστει πεποίηκεν τὸ πάσχα καὶ τὴν πρόσχυσιν τοῦ αἵματος, ἵνα μὴ ὁ ὀλοθρεύων τὰ πρωτότοκα θίγῃ αὐτῶν. [SBLGNT]

King James Version

23 By faith Moses, when he was born, was hid three months of his parents, because they saw he was a proper child; and they were not afraid of the king's commandment. 24 By faith Moses, when he was come to years, refused to be called the son of Pharaoh's daughter; 25 choosing rather to suffer affliction with the people of God, than to enjoy the pleasures of sin for a season; 26 Esteeming the reproach of Christ greater riches than the treasures in Egypt: for he had respect unto the recompence of the reward. 27 By faith he forsook Egypt, not fearing the wrath of the king: for he endured, as seeing him who is invisible. 28 Through faith he kept the passover, and the sprinkling of blood, lest he that destroyed the firstborn should touch them.

New Rendition

23 By faith Moses, after he was born, was hidden for three months by his parents, because they saw that the child was handsome, and they did not fear the king's edict. 24 By faith Moses, after he grew up, refused to be called the son of Pharaoh's daughter, 25 choosing rather to endure persecution together with the people of God than to enjoy the short-lived pleasures of sin. 26 He regarded disgrace suffered for Christ to be greater wealth than the treasures of Egypt, for he fixed his attention on the reward. 27 By faith he left Egypt, not fearing the king's anger, for he persevered, seeing as it were the one who is unseen. 28 By faith he kept the Passover and the sprinkling of blood, so that the destroyer of the firstborn did not touch them.

Translation Notes and Comments

11:23 ***By faith Moses, when he was born, was hid three months of his parents / By faith Moses, after he was born, was hidden for three months by his parents:*** The reference here is to Exodus 2:1–3. It is of note that though

Moses is the subject of the sentence, the faith referred to is that of his parents, Jochebed and Amram. They defied Pharaoh's order demanding the death of all Hebrew males born in Egypt.

because they saw he was a proper child / because they saw that the child was handsome: The adjective ἀστεῖος (*asteios*), "handsome," is derived from the noun τὸ ἄστυ (*to astu*), "the city," and refers to the contrast between the urbane inhabitants of the city and the unrefined country folk. It denotes "good breeding and refinement" as well as "personal grace and charm" and, in a physical sense, being beautiful or handsome.[224] Some sources use it to connote "good character," especially that of one who rejects the wealth and pleasures of the world rather than depart from godly ways.[225] As such it is an excellent description of Moses.

The NIV translates the phrase as Moses' parents "saw that he was no ordinary child." This interpretation pushes the more literal definitions and nuances of the Greek word a bit far. It does, however, catch a view consistent with the theme of Hebrews that faith's power opens the eyes to spiritual reality. Thus, Moses' parents "saw," likely through inspiration, his potential and risked their lives to save him. The martyr Stephen noted that Moses was ἀστεῖος τῳ θεῷ (*asteios tō theō*), "beautiful to God" (Acts 7:20), and thus the Father took care to preserve him. Even so, we have felt it best to translate the term more conservatively in our Rendition as "handsome," a quality that would have attracted Pharaoh's daughter to him.

The JST changes the adjective given as "proper" (ἀστεῖος, *asteios*) in the KJV to "peculiar." In the present context, the word does not carry the nuances of odd, eccentric, or strange but that which is distinctive or out of the ordinary and points to what comes under God's special care.[226] By changing the word, the JST switches the focus from Moses' comeliness to his uniqueness in being favored by God and suggests his parents sensed this and worked to preserve him.

---

224. BDAG, 145.

225. Philo, *Alleg. Interp.* 3.23; *Posterity* 101; *Good Person* 72. See also Koester, *Hebrews,* 501.

226. *Collegiate Dictionary,* s.v. "peculiar." The Hebrew verb סְגֻלָּה (sĕgullāh), translated as "peculiar" in the KJV (see Ex. 19:5; Deut. 14:2; 26:18; Ps. 135:4; and Eccl. 2:8), denotes "a private possession that one personally acquired and carefully preserves" and connotes particularly Jehovah's relation with Israel. *HAL,* 742; BDB, 688; *TWOT,* 1460a. The Greek adjective περιούσιος (*periousios*) found in Titus 2:14 means "beyond the usual" and nuances those people that God has selected to be his own. BDAG, 802–3. The noun περιποίησις (*peripoiēsis*), found in 1 Pet. 2:9, denotes an acquired possession and specifically a people that has become God's own possession. BDAG, 804.

they were not afraid of the king's commandment / they did not fear the king's edict: The Greek noun διάταγμα (*diatagma*) denotes an official ordinance such as a command or edict. According to Exodus 1:22, Pharaoh, fearing that the Hebrews might take over the land, commanded his people to destroy all the Hebrew male babies. The command suggests there would have been severe consequences to any Hebrews who resisted.[227]

The verb φοβέω (*phobeō*), "to fear,"[228] is found here as an aorist passive. That Moses' parents were unafraid does not mean that they were not in an apprehensive state but rather they did not give into that fear.[229] Indeed, it suggests they were willing to resist Pharaoh's will because of what they saw in the child.

11:24 ***By faith Moses, when he was come to years, refused to be called the son of Pharaoh's daughter / By faith Moses, after he grew up, refused to be called the son of Pharaoh's daughter:*** The verb ἀρνέομαι (*arneomai*) means not only to refuse something offered but also to repudiate and disdain it.[230] The word reveals the strength of Moses' rejection. It amounted to a complete renouncement of all that Egypt offered.[231]

The JST adds to the phrase "was come to years" the words "of discretion." In doing so, it shows that Moses made his decision when he reached an age where he had the ability to make responsible decisions. As such it suggests an age over seven, since one can discern right from wrong at the age of eight.[232] The story of Moses, however, suggests he was considerably older since he did not leave Egypt until he was forty.

11:25 ***choosing rather to suffer affliction with the people of God / choosing rather to endure persecution together with the people of God:*** The verb αἱρέω (*haireō*), "to choose," is found here as an aorist middle participle. The tense and the voice are important because they allow the author to emphasize the definitive nature of Moses' act. The middle voice stresses the prophet's personal involvement in the choice.[233]

---

227. The verb צִוָּה (*ṣiwwāh*) means "to command, instruct, order." *HAL*, 1011.

228. BDAG, 1060–61.

229. Lane, *Hebrews 9–13*, 370; Cockerill, *Epistle to the Hebrews*, 567; McConkie, *Doctrinal New Testament Commentary*, 3:211–12.

230. Louw-Nida, §§30.52; 33.277; 34.48; BDAG, 132–33.

231. Ellingworth, *Epistle to the Hebrews*, 611.

232. See C. Terry Warner, "Accountability," in Ludlow, *Encyclopedia of Mormonism*, 1:13. Extrapolating from Moro. 8:10; and D&C 29:47; 68:25, accountability begins at the age of eight.

233. Lane, *Hebrews 9–13*, 370; McConkie, *Doctrinal New Testament Commentary*, 3:212.

Moses walked away from wealth and ease into a condition the author describes with verb συγκακουχέομαι (*synkakoucheomai*). The word means "to suffer" or "be mistreated" together with others and carries the nuance of enduring persecution.

The phrase τῷ λαῷ τοῦ θεοῦ (*tō laō tou theou*), "the people of God," is important here because it unites the author's readers with the faithful of the former generations and suggests not only a oneness between them but also a bonding through faith.[234]

than to enjoy the pleasures of sin for a season / than to enjoy the short-lived pleasures of sin: The phrase πρόσκαιρον ἔχειν ἁμαρτίας ἀπόλαυσιν (*proskairon echein hamartias apolausin*) translates literally as "to have the temporary enjoyment of sin." The adjective πρόσκαιρος (*proskairos*) denotes something "lasting only for a time," thus "temporary, transitory."[235] As the Book of Mormon makes clear, "wickedness never was [that is, results in] happiness" (Alma 41:10).

The noun ἀπόλαυσις (*apolausis*) means "enjoyment, pleasure."[236] Given the context here, "profit" or "advantage" would also work.[237] Moses was in a position to take full advantage of all the benefits that Hebrew slavery brought the Egyptians, but he would not enter into such sin.

11:26 *Esteeming the reproach of Christ greater riches than the treasures in Egypt / He regarded disgrace suffered for Christ to be greater wealth than the treasures of Egypt:* The verb ἡγέομαι (*hēgeomai*) denotes careful and thoughtful consideration of a matter, thus to regard something carefully. Here the author uses it to show that Moses' decision to reject Egypt was not done as a whim but after careful consideration.

The noun ὀνειδισμός (*oneidismos*) denotes the act of speaking unjustified and disparaging words of a person, often with the intent of bringing disgrace upon them.[238] The phrase τὸν ὀνειδισμὸν τοῦ Χριστοῦ (*ton oneidismon tou Christou*), "the disparaging of Christ," can be taken two ways. It

---

234. Attridge, *Epistle to the Hebrews,* 340 n. 34; Ellingworth, *Epistle to the Hebrews,* 612. Israel was the chosen race to be Jehovah's own. McConkie, *Doctrinal New Testament Commentary,* 3:212.

235. BDAG, 880–81.

236. BDAG, 115.

237. LSJ, 205; Franco Montanari, *The Brill Dictionary of Ancient Greek,* ed. Madeline Goh and Chad Schroeder (Leiden, Neth.: Brill, 2015), s.v. "ἀπόλαυσις"; Johnson, *Hebrews,* 300.

238. Louw-Nida, §33.389; BDAG, 710. Such is often the case with the people of Christ. The word suggests "the scorn and contempt in which the saints are always held by worldly people." McConkie, *Doctrinal New Testament Commentary,* 3:212.

could refer to the abuse the Savior himself suffered in behalf of his people, or it could refer to the abuse one receives by standing for the cause of Christ.[239] Given the context, we felt the latter was the stronger nuance, and we follow that in our Rendition.

for he had respect unto the recompence of the reward / for he fixed his attention on the reward: The verb ἀποβλέπω (*apoblepō*), found here in the imperfect tense, means to "look at" or "pay attention to" and suggests the spiritual vision that propelled Moses to act as he did.[240] The tense is important because it shows that Moses had his eye fixed continually on the reward. He seems to have been ever conscious of the promises of God and worked to see them fulfilled.

The noun μισθαποδοσία (*misthapodosia*) denotes a "reward" or "recompense" and, in this case, refers to the eternal, not a temporal, reward God promises the righteous.[241]

11:27 ***By faith he forsook Egypt, not fearing the wrath of the king / By faith he left Egypt, not fearing the king's anger:*** At this point, the author looks ahead to Moses' return to Egypt from Midian and his leading the children of Israel out of that land.[242] The verb καταλείπω (*kataleipō*) means "to leave behind." It carries the implication of finality and therefore the nuance of abandonment.[243] Moses left with no thought of ever returning.[244]

The phrase μὴ φοβηθεὶς (*mē phobeithēs*), "not fearing," is important because it suggests the utter fearlessness felt by Moses toward the most powerful individual in much of the Near East at the time. It echoes the faith of Moses' parents, who also did not fear the anger of Pharaoh.[245]

for he endured, as seeing him who is invisible / for he persevered, seeing as it were the one who is unseen: This is a key phrase in the author's argument, and the verb καρτερέω (*kartereō*) is very important because it means "to continue without wavering," thus "to hold steadfast" and "to

---

239. Lane, *Hebrews 9–13,* 368 note k; Bruce, *Epistle to the Hebrews,* 311–12; compare Vanhoye, *Letter to the Hebrews,* 188–89.

240. BDAG, 107.

241. Vanhoye, *Letter to the Hebrews,* 189; Johnson, *Hebrews,* 301.

242. Ex. 2:13–15 tells of Moses' flight out of Egypt caused by his fear of Pharaoh's punishment for killing an Egyptian. Such fear he did not exhibit forty years later when he returned to demand the freedom of the Hebrew slaves. See O'Brien, *Letter to the Hebrews,* 433–34.

243. BDAG, 520–21, but taking the aorist with culminative force.

244. His attitude stands in marked contrast to that of many of the Hebrews, who continually desired to go back to Egypt. For examples, see Ex. 14:12; 16:3; 17:3.

245. Johnson, *Hebrews,* 302.

persevere."[246] The KJV translation as "endure," denoting resistance to destructive forces or agents over a period longer than expected, does not catch the correct nuance. The force of the Greek is more of a refusal to be discouraged coupled with a dogged determination in pursuit of a goal when met with opposition. Thus, "persevere" works best.[247]

The subordinating conjunction ὡς (*ōs*), translated as "as it were," qualifies the circumstances referred to and shows that it takes a special condition, namely faith, to see he who is otherwise unseen. By the time Moses went back to Egypt, he had already encountered Jehovah on several occasions, even seeing him "face to face,"[248] and through his faith he never lost sight of the divine.

The verb ὁράω (*horaō*), "to see," is found here as a present participle, the tense indicating the perennial habit of the prophet of "seeing" the Lord and thereby being able to persevere in all that God demanded of him.[249]

The adjective ἀόρατος (*aoratos*) denotes the property of not being seen.[250] The Greek phrase has no object, so "one" is supplied in both the KJV and Rendition. Since the adjective's gender is masculine, the reference is to God.[251] Although God is invisible to most mortals, Moses "saw" him initially through the eye of faith, which enabled Moses to see God "face to face." These encounters fortified Moses to persevere in the trials he had to meet, including facing Pharaoh.

11:28 *Through faith he kept the passover / By faith he kept the Passover:* The reference here is to the events recorded in Exodus 12–13. Though the noun πάσχα (*pascha*), "Passover,"[252] usually refers to the formal celebration held annually among the Jewish people, here it refers to Moses preparing the people for the coming of the destroying angel so they would not be touched by the imminent plague.

Nonetheless, in his preparation, Moses established the ordinance and process of celebration that Israel would practice in the promised land. The

---

246. BDAG, 510; Louw-Nida, §25.178.

247. *Webster's New Dictionary of Synonyms,* s.v. "continue"; "persevere." The time frame for Moses' perseverance is vague. It could refer to his time in Egypt or in Sinai. However, since the author's focus is on a specific kind of faith rather than a specific event, precision is unnecessary. Johnson, *Hebrews,* 302.

248. Over the course of his life, Moses encountered Jehovah a number of times. See Ex. 3:4; 19:20; 24:9–11; 33:11; 34:27–35; Num. 12:4–10; Deut. 34:10; and Moses 1.

249. Lane, *Hebrews 9–13,* 376; Cockerill, *Epistle to the Hebrews,* 577.

250. BDAG, 94–95.

251. Vanhoye, *Letter to the Hebrews,* 189.

252. BDAG, 784–85; McConkie, *Doctrinal New Testament Commentary,* 3:213.

author indicates this by using the perfect tense of the verb ποιέω (*poieō*), "to do, make," showing that what Moses did was to be permanent. Thus, the verb carries the nuance of establishing a procedure that was to be followed ever after. Noteworthy is Jehovah's revealing the whole of the celebration even before the Israelites left Egypt (see Ex. 12),[253] suggesting the celebration's importance right from the beginning.

and the sprinkling of blood: The reference here is to Exodus 12:21–24, where Moses tells the people, using hyssop as an aspergillum, to sprinkle the blood of the lamb they will use for Passover on the lintel and frames of their doors so the destroying angel will pass over them.

lest he that destroyed the firstborn should touch them / so that the destroyer of the firstborn did not touch them: The noun ὀλοθρεύω (*olothreuō*) means "to destroy" and carries the nuance of utter or full ruin.[254] Here it is a present active participle in form with a definite article, ὁ ὀλοθρεύων (*ho olothreuōn*), that makes it substantive and therefore translated as "the destroyer" in our Rendition.

The verb θιγγάνω (*thinganō*) means "to touch."[255] Its use by the author is instructive in revealing how he saw the event. In LXX Exodus 12:12, the text notes that the destroyer will not "strike" (πατάσσω, *patassō*) the Hebrews. Here, the angel will not even "touch" (θίγῃ, *thigē*) them.[256]

Analysis and Summary

These verses continue the historical progression moving from Abel through Abraham and his descendants to arrive at Moses. This prophet's section is, along with Abraham's, one of the longest and most important parts of Hebrews 11. With Moses, the author moves chronologically from the book of Genesis to Exodus.

This section contains themes the author has already developed: faith as the means of seeing what is not naturally visible (11:27); Jehovah as the giver of rewards (11:26); and the escape from mortal death or near death (11:23, 28). The material in this section is, however, distinctive in showing "the necessity for faith to make hard choices for God in the face of danger

---

253. Ellingworth, *Epistle to the Hebrews*, 617.

254. BDAG, 703.

255. BDAG, 456.

256. It is possible to take "firstborn" as the object of the participle "destroyer" and thus to cast the sentence as saying that the destroying angel would "not touch their firstborn." To do so, however, would mean that the author put "firstborn" directly after "the one destroying" for emphasis, and this hardly seems likely. See Cockerill, *Epistle to the Hebrews*, 580 n. 63.

(although that certainly was the case for Abraham as well!), human wrath, and dishonor (11:23, 25–26, 27, 31). Faith demands fearing God rather than human rulers (11:23, 27)."[257]

Hebrews 11:23 further emphasizes the faith the author wants to teach about. In discussing Moses, the author notes that "by faith Moses, when he was born, was hid three months of his parents." The way the KJV reads, it appears that Moses was exercising faith "when he was born." The Greek text makes it clear, however, that it was his parents who were exercising faith and gives the reason why: they could "see" he was "handsome" (ἀστεῖος, *asteios*).[258] The word connotes a person of class and good breeding as well as one who has good features and charm. But under the word lies the suggestion that his parents "saw" his divine potential.[259] Indeed, they seemed to have sensed in him one who could resist all that Egypt offered in order to follow God (compare 11:24–26).

Focusing on Moses, the author notes that by faith, Moses gave up the riches of Egypt with its accompanying sinful lifestyle (11:24–26). Note the author equates Egyptian rule with sin, likely because it meant the persecution of God's people. This verse affirms that the faith that allowed Moses' parents to "see" his potential proved true. Like them he could choose how to act in the present—here, giving up a life of ease—because he possessed the vision that faith gives.[260]

The author does not mention the singular act through which Moses forcefully separated himself from all things Egyptian. It was by killing an Egyptian in defense of two Hebrews who were being threatened by this taskmaster (Ex. 2:11–12). The book of Exodus and the Epistle to the Hebrews come together on this matter by noting that the event took place "when [Moses] was grown" (μέγας γενόμενος, *megas genomenos*).[261] Moses' action made reconciliation between himself and Pharaoh impossible. It also shows the disdain in which Moses held the Egyptian taskmasters.

At some point as Moses grew to maturity, through faith he came to "see" and desire what Jehovah promised. Motivated by this vision, he not only rejected Egypt and all it offered but viewed it as sin. Further, he willingly suffered with his people for the cause he knew was right (11:26). The

---

257. Johnson, *Hebrews,* 297–98.

258. It is interesting that Hebrews should have "parents" here. According to the account in Exodus, it was primarily the work of Moses' mother, Jochebed, and sister, Miriam.

259. BDAG, 145; Cockerill, *Epistle to the Hebrews,* 566; Lane, *Hebrews 9–13,* 370.

260. Cockerill, *Epistle to the Hebrews,* 568.

261. Lane, *Hebrews 9–13,* 370–71.

author's intent comes out clearly here, showing that Moses, through the vision faith brings, understood that by suffering he identified with the Messiah who was to come. The author's readers would have understood this was Jesus. Through Moses' example, the author encourages them to imitate both Moses and the Savior. They too had to endure in faithful obedience the present distress for the cause of Jesus.[262]

Being able to continually "see" Jehovah, as it were, gave Moses the incentive not only to face Pharaoh but also to do so without fear. Moses knew that the earthly ruler's power was no match for the invisible God (11:27). Moses had indeed experienced that power sometime before when he was "caught up into an exceedingly high mountain" and there "saw God face to face, and he talked with him, and the glory of God was upon Moses; therefore Moses could endure his presence" (Moses 1:1–2). At that time, the Lord revealed to him much of the history of the earth along with a glimpse of God's creative power. When the vision was over, Moses concluded, "Man is nothing" (Moses 1:10), and that included Pharaoh.

With the eye of faith, Moses commanded the Israelites to sprinkle blood on the lintels and posts of their doors. In doing so, he assured the Hebrews the destroying angel would pass over them, not taking their first born (11:28). Of all the signs of Jehovah's power executed by Moses and Aaron, this final one was the greatest in two respects. First, it did what none of the other signs did: it humbled the Egyptian Pharaoh to the point of letting Israel go. Second, and more importantly, it displayed Jehovah's power to save his people through their faith.[263]

There was yet one more even greater sign that Jehovah would enact: splitting the Red Sea, allowing Israel to cross on dry ground (11:29). Both of these acts highlight the author's point that faith is the ability to "see" what is coming and to appropriately respond to the will of God. When Moses commanded the Israelites to mark their homes, he did so because, through faith, he could "see" what was about to happen. When he brought them to the shores of the Red Sea, it was because he, through faith, could "see" what needed to be done. Giving insight to this moment of history, D&C 8:2–3 states, "Yea, behold, I will tell you in your mind and in your heart, by the Holy Ghost, which shall come upon you and which shall dwell in your heart. Now, behold, this is the spirit of revelation; behold, this is the spirit by which Moses brought the children of Israel through the Red

262. Cockerill, *Epistle to the Hebrews,* 572–73 and n. 35.
263. Ellingworth, *Epistle to the Hebrews,* 618.

Sea on dry ground." It is responding to the Holy Ghost's enlightening the mind and heart that constitutes revelation—"seeing," as it were, through God's eyes and knowing what to do.

Note the author, as in a number of incidences in this chapter, does not draw any Christological inferences from the examples he gives. This omission serves his purpose well because he does not seem to want to take the readers' focus off the power of personal faith.

The author shows that because of Moses' faith, Israel received reward after reward.[264] Earlier in the Epistle, the author shows that Jesus is superior to Moses (3:1–6). In this section, Jesus' superiority is tacitly heightened by emphasizing Moses' own great faith.

Through Moses' willingness to give up all the wealth of Egypt, the author highlights some aspects of faith that he has emphasized before. Here it is that faith allows one to "see" a better world than the ordinary one we inhabit. The author is clear that Moses esteemed "the reproach of Christ greater riches than the treasures in Egypt" (11:26).

Verses 26–28 are significant for a number of reasons.[265] First, they show that for the author, faith was anchored in Jesus Christ, even by those who lived under the previous covenant.[266] This is an important consideration for Latter-day Saints, especially with the strong statements in the Book of Mormon that all the prophets knew of Jesus Christ, because he was the only means of salvation (see Jacob 4:4–5).

Second, these verses continue the theme that faith involves a broader perspective than simply this world, for a trusting relationship with God does create a hope for a better world. Within Hebrews' interpretative world, Moses gave up an easy existence to live according to his faith for a higher reward that only the invisible God could give.

---

264. The author does not mention the forty-year journey that tried Moses to the core. The omission allows the author to focus not on the faithlessness of Israel, which he has already done (3:7–16), but on the faith of Moses and its result. Vanhoye, *Letter to the Hebrews,* 187.

265. Much of the material in this section of the analysis is taken from an unpublished paper by Nathaniel Pribil, in possession of the authors.

266. This relates to A of F 4, which indicates the first principle of the gospel is "faith in the Lord Jesus Christ." It should also, perhaps, be noted that the language "first principles" that Joseph Smith used in the Articles of Faith derives in part from this Epistle, especially 5:12 and 6:1–3. See in particular the JST on 6:1, and Joseph Smith's remarks on his difficulties with 6:1 in "Discourse, 15 October 1843, as Reported by Willard Richards," 130, Joseph Smith Papers, https://www.josephsmithpapers.org/paper-summary/discourse-15-october-1843-as-reported-by-willard-richards/3, and the Translation Notes and Analysis for these verses.

Third, they reiterate a point first made in the example of Enoch (11:5) that faithful trust in God yields great blessings. The reason that blessings flow through faith is that it motivates people to do as God requests. As noted above, the author states that Moses "fixed his attention on the reward" (NR 11:26). In other words, one of the reasons why Moses had the strength and the willingness to forsake Egypt and to endure the hardships that were placed upon him was because of his explicit faith that God would give blessings far greater than Egypt ever could.

Finally, the context makes an explicit distinction between the Israelites (simply called "they" by the author), who succeeded in crossing the Red Sea, and the Egyptians, who did not. Admittedly, the reason for the Egyptians' failure is not explicitly stated, but it is apparent that, unlike the Israelites, the Egyptians had no faith. Through this comparison, the author makes it very clear that success is tied to faithfulness. This emphasis is, in some ways, not surprising, since the Exodus, and especially the salvation of Israel at the Red Sea, was the primary salvific event in the history of ancient Israel, as witnessed by the numerous references to it in both the Old and New Testament. Early in his Epistle, the author quoted from Psalm 95, which alludes to and connects his audience to the Exodus and the "rest of the Lord" (4:1–16).

But with all the elements the author highlights, what is conspicuously absent is a mention of Moses receiving the law. In the biblical account, this was the primary activity that Moses accomplished "by faith." Its absence is especially noticeable in light of the Epistle's emphasis on law. It is likely, however, because the emphasis in Hebrews 11 is on the personal activities and actions that are derived from faith in God that the author wants the focus to remain here rather than on God's response to that faith.

Through the example of Moses, the author is able to focus on the reality of the "unseen" power that attends and sustains the righteous and enables them to do God's will despite threat or opposition. That is not to say the author has lost sight of his theme of the future fulfillment of God's promises. He has not, but his focus is different here—it allows him to show how faith can assist his readers in their present difficult circumstances. Using these examples from Moses' life, the author strives to stimulate and encourage his audience to continue living with faith in God in face of persecution with its accompanying shame and rejection.[267]

---

267. Cockerill, *Epistle to the Hebrews,* 564–65, 576–77. Koester, *Hebrews,* 507, entitles this section of his essay "Faith in the Face of Adversaries."

The author constructed this section to emphasize the above point.[268] With great care and excellent execution, the author parallels four examples of faith as displayed by Abraham (11:8–12, 17–19) with four as displayed by Moses (11:23–29). In each case, the climax of faith appears in the fourth example: the binding of Isaac and the preserving of Israel from the destroying angel. The examples the author uses from Moses are, however, not mere repetitions. With Moses, faith enters a new era in which God's promises to Abraham begin to find their earthly fulfillment. The "sight" engendered by Abraham's faith begins to be literally fulfilled with the Exodus. The author has been careful, however, to keep his readers' vision focused not on earthly but in heavenly horizons, where the ultimate fulfillment of God's promises will be realized not in possessing the promised land but through an inheritance in the eternal city. Even so, with Moses, Israel experienced God's power as never before. "Thus, without losing sight of faith's focus on the future ultimate fulfillment of God's promise [11:1a], these verses emphasize the reality of his 'unseen' power to sustain the faithful in the present [11:1b]."[269] The author's readers would not have missed the message and promise therein that by emulating their progenitors' faithful endurance they too would find God's power sustaining them.

The chiastic structure used by the author in this section allowed him to subtly but forcefully point to the object of the faith of both Moses and Abraham, namely, the God who raises the dead.

A. 11:8
  B. 11:9–10 Faith That Awaits the Promises of God.
    C. 11:11–12
      D. 11:13–16
        E. 11:17–19 Faith in a God "Who Raises the Dead."
      D1. 11:20–22
    C1. 11:23
  B1. 11:24–26 Faith That Endures through the Power of God.
A1. 11:27[270]

This structure shows that the faith of Abraham, and more subtly that of Moses, was on God's power over death. The author desires his readers

---

268. The material in this section is taken from Garth Lee Cockerill, "The Better Resurrection (Heb. 11:35): A Key to the Structure and Rhetorical Purpose of Hebrews 11," *Tyndale Bulletin* 51, no. 2 (2000): 215–34; and Cockerill, *Epistle to the Hebrews*, 564–66, 578–80.

269. Cockerill, *Epistle to the Hebrews*, 564–65.

270. Cockerill, *Epistle to the Hebrews*, 578.

to emulate that kind of faith. The tacit message is if their forebears could exhibit such faith under tremendous opposition, so could they. In the face of such faith, God would sustain them in the present and more—he would bring them alive into his eternal city.

The Faith of Other Israelite Heroes (11:29–40)

Greek Text

29 Πίστει διέβησαν τὴν Ἐρυθρὰν Θάλασσαν ὡς διὰ ξηρᾶς γῆς, ἧς πεῖραν λαβόντες οἱ Αἰγύπτιοι κατεπόθησαν. 30 πίστει τὰ τείχη Ἰεριχὼ ἔπεσαν κυκλωθέντα ἐπὶ ἑπτὰ ἡμέρας. 31 πίστει Ῥαὰβ ἡ πόρνη οὐ συναπώλετο τοῖς ἀπειθήσασιν, δεξαμένη τοὺς κατασκόπους μετ᾽ εἰρήνης. 32 Καὶ τί ἔτι λέγω; ἐπιλείψει με γὰρ διηγούμενον ὁ χρόνος περὶ Γεδεών, Βαράκ, Σαμψών, Ἰεφθάε, Δαυίδ τε καὶ Σαμουὴλ καὶ τῶν προφητῶν, 33 οἳ διὰ πίστεως κατηγωνίσαντο βασιλείας, εἰργάσαντο δικαιοσύνην, ἐπέτυχον ἐπαγγελιῶν, ἔφραξαν στόματα λεόντων, 34 ἔσβεσαν δύναμιν πυρός, ἔφυγον στόματα μαχαίρης, ἐδυναμώθησαν ἀπὸ ἀσθενείας, ἐγενήθησαν ἰσχυροὶ ἐν πολέμῳ, παρεμβολὰς ἔκλιναν ἀλλοτρίων· 35 ἔλαβον γυναῖκες ἐξ ἀναστάσεως τοὺς νεκροὺς αὐτῶν· ἄλλοι δὲ ἐτυμπανίσθησαν, οὐ προσδεξάμενοι τὴν ἀπολύτρωσιν, ἵνα κρείττονος ἀναστάσεως τύχωσιν· 36 ἕτεροι δὲ ἐμπαιγμῶν καὶ μαστίγων πεῖραν ἔλαβον, ἔτι δὲ δεσμῶν καὶ φυλακῆς· 37 ἐλιθάσθησαν, ἐπρίσθησαν, ἐν φόνῳ μαχαίρης ἀπέθανον, περιῆλθον ἐν μηλωταῖς, ἐν αἰγείοις δέρμασιν, ὑστερούμενοι, θλιβόμενοι, κακουχούμενοι, 38 ὧν οὐκ ἦν ἄξιος ὁ κόσμος ἐπὶ ἐρημίαις πλανώμενοι καὶ ὄρεσι καὶ σπηλαίοις καὶ ταῖς ὀπαῖς τῆς γῆς· 39 καὶ πάντες μαρτυρηθέντες διὰ τῆς πίστεως οὐκ ἐκομίσαντο τὴν ἐπαγγελίαν, 40 τοῦ θεοῦ περὶ ἡμῶν κρεῖττόν τι προβλεψαμένου, ἵνα μὴ χωρὶς ἡμῶν τελειωθῶσιν. [SBLGNT]

King James Version

29 By faith they passed through the Red sea as by dry land: which the Egyptians assaying to do were drowned. 30 By faith the walls of Jericho fell down, after they were compassed about seven days. 31 By faith the harlot Rahab perished not with them that believed not, when she had received the spies with peace. 32 And what shall I more say? for the time would fail me to tell of Gedeon,

New Rendition

29 By faith they crossed the Red Sea as if on dry land, but when the Egyptians attempted to cross it, they were drowned. 30 By faith the walls of Jericho fell after the Israelites had marched around them for seven days. 31 By faith Rahab, the prostitute, was not destroyed with those who were disobedient, because she had welcomed the spies in peace.

and of Barak, and of Samson, and of Jephthae; of David also, and Samuel, and of the prophets: 33 Who through faith subdued kingdoms, wrought righteousness, obtained promises, stopped the mouths of lions, 34 Quenched the violence of fire, escaped the edge of the sword, out of weakness were made strong, waxed valiant in fight, turned to flight the armies of the aliens. 35 Women received their dead raised to life again: and others were tortured, not accepting deliverance; that they might obtain a better resurrection: 36 And others had trial of cruel mockings and scourgings, yea, moreover of bonds and imprisonment: 37 They were stoned, they were sawn asunder, were tempted, were slain with the sword: they wandered about in sheepskins and goatskins; being destitute, afflicted, tormented; 38 (Of whom the world was not worthy:) they wandered in deserts, and in mountains, and in dens and caves of the earth. 39 And these all, having obtained a good report through faith, received not the promise: 40 God having provided some better thing for us, that they without us should not be made perfect.

32 And what more might I say? For there would not be enough time for me to go into detail about Gideon, Barak, Samson, Jephthah, David, Samuel, and the other prophets, 33 who by faith conquered kingdoms, acted righteously, obtained promises, shut the mouths of lions, 34 quenched the power of fire, escaped the edge of the sword, were strengthened in weakness, were made mighty in battle, caused enemy armies to retreat. 35 Women received their dead raised again to life.

But others were tortured having refused deliverance so that they might attain a better resurrection. 36 Still others experienced derision, floggings, and even chains and imprisonment. 37 They were stoned, sawn in two, murdered by the sword. They wandered about wearing sheepskins and goatskins, impoverished, oppressed, maltreated—38 the world was not worthy of them—wandering in deserts and mountains and caves and holes in the ground.

39 And although they were all commended by God because of their faith, they did not obtain what was promised, 40 since God had provided something better with regard to us, so that without us they could not be made perfect.

Translation Notes and Comments

11:29 ***By faith they passed through the Red sea as by dry land / By faith they crossed the Red Sea as if on dry land:*** The reference here is to Exodus 14. This phrase in the Greek text has no stated subject. It is implied by the plural form of the verb διαβαίνω (*diabainō*), which means "to cross over,"[271] and by inference "they" refers to the Israelites.

---

271. BDAG, 226.

The faith the author refers to here largely belongs to Moses rather than corporate Israel, which faith both Hebrews and Exodus show they greatly lacked. Even so, these people did follow him into the sea, thus showing a modicum of faith.[272]

which the Egyptians assaying to do were drowned / but when the Egyptians attempted to cross it, they were drowned: The noun πεῖρα (*peira*) denotes an attempt at something,[273] in this case the crossing of the Red Sea by the Egyptian army. The phrase ἧς πεῖραν λαβόντες (*hēs peiran labontes*) is idiomatic in Greek, and its literal translation is quite awkward: "of which attempt taking." In our Rendition, we have translated it as "but when the Egyptians attempted to cross it" to better express the sense in English.

The verb καταπίνω (*katapinō*), here in the passive voice, means "to be completely swallowed up." The sense of the prefix is intensive,[274] hence the Egyptians did not just drown, they were destroyed completely by means of drowning. The aorist tense that the author uses here suggests the once-and-for-all finality of the act. Because the Egyptians' attempt was faithless, unlike that of the Hebrews, it proved utterly fatal.[275]

11:30 ***By faith the walls of Jericho fell down / By faith the walls of Jericho fell:*** The reference here is to Joshua 6. Though in 11:29 the faith the author refers to is primarily that of Moses, here it appears to be that of Israel in general. The whole congregation obeyed strictly the Lord's commands. Their obedience expressed a kind of faith that their parents never developed. It led to Jericho's walls falling by divine action, thus negating any need for a long siege on Israel's part.

after they were compassed about seven days / after the Israelites had marched around them for seven days: The verb κυκλόω (*kykloō*) means to move or march around an object.[276] We have translated the passive participial phrase κυκλωθέντα ἐπὶ ἑπτὰ ἡμέρας (*kyklōthenta epi hepta hēmeras*), literally "[the walls] having been encircled for seven days," as "after the Israelites had marched around them for seven days." The noun "Israelites" is not present in the text, but we added it for clarity.

11:31 ***By faith the harlot Rahab perished not with them that believed not, when she had received the spies with peace / By faith Rahab, the prostitute,***

---

272. Attridge, *Epistle to the Hebrews,* 344.

273. BDAG, 729.

274. BDAG, 524; Smyth, *Greek Grammar,* §1690.3.

275. Attridge, *Epistle to the Hebrews,* 344.

276. BDAG, 574.

was not destroyed with those who were disobedient, because she had welcomed the spies in peace: The reference here is to Joshua 2:1–21; 6:21–23. The noun πόρνη (*pornē*) refers to a prostitute.[277] Rahab expressed her faith by protecting the Israelite spies. She believed the reports she had heard about Israel crossing the Red Sea and their taking of the Ammonite lands. She acted on that belief to her salvation.

The verb ἀπειθέω (*apeitheō*), "disobey, be disobedient," in the New Testament always refers to disobedience to God.[278]

11:32 ***And what shall I more say? / And what more might I say?:*** The question is double edged. First, it implies that the evidence the author has already provided is enough to establish his case. Second, it acts to introduce the overwhelming evidence the rest of the Old Testament provides.[279]

for the time would fail me to tell / For there would not be enough time for me to go into detail: The verb διηγέομαι (*diēgomai*), "to relate, detail," carries the nuance of giving a thorough account of an event.[280] The author's point is that the Old Testament is simply too full of examples for such an attempt.

Gideon: See Judges 6–8.

Barak: See Judges 4–5.

Samson: See Judges 13–16.

Jephthae: See Judges 11–12.

David: See 1 Samuel 17–30.

Samuel: See 1 Samuel 2, 8–16.

the prophets / other prophets: The reference here is to both the major and minor prophets whose writings are found in the Old Testament.

11:33 ***Who through faith subdued kingdoms / who by faith conquered kingdoms:*** The reference, among others, is to the conquests of the Israelites from Joshua through David.

wrought righteousness / acted righteously: This phrase can be taken in more than one way. The verb ἐργάζομαι (*ergazomai*) means "do, accomplish, carryout,"[281] while the noun δικαιοσύνη (*dikaiosynē*) denotes not only "justice" and "fairness" but also "upright behavior" and "righteousness."[282]

277. BDAG, 854.
278. BDAG, 99; LSJ, 181.
279. Cockerill, *Epistle to the Hebrews,* 587.
280. BDAG, 254; Louw-Nida, §33.201.
281. BDAG, 389.
282. BDAG, 247–48.

Thus εἰργάσαντο δικαιοσύνην (*eirgasanto dikaiosynēn*), in a more restricted sense, could refer to rulers and judges who "administered justice." In a broader sense, it could point to the people who "accomplished righteousness." We have assumed this latter sense is meant here and have translated it as "lived righteously."

obtained promises: From the period of the judges to those of the kings, Jehovah continually made provisional promises to Israel's leaders and others,[283] but the force of the verb ἐπιτυγχάνω (*epityngchanō*), "to obtain," focuses on those who actually realized them.[284]

stopped the mouths of lions / shut the mouths of lions: See Daniel 6.

11:34 ***Quenched the violence of fire / quenched the power of fire:*** See Daniel 3:1–30.[285]

escaped the edge of the sword: This reference could be to a number of individuals, but note David in 1 Samuel 17:45–47; Elijah in 1 Kings 19:1–3; Elisha in 2 Kings 6:26–32; and Jeremiah in Jeremiah 26:7–24.

out of weakness were made strong / were strengthened in weakness: With the many examples the Old Testament provides, the author could have had any number of people in mind.

waxed valiant in fight, turned to flight the armies of the aliens / were made mighty in battle, caused enemy armies to retreat: Again, the Old Testament provides many examples, so it is impossible to know if the author has specific individuals in mind or is taking them all together.

11:35 ***Women received their dead raised to life again / Women received their dead raised again to life:*** See the example of the widow of Zarephath in 1 Kings 17:17–24 and the Shunammite mother in 2 Kings 4:18–37.

and others were tortured, not accepting deliverance / But others were tortured having refused deliverance: The phrase ἄλλοι δέ (*alloi de*), "but others," is important here because it signals that the author is now changing his focus. He is still looking at those who showed great faith, but this time it is toward those who chose to accept what life handed out without asking God to intervene. His first example is extreme, looking as it does to martyrdom.

The verb τυμπανίζω (*typanizō*) means literally "to beat a drum" but had the derived sense of beating or torturing someone, perhaps with a τύμπανον (*tympanon*), "some instrument of torture or execution."[286] That

283. Koester, *Hebrews,* 513; Lane, *Hebrews 9–13,* 386.

284. BDAG, 385.

285. Compare 1 Macc. 2:59–60; and 4 Macc. 16:21–22.

286. BDAG, 1019; LSJ, 1834.

these people were willing to suffer the worst the world had to offer rather than renounce and forsake their religion reveals a faith that truly does look beyond the transitory present to the eternal future.

that they might obtain a better resurrection / so that they might attain a better resurrection: The verb τυγχάνω (*tungchanō*), "to obtain, attain," explains why they were willing to suffer. The word denotes attaining or gaining an objective.[287]

The noun ἀνάστασις (*anastasis*), literally "a rising up," was the common term denoting the resurrection.[288]

The comparative adjective κρείττων (*kreittōn*), "better," denotes not only something that is of higher status but also something that is more advantageous to a person.[289]

The JST changes "a better" to "the first" and in doing so suggests that the idea of a "first resurrection" was known to the people. That Revelation 20:5–6 refers to a "first resurrection" shows that the idea was circulating during the time of the nascent Church. According to that text, "Blessed and holy is he that hath part in the first resurrection: on such the second death hath no power, but they shall be priests of God and of Christ, and shall reign with him a thousand years."[290]

11:36 ***And others had trial of cruel mockings / Still others experienced derision:*** The phrase ἕτεροι δέ (*heteroi de*), "still others," shows that the author is referring to yet another group from all those whom he has mentioned before. Whether saved through their faith or choosing death in hopes of "a better resurrection," this group had in common an exquisite faith.

The noun ἐμπαιγμός (*empaigmos*) denotes derision, the use of scorn and especially ridicule to show contempt of an especially painful kind.[291]

---

287. BDAG, 1019.

288. BDAG, 71–72.

289. BDAG, 566.

290. A fuller development of the idea is found, however, in the writings of the Book of Mormon. See Mosiah 15:21–26; and Alma 40:15–17. The idea is also mentioned in D&C 132:19, 26. Joseph Smith used this verse to make a distinction between translation and resurrection. He stated that the term "a better resurrection" did not refer to translation. The latter means "deliverance from the tortures and sufferings of the body." The Prophet went on to explain that, concerning those who are translated, "their existance will [be] prolong[ed] as to their labors and toils of the ministry." Their work takes place "before they can enter in to so great a rest and glory" referring to "a better resurrection." "Instruction on Priesthood," 7.

291. BDAG, 323; Mickaelis, *TDNT,* 5:364–66.

scourgings / floggings: The noun μάστιξ (*mastix*) refers to a whip, scourge, lash, or switch used for coercion or punishment.[292] Though very painful, this was a short-term punishment and one of the favorites in both the Jewish and Greco-Roman world to discourage deviant behavior. Lashings were a public affair often accompanied by jeering and mocking crowds and designed to bring stigma and shame upon the person (see 1 Kgs. 22:27; and Jer. 20:2, 7; 29:26; 37:15).

bonds and imprisonment / even chains and imprisonment: This punishment could be of short or long duration, but a Roman prison—designed for punishment, not reform—was not a place a person wanted to stay for long.

11:37 ***They were stoned:*** The verb λιθάζω (*lithazō*) means "to stone" someone as a means of capital punishment, often used by the Jews for sins such as adultery, blasphemy, and idolatry. The technical term is lapidation. According to Jewish oral law, the convicted person was thrown from a height of about eighteen feet. Two witnesses then together picked up a bolder and dropped it upon the person. If that did not kill the person, they dropped a second.[293] The unjustified stoning of the prophet Zachariah son of Jehoiada is recorded 2 Chronicles 24:20–22.

they were sawn asunder / sawn in two: Legend has it that Isaiah died by this horrible means.[294]

were tempted / —: The verb ἐπειράσθησαν (*epeirasthēsan*), "they were tempted," is not found in the early papyrus 𝔓[46] (c. AD 175–225). Other early manuscripts include it, but sometimes before and sometimes after ἐπρίσθησαν (*epristhēsan*), "they were sawn in two." These inconsistencies suggest it was likely an early scribal error and thus is not included in our Rendition.[295]

were slain with the sword / murdered by the sword: The verb φόνος (*phonos*) denotes a murder or unjustified killing.[296]

they wandered about in sheepskins and goatskins / They wandered about wearing sheepskins and goatskins: The verb περιέρχομαι (*perierchomai*), "to wander about,"[297] connotes the final state of certain faithful persons who were ostracized from society and deprived of the necessities of life, including shelter and clothing. Banishment of this kind was

---

292. Montanari, *Brill Dictionary of Ancient Greek,* s.v. "μάστιξ."
293. *M. Sanh.* 6.
294. *Mart. Isa.* 5:1–11*; Liv. Pro.* 1:1; compare Sus. 59.
295. Metzger, *Textual Commentary,* 603–4; Ogden and Skinner, *Verse by Verse,* 261.
296. BDAG, 1063.
297. BDAG, 800.

considered a fate worse than death.[298] It is of note, however, that some prophets chose to wear sheep- or goatskins likely to stress their break with worldly society (see 1 Kgs. 19:13, 19; and 2 Kgs. 2:8, 13–14).[299]

being destitute, afflicted, tormented / impoverished, oppressed, maltreated: The verb ὑστερέω (*hystereō*), "to be destitute, poor," denotes a lack of basic needs and suggests more specifically a deficiency of food.[300]

The verb θλίβω (*thlibō*) in the passive means "to be afflicted, oppressed," and carries the idea of being physically crushed and by analogy suffering great physical distress due to pressure brought on by others.[301] For this reason, we translate it as "oppressed" in the Rendition.

The verb κακουχέω (*kakoucheō*) in the passive means to be maltreated or tormented.[302] "Torment" carries the idea of being acutely and repeatedly misused. "Maltreat" implies an evil motive on the part of society that causes the action and is therefore used in our Rendition.

Taken together, all these conditions describe the depth to which society had gone. The phrase shows that these wicked people not only ostracized the faithful but also went far out of their way to abuse them. Good examples would be Elijah and Elisha (see 1 Kgs. 17:2–16; 19:1–19; and 2 Kgs. 1:3–15; 2:23; 4:1–2, 8–12, 38–43; 8:1–2).

11:38 ***Of whom the world was not worthy / the world was not worthy of them:*** Though the author adds this as an aside, it is quite revealing. The noun κόσμος (*kosmos*), "world," often refers to the earth, but here it is the unrighteous.[303]

The adjective ἄξιος (*axios*), "worthy," denotes a state of fitness and deservedness. It carries the sense of comparative value.[304] This world met none of these conditions. In short, nothing in the world had any comparative value matched to the lives and testimonies of these faithful people. These righteous men and women were simply too good for this world.[305]

---

298. Lane, *Hebrews 9–13,* 391–92.

299. See also Koester, *Hebrews,* 515; and Lane, *Hebrews 9–13,* 391.

300. BDAG, 1043–44; Cockerill, *Epistle to the Hebrews,* 595.

301. BDAG, 457; Louw-Nida, §22.21.

302. BDAG, 502.

303. Lane, *Hebrews 9–13,* 392. The word here has the same connotation as that found in JS–M 1:4 where Jesus' disciples spoke of the "end of the world, or the destruction of the wicked, which is the end of the world."

304. Louw-Nida, §65.17.

305. BDAG, 93–94; Foester, *TDNT,* 1:379–80.

they wandered in deserts, and in mountains, and in dens and caves of the earth / wandering in deserts and mountains and caves and holes in the ground: Again, just who the author has in mind cannot be identified, but often the destitute sought shelter in the wilderness (Judg. 6:2). Many areas of Israel are pitted with limestone caves and grottos, and they were not hard to find and hide in. This is what David (1 Sam. 23:14), Elijah (1 Kgs. 17:3), and the Maccabees (1 Macc. 2:28, 31; 2 Macc. 5:27; 10:6) all did. The point is that whomever the author has in mind, the wicked deprived them of shelter and forced them to live in the most primitive of conditions.

11:39 ***And these all, having obtained a good report through faith / And although they were all commended by God because of their faith:*** This phrase forms an *inclusio* with 11:2—the chapter opens and closes with a reference to people being commended because of their faith. As already discussed in the Translation Notes to 11:2 above, this commendation comes from God, and so we have added "by God" in our Rendition.

received not the promise / they did not obtain what was promised: This phrase, though agreeing with the statement the author makes in 11:13, stands in contradiction to the point the author has made in 11:33. In that verse, he clearly states his subjects did obtain the promises. How then can he state here that none of them did? The answer seems to be that 11:33 refers to promises made during the period of Old Testament history, such as occupying the Holy Land and finding protection through obedience, while 11:13 and 39 refer to the broader promises such as eternal life that Jehovah made that could only be realized after mortality. The author has clearly stated in 10:36 and will reassure his readers in 11:40–12:2 that receiving the reward of the promises is yet a matter of confident hope coupled with enduring to the end.[306]

11:40 ***God having provided some better thing for us / since God had provided something better with regard to us:*** The verb πορβλέπω (*problepō*) denotes "seeing beforehand," but in the middle voice, as found here, it means "to make provisions for."[307] The implication is that God foresaw a need and made provisions to meet that need in advance.

That need is defined by the phrase κρεῖττόν τι (*kreitton ti*), "something better." The reason that the Old Testament righteous did not receive their final blessing was they had to wait until the Christian era began. The author

306. Ellingworth, *Epistle to the Hebrews*, 559.

307. BDAG, 866. Louw-Nida, §35.35 notes that the word carries the nuance of providing for the needs of others "with the implication of anticipating such a need."

notes why this is so in the next phrase, but with this phrase, he makes it clear his readers were a part of bringing the blessing to their forebears.

that they without us should not be made perfect / without us they could not be made perfect: The verb τελειόω (*teleioō*) means "to make complete, whole, or perfect."[308] The author has already clarified that "the law made nothing perfect" (NR 7:19) and further "the law . . . can never . . . perfect those who come to worship" (NR 10:1). The faithful of the old covenant are dependent on those of the new to reach this state and realize the ultimate promise.

The JST makes a substantial change to this verse: "God having provided some better things for them through their suffering, for without suffering they could not be made perfect." The change redirects the focus of the verse away from the author's present and looks back at the period of suffering that some of the Old Testament faithful had to endure. Suffering, properly endured, provides humility and dependence on God. It also acts to verify faith. The result is "perfection" as understood in Hebrews. Even the Savior found perfection in this way (2:10). This change would have provided hope and purpose to Joseph Smith and his followers, giving them as it did a good reason for the difficulties and persecution that they did and would face.[309]

Analysis and Summary

As noted above, the author of Hebrews is moving his audience historically, albeit not strictly chronologically, through the Bible. He begins in 11:29–31 with the Exodus and stories from the book of Joshua. The first two examples break with the author's pattern of naming individuals, instead simply looking at the deeds done "by faith." The first act of faith was that of Israel as they followed Moses into the Red Sea (Ex. 14).[310] Though they began the journey by fearing Pharaoh, they ended reverencing Jehovah.[311] The second act of faith was that of Israel before the fortress Jericho, where their faith prompted Jehovah to fell the walls (Josh. 6). The juxtaposition of the examples, though following chronological order, also tacitly suggest that as the new generation of Israelites entered the promised land, their faith had become more Moses-like.

308. BDAG, 996.
309. Compare Ogden and Skinner, *Verse by Verse,* 261.
310. Bruce, *Epistle to the Hebrews,* 316.
311. Lane, *Hebrews 9–13,* 377.

These and the verses that follow emphasize the aspect of faith that expresses itself as confidence in God's real power that, though unseen, will and does manifest itself in the present as the people remain true. In doing so, the author is not depersonalizing the power but stressing the extent of its results. There is a tacit contrasting lesson to be learned here. When the Egyptian army, in a determined faithlessness that despised Jehovah's power, tried to cross the Red Sea, the sea "swallowed [them] up" (καταπίνω, *katapinō*).[312] The lesson anticipates God's final judgment (see 12:25–29) and clearly warns all that those who do not live by faith, but spurn God, will face the judgment of him who is an all-consuming fire (12:29).[313]

The author knows how to craft his argument. Interrupting his long series of examples of those who overcame "by faith," he uses an excellent rhetorical device called *preterition*—first listing a few specific people and then noting he has no further space to present them in any detail. He then, with eloquence, presents an overview first of the faithful's successes and then of their trials.[314]

In 11:30–31, the author focuses on the fall of Jericho, reminding his readers of two associated events. The first is the walls of Jericho fell by faith and not as a consequence of the Israelite siege (11:30). Note the author gives credit for the faith not to Joshua alone, even though he led the people, but to the people as a whole. After all, the walls fell down "after they were compassed about [by the Israelites] seven days," tacitly giving Jehovah the credit but in response to the people's corporate faith.

The second of the two associated events we find in 11:31. Here the author returns to his pattern of using specific individuals as examples. Here he notes the acts of Rahab. According to the text of Joshua 6:17, she was a harlot (זוֹנָה, *zônāh*; πόρνη, *pornē*), but one that was not devoid of faith.[315] The author notes she did not perish "with those who were disobedient." The word translated as "disobedient" (ἀπείθεω, *apetheō*) carries the nuance of defiance in face of persuading evidence.[316] The disobedient in this passage are,

312. BDAG, 524; Ellingworth, *Epistle to the Hebrews,* 620.

313. Cockerill, *Epistle to the Hebrews,* 581–83.

314. Vanhoye, *Letter to the Hebrews,* 190.

315. Some ancient Jewish authorities have tried to sanitize her reputation by stating she was an "innkeeper" and have made her the model of hospitality. For examples, see Josephus, *Ant.* 5.2, 7. Johnson, *Hebrews,* 304, lists the rabbinic traditions surrounding her. These are all unconvincing. The LXX of Joshua 2:1 and 6:25 as well as the MT all designate her as a prostitute.

316. BDAG, 99; LSJ, 90. The noun is an alpha privative of πείθω, the verb meaning "to persuade" or to "to be won over," depending on the voice.

therefore, those who were unwilling to be persuaded of Jehovah's power. Rahab believed and therefore assisted the Israelite spies, likely repenting of her past life as she became one with God's people.

The text in Joshua 2:9–11 reveals the reason and depth of Rahab's faith. When talking to the Israelite spies, she stated, "I know that the Lord hath given you the land, and that your terror is fallen upon us, and that all the inhabitants of the land faint because of you. For we have heard how the Lord dried up the water of the Red sea for you, when ye came out of Egypt; and what ye did unto the two kings of the Amorites, that were on the other side Jordan, Sihon and Og, whom ye utterly destroyed." Her testimony falls into two parts: that of the community in general and that of her own.

The community was well aware Jehovah's power was with Israel, and that knowledge frightened them. As Rahab said, "Your terror is fallen upon us, and . . . all the inhabitants of the land faint because of you" (Josh. 2:9). Even so, they refused to repent. The effort to persuade them to God's side had been going on for some time. According to the Book of Mormon, God made Israel "mighty unto the driving out of the children of the land, yea, unto the scattering them to destruction" because "this people had rejected every word of God." This suggests that some form of missionary work had been going on among them for some time. By rejecting the effort, "they were ripe in iniquity; and the fulness of the wrath of God was upon them; and the Lord did curse the land against them, and bless it unto our fathers; yea, he did curse it against them unto their destruction, and he did bless it unto our fathers unto their obtaining power over it" (1 Ne. 17:32–35).[317]

Rahab, like the community, was well informed, but unlike them she had faith. She believed that "the Lord hath given you the land" because "the Lord your God, he is God in heaven above, and in earth beneath" (Josh. 2:9, 11). She acted on that testimony even before the promise was realized. Again, the author makes his point clear that faith is the ability to see beyond the present horizon.[318]

Rahab is significant in the context of the author's discussion for five reasons: First, with Sarah, she represents the female side of faith. Second, she is not an Israelite but rather a Canaanite (and therefore outside of the Mosaic covenant).[319] This suggests that, for the author, faith is not spe-

317. See also Cockerill, *Epistle to the Hebrews,* 584–85 n. 79.

318. Johnson, *Hebrews,* 297–98.

319. Abel and Enoch were also outside both the Noachian and Mosaic covenants. They, however, did share in that of Adam. Rahab, on the other hand, had no covenantal ties of any kind.

cifically bound to Hebrew descent; what counts is not ethnicity but one's response to God's word. Although this epistle is addressed to a Jewish Christian audience, it was likely an audience with quite a number of Gentile converts; these would have resonated with this example. Third, Rahab's former life shows that faith and its blessings are not contingent on previous merit. When she heard, she believed, accepted God's will, and acted on her belief. In the end, that faith not only saved her but also her whole family (Josh. 2:12–13; 6:25). Fourth, like Moses, she identified with the children of Israel. When she met the spies, she welcomed them with "peace," a salutation used by God's own people[320] and one that showed she was one with them. Finally, she is an excellent example of the aspect of faith the author is highlighting in this section. She "believed both that God's power was real and his promises were certain" and acted accordingly.[321]

The final section begins with 11:32 and runs through verse 40. These verses are different than the previous ones in that they are not introduced by the phrase "through faith." By dropping the phrase, the author is able to quickly and pointedly push his argument by listing person after person who exercised the kind of faith he wants his readers to emulate.

The section begins with a list of the faithful taken largely from the books of Judges and 1 Samuel. These are Gideon (Judg. 6–8), Barak (Judg. 4–5), Samson (Judg. 13–16), Jephthah (Judg. 11–12), David (1 Sam. 17–30), and Samuel (2 Sam. 2, 8–16). The subjects are not mentioned in canonical order. Barak was not a judge but the war leader of the prophetess Deborah, who was the judge. Listing Samuel last acts as the author's bridge to mentioning all the rest of the prophets in general (11:33). The author of Hebrews states why he lumped all the others together: he simply does not have the time to detail the faithfulness of the many individuals found in the Hebrew Bible (11:32).

Beginning with 11:33, he gives nine examples of the products of faith. The first two and the last two describe political successes: these people "conquered kingdoms, acted righteously, . . . were made mighty in battle, caused enemy armies to retreat" (NR 11:33–34). Along the way they "obtained [that is, realized] promises" (NR 11:33). Three refer to those who escaped death: these "shut the mouths of lions, quenched the power of fire, escaped the edge of the sword" (NR 11:34). Then comes the general description of those who "were strengthened in weakness" (NR 11:34). The section ends climactically with a standalone example, this one not of powerful men and marching

320. Bruce, *Epistle to the Hebrews,* 315 n. 213; compare Koester, *Hebrews,* 505–6.
321. Cockerill, *Epistle to the Hebrews,* 584–85.

armies but of humble women whose faith overcame death and brought their children back to life.[322]

Thus, we see the author briefly focuses on a number of remarkable, even miraculous activities these people did because of their faith. He notes they "subdued kingdoms" (likely a reference to the success of Israel's various rulers who subdued the various peoples who fought against them during the period of the judges and kings), "wrought righteousness," and realized God-given promises (NR 11:33). Because of the number of possibilities the author could have had in mind, it is impossible to determine exactly who they might have been. It should be noted, however, that the actions he does enumerate reflect one of the major themes: faithfulness brings the realization of the covenantal promises that come through Jehovah.

The author includes one who "stopped the mouths of lions." This is likely Daniel, whose story of being tossed into the den of lions is told in Daniel 6. In fact, Daniel 6:22 uses language echoed in Hebrews 11:33 when Daniel says that God sent an angel who "shut the lions' mouths." The author next mentions those who "quenched the violence of fire" (11:34). He appears to have Daniel's three friends, Shadrach, Meshach, and Abed-nego, in mind here. Because they would not bow to the king's idol, they were thrown into a great burning furnace. Instead of being burned, they walked "in the midst of the fire, and they [had] no hurt" (Dan. 3:25).

The other acts of faith the author notes briefly seem to refer to other faithful people whose actions are recorded not only in the book of Judges but also in other places as well. These "escaped the edge of the sword, were strengthened in weakness, were made mighty in battle, [and] caused enemy armies to retreat" (11:34).[323]

In 11:35, the author mentions that faith-filled "women received their dead raised to life again." The allusion is likely to the miracles of Elijah and Elisha, who both responded to the faith of women and restored each of their children to life (1 Kgs. 17:17–24; 2 Kgs. 4:18–37).

We must emphasize that the author of Hebrews is realistic enough to know faith does not always result in miracles. In 11:35, he tells of biblical heroes who "were tortured, not accepting deliverance; that they might

322. Vanhoye, *Letter to the Hebrews*, 192.

323. It is a compelling statement about the generality of God's faithfulness that almost everything that the author of Hebrews indicates for these heroes of the Old Testament also applies to those whose lives and ministries are recorded in the Book of Mormon. See discussion below on Moroni's writings in Ether 12.

obtain a better resurrection." The word for torture (τυμπανίζω, *tympanizō*) refers to being beaten to death.[324] The reference could be to the martyrdom of the scribe Eleazar who endured such a death as recorded in 2 Maccabees 6:18–31.

The remainder of the references in chapter 11 note traditions that are not in the Bible as we have it. They do have connections through the Old Testament apocrypha, which is part of the LXX, thus supporting the idea that the author is referring to stories contained there.[325] For example, the note in 11:37 that some were "sawn asunder" may refer to the tradition that the prophet Isaiah was martyred in this way.[326]

The author's aside in 11:38, that the world was not worthy of these people, is full of irony. The worldly he has in view went out of their way to judge, ostracize, and make miserable the lives of the faithful. But the unrighteous' complete condemnation of the faithful will prove a mirror of God's complete condemnation of them. The misery they invoked on the righteous will be but an echo of the pain that they will suffer in hell. The Book of Mormon carries a severe warning to the wicked who would abuse the people of God. It states that when they are fully ripe in iniquity, they shall be destroyed (2 Ne. 28:16). It gives three conditions that constitutes being "fully ripe": first, when "the voice of this people [that is, the majority] should choose iniquity" (Alma 10:19); second, when these people "turn aside the just for a thing of naught and revile against that which is good, and say that it is of no worth" (2 Ne. 28:16); and third, "when [they] cast out the righteous from among [them], then shall [they] be ripe for destruction" (Hel. 13:14).

The author then concludes his treatise on faith. Looking back at those who suffered even though their faith was well attested, his statement that they did not receive what was promised (11:39) is a bit startling. When we realize, however, that one of the overall themes of this Epistle is the superiority of Jesus and his new covenant over Moses and the old one, then we

---

324. BDAG, 1019; see also the work of the nineteenth-century commentator Heinrich Meyer at Bible Hub, accessed October 11, 2015, https://biblehub.com/commentaries/hebrews/11-35.htm.

325. See Vanhoye, *Letter to the Hebrews,* 193, for discussion.

326. *Mart. Isa.* 5:1–11; *Liv. Pro.* 1:1; compare Sus. 59. The former text dates to between the second century before Christ and the first century after him. The text is available in R. H. Charles, *The Apocrypha and Pseudepigrapha* (Oxford: Clarendon Press, 1913), and online at Wesley Center Online, http://wesley.nnu.edu/sermons-essays-books/noncanonical-literature/the-martyrdom-of-isaiah/. Compare Holzapfel and Wayment, *Making Sense,* 456.

see why the author makes this point. In sum, his readers must not confuse the fulfillment of promises (11:11, 33) with the fulfillment of *the* promise. Although many of the biblical heroes he refers to not only received promises but also saw them fulfilled, none realized what the author refers to as *the* promise of "some better thing" (κρεῖττών τι, *kreitton ti*; 11:40). According to his statement in 9:15, the promise consisted of obtaining an "eternal heritage."

That these righteous people received divine commendation shows the fact that they suffered was not their fault. It was because something more had to be done before they could realize the promise. But so strong was their faith that they were willing to endure all the unfair abuses of life and temporarily forego receiving the promise until the necessary conditions were met. That happened with the Atonement of Christ and the possibilities it opened.[327]

What they had not yet received, then, was the ultimate blessing. Those heroes the author lists are the ones who looked beyond mortality toward that eternal blessing. That they did not realize their hope then was because God "provided something better with us in mind."[328] In the author's day, Christ established the age of the new covenant, a day the Old Testament Saints looked forward to with eagerness. What the "something better" was, the author identifies with the statement "so they without us should not be made perfect" (11:40). The Old Testament faithful "were denied the historical experience of the messianic perfection until Christians could share in it. In short, God in his providence deferred the bestowal of the final reward until the advent of Christ and the enactment of the new covenant."[329]

As the author has clearly pointed out, Christ is now in position to assist the faithful in realizing the fulness of the promise (Moro. 7:27–28) because of his Atonement, his station as Savior and High Priest, and his place on the right hand of God. The delay had to do with the perfection of the Saints. To make that effective, all had to wait until the ministry of the Savior reached its completion in the Resurrection (7:19; 10:10, 14).[330] Through

327. Bruce, *Epistle to the Hebrews,* 330; Lane, *Hebrews 9–13,* 392.

328. Lane, *Hebrews 9–13,* 392.

329. Lane, *Hebrews 9–13,* 393. Joseph Smith noted, "The Spirits of the just are exalted to a greater and more glorious work—hence they are blessed in their departure to the world of Spirits. Enveloped in flaming fire, they are not far from us, and know and understand our thoughts, feelings, and motions, and are often pained therewith." "History, 1838–1856, Volume E-1," 1751.

330. Koester, *Hebrews,* 520; Vanhoye, *Letter to the Hebrews,* 194.

that means the Lord procured the "perfection" for both the old covenant Saints and the new covenant Christians (11:40). As one Bible translation puts it, "With us in mind, God had made a better plan, that only in company with us should they reach their perfection" (NEB 11:40). Because of him, all "now enjoy unrestricted access to God through Christ, as fellow-citizens of the heavenly Jerusalem."[331]

The author's audience had reached a state of "perfection" in their lifetime because the grace of Christ had purged their sins and purified and prepared them for priestly service. Thus, in this sense they had, in the present, reached the state of perfection necessary to receive place in the heavenly Jerusalem. Having done so, it was now their responsibility to assist the faithful who came before to reach this same state.

Although all of these souls were faithful in their day, their final salvation and promised rewards had to wait until the ministry of Jesus Christ was finished. Though they labored under God's authority, it was bound by the Mosaic law and governed by the Aaronic order of the priesthood and therefore did not have the Melchizedek ordinances necessary for salvation.[332] Only after the Lord made the Atonement was the way prepared for all to receive these ordinances and thus have the door opened to exaltation.[333] As is the usual case in the Epistle to the Hebrews—even this long segment that draws example after example from the Old Testament—the final purpose of this pericope is to point toward Jesus and his saving work.[334]

As in the Translation Notes above, the JST of 11:40 puts a different emphasis on this verse by noting that it was through suffering that the ancient Saints found perfection. By 1842, however, Joseph Smith had learned more

331. Bruce, *Epistle to the Hebrews,* 330.

332. J. Reuben Clark Jr., *On the Way to Immortality and Eternal Life* (Salt Lake City: Deseret Book, 1950), 413–14, taught that many of the prophets down to Elijah held the Melchizedek Priesthood. So, too, did Joseph Fielding Smith, *Answers to Gospel Questions,* 1:50. He noted that the prophets did so only by special ordination. It was generally not held by the priests or Levites. This was also the case with the Book of Mormon prophets—even though they held the Melchizedek Priesthood, they were still bound by the keys of the Aaronic order and therefore could not perform the ordinances of salvation associated with the keys of the Melchizedek order. For discussion, see Smith, *Gospel Questions,* 1:123–128.

333. For a full discussion, see Draper and Rhodes, *Paul's First Epistle to the Corinthians,* 779–80, dealing with 1 Cor. 15:29.

334. In a letter now canonized as section 128 of the Doctrine and Covenants, Joseph Smith takes this final point a little bit further by noting they cannot be saved without us and we cannot be saved without them. This point underscores the importance of proxy work carried out in Latter-day Saint temples. See D&C 128:15.

and therefore modified his view. He notes that the phrase "they without us should not be made perfect" referred to the necessity for the work of baptism for the dead. He explained, "For we without them cannot be made perfect; neither can they without us be made perfect. Neither can they nor we be made perfect without those who have died in the gospel also; for it is necessary in the ushering in of the dispensation of the fulness of times, which dispensation is now beginning to usher in, that a whole and complete and perfect union, and welding together of dispensations, and keys, and powers, and glories should take place, and be revealed from the days of Adam even to the present time" (D&C 128:18).[335]

On March 10, 1844, Joseph Smith explained further:

> What is this office and work of Elijah? It is one of the greatest and most important subjects that God has revealed, [that] He should send Elijah to seal the children to the fathers, and the fathers to the children. Now was this merely confined to the living, to settle difficulties with families on earth? By no means, it was a far greater work. Elijah! what would you do if you were here? Would you confine your work to the living alone? No. I would refer you to the Scriptures [11:40], where the subject is manifest that is, without us they could not be made perfect, nor we without them; the fathers without the children, nor the children without the fathers.[336]

In this light, it would appear the author of Hebrews understood that cleansing, perfecting, and preparing people for eternal life had to wait until the new covenant had been initiated and work for the dead begun. The Atonement activated the new covenant and allowed, at last, forgiveness of sins, justification, sanctification, and eternal salvation to be fully realized for those not only under the new covenant but also the old.[337]

Taking the chapter as a whole, the author shows faith in God can be expressed in complex and manifold ways but always with the same end—blessings from the Divine. Abel's sacrifice, Enoch's translation, Sarah's bearing of Isaac, the patriarchs' prophesying of future generations, and Moses' rejection of the wealth of Egypt are all examples of things done "by faith." The phrase as rendered in the KJV that faith is "the evidence of things not seen" connotes a state of mind free from any doubt that the blessing God has promised will be realized. In short, these Saints continually act upon

---

335. Compare McConkie, *Doctrinal New Testament Commentary,* 3:220–21.

336. "History, 1838–1856, Volume E-1," 1920.

337. Cockerill, *Epistle to the Hebrews,* 598–99; Ellingworth, *Epistle to the Hebrews,* 635–36.

their faith, whatever happens in life, because of their conviction on the reliability of God's promise. Strong faith makes the future world, the "things not seen," a present, almost tangible reality. Taken in this way, 11:1 is not, as the whole chapter shows, a definition of faith as much as "a summary of what faith does; faith binds the believer securely to the reality of what he does not (yet) see, but for which he hopes."[338] That the blessings are to be fully realized only in the future means that they are not presently attainable; indeed, they are so far off they are invisible to those without faith. But belief in the blessings' reality causes a person to follow the will of God and thus repudiate the allure of the world. In doing so, the manifestations of faith—primarily as the gifts of the Spirit—act as assurances that the fulness of the promise will be realized. Through continually acting in faithful obedience they are assured of a place in the eternal city whose architect and builder is God.

338. Ellingworth, *Epistle to the Hebrews*, 566.

Chapter 12

The Need to Endure in Faith; God's Discipline

Introduction

Having established that many of the people under the old covenant endured in faith and thereby proved it was possible, the author now begins his admonition that his readers follow their spiritual predecessors' example. To bolster his point, he cites a better and more contemporary example, namely that of the Savior himself. Using athletic imagery, the author asks his readers to run the race with endurance by keeping their eye on the Lord who is the "founder and perfecter of our faith." He holds this position not only because he won his race but also because he is now empowered to help them run theirs (NR 12:1–2; compare Moro. 6:4).

The author, with great skill, brings together here what he set in motion in 3:1–6. In that passage, he established the unity his readers had with Moses and the household of faith. That unity tied those Saints to all who endured during Israel's long history. It is on the basis of that link with the ancient faithful that the author admonishes his readers to run with endurance their race as the ancients ran theirs (12:1). They can succeed because of what Christ had become. In 4:14–10:18, the author made perfectly clear the faithfulness of the Son and thus his role as the High Priest and Apostle (of whom his readers bear testimony) and who now sits at the right hand of the Father wielding godly power. Christ has become the "founder and perfecter of our faith" because he has prepared the way for all who will run the race to win the prize of entering the presence of God. But the Christians must do their part by running the race.

The author begins his admonition by encouraging his readers to not only follow Jesus' example but also to rely on him (12:1–4). The author stresses the importance of being disciplined and that, although it may seem difficult and even painful at the time, seen properly, it reveals the love of God, strengthens the individual in righteousness and peace, and moves her or him to holiness (12:5–13). The author then gives a clear and powerful warning against refusing what God offers and the consequences that would follow (12:14–27). He concludes by again admonishing his readers to worship the Father with reverence and awe, knowing that "our God is a consuming fire" (12:28–29).

God Disciplines His Children (12:1–13)

Greek Text

Τοιγαροῦν καὶ ἡμεῖς, τοσοῦτον ἔχοντες περικείμενον ἡμῖν νέφος μαρτύρων, ὄγκον ἀποθέμενοι πάντα καὶ τὴν εὐπερίστατον ἁμαρτίαν, δι᾽ ὑπομονῆς τρέχωμεν τὸν προκείμενον ἡμῖν ἀγῶνα, 2 ἀφορῶντες εἰς τὸν τῆς πίστεως ἀρχηγὸν καὶ τελειωτὴν Ἰησοῦν, ὃς ἀντὶ τῆς προκειμένης αὐτῷ χαρᾶς ὑπέμεινεν σταυρὸν αἰσχύνης καταφρονήσας, ἐν δεξιᾷ τε τοῦ θρόνου τοῦ θεοῦ κεκάθικεν.

3 Ἀναλογίσασθε γὰρ τὸν τοιαύτην ὑπομεμενηκότα ὑπὸ τῶν ἁμαρτωλῶν εἰς ἑαυτὸν ἀντιλογίαν, ἵνα μὴ κάμητε ταῖς ψυχαῖς ὑμῶν ἐκλυόμενοι. 4 οὔπω μέχρις αἵματος ἀντικατέστητε πρὸς τὴν ἁμαρτίαν ἀνταγωνιζόμενοι, 5 καὶ ἐκλέλησθε τῆς παρακλήσεως, ἥτις ὑμῖν ὡς υἱοῖς διαλέγεται, Υἱέ μου, μὴ ὀλιγώρει παιδείας κυρίου, μηδὲ ἐκλύου ὑπ᾽ αὐτοῦ ἐλεγχόμενος· 6 ὃν γὰρ ἀγαπᾷ κύριος παιδεύει, μαστιγοῖ δὲ πάντα υἱὸν ὃν παραδέχεται. 7 εἰς παιδείαν ὑπομένετε· ὡς υἱοῖς ὑμῖν προσφέρεται ὁ θεός· τίς γὰρ υἱὸς ὃν οὐ παιδεύει πατήρ; 8 εἰ δὲ χωρίς ἐστε παιδείας ἧς μέτοχοι γεγόνασι πάντες, ἄρα νόθοι καὶ οὐχ υἱοί ἐστε. 9 εἶτα τοὺς μὲν τῆς σαρκὸς ἡμῶν πατέρας εἴχομεν παιδευτὰς καὶ ἐνετρεπόμεθα· οὐ πολὺ μᾶλλον ὑποταγησόμεθα τῷ πατρὶ τῶν πνευμάτων καὶ ζήσομεν; 10 οἱ μὲν γὰρ πρὸς ὀλίγας ἡμέρας κατὰ τὸ δοκοῦν αὐτοῖς ἐπαίδευον, ὁ δὲ ἐπὶ τὸ συμφέρον εἰς τὸ μεταλαβεῖν τῆς ἁγιότητος αὐτοῦ. 11 πᾶσα δὲ παιδεία πρὸς μὲν τὸ παρὸν οὐ δοκεῖ χαρᾶς εἶναι ἀλλὰ λύπης, ὕστερον δὲ καρπὸν εἰρηνικὸν τοῖς δι᾽ αὐτῆς γεγυμνασμένοις ἀποδίδωσιν δικαιοσύνης.

12 Διὸ τὰς παρειμένας χεῖρας καὶ τὰ παραλελυμένα γόνατα ἀνορθώσατε, 13 καὶ τροχιὰς ὀρθὰς ποιεῖτε τοῖς ποσὶν ὑμῶν, ἵνα μὴ τὸ χωλὸν ἐκτραπῇ, ἰαθῇ δὲ μᾶλλον. [SBLGNT]

King James Version

1 Wherefore seeing we also are compassed about with so great a cloud of witnesses, let us lay aside every weight, and the sin which doth so easily beset us, and let us run with patience the race that is set before us, 2 Looking unto Jesus the author and finisher of our faith; who for the joy that was set before him endured the cross, despising the shame, and is set down at the right hand of the throne of God. 3 For consider him that endured such contradiction of sinners against himself, lest ye be wearied and faint in your minds. 4 Ye have not yet resisted unto blood, striving against sin. 5 And ye have forgotten the exhortation which speaketh unto you as unto children, My son, despise not thou the chastening of the Lord, nor faint when thou art rebuked of him: 6 For whom the Lord loveth he chasteneth, and scourgeth every son whom he receiveth. 7 If ye endure chastening, God dealeth with you as with sons; for what son is he whom the father chasteneth not? 8 But if ye be without chastisement, whereof all are partakers, then are ye bastards, and not sons. 9 Furthermore we have had fathers of our flesh which corrected us, and we gave them reverence: shall we not much rather be in subjection unto the Father of spirits, and live? 10 For they verily for a few days chastened us after their own pleasure; but he for our profit, that we might be partakers of his holiness. 11 Now no chastening for the present seemeth to be joyous, but grievous: nevertheless afterward it yieldeth the peaceable fruit of righteousness unto them which are exercised thereby.

New Rendition

1 Therefore, since we have such a great cloud of witnesses surrounding us, let us put aside every impediment and hindering sin, and with steadfast endurance, run the race that is set before us, 2 fixing our eyes on Jesus, the founder and perfecter of our faith, who for the joy that was placed before him endured the cross, disregarding its shame, and

> "sat down on the right hand of God's throne." [Ps. 110:1; LXX Ps. 109:1]

3 Indeed, consider him who endured such hostility towards himself by sinners, so that you will not grow weary and lose heart. 4 You have not yet resisted unto the shedding of your blood as struggle against sin. 5 And you have completely forgotten the encouragement that is spoken to you as children,

> "My child, do not disregard the Lord's discipline, nor give up when you are corrected by him. 6 For the Lord disciplines the one he loves, and chastises every child he accepts." [Prov. 3:11–12]

7 Endure these things for the sake of discipline, God is treating you as children. For what child is not disciplined by his father? 8 But if you are not disciplined, as all children are, then you are illegitimate and not children. 9 Furthermore, we have had fathers of our bodies who corrected us, and we treated them with respect. Should we not then even more so submit ourselves to the Father of our spirits and live? 10 For our earthly fathers corrected us for a short time as seemed best to them, but our Heavenly Father corrects us for our benefit so that we can share in his holiness. 11 Now all discipline does not seem pleasant at

12 Wherefore lift up the hands which hang down, and the feeble knees; 13 And make straight paths for your feet, lest that which is lame be turned out of the way; but let it rather be healed.

the time, but painful. Later, however, it yields the peaceful fruit of righteousness to those who have been trained by it. 12 Therefore,

> "strengthen your weak arms and your feeble knees" [Isa. 35:3],

13 and

> "prepare straight paths for your feet" [LXX Prov. 4:26],

so that you do not make worse what is already lame, but instead let it be healed.

Translation Notes and Comments

12:1 ***Wherefore seeing we also are compassed about with so great a cloud of witnesses / Therefore, since we have such a great cloud of witnesses surrounding us:*** The conjunction τοιγαροῦν (*toigaroun*), "therefore," signals that the author is now going to make his point and set up his exhortation based on the examples he has already given.[1]

The noun νέφος (*nephos*), "cloud," was often used figuratively to designate a large group of people.[2] Here it looks to the large number the author designates as μαρτύρων (*martyrōn*), "witnesses,"[3] referring to those whose lives have proven the value of faith and stand as once living examples of its effect and worth. The author does a little role reversal here: the biblical heroes are not the ones his readers look to but are the audience who are interested in and follow the efforts of his readers.[4]

The verb περίκειμαι (*perikeimai*), "to surround,"[5] gives the imagery of people gathered in a large athletic center watching the games.

---

1. For a discussion of this verse in its setting, see Carolyn Osiek, "The Great Cloud of Witnesses," *Bible Today* 50, no. 2 (2012): 95–100. For a general study of this section (12:1–12), see N. C. Croy, *Endurance in Suffering: Hebrews 12:1–13 in Its Rhetorical, Religious, and Philosophical Context* (Cambridge: Cambridge University Press, 1998).

2. BDAG, 670; Lane, *Hebrews 9–13*, 408.

3. BDAG, 618–19. The word can denote, in a very technical and forensic sense, a witness in a trial, or more generally, anyone who witnesses any event, that is, a spectator. In the most Christian sense, the word denotes one who witnesses for Christ under the most threatening of circumstances. See Attridge, *Epistle to the Hebrews,* 354–55.

4. Vanhoye, *Letter to the Hebrews,* 195.

5. BDAG, 801–2.

let us lay aside every weight, and the sin which doth so easily beset us / let us put aside every impediment and hindering sin: The verb ἀποτίθημι (*apotitheimi*) taken literally means "to put off" and can refer to removing one's clothes. In a figurative sense, it means "to lay aside, rid oneself" of something—in this case any "impediment."[6]

The noun ὄγκος (*onkos*), "impediment," denotes a bulky, heavy weight, but figuratively it points to anything that hinders or slows a person's progress.[7] Its coupling with the adjective πάντα (*panta*), "all, every," suggests ridding oneself of anything that impedes progress, which the author identifies as sin. For that reason, the phrase is translated as "every impediment" in our Rendition.

The adjective εὐπερίστατος (*euperistatos*) has two nuances. One points to that which is distracting, the other to that which constricts, hinders, obstructs, or ensnares.[8] It is an excellent adjective to describe ἁμαρτία (*hamartia*), "sin," that, in the singular, suggests the entire range of sins from commission to omission.[9] Based on context and external textual evidence,[10] we use the more negative sense in our Rendition.

let us run with patience the race that is set before us / with steadfast endurance, run the race that is set before us: The operative word in this phrase is ὑπομονή (*hypomonē*), "patience, endurance." For a fuller discussion, see Translation Notes for 10:36 with the associated Analysis. For our purposes here, the word refers to holding out or bearing up in the face of difficulty[11] and carries the force of steadfastness to a cause. It denotes a continued resistance especially to destructive forces or agencies that exceed what is normal or expected.[12] To catch the full nuance of the word, we have translated it as "steadfast endurance" in our Rendition. The term is

6. BDAG, 123–24; see Lane, *Hebrews 9–13,* 409; compare 2 Ne. 4:17–18; and Alma 7:15.

7. BDAG, 689.

8. BDAG, 410; Louw-Nida, §§30.22; 37.6. For discussion, see Ellingworth, *Epistle to the Hebrews,* 638–39.

9. Cockerill, *Epistle to the Hebrews,* 604.

10. Moulton and Milligan, *Vocabulary,* 264.

11. BDAG, 1039–40. The noun refers to a temper that refuses to succumb under social pressure no matter how strong. At 6:12, the author called on his readers to exercise patience. The word he used there, μακροθυμία (*makrothymia*), denotes "a state of remaining tranquil while awaiting an outcome, patience, steadfastness, endurance." BDAG, 612. On the other hand, ὑπομονή (*hypomonē*) denotes enduring, "the capacity to hold out or bear up in the face of difficulty, patience, endurance, fortitude, steadfastness, perseverance." BDAG, 1039.

12. Louw-Nida, §§25.174; 29.20; *Webster's New Dictionary of Synonyms,* s.v. "continue."

important because it sets the standards for the race: it is not just the swift that win but all that cross the finish line.[13]

12:2 *Looking unto Jesus the author and finisher of our faith / fixing our eyes on Jesus, the founder and perfecter of our faith:* The verb ἀφοράω (*aphoraō*) has two related meanings, "to direct one's attention without distraction, fix one's eyes trustingly on someone" and "to develop more precise knowledge about something in the offing."[14] Here the author's emphasis is on concentrating or fixing one's sight on Jesus.

The noun ἀρχηγός (*archēgos*) describes one who begins something, an "originator" or "founder."[15] We translate it as "founder" in our Rendition.

The noun τελειωτής (*teleiōtēs*) refers to one who brings something to its highest possible level.[16] Thus, we have translated it as "perfecter" in our Rendition. Christ not only makes it possible for us to have faith; he also, through his Atonement, ensures that our faith in him will result in the salvation and exaltation we hope for. He is thus both "the founder and perfecter" of our faith (compare Moro. 6:4).

who for the joy that was set before him endured the cross, despising the shame / who for the joy that was placed before him endured the cross, disregarding its shame: The author's use of the preposition ἀντί (*anti*) has caused some debate as to the point he is making.[17] The word can mean "instead of, in place of" but also "in behalf of" or "for" someone and "in exchange for" something.[18] Its object is χάρα (*chara*), a word meaning "gladness, delight, joy."[19] If *anti* is understood as "instead of," then the author's point seems to be that Jesus surrendered the possibility of earthly joy that was within his reach and instead faced the pain and shame of the cross.[20] If *anti* is taken as "in exchange for," then the author is saying that for the joy Jesus could see coming from facing the cross—salvation for

13. The idea comes from Ecc. 9:11. There the phrase "the race is not to the swift, nor the battle to the sure" is used as evidence of the unfairness of life. Some Church leaders, however, have put a positive spin on it. They use it to teach that those who endure to the finish line, not just the swift, gain the prize. For examples, see Brigham Young, in *Journal of Discourses,* 1:89; and Monson, *Invitation to Exaltation,* 9–11.

14. Strong, "New Strong's Expanded Dictionary ... Greek," s.v. "ἀφοράω"; BDAG, 158; Louw-Nida, §§27.6, 30.31.

15. BDAG, 138–39.

16. BDAG, 997; Vanhoye, *Letter to the Hebrews,* 196; Delling, *TDNT,* 8:86–87.

17. For a discussion, see Ellingworth, *Epistle to the Hebrews,* 641.

18. BDAG, 87–88; Louw-Nida, §§89.24, 133; 90.37; Johnson, *Hebrews,* 318.

19. BDAG, 1077.

20. *NID,* s.v. "χαίρω."

all humankind—he endured both his suffering and its shame. Given the author's point that Jesus did what he did for joy, the second alternative seems the better. Because joy seems too strong a word for what the world had to offer Jesus (see Analysis below), we follow the majority of translators in our Rendition.

As nearly always, the noun σταυρός (*stauros*), "cross," refers to crucifixion.[21] The author associates such a death with αἰσχύνη (*aischynē*), "shame." In the present context, the noun denotes "the experience of ignominy" associated with this particular form of death.[22] The Romans generally reserved crucifixion for the most offensive of crimes of the lower class, particularly thievery, murder, and high treason. The Jewish historian Josephus described it as "the most pitiable of deaths" (θάνατον τὸν οἴκτιστον, *thanatōn ton oiktiston*).[23] The reason was twofold: it was a most severe type of torture, lasting up to days, and it was designed to be publicly humiliating in that the person was crucified naked, generally along a very busy street. Because those who were crucified were viewed as the dregs of society and because of the public humiliation, such a death carried a heavy burden of shame.[24]

and is set down at the right hand of the throne of God / and "sat down on the right hand of God's throne": The reference is to LXX Psalm 109:1, which the author has referred to in 1:3 and 10:12. For a discussion, see Translation Notes for 1:3 with the associated Analysis. Here we need but note that because the right hand was a natural metaphor for power, to sit on God's right hand connoted a sharing in and wielding of his power without limitation. The author's point is not Jesus' station but what having that station does for the faithful: the Lord is in the utmost position of power to assist them (compare D&C 66:12; 76:23–24).

12:3 ***For consider him that endured such contradiction of sinners against himself / Indeed, consider him who endured such hostility towards himself by sinners:*** The conjunction γάρ (*gar*) marks a strong affirmation and ties what the author has said about Jesus to what the author is going to say next. It is therefore translated as "indeed" in our Rendition.

---

21. BDAG, 941.

22. BDAG, 29–30; Ogden and Skinner, *Verse by Verse,* 261–62. For a study, see Martin Hengel, *Crucifixion in the Ancient World and the Folly of the Message of the Cross* (Philadelphia: Fortress Press, 1977).

23. Josephus, *J.W.* 7.203.

24. For a study, see Schneider, *TDNT,* 7:572–84.

The verb ἀναλογίζομαι (*analogizomai*), "consider," means "to reason with careful deliberation"[25] and is the author's way of encouraging his readers to take Jesus' example very seriously.

The key word in the sentence is ἀντιλογία (*antilogia*), "hostility." The noun denotes the act of speaking against someone and carries the nuance of strong opposition and even defiance on the part of the hostile element.[26] It is modified by the adjective τοιοῦτος (*toioutos*), "such," and implies the intensity of the hostility.[27] Together they suggest the depth of hatred some felt toward Jesus and reveal the pains they went to in expressing it.[28]

It is therefore not surprising that the author refers to Jesus' opponents as ἁμαρτολοί (*hamartōloi*), "sinners." The noun connotes any and all activities that do not measure up to a moral standard and was applied to persons who did these activities.[29]

lest ye be wearied and faint in your minds / so that you will not grow weary and lose heart: The coordinating conjunction ἵνα (*hina*), "so that,"[30] serves as a marker showing purpose and gives the reason why the author wants his readers to keep their attention fixed on Jesus.

The phrase ταῖς ψυχαῖς (*tais psychais*), "with respect to the souls" (a dative of reference/respect),[31] can grammatically modify either the verb κάνητε (*kanēte*), "grow weary,"[32] or the participle ἐκλυόμενοι (*ekluomenoi*), "becoming weary."[33] In our Rendition, we assumed that it modifies the participle, that is, "becoming weary with respect to your souls," and have translated it as "lose heart."[34]

12:4 ***Ye have not yet resisted unto blood, striving against sin / You have not yet resisted unto the shedding of your blood as struggle against sin:***

25. BDAG, 67.

26. BDAG, 89.

27. BDAG, 1009–10; Ellingworth, *Epistle to the Hebrews,* 643.

28. Variant readings exist for the phrase with some text having εἰς ἑαυτόν (*eis heauton*), "against himself," and others having εἰς ἑαυτούς (*eis heautous*), "against themselves." The latter suggests that the sinners' hostility actually acted against them by exposing their hatred. This idea is, however, forced. The better understanding comes from the first reading, showing that the hostility was toward Jesus. See Metzger, *Textual Commentary,* 604–5; Ellingworth, *Epistle to the Hebrews,* 643; Lane, *Hebrews 9–13,* 415–16; and Cockerill, *Epistle to the Hebrews,* 611 and n. 48.

29. BDAG, 51.

30. BDAG, 475–76.

31. Wallace, *Greek Grammar,* 144–46.

32. BDAG, 1098–100.

33. BDAG, 306.

34. BDAG, 306; Lane, *Hebrews,* 400 note w.

The verb ἀντικαθίστημι (*antikathistēmi*) denotes resistance against opposition[35] and echoes the opposition felt by the Lord on account of his enemies.

The noun αἷμα (*haima*) means "blood," but here in a metaphorical sense, the life of a person.[36] In the phrase μέχρις αἵματος (*mechris haimatos*), literally "until blood," it designates violent death[37] and will have drawn the readers' attention to the Lord's agony in the garden and then on the cross (12:2) as well as the possibility of martyrdom on their part. Indeed, the adverb οὔπω (*oupō*), "not yet,"[38] suggests that such may be in their future.

The verb ἀνταγωνίζομαι (*antagōnizomai*) means "to struggle" but carries the nuance of the hard work associated with athletic games.[39] Here the author uses a present participle suggesting he has in view a persistent spiritual disposition to resist evil.[40] The nuance of the word is that his readers have put up a good fight against sin but need to continue the fight and not give in. They are to keep in mind that the Lord never gave up the struggle, resisting even to his death.

With the use of the verbs ἀντικαθίστημι (*antikathistēmi*), "to resist," and ἀνταγωνίζομαι (*antagōnizomai*), "to struggle," the author's readers likely heard strong echoes of a boxing match and each contender's effort during such bouts.[41] The imagery carries the author's athletic associations forward.

What must be resisted and fought against is "sin." The noun ἁμαρτία (*hamartia*) generally denotes any kind of trespass against God and his laws.[42] Here the absence of a definite article and the singular number suggest the author is not looking at personal sins but at sin specifically as an evil destructive power,[43] one that is embodied in "sinners" and that expressed itself in the past as opposition against Jesus and now as persecution against righteousness.[44] The author's readers have and are experiencing such an expression of sin.

---

35. BDAG, 88.

36. BDAG, 26–27.

37. Ellingworth, *Epistle to the Hebrews,* 645.

38. BDAG, 717.

39. BDAG, 86; Moulton and Milligan, *Vocabulary,* 46.

40. Cockerill, *Epistle to the Hebrews,* 619 n. 22.

41. Both verbs are found only here in the Bible but are associated with athletics in secular literature. See Lane, *Hebrews 9–13,* 417. The verb ἀνταγωνίζομαι (*antagōnizomai*) evokes ἀγων (*agōn*), the noun used for "race" in 12:1. Cockerill, *Epistle to the Hebrews,* 618 n. 18.

42. Louw-Nida, §§88.118 289.

43. BDAG, 50–51.

44. Lane, *Hebrews 9–13,* 418–19.

12:5 ***And ye have forgotten the exhortation which speaketh unto you as unto children / And you have completely forgotten the encouragement that is spoken to you as children:*** In these verses, the author explains, at least partially, the reason for his readers' discouragement. The verb ἐκλανθάνομαι (*eklanthanomai*) means "to forget entirely"[45] and points to the root cause of the Christians' problem: what they once knew, they can no longer remember. The implication is that if they could, they would not be having their current problems. He is, therefore, going to restore that knowledge.

The noun παράκλησις (*paraklēsis*) denotes the act of encouraging or exhorting another to action.[46] In this case, God is doing the exhorting. He is willing to do so because of the special relationship he has with these people: they are his children.

My son, despise not thou the chastening of the Lord, nor faint when thou art rebuked of him / "My child, do not disregard the Lord's discipline, nor give up when you are corrected by him: To make his point, the author quotes Proverbs 3:11–12. The central issue here is caught in the phrase παιδείας κυρίου (*paideias kyriou*), the "Lord's discipline." The noun παιδεία (*paideia*) refers to training that includes instruction, correction, and discipline.[47] Of these, the emphasis is on discipline, that aspect of training focused on the honing of mental faculties and moral character.

The author warns his readers that they can disregard the Lord's instruction in two ways. The first, expressed by the verb ὀλιγωρέω (*oligōreō*), means to take something lightly because it is viewed as having little esteem. In sum, to disregard its value.[48] The second is expressed by the verb ἐκλύω (*ekluō*), "to become weary" and so "to give up" (see 12:3).[49]

Because the thrust of this scripture looks at "sons" coupled with the usual practice of the day in writing to the public, the author does not include females in his discussion. Nonetheless, what applies to sons applies to daughters as well.[50] For this reason, we have translated the noun υἱός (*huios*) as "child."

12:6 ***For whom the Lord loveth he chasteneth, and scourgeth every son whom he receiveth / For the Lord disciplines the one he loves, and***

---

45. Louw-Nida, §29.15.

46. BDAG, 766.

47. BDAG, 748–49.

48. BDAG, 703; Vanhoye, *Letter to the Hebrews*, 201.

49. BDAG, 306.

50. For a study, see Judith P. Hallett, *Fathers and Daughters in Roman Society: Women and the Elite Family* (Princeton: Princeton University Press, 1984).

chastises every child he accepts": This phrase concludes the author's quotation of Proverbs 3:11–12. He uses it to show why the Lord disciplines his children. The key word is ἀγαπάω (*agapaō*), "to love." Behind all that God does stands this motivating virtue. As noted above, this includes his παιδεία (*paideia*), "disciplining."

This phrase can also include something even harsher. The verb μαστιγόω (*mastigoō*), "chastise," carries the rather severe meanings of "whipping" and "flogging." Softening this is the nuance of doing so not as a means of punishment but as a correction.[51] In the context here, the emphasis seems to be more on the harsh treatment the Church's enemies are imposing on its members rather than on any actual beatings.

The verb παραδέχομαι (*paradechomai*), "accept," can mean to receive someone in a hospitable manner, but in the present context, it denotes doing so because of a fatherly love.[52] There is a nuance here that must be noted: not everyone is accepted. There are those who put themselves outside the divine family and thereby the Father's acceptance. The scripture refers to these as the "filthy still"—those who can go through the refining fires of hell and resist their cleansing power (see Rev. 22:11; Morm. 9:4, 14; and D&C 88:35). They are known as the sons of perdition (D&C 76:43).

12:7 *If ye endure chastening / Endure these things for the sake of discipline:* The Greek phrase is very compressed: εἰς παιδείαν ὑπομένετε (*eis paideian hypomenete*), literally "for discipline endure." The preposition εἰς (*eis*) could be a marker of reference, making παιδείαν (*paideian*) a predicated accusative, thus reading "endure as discipline."[53] Or it could express purpose, thus reading "endure for the sake of discipline," that is, for the good that can come out of it.[54] In our Rendition, we chose the latter translation as better fitting the overall context of this section. The phrase "these things" is not in the Greek text, but we have added it for clarity.

---

51. BDAG, 620. The Mosaic law demanded this kind of correction for certain offenses. The executor administered the punishment using a whip with three thongs and striking the person thirteen times upon the chest and each shoulder. Paul suffered such punishment five times. See 2 Cor. 11:24.

52. BDAG, 761.

53. Lane, *Hebrews 9–13,* 397. REB reads this way.

54. Ellingworth, *Epistle to the Hebrews,* 650; NRSV reads this way. In his study, Philip A. Davis Jr., *The Place of Paideia in Hebrews' Moral Thought* (Tübingen: Mohr Siebeck, 2018), posits that because much of ancient education used physical punishment as a means of achieving the objective of moral development, the author of Hebrews plays on this to show his readers their suffering is a concomitant part in their moral growth the gospel demands. Compare Ogden and Skinner, *Verse by Verse,* 262; and Holzapfel and Wayment, *Making Sense,* 457.

God dealeth with you as with sons / God is treating you as children: The verb προσφέρω (*prospherō*) in the passive, as used here, has the sense "to behave or deal with someone."[55]

The author's use of the phrase ὡς υἱοῖς (*hōs huiois*), "as children," shows that, from his point of view, these people have the status of children of God.[56]

for what son is he whom the father chasteneth not? / For what child is not disciplined by his father?: The question is rhetorical, designed to bolster the author's point.

12:8 ***But if ye be without chastisement, whereof all are partakers, then are ye bastards, and not sons / But if you are not disciplined, as all children are, then you are illegitimate and not children:*** The first occurrence of the noun "children" in this verse is not in the Greek text but is implied from context. We added the word to the Rendition for clarity. The author's point is that all children belonging to a household would be held to the standards of that house and the society of their parents.[57]

The adjective μέτοχος (*metochos*) denotes sharing or participating in something.[58] The relative clause ἧς μέτοχοι γεγόνασιν πάντες (*hēs metochoi gegonasin pantes*) reads literally "of which all [children] have been sharing." In our Rendition, we have translated this "as all children are" for clarity in English. The force of the word is that a family member does not stand alone. The Father disciplines all his children. No one escapes. Each child, therefore, has a common bond with the other children.

The noun νόθος (*nothos*), "illegitimate," means to be born either out of wedlock or of servile origin.[59] Either way, the term denotes a person who has neither legal status nor civil or filial rights.[60] Being without a legal father, such a person would have no male supervisor invested in their wellbeing or concerned with their upbringing.

---

55. BDAG, 887; K. Weiss, *TDNT,* 9:65–66; Ellingworth, *Epistle to the Hebrews,* 650.

56. Ellingworth, *Epistle to the Hebrews,* 650. In the restored gospel, we often use the phrase "children of God" to refer to those who have, through overcoming trials and temptations and enduring in faith, become like our Heavenly Parents. See Gladys Clark Farmer, "Chastening," in Ludlow, *Encyclopedia of Mormonism,* 1:264–65. The Lord called Emma Smith his daughter and stated, "All those who receive my gospel are sons and daughters in my kingdom" (D&C 25:1).

57. O'Brien, *Letter to the Hebrews,* 466. The examples the author has cited from Israel's past clearly demonstrate this point.

58. BDAG, 643.

59. Michel, *TDNT,* 4:683–94.

60. Ellingworth, *Epistle to the Hebrews,* 651, noting Kliene Pauly 1.1269.

12:9 *Furthermore we have had fathers of our flesh which corrected us / Furthermore, we have had fathers of our bodies who corrected us:* The author again unites himself with his readers by using the first person plural form of the verb ἔχω (*echo*), "we have," and the first person plural pronoun ἡμων (*hēmōn*), "our." With the adverb εἶτα (*eita*), "furthermore," the author signals his readers he is continuing to build his case with a new example.[61]

The noun σάρξ (*sarx*) denotes the flesh and also "the body as a functioning entity."[62] Here the nuance is on the personal and intimate association a child has to a father.

The noun παιδευτής (*paideutēs*), "corrector, one who disciplines,"[63] is here used as a predicate accusative, literally "we had fathers . . . [as] correctors," which is rather awkward in English. We have translated it as the relative clause "who corrected us" in our Rendition.

we gave them reverence / we treated them with respect: The verb ἐντρέπω (*entrepō*), found here in the form of an imperfect passive, denotes showing "deference to a person in respect for her or his special status."[64] In this case, the respect revealed itself in accepting the correction. The author's use of the imperfect tense suggests that the respect manifested itself over a long period.

shall we not much rather be in subjection unto the Father of spirits, and live? / Should we not then even more so submit ourselves to the Father of our spirits and live?: The question is rhetorical and is used to gain readers' acceptance of the point. The verb ὑποτάσσω (*hypotassō*), "submit,"[65] in the passive voice, as found here, means "to subject oneself."[66] The author has already used the term in 2:5–8 to show that submission should be to Christ. See Translation Notes for 2:5.

61. Ellingworth, *Epistle to the Hebrews,* 652; BDAG, 295.

62. BDAG, 914–15.

63. BDAG, 749. Hellenistic writers associated the term with teachers, where it had the connotation of direction rather than punishment. Croy, *Endurance,* 202. For a father's duties, see Johnson, *Hebrews,* 312.

64. BDAG, 341.

65. BDAG, 1042.

66. BDAG, 1042; *NID,* s.v. "ὑποτάσσω"; Delling, *TDNT,* 8:27–48. A constant theme in this work is the idea of yielding oneself to God's will. There is no room for coercion. See Ellingworth, *Epistle to the Hebrews,* 145.

The phrase πολὺ μᾶλλον (*poly mallon*) means "much more" or "even more so." The author's use of it emphasizes the importance of submitting to God's discipline.[67]

The phrase τῷ πατρὶ τῶν πνευμάτων (*tō patri tōn pneumatōn*), "the Father of our spirits," is arresting because it reveals something of the author's understanding of God. He is the author of all human life and thus stands as the creative (or even procreative) force behind it.[68]

The last word in the phrase, ζάω (*zaō*), "to live," is key. Though it denotes physical life in general, it also carries the idea of the transcendent and sanctified life of a child of God.[69] It is to the latter that the author is pointing. That the verb is found in the future tense suggests that the author is looking at that quality of life the heirs of the celestial glory will enjoy. His point is that submission places one in a position to live in the fullest sense of the term by sharing in God's own existence, exaltation, and glory.[70] As such, it puts a premium on his readers placing themselves under divine discipline.

12:10 ***For they verily for a few days chastened us after their own pleasure / For our earthly fathers corrected us for a short time as seemed best to them:***[71] The phrase "earthly fathers" is not found in the Greek text but it is implied by οἱ μὲν (*hoi men*), "they, on the one hand," and is added to our Rendition for clarity. Again, the emphasis is on παιδεία (*paideia*), "instruction, correction,"[72] but here on its application by earthly fathers.

The phrase ὀλίγας ἡμέρας (*oligas hēmeras*), literally "for a few days," denotes a short period of time,[73] but given the customs of the day, that period lasted from birth to maturity at about age fifteen.[74]

---

67. The author again uses the rabbinic rhetorical device *qal waḥomer* in which a comparison with a lesser matter is used to stress the importance of a much greater one. On the nature and use of the *qal waḥomer* or *a fortiori* argument, see discussion in the introduction on page 30.

68. BDAG, 786–88.

69. BDAG, 424–26.

70. O'Brien, *Letter to the Hebrews,* 467; Johnson, *Hebrews,* 322. For the author, to live means to exist as God does. See 3:12; 4:12; 7:3, 8, 16, 25; 9:14, 17; 10:20, 31.

71. To make this sentence flow in English, of necessity we have obscured the author's use of four prepositional phrases: "for a few days," "as seemed good to them," "for the benefit," and "for the sharing of holiness."

72. BDAG, 748.

73. Louw-Nida, §67.106.

74. For a study, see Beryl Rawson, *Children and Childhood in Roman Italy* (Oxford: Oxford University Press, 2003).

The phrase we render "as seemed best to them" (κατὰ τὸ δοκοῦν αὐτοῖς, *kata to dokoun autois*) translates literally as "according to the seeming to them." To make sense in English, to the verb δοκέω (*dokeō*), "to seem, think,"[75] we added the adverb "best." The author's point is that earthly fathers were under no constraint in their disciplining other than what they felt was best for the child. The inference is that the child had no right to question the actions of the father but to learn from them.

but he for our profit, that we might be partakers of his holiness / but our Heavenly Father corrects us for our benefit so that we can share in his holiness: The phrase "Heavenly Father" does not appear in the Greek text, but it is implied by the masculine singular definite article ὁ (*ho*) and is supplied in our Rendition for clarity.

The verb συμφέρω (*sympherō*) means "to be of benefit, to be useful,"[76] and the verb μεταλαμβάνω (*metalambanō*) means "to have a share in" something and thus to take possession of or ownership of at least a portion of it.[77]

To denote the benefit that his readers can have a share in, the author uses the noun ἁγιότης (*hagiotēs*), "holiness."[78] The word connotes a state of perfection in goodness and righteousness. This attribute is a primary quality of Jehovah (Lev. 11:45; 19:2; 20:26; 1 Pet. 1:16) and necessary for one to have in order to enter and remain in his presence (see Moses 6:57; 7:35). An unsanctified person simply cannot abide there (see 1 Cor. 6:9; 1 Ne. 10:21; 15:33; Alma 11:37; 40:26; and 3 Ne. 27:19).

The author's point is that, properly seen, God's correction has but one main purpose: to benefit the child. Through accepted correction, the transformative power of God's grace can bring the child into the same state of holiness that the Father enjoys.

12:11 ***Now no chastening for the present seemeth to be joyous, but grievous / Now all discipline does not seem pleasant at the time, but painful:*** Here the author looks to practical earthly experience to make his point. His expression πρὸς τὸ παρόν (*pros to paron*), "for a time," indicates that the discipline is temporary and suggests, from that perspective, his readers should take heart and endure it.

---

75. BDAG, 254–55.
76. BDAG, 960.
77. BDAG, 639.
78. BDAG, 11; Louw-Nida, §88.25.

nevertheless afterward it yieldeth the peaceable fruit of righteousness unto them which are exercised thereby / Later, however, it yields the peaceful fruit of righteousness to those who have been trained by it: Here the author reveals the results of accepting God's discipline. The noun καρπός (*karpos*), "fruit," refers not only to the product of a plant but also to what an activity or effort produces.[79]

The adjective εἰρηνικός (*eirēnikos*) denotes that which is peaceful, serene, and without worry. Therefore, the phrase refers to "the peaceful reward of a righteous life."[80]

The verb γυμνάζω (*gymnazō*), "to train," connotes the discipline necessary to master a skill.[81] The perfect tense of its participle, as found here, points to training that extends from the past into the present. Again, we hear an athletic echo.

12:12 ***Wherefore lift up the hands which hang down, and the feeble knees / Therefore, "strengthen your weak arms and your feeble knees":*** This is a close paraphrase of Isaiah 35:3. The referential conjunction διό (*dio*), "therefore," acts here to tie what the author has said before with the instruction that he will now give and works to emphasize the reason for that instruction.[82] It suggests that because of what discipline can produce—both peaceable fruit and holiness—the person should press forward.

This sentence can be taken two ways. Either it is the end of the admonition the author has just given and therefore asks the reader to strengthen their own hands and knees, or it introduces what comes next, in which case it is asking the readers (who have placed themselves under the discipline) to encourage and strengthen those in need.[83] We have chosen the first interpretation in our Rendition because the next verse begins with a citation from Proverbs 4:26, "prepare straight paths for your feet," that explicitly uses the second person plural possessive pronoun ὑμῶν (*hymōn*), "your." This implies strongly that this verse also is referring to "your" arms and feet.

The verb ἀνορθόω (*anorthoō*), found here in the imperative mood, means to straighten what has become bent and, by extension, to strengthen an area of weakness,[84] in this case both the arms and the knees.

---

79. BDAG, 509–10; Louw-Nida, §§3.33; 42.13. The author echoes James 1:2–3 and 1 Pet. 1:6–7.

80. BDAG, 509–10; Louw-Nida, §25.249.

81. BDAG, 208.

82. BDAG, 250.

83. For discussion, see Ellingworth, *Epistle to the Hebrews*, 657–58.

84. Louw-Nida, §§17.33; 45.4.

The verb παρίημι (*pariēmi*) means "to be weak"[85] and suggests the weakness is the result of great exertion. The verb παραλύω (*paraluō*) means "to be disabled, feeble"[86] and also suggests a condition that has resulted from strenuous effort. Taken together, the words paint a picture of a person who has, through great exertion, pushed his body to the point of exhaustion.

The JST changes the phrase to read, "lift up the hands that hang down and *strengthen* the feeble knees" (italicized word showing the change). The addition resolves the tension of the KJV where the admonition is to "lift up" both the hands and knees. It makes much better sense to lift the hands but to strengthen the knees. This reading conforms to the wording given in a revelation on March 15, 1832, and found in D&C 81:5.

12:13 Just what the author means in this verse is sufficiently oblique that any translation must be tentative. It is even hard to determine if his target audience is the strong members of the Church or the weak. Whomever he is addressing, he is admonishing them to press forward but to be careful not to make conditions more difficult for themselves and others than they already are. In the context of the Epistle as a whole, it would seem that the author is concerned about the weak members of the Church. These "must either progress to maturity, or fall back to a state worse than that in which they began their Christian life."[87]

make straight paths for your feet / "prepare straight paths for your feet": This is a quote from LXX Proverbs 4:26. The verb ποιέω (*poieō*) means "to make or prepare something for oneself."[88]

The noun τροχιά (*trochia*) denotes a path or way,[89] but in a metaphorical sense, it connotes an appropriate course of life that a person should follow.[90]

Taken literally, the proverb is a command for a person to prepare a path that both leads directly to an objective and allows for swift passage toward it.[91] The statement is, however, a biblical idiom that admonishes a person to "behave in strict conformance to a predetermined model of behavior."[92]

---

85. BDAG, 777. The word is found here as a perfect passive participle.

86. BDAG, 768–69. The word is found here as a perfect passive participle. The Greek phrase is an idiom that reads literally "straighten the paralyzed knees" but means to encourage oneself through a strong resolve. Louw-Nida, §25.152.

87. Ellingworth, *Epistle to the Hebrews,* 660.

88. BDAG, 839–42.

89. It denotes specifically wheel tracks for a cart or wagon. BDAG, 1017.

90. Cockerill, *Epistle to the Hebrews,* 630 n. 71.

91. BDAG, 1017.

92. Louw-Nida, §41.30.

lest that which is lame be turned out of the way / so that you do not make worse what is already lame: The adjective χωλός (*chōlos*) refers to a lame or crippled leg.[93] In this instance, however, the author is using the term metaphorically. That he uses the neuter singular form suggests he is not referring to an individual "who is crippled" but to "what is crippled."[94]

The verb ἐκτρέπω (*ektrepō*), in the passive form as found here, primarily means "to be turned out of the way" thus leaving a path or road. In a secondary and medical sense, it means "to dislocate or sprain an ankle or knee."[95] The context suggests the author is referring to the latter, and he is admonishing his readers to make the way as easy as possible so as to not damage further what is already sprained.

but let it rather be healed / but instead let it be healed: The adverbial phrase δὲ μᾶλλον (*de mallon*) acts as a marker for an alternative, thus, "but rather" or "but instead."[96]

The verb ἰάομαι (*iaomai*), found here as a passive subjunctive, is dependent on the conjunction ἵνα (*hina*) and means "so that it be healed,"[97] suggesting that walking the straight path has healing effect.

Analysis and Summary

In this section, the author begins his exhortation. In verse 12:1, he creates the imagery of a large coliseum filled with spectators watching an athletic contest. These spectators are witnesses (μάρτυρες, *martyres*) to the power of faith for, through that means, they have already participated successfully in the games. But their role in this instance is passive. It is the author's readers who have the active part, for they are the ones who must now run the race.[98] The audience, however, plays an important role: they show the race can be won, their vast number emphasizing the point. The witnesses act as the cheering section energizing those who must now run.[99] They empower

93. BDAG, 1085–86.

94. Vanhoye, *Letter to the Hebrews,* 204.

95. BDAG, 311; Moulton and Milligan, *Vocabulary,* 199. See also Bruce, *Epistle to the Hebrews,* 348; and O'Brien, *Letter to the Hebrews,* 471.

96. BDAG, 613–14.

97. BDAG, 465.

98. Ellingworth, *Epistle to the Hebrews,* 638; Johnson, *Hebrews,* 315.

99. Markus Cromhout, "The 'Cloud of Witnesses' as Part of the Public Court of Reputation in Hebrews," *HTS Teologiese Studies/Theological Studies* 68, no. 1 (2012), accessed March 10, 2017, https://hts.org.za/index.php/HTS/article/view/1151/2446. The author of this article points out that the witnesses/spectators played a very dynamic role in the

the new athletes by giving them assurance and hope that, if they will run, they too will succeed.

Continuing his analogy, the author advises his readers to strip themselves of sin as a runner removes everything that will impede his speed. Given that Olympic athletes competed without any clothing,[100] the imagery suggests putting off all sin. The author is a realist, recognizing that sin is "an impediment" that "hinders" (εὐπερίστατος, *euperistatos*) progress by standing in the way of securing the reward.[101]

With encouragement, the author relates what is necessary to win the prize. The key is "steadfast endurance" (ὑπομονή, *hypomonē*). By the rules of this game, the race is not just to the swift but to the sure.[102] Everyone who crosses the finish line, no matter how long it takes, wins the full prize. For that reason, the author admonishes his readers "with steadfast endurance, [to] run the race that is set before us" (NR 12:1). He has already shown that it can be done because Christ, the great "forerunner," has opened the way (6:19–20). This race has an unusual advantage because it will allow all who endure to win the promised prize. It is, however, self-selecting, because any who desire are admitted.

From 3:1–6, the author has prepared his readers to look to Jesus as the founder and perfecter of faith. Here in 12:2, the author admonished them to look away from the world and fasten their eyes exclusively (ἀφορέω, *aphoreō*) on this founder and perfecter.[103] Jesus has already successfully run the race of faithful endurance. In doing so, he not only has shown it is possible but also can assist those who are now running. Because he has become High Priest and Savior, sitting on the right hand of God (4:14–5:11), they can look to him to receive the promised rewards in mortality (as the many examples the author has given act as witnesses) and the final reward in the eternal city. In short, Jesus makes winning the race not only possible but sure.[104] The author makes it abundantly clear that this "race" is one of

---

community to which this Epistle was addressed. They formed a part of the public reputation all shared as fellow believers in God. Further, it grounded the Epistle's readers' identity with Old Testament faithful.

100. "Ancient Olympia History: Athletic Contests," Olympia Greece, accessed March 10, 2017, http://www.olympia-greece.org/contests.html.

101. Cockerill, *Epistle to the Hebrews,* 603.

102. The idea comes from Ecc. 9:11. On the phrase "the race is not to the swift, nor the battle to the sure," see note 13 in this chapter.

103. McConkie, *Doctrinal New Testament Commentary,* 3:222.

104. Ellingworth, *Epistle to the Hebrews,* 640.

"moral and religious transformation in which the 'faithful' Jesus (3:1) and the believers are intimately linked."[105]

Both of the Lord's positions—author and perfecter—give reason why the faithful can depend on him. His job as author is critical, for through this means he engenders faith. According to the Book of Mormon,

> after God had appointed that [the gospel plan] should come unto man, behold, then he saw that it was expedient that man should know concerning the things whereof he had appointed unto them; Therefore he sent angels to converse with them, who caused men to behold of his glory. And they began from that time forth to call on his name; therefore God conversed with men, and made known unto them the plan of redemption, which had been prepared from the foundation of the world; and this he made known unto them according to their faith and repentance and their holy works. (Alma 12:28–30; compare D&C 29:42)

The passage does not mention the role of Jesus in the revelatory process; nonetheless he is central. As John testified, "No man hath seen God at any time, except he hath borne record of the Son; for except it is through him no man can be saved" (JST John 1:18). Thus, it has fallen to the Son to reveal the gospel to humankind. In this light, the Apostle also testified Jesus is God's "Word" and "in him was life; and the life was the light of men" (John 1:4). Speaking of his ministry, the Savior taught his disciples that he came to preach "the gospel of the kingdom of God" (Mark 1:14), indeed, "for therefore came I forth" (Mark 1:38; compare Luke 4:43). He assured his hearers, "He whom God hath sent speaketh the words of God: for God giveth not the Spirit by measure unto him. The Father loveth the Son, and hath given all things into his hand. He that believeth on the Son hath everlasting life" (John 3:34–36). He could, therefore, assure them, "My doctrine is not mine, but his that sent me. If any man will do his will, he shall know of the doctrine, whether it be of God, or whether I speak of myself" (John 7:16–17). Thus, D&C 93:8 can summarize, "In the beginning the Word was, for he was the Word, even the messenger of salvation."[106] As such, then, he is the founder of salvation.

Christ's role as perfecter of faith is also critical. As the many examples the author of Hebrews gives, faith is realized in the present by receiving Christ's power into the Christian's life. On the one hand that reception can

---

105. Johnson, *Hebrews,* 317.

106. Bruce, *Epistle to the Hebrews,* 337, notes the Savior "led all the people of God, from earliest times, along the path of faith."

be as little as a divinely inspired steadfast belief in him. As D&C 46:13–14 notes, "To some it is given by the Holy Ghost to know that Jesus Christ is the Son of God, and that he was crucified for the sins of the world. To others it is given to believe on their words, that they also might have eternal life if they continue faithful." On the other hand, that power may be displayed by working miracles and prophesying (D&C 46:21–22). Nonetheless, "all these gifts come from God, for the benefit of the children of God" (D&C 46:26).

The realization of these powers in the Christians' lives increases faith in the Lord Jesus Christ. When a person exhibits ever-growing faith in him, through the Lord's grace, he gives them even more power. Thus, faith and power keep growing level by level until the person's faith is perfected in realizing all the power that God has to give. At the same time, the person him- or herself is also perfected. As the Book of Mormon admonishes, "Come unto Christ, and be perfected in him, and deny yourselves of all ungodliness; and if ye shall deny yourselves of all ungodliness, and love God with all your might, mind and strength, then is his grace sufficient for you, that by his grace ye may be perfect in Christ; and if by the grace of God ye are perfect in Christ, ye can in nowise deny the power of God" (Moro. 10:32). In sum, a person cannot deny that Christ has perfecting power when, through his grace, it has been the means of that person's perfection. At that point, he or she can have perfect faith in Christ, knowing he has fulfilled and can continue to fulfill his promises. Thus, the Savior is the perfecter of both faith and of the individual. The author assures his readers this is possible if they will but continue in faithful steadfastness.

With his statement that Jesus "endured the cross, disregarding its shame, and 'sat down on the right hand of God's throne'" (NR 12:2; compare 2 Ne. 9:18), the author shows precisely not only what Jesus did to perfect faith but also what he did to perfect faith-filled individuals. His motivation was to make them fit to receive the reward he has for them. The author notes three things the Lord did specifically: he endured the suffering of the cross, disregarded its shame, and took his place at God's side. Because of these he is in the perfect position to act as Savior.

The author shows that joy played an important part in the Atonement, for it motivated Jesus to take upon himself the full weight of the cross. But what is joy, and how did it serve to motivate the Savior to endure crucifixion?[107] According to the prophet Lehi, gaining joy is the central purpose of life. He

---

107. For a study, see Conzelmann, *TDNT,* 9:359–72.

states, "Adam fell that men might be; and men are, that they might have joy" (2 Ne. 2:25). The prophet's thought is so succinct that it is easy to dismiss or pass over with little awareness of its importance. Here, in just fourteen words, Lehi answers the age-old question, what is the purpose of life? His point needs examination. Adam made a decision to fall, and he made it consciously and deliberately. His objective was to bring humankind into being. If Adam had not made that choice, there would have been no mortals on this planet—ever. But he did, and humankind entered this transient world (see 2 Ne. 2:25; and Moses 5:11). Still, all die. Was death to be the end of existence? If so, why bother bringing humans into being at all? The answer is that only the physical part of "men" was mortal, and even that will not be the case after the resurrection. So, Lehi looked more broadly than merely at mortality to find a meaning and purpose of existence as a whole. In so doing, he taught us that we are moving toward a grand objective. God has a greater purpose for his children than experiencing a mere flash of mortality. Lehi taught us that the purpose for existence, both in mortality and beyond, is to gain joy.

Joseph Smith, the translator of Lehi's words, paraphrased the prophet's thought this way: "Happiness is the object and design of our existence, and will be the end thereof, if we pursue the path that leads to it."[108] So what does "happiness" mean? It, along with the related words blessedness, felicity, beatitude, and bliss, denotes the pleasurable satisfaction that arises from a state of well-being. "Happiness" is the more generic term and, while it can apply to almost any state of pleasurable enjoyment or well-being, more particularly describes the feeling arising from security, accomplishment, or obtaining a wish or goal.

But under inspiration, the prophet Lehi said that "men are that they might have joy." He did not use the word "happiness." Is there a difference? Care must be taken not to place too much emphasis on the use of any particular word in the Book of Mormon. Unlike the Bible, we cannot check the original language to see just how broadly or narrowly a term could have been translated. As noted above, Joseph Smith paraphrased Lehi's statement by saying, "Happiness is the object and design of our existence." In the Prophet's context, joy and happiness are synonyms. Even so, there are differences in nuance which deserve exploration.

Happiness describes the feeling associated with a state of well-being.[109] When that state is unachieved, threatened, or disrupted, we are not happy.

---

108. "History, 1838–1856, Volume D-1," 3 [addenda].
109. *Webster's New Dictionary of Synonyms,* s.v. "happiness."

Joy is the agreeable emotion which accompanies the possession, acquisition, or expectation of something good or very desirable.[110] Joy can, but does not necessarily, arise out of the present. A person can feel joy over something he or she anticipates. In this light, consider the well-known question God asked Job: "Where wast thou when I laid the foundations of the earth? declare, if thou hast understanding. Who hath laid the measures thereof, if thou knowest? or who hath stretched the line upon it? Whereupon are the foundations thereof fastened? or who laid the corner stone thereof; When the morning stars sang together, and all the sons of God shouted for joy?" (Job 38:4–7). In this case, it was not just the creation but its anticipation that brought joy to the children of God.

Happiness relies heavily on the present; joy much less so. Joy adds the dimensions of acquisition and continuance to happiness. "Those who have died in Jesus Christ," taught Joseph Smith, "may expect to enter in to all that fruition of Joy when they come forth. which they have possessed [or anticipated] here."[111] Thus, the future bequeaths a fulness of the joy either won or anticipated in the present. Joy is closely akin to pleasure and delight when these words are taken in a positive sense.[112] But "a fullness of joy" implies an emotion that is "so great as to be almost painful in its intensity."[113] Thus, joy should never be divorced from either pleasure or happiness, but it is not dependent on them either. Joy can thrive outside a state of well-being, for it is the extreme feeling which comes from the realization and fulfillment of all that one has striven for and the anticipated results of all that one strives for.[114] Heaven is the place where joy is found in its fulness.

It is in this light that we should understand the statement in Hebrews that the Savior himself endured all things, including the cross, "for the

---

110. *Webster's New Dictionary of Synonyms,* s.v. "joy."

111. "Discourse, 16 April 1843, as Reported by Willard Richards," [143], Joseph Smith Papers, https://www.josephsmithpapers.org/paper-summary/discourse-16-april-1843-as-reported-by-willard-richards/5. The phrase "or anticipated" appears in *Teachings of the Prophet Joseph Smith,* comp. Joseph Fielding Smith (Salt Lake City: Deseret Book, 1974), 295, and was likely added by Joseph Fielding Smith to clarify.

112. David O. McKay, in *Gospel Ideals: Selections from the Discourses of David O. McKay* (Salt Lake City: Improvement Era, 1953), 491–92, notes the negative side of pleasure when he admonished the Saints, saying, "Let us in life distinguish between the joy that the Prophet Lehi had in mind when he said, 'Men are that they might have joy,' and the pleasure that the world is seeking by indulging in appetites and passions, vainly hoping to find happiness. Happiness springs from within. . . . Pleasure is not the purpose of man's existence. Joy is."

113. *Webster's New Dictionary of Synonyms,* s.v. "pleasure."

114. *Webster's New Dictionary of Synonyms,* s.v. "pleasure."

joy that was set before him" (12:2). With the author of Hebrews, the Apostle Paul was well aware of the shame that was associated with the cross. The Apostle noted the idea of the Messiah being crucified was a "stumblingblock" to the Jews and "foolishness" to the Gentiles (1 Cor. 1:23). The Greek noun translated "stumblingblock" (σκάνδαλον, *skandalon*) is hard to translate precisely, but the English term "scandal" is derived from it and connotes the trap in which politicians and celebrities sometimes find themselves, and this hints at its Greek meaning. Certainly, the nuance as something that blocks progress is too weak. The Greek word literally denotes either the trigger or the actual trap used to catch animals alive, thus, "a snare." Metaphorically, it denotes "an action or circumstance that leads one to act contrary to a proper course of action or set of beliefs," thus "temptation or enticement."[115] The word also connoted any action or belief in one person that caused another person to take offense to the point of anger.[116] The English word "affront," in the sense of deliberately doing something that annoys, humiliates, or vexes another person, carries that idea.[117] Thus, the Jews were affronted by the Christian preaching of a crucified Messiah.[118] They joined with the Gentiles in viewing Jesus as a person of the lowest possible social status, namely, a crucified low-class criminal, an instigator or political revolutionary.[119] For the Jews, to be asked to accept the humiliating and disgraceful execution of a Jewish teacher by a foreign sovereignty as a heavenly sign of God's saving power was an affront. They wanted a victorious Messiah heralded by a display of divine power. For the Gentiles, to be asked to accept as a God one whose suffering and death shouted dishonor, shame, and failure was nothing short of foolishness.[120] They wanted a philosopher king whose wisdom and intellect none could challenge. In these ways, "both Jew and Greek become adversaries

---

115. BDAG, 926.

116. Louw-Nida, §25.181.

117. Thiselton, *First Epistle*, 171.

118. This was not the only thing about Jesus that offended them. See George Q. Cannon, in *Journal of Discourses*, 22:262; and Wilford Woodruff, in *Journal of Discourses*, 18:188.

119. Stephen M. Pogoloff, *Logos and Sophia: The Rhetorical Situation of 1 Corinthians*, SBL Dissertation Series 134 (Atlanta: Society of Biblical Literature, 1992), 156.

120. Thiselton, *First Epistle*, 170. For a study from a Latter-day Saint perspective, see Gaye Strathearn, "Christ's Crucifixion: Reclamation of the Cross," *Religious Educator* 14, no. 1 (2013): 45–57.

of the crucified Christ."[121] The author of Hebrews makes it abundantly clear that Jesus understood the weight of ignominy of being hung on the cross but nevertheless submitted, motivated by "the joy that lay before him." He was able to bear the shame of the cross because he "looked to God as the source of his honor and glory, rather than to the court of human opinion."[122]

Having faced the cross, Christ took the final step necessary to be the Savior. The imagery taken from LXX Psalm 109:1 of sitting at God's right hand emphasizes the idea of the power the Savior now wields. All that God has is his to execute in behalf of the righteous.

In 12:3, the author explains why he wants his readers to keep their eyes fixed on Jesus: so they will follow his example and not become weary or lose motivation in face of the opposition they are going through. The author's admonition echoes athletic training in which participants push themselves so they do not become overly weak or unduly fatigued during the actual contest.[123] But as difficult this training is for the author's readers, it was harder for the Lord. He faced not only outright and personally painful hostility (ἀντιλογία, *antilogia*) but also death. The Christians are not to consider him only on the basis of the example he set for them, however, but on what, through his endurance, he became—the one having full power to sustain them through their present trials.[124]

Unlike the Lord, the author notes, his readers have not yet resisted unto blood (μέχρις αἵματος, *mechris haimatos*) in their struggle against sin. The verbs "resist" (ἀντικαθίστημι, *antikathistēmi*) and "struggle" (ἀνταγωνίζομαι, *antagōnizomai*) were associated with athletic contests and particularly boxing. This sport was especially brutal and bloody because the participants' gloves were inlaid with bits of metal.[125] Such stark imagery likely reminded the author's readers of the lengths they needed to go in order to endure in faith and to defend the kingdom.

---

121. Joseph A. Fitzmyer, *First Corinthians: A New Translation with Introduction and Commentary,* vol. 32 of Anchor Yale Bible (New Haven, Conn.: Yale University Press, 2008), 160.

122. Johnson, *Hebrews,* 317.

123. The verb ἐκλύομαι (*ekluomai*), "to become very weary," is associated with athletes that have not trained well and are, therefore, in bad condition. Attridge, *Epistle to the Hebrews,* 358 n. 80.

124. Cockerill, *Epistle to the Hebrews,* 612.

125. Cockerill, *Epistle to the Hebrews,* 618 n. 19.

The focus of their resistance is against "sin" (ἁμαρτία, *hamartia*). Here (12:4) that focus is not on sin in general but on sin as expressed in opposition to God and his people. Against this the author encourages his readers to struggle. The present participle he uses denotes the need for continual striving against those forces battering the Saints. To bolster them, he appeals to the Savior's own struggle against his adversaries even to death. There is a hint here, however, that his ultimate victory will also be theirs.[126]

The rest of this section of the author's work rests on Proverbs 3:11–12, which deals with the need to accept discipline (παιδεία, *paideia*). In 12:5–6, he quotes it; in 12:7–11, he interprets it; and in 12:12–13, he applies it.[127] His purpose is to encourage his readers to continue their faithful endurance. The term he used often refers to the discipline a good father must impose on a wayward child (Deut. 21:18; Prov. 13:24; 19:18; 23:3; 29:17). God put Israel under his discipline (Deut. 4:36; Hosea 7:12; 10:10) and was not above using severe disciplinary measures to correct them.[128]

Over time, the negative aspect of "chastisement" fell behind the more positive aspect of "instruction." Jehovah gave instructions to Israel so that they would realize they owed their very existence to his saving will and, therefore, should give their full allegiance to their divine instructor (Deut. 8:1–6). The Wisdom literature brings together both the moralizing and humanizing tendency that thus unites faith and reason.[129] The purpose of discipline was to produce a people who lived according to God's will. His will was expressed in the law, viewed as having a timeless dimension unaffected by history, and could therefore continually form the basis of the people's relationship with him.[130]

After Judah's return from Babylonian bondage, the idea of discipline developed another dimension. This was that Jehovah's teachings and loving hand was to be experienced through suffering. It was by this that righteousness and

---

126. Croy, *Endurance,* 194; Cockerill, *Epistle to the Hebrews,* 619.

127. Cockerill, *Epistle to the Hebrews,* 615. For studies, see *NID,* s.v. "παιδεύω"; Bertram, *TDNT,* 5:596–625; and Ched E. Spellman, "When Hope Screams: Learning How to Suffer as Sons from the Book of Hebrews," *Southwestern Journal of Theology* 53, no. 2 (Spring 2011): 112–34.

128. The same is true for modern Saints. See McConkie, *Doctrinal New Testament Commentary,* 3:223.

129. Bertram, *TDNT,* 5:608.

130. *NID,* s.v. "παιδεύω."

perfection could be achieved.[131] The author picks up this theme to show his readers that suffering is a sign of God's love and, therefore, is no reason to lose courage. Indeed, it is a sign of their legitimacy in the divine family and that they are accepted by him (12:6). The author has already taught that it was "fitting" that the Father perfect his Son through suffering (2:10). Here the author shows that it is also appropriate for the rest of God's children to so suffer in order to reach the same end. Such suffering is, therefore, not a chastening for an individual's sins (indeed, of these Christ has already cleansed him or her).[132] Though the word "discipline" carries the idea of "training" and "instruction," it transcends these, marking the Father's use of opposition as the means to strengthen and fortify his children. He does this so they can both stay on and progress along his path. The Father's discipline betokens their legitimacy as it did that of his Only Begotten and in doing so unites children with Son.[133]

The author makes the point that his readers should have concerns if they do not come under God's discipline. In 12:7–10, he uses the example of human upbringing. As mortal fathers are willing to chastise their children for their own good and growth, so too does God. The discipline can carry harsh measures as 12:6 shows, including that of being chastised (μαστιγόω, *mastigoō*). The noun carries the idea, however, that it is the means to further the person's wellbeing rather than punishment.[134] If they resist such discipline, they are not only defying God and rejecting his love but also cutting themselves off from the growth such can produce.[135]

The author makes an arresting point. In his example, a person has either a legitimate or an illegitimate status with God. The latter would be those "who have not been adopted into the family of God as joint-heirs

---

131. This idea was not new; hints are found in Old Testament. For examples, see Deut. 8:5; 11:2; and 2 Sam. 7:14.

132. By placing emphasis on the positive aspects of παιδεία (*paideia*), "discipline," the author actually breaks with the thrust of Prov. 3:12. There the emphasis is on reproving (ἐλέγχω, *elengchō*) and chastising (μαστιγόω, *mastigoō*) a child for wrongdoing. It nuances a Hebraic background that is concerned with rebellion and broken covenants and their results. Thompson, *Hebrews,* 254. The author of Hebrews is coming at suffering from the perspective of God's love and training. See Croy, *Endurance,* 197–98. Therefore, the author does not repeat the idea of reproving or chastising in his analysis of the scripture.

133. Cockerill, *Epistle to the Hebrews,* 616. The author's point is that God is treating them no differently than he did his own Son. Johnson, *Hebrews,* 321.

134. BDAG, 620. The Mosaic law demanded this kind of correction for certain offenses. See note 51 in this chapter.

135. *NID*, s.v. "παιδεύω."

with Christ."[136] Concerning an illegitimate status, because of the mores of the day, the father was not responsible for one "baseborn" (νόθος, *nothos*) under Roman law. These children, from a civic or familial standpoint, had no place in the family and, therefore, need not be accepted. The author's point is that if children had no one to discipline them, it meant they had no head of household to be concerned about them. On the other hand, if they were disciplined, it meant they were legitimate and had a place in the family.

The analogy suggests that these Saints were going through a period of persecution, not one that yet yielded martyrdom but was nonetheless very difficult.[137] The harsh times were a sign they were in God's family—indeed, that they had status as children—suggesting a connection with Christ who was the Son par excellence and who also suffered greatly for the faith.[138]

In 12:9, the author refers to "fathers of our flesh" and the "Father of spirits." The noun "father" (πατήρ, *patēr*) carries a strong nuance. In the patriarchal societies, the father had two primary responsibilities. First, he was the head of the household and therefore commanded respect due to his absolute authority.[139] Second, he was responsible for providing for and guarding his family. This included inculcating his children with both moral and intellectual ideals. Theologically, when applied to God, the term enforced not only the idea of his absolute authority but also his merciful love and served as background for his law and the discipline it demanded.[140]

Normally in both the Old and New Testaments, being a child of God was not a natural quality or state but was brought about by the divine action of grace through which the child entered into God's spiritual family and became an heir of eternal life (Ex. 4:22; Deut. 14:1–2; Hosea 11:1–4; Rom. 8:14–17; Gal. 4:1–7).[141] In this passage, however, the author looks more broadly, seeing God as the originator of not just a person's earthly life but of his or her spirit life as well. The author appears to be following the Apostle Paul, who referred to the "one God and Father of all, who is above all, and through all, and in you all" (Eph. 4:6). The words of these two Church leaders suggest a paternal bond that, from a Latter-day Saint perspective,

136. McConkie, *Doctrinal New Testament Commentary,* 3:224.

137. The author may be preparing them for a more severe struggle yet to come. Attridge, *Epistle to the Hebrews,* 360.

138. Ellingworth, *Epistle to the Hebrews,* 651.

139. Under the Mosaic law, rebellion against one's father was a capital offense. See Deut. 21:18–21.

140. *NID,* s.v. "πατήρ."

141. McConkie, *Doctrinal New Testament Commentary,* 3:224–25.

originated in the premortal sphere of the Father's eternal plan. As "The Family: A Proclamation to the World" states, "All human beings—male and female—are created in the image of God. Each is a beloved spirit son or daughter of heavenly parents, and, as such, each has a divine nature and destiny. . . . In the premortal realm, spirit sons and daughters knew and worshipped God as their Eternal Father."[142]

As the author of Hebrews notes in 12:10, God disciplines to bring about one condition, that of holiness (ἁγιότης, *hagiotēs*). This condition is necessary for a person to abide in God's presence. For further discussion, see Analysis in the next section.

Though admitting in 12:11 that undergoing discipline is not at all pleasant, the author points out there is great reward for those who yield themselves to God's training hand. These souls eventually partake of the fruit of their continual effort, which is the peaceful quality of life shared by the righteous.

The author concludes this section of his discourse (12:12–13) with an admonition that his readers push forward directly toward the eternal city. In doing so, he has come back to the beginning of his discussion in which he urged his readers to "run the race that is set before [them]" (NR 12:1). In doing so, they will confirm the road that the "lame," that is, the spiritually weak, should also take. Whether the term "lame" refers to the weak within the Christian community or to the community itself,[143] those who walk the path will set an encouraging example for the weak to follow. For those who do run by making the path either "for their feet," by moving obstacles out of the way, or "with their feet," by walking in a straight course,[144] the Saints will show the "lame" that the walk can be done and also provide the way not only to safeguard the weak against any further injuries but also to allow healing to occur.

---

142. The First Presidency and the Council of the Twelve Apostles of The Church of Jesus Christ of Latter-day Saints, "The Family: A Proclamation to the World," *Ensign* 25, no. 11 (November 1995): 102. For a broad study of the concept of fatherhood in the ancient Near East and more especially in the Old and New Testament, see Schrenk, *TDNT,* 5:945–59; Quell, *TDNT,* 5:959–74; and Schrenk, *TDNT,* 5:974–1022. For the premortal relationship between God and humankind from a Latter-day Saint perspective, see Gayle Oblad Brown, "Premortal Life," in Ludlow, *Encyclopedia of Mormonism,* 3:1123–25; B. H. Roberts, *Mormon Doctrine of Deity: The Roberts–Van Der Donckt Discussion* (Salt Lake City: Deseret News, 1903), 259–65; and McConkie, *Doctrinal New Testament Commentary,* 3:224–26. For a study of the meaning of premortality and the ultimate issue of human existence, see Truman G. Madsen, *Eternal Man* (Salt Lake City: Deseret Book, 1966).

143. For discussion, see Cockerill, *Epistle to the Hebrews,* 630 and n. 72.

144. Cockerill, *Epistle to the Hebrews,* 630 n. 73.

Warnings against Rejecting God's Grace (12:14–17)

Greek Text

14 Εἰρήνην διώκετε μετὰ πάντων, καὶ τὸν ἁγιασμόν, οὗ χωρὶς οὐδεὶς ὄψεται τὸν κύριον, 15 ἐπισκοποῦντες μή τις ὑστερῶν ἀπὸ τῆς χάριτος τοῦ θεοῦ, μή τις ῥίζα πικρίας ἄνω φύουσα ἐνοχλῇ καὶ δι' αὐτῆς μιανθῶσιν πολλοί, 16 μή τις πόρνος ἢ βέβηλος ὡς Ἠσαῦ, ὃς ἀντὶ βρώσεως μιᾶς ἀπέδετο τὰ πρωτοτόκια ἑαυτοῦ. 17 ἴστε γὰρ ὅτι καὶ μετέπειτα θέλων κληρονομῆσαι τὴν εὐλογίαν ἀπεδοκιμάσθη, μετανοίας γὰρ τόπον οὐχ εὗρεν, καίπερ μετὰ δακρύων ἐκζητήσας αὐτήν. [SBLGNT]

King James Version

14 Follow peace with all men, and holiness, without which no man shall see the Lord: 15 Looking diligently lest any man fail of the grace of God; lest any root of bitterness springing up trouble you, and thereby many be defiled; 16 Lest there be any fornicator, or profane person, as Esau, who for one morsel of meat sold his birthright. 17 For ye know how that afterward, when he would have inherited the blessing, he was rejected: for he found no place of repentance, though he sought it carefully with tears.

New Rendition

14 Seek for peace with everyone, and for holiness, without which no one will see the Lord. 15 See to it that no one fails to obtain God's grace, and that

> "no bitter root sprouts up" [Deut. 29:18]

to cause trouble by which many become defiled. 16 And see to it that there is no immoral or worldly person like Esau, who

> "sold his own birthright for a single meal" [Gen. 27:29–34].

17 For you know that afterwards, when he wanted to inherit the blessing, he was rejected, for he found no opportunity for repentance even though he sought for it with tears.

Translation Notes and Comments

12:14 *Follow peace with all men / Seek for peace with everyone:* The verb διώκω (*diōkō*), "to seek," carries the idea of rapidly and decisively moving toward an objective.[145]

In this case, that objective is expressed by the noun εἰρήνη (*eirēnē*), "peace."[146] The word carries a heavy theological meaning (see Analysis below) but in general denotes well-being based on health and safety.

145. BDAG, 254.
146. BDAG, 287–88.

However, because of its positive nuance in the Hebrew Bible, where it is closely associated with the Divine, many saw in it a condition that transcended mere earthly security and rest. Instead, the word described the "eschatological salvation of the whole man."[147]

The phrase μετὰ πάντων (*meta pantōn*), literally "with all," is vague. It could indicate striving for a peaceful relationship with "all whom one is associated"[148] or "in company with one's fellows."[149] The broader meaning would include even those who were persecuting the Saints. Given Christ's admonition to love and even pray for one's enemies (Matt. 5:44), seeking peace with them would be a proper activity for the Saints. The context of this part of the Epistle suggests the author had this broader view in mind. There is no doubt that his major concern is with the community of the Saints, not with society in general. His fear is that some may rebel and end up like the wilderness generation, losing the promise of a place in the heavenly city. But playing in the background is the tension that exists between the Church and its neighbors, and relieving that tension would go a long way to ameliorating the problems the Saints were facing. If that is the case, then the *meta pantōn* refers to the whole of the community in which the Church moved, and the author is requesting his readers build up peace among those who are part of that community.[150]

and holiness, without which no man shall see the Lord / and for holiness, without which no one will see the Lord: The noun ἁγιασμός (*hagiasmos*), "holiness," in the author's context does not represent a process of moral development as it does in some contexts. For him it is always a gift of God provided by Christ for the community of believers that comes because of the Atonement (10:10, 14[151]). Also, it is not a onetime gift but a continual state in which the recipient lives sin free.[152] It results in close spiritual association with the Father and Son.[153]

---

147. Foester, *TDNT,* 2:412–13.

148. Attridge, *Epistle to the Hebrews,* 367; Bruce, *Epistle to the Hebrews,* 348; Johnson, *Hebrews,* 323.

149. Lane, *Hebrews 9–13,* 438 note b; Cockerill, *Epistle to the Hebrews,* 634.

150. For discussion, see Ellingworth, *Epistle to the Hebrews,* 661–62.

151. In these verses, the word "sanctified" is translated from the verb ἁγιάζω (*hagiazō*), "to make holy." Vanhoye, *Letter to the Hebrews,* 206.

152. The theological term for this state is δίκαιος (*dikaios*), "justified." It describes the quality or character of being right with God and thereby having a close relationship with him. It comes as a gracious gift from Christ that makes the person sin free and keeps her or him that way as long as they strive to live the covenantal life. See the Translation Notes and the associated Analysis for 4:16.

153. Cockerill, *Epistle to the Hebrews,* 634 and n. 13. Compare Lane, *Hebrews 9–13,* 450.

The verb ὁράω (*horaō*), "to see," that is, "to perceive with the eye," also means "to experience."[154] That the author uses the future tense suggests he understands that, without first obtaining the state of holiness, fellowship with God in the next life will be impossible.

12:15–16 To make the very long sentence that comprises 12:15–16 read more easily, we have divided it into two sentences at the end of 12:15 and repeated the phrase "see to it" at the beginning of 12:16. Note the author draws on Deuteronomy 29:16–20 to make his points. Those verses deal with apostasy from Jehovah and express concerns similar to those the author is addressing.[155]

12:15 ***Looking diligently lest any man fail of the grace of God / See to it that no one fails to obtain God's grace:*** In this verse, the author continues his admonition. The verb ἐπισκοπέω (*episkopeō*) means "to see that something is done." Its nuance has a warm personal flavor connoting as it does the acceptance of responsibility for someone and seeing to his or her care.[156] A more full nuance would include an acute awareness on the part of the caregiver of any danger that might befall the person in need.[157] Found here as a present active participle, it carries on the sense of the imperative διώκετε (*diōkete*), "seek for," in the previous verse. It reveals the author's intent to have his readers understand their responsibility to care for their fellow Christians.

The verb ὑστερέω (*hystereō*) denotes "to miss out on something through one's own fault," "to fail to obtain." The use of the word by the author in the present context reveals his position on the matter. He asks his readers to overlook the weakness of others and accept the responsibility of assisting them toward a specific end.

The noun χάρις (*charis*) means "grace." In the present context, the noun designates the Father's favorable predisposition toward his children expressing itself in compassion and understanding. The term nuances the outreach of his divine love as revealed through the ministry of the Son. It looks more particularly to the enabling gift he freely and lovingly gives to those who strive to do his will. It must also be noted this gift empowers them to do what they could not otherwise do.[158] Since all are subject to

---

154. BDAG, 719–20.

155. For discussion, see Cockerill, *Epistle to the Hebrews,* 635–36 and n. 19.

156. BDAG, 379. Note that the noun derived from this verb, ἐπίσκοπος (*episkopos*), is the New Testament word for the ecclesiastical office of "bishop." BDAG, 379.

157. Ellingworth, *Epistle to the Hebrews,* 663.

158. BDAG, 1079–81; Conzelmann, *TDNT,* 9:372–76; *NID,* s.v. "χάρις." For an extended study from a Latter-day Saint perspective, see Draper and Rhodes, *Paul's First Epistle to the Corinthians,* 74–100.

sin, members of the Church should do all they can to help others to take advantage of God's grace.

lest any root of bitterness springing up trouble you, and thereby many be defiled / and that "no bitter root sprouts up" to cause trouble by which many become defiled: The phrase contains a reference to Deuteronomy 29:18. The author's concern is with the ῥίζα πικρίας (*riza pikrias*), a "root of bitterness." The noun ῥίζα (*riza*), "root," refers primarily to the underground part of a plant but in a secondary sense to the "shoot" it sends up that can grow into a full plant.[159]

The noun πικρία (*pikria*), "bitterness," refers not just to a bitter taste but, in a more metaphorical sense, to harshness, animosity, and anger.[160] The latter particularly can lead a person away from peace and therefore away from God. The ῥίζα πικρίας (*riza pikrias*) the author asks his readers to watch out for could refer to either rebellious persons themselves or to their "evil, unbelieving heart" that leads them to "rebel against the living God" (3:12).[161]

The author understands what bitterness can cause. He uses the verb ἐνοχλέω (*enochleō*), "to trouble," to articulate it. In an abstract sense, the word means "to cause trouble"[162] and points to what bitterness, full grown, can do not only to the acrimonious person but also to the community in which she or he has place.

The verb μιαίνω (*miainō*), "to defile,[163] describes the end result. A person filled with bitterness can act to defile him- or herself and those nearby. Taken in the Judeo-Christian context, the term carried the idea of breaking one's relationship with God. But within the broader religious culture of the day, it carried more than a concern for the wellbeing of the individual. "Harmonious relations with the transcendent realm were understood to be dependent on the careful observance of certain moral and ritual proprieties. Individuals were subordinate to the interests of the community and violations of standard moral and ceremonial expectations could jeopardize the delicate balance between the entire populace and their deities."[164] This idea was close to the Jewish concept concerning their dealings with Jehovah and thereby played a part in the psyche of the Christians as well.

---

159. BDAG, 905–6.
160. BDAG, 813.
161. Cockerill, *Epistle to the Hebrews,* 637.
162. BDAG, 338.
163. BDAG, 650.
164. BDAG, 650.

The author is concerned with the potential that πολλοί (*polloi*), "many," may become defiled. The adjective πολύς (*polys*), "much," in the plural, "many,"[165] shows the possible extent of the damage a bitter person can cause.[166] Thus, the actions of one person could lead to defilement of many and cost them their relationship with God, forfeiting his grace. Once again, we see echoes of the rebellious wilderness generation who lost Jehovah's grace and died both physically and spiritually out of his presence.

12:16 ***Lest there be any fornicator / see to it that there is no immoral [person]:*** The root of bitterness unchecked leads to breaking the covenant. The noun πόρνος (*pornos*) denotes a sexually immoral person or a prostitute.[167] It also shows what potentially can happen when people leave the Lord: having lost Christ's grace, they become apostate and, in their bitterness, deliberately violate the conditions of the new covenant by committing one of the most grievous of sins, that of sexual sin (Alma 39:5). In doing so, they become an immoral person.

profane person / worldly person: The adjective βέβηλος (*bebēlos*) denotes a person who is "worldly as opposed to having an interest in transcendent matters."[168] The word describes a profane person who is far from God and is ethically deficient.[169] Such a person is the epitome of godlessness.

Esau, who for one morsel of meat sold his birthright / Esau, who "sold his own birthright for a single meal": The reference is to Genesis 27:29–34. Esau, the son of Isaac, was infamous for selling his birthright. The numerical adjective μιᾶς (*mias*), "one,"[170] connotes a single meal and nuances the cheap price Esau was willing to trade for his birthright. Further, the idea underscores the total lack of care he had for God's blessing.

The noun πρωτοτόκια (*prōtotokia*), "birthright,"[171] refers to the privileged position of the firstborn son. Due to Esau's position, he had preeminence and authority over his siblings and also received a double portion of his father's property (Gen. 27:29; 49:3; Deut. 21:17).

---

165. BDAG, 847–50.

166. Attridge, *Epistle to the Hebrews,* 368.

167. BDAG, 855.

168. BDAG, 173.

169. Hauck, *TDNT,* 1:605; *NID,* s.v. "βέβηλος."

170. This is the genitive, feminine, singular form of the cardinal εἷς (*heis*), "one." BDAG, 291–93.

171. BDAG, 894."

Whether the author refers to Esau as an example of both an immoral and a profane person is not clear. The ground for thinking the author has two different people in mind is that Genesis never describes Esau as being immoral, and the focus of the author is on Esau's lack of regard for his birthright, not on any immorality on his part. On the other hand, the ground for thinking he has only Esau in mind is that there was an ancient Jewish tradition suggesting Esau was a profane and lustful man not above forcing women to yield to his desires, and also his relationship to the Hittite women involved fornication.[172] The author was likely aware of this tradition. Further, he was well aware that the Hebrew Bible consistently uses immorality as the primary symbol for idolatrous apostasy. No firm conclusion can be drawn on this issue, but that the author uses *pornos* and *bebēlos* in close proximity gives some weight to the idea he saw Esau as an example of both an immoral and a worldly person.[173]

12:17 ***For ye know how that afterward, when he would have inherited the blessing, he was rejected / For you know that afterwards, when he wanted to inherit the blessing, he was rejected:*** The author alludes to Genesis 27:30–40. The phrase ἴστε γὰρ (*iste gar*), "for you know," points to a well-known fact against which none should argue.

The adverb μετέπειτα (*metepeita*), "afterwards," denotes the point in time at which Esau should have received his birthright.

The verb θέλω (*thelō*), "wish, desire, want,"[174] shows there came a point when Esau decided he wanted the birthright (referred to as the εὐλογία [*eulogia*], "blessing"[175]) and determined to renege on his covenant with Jacob.

The verb ἀποδοκιμάζω (*apodokimazō*) denotes that which is rejected either because it is unfit or unworthy.[176] Esau fits both criteria.

for he found no place of repentance, though he sought it carefully with tears / for he found no opportunity for repentance even though he sought for it with tears: The noun τόπος (*topos*), "place, opportunity," in this context denotes a favorable point in time to do something and thus connotes "an opportunity."[177] For Esau, none existed.

---

172. *Jub.* 25.1. Philo, *Virt.* 208, connects Esau's disregard for his birthright with his inability to control both his physical and sexual urges.

173. For a discussion, see *NID*, s.v. "βέβηλος."

174. BDAG, 447–48.

175. BDAG, 408–9.

176. BDAG, 110.

177. BDAG, 1011–12.

The noun μετάνοια (*metanoia*), "repentance," denotes changing one's mind, disposition, and attitude such that one's very lifestyle changes. Even so, among the Jews and Christians, the thought never lost the Semitic sense of turning away from something.[178] In the present context, it seems the force is on the latter. The reason is that Esau definitely changed his mind,[179] but it did no good because he could not find a way to turn away from his deal with Jacob. The phrase τόπος μετανοίας (*topos metanoias*), literally "a place of repentance," is an idiom meaning "to have the opportunity for repentance,"[180] and is therefore used in our Rendition.

The noun δάκρυον (*dakryon*) denotes "a tear," but in the plural, as here, "tears."[181] The phrase μετὰ δακρύων (*meta dakryōn*), "with weeping," shows the intensity with which Esau sought the birthright.[182] But he had already covenanted it away, and there was no getting it back.

The feminine pronoun αὐτήν (*autēn*), "it," can be taken two ways. Its antecedent could be either "repentance" or "blessing" because both are feminine. However, though in the sentence "repentance" is closer to the pronoun than "blessing," the former is associated with the masculine noun "place" in the phrase "a place of repentance." Since the author is very skilled with his Greek, it is likely, if he were referring to repentance, he would have made the pronoun masculine to match repentance's associated noun "place." Also, the verb ἐκζητέω (*ekzēteō*), "to seek," works better with "blessing" than with "repentance." In light of these, the author was most likely referring to the blessing Esau had lost.[183]

Analysis and Summary

The author begins this section (12:14) of his argument with an imperative to "seek" (διώκετε, *diōkete*) that carries the nuance of rapidly and decisively moving toward an objective.[184] In this case, there is not one but three

178. BDAG, 640–41. For a discussion on the ways the idea can be taken, see Ellingworth, *Epistle to the Hebrews,* 668–69.

179. Though it has been speculated that Esau sought to change the mind of either God or Isaac, the regular use of the noun always points to the person himself. See Lane, *Hebrews 9–13,* 440 note r; and Ellingworth, *Epistle to the Hebrews,* 668.

180. For references, see O'Brien, *Letter to the Hebrews,* 476 n. 163; and Lane, *Hebrews 9–13,* 440 note r.

181. BDAG, 211.

182. LXX Gen. 27:34 does not mention weeping, but it does say he "cried out with a loud cry and great bitterness."

183. For discussion, see Lane, *Hebrews 9–13,* 440 note t; and Cockerill, *Epistle to the Hebrews,* 640.

184. BDAG, 254.

objectives. The first is peace, the second is holiness, and the third is guarding against bitterness.

The noun "peace" (εἰρήνη, *eirēnē*) carries a heavy theological nuance. Among the Jewish Christians it ever echoed the Hebrew שָׁלוֹם (*šālôm*),[185] meaning "well-being," and denoted the ideas of safety and good health. Behind it stood the idea of a godly gift that directly affected, in a very positive way, human relationships. The Hebrew Bible views it as one of the greatest gifts Jehovah could bestow upon his people. From there the Jews derived a very comprehensive meaning describing "the experience of the person who fully enjoys the presence of [Jehovah], being blessed, guarded, and treated graciously by him."[186] The word came to further indicate "a comprehensive kind of fulfilment or completion, indeed of a perfection in life and spirit which quite transcends any success which man alone, even under the best of circumstances, is able to attain."[187] From there it was only a step to equate the word with salvation and the nature of heaven itself.

Among the Christians, the term suggested the goal and content of the gospel message. Indeed, Paul called his preachment "the gospel of peace" (Eph. 6:15; compare Acts 10:36; and Eph. 2:17). In the Christian context, "peace" was a gift that was bestowed by both the Father and the Son (for example, see Rom. 1:7; 1 Cor. 1:3; and Col. 3:15) and was maintained and deepened through communion with the Savior (John 16:33; Philip. 4:7; 1 Pet. 5:14). As noted above, the author of Hebrews sees it as a product of discipline through which one receives the "fruit of righteousness" (12:11).

The second state the author admonished his readers to attain is "holiness." The author is anxious that his readers attain this state because of its necessity if one is to "see" God (12:14). The verb "to see" (ὁράω, *horaō*) denotes not only viewing but also experiencing something. In this case that is an association with the Father. Jesus had already made it abundantly clear that only the pure in heart (a condition of holiness) can see God (Matt. 5:8). The pure not only have the opportunity to partially experience God while in the flesh but fully in the world to come. According to a revelation to Joseph Smith, "it shall come to pass that every soul who forsaketh his sins and cometh unto me, and calleth on my name, and obeyeth my voice, and keepeth my commandments, shall see my face and know that I am" (D&C 93:1). Another

---

185. The phenomenon is called "semantic borrowing."

186. John I. Durham, "שָׁלוֹם and the Presence of God," in *Proclamation and Presence: Old Testament Essays in Honour of Gwynne Henton Davies,* ed. John I. Durham and J. R. Porter (Richmond, Va.: John Knox Press, 1970), 280.

187. Durham, "שָׁלוֹם and the Presence of God," 280.

revelation admonishes the Saints to "strip yourselves from jealousies and fears, and humble yourselves before me . . . [and] you shall see me and know that I am" (D&C 67:10). All the attributes these revelations mention are necessary aspects of holiness and prepare the person to experience fully an association with the Father and the Son.[188]

The idea of holiness is important throughout the Bible[189] as an attribute associated with God but one he shares with others. Indeed, it is he "who invests a person, place or object with holiness."[190] In the Old Testament, the noun "holiness" denotes a state opposite of that which is profane or common. It connotes that which is devoid of any competing elements and is therefore pure. The term also carries the idea of a complete separation from false religious practices and an exclusive devotion to Jehovah. Holiness is a state necessary to properly approach the Divine, because it is one of God's major attributes and, to be comfortable being around him, one must also have this attribute.

The New Testament adds another dimension. Whereas among the Israelites, holiness belonged to objects, places, and rites, among the Christians, it belongs more to the prophetic sphere in which the Holy Ghost dominates a person's life. It is the possession of this divine Spirit that makes one holy. Thus, its acquisition is more than mere moral transformation necessary for fellowship with God but rather a participation in the very nature of divine life through an intimate association with the Father of spirits.[191] It is hallowing God—that is, glorifying him through obedience to his commandments—that opens the door to the reception of the Spirit and thereby to holiness.

The author of Hebrews uses the concept of holiness in a highly specialized way. He ties it to Christ as High Priest and particularly to his priestly service. The Savior's self-sacrifice coupled with his priesthood authority is the means by which the Saints secure that state of holiness for themselves and achieve eternal redemption. Once people come under the "blood of the covenant" (10:29), they are sanctified, that is, they enter into a state of holiness. For this reason, the author of Hebrews admonishes his readers to "seek for peace with everyone, and for holiness, without which no one will see the Lord" (NR 12:14). He emphasizes that the Father disciplines in order to make

188. McConkie, *Doctrinal New Testament Commentary,* 3:227.

189. For studies, see Procksch and Kuhn, *TDNT,* 1:88–115; *NID,* s.v. "ἅγιος"; and Bell, "Holiness," in Ludlow, *Encyclopedia of Mormonism,* 2:648–49.

190. Bell, "Holiness," in Ludlow, *Encyclopedia of Mormonism,* 2:648–49.

191. Lane, *Hebrews 9–13,* 425.

his followers holy so they are, as the author has already pointed out (11:10), prepared for a place in God's eternal city.

The attributes of holiness and peace serve the community of Saints, acting as uniting forces and should never be separated. The peace of Christ (John 14:27) that binds the Christians together is one of the achievements of the cross and the holiness that identifies them as Christ's own is another (compare Moro. 7:41).[192]

In 12:15, the author continues his admonition with a stiff warning. Though speaking to his readership as a whole, he shows concern for a specific group: those who are struggling with their faith. In this verse, he admonishes the members to take responsibility for one another and see to it (ἐιπισκοπέω, *episkopeō*) that struggling souls do not fall from grace (χάρις, *charis*). If members did fall, it would mean losing grace's empowerment, which would leave these vulnerable Saints without the additional spiritual strength they desperately need.

The third state the author wants his readers to watch out for is bitterness (πικρία, *pikria*) that, if it took root in the community, could defile the whole (μιαίνω, *miainō*). Bitterness often expresses itself in animosity and anger.[193] The latter particularly can stand in the way of peace and can easily cause trouble (ἐνοχλέω, *enochleō*) as the author warns. That trouble could express itself in strained relationships between members of the Church, their gentile associates and antagonists, and even with God and Christ. The author's use of the adjective "many" (πολλοί, *polloi*) suggests he is not concerned that, due to the bitterness of a few members, the majority of the congregation would apostatize, but that they could be negatively affected by the poisonous attitude of a single member and lose the peace that binds them together.[194] The result would weaken the community as a whole and could lead others into apostasy.

The author's real concern, however, focuses more on the individual than on the community. He fears open apostasy that would result from the member's losing the grace of God, that enabling power that finds victory in spite of opposition (compare 4:16). Since those running the race do not do so fully on their own power, "falling short" (ὑστερων, *hysterōn*) of grace guarantees their failure.[195] The result could lead to outright rebellion in

192. Lane, *Hebrews 9–13,* 450.

193. BDAG, 813.

194. Attridge, *Epistle to the Hebrews,* 368; Ellingworth, *Epistle to the Hebrews,* 665.

195. The verb is not associated with races but does carry the nuance of lagging behind and falling short of reaching a goal. BDAG, 1043–44.

which the person throws off the constraints of virtue and becomes immoral and profane. These take up both the attitude and actions of the wilderness generation and come under God's censure as those rebellious souls did and thus lose their reward. All too often, the loss of grace allows apostates to drift further away from the Lord's kingdom and react not only by throwing away all that they had but also hating the Lord. Such are only a breath away from crucifying "to themselves the Son of God afresh, and [putting] him to an open shame" (6:6).

Based on this, the author gives clear instructions to his readers (12:16) to safeguard the community of believers from immoral and profane people. He uses as his example Esau. Jacob's brother became the epitome of a profane, thus godless, man. Such a person lives without the godly fear so manifest in the faithful (5:7; 11:7; 12:28). Though such is aware of God's promises, he or she rejects the idea that God has power and spurn the promised reward. Such was Esau. For a single meal of bread and lentil soup, he sold his birthright to Jacob and after eating simply got up and walked away without a single shred of remorse (Gen. 25:34). How different he is from Moses, who considered "the reproach of Christ greater than" all the pleasures and advantages Egypt had to offer (11:26).[196] Little wonder then that the author uses Esau as a prime example of the profane and warned his readers not to allow such individuals to have place in the community of the Saints.

In 12:17, the author gives a severe warning again using Esau as an example. The hunter had the great blessing of the birthright. It was his alone and could not be contested by heaven or earth. However, in his younger years, he had no regard for it. Jacob took advantage of his brother's disregard, exchanging the blessing for "bread and pottage of lentiles" (Gen. 25:34). Noteworthy is how easily Esau give the birthright away, including swearing a solemn oath (Gen. 25:33) that likely invoked the name of Jehovah as witness. Making an oath was a potential self-curse because the procedure usually called on the divine to take action against the oath-maker if he broke it.[197] Esau's actions gave the birthright to Jacob (Gen. 25:33), and God stood behind it. By making the oath, Esau forfeited any and all rights to the birthright even if he changed his mind. In sum the oath could not be broken. In this sense, Esau could not find an opportunity for repentance (μετάνοια, *metanoia*). Once he swore the oath, he put himself in a position where he could under

196. Cockerill, *Epistle to the Hebrews*, 638–39.
197. For a discussion, see Schneider, *TDNT*, 5:457–67.

no circumstances get the birthright back. His later grief and weeping could not undo his actions. He had willing placed himself beyond the reach of repentance, that is, turning back even if he changed his mind, and therefore could never go back to the original condition.[198]

Though unstated, the author's warning is clear. What happened to Esau could also happen to any of the Saints. By having disrespect for God's grace, they too could put themselves beyond repentance's grasp and eternally lose their place in the heavenly Jerusalem. Noting the role such persons play in their own self-cursing, President Joseph F. Smith asked,

> "Can [God] be just and yet inflict such punishment upon His own children?" Let me tell you that God does not and will not inflict it upon them. Those who enter into this death will find that they have inflicted it upon themselves, and that God has not done it. They have done it because they loved unrighteousness, they loved not the truth, and abode not in the truth. And their judgment will be just, and they will be conscious that it is just. No one perhaps will feel more sorrowful over their dreadful fate than the loving God who gave them life and being in the world.[199]

Mount Sinai and Mount Zion Contrasted (12:18–24)

Greek Text

18 Οὐ γὰρ προσεληλύθατε ψηλαφωμένῳ καὶ κεκαυμένῳ πυρὶ καὶ γνόφῳ καὶ ζόφῳ καὶ θυέλλῃ 19 καὶ σάλπιγγος ἤχῳ καὶ φωνῇ ῥημάτων, ἧς οἱ ἀκούσαντες παρῃτήσαντο μὴ προστεθῆναι αὐτοῖς λόγον· 20 οὐκ ἔφερον γὰρ τὸ διαστελλόμενον· Κἂν θηρίον θίγῃ τοῦ ὄρους, λιθοβοληθήσεται· 21 καί, οὕτω φοβερὸν ἦν τὸ φανταζόμενον, Μωϋσῆς εἶπεν· Ἔκφοβός εἰμι καὶ ἔντρομος. 22 ἀλλὰ προσεληλύθατε Σιὼν ὄρει καὶ πόλει θεοῦ ζῶντος, Ἰερουσαλὴμ ἐπουρανίῳ, καὶ μυριάσιν ἀγγέλων,

---

198. It is noteworthy that it was Esau, not Jehovah, who placed himself in a position where repentance was no longer possible. Such is always the case, for neither the Father nor the Son will ever shut the gate to the entrance of the Holy City against a person. That act the person must do himself or herself. Though repentance can retrieve one from the fires of hell, neither those who have chosen to live a terrestrial nor a telestial law are willing to repent sufficiently to gain a celestial mansion. See D&C 76:30–113; 88:17–31. The scriptures are replete with examples showing that many, like Esau, put themselves in this position.

199. Arthur Winter, "Discourse Delivered at the Oneida Stake Conference, Franklin, Idaho, Sunday Afternoon, January 20th, 1895, by President Joseph F. Smith," *Deseret Weekly,* February 16, 1985, 258.

πανηγύρει 23 καὶ ἐκκλησίᾳ πρωτοτόκων ἀπογεγραμμένων ἐν οὐρανοῖς, καὶ κριτῇ θεῷ πάντων, καὶ πνεύμασι δικαίων τετελειωμένων, 24 καὶ διαθήκης νέας μεσίτῃ Ἰησοῦ, καὶ αἵματι ῥαντισμοῦ κρεῖττον λαλοῦντι παρὰ τὸν Ἄβελ. [SBLGNT]

King James Version

18 For ye are not come unto the mount that might be touched, and that burned with fire, nor unto blackness, and darkness, and tempest, 19 And the sound of a trumpet, and the voice of words; which voice they that heard entreated that the word should not be spoken to them any more: 20 (For they could not endure that which was commanded, And if so much as a beast touch the mountain, it shall be stoned, or thrust through with a dart: 21 And so terrible was the sight, that Moses said, I exceedingly fear and quake:) 22 But ye are come unto mount Sion, and unto the city of the living God, the heavenly Jerusalem, and to an innumerable company of angels, 23 To the general assembly and church of the firstborn, which are written in heaven, and to God the Judge of all, and to the spirits of just men made perfect, 24 And to Jesus the mediator of the new covenant, and to the blood of sprinkling, that speaketh better things than that of Abel.

New Rendition

18 For you have not come to something that can be touched, to a burning fire, darkness, gloom, and a whirlwind, 19 to the sound of a trumpet and a voice speaking words which those who heard it pleaded that no further words be spoken to them, 20 for they could not endure what it commanded, namely:

> "If even an animal touches the mountain, it will be stoned" [Ex. 19:12–13].

21 Indeed, the scene was so frightening that Moses said,

> "I am terrified and trembling" [Deut. 9:19].

22 But you have come to Mount Zion even the City of the Living God, to the heavenly Jerusalem, and to myriads of angels, 23 to a festal gathering, even the church of those who are firstborn, whose names are recorded in heaven, to God the Judge of all people, to the spirits of righteous people who have been perfected, 24 to Jesus, the guarantor of the new covenant, and to the blood of sprinkling which proclaims something better than the blood of Abel.

Translation Notes and Comments

12:18–21 In the first section of this pericope, the author's discourse lacks his usual clarity, making it a bit more difficult to translate. The contrast he makes between two pictures, however, is clear. The first one is very somber—even frightening—and one that his hearers have not experienced. The second one is very joy-filled and easy and one that his readers have experienced (12:22–24). It is the first picture that is obscure. The author does not even mention the location of the events he describes but leaves it up to the readers to determine. In doing so, he downplays the Sinaitic theophany and instead redefines the event as one of judgment and separation. As the author notes, such has not been the Christian experience.[200]

12:18 ***For ye are not come unto the mount that might be touched / For you have not come to something that can be touched:*** The verb προσέρχομαι (*proserchomai*), "to come, approach,"[201] is found here in the perfect tense and, coupled with the negative particle οὐ (*ou*), "not," shows that the author's readers have never approached something, as did Israel, that was so holy it could not be touched or realized.

The verb ψηλαφάω (*psēlaphaō*), "to touch,"[202] denotes feeling or handling something. What that something is the author does not directly state.[203] His imagery, however, leaves no doubt but that he is referring to Mount Sinai at the time the Israelites camped before it after the Exodus (Ex. 19:9–20:23).[204] As shown by his descriptions below, the author uses it to represent exclusion from God and a place of terrible judgment. That it can be touched only when conditions are right emphasizes the palpable reality of the scene of exclusion and judgment.[205] To such a place the author's readers have not yet come, and he wants to keep it that way.

and that burned with fire, nor unto blackness, and darkness, and tempest / to a burning fire, darkness, gloom, and a whirlwind: This is a paraphrase of LXX Deuteronomy 4:11.[206] In the phrase καὶ κεκαυμένῳ πυρί (*kai kekaumenō pyri*), literally "and having been ignited with fire," the verb καίω (*kaiō*), "to ignite, to burn," is found here in the form of a perfect passive participle. Both the voice and tense suggest the consuming fire had been lit at some point in the past by an unseen agent, namely God, and that it

---

200. Vanhoye, *Letter to the Hebrews,* 210.

201. Louw-Nida, §15.77; BDAG, 878.

202. BDAG, 1097–98.

203. In some manuscripts, scribes have added the noun ὄρει (*orei*), "mount," for clarity. Metzger, *Textual Commentary,* 605; Koester, *Hebrews,* 543. The addition actually takes away from what the author is trying to do by making his deliberately abstract reference too concrete.

204. Moses notes their unwillingness to commune directly with God in Deut. 5:5–6, 25.

205. Johnson, *Hebrews,* 330.

206. This verse reads, τὸ ὄρος ἐκαίετο πυρὶ ἕως τοῦ οὐρανοῦ, σκότος, γνόφος, θύελλα, φωνὴ μεγάλη (*to oros ekaieto puri heōs tou ouranou, skotos, gnophos, thyella, phōnē megalē*), "the mountain burned with fire up to heaven: there was gloom, darkness, and a whirlwind" (our translation). For other possibilities for the source, see Ex. 19:16–22; 20:18–21; and Deut. 5:22–27; 9:1–9.

continued to rage.[207] Even so, this fire brings no light, for the place remains one of darkness and gloom; it does however, bring great fear and pain.

Both the nouns γνόφος (*gnophos*), "blackness,"[208] and ζόφος (*zophos*), "darkness,"[209] denote partial to full blockage of light. The latter noun, *zophos,* was especially used to describe the darkness of the nether regions.[210]

The noun θύελλα (*thuella*) refers to any kind of violent atmospheric disturbance, thus a "tempest," "whirlwind," or "strong storm."[211] Moses used the images to give his listeners, only two of whom were present at Sinai, a sense of the frightful power that emanated from the heights of the mountain (Deut. 4:11).

12:19 ***And the sound of a trumpet / to the sound of a trumpet:*** The phrase echoes Exodus 19:13. The noun σάλπιγξ (*salpingx*) designates an instrument used to call people together or to signal instructions during a battle.[212] Among the Israelites, it was a specially prepared ram's horn known as a שׁוֹפָר (*šôphār*).[213]

the voice of words / a voice speaking words: The noun φωνή (*phōnē*) denotes any sound, tone, or noise,[214] but here it is associated with the noun ῥῆμα (*rhēma*) that refers to an oral statement or expression.[215] Taken together, the phrase suggests a supernatural, almost overpowering communication. Tacitly, it also suggests that, though the Israelites heard God's voice, they could not see him, and therefore there was yet a barrier that separated them.

which voice they that heard entreated that the word should not be spoken to them any more / which those who heard it pleaded that no further words be spoken to them: The verb παραιτέομαι (*paraiteomai*), "entreat, plead," carries the idea of not just asking someone to stop speaking but also of refusing to listen.[216]

---

207. Ellingworth, *Epistle to the Hebrews,* 671.

208. BDAG, 292.

209. BDAG, 429. LXX Deut. 4:11 uses σκότος (*skotos*), "gloom, darkness," rather than ζόφος (*zophos*), "gloom," but the two are synonyms.

210. It was associated with the netherworld and the gloom that prevails there. BDAG, 429; Louw-Nida, §§1.14; 14.57; Ellingworth, *Epistle to the Hebrews,* 672.

211. BDAG, 461.

212. BDAG, 911.

213. In Ex. 19:13, the instrument is described as a יוֹבֵל (*yôbēl*), but the term is synonymous with a שׁוֹפָר (šôphār).

214. BDAG, 1071–72.

215. BDAG, 905.

216. BDAG, 764. On the idea that the Israelites not only begged that God not speak to them but even refused to listen any further, see Johnson, *Hebrews,* 326–27; and Koester,

The verb προστίθημι (*prostihēmi*) denotes adding more to something that is already present. Here it refers to the words the voice was speaking. With the negative particle *mē* (*μὴ*), "not," the verb means "to speak no further."[217]

12:20 ***(For they could not endure that which was commanded, And if so much as a beast touch the mountain, it shall be stoned / for they could not endure what it commanded, namely: "If even an animal touches the mountain, it will be stoned":*** The reference here is to Exodus 19:12–13. The verb φέρω (*pherō*) in this context means to hold out in the face of difficulty and thus "to endure" something.[218] The verb is found here in the imperfect tense with the negative particle οὐ (*ou*), "not," denoting resistance or refusal.[219] Thus these people simply could not endure what was set before them.

The verb διαστέλλω (*diastellō*) means "to give a command or order" that defines precisely what one wishes another to do. Here it points to Jehovah's demand for the death of anything that approached the mountain. The adverbial particle κἄν (*kan*), "if even," exposes the real fear of the people.[220] Though the immediate focus is on the noun θηρίον (*thērion*), "animal,"[221] the implication is much broader. The idea behind the whole phrase is that any and all things that touch the mountain prematurely must die *even if* (*kan*) it is a mere animal, but how much more so if a human should trespass over the boundary?

or thrust through with a dart: This phrase is found in only a few variants and is likely not part of the original.[222] It is therefore not included in our Rendition.

12:21 ***And so terrible was the sight, that Moses said, I exceedingly fear and quake:) / Indeed, the scene was so frightening that Moses said, "I am terrified and trembling":*** The reference is to Deuteronomy 9:19. The adjective φοβερός (*phoberos*) denotes that which causes fear. The adverb οὕτως (*houtōs*), "so,"[223] serves to intensify the depth of the fear.

Hebrews, 543. As appealing and revealing as this approach is, because of the negative particle μή (*mē*), "not," it seemed more natural to us to translate the word as "plead." Compare Lane, *Hebrews 9–13,* 441 note cc.

217. BDAG, 885.

218. BDAG, 1051–52.

219. Smyth, *Greek Grammar,* §1855.

220. Johnson, *Hebrews,* 330.

221. The word usually refers to undomesticated animals, but it can denote any living creature that is subhuman. Louw-Nida, §4.3, 4; BDAG, 455–56.

222. Lane, *Hebrews 9–13,* 441 note dd.

223. Louw-Nida, §78.4.

The verb φαντάζω (*phantazō*) in the passive as is found here means "to appear, become visible," referring to what a person sees, thus "a sight" or "spectacle." It carries the nuance of seeing something extraordinary and more especially a theophany.[224] We have translated it as "scene" in our Rendition.

The author describes the scene's effect on Moses with two words. The adjective ἔκφοβος (*ekphobos*) means "terrified,"[225] and the adjective ἔντρομος (*entromos*) means "trembling" because of "exposure to an overwhelming or threatening circumstance."[226] Taken together, the author uses the effect on Moses, who stood in terror of Jehovah due to the display of his power as it rested on Mount Sinai, to both put the reaction of the rest of the Israelites in a more sympathetic light[227] and to stress how terrifying the experience really was.

12:22 ***But ye are come unto mount Sion / But you have come to Mount Zion:*** The conjunction ἀλλά (*alla*), "but," sets off and signals a contrast with what the author has said above with what he is about to say below.

Again, the author uses the verb προσέρχομαι (*proserchomai*), "to come," in the perfect tense. Here it separates his readers from the Israelites who "could not come" to the mount. The perfect tense shows that there are those among his readers who have already realized the promise of the heavenly blessings by associating with angels and perfected spirits.[228]

The phrase Σιὼν ὄρος (*Ziōn oros*), "Mount Zion," as the associated descriptions show, does not refer to the physical hill but to a real yet heavenly place.[229]

---

224. BDAG, 1049; Lane, *Hebrews 9–13,* 441 note ee.

225. BDAG, 312.

226. BDAG, 341. Nowhere in the Hebrew Bible is ἔντρομος (*entromos*), "trembling," associated with Moses. The author likely added it to intensify the effect he was striving for. See Lane, *Hebrews 9–13,* 464. The author has used it twice before, once to describe that which God will mete out against his foes (10:27) and the result of falling into the hands of an angry God (10:31). See Johnson, *Hebrews,* 330.

227. The context actually works better for Moses' reaction to Israel's kindling God's anger due to their worshiping the golden calf as recorded in Ex. 32. The author, however, as shown in 12:18–20, does not seem to feel constrained to stay within the biblical context in order to make his point. He may have felt justified since all the events he refers to happened while Israel was at Sinai. See Ellingworth, *Epistle to the Hebrews,* 676.

228. Vanhoye, *Letter to the Hebrews,* 212.

229. In Latter-day Saint theology, the term is sometimes associated with the New Jerusalem that will be established in Jackson County, Missouri. D&C 84:2, 32; 133:18, 56. See McConkie, *Doctrinal New Testament Commentary,* 3:230.

and unto the city of the living God / even the City of the Living God: The author uses this phrase to ensure his readers do not misunderstand his point. The noun πόλις (*polis*), "city,"[230] refers to an actual as opposed to a metaphorical, philosophical, or symbolic place (see D&C 76:66).[231] It is the city where God is the architect and builder (11:16). Though it is in the heavenly realm, it is nonetheless real and therefore reachable. It is the abode of the God whom these people worship (11:10), one that is cognizant, personal, and active. He is the one who continues to direct the Church albeit through his Son (1:2). His immediacy also means he knows all that goes on. For the righteous, these words promise high reward, but for the wicked they bode ill for, as the author states, "It is a fearful thing to fall into the hands of the living God" (10:31).[232]

the heavenly Jerusalem / to the heavenly Jerusalem: This phrase refers to the resplendent eternal city where God and Christ will dwell with the redeemed. It is also referred to as the New Jerusalem (compare Rev. 3:12; 21:2, 10). That John the Revelator saw it uniting with the celestialized earth suggests it has a present reality that will, in the future, be transferred to the new earth.[233]

to an innumerable company of angels / and to myriads of angels: Though the noun μυριάς (*myrias*) means literally "ten thousand," it was often used to designate a very large but not precisely defined number.[234] That the noun is in the plural here emphasizes the vast number of angels

230. BDAG, 844–85.

231. The author shows no influence here of Platonism. His use of concrete terms argues against any reference to Platonic ideals where God exists both beyond time and place. For the author, heaven is not just a real though spiritual place but an actual *polis* that includes individuals, their society, and government. John, too, speaks of the city of God. See Rev. 21:2–3. Elder Orson Pratt noted that heaven would have "lands, houses, cities, vegetation, rivers, and animals; with thrones, temples, palaces, kings, princes, priests, and angels," all of which would be material. "Indeed," he states, "the Saints' heaven is a redeemed, glorified, celestial, material creation, inhabited by glorified material beings, male and female, organized into families, embracing all the relationships of husbands and wives, parents and children." "Past and Future Existence," *Millennial Star* 28 (November 17, 1866): 721–22.

232. Johnson, *Hebrews,* 331; compare Vanhoye, *Letter to the Hebrews,* 211.

233. The designation should not be confused with the "New Jerusalem" that will be built on the American Continent in the near future (A of F 10; 3 Ne. 20:22; Ether 13:2–6). For discussion, see Graham W. Doxey, "New Jerusalem," in Ludlow, *Encyclopedia of Mormonism,* 3:1009–10.

234. BDAG, 661. The English word "myriad" is a direct borrowing from the Greek.

that will inhabit the city. Their primary role in scripture is to praise and glorify God (Rev. 5:11–12) as well as serve as his ministers (1:14).[235]

12:23 ***To the general assembly and church of the firstborn / to a festal gathering, even the church of those who are firstborn:*** The noun πανήγυρις (*panēgyris*), describes "an assemblage of many persons for a special occca-sion, festal gathering."[236] Here it points to a solemn assembly of those who have gathered for festal rejoicing because the toils and sorrows of earth life have forever passed away.[237] There is a touch of irony here, for the very people who will compose such an august body are the very ones who are being rejected from festal celebrations on earth.[238]

Just what this noun modifies is vague, leaving three possible translations. If *panēgyris* qualifies the angels, then it is these beings who compose the festal gathering. If the noun stands in opposition to the angels, then it refers to some festal gathering whose members are not indicated but may include all the heavenly hosts. If it is construed with the firstborn, then they are the ones who compose the festal gathering. We have chosen the second option only because it gives a flavor of joy to the whole of the assembled people.

The noun ἐκκλησία (*ekklēsia*), "church," denotes a gathering or assembly of people with shared beliefs. Here it points to the heavenly community of the saved.[239]

The title πρωτότοκος (*prōtotokos*), "firstborn," is one of the titles for Christ (1:6; Col. 1:15, 18). The adjective found here however is plural and, therefore, refers not to Christ but to all those who take advantage of Christ's Atonement and become "heirs of God, and joint-heirs with Christ" (Rom. 8:17). Each heir will receive "my Father's kingdom; therefore all that my

---

235. Vanhoye, *Letter to the Hebrews,* 211; Attridge, *Epistle to the Hebrews,* 374–75 and nn. 56, 57; Lane, *Hebrews 9–13,* 467. These are likely not spirit messengers of God but resurrected beings. If that is the case, they would fit nicely under Joseph Smith's defini-tion of angels as having a body of "Flesh and Bones." "History, 1838–1856, Volume C-1," 13 [addenda]; see also "Minutes of a Conference of the Church of Jesus Christ of Latter Day Saints, held in Nauvoo, Ill, Commencing Oct. 1st, 1841," *Times and Seasons* 2 (October 15, 1841): 577, online as "Discourse, 3 October 1841, as Reported by *Times and Seasons,*" Joseph Smith Papers, https://www.josephsmithpapers.org/paper-summary/discourse-3-october-1841-as-reported-by-times-and-seasons/1; "History, 1838–1856, Volume E-1," 1750.

236. BDAG, 753–54.

237. Cockerill, *Epistle to the Hebrews,* 653 n. 53. For discussion, see Ellingworth, *Epistle to the Hebrews,* 678–79; and Lane, *Hebrews 9–13,* 441–42 note jj; see also Cockerill, *Epis-tle to the Hebrews,* 654 n. 54.

238. Koester, *Hebrews,* 551.

239. BDAG, 303–4.

Father hath shall be given unto him" (D&C 84:38). The firstborn's inheritance is to obtain all that his or her father has, but in the celestial realm this is not restricted to just one person; it is available to all. These make up the heavenly community or "Church" that belongs to the Savior (D&C 76:54; 93:22–23).[240]

which are written in heaven / whose names are recorded in heaven: The verb ἀπογράφω (*apographō*) means "to register" in an official capacity, usually for tax purposes, and thereby gain recognition in a community, assembly, or association.[241] Those who belong to the Church of the Firstborn have this unique status. Their names have been recorded in heaven, thus making them official members of that community (compare D&C 76:68).[242] Importantly, the term is found here in the form of a perfect passive participle, suggesting that at some time in the past, likely during their mortal lives, these Saints' names were made a part of the heavenly register and that they are still there.

to God the Judge of all / to God the Judge of all people: The noun κριτής (*kritēs*), though it can refer to a theocratic ruler, most often denotes a "judge," that is, a person who has legal authority to decide cases.[243] The author focuses on this one aspect of the Father. He is the final and ultimate judge who decides all cases and through whom all blessings and punishments are determined. He, however, exercises this authority through the Son (John 5:27; Acts 10:42; 2 Tim. 4:1; 1 Pet. 4:5; Moro. 10:34).

---

240. The genesis of this Church begins on earth among those who devote themselves to righteousness and receive the higher ordinances of the temple including celestial marriage. These compose the earthly side of the celestial Church (see D&C 76:54; 77:10–11; 78:21; 93:20–22), which continues in heaven (see D&C 76:71, 94; 88:1–5). For discussion, see Smith, *Doctrines of Salvation,* 2:9, 41–43.

241. BDAG, 108; Moulton and Milligan, *Vocabulary,* 59–60. Little wonder, then, that Jesus told his disciples, "Rejoice not, that the spirits are subject unto you; but rather rejoice, because your names are written in heaven" (Luke 10:20).

242. Helyer, "*Prōtotokos* Title," 15. While in the author's culture, having one's name recorded in a register marks one as an official member of a community, in Latter-day Saint theology, this act occurs while one is yet in mortality and secures eternal life to the individual. Rev. 3:5; 13:8; 17:8; 20:12, 15 speak of the Lamb's "book of life," noting that those whose names are placed there are assured of eternal life. The phrase "book of the living" appears biblically first in Ps. 69:28, and a number of passages refer to this heavenly ledger. See, for example, Ex. 32:32–33; Isa. 4:3; 65:6; and Dan. 7:10; 12:1; see also Philip. 4:3; and Rev. 3:5; 13:8; 21:27. For discussion, see J. Lewis Taylor, "Book of Life," in Ludlow, *Encyclopedia of Mormonism,* 1:138–39.

243. BDAG, 570.

to the spirits of just men made perfect / to the spirits of righteous people who have been perfected: The phrase refers to "an individual who [has] completed his mortal existence but whose labors continue in the spirit world while he awaits the resurrection of the body."[244]

Such a person is described as δίκαιος (*dikaios*), "just, righteous."[245] The word denotes the state of those who have come under the power of Christ's grace and been cleansed by him and thereby meet the requirements for redemptive action.[246]

On the verb τελειόω (*teleioō*), "to be perfect," see Translation Notes for 2:10–11 with the associated Analysis. Noteworthy is that the word does not carry the idea of flawlessness and faultlessness as it does in English. Rather, it stresses the idea of wholeness, completeness, and maturity, especially as spiritual qualities.[247] That it is found here as a perfect passive participle is important. The voice marks God as the transforming agent,[248] the one who has made these people whole, complete, and who has bestowed upon them the full measure of this celestial quality. The tense shows God imparted the condition of perfection at some point in the past, and that condition continues into the present. The author describes these righteous and celestial beings as "ministering spirits who are sent forth to serve those who will inherit salvation" (NR 1:14).

12:24 ***And to Jesus the mediator of the new covenant / to Jesus, the guarantor of the new covenant:*** For a study of the noun μεσίτης (*mesitēs*), "mediator, guarantor," see Translation Notes for 8:6 with the associated Analysis. Here we need but note that the term usually carries the basic sense of "one who mediates between two parties to remove a disagreement or reach a common goal."[249] But important for the present context, it was also used in a legal setting to describe one involved in a legal transaction who guaranteed that the terms of the agreement would be carried out, thus a "guarantor." It is the Savior, through his own blood (2:14; 9:13, 19, 22, 25;

---

244. Oscar W. McConkie, "Angels," in Ludlow, *Encyclopedia of Mormonism,* 1:41; see also Attridge, *Epistle to the Hebrews,* 376; D&C 76:69; 129:1–3; and "History, 1838–1856, Volume E-1," 1750.

245. BDAG, 246–47.

246. Colin B. Douglas, "Justification," in Ludlow, *Encyclopedia of Mormonism,* 2:776–77; Lane, *Hebrews 9–13,* 470–72.

247. BDAG, 996; Delling, *TDNT,* 8:79–84.

248. Wallace, *Greek Grammar,* 437–38.

249. BDAG, 634.

10:4, 19, 29), who not only effects the new covenant but also guarantees its full reward to the faithful (compare John 14:6; 1 Tim. 2:5; 2 Ne. 2:28; and D&C 107:19) by perfecting them (D&C 76:69).

to the blood of sprinkling: The reference here takes on an Old Testament cast where the blood of the sacrificial animal was sprinkled at the altar (Lev. 1:11; 3:2; 4:6, 17; 7:2), bringing God's forgiveness and blessings to the people. The author uses it to refer to that aspect of the Atonement (9:13, 19, 21; 10:22). It was this giving of himself through which the Lord became the guarantor of the new covenant.[250]

that speaketh better things than that of Abel / which proclaims something better than the blood of Abel: The verb λαλέω (*laleō*), "to speak, proclaim," describes any form of oral communication. Because the English word "proclaim" means to both declare and praise something openly and proudly,[251] we have used it in our Rendition. The present tense of the verb stresses that the Father has procured these blessings "once for all" (10:10) through the ministry and sacrifice of his Son and continues to offer them via the Son's power to those in present distress.[252]

The comparative adverb κρεῖττον (*kreitōn*) points to that which is not only of a higher quality but also of more advantage.[253] Here it refers to the blood of Christ.

The blood of Abel, the first martyr, cried to Jehovah for vengeance against Cain (Gen. 4:1–10), and God made recompense upon the recalcitrant brother by judgment, cursing, and separation (Gen. 4:9–16).[254] In contrast, Christ's blood brings cleansing and release from sin with the accompanying acceptance and inclusion.[255]

---

250. See Kevin B. McCruden, "The Eloquent Blood of Jesus: The Neglected Theme of the Fidelity of Jesus in Hebrews 12:24," *Catholic Biblical Quarterly* 75, no. 3 (July 2013): 504–20.

251. *Collegiate Dictionary,* s.v. "proclaim."

252. Ellingworth, *Epistle to the Hebrews,* 683.

253. BDAG, 566.

254. Lane, *Hebrews 9–13,* 473; Bruce, *Epistle to the Hebrews,* 361; compare McConkie, *Doctrinal New Testament Commentary,* 3:231–32. The JST of Gen. 17:3–7 notes that a heresy arose among some in Abraham's day in which certain apostates began "washing of children" as a saving ordinance and, it would appear, sprinkling them with sacrificial blood representing that shed by Abel, which they believed "was shed for sins." See McConkie, *Doctrinal New Testament Commentary,* 3:231–32. There is no hint that the author of Hebrews had this in mind.

255. McConkie, *Doctrinal New Testament Commentary,* 3:232.

Analysis and Summary

At this point, the author brings to a climax the rhetorical elements to his Epistle. He divides the climax into two distinct sections, the first indicated by "you have not come . . ." (12:18) and the second by "you have come . . ." (12:22). Though the author bunches up items in two lists to emphasize his point, the two lists are not parallel. Their purpose is to emphasize the difference between the conditions faced by the rebellious Hebrews and faithful Christians. Impersonal, climatic, and terrifying features dominate the first list while personal, warm, and joyous features dominate the second.[256] Taken together, the two lists make yet another warning (although this one is quite subtle) and appeal. The author is fearful that his readers are in danger of missing out on the great blessing that the Father has bestowed and will bestow because of the sacrifice of the Son, and the author's concern colors his exhortation. Even so, encouragement dominates the pericope.[257]

To grasp the author's point in this section, we must keep in mind that he saw two ways in which the Savior fulfilled the law of Moses. First, through his Atonement, the Lord proved the old covenant's validity and proficiency by showing its various sacrifices and rites were similes and types revealing and testifying to his sacrifice. Second, the Lord's teachings show that the Sinaitic prohibition against sin continued to be valid albeit now with even greater breadth and intensity. Having up to this point established the first way, the author turns to a passionate development of the second.

Though he develops a contrast between the Old Testament past and the New Testament present,[258] the author is not actually pitting the old order against the new or the lower earthly against the higher heavenly. With great skill, "he is describing two present possibilities for the professed people of God. He is not concerned with old and new, before and after, but with belief and unbelief, with apostasy and faithfulness, with judgment and blessing. Sinai depicts the terrible exclusion of the apostate from the presence of God; Zion, the present joy of the faithful in the divine presence."[259] In this section, the author is reaching out to his readers in a

256. Vanhoye, *Letter to the Hebrews,* 210.

257. Ellingworth, *Epistle to the Hebrews,* 670.

258. Koester, *Hebrews,* 549; Johnson, *Hebrews,* 329.

259. Cockerill, *Epistle to the Hebrews,* 643. J. M. Casey, "Christian Assembly in Hebrews: A Fantasy Island?" *Theology Digest* 30 (1982): 332–33, also notes that the author of Hebrews is presenting his readers with two different and competing scenes either of which is open to them.

climatic synthesis, exhorting them to persevere in faith so they do not lose what they have gained or worse, find themselves condemned before God.[260] As author, High Priest, and guarantor of the new covenant, Christ has opened the way to the heavenly Mount Zion for those who believe. On the other hand, he has also intensified the peril of Mount Sinai for those who follow the way of the unfaithful Israelites. The old covenant brought its penalties for apostasy, and the new covenant is even harsher (2:1–4). These possibilities undergird and give force to the author's heart-felt appeal to his readers. In 12:18–21, he reviews the nature of judgment against the faithless. In 12:22–24, he states the privileges Christ's salvation affords the faithful.[261] It is therefore not surprising the author concludes this section (12:25–28) with a graphic description of the final judgment and a reminder that "our God is a consuming fire" (12:29).

In 12:18 and 22, the author uses the verb "to come" (προσέρχομαι, *proserchomai*) with good effect. The verb carries the nuance of not only approaching something but also of having association with it.[262] In this case, this could be an indirect reference to the belief that cultic worship is not merely approaching Deity but also entering into a relationship with him. The point is, unlike the experience of Israel at Sinai, there is no longer a restraining barrier that keeps God's people from seeing and communing with him.[263]

The letter's recipients were well aware that the barrier was now gone, having had deep spiritual experiences themselves. The question arises when these would have happened. Their initial experience would likely have been at the time of their conversion. The author notes there were many who have "been enlightened, who have tasted the heavenly gift, who have become partakers of the Holy Ghost, and who have tasted the good word of God and the wonders of the world to come" (NR 6:4–5). Thus, they have actually come to, that is, experienced, the Divine.

The phrase "you have come" seems to reflect the delicate position in which the author's readers live. They have already received the assurance that they have place in the "unshakeable kingdom" (NR 12:28). Even so,

---

260. O'Brien, *Letter to the Hebrews,* 477; Ellingworth, *Epistle to the Hebrews,* 669. Though the author was influenced by traditional materials, he has skillfully arranged them to suit his own purposes. Lane, *Hebrews 9–13,* 447–48, 461.

261. Lane, *Hebrews 9–13,* 448; Cockerill, *Epistle to the Hebrews,* 664–65.

262. Louw-Nida, §34.23.

263. Bultmann, *TDNT,* 3:21–22.

they need both negative and positive exhortation because they can still fall into apostasy.[264]

As noted, the author develops his argument with both care and skill. He sets his foundation on the events that occurred at Mount Sinai. According to Exodus 19, the Lord demanded that nothing, neither human nor animal, approach the mountain until a long trumpet blast sounded. At that point, conditions were such that the people could come before the Lord. The LXX account of Exodus 19:13 differs in what that sign was—it was when the sound of the trumpet ceased and the darkness dissipated. The MT notes that this occurred not at that time but two days later. It was then the Israelites reported to Moses they did not want Jehovah to speak to them directly anymore. Rather, they asked the prophet to be their intermediary. The author, for his purposes, changes the events to emphasize the points he wishes to make. One of these was that the people feared because of the command that whatever touched the mountain prematurely had to be killed. That included not only animals but people as well. The idea that Jehovah demanded such a high regard frightened the Israelites so much they did not want to hear any more directly from him. Rather, they wanted communication diluted through a human agent.[265]

The author has so shaped his use of the Old Testament narrative that it accentuates his point. Noteworthy is that he does not even name the mountain but calls it a place "that can be touched" (NR 12:18). By doing so, he acknowledges it has an actual geographical location, but underplays its name and site so that he can concentrated on its terrible majesty and forbidding nature. Both qualities are emphasized by Jehovah's command that if anything, whether beast or human, approached the mount, it was to be killed. Thus, the author has skillfully made Sinai a symbol of both exclusion from Jehovah's presence and of his dreadful judgment.[266] The images of burning fire, darkness, foreboding gloom, and finally, roiling tempest create a terrifying picture. As the author tells it, even Moses both feared and trembled (12:21).[267] Due to the author's skill, Sinai has become

264. Ellingworth, *Epistle to the Hebrews,* 671.

265. Ellingworth, *Epistle to the Hebrews,* 673–75.

266. Cockerill, *Epistle to the Hebrews,* 646.

267. In the biblical accounts of Deut. 9:15–20, recorded in both the MT and LXX, Moses did not fear and tremble before God until he came down from Sinai and caught the people worshiping the golden calf. At that moment, he greatly feared that God's wrath would be unleashed against these faithless and rebellious souls.

a "fear-engendering event."[268] In this way, he has made it a foreshadowing of the result of apostasy, and thus serves as a tacit warning to his readers.

Having built his case against Mount Sinai, the author introduces Mount Zion. Initially, the geographical Mount Zion was the Jebusite fortress that occupied the Ophel ridge, the tongue of land extending southward between the Tyropoean and Kidron Valleys.[269] David conquered this city and made it his capitol, and thus it became known as the "City of David" (2 Sam. 5:7, 9; 1 Chr. 11:5). Later the name "Mount Zion" was applied to Mount Moriah, the next rise above the Ophel to the north. On this higher spot, the temple of Solomon stood (Ps. 48:2; 74:2; Isa. 60:14). Finally, the term came to denote all of Jerusalem (Isa. 10:12; 18:7; 29:8; Obad. 1:17).

The metaphorical Mount Zion referred less to a location and more to the environment of righteousness associated with God's people and his sanctuary, shedding the often negative and sometimes scathing nuances associated with the earthly Jerusalem. The antithetical relationship between city and mount, though not fully consistent in all the prophetic writings, remains ever more positive for Mount Zion. The term nuanced the place that enjoyed God's blessing and peace. More fully, it figuratively referred to the cultic center and the community of the righteous as covenant keepers. Even so, Jerusalem, in spite of its association with rebellion and judgment, held both hope and promise. The prophets saw a future day when it would again be God's city and the center of his heavenly reign—it would become Mount Zion.[270]

The author of Hebrews points out that though Christ has done away with the old covenant with its Sinaitic attachments, he left joined, under the new covenant, the heavenly mount and heavenly city. By describing the place with three names, "Zion," "the city of the living God," and "Jerusalem," the author indicates it is a real place, one that needs multiple terms to catch its manifold dimensions. One image simply cannot catch its breadth, majesty,

---

268. Cockerill, *Epistle to the Hebrews,* 647 n. 24.

269. The etymology of the Hebrew term translated "Zion" is unsure, but it seems to point to a stronghold or fortress. BDAG, 925; BDB, 851; *HAL,* 1022.

270. For a study of the physical Mount Zion/Jerusalem, see W. Harold Mare, *The Archaeology of the Jerusalem Area* (Grand Rapids, Mich.: Baker Book House, 1987), 15–117; for a study of Zion and its relationship to Jerusalem in the Hebrew Bible, see Fohrer, *TDNT,* 7:292–319; for the same in the New Testament, see Lohse, *TDNT,* 7:319–38; for a Latter-day Saint view of Zion, see A. D. Sorensen, "Zion," in Ludlow, *Encyclopedia of Mormonism,* 4:16254–26; and for an extended study for how the concept applies to modern life, see Nibley, *Approaching Zion.*

and power. All the descriptions, however, point not just to the dwelling place of God but also to the place of "rest" for his people (3:1–4:11).

Zion, however, is not a city where residence can be achieved only in the future. Though the city is heavenly, membership therein can still be realized by mortals. Indeed, the author insists these Christians have already come to Mount Zion and the heavenly Jerusalem (12:22). They have done so by entering into the new covenant, which has provided for each member a key to a heavenly home in the eternal city. The possibility has become a reality for them because of the self-sacrifice of their Savior. That reality has been vouchsafed by their association with those who already dwell there—angels and just men and women made perfect in Christ (12:23; compare D&C 76:54, 68, 69; 77:11; 78:21; 88:5; 93:22; 107:19; 129:3). Thus the city is for the Saints both a present reality and also their ultimate future destiny.[271] The author's concern is that, though they now possess the very key to an eternal home, they can, if they do not endure in faithfulness, lose it and its attendant blessings.[272]

He shows the new celestial center to be the home of myriads of angels and the assembly of the firstborn ones (πρωτοτόκων, *prōtotokōn*). The picture is one of a vast congregation in a celebration of joyful worship (πανήγυρις, *panēgyris*). It echoes the "Sabbath rest" and joy the author stated would be the destiny of the people of God (4:9).[273] The author speaks of the "firstborn ones" as an exclusive group. It consists of all of God's children from Adam and Eve on who willingly accept Jesus Christ (the Firstborn of the Father) as their savior and redeemer, and who through obedience to his gospel become "heirs of God, and joint-heirs with Christ" (Rom. 8:17). Each will obtain in heaven "all that [the] Father hath" (D&C 84:38). In modern revelation, the Lord has declared, "I say unto you, I was in the beginning with the Father, and am the Firstborn; And all those who are begotten through me are partakers of the glory of the same, and are the church of the Firstborn" (D&C 93:21–22).

There were those among the author's readers who had communed with this special group. Joseph Smith asked,

> What did they learn by coming to the spirits of just men made perfect? Is it written? No; what they learned has not been, and could not have been written. What object was gained by this communication with the spirits of

271. Cockerill, *Epistle to the Hebrews,* 652–53.

272. Compare Holzapfel and Wayment, *Making Sense,* 458.

273. Lane, *Hebrews 9–13,* 467.

> the just? It was the established order of [the] kingdom of God—the keys of power and knowledge were with them to communicate to the Saints:—hence the importance of understanding the distinction between the spirits of the just, and angels. . . . The spirits of just men are made ministering servants to those who are sealed unto life eternal, and it is through them that the sealing power comes down.[274]

This statement gives insight into what it means to be "begotten" through Christ: to "be sealed unto eternal life" through the keys possessed by these just men and thus to make one's calling and election into the celestial realm sure. Being "born again" through baptism and the reception of the gift of the Holy Ghost opens the way (John 3:1–6). By this means, people enter the "strait and narrow path" that leads to eternal life. They must, however, "press forward with a steadfastness in Christ" with "unshaken faith in him, relying wholly upon the merits of him who is mighty to save," gain "a perfect brightness of hope, and a love of God and of all men," and continually feast "upon the word of Christ, and endure to the end." By this means the Father assures them, "Ye shall have eternal life" (2 Ne. 31:19–20).

That promise, however, can be realized before one dies. It happens when people meet the requirements God places upon them.[275] They are then "sealed up . . . through the power of the Holy Priesthood" and thus receive the "more sure word of prophecy" (D&C 131:5;[276] see also 1 Pet. 1:4–5; 2 Pet. 1:10, 19), thus guaranteeing their place in the heavenly city.[277]

---

274. "History, 1838–1856, Volume E-1," 1750; see also Joseph Smith, discourse October 9, 1843, reported in "Minutes of a Special Conference," *Times and Seasons* 4 (September 15, 1843): 331.

275. The requirements are very demanding. Joseph Smith taught that "when the Lord has thoroughly proved [a person] & finds that the [person] is determine to serve him at all hazards then the [person] will find his [or her] calling & Election made sure." "Discourse, between circa 26 June and circa 2 July 1839, as Reported by Willard Richards," 19, Joseph Smith Papers, https://www.josephsmithpapers.org/paper-summary/discourse-between-circa-26-june-and-circa-2-july-1839-as-reported-by-willard-richards/5.

276. This sealing power can be delegated to an exclusive group of priesthood holders chosen by the current Church president. See D&C 68:12.

277. Joseph Smith admonished the Latter-day Saints to "go on & continue to call upon God until you make your calling & election sure for yourselves by obtaining this more sure word of prophescy & wait patiently for the promise untill you obtain it." "Discourse, 14 May 1843, as Reported by Wilford Woodruff," [33], Joseph Smith Papers, https://www.josephsmithpapers.org/paper-summary/discourse-14-may-1843-as-reported-by-wilford-woodruff/4. For studies of this doctrine, see McConkie, *Doctrinal New Testament Commentary,* 3:323–55; Marion G. Romney, in CR, October 1964, 48–52; and Andrus, *Principles of Perfection,* 331–65.

> Those who compose the Church of the Firstborn
>
> overcome [the world] by faith, and are sealed by the Holy Spirit of promise, which the Father sheds forth upon all those who are just and true. . . . They are they into whose hands the Father has given all things—They are they who are priests and kings, who have received of his fulness, and of his glory; And are priests of the Most High, after the order of Melchizedek, which was after the order of Enoch, which was after the order of the Only Begotten Son. . . . These are they who are come unto Mount Zion, and unto the city of the living God, the heavenly place, the holiest of all. These are they who have come to an innumerable company of angels, to the general assembly and church of Enoch, and of the Firstborn. These are they whose names are written in heaven, where God and Christ are the judge of all. These are they who are just men made perfect through Jesus the mediator of the new covenant, who wrought out this perfect atonement through the shedding of his own blood. These are they whose bodies are celestial, whose glory is that of the sun, even the glory of God, the highest of all, whose glory the sun of the firmament is written of as being typical. (D&C 76:53, 55–56, 66–70)

Note God holds the central position in this pericope. Of the five persons or groups the author lists as inhabitants of the heavenly Jerusalem, God is third, right in the middle. Also note these Christians have not only approached the city but also God himself. All nonpersonal barriers have indeed been removed.[278]

The text is clear that the heavenly Jerusalem is God's city and all have position and place according to him. He acts as "judge" (12:23; compare D&C 76:68). Due to the effects of his judgment, the idea of "Vindicator," "Redeemer," or "Deliverer" come to mind.[279] The description as "judge," however, fits the author's purposes best for three main reasons: first, it emphasizes the work of the Mediator and the benefits of his "blood of sprinkling" that allows judgment to carry an aspect of mercy; second, it keeps the author's thread of warning and comfort ever before his readers; third, "it also provides the most compelling motivation for the perseverance of the [author's readers], both ancient and modern."[280]

Appropriately, the author next focuses on those who have come under the power of that judgment (12:23). These are the spirits of righteous men and women who have been perfected through the grace of Christ (7:19;

---

278. Vanhoye, *Letter to the Hebrews,* 213.

279. Attridge, *Epistle to the Hebrews,* 376 and n. 80.

280. Cockerill, *Epistle to the Hebrews,* 656.

9:9; 10:1, 14). The Father made the Son perfect through the vehicle of the Son's suffering (2:10; 5:9). The Son now communicates that perfection to those who endure in faith as he did.[281] Among these are the Old Testament heroes listed in chapter 11. The faith of these noble men and women brought upon them the cleansing power of the Lord's Atonement and gave them not only access to the heavenly Jerusalem but also the ability to confidently approach the throne of grace and partake of God's full reward (4:14–16; compare 10:19–24).

With 12:24, the author reaches the climax of this pericope. The focus is on "Jesus, the guarantor of the new covenant." He has made possible all the blessings the author has described in 12:22–23 and acts as guarantor for the faithful (7:23–25; 9:14–15; 10:15–18). It is he, and he alone, who "is able to cleanse the heart from sin, implant God's law within, and remove every barrier that has separated God's people from his presence."[282] Thus, the blood Jesus shed is "better" (κρεῖττον, *kreittōn*) than that of Abel (12:24), for while the latter demanded vengeance and separation, the former makes possible forgiveness and oneness.[283] The Lord's blood is better for at least three reasons. "First, it speaks more clearly than any word expressed in the story of Scripture. Second, it speaks more powerfully, for it reaches all humans. Third, it speaks from and of a greater reality," namely that of eternal salvation.[284]

With the mention of Abel, the author has brought this portion of his argument full circle (see 11:4). The opening of the circle began with reference to the blood of this righteous soul and the closing of that circle now brings that blood again to the attention of the author's readers. He does so, however, to make a point of contrast that allows him to stress what other and better blood has done, namely that of Jesus. It has made the blessing of having place on Mount Zion and in the heavenly Jerusalem possible. Further, those who come under its effects are thus made not only righteous but also perfect, meeting all the requirements of celestial glory. Thus, they become members of the Church of the Firstborn and can commune with just men and women who also have been made perfect, becoming part of the "festal assembly" (πανήγυρις, *panēgyris*) who rejoice because of what the Savior has done in putting all weakness, care, sorrow, suffering, and sin behind them (12:22).

---

281. Vanhoye, *Letter to the Hebrews,* 213.
282. Cockerill, *Epistle to the Hebrews,* 658.
283. McConkie, *Doctrinal New Testament Commentary,* 3:232.
284. Johnson, *Hebrews,* 333.

The author's words "you have come" are ripe with meaning. He uses the perfect tense of the second person plural verb προσέρχομαι (*proserchomai*) and in doing so shows that some among his readership have achieved communion with the Divine and with "just men made perfect" (12:23). Further, some already have claim to a place on Mount Zion and in "the city of the living God" (12:22). Though they have, in Peter's words, made their "calling and election sure" (2 Pet. 1:10), they can still fall. The author of Hebrews aligns with the teachings of the Prophet Joseph Smith in seeing that there is a reserve made in the sealing keys.[285] Some sins produce such a transformation in the core of the sinner, the hardening the heart, that repentance becomes impossible. Such sins, however, come only after a person has had the most sublime of spiritual experiences and then turns from and spurns them.[286] Knowing that such can happen to some of his readers (6:4–8), the author of Hebrews is most anxious that they do not fall. Thus, he now moves to a stern warning.

A Warning against Refusing God (12:25–29)

Greek Text

25 Βλέπετε μὴ παραιτήσησθε τὸν λαλοῦντα· εἰ γὰρ ἐκεῖνοι οὐκ ἐξέφυγον ἐπὶ γῆς παραιτησάμενοι τὸν χρηματίζοντα, πολὺ μᾶλλον ἡμεῖς οἱ τὸν ἀπ᾽ οὐρανῶν ἀποστρεφόμενοι· 26 οὗ ἡ φωνὴ τὴν γῆν ἐσάλευσεν τότε, νῦν δὲ ἐπήγγελται λέγων· Ἔτι ἅπαξ ἐγὼ σείσω οὐ μόνον τὴν γῆν ἀλλὰ καὶ τὸν οὐρανόν. 27 τὸ δὲ Ἔτι ἅπαξ δηλοῖ τῶν σαλευομένων μετάθεσιν ὡς πεποιημένων, ἵνα μείνῃ τὰ μὴ σαλευόμενα. 28 διὸ βασιλείαν ἀσάλευτον παραλαμβάνοντες ἔχωμεν χάριν, δι᾽ ἧς λατρεύωμεν εὐαρέστως τῷ θεῷ μετὰ εὐλαβείας καὶ δέους, 29 καὶ γὰρ ὁ θεὸς ἡμῶν πῦρ καταναλίσκον. [SBLGNT]

---

285. Joseph Smith noted that "if men have received the good word of God, and tasted of the powers of the world to come, if they shall fall away, it is impossible to renew them again, seeing they have crucified the son of God afresh, and put him to an open shame, so there is a possibility of falling away, you could not be renewed again, and the power of Elijah cannot seal against this sin." "History, 1838–1856, Volume E-1," 1921.

286. Joseph Smith noted that such a person "has got to say that the sun does not shine while he sees it—he has got to deny Jesus Christ when the heavens have been opened unto him, and to deny the plan of salvation with his eyes open to the truth of it; and from that time he begins to be an enemy." "History, 1838–1856, Volume E-1," 1976.

King James Version

25 See that ye refuse not him that speaketh. For if they escaped not who refused him that spake on earth, much more shall not we escape, if we turn away from him that speaketh from heaven: 26 Whose voice then shook the earth: but now he hath promised, saying, Yet once more I shake not the earth only, but also heaven. 27 And this word, Yet once more, signifieth the removing of those things that are shaken, as of things that are made, that those things which cannot be shaken may remain. 28 Wherefore we receiving a kingdom which cannot be moved, let us have grace, whereby we may serve God acceptably with reverence and godly fear: 29 For our God is a consuming fire.

New Rendition

25 See that you do not reject the one who is speaking. For if those who rejected him who warned them on earth did not escape, how much less will we escape, if we repudiate him who is speaking from heaven. 26 At that time his voice shook the earth, but now he has promised, saying:

> "Once more I will shake not only the earth but also heaven" [Hag. 2:6].

27 Now the phrase "once more" means the removal of the things that are shaken, that is, of things which have been made, so that the things which are not shaken may remain. 28 Therefore, since we are receiving an unshakeable kingdom, let us give thanks, by which we may acceptably serve God with reverence and awe, 29 for indeed

> "our God is a consuming fire" [Deut. 4:24; 9:3].

Translation Notes and Comments

12:25 ***See that ye refuse not him that speaketh / See that you do not reject the one who is speaking:*** The imperative βλέπετε (*blepete*), "see to it," repeats the author's earlier warning concerning imitating the faithless wilderness generation and thereby falling under the same consequences (3:12).

The verb παραιτέομαι (*paraiteomai*), "to reject," means to forcefully decline to do what another wishes. In connection with the Divine, it carries the idea of willful disobedience.[287]

The present active participial phrase τὸν λαλοῦντα (*ton lalounta*), "the one who is speaking," refers to God, the one who spoke from Sinai and will speak from Mount Zion but is now speaking through the Son (1:1–2).[288] The

287. BDAG, 764; Louw-Nida, §§34.35; 36.27. The word can mean "to beg," but here it takes on the stronger connotation of refusal and rejection. Lane, *Hebrews 9–13,* 475. Israel's rejection of God was nothing less than a refusal to obey his word. Johnson, *Hebrews*, 334.

288. Because the author states the Father speaks through his Son, the reference could be to the "blood" of the Son that "speaks better than that of Abel." However, the context

tense is important because it stresses that God is presently active in directing his people. In sum, revelation continues.

For if they escaped not who refused him that spake on earth / For if those who rejected him who warned them on earth did not escape: The conjunction εἰ (*ei*), "if," applies to a real situation, that of the rebellious Israelites at Sinai. The plural demonstrative adjective ἐκεῖνοι (*ekeinoi*), "those," refers to the same people. They were guilty of rejecting Jehovah's word and, therefore, of rejecting him.

The verb χρηματίζω (*chrēmatizō*) refers to making known a divine injunction or warning.[289] The law of Moses carried very clear warnings to the people if they disobeyed God's commandments (for examples, see Deut. 8:20; 11:28; 28:15, 45, 62).

The phrase ἐπὶ γῆς (*epi gēs*), "on earth," refers to the revelations Moses received while at Sinai. At that time, God had come to earth to reveal his will and was therefore not far from the people. This makes those who rejected his word all the more culpable. Nonetheless, the giving of the law was still an earthly event with carnal commandments (9:10) given because the people would not endure a more heavenly order (Mosiah 13:29–30).

The verb ἐκφεύγω (*ekpheugō*) means "to escape danger or peril" and in this case refers to the judgments of God upon these rebellious souls.

much more shall not we escape, if we turn away from him that speaketh from heaven / how much less will we escape, if we repudiate him who is speaking from heaven: The adverbial phrase πολὺ μᾶλλον (*poly mallon*) means "how much greater" and acts here to contrast a lesser outcome to a larger one. Here, because of the nature of the contrast, the idea is that if Israel could not escape the consequences of its rebellion, how much less a chance does the apostate Christian?[290]

The verb ἀποστρέφω (*apostrephō*), "repudiate," means literally "to turn aside,"[291] and the nuance in this case, "to turn away from by rejecting,"[292] is

---

suggests the author wants to keep the active nature of the Father before his readers. See Vanhoye, *Letter to the Hebrews,* 215; and Ellingworth, *Epistle to the Hebrews,* 684; for a discussion, see Gene Smillie, "'The One Who Is Speaking' in Hebrews 12:25," *Tyndale Bulletin* 55, no. 2 (2004) 275–94, accessed April 4, 2017, https://legacy.tyndalehouse.com/tynbul/Library/TynBull_2004_55_2_07_Smillie_Heb12_25Speaker.pdf.

289. BDAG, 1089.

290. Johnson, *Hebrews,* 334, notes that because of the context the phrase must be translated as "how much less."

291. BDAG, 122–23. The nuance of the word is to take something of value from another by fraud, deception, or robbery.

292. BDAG, 122–23.

to apostatize. Since the English word "repudiate" carries the idea of refusing to have anything to do with someone and rejecting him as having no authority,[293] we use it in our Rendition.

The phrase ἀπ' οὐρανῶν (*ap ouranōn*), "from heaven," contrasts God speaking through Moses at Sinai to his speaking more directly to the Christians "from heaven." There is no longer any need for a mortal intercessor nor has there been since God has spoken and continues to speak through his Son.[294] The effect places heavy obligation on the Christian to obey or suffer severe consequences.

12:26 ***Whose voice then shook the earth / At that time his voice shook the earth:*** The reference is to Exodus 19:18, where Sinai quaked due to the presence of Jehovah. The verb σαλεύω (*saleuō*) means "to be made to move to and fro," thus "to shake, totter," which the author attributes to the effect of God's voice.[295]

but now he hath promised, saying, Yet once more I shake not the earth only, but also heaven / but now he has promised, saying: "Once more I will shake not only the earth but also heaven": To bolster his point, the author uses Haggai 2:6.[296] For emphasis, the author chooses ἐπαγγέλλομαι (*epangellomai*), "to promise," found here in the perfect tense. The word carries the nuance of fully intending to bring something to pass. In this case, it stresses God's intent to shake both the created and uncreated spheres. The perfect tense of the verb highlights that the promise God made in the past is still in effect and will, therefore, be carried out.

The verb σείω (*seiō*), "to shake, agitate," especially of natural phenomena.[297] The author so constructs his sentence to contrast the shaking of the earth at Sinai, a very local event, to the eschatological shaking of heaven and earth, a broad, even cosmic, event. This shaking is likely symbolic of the breadth of God's final judgment.[298]

---

293. *Collegiate Dictionary,* s.v. "repudiate."

294. For the sake of his argument, the author here neglects the role of prophets and apostles as Christ's spokesmen to the Church.

295. BDAG, 911.

296. BDAG, 356; Vanhoye, *Letter to the Hebrews,* 216.

297. BDAG, 918.

298. Koester, *Hebrews,* 547. According to D&C 45:48, both heaven and earth will shake at the time of the Lord's Second Coming. At that time, "every corruptible thing . . . shall be consumed" (D&C 101:24), "and there shall be a new heaven and a new earth" (D&C 29:23) "wherein dwelleth righteousness" (2 Pet. 3:13). The Savior has been very specific in stating that "everything that is in the world, whether it be ordained of men, by thrones, or principalities, or powers, or things of name, whatsoever they may be, that are not by me or by my word, saith the Lord, shall be thrown down, and shall not

As is his wont, the author adjusts the passage from Haggai to fit his needs. Here he does not use the full quote that also notes Jehovah will also shake sea and dry land in addition to heaven and earth. Haggai's emphasis was on the effect upon the earth and its sky. By leaving out the rest, the author was able to reinterpret "heaven" not as earth's sky, but as the divine realm. This refocus allows the author to give scriptural weight to his point.

12:27 ***And this word, Yet once more, signifieth the removing of those things that are shaken / Now the phrase "once more" means the removal of the things that are shaken:*** The author's focus is on the phrase ἔτι ἅπαξ (*eti hapax*), "yet once more," found in Haggai 2:6. The adverb *hapax* refers to a single, decisive, and unique occurrence. In this case, it is God's shaking of earth and heaven.

The noun μετάθεσις (*metathesis*) means "removal, taking away,"[299] and refers to all things that cannot pass God's judgment. That which does not measure up will be removed so as not to affect what will remain.[300]

as of things that are made / that is, of things which have been made: The verb ποιέω (*poieō*), "to make,"[301] found here as a perfect passive participle, refers to the created order, that which is earthly and transitory, specifically those things God put in place and that have remained into the present for the purpose of advancing his earthly children. Once these things have served their purpose, they will pass away because they are no longer necessary.

that those things which cannot be shaken may remain / so that the things which are not shaken may remain: The "things" that cannot be

---

remain after men are dead, neither in nor after the resurrection, saith the Lord your God. For whatsoever things remain are by me; and whatsoever things are not by me shall be shaken and destroyed" (D&C 132:13–14). Only that which meets millennial standards will remain. McConkie, *Doctrinal New Testament Commentary,* 3:233.

299. BDAG, 97.

300. Some have argued that the author is not talking about the final judgment but is lamenting the changeability of the natural order and praising the permanence of the eternal one. They see Platonic dualism influencing the author. For example, see Lincoln D. Hurst, "Eschatology and 'Platonism' in the Epistle to the Hebrews," in *Society of Biblical Literature Seminar Papers,* ed. Kent H. Richards (Atlanta: Scholars Press, 1984), 41–74. To bolster their position they place a lot of emphasis on the meaning of *metathesis* as "changeable, transformable." Though that translation is possible (see BDAG, 639), the context of this whole pericope (11:1–12:28) deals with judgment and warns against apostasy and its result, namely, being removed from God's presence. Therefore, the translation of *metathesis* as "removal" is more consistent with the context. For discussion, see Cockerill, *Epistle to the Hebrews,* 666–67.

301. BDAG, 839–40.

shaken, to use the author's metaphor, are those that have a permanent foundation. The verb μένω (*menō*) means to "stay, wait" and "to continue to exist" and therefore "to remain."[302] Here it refers to the permanent city where God dwells (13:14). Here the author explains both the reason and result of the shaking, that is, what passes the test will remain forever. Thus, the shaking is a metaphor for the Final Judgment.[303]

12:28 *Wherefore we receiving a kingdom which cannot be moved / Therefore, since we are receiving an unshakeable kingdom:* The conjunction διό (*dio*), "therefore,"[304] signals that the author is making his conclusion and also giving his reason for the admonition that follows.

The verb παραλαμβάνω (*paralambanō*), "to receive,"[305] is found here as a present active participle used circumstantially in a causative sense. Hence, we have translated it "since we are receiving" in our Rendition. The present tense of the participle is important here because it shows that these Saints are actually, in their present mortal condition, in the process of receiving a place in the "unshakable kingdom." Though full enjoyment must wait until after the Final Judgment, they are already enjoying some of the kingdom's benefits and the accompanying assurance that they will receive the rest.[306]

let us have grace / let us give thanks: The noun χάρις (*charis*), translated as "grace" in other passages in Hebrews (2:9; 4:16; 10:29; 12:15), is here rendered as "thanks"[307] because in the present context, the word expresses a deep feeling of thankfulness for what God is not only going to do but also for what he has already done and is doing.[308]

The JST makes an interesting modification to this phrase, eliminating the words "let us" before "have grace" and in so doing moving the context from an admonition to a command. Thus, it stresses the importance of this worshipful act as a needful precursor to giving "acceptable service" to God.

whereby we may serve God acceptably with reverence and godly fear / by which we may acceptably serve God with reverence and awe: With the phrase δι' ἧς (*di hēs*), "by which," the author notes the result of heartfelt thankfulness.

---

302. BDAG, 630–31.

303. Cockerill, *Epistle to the Hebrews,* 665–66.

304. BDAG, 250.

305. BDAG, 768.

306. Lane, *Hebrews 9–13,* 484.

307. Louw-Nida, §33.350.

308. BDAG, 1079–81, notes that the word expresses, among other things, a genuine "response to generosity or beneficence," therefore "thankfulness."

The verb λατρεύω (*latreuō*), "to serve," denotes religious service specifically.[309] The author modifies it with the adverb εὐαρέστως (*euarestōs*), "acceptably,"[310] pointing to service done in such a way that God finds it acceptable and is therefore willing to recognize and honor it.

The author notes two attributes that make service acceptable to God.[311] The first he expresses with the noun εὐλάβεια (*eulabeia*), which in the New Testament refers to "reverent awe in the presence of God."[312] While the Old Testament places its emphasis on fear, the New Testament does so on love. However, given that the author bases his arguments and exhortations on the Old Testament nuances, the undercurrent of fear continues to give color to that love.[313]

The second attribute the author expresses with the noun δέος (*deos*), "awe." The word denotes a feeling "of profound respect and reverence for deity."[314] Indeed, it carries the idea of an almost overwhelming emotion due to one's sense of the superiority, greatness, power, and majesty possessed by Deity.[315]

12:29 ***For our God is a consuming fire / for indeed "our God is a consuming fire":*** The reference here is to Deuteronomy 4:24; 9:3. The verb καταναλίσκω (*katanaliskō*), found here in the form of a present participle, means "to consume"[316] and, by modifying "fire," emphasizes its power to

---

309. BDAG, 587. The verb as used in 8:5; 9:9; 13:10, is associated with temple worship and therefore carries the idea of covenantal responsibility. *NID,* s.v. "λατρευω."

310. BDAG, 403.

311. However, Ellingworth, *Epistle to the Hebrews,* 691, suggests we are dealing with a hendiadys and suggests translating the phrase as "reverent fear."

312. BDAG, 407.

313. The primary meaning of the noun εὐλάβεια (*eulabeia*) relates to being prudent and precise "in dealing with the transcendent realm." Indeed, in the Greco-Roman culture, "one must be [especially] cautious about giving offense to deities, hence, 'reverence, piety.'" In the New Testament, it takes on the more positive cast of reverent awe for the Divine. BDAG, 407. For a study, see Bultmann, *TDNT,* 2:751–54.

314. BDAG, 218.

315. Because the noun δέος (*deos*) appears only here in the New Testament, the exact nuance the author intended is harder to identify. However, given that the term in 2 Macc. 3:17; 12:22; 13:16; 15:23 connotes fear and anguish, it most likely continued to carry some of the weight of that negative nuance into the author's use. That the noun is treated under the category of words associated with φοβέω (*phobeō*), "to fear" in Balz and Wanke, *TDNT,* 9:189–219, suggests its close association with the idea of dreadful respect. That being the case, εὐλάβεια (*eulabeia*) would also carry that nuance and, therefore, the idea of "godly fear." This force must stand behind the idea of "reverence." See also Lane, *Hebrews 9–13,* 444 note jjj.

316. BDAG, 522.

destroy utterly. The tense shows that the aspect of God of which Moses testified still operates. The author emphasizes this point by beginning the phrase with "καὶ γάρ (*kai gar*), "for indeed."

Analysis and Summary

The author, leaving the positive vision of Mount Zion, again returns to the major purpose of his Epistle: to warn against apostasy.

He begins his dissuasion by admonishing his readers to not reject the clear instructions coming from the Father through the Son (12:25). Though him—the faithful, obedient, self-sacrificing High Priest who presides over his people—the Father now speaks from heaven. The author's use of the present tense emphasizes the continuing nature of the revelation and inspiration that as yet continues to flow through the Church. The author's words show that both the Father and the Son are as active and as present as Jehovah was at Sinai. To the Christian generation, they are extending the same heavenly calling (3:1) to be God's people and receive the associated blessings.[317]

However, God's closeness brings both responsibility and consequences. Readers must listen to God and not refuse (παραιτέομαι, *paraiteomai*) his word or "turn away" (ἀποστρέφομαι, *apostrephomai*) from him as did the faithless wilderness generation. To do so would put readers under the same divine censure as the rebellious Israelites who refused to listen to the voice of God at Sinai. Accessibility to God's word means greater accountability (4:12–13), as the early Hebrews found out to their sorrow. The author assures his readers he does not want such sorrow to happen to them. To make his point, the author again uses a *qal waḥomer* argument in which what applies to a lesser point will most assuredly apply to a greater one and with heavier consequences.[318] The rhetorical device gives potent moral force to the author's point: "the greater the gift, the greater the peril involved in its rejection."[319] In this case the rejected gift brought a curse upon the rebellious Israelites that prevented them from entering the promised land (3:16–18).[320] The greater, surer, and more terrible curse that will

317. Cockerill, *Epistle to the Hebrews,* 661–62.

318. On the nature and use of the *qal waḥomer* or *a fortiori* argument, see discussion in the introduction on page 30.

319. Johnson, *Hebrews,* 334.

320. The author refers to these as "those who heard" but begged God to quit speaking to them (NR 12:19). The author's use of the term should be taken in a broader context as a prototype for all who rebel. Ellingworth, *Epistle to the Hebrews,* 684.

fall on the faithless Christians will prevent them from entering into God's eternal rest.[321]

The author unites with his readers in the warning by stating, "If we repudiate him [God]," we will not escape."[322] In doing so, he is able to give his stiff warning without offending his readers.

At 12:26, the author introduces his second *qal waḥomer* argument. He focuses on the verb "to shake" (σαλεύω, *saleuō*), referring to the time when God's presence shook the earth. Here he contrasts "at that time," referring to when the earth shook at Sinai, with "but now," referring to when heaven and earth will shake due to God's coming judgment.[323] To bolster his point, the author references Haggai 2:6, stating that God will shake earth and heaven (compare D&C 43:18; 84:118). He interprets the warning found there as God's promise for the future. It seems at first puzzling that the author would refer to judgment by the positive word "promise" (ἀπαγγελλομαι, *apangellomai*), but in this context we can see that the author's thrust is to encourage his readers to ever greater faithfulness even during times of anxiety and fear. That God will shake heaven and earth should hold no fear for the Christian because their abode is not in the weak, transitory arena that cannot withstand the shaking but in Mount Zion and the heavenly City that are impervious to such (compare D&C 45:32).[324]

In 12:27, the author interprets for his readers the message of Haggai. The phrase "yet once more" ("Ετι ἅπαξ, *Eti hapax*) found there, as the author understands it, is critical to his message. The phrase refers to a single, decisive, and unique occurrence. The author has already used it to refer to the Son's self-sacrifice "once for all" (9:26; 10:10).[325] So too will be God's final judgment, and it can be fully implemented with both justice and mercy at play because of the Son.

That "shaking" will be a once-for-all event and anything that cannot stand up to it will suffer removal (μετάθεσις, *metathesis*). The author is

---

321. Cockerill, *Epistle to the Hebrews,* 662–63.

322. The author puts stress on the idea by making it emphatic: "we . . . who turn away." Attridge, *Epistle to the Hebrews,* 378 n. 4. Refusing God is tantamount to turning away or repudiating (ἀποστρέφομαι, *apostrephomai*) him. Lane, *Hebrews 9–13,* 475; O'Brien, *Letter to the Hebrews,* 492–94.

323. The author does not use the verb "to shake" as found in Haggai (σειω, *seiō*), but a close synonym (σαλευω, *saleuō*). The reason may be that the latter word has a closer association with God's judgments. See LXX 2 Kgs. 17:20; and LXX Ps. 47:6.

324. Ellingworth, *Epistle to the Hebrews,* 687; compare Vanhoye, *Letter to the Hebrews,* 216.

325. The author describes both the Lord's sacrifice as well as his entrance into heaven as "once for all" (ἐφάπαξ, *ephapax*) in 7:27 and 9:12 respectively.

most specific that this applies to all things "that have been made," that is, to the created or temporal order, both physical and spiritual. Nothing that does not have a permanent foundation can withstand the final shaking, including things both on earth and in heaven. These will be permanently removed from God's presence.[326]

Isaiah 65:17 described the aftermath of this moment with telling imagery. It refers to "new heavens and a new earth," stating that when God creates this new order, "the former shall not be remembered." The author of Hebrews assures his readers that what Isaiah promised will become a reality. But what exactly, in Isaiah's imagery, is made new?[327] The Greek phrase οὐρανὸν καινὸν καὶ γῆν καινήν (*ouranon kainon kai gēn kainēn*), "a new heaven and a new earth," can be seen as describing the whole of the created order brought into existence by God. This echoes the very first verse of Genesis: "In the beginning God created the heaven and the earth" (Gen. 1:1). However, in being shaken, the old earth is not so much annihilated as reconstituted to become a new celestial orb, but so drastic is the change the result can be described as nothing short of "new." The same is true of heaven, here likely referring to the spirit world, consisting of both paradise and hell. As a result of the final judgment, both will pass away having served their purpose (see Rev. 20:12–14; 2 Ne. 9:12; D&C 19:1–12; 128:22; Moses 7:38, 57).

The author's report confirms a long-established Judeo-Christian tradition: salvation, in the biblical sense, is not just for mankind but for all creation (see, for example, Rom. 8:21; and 2 Cor. 5:17). All things are to be saved both on earth and in heaven. The Doctrine and Covenants also affirms this view: "And the end shall come, and the heaven and the earth shall be consumed and pass away, and there shall be a new heaven and a new earth. For all old things shall pass away, and all things shall become new, even the heaven and the earth, and all the fulness thereof, both men and beasts, the fowls of the air, and the fishes of the sea; and not one hair, neither mote, shall be lost, for it is the workmanship of mine hand" (D&C 29:23–25).

The Lord, through modern revelation, has given a clear understanding of the final state of the earth: it is to be the home of those who have lived the celestial law and received a fulness of God's glory. As the Lord

326. The author is not, therefore, looking at total annihilation but at removal from association. See Ellingworth, *Epistle to the Hebrews,* 688; and Cockerill, *Epistle to the Hebrews,* 668 and n. 34.

327. The Hebrew חָדָשׁ (*ḥādāš*) refers to not only what is "new" but also to what is renewed or refreshed. BDB, 294.

stated, "the poor and the meek of the earth shall inherit it" (D&C 88:17; compare Matt. 5:5). "Therefore, it must needs be sanctified from all unrighteousness, that it may be prepared for the celestial glory; For after it hath filled the measure of its creation, it shall be crowned with glory, even with the presence of God the Father; That bodies who are of the celestial kingdom may possess it forever and ever; for, for this intent was it made and created, and for this intent are they sanctified" (D&C 88:18–20). Joseph Smith stated, "This earth will be rolled back into the presence of God, and crowned with celestial glory."[328] After its cleaning, the earth will be as a crystal and a Urim and Thummim for those who would dwell upon it (D&C 77:1; D&C 130:9).

No taint should be attached to the "things that are made" and that will pass away. They were, after all, created by God. His purpose in making them was, however, only for a given time, and once they have served their purpose, they shall be removed (1:11–12). That which remains will be all things that share in the Father's holiness (12:10).[329] In the author's model, it is the city, called the Heavenly Jerusalem and Mount Zion, whose architect and builder is God (11:10). It is this that holy men and women have sought for from time immemorial (11:13–19). According to Joseph Smith,

> The building up of Zion is a cause that has interested the people of God in every age; it is a theme upon which prophets, priests, and kings have dwelt with peculiar delight; they have looked forward with joyful anticipation to the day in which we live; and fired with heavenly and joyful anticipations they have sung, and wrote, and prophesied of this our day;—but they died without the sight; we are the favored people that God has made choice of to bring about the Latter Day glory, . . . a work that God and angels have contemplated with delight, for generations past; that fired the souls of the ancient patriarchs and prophets—a work that is destined to bring about the destruction of the powers of darkness, the renovation of the earth, the glory of God, and the salvation of the human family.[330]

For the author of Hebrews, Mount Zion is the real and eternal place where the Father and Son dwell and the eventual home of the righteous where they

---

328. "Discourse, [5 January 1841], as Reported by Unknown Scribe–A," 1, Joseph Smith Papers, https://www.josephsmithpapers.org/paper-summary/discourse-5-january-1841-as-reported-by-unknown-scribe-a/1. For discussion, see Thomas J. Riskas Jr., "New Heaven and New Earth," in Ludlow, *Encyclopedia of Mormonism,* 3:1009.

329. Johnson, *Hebrews,* 335–36.

330. "The Temple," *Times and Seasons* 3 (May 2, 1842): 776, https://contentdm.lib.byu.edu/digital/collection/NCMP1820-1846/id/9843/rec/4.

will at last enter into God's full rest. "The essential difference, then, between what can be shaken and what cannot, lies in their respective relationship to God and his purposes."[331]

In sum, the author using the *qal waḥomer* rhetorical argument presents two scripture-based reasons why his readers should "not reject the one who is speaking" (NR 12:25).[332] "First, if God's judgment on those who heard him speak at Sinai was certain, his judgment on those who refuse his gracious word, spoken from heaven through the exalted Son, is much more certain [12:25]. Second, as he once caused Sinai to tremble, so [God] will shake 'heaven and earth' at the final Judgment. That Judgment will leave those who have no part in the eternal City without a place to stand [12:26–27]."[333]

The author finishes this pericope with an admonition (12:28). It is built on the sure promise that Haggai's prophecy will be fulfilled. For the righteous, that promise will bring about their entrance into the Holy City and final rest.[334] Because they are receiving benefits from being its members, the author assures them, the faithful have nothing to fear when heaven and earth are shaken in final judgment.

In the meantime, his readers are to show their faithfulness through worshipful service to one another. The author puts stress on what will allow his readers to "acceptably serve God," expressed with the admonition "let us give thanks." The phrase refers to an expression of a deep feeling of gratitude for all God has done, is doing, and will do.[335] The author notes two emotions that guarantee acceptable service to God. These are "reverence" (εὐλάβεια, *eulabeiai*) and "awe" (δέος, *deos*). Both words carry the idea of an emotion inspired by something that arouses one's deep respect and veneration. That emotion is built on a recognition of the sacredness and inviolability of Deity coupled with full reverence and deep humility before the power and majesty of the Father and Son. It stems from the recognition of what they, through their grace, have done to open the way to eternal life for humankind. That deep emotion generates heartfelt thankfulness.

---

331. Cockerill, *Epistle to the Hebrews,* 669; see also O'Brien, *Letter to the Hebrews,* 496.

332. On the nature and use of the *qal waḥomer* or *a fortiori* argument, see discussion in the introduction on page 30.

333. Cockerill, *Epistle to the Hebrews,* 669–70.

334. O'Brien, *Letter to the Hebrews,* 498.

335. BDAG, 1079–81, notes that the word expresses, among other things, a genuine "response to generosity or beneficence," therefore "thankfulness." See also Vanhoye, *Letter to the Hebrews,* 217.

Standing behind and motivating these emotions is "godly fear" (δέος, *deos*). During his lifetime, the Savior expressed his godly fear through obedience (5:7–8). This same reverence characterized Abel, Noah, Abraham, and the rest of the Old Testament heroes and was the ground of their humility and reverence before God. It also generated the deep feeling of gratitude that the author so desires his readers to feel. Service based on such feelings of thankfulness can be described as nothing less than worship. Such a life is devoted to good works, as the author will discuss in chapter 13.[336]

To reinforce the importance of service and thankfulness, the author ends this pericope with a stern reminder that focuses not on God's majesty but on his power to destroy utterly (12:29). The author has already noted it is "a fearful thing to fall into the hands of the living God" (10:31). Here he identifies why. He has already appealed to Deuteronomy 4:11–12; 5:22–24, which describe the power of God felt by the Israelites and the force of the judgment that Jehovah meted out against them. Because of what God did then, the author's readers must ever keep in mind Moses' testimony: "your God is a consuming fire." The author brings force for his audience by changing the text from reading "your God" to reading "our God." His point is if those who rejected Jehovah's laws at Sinai fell under God's judgment, how much more shall those who reject the new covenant? For such unfaithful souls, God's fire awaits. Joseph Smith confirmed that God is, among other things, "a consuming fire." He noted, "God Almighty himself dwells in eternal fire; flesh and blood cannot go there, for all corruption is devoured by the fire. . . . When our flesh is quickened by the Spirit, there will be no blood in the tabernacle," making it possible to dwell with God in "everlasting burnings."[337] For those not prepared, the threat of the consuming fire will drive them away. This warning the author takes seriously not only for his readers but also for himself. There is always a danger of falling. His emphasis, however, is on guarding against this through a life of devoted, worshipful service grounded in reverence and awe.

---

336. Compare Lane, *Hebrews 9–13,* 487; Cockerill, *Epistle to the Hebrews,* 672.

337. "History, 1838–1856, Volume F-1," 20, punctuation and spelling standardized. See also Ogden and Skinner, *Verse by Verse,* 262–63. For discussion, see Roberts, *Mormon Doctrine of Deity,* 68–79; and Dale C. Mouritsen, "Transfiguration," in Ludlow, *Encyclopedia of Mormonism,* 4:1484–85.

Chapter 13

A Life of Thanksgiving and Godly Fear

Introduction

This chapter is the author's peroration, a rhetorical device used by orators as a final attempt to persuade an audience to accept the position the orator has set forth. In the case of our author, he uses it to further encourage his readers to a life of faithful endurance. Because this last section marks a rather abrupt change in style, some have suggested that it did not belong to the original document but was added later either by the author or someone who forwarded the work to others. Though it is true that this section is unique, given the sophistication of the literary bravura and its concrete application of the key themes the author developed throughout his Epistle, the strongest evidence suggests this section was part of the original.[1] We see this particularly in 13:1–17, where he uses short exhortations coupled with vivid imagery to move his readers to action. This peroration plays an important role in his efforts. Without it, the author "would not have been able to effectively conclude the appeal for perseverance through wholehearted reliance on Christ that he has so diligently pursued since the beginning of his [Epistle]."[2]

His emphasis in this last section is no longer on establishing a relationship with God through holiness. Instead the author focuses on relationships between people. He has already broached this subject when he admonished his readers to "seek peace with everyone" (NR 12:14). He now commends them to let brotherly love continue among them (13:1).

---

1. For discussion, see Lane, *Hebrews 9–13*, 496–97; Cockerill, *Epistle to the Hebrews*, 673–75; Attridge, *Epistle to the Hebrews*, 384–85.

2. Cockerill, *Epistle to the Hebrews*, 675.

The transition between chapters 12 and 13 appears to be very abrupt. The author closed the previous section with a stern warning concerning the fear of God that readers should have. He opens this section with an appeal to love. The transition, however, is not as abrupt as it first seems. One aspect of the old covenant contends that godly fear was the guarantee of good relations between people (for example, see Lev. 19:14, 18), thus the fear of God and love of neighbor find a close connection.

The author's new focus centers on how God is to be worshiped under current circumstances—through loving care and selfless service to one's fellows.[3] Here the author aligns with the teaching in the Book of Mormon that "when ye are in the service of your fellow beings ye are only in the service of your God" (Mosiah 2:17). The point is clearly that choosing the Christian way of life has notable consequences in "daily living, in love and mutual support, and in faithfulness in marriage. This is what it means to be the people of the new covenant, and to allow God to work his perfect will in the midst of his people."[4]

The material in this last portion of the Epistle can be split into three sections.[5] In 13:1–6, the author explains how his readers can live a faithful life of thanksgiving coupled with reverence toward God within the community of the Saints. He closes the first section with an appeal that his readers join him in affirming their trust in God, as defined by the selfless obedience of Christ that the author has been advocating. The style of this section differs remarkably from the sections that comes before (12:14–29) and after (13:7–17), marked by three differences. First, the rhythm is swift, almost staccato (the first sentence in Greek has but three words, and one of those is a definite article). Second, a verb is missing from several sentences and must be supplied. And third, with rapidity and no development, the author moves from one theme to another.[6] The change of pace helps keep the readers' attention on the author's message.

In 13:7–17, the author begins by asking his readers to imitate both their former and present leaders who have fearlessly proclaimed the word of God, and he closes by reminding readers that these rulers "watch over

3. Vanhoye, *Letter to the Hebrews,* 218–19.

4. Ellingworth, *Epistle to the Hebrews,* 692.

5. This breakdown follows Cockerill, *Epistle to the Hebrews,* 676–77. For other arrangements, see Vanhoye, *Letter to the Hebrews,* 217–38; Lane, *Hebrews 9–13,* 497; and Attridge, *Epistle to the Hebrews,* 390. However commentators break down this section, the overall message remains the same.

6. Vanhoye, *Letter to the Hebrews,* 218; see also Holzapfel and Wayment, *Making Sense,* 458.

[their] souls." In between, he reiterates his earlier appeal that his readers remember the Lord's suffering done so that "he might sanctify the people" (13:12). The author admonishes them to identify with this suffering so they will offer their own acceptable sacrifice of praising God and doing good works. In doing so, they will offer the appropriate response to the Savior's atoning work and not only live in thanksgiving and godly fear[7] but also find their sacrifice well pleasing to God. In the final section (13:18–25), the author askes his readers to sustain him through their prayers, pronounces his own blessing upon them, and closes the letter.

Living a Life of Thanksgiving and Reverence (13:1–6)

Greek Text

1 Ἡ φιλαδελφία μενέτω. 2 τῆς φιλοξενίας μὴ ἐπιλανθάνεσθε, διὰ ταύτης γὰρ ἔλαθόν τινες ξενίσαντες ἀγγέλους. 3 μιμνῄσκεσθε τῶν δεσμίων ὡς συνδεδεμένοι, τῶν κακουχουμένων ὡς καὶ αὐτοὶ ὄντες ἐν σώματι. 4 τίμιος ὁ γάμος ἐν πᾶσιν καὶ ἡ κοίτη ἀμίαντος, πόρνους γὰρ καὶ μοιχοὺς κρινεῖ ὁ θεός. 5 ἀφιλάργυρος ὁ τρόπος· ἀρκούμενοι τοῖς παροῦσιν· αὐτὸς γὰρ εἴρηκεν· Οὐ μή σε ἀνῶ οὐδ' οὐ μή σε ἐγκαταλίπω· 6 ὥστε θαρροῦντας ἡμᾶς λέγειν· Κύριος ἐμοὶ βοηθός, οὐ φοβηθήσομαι· τί ποιήσει μοι ἄνθρωπος; [SBLGNT]

King James Version

1 Let brotherly love continue. 2 Be not forgetful to entertain strangers: for thereby some have entertained angels unawares. 3 Remember them that are in bonds, as bound with them; and them which suffer adversity, as being yourselves also in the body. 4 Marriage is honourable in all, and the bed undefiled: but whoremongers and adulterers God will judge. 5 Let your conversation be without covetousness; and be content with such things as ye have: for he hath said, I will never leave thee, nor

New Rendition

1 Keep on loving each other as brothers and sisters. 2 Do not neglect hospitality, because by so doing, some have entertained angels without knowing it. 3 Remember those who are in prison as though you were fellow-prisoners, and those who are mistreated as though you were also suffering mistreatment. 4 Marriage should be held in honor by all, and the marriage bed kept undefiled, for God will condemn all fornicators and adulterers. 5 Your conduct should be free of the love of money,

7. Koester, *Hebrews,* 577; Lane, *Hebrews 9–13,* 497–98.

forsake thee. 6 So that we may boldly say, The Lord is my helper, and I will not fear what man shall do unto me.

being content with what you have. For God himself has said,

> "I will never desert or abandon you" [Josh. 1:5],

6 so that we can confidently say,

> "The Lord is my helper, I will not be afraid. What can anyone do to me?" [Ps. 118:6].

Translation Notes and Comments

13:1 ***Let brotherly love continue / Keep on loving each other as brothers and sisters:*** With this verse the author begins eight admonitions. The noun φιλαδελφία (*philadelphia*), "love of brother/sister," denotes the special kind of affection that is shared by family members. Within the Christian community, it expresses the commitment each member feels toward the other members belonging to the same household of faith.[8]

The verb μένω (*menō*), found here in the form of a third-person-singular imperative, means "to stay, remain" or "to continue" in the sense of maintaining a state or quality.[9] Here both state and quality apply to love. The Saints are to maintain the high degree of love they have achieved. The force of the imperative suggests such love was extensive among the Christians but needed to be guarded and promoted.

13:2 ***Be not forgetful to entertain strangers / Do not neglect hospitality:*** This verse contains the author's second exhortation. The verb ἐπιλανθάνομαι (*epilanthanomai*), "forget," found here as an imperative, means not just to forget someone but to neglect them because one does not care the least bit about them.[10] The negative particle μή (*mē*), "not," shows such a condition should never be found among the Saints.

The noun φιλοξενία (*philoxenia*), literally "love of a stranger," denotes "hospitality" and points to the kind of graciousness that a Christian should bestow upon those who are not in her or his immediate circle of extended

---

8. BDAG, 1055. The concept of brotherly love under the old covenant was exclusively pointing to "the children of thy people" as one's neighbors and toward whom love should be directed (Lev. 19:17–18). The new covenant redefined the concept by bringing all, through rebirth by water and spirit (John 3:1–7), into the same family as equal brothers and sisters (Acts 15:23; Gal. 3:26–28). Vanhoye, *Letter to the Hebrews,* 219.

9. BDAG, 630–31.

10. Louw-Nida, §29.14, 17; BDAG, 374.

family and close friends.[11] The word "stranger" is not in the Greek text, and therefore we have left it out of our Rendition.[12] The nuance is broad enough that whether the author is thinking only in terms of other Christians or of those outside the community is not clear. Given, however, the Old Testament roots on which this Epistle draws its support, the broader interpretation seems best.[13]

for thereby some have entertained angels unawares / because by so doing, some have entertained angels without knowing it: The verb ξενίζω (*xenizō*) means "to show hospitality," often in the form of entertainment.[14]

The noun ἄγγελος (*angelos*) here denotes a God-sent "messenger," whether a mortal, spirit, or resurrected being.[15] Given their nature, these messengers can appear to be ordinary people. For that reason, a person could show hospitality to such beings not knowing who they were.[16]

13:3 ***Remember them that are in bonds, as bound with them / Remember those who are in prison as though you were fellow-prisoners:*** This verse contains the author's third and fourth exhortations. The verb μιμνῄσκομαι (*mimnēskomai*), found here in the form of a present imperative, denotes remembering someone, but given the present tense, it carries the nuance of "continually remembering" and in doing so responding in an appropriate manner to the circumstances of the one remembered.[17]

The noun δέσμιος (*desmios*) denotes "a prisoner"[18] while συνδέω (*syndeō*), found here in the form of a perfect passive participle, though referencing imprisonment in general, in this passive context means "to be bound with" someone, that is, to share the weight of their bondage. Generally, this took

---

11. Louw-Nida, §34.57; BDAG, 1058.

12. The idea is implied in the compound noun, the latter part being related to the noun ξένος (*xenos*), "stranger." The term can refer to a stranger in general but more often to one who is an invited guest. For discussion of "hospitality," see Stählin, *TDNT,* 5:1–36.

13. Abraham (Gen. 18:1–8), Lot (Gen. 19:1–3), and even Rahab (Josh. 2:1–6) would have modeled a very inclusive kind of hospitality.

14. Louw-Nida, §34.57; BDAG, 683–84.

15. BDAG, 8–9.

16. McConkie, *Doctrinal New Testament Commentary,* 3:234–35; McConkie, "Angels," in Ludlow, *Encyclopedia of Mormonism,* 1:40–41. Joseph Smith did make the distinction between messengers who are spirits and those who are resurrected beings, stating that "spirits can only be revealed in flaming fire, or glory. Angels have advanced farther—their light and glory being tabernaccled; and hence they appear in bodily shape." "History, 1838–1856, Volume E-1," 1750. For an extended study, see Oscar W. McConkie Jr., *Angels* (Salt Lake City: Deseret Book, 1975).

17. BDAG, 652; Louw-Nida, §29.16; Ellingworth, *Epistle to the Hebrews,* 696.

18. BDAG, 219.

the form of not only visiting someone but also taking items to make their imprisonment more bearable.

and them which suffer adversity, as being yourselves also in the body / and those who are mistreated as though you were also suffering mistreatment: The verb κακουχέω (*kakoucheō*), found here in the form of a perfect passive participle, means "to be maltreated" and even "tormented."[19] The tense of the participle suggests some people have been suffering under this condition for some time.

The phrase ἐν σώματι (*en sōmati*), "in the body," means to be subject to mortal ills and therefore to the maltreatment of others. The author uses the phrase to encourage charity toward sufferers because Christians themselves may someday need it.[20]

13:4 ***Marriage is honourable in all, and the bed undefiled / Marriage should be held in honor by all, and the marriage bed kept undefiled:*** This verse contains the author's fifth and sixth admonitions. These two phrases do not have a stated verb, and therefore one must be supplied. There are two choices. If the supplied verb is ἐστίν (*estin*), "is," as in the KJV, then the two phrases are statements. If, on the other hand, the supplied verb is ἔστω (*estō*), "let [it] be" (a third-person singular imperative), then the two phrases, as in our Rendition, are commands.[21] We have taken this view because of the author's construction of the whole phrase. He has adopted the style of definite nouns ("marriage" and "marriage bed") being qualified by predicate adjectives ("honored" and "undefiled"). This form of construction implies a missing third-person impetrative.[22]

The noun γάμος (*gamos*), "marriage,"[23] as used in the scriptures, can refer to only one legal, moral, and religious relationship—one that was set up by God in the beginning, namely, the divine union between a man and a woman (Gen. 2:23–24).

The adjective τίμιος (*timios*), "honorable, esteemed," denotes something of exceptional worth and therefore "valuable" or "precious."[24] The term is

---

19. BDAG, 502.

20. The phrase should be understood to refer neither to the Church and the union between the persons therein nor to the philosophical sense of the body being the seat of evil. The author is referring to each person's vulnerability while in mortality. Ellingworth, *Epistle to the Hebrews,* 696.

21. Lane, *Hebrews 9–13,* 508 notes i, k; Ellingworth, *Epistle to the Hebrews,* 697; Attridge, *Epistle to the Hebrews,* 387.

22. Cockerill, *Epistle to the Hebrews,* 682.

23. BDAG, 188–89.

24. BDAG, 1005–6; Moulton and Milligan, *Vocabulary,* 635.

most often used to describe gems of unusual value (1 Kgs. 7:9–11; Rev. 18:12, 16). Only here in scripture is the word used to describe marriage; in doing so, it stresses the author's high view of the institution as something unusually precious.

The noun κοίτη (*koitē*), literally "bed," also refers to the "marriage bed" and is a euphemism for marital intimacy.[25]

The adjective ἀμίαντος (*amiantos*), "undefiled," means "pure" in a religious and moral sense,[26] and this quality was closely associated with the requirements necessary for acceptable temple worship.[27] As such, the nuance casts a covenant light on marriage and the sexual relations that are associated therewith (compare 1 Cor. 7:3–5).

The phrase ἐν πᾶσιν (*en pasin*), "in all," as in the KJV, is problematic because the adjective *pas*, "all," can be construed as either masculine or neuter. If it is taken as neuter, then the phrase is instrumental and means "by all,"[28] thus connoting that everyone should honor marriage. If it is taken as masculine, then the phrase is local and means "among all," thus connoting the Christian community should view marriage that way. Either way, the point is that among the Christians, at least, there are no exceptions to this command.[29]

but whoremongers and adulterers God will judge / for God will condemn all fornicators and adulterers: The conjunction γάρ (*gar*), "for," emphasizes the threat of judgment that God will mete out upon two sets of people, both of whom, in their own way, are guilty of defiling the wedding bed.

The noun πόρνος (*pornos*), "fornicator," is the general term for anyone who indulges in illicit sexual activity,[30] while the noun μοιχός (*moichos*), "adulterer," denotes anyone who betrays his or her spouse through sexual relations with another.[31] The author assures both of these will face godly

---

25. BDAG, 554; Louw-Nida, §§6.108; 23.62. The term can also refer to gross immorality. Louw-Nida, §88.273.

26. BDAG, 54.

27. *NID*, s.v. "μιαίνω." The author uses the term *amiantos,* along with "holy" (ὅσιος, *hosios*) and "blameless" (ἀκακός, akakos), to describe the qualifications of Jesus as High Priest (7:26).

28. It is also possible that, if construed as a neuter, the phrase could mean "in every way," suggesting that all aspects of the marriage relationship are proper and good so long as they follow within the bounds set by the Lord.

29. Cockerill, *Epistle to the Hebrews,* 683. Attridge, *Epistle to the Hebrews,* 387, notes that there is little difference between the two ideas.

30. BDAG, 855. To see the range of illicit sexual acts covered by the word, see 1 Cor. 5:9–11; 6:9; Eph. 5:3–5; 1 Tim. 1:10; and Rev. 21:8; 22:15.

31. BDAG, 657.

judgment. "Their home in the spirit world shall be hell (2 Ne. 9:36), and their inheritance in eternity the lowest kingdom God has provided for men."[32]

13:5 ***Let your conversation be without covetousness / Your conduct should be free of the love of money:*** This verse contains the author's seventh and eighth admonitions. The noun τρόπος (*tropos*), "custom, conduct," denotes the proper decorum that should govern members of a group or society.[33] During the period when the KJV was translated, the term "conversation" referred not to speaking with someone but to one's conduct or behavior.[34]

The adjective ἀφιλάργυρος (*aphilargyros*), literally "not loving money," here suggests a generous nature.[35] The scriptures condemn the vice φιλαρυρία (*philargyria*), "love of money," that stands opposite this virtue, noting it is the root of much that is evil (Luke 16:14; 1 Tim. 6:10; 2 Tim. 3:2).[36] Thus, the virtue of having a generous nature guards against a vast variety of sins.

The JST changes the word "conversation" to "consecrations" and in doing so redirects the modern nuance of the KJV from one person's chatting with another to that of a person's religious donations. The change shows a person can covet his or her own property but warns against such (note D&C 19:26).

be content with such things as ye have / being content with what you have: The verb πάρειμι (*pareimi*), found here in the form of a present participle, denotes all that is at one's disposal but more specifically one's possessions.[37] The force of the participle is imperative, qualifying the previous exhortation, and thereby gives the means or reason for the act, namely practicing generosity.[38]

---

32. McConkie, *Doctrinal New Testament Commentary*, 3:237.

33. BDAG, 1016–17. In English at the time the KJV was written, "conversation" denoted a person's way of life, conduct, and social interactions.

34. The Latin root of the word *conversari* denoted "to associate with" but nuanced proper behavior toward others. *Collegiate Dictionary*, s.v. "conversation."

35. BDAG, 157. The phrase ἀφιλάργυρος ὁ τρόπος (*aphilargyros ho tropos*), literally "not-loving-money the way," illustrates the remarkable economy of words the Greek language is capable of. In our Rendition, we have expanded this to be clear in modern English.

36. Johnson, *Hebrews*, 343.

37. BDAG, 773–74. The phrase ἀρκούμενοι τοῖς παροῦσιν (*arkoumenoi tois parousin*), "being content with the things available," is another example of the compactness of Greek.

38. Cockerill, *Epistle to the Hebrews*, 685; McConkie, *Doctrinal New Testament Commentary*, 3:237.

The verb ἀρκέω (*arkeō*) denotes that which is sufficient but carries the idea of being satisfied or content with what is allotted to one in both time and means.[39]

for he hath said, I will never leave thee, nor forsake thee / For God himself has said, "I will never desert or abandon you": The quote is from Joshua 1:5 (compare Deut. 31:6, 8). Both the verbs ἀνίημι (*aniēmi*), "leave, desert," and ἐγκαταλείπω (*engkataleipō*), "forsake, abandon," carry the force of abandoning, deserting, and forsaking something or someone. The latter stresses more the severing of relationships, while the former more the rejection of the individual.[40]

The sentence contains the double negative οὐ μή (*ou mē*), "not," with the verb in the subjunctive, which is the strongest way in Greek to negate something. Here God uses it to assure his people that he will never sever his relationship with them or abandon them in time of need. He really will be with them through both the good times and the bad.

13:6 *So that we may boldly say, The Lord is my helper / so that we can confidently say, "The Lord is my helper:* The quote is from Psalm 118:6.

The verb θαρρέω (*tharreō*) means "to be bold, confident."[41] It is here found as a present active participle agreeing with ἡμᾶς (*hēmas*), "we." The phrase ὥστε θαρροῦντας ἡμᾶς λέγειν (*hōste tharrountas hēmas legein*) is an example of the use of the conjunction ὥστε (*hōste*) with an infinitive to express actual results, "so that." Thus, the phrase can be translated, "so that we can confidently say."

Though this phrase introduces a quote, it expresses the Christian's faith in God and the sureness of his promises. With the use of the first-person plural, the author seeks to have his readers identify together with him in this heartfelt and faith-filled declaration.

The adjective βοηθός (*boēthos*), "helpful," when used as a substantive, denotes one who plays a responsible role as an assistant, thus, "helper."[42] In the LXX, the word is often used in a military context (for example, see Josh. 10:4; 2 Sam. 8:5; 1 Chr. 12:1; and Isa. 31:3) and denotes the aid a willing ally gives to another. The term is often used to describe the association that Jehovah has with his people. He is the willing helper who delivers them

39. BDAG, 131–32.

40. BDAG, 82–83; 273.

41. Louw-Nida, §25.156; BDAG, 444.

42. BDAG, 180. The word is a combination of βοή (*boē*), "to cry," and θέω (*theō*), "to run," and carries the idea of running to one who cries out for help. *NID*, s.v. "βοηθέω."

from their enemies (for examples, see Ps. 9:9; 19:14; 20:3; 30:10). Indeed, Israel is to seek help from no other source (for example, see Ps. 60:11).

In the present context, the word refers to Christ as the one who helps overcome weakness and trials. The word has strong echoes to 2:18, where the author states that Christ is the one who can βοηθέω (*boētheō*), "succor," his people, and 4:16, where the author notes that Jesus is the one with whom the faithful can "find grace to help [βοήθεια, *boētheia*] in time of need."[43]

I will not fear what man shall do unto me / I will not be afraid. What can anyone do to me?": The quote is from Psalm 118:6, though the idea is also found in Psalm 56:11. Note this quote is the only one the author chooses that do not have God as the speaker. The uniqueness serves to give them additional punch. Though the Greek phrase can be construed as a single sentence, as in the KJV, the better choice is to make it two declarative sentences.[44] Though the righteous will go through tribulations and trials, the Lord's sustaining power will assist them to victory, and therefore they have nothing to fear.

Analysis and Summary

This section contains a carefully composed peroration, a common rhetorical device the author adopts in his final endeavor to motivate his readers to Christian service. It is composed of eight exhortations. The author begins with an admonition to love (13:1). He chooses the noun "brotherly love" or, more accurately, "love of one's brother or sister" (φιλαδελφία, *philadelphia*) to express his desire.[45] Though the word has a sense similar to the more popular scriptural word for love, ἀγάπη (*agape*),[46] *philadelphia* carried the added nuance of love between family members. The Savior used this family-oriented affection to express the kind of love he wanted his disciples to direct toward himself and others (Matt. 10:37). Further, it also expressed the kind of love the Father has for both his Son (John 5:20) and his other children (John 16:27). Indeed, the Father insists, "Those whom I love [φιλέω, *phileō*], I discipline" (Rev. 3:19, our translation). No one under his love escapes his correction; correction is an expression of his deep love.

---

43. For a study, see Büchel, *TDNT,* 1:628–29.

44. Ellingworth, *Epistle to the Hebrews,* 701.

45. BDAG, 1055; LSJ, 1931.

46. Hebrews makes little distinction between φιλαδελφία (*philadelphia*) and ἀγάπη (*agapē*). Both exhibit the same human emotion that generates godly service toward all those in the community of faith. Ellingworth, *Epistle to the Hebrews,* 694.

Love of and for the Father and Son is a *sine qua non* of salvation.[47] This is because the expression of love toward God and his children sanctifies all a person does. Paul expressed this idea: "Greet those that love us in the faith" (Titus 3:15). The idea behind his request is that brotherly love is correctly understood only when it is "reinterpreted in light of God's love in the revelation of his Son."[48] In this way, human love is transformed as love in faith. Therefore, the word must be understood more broadly than the figurative sibling-like love, "but as the mutual love of those who are united" in the Christian bond.[49] Non-Christians also understood the nuance of the word as more than "a matter of sentiment . . . but mutual sharing of possessions and activities. That is why some of the New Testament passages calling for brotherly love modify it with language about feelings" (for example, see Rom. 12:10; and 1 Pet. 1:22).[50]

Further, as distinctively noted by the author, Christians are not brothers and sisters only of one another but also of Christ himself.[51] Together the Lord and his people compose the divine and eternal family of the Father and are joint heirs together of all that he has (6:17; Rom. 8:17; Gal. 3:29).

In 13:2, the author gives his second exhortation, defining the kind of love that should be directed to those outside the immediate community of faith—"hospitality" (φιλοξενία, *philoxenia*). As with the old covenant, the new one is also concerned with those outside its protective constraints. These, the author admonishes, God's people are not to forget, for they are to be concerned not only with the well-being of one another but also of others. All are to be offered friendship and assistance (see Gen. 19:13; Lev. 19:34; Deut. 10:19; 31:12; 2 Sam. 12:4; and Isa. 58:7). The Lord, during his earthly ministry, stressed hospitality's importance for the Christian community (Luke 10:25–35; 11:5–6; 14:12–21), and it was generally adopted by the Church (Rom. 12:13–14; 1 Tim. 3:2; Titus 1:8; 1 Pet. 4:9).[52]

The author gives an interesting reason for extending such hospitality. He references those who have unknowingly entertained angels. He could have had Abraham and Sarah (Gen. 18:2–15), Lot (Gen. 19:1–22), or Manoah (Judg. 13:2–23) in mind. Indeed, in Manoah's case, the scripture is clear

47. This is so much so that Paul can say, "If anyone does not love the Lord, let him be accursed" (NR 1 Cor. 16:22).

48. *NID,* s.v. "φιλέω."

49. Ellingworth, *Epistle to the Hebrews,* 694.

50. Johnson, *Hebrews,* 339.

51. Ellingworth, *Epistle to the Hebrews,* 694.

52. Vanhoye, *Letter to the Hebrews,* 219–20.

that only after he interacted with the stranger did he know "that he was an angel of the Lord" (Judg. 13:21).

In 13:3, the author gives his third and fourth exhortations. Here the author uses the more positive "remember" (μιμνήθσκω, *mimnēthskō*) rather than the negative "do not forget," which he used in the previous verse. To remember carries the nuance of not simply calling those who are suffering to mind but of having concern for them expressed by giving them appropriate care.[53]

The author admonishes his readers to first remember those incarcerated. The living conditions in many Greco-Roman prisons were rather severe. Prisons themselves were often dark, dank, filthy places, often overly hot or cold. Prisoners were supplied with no clothing and often no bedding. Food was often infrequent and unsatisfying. Worse, some jailors had a propensity for sadism, and many were out for a bribe, and when such was not forthcoming, they were extra hard on an inmate. Prisoners could receive help and benefaction from those outside, and such care often relieved much of the suffering prisoners had to endure.[54]

The author's context suggests that the people he has in mind are those who have been unjustly imprisoned due to the faith. To openly associate with them could easily put ministering Christians in danger. These faithful people have, however, already shown such bravery (10:33–34), and the author wants them to continue to do so.

The author's fourth admonition is more comprehensive than the third, looking to all those who presently suffer. The verb he uses, κακουχέω (*kakoucheō*), denotes not only maltreatment but also torture and suggests the harsh treatment that some are experiencing. Whether or not the author has only Christians in mind cannot be determined from the context. Certainly, Christian love should know no bounds. Even so, the Christian community is likely whom the author has in mind. Seeing the sometimes severe maltreatment happening to others could make some balk at giving assistance. Thus, the author reminds them they are yet "in the body" (ἐν σώματι, *en sōmati*). In that condition, they are not immune from similar suffering; at some future time, they might find themselves also needing care and assistance. The author, in his list of Old Testament heroes, has already cited the example of those

53. Louw-Nida, §29.16; Vanhoye, *Letter to the Hebrews*, 220.

54. Koester, *Hebrews*, 564–65; for a study, see Craig S. Wansink, *Chained in Christ: The Experience and Rhetoric of Paul's Imprisonments* (Sheffield, Eng.: Sheffield Academic Press, 1996), 27–95.

who were fearless during periods of opposition. They "experienced derision, floggings, and even chains and imprisonment. They were stoned, sawn in two, murdered by the sword. They wandered about wearing sheepskins and goatskins, impoverished, oppressed, [and] maltreated." Of these the "world was not worthy" (11:36–38). The implication of this verse is to warn the author's readers that they must not assume they are above such trials. Indeed, many, even among them, will still have such trials, and therefore they should develop empathy and compassion for those of whom the world is still not worthy.

In 13:4, the author gives his fifth admonition, emphasizing the highly prized state marriage should have. The author exhorts his readers to ensure that marriage maintains its supernal and holy state. He uses an adjective that means "precious, honorable, esteemed" (τίμιος, *timios,* which could refer to expensive gems[55]) to describe how the Saints should view marriage, stressing the extraordinarily significant state of marriage as viewed by God. So great is the marriage commitment that it excludes all other earthly obligations including one's duties to parents (Gen. 2:24). "By beginning with the covenant of marriage rather than with individual chastity [which he treats in the next phrase], the [author] confirms the fact that sexual misconduct is not merely a matter of private concern but has implications for the common life of the people of God."[56]

The author's next exhortation, let "the marriage bed be kept undefiled" (13:4), makes the former one more specific. His point is the Christian should not let anything despoil the intimacy God designed marriage to have. The author assures his readers that God's judgment hangs over those who violate the law of chastity. This includes not only the adulterer (μοιχός, *moichos*) but also the fornicator (πόρνος, *pornos*). Indeed, expressed lust desecrates the union either before or after marriage by forfeiting the oneness God designed intimacy to create. All the lecherous will face the power of the living God who, as the author notes, is "a consuming fire" (12:29).[57] The lascivious need remember that it is indeed "a frightening thing to fall into the hands of the living God" (NR 10:31), but it is also, paradoxically, for the righteous, "the safest of all places to be."[58]

---

55. BDAG, 1005–6.
56. Cockerill, *Epistle to the Hebrews,* 683.
57. See Lane, *Hebrews 9–13,* 2:508 note l.
58. Johnson, *Hebrews,* 344.

In Genesis, intimacy is described as being of "one flesh" (Gen. 2:24). Part of being "one flesh" is procreation. Indeed, Adam and Eve were told to "be fruitful and multiply and fill up the earth" (Gen. 1:28, our translation). But there is more to it than that. According to D&C 49:15–17, "marriage is ordained of God unto man . . . that he should have one wife, and they twain shall be one flesh, and all this that the earth might answer the end of its creation; and that it might be filled." And what is the end of that creation? The Lord declared, "We will go down, for there is space there, and we will take of these materials, and we will make an earth whereon these may dwell; and we will prove them herewith, to see if they will do all things whatsoever the Lord their God shall command them; . . . and they who keep their second estate shall have glory added upon their heads for ever and ever" (Abr. 3:24–26). Marriage plays an indispensable role in gaining that glory. According to Elder Bruce R. McConkie, "The whole plan of salvation and exaltation centers in and revolves around the family unit." For that reason, "to deliberately refrain from assuming marital or parental obligations is to fail the most important test of this mortal probation."[59]

The Savior used the term "one flesh" to teach the Pharisees the importance and purpose of marriage, stating that through marriage "they [the couple] are no more twain, but one flesh," and then commanding, "What therefore God hath joined together, let not man put asunder" (Matt. 19:6). That Jesus would give such a strong command is of little wonder given what the scriptures teach about marriage. According to D&C 131:2–3, exaltation is contingent upon marriage. Indeed, "in order to obtain [celestial glory], a man [and woman] must enter into this order of the priesthood [meaning the new and everlasting covenant of marriage]; And if [they do] not, [they] cannot obtain it."[60] These words embody the divinely appointed result of marriage. God intended it to have the deepest corporeal and spiritual unity of any interpersonal association and transcend the demands of any other relationship, including that of child toward parents. The vital oneness of the husband and the wife includes a spiritual union of both the body and the heart. Indeed, Adam was to "cleave unto" Eve (Gen. 2:24).

The Hebrew word דָּבַק (*dābaq*) means "to stick to, cling to," or "adhere to." The Greek word used by Matthew (κολλάω, *kollaō,* derived from κόλλα, *kolla,* "glue") nicely expresses the idea of the Hebrew. The word

59. McConkie, *Doctrinal New Testament Commentary,* 3:236.

60. For a discussion, see Carlfred Broderick, *One Flesh, One Heart: Putting Celestial Love into Your Temple Marriage* (Salt Lake City: Deseret Book, 1986).

means "to join together, bind, or weld" and stresses making two things into one.[61] The man and woman are to be regarded as one entity—no longer considered two persons but one body.[62] In other words, the Savior emphasizes that God created males and females to be re-created in an inviolable union through marriage. In doing so, God creates a new spiritual and physical relationship marked by the words "one flesh" (σάρξ μία, *sarx mia*). Underscoring the point, Genesis 5:2 declares that God created male and female "and blessed them, and called *their name Adam*" (emphasis added). God no longer regarded them as two beings but rather as one unit, הָאָדָם (*hā'ādām*), "the Adam." Paul understood this, stating, "So ought men to love their wives as their own bodies. He that loveth his wife loveth himself" (Eph. 5:28). He verified that "they two shall be one flesh" (Eph. 5:31) but admitted the latter statement "is a great mystery" (Eph. 5:32).

It is of importance that Paul juxtaposes marriage and mystery. The Greek understanding of the word "mystery" (μυστήριον, *mysterion*) does not denote something that cannot be understood but rather something that should not be spoken of commonly.[63] The Greeks used the word "mystery" to describe the sacred rites associated with certain aspects of temple worship. As a technical term, it denoted those sacred doctrines that could only be known to the initiates who were sworn never to reveal them to outsiders.[64] For Paul and other early Christians, it denoted God's work of salvation which was to be disclosed to the Christian community but not to the world (see 1 Cor. 2:7–10).

The scholar and religious writer C. S. Lewis caught this significance of the Savior's teachings. Lewis noted that single humans are but half beings whom God designed to be combined in pairs. The combination, as noted above, is designated as "one flesh" in the scriptures. Lewis nicely illustrated the meaning of the word "one flesh" by comparing a man and a woman to a violin and its bow that make but one musical instrument, just as a lock with its key are but one mechanism.[65] Only when the two work together do we have a whole. So it is with *hā'ādām*.

One point the author makes very clear is that the wedding bed must remain undefiled. He has already referred to Esau as an example of one

61. Schmidt, *TDNT,* 3:822–23.
62. C. S. Mann, *Mark* (New York: Doubleday, 1986), 391.
63. BDAG, 661–62.
64. Moulton and Milligan, *Vocabulary,* 420.
65. Lewis, *Mere Christianity,* 88–89.

who was willing to sell his future for current gratification. This wayward son thus becomes a prime example of those who disregard God's laws because, in their faithlessness, they take no thought of the future.[66] As one scholar noted, "Married couples are to keep themselves exclusively for one another, or incur God's judgment."[67] That judgment will be severe for the unrepentant. According to Elder Joseph Fielding Smith,

> Every soul is entitled to the right to come into this world in a legitimate way—in the way the Father has willed that souls should come. Whosoever takes a course contrary to this is guilty of an almost irreparable crime.
>
> Is there any wonder, then, that the Lord places the violation of this covenant of marriage and the loss of virtue as second only to the shedding of innocent blood? Is there not, then, sufficient reason for the severity of the punishment which has been promised to those who violate this eternal law? Moreover, have we not forgotten in large measure the enormity of the crime of unchastity and breaking of marriage vows? Do those who are guilty think the enormity of the offense of maliciously or wickedly tampering with the laws of life will be overlooked by a just God? Do they think that only a few stripes, if any punishment at all, will amend this broken law?
>
> The demand for personal purity is made by the Church upon both men and women equally. There is no double standard of judgment. "If purity of life is neglected," President Joseph F. Smith once said, "all other dangers set in upon us like the rivers of water when the flood gates are opened." Sexual impurity is a most deadly sin. Anciently it was considered so, and according to the law of God, those who were guilty were in danger of being put to death [Lev. 20:10].[68]

The author follows his sixth exhortation with a seventh having a connected theme: generosity (13:5). The Greek he uses (ἀφιλάρυρος, *aphilargyros*) means literally "not loving money"[69] and connotes a kind and giving nature. This virtue stands opposite the vice "greed" (φιλαρυρία, *philargyria,* literally "love of money"), the very root of evil (1 Tim. 6:10).[70]

The vices lust and greed have a natural connection—many afflicted with one are also afflicted with the other.[71] Both are grounded in acute selfishness

66. Thompson, *Hebrews,* 279; Attridge, *Epistle to the Hebrews,* 388.

67. Ellingworth, *Epistle to the Hebrews,* 697.

68. Smith, *Doctrines of Salvation,* 2:92.

69. BDAG, 157.

70. Johnson, *Hebrews,* 343.

71. Attridge, *Epistle to the Hebrews,* 387 nn. 45–47. See also Luke 16:9–18; 1 Cor. 5:1–6:11; Eph. 5:3–5; Col. 3:5; and 1 Thes. 4:3–7, where the two are connected.

and block out love and loyalty to others. Indeed, the love of money stands directly opposite the love of others.[72] Further, the two are found juxtaposed in the seventh and eighth commandments (Ex. 20:14–15). Each alone was bad enough, but together they destroy the oneness and unity of both the marriage relationship and the Christian community and lead to God's withdrawal of his association and power. As the Savior said, "If ye are not one ye are not mine" (D&C 38:27). High moral behavior coupled with its associated generosity expressed as caring service, on the other hand, promotes trust, unity, and oneness. "If stoics counseled people to be content for the sake of self-sufficiency, Hebrews urges [its readers] to be content for the sake of serving others in the confidence that God will give them a future reward (Heb. 10:35; 11:26)."[73]

The author clearly understood the proper response for finding security in one's life during periods of trial. It is not a grasping greed but a continued reliance upon the Father. As the author makes clear, God himself has promised that he will never desert or abandon the faithful (13:5). The intensive "himself" (αὐτός, *autos*), as used by the author, stresses that this is God's decree and that he will in very deed keep it.[74]

Note the absence of a promise that the faithful person's life will be without trials. Rather, the promise is that God will be the Saint's companion during those times of particular need and assist her or him to come through victorious.

The author uses Jehovah's declaration that he will never break relations with or abandon the faithful with telling effect. It enables the author to bring together all of the quotations he has mustered from his biblical sources, where God has spoken to his people, to one grand conclusion. The God who continually warned, rebuked, and chastised the faithless will also continually sustain, lift, and strengthen the faithful with the same if not more energy and certainty. Thus, the author assures his readers that they can and must depend on their God rather than anything the world can offer.[75] In 13:6, the author, quoting portions of LXX Psalm 117:6 and 55:12,

72. Vanhoye, *Letter to the Hebrews,* 220.

73. Koester, *Hebrews,* 559.

74. Lane, *Hebrews 9–13,* 519; Ellingworth, *Epistle to the Hebrews,* 699–700. The nuance the author gives this scripture does not actually appear in the Old Testament. Indeed, to make his point, the author has combined a promise that God made to Joshua (Josh. 1:5) with a pronouncement that Moses made in Jehovah's name "to all Israel" (Deut. 31:1, 6). Nonetheless, the author's point is well taken: God does not forsake the faithful. Vanhoye, *Letter to the Hebrews,* 220–21.

75. Cockerill, *Epistle to the Hebrews,* 686.

gives the result: the faithful can say with assurance that the Lord is their helper and will sustain them through all trials and tribulations. Therefore, they need never fear anything the world can do to them.

In sum, the author has carefully identified and explained the importance and ramifications of Christ's work as High Priest to prepare readers for what it means to say, "The Lord is my helper." Because of him, and only because of him, they can "draw near" (10:22) and find "grace to help" (4:16) them during this time of heavy trial. Thus, the expressions of faith in LXX Psalm 117:6 and 55:12 are an excellent conclusion not only for the final chapter of Hebrews but also for the theme of the Epistle as a whole. Christians are to live with full confidence in God's active awareness and assistance. They must have faith that these will carry them through the difficult times and more. Through his power, all his promises will be realized both temporally and spiritually (11:1–6). That saving power is wielded by the Savior due to his ministry, self-sacrifice, and present and eternal station and is presently activated by him. In and through him, the Father has provided all the help the faithful will ever need to succeed in life and to have place in the eternal city.[76]

Further Counsel and Admonitions (13:7–17)

Greek Text

7 Μνημονεύετε τῶν ἡγουμένων ὑμῶν, οἵτινες ἐλάλησαν ὑμῖν τὸν λόγον τοῦ θεοῦ, ὧν ἀναθεωροῦντες τὴν ἔκβασιν τῆς ἀναστροφῆς μιμεῖσθε τὴν πίστιν. 8 Ἰησοῦς Χριστὸς ἐχθὲς καὶ σήμερον ὁ αὐτός, καὶ εἰς τοὺς αἰῶνας. 9 διδαχαῖς ποικίλαις καὶ ξέναις μὴ παραφέρεσθε· καλὸν γὰρ χάριτι βεβαιοῦσθαι τὴν καρδίαν, οὐ βρώμασιν, ἐν οἷς οὐκ ὠφελήθησαν οἱ περιπατοῦντες. 10 ἔχομεν θυσιαστήριον ἐξ οὗ φαγεῖν οὐκ ἔχουσιν ἐξουσίαν οἱ τῇ σκηνῇ λατρεύοντες. 11 ὧν γὰρ εἰσφέρεται ζῴων τὸ αἷμα περὶ ἁμαρτίας εἰς τὰ ἅγια διὰ τοῦ ἀρχιερέως, τούτων τὰ σώματα κατακαίεται ἔξω τῆς παρεμβολῆς· 12 διὸ καὶ Ἰησοῦς, ἵνα ἁγιάσῃ διὰ τοῦ ἰδίου αἵματος τὸν λαόν, ἔξω τῆς πύλης ἔπαθεν. 13 τοίνυν ἐξερχώμεθα πρὸς αὐτὸν ἔξω τῆς παρεμβολῆς, τὸν ὀνειδισμὸν αὐτοῦ φέροντες. 14 οὐ γὰρ ἔχομεν ὧδε μένουσαν πόλιν, ἀλλὰ τὴν μέλλουσαν ἐπιζητοῦμεν· 15 δι᾽ αὐτοῦ οὖν ἀναφέρωμεν θυσίαν αἰνέσεως διὰ

76. Cockerill, *Epistle to the Hebrews,* 688; McConkie, *Doctrinal New Testament Commentary,* 3:237.

παντὸς τῷ θεῷ, τοῦτ᾽ ἔστιν καρπὸν χειλέων ὁμολογούντων τῷ ὀνόματι αὐτοῦ. 16 τῆς δὲ εὐποιΐας καὶ κοινωνίας μὴ ἐπιλανθάνεσθε, τοιαύταις γὰρ θυσίαις εὐαρεστεῖται ὁ θεός. 17 Πείθεσθε τοῖς ἡγουμένοις ὑμῶν καὶ ὑπείκετε, αὐτοὶ γὰρ ἀγρυπνοῦσιν ὑπὲρ τῶν ψυχῶν ὑμῶν ὡς λόγον ἀποδώσοντες, ἵνα μετὰ χαρᾶς τοῦτο ποιῶσιν καὶ μὴ στενάζοντες, ἀλυσιτελὲς γὰρ ὑμῖν τοῦτο. (SBLGNT)

King James Version

7 Remember them which have the rule over you, who have spoken unto you the word of God: whose faith follow, considering the end of their conversation. 8 Jesus Christ the same yesterday, and to day, and for ever. 9 Be not carried about with divers and strange doctrines. For it is a good thing that the heart be established with grace; not with meats, which have not profited them that have been occupied therein. 10 We have an altar, whereof they have no right to eat which serve the tabernacle. 11 For the bodies of those beasts, whose blood is brought into the sanctuary by the high priest for sin, are burned without the camp. 12 Wherefore Jesus also, that he might sanctify the people with his own blood, suffered without the gate. 13 Let us go forth therefore unto him without the camp, bearing his reproach. 14 For here have we no continuing city, but we seek one to come. 15 By him therefore let us offer the sacrifice of praise to God continually, that is, the fruit of our lips giving thanks to his name. 16 But to do good and to communicate forget not: for with such sacrifices God is well pleased. 17 Obey them that have the rule over you, and submit yourselves: for they watch for your souls, as they that must give account, that they may do it with joy, and not with grief: for that is unprofitable for you.

New Rendition

7 Remember your leaders who spoke the word of God to you. Carefully consider what they have accomplished in their lives and emulate their faith. 8 Jesus Christ is the same yesterday, today, and forever. 9 Do not be misled by deceitful and strange teachings, for it is well for the heart to be made firm by grace, not by ceremonial meals that have not been of benefit to those who participate in them. 10 We have an altar from which they who serve in the tabernacle have no right to eat. 11 For the bodies of the animals whose blood is brought into the tabernacle by the high priest for a sin offering are burned outside the camp. 12 Therefore Jesus also suffered outside the city gate so that he might sanctify the people by his own blood. 13 So let us go out to him outside the tabernacle, enduring his reproach. 14 For we do not have here an enduring city, but we seek the city that is to come. 15 Therefore through him let us continually offer up a sacrifice of praise to God, that is, the fruit of our lips confessing his name. 16 And do not neglect good works and generosity, for God is pleased with such sacrifices. 17 Obey your leaders and submit to them, for they keep watch over your souls as men who will give account of their responsibilities, so that they may do it joyfully without groaning, for that would be of no help to you.

Translation Notes and Comments

13:7 ***Remember them which have the rule over you / Remember your leaders:*** In this section, the author gives five more admonitions. These differ from the ones he has already given in that they are more fully developed.

On "remember," see Translation Notes for 13:3 above.

The verb ἡγέομαι (*hēgeomai*), found here in the form of a present participle, means "to guide, lead," the participial phrase referring to Church leaders and stressing the need to lead continually.[77]

who have spoken unto you the word of God / who spoke the word of God to you: The verb λαλέω (*laleō*), "to speak,"[78] found here in the aorist tense, suggests the reference is to former leaders who had been known to at least some of the members of the community and had since died.

The phrase τὸν λόγον τοῦ θεοῦ (*ton logon tou theou*), "the word of God," refers to the gospel or, in the author's terms, the "great salvation" (2:3) and suggests the leaders he refers to had at one time visited and spoken to members of this Christian community. It is not clear if the author is referring to those who first brought the gospel to the area or to those who visited afterward to strengthen and give further instructions as seen in the book of Acts and the writings of Paul and others.

whose faith follow, considering the end of their conversation / Carefully consider what they have accomplished in their lives and emulate their faith: This phrase contains the author's second admonition.

The verb μιμέομαι (*mimeomai*), found here as an imperative, means "to imitate" but more particularly "to emulate" what others have done.[79]

This phrase contains two nouns, ἔκβασις (*ekbasis*), "end, outcome, result,"[80] and ἀναστροφή (*anastrophē*), "way of life, conduct, behavior,"[81] and can be translated literally as "the result of the behavior," referring to the end product of the past leaders' lives. These people are good examples not only of those who have striven to implement the principles of Christ's gospel in

---

77. BDAG, 434. The word does not have an exclusively religious meaning. It is most often applied to the top leadership of a community or organization. Ellingworth, *Epistle to the Hebrews,* 702; Vanhoye, *Letter to the Hebrews,* 223.

78. BDAG, 582–83.

79. Louw-Nida, §44.41; BDAG, 651. The expression does leave open the possibility of martyrdom, but it more likely refers to faithfulness endured to the end. Vanhoye, *Letter to the Hebrews,* 223.

80. BDAG, 299.

81. BDAG, 72–73.

their lives but also of those who have received the reward of so doing. Thus, they should be emulated. In the KJV, *anastrophē* is translated as "conversation," which had the sense "behavior, conduct" in seventeenth-century English.[82]

13:8 *Jesus Christ the same yesterday, and to day, and for ever / Jesus Christ is the same yesterday, today, and forever:* The author gives punch to his declaration by using both the Lord's name and title.

The adjective αὐτός (*autos*), "self, same," indicates something that is identical with or related to its object.[83] With the phrase ὁ αὐτός (*ho autos*), "the same," the author emphasizes the constancy of the Lord through all aspects of time and in doing so reflects his witness in 1:12.

13:9 *Be not carried about with divers and strange doctrines / Do not be misled by deceitful and strange teachings:* The noun διδαχαί (*didachai*), "teachings," expresses the author's central concern. That the word comes first in the Greek sentence emphasizes its importance. In the New Testament as a whole, the noun denotes authentic doctrines concerning Christ and his message. The force of the word is generally not on intellectual understanding as much as it is on personal application.[84] In Hebrews, however, it takes on a negative cast, pointing to principles so elementary the author refers to them as "milk" that get in the way of developing spiritual maturity (5:12; 6:1). Here he focuses on yet another aspect.

The adjective ποίκιλος (*poikilos*) denotes something that exists in various aspects and is therefore diverse or manifold. Here it carries the nuance of teachings that are ambiguous or, more especially, deceitful.[85]

The adjective ξένος (*xenos*) means "strange, foreign," specifically that which comes from outside a community. Here it refers to teachings that have not originated with Christ and his leaders and are therefore false.[86]

The verb παραφέρω (*ropapherō*), found here as an imperative, means "to be carried away, mislead."[87] The force of the word suggests a power that can deceive and implies these false doctrines had a certain appeal that caused some to be enthused about them and therefore to promulgate them. Taking

82. See note 33 in this chapter.

83. BDAG, 152–54.

84. *NID,* s.v. "διδάσκω."

85. BDAG, 842.

86. BDAG, 684.

87. Louw-Nida, §§15.162; 31.75; BDAG, 772. For the meaning of being misled by error, see Johnson, *Hebrews,* 346.

the present tense with iterative force suggests that the author is directing his readers to reject these teachings whenever and wherever they arise.[88]

For it is a good thing that the heart be established with grace / for it is well for the heart to be made firm by grace: The verb βεβαιόω (*bebaioō*) means both "to put something beyond doubt" and "to make a person firm in commitment."[89]

For the word καρδία (*kardia*), "heart," see Translation Notes for 3:8 with associated Analysis. Here we need but note that it refers to the complete moral and mental center of an individual.[90]

The adjective καλός (*kalos*), "good," is rich with theological nuances. In the present context, it carries the idea of that which is "useful" or "proper," pointing particularly to that which is "good, noble, praiseworthy, contributing to salvation."[91] It looks to the importance of χάρις (*charis*), "grace" (here, based on the context of the Epistle as a whole,[92] the word refers to the Lord's self-sacrifice and the power that flows from it to individuals), as the means of making firm a person's commitment to the gospel.

not with meats / not by ceremonial meals: The noun βρῶμα (*brōma*) refers to food in general. Here the word is found in the plural, "foods," and could refer to Greco-Roman sacrificial banquets. Given the context of the Epistle as a whole as well as within this section, however, the author likely had one of two items in mind. The first could be Jewish sacrifices. Few of these where wholly burned. Parts of most were given to the priests and Levites to eat, and parts of some were retained by the individual to be used in a covenant-renewing meal.[93] The other item could be Jewish dietary regulations. Disputes over eating certain foods was rife in areas where Paul (for example, see Mark 7:1–8; Acts 10–11; Rom. 14; and 1 Cor. 8–10) and John (Rev. 2:14, 20) taught.[94]

which have not profited them that have been occupied therein / that have not been of benefit to those who participate in them: The verb

88. Lane, *Hebrews 9–13,* 522 note g.

89. BDAG, 172–73.

90. BDAG, 508–9.

91. BDAG, 504–5; Grundmann, *TDNT,* 3:536–50.

92. See specifically Translation Notes on 2:9; 4:14, with associated Analysis.

93. "Bible Dictionary," s.v. "Sacrifices."

94. Johnson, *Hebrews,* 347. Lane, *Hebrews 9–13,* 532–35, argues that the reference is to Jewish ceremonial meals practiced throughout the Greco-Roman world. See also Ellingworth, *Epistle to the Hebrews,* 709–10.

ὠφελέω (*ōpheleō*) means "to provide assistance" and therefore "to be of benefit to" or "of profit to" an individual.[95] Here with the negative particle οὐκ (*ouk*), "not," it suggests that which is totally worthless.

The verb περιπατέω (*peripateō*), literally "to walk around," denotes a person's comportment or behavior.[96] Here it seems to refer to those who are trustful of and therefore participate in the Mosaic sacrificial system without seeing it as an introduction, revelation, and exposition to the Lord and his ministry. Though the scriptures often use the term of walking in or around something metaphorical (for example, walking in darkness or walking in the light), the imagery here of "walking in foodstuffs" is hard to grasp. The best solution is to see it as the author's reference to a person's positive attitude toward Mosaic sacrifices or dietary restrictions.[97]

13:10 ***We have an altar, whereof they have no right to eat which serve the tabernacle / We have an altar from which they who serve in the tabernacle have no right to eat:*** The noun ἔχω (*echō*), "to have," found here in the form of a first-person plural, translates as "we have." In the present context, it refers to the whole of the Christian community to whom the author is writing.[98]

The noun θυσιαστήριον (*thysiastērion*), "altar," generally refers to either the altar of incense inside the sanctuary or to the one in the inner court of the tabernacle or temple.[99] Since there is no known Christian altar, exactly what the author is referring to is vague. It could be referring to the sacramental table,[100] but since the author has not developed a theme dealing with the Lord's Supper, that seems unlikely.[101] More likely he is referring to the cross and the blessings that flow from the Lord's Atonement.[102]

The noun ἐξουσία (*exousia*), "right, authority," denotes a person's comprehensive authority or absolute power over something.[103] Under the Mosaic law, the term describes exactly the position of both priest and Levite in dealing with cultic issues and rites. The author's use of the negative

---

95. BDAG, 1107–8.

96. Louw-Nida, §41.11; BDAG, 803.

97. Ellingworth, *Epistle to the Hebrews,* 708.

98. BDAG, 420–22.

99. BDAG, 463.

100. For a list of those who adopt this view, see Cockerill, *Epistle to the Hebrews,* 696 n. 36.

101. Ellingworth, *Epistle to the Hebrews,* 711; Cockerill, *Epistle to the Hebrews,* 696.

102. McConkie, *Doctrinal New Testament Commentary,* 3:241; O'Brien, *Letter to the Hebrews,* 521; Attridge, *Epistle to the Hebrews,* 396; Lane, *Hebrews 9–13,* 538–39.

103. BDAG, 352–53; *NID,* s.v. "ἐξουσια."

particle οὐκ (*ouk*), "not," stresses that under the new covenant, their exclusive rights have been annulled and are therefore of no further effect.

The term σκηνή (*skēnē*), literally "tent," refers to the Mosaic tabernacle,[104] but the author seems to be using it to designate the full range of Mosaic practices.

13:11 ***For the bodies of those beasts, whose blood is brought into the sanctuary by the high priest for sin, are burned without the camp / For the bodies of the animals whose blood is brought into the tabernacle by the high priest for a sin offering are burned outside the camp:*** The reference is to Exodus 30:10; Leviticus 4:1–21; and more specifically to Leviticus 16:27. All these address the handling of sacrifices on the Day of Atonement.[105] For discussion, see Translation Notes for 9:6–7 and related Analysis along with the "Excursus on the Ritual of the Day of Atonement" also found in that chapter.

The author uses the noun ζῷον (*zōon*), "animal,"[106] here specifically to denote the bullock and goat that were sacrificed as the sin offering on this holy day.[107] The sacrifice was used to purge the sins of both the high priest and the people as a whole and thereby reconcile them to Jehovah. This offering was unique in that it was the only one where the animal's body was burned not on the temple altar but outside the camp of Israel (Lev. 16:27).[108]

For the noun ἁμαρτία (*hamartia*), "sin," see Translation Notes for 3:13 with associated Analysis. In connection with this sacrifice, sin is shown to have two aspects. First, it is preeminently and exceedingly hateful and evil before God and therefore of an absolutely abhorrent nature. Second, it is

---

104. BDAG, 928.

105. For discussion, see David P. Wright, "Day of Atonement," in Freedman, *Anchor Bible Dictionary*, 2:72–76; for a typological study, see Jukes, *Law of the Offerings*, 137–71.

106. The term generally refers to any creature in the genus "animal" whether domesticated or wild. BDAG, 431.

107. Ellingworth, *Epistle to the Hebrews*, 713.

108. There were two other aspects that made the offering unique. First, it was an offering specifically for sin in general, including iniquity of every kind and on every level: sins of omission and commission both inadvertent and deliberate. Second, it carried nothing of a "sweet savour" as did all the other sacrifices. The phrase is a translation of רֵיחַ נִיחֹחַ (*rēaḥ nîḥōaḥ*) (in the LXX, ὀσμὴ εὐωδίας, *osmē euōdias*), a technical term referring to sacrifices that were acceptable to Jehovah (see Lev. 1:9, 13, 17). The phrase can be translated as "the smell of compliance" or "of satisfaction" and carries the nuance of that which produces calmness and restfulness and is acceptable to God. See BDB 629b; 926b. Typologically, the offering points to the condition of the heart of the individual making the offering. It is this that makes the offering acceptable to the Lord. That this sacrifice carried no "sweet savour" stresses the repulsion God feels toward sin of every kind. For a study, see Jukes, *Law of the Offerings*, 137–71.

"confessed sin, judged sin, sin requiring sacrifice and blood-shedding; yet sin atoned for, blotted out, and pardoned."[109] This offering stresses the idea that no sin is so egregious that it cannot be overcome and forgiven by the Savior through repentance.

The noun ἅγιος (*hagios*) denotes that which is holy, and the phrase τὰ ἅγια (*ta hogia*), "the holy [things]," referred to the tabernacle. Here, however, the author uses it to refer to the Holy of Holies within the tabernacle where the sacrificial blood was sprinkled before the ark of the covenant.[110]

Note the blood of the animal carries the sin. The wages of sin are death (Rom. 6:23). The blood represents the kind of death that expiates sin and puts the offender in a position to be forgiven. Only one kind of blood does that, and it takes the sacrifice of nothing less than a God (Mosiah 3:11, 16, 18; Alma 5:21, 27; 34:13; Hel. 5:9; 3 Ne. 18:11; 27:19; Morm. 9:6; Ether 13:10–11; Moro. 10:33).

13:12 ***Wherefore Jesus also . . . suffered without the gate / Therefore Jesus also suffered outside the city gate:*** The inferential conjunction διό (*dio*), "therefore,"[111] is telling. With it the author informs his readers that he is going to make a typological connection between an aspect of the ritual of the Day of Atonement and the Savior's death.

The verb πάσχω (*paschō*), "to suffer,"[112] in this context means "to die"[113] and therefore looks more specifically at the Crucifixion of the Lord rather than at all the suffering he endured before meeting death.

The noun πύλη (*pylē*) denotes a "gate."[114] In the phrase ἔξω τῆς πύλης (*exō tēs pylēs*), literally "outside the gate," it means "outside the city,"[115] the usual place where crucifixions took place. In 13:11 and 13, the author uses the term "outside the encampment" (ἔξω τῆς παρεμβολῆ, *exō tēs parembolēs*). The change in this verse, though lining up with the Gospel writers that Jesus died outside the walls of Jerusalem,[116] is likely stylistic

---

109. Jukes, *Law of the Offerings,* 137.

110. Ellingworth, *Epistle to the Hebrews,* 713.

111. BDAG, 250.

112. BDAG, 784–86.

113. Lane, *Hebrews 9–13,* 523 note s.

114. Louw-Nida, §7.48.

115. BDAG, 897.

116. All the Gospel writers note that Jesus was crucified on Golgotha. Matt. 27:33; Mark 15:22; Luke 23:33; John 19:17. This hill was located just outside one of the main gates of Jerusalem. See Virgilio C. Corbo, "Golgotha," in Freedman, *Anchor Bible Dictionary,* 2:1071–73. Johnson, *Hebrews,* 348, calls this verse a "stunning turn" because the author, at last, "merges literary and historical horizons" that show the intersection between the

because the author did not want to repeat the word παρεμβολή (*parembolē*) three times in a row.[117]

that he might sanctify the people with his own blood / so that he might sanctify the people by his own blood: On the verb ἁγιάζω (*hagiazō*), "sanctify," see Translation Notes for 2:11 and the associated Analysis. Here we need but note that the word points to a state of soul that is not only sin free but also godlike.

The phrase διὰ τοῦ ἰδίου αἵματος (*dia tou idiou haimatos*), "through his own blood," identifies the operative sanctifying power. The adjective ἴδιος (*idios*), "his own,"[118] is important because it stresses that only the blood of the Lord could do the job (see 13:11 above).

13:13 *Let us go forth therefore unto him without the camp, bearing his reproach / So let us go out to him outside the tabernacle, enduring his reproach:* Some of the particulars of what the author has in mind in this sentence are vague. The role of the inferential particle τοίνυν (*toinyn*), "therefore, hence," does not seem to play its usual role of indicating a logical sequence. If taken as a logical sequence, it would mean that because Jesus suffered outside the gate, so should we. More likely it suggests a point of comparison between what Jesus had to endure and what the author is admonishing his readers to endure.[119]

Further, the phrase ἐξερχώμεθα πρὸς αὐτόν (*exerchōmetha pros auton*), "let us go unto him," is also vague. It is unclear in the present context where the author sees Jesus as being. A point of emphasis for the author is that Jesus sits on the right hand of God in heaven, but here he seems to be more on the mortal plane. The meeting the author is referring to is likely not personal but experiential, that is, suffering the Lord's humiliation and rejection and thereby meeting him on that ground.[120]

Additionally, what the term παρεμβολή (*parembolē*), "camp,"[121] represents is also hard to determine. Does it represent the world, materialism, the old covenant, or Judaism? Any or all of these, and others, are possibilities.[122]

---

prophetic element of the old cult and its fulfillment in Jesus. Johnson recognizes that some elements of the Day of Atonement ritual do not line up exactly, but the overall theme matches well. See also Vanhoye, *Letter to the Hebrews,* 225.

117. Ellingworth, *Epistle to the Hebrews,* 715.

118. BDAG, 466–67.

119. Ellingworth, *Epistle to the Hebrews,* 716.

120. Cockerill, *Epistle to the Hebrews,* 702 n. 57.

121. BDAG, 775.

122. For various views on the meaning of the phrase, see the references in Ellingworth, *Epistle to the Hebrews,* 716–17.

The context does not provide much help. That the author exhorts his readers to remember they have no real home here but should seek an eternal city (13:14) suggests he is asking them to leave the world and its materialism behind. On the other hand, his request that they do much good and share with others (13:16) suggests they are to work in the world and not seek to escape it. The author most likely intends that the term be taken in the broadest degree possible and therefore that it represent faithless society, whether it expresses opposition by Jews or Gentiles or the seductive allure presented by the worldly.[123] There is, however, the author's continuing concern with the ever-present appeal that pulls some to return to the security and acceptance of some form of Judaism.[124]

Though all these details are vague, the author's main point is not. He expresses it with the phrase τὸν ὀνειδισμὸν αὐτοῦ φέροντες (*ton oneidismon autou pherontes*), literally "the reproach of him enduring." The verb φέρω (*pherō*) means "to bear, carry," but also "to endure."[125] Because the idea of bearing or carrying something is external to the self, the idea of enduring seems better because it is internal and therefore more personally felt.

The noun ὀνειδισμος (*oneidismos*) denotes a "reproach, disgrace," and even "a reviling,"[126] but more importantly it carries the nuance of a denunciation that is unjustified and therefore connotes a particularly bitter sting.[127]

In short, the author is asking his readers to make a full identification with the Lord including accepting the necessary stigma and public humiliation heaped upon him by those within "the camp."

13:14 *For here have we no continuing city / For we do not have here an enduring city:* The causal conjunction γάρ (*gar*), "for," is important because it signals the reader that the author is going to give his reason for the above admonition.

---

123. Cockerill, *Epistle to the Hebrews,* 700; Vanhoye, *Letter to the Hebrews,* 225. Elder McConkie viewed it as Judaism and its trust in animal sacrifices. McConkie, *Doctrinal New Testament Commentary,* 3:241.

124. The image of the παρεμβολή (*parembolē*), "camp," echoes Israel's wilderness encampment and the continual rebellion that took place there. By his reference to the current "camp," the author is likely looking at those forces that would cause some among his readership to follow their forebears' lead and rebel against the Savior. Cockerill, *Epistle to the Hebrews,* 702–3.

125. BDAG, 1051–52.

126. BDAG, 710.

127. Louw-Nida, §33.389.

His admonition is grounded on the adverb ὧδε (*hōde*), "here," which points to the world and all it contains. Using his imagery, the impermanent "city" must be left behind.[128]

The verb μένω (*menō*), "to stay, remain," found here in the form of a present participle, carries the nuance of that which continues in a certain state and is therefore permanent.[129] It is coupled with the negative particle οὐ (*ou*), "not," and both modify πόλις (*polis*), "city." The phrase shows that for the Christian, there *is* no permanent place in this world and therefore no security.

but we seek one to come / we seek the city that is to come: The conjunction ἀλλά (*alla*), "but," is important because it signals that there is another alternative to remaining in the instable and tottering city.

The verb ἐπιζητέω (*epizēteō*), "to search for, seek after," can also have the sense "to desire" or "to wish for" something and implies putting effort into gaining it.[130] Here it refers to the heavenly city. The present tense shows that the author and at least some of his readers are at that very time earnestly seeking membership in the eternal city.

The verb μέλλω (*mellō*), "to be about to, to come (in the future)," found here in the form of a present active participle, denotes something will happen in the future. It can carry a nuance of inevitability.[131]

13:15 ***By him therefore let us offer the sacrifice of praise to God continually / Therefore through him let us continually offer up a sacrifice of praise to God:*** The conjunction οὖν (*oun*), "therefore, consequently,"[132] plays an important role here giving readers notice as to why they should do something. In this case, the reason for action is because of what Christ has done for them.

---

128. Jason A. Whitlark suggests this is an oblique reference and repudiation of Roman propaganda that extols the capitol or the "eternal city." See Jason A. Whitlark, "'Here We Do Not Have a City That Remains': A Figured Critique of Roman Imperial Propaganda in Hebrews 13:14," *Journal of Biblical Literature* 131, no. 1 (2012): 161–79, accessed May 2, 2017, https://muse.jhu.edu/article/470018.

129. Louw-Nida, §§13.89; 85.60; BDAG, 630–31.

130. BDAG, 371; Louw-Nida, §25.13. The author is not admonishing his readers to search out information on the eternal city but rather to earnestly strive for entrance into it. Cockerill, *Epistle to the Hebrews*, 704 n. 65.

131. Louw-Nida, §71.36. Mainly, the verb denotes what is about to happen shortly (Louw-Nida, §67.62), but in the form of a present participle, it points well into the future. BDAG, 627.

132. BDAG, 736–37. Though the particle is missing in some important variants, the best evidence suggests that it is original. Metzger, *Textual Commentary*, 605.

The phrase δι' αὐτοῦ (*di' autou*), "through him," is instructive. The preposition διά (*dia*) acts as a marker of instrumentality pointing to that which made something possible.[133] The nuance here is to mediation by which the Savior makes possible both praise and access to God and his eternal city.[134]

The phrase θυσίαν αἰνέσεως (*thysian aineseōs*), "sacrifice of praise,"[135] stands in contrast to animal sacrifices, including the "thank-offering" used to express gratitude to Jehovah (LXX Lev. 7:12, 13, 15; 2 Chr. 29:31; 33:16). The author clarifies that praise is the sacrifice. The author's intent is likely to show that an acceptable sacrifice must be based on recognition of what the Father and Son have done. This recognition constitutes the subject matter of the praise-offering.

The phrase διὰ παντός (*dia pantos*), literally "through all," means "continually" and suggests that the seat of the Christian's praise is in the constancy of his or her lifestyle (compare Alma 34:27).[136]

that is, the fruit of our lips giving thanks to his name / that is, the fruit of our lips confessing his name: The phrase τοῦτ' ἔστιν (*tout' estin*), "that is," makes it clear that the author's reference is to the praise-offering, not to any animal sacrifice.[137]

The phrase καρπὸν χειλέων (*karpon cheileōn*), "fruit of our lips," defines the sacrifice.[138] The nuance of the noun καρπός (*karpos*), "fruit,"[139] used here figuratively, points to the product of one's praise. The "lips" are modified by the present participle of the verb ὁμολογέω (*homologeō*), "to confess" or "bear witness," with the connotation of a public declaration.

The object of that praise is τῷ ὀνόματι αὐτοῦ (*tō onomati autou*), "to his name." The noun ὄνομα (*onoma*), "name,"[140] in the present context stands for the Father himself. Here the phrase likely refers to what lay behind the

---

133. BDAG, 223–26.

134. Vanhoye, *Letter to the Hebrews,* 226. Ellingworth, *Epistle to the Hebrews,* 719–20.

135. BDAG, 27. The noun αἰνέσεως (*aineseōs*), "of praise," an attributive genitive, defines the nature of the sacrifice. Lane, *Hebrews 9–13,* 549. The author may have in mind LXX Ps. 49:14, where the phrase "sacrifice of praise" is found in the context not of blood offerings but of making and keeping vows with Jehovah. Vanhoye, *Letter to the Hebrews,* 227–28.

136. Note the use of the phrase διὰ παντός (*dia pantos*) in 9:6 where it describes the continuing necessity of the sacrifices performed by Levitical high priest. The LXX uses the phrase to denote the perpetual repletion of blood sacrifices. See Lane, *Hebrews 9–13,* 548–49, for the relationship of this idea with both Jewish and biblical writings.

137. Ellingworth, *Epistle to the Hebrews,* 720.

138. The author may have LXX Hos. 14:2 in mind for this exact phrase. The "'sacrifice of praise' means 'offering thanks.'" Vanhoye, *Letter to the Hebrews,* 226.

139. BDAG, 509–10.

140. BDAG, 711–14.

praise the Saints were to continually render: their love and appreciation for the Father's work in their behalf.[141]

13:16 ***But to do good and to communicate forget not / And do not neglect good works and generosity:*** The verb ἐπιλανθάνομαι (*epilanthanomai*), "to forget, neglect,"[142] is in the form of a present imperative and is coupled with the negative particle μή (*mē*), "not." Together, they show the author's readers have been and currently are doing as he asks.

The author's admonition focuses on two commendable practices. The noun εὐποιΐα (*eupoiia*) denotes both "a laudable service" and "a good deed."[143] Here, the context shows it is the latter the author has in mind.[144]

The noun κοινωνία (*koinōnia*) refers to an "attitude of good will that manifests an interest in a close relationship with others" expressed by "generosity, fellow-feeling," and "altruism."[145]

The relationship between the two nouns is very close and looks to the service one Christian should provide for another.[146] Though the idea conveyed by the words does not exclude those outside the community, the admonition suggests a more exclusive benefaction by one Saint toward another. The phrase, therefore, precludes organized philanthropy and puts force on individual good deeds.[147]

for with such sacrifices God is well pleased / for God is pleased with such sacrifices: Again, the conjunction γάρ (*gar*), "for," introduces why an act should be done.[148] Here the verb εὐαρεστέω (*euaresteō*), "to be pleased, find acceptable,"[149] expresses the reason.[150]

---

141. The noun in the New Testament generally refers to the Father. Ellingworth, *Epistle to the Hebrews*, 721. To do something εἰς τὸ ὄνομα αὐτοῦ (*eis to onoma autou*), "in his name," means "with regard to him" or "to his account" and by extension "by his authority." See Moulton and Milligan, *Vocabulary*, 451; and Ellingworth, *Epistle to the Hebrews*, 331. Here the phrase uses the dative preposition *tō* meaning "to" or in other words "for" or "because of."

142. BDAG, 374.

143. Louw-Nida, §88.7; BDAG, 410. Some suggest it is equivalent to φιλαδελφία (*philadelphia*), "brotherly love," as found in 13:1, since this force stands behind divinely acceptable good deeds. See Cockerill, *Epistle to the Hebrews*, 707 n. 80. For a study of aspects of this kind of love within the Christian community, see Johnson, *Hebrews*, 350–51.

144. BDAG, 410; Ellingworth, *Epistle to the Hebrews*, 721.

145. BDAG, 552–53.

146. Vanhoye, *Letter to the Hebrews*, 227, translates them as "benefice" and "solidarity."

147. Ellingworth, *Epistle to the Hebrews*, 721–22.

148. The phrase shows that pleasing God is the motivation for those who give this kind of service. Cockerill, *Epistle to the Hebrews*, 707 n. 84.

149. BDAG, 403.

150. Both Greco-Roman and Jewish piety viewed the virtues of godly praise and good works as pleasing sacrifices to Deity. For references, see Johnson, *Hebrews*, 349.

The author refers to the deeds of "doing good" and "generous giving" by the noun θυσία (*thysia*), "sacrifice."[151] He uses it here in a figurative sense and is likely contrasting the freewill offerings the Christian should make with the sacrifices of the old covenant. The nuance behind this kind of sacrifice precludes the often-associated negative idea of a painful forfeiting of something. Rather, it suggests an offering given without reservation, perhaps even with delight. It is the condition of the heart that makes the offering not just acceptable but pleasing to God. Assistance to fellow Christians constitutes such sacrifices offered to God.[152]

13:17 ***Obey them that have the rule over you / Obey your leaders:*** The verb πείθω (*peithō*) in the middle voice as found here means "to obey, follow" and carries the nuance not of forced compliance due to authority but of deference due to care and concern.[153] The present imperative, found here, suggests the need for continuous action.[154]

On the verb ἡγέομαι (*hēgeomai*), "to lead, guide," see Translation Notes for 13:7 above. Here we need but note that the word refers to the leaders of the Church. The nuance of the word is, however, instructive. It refers less to rule and more to leadership. The verb does show these people had ruling power and authority but they implemented it primarily by winning the support of those under them.[155]

and submit yourselves / and submit to them: The verb ὑπείκω (*hypeikō*), "to submit,"[156] is found only here in the New Testament but is a common verb in classical Greek, its use going back to Homer.[157]

for they watch for your souls / for they keep watch over your souls: The verb ἀγρυπνέω (*agrypneō*), "to watch over, care for," carries with it the nuance of being alert and on guard due to present or perceived danger.[158] The author's use of the word stresses the nature of the leader's attentive and caring concern for the Saints. The intensive pronoun αὐτοί (*autoi*) at the beginning of this phrase emphasizes the importance of the role played by Church leaders, "for *they* keep watch over your souls."

The noun ψυχή (*psyche*), "soul," in the present context, refers to the seat and center of life that both encompasses and transcends the mortal

---

151. BDAG, 462–63.
152. Vanhoye, *Letter to the Hebrews,* 227–28.
153. BDAG, 791–92; Louw-Nida, §33.301.
154. Ellingworth, *Epistle to the Hebrews,* 723.
155. BDAG, 434; Louw-Nida, §§36.1; 37.58.
156. Louw-Nida, §36.18; BDAG, 1030; Moulton and Milligan, *Vocabulary,* 651.
157. LSJ, 1855–56.
158. Louw-Nida, §§27.57; 35.41; BDAG, 16.

plane[159] and shows the breadth of the concern of the Christian leaders for their people.

as they that must give account / as men who will give account of their responsibilities: The comparative particle ὅς (*hōs*), "as," in the present context, acts as a marker showing both why the Church leadership has such a concern for the Saints and what is entailed upon them due to their position.[160]

The verb ἀποδίδωμι (*apodidōmi*), "to give," denotes the fulfilling of responsibility.[161] It is here found as a future participle and is thus translated with a future tense in our Rendition.

The noun λόγος (*logos*) here has the sense "account, reckoning"[162] and looks not at a self-report on how well leaders have done but on how well their charges have done. The author does not state when, where, or to whom this account will be given. The implication, however, is that it will be at judgment day.

that they may do it with joy, and not with grief / so that they may do it joyfully without groaning: The phrase explains why the author's readers should obey their leaders. In the subjunctive phrase τοῦτο ποιῶσιν (*touto poiōsin*), "that they may do it," "it" most likely refers to the leadership's task of watching over the souls of those under their care rather than their giving an account of their responsibilities. If those over whom they have stewardship are obedient, the leaders' task will be filled μετὰ χαρᾶς (*meta charas*), "with joy,"[163] μὴ στενάζοντες (*mē stenazontes*), "without sighing, groaning," where the verb στενάζω (*stenazō*) means "to express oneself involuntarily in the face of an undesirable circumstance, sigh, groan."[164]

for that is unprofitable for you / for that would be of no help to you: The demonstrative pronoun τοῦτο (*touto*), "that," refers to the disobedience that would cause the leaders' distress.

The adjective ἀλυσιτελής (*alysitelēs*), "unprofitable,"[165] is another word that appears only here in the New Testament, and therefore the author's exact meaning is uncertain. It appears to connote that which is unhelpful and, more negatively, what is harmful or detrimental.[166] Even so, the

---

159. BDAG, 1098–1100. Lane, *Hebrews 9–13,* 524 note jj, nuances the phrase as "eternal life."
160. BDAG, 1103–6; Ellingworth, *Epistle to the Hebrews,* 723.
161. BDAG, 109–10.
162. BDAG, 598–601.
163. BDAG, 1077.
164. BDAG, 942.
165. BDAG, 48.
166. Lane, *Hebrews 9–13,* 525 note mm.

echo of the language of commerce can still be heard behind it. The author bases his appeal not on the coming judgment that all will face but on the valuelessness of disobedience. Here the language of the market suits well his point. Since rebellion would "not be profitable," it behooves each of his readers to take care of their own spiritual bottom line.[167] The rather obvious understatement of his point actually serves to give it even more impact.

Analysis and Summary

This section, beginning and ending as it does with an appeal to follow Church leaders, forms an inclusion that focuses on the inner life of the Christian community. The section links to the former section with its multiple admonitions "to remember." Here the focus is on leaders, both past (13:7) and present (13:17). In between, to give his exhortations force, the author references points he has already made as a "forceful synthesis of the doctrine and paraenesis of the whole text."[168] A major theme is the need to persevere in faith (13:7) and to follow Christ's example (13:13–16).[169]

The author of Hebrews bases his appeal on the lives of past leaders whom at least some of those in the congregation knew (13:7). Though he does not say so, apparently these past leaders had both run the course and finished the fight in faithfulness and in doing so left an example that the author wants his readers to follow. Tacitly, he unites the heroes of the old covenant with those of the new as examples of endurance in faith. He also hints at God's faithfulness in sustaining them.[170]

His admonition "to remember" (μιμνῄσκομαι, *mimnēskomai*) these former leaders is not a call to sentimental recollection but an entreaty to consider not just the course and faithfulness of these leaders' lives but more especially to contemplate their lives' outcome (ἔκβασις, *ekbasis*). They, as did the heroes the author listed in chapter 11, show the faithful life both is possible and brings great reward.[171] Whether any of those leaders to whom the author refers had suffered martyrdom is unknown, but all lived lives of faith. For this reason, the author admonishes his readers to emulate (μιμνέομαι, *mimneomai*) them.

---

167. Cockerill, *Epistle to the Hebrews,* 709.

168. Attridge, *Epistle to the Hebrews,* 391.

169. Ellingworth, *Epistle to the Hebrews,* 701–2. In biblical criticism, a "paraenesis" denotes a series of moral admonitions.

170. Bruce, *Epistle to the Hebrews,* 374–75.

171. Cockerill, *Epistle to the Hebrews,* 690.

In 13:8, with no obvious connection to what he has said before or what he will say after, the author declares the constancy of the Lord as "the same" throughout time.[172] The declaration is a bit startling since it seems to sit independent of other syntactical connections. However, the statement is the ground upon which the entire Epistle sits. Christ's constancy and eternity as God, Savior, and High Priest are the mooring that tied the faithfulness of those in both the past and present generations. The statement has two important implications. First, it shows Christ as the perpetual facilitator of God's will whose effectiveness is a declaration and guarantee of God's own personal effectiveness. Second, it suggests that the availability of Christ's assistance to the faithful in past generations is just as readily available to those of the present.[173]

Having declared the constancy of Jesus, the central and pivotal doctrine of his text, the author next warns his readers against false doctrine (13:9). He does not identify just what these pseudo-teachings are but certainly viewed them as "all sorts of outlandish teachings."[174] That he did not need to explicitly state what they were suggests they were familiar to his readers. Unfortunately, that is not the case today, and therefore the full range of his concerns can only be surmised. Even so, his cautions provide a clue, as shown below, as to what at least some of these may have been.[175]

---

172. Holzapfel and Wayment, *Making Sense,* 458, calls this "a brilliant insight." The statement likely does not apply to the Lord's mortal state wherein he condescended to become fully mortal (2 Ne. 9:53; Jacob 4:7), laying aside his glory and having to be "made perfect" through his suffering (2:10; 5:8–9: 7:28). Rather, it refers to the state he returned to after his suffering being reunited with and reglorified by his Father (John 17:5) and "crowned with glory and honour" (2:9) and retaking his place as the High Priest (7:16–25). Vanhoye, *Letter to the Hebrews,* 223.

173. Cockerill, *Epistle to the Hebrews,* 691.

174. Ellingworth, *Epistle to the Hebrews,* 707; Attridge, *Epistle to the Hebrews,* 394–95. See also Vanhoye, *Letter to the Hebrews,* 223–24, who notes the author was not alone in confronting errant doctrines. The Apostle Paul was concerned with those preaching "another gospel" (2 Cor. 11:4; Gal. 1:6) and those who followed "another spirit" (2 Cor. 11:4) and preached "commandments and doctrines of men" (Col. 2:22). He warned Timothy concerning those preaching "doctrines of devils" (1 Tim. 4:1). Both Peter and John were concerned with false prophets who promulgated false doctrines (2 Pet. 2:1; 1 John 4:1–6; 2 John 7; Rev. 2:14–16, 20–21).

175. This section of Hebrews, 13:9–14, constitutes one of the most difficult passages to interpret and understand in the whole Epistle. Due to his succinctness, many of the author's references are lost to us. As a result, speculations on what his images, examples, and warnings refer to are wide and varied. For discussion of the problem, see Lane, *Hebrews 9–13,* 530; and Ellingworth, *Epistle to the Hebrews,* 705–6. As writers, we have set

But first we must note his declaration on what testimony and commitment should be based. Simply put, it is "grace" (χάρις, *charis*). Based on teachings earlier in the Epistle, the term looks most specifically at the gift that flows to the individual from the Lord's Atonement and confirms to the soul the reality and truthfulness of the gospel message.

The author's insistence that a person's moral and intellectual center, the heart (καρδία, *kardia*), should be "made firm" (βεβαιόω, *bebaioō*) with grace suggests there were those who were basing their testimony and therefore their salvation on things that were not spiritual. Perhaps these were such things as philosophical speculations, external evidences, or appealing practices of those around them. He speaks specifically of those who trust in partaking of certain foods (βρῶμα, *broma*), likely referring to participants in Mosaic sacrifices or followers of Jewish dietary practices.[176] He firmly proclaims that such has proved itself totally useless to all those who adhere to the practice.

In 13:10, to drive home his point, the author focuses on the imagery of the "altar" (θυσιαστεηριον, *thysiastērion*) and notes that the whole of the Christian community can partake of its benefits. He contrasts that with those who "serve the tabernacle," referring not just to the Levitical Priesthood but to all who practice the ways of Judaism, and declares that they have no right to partake of the benefits of the Christian altar. His words should not be construed as indicating that certain Jews were trying to participate in Christian services without accepting the Lord as Messiah and Savior. Rather, he was indicating that the new and old covenants were distinct from each other in serving God's purposes and that the old covenant and its ways were not to be imposed in the new covenant and its rites. Though Levitical priests did indeed at one time have the priesthood, that did not give them authority to participate in the ordinances of the new covenant. In sum, the author is insisting there must be a complete break between the two orders.[177] He therefore sets up a contrast not between

---

our task as viewing the varied discussions and drawing what we can from them in light of the Restoration and writings of Latter-day Saint leaders and scholars.

176. Lane, *Hebrews 9–13,* 523 note i; for discussions, see Helmut Koester, "'Outside the Camp': Hebrews 13.9–14," *Harvard Theological Review* 55, no. 4 (1962): 299–315; and Norman H. Young, "'Bearing His Reproach' (Hebrews 13.9–14)," *New Testament Studies* 48, no. 2 (2002), 243–61.

177. Ellingworth, *Epistle to the Hebrews,* 710. The author is undoubtedly extending the contrast between the old and new covenants and the old and new Israel that he developed earlier. See Koester, *Hebrews,* 569–70; and Johnson, *Hebrews,* 347. However, the

the Old and New Testament faithful (whom he sees as one people) but between "we who have the true altar" (correct doctrine) and "those who serve the tabernacle" and promulgate "divers and strange teachings."[178]

But what is the Christian altar? The context suggests that it is the cross on which Jesus made the Atonement and therefore a metaphor for the Atonement itself (note 13:12). The following verses strengthen this idea by refering to the sacrifice (θυσία, *thysia,* "sacrifice," related to θυσιαστήριον, *thysiastērion,* "sacrificial altar") Christians are to make of both "praise to God" (13:15) and their acts of care and sharing (13:16).[179] Elder McConkie noted, "We Christians have an altar, the cross of Christ, whereon he offered himself for the sins of the world; but the full blessings of this atoning sacrifice are reserved for members of the Church; they do not come to those without the fold, those who serve the tabernacle, those who put their trust in the dead ordinances of the Mosaic Law."[180]

The author, having mentioned the tabernacle in 13:10, now returns to the ritual of the Day of Atonement and the typological lesson that it can teach the Christians (3:11). Though the old covenant had been superseded by the new, the elements of the Savior's ministry it foreshadowed and the lessons the Christians were to learn should not be overlooked. The author makes double conclusions: one for Jesus (13:12) and one for the readers (13:13).

The author clearly sees the prophetic aspect of the sacrifice offered on the Day of Atonement that was burned outside the camp as that of Jesus being crucified there. Because of the author's focus on what happened "outside the gate" and the lesson he wants his readers to learn, he leaves out certain aspects of the ritual. For example, he does not mention the animal was actually killed in the tabernacle precinct before its body was removed. Further, he does not mention the critical role the high priest played in the

---

context suggests he is not concerned with problems of the past but is addressing contemporary false teachings that are affecting members of his community. Cockerill, *Epistle to the Hebrews,* 692.

178. Cockerill, *Epistle to the Hebrews,* 693. It is possible that this is an oblique reference to a nascent movement that would eventually express itself in the Ebionite faction within Christianity. A central doctrine was that the man Jesus was invested by the power of the angelic Christ who then left him at the time of the crucifixion. See Stephen Goranson, "Ebionites"; and Freedman, *Anchor Bible Dictionary,* 2:260–61. For a possible connection to Hebrews, see Michael Goulder, "Hebrews and the Ebionites," *New Testament Studies* 49, no. 3 (2003): 393–406.

179. Ellingworth, *Epistle to the Hebrews,* 719–21.

180. McConkie, *Doctrinal New Testament Commentary,* 3:241; See also Vanhoye, *Letter to the Hebrews,* 224–25.

ritual or that the whole procedure was for the remission of sins. By not cluttering his reference with these items, he lets fall the full force of his argument and the exhortation he uses it to give.[181]

Besides the location of the sacrificial animal's burning and the Savior's crucifixion, the author focuses on one more point of contact: blood. Both the blood of the animal and that of Christ were shed. However, the author makes a point of contrast. The blood of the animal was shed for, that is, on account of, sin. His focus is on what made the sacrifice necessary, namely because the high priest and the people sinned. On the other hand, the blood of the Savior was shed for the purpose of sanctification. The author's focus is again on what made this sacrifice necessary, but in this case it was to make the people sinless and pure. His contrast again speaks to his insistence that the death of the thousands of animals sacrificed over hundreds of years did nothing to change the hearts of the people and therefore left them unsanctified. On the other hand, the blood of Jesus, shed but once, opened the way such that people's hearts could be changed, their lives purified, and their souls made holy.

Because of what Christ has done, the author in 13:13 admonishes his readers to go outside the camp as Jesus did and take upon them the "reproach" (ὀνειδισμός, *oneidismos*) he suffered there. The author's admonition is but a reminder of what he has already taught about the suffering of the Son (8:1–10:18) wherein he "endured the cross, disregarding its shame" (NR 12:2). The author now asks them to follow suit. Like Abraham who lived as a nomad, Moses who left the fleshpots of Egypt, and other Old Testament heroes, readers must withdraw from an unbelieving and faithless society that unjustly heaps scorn upon those who reject their low moral standards. In doing so, Christians will find, as did the Son, that their suffering will be the means of gaining oneness with God and Christ and a place in the Holy City (13:14).[182]

Based on the above, the author admonishes his readers, like those who have gone before, to make sacrifices (13:14–15). In 13:14, the author reminds his readers that they have no place in the present earthly, faithless "camp," primarily because its inhabitants have rejected the Lord but also because it has no permanent foundation. Because of its transient nature, to place one's trust and confidence in it would be foolish. Rather, the Saints must continue to earnestly seek for (ἐπιζητέω, *epizēteō*) the "enduring city" God

181. Ellingworth, *Epistle to the Hebrews*, 715.

182. Johnson, *Hebrews*, 349; Cockerill, *Epistle to the Hebrews*, 701–3.

has built (11:10; 12:22). As Elder McConkie notes, "Why should we worry about any temporal loss entailed by such a course; the things of this world are fleeting and transitory anyway; what we seek, through Christ, is eternal and enduring; it is an inheritance in the heavenly city."[183]

Earnest seeking rests on and is motivated by the "altar" of Christ—the Atonement—and the power Christians have enjoyed because of it. This experience brings assurance they can achieve what they do not yet have (11:1–6). Perseverance based on what they do have is the sure way to achieve what they do not yet have.[184]

The author next turns to those deeds that will assure his readers a place in the heavenly Jerusalem (13:15–16). He refers to these as "sacrifices" (θυσία, *thysia*), likely to contrast what the Christian is to do with what the Levitical system practiced. He sets the Christian sacrifices on the foundation of the "praise of God continually" and defines this as the open and verbal giving of acclaim for what Christ has done. "The Christian life must be continually permeated with thanksgiving," as one scholar noted. "God is continually bestowing grace upon us; we must continually give him thanks. Christian life is a life of grateful love."[185]

The author desires his readers to persevere in confessing Christ to an unbelieving world (3:1; 4:14; 10:23), thereby making the "sacrifice of praise" (13:15) that is so "pleasing to God, and thus the ultimate act of worship."[186]

The author shows, however, there is more to such sacrifices than heartfelt witnessing. They also include continuous service in doing good (εὐποιΐα, *eupoiia*) coupled with an attitude of good will expressed by generosity (κοινωνία, *koinōnia*) to members within the Christian community. Christian concern and fellowship include sharing material goods with those in need.[187] The reason these acts of mutual concern are of benefit is because they are pleasing (εὐαρεστέω, *euaresteō*) to God. "What then are the sacrifices of the true Christian?" asks Elder McConkie. "They are unending praise and thanksgiving to the Father who gave his Only Begotten Son as a ransom for our sins; they are everlasting praise to the Son for the merits and mercies and grace of his atoning sacrifice; they are obedience to the laws of the Lord; these are the sacrifices that please God."[188]

---

183. McConkie, *Doctrinal New Testament Commentary,* 3:241.

184. Cockerill, *Epistle to the Hebrews,* 704.

185. Vanhoye, *Letter to the Hebrews,* 227. Note the Apostle Paul's admonition to this same end in Eph. 5:2 and 1 Thes. 5:18.

186. Cockerill, *Epistle to the Hebrews,* 706.

187. Lane, *Hebrews 9–13,* 552.

188. McConkie, *Doctrinal New Testament Commentary,* 3:242.

Concerning what constitutes the sacrifice of the new covenant, the Lord himself has said, "And ye shall offer up unto me no more the shedding of blood; yea, your sacrifices and your burnt offerings shall be done away, for I will accept none of your sacrifices and your burnt offerings. And ye shall offer for a sacrifice unto me a broken heart and a contrite spirit. And whoso cometh unto me with a broken heart and a contrite spirit, him will I baptize with fire and with the Holy Ghost" (3 Ne. 9:19–20). The Hebrew Bible was no stranger to this idea. According to the Psalmist, Jehovah "delightest not in burnt offering." Rather, "the sacrifices of God are a broken spirit: a broken and a contrite heart." Indeed, these will God "not despise." For this reason, the Psalmist can promise his readers that God will "do good in [his] good pleasure unto Zion" and notes that, when these conditions are met, God will "be pleased with the sacrifices of righteousness, with burnt offering and whole burnt offering" (Ps. 51:16–19; compare Isa. 57:15).

The psalm focuses on acceptable personable praise toward Jehovah grounded in repentance and the suitable attitude of worship, that is, the proper condition of the heart and spirit (Ps. 51:15–17). Nowhere in the psalm is the principle and practice of sacrifice denied.[189] Rather, the focus is on what made the sacrifice beneficial. Here the old and new covenants find the common foundation upon which both rest and to which the author of Hebrews appeals. That foundation is the condition of the soul that sanctifies the offering, whether it be an animal or a prayer. The problem the author of Hebrews has with the old system is that a sacrifice could be, and all too often was, offered without the necessary sanctifying power of the proper attitude. As he saw, it is the penitent person's reaching for righteousness through the humble heart and repentant spirit (hopefully evidenced in making the sacrifice of a "burnt offering") that pleases God (Ps. 51:19). For that reason, the nascent Church in the Holy Land did not initially abandon the sacrificial system for Jewish converts. For gentile converts, however, the Church determined to put emphasis on the ground that made the sacrifices acceptable and to forgo the sacrifices themselves. In the Book of Mormon, due to the Church's unique circumstances, the Lord did the same (3 Ne. 9:19–20).

The author uses the psalm as the means of summarizing the life of faithful righteousness forcefully advocated throughout his Epistle.[190] Unlike the Levitical sacrifices that had to be continually performed due to sin,

---

189. Guthrie and Motyer, *New Bible Commentary,* 484.

190. Lane, *Hebrews 9–13,* 548, calls it the "theological and practical synthesis of Hebrews."

the humble and heartfelt free offerings of the new covenant are made in recognition of and in grateful response for the sin-removing and cleaning power that flows from the once-for-all self-sacrifice of the Son (12:28).[191] In other words, "the sacrifices of the Old Covenant were offered perpetually because they were never effective in removing sin (10:1–4). The sacrifices of praise and right living described in these verses are to be offered perpetually because Christ's obedient self-offering has effectively done away with sin."[192] The author's point is that "having a share in Christ's altar means finally to follow him on the road of suffering, to worship God through sacrifices of praise, and to devote oneself to loving service of other members of the covenant community."[193]

The author now (13:17) turns his attention to the respect his readers should show for their current leaders and in doing so throws his complete support and confidence behind them. That respect, he insists, should express itself in obedience (πείθω, *peithō*) and willful self-submission (ὑπείκω, *hypeikō*) to those in authority. His admonition to follow the leaders likely centers on his concern about the false doctrine and incorrect practices he has already warned against (13:9–10). The force of the two terms "obedience" and "submission" combine to stress the absolute need for faithful adherence to Church leadership. His use of the present imperative expresses his desire that his readers continue the obedience they have already rendered but to now do it with renewed and determined effort.[194]

The author gives three reasons why these people should make obedience to Church leadership a lifelong habit. First, the leaders, with care and alertness, watch over the Saints' temporal and spiritual welfare ever guarding them against danger.[195] Second, the leaders' duty demands that they give an account (λόγος, *logos*) of the lives of those under their stewardship.[196] And third, leaders' negative reports would prove "unprofitable"

191. Compare Lane, *Hebrews 9–13*, 549.

192. Cockerill, *Epistle to the Hebrews*, 705.

193. Attridge, *Epistle to the Hebrews*, 391.

194. Cockerill, *Epistle to the Hebrews*, 707–8.

195. The verb ἀγρυπνέω (*agrypneō*) suggests a continued vigilance against "threatening peril." BDAG, 16. Certainly, based on 10:39 (compare 2 Cor. 12:15), the author's primary concern is with their eternal welfare.

196. This demand goes well back into Old Testament times (see Ezek. 33:7–9) and shows that the reckoning is before God. McConkie, *Doctrinal New Testament Commentary*, 3:242.

(ἀλυσιτελής, *alysitelēs*) for the faithless, leaving them spiritually bankrupt before God. The author concludes this admonition asking readers to obey so their leaders can give their report on each person with joy (χάρα, *chara*) and without complaining (στενάζω, *stenazō*). That the leaders would feel these emotions toward those under their charge suggests the depth of their care.

The Final Benediction (13:18–21)

Greek Text

18 Προσεύχεσθε περὶ ἡμῶν, πειθόμεθα γὰρ ὅτι καλὴν συνείδησιν ἔχομεν, ἐν πᾶσιν καλῶς θέλοντες ἀναστρέφεσθαι. 19 περισσοτέρως δὲ παρακαλῶ τοῦτο ποιῆσαι ἵνα τάχιον ἀποκατασταθῶ ὑμῖν. 20 Ὁ δὲ θεὸς τῆς εἰρήνης, ὁ ἀναγαγὼν ἐκ νεκρῶν τὸν ποιμένα τῶν προβάτων τὸν μέγαν ἐν αἵματι διαθήκης αἰωνίου, τὸν κύριον ἡμῶν Ἰησοῦν, 21 καταρτίσαι ὑμᾶς ἐν παντὶ ἀγαθῷ εἰς τὸ ποιῆσαι τὸ θέλημα αὐτοῦ, ποιῶν ἐν ἡμῖν τὸ εὐάρεστον ἐνώπιον αὐτοῦ διὰ Ἰησοῦ Χριστοῦ, ᾧ ἡ δόξα εἰς τοὺς αἰῶνας· ἀμήν. [SBLGNT]

King James Version

18 Pray for us: for we trust we have a good conscience, in all things willing to live honestly. 19 But I beseech you the rather to do this, that I may be restored to you the sooner. 20 Now the God of peace, that brought again from the dead our Lord Jesus, that great shepherd of the sheep, through the blood of the everlasting covenant, 21 Make you perfect in every good work to do his will, working in you that which is wellpleasing in his sight, through Jesus Christ; to whom be glory for ever and ever. Amen.

New Rendition

18 Continue to pray for us, for we are certain that we have a clear conscience and desire to conduct ourselves well in all things. 19 And I especially urge you to do this so that I may quickly be restored to you. 20 Now may the God of peace, who brought back from the dead the great shepherd of the flocks through the blood of the eternal covenant, even our Lord Jesus, 21 make you complete in every good thing to do his will, working in us that which is pleasing before him through Jesus Christ, to whom be glory forever, amen.

Translation Notes and Comments

13:18 ***Pray for us / Continue to pray for us:*** The verb προσέρχομαι (*proserchomai*), "to pray,"[197] is found here in the form of a present imperative, which gives it durative force, and is therefore translated as "continue to pray for us" in our Rendition.[198]

The author's use of the plural pronoun ἡμῶν (*hēmōn*), "us,"[199] juxtaposed as it is with his request that his readers follow their leaders, suggests that he is one of them, although he differs from the others in that his labors extend beyond this specific community. Whether or not that would entail apostolic authority cannot be determined since there were a number of nonapostolic itinerate missionaries working at the time.

for we trust we have a good conscience / for we are certain that we have a clear conscience: The conjunction φάρ (*gar*), "for," again serves to give reason for an action.[200]

The verb πείθω (*peithō*), "to trust," carries the nuance of being persuaded to take a particular position. In this case, it means "to be convinced, sure, certain" of a state or position.[201]

The noun συνείδησις (*syneidēsis*), "conscience," as used here, denotes "the inward faculty of distinguishing right and wrong" and connotes a heightened "moral sensitivity" with an accompanying purity of mind.[202] For a study, see Translation Notes for 9:9 and the associated Analysis. That the author modifies the noun with the adjective καλός (*kalos*), "good,"[203] stresses the high quality of the state of the conscience. The phrase shows that the author feels he can ask for his readers' support because the leaders have a clear conscience in what they do for the Saints.[204]

in all things willing to live honestly / and desire to conduct ourselves well in all things: The phrase ἐν πᾶσιν (*en pasin*) is vague due to an unclear gender reference. If it is taken as masculine, then it means "among all people," but if it is taken as a neuter, it means "in all things," that is, "in every way."[205] Since the author has just described the leaders' state of mind, the latter seems the more likely and is used in our Rendition.

---

197. BDAG, 879.
198. Lane, *Hebrews 9–13,* 525 note nn; Johnson, *Hebrews,* 353.
199. BDAG, 275.
200. Cockerill, *Epistle to the Hebrews,* 712 n. 12.
201. Lane, *Hebrew 9–13,* 525 note oo.
202. BDAG, 967–68; Louw-Nida, §26.13; Maurer, *TDNT,* 7:898–911.
203. BDAG, 504–5.
204. Ellingworth, *Epistle to the Hebrews,* 726.
205. Ellingworth, *Epistle to the Hebrews,* 726.

The verb θέλω (*thelō*), "to desire," can imply not just a willingness but a resolve to do something.[206]

The verb ἀναστρέφω (*anastrephō*), "to live," denotes comportment and, coupled with the adverb καλῶς (*kalōs*), "commendably," connotes living in a state of personal excellence.[207]

13:19 ***But I beseech you the rather to do this / And I especially urge you to do this:*** The verb παρακαλέω (*parakaleō*) means "to make a strong request" and therefore "to urge, implore, beseech";[208] when coupled with the adverb περισσοτέρως (*perissoterōs*), which means "to a much greater degree, especially,"[209] together they suggests the great urgency and need the author puts behind his request.

The phrase τοῦτο ποιῆσαι (*touto poiēsai*), "to do this," refers to the request for an earnest prayer he made in 13:18.

that I may be restored to you the sooner / that I may quickly be restored to you: The conjunction ἵνα (*hina*), "that," usually signals purpose but here is used to specify the content of the prayer the author is asking for.[210]

The verb ἀποκαθιστάνω (*apokathistanō*), found here as an aorist subjunctive, means "to be restored" and carries the idea of coming back to an earlier pleasant state or condition.[211] The whole phrase reveals the warm relationship the author has with his readers.

The adverb τάχιον (*tachion*), "quickly, soon,"[212] can be taken two ways: simply as "quickly, soon," or as a comparative meaning "sooner than if you did not pray."[213] The former definition seems less strained and so is used in our Rendition.[214]

13:20–21 constitute one long sentence that consists of a benediction on the part of the author for his readers' spiritual wellbeing. In order to make his thoughts read smoothly in English, we have broken this section into smaller sentences.

---

206. BDAG, 447–48; Schrenk, *TDNT,* 3:44–62.

207. BDAG, 505–6.

208. BDAG, 764–65.

209. Louw-Nida, §78.31; BDAG, 806.

210. Ellingworth, *Epistle to the Hebrews,* 727.

211. BDAG, 111–12. This verse echoes the condition in which Paul found himself when he wrote to Philemon (1:22), asking for a speedy reunion through prayer. Vanhoye, *Letter to the Hebrews,* 229.

212. BDAG, 993.

213. Lane, *Hebrews 9–13,* 525 note uu; Attridge, *Epistle to the Hebrews,* 403. Note RSV, [N]JB.

214. Ellingworth, *Epistle to the Hebrews,* 727. Note NIV, NRSV.

13:20 *the God of peace / may the God of peace:* For a discussion on the noun εἰρήνη (*eirēnē*), "peace," see Translation Notes for 12:14 with the associated Analysis. Here we need only note that the word in its broadest sense came to denote not only well-being based on health and safety but also the partaking of all that was moral and ethical, thus including the enjoyment of "every good work" or "to all that is good."[215] In addition, because of its positive nuance in the Hebrew Bible, where it is closely associated with the Divine, it came to connote a condition that transcended mere earthly security and rest and suggest a heavenly amity and oneness.[216] In this phrase, the author shows that it is an attribute of the Father.

that brought again from the dead our Lord Jesus / who brought back from the dead . . . even our Lord Jesus: The verb ἀνάγω (*anagō*) means "to bring up from a lower to a higher point" and in this instance refers to restoring Jesus from the realm of the dead.[217]

The author gives emphasis to the role of the Father as the one who did this work. It is of note, however, that according to the view found in the Gospel of John, the Father did this not by bestowing his life-giving power upon the Son after his death but by bestowing it when the Son was born (John 5:26). The Savior's power over death included the key of his own resurrection: "No man taketh [my life] from me, but I lay it down of myself. I have power to lay it down, and I have power to take it again. This commandment have I received of my Father" (John 10:18). Thus, Jesus apparently held the power over death throughout his life and took it with him into the spirit realm. It was by exercising this self-held but divinely bestowed power that the Savior then overcame his own death and opened the way of universal resurrection.[218] The author, however, looks to the seat of Jesus' power and therefore rightly gives credit to the Father.[219]

---

215. *NID,* s.v. "εἰρήνη." On the traditional idea of the Father as a God of peace, see Attridge, *Epistle to the Hebrews,* 405. The expression is very Pauline. See Rom. 15:33; 16:20; 1 Thes. 5:23; and Philip. 4:9.

216. That the author uses the phrase "God of Peace" reinforces his admonition that his readers live in harmony and peace with those around them, thus expressing this same attribute. Attridge, *Epistle to the Hebrews,* 405; Lane, *Hebrews 9–13,* 560.

217. BDAG, 61–62.

218. Taylor, *Mediation and Atonement,* 146–47; James B. Mayfield, "Covenant Israel, Latter-day," in Ludlow, *Encyclopedia of Mormonism,* 1:330–31; Wouter Van Beek, "Covenants," in Ludlow, *Encyclopedia of Mormonism,* 1:331–33; George S. Tate, "Covenants in Biblical Times," in Ludlow, *Encyclopedia of Mormonism,* 1:333–35; Smith, *Doctrines of Salvation,* 1:127.

219. According to President Brigham Young, in *Journal of Discourses,* 15:137, resurrection is an ordinance performed through the operation of the keys of the priesthood.

The author gives Jesus the title κύριος (*kyrios*), "Lord." In this context, it is a reverential title for Jesus denoting both his rulership and divinity.[220]

that great shepherd of the sheep / the great shepherd of the flocks: The noun ποιμήν (*poimēn*) denotes a shepherd. Though shepherds composed a low class among the Jews of Jesus' day,[221] the Jewish Christians, likely based on Old Testament imagery, viewed the profession very positively, seeing such nuances in it as a caring, selfless attitude and devotion even to the point of personal danger (for examples, see Matt. 18:12–14; Luke 15:4–7; and John 10:3–4). The Hebrew Bible contains a host of references to this imagery. The work describes the Davidic line as well as the Messiah as shepherds to whom God gave the responsibility for the care of his people.[222]

The adjective μέγας (*megas*), "great," in this context denotes that which not only exceeds a given standard in quality but also attains a high degree of superiority.[223] By using the term "great shepherd," the author separates the Lord from all other shepherds by the degree of his supremacy and yet retains all the positive attributes associated with the image.

The noun πρόβατον (*probaton*), "sheep,"[224] here in the plural, denotes in figurative terms those who belong to the Christian flock and thereby come under the Lord's watchful and protective care.[225]

through the blood of the everlasting covenant / through the blood of the eternal covenant: This phrase can be understood two ways depending on how the preposition ἐν (*en*) is construed. If the phrase denotes

---

These keys "will be given to those who have passed off this stage of action and have received their bodies again. . . . They will be ordained, by those who hold the keys of the resurrection."

220. BDAG, 576–79. Isaiah 40:3 used the term to denote the governor of the new community for whom the people were to prepare the way. That nuance seems to have been picked up by the synoptic writers. For example, see Matt. 3:3; Mark 1:3; Luke 3:4; and John 1:23.

221. After the exile, the rabbis showed a strong dislike for members of the occupation, even forbidding faithful Jews from purchasing milk, meat, and wool from them. By the time of Jesus, they could not function as judge or witness. This very negative view of the shepherd did not affect Christianity likely because of the highly positive imagery used by the Lord. See Jack W. Vancil, "Sheep, Shepherd," in Freedman, *Anchor Bible Dictionary,* 5:1187–90.

222. Johnson, *Hebrews,* 355, develops this idea.

223. BDAG, 623–24.

224. BDAG, 866. One of the major nuances of the term is that of "the people of God."

225. Throughout the Hebrew Bible, the "flock" denotes the people of God exclusively. For example, see Ps. 100:3; Jer. 13:17; Ezek. 34:31; and Zech. 10:3. Seeing themselves in this position, the Christians easily adopted the imagery.

accompaniment, then it means "along with the blood." If the phase is taken instrumentally, then it means "by means of the blood."[226]

Taking the preposition as indicating accompaniment, then the idea is that the Father led Jesus from the dead "along with the blood." The imagery does not mean Jesus was resurrected with a body having blood, but the effects of the Atonement came through the Resurrection with him and would therefore carry forward, making the new covenant eternal.

Taking the preposition as indicating means or instrument, then the phrase shows the Father led Jesus from the dead "by means of the blood"—Jesus' Atonement allowed the powers of the Father to operate such that he could restore the Son to life in accordance with the conditions of the new covenant.

The author seems to have taken his imagery from LXX Zechariah 9:11, which states, "By the means of the blood of your [that is, God's] covenant, you have sent forth the prisoners out of the pit that has no water" (our translation). If this is the case, then the preposition should be taken instrumentally. Given the author's broad biblical knowledge, he was very likely influenced by this verse and therefore saw in it the means through which God operated. In the author's model, "Jesus died on the cross as a covenant sacrifice and [then] entered the heavenly sanctuary and there sprinkled his own blood, prior to the resurrection" (9:11–15; 10:5–10).[227] His Resurrection then occurred, having been initiated by virtue of this sprinkling of blood through which he established the new covenant.

The "blood of the covenant" refers to the act that sealed the covenant and thereby made it effective.[228] Though the Savior's self-sacrifice on the cross stands out here, it is the whole of his life of perfect obedience culminating in his self-sacrifice that fully constitutes the "blood of the covenant."[229]

On the noun διαθήκη (*diathēkē*), "covenant," see Translation Notes for 9:16–17 with the associated Analysis. In the present context, we need only note that the term designates a contract initiated by God in behalf of his people that they can accept for their good or reject to their ill.[230]

---

226. For discussion, see Lane, *Hebrews 9–13,* 559 note b; and Ellingworth, *Epistle to the Hebrews,* 727–28.

227. Lane, *Hebrews 9–13,* 563.

228. Note Ex. 24:8, where the blood established the Mosaic covenant, and Heb. 10:29, which shows the blood is the sanctifying power.

229. Cockerill, *Epistle to the Hebrews,* 717.

230. BDAG, 228–29. For discussion, see Smith, *Doctrines of Salvation,* 1:152–58.

Here, for the only time, the author defines the covenant by the use of the adjective αἰώνιος (*aiōnios*), "everlasting."[231] In doing so, he contrasts the new but everlasting covenant with the old one that had passed away (8:13). A major theme of Hebrews is the permanent nature of Christ's work (9:25–28; 10:12–14), including his revelation and implementation of a new covenant, one that would last forever. Its permanence would derive from where it was written—on the hearts of the people (10:8; Jer. 31:33; compare Prov. 7:3; and 2 Cor. 3:3).

13:21 ***Make you perfect in every good work to do his will / make you complete in every good thing to do his will:*** In this verse the author continues his benediction and blessing of his readers.

The verb καταρτίζω (*katartizō*) means to put someone in a proper condition to bring about a certain task, thus, "to make full, complete, adequate," or "to fully equip."[232]

The adjective ἀγαθός (*agathos*), "good,"[233] generally denotes positive moral qualities of the most general nature,[234] but as a substantive, as in this case, it points to "good deeds" and suggests the possession of those useful and helpful characteristics so necessary in doing the will of God in a fully satisfactory way.[235] When modified by πᾶς (*pas*), "every," the word encapsulates all those works that are pleasing to God and, therefore, of utmost benefit to the Saints and the people they serve.

working in you that which is wellpleasing in his sight / working in us that which is pleasing before him: The verb ποιέω (*poieō*), "to do, work," found here in the form of a present participle, points to continuing divine activity that brings a state or condition into being.[236]

That state or condition the author describes as εὐαρσετός (*euarestos*), "acceptable, pleasing." The emphasis here is on the latter, for the phrase points to deeds that are not only acceptable but also delightful in the eyes of God.[237]

---

231. BDAG, 33.

232. BDAG, 526; Louw-Nida, §75.5; Ellingworth, *Epistle to the Hebrews,* 730.

233. BDAG, 3–4. The adjective is missing from a number of important texts, but it is implied by the dative, neuter adjective παντί (*panti*), "everything." Metzger, *Textual Commentary,* 605.

234. Louw-Nida, §88.1.

235. Louw-Nida, §65.20. Manuscripts vary on this phrase, some having ἡμῖν (*hēmin*), "us," instead of ὑμᾶς (*hymas*), "you." Metzger, *Textual Commentary,* 606. If the correct reading is *hēmin,* the author joins with his readers in coming under the Lord's enabling power. Johnson, *Hebrews,* 354.

236. BGAG, 839–42; Louw-Nida, §§13.9; 42.29, 41.

237. BDAG, 403.

The preposition ἐνώπιον (*enōpion*), "before," means "in the judgment of"[238] and points to divine action. The Father is doing what he sees as best for the individual.

through Jesus Christ: The preposition διά (*dia*), "through," in this instance is comprehensive, showing the agent, means, and benefactor who brings about a given state or condition.[239] The preposition sums up nicely the work of Christ as the instrument enabling people to do God's will both sufficiently and satisfactorily.

to whom be glory for ever and ever / to whom be glory forever: The antecedent of the relative pronoun ᾧ (*hō*), "whom," is vague. The word stands closest to "Jesus," and it would be natural for it to reference him. On the other hand, since the Father is the subject of the whole sentence, it would be logical for the author to end by again referencing him. The author has already explained that the Son reflects the Father's glory (1:3) and that the Father glorifies the Son (2:7–10), so it seems the author most likely had the Father in mind.[240]

On the noun δόξα (*doxa*), "glory," see Translation Notes for 1:3 with associated Analysis. In the present context, the word denotes the praise and honor that is God's due because of all he has done in the redemption process.[241]

The plural noun αἰῶνας (*aiōnas*) refers to the endless age to come and therefore nuances that which is eternal and thereby lasts "forever."[242]

Analysis and Summary

The author's closing (13:18–25) follows the usual form of a conclusion and benediction consistent with many of the New Testament Epistles. The author's closing, however, is not a perfunctory following of tradition. Rather, using his considerable skills, the author crafts his conclusion to reinforce important elements in his letter. By saving them until this point, he addresses personal issues and concerns that would have detracted from his message elsewhere.[243]

---

238. Louw-Nida, §90.20; BDAG, 342.

239. Cockerill, *Epistle to the Hebrews,* 718 n. 47; Louw-Nida, §§89.76; 90.4, 8, 38.

240. For discussion, see Ellingworth, *Epistle to the Hebrews,* 731; and Vanhoye, *Letter to the Hebrews,* 233.

241. BDAG, 256–58.

242. BDAG, 32–33.

243. Cockerill, *Epistle to the Hebrews,* 710–11.

The author's request that his readers pray for him and the other leaders (13:18) reveals the weight they feel for the responsibilities that are theirs and also the confidence they have in the Father's willingness to assist them due to the appeals of those they serve. The author assures his readers he and the other leaders feel they can make this request due to their determination to live exemplary lives demonstrated by how they have lived up to this point. Indeed, he assures his readers that the leaders' consciences are clear in the service they have rendered and are therefore worthy of divine blessing. However, he wants his readers to pray urgently and earnestly for a specific outcome (13:19): that he might be restored (ἀποκαθιστάνω, *apokathistanō*) quickly to the pleasant associations he enjoyed when he was once with them.

Beginning with 13:20, the author both makes another appeal to and expresses a heartfelt wish for his fellow Saints. Note his urgent appeal for a prayer in his behalf is now followed by a wish in his readers' behalf.[244] His hope for the realization of his wish is based on the work of the Father, who "through the blood of the everlasting covenant" brought Jesus "back from the dead." Also noteworthy is that although the author has addressed the Lord's ascension and his place on the right hand of God (1:3; 8:1; 10:12; 12:2), this is the first time in the entire Epistle that the author has referenced the Lord's Resurrection. Further, he does not use the usual word for denoting resurrection (ἐγείρω, *egeirō*) but instead one that was much rarer (ἀνάγω, *anagō,* meaning "to raise up, lead forth").[245] He may have been influenced by LXX Isaiah 63:11, which speaks of one who is "the shepherd of the sheep" whom God "raised up" (*agagō*) from the deep and into whom he "put his Holy Spirit."[246] The author, however, separates Jesus from Moses by calling the former "the great shepherd."

Importantly, the author does not depict the Resurrection "as an individual glorification that would only concern Jesus himself, but as a decisive event for the destiny of all the flock of which Jesus is 'the great shepherd.'"[247]

---

244. The conjunction δέ (*de*), "and," in this verse connects this request with the request for a prayer in 13:18. Lane, *Hebrews 9–13,* 560. The context here makes the author's appeal less a formal prayer then a heartfelt wish. Nonetheless, entreaty to the Divine stands behind it. Vanhoye, *Letter to the Hebrews,* 230.

245. BDAG, 61–62. Paul used this word once (Rom. 10:7) to denote the Resurrection, but otherwise he used the common ἐγείρω (*egeirō*).

246. Both Lane, *Hebrews 9–13,* 560–62, and Vanhoye, *Letter to the Hebrews,* 231, accept the idea, but Attridge, *Epistle to the Hebrews,* 406, thinks it is a reach.

247. Vanhoye, *Letter to the Hebrews,* 231.

The author's words suggest that the "blood of the covenant" made the Resurrection possible—an important idea in Latter-day Saint theology. Joseph Smith taught that an "everlasting covenant was made between three personages before the organizations of the earth, and relates to their dispensation of things to men on the earth, these personages . . . are called God the first, the Creator; God the second, the Redeemer, and God the third, the witness or Testator."[248] The Prophet's statement shows that the "everlasting covenant" the Father made with the Son centered on his work of redemption. In order to carry that out, according to the view found in the Gospel of John, the Father extended to the Son the power of life. The Savior noted that "as the Father hath life in himself; so hath he given to the Son to have life in himself" (John 5:26). He could therefore affirm, "No man taketh it from me, but I lay it down of myself. I have power to lay it down, and I have power to take it again. This commandment have I received of my Father" (John 10:18). Thus, even as a mortal, the Lord had power over death, which he exercised after dying in order to return from the dead. Nonetheless, that power of life originated with the Father, and he gave it to the Son so he could carry out his portion of the everlasting covenant. When he completed the Atonement, he also fulfilled that part of the covenant. Indeed, the Savior's Resurrection clearly demonstrates God's acceptance of the Lord's self-sacrifice and of the fulfilling of that part of their agreement.[249] All was not done, however, until the Savior instituted the "new and everlasting covenant" promised by Jeremiah (Jer. 31:31–33) as stressed by the author (8:10; 10:16).

In his view, it was the Father who directly performed the Resurrection. With extreme brevity, the author identifies three key factors operating in the Father's work and in doing so states the experiential and confessional basis underlying the author's complex arguments and supporting his exhortations. First and most important, God raised Jesus from the dead (compare Rom. 4:24; 10:9). The word the author chose, ἀνάγω (*anagō*), means literally "to lead one from a lower to a higher place" and more metaphorically "to bring back from the dead" (see 1 Sam. 2:6; and Ps. 71:20).[250] Thus, the Father holds all power over death and exercised that power in

248. "Discourse, circa May 1841, as Reported by Unknown Scribe–A," 1, Joseph Smith Papers, https://www.josephsmithpapers.org/paper-summary/discourse-circa-may-1841-as-reported-by-unknown-scribe-a/1.

249. Bruce, *Epistle to the Hebrews,* 388.

250. BDAG, 61–62.

behalf of the Son. Second, the one who God raised up is "Lord" (κύριος, *kyrios*), the title showing both the divinity of Jesus and his right to rule. He is the one who sits on the right hand of God and to whom the Father delegated all power necessary for the salvation of humankind. And third, by virtue of the blood of the Son, the Father instituted a new and eternal covenant with his people, one that would bring them under the power of Jesus so that he, like his Father, could bring them from the place of death to that of eternal life.[251] On these three facts the author hangs his entire discourse.

This last point is central to the author's theses. The Savior gave his life—"the blood of covenant"—"out of filial obedience to God and out of fraternal solidarity toward humankind; it therefore established the union between humanity and God."[252] Through this means, the Savior became both the establisher and "mediator of the new covenant" (9:15; 12:24) and because he offered his own blood, he also became a "priest forever" (5:6) "according to the power of an indestructible life" (7:16). Because he now possesses this kind of life, the covenant he has established is also indestructible.[253]

The author, for the first and only time in his Epistle, uses the term "shepherd" (ποιμήν, *poimēn*) to describe the Lord, likely to stress the Lord's present intercession in behalf of his people in protecting them and leading them to the eternal city.[254] The connection between the imagery and the Divine goes back even into Old Testament times.[255] Noteworthy is that the term became associated with the coming Messiah (Jer. 3:15; 23:4; Ezek. 34:23; 37:24) and the idea that he would be rejected and suffer (see Zech. 13:7 in light of Heb. 12:10).[256] The Gospel writers saw Jesus as fulfilling this function as he began to gather the flock into the kingdom of God (Matt.

---

251. Johnson, *Hebrews,* 355.

252. Vanhoye, *Letter to the Hebrews,* 232.

253. Vanhoye, *Letter to the Hebrews,* 232.

254. Attridge, *Epistle to the Hebrews,* 406.

255. See specifically Gen. 49:24; and Ps. 80:1; and generally Gen. 48:15; Deut. 26:5–8; Jer. 13:17; and Micah 7:14; and most beautifully in Ps. 23. The imagery of the Divine as the caring, protecting, and self-giving shepherd is prominent in the psalms (for example, see Ps. 28:9; 74:1; 77:20; 78:52–53; 95:7) and in the later prophets (for example, see Jer. 23:2; 31:10; 50:17; and Ezek. 34:11–12).

256. For discussion, see J. Jeremias, *TDNT,* 6:485–502. This is likely because of the broad ancient Near Eastern use of the metaphor as referring to kings. It was very common for Mesopotamian kings to refer to themselves as "good shepherds." Since the Messiah is fundamentally about kingship, it is no wonder that the Messiah is characterized in this way. The Egyptian pharaohs were also considered shepherds of their people. They held a shepherd's crook in one of their hands to symbolize this responsibility.

9:36; 10:6; 15:24; see also Luke 19:10 with Ezek. 34:15). The Lord took upon himself the title, stressing he was the "good shepherd" who would lay down his life for the sheep (John 10:1–30). This duty he passed on to Peter (John 21:16), telling him to "shepherd my sheep" (ποίμαινε τὰ πρόβατά μου, *poimaine ta probata mou*). This duty Peter passed on to other Church leaders (1 Pet. 5:1–2), promising them when the "chief shepherd" (ἀρχιποίμην, *archipoimēn*) comes again, he will reward them with a crown of glory (1 Pet. 5:3–4).[257]

Though the author was likely well acquainted with the imagery in the Hebrew Bible, to what degree he knew of the Christian usage of "shepherd" cannot be determined, but he certainly follows the pattern: he describes Jesus as the "great shepherd," or overseer of all other shepherds, echoing Ezekiel 34 where Jehovah places himself in this very position. Further, when the author identifies the "great shepherd" as the "Lord Jesus," his Greek-speaking readers would have likely recalled the opening lines of Psalm 23, "The Lord is my Shepherd." By evoking the imagery at this point in his Epistle, the author reinforces, albeit from another perspective, the caring and guarding aspect of the Savior. The author also tacitly opens the door to the image of sacrifice, that is, of Jesus not as the shepherd but as the sheep.

The instrument that has made everything possible, including the Lord's own Resurrection, as the author explains, is "the blood of the everlasting covenant." The imagery points to that sacrifice that put the covenant into effect. That sacrifice culminated but did not begin at Golgotha; it began the moment Jesus determined he would do the Father's will and bend himself to that task no matter the personal cost. For that reason, the sacrifice's roots reach back into the premortal period when the Savior said, "Father, thy will be done, and the glory be thine forever" (Moses 4:2). It evidenced itself during his mortal ministry when Jesus went about his "Father's business" (Luke 2:49) and continued in Gethsemane when he cried, "Abba, Father, all things are possible unto thee; take away this cup from me: nevertheless not what I will, but what thou wilt" (Mark 14:36). All this made the "blood of the covenant" effective and opened the way for it to be both implemented and written "on the tables of the heart" of the faithful (2 Cor. 3:3; compare 8:8–10; and Jer. 31:31–33).[258]

---

257. For discussion, see *NID*, s.v. "ποιμήν."

258. Cockerill, *Epistle to the Hebrews*, 717. The Lord states in Jer. 32:38–40 these dynamics: "They shall be my people, and I will be their God: And I will give them one

The author contrasts the old covenant that had now been fulfilled and passed away with the new covenant that he describes as "everlasting" (αἰώνιος, *aiōnios*).[259] There are a number of places where God made an everlasting covenant with either a person or a people (for example, see Gen. 9:16; 17:7, 13, 19; Ex. 31:16; Lev. 24:8; and Num. 18:19). In each case, the Hebrew Bible uses the noun עוֹלָם (*ʿôlām*) in a construct state,[260] which has the sense "long time" (usually eternal or eternity, but not in a philosophical sense).[261] The LXX uses the adjective αἰώνιος (*aiōnios*), which can refer to "a long period of time" as well as "a period of unending duration, without end" but differs from the noun ἀΐδιος (*aidios*), which denotes a quality of time. The word excludes any interruption and stresses permanence and unchangableness.[262] Thus, *aiōnios* can refer to a shorter period of time such as an age or even a lifetime.[263] The nuance that is important here, however, denotes a state or relationship that lasts so long as certain conditions exist.[264] For example, Jehovah made a covenant with Aaron and his descendants that they would have specific priesthood duties "forever" (Ex. 29:9; 1 Chr. 15:2; 23:13). Thus, it would befall them, and no others, to perform these ordinances but only so long as it was part of the Lord's program. When the program changed, the need would be no longer necessary. The Levites' rights to do them, however, would not cease, for it was theirs forever. Joseph Smith taught that at some time in the future the offering of animal sacrifices that were done before the Mosaic period will again be ministered, and "then shall the sons of Levi offer an acceptable sacrifice to the Lord."[265] As the author explains, when there is a change of the priesthood, there is

---

heart, and one way, that they may fear me for ever, for the good of them, and of their children after them: And I will make an everlasting covenant with them, that I will not turn away from them, to do them good; but I will put my fear in their hearts, that they shall not depart from me."

259. BDAG, 33.

260. Hebrew often used a noun in the construct state instead of an adjective, hence בְּרִית עוֹלָם (*bĕrît ʿôlām*), "a covenant of eternity," equates with "an eternal covenant." See Wilhelm Gesenius, *Gesenius' Hebrew Grammar,* ed. and enl. E. Kautzsch, trans. A. E. Cowley (Mineola, N.Y.: Dover Publications, 2006), §128.o–p.

261. HAL, 798; BDB, 761–62; Sasse, *TDNT,* 1:208–9.

262. BDAG, 33; Sasse, *TDNT,* 1:208–9.

263. *NID,* 1:193–200.

264. For example, the word refers to the period a slave must remain in service (Ex. 21:6; Deut. 15:17) and the time that Samuel was to remain in the service of the tabernacle (1 Sam. 1:22).

265. "Instruction on Priesthood," 9. See also Ehat and Cook, *Words of Joseph Smith,* 42, 52 n. 15.

also a change in the law (7:12). In this case, that included the cessation of those ordinances and rites associated with the Mosaic sacrifices of the Levitical order of the priesthood. Still, the new covenant would include any portions of the old one that had not been fulfilled by Christ (Matt. 5:17–18).

From a Latter-day Saint perspective, "the new and everlasting covenant is the gospel of Jesus Christ. The sum of all gospel covenants that God makes with mankind is called '*the* new and everlasting covenant' and consists of several individual covenants, each of which is called '*a* new and *an* everlasting covenant.' It is 'new' when given to a person or a people for the first time, and 'everlasting' because the gospel of Jesus Christ and Plan of Salvation existed before the world was formed and will exist forever."[266] Concerning implementation of the covenant in this latter day, the Lord stated, "I have sent mine everlasting covenant into the world, to be a light to the world, and to be a standard for my people, and for the Gentiles to seek to it, and to be a messenger before my face to prepare the way before me" (D&C 45:9). It is likely that these reasons were also why he established it during the New Testament era.

Having laid the background of the initiation of the covenant in the previous verse, the author now (13:21) pronounces his sincere benediction upon his readers, desiring that they reap the full benefit that can flow from covenant keeping. To understand what he does here, background is important. The author has warned his readers about the consequences of not following the Lord and of resisting God's will (6:4–6). The author has also upheld the Savior's complete submission to the Father's will as the perfect example for readers to follow (10:5–10) in order to partake fully of the blessings of the new covenant. With this verse, the author touches on a very important point: how God uses the product of the Savior's submission to work "his will within the human will, without destroying its freedom."[267]

The enabling process begins when an individual comes to understand who Christ is and what he has done for them and begins to desire, magnified by the help of the Spirit, to do the Father's will. At that point, further benefits of the Atonement kick in and the Father equips them further to

266. D. Cecil Clark, "New and Everlasting Covenant," in Ludlow, *Encyclopedia of Mormonism,* 3:1008–9.

267. Ellingworth, *Epistle to the Hebrews,* 730. It is the obedience of the Lord that not only sets the example but also empowers obedience in the Saints. O'Brien, *Letter to the Hebrews,* 536; Johnson, *Hebrews,* 356.

do his will—defined as doing that which is "pleasing in his sight" (13:21). The emphasis of the phrase shows the Saints do not live this kind of life on their own; they rely on the grace and enabling power of their great High Priest to draw ever nearer to him and the Father. "This life of trust in God's power and promises (11:5–6), of filial awe and thanksgiving (12:28), of praise and brotherly love (13:15–16; cf. 13:1–6), is the only life that is 'pleasing before him.'"[268] And it reaps a great reward. It is through the "grace of God" that one becomes "perfect in Christ"; only through that power are they "sanctified in Christ . . . through the shedding of [his] blood . . . which is in the covenant of the Father unto the remission of [their] sins, that [they] become holy, without spot" (Moro. 10:33). To stress the author's point, it is "through Jesus Christ" (13:21) the perfect life is made possible. The idea behind the phrase is not that the enabling power comes just *by* the Savior, but *because of* him.[269] He is the center of the whole operation.

From the author's teachings, we see how God operates on the Saints to do his will within the context of their moral agency—by equipping (καταρτίζω, *katartizō*) them to do as they want when it is in line with what the Father views (ἐνώπιον, *enōpion*) as best. By equipping the soul to do what he wants—but neither overwhelming nor overriding it—God both protects agency and works within its bounds to bring about his will.

Note that what they are equipped to do is "every good thing" (ἀγαθός, *agathos*), meaning whatever is "pleasing" (εὐαρεστός, *euarestos*) to God. Such equipping does not demand that the person first be perfect, meaning flawless, faultless, and impeccable, but rather that he or she desires to do as the Father wishes (see D&C 46:8–9). Such a desire opens the way for the enabling power to assist them in doing the task at hand and also, by this means over time, to acquire the attributes of perfection and holiness so necessary to be one with the Father and the Son. Note that God prepares the Saints to move to that end—perfection—by equipping them to do the tasks at hand.

God writes the new law not externally on tablets of stone but internally upon the heart, evidencing his divine action upon the individual. Here the author echoes Paul, who taught, "God works in you, both to will and to work his good pleasure" (Philip. 2:13, our translation). These words show the Father's work is "not a question of a divine action done once and for all; it is about an ongoing activity of God in the hearts of believers. Like

---

268. Cockerill, *Epistle to the Hebrews,* 718.

269. The preposition εἰς (*eis*), as used here, denotes "means, manner, and cause."

Jesus, who continually received the work that his Father 'gave' him (see John 5:17, 20, 36; 17:4), believers are called upon to receive constantly in them, through the mediation of Jesus Christ, the activity of God, full of intense love."[270]

Having pronounced his benediction, the author closes the formal portion of his Epistle and next turns to more personal matters. Even in these closing remarks—so reminiscent of the close of many letters written in his day—he skillfully continues to encourage his readers to wholehearted compliance to God's will.[271]

Concluding Matters (13:22–25)

Greek Text

22 Παρακαλῶ δὲ ὑμᾶς, ἀδελφοί, ἀνέχεσθε τοῦ λόγου τῆς παρακλήσεως, καὶ γὰρ διὰ βραχέων ἐπέστειλα ὑμῖν. 23 γινώσκετε τὸν ἀδελφὸν ἡμῶν Τιμόθεον ἀπολελυμένον, μεθ' οὗ ἐὰν τάχιον ἔρχηται ὄψομαι ὑμᾶς. 24 ἀσπάσασθε πάντας τοὺς ἡγουμένους ὑμῶν καὶ πάντας τοὺς ἁγίους. ἀσπάζονται ὑμᾶς οἱ ἀπὸ τῆς Ἰταλίας. 25 ἡ χάρις μετὰ πάντων ὑμῶν. [SBLGNT]

King James Version

22 And I beseech you, brethren, suffer the word of exhortation: for I have written a letter unto you in few words. 23 Know ye that our brother Timothy is set at liberty; with whom, if he come shortly, I will see you. 24 Salute all them that have the rule over you, and all the saints. They of Italy salute you. 25 Grace be with you all. Amen.

New Rendition

22 And I urge you, brothers and sisters, to bear with my word of exhortation, for I have written you briefly in a letter. 23 Know that our brother Timothy has been set free, with whom, if he comes soon, I will see you. 24 Greet all your leaders and all the Saints. Those from Italy send you greeting. 25 May grace be with all of you. Amen.

Translation Notes and Comments

13:22 ***I beseech you, brethren / I urge you, brothers and sisters:*** For the use of the phrase "brothers and sisters," see Translation Notes for 3:1.

270. Vanhoye, *Letter to the Hebrews,* 233.
271. Cockerill, *Epistle to the Hebrews,* 719.

The verb παρακαλέω (*parakaleō*) means "to appeal to, urge, beseech"[272] and shows the urgency in the author's request.

suffer the word of exhortation / to bear with my word of exhortation: The verb ἀνέχω (*anechō*) means "to regard something with tolerance" and therefore "bear with, put up with"[273] and carries an apologetic tone. The reason the author feels to apologize is given in the next phrase.

The noun παράκλησις (*paraklēsis*), related to the verb above, denotes the act encouraging someone to take a course of action, thus, "encouragement, exhortation."[274] That the author identifies his work simply as "my word" should not be taken to mean he did not see it as containing solid doctrine. The same expression is found in Acts 13:16–41, yet the content there is definitely an explication of God's work among his people centering on the doctrine of the Lord's Resurrection coupled with an exhortation to not reject the message. The same is true here—the Epistle's center is doctrinal, and the author builds his exhortations upon that likely because the doctrine gives reason for and makes a requested action understandable and desirable.

for I have written a letter unto you in few words / for I have written you briefly in a letter: The phrase καὶ γάρ (*kai gar*), "for indeed," introduces the author's apology for making his readers "endure" what he has written. It is revealed in his use of the adjective βραχύς (*brachys*), which denotes something that is brief or short and of low quality.[275] In the present context, the word expresses the author's humility and concern and implies he could have written much more on the subject that would have been of greater value and liking.[276]

13:23 *Know ye that our brother Timothy is set at liberty / Know that our brother Timothy has been set free:* The challenge with this phrase centers on the word γινώσκω (*ginōskō*), "to know." The form can be construed in either the indicative or imperative mood. If it is the former, then the author

---

272. BDAG, 764–65.

273. BDAG, 78.

274. BDAG, 766.

275. BDAG, 183.

276. From our perspective, given the beauty of the Epistle's language, the careful development of its thoughts, and the power of its witness, how the author felt anyone would have to "endure" his words is beyond us. However, false humility on the part of the author does not fit the sobriety of his message, and therefore we must take his tacit apology as sincere. We can only wonder about his power of persuasion if he had had the time and means to fully develop his theses. His words seem to echo those of Nephi (2 Ne. 33:1) and Moroni (Ether 12:23–26), who also felt to apologize for being unable to fully and powerfully express their witness in writing.

is reminding his readers of something they already knew. If the latter, he is giving them new information. Because of the weight of context, we have taken the latter view for the Rendition.

The scriptures mention only one Timothy, the convert and companion of the Apostle Paul.[277] Though the name was common in the Greco-Roman world, it is likely this is the same person.

The verb ἀπολύω (*apolyō*) has a broad range of meaning, including "to depart" and "to be released."[278] The latter is likely at play here since the word's primary meaning is "to be set free."[279] In that case, it points to a former imprisonment of this leader, a circumstance not mentioned elsewhere in the New Testament.[280]

with whom, if he come shortly, I will see you / with whom, if he comes soon, I will see you: The verb ἔρχομαι (*erchomai*) means both "to go" and "to come,"[281] and either could be at play here. If it means the former, then it suggests that Timothy will go to the readers' location where the author will meet all of them. If it is the latter, then the author will wait for Timothy for a short time so they can travel together. This is the more logical sense, and we have used it in our Rendition, though the former idea cannot be ruled out.

13:24 ***Salute all them that have the rule over you / Greet all your leaders:*** The verb ἀσπάζομαι (*aspadzomai*) means "to greet another in hospitable recognition" and nuances a feeling of warmth.[282]

The verb ἡγέομαι (*hēgeomai*), "to lead," found here in the form of a nominalized, plural participle, denotes being in a supervisory capacity,[283] hence "leaders." The author's use of πᾶς (*pas*), "all," suggests that the Christian organization had some size. Whether or not his words refer to a single large congregation or multiple smaller congregations cannot be determined.

Taking the words as they stand, they seem to suggest that the author's target audience is not among the leadership of the local congregation. The question then arises, who are they? An answer is that he has directed remarks to a particular subset of the community, that is, those tempted to

---

277. "Bible Dictionary," s.v. "Timothy."

278. Other meanings include "to dismiss, send, divorce, and forgive." Louw-Nida, §2.30.

279. BDAG, 117–18.

280. For discussion, see Ellingworth, *Epistle to the Hebrews,* 734.

281. BDAG, 393–94.

282. BDAG, 144; Louw-Nida, §§25.130; 33.30; 34.55.

283. BDAG, 434.

return to some form of Judaism. That he does not ask them to read his letter to the community at large seems to bear out this idea. On the other hand, he may be making a request and thus be saying, "'Greet all your leaders and all the Saints' in my behalf."[284] This, however, seems the weaker position.

and all the saints / and all the Saints: The adjective ἅγιος (*hagios*), "holy," carries the idea of that which is dedicated to God and, when used as a substantive, designates the followers of Christ and is thus translated as "Saint."[285] The importance of the term in the context of Hebrews is that it should act as a double reminder for the author's readers: first, to the cleansing and purifying power of the Savior of which at least some of the Epistle's readers have partaken (2:11; 9:11–14; 10:10, 14, 29; 13:12), and second, to the complete holiness that the readers are to pursue (12:14).[286]

They of Italy salute you / Those from Italy send you greeting: The noun Ἰταλία (*Italia*), "Italy," by the Christian era, denoted basically the modern geographical area.[287] The author's brief comment shows that he was currently among those to whom he referred, and they were aware of his sending the letter.

Though it may appear that this phrase could illuminate some broader context for the Epistle, such is not the case. The reason is that two completely opposite meanings can be construed from this sentence. Either it refers to "those in Italy," that is, resident Italians, or to "those from Italy," that is, expatriates. In the former case, the author is sending greetings from Church members residing in Italy, which would suggest he is in Italy and sending the Epistle outside that area. In the latter case, he is sending greetings from expatriate Italians to members who could be living anywhere in the Greco-Roman area but likely in Italy, because they would have known those to whom the author referred.[288] The source of this ambiguity stems from the preposition ἀπό (*apo*), which usually meant "of" but during the Koine period was in the process of absorbing ἐκ (*ek*), "out of, from."[289] Some fairly early manuscripts (fifth and sixth century) have a subscription stating the Epistle was written from Italy. This subscription shows that at least some early Christians interpreted the phrase to mean these members were currently within Italy. However, the gloss is

---

284. Cockerill, *Epistle to the Hebrews,* 721.
285. BDAG, 10–11.
286. Cockerill, *Epistle to the Hebrews,* 721.
287. *Oxford Classical Dictionary,* 773.
288. Lane, *Hebrews 9–13,* 571.
289. Lane, *Hebrews 9–13,* 567 note i.

an addition to the text that likely represents some scribe's best guess of the Epistle's origin.[290] The only other place in the New Testament that has a parallel phrase is Acts 18:2, where the context is clear that ἀπό (*apo*) means "from," not "in."[291] This may be the most natural way of reading 13:24 as well, but Acts was written by Luke and not our author, and their understandings of the preposition may have varied. What is clear and significant is, however, that this reference "shows that the circle in which Hebrews originated included Christians who lived outside of Palestine in the Greco-Roman world."[292]

13:25 *Grace be with you all. Amen / May grace be with all of you. Amen:* The noun χάρις (*charis*), "grace," in this context, denotes the peace and power that come from God and Christ. The sentence constitutes a prayer and follows the common formula used by Paul in his Epistles (compare Rom. 16:24; 2 Cor. 13:14; 2 Thes. 3:18; and Titus 3:15). In the context of Hebrews, however, the prayer points to the result of the supernal act of Christ through which sin can be purged and peace, holiness, and union with the divine achieved (2:17–18; 4:14–16; 10:19–25; 12:15; 13:12).

Analysis and Summary

By calling his Epistle an "exhortation" (παράκλησις, *paraklēsis*), given both the letter's themes and development, the author appropriately identifies what he has produced (13:22). His work consists of appeals from God, Christ, and a host of Old Testament prophets as well as the recently past and current leaders of the Church to endure in faith and trust in the care of the Divine. The author's appeal (παρακαλέω, *parakaleō*) that his readers pay careful attention to what he has written together with his self-effacing suggestion that his work could have been better, as one scholar noted, likely "were a polite way of showing deference, and thus gaining his [readers'] compliance." Further, this scholar notes, "even the claim of brevity, which might seem inappropriate for a book as long as Hebrews, is meant to reinforce the sermon's message by implying [correctly] that there was much more that could have been said in its defense."[293] Thus, from

290. Metzger, *Textual Commentary,* 607.

291. The scripture refers to Aquila and his wife Priscilla, who were currently in Corinth; they had sailed "from Italy" (ἀπο τῆς Ἰταλίας, *apo tēs Italias*) when Emperor Claudius issued a decree expelling Jews from Rome.

292. Koester, *Hebrews,* 581.

293. Cockerill, *Epistle to the Hebrews,* 720.

beginning to end, this masterwork is an exhortation. Nonetheless, it is an exhortation built on a solid doctrinal foundation that centers on the teachings, mission, Atonement, Resurrection, and enthronement of the Savior, Jesus Christ. By placing his petitions on this foundation, the author gives them reason and meaning, thus making them both relevant and appealing.

At this point (13:23), the author shares some good news with his readers. The well-known and respected leader Timothy has been released from prison. Though the text is ambiguous, it appears the author is going to wait to see if Timothy joins him, at which time they will travel together to meet with these Saints. The text does make two points clear. First, the author is going to travel to the readers' location, regardless of what Timothy does. Second, the author use of the adverb τάχιον (*tachion*), "shortly," shows that he plans his visit for the near future, thus his request for the prayer in 13:19 that nothing impede him.[294]

He closes asking his readers to give his best regards to both the leadership and membership of the congregation (13:24). He has asked his readers to give due respect to their current leaders (13:17), showing the author's own appreciation and respect for these men and women. Note the author's words suggest his Epistle was not directed to the Saints in the area as a whole but to a specific group within the community of believers. He is likely addressing specific problems meant for a particular group of people.[295] In a remarkable way, these "early Christian communities joined themselves together through a network of personal and written communication, even in circumstances that made such communication difficult."[296]

Having asked his readers to give his best to other members of the Christian community, the author notes others want to send their regards as well. These he identifies as "those from Italy." Whether or not his reference is to Saints living in Italy or those who once resided there, it shows the broad concern Christians as a whole had for one another, and that they were aware of each other's situations.

With a final prayer—a benediction that the all-sufficient power of Christ, expressed in the bequeathing of his grace, be upon his readers—the author closes a most magnificent and in-depth witness to the work, necessity, and power of the Father and the Son to whom glory be given forever.

---

294. Ellingworth, *Epistle to the Hebrews,* 735.

295. For discussion, see Cockerill, *Epistle to the Hebrews,* 721–22.

296. Johnson, *Hebrews,* 352.

Selected Bibliography

Anderson, Gary. *Sin: A History*. New Haven: Yale University Press, 2010.

Anderson, Richard Lloyd. *Guide to Acts and the Apostles' Letters*. Provo, Utah: FARMS reprint, 1999.

———. "Paul's Witness to the Early History of Jesus' Ministry." In *The Apostle Paul: His Life and His Testimony: The 23rd Annual Sidney B. Sperry Symposium*, 1–33. Salt Lake City: Deseret Book, 1994.

———. *Understanding Paul*. Salt Lake City: Deseret Book, 1983.

Andrus, Hyrum L. *Doctrinal Commentary on the Pearl of Great Price*. Rev. ed. Salt Lake City: Deseret Book, 1967.

———. *The Glory of God and Man's Relation to Deity*. Provo, Utah: Extension Publications, Brigham Young University, 1964.

———. *God, Man, and the Universe*. Salt Lake City: Bookcraft, 1968.

———. *Principles of Perfection*. Salt Lake City: Bookcraft, 1970.

Ashton, Marvin J. "Adversity and You." *Ensign* 10, no. 11 (November 1980): 54–60.

Attridge, Harold W. *The Epistle to the Hebrews: A Commentary on the Epistle to the Hebrews*. Philadelphia: Fortress Press, 1989.

———. "'Let Us Strive to Enter That Rest': The Logic of Hebrews 4:1–11." *Harvard Theological Review* 73, nos. 1–2 (1980): 279–88.

———. "The Uses of Antithesis in Hebrews 8–10." *Harvard Theological Review* 79, nos. 1–3 (1986): 1–9.

Aune, David E. *Revelation*. Vol. 52 of Word Biblical Commentary. Edited by Bruce M. Metzger. 3 vols. Dallas: Word Book, 1997–98.

Austin, Michael. *Re-reading Job: Understanding the Ancient World's Greatest Poet*. Salt Lake City: Greg Kofford Books, 2014.

Bacher, Wilhelm, and Jacob Zallel Lauterbach. "Talmud Hermeneutics." In *Jewish Encyclopedia*. Accessed March 11, 2016. http://www.jewishencyclopedia.com/articles/14215-talmud-hermeneutics.

Bailey, Arthur A. "A Message of Judgment from the Olivet Sermon." In *The Lord of the Gospels: The 1990 Sperry Symposium on the New Testament*, edited by Bruce A. Van Orden and Brent L. Top, 8–22. Salt Lake City: Deseret Book, 1991.

Barnard, Jody A. "Anti-Jewish Interpretations of Hebrews: Some Neglected Factors." *Melilah: Manchester Journal of Jewish Studies* 11 (2014): 25–48.

Barnhart, D. "The Life of No Retreat: An Exegetical Study of Hebrews 6:1–12." *Central Biblical Quarterly* 19 (1976): 16–31.

Barrett, C. K. "The Eschatology of the Epistles to the Hebrews." In *The Background to the New Testament and its Eschatology,* edited by W. D. Davis and D. Daube, 363–92. Cambridge: Cambridge University Press, 1956.

Bauckham, Richard. *Jesus and the Eyewitnesses: The Gospels as Eyewitness Testimony.* Grand Rapids, Mich.: Wm. B. Eerdmans, 2017.

Beale, G. K. *The Temple and the Church's Mission: A Biblical Theology of the Dwelling Place of God.* Downers Grove, Ill.: InterVarsity Press, 2004.

Beavis, Mary Ann, and HyeRan Kim-Cragg. *Hebrews.* Edited by Linda Maloney. Vol. 54 of Wisdom Commentary. Edited by Barbara E. Reid. Collegeville, Minn.: Liturgical Press, 2015.

Bednar, David A. "The Hearts of the Children Shall Turn." *Ensign* 41, no. 11 (November 2011): 24–27.

Benson, Ezra Taft. "I Testify." *Ensign* 18, no. 11 (November 1988): 86–87.

Berardino, Angelo Di, ed. *Encyclopedia of the Early Church.* Translated by Adrian Walford. 2 vols. Oxford: Oxford University Press, 1992.

Berrett, William E. *Blessed Are They Who Come unto Me.* Provo, Utah: Ensign Publishing, 1979.

Bonfiglio, Ryan. "Priests and Priesthood in the Hebrew Bible." *Oxford Biblical Studies Online.* Accessed February 8, 2016. http://www.oxfordbiblicalstudies.com/resource/priests.xhtml.

Bousset, Wilhelm. *Kyrios Christos: A History of the Belief in Christ from the Beginnings of Christianity to Irenaeus.* Translated by John E. Steely. Nashville: Abingdon Press, 1970.

Boyarin, Daniel. "Beyond Judaism: Meṭaṭron and the Divine Polymorphy of Ancient Judaism." *Journal for the Study of Judaism* 41, no. 3 (2010): 323–65.

———. "Rethinking Jewish Christianity: An Argument for Dismantling a Dubious Category." *Jewish Quarterly Review* 99, no. 1 (Winter 2009): 7–36.

Brady, Cora. "The World to Come in the Epistle to the Hebrews." *Worship* 39 (1965): 329–39.

Broderick, Carlfred. *One Flesh, One Heart: Putting Celestial Love into Your Temple Marriage.* Salt Lake City: Deseret Book, 1986.

Brough, Monte J. "Between Two Gardens: The Law of Sacrifice." In *Speeches: Brigham Young University 1995–96,* 157–65. Provo, Utah: Brigham Young University Press, 1996.

Brown, S. Kent. "The Dead Sea Scrolls: A Mormon Perspective." *BYU Studies* 23, no. 1 (Winter 1983): 49–66.

Bruce, F. F. *The Epistle to the Hebrews.* Rev. ed. The New International Commentary on the New Testament. Grand Rapids, Mich.: William B. Eerdmans, 1990.

———. "The Kerygma of Hebrews." *Interpretation* 23, no. 1 (1969): 3–19.

Buchanan, George Wesley. *To the Hebrews.* Vol. 36 of the Anchor Bible. New York: Doubleday, 1972.

Brumm, Ursula. *American Thought and Religious Typology.* Translated by John Hoaglund. New Brunswick, N.J.: Rutgers University Press, 1970.

Caird, G. B. *A Commentary on the Revelation of St. John the Divine*. Peabody, Mass.: Hendrickson Publishers, 1966.

———. "Son by Appointment." In *The New Testament Age: Essays in Honor of Bo Reicke,* edited by William C. Weinrich, 1:73–81. 2 vols. Macon, Ga.: Mercer University Press, 1984.

Callister, Tad R. *The Infinite Atonement.* Salt Lake City: Deseret Book, 2009.

Cannon, George Q. *Gospel Truth: Discourse and Writings of George Q. Cannon.* Edited by Jerreld L. Newquist. Salt Lake City: Deseret Book, 1987.

Carlston, C. E. "The Things That Defile (Mark VII. 14) and the Law in Matthew and Mark." *New Testament Studies* 15, no. 1 (1968–69): 75–96.

Casey, J. M. "Christian Assembly in Hebrews: A Fantasy Island?" *Theology Digest* 30 (1982): 323–34.

Caspi, Mishael, and John T. Greene. *Unbinding the Binding of Isaac.* Lanham, Md.: University Press of America, 2007.

Charlesworth, James H. *The Pesharim and Qumran History: Chaos or Consensus?* Grand Rapids, Mich.: Wm. B. Eerdmans, 2002.

Choi, Sungho. *The Messianic Kingship of Jesus: A Study of Christology and Redemptive History in Matthew's Gospel with Special Reference to the Royal Enthronement Psalms.* Eugene, Ore.: Wipf and Stock, 2011.

Christofferson, D. Todd. "That They May Be One in Us." *Ensign* 32, no. 11 (November 2002): 71–73.

Chrysostom, John. *Discourses against Judaizing Christians.* Translated by Paul W. Harkins. Vol. 68 of Fathers of the Church, edited by Hermigild Dressler, Robert P. Russell, William R. Tongue, Thomas P. Halton, and M. Josephine Brennan. Washington, D.C.: Catholic University of America Press, 1979.

Clark, J. Reuben, Jr. *On the Way to Immortality and Eternal Life.* Salt Lake City: Deseret Book, 1950.

Clines, D. J. A. "The Image of God in Man." *Tyndale Bulletin* 19 (1968): 53–103.

Coats, G. W. *Rebellion in the Wilderness: The Murmuring Motif in the Wilderness Traditions of the Old Testament.* Nashville: Abingdon Press, 1968.

Cockerill, Gareth Lee. "The Better Resurrection (Heb. 11:35): A Key to the Structure and Rhetorical Purpose of Hebrews 11." *Tyndale Bulletin* 51, no. 2 (2000): 215–34.

———. *The Epistle to the Hebrew.* The New International Commentary on the New Testament. Grand Rapids, Mich.: Wm. B. Eerdmans, 2012.

———. "Hebrews 1:6: Source and Significance." *Bulletin for Biblical Research* 9 (1999): 51–64.

Cody, Aelred. *Heavenly Sanctuary and Liturgy in the Epistle to the Hebrews: The Achievement of Salvation in the Epistle's Perspectives.* St. Meinrad, Ind.: Grail Publications, 1960.

Conklin, Blane. *Oath Formulas in Biblical Hebrew.* Warsaw, Ind.: Eisenbrauns, 2011.

Coogan, Michael D. *A Brief Introduction to the Old Testament.* Oxford: Oxford University Press, 2009.

Cook, Gene R. "Receiving Divine Assistance through the Grace of the Lord." *Ensign* 23, no. 5 (May 1993): 79–81.

Compton, Jared M. "The Origin of Σῶμα in Heb. 10:5: Another Look at a Recent Proposal." *Trinity Journal* 32, no. 1 (Spring 2011): 19–29.

Cornish, J. Devan. "Learning How the Atonement Can Change You." *Ensign* 32, no. 4 (April 2002): 20–23.

Croy, N. C. *Endurance in Suffering: Hebrews 12:1–13 in Its Rhetorical, Religious, and Philosophical Context*. Cambridge: Cambridge University Press, 1998.

Cullimore, James A. "The Importance of a Personal Testimony." *Ensign* 2, no. 7 (July 1972): 56–58.

Dahl, Larry E., and Charles D. Tate Jr., eds. *The Lectures on Faith: In Historical Perspective*. Provo, Utah: Religious Studies Center, Brigham Young University, 1990.

Dahl, N. A. "A New and Living Way: The Approach to God according to Hebrews 10:19–25." *Interpretation* 5, no. 4 (1951): 401–12.

Daley, Brian E. *The Hope of the Early Church: A Handbook of Patristic Eschatology*. New York: Cambridge University Press, 1991.

Dana, H. E. *Jewish Christianity: An Expository Survey of Acts I to XII, James, I and II Peter, Jude, and Hebrews*. New Orleans: Bible Institute Memorial Press, 1937.

Davidson, Karen Lynn, David J. Whittaker, Mark R. Ashurst-McGee, and Richard L. Jensen, eds. *Histories, Volume 1: Joseph Smith Histories, 1832–1844*. Vol. 1 of the Histories series of The Joseph Smith Papers. Edited by Dean C. Jessee, Ronald K. Esplin, and Richard Lyman Bushman. Salt Lake City: Church Historian's Press, 2012.

Davidson, Richard M. "Christ's Entry 'Within the Veil' in Hebrews 6:19–20: The Old Testament Background." *Andrews University Seminary Studies* 39, no. 2 (Autumn 2001): 175–90.

Davis, John J. *Moses and the Gods of Egypt: Studies in Exodus*. Grand Rapids, Mich.: Baker Book House, 1986.

Davis, Philip A., Jr. *The Place of Paideia in Hebrews' Moral Thought*. Tübingen: Mohr Siebeck, 2018.

Desilva, David A. "Hebrews 6:4–8: A Socio-rhetorical Investigation (Part 1)." *Tyndale Bulletin* 50, no. 1 (1999): 33–57.

———. *Perseverance in Gratitude: A Socio-rhetorical Commentary on the Epistle "to the Hebrews."* Grand Rapids, Mich.: Wm. B. Eerdmans, 2000.

Dew, Sheri. *Amazed by Grace*. Salt Lake City: Deseret Book, 2015.

Dillon, John M. *The Middle Platonists, 80 B.C. to A.D. 220*. Ithaca, N.Y.: Cornell University Press, 1977.

Draper, Richard D. "Babylon in Zion: The LDS Concept of Zion as a Cause for Mormon-Gentile Conflict, 1846–1857." Master's thesis, Arizona State University, 1974.

———. "Light, Truth, and Grace: Three Themes of Salvation (D&C 93)." In *Sperry Symposium Classics: The Doctrine and Covenants,* edited by Craig K. Manscill, 234–47. Provo, Utah: Religious Studies Center, Brigham Young University, 2004.

———, and Michael D. Rhodes. *The First Epistle of Paul to the Corinthians*. Brigham Young University New Testament Commentary Series. Provo, Utah: BYU Studies, 2015.

Dumbrell, William J. *Covenant and Creation: A Theology of the Old Testament Covenants*. 2d ed. Milton Keynes, Eng.: Paternoster Publishing, 2002.

Dunnill, John. *Covenant and Sacrifice in the Letter to the Hebrews.* Vol. 75 of Society for New Testament Studies Monograph Series. New York: Cambridge University Press, 1992.

Durham, John I. "שָׁלוֹם and the Presence of God." In *Proclamation and Presence: Old Testament Essays in Honour of Gwynne Henton Davies,* edited by John I. Durham and J. R. Porter, 272–93. Richmond, Va.: John Knox Press, 1970.

Du Toit, Andries. "Ta pros ton theon in Romans and Hebrews: Towards Understanding an Enigmatic Phrase." *Zeitschrift für die Neutestamentliche Wissenschaft* 101, no. 2 (2010): 241–51.

Easter, Matthew C. *Faith and the Faithfulness of Jesus in Hebrews.* The Society for New Testament Studies Monograph Series 160. Cambridge: Cambridge University Press, 2014.

Ehat, Andrew F., and Lyndon W. Cook. *The Words of Joseph Smith: The Contemporary Accounts of the Nauvoo Discourses of the Prophet Joseph.* Provo, Utah: Religious Studies Center, Brigham Young University, 1980.

Eilberg-Schwartz, Howard. "Myth, Inference, and the Relativism of Reason: An Argument from the History of Judaism." In *Myth and Philosophy,* edited by Frank E. Reynolds and David Tracy, 247–85. Albany: State University of New York Press, 1990.

Eisenbaum, Pamela. "Hebrews, Supersessionism and Jewish-Christian Relations." Presentation at the SBL Annual Meeting, Philadelphia, 2005. Accessed April 23, 2017. https://www.hebrews.unibas.ch/documents/2005Eisenbaum.pdf.

Ellingworth, Paul. *The Epistle to the Hebrews: A Commentary on the Greek Text.* The New International Greek Testament Commentary. Grand Rapids, Mich.: Wm. B. Eerdmans, 1993.

Ellis, E. Earle. *The Old Testament in Early Christianity.* Tübingen: J. C. B. Mohr, 1991.

Emmrich, Martin. "*Pneuma* in Hebrews: Prophet and Interpreter." *Westminster Theological Journal* 64 (2002): 55–71.

Erlandsson, Seth. "The Wrath of God." *Tyndale Bulletin* 23 (1972): 111–16.

Fairhurst, A. M. "Hellenistic Influence in the Epistle to the Hebrews." *Tyndale Bulletin* 7–8 (1961): 17–27.

Farley, Brent S. "The Baptism and Temptations of Jesus." In *Studies in Scripture, Volume 5: The Gospels,* edited by Kent P. Jackson and Robert L. Millet, 175–87. Salt Lake City: Deseret Book, 1986.

Faulconer, James E. *Romans 1: Notes and Reflections.* Provo, Utah: Foundation for Ancient Research and Mormon Studies at Brigham Young University, 1999.

Faust, James E. *Reach Up for the Light.* Salt Lake City: Deseret Book, 1990.

Fitzmyer, Joseph A. *First Corinthians: A New Translation with Introduction and Commentary.* Vol. 32 of Anchor Yale Bible. New Haven, Conn.: Yale University Press, 2008.

———. Review of *The Melchizedek Tradition: A Critical Examination of the Sources to the Fifth Century A.D. and in the Epistle to the Hebrews,* by Fred L. Horton Jr. *Catholic Biblical Quarterly* 39, no. 3 (July 1977): 436–38.

———. "'Now This Melchizedek . . .' (Heb 7,1)." *Catholic Biblical Quarterly* 25 (July 1963): 305–21.

Frankowski, Janusz. "Early Christian Hymns Recorded in the New Testament: A Reconsideration of the Question in Light of Hebrews 1:3." *Biblische Zeitschrift* 27 (1983): 183–94.

Gallos, Erhard. "Κατάπαυς and Σαββατισμός in Hebrews 4." *Andrews University Seminary Studies* 50 (Spring 2012): 67–68.

Garrett, H. Dean. "The Three Most Abominable Sins." In *The Book of Mormon: Alma, the Testimony of the Word,* edited by Monte S. Nyman and Charles D. Tate Jr., 157–71. Provo, Utah: Religious Studies Center, Brigham Young University, 1992.

Gordon, Robert P. *Hebrews.* 2d ed. Readings: A New Biblical Commentary, edited by John Jarick. Sheffield, Eng.: Sheffield Phoenix Press, 2008.

Goulder, Michael. "Hebrews and the Ebionites." *New Testament Studies* 49, no. 3 (2003): 393–406.

Gray, Patrick. "Brotherly Love and the High Priest Christology of Hebrews." *Journal of Biblical Literature* 122, no. 2 (Summer 2003): 335–51.

Greer, Rowan A. "The Jesus of Hebrews and the Christ of Chalcedon." In *Reading the Epistle to the Hebrews: A Resource for Students,* edited by Eric F. Mason and Kevin B. McCruden, 231–49. Atlanta: Society of Biblical Literature, 2011.

Gower, Ralph. *The New Manners and Customs of Bible Times.* Chicago: Moody Press, 1987.

Guthrie, D., and J. A. Motyer, eds. *The New Bible Commentary, Revised.* Grand Rapids, Mich.: Wm. B. Eerdmans, 1970.

Guthrie, George H. "Hebrews." In *Commentary on the New Testament's Use of the Old Testament,* edited by D. A. Carson and G. K. Beale, 919–56. Grand Rapids, Mich.: Baker Academic, 2007.

———. *The Structure of Hebrews: A Text-Linguistic Analysis.* Reprint, Grand Rapids Mich.: Baker Book, 1998.

Haight, David B. "The Keys of the Kingdom." *Ensign* 10, no. 11 (November 1980): 73–75.

———. *A Light unto the World.* Salt Lake City: Deseret Book, 1997.

Hallett, Judith P. *Fathers and Daughters in Roman Society: Women and the Elite Family.* Princeton: Princeton University Press, 1984.

Hamerton-Kelly, R. G. *Pre-existence, Wisdom, and the Son of Man: A Study of the Idea of Pre-existence in the New Testament.* Vol. 21 of the Society for New Testament Studies Monograph Series. Cambridge: Cambridge University Press, 1983.

Harris, J. Rendel. *The Origin of the Prologue to St. John's Gospel.* Cambridge: Cambridge University Press, 1917.

Harris, Murray J. "The Translation and Significance of ὁ θεός in Hebrews 1:8–9." *Tyndall Bulletin* 36 (1985): 129–62.

Heath, David M. "Chiastic Structures in Hebrews: With a Focus on 1:7–14 and 12:26–29." *Neotestamentica* 46, no. 1 (2012): 61–82.

Helyer, Larry R. "The *Prōtotokos* Title in Hebrews." *Studies in Biblical Theology* 6 (1976): 3–28.

Hezser, Catherine. *Jewish Literacy in Roman Palestine.* Tübingen: Mohr Siebeck, 2001.

Hilgert, Earle. *The Ship and Related Symbols in the New Testament.* Assen, Neth.: Royal Van Gorcum, 1962.

Hill, Craig Allen. "The Use of Perfection Language in Hebrews 5:14 and 6:1 and the Contextual Interpretation of 5:11–6:3." *Journal of the Evangelical Theological Seminary* 57, no. 4 (2014): 727–42.

Hinckley, Gordon B. "God Grant Us Faith." *Ensign* 13, no. 11 (November 1983): 51–53.

Holzapfel, Richard Neitzel, and Thomas A. Wayment. *Making Sense of the New Testament: Timely Insights and Timeless Messages.* Salt Lake City: Deseret Book, 2010.

Horbury, William. "The Aaronic Priesthood in the Epistle to the Hebrews." *Journal for the Study of the New Testament* 19 (1983): 43–71.

Horgan, Maurya P. *Pesharim: Qumran Interpretations of Biblical Books.* Catholic Biblical Quarterly Monograph Series 8. Washington, D.C.: Catholic Biblical Association of America, 1979.

Hoskisson, Paul Y. "Looking beyond the Mark." In *A Witness of the Restoration: Essays in Honor of Robert J. Matthews,* edited by Kent P. Jackson and Andrew C. Skinner, 149–64. Provo, Utah: Religious Studies Center, Brigham Young University, 2007.

Hovorka, Janet. "Sarah and Hagar: Ancient Women of the Abrahamic Covenant." In *Astronomy, Papyrus, and Covenant,* edited by John Gee and Brian M. Hauglid, 147–66. Provo, Utah: Foundation for Ancient Research and Mormon Studies, Brigham Young University, 2005.

Hughes, Graham. *Hebrews and Hermeneutics: The Epistle of Hebrews as a New Testament Example of Biblical Interpretation.* Vol. 36 of Society for New Testament Studies Manuscript Series, edited by Paul Trebilco. Cambridge: Cambridge University Press, 1979.

———. "The Blood of Jesus and His Heavenly Priesthood in Hebrews: Part III, The Meaning of 'The True Tent' and 'The Greater and More Perfect Tent.'" *Bibliotheca Sacra* 130 (October 1973): 305–14.

———. "Hebrews 6:4–6 and the Peril of Apostasy." *Westminster Theological Journal* 35, no. 2 (1973): 137–55.

Hunter, Howard W. "Faith—the First Step." *Ensign* 5, no. 5 (May 1975): 37–39.

———. "The Temptations of Christ." *Ensign* 6, no. 11 (November 1976): 17–19.

———. "To Know God." *Ensign* 4, no. 11 (November 1974): 96–97.

Hurst, L. D. *The Epistle to the Hebrews: Its Background of Thought.* Cambridge: Cambridge University Press, 2005.

Hurst, Lincoln D. "Eschatology and 'Platonism' in the Epistle to the Hebrews." In *Society of Biblical Literature Seminar Papers,* edited by Kent H. Richards, 41–74. Atlanta: Scholars Press, 1984.

Hurtado, Larry W. *Lord Jesus Christ: Devotion to Jesus in Earliest Christianity.* Grand Rapids, Mich.: Wm. B. Eerdmans, 2003.

Jackson, Kent P. *Joseph Smith's Commentary on the Bible.* Salt Lake City: Deseret Book, 1994.

Janowitz, Naomi, and Andrew J. Lazarus. "Rabbinic Methods of Inference and the Rationality Debate." *Journal of Religion* 72, no. 4 (October 1992): 491–511.

Jastrow, Marcus, comp. *A Dictionary of the Targumim, the Talmud Babli, and Yerushalmi, and the Midrashic Literature.* 2 vols. 1943; New York: Judaica Press, 2004.

Jensen, Robert Scott, Richard E. Turley Jr., and Riley M. Lorimer, eds., *Revelations and Translations, Volume 2: Published Revelations*. The Joseph Smith Papers. Salt Lake City: Church Historian's Press, 2011.

Jipp, Joshua W. "The Son's Entrance into the Heavenly World: The Soteriological Necessity of the Scriptural Catena in Hebrews 1.5–14." *New Testament Studies* 56, no. 4 (October 2010): 557–75.

Johnson, Luke Timothy. *Hebrews: A Commentary*. Louisville: Westminster John Knox Press, 2006.

Johnsson, William G. "The Cultus of Hebrews in Twentieth-Century Scholarship." *Expository Times* 89, no. 4 (1978): 104–8.

———. "Defilement/Purification in Hebrews 9:23." In *Issues in the Book of Hebrews*, edited by Frank B. Holbrook, 79–103. Vol. 4 of Daniel and Revelation Committee Series. Silver Springs, Md.: Biblical Research Institute, 1989.

Johnston, George. "Οἰκουμένη and κόσμος in the New Testament." *New Testament Studies* 10, no. 3 (1964): 352–54.

Joslin, Barry. *Hebrews, Christ, and the Law: The Theology of the Mosaic Law in Hebrews 7:1–10:18*. Milton Keynes, Eng.: Paternoster Publishing, 2008.

Jukes, Andrew. *The Law of the Offerings*. Grand Rapids, Mich.: Kregel Publications, 1976.

Kaiser, Walter C., Jr., "The Abolition of the Old Order and Establishment of the New: Psalm 40:6–8 and Hebrews 10:5–10." In *Tradition and Testament: Essays in Honor of Charles Lee Feinberg*, edited by John S. Feinberg and Paul D. Feinberg, 19–37. Chicago: Moody Press, 1981.

———. "The Old Promise and the New Covenant: Jeremiah 31:31–34." *Journal of the Evangelical Theological Society* 15, no. 1 (Winter 1972): 11–23.

Keener, Craig S. *The Historical Jesus of the Gospels*. Grand Rapids, Mich.: Wm. B. Eerdmans, 2010.

Kelly, J. N. D. *Early Christian Creeds*. 3d ed. London: Bloomsbury Academic, 2006.

Kimball, Spencer W. *The Miracle of Forgiveness*. Salt Lake City: Bookcraft, 1969.

———. *The Teachings of Spencer W. Kimball*. Edited by Edward L. Kimball. Salt Lake City: Deseret Book, 1982.

Kistemaker, Simon J. *The Psalm Citations in the Epistle to the Hebrews*. 1961; Eugene, Ore.: Wipf and Stock, 2010.

Kline, Meredith G. "Canon and Covenant." *Westminster Theological Journal* 32, no. 1 (1969): 49–67. Accessed March 3, 2016. https://meredithkline.com/files/articles/Canon-and-Covenant-1.pdf.

Koester, Craig R. "Conversion, Persecution, and Malaise: Life in the Community for Which Hebrews was Written." *Hervormde Teologiese Studies* 61, nos. 1–2 (2009): 231–51.

———. *Hebrews*. Vol. 36 of the Anchor Yale Bible Commentary Series. New Haven, Conn.: Yale University Press, 2001.

Koester, Helmut. "'Outside the Camp': Hebrews 13.9–14." *Harvard Theological Review* 55, no. 4 (1962): 299–315.

Komatsu, Adney Y. "Looking to the Savior." *Ensign* 17, no. 5 (May 1987): 78–79.

Kurianal, James. *Jesus Our High Priest: Ps 110,4 as the Substructure of Heb 5,1–7,28.* Frankfurt am Main: Peter Lang, 2000.

Laansma, Jon. *"I Will Give You Rest": The Rest Motif in the New Testament with Special Reference to Mt 11 and Heb 3–4.* Tübingen: Mohr Siebeck, 1997.

Ladd, George Eldon. *The Pattern of New Testament Truth.* Grand Rapids, Mich.: Wm. B. Eerdmans, 1968.

Lane, Janet. "The Redemption of Abraham." In *Astronomy, Papyrus, and Covenant,* edited by John Gee and Brian M. Hauglid, 167–74. Provo, Utah: Foundation for Ancient Research and Mormon Studies, 2005.

Lane, William L. *Hebrews 1–8.* Vol. 47a of Word Biblical Commentary, edited by David A. Hubbard and Glenn W. Barker. Dallas: Word Book Publishers, 1991.

———. *Hebrews 9–13.* Vol. 47b of Word Biblical Commentary, edited by David A. Hubbard and Glenn W. Barker. Dallas: Word Book Publishers, 1991.

Largey, Dennis L., ed. *Book of Mormon Reference Companion.* Salt Lake City: Deseret Book, 2003.

———. and Larry H. Dahl. *Doctrine and Covenants Reference Companion.* Salt Lake City: Deseret Book, 2012.

Law, Timothy Michael. *When God Spoke Greek.* New York: Oxford University Press, 2013.

Lee, E. Kenneth. "Words Denoting 'Pattern' in the New Testament." *New Testament Studies* 8, no. 2 (1962): 166–73.

Lee, John A. L. "Hebrews 5:14 and ΕΞΙΣ: A History of Misunderstanding." *Novum Testamentum* 39, no. 2 (1997): 151–76.

Lewis, C. S. *Mere Christianity: An Anniversary Edition of the Three Books The Case for Christianity, Christian Behavior, and Beyond Personality.* New York: Macmillan, 1981.

Long, D. Stephen. "Sources as Canons: The Question of Canonical Coherence." *Modern Theology* 28, no. 2 (April 2012): 229–51.

Louw, Johannes P., and Eugene A. Nida, eds., *Greek-English Lexicon of the New Testament Based on Semantic Domains.* 2 vols. New York: United Bible Society, 1989.

Ludlow, Daniel H. *A Companion to Your Study of the New Testament.* Salt Lake City: Deseret Book, 1982.

———, ed. *The Encyclopedia of Mormonism.* 4 vols. New York: Macmillan, 1992.

Mackie, Scott D. *Eschatology and Exhortation in the Epistle to the Hebrews.* Tübingen: Mohr Siebeck Press, 2007.

MacRae, George W. "Heavenly Temple and Eschatology in the Letter to the Hebrews." *Semeia* 12 (1978): 179–99.

Madsen, Ann Nicholls. "Melchizedek, the Man and the Tradition." Master's thesis, Brigham Young University, 1975.

Madsen, Truman G. *Eternal Man.* Salt Lake City: Deseret Book, 1966.

———. *The Temple: Where Heaven and Earth Meet.* Salt Lake City: Deseret Book, 2008.

Mare, W. Harold. *The Archaeology of the Jerusalem Area*. Grand Rapids, Mich.: Baker Book House, 1987.

Marsh, W. Jeffrey. *A Child Is Born*. Springville, Utah: Cedar Fort, 2008.

———. *His Final Hours*. Salt Lake City: Deseret Book, 2000.

———. "The Living Reality of the Savior's Mercy." In *Jesus Christ: Son of God, Savior*, edited by Paul H. Peterson, Gary L. Hatch, and Laura D. Card, 152–75. Provo, Utah: Religious Studies Center, Brigham Young University, 2002.

Marshall, I. Howard. "The Problem of Apostasy in New Testament Theology." *Perspectives in Religious Studies* 14, no. 4 (1987): 65–80.

Mason, Eric F. "Cosmology, Messianism, and Melchizedek: Apocalyptic Jewish Traditions and Hebrews." In *Reading the Epistle to the Hebrews: A Resource for Students*, edited by Eric F. Mason and Kevin B. McCruden, 53–77. Atlanta: Society of Biblical Literature, 2011.

Matthews, Robert J. "Great Faith Obtained Only through Personal Sacrifice." In *Lectures on Faith in Historical Perspective*, edited by Charles D. Tate and Larry E. Dahl, 241–62. Salt Lake City: Deseret Book, 1990.

———. "I Have a Question." *Ensign* 17, no. 8 (August 1987): 21.

Maxwell, Neal A. "The New Testament—a Matchless Portrait of the Savior." *Ensign* 16, no. 12 (December 1986): 20–27.

———. "Our Acceptance of Christ." *Ensign* 14, no. 6 (June 1984): 69–74.

———. *We Talk of Christ, We Rejoice in Christ*. Salt Lake City: Deseret Book, 1984.

MacLeod, David J. "The Cleansing of the True Tabernacle." *Bibliotheca Sacra* 152 (January–March 1995): 60–71.

McConkie, Bruce R. *Mormon Doctrine*. 2d ed. Salt Lake City: Bookcraft, 1966.

———. *A New Witness for the Articles of Faith*. Salt Lake City: Deseret Book, 1985.

———. *The Promised Messiah: The First Coming of Christ*. Salt Lake City: Deseret Book, 1978.

McConkie, Joseph Fielding "Jesus Christ, Symbolism, and Salvation." In *Studies in Scripture Volume 6: Acts through Revelation*, edited by Robert L. Millet, 192–206. Salt Lake City: Deseret Book, 1987.

———. *Witnesses of the Birth of Christ*. Salt Lake City: Bookcraft, 1998.

McConkie, Oscar W., Jr. *Angels*. Salt Lake City: Deseret Book, 1975.

McCruden, Kevin B. "The Concept of Perfection in the Epistle to the Hebrews." In *Reading the Epistle to the Hebrews: A Resource for Students*, edited by Eric F. Mason and Kevin B. McCruden, 209–29. Atlanta: Society of Biblical Literature, 2011.

———. "The Eloquent Blood of Jesus: The Neglected Theme of the Fidelity of Jesus in Hebrews 12:24." *Catholic Biblical Quarterly* 75, no. 3 (July 2013): 504–20.

McKay, David O. *Gospel Ideals: Selections from the Discourses of David O. McKay* (Salt Lake City: Improvement Era, 1953.

McNamara, Martin. "Melchizedek: Genesis 14, 17–20 in the Targums, in Rabbinic and Early Christian Literature." *Biblica* 81, no. 1 (2000): 1–31.

Meier, John P. "Symmetry and Theology in the Old Testament Citations of Heb 1,5–14," *Biblica* 66, no. 4 (1985): 504–33.

Merriam Webster's Dictionary of Synonyms. Springfield, Md.: Merriam-Webster, 1984.
Metzger, Bruce M. *A Textual Commentary on the Greek New Testament*. 2d ed., 9th printing. Stuttgart, Ger.: Deutsche Bibelgesellschaft/German Bible Society, 2012.
Millet, Robert L. "The Holy Order of God." In *The Book of Mormon: Alma, the Testimony of the Word,* edited by Monte S. Nyman and Charles D. Tate Jr., 61–88. Provo, Utah: Religious Studies Center, Brigham Young University, 1992.
———. *Grace Works*. Salt Lake City: Deseret Book, 2003.
———. *Jesus Christ, the Only Sure Foundation*. Salt Lake City: Bookcraft, 1999.
———. *Selected Writings of Robert L. Millet*. Gospel Scholars Series. Salt Lake City: Deseret Book, 2000.
Mitchell, Alan C. *Hebrews*. Collegeville, Minn.: Liturgical Press, 2007.
Moffatt, James A. *A Critical and Exegetical Commentary on the Epistle to the Hebrews*. New York: Charles Scribner's Sons, 1924.
Moffitt, David. "The Interpretation of Scriptures in the Epistle of Hebrews." In *Reading the Epistle to the Hebrews: A Resource for Students,* edited by Eric F. Mason and Kevin B. McCruden, 77–97. Atlanta: Society of Biblical Literature, 2011.
Monson, Thomas S. *An Invitation to Exaltation*. Salt Lake City: Deseret Book, 1997.
———. "The Paths Jesus Walked." *Ensign* 4, no. 5 (May 1974): 48–50.
———. "A Royal Priesthood." *Ensign* 37, no. 11 (November 2007): 59–61.
Morris, Leon. "Theories of the Atonement." Monergism.com. Accessed March 15, 2016. http://www.monergism.com/thethreshold/articles/onsite/atonementmorris2.html.
Moulton, James Hope, and George Milliagan. *The Vocabulary of the Greek New Testament: Illustrated from the Papyri and Other Non-literary Sources* (Grand Rapids, Mich.: Wm. B. Eerdmans, 1952.
Mugridge, Alan. "Warnings in the Epistle to the Hebrews: An Exegetical and Theological Study." *Revue de théologie et de philosophie* 46 (1987): 74–82.
Nelson, Russell M. "Combating Spiritual Drift—Our Global Pandemic." *Ensign* 23, no. 11 (November 1993): 102–8.
———. "Doors of Death." *Ensign* 22, no. 5 (May 1992): 72–74.
———. "Perfection Pending." *Ensign* 25, no. 11 (November 1995): 86–88.
Neusner, Jacob. *Messiah in Context: Israel's History and Development in Formative Judaism*. Philadelphia: Fortress Press, 1984.
———, Alan J. Avery-Peck, and William Scott Green. *Encyclopedia of Judaism*. 5 vols. Lieden, Neth.: Brill Publishers, 2004.
Neyrey, Jerome H. "Jesus as Broker in Hebrews: Insights from the Social Sciences." In *Reading the Epistle to the Hebrews: A Resource for Students,* edited by Eric F. Mason and Kevin B. McCruden, 145–70. Atlanta: Society of Biblical Literature, 2011.
Nibley, Hugh. *Approaching Zion*. Edited by Don E. Norton. Vol. 9 of The Collected Works of Hugh Nibley. Salt Lake City: Deseret Book, 1989.
———. "The Atonement of Jesus Christ." *Ensign* 20, no. 7 (July 1990): 18–23; no. 8 (August 1990): 30–34; no. 9 (September 1990): 22–26; no. 10 (October 1990): 26–31.
———. "Baptism for the Dead in Ancient Times." In *Mormonism and Early Christianity,* edited by Todd M. Compton and Stephen D. Ricks, 100–167. Vol. 4 of The

Collected Works of Hugh Nibley. Provo, Utah: Foundation for Ancient Research and Mormon Studies, 1987.

———. *Enoch the Prophet.* Edited by Stephen D. Ricks. Vol. 2 of The Collected Works of Hugh Nibley. Salt Lake City: Deseret Book; Provo, Utah: Foundation for Ancient Research and Mormon Studies, 1986.

———. *Nibley on the Timely and Timeless.* Vol. 1 of Religious Studies Monograph Series. Provo, Utah: Religious Studies Center, Brigham Young University, 1978.

———. *Teachings of the Book of Mormon, Semester 1: Transcripts of Lectures Presented to an Honors Book of Mormon Class at Brigham Young University, 1988–1990.* Provo, Utah: Foundation for Ancient Research and Mormon Studies, 2004.

———. *Temple and Cosmos.* Edited by Don E. Norton. Salt Lake City: Deseret Book, 1992.

Nongbri, Brent. "A Touch of Condemnation in a Word of Exhortation: Apocalyptic Language and Graeco-Roman Rhetoric in Hebrews 6:4–12." *Novum Testamentum* 45, no. 3 (2003): 265–79.

Oaks, Dallin H. "The Godhead and the Plan of Salvation." *Ensign* 47, no. 5 (May 2017): 100–103.

———. *His Holy Name.* Salt Lake City: Bookcraft, 1998.

———. "The Keys and Authority of the Priesthood." *Ensign* 44, no. 5 (May 2014): 49–52.

———. "Scripture Reading and Revelation." *Ensign* 25, no. 1 (January 1995): 6–9.

———. "Taking Upon Us the Name of Christ." *Ensign* 15, no. 5 (May 1985): 80–82.

Oberholtzer, T. K. "The Eschatological Salvation of Hebrews 1:5–2:5." *Biblia Sacra* 145 (1988): 83–97.

O'Brien, Peter T. *The Letter to the Hebrews.* Grand Rapids, Mich.: Wm. B. Eerdmans, 2010.

Ogden, D. Kelly, and Andrew C. Skinner. *Verse by Verse: Acts through Revelation.* Salt Lake City: Deseret Book, 2006.

Osiek, Carolyn. "The Great Cloud of Witnesses," *Bible Today* 50, no. 2 (2012): 95–100.

Ounsworth, Richard. "Faith in the Epistle to the Hebrews." *Scripture Bulletin* 43 (January 2013): 22–32.

———. "On the Threshold of the Promised Land—Psalm 95 in the Letter to the Hebrews." *Religious Life Review* 50 (2011): 69–78.

Oyetade, M. O. "Eschatological Salvation of Hebrews 1:5–2:5." *Ilorin Journal of Religious Studies* 3, no. 1 (2013): 69–82.

Packer, Boyd K. *The Holy Temple.* Salt Lake City: Bookcraft, 1980.

———. "Little Children." *Ensign* 16, no. 11 (November 1986): 16–18.

Parrish, Alan K. "Doctrine and Covenants Section 76 and the Visions of the Resurrected Life in the Teachings of Elder B. H. Roberts." In *Doctrines of Exaltation: The 1989 Sperry Symposium on the Doctrine and Covenants,* 201–23. Salt Lake City: Deseret Book, 1989.

Parry, Jay A., and Donald W. Parry. "The Temple in Heaven: Its Description and Significance." In *Temples of the Ancient World: Ritual and Symbolism,* edited by Donald W. Parry, 515–32. Salt Lake City: Deseret Book; Provo, Utah: Foundation for Ancient Research and Mormon Studies, 1994.

Paulsen, David L. "The Redemption of the Dead: A Latter-day Saint Perspective on the Fate of the Unevangelized." In *Salvation in Christ: Comparative Christian Views,* edited by Roger R. Keller and Robert L Millet, 263–98. Provo, Utah: Religious Studies Center, Brigham Young University, 2005.

Penrose, Charles W. *Blood Atonement, as Taught by Leading Elders of The Church of Jesus Christ of Latter-day Saints.* Salt Lake City: Deseret News, 1916.

Petersen, Mark E. *Abraham: Friend of God.* Salt Lake City: Deseret Book, 1976.

———. "The Message of Elijah." *Ensign* 6, no. 5 (May 1976): 14–16.

Peterson, David. *Hebrews and Perfection: An Examination of the Concept of Perfection in the Epistle of Hebrews.* Cambridge: Cambridge University Press, 1982.

———. "The Prophecy of the New Covenant in the Argument of Hebrews." *Reformed Theological Review* 38, no. 3 (September–December 1979): 74–81.

Pillai, C. A. J. "In Many and Various Ways." *Bible Today* 21 (1965): 1385–89.

Pinegar, Patricia P. "Increase in Faith." *Ensign* 24, no. 5 (May 1994): 94–96.

Pogoloff, Stephen M. *Logos and Sophia: The Rhetorical Situation of 1 Corinthians.* SBL Dissertation Series 134. Atlanta: Society of Biblical Literature, 1992.

Proctor, J. "Judgement or Vindication? Deuteronomy 32 in Hebrews 10:30." *Tyndale Bulletin* 55, no. 1 (2004): 65–80.

Rapske, Brian. *The Book of Acts and Paul in Roman Custody.* Grand Rapids, Mich.: Wm. B. Eerdmans, 1994.

Rasmussen, Dennis F. "What Faith Is." In *The Lectures on Faith: In Historical Perspective,* edited by Larry E. Dahl and Charles D. Tate Jr., 163–77. Provo, Utah: Religious Studies Center, Brigham Young University, 1990.

Rawson, Beryl. *Children and Childhood in Roman Italy.* Oxford: Oxford University Press, 2003.

———. "The Melchizedek Traditions." *Scandinavian Journal of the Old Testament* 26, no. 2 (2012): 259–65.

Roberts, B. H. *Mormon Doctrine of Deity: The Roberts–Van Der Donckt Discussion* (Salt Lake City: Deseret News, 1903.

———. *Seventies Course in Theology.* 2 vols. Salt Lake City: Deseret News, 1907–12.

Robertson, A. T. *A Grammar of the Greek New Testament in the Light of Historical Research.* 4th ed. Nashville, Tenn.: Broadman Press, 1934.

Robinson, Stephen E. *Believing Christ: The Parable of the Bicycle and Other Good News.* Salt Lake City: Deseret Book, 1992.

Robison, Elwin C. *The First Mormon Temple: Design, Construction, and Historic Context of the Kirtland Temple.* Provo, Utah: Brigham Young University Press, 1997.

Romney, Marion G. *Look to God and Live.* Salt Lake City: Deseret Book, 1971.

Rudolph, Kurt. "Early Christianity as a Religious-Historical Phenomenon." In *The Future of Early Christianity: Essays in Honor of Helmut Koester,* edited by B. A. Pearson, 9–19. Minneapolis: Fortress Press, 1991.

Ruether, Rosemary R. *Faith and Fratricide: The Theological Roots of Anti-Semitism.* New York: Seabury Press, 1974.

Rushdoony, Rousas John. *The Institutes of Biblical Law.* n.p.: Presbyterian and Reformed Publishing, 1973.

Saints: The Story of the Church of Jesus Christ in the Latter Days. Volume 1, *The Standard of Truth, 1815–1846.* Salt Lake City: The Church of Jesus Christ of Latter-day Saints, 2018.

Sanders, Jack T. *The New Testament Christological Hymns: Their Historical Religious Background.* Vol. 15 of Society for New Testament Studies Monograph Series. Cambridge: Cambridge University Press, 1971.

Sanders, James A. "Cave 11 Surprises and the Question of Canon." In *New Directions in Biblical Archaeology,* edited by David Noel Freedman and Jonas C. Greenfield, 113–30. Garden City, N.Y.: Doubleday, 1971.

Schenck, Kenneth. *Understanding the Book of Hebrews: The Story behind the Sermon.* Louisville, Ky.: Westminster John Knox Press, 2003.

Schmidt, Brent L. *Rational Grace: The Reciprocal and Binding Covenant of* Charis. Provo, Utah: BYU Studies, 2015.

Schofield, John. *Philip Melanchthon and the English Reformation.* Farnham, Eng.: Ashgate Publishing, 2006.

Seely, David Rolph, and Jo Ann H. Seely. "Jesus as Messiah: Prophet, Priest, and King." In *Jesus Christ: Son of God, Savior,* edited by Paul H. Peterson, Gary L. Hatch, and Laura D. Card, 248–69. Provo, Utah: Religious Studies Center, Brigham Young University, 2002.

Silva, Moises. "Perfection and Eschatology in Hebrews." *Westminster Theological Journal* 36, no. 1 (1976): 60–71.

Skemp, J. B. *The Greeks and the Gospel.* London: Carey Kingsgate Press, 1964.

Skinner, Andrew C. *Gethsemane.* Salt Lake City: Deseret Book, 2002.

———. *Prophets, Priests, and Kings: Old Testament Figures who Symbolize Christ.* Salt Lake City: Deseret Book, 2005.

Smalley, S. S. "The Atonement in the Epistle to the Hebrews." *Tyndale Bulletin* 7–8 (1961): 28–35.

Smillie, Gene R. "'Ο Λογοσ Του Θεου' in Hebrews 4:12–13." *Novum Testamentum* 46, no. 4 (2004): 338–52.

———. "'The One Who Is Speaking' in Hebrews 12:25." *Tyndale Bulletin* 55, no. 2 (2004): 275–94.

———. "'The Other λόγος' at the End of Heb. 4:13." *Novum Testamentum* 47, no. 1 (2005): 19–25.

Smith, Eliza R. Snow. *Biography and Family Record of Lorenzo Snow.* Salt Lake City: Deseret News, 1884.

Smith, Joseph F. *Gospel Doctrine.* 11th ed. Salt Lake City: Deseret Book, 1959.

Smith, Joseph Fielding. *Answers to Gospel Questions.* 5 vols. Salt Lake City: Deseret Book, 1957–66.

———. *Doctrines of Salvation.* Compiled by Bruce R. McConkie. 3 vols. Salt Lake City: Bookcraft, 1954–56.

Soulen, Richard N. *Handbook of Biblical Criticism.* 2d ed. Atlanta: John Knox Press, 1981.

Sowers, Sidney G. *Hermeneutics of Philo and Hebrews: A Comparison of Interpretation.* Richmond: John Knox Press, 1965.

Spackman, T. Benjamin. "The Israelite Roots of Atonement Terminology." *BYU Studies Quarterly* 55, no. 1 (2016): 39–64.

Spellman, Ched E. "When Hope Screams: Learning How to Suffer as Sons from the Book of Hebrews." *Southwestern Journal of Theology* 53, no. 2 (Spring 2011): 112–34.

Stanley, Steven K. "A New Covenant Hermeneutic: The Use of Scripture in Hebrews 8–10." *Tyndale Bulletin* 46, no. 1 (1995): 204–6.

Stapley, Delbert L. "Easter Thoughts." *Ensign* 6, no. 5 (May 1976): 76–78.

Stott, Wilfrid. "The Conception of 'Offering' in the Epistle to the Hebrews." *New Testament Studies* 9, no. 1 (October 1962): 62–67.

Strathearn, Gaye. "Christ's Crucifixion: Reclamation of the Cross." *Religious Educator* 14, no. 1 (2013): 45–57.

Swetnam, James. "The Crux at Hebrews 2,9 in Its Context." *Biblica* 91, no. 1 (2010): 103–11.

———. "Hebrews 10,30–31: A Suggestion." *Biblica* 75, no. 3 (1994): 388–94.

———. "The Meaning of τοῖς ἀκούσασιν at Hebrews 4:2." *Biblica* 93, no. 4 (2012): 601–8.

———. "On the Imagery and Significance of Hebrews 9,9–10." *Catholic Biblical Quarterly* 28, no. 2 (1966): 155–73.

Synge, F. C. *Hebrews and Scripture*. London: SPCK, 1959.

Szink, Terrence L. "Authorship of the Epistle to the Hebrews." In *How the New Testament Came to Be: The 35th Annual Brigham Young University Sidney B. Sperry Symposium,* edited by Kent P. Jackson and Frank F. Judd Jr., 243–59. Salt Lake City: Deseret Book, 2006.

Talmage, James E. *The Vitality of Mormonism*. Boston: n.p., 1919.

Talmon, S. "The Concepts of *Māšîaḥ* and Messianism in Early Judaism." In *The Messiah: Developments in Earliest Judaism and Christianity,* edited by James H. Charlesworth, 79–115. Minneapolis: Fortress Press, 1992.

Taylor, John. *Mediation and Atonement*. Salt Lake City: Deseret News, 1882.

Taylor, Vincent. "Does the New Testament Call Jesus God?" *Expository Times* 73, no. 4 (1961–62): 116–18.

Thiessen, Matthew. "Hebrews and the End of the Exodus." *Novum Testamentum* 49, no. 4 (October 2007): 353–69.

Thiselton, Anthony C. *The First Epistle to the Corinthians: A Commentary on the Greek Text*. New International Greek Testament Commentary. Grand Rapids, Mich.: Wm. B. Eerdmans, 2000.

Thomas, M. Catherine. "Hebrews: To Ascend the Holy Mount." In *Temples of the Ancient World: Ritual and Symbolism,* edited by Donald W. Parry, 479–91. Salt Lake City: Deseret Book; Provo, Utah: Foundation for Ancient Research and Mormon Studies, 1994.

Thompson, J. A. *The Ancient Near Eastern Treaties and the Old Testament*. London: Tyndale Press, 1964. Accessed March 26, 2016. http://biblicalstudies.org.uk/pdf/tp/treaties_thompson.pdf.

Thompson, J. W. "The Structure and Purpose of the Catena in Hebrews 1:5–13." *Catholic Biblical Quarterly* 38 (1976): 352–63.

Thompson, James W. "*Ephapax*: The One and the Many in Hebrews." *New Testament Studies* 53, no. 4 (October 2007): 566–81.
———. *Hebrews*. Paideia: Commentaries on the New Testament. Grand Rapids, Mich.: Baker Academic, 2008.
———. "What Has Middle Platonism to Do with Hebrews?" In *Reading the Epistle to the Hebrews: A Resource for Students,* edited by Eric F. Mason and Kevin B. McCruden, 31–52. Atlanta: Society of Biblical Literature, 2011.
Thornton, T. C. G. "The Meaning of *αἱματεκχυσία* in Heb. IX. 22." *Journal of Theological Studies* 15, no. 1 (April 1964): 63–65.
Tongue, D. H. "The Concept of Apostasy in the Epistle to the Hebrews." *Tyndale Bulletin* 5–6 (1960): 19–26.
Turner, Rodney. "Grace, Mysteries, and Exaltation." In *Studies in Scriptures Volume 6: Acts to Revelation,* edited by Robert L. Millet, 107–24. Salt Lake City, Deseret Book, 1987.
———. "The Imperative and Unchanging Nature of God." In *The Lectures on Faith in Historical Perspective,* edited by Larry E. Dahl and Charles D. Tate Jr., 199–220. Provo, Utah: Religious Studies Center, Brigham Young University, 1990.
Uchtdorf, Dieter F. "Fourth Floor, Last Door." *Ensign* 46, no. 11 (November 2016): 15–18.
———. "How Great the Plan of Our God." *Ensign* 46, no. 11 (November 2016): 19–22.
———. "The Infinite Power of Hope." *Ensign* 38, no. 11 (November 2008): 21–24.
Vanhoye, Albert. *Letter to the Hebrews: A New Commentary.* Translated by Leo Arnold. New York: Paulist Press, 2015.
———. *Old Testament Priests and the New Priest according to the New Testament.* New ed. Translated by J. Bernard Orchard. Leominster, Eng.: Gracewing, 2009.
Van Orden, Bruce A. "The Pastoral Epistles." In *Studies in Scripture Volume 6: Acts through Revelation,* edited by Robert L. Millet, 178–91. Salt Lake City: Deseret Book, 1987.
Vermes, G. *The Dead Sea Scrolls in English.* 3d ed. London: Penguin Books, 1987.
Vos, Geerhardus. "The Priesthood of Christ in the Epistle to the Hebrews." *Princeton Theological Review* 5, no. 3 (1907): 423–47, 579–604.
Walker, Peter. "Jerusalem in Hebrews 13:9–14 and the Dating of the Epistle." *Tyndale Bulletin* 45, no. 1 (1994): 39–71.
Walton, John. *Genesis 1 as Ancient Cosmology.* State College, Penn.: Eisenbrauns, 2011.
Wansink, Craig G. *Chained in Christ: The Experience and Rhetoric of Paul's Imprisonments.* Sheffield, Eng.: Sheffield Academic Press, 1996.
Warfield, Benjamin B. "The Divine Messiah in the Old Testament." In *Christology and Criticism* (New York: Oxford Press, 1929), 3–49.
Webb, Stephen H. "Toward a Mormon Systematic Theology." *BYU Studies Quarterly* 54, no. 1 (2015): 141–48.
Welch, John W. *Chiasmus in Antiquity: Structures, Analyses, Exegesis.* Provo, Utah: Research Press, 1999.
———. *An Epistle from the New Testament Apostles: The Letters of Peter, Paul, John, James, and Jude, Arranged by Themes, with Readings from the Greek and the Joseph Smith Translation.* Salt Lake City: Bookcraft, 1999.

———. “The Melchizedek Material in Alma 13:13–19.” In *By Study and Also by Faith: Essays in Honor of Hugh W. Nibley on the Occasion of His Eightieth Birthday, 27 March 1990,* edited by John M. Lundquist and Stephen D. Ricks, 2:238–72. 2 vols. Salt Lake City: Deseret Book; Provo, Utah: Foundation for Ancient Research and Mormon Studies, 1990.

———, and James V. Garrison. “The ‘Hymn of the Pearl’: An Ancient Counterpart to ‘O My Father.’” *BYU Studies* 36, no. 1 (1996–97): 127–38.

Wengert, Timothy. “The Priesthood of All Believers and Other Pious Myths.” In *Saying and Doing the Gospel Today: Mass, Ministry, Mission,* edited by Rhoda Schuler, 92–115. Institute of Liturgical Studies Occasional Papers no. 12. Valparaiso, Ind.: Institute of Liturgical Studies, 2007. Accessed November 24, 2016. https://scholar.valpo.edu/cgi/viewcontent.cgi?referer=&httpsredir=1&article=1118&context=ils_papers.

Wenkel, David H. “Gezerah Shawah as Analogy in the Epistle to the Hebrews.” *Biblical Theology Bulletin: Journal of Bible and Culture* 37, no. 2 (May 2007): 62–68.

Westfall, Cynthia Long. *A Discourse Analysis of the Letter to the Hebrews: The Relationship between Form and Meaning.* London: T&T Clark International, 2005.

Widtsoe, John A. *Priesthood and Church Government.* Salt Lake City: Deseret Book, 1939.

Wiessenberg, Hanne von. “Gods, Angels, and Demons in the Dead Sea Scrolls.” Accessed August 7, 2016. http://www.academia.edu/1499534/God_s_Angels_and_Demons_in_the_Dead_Sea_Scrolls.

Wilken, Robert L. *The Christians as the Romans Saw Them.* New Haven, Conn.: Yale University Press, 1984.

Williamson, Ronald. *Philo and the Epistle to the Hebrews.* Leiden, Neth.: E. J. Brill, 1970.

Wilson, Andrew J. “Hebrews 3:6b and 3:14 Revisited.” *Tyndale Bulletin* 62, no. 2 (2011): 247–69.

Wilson, Stephen G. *Related Strangers: Jews and Christians, 70–170 C.E.* Minneapolis: Fortress Press, 1995.

Witherington, Ben, III. *Letters and Homilies for Jewish Christians: A Socio-rhetorical Commentary on Hebrews, James, and Jude.* Downers Grove, Ill.: InterVarsity Press, 2007.

Witt, R. E. “ΨΠΟΣΤΑΣΙΣ.” In *Amicitiae Corolla: A Volume of Essays Presented to James Rendel Harris.* Edited by H. G. Wood, 319–43. London: University of London Press, 1933.

Wolmarans, Johannes L. P. “The Text and Translation of Hebrews 8:8.” *Zeitschrift für die neutestamentliche Wissenschaft* 75 (1984): 139–44.

Young, Norman H. “Αἱματεκχυσία: A Comment.” *Expository Times* 90, no. 6 (1979): 180.

———. “‘Bearing His Reproach’ (Hebrews 13.9–14).” *New Testament Studies* 48, no. 2 (2002): 243–61.

———. “The Day of Dedication or the Day of Atonement? The Old Testament Background to Hebrews 6:19–20 Revisited.” *Andrews University Seminary Studies* 40, no. 1 (Spring 2002): 61–68.

———. “The Gospel according to Hebrews 9.” *New Testament Studies* 27, no. 2 (1981): 198–209.

———. “‘Where Jesus Has Gone as a Forerunner on Our Behalf’ (Hebrews 6:20).” *Andrews University Seminary Studies* 39, no. 2 (Autumn 2001): 165–73.

Scripture Index

This index is ordered by book under Old Testament, New Testament, Book of Mormon, Pearl of Great Price, Other Ancient Sources, and Doctrine and Covenants.

Old Testament

Genesis

Numbers

Deuteronomy

Joshua

Judges

1 Samuel

2 Samuel

1 Kings

2 Kings

1 Chronicles

2 Chronicles

Ezra

Nehemiah

Job

Psalms

Proverbs

Isaiah

Jeremiah

Lamentations

Ezekiel

Daniel

Hosea

Joel

Amos

Obadiah

Micah

Habakkuk

Haggai

Zechariah

Malachi

New Testament

Matthew

Mark

Luke

John

Acts

Romans

1 Corinthians

2 Corinthians

Galatians

Ephesians

Philippians

Colossians

1 Thessalonians

2 Thessalonians

1 Timothy

2 Timothy

Titus

Hebrews

Numbers in ***bold italics*** indicate the main discussion of the scriptural passage.

James

1 Peter

2 Peter

1 John

Jude

Revelation

Book of Mormon

1 Nephi

2 Nephi

Jacob

Enos

Jarom

Mosiah

Alma

Helaman

3 Nephi

Mormon

Ether

Moroni

Pearl of Great Price

Moses

Subject Index

A

D

E

F

G

Q

R

T